Robert Campbell

Spring 1987

D1540157

THE CANADIAN POLITICAL SYSTEM

Environment, Structure and Process

THE CANADIAN POLITICAL SYSTEM

Environment, Structure and Process

Fourth Edition

Richard J. Van Loon
Professor, Faculty of Administration
University of Ottawa

Michael S. Whittington
Professor, Political Science
Carleton University

McGraw-Hill Ryerson Limited

Toronto Montreal New York Auckland Bogotá Cairo Caracas
Hamburg Lisbon London Madrid Mexico Milan New Delhi Panama
Paris San Juan São Paulo Singapore Sydney Tokyo

THE
CANADIAN
POLITICAL
SYSTEM

Environment, Structure & Process
Fourth Edition

ISBN: 0-07-549073-0

1 2 3 4 5 6 7 8 9 0 THB 6 5 4 3 2 1 0 9 8 7

Cover Design by Daniel Kewley

Printed and bound in Canada

Canadian Cataloguing in Publication Data

Van Loon, Richard J., date
The Canadian political system

Bibliography: p.
Includes index.
ISBN 0-07-549073-0

1. Canada — Politics and government. I. Whittington, Michael S., date   . II. Title.

JL15.V3 1987   320.971   C87-093381-7

CONTENTS

PREFACE

Some six years have passed between the third and the fourth editions of this text. They could as easily have been a whole political generation. Pierre Trudeau, whose term as prime minister was the third longest in Canadian history, has left political life. The Liberal party, which held power for twenty-one years with a hiatus of only a few months, was crushingly defeated in 1984 and the Progressive Conservatives took office with the largest majority in Canadian history. The Constitution Act of 1982 patriated the Canadian Constitution and gave Canada a Charter of Rights and Freedoms, fundamentally changing the relationship between Canadians and their governments.

The federal government was forced to struggle with the largest peace-time deficit in Canadian history, brought on in no small part by the most severe recession since the Great Depression of the 1930s. In the provinces, the Parti Québécois, the keeper of the separatiste dream in Quebec, was replaced by the Liberal party, led by a premier who had left political office in disgrace nearly a decade earlier. The longest standing government in any parliamentary democracy, the Conservative party in Ontario, fell to the provincial Liberals. Alberta and British Columbia, the two fastest growing and richest provinces of the 1970s, fell upon more difficult times.

These rapid political changes carry with them difficulties for intrepid political science textbook writers, for the examples we use today can be rapidly outmoded tomorrow. But they are underlain by patterns in Canadian politics which change much more slowly. It is these which ultimately determine the rapidly shifting patterns of day-to-day political life. There are enduring features to federal-provincial relations, to the nature of the policy process within government, to the relationship of citizen and state, to the behaviour of government bureaucracies, to the relationships between the governments of Canada and their economic and social environment, to the nature of interest group activity, and to the peregrinations of political parties. The real test of a textbook must be how well it presents these complex patterns, thus allowing the student to understand the underlying realities of political life in a nation. It is our hope that in this, the fourth edition of *The Canadian Political System*, we have provided that sort of enduring perspective.

In common with all the earlier editions of *The Canadian Political System*, this is an enterprise which has benefited from the help of many people. The word processing was done by the secretarial staff at Carleton University and by Sandy Mooney and Brenda Taylor at Word Magic in Ottawa. Gail Mordecai of the political science department at Carleton University helped with much of the administration involved and suffered through the difficult process of cleaning up the bibliography. Bibliographical research was carried out by Susan Phillips of Carleton University. Extensive research assistance was provided by Susan Gates. Many public servants, party workers, and members of interest groups helped by reviewing parts of the manuscript, often providing extensive comments and saving us from errors. We are indebted to Jay Smith of Athabasca University and to Rand Dyck of Laurentian University for comments on drafts of the text. Professor Dyck's comments were particularly detailed and helpful. In addition, we appreciate receiving comments and corrections from our colleagues who use this text. Those of you who have communicated with us in the past may recognize the fruits of your efforts herein.

Michael Whittington, Carleton University, Ottawa
and Government of the Northwest Territories,
Yellowknife

Richard Van Loon, University of Ottawa, and
Government of Canada, Ottawa

C H A P T E R 1

INTRODUCTION

THE POLITICAL FUNCTION: CONFLICT RESOLUTION
■ Limited Environment ■ Competition and Cooperation
■ Conflict Resolution by Resource Allocation ■ Authority and Legitimacy
THE POLITICAL SYSTEM: STRUCTURE AND ENVIRONMENT
THE POLITICAL PROCESS
■ Inside the System: Policy Making ■ Goal Attainment and System Maintenance
■ The Policy Concept
■ The Policy Process in a Technological Age
THE POLICY PROCESS IN CANADA: A MODEL
■ The Initiation of Policies ■ The Establishment of Policy Priorities
■ The Formulation of Policy ■ The Refinement of Policy
■ Limitations of the Model

I f it is true as one prominent Canadian public figure once stated that "the government has no place in the bedrooms of the nation," it is clear that government has surely found a place in every other room of the house. Picture for a moment a middle-aged political scientist standing in front of his bathroom mirror about to scrape the excess hair from his haggard features. "In here," he might be overheard to say with satisfaction, "the government certainly has no place."

But then he might pause and ponder his immediate surroundings. He notices that there is a little note etched on the corner of the mirror, which indicates that this particular piece of glass meets a certain government standard. The label on the aerosol can containing his shaving cream warns him, "Do not puncture or incinerate." A government agency somewhere has decided that such warnings are necessary. The same label tells him that the can contains "350 mL" (however much that is!), because still another government agency has abolished fluid ounces; moreover, the government requires that the information on the label be repeated in the two official languages. As he brushes his teeth, our hero, by now on the verge of paranoia, remembers that the electricity and the water in the small room are supplied by public utilities, and that the municipality puts various chemicals in the water to protect him from typhoid, dysentery, tooth decay, and sundry

1

other public health horrors. Trembling with the embarrassment of how public his bathroom has become, he glances out the window and notices an elderly gentleman walking his dog along the municipally owned and operated sidewalk. The dog is on a leash because a municipal by-law decrees it; and, as if to add insult to injury, the man is carrying a small shovel and a little plastic "doggie bag" because the municipality is very concerned about keeping its streets clean.

The point of this little vignette is that governments in the 1980s touch upon literally every aspect of our day-to-day existence. What is still more significant, perhaps, is that most of the examples of government's ubiquity cited in our brief fable are fairly recent in their origins. Governments are not only very prominent actors in our lives today, but trends in the past two decades indicate that government is increasing the extent to which its decisions touch upon our daily routines. We exclaimed in an earlier edition of this text that in 1971 *all* governments in Canada spent a total of $35 billion. In the 1982–83 fiscal year, however, the federal government *alone* spent about $70 billion, and the 1986–87 fiscal plan indicates a planned federal expenditure budget of about $117 billion. Even if we try to reduce the enormity of the federal budget by taking into account a decade of inflation, we would still see that the total expenditures of federal, provincial, and municipal levels of government have continued to rise steeply: in 1971 they were about 38% of the gross national product, in 1980 they had risen to 45% of the GNP, and by 1986 total government expenditures were more than 50% of Canada's economy. Indeed, government is a dominant actor in our day-to-day affairs, and its presence in society and the economy is growing at a very rapid pace[1].

Governments in Canada today provide myriad services ranging from the defence of our borders to the redistribution of income. Government regulates industry, labour, and the professions; it provides the roads we drive on, the water we drink, national communications networks, public education, medical care, and low-cost housing; it engages in commercial enterprises ranging from running airlines to producing synthetic rubber to running multinational oil companies. The scope of government's activities ranges from the attempted manipulation of the national economy through fiscal, monetary, and exchange rate policies, to the more mundane hosting of an annual first of July "bash" on Parliament Hill. Finally, government with one hand preserves peace and order in our society, and with the other hand opens our mail, taps our phones (after obtaining a warrant), and decides what films and videos (or, in Ontario, what parts of them) we will be permitted to see.

Beyond the provision of goods and services and the redistribution of material resources, governments are also important symbolic reference points to their citizens. They provide symbols such as flags, anthems, and a political apparatus with which we can identify, or against which we can vent hostility. Moreover, through their antics, posturings, and sincere concerns, our politicians provide us with psychological stimuli, which may have little direct relevance to the political

---

[1] See: Economic Council of Canada, *Eighth Annual Review: Design for Decision Making* (Ottawa: Information Canada, 1971), especially pp. 5–16, for a brief but succinct discussion of the increased role of government.

system, but which add a significant and often entertaining dimension to modern life.

In sum, governments are the dominant actors on the world's stage, and their activities constantly affect the economic, social, and psychological dimensions of our everyday lives. This book is about how government works at the national level in Canada. The relevance of this inquiry is clear enough, given the importance of government in the modern world. But, if this is not reason enough for such a study, the subject and the questions it poses are also inherently fascinating: What is the real meaning of our electoral process? How do our political parties work? What is the nature and importance of relations between the provinces and Ottawa? How do other Canadians think and feel about our political process? What difference does it make whether the government has a majority? And, most important of all, how do the needs of society become translated into the policies of government? Before attempting to answer any of these questions, it is necessary to provide some framework within which such processes can be systematically described and analyzed.

THE POLITICAL FUNCTION: CONFLICT RESOLUTION

All societies,[2] however primitive, possess some form of government. It is logical, therefore, to assume that there must be some common underlying function[3] (or set of functions) that is performed by such institutions. There are two simple reasons for the existence and nature of the governmental or political function: first, human beings have a multitude of basic needs and wants that must be satisfied if the species is to survive and if individuals are to attain happiness and live long and healthy lives; second, the resources necessary for the satisfaction of these needs and wants must be extracted from an environment that is finite, and thus limited. The combination of virtually unlimited human wants and limited resources produces a situation where individuals or groups of individuals must compete with others to maximize personal or collective satisfaction. The function of government is to *resolve the conflict* which arises over who gets what resources in a given society.

The Limited Environment

Canadians are immensely lucky in terms of where they live. Although our climate is hard on people, automobiles, and brass monkeys, and although non-renewable resource depletion will eventually face Canada as well as other countries

---

[2] By "society" we mean the network of social relationships that exist among individuals and is continuous through successive generations. This rather perfunctory definition is intended merely as a starting point for the reader, and will be elaborated as the discussion unfolds. See: Marion J. Levy, *The Structure of Society* (Princeton: Princeton University Press, 1952), p. 113; and J. W. Vander Zanden, *Sociology* (New York: The Ronald Press, 1965), p. 153.

[3] Marion Levy defines the term as well as anybody: "A function is a condition or state of affairs resultant from the operation. . . . of a structure through time . . . A structure is a pattern, i.e., an observable uniformity of action or operation." The quotation is in Roland Young, *Approaches to the Study of Politics* (Evanston: Northwestern, 1958), p. xv.

in the world, the natural resources available to Canadians are relatively so abundant that our material standard of living and the general quality of life is among the highest in the world. No matter how abundant our resources are in relative terms,however, they are still limited in absolute terms. No one would argue that the Canadian economy produces enough material goods to completely satisfy every Canadian, and, in fact, because our expectations tend to rise with our standard of living, the total elimination of material scarcity may be an impossible dream. Furthermore, as we will see in the next chapter, our material well-being in the aggregate is offset by significant inequalities in the distribution of our national wealth.

But material scarcity is only one dimension of the limited environment. Even if there were no limit to the *material* resources of a society, there are other situations where scarcity cannot be eliminated or even significantly reduced. *Status*, for instance, is a psychological need that can be satisfied only relative to other people.[4] One's status is high because that of others is low. It is illogical, therefore, to speak of "eliminating" scarcity in such a resource. The inequality in the distribution of psychological goods such as status can be reduced only if people can be conditioned to need them less.

Competition and Cooperation

The result of a limited environment is that in Canada, as in all societies, people must compete with others for the resources they require to survive and to be content. This competition occurs at several levels. At one level, one may compete directly with others. In spite of some halting evidence of changing values in North America, getting a promotion or raise, finding a job in the first place, winning a scholarship, and, in general, "keeping up with the Joneses" is still a central concern of life. But competition often transcends the individual level. Groups of people with interests in common are also in competition with other groups; labour unions compete with management, farmers compete with non-agricultural occupational groups, and dentists compete with denturists. Intergroup competition is a sort of bargaining game where the "prize" is the larger share of an available but limited resource.

But competition among groups in society is transcended by an even broader "intersector" conflict. In our post-industrial society, some would argue that traditional interpersonal and intergroup conflict has been superseded by a "balance of bigness," with big business, big labour, and big government as the main protagonists.[5] Moreover, in systems such as Canada's, intergovernmental con-

---

[4] Whether the need for status is biologically determined and common to other animals than humans or whether it is a culturally determined feature of human society is an interesting debate, but is not really germane here. The point here is that Canadians do seem to have a need for status, and that their political behaviour is influenced by this need. Those interested in the debate itself may wish to peruse Robert Ardrey, *The Social Contract* (New York: Delta, 1970).

[5] This thesis is set forth most succinctly in J. K. Galbraith's *The New Industrial State* (Boston: Houghton Mifflin, 1969); and in *Economics and the Public Purpose* (New York: Thomas Allen and Sons, 1973). For a different perspective, see articles in M. D. Hancock and G. Sjoberg, eds., *Politics in the Post-Welfare State* (New York: Columbia University Press, 1972), especially pp. 37–55.

flict itself is an important dimension of the competition for the scarce resources of the federation.

At another level, whole societies are perpetually in conflict, not only in the international arena, where governments are the actors and the ultimate manifestation of conflict is war, but also even within the confines of a single state, where, for example, large national, cultural, or regional groups are the adversaries. The French-English conflict that colours so much of Canadian politics or the growth of "western alienation" in the 1970s are obvious examples of this, and the increasing demands of our native peoples for the settlement of land claims and greater opportunities for self-government might also be viewed in this way.

Finally, it is also argued by some that *the* pre-eminent conflict in Canada is the direct and necessary product of fundamental structural flaws in our advanced capitalist society. Here the mainspring of political change is seen to be conflict between "classes" — working class vs. capitalist class, proletariat vs. bourgeoisie, or simply rich vs. "not rich." The immediate cause of such conflict is simply the unequal distribution of economic resources and opportunities among the members of society and the ultimate cause is seen to be the capitalist system that makes such inequality inevitable and perpetual.

So far conflict has been our central focus. Conflict is inherently neither good nor bad, but simply an inevitable state of affairs that occurs when people's boundless appetites are loosed on a limited environment. However, *cooperation* is as inevitable as conflict in society. The very fact that human beings do live in societies and not alone testifies to the fundamentally cooperative side of human nature. Cooperation is thus inevitable, because human beings are naturally sociable and gregarious and it is useful because one can accomplish more through combined effort with others than one can alone. Within the context of a modern industrial society, this has led to highly developed systems of cooperation called *organizations*, which permit a high division of labour and increase the capacity of a society to reduce material scarcity. Furthermore, as pointed out earlier, many of an individual's psychological needs can be satisfied only in relation to others. While the drive to satisfy these needs results in interpersonal competition, without cooperation there would be no social resources for which to compete. In sum, while conflict often seems more interesting and more visible, the cooperative mechanisms and instincts that permit a society to come into existence in the first place are at least equally significant and form the cornerstone — a given — of all social science.[6] In fact, once we understand the logical interrelatedness of the concepts of conflict and cooperation, it is possible to see the political functions as *either* the "resolution of conflict" or the "optimization of cooperation" — or both.

Finally, because most conflict in a society occurs between groups, organizations, or classes — in essence, among and between *aggregations* of individuals — one of the direct results of such conflict is to encourage cooperative effort *within* the

---

[6] When we come to analyse the bases of conflict and cooperation within Canadian society, we will use the terms *cleavage* and *consensus*. A cleavage is a line of conflict between two groups that are in competition for the same resources. Hence, for example, we will often speak of French-English cleavage, class cleavage, or regional cleavage. *Consensus* is a state of agreement among a group of people over the desirability of some end. Consensus is the foundation for cooperation among individuals, within groups, and within societies.

aggregate. The need to compete effectively with other aggregations of individuals fosters group cohesiveness, and coordination of organizational effort, both of which are important integrative mechanisms. Thus, conflict and cooperation are not only inevitable in human societies, but these apparently opposite forces, in fact, are mutually reinforcing in the real world.

Conflict Resolution by Resource Allocation

Because all societies can persist only if internal conflicts are minimized and cooperation is facilitated, mechanisms for resolving conflict must be developed. The basic mechanisms of conflict resolution in society are *systems*[7] which take the potential disputes over the disposition of scarce resources out of the realm of uncertainty and *allocate* those resources among the members of that society.

In any society there are a number of different systems or sets of human relationships that perform the function of *resource allocation*. For example, in Canadian society the economic system, through a medium of exchange we call money and by a complex process of bargaining we call the price system, does much to determine what material resources individuals and groups will possess. Resources may also be allocated by our system of beliefs and values. For example, the value our society places upon competitive sports means that an outstanding athlete receives greater rewards in terms of status and money than an outstanding clergyman or professor (damn it!). While the way in which these different systems interact in the process of resource allocation will vary from society to society and from time to time, the allocative function is always performed.

Government too is a system for allocating resources, but it is unique. Unlike the other allocative systems in society, it can be viewed as the master system and there are very few limits on what resources government can allocate.[8] Furthermore, *all* persons in a given society are subject to the allocative decisions of government, like it or not. By choosing to be a member of a given society, an individual has automatically agreed to live by the rules of that society as determined by its government. In this sense — that governments allocate a wide range of resources among *all* of the people in a given territorial space — the jurisdiction of governments, unlike that of other allocative systems, is general rather than specific, comprehensive rather than limited.

A further practical manifestation of the comprehensiveness of government's jurisdiction is that it is thus empowered to control the functioning of all other allocative systems. For example, the family may be regarded as an allocative system. In most societies, the head of the family will be permitted to distribute allowances to the children, but prohibited by laws enacted by government from, for instance, killing unwanted infants. Similarly, the operation of the economic

---

[7] The examination of society as a group of systems and sub-systems has a history too long to be traced in a footnote. Most recently, the concept has been promoted by Talcott Parsons in most of his voluminous writings, and in political science by Gabriel Almond, David Easton, and Karl Deutsch, among others. A listing of the relevant books is to be found in the bibliography and in other footnotes in this chapter.

[8] In Canada, governments have chosen to place limits on themselves through simple restraint in areas where the intervention of the state is seen as illegitimate, and explicitly through a constitution that includes a Charter of Rights and Freedoms.

system is limited by a host of laws prohibiting such things as misleading advertising, undue restriction of competition, or unfair employment practices, and regulating matters as disparate as labour relations or the emission of pollutants into the environment. Thus, government is different from other allocative systems in a society in that its jurisdiction or sphere of control, while perhaps limited territorially by national boundaries, is all-inclusive.

However, there are reasons for not taking this description of the government as the "master" system too far. Governments in Canada may be formally omnipotent, but they are constrained by the distribution of economic power, the prevailing value system of the society, by the values and beliefs of the decision makers themselves, and by the 1982 Charter of Rights and Freedoms. For example, while it is theoretically conceivable that a government in Canada could decree that all Roman Catholics be summarily executed or that all corporations be summarily nationalized, the prevailing value system and the prevailing distribution of economic power would obviously prohibit the untrammelled exercise of governmental power in these areas. Finally, because Canada's is a federal system with a constitutionally defined division of power between the federal and provincial governments, governments constrain each other, as well. We will discuss in depth later the realistic limitations on government activity in Canada, but we can conclude at this point that government, while certainly not omnipotent, is far and away the single most powerful and ubiquitous allocative system in any modern society.

Authority and Legitimacy

Another distinguishing characteristic of governments is that the decisions they make are *authoritative*.[9] In part, this means that government possesses a monopoly over the legitimate use of the collective coercive power of the society to back up its decisions. The exclusive ability to employ coercion obviously lends a great deal of authority to governmental enactments; but a system that relied only on coercion in order to make its allocations effective would be neither stable nor efficient. Too large a percentage of the available resources would be utilized in merely keeping the citizenry in line, and the slightest let-up in the use of force would leave the system vulnerable to overthrow or collapse. For a governmental system to persist, it must acquire *legitimacy*. The members of the society must accept the system not merely because they have to, but also because there is some agreement that it is good, or at least adequate.

A system becomes legitimate in many ways. Often it happens simply because people accept it out of habit or because it is easier to accept the existing regime than to rebel against it. But whatever the origins of a system's legitimacy, it can persist only if the values and norms the system reflects through its actions are basically acceptable to the society as a whole. It must do its job in such a way as to gain and retain the support of most of the members of society, most of the time.

[9] David Easton, *A Systems Analysis of Political Life* (New York: John Wiley and Sons, 1965), chapter 1.

Our original conception of the political function as the resolution of conflict can now be filled out somewhat in light of what has been said about the allocative role of government, the authoritative nature of governmental decisions, and the comprehensiveness of the sphere of control of government. A more complete statement of the political function is: *conflict resolution through the authoritative allocation of the scarce resources of a society.* "Politics" can then be defined as the process[10] by which the political function is performed; it is the way that authoritative decisions concerning the allocation of scarce resources are made and carried out in a society.

THE POLITICAL SYSTEM: STRUCTURE AND ENVIRONMENT

The political system is essentially an elaborate social structure or set of institutions that perform the political function. Because the basic unit of social structure is the *role*, it follows that the political system must be seen ultimately as a complex of interrelated roles.[11]

A role is a pattern of behaviour that is defined either formally or informally by the expectations a society has of one who is occupying a certain position. Thus, the prime minister performs a set of interrelated roles that include, among other things, acting as chairman of Cabinet meetings, chief advisor to the Governor General, Privy Councillor, party leader, Member of Parliament, and chief representative of Canada in international summit conferences. The way in which a prime minister behaves in each of these roles is determined largely by what society determines is appropriate and desirable. Sometimes, as in the case of the prime minister's more formal roles, the society has made its expectations explicit through the constitution and statutes. The prime minister is, in this manner, constrained to behave according to guidelines explicit to the role itself — by the "job description" or positional mandate — and not according to personal predispositions.

However, role theory is not as neat in practice as it seems in the abstract. In the first place, most roles are defined partly by the person playing them. It is only roles that are defined legally or constitutionally that leave little room for improvisation on the part of the incumbent. Moreover, each person occupies many roles in life, and all of these overlap and become interrelated. For example,

---

[10] It is necessary to make an analytical distinction here between the concepts of function and process. *Function* is viewed as outcome, effect, or result of organizational activity. *Process* is viewed as the activity that produces outcomes, effects, or results. The political function is thus conflict resolution, and the political process is resource allocation, according to our definition.

[11] We use the term "political system" because it is less associated with a particular view of politics than is the term "the state," which has been appropriated in large measure by the left in political analysis. "Political system" is also our preferred term over "the government" because the latter term can also mean the government, in the sense of the specific set of current incumbents, that is, the government of the day. However, in practice we will use "political system," "the state," "the government" and "the polity" to refer interchangeably to the same structural entity.

the fact that Prime Minister Mulroney's wife, Mila, accompanied him to the "Shamrock Summit" meeting with U.S. President Reagan in Quebec City, certainly modified his behaviour and that of his distinguished guests, even though, strictly speaking, his role as "husband" has little connection with his role as Canada's prime minister. The roles themselves may not be connected, but the fact that the same person occupies all of them will probably cause them to impinge on each other in many subtle ways. Nevertheless, despite the limitations of role theory, it is still useful to refer to the political system, structurally, as a complex of interrelated political roles. Of course, what makes a role *political* is the fact that it directly concerns the authoritative allocation of resources.

There are also roles such as "voter," "party member," "political activist," etc., which are relevant to politics but that cannot be said to affect the authoritative allocation of resources directly and immediately. Such *politically relevant* roles are probably best considered as part of the environment of the political system, and not part of the system itself. However, the boundary between the political and the politically relevant cannot be drawn distinctly, and the boundary between the politically relevant and the apolitical is similarly difficult to define.

While recognizing this thorny problem of boundaries, it is still possible to say that certain roles and complexes of roles that we refer to as *institutions* are definitely political, and that certain others definitely are not. By looking at the roles and institutions of the "gray area" in terms of their relationship to roles and institutions that are either clearly political or clearly not, we will come to understand their overall significance for the political process. It does not matter, for instance, whether we decide categorically that an interest group is a part of the political system or a politically relevant part of the environment — we will come to understand the political functions of interest groups through looking at their place in the process of politics. Thus, in our discussion of interest groups, we will point out that they perform both political and nonpolitical activities: they are acting politically when their agents attempt to "lobby" Cabinet ministers or bureaucrats, but they are acting apolitically when they publish a monthly newsletter devoted to new methods and techniques that may assist their members in the day-to-day performance of their jobs. The key to the subsequent analysis of the Canadian political system is that it is to be viewed both in terms of processes and in terms of structures: the latter are significant as the institutional context within which the political process occurs.

But the political process occurs within a context that is much wider than the institutions that make up the political system. In fact, one of the reasons we describe our governmental structure as a "system" is that it is located within and interacts with an external *environment* — in other words, it is *open* and responsive to its environment.[12]

---

[12] While open-system theory has been popularized for political scientists, most notably by the works of David Easton and Gabriel Almond, it has been far more completely developed in other disciplines. See particularly: L. von Bertalanffy, "The Theory of Open Systems in Physics and Biology," *Science III* (1950): 23–28; J. G. Miller, "Toward a General Theory for the Behavioral Sciences," *American Psychologist* 10 (1955): 513–531; T. Parsons, *The Social System* (New York: Free Press, 1951); and, more recently, D. Katz and R. L. Kahn, *The Social Psychology of Organizations* (New York: John Wiley and Sons, 1966).

In the widest conceptual sense, the environment of the political system includes everything that is "other" than the institutions and actors we might include in our definition of "the political," the state, the government, or the political system. We have already spoken of the difficulty in determining the boundary between the political system itself and its environment. Now, when we come to look at the environment itself we must determine how much of the environment is even remotely relevant to an understanding of the nature and scope of politics in Canada (see Figure 1). Clearly, in a technical sense, sunspots, quasars, and Halley's Comet are all part of the environment of the Canadian political system, but we can likely come to understand Canadian politics fairly well without much grounding in astrophysics. However, as we move inwards from the ontological outer limits of this "environment" of politics, we can conceptualize the environment as a series of concentric rings, each of which includes variables of ascending importance to the political process.

FIGURE 1:
THE ENVIRONMENT

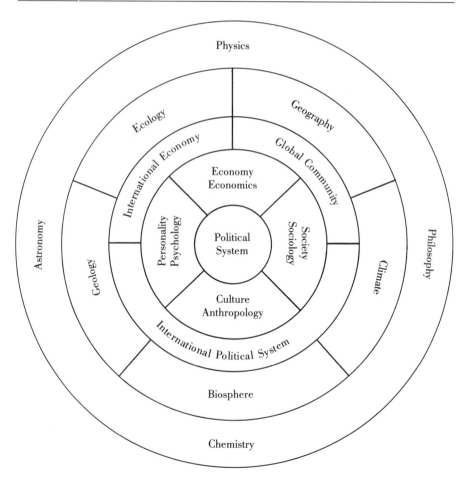

It is interesting and important that each of these concentric rings tends to provide a specific focus for a different academic discipline. One implication of this fact is that students of politics must acquire at least some familiarity with a number of sister disciplines in order to fully understand the political phenomena that are the immediate concern of their research. Thus, while a political scientist can likely get by without a great deal of sophistication in the sciences of physics, chemistry, or microbiology, he may from time to time require some understanding or familiarity with the basic concepts of geology, physical geography, macrobiology, and ecology. Geology tells us, among other things, about the location and commercial value of mineral resources, all of which can become the focus of political discourse in, for example, the intergovernmental arena, or in the development of a national industrial strategy. Physical geography can determine, in part, the nature and scope of regional conflicts in Canada, and the physical location of geographical features can become a determinant of political decisions: the existance of a pingo in the Mackenzie Delta may not have any intrinsic political relevance, but may acquire a relevance if, for instance, there is oil and gas underneath it, it is the subject of aboriginal land claims, or the federal government decides it should be part of a national park or wildlife preserve. Biology, ecology, and climate can similarly become significant considerations in political debate because such variables help to determine the nature and viability of renewable resource industries such as agriculture, fisheries, and furs.

However, it is with respect to the phenomena that comprise the "inner ring" of the environment — the disciplinary foci of the social-science disciplines of psychology, sociology, anthropology, and economics[13] — that the political scientist must be most directly concerned. Individual personality, socioeconomic factors, and culture are all variables that set the agenda for political discourse in Canada: they are the determinants of the specific conflicts that the system must resolve — the "stuff" of Canadian politics.

The basic point that we are making with respect to the environment of the political system is that it is the environment that determines what the political decision makers within our governmental institutions must address — it defines the conflicts over how the scarce resources of the society should be allocated. The secondary point is that there is a *multitude* of variables in the environment that determines the nature and focus of the political process. Unfortunately, the discipline of political science goes through phases or cycles where various academic practitioners come to champion the importance of one set of variables over the others — arguing that some of the environmental factors have a "primacy" that makes them more important than the others. In the 1950s, political science in Canada tended to be dominated by those who felt that knowing the institutions

---

[13] We have not explicitly mentioned the important discipline of human geography here simply because, as with political science, it is not a discrete discipline but a hybrid that looks at culture, society, and economics within a specifically *spatial* context. Similarly, we have placed philosophy in the outer ring of our map of the environment because ultimately it is concerned with the nature of being and hence shares the ontological concerns of astrophysicists, who are exploring the limits of the universe. The specific field of *political* philosophy we see as the prescriptive branch of political science itself, and hence it forms part of the immediate ideational context of the political process.

of government themselves was sufficient to gain an understanding of the political process. This *institutional* approach was supplanted in the 1960s by scholars in the discipline who espoused the view that psychological and sociological factors were the key determinants of politics, because, at root, institutions were only important as a venue within which various human actors behave. This *behavioural* approach was complemented, and, in some cases, supplanted by the view that behaviour is in turn caused by the attitudes and values of Canadians, both élite and non-élite. This *political-culture* approach was in turn complemented by scholars who preferred to focus on the manner in which values and attitudes are acquired by individuals and transmitted from one generation to the next — the process of *political socialization*. We think *all* of these approaches are important and that sub-disciplinary chauvinism, while fostering the development of new and expanded approaches to the study of the Canadian political process, can also serve to artificially narrow our understanding of the subject. Hence, we consciously attempt to utilize the full range of approaches in this text.

The most recent era in the discipline has been dominated by those who espouse the *political-economy* approach, and many of our friends and colleagues in the discipline have urged us to "get with it" in this incarnation of *The Canadian Political System*. Our response is that we *already* utilize a political-economy approach, but that we cannot focus on economic determinants of politics to the exclusion of others that we continue to see as important. We agree that, in a sense, economic variables underlie and to a considerable extent determine our basic values and attitudes — the Canadian political culture, indeed, is reflective of the values implicit in a capitalist system. We agree that the distribution of wealth among regions and among individuals in Canadian society is a critical determinant of the lines of cleavage in Canadian society and an immediate modifier of the political behaviour of voters, interest groups, and politicians. We also agree that the very structures of the Canadian political system — our institutions of government — are the way they are to a large extent because of certain structural givens in the Canadian economy. However, political culture, patterns of political behaviour, and political institutions also take on a life of their own and assume a role that is independent of economics and that is, or can be, self-sustaining.

Thus, in our view, while economics can be looked upon as a sort of "primal ooze" of political life, environmental factors such as ethnicity, language, religion, culture, individual personality, and institutions all are independently important and in fact reciprocally alter and attenuate the economic forces that underlie them. Hence, in discussing the environment of the political system in chapters two to five, while we have identified economic factors as among the most important determinants of political forces and institutions, we have also continued to view non-economic factors as having a profound and independent causative role.

Finally, before leaving this discussion of the environment and our treatment of it in the text, we feel it necessary to respond to one further criticism of our approach in previous editions. This type of criticism flows generally from a particular branch of the political-economy school, which favours class analysis and which utilizes the vocabulary and paradigms of what has come to be referred to as neo-Marxism.

Perhaps the leading scholar in this school in Canada is Leo Panitch, a close colleague and friend (with whom we disagree almost daily). Panitch argues that what is wrong with our modified "system" approach is not so much that the system itself is portrayed as a "black box" — approximately half the chapters in the previous edition of *The Canadian Political System* are devoted to opening up and explaining the contents of the black box — but that the environment is presented as a "black hole":

> We are told that scarcity prevails here and that demands are generated by conflicts over resources, but a systematic examination of the way in which our economy is structured to cope with material scarcity, of the social relations that result between people, and thus of the concrete material clash of social forces that goes on is seldom undertaken.[14]

The fact that previous editions of this text devote approximately one-third of the chapters to illuminating the "black hole" does not impress Leo Panitch — for him, the hole is as black as ever because the categories of analysis that we employ are "abstractions," taken

> from the concrete social relationships between people in a capitalist society such as Canada's [and] they do not contribute enough to our understanding of what is acknowledged to be the determinant element of politics — the socioeconomic system in which politics is embedded.[15]

For Panitch, a real understanding of politics involves:

> getting down to the material social relationships between people, their common experiences in terms of these relationships, and the actual collectivities they form and the struggles they enter into in handling these experiences. This is what *class analysis* . . . is designed to do.[16]

Thus, to Leo Panitch and his confrères, we can never explain the dynamics of Canadian society unless we employ class analysis. But, in response to this critique, we can argue that we *do* see class as an important determinant of political phenomena, and we admit the *inevitability* of at least some class conflict in a society that is based on the capitalist mode of production. Where we differ with the proponents of the neo-Marxist class-analysis approach is in the importance to be accorded to other categories of social and economic differentiation in society. From the perspective employed in this book, ethnicity, culture, religion, language, occupation, economic sector, region, level of income, gender, and ideology are all important determinants of political phenomena, independent of the class structure. Although most labels to some extent distort the true picture, we can say that our approach is a *liberal-pluralist* approach — liberal because we prefer the individual over class as the basic unit of political analysis, and pluralist because to the extent that individuals operate within the context of categoric groups, they

---

[14] Leo Panitch, "Elites, Classes and Power in Canada," in Michael Whittington and Glen Williams, eds., *Canadian Politics in the 1980s* (Toronto, Methuen, 1984), p. 230.

[15] "Elites," p. 230.

[16] "Elites," p. 230.

do so from a multitude of groupings and not just as members of classes or class fragments.

Finally, it should also be pointed out that we differ with the neo-Marxist approach to the extent that it is prescriptive as well as analytic. Not that prescription is itself to be avoided — everyone has a point of view — but because the specific prescription that the capitalist system is fundamentally bad and should be replaced is one with which we disagree. In the first place, we cannot think of a non-capitalist system in the world that is very attractive in terms of quality of life, and in the second, neo-Marxism offers no practical alternatives to capitalism. Finally, in their heart of hearts, "Van Loon and Whittington, as with most Canadians, essentially either are capitalists or would like to be!"[17]

By way of concluding this section, it is important to point out that while we do not explicitly adopt neo-Marxist class analysis as the overall approach to this text, we do indeed recognize the value of this and other critical approaches to understanding Canadian politics. By better understanding the role of capitalism in determining the "battle lines" in much of the political debate that goes on in Canada, we are in a better position to identify the warts and flaws in the existing system with an eye to adapting and improving upon the performance of the political function in this country.

What follows is an overview or model of the political process that will be utilized as a framework for our detailed description of the Canadian system. This model has a purely pedagogical function. It should be used as a mental peg board on which to organize information. To use another metaphor, this chapter provides a rough map of the Canadian political process, without which the subsequent masses of information might be but an array of disjointed facts. Later chapters can be regarded as the "real-world" topography, which is rather imperfectly represented and oversimplified on our map.

THE POLITICAL PROCESS

As we have already seen, the political system is located in and open to its environment. It is the environment that provides the stuff of political conflict, that sets the agenda for the allocative decisions of the government. However, for the environment to have this result, there must be a continuing flow of information from the environment to the relevant people in positions of authority within the system. Thus, the input of information is the link between the conflicts and potential conflicts in the real world and the institutions whose function it is to reduce or resolve those conflicts.

Similarly, in order to have the effect of resolving societal conflicts, the system must first make decisions and then communicate those decisions to the relevant individuals and groups in Canadian society. Thus, the output of information to actors in the real world is the link between decisions taken in the system and the

---

[17] Charlie Logue, Senior Partner, Geo. A. Welch and Company (after three beers), Holden's Bar, September 1985.

ultimate effect of those decisions. The basic form of outgoing communication from the system to the environment is the *allocative* output. This takes the form of information that produces allocations of resources in the environment.

Allocative outputs, however, are of two basic types. First there are general statements known as *laws*. Laws state who gets what, when, and how in general terms. Second, there are outputs that apply the laws to individuals in society — statements that tell an individual how one is affected by the law and what one's rights and obligations are *vis-à-vis* that law. These two basic types of allocative output correspond roughly to the more traditional classification of governmental functions: the first kind of allocative output corresponds to *rule making*, the latter to *rule application*, which includes both the executive and adjudicative functions.

There is a second form of output of the political system that is not allocati̇ e in any direct sense. This is an output of information aimed at educating, inform ng, or propagandizing, and which can be styled a *symbolic output*. The usual function of symbolic outputs is to communicate additional information about the allocative outputs of the system to those who might be affected by them. In this sense, symbolic outputs reinforce the impact of allocative ones. However, another important function of symbolic outputs is to increase support for the system without having to make any new allocative decisions. In this sense the government attempts to convince us of the goodness and legitimacy of the system simply by extolling its virtues to us.

Another way of looking at outputs of the system is to see them as instruments of government — as a range of devices through which the allocative decisions of the government are carried out. Bruce Doern and Richard Phidd see *governing instruments* as falling along a continuum according to the degree of coercion that must be employed by the state to carry them into effect. At the least coercive extreme they cite "exhortation" as a means of governing:

> To govern by exhortation is to engage in a whole series of potential acts of persuasion and voluntary appeals to the electorate as a whole or to particular parts of it. In this sense many would properly view exhortation as democratic government in its highest and most ideal form.[18]

Thus, exhortation is essentially a symbolic output of the system, but with an allocative intent. Campaigns against smoking, drunk driving, or racism are recent examples of the use of exhortation in an attempt to alter our attitudes or behaviour directly or as a supplement to more coercive instruments.

The next level of governing instrument in terms of coerciveness is the simple *expenditure* of public moneys. Expenditures can be either *distributive* or *redistributive*. The former are directed to the creation of a public good, such as the construction of a highway, the establishment of a national park, or the erection of a school, any of which are open for the potential benefit of all Canadians. Redistributive expenditures, by contrast, are measures such as old-age pensions or welfare programs, which have the effect of transferring wealth from all taxpayers

[18] G.B. Doern and R.W. Phidd, *Canadian Public Policy: Ideas, Structure, Process* (Toronto, Methuen, 1983), p. 124.

to a special category of citizens deemed to be more needy than the rest of us. Public expenditure is

> only moderately coercive in that governments, when they spend, are distributing the funds as benefits or services. . . . Actual coercion occurs when the revenue is extracted, from the taxpayer, but when it is spent the coercive edge has disappeared.[19]

Taxation is a governing instrument to the extent that the tax system can be employed to effect the redistribution of wealth. By allowing a large corporation a big tax write-off, for instance, the government can thereby encourage growth within such organizations or in specific industries. Sometimes this style of governing instrument is referred to as *tax expenditures*, because the net effect is that there is less money in the public coffers to go around. This instrument is no more or less coercive than simple expenditure of public moneys, but is certainly less visible and hence a useful device if the government wishes to provide financial assistance to a particular industry, but would rather not let the average taxpayer know about it.

Regulation is the governing instrument that is most familiar to us. Most laws passed by the government have the effect of regulating our behaviour. Regulation can range from outright prohibition, as with matters in the Criminal Code, to the setting of freight rates or air fares, or to requiring licences for engaging in certain kinds of enterprises. Regulation is more coercive than the instruments discussed up to this point because regulations are enforced in such a way that non-compliance can result in penalties such as revoking of a licence, fines, or even imprisonment.

Finally, *public enterprise* is a governing instrument that is especially characteristic of our political system. The vast number of Crown corporations at both the federal and provincial levels in Canada provide ample examples of the use of this sort of governing instrument. While it is in some ways less coercive than regulation, public ownership does have an impact on a very wide range of Canadians as well as the private-sector individuals and corporations who must compete with the public enterprise. We will return to the discussion of these various types of governing instruments later in the book when we are dealing with the policy process.

Once an output occurs there will normally be some sort of reaction to it from people in the environment. As time passes, it will become apparent whether the policy has had the desired effect and the decision makers in the system are able to modify their future decision making accordingly. This process is known as *feedback*. In a primitive system this is a simple process, because direct personal contact is possible between decision makers and the environment. Indeed, in a simple system the decision maker leaves a meeting and becomes a major part of the social environment. In Canada the decision maker also has roles — such as the role in one's family — that make one a part of the environment, and there will be some limited opportunity to gain feedback in that way. However, our political system relies primarily on those parts of its institutions that operate on

---

[19] *Canadian Public Policy*, p. 112.

the input side of the process to gather information about the impact of its policies on society. In fact, as we will see when we look at the policy process, a major activity in which policy makers become involved is the evaluation of the impact of their decisions on the real world.

Inside the System: Policy Making

While we have briefly described how the political system interacts with its environment, we have so far left untouched what is ultimately the core concern of the political scientist: the *policy process*, whereby the decision makers in the political system decide what the system should do. The resolution of conflicts that arise over the distribution of resources is the operational goal of the political system, and the activities that directly contribute to the attainment of that goal are the central process of politics. The part of the process that is internal to the system is the making of public policy, and it forms the dominant focus of this book.

However, in selecting policy making as our central theme, we must recognize that other processes of politics have great relevance as well. For the political system to pursue effectively its operational goal of conflict resolution, it must persist over time. Thus, while the attainment of operational goals is the "job" government does on a day-to-day basis, there are functions related directly to the maintenance of the system that must be performed first.

Goal Attainment and System Maintenance

In one sense, the maintenance of the system is very closely related to its effectiveness in attaining operational goals, for if the "clients"[20] of the system are not satisfied with the standard of service being performed for them they will not continue to support it. In this way the legitimacy of a system is achieved, at least in part, through effective goal attainment. Similarly, if the system is to continue to perform its allocative function effectively, it will be necessary from time to time for the system to initiate structural changes and sometimes even to redefine goals[21] in response to environmental changes. It is the *adaptive mechanisms* of a political system that permit it to persist even when faced with large-scale social

---

[20] The term "clientele" has been developed and utilized most in the literature of administrative theory and policy analysis, although the concept is implicit in the notion of legitimacy. See: L.C. Freeman *et al.*, "Role of Community and Clientele Leaders: Identifying Community Leaders in Decision-Making," B.L. Bible and E.J. Brown, "Role of Community and Clientele Leaders: Coopting Clientele in Decision-Making," and R.G. Mason, "Securing Clientele Acceptance and Cooperation," all articles in F.J. Lyden *et al.* eds., *Policies, Decisions and Organization* (New York: Appleton-Century-Crofts, 1969), pp. 66–76, 77–87, and 214–228.

[21] While Roberto Michels is normally credited with originating the concept of *goal displacement*, there is a large body of literature that has developed the concept and applied it to specific organizations. This phenomenon is discussed briefly and clearly in A. Etzioni, *Modern Organizations* (Englewood Cliffs: Prentice-Hall, 1964), pp. 10–14. See also R.J. Merton, *Social Theory and Social Structure* (Glencoe: Free Press, 1957), pp. 197ff.; and P. Selznick, "An Approach to a Theory of Bureaucracy," *American Sociological Review*, vol. 8, no. 1 (1943), pp. 47–54. The redefinition of goals in the interest of the survival of the organization is elaborated in a case study of the Salvation Army. See S.D. Clark, *Church and Sect in Canada* (Toronto: University of Toronto Press, 1948).

and economic changes or major shifts in the predominant value system of a population.[22]

Other aspects of the process of system maintenance, however, are linked less closely to policy making. For instance, because the political system is goal directed, the persons who occupy roles must be induced to engage in activity that is directed at the attainment of system goals. Because the goals of the system will likely not be identical to the personal goals of the occupants of system roles, the actors within the system must be made willing to put off the satisfaction of their immediate preferences in the interest of working towards the attainment of system goals. This *integrative function* is a critical dimension of system maintenance, and it is achieved through a number of processes related to political recruitment, socialization, and the manipulation of material and non-material rewards, and, in the bureaucracy, through the process of management. All of these facets of system maintenance will be discussed in the chapters that follow.

Finally, while we can say that there are mechanisms by which the system maintains itself, ultimately the persistence of the system depends upon the continued support of most of its citizens. There are three objects or aspects of the political system towards which individuals can give support. The basic object of support is the *political community*, or the society itself. In the case of the Canadian system, for instance, the political community is the Canadian nation and its significance is that it permits Canadians to identify themselves as politically "other" than the rest of the world. Support for the political community involves the attitude that the social unit and geopolitical boundaries on which the political system is built are viable — that there is indeed a true community and not merely an artificial or coerced unity.

A second fundamental object of support is the *regime*. The regime is the set of structures, norms, and values that define the form of the state. It not only sets broad system goals and defines the limits of legitimate governmental activity, but it also provides the institutional mechanisms and the rules of the game of politics in a given country. In Canada the regime is composed of our political institutional arrangements, such as federalism, parliamentary government, and Cabinet responsibility. Support for the regime involves the acceptance that the values implicit in the particular form of political system are good.

Finally, the *authorities* of the system can be an object of support as well. Support for the authorities means support for the individuals occupying the positions or roles of the political system — the incumbents to whom we have been referring as the political decision makers.

---

[22] Note here that there are some value limits beyond which a system may not adapt without becoming a new system entirely. The maintenance of these is referred to as "pattern maintenance" and is described as protecting "the basic ordering principles of the system with regard to both the value of such patterns and the commitment of system units to them." T. Parsons, "The Political Aspect of Social Structure and Process," in D. Easton, ed., *Varieties of Political Theory* (Englewood Cliffs: Prentice-Hall, 1966), p. 105. In other words, whereas adaptation is the dynamic element in the system, pattern maintenance is the conservative element. The "raw material" of pattern maintenance can be found in the fundamental values of the members of the society, and/or in the "clientele" of the system.

For a society to be stable, it is important that support for the political community and the regime be sustained at a relatively high level. If there is a withdrawal of support for the political community, one of the results can be separation of the dissatisfied section. For example, separatist activities in the province of Quebec in the 1970s reflected a lack of support for the political community of Canada by some of its members. Similarly, if there is withdrawal of support for the regime, the result can be the destruction or radical alteration of the existing system. The Communist Party of Canada, for instance, accepts the Canadian political community but rejects the liberal democratic form of the regime. This party would like to see the present regime supplanted by one similar in principle to that of the Soviet Union.

While the stability and persistence of a political system depends on the retention of support for the political community and the regime, in liberal democratic systems the regime explicitly provides institutional devices such as elections for expressing the withdrawal of support from the authorities. In fact, such systems could be said to encourage the periodic withdrawal of support for one set of authorities and their replacement by another set through elections and the party system.

To summarize, our aim is to look at political institutions and processes primarily in terms of their relationship to goal attainment. Because goal-attainment activity within the context of the political system amounts to policy making, that will be our central concern. While it is our intention neither to ignore nor to de-emphasize the processes of politics related to the maintenance of support for the system, these will be viewed primarily in terms of their relationship to effective policy making.

The Policy Concept

A *policy* can best be defined as the stated intention to produce a certain allocative or symbolic output, and the process of policy making involves deciding what that output should be. However, while such a definition is simple enough on the surface, it includes a number of implications that need elaboration.

In the first place, it is possible to think of policy and the process of policy making within the context of any organization, not just the political system. For example, it is quite reasonable to speak of "company policy" without implying any connection to the political system, and if the structural focus is specified, the above definition of policy is compatible with all of these usages of the term.[23] However, unless otherwise specified, the term "policy" within the context of this book will refer only to public policy or governmental policy.

The second implication of this definition of policy is that the policy process consists of decision-making activity. Because political decision making is, in the end, the prerogative of individual minds acting in complex organizations, in order to

---

[23] "Company policy," for instance, may be viewed as decisions by the people who occupy authority positions within a company that a certain course of action should be expressed as an organizational "output."

understand the policy process completely it would be necessary to consider social-psychological factors, as well as a host of influences that arise because of the organizational context within which decisions are made. But our concern is more with the question of which people occupying which political roles have the power to make various kinds of political decisions, rather than with the process whereby a human mind in the organizational setting perceives a problem, looks for alternative solutions to the problem, and then chooses one of the alternatives.[24] This is not to assert that the social-psychological and organizational imperatives are not vital, but rather that they are too complex to be discussed extensively in a basic text on government.

Finally, this definition of policy recognizes that there is a distinction between "policy" and "output." While the outputs of a political system are always a reflection of decisions taken within the system, the transformation of a policy into an output often requires formal steps that legitimize or render authoritative the internal decisions. For example, a bill passed by Parliament does not become a legislative output until it has been assented to by the Governor-General, proclaimed, and printed in the *Canada Gazette*. Because "being the government" in Canada to a large extent means having control over these formal legitimizing procedures, the conversion of government policy to outputs is a routine matter. The decision to employ those procedures is in reality the final step in the policy process; what occurs subsequently is virtually automatic and not strictly a part of policy making. Thus, while we will occasionally speak of "outputs" and "policies" as almost synonymous terms, and while it would be rare empirically for one to occur without the other, it must be recognized that there is an analytical distinction.

There have been many attempts to define policy in more restrictive terms than ours. For instance, policy decisions are frequently viewed as those more properly taken by politicians than by administrators, judges, or bureaucrats. In this view a distinction is made between "political" decisions, which involve "policy," and "administrative" or "judicial" decisions, which do not.[25] While the distinction between policy making and policy implementation or between deciding and doing may be analytically appealing, empirically the distinction very quickly breaks down. The decision to pass a piece of major legislation may be more important than the decision of a customs official who sets guidelines as to when to inspect or not to inspect someone's luggage, but each of these activities does involve making a governmental decision and each results in an output. To say that one process is policy and the other is not is to introduce an artificial distinction.

---

[24] Herbert Simon refers to these stages of decision making as "intelligence activity," "design activity," and "choice activity." See Herbert Simon, *The Scope of Automation: For Men and Management* (New York: Harper and Row, 1965), pp. 53–54. See also J.G. March and H.A. Simon, *Organizations* (New York: John Wiley and Sons, 1958), chapters 6 and 7. We will make extensive use of organization theory when discussing the Cabinet and the bureaucracy in Canada.

[25] Peter Drucker speaks of a split between the "deciders and the doers" in the political system and sees a clear delineation of these functions as a solution to some of the problems of the "age of discontinuity." See Peter Drucker, *The Age of Discontinuity* (New York: Harper and Row, 1969), p. 233.

While it is artificial to attempt to classify "political" decisions as policy and administrative decisions as some lower species, it is useful to classify policy into different types. The simplest, yet one of the most useful, classifications is to divide outputs into those generated by the legislative process, those generated by the executive or administrative process, and those generated by the judicial process. By describing legislative, executive, and adjudicative decisions by the common term "policy," we can avoid a good deal of semantic debate about what is a policy, while still being able to relate each type of output back to a particular, analytically distinct process.

These three types of process and output are themselves very closely interrelated. Both the executive and adjudicative outputs depend upon the pre-existence of *laws*, with the former having the effect of implementing and the latter of interpreting them. Consequently, there is a certain primacy about legislation that has caused the law-making process to be viewed traditionally as the "master" allocative function of government. In conformity with this, our analysis of the Canadian political system will focus primarily on the decision-making processes that result in the formation of legislation and secondarily on the processes that result in the executive and judicial implementation and interpretation of law.

Our presumption of the primacy of the legislative policy process is not intended to minimize the importance of executive or judicial processes. Because the effectiveness of the political system in meeting the demands of a diverse clientele to a large extent depends upon the details of how the vast tax revenues of the system are spent, executive decision making within the political system, particularly that related to the preparation of the budget and the expenditure of public funds, is an increasingly important dimension of policy making. More than 90% of the money spent by the Canadian government each year is spent on already existing programs, and a large part of this money is allocated primarily through executive and administrative decisions. Similarly, we see how judicial decisions not only mediate the relationship between the individual and the state, but that judicial interpretations have in fact shaped the institutional framework of the Canadian federal system. Thus judicial and administrative decision making must be viewed as important categories of policy making. Nevertheless, because each of the continuing programs was generated originally by new legislation, and because the key issues of politics today still involve new policies more than the ongoing ones, our initial analytical departure point is the process whereby decisions about new legislation are taken.

The Policy Process in a Technological Age

The theory of parliamentary democracy posits an ideal system of government where legislative outputs prevail over all other outputs of the system and where the power to legislate is vested in an elected parliament. Furthermore, the executive power in a perfect parliamentary system resides with the prime minister and the cabinet, who are in turn responsible directly to parliament. Thus, in an ideal parliamentary democracy, ultimate power rests with the people who elect the parliament, which in turn controls the prime minister and the cabinet. The administrative arm of the government, the bureaucracy, is responsible directly to the cabinet, and indirectly, through the budgetary process, to parliament. The bureaucracy is responsible for the implementation or application of the laws passed by parliament, and such responsibilities are totally divorced from the legislative process.

While it seems unlikely that this theoretical version of parliamentary democracy was ever a fact, it is part of the conventional wisdom that there was a "golden age" of parliamentary democracy when reality conformed much better to the ideal than it does today. One major factor associated with this trend away from the hypothetical ideal of parliamentary democracy is technological change, although in large part it is not technology but the social and economic consequences of technology that have altered the policy process most startlingly.

Technological advances precipitated industrialization, which has been the single most important variable in determining the nature of modern societies. The movement from a pre-industrial or agricultural society produced social discontinuities, which were so great that existing mechanisms of social adaptation could not cope. Industrialization, for instance, created in Canada the phenomenon of the employable unemployed. The problem of welfare within the pre-industrial system had concerned the care of those unable to find employment because of physical or mental disability, a problem that could be dealt with by agencies such as the church and local charities. With the massive unemployment that resulted from economic fluctuations in industrial society, the traditional agencies were no longer capable of carrying the burden of welfare. By default, more than anything else, government was forced to step into the field of income redistribution and social insurance in order to alleviate the intense economic hardships of depression and unemployment.

Similarly, because an industrial society is complex and very sensitive to the activities of individuals who control large amounts of capital, economic stability can be maximized only if there is a degree of control and planning of the economy. Governments were the natural structures in society with sufficient resources and the ability to use coercion legitimately to step in and regulate the economic system, using such techniques as anti-combines and labour-relations legislation and legislated, fair-employment practices and fiscal and monitary policy. The "unseen hand" of Adam Smith did not effectively keep the economy in a state of equilibrium, and government stepped in to attempt to restore the balance.

Technology not only made industrialization possible in the first instance but, through developments in the field of economics, also made possible the intervention of government as a planner and regulator of the industrial economy: "Even in the most conservative of the industrial states, technology has steadily expanded governmental activity in the fields once left exclusively to the private entrepreneurs."[26] Technology and industrialization thus stimulated a change in the role of the political system in society. Where governments had once been very

---

[26] E.G. Mesthene, *Technological Change* (Cambridge: Harvard University Press, 1970), pp. 64–65; and V.C. Ferkiss, *Technological Man* (New York: Braziller, 1969), p. 177.

passive and negative, they assumed positive and active roles in society. Where the public attitude to the role of government had once been that the government that governed least was the best form of government, the political system was now expected, as a matter of course, to perform broad regulatory and redistributive functions heretofore left to economic and social mechanisms, or not performed at all.

The immediate implications of this changing role of government for the political system were three. First, the number of outputs of government increased because the role of government expanded. The increase in the amount of governmental activity means that the number of policies considered in any given year will normally be greater than in the year before.[27]

Second, the complexity of legislation increased enormously after the turn of the century. The amount of detail required in legislation that spells out the procedures and formulae in a national pension plan, for instance, is much greater than that required in legislation to amend a criminal code, and an increasing percentage of legislation deals with subjects like pension plans and welfare schemes.

Finally, not only have governmental outputs increased in number and the amount of detail they encompass, but their content has increased in technological sophistication, as well. Policies dealing with subjects such as economic planning, scientific research, and taxation must of necessity be highly technical, reflecting as they do the most advanced levels of knowledge in the given field. The combination of increased volume, complexity, and technological sophistication of governmental activity has made a high level of specialization and technical expertise necessary for effective policy making. This has had important consequences for the ideal of parliamentary democracy.

In the first place, parliament, being neither specialized nor highly expert, is disqualified, in practical terms, from taking the central part in the policy process. In part, the law-making power in the Canadian political system has shifted to the Cabinet, for it is this body that has acquired and retains the *de facto* authority to set goals or establish priorities for governmental action. Through party discipline and through the Cabinet's access to the expertise within the various government departments, Cabinet members are placed in a position of considerable advantage over the back-bench MP.

In part, however, the policy function has moved out of the Cabinet as well, and into the hands of the thousands of experts throughout the public service. These experts are entrusted with the responsibility of tendering policy advice to the ministers. The power to advise becomes a very real political power when the advice given is highly technical in nature and when the person being advised is not an expert. In Peter Drucker's terms, knowledge has become power; it is the "central capital" of modern society: "Scientists and scholars are no longer merely 'on tap' they are 'on top.' . . . They largely determine what policies can be considered seriously in such crucial areas as defence or economics."[28]

---

[27] *Technological Man*, p. 178.

[28] *The Age of Discontinuity*, p. 372.

While the power to decide policy still resides with political office holders such as the prime minister and the Cabinet, this is in many ways *positional* power. That is to say, it derives from the role an individual occupies and is only secondarily affected by the character and ability of the individual. Because rational decision making in a modern system necessitates the use of specialized and technical information that politicians do not possess, the real power that accrues to them through their positions is significantly reduced. As E.G. Mesthene has pointed out:

> The task of the expert is to furnish the politician with information and estimates on which he can base a decision. . . . When the expert has effectively performed his task of pointing out the necessary ways and means, there is generally only one logical and admissible solution. The politician will then find himself obliged to choose between the technician's solution, which is the only reasonable one, and other solutions which he can indeed try out at his own peril, but which are not reasonable. . . . In fact, the politician no longer has any real choice; decision follows automatically from the preparatory technical labours.[29]

Finally, it is also a fact of modern government that senior bureaucrats are the central contact point between the technocrats and the politicians. Lacking the positional authority of the politician and the expertise of the technocrats, the senior public servants gain their power as the "managers" of expertise. They are the men and women who try to translate the technical information into terms the politician in the cabinet can understand, and through this role they have maintained a high level of power in the system as well.

While the above generalizations likely apply fairly accurately to the Canadian situation, the fact remains that Cabinet ministers and the prime minister will not infrequently make decisions that go contrary to the advice of their technical hired hands. Whether they are inspired by sincere doubts about the validity of the advice tendered, by the conviction that non-technical considerations outweigh the technical, by political opportunism, or by simple whim, our politicians still possess the positional power to make policy decisions against the advice of technicians and senior bureaucrats. However, for the most part, technical advice to our political leaders does have a profound influence on their decisions.

The outcome of the shift in policy-making power from those who occupy political-authority roles to those who possess technical knowledge or information is that the institutions that concentrate expertise, such as bureaucratic agencies, will tend to dominate the institutions, such as Parliament, that do not. *Prima facie*, there is no reason that concentrations of expertise in non-governmental locales such as industry, the universities, and pressure groups could not provide important sources of policy influence to compete with the governmental bureaucracy. In some instances they do. However, two factors intervene. First, "the development and the application of technology seem necessarily to require large scale and complex social concentration,"[30] which occurs most commonly, at least with

---

[29] *Technological Change*, pp. 64–65.

[30] J. Ellul, *Technological Society* (New York: Alfred A. Knopf, 1965) pp. 258–259.

respect to social programs and general economic management, in government. There are few non-governmental organizations that control sufficient resources to gather expertise and technological information on a scale that would permit them to compete effectively with the governmental bureaucracy.[31] Those that might, the multinational corporations, are so large and diversified that they must be analyzed as "proto governments" rather than as private enterprise. This means that the relationship between multinationals and government is more akin to the relationships among sovereign states than between a sovereign government and its domestic corporations.

Second, the number of sources of information that the harried formal or positional decision makers in the Cabinet and its support agencies can deal with is limited. There is simply not time to consider a larger number of alternative viewpoints. The decision maker therefore "satisfices," to use Herbert Simon's now famous term, by selecting the first passable solution, and since it is the public service that for the most part screens the information flowing to ministers, it is their selection of information that tends to be dominant.

Public servants can also influence governmental outputs more directly through the instrument of delegated power. It is frequently necessary, because of the complexity of the matters being dealt with by government, for legislation to leave a great deal of discretion to the public servants who implement it. The power to work out the details of a particular government program is often delegated to the administrative agency charged with the responsibility for administering it in such a way that the administrators become, in a limited way, legislators. This presents serious problems of political control. The bureaucrats, unlike the politicians, are not elected. Although Parliament attempts to control this problem through its Statutory Instruments Committee, perhaps the most effective way of preventing the abuse of delegated power today is through judicial process, which provides remedies through civil action for an individual who is harmed by misuse of administrative discretion.

The foregoing paints a picture quite different from the traditional one of a supreme parliament, responsible to an informed and active electorate, making policy on the basis of a grand concept of "national interest." Nevertheless, while the policy process in the positive state does not match our classical image of parliamentary democracy, the system does seem to work after a fashion. Furthermore, it is important to emphasize that there is no blame to be assigned for this shift in power within our system. Power is moving from Parliament to the Cabinet and from the Cabinet to the bureaucracy simply because the environment of the political system is such that experts in large information-gathering organizations are the ones most likely to find solutions to current problems. The bureaucrats and technocrats have not deliberately wrested policy-making power from the hands of those who should rightfully possess it. There has been no *coup d'état*, but, in a technological society, those with technological know-how will inevitably wield power that exceeds what is implicit in their slot in an organization chart.

---

[31] For an opposite point of view, see M. Lamontagne, "The Influence of the Politician," *Canadian Public Administration*, vol. 11, no. 3 (1968), pp. 263–271.

THE POLICY PROCESS IN CANADA: A MODEL

The Initiation of Policies

The policy process has been defined as internal to the political system. It is the process whereby persons "inside" the system decide what should become system outputs. A distinction has already been made between policy and output, but little has been said about the input side of the process. The authorities do not make policy decisions on a purely random or whimsical basis (even though this sometimes appears to be the case). The policy process is triggered by information from outside the system, specifically by information about problems that can be solved by governmental action. Hence, given that the origins of public policy lie in information about environmental circumstances, the process whereby that information comes to the attention of the policy makers is the first stage in the formation of policy.

The key problem in initiating or triggering the policy process is in finding channels through which demand inputs can be brought to the attention of people occupying policy roles. Points of access occur naturally where people within the system are paying attention to what is going on outside; in order to ensure continued attentiveness, MPs and Cabinet ministers are subject to periodic evaluation through the institutional device of elections. Institutions such as political parties and pressure groups have come to play a key role in rationalizing and articulating to Parliament and Cabinet the wants and needs of people in the environment. However, given the diversity of problems that exist in modern societies, and given the overall movement of decision-making power from the purely political institutions to the executive ones, newer, less traditional channels of access to the political system have developed at the Cabinet and the bureaucratic levels.

Many government departments have as their organizational *raison d'être* a specific clientele. For instance, the Department of Agriculture exists to serve agricultural interests and to solve agricultural problems, and the Department of Veterans' Affairs exists to serve the interest of ex-servicemen. The survival and growth of these departments depends almost entirely on their success in representing the interest of their clienteles. The more problems they can define and begin to solve, the greater will be their budgetary allocations and manpower establishment. Conversely, the stronger their rapport with their clientele, the more likely are they to be able to mobilize their public against cuts when the time comes for government reductions. As a result, clientele-oriented departments constantly seek environmental information in an effort to anticipate the needs and problems of their clientele. Because of this attentiveness, important channels of access to the policy process have been created within the public service, and channels of access through ministers responsible for clientele-oriented departments have been reinforced.

Today, even large interest groups focus their attention on executive and bureaucratic channels, frequently by seeking the establishment of a separate department that will serve their clientele. Close symbiotic relationships exist today between organizations such as the Canadian Petroleum Association or the Canadian Manufacturers' Association and departments such as Energy, Mines, and Resources or Regional Industrial Expansion. While bureaucratic and ministerial channels of access have not completely replaced the traditional ones, they are often more effective for policy initiation. Because so many agencies are clientele-oriented, and because they possess the expertise that makes them more effective than purely political institutions in ferreting out problems among their clientele, the traditional political channels are increasingly in competition with the newer executive-based ones.

Nor is this situation confined to the federal government. There are similar points of access at the provincial level in Canada. The trends there are similar to those at the federal level: decision-making power generally has been moving from the political to the bureaucratic institutions, with the consequent increase in the importance of provincial departments as channels of policy initiation. The trend is more marked in large provinces than in smaller ones, but it exists everywhere.

The Establishment of Policy Priorities

The inflow of information from the environment is a necessary condition for policy making. If that flow of information should cease for some reason, the policy process would grind to a halt. In the modern political system, however, the central problem is not in garnering information but in coping with vast amounts of it. The problems of modern societies are so numerous and so complex that the greatest threat to the stability of the system may well lie in *information overload*. The first internal step in the policy process, therefore, involves weeding out, reducing, and ordering in importance the vast quantity of information with which the priority setters are constantly bombarded.[32]

The core institutions or the key authorities involved in the establishment of policy priorities in the Canadian system are the Cabinet, the prime minister, and federal-provincial conferences. It is the Cabinet that possesses the formal authority to set the broadest directions of public policy. Because of the vast bulk of inputs, however, much of the initial reduction of policy demands and the preliminary weeding-out of information must be performed elsewhere. The channels of input themselves act as "gatekeepers" in filtering, integrating, and ordering policy information even before it comes to the attention of the Cabinet and the prime minister. Pressure groups, for instance, establish priorities among the objectives of their membership in order to maximize policy influence. Not all of the needs of the entire clientele of an interest group can be met simultaneously, so the organizational leaders must decide which policy objectives are most important and which, within a given time, are achievable. Similarly, a clientele-oriented government department must limit and order the policy demands of its clientele; in doing so, it reduces the number of choices facing the political decision makers.

---

[32] Victor Thompson speaks of "the knowledge explosion" and of "information affluence." See: *Bureaucracy and Innovation* (Montgomery: University of Alabama, 1969), pp. 1–6.

At a point closer to the Cabinet and the prime minister, still more reduction and ordering of information occurs. The gatekeepers here are found among the advisory staff of the prime minister and Cabinet, located primarily in the Prime Minister's Office (PMO), the Privy Council Office (PCO), and the political staffs in the offices of individual ministers. While the prime minister and the Cabinet can bypass the PMO and PCO and ministerial staffs in seeking information, most information flowing from the bureaucracy and interest groups is in fact filtered through these offices. By deciding which of the information they receive is important enough to be passed on to their Cabinet "masters," by summarizing information so as to brief the ministers, and by helping to set the agenda for Cabinet and Cabinet-committee meetings, the people in these agencies play a significant role in determining what policy demands will even be considered by the priority setters. However, whether gleaned independently, or filtered through the various information gatekeepers, a great many policy ideas ultimately do come to the attention of the Cabinet; it is these that make up the raw material of Cabinet-level priority decisions.

The initial Cabinet-level decision in the process is whether to reject a policy idea outright or to consider it further. For those ideas deemed important enough to be considered further, the Cabinet must then decide which should be dealt with first and which government agency should be given the responsibility for formulating specific operational alternatives. The rejection of a policy idea outright can be considered as a negative output of the system and can have important consequences not only in terms of support for the system but also in terms of future inflow of information.

Most policy decisions at this stage will inevitably be negative ones. Although the number of demands being made on the system is potentially limitless, the resources of the system are severely limited. These resources, calculated in terms of human energy and finance, must be parsimoniously allocated to a very few policy suggestions that are deemed most worthy. These negative priority decisions are often not noticed by the media or the public, but they are important since they are effectively the same as opting for the status quo.[33]

While these Cabinet-level choices as to what should be done and when may seem relatively simple, given the reduction and ordering that has already taken place, they may not be so. Because of the complex and technical nature of most subjects of government concern today, further information is usually necessary, first in order to establish general principles and standards, and second, to measure the various choices against those standards. This information can be examined within a fourfold classification system.

i) The first type is *normative information*. This involves knowledge about the basic values of the system, which set the broadest limits for governmental action. Such information will be possessed by virtually all participants in the policy process as part of their personal value systems, acquired through the process of socialization. It is this type of information that provides vague criteria such as

---

[33] See: P. Bachrach and M.S. Baratz, *Power and Poverty* (New York: Oxford University Press, 1970), pp. 39–51.

justice, human dignity, freedom, and equality, against which people in modern western democracies automatically measure all policies. The problem with normative information is that it sets only very broad limits on governmental activity. Thus, for example, if someone suggests that we exterminate the Jews, the basic values of Canadian policy makers will prohibit consideration of such a policy alternative. However, if someone suggests nationalizing automobile insurance, the answer is not implicit in a set of shared values, but must be weighed against less fundamental criteria.

Normative information is not drawn from specialized institutions but from the shared values of virtually all Canadians and from what is often only implicit in our constitution. This means that at this level of policy determination, the political authorities in the Cabinet and Parliament do possess real decision-making power. This is more an apparent than a real power, however, since such fundamental decisions arise only very infrequently.

ii) *Political information* is the second type of information necessary in establishing policy priorities. This is information concerning the political feasibility or advisability of undertaking various policies. The criteria that must be employed in measuring the political advisability of a policy are shaped by the political institutions themselves. Thus, in the Canadian system, which features elections with a "universal" franchise, the criterion is simply how many votes a policy will ultimately win and lose for the current political office holders.

The main institutions tendering political advice to the Cabinet are the Prime Minister's Office and the political-party organization. By monitoring information flowing from political parties, pressure groups, the press, and the provincial governments, the people in the PMO and party organizations keep themselves attuned to political developments across the country. The bureaucracy also pays considerable attention to political information, for senior bureaucrats are well aware that there is no point in tendering politically unrealistic advice to the Cabinet and the prime minister. Political information is very often intuitive information based on the gut feelings of politicians or senior officials, but in the 1960s and 1970s techniques of data gathering began to replace at least some of the more intuitive methods used in the past.

iii) *Technical information* is that possessed by the policy branches within the public service. Here, technocrats are called upon to advise the politicians of the technical feasibility of various possible policy suggestions and to make estimates of cost. While technical information may be available from non-governmental sources, at the level of Cabinet decisions concerning broad policy priorities, the most significant competition for the federal departments will come from the federal central agencies such as the Treasury Board or the Department of Finance, or from the provincial bureaucracies, through the provincial cabinets and senior provincial bureaucrats.

iv) *Financial information* is relevant to the fundamental problem of funding governmental projects. When an estimate of the cost of undertaking a certain policy is provided by a line department, the financial advisors to the government in the Department of Finance, the Treasury Board Secretariat, and within individual departments must provide information as to the financial feasibility of the suggested policy. In broad terms, the financial experts within the bureaucracy must advise the government of the day whether they can afford the suggested policy and whether implementing this policy will necessitate the increase of taxes, a bigger deficit, or the cancellation of existing programs. Moreover, as governments throughout Canada have moved to limit sharply the growth of government expenditures, the financial information forwarded to Cabinet has become more and more important.

Having obtained political, technical, and financial information about the policy proposal under consideration, the Cabinet must ultimately decide whether to act at all. When there is conflicting advice, the Cabinet must make a choice. If the experts do not agree as to the feasibility of the policy suggestion, or if political exigencies conflict with substantive and technical concerns, it is a common response for the Cabinet simply not to act at all. The immediate effect here is the same as if a negative decision had been taken.

Another common response to conflicting technical information is for the Cabinet to refer the matter to a specialized body for further study. Royal commissions and task forces can often provide a vehicle through which difficult decisions can be postponed while new technical information is gathered.

Perhaps the most common occurrence of conflicting advice at the level of priority setting is that between political and technical information. In private, technocrats are very quick to accuse the politicians of "playing politics" when their advice has been rejected. What often has happened, of course, is that their technical advice has been rejected because of competing advice from the "political technocrats." In that case, sometimes, as Jacques Ellul points out, "the conflict is not between politicians and technicians, but among technicians of differing categories."[34] If the advice of the various categories of experts does point in generally the same direction, the Cabinet will usually follow that advice. While it is always conceivable that a prime minister and Cabinet can assert their positional power and refuse to heed advisors, most evidence indicates that prime ministers and Cabinets do, with a few exceptions, act according to the consensus of their advisors.

Once a number of policy ideas is adopted by the Cabinet, the next step is determining which of the policies should be tackled first. Finally, the decision must be made as to who will formulate the specific alternatives for putting the policy idea into effect. In other words, the Cabinet must decide which department or agency will take the responsibility for the next stage in the process, *policy formulation*.

The Formulation of Policy

Until this stage, the concern has been with the broad directions of public policy rather than with the specifics. At the formulation stage of the process, the object is to narrow down the number of specific choices to a few "best" ones from which the final choice can be made.

There are two analytically separate steps in the formulation of policy alternatives.

---

[34] *Technological Society*, p. 257.

First, the myriad experts within the public service must design a few workable schemes and come up with proposals as to the most effective *governing instrument* for bringing the programs into effect; second, the politicians must choose the one that appears to be the best.

Design activity initially involves narrowing down the number of possible approaches to a workable few; this becomes the responsibility of the more senior "generalists" in a department, likely in consultation with other departments and possibly with other levels of government as well. Then, those few viable choices must be "fleshed out" through the activity of a great many technocrats often with very specialized expertise. In Galbraith's terms: "Knowledge is brought to bear on the ultimate microfraction of the task; then on that in combination with some other fraction; then, on some further combination and thus on to final completion."[35]

In this sense, only very broad direction is given at the more senior bureaucratic and ministerial levels. The bulk of the responsibility for the ultimate detail of policy resides with the many highly specialized technocrats at lower levels of the hierarchy. The end product is produced incrementally as many individuals make small technical decisions that are aggregated at higher levels.

Given the incremental and aggregative nature of the process of policy design, the choice of the politician can be seriously curtailed. Departmental proposals have been produced through a hierarchy of decisions, beginning with the most highly specialized at the middle levels, and proceeding to ever more general ones at the higher levels. At each higher level of decision making, there is less choice than at the previous one, because there is proportionately less information transmitted with the proposals. By the time the politician, who is at the top of the hierarchy, comes to make the choice, it often will be simply to accept or reject the incrementally generated and monolithic conclusion of the department, which is presented to the Cabinet in the form of a three- or four-page "Ministerial Recommendation" and a seven- or eight-page "Memorandum to Cabinet." The choice, in other words, will be determined largely through the design process itself.

Politicians sometimes appear to reject "irrationally" a detailed policy proposal that has been meticulously produced by the technocrats in a department. Normally, however, policies are significantly altered or rejected at this stage only because of new political circumstances. But while a policy must continue to meet important political criteria, and while political or budgetary circumstances may temporarily stall the process, in most cases some form of output is eventually inevitable once the formulation process has commenced.

The complicated process we have spelled out here is, in fact, a simplified version of reality; at both the priority and the formulation stages of the policy process, innumerable complications can occur. The most pervasive of such complications result from the unavoidable lack of clarity in the jurisdictional boundaries between the federal and the provincial governments and among departments within those governments. As we discuss the policy process in more detail we

---

[35] *The New Industrial State*, p. 13.

will see that the Canadian political system has developed an array of devices to handle these complications as well as those already mentioned here.

The Refinement of Policy

At this stage in the policy process, the detailed policy proposal formulated by the bureaucracy and approved formally by the Cabinet must be translated into "legalese." The technical details of the policy proposal must be put into the language of legislative outputs. This task is performed by legislative drafters in the Department of Justice, after which the draft legislation must be introduced in Parliament as a bill.

The basic problem at this stage of the process is to ensure that the legislative proposal accurately reflects the aims of the priority setters, and that there are no ambiguities in the bill that might lead to administrative problems in its implementation. In addition to the legal drafters, the Standing Committees in the House of Commons play a major role in refining the legislation before it is converted to output. As well, at this time, through discussion and through Opposition probing, the government is forced to justify its policy publicly. The legislation is thus legitimized by receiving the "seal of approval" of the people's representatives.

Because of party discipline and because of the complex and technical nature of most legislation, the MP can have relatively little impact on the substance of policy at this stage. Faced with a proposal that has taken years of full-time attention on the part of perhaps a few hundred specialists of different types, the overworked MP, who is not an expert in the field in question, and who must deal with a large number of proposals per session, is unlikely to be able to make substantive criticisms that cannot be answered by the government and its advisors. There has never been a piece of government legislation defeated by the House of Commons in a majority situation, and even with a minority government, government legislation has only been defeated on rare occasions.

Members of parliament do, however, have a significant negative power at this stage. It is far from unknown for a government to withdraw legislation previously approved by Cabinet in the face of concerted opposition from members of its own caucus, and more than one significant piece of government legislation has been withdrawn in the face of concerted Opposition threats to hold up the business of the House until the government backs down. However, one should not make too much of this power. While the Opposition may stall government legislation temporarily because of their control over a considerable amount of time in the House of Commons, this does not happen often; and while the government caucus may occasionally be obstreperous, it will always, in the end, rally to the support of its leaders in Cabinet. Furthermore, even granting that a Parliament could, in legal terms, reject a government policy proposal, the power here is only negative; the *initiative* to introduce legislation still resides with the Cabinet, and if a majority government is really determined that a piece of legislation will pass, it will indeed pass Parliament.

Limitations of the Model

Any model abstracts from reality. Accordingly, it distorts some of the features of that reality. One weakness of the policy model posited above is that it attempts to represent a complex and multidimensional process in what is admittedly a linear framework. The "stages" in the policy process are established arbitrarily. In the real world, formulation begins while priorities are being established, new policy ideas emerge in the process of formulating other ones, and governmental priorities occasionally change so drastically during the process of formulation that a policy proposal may die at an advanced stage in its development. Government and, by implication, the governmental policy process is so complex that it cannot accurately be described in such simple terms. A second major weakness of the policy model is that it fails to deal adequately with the policy process in multi-jurisdictional systems. That is a failing we will attempt to rectify as we discuss the process in more detail.

But though our model oversimplifies, it does direct our attention to certain patterns that can be observed in the real world. Most of the phenomena we have described as clustering in "stages" do occur at some point in the evolution of any policy, and almost always in the order presented here. To understand the whole panorama at once would be an impossible task. It is quite simply convenient to view logically related activities as occurring at distinct stages. We are distorting reality in order to understand it! The rest of this text is, in effect, an elaboration of this model in the direction of greater reality.

PART 1

THE CULTURAL AND DEMOGRAPHIC ENVIRONMENT

ENVIRONMENT: SOCIAL AND ECONOMIC CONTEXT

The summer of 1973 was a period of rapidly rising food prices in Canada and throughout the western world. The price of steak rose from $1.29 a pound a year earlier to as high as $2.49, and hamburger meat rose from 69¢ to $1.09 a pound. The price of wheat more than doubled in a short time, and the price of a loaf of bread rose by over 33%. Gasoline which had been available for 40¢ a gallon in June rose to 55¢ in September and to over 60¢ in December. Canada — and indeed all of the western world — was caught in the initial grip of a spiralling inflation. The cry for the government to "do something" grew louder as individual Canadians felt more and more alarmed by the escalating price increases.

T hus went the introductory paragraph of this chapter in the second edition of this book. It went on to point out that the economy was booming and Canada's trade picture had seldom looked better. Many companies were enjoying record levels of revenues produced by rapidly growing personal incomes, and the rate of unemployment had declined to 5.5% from 6.2% a year earlier.

How different the world seems in the 1980s, how rapidly shifting the environment within which the political system must operate. In the ensuing fifteen years Canada has seen inflation climb to more than 12% in the early 1980s and then decline again to less than 4% in 1986. The declining inflation rates accompanied the most serious recession since the depression of the 1930s. In the recession, from 1981 to 1983, unemployment rose rapidly, from 7.5% to the 12% range, and remained stubbornly at double-digit levels until the late 1980s. The recession was brought on, and certainly made worse, by interest rates that rose in 1981 to more than 20% even for the most creditworthy borrowers; while the rates have declined from those astronomical levels, they have remained at historically high real levels into the middle of the decade. About the only sure economic prediction we can make concerning the rest of the 1980s is that, by 1990, all of these patterns will have changed again.

The ideological background in which government operates has also changed significantly. From the 1960s through the mid-1970s, there was broad agreement that government was the appropriate tool to solve most major social and economic problems. "More government" was the most frequently prescribed nostrum for our ills, and one of the major uses to which government was to be put was to defend Canada against foreign ownership and cultural domination. The neo-conservatism that constitutes the orthodoxy of many opinion leaders in the 1980s is founded on virtually the opposite point of view. Now business, particularly small business, is to be the solution to our economic problems, and, to that end, the individual entrepreneur is to be freed of the heavy hand of government. The nationalism of the 1970s has turned to continentalism. The free-trade negotiations with the United States, in progress in the mid-1980s, would have been utterly unthinkable a decade earlier.

Consider the conflicting sets of demands on Canadian governments created by the shifting social and economic environments of the mid-1980s. For example, many of the nearly one million unemployed badly need government assistance and would hardly agree that cutbacks in government expenditures could be beneficial — yet it is the economic orthodoxy of the business community that our economic troubles, including high unemployment, can be traced directly to excessive levels of government spending. Similarly, female members of the labour force are consistently paid far less than their male counterparts, even when they perform comparable jobs, and they are often isolated from advancement in female job ghettos. That situation may not change much without considerable government intervention — yet such intervention may create other distortions in the labour market (perhaps even including increased female unemployment), and such intervention is, in any case, difficult for a government to undertake in an era when bigger government is not in style. The issue in this case is joined by women's groups on one side and by business groups on the other, each pressing their claims on government with an equal vehemence; indeed, this issue, like so many others in the 1980s, is characterized by strong interests promoting strong cases on either side of an issue and with great political skills.

By early 1986, the annual federal government deficit was running at $31 billion, and the accumulated federal deficit had risen to more than $200 billion, 45% of the GNP. The accumulated deficit had become so large that paying the interest on it was itself causing the deficit to increase as a proportion of GNP. According to orthodox economic theory, that situation was causing the high interest rates that were contributing to the growth of the deficit. This Gordian knot, many analysts suggested, could be cut only if we made massive cuts in government expenditures, very large tax increases, or both.[1] Yet these "solutions" promised to worsen unemployment and would, according to that same economic theory, slow the very economic growth the government sought to foster. At the same time, other equally reputable economists could be found who would attest that the size of the deficit was not a major problem; during the Second World War, the accumulated federal deficit had been more than 100% of GNP, and yet we had handled it easily enough. Moreover, the standard ways of expressing the size of deficits did not take account of inflation, and so greatly overstated its magnitude. In addition, the "structural deficit" — the level of the deficit we would have at full levels of economic activity — was much lower than the stated deficit, and some provincial governments were even in a surplus position. According to that line of reasoning the deficit problem, while not trivial, was vastly overstated, and any attempt to reduce it precipitously would create major problems.

The conflicting demands of economic management can be multiplied almost infinitely. Consumers applaud lower oil prices; oil companies demand assistance because of them. The governments of oil-producing provinces feel far differently about oil prices than do the governments of consuming provinces. Western farmers have traditionally claimed the importance of freight-rate subsidies for grain, yet will cry foul at tariff protection for manufactured products or bail-outs of manufacturers. Corporation presidents decry government expenditures, yet line up for subsidies for their firm — "just this once, to tide us over a critical situation and save the jobs of our employees."

Now consider the underlying sources of these competing demands. In the early 1980s, inflation was endemic throughout the world and frequently higher among Canada's major trading partners than in Canada. When those trading partners, particularly the United States, raised interest rates to record levels, Canada probably had little choice but to follow. After all, there is nothing so readily transportable as money and it will tend to flow to the place where it gets the highest interest. The effect on Canada's already depressed currency could have been devastating and, since Canada imports such a large proportion of what it consumes, the effect on inflation would have been very severe. The recession created by the high interest rates of the early 1980s also afflicted all other western nations, and it seems doubtful that any economic policies undertaken by the Canadian government could have prevented it here.

Oil prices are established by a world market over which Canadian govern-

---

[1] The clearest statement of this line of reasoning is to be found in the government's own publication, *A New Direction for Canada* (Ottawa: Department of Finance, November 8, 1984).

ments have no influence. The weather in China or Russia is far more important in determining the prices received by prairie farmers for their grain than is anything that happens in Canada, and hog prices in Canada depend largely on how many hogs U.S. midwestern farmers raise and how successful they may be in lobbying the U.S. government to apply quotas to Canadian meat imports. Mineral and forest-product prices are established in world-wide markets in which even large producers such as Canada cannot assert a dominant influence. Unemployment in our resource-producing regions is determined far more by those world markets and by the behaviour of the United States, than by domestic Canadian forces.

We have spoken so far mainly of economic pressures, but other forces in the environment can create at least equally difficult demands. Consider the impact on the federal government of pressures from French Canada and in particular from Quebec. For a hundred years after Confederation, the federal public service was basically unilingual and rather few Francophones ever arrived in the upper levels. This not only made it difficult for French-speaking Canadians to communicate with the federal public service, but also under-represented French-Canadian cultural values in public administration and in the provision of policy advice. These factors were thought by federal politicians to be partially responsible for the increase in unrest in Quebec in the 1960s and 1970s. No one attributed French Canada's "Quiet Revolution" and the growth of its unquiet aspects solely to this cause, but the situation in Quebec did put pressure upon federal political decision makers. One resulting change was that the federal government decided to make the federal public service bilingual by establishing training programs for its employees and by emphasizing bilingualism in its recruitment programs. Later Parliament passed the Official Languages Act, intended to make it possible for Canadians to deal with the federal government in either official language. The representation of Francophones in the upper levels of the public service has also been greatly increased, as has the attention paid to Quebec issues in government in Ottawa. Whether these changes have been a crucial factor in the decline of separatism in Quebec may never be answered; but the programs demonstrate the type of change that may be induced within a political system through stress generated by its own social environment. The sometimes negative response engendered in other parts of Canada by what is occasionally felt to be an excessive federal concern with the problems of Quebec also illustrates that dealing with one set of problems may create others for a political system.

Few of the stresses generated by the environment of a political system are simple. What pleases French-speaking Quebeckers may not please English-speaking Albertans, and what pleases farmers may not please consumers. The reconciliation of these various demands, the balancing of one against another, is at the heart of the political process. In many cases, the competition can be reconciled through the economic system or other social systems, but in Canada today it is more and more often the political system that is called upon to allocate the limited available resources among the multitude of competing groups that make up the socioeconomic environment.

CLEAVAGE AND CONSENSUS

In all nations, some differences in the environment are of particular and long-standing importance in generating conflicting demands for governments. We refer to these as *cleavages*. In Canada they include such factors as regional disparities, income differentiation, or Francophone-Anglophone divisions.

Cleavages created by one factor are often reinforced by another. For example, the cultural cleavage between French- and English-speaking Canadians is reinforced because most Francophones live in one province (creating a geographical cleavage), and because that province is one of the less well developed in Canada (creating an economic cleavage). When cleavages are reinforced by a number of factors in this way they become more difficult for the political system.

We have described politics as a process of conflict and cooperation. The conflict arises from cleavage, but from what does the cooperation arise? Consider for a moment what happens within a group that is in conflict with another group over some issue. *Consensus*, which we define as a state of agreement among a group of people over the desirability of some end, may well form within each group over the issue in question. For instance, among residents of the western provinces there was near-unanimous agreement that the National Energy Policy of 1981 — intended to encourage greater Canadian ownership of oil and gas resources, more money for the federal government from oil and gas taxes, and gradual price changes for petroleum products—was highly undesirable. In eastern oil-consuming provinces, by contrast, there was a considerable agreement that the policy was a good one. The consensus within each group was further strengthened by the fact that several other issues based upon geographic and economic cleavages divided the residents of the western provinces from those in the east.

The term consensus is often used to refer to agreement over a particular issue. It is therefore not simply the opposite of a cleavage, because there may be substantial disagreement within the group over a wide range of other issues. While westerners were nearly unanimous on the subject of the federal energy policy in the early 1980s, they evinced broad disagreements among themselves on issues like agricultural policy or the desirability of a Charter of Rights and Freedoms in the Constitution. However, the consensus created by one issue may spill over into other areas as well, simply because the people involved come to know each other or because their leaders find the coalitions so created to be useful over longer periods of time. Moreover, conflict between large groups tends to create large areas of consensus. A war against an external enemy can do wonders to unify a divided nation.

There is, however, a second and more comprehensive sense of the term consensus, which, for the political process, is more important than that within sub-groups of a society about particular issues. It is a consensus about *how* political decisions are to be made, rather than about what those specific decisions should be. This "procedural consensus" is particularly important because it means that even if people do not agree with political decisions they will abide by them because the decisions were made in keeping with the accepted rules of the game.

Finally, in the Canadian context we can speak of consensus with respect to the legitimate ends of government. Here what we mean is that there is agreement over the basic political values that underlie our system and that set limits on the extent to which government can interfere with individual freedoms. It is this broad agreement about basic political values coupled with procedural consensus that establishes the legitimacy of the Canadian political system. If the system is viewed as legitimate by Canadians, they will abide by its rules even if they might disagree with the specific enactment. This lends an important element of stability not present in systems that lack procedural and basic-value consensus. Canadian governments are fortunate in enjoying a high degree of legitimacy, a situation that makes Canada among the easiest of nations to govern.[2]

To sum up, where there is unity over either one item or a broad range of items or procedures, we speak of a *consensus*. Where there is a disagreement concerning appropriate policies that persists over time, we speak of an *issue*. A *cleavage* is a division in society caused by long-standing cultural, economic, or geographical factors that may cause differences over any number of issues. It is the environment of a political system that generates cleavages, issues, and consensus. It is important for a political system to manage issues and cleavages in such a way as to maintain sufficient consensus for the political community to persist.

In the rest of this chapter and in the next, we will look at the global context within which the Canadian system must operate, concentrating first on the economic environment and then on Canada's relations with the United States, because those features have the greatest impact on internal political action. We will then look at the three most important types of internal cleavage in the environment of Canadian politics: geographical and general economic cleavages, cleavages based on socioeconomic stratification, and ethnic cleavages. In each case we shall first consider the underlying nature of the cleavage, and then its consequences for Canadian politics. Perhaps by the end of chapter 3 we will recognize that the Canadian political system exists in spite of quite considerable difficulties generated by its environment, and that its persistence and relative placidity are a tribute to the political skills of Canadians in building consensus in difficult circumstances.

CANADA'S INTERNATIONAL ENVIRONMENT

Canada is unique among nations in that it shares a land border with only one other nation — a giant ten times her size. It is separated from most of the rest of the world by thousands of miles of water, land, or ice. This geographic situation has led to trade patterns which are overwhelmingly dominated by exchanges

---

[2] See the report of the Macdonald Commission — the Royal Commission on the Economic Union and Development Prospects for Canada (Ottawa: Supply and Services, 1985), vol. 1, p. 7. The commissioners note: "To look out at the more than 150 member states of the United Nations should also halt any expression Canadians might give to the platitude that Canada is a difficult country to govern. . . . We should cease to strain the credulity . . . of most of the rest of the world's nations by implying that our governing task is especially arduous. The reverse is true. . . . We are a tolerant people, skilled at compromise and we have inherited a relatively peaceful society."

with the United States. Thus, in 1984, 76% of Canada's exports went to the United States and 72% of our imports came from there. Our next biggest trading partner was the European Economic Community, which took 6% of Canada's exports, while Japan took only 5% of Canadian exports and supplied 6% of our imports.[3] Canada has had a balance-of-trade surplus in every year but one since 1961, but that surplus is counterbalanced by the outflow of Canadian dollars in the form of dividends and interest payments to foreign sources, particularly in the United States.[4]

Canada is the sixth-largest trading nation in the western world, ranking behind the United States, West Germany, Great Britain, Japan, and France. About 30% of Canadian income is generated directly by exports. In terms of trade per capita, it ranks tenth. Less populous countries tend to have higher per-capita trade figures, so that in this respect Canada is outranked by such nations as Switzerland and Austria, which generate 33% and 40% of their income respectively from trade. In contrast, larger economies, such as the United States and Japan, rely on exports for 10% and 15% respectively of their GNP.[5]

Canada is in a more difficult position than most other major trading nations in two important respects. First, it does not belong to any regional trading block. Canada thus has historically lacked access to large and stable markets with relatively low or nonexistent trade barriers. This in turn has made it somewhat more difficult for Canadian industry to develop new and specialized products secure in the knowledge of a substantial market in which to sell them. In part this problem has been overcome through the negotiation of a series of special arrangements, such as the automotive trade agreements with the United States. These agreements are far more important to Canada than to the United States. About 22% of Canada's gross national product is generated by trade with the United States, and one out of every two jobs in goods-producing industry depends upon that trade.[6] By contrast, less than 3% of the U.S. GNP is directly dependent on trade with Canada.

Although the balance has been shifting towards Canadian export of secondary or manufactured goods, Canada remains principally an exporter of primary goods, such as lumber, agricultural products, and metals, and an importer of manufactured end products. Thus in 1984, 42.4% of Canadian exports were fully manufactured end products, whereas 66% of imports were fully manufactured. American exports are usually about 37% primary goods, and European Eco-

[3] Statistics Canada, *Exports: Merchandise Trade*, and Department of Finance data. Canada's trade ties with the United States have been growing in recent years and the balance of trade has reversed in Canada's favour. In 1964, the United States provided 68.9% of Canada's imports and took only 52.7% of Canadian exports; in that year, Britain bought 14.8% of Canadian exports. By 1974 the balance was essentially even, while the 1984 figures cited above show a balance in Canada's favour.

[4] Department of External Affairs, "International Trade," a paper prepared for the National Economic Conference, March, 1985. Trade-balance data is available in the Statistics Canada series and, with some time delay, in the Statistics Canada *Canada Year Book* (Ottawa: Supply & Services).

[5] M.G. Smith and Wendy Dobson, "Canada's Access to International Markets," a paper for the National Economic Conference, March 1985.

[6] Standing Senate Committee on Foreign Affairs, Canada–United States Relations, vol. 2 (Ottawa: Queen's Printer, 1978), p. 5. Data updated to reflect increased trade figures in 1985.

nomic Community exports are usually about 33% primary goods.[7] Primary goods are far more susceptible to international competition and price fluctuations than are manufactured goods, because the latter often depend upon specialized knowledge and techniques specific to one particular nation. Exports of primary goods may be suddenly and drastically affected by unpredictable factors, such as rainfall in Russia and China or the discovery of nickel deposits in New Caledonia. For example, the effects of the Depression were worsened in Canada not only by a prolonged drought in our own wheat-growing area but by good growing conditions in some other wheat-producing areas of the world. The 1981–82 recession was deeper in Canada than in the United States in large part because it was accompanied by falling value of Canadian resource exports, the prices of which are set in world markets beyond Canadian control. Over time, of course, natural resources may become more scarce, to Canada's advantage, but we should continue to anticipate wide fluctuations in price with concomitant destabilizing effects on the Canadian economy.

The whole international environment within which Canada is situated is becoming a more open one. Among all countries, in the Organization for Economic Cooperation and Development (OECD) the proportion of Gross Domestic Product (GDP) accounted for by exports has risen from 11.6% in 1960 to 20.2% in 1980.[8] In effect, nearly twice as much of the economic activity in the industrialized world is generated by trade as was the case twenty years ago.

While we lay great emphasis on Canada's relationships with the United States, it is important also to recognize that the increasingly open nature of the global environment has meant the growth of multilateral institutions and processes and the corresponding growth of Canada's participation in them. Much of the extensive growth of Canadian trade over the past decade has occurred under the aegis of the General Agreement on Tariffs and Trade (GATT), a multi-country agreement with respect to tariff levels and trade patterns. To the end of maintaining an open international environment, Canada accords very great attention to the United Nations and its associated agencies, participating more actively than some of the larger western nations. Given our high degree of exposure to the international environment and to our giant neighbour, and given the lack of any permanent formalized economic ties to other nations, such as is available to the smaller European Economic Community countries, the attention given by successive Canadian governments to the support of multilateral international institutions is readily understandable. As the Royal Commission on the Economic Union and Development Prospects for Canada (the Macdonald Commission) noted:

> Canadians have been preoccupied historically with the problem of maintaining the freedom of manoeuvre we need to preserve a separate and satisfying political identity. For these reasons we have been exceptionally open to arguments in favour of conducting international relations multilaterally. . . . These arguments were all

---

[7] 1984 Canadian figures are from Statistics Canada, *Summary of External Trade*, December 1984, Table 3. Comparative data is available in United Nations, *Yearbook of International Trade Statistics*.

[8] Organization for Economic Cooperation and Development, *Historical Statistics 1960–1981*, (OECD, Paris, 1983). The "OECD countries" are the most advanced non-Communist-bloc industrialized countries.

the more attractive because they offered a happy way of combining altruism with enlightened self-interest.[9]

Middle or Major Power?

This concentration upon multilateralism has been, to some degree, a reflection of our concept of Canada as a middle power, a concept that some have argued tends to obscure Canada's real place in the global environment and to underestimate (in characteristic Canadian fashion) our potential importance in world affairs. At the end of World War Two, Canada probably ranked fourth among world powers in economic and military capability. That was a position that could hardly have been expected to last, and it did not. The Canadian role was further obscured by the emergence of the large number of new nations resulting from the decline of colonialism and by the consequent dilution of any one nation's visibility on the world stage. For a period in the 1960s, a very high level of visibility and importance was provided for Canada in the world of international politics by our peace-keeping role, the use of Canadian military forces to buffer international conflict in such hot spots as Cyprus and the Middle East. With the presence of peace-keeping forces, which were vital in keeping some semblance of international order in the northern hemisphere in the 1960s, also went considerable diplomatic influence.

The peace-keeping role was a pragmatic response to a particular set of circumstances. It could not last beyond those circumstances and it could not be built into a perpetual foundation of Canadian world influence and diplomacy. However, the high visibility it had both at home and abroad led Canadians, and others in the diplomatic community, to equate its disappearance with a presumed decline in Canada's international role. From the late 1960s on, Canada has generally been viewed as one of a large number of "middle powers" on the world stage.

This perspective has not gone unchallenged. In 1975, James Eayrs looked at Canada's attributes, including a robust economic base and abundant natural and technological resources, and argued that these, plus the weakening of the United States' global influence, meant that Canada had the potential to be not merely a middle power, but a "foremost" power.[10] Later, in 1979, Peyton Lyon and Brian Tomlin attempted to located Canada on an international scale of capabilities — measured by military and economic strength, availability of natural resources, and diplomatic representation — and concluded that Canada should be ranked not with middle powers such as Australia or Sweden but with major powers such as Britain, France, and West Germany.[11] Table 2-1 backs up this assertion by noting that Canada's GDP ranks seventh among OECD nations, and is

---

[9] *Royal Commission on the Economic Union*, vol. 1, p. 199. (Privy Council of Canada). The analysis that follows draws from pp. 199–206 of the report. Reproduced with permission of the Minister of Supply and Services Canada.

[10] James Eayrs, "Defining a New Place for Canada in the Hierarchy of World Powers," *International Perspectives* (May–June 1975).

[11] P.V. Lyon and B. Tomlin, *Canada as an International Actor* (Toronto: Macmillan, 1979).

TABLE 2-1
SHARES IN OECD TOTALS OF GDP:
in current dollars at current exchange rates (%)

	Percentage Share
Canada	4.14
United States	41.84
Japan	14.76
Australia	1.99
New Zealand	.29
Austria	.86
Belgium	1.02
Denmark	.72
Finland	.63
France	6.63
Germany	8.34
Greece	.44
Iceland	.03
Ireland	.23
Italy	4.51
Luxembourg	.04
Netherlands	1.69
Norway	.70
Portugal	.26
Spain	2.02
Sweden	1.17
Switzerland	1.24
Turkey	.64
United Kingdom	5.81
Yugoslavia	—

On an OECD total of 7,829.92 billion U.S. dollars.

Source: OECD, *National Accounts, 1960–1983* (Paris: Department of Economics and Statistics, 1984),
   vol. 1, pp. 114, 124.

far larger than the "middle powers" such as Sweden, Norway, or Australia, to which it is often compared. For example, the Canadian economy is three and one-half times as large as that of Sweden, more than twice as large as Australia's and five times as big as that of Austria. It is also seldom recognized by Canadians that the Canadian economy is more than 70% as large as that of Britain and half the size of that of West Germany. As Lyon and Tomlin discovered, neither diplomats nor independent foreign-policy analysts recognized this situation, in large part perhaps because of Canadian diffidence about claiming a position onstage. More recently still, David De Witt and and John Kirkton have concluded that, by the early 1980s, the expansion of Canada's relative capabilities had led to the adoption of a more independent and autonomous foreign policy reflecting an ability to pursue Canadian interests bilaterally and, if necessary, in competition with other states.[12]

[12] David B. De Witt and John J. Kirkton, *Canada as a Principal Power* (Toronto: Wiley, 1983).

Certainly these analyses turn the conventional view of Canada as a "middle power" on its head, but they are compellingly backed up by analyses of human and natural resources and of economic power and potential. It is important for Canadians to recognize this power and potential as they operate in world forums. It would be singularly unfortunate to minimize Canada's power and opportunities to serve both its own and broader international interests.

Canada and the United States

Whatever the appropriate assessment of Canada's potential influence in the world, its preoccupation with the United States is readily understandable. During a visit to Washington early in 1969, Pierre Trudeau suggested to his U.S. audience, "Living next to you is in some ways like sleeping with an elephant, no matter how friendly and even-tempered is the beast . . . one is affected by his every twitch and grunt."[13] The elephant in this case has a population ten times as large as Canada's and generates twelve times the gross national product. More than 90% of Canadians live within three hundred miles of the United States, and most live in a narrow strip within a hundred miles of the border.[14]

Trade and Trade Policy   Some further measure of the importance of Canada-United States trade relations can be taken from the following:

> The largest trade flow that has ever taken place between two countries is the one now occurring across the Canada-U.S. border; this trade is almost 50 per cent larger than the next largest trade flow — that between the U.S. and Japan. Three-quarters of Canadian exports go to the U.S.; and consequently, about one-fifth of Canadian GNP and employment is generated by sales to the U.S. From the American point of view, this Canada-U.S. trade relationship is not as critical, but it is still extremely important. Not only does the U.S. trade more with Canada than with second-place Japan or any other country; the U.S. exports more to the province of Ontario alone than to Japan (1983 estimate: $27.0 vs. $21.9 billion). Therefore, maintaining a healthy trade relationship is a priority concern for the U.S. as well.[15]

Periodically during Canadian history, the deep trading relationship with the United States, combined with some degree of dissatisfaction with Canada's economic

---

[13] Prime Minister Trudeau in a speech to the Washington Press Club, March 25, 1969.

[14] In addition to specific sources cited in the chapter, the reader should consult Janet Morchain, ed., *Sharing a Continent* (Toronto: McGraw-Hill Ryerson, 1973); J. Pammett and B. Tomlin, eds., *The Integration Question* (Toronto: Addison-Wesley, 1984); Andrew Axline *et al.*, eds., *Continental Community* (Toronto: McClelland & Stewart, 1974); J.S. Dickey, *Canada and the American Presence* (New York: New York University Press, 1975); J. Hutcheson, *Dominance and Dependence* (Toronto: McClelland and Stewart, 1978); C.F. Foran, *Economic Interdependence, Autonomy and Canadian American Relations* (Montreal: Institute for Research on Public Policy, 1983); Maureen Appel Molot and Glen Williams, "The Political Economy of Continentalism," in M.S. Whittington and G. Williams, *Canadian Politics in the 1980s* (Toronto: Methuen, 1984); Michael Tucker, *Canadian Foreign Policy* (Toronto: McGraw-Hill, 1980); Stephen Clarkson, *Canada and the Reagan Challenge* (Ottawa: Canadian Institute for Economic Policy, 1982); Joseph Nye and Robert Keohane, *Power and Interdependence* (Boston: Little, Brown, 1977); and John H. Redekop, "Continentalism: The Key to Canadian Politics" in J. Redekop, ed., *Approaches to Canadian Politics* (Toronto: Prentice-Hall, 1983). Redekop has also provided a valuable annotated bibliography on the subject.

[15] R.J. Wonnacott, "Trade Liberalization," a paper prepared for the National Economic Conference, Ottawa, March 1, 1985, p. 1.

performance, combines to push the issues of freer trade with the United States to the forefront of Canadian politics. High points of Canadian interest within this idea have been reached in 1910–11, immediately after World War Two, and again during the mid-1980s. Canadians are perpetually ambivalent about this relationship with the United States, an ambivalence reflected in trade matters no less than elsewhere.[16]

However, the tendency has been towards freer trade relations over the past three decades, to the point where, by 1985, successive rounds of tariff-cutting have meant that 80% of Canadian exports to the United States enter tariff-free. It is important to note, however, that up to the mid-1980s, and with some significant exceptions such as the automotive trade agreement, most of the reductions in tariff have occurred as a result of multilateral exercises, particularly the General Agreemeent on Tariffs and Trade (GATT), rather than because of bilateral arrangements. Conspicuously absent has been any across-the-board arrangements similar to those of the European common market.

Of particular concern for Canadians in the mid 1980s were two factors. One was the failure of the Canadian economy to recover rapidly and fully from the deep recession of 1981–82, with the resulting persistence of very high levels of unemployment. The second was the increasing tendency towards protectionist trade policies in the United States. While most of these were not aimed directly at Canada, the overwhelming importance of Canada-U.S. trade has meant that such policies have a very strong effect in Canada.

The belief that Canadian industrial growth can best be enhanced through direct access to the huge markets south of the border is a strongly held one among Canadian economists and business people. The fear of the effects of further U.S. protectionist measures is at least equally great. These beliefs and concerns have constituted a powerful force to encourage Canadian governments to look with great interest at some closer form of bilateral trading arrangements.

However, the ambivalence of Canadians about closer ties to the United States deserves emphasis. The fear of U.S. cultural domination, described below, is a strong one. So is the concern that Canadian foreign policy could become totally

---

[16] There is a vast economic literature on Canadian trade policy and trade relations with the United States. The Royal Commission on the Economic Union and Development Prospects for Canada has covered the issues extensively, and has published several summary research papers on the subject. Two of the papers are: John M. Curtis, "Which Way: Canadian Trade Policy in a Changing World Economy," and R.J. Wonnacott, in "Canada/U.S. Free Trade: Problems and Opportunities" (in volume 1 of the commission report, pp. 297–377). The report was published in 1985 in Toronto by the University of Toronto Press. Other comprehensive studies include Donald J. Daly, *Canada in an Uncertain World Environment* (Montreal: Institute for Research on Public Policy, 1982); Richard G. Harris and David Cox, *Trade, Industrial Policy and Canadian Manufacturing* (Toronto: Ontario Economic Council, 1983); Frank Stone, *Canada, the GATT and the International Trade System* (Montreal, Institute for Research on Public Policy, 1984); Government of Canada, *Canadian Trade Policy for the 1980s* (Ottawa: Supply and Services, 1983); Keith A.J. Hay, "Canadian Trade Policy in the 1980s," *International Perspectives*, July–August, 1982; Glen Williams, *Not for Export: The Political Economy of Canada's Arrested Industrialization* (Toronto: McClelland and Stewart, 1983); Paul and Ronald Wonnacott, "Free Trade Between the United States and Canada: Fifteen Years Later," *Canadian Public Policy*, vol. 7, October 1982; B.W. Wilkinson, "Canada-U.S. Trade Policy Relations," *Canadian Public Policy*, vol. 10, March 1984; and Senate of Canada, Standing Committee on Foreign Affairs, *Canada-United States Relations, Vol. 3: Canada's Trade Relations with the United States* (Ottawa, 1982).

dominated by the United States. There would be major economic adjustments and, while some industries could experience rapid growth, others could well decline. The regional impacts of freer trade would be uneven and unpredictable. Once the Canadian economy had adjusted to freer trade, the United States could still abrogate any arrangement with little damage to itself but with catastrophic consequences for Canada. Ultimately, some people fear that even Canadian political sovereignty could be threatened if the relationship were successful and grew deeper. Little wonder then that Donald Macdonald, former Finance Minister and chairman of the Royal Commission on the Economic Union, while advocating freer trade arrangements, described them as a "leap of faith." How the issue will be resolved in the immediate future we cannot determine at the time of this writing. That it will be a persisting one in Canadian politics we can be certain.[17]

Defence and Foreign Affairs Sharing a continent with the United States has significant consequences for Canada's military posture as well. As recently as 1905 the Canadian military made substantial defence preparations against the United States. Even between the two world wars, the only defence plans drawn up by the Canadian military were for an attack from the south. Fears of a direct attack have finally vanished or, at least, Canadians have recognized the dubious benefits of defence against an immensely improbable military enemy, which, in any case, could not be resisted.

In a more significant sense, however, Canada's proximity to the United States still shapes Canadian defence policy. It makes Canada strategically one target with the United States; an attacker would hardly discriminate between these two parts of North America. The clearest evidence of the impact of that feature of Canada's global position is participation in NORAD, the North American Aerospace Defence Command. Under the terms of NORAD, the effective commander of Canadian air forces in time of international crisis is the American NORAD commander. Canadian participation in NORAD is not really optional: the American presence on our doorstep would make abstention difficult and withdrawal impossible. That does not mean that there is no room for independent manoeuvre in defence policy, but it does mean that the room is very sharply circumscribed.

In fact, most western countries seem to move broadly together in defence policy. The early Liberal governments of Prime Minister Pierre Trudeau were less than enthusiastic about defence expenditures, and, as a result, those constituted a steadily diminishing proportion of federal budgets during the first decade of his government. However, this was also true of many other countries, including even the United States, during the early 1970s, as social programs took up a larger share of public expenditures. While the Conservative government of Prime Minister Brian Mulroney is widely viewed as having responded to the urgings of the U.S. government by initiating increases in Canadian defence expenditures, in fact its Liberal predecessor had already made a commitment to make defence the

---

[17] A valuable summary of current ideas from Canadian political scientists may be found in Charles Pentland, "North American Integration and the Canadian Political System," published as a research paper by the Royal Commission on the Economic Union and Development Prospects for Canada, Ottawa, 1985.

fastest-growing area of government expenditures two years before it left office, and at about the same time as most NATO allies began to make similar increases. While the newly elected Conservative government at first appeared to embrace President Ronald Reagan's "Star Wars" initiatives with enthusiasm, before long it appeared to develop considerable reservations about going too far in active support of the initiative, a stance close to that of Canada's European allies. Overall, however, limited manoeuvrability within the American sphere of influence and in the broad context of NATO policies is likely the most appropriate description of the range of the possible with regard to Canadian defence policy.[18]

Cultural Domination Perhaps more important in the long run than the various military and foreign-policy ramifications of American proximity to Canada is cultural domination. A number of factors facilitate the impact of American culture on Canada.[19] American television reaches almost everyone in Canada. English-Canadian stations carry a great deal of American programming, and, more important, some 55% of Canadians are in direct range of American television stations; 90% can receive them on cable systems; and everyone is within the range of satellite systems. Thus, of fifty-one viewing options on cable television in central Ontario between eight and eleven PM on Thursday, May 2, 1985, thirty-four were American in origin, six were British imports running on U.S. channels, and eleven were Canadian. Most of the Canadian shows were news or talk programs and none were dramas.[20] In areas where both Canadian and American sources are available, the latter are generally preferred. Bureau of Broadcast Measurement statistics for the week of March 14 to 20, 1985, showed that not one of the top-ten viewing choices in Canada was a Canadian program.[21] In 1973, a survey in Toronto showed only 13% of evening viewers watching Canadian programs, and in prime time only 9%.[22]

Children and adults alike pick up cultural images from television. "How many . . . Canadians want to concern themselves with the special concerns of Quebec or the Inuit when their eyes are fixed on Dallas?" asked one veteran Canadian broadcaster.[23] John Meisel, at the time chairman of the Canadian Radio-television and Telecommunications Commission, remarked in a speech in 1981

[18] For further discussions and elaborations of Canada's defence posture, and in particular her place in NORAD and NATO see: J.W. Holmes, *Canada and the United States: Political and Security Issues* (Toronto: Canadian Institute of International Affairs, 1970); Jan B. McLin, *Canada's Changing Defence Policy, 1957–63* (Toronto: Copp Clark, 1967); L. Hertzman, John Warnock, and Thomas Hockin, *Alliances and Illusions: Canada and the NATO-NORAD Question* (Edmonton: Hurtig, 1969); and N. Hillmer and G. Stevenson, *Foremost Nation: Canadian Foreign Policy and a Changing World* (Toronto: McClelland and Stewart, 1977).

[19] For an extensive discussion, see S.M. Crean, *Who's Afraid of Canadian Culture* (Toronto: General Publishing, 1970). The underlying factors have remained the same since 1970.

[20] David Wesley, editorial, *TV Guide*, week of May 11–18, 1985, n. p.

[21] Wesley, *TV Guide.*

[22] Redekop, *Approaches to Canadian Politics*, p. 51.

[23] F.W. Peers, "Canada and the U.S.: Comparative Approaches to Broadcasting Policy," Canadian-U.S. Conference on Communication Policy, Centre for Inter-American Relations, New York, 1983; cited in "The Mass Media and Politics: An Overview," F.J. Fletcher and Daphne Gotlieb Taras, in M.S. Whittington and G. Williams, eds., *Canadian Politics in the 1980s* (Toronto: Methuen, 1984), p. 201.

that television "has contributed significantly to the loss of regional and national identities" and to the "Americanization of Canada."[24]

Much of French Canada is also within range of American television, but fewer French Canadians watch American channels because of the language barrier. The Canadian content of the French network of the CBC is much higher than that of the English network, so the television exposure of French Canadians to foreign culture has been less than that of English Canadians. The language barrier has been instrumental in helping to preserve French-Canadian culture from the overwhelming geographical proximity of the United States.

The problems of preserving a cultural identity in English-speaking Canada are compounded when the effects of radio, magazines, and other segments of the mass media are added. In 1969, 95% of all the various magazines available in Canadian retail outlets were American imports. For decades, the two American giants — *Time* and *Reader's Digest* — took about 40% of total magazine advertising in Canada. By the mid-1970s, *Reader's Digest* had a monthly circulation of 1,250,000, and *Time* of 550,000. In 1976, Canadian-content legislation brought about the demise of the Canadian edition of *Time*, at least temporarily, but many subscribers simply switched to the U.S. edition, and so did the advertisers while the Senate Committee on the Mass Media noted, "We spend more money buying American comic books than we do on seventeen leading Canadian-owned magazines."[25] Nonetheless the situation has improved during the 1980s. The circulation of *Reader's Digest* has remained constant. That of *Time* magazine has declined to 335,000 while *Maclean's* has risen steadily to a paid circulation of 650,000 by 1986 and, in combination with its French language sister publication *L'actualité*, sells over 900,000 copies weekly.[26]

While the military implications of proximity to the United States are often viewed by Canadians with resignation if not applause, and while cultural domination is frequently decried, it is the economic dimension of United States-Canadian relations that receives the most attention. We have already indicated the closeness of trade ties between the two neighbours, but there are other crucial aspects of Canadian-United States economic relations that deserve attention. The most important of these is the issue of foreign investment.

The Foreign Investment Question

In the late 1960s and throughout the 1970s, one of the dominant issues of Canadian politics was foreign ownership of Canadian industry. Concerns about foreign ownership have abated, at least temporarily, with trade rather than ownership patterns tending to dominate the agenda. Indeed, in the 1980s the government

---

24 J. Meisel, cited in Whittington and Williams. There is recognition of this fact at many levels in Canadian government, and there are even occasional attempts to counteract the problem. For example, in 1970 the Canadian Radio-television and Telecommunications Commission (CRTC) announced a series of steps to increase the Canadian content of radio, prime-time television, and cablevision services. This has no doubt helped, but what viewers watch cannot be dictated, and English-Canadian viewers still watch American television.

25 Cited in Redekop, *Canadian Politics*, p. 48.

26 Data are from *Canadian Advertising Rates and Data*, July, 1986.

TABLE 2-2
CANADIAN BALANCE OF INTERNATIONAL INDEBTEDNESS,
1926-1975 (PORTFOLIO AND DIRECT INVESTMENT)

	1926	1939	1949	1959	1969	1975	1980
Gross liabilities (in billions of dollars)	6.4	7.4	9.3	23.8	46.9	75.6	129.0
Per cent held in U.S.	55.0	61.0	69.0	71.0	74.0	75.0	69.0
Per cent held in U.K.	42.0	35.0	19.0	14.0	10.0	8.0	6.6
Gross National Product (in billions of dollars)	5.1	5.6	16.3	32.3	79.8	165.4	298.0
Foreign indebtedness as percent of GNP	125.0	132.0	57.0	74.0	59.0	46.0	43.0

Source: *Canada Year Book*, 1972, pp. 1177 and 1211; *Canada Year Book*, 1978–79, pp. 871–872; and Statistics Canada, *Canada's International Investment Position*, 1979–1980.

of Canada has tended to define the problem as one of too little rather than too much foreign investment. That change is motivated in part by a concern to create jobs through investment in a period of relatively high unemployment, and partially by a quite substantial change that occurred in the 1970s in the flow of investment into and out of Canada.[27]

Table 2-2 indicates two basic trends in foreign investment in Canada. First, the ratio of foreign investment to Gross National Product has been decreasing. Second, the proportion of holdings by Americans has steadily increased as a proportion of foreign investment but has been decreasing through the 1970s and 1980s as a proportion of all Canadian industrial investment.

Over the long term, the first point is somewhat deceptive because the nature of foreign investment has changed significantly since 1926. The normal form of investment before World War Two was "portfolio" investment — primarily in bonds or debentures, which gave the investor little managerial control over the firm. Since 1945, holdings have increasingly been in the form of direct or equity investment, that is, in the shares of a firm, which may give the investor control over what the company actually does.[28] Moreover, in accounting for the amount of international indebtedness, Statistics Canada uses the "book value" of foreign-controlled assets — a value reflecting the original cost of assets rather than their

[27] There is an immense economic literature on the effects of foreign ownership in Canada, and it cannot all be cited here. The classic works are: *The Report of the Task Force and Foreign Ownership and the Structure of Canadian Industry* (Ottawa: Queen's Printer, 1965); A.E. Safarian, *Foreign Ownership of Canadian Industry* (Toronto: McGraw-Hill, 1965); Kari Levitt, *Silent Surrender* (Toronto: 1970); and A.E. Litvak, *Dual Loyalty: The Government of Canada, Foreign Direct Investment in Canada* (Ottawa: Queen's Printer, 1972). A balanced assessment of the current situation may be found in A.E. Safarian, "Government Control of Foreign Business," published by the Royal Commission of the Economic Union in 1986. Safarian's study also contains an extensive current bibliography.

[28] See I.A. Litvak, C.J. Maule, and R.D. Robinson, *Dual Loyalty* (Toronto: McGraw-Hill Ryerson, 1971), p. 2. In 1926 there was twice as much portfolio investment as direct investment. The situation is now reversed.

TABLE 2-3
NON-RESIDENT CONTROL* AS A PERCENTAGE OF SELECTED
CANADIAN INDUSTRIES, 1926–1981

	1926	1939	1948	1963	9169	1976	1981
Percentage of Total Controlled by All Non-Residents							
Manufacturing	35	38	43	60	60	57	50
Petroleum and natural gas	—	—	—	74	74	73	44
Mining and smelting	38	42	40	59	70	57	46
Railways	3	3	3	2	2	1	—
Other utilities	20	26	24	4	6	4	—
TOTAL	17	21	25	34	35	33	26
Percentage of Total Sector Controlled by U.S. Residents							
Manufacturing	30	32	39	46	47	43	38
Petroleum and natural gas	—	—	—	62	60	57	34
Mining and smelting	32	38	37	52	59	44	31
Railways	3	3	3	2	2	1	1
Other utilities	20	26	24	4	4	4	4
TOTAL	15	19	22	27	28	26	20

*Control is computed as percentage of total output in that sector from companies more than 50% foreign-owned.

Source: *International Investment Position, 1975* (Ottawa: Statistics Canada, 1979), p. 35. The 1981 figures are adapted from a Statistic Canada Bulletin, 26 January, 1983, cited in A.E. Safarian, "Government Control of Foreign Business Investment," a research report prepared by the Royal Commission on the Economic Union (Toronto: University of Toronto Press, 1985).

value after inflation — whereas GNP figures reflect the full impact of inflation. Thus, when uninflated book values are compared to inflated GNP figures, the magnitude of direct foreign investment is understated. However, even with these caveats, the fact remains that foreign investment is not now as great as it once was: it has been decreasing consistently for more than a decade.

Table 2-3 indicates the changes in the percentage of Canadian industry controlled by non-residents and by United States residents. The table again indicates that the extent of foreign control over Canadian industry peaked in the mid to late 1960s. The table also demonstrates that not all Canadian industries have fallen under foreign control. For example, at various times Canadian governments have decided that banking and finance, railways, communications, insurance, and uranium mining were too vital to be allowed to fall into the hands of foreigners.[29] Other industries, particularly petroleum, once heavily foreign-controlled, have shifted to Canadian hands during the past decade.

Another indication of the change over time in the flows and patterns of investment can be seen by considering the Canadian situation in comparative perspective. In the early 1960s, Canada accounted for 16% of the flow of inward investment among OECD countries. By the later 1970s, that figure had declined to 3%, and by the mid-1980s, Canada had become a net exporter of capital. By contrast, the proportion of OECD capital inflows going to the United States has

[29] Litvak, *Dual Loyalty*, p. 7.

increased from 3% to 41% since the 1960s. It is also important to emphasize that the Canadian situation is not unique: several large developed nations, including Italy, France, West Germany, and Britain, have between 20% and 30% of the capital in their manufacturing sector owned abroad, compared to Canada's 26%. At the lower end of the scale are Sweden and Norway, in the 10% range, and the United States and Japan, in the 5% range.[30]

Paradoxically, some responsibility for the high degree of U.S. ownership in the Canadian economy must be laid squarely on a policy that was designed to avoid American domination, Sir John A. Macdonald's famous "National Policy" of the nineteenth century. The national policy had three prongs: build railways, encourage immigration, and erect tariff barriers. The first two components of the policy did serve the purpose of pre-empting United States settlement in the northwest and preserving that territory for Canada. The third, designed to encourage Canadian industry, may have been successful in the short run but ultimately backfired. Foreign firms — first British and later American — seeing a lucrative territory for their investments, moved in behind the tariff barriers that protected them from competition. They then set up miniature replicas of their home operations, or "branch plants," but without any attempt to develop and implement new technology or to develop markets outside Canada; those markets were reserved for the parent firms. To add to the problem, most of the plants they established were too small to take advantage of economies of scale, reducing the potential level of productivity in Canada. Meanwhile, other foreign entrepreneurs, who must sometimes be given credit for seeing more possibilities in Canadian resource industries than did Canadians themselves, invested in primary industry and exported the primary goods to their own home basis to be made into manufactured goods, thus providing jobs for workers in other nations. It is extremely difficult for governments to foresee all the consequences of the policies they make, and in this case, one consequence of Macdonald's national policy was, ironically, exactly the opposite of what was intended.

Another argument often advanced to explain the prevalence of American ownership in the Canadian economy is that Americans have provided necessary capital that was not otherwise available. Table 2-4 indicates, however, that Canada's need for foreign capital is not nearly as great as often believed; the capital that has been used by foreign entrepreneurs to expand Canadian history is mainly Canadian, not foreign. Moreover, Canadians are themselves large foreign investors. Canadian individuals and firms now invest more abroad and in the United States than foreigners invest in Canada. At no time since records have been kept has foreign capital ever accounted for more than 30% of total new investment in a given year.[31] In 1980, only about 15% of the capital used to expand Canadian industry came from foreign sources. Kari Levitt has put the case bluntly:

> It is simply not true that Canada is short of capital. The expensive infrastructure required by her peculiar geography has long been put in place and paid for. . . .

[30] Data are from A.E. Safarian, "Government Control of Foreign Business Investment."

[31] Litvak, *Dual Loyalty*, pp. 21–22; and Statistics Canada, *The Canadian Balance of International Payments.* Data is usually available only after four- to five-year delay.

The brutal fact is that acquisition of control by U.S. companies over the commodity-producing sectors of the Canadian economy has largely been financed from corporate savings deriving from the sale of Canadian resources, extracted and processed by Canadian labour, or from the sales of branch plant manufacturing businesses to Canadian consumers at tariff-protected prices. Thus, over the period of 1957 to 1964, U.S. direct investments in manufacturing, mining, and petroleum secured 73 per cent of their funds from retained earnings and depreciation reserves, a further 12 per cent from Canadian banks and other intermediaries and only 15 per cent in the form of new funds from the United States. Furthermore, throughout the period, payout of dividends, interest, royalties, and management fees exceeded the inflow of new capital.[32]

TABLE 2-4
USE OF FOREIGN AND DOMESTIC RESOURCES IN GROSS CAPITAL
FORMATION IN CANADA, SELECTED YEARS 1950–1977

	1950	1955	1960	1965	1977	1980
Gross capital formation (in billions of dollars)	4.5	6.6	8.7	13.7	47.6	69.0
Per cent from domestic sources	84.0	74.0	74.0	79.0	80.0	85.0

Source: Adapted from Statistics Canada, *The Canadian Balance of International Payments and International Investment Position, 1963, 1964, 1965, 1979, 1980* (Ottawa: Queen's Printer), p. 76; cited in Litvak, *Dual Loyalty*, p. 3. The 1977 and 1980 figures are from Statistics Canada, *Canada's International Investment Position, 1979 and 1980* (July 1984), p. 91.

What is the impact of foreign, largely U.S., control of large segments of Canadian industry? Some analysts have argued that foreign control may be undesirable for reasons related to both economic growth and economic stability.[33] To the extent that Canada depends on the investment decisions of foreign-controlled corporations, the economy and the jobs of Canadians are vulnerable to changes in the growth patterns of those firms. Those patterns will depend in turn on how the firms view their growth prospects elsewhere in the world. Since 1950 foreign corporations have concentrated their investments (some of which are financed by the earnings of Canadian subsidiaries) in Europe, and later in developing areas such as Korea, Hong Kong, or Taiwan, which have low labour costs, rather than in Canada.

Concern has also been expressed that foreign-owned firms do not carry out research and development activities in Canada; that insufficient numbers of Canadians have access to management roles; that exports to third countries are usually from the home-base plant; that supplies are not purchased in Canada; and that the firms evade taxation by various subterfuges.[34] Yet it bears emphasis that "with regard to most of these activities, researchers have found that, in fact, American affiliates perform as well, if not better, than comparable Canadian

[32] Levitt, *Silent Surrender*, (New York: Liverright, 1970) pp. 63–64.

[33] Litvak, *Dual Loyalty*, pp. 21–22.

[34] Litvak, *Dual Loyalty*, p. 22.

firms but worse than comparable American firms in the U.S."[35] Nonetheless, after considering all these factors, a 1972 federal government study, *Foreign Direct Investment in Canada* (The Gray Report), was introduced by the statement that:

> The high and growing degree of foreign and, particularly, U.S. control of Canadian business activity has led to a Canadian industrial structure which largely reflects the growth priorities of foreign corporations [and has] . . . led to the establishment of "truncated" firms for which many important functions are performed abroad by the parent company with the result that Canadian capacities or activities in these areas is stultified. . . . These developments have made it more difficult for the government to control the domestic national economic environment. They have also influenced the development of the social, political, and cultural environment in Canada.

However, the other side of the story, too, deserves emphasis. Many Canadian corporations are not truncated at all, being instead major multinational enterprises. Some foreign multinationals may be truncated, but others have chosen to concentrate production of goods in Canada, which are then distributed worldwide. The technology that is brought into Canada through multinational enterprises is an important contributor to Canadian growth and productivity.

A.E. Safarian states:

> From the viewpoint of a developed host country such as Canada, both theory and evidence suggest that the most likely outcome of such investment is macroeconomic benefits, with their size depending on the policies followed by the host country in terms of taxation and competition in particular. . . . There is not strong evidence for a view, widely held in Canada, that foreign control in itself leads to truncated subsidiaries. In brief, macro-economic analysis suggests that gains are likely, micro-economic analysis that gains are possible and sovereignty costs are not inevitable. . . . Everything depends on the [government] policy response to such firms.[36]

Extra-Territoriality The problems posed by foreign subsidiaries cannot be understood or dealt with solely in economic terms, however. There are also issues of sovereignty and the control by a nation of its own economy, society, and territory.[37] Perhaps the major political problem created by the more than ten thousand American-owned factories in Canada is that of extra-territoriality — the application of the laws of one nation within the boundaries of another. In 1957 a Canadian trader charged that Ford Canada had refused to ship trucks to China because of fear that the parent company would be penalized under the United States Treasury's Foreign Assets Control Regulations and the United States' Trading with the Enemy Act. That case was never satisfactorily resolved, in part because the order itself was mysteriously withdrawn by the Chinese when it began to

---

[35] Litvak, *Dual Loyalty*, p. 22.

[36] A.E. Safarian, "Government Control of Foreign Business Investment," p. 1.

[37] This issue receives extensive treatment in Glen Williams, *Not For Export* (Toronto: McClelland and Stewart, 1983).

appear possible that it would be filled. In 1958 John Diefenbaker obtained assurance from President Eisenhower that, to quote Diefenbaker:

> If cases arose in the future where the refusal of orders by companies operating in Canada might have an effect on Canadian economic activity, the U.S. government would consider favourably exempting the parent company in the U.S. from the application of foreign asset control regulations with respect to such orders.[38]

Yet incidents continued, and some Canadian subsidiaries shied away from trade with North Vietnam, North Korea, and Cuba in the 1960s and 1970s, for fear of the U.S. Trading with the Enemy Act or adverse U.S. reaction, which might affect their markets.[39] The United States regulations were changed in 1969 to permit U.S. subsidiaries to trade with China, but, as some analysts point out: "This change in policy clearly confirms that these policies do have an extraterritorial reach."[40]

More recent examples confirm that the Trading with the Enemy Act may still potentially hamper the activity of Canadian subsidiaries of American firms. In 1974, a Montreal locomotive company, MLW-Worthington Ltd., had arranged to build twenty-five locomotives for Cuba. Trouble arose, however, when the American parent company, Studebaker-Worthington, Inc., felt obliged under the Trading with the Enemy Act to seek a licence for the transaction from the American government.[41] Ultimately, after considerable controversy in the Canadian press and very substantial pressure from the Canadian government, the board of directors of the Canadian subsidiary did vote to go ahead with the sale, although the American members of the board voted against it in the hope of avoiding personal prosecution by the U.S. government.[42] The U.S. government chose not to intervene directly to block the sale to Cuba, but it was clear that the Act could indeed still affect the behaviour of the Canadian company.

In 1983 and 1984, in an action with more impact in Europe than in Canada, the U.S. government attempted to use the Act to block the export of gas pipeline technology to the USSR via subsidiaries located abroad. In 1985, U.S. Treasury officials threatened to monitor Canadian subsidiaries of U.S. firms for trade with Nicaragua, which the U.S. administration had decided was "the enemy."[43] No action resulted, however, after the minister of external affairs made clear that Canada considered this threat unacceptable.

In application, the Trading with the Enemy Act has tended to be rather a paper tiger; whenever the affected country has protested loudly enough, the American administration has tended to back down. It should therefore probably be viewed more as an annoyance than a real day-to-day threat.

[38] The quotation is from the House of Commons debates (Hansard), July 14, 1958, p. 2142, and is quoted in Litvak, *Dual Loyalty*, p. 25.

[39] Litvak, *Dual Loyalty*, pp. 25–26.

[40] Litvak, *Dual Loyalty*, p. 26.

[41] Geoffrey Stevens, "Like the Bad Old Days," *Globe and Mail*, February 27, 1974, p. 6.

[42] *Globe and Mail*, Saturday, March 9, 1974.

[43] *Globe and Mail*, May 8, 1985.

There have been several other instances when other U.S. regulations have been applied to the Canadian political system through U.S.-controlled firms operating in Canada. In January 1968 the United States introduced mandatory controls on foreign investment by U.S. companies. This resulted in an outflow of Canadian funds to the United States, and it was not until March that Canada was able to gain some exemptions to avoid too much damage to the economy. Despite the existence of a U.S.-Canada consultative committee to discuss problems such as these, the Canadian government had no warning of the move or of similar and even more drastic moves by the United States in August 1971. Balance-of-payment difficulties in the United States can thus be transmitted to Canada via subsidiaries of U.S. firms.

More broadly, U.S. antitrust legislation applies to all aspects of the operations of U.S.-controlled firms. In some cases the U.S. legislation may conflict with Canadian government policy when Canada attempts to encourage the creation of firms of sufficient size to be internationally competitive. A detailed study of twenty-one such cases between 1945 and 1971 concluded that the Canadian government was eventually satisfied with the outcome in the majority. However, there is no comparable study for the post-1974 period.[44]

Throughout the 1970s and in the early 1980s, Canada attempted to counter the problems created by foreign investment. There are laws, already mentioned, relating to the level of foreign investment in key sectors, there is a 15% withholding tax on interest and dividends to foreigners, and, such as it is, much of the financial-disclosure legislation currently on the books in Canada is aimed at foreign companies. In December 1973 the federal government passed legislation that set up a Foreign Investment Review Agency (FIRA) to advise Cabinet on the acceptability of the takeover of Canadian companies or the expansion into Canada by foreign corporations. The National Energy Program of 1980 was aimed at greatly reducing foreign (U.S.) ownership of Canadian petroleum resources.

There have also been several bilateral agreements with the U.S. government, such as that made by John Diefenbaker and Dwight Eisenhower in 1958. With the exception of the automobile agreements, which, in any case, deal with trade rather than directly with investment, the effects of these have been judged by some commentators to be a mixed success.

> To date the bilateral consultations and arrangements between Canada and the U.S. have rarely realized Canadian objectives because the political bargaining takes place between two very unequal partners. Canada is fully able to articulate the problems to the U.S. government but it lacks the political power to negotiate mutually beneficial solutions. . . . In short, as the two economies become more closely integrated along "continentalist" [North American] lines, the threat to Canadian political sovereignty is escalated. . . . Experience to date has shown that Canada alone has little political bargaining power, vis-à-vis the U.S. in cases where the loci of decision-making power are centered in U.S. multinational corporations,

---

[44] David Leyton-Brown, "The Multi-National Enterprise and Conflict in Canadian-American Relations," *International Organization* 4, 1974, pp. 733–53.

and where the U.S. government had been unwilling to renounce the extraterritorial reach of its laws.[45]

However, there is another side to the story. In *Power and Interdependence*, Joseph Nye and Robert Keohane have attempted to "score" Canada-U.S. agreements in the post-war era to determine which country has most often come out ahead, and then they compared the Canada-U.S. scores with similar results from Australia-U.S. relationships.[46] Surprisingly, they found that, more often than not, Canada came out ahead in economic terms and that Canada did much better than Australia in relations with the United States. It seems, then, that reality may not always fit initial perceptions. Given Canadian tenderness on the issue of Canada-U.S. relations, the Canadian press and public may tend to make a major issue out of cases where Canadian interests are imperilled while taking little note of the majority of cases where Canada's interests are well served.

It is also worth emphasizing that, while the multinational enterprises may be themselves a problem with respect to sovereignty simply because of their vast size and their autonomy, they may also be the unwilling instruments of conflict that is really between governments. The Trading with the Enemy Act is, after all, U.S. government legislation, the effects of which are carried into Canada by U.S. firms, sometimes quite against the firms' wishes. In general, corporations would prefer harmonious tax and trade relations and they dislike international discord. It can be a futile policy to shoot the messenger, who may carry benefits as well as bad news, in an effort to deal with differences between governments. Ultimately the issue with respect to any enterprise is not whether it is owned by domestic or foreign capital; it is how the enterprise behaves. The policy problem is not therefore one of eliminating or even sharply reducing foreign investment *per se*, but rather one of attempting to maximize its benefits for Canada by industrial policies that make all firms, Canadian or foreign-owned, develop strongly and behave well.

Canadian concern with foreign investment tends to increase with economic prosperity, while economic recession, and, particularly, high levels of unemployment, make Canadian governments much more sympathetic to job-creating investment no matter what its source. Thus in the mid-1980s, the combination of persistent high levels of unemployment and a recognition that the flow of foreign investment that has characterized the first three-quarters of the twentieth century had reversed led to a turnaround in the policy stance of the government of Canada. Although the policy shift was accompanied by a change from a Liberal to a Conservative government, it is quite likely that a government of either partisan stripe would have made similar changes; indeed, John Turner, who briefly replaced Pierre Trudeau as Liberal prime minister in 1985, had already signalled the change. Thus by mid-1986, the National Energy Program had been essentially dismantled and FIRA had become Investment Canada, charged not with screening foreign investment but with encouraging it. The prime minister was enthusiastically embracing the U.S. president and the Minister of Finance

[45] Litvak, *Dual Loyalty*, p. 154.

[46] Joseph Nye and Robert Keohane, *Power and Interdependence* (Boston: Little, Brown, 1977).

was declaring Canada "open for (foreign) business" once more. Free-trade negotiations between Canada and the United States were underway and the rhetoric
of economic nationalism was shelved, at least for the time being. Like so much
else in Canadian politics, the issues of foreign investment and control are cyclical,
with the reality oscillating, sometimes quite widely, around a centre line.

Canada's Internal Geographical and Economic Environment

In the years between Confederation and 1986, Canada's population has risen
from 3.5 million to 24.5 million. Many features of the population have changed,
but many have remained the same. For example, in 1867, 75% of all Canadians
lived in that part of southern Ontario and Quebec called the St. Lawrence lowlands;
in 1986, more than 60% still did. Within these regions, as elsewhere in Canada,
there has been a general movement off the farms and into urban centres. In
1871 only 3.3% of Canadians lived in centres of more than 100,000 population.
(Montreal was the only one.) By 1981 there were 27 urban areas larger than
Montreal had been in 1871, and more than 70% of Canadians lived in such
centres.[47] By 1983 only 2.8% of the gross domestic product came from agriculture.[48] By 1985, only 4.1% of the Canadian labour force worked on producing farms.[49]

In short, Canada has changed over the past century from a rural agricultural
society to an urban industrialized one, and is now one of the most highly urbanized of western societies.[50] The rapid adjustments necessary have often put strains
on the political system as people moved from farms to cities faster than the urban
structures and governments could adapt. Yet although Canada is an urban society with manufacturing and service industries accounting for the largest portion
of its GNP, it is still in many ways a resource-based society.[51] Many of Canada's
larger industrial complexes are still in the primary sector of the economy, in
industries like mining or pulpwood production. In terms of numbers of workers,
secondary and service industries far outrank primary industries, but Canadian
exports have always included a high proportion of primary and semi-manufactured
goods. In 1984, 58% of Canadian exports were agricultural, raw or semi-
manufactured goods, while only 34% of its imports were in that category. This
situation has been changing. In 1954, only 8.6% of Canadian exports were fully

---

[47] Statistics Canada, *Census Metropolitan Areas*, 1981 Census.

[48] Statistics Canada, *National Income and Expenditure Accounts*, 1969–1983, p. 36.

[49] Statistics Canada, *The Labour Force*, April 1985, p. 41.

[50] Agriculture remains a very important industry in Canada. In one way or another, food- and agriculture-
related service and manufacturing activities account for more than 25% of the country's economic activity,
and agricultural exports accounted for more than 20% of the value of the country's total exports in 1977. In
1985, 1.6 times as many workers were engaged in agriculture as in all other primary industries combined.
See Statistics Canada, *The Labour Force*, April 1985, p. 41.

[51] In 1983, 9.9% of Canada's domestic product came directly from primary industries, while 17.6% came
from manufacturing and 50% from service industries and retail trade. See: Statistics Canada, *National
Income and Expenditure Accounts, 1969–1983*, p. 36.

manufactured end products.[52] Nonetheless, the standard of living enjoyed by Canadians is still substantially dependent on her natural resources.[53]

The past three decades have also been characterized in Canada by major changes in the nature of the Canadian labour force. Until 1960, the rate of growth of the labour force approximately paralleled the rate of growth of the population. Since that time the rapid influx of women into the labour force has created labour-force growth that has been very rapid by historical standards. In 1966, 38% of Canadian women aged twenty-five to fifty-four were in the labour force. By 1985, the figure was slightly more than 60% and women in that age range made up one-third of the entire labour force. The years from the mid-1960s to the late 1970s were characterized by particularly rapid labour-force growth as the baby boomers entered the labour force at the same time as the participation rates of women continued to increase.[54] In response to these trends, the rate of job creation was also extremely rapid in those years — the most rapid in the western world — so that until the recession of 1982–83, the rate of unemployment remained less than 7%. While that figure was high by historical standards, it is low in comparison to the experience of the 1980s, and did not appear to create unusual strains for the political system.

Paralleling these changes in labour-force composition were two other broad sets of changes. One was in the composition of employment by type of industry. The three decades saw a massive shift from blue-collar to white-collar employment and from primary and secondary industrial employment to tertiary or service-sector employment. In one typical period, from 1973 to 1979, primary industries contributed less than 3% to employment growth, manufacturing and construction contributed less than 20%, and service-sector growth contributed more than three-quarters of all new jobs.[55]

The second set of changes was in the proportion of the labour force that was organized into collective bargaining units. In 1945 less than 25% of the Canadian labour force was unionized. By 1961 the figure was 29.5% and by 1983 it was nearly 40%. These figures are in sharp contrast to those in the United States, where the trend has been in the opposite direction. There, where the end of World War Two saw nearly 35% of the labour force unionized, the proportion of U.S. workers who belong to unions has decreased quite steadily since to a figure

---

[52] Report of the Royal Commission on Economic Development, vol. 1, p. 236.

[53] There is a continuing debate among economic historians as to whether it was inevitable that Canada's economic growth would be based on primary industries. See J.K. Galbraith, "The Causes of Economic Growth: The Canadian Case," *Queen's Quarterly*, Summer, 1958, pp. 169–82. The argument that Canada's growth did depend on resource industries is referred to as "the staple-products theory." The numerous works of H.A. Innis represent the most complete statement of the theory. See also M.H. Watkins, "A Staple Theory of Canada's Economic Growth," *Canadian Journal of Economics and Political Science*, May, 1963, pp. 141–58, in favour of the theory; and K. Buckley, "The Role of Staple Industries in Canada's Economic Development," *The Journal of Economic History*, vol. 18, 1958, pp. 439–52, against it. There is a succinct summary of the staple-products theory in L.R. Marsden and E.B. Harvey, *Fragile Federation* (Toronto: McGraw-Hill Ryerson, 1979).

[54] Labour-force composition data are from the Report of the Royal Commission on the Economic Union, vol. 2, pp. 16–18.

[55] Royal Commission on Economic Union, p. 18.

of less than 25% by the early 1980s.[56] However, the consequences of these trends in union membership for the Canadian political system are quite unclear. We will see later that, for a variety of reasons, Canadian unions have not been nearly so significant a force in Canadian politics as have European unions in the politics of European nations. For the most part, North American unions have tended to concern themselves more with the "bread and butter" issues of wages and working conditions than with the broader issues of politics.

It will hardly seem a surprising observation to most who live here that Canada has a climate more severe than that of most industrialized countries. This, together with a landscape whose largest areas are covered with rock, water, tundra, or permafrost, has led to the concentration of population along the southern boundary. It has also created a number of stresses with which the political system must cope. Seasonal unemployment in outdoor and construction industries, although today a less significant factor than it was two decades ago, can add a quarter of a million to the list of Canada's jobless; a shortened construction season adds to the cost of large projects; low-cost transportation of bulk cargoes to and from the interior depends on the St. Lawrence Seaway, a route that is closed by ice for four months of the year; and it costs more than eighty dollars a year per capita just to scrape the snow off our streets and highways.[57]

As well, the sheer physical dimensions of the country create difficulties. Distances between the major industrial centres in the St. Lawrence lowlands are relatively small, but in the rest of the country Canadians must maintain communication links between units of population separated by vast distances. Indeed, paradoxically, one reason for the high level of urbanization in Canada may be its vast size. The maintenance of adequate communications and services in small population centres widely separated from each other is much more costly per capita than the maintenance of similar services in centres that are close together. One way around this problem is to concentrate population in large centres that can collectively afford the costly communication links involved. Thus small, densely populated nations can afford to be less urbanized than Canada.

From what has been said so far, we can piece together a partial picture of the internal geographical and economic environment within which the Canadian political system must operate. It functions in a highly urbanized context with at least half of its economic output generated in the retail and service sectors, yet serving a nation that still depends significantly on resources found far from the urban centres. The climate and the topography combine to make much of the land scenic, but not well suited to permanent habitation, and to make transportation and construction very expensive.

The consequences of all this for the political system are immense. Major transportation projects have always required government assistance; indeed, much of the politics of the first fifty years of Confederation was concerned directly with

---

[56] Royal Commission on Economic Union, pp. 674–675.

[57] Roy I. Wolfe, "Economic Development," in Warkentin, ed., *Canada: A Geographical Interpretation*, pp. 189–191. Wolfe's information has been updated by using for 1969–1985 increase in the Statistics Canada implicit price index for government services.

railway construction.[58] Settlement and development of our territory have depended on vast expenditures and intervention by all levels of government, for only governments have had sufficient resources to be able to take on the risks involved. The harsh climate produces cyclical economic effects that only the efforts of very large governmental units can hope to overcome. In short, the scattering of a small population over a large area accustomed Canadians early to big government and prepared the way naturally for the further growth of government in the mid-twentieth century.

Regional Disparity in Canada   So far, the focus has been on factors that are common to most of Canada. Now the discussion will turn to cleavages in the geographical and economic environment — in particular those regional differences that may generate conflicting demands on the political system. Table 2-5 gives some indication of the great discrepancies in income across Canada. A person living in Ontario is likely to have an annual income 61% greater than a person living in Newfoundland and 47% greater than someone living in New Brunswick. The Atlantic provinces, as a whole, have levels of income only about 75% of the national average, while those of British Columbia, Ontario, and Alberta are significantly above it. In previous editions we remarked upon the "stubborn resistance of these patterns to change," and noted that the relative positions of provinces had remained basically unchanged as long as records had been kept. A comparison of the 1978 and 1983 numbers in Table 2-5 will tend to confirm this impression. Over the longer run, however, changes do occur in the direction of moving all provinces closer together. The most striking of these has been the movement of Alberta from a situation of slightly below-average-per capita-income at the start of the 1970s to some 8% above that average in 1983. Moreover, there has been an overall tendency for disparities to diminish. For example, in 1970 the per-capita income in Ontario was some 76% greater than that in Newfoundland, but this discrepancy dropped by some fifteen percentage points by 1983. By 1982 the balances in government access to revenue had shifted to such an extent that if revenues from land sales and leases for oil exploration were included as a standard source of government revenue, Ontario was actually eligible for federal equalization payments.

Regardless of their relative decline, these regional economic cleavages continue to put stress on the Canadian political system, and overcoming them is a constant preoccupation of the federal government. Thus, for example, there is a constant cry expressed at every federal-provincial finance ministers' conference that the governments of Canada's poorer provinces require larger transfers from the federal government, a cry not always echoed by the richer regions. With the exception of the Atlantic provinces, the poorer regions have frequently spawned protest movements — often in the form of minor political parties — and in their protests usually accuse the richer regions of exploiting the poorer. "The barons

---

[58] See Pierre Berton, *The National Dream* (Toronto: McClelland and Stewart, 1971), and *The Last Spike* (Toronto: McClelland and Stewart, 1972); W.T. Easterbrook and M.G. Aitken, *Canadian Economic History* (Toronto: Macmillan, 1965), chapter 18; and D. Creighton, *The Old Chieftain* (Toronto: Macmillan, 1955).

TABLE 2-5
GEOGRAPHICAL DISTRIBUTION OF PER-CAPITA INCOME IN CANADA

Province	Per Cent of National Average		$ Per Capita Per Year (1983)
	1978	1983	
Newfoundland	66	68	9179
Prince Edward Island	69	74	10056
Nova Scotia	80	80	10889
New Brunswick	74	74	10040
Quebec	95	93	12531
Ontario	109	109	14784
Manitoba	93	93	12603
Saskatchewan	92	94	12686
Alberta	105	108	14652
British Columbia	109	106	14339
TOTALS	100	100	13541

Source: Statistics Canada, *National Income and Expenditure Accounts 1969–1983* Number 13-001 (November 1, 1984). p. 47. Figures include government transfer payments. Reproduced with permission of the Minister of Supply and Services Canada.

of Bay Street," "the robbers of St. James Street," and, more recently, "the "blue-eyed sheikhs of Alberta" are familiar Canadian villains.

To some extent Canadian public policies *have* favoured the central regions over the periphery. For instance, corporation tax collected from a firm whose head office is in Toronto is split only between the federal and Ontario governments, in spite of the fact that the earnings of the corporation may come from anywhere in Canada. The effects of this are now mitigated by equalization payments from the federal government to poorer provinces and by the regional redistributive effects of massive federal transfers to individuals and the provinces. This has not always been the case, however, and poorer regions claim that the head start given the richer central areas cannot be overcome by the payment of present-day equalization settlements. Too, the maritimes and the prairies claim, with considerable justification, that the tariff barriers that prevailed in Canada from the mid-nineteenth to the mid-twentieth centuries protected industry in the central provinces but did nothing to protect the resources of the poorer areas from the fluctuations of world markets. The central provinces counter by suggesting that their own resource industries do not appear to have been badly harmed by world competition, and that their citizens also paid tariff-protected prices for manufactured products.

Part of the problem in poorer areas in Canada stems from the type of industry located there. Relative to the rest of Canada, the Atlantic provinces have less manufacturing and a higher concentration of primary industries such as mining, fishing, and forestry. These industries are less likely to create new jobs and more likely to foster underemployment of people.[59]

[59] Economic Council of Canada, *Living Together* (Ottawa: 1978), pp. 31–60.

However important government policies may have been in creating regional disparities, geographical factors have been much more important.[60] Differences of terrain, climate, and the distribution of mineral and forest resources by themselves create regional disparities. Of these three factors, climate is probably the least troublesome for, in spite of the overall harshness of the weather, there are fairly large areas of Canada where rainfall and mean temperatures are sufficient to grow productive crops if the soil is fertile enough.[61] Growing seasons vary greatly from region to region, but if climate were the only determinant, regional disparities would not be as great as they are.

Another of Canada's problems is that most of the country has only shallow young soil spread thinly over rocky terrain. In the west, the Cordillera rises to spectacular heights more suited to viewing and skiing than to farming. Most of Manitoba, Ontario, Quebec, and the Northwest Territories and much of Saskatchewan are covered by the Canadian Shield, whose old low hills and valleys were scoured nearly clean of soil during the last Ice Age. Much of the Atlantic region is covered by the rocky northern extension of the Appalachian mountains. Only on the prairies and near the Great Lakes, in the St. Lawrence lowlands, are there extensive regions of fertile soil combined with a climate suitable to agriculture.

Whatever the difficulties of topography and climate, Canada does have an abundance of at least four crucial resources — water, forests, petroleum, and minerals. Water has enabled Canada to generate large amounts of electricity inexpensively and has consequently made electrical energy one of her most plentiful commodities. This in turn has provided the basis for industrial development and helped to temper the effects of the energy shortages of the 1970s. Water has also provided the basis for one of Canada's largest industries, tourism, and has been talked about, from time to time, as an exportable commodity. The oil and gas reserves in the western provinces helped Canada avoid the brunt of the oil shortages that afflicted most industrial nations in the seventies, even if they have exacerbated regional economic disparities. Reserves off the east coast and in the far north may similarly protect Canadians in the future. Trees have made Canada the western world's largest producer of newsprint and one of the largest producers of paper and lumber. Mineral deposits have made isolated areas of the Canadian Shield and the Cordillera pockets of prosperity.

However, Canada's primary resources are not evenly distributed. Significant amounts of hydroelectric power can be generated only in large watersheds, and mineralization occurs in isolated pockets in the rock. The best forest stands are concentrated in only four provinces. Ontario, whose secondary industries are Canada's largest, also has the largest mineral production. British Columbia, with fertile interior valleys and a congenial climate, also has large deposits of minerals and the best timber stands; and Alberta, already agriculturally advanced,

---

[60] For a general description, see P.B. Clibbon and L.E. Hamelin, "Landforms," in Warkentin, ed., *Canada: A Geographical Interpretation*, pp. 57–77. See also the more general description in C.F.J. Whebell, "Geography and Politics in Canada; Selected Aspects," in J.H. Redekop, ed., *Approaches to Canadian Politics*, 2nd edition (Toronto: Prentice-Hall, 1983), pp. 3–28.

[61] See F.B. Watts, "Climate, Vegetation, Soil," in Warkentin, *Canada*, pp. 77–111.

has the largest proven reserves of oil. The Atlantic provinces, with poor agricultural prospects, also lack the large mineral deposits, readily accessible petroleum reserves, stands of timber, and hydroelectric-power resources of central and western Canada.

Geography has conspired as well to cut sections of Canada off from one another. The maritimes are separated from the rest of Canada by the Northern Appalachians, and the Canadian Shield cuts off Ontario and Quebec from the prairies, which are, in turn, separated from British Columbia by the Cordillera. This often leads to the observation that Canada is really five distinct regions, and that Canadian nationhood has been achieved in spite of physical barriers that should have lined us up along a north-south rather than an east-west axis. The difficult geographical environment has meant that the building of communication lines has had to be a cooperative venture, national in scope. The lessons learned about cooperation and about the uses to which the state can be put to overcome big obstacles may have done much to help in building Canadian attitudes towards government.

For those who must make political decisions, the difficulties posed by regional economic disparities are intensified by uncertainty about how to improve regional performance and how to achieve an appropriate balance between national and regional economic growth. For example, can the Atlantic provinces best be helped by freer trade arrangements with the United States? Should governments support existing industries, or would economic growth be increased by encouraging new and growing industries to locate in underdeveloped areas while letting the older ones die a natural death? Or might everyone be made better off by encouraging greater mobility of the labour force while leaving industry alone to locate where it can grow fastest — usually in southern Ontario or Quebec?[62]

In general, policy makers have adopted the policy of encouraging growth in certain "designated areas," which are at present depressed but in which the application of capital might be expected to produce significant growth. The Agricultural and Rural Development Act (ARDA), the Fund for Rural Economic Development, the Atlantic Development Board, the Area Development Agency, and more recently the amalgamation of many of these plans under the Department of Regional Economic Expansion, later retitled Regional Industrial Expansion, have all been variants of this approach.[63] The most important of the federal responses, however, has been the provision of transfer and equalization payments to provincial governments and transfer payments to individuals. We deal with these extensively later.

Finally, it should be re-emphasized that in a very large and very sparsely settled territory like Canada, solutions that may be appropriate elsewhere do not

---

[62] Two articles epitomizing the different sides of this debate are: W.J. Woodfine, "Canada's Atlantic Provinces: A Study of Regional Economic Retardation," *The Commerce Journal*, 1962; and T.W. Wilson, "Financial Assistance with Regional Development," in J.H. Deutsch *et al.*, eds., *The Canadian Economy* (Toronto: Macmillan, 1965), pp. 402ff. The Report of the Royal Commission on the Economic Union and Development Prospects for Canada deals extensively with the policy problems involved in volume 3.

[63] See T.N. Brewis, "Regional Development," in T.N. Brewis, *et al.*, *Canadian Economic Policy* (Toronto: Macmillan, 1965), pp. 316ff. Equalization devices are described more extensively in Chapter 9 of this book.

always fit. For example, private-sector development of transportation, which was successful in the United States, could not be applied in Canada. Because transportation links to remote areas of low population density do not pay, most major developments in Canada have been carried out by government alone or by private enterprise with huge government subsidies. Examples include the national railways, airlines, and pipelines. Later, when the links themselves create a market for their own use, it may be possible to make a profit, and then private business can be induced to invest capital; but for many such projects, private enterprise in Canada is shored up by huge government subsidies. Broadcasting constitutes another example: in the early days of radio, there were not enough customers to allow a national network to pay its own way, yet a national network could obviously be useful in fostering national unity. The solution adopted was for the government to step in to create the Canadian Radio Broadcasting Commission. In fact, the commission and its successor, the Canadian Broadcasting Corporation, have never been operated as profit-seeking enterprises because they have had to provide services to remote areas and because they have often dealt with topics with little sponsor appeal. The Canadian situation, in this respect, can be contrasted with the situation in the United States, where there are no publicly owned railways (although the U.S. government has recently moved into the operation of rail passenger services), and where public broadcasting is relatively young.

SOCIAL STRATIFICATION: CLASS CLEAVAGE IN CANADA

In addition to the regional cleavages we have discussed, societies have other lines of cleavage deriving from class differences or social stratification.[64] There are a number of criteria that may be used to measure socioeconomic status.[65] One scale proposed for the Canadian setting depends upon a ranking of occupations based on a combination of factors such as years of education or annual income. Another depends upon a survey of people's perceptions of other people's occupations.[66] These "objective" systems of measurement can be buttressed by subjective systems, in which people are asked to rate their own status. No one of these scales is perfect, and occasionally someone like the priest, who ranks fairly low on the income scale, will rank fairly high on some of the other scales. For the most part, however, rankings on the scales are highly correlated. For this reason it is fairly safe to use any scale, whether of occupation, education, or income, as an index of social class in Canada. Since income data are the most readily col-

---

[64] We will use the terms "class cleavage," "vertical cleavage," and "social stratification" virtually synonymously, although there may be subtle distinctions among them.

[65] Bernard R. Blishen, "A Socio-Economic Index for Occupations in Canada," *Canadian Review of Sociology and Anthropology*, vol. 4, No. 1, February 1967, pp. 41–54.

[66] Peter C. Pineo and John Porter, "Occupational Prestige in Canada," *Canadian Review of Sociology and Anthropology*, vol. 4, No. 1, February 1967, pp. 24–40. With respect to stratification in general, and particularly with respect to Canada, see: Dennis Forcese, *The Canadian Class Structure* (Toronto: McGraw-Hill Ryerson, 1980).

lected and the most widely available, we will base most of our discussions on the income scale.

Poverty in Canada[67]

By 1987, the average family income in Canada was more than $36,000 and, while the rapid rises in income that characterized the 1970s have been conspicuously absent since 1981, the mythical "average family" lives in relative comfort and security compared both to earlier generations in Canada and to the vast majority of the world's population. While international comparisons of living standards are always treacherous, the Organization for Economic Cooperation and Development reported in 1984 that Canada's real Gross Domestic Product per capita ranked second in the world, with only the United States ranking higher.[68]

A relatively satisfactory overall picture, however, can mask very substantial hardships for many people. From Table 2-6 it can be seen that in 1983, the lowest 20% of families and unattached individuals in Canada received only 4.4% of all income. Put otherwise, this means that the lowest 20% of the population received only about one-tenth the income of the highest 20%.

The situation is highly resistant to change. The distribution of income in Canada today is little different from what it was in 1945, although it has improved since the 1920s. Table 2-6 indicates the distribution of income in Canada in a sampling of four post-war years.[69] It can be seen that these figures have changed only slowly, and sometimes for the worse, over the thirty-two-year period covered. The right-hand set of columns of the table indicate the highest income per family or individual for those in each group. Thus, for example, in 1983 the highest income of families in the fourth group (having that income below which 80% of families fall) was $43,770. Expressed otherwise, the most "affluent" family in the lowest 20% of the population received about $10,648 in 1983, while no family or individual in the highest 20% received less than $43,770.

Table 2-6 shows the picture in broad outline. More detailed figures reveal that in 1983, 14.6% of families and 41% of unattached individuals were living below the Statistics Canada low-income cutoff—the point at which more than 58.5% of income must be spent to obtain adequate food, shelter, and clothing.[70]

Judged by these figures, in the mid-1980s, some 4.3 million people in Canada were living in, at best, difficult economic circumstances. These figures vary with time and particularly with the point in the economic cycle, but even by the

[67] The "discovery" by social scientists in the mid-1960s that the affluent society hid a great deal of poverty produced a deluge of literature on the subject in Canada. See, for example: Special Senate Committee on Poverty, *Poverty in Canada* (Ottawa: Information Canada, 1971); Ian Adams, *et al.*, *The Real Poverty Report* (Edmonton: Hurtig, 1971); and T.E. Reid, *Canada's Poor* (Toronto: Holt, Rinehart and Winston, 1972).

[68] OECD, Economics and Statistics Department, *Real GDP in OECD Countries and Associated Purchasing Power Parities* (Working Paper No. 17, Paris, 1984).

[69] A percentile is defined as the figure below which that percentage of cases lies. Thus the twentieth percentile of family income is that income below which 20% of the incomes in Canada lie.

[70] Statistics Canada, *Income Distributions by Size in Canada, 1983*, p. 17.

TABLE 2-6
LOW-INCOME FAMILIES AND UNATTACHED INDIVIDUALS IN CANADA

Percentile	Per Cent of Total Income					Upper Limit of Quintile		
	1951	1967	1975	1980	1983	1975	1980	1983
1 to 20	4.4	4.2	4.0	4.1	4.4	5038	8243	10648
21 to 40	11.2	11.4	10.6	10.5	10.3	9793	16000	19762
41 to 60	18.3	17.8	17.6	17.7	17.1	14545	23292	30032
61 to 80	23.3	24.6	25.1	25.6	24.0	20598	33753	43770
81 to 100	42.8	42.0	42.6	42.4	43.2	–	–	–

Source: Statistics Canada, *Income Distribution by Size in Canada*, Ottawa, August 1985.

somewhat conservative definition implied in Statistics Canada's low-income cutoff, poverty is very widespread in Canada.

The poor in Canada do not live only in depressed areas of the country. We often think of the Atlantic provinces and eastern Quebec as being Canada's poorest regions, and indeed the concentration of poor people is higher in those areas, but 60% of low-income families live in urban regions with populations of more than 100,000, and more than 45% live in supposedly affluent metropolitan areas. While we think of the poor as being unemployed, the heads of 58% of poor families were active in the labour force at least part of the year. The heads of 24% of low-income families worked more than forty weeks in 1983. Of poor families, 66% are headed by men, although 47% of female-headed households are below the low-income cutoff, as opposed to only 10% of male-headed households.[71]

Many of Canada's poor are children. More than one million, or one-fifth of all Canadian children, live in low-income families. Many of these live in single-parent female-headed families. Children from those families have a 50% chance of being poor. One-quarter of the elderly in 1983 were below low-income cut-offs, and almost all of these, some 600,000, were single. Indeed, in 1983, 58% of the elderly unattached lived with incomes below the poverty line; 90% of them lived alone; and women outnumbered men by four to one. Increases in the Guaranteed Income Supplement in 1984 improved the income of most single elderly to above the low-income cut off, but without these payments many of this group would be destitute. Conversely, if you are reading this book, your chances of having an above-average income are relatively good, particularly if you pass the course. The average family income for families headed by university graduates in 1983 was $52,000, compared to $26,000 for families whose heads had less than eight years of education.

In Canada, one of the highest incidences of poverty is found among native peoples.[72] In 1980, more than 40% of native Indian families were living with at

---

[71] All figures in this paragraph and the next are from Statistics Canada, *Income Distributions by Size, 1983*.

[72] Statistics Canada census data indicated that there were 23,200 Inuit, 313,600 Indians, and 75,600 Métis in 1981. With the exception of Status Indians and Inuit, census data on natives are not considered very reliable.

lest two families in a dwelling unit and half of all Indian housing had inadequate sewage disposal and unsafe water supplies.[73] Less than one-third of present reservation lands could be made capable of supporting even their present populations in reasonable fashion, and 45% are accessible only by water or seaplane. This poverty translates directly into other social problems. The death rate for Indians in the twenty-two-to-forty-four-year age group is four times the national average. Violent deaths are also four times the national average, while Indians in the fifteen-to-twenty-four-year age group commit suicide at six times the rate of other Canadians. Some 50% to 60% of Indian deaths and illnesses are alcohol-related. Seven times as many Indians as non-Indians per capita are in penitentiaries. In spite of all this, the Indian population is the fastest growing in Canada.

Undoubtedly the greatest handicap the poor face in modern society is simply low income. The problem goes deeper, however, for poverty creates a subculture within the larger Canadian culture — a subculture with its own norms and values. Some of these norms, such as a lack of belief in the value of education, make it extremely difficult for the poor to escape their situation. Poverty leads as well to crime, disease, and low productivity, and constitutes a vast waste of potential talent within Canadian society.[74]

The Canadian Economic Elite

So far our discussion of stratification in Canada has been far from complete. If 15% to 20% of Canadians are below the poverty line, then some 80% are above it; and these constitute a heterogeneous group. On the top end of the scale is a very small group holding the top positions in industry, business, the professions, and the bureaucracy. Estimates of the size of this élite vary depending on the criteria used to describe it, but at most it comprises some 2% or 3% of the population.

For many years now, the key works in the study of Canadian élites have been John Porter's classic *The Vertical Mosaic* and Wallace Clement's *The Canadian Corporate Elite*.[75] Porter first addresses himself to the question of whether there is a Canadian élite, and, having decided that there is, he examines its characteristics. His data, from 1965, indicate that the 985 occupants of the top positions in a number of hierarchies, such as those of business, religion, education, politics, and the bureaucracy, are likely to share similar backgrounds. These include Charter-group (British or French) ethnic origin, a middle- or upper-class upbringing, and Catholic, Anglican, or United Church religious affiliations. There are also similarities in educational background in this group, and there exists among them a web of social interconnections. Clement's more recent data, from 1973, tend to corroborate Porter's initial conclusions, with the significant exception that Clement finds a much higher proportion of non-Canadian residents

---

[73] 1980 data were supplied by the Federal Department of Indian and Northern Affairs. See also Chapter 3 infra.

[74] See Ian Adams, *The Poverty Wall* (Toronto: McClelland and Stewart, 1970); and W.E. Mann, ed., *Poverty and Social Policy in Canada* (Toronto: Copp Clark, 1970).

[75] John Porter, *The Vertical Mosaic* (Toronto: University of Toronto Press, 1965); and Wallace Clement, *The Canadian Corporate Elite* (Toronto: McClelland and Stewart, 1975).

among the corporate élite than did Porter. In firms with more than $25 million in assets, Clement finds that 62% of directors come from outside Canada; for the earlier period in which Porter worked, the figure was only 27%.[76] Clement's research was conducted at the time of maximum foreign ownership of Canadian industry, so that a similar study in the 1980s might find a higher proportion of Canadians in the corporate élite.

But if these people are potentially a ruling class, do they actually behave as one? As the rest of this text indicates, the great complexity of the decision-making process in Canada ensures that control by any one small group is extremely difficult. Furthermore, the fact that members of the various élites may share a similar outlook on life is no guarantee that, under the complex pressures that come to bear on any particular decision, they will act as a uniform class. On the other hand, given that the decision makers are primarily middle- and upper-class in origin, and that most inputs from the environment are channelled through middle-class organizations, it seems probable that the voice of lower-class citizens is, at best, muffled.[77]

The Swollen Middle

If the various élites make up only 2% or 3% of the population and those below the poverty line about 20%, obviously the middle-income group of the population, made up of the middle class and the better-off members of the working class, constitutes the majority. It must not be supposed that this group is by any means homogeneous, for there are wide variations in behavioural patterns that may lead to differences in political behaviour and in the type of demands fed into the political system.

Within this middle-income group, the dividing line between the middle class and the working class depends not so much on income as on type of occupation. Many skilled tradespeople, such as plumbers or electricians, earn more money than many junior executives, yet the junior executive tends to emulate the lifestyle of corporate seniors while the tradesperson does not.[78] The differences in behaviour appear to derive mainly from family traditions, for working-class families tend to remain working class for many generations, and from job security, for the junior executive is less subject to the vagaries of the business cycle than is the tradesperson or industrial worker.

---

[76] Wallace Clement, *Continental Corporate Power* (Toronto: McClelland and Stewart, 1977). In a dynamic society, the composition of élites may shift relatively rapidly. New research in this area is needed every decade, so the reader should be on the lookout for new sources not cited here.

[77] The whole question of élites and political decision making is discussed in much more detail in chapter 14. This text is primarily informed by the liberal-pluralist perspective. For a Marxist class-analysis perspective, see: Leo Panitch, ed., *The Canadian State* (Toronto: University of Toronto Press, 1977).

[78] There is an extensive discussion of the impact of stratification on life-styles in Forcese, *The Canadian Class Structure*, chapters 3 and 4.

Stratification and Canadian Politics

There are empirical reasons to suggest that class-based cleavages are important to the Canadian political system for, as we will see when we discuss political participation, lower-class Canadians take little interest in the political system, have little awareness of its relevance to them, and do very little to attempt to influence it. The further up the economic hierarchy we go, the greater the amount of interest, participation, and actual influence in the political process. We will see as well, however, that class is not a vital determinant of Canadian voting behaviour or party identification. There have been attempts to establish class-based parties in Canada, but these have been less than successful. The Independent Labour Party flashed briefly across Ontario politics in the 1920s and died. The Communist Party of Canada has never been anything but a token presence, and even the more broadly based CCF-NDP has had trouble establishing itself as a credible threat to gain national power. In fact, the CCF-NDP had tended to succeed in inverse proportion to the amount of attention it has devoted to class-related issues and cleavages.

Whatever the influence of social class on the political behaviour of Canadians, the presence of inequalities of opportunity and of large disparities in the distribution of wealth has called forth many responses from the political decision makers. Thus in 1986, income-transfer expenditures and related tax measures by Canadian governments totalled more than $6.6 billion, and direct-income transfer programs accounted for more than 30% of all expenditures by all levels of government that year.[79] There are literally hundreds of federal, provincial, and municipal welfare programs, ranging from the Old Age Security payments, which resulted in the payment of $11.4 billion in 1984–85, down to local welfare programs in the smallest municipal governments.[80] If these programs have not significantly reduced income disparities, they have at least helped to insure that fewer Canadians live in absolute poverty than was previously the case.[81] The public expenditures on this problem suggest that our political system will respond, even if slowly and with some considerable inefficiency, to the poverty problem. However, it

[79] Figures are from Statistics Canada, Consolidated Expenditure Accounts, updated annually, and supplemented by tax figures from the Department of Finance. Expenditures include Unemployment Insurance, Family Allowances, Canada/Quebec Pension Plans, Old Age Security and Guaranteed Income Supplements, the Canada Assistance Plan, provincial and municipal social-security expenditures, the Child Tax Credits and deductions, married exemptions, and an array of smaller programs.

[80] Unlike their American counterparts, Canadian governments are fairly proud of their welfare programs and go to great lengths to describe them to the public. Thus, detailed information on the structure of welfare programs can be found in any bookstore selling government publications. Useful brief descriptions are available in Statistics Canada, *The Canada Year Book* or in the Canadian Tax Foundation's annual review, called *The National Finances*, or in a Health and Welfare annual publication, *Income Security Programs in Canada*, Supply and Services, Ottawa.

[81] There is an ongoing debate about the efficacy of income-transfer programs. Without them, in 1981 the bottom one-fifth of the Canadian population would have received two-thirds less income than even their current levels. There remains constant controversy as to whether the money could be distributed more effectively. See, for example, the Report of the Royal Commission on the Economic Union, vol. 7, chapter 19, "Income Security Programs in Canada."

has also been argued that welfare policies tend simply to legitimize the existing system, with all of its inequities, rather than to reduce the inequities themselves. According to this reasoning, welfare programs function as an inoculation against demands for more radical economic reforms that would be heard if the lot of the poor were permitted to deteriorate in absolute terms.[82]

Conclusions

We have dealt in this chapter with a number of the major features of the environment of the Canadian political system. Up to this point, we have been concerned primarily with economic, geographic, and demographic factors. There are, however, many other aspects of Canadian society that have very great influence on the structure and functions of governments in Canada. These include the particularly important cleavage between Francophone and Anglophone Canadians, and between Quebec and the rest of Canada. They also include the opinions or ideas Canadians hold about their governments and the things those governments ought to do, and they include the ways in which Canadians participate in politics. In the next chapter we will deal with French-English relations in Canada, and in the following chapters with political values, public opinion, and political participation in Canada.

---

[82] This argument is put in Leo Panitch, "The Role and Nature of the Canadian State," in Panitch, *The Canadian State*, p. 8.

ENVIRONMENT: ETHNIC CLEAVAGE IN CANADA

F or more than two hundred years the dominant political conflict in Canada has been that surrounding the relationship between the French- and the English-speaking "charter groups" in the federation. Through severe economic depression, and even through world wars — crises that have threatened the very survival of our way of life — the issues of French-English relations have continued to occupy a place at the top of the agenda for political discourse in both national and provincial forums. Moreover, there is little in our recent history to indicate that this, our national obsession, is about to fade away. Despite some encouraging indicators that the most recent ethnic crisis, that of separatism in Quebec, has gone into remission, other French-English battle lines have been drawn up, in Manitoba over separate language education and in New Brunswick, the Yukon, and the Northwest Territories over official bilingualism. It would seem that French-English cleavage in Canada is one of the strongest affirmations of the old aphorism that, in politics, the more things change, the more they remain the same. As an illustration of this point, and by way of setting the stage for a more general attempt at an explanation of the current status of ethnic conflict in Canada today, let us look briefly at the major events or crises in French-English relations in Canada since Confederation.

FRENCH-ENGLISH RELATIONS IN CANADA: 1876–1980[1]

History must be seen both as a reflection of the fundamental cleavages that exist between French and English groups in Canada, and, as well, as one of the causes or roots of the phenomenon. Thus the events described in the following section can be seen as the direct result of deep-seated differences between the two charter groups; as well, each of these "crises" comes to be remembered as still one more piece of evidence to justify the continued significance of French-English cleavage and to legitimize future manifestations of such conflict.[2]

The Riel Rebellion

The period immediately following Confederation could be called a honeymoon period in ethnic relationships in Canada. Upper Canadians had achieved their goal of "representation by population" and French Canadians had a government in Quebec that they felt they could call their own. The coalition of John A. Macdonald and Georges E. Cartier seemed to be working well at the federal level, and the two ethnic groups seemed more concerned with internal than external problems. There was a brief uprising of the Métis people in Manitoba in 1870, in which an Ontario Orangeman died, but Louis Riel, the leader of the rebellion, fled to the United States and little more was heard of the incident. Riel, however, returned to Canada in 1885, and Canada's first major post-Confederation ethnic quarrel broke around him. On his return, he regrouped his Métis and Indian forces and led them in a second rebellion. Troops were sent from eastern Canada to put down the insurrection, and Riel was captured, with several of his followers, and sentenced to death for treason. He became a symbol for anti-Catholic Protestants in Ontario and even more so for anti-Protestant Catholics in Quebec, who were disturbed that the originally Catholic and French-speaking communities of Manitoba were being swamped by English-speaking settlers. Mass rallies swept both provinces. In Montreal, *La Presse* screamed, "Henceforward there are no more Liberals nor Conservatives nor Castors. There are only PATRIOTS

---

[1] We were assisted in the preparation of earlier versions of this section by Professor Richard Simeon of Queen's University. We have not considered the first of Canada's ethnic crises, the pre-Confederation rebellion led by Louis Joseph Papineau. For a more extensive general description of French-English relations in Canada from a more French-Canadian perspective, see André Bernard, *What Does Quebec Want?* (Toronto: James Lorimer, 1978).

[2] For historical perspective on the roots and current status of French-Canadian nationalism, see: Marcel Rioux, *La Question du Québec* (Paris: 1969); Leon Dion, *Quebec: The Unfinished Revolution* (Montreal: McGill-Queen's Press, 1976); R. Whitaker, "The Quebec Cauldron," in Whittington and Williams, eds., *Canadian Politics in the 1980s*, (Toronto: Methuen, 1984); F.P. Gingras, and N. Nevitte, "The Evolution of Quebec Nationalism," in A. Gagnon, ed., *Quebec: State and Society*, (Toronto: Methuen, 1984); and R. Gibbins, *Conflict and Unity* (Toronto: Methuen, 1985), chapters one to four.

and TRAITORS." For Quebec, the issue was one of the execution or pardon of a patriot; for Ontario, one of the execution or pardon of a traitor and murderer. Riel was executed, but the bitter dispute did not end with his death. Even today, he is often presented in French Canada as a hero and in English Canada, if not as a traitor, at least as an addled, misguided, and vaguely dishonest mystic.

The Riel Rebellion controversy illustrates a number of important aspects of ethnic conflict in Canada. The first is the role played by the incumbent political leaders in dealing with the political results of cleavage. In this case, the conflict had originated in large measure from various religious and ethnic organizations, and politicians of both major parties had tried to moderate it. Macdonald tried to delay Riel's execution, but was forced to give in to pressure from Ontario and particularly from the Orange Lodge, that most potent of forces in early Ontario politics. The French-Canadian members of Macdonald's cabinet, while privately opposed to the execution, refused to break with Macdonald and urged calm in Quebec. Sir Wilfrid Laurier, then Leader of the Opposition, opposed the government's handling of the matter, but urged his countrymen to adopt a moderate approach. The higher clergy of the Catholic Church also played a moderating role, and Bishop Taché even urged French-Canadian Conservative MPs not to vote against their own party.

Another set of leaders, however, acted to foster and exacerbate the conflict. In Ontario, the Orange Lodge and other Protestant groups played an important role in condemning the French-Canadian "papists." The Ontario press also played on ethnic hostilities. For example, the Toronto *Mail and Empire* declared: "As Britons, we believe that the conquest will have to be fought over again. Lower Canada may depend on it, there will be no new treaty of 1763. The victors will not capitulate the next time."

In Quebec, on the other hand, the "out" political leaders seized this opportunity to overthrow and virtually destroy the provincial Conservative party. Playing on the same sort of ethnic hostility as that used by Ontario's Orangemen, Honoré Mercier formed the Parti national, which was aimed at uniting all French Canadians in all provinces into a single party. The Parti national was never successful at the federal level, but it did gain power provincially in spite of the fact that it was opposed both by the church hierarchy (though not necessarily the lower clergy) and by the incumbent political leaders.

A pattern can be discerned here that recurs frequently in Canadian politics. The incumbent leaders and some important community institutions acted to minimize intergroup conflict. Other potential leaders, currently out of power, built up the hostilities on either side. From another perspective, the "outs" were attempting to use the crisis to gain political power, while the entrenched "ins" tried to save the status quo.[3]

---

[3] An often unrecognized irony of the Riel Rebellion is that it was seen as an issue of French vs. English and Catholic vs. Protestant, where what was really at stake was the survival of a separate and distinctive ethnic group, the Métis. It is only recently that Riel has been recognized as a symbol of the people of mixed Indian and white blood, and that the Métis have been recognized constitutionally as aboriginal people with special rights in the federation.

The Manitoba School Crisis

The bitterness left by the Riel affair and the hostilities raised in English Canada by many of the actions of the Mercier government in Quebec inspired a general climate of distrust, especially among middle levels of the elites of both sides. It was against this background that the Manitoba-schools crisis erupted and, in fact, conflicts over minority-education rights have provided a focal point for ethnic disagreements in that province ever since.

In 1890, Manitoba passed a law establishing a completely non-sectarian educational system, replacing a system where Catholic schools had received provincial funding.[4] The bitter debate that ensued placed the opponents of the legislation, most of whom were French, Roman Catholic, and from Quebec, in an anomalous position. To oppose Manitoba's school law was to demand that the federal government use its power under section 93 of the BNA act to disallow the provincial legislation. However, this would obviously constitute a case of direct federal interference in provincial matters, a state of affairs that Quebec was opposed to on principle. Provincial politicians in Quebec squirmed uncomfortably while the church pressured the federal government to disallow the legislation, and while Sir Wilfrid Laurier, still Leader of the Opposition, took his stand on the side of provincial rights. The courts declared the Manitoba legislation to be within provincial powers, but affirmed that the federal government could use its power to disallow it, and the Conservative government finally did introduce a bill to invalidate the law. An election intervened and the subsequent campaign was fought largely on the school issue.

For once, ethnic and religious divisions did not coincide, since the church, demanding that the Manitoba legislation be killed, supported its traditional ally, the Conservative party, while Laurier, the first French Canadian to lead a major national party, appealed to the Quebec electorate on ethnic grounds. Quebeckers could vote for either their church or their ethnic group, and they appear to have opted for the latter. The result was a Liberal victory nationally; in Quebec, Laurier received 54% of the popular vote. The Liberals were not to drop below 50% of the vote in that province again until 1958.

It has been pointed out that conflicts may be made worse by *coincident* cleavage lines, and conversely may be muted when cleavage lines overlap or cross cut.[5] The cross-cutting of two major cleavages did much to reduce the bitterness of this particular issue, and it was ultimately settled by negotiations between Laurier and the provincial government in 1897, with the substance of the legislation basically unchanged. However, the crisis left the Canadian party system altered permanently.

---

[4] Similar situations arose in New Brunswick, in Alberta and Saskatchewan when they became provinces in 1905, and, most ominously, in Ontario just before World War One.

[5] See pp. 66–72.

Regulation Seventeen, Conscription, and
Quebec Nationalism to the 1920s

In the early part of the twentieth century, several nationalist movements appeared in French Canada. The most important of these was led by Henri Bourassa. At the time, the term "nationalist" implied more power for the government of Quebec in cultural matters and more independence of Canada from the British connection. Although Bourassa stopped short of any call for the separation of Quebec from Canada, this was not necessarily true of his followers, just as it had not been true of several members of the previous nationalist movement, the Parti nationale, in the 1880s. The new movements posed a threat to Laurier, as the nationalist demands generally ran counter to the Liberal policy of moderation and compromise. The movements may have been partially a response to defeats on the question of language and education; but, ironically, it was the defection of Bourassa and his followers from the Quebec Liberal party that led to the election of the English-Canadian-dominated and strongly pro-British Robert Borden government in 1911. Bourassa and the other nationalists supported the Conservatives in that election campaign, and this led to a 6% decline in Liberal votes in Quebec. The campaign was unscrupulous on both sides and left a further residue of bitterness as Canada approached one of the greatest ethnic crises of its national life.[6]

That crisis came during World War One, and perhaps Canada came closer to civil war then than at any other time in its history, as two issues combined to bring ethnic tensions to the boiling point. The first was yet another school crisis, brought on by a 1913 Ontario regulation limiting the use of French in Ontario schools. The second was the battle over conscription for war service.

At a time when national unity was most vital, the agitation about schools made it impossible. For Quebec, traditionally inward-looking, the educational issue was far more important than fighting a foreign war. There were frequent mass rallies and demonstrations in the province. Quebec schoolchildren and school boards contributed money to maintain the French schools in Ontario, as did many municipal governments in Quebec. A petition asking for disallowance of the Ontario regulation, signed by six hundred thousand people, was presented to the federal government. Virtually all elements of the Quebec population supported the attack on Ontario's "Regulation Seventeen." As *Le Soleil*, a Quebec City newspaper, put it: "The hour of mobilization of the French-Canadian race has come." This agitation had its counterpart in Ontario. The Orange Lodge, predictably, demanded an end to *all* teaching of French in Ontario schools, and English-Canadian newspapers presented the issue as a question of "papist" domination and as a French-Canadian conspiracy to dominate English Canada. Said one overwrought and undoubtedly unilingual Member of Parliament: "Never shall we let the French Canadians plant in Ontario the disgusting speech they use." How widespread such feelings were on either side will never be known, but it appears they were general.

---

[6] See J. Schull, *Laurier* (Toronto: Macmillan, 1965), for an excellent and balanced discussion of this period.

It was in this already tense atmosphere that the conscription crisis arose. At first all elements of the population had enthusiastically supported Canadian participation in the war, though some nationalist leaders, like Henri Bourassa, advocated only limited activity. As the war went on, however, enlistments from Quebec, which had never been high, dwindled. There were many reasons for this besides the obvious one, that if you went over to Europe, a bunch of Germans would try to kill you. French Canadians could not help but be put off by the overwhelmingly English nature of the armed forces, the lack of French-speaking units, and the failure to give French Canadians equal opportunities for promotion. These feelings were reinforced by the feelings of hostility arising out of the school issue and the contrast in outlook between Quebeckers, who had been cut off from Europe completely since 1759, and English Canadians, many of whom had only recently arrived from England and retained a sense of duty to the mother country.

As Canadian casualties in Europe mounted, the need became more and more urgent for new recruits to maintain Canada's commitments. In efforts to stave off the possibility of conscription, political leaders like Wilfrid Laurier, and even the church hierarchy, campaigned for French Canadians to volunteer. There was widespread resentment among English Canadians who felt that the Québécois were not "pulling their weight." Finally, in 1917, after a visit to the troops in Europe, Robert Borden became convinced that conscription was indeed necessary and announced in May that selective conscription would soon be introduced.

The Quebec reaction included riots, attacks on pro-government newspapers, and mass demonstrations. Laurier, still playing the mediating role, warned that if the Liberals agreed to conscription, they would, in effect, be handing Quebec over to the nationalists. He pointed out that the Liberals were the only political representatives of the majority in a province that was both pro-Canadian and anti-conscription, and Laurier judged that anti-conscription feelings were stronger than pro-Canadian sentiment. Conscription would, he said, "create a line of cleavage within the population, the consequence of which I know too well, and for which I will not be responsible." But he also signified his continuing Canadianism by asserting that, if the English-Canadian majority passed a conscription law, he would attempt to secure Quebec's compliance. All but one French-Canadian Cabinet minister resigned from Borden's Conservative government, as did the Deputy Speaker and the chief government whip from Quebec. The depth of feeling was revealed in speeches by French-Canadian members of parliament. Said Louis-Joseph Gauthier: "My people are willing to go the limit if you impose on them such a piece of legislation." Another MP warned that conscription might mean civil war and the end of Confederation. When the vote on conscription came, party lines were crossed and ethnic lines maintained: most English-speaking Liberals supported it; virtually all French-speaking Conservatives voted against it.

The extreme polarization of the electorate was revealed in the bitter election fight that followed passage of the bill and there was serious threat of civil disobedience in Quebec. English Liberals united with the Conservatives to form a Union government, which ran Union candidates in the 1917 election. The French-

Canadian nationalists this time supported the Laurier Liberals in Quebec and the Laurier followers won 84% of the vote and 62 of the 65 seats in the province. The Unionists, by contrast, won only 3 seats and 15% of the provincial popular vote. Outside Quebec, the split in popular vote was not so glaring, as the Laurier Liberals won 35% versus the Unionists' 65%, but the Liberals won only 20 seats while the Union government won 150. In terms of parliamentary seats, a united Quebec faced a united English Canada and the split Laurier had always feared, and which he had worked all his life to avoid, was a fact.

Fortunately, the war ended soon thereafter. Few people were ever actually drafted and the conscription crisis blew over, but the bitterness remained and served to nourish a new movement, which was distinctly provincialist and sometimes separatist in outlook. In the first post-war election, in 1921, the Unionist government broke up, and the Liberals again formed the government, winning all sixty-five Quebec seats and fifty-three seats elsewhere in Canada. In the first Quebec provincial election after the war, the Conservatives were so weak that they did not even bother to run candidates in forty-one of the eighty-three Quebec constituencies and, with the exception of the 1958 and 1984 federal elections, they have never since been a strong force in Quebec politics at either level of government.

Nationalism and the Duplessis Years

During the 1920s and 1930s nationalist agitation grew in Quebec, partly as a result of the wartime hostility and partly in response to the economic factors that were discussed earlier. It gained strength under the impact of the Depression and found expression in the rise of a new Quebec provincial party, l'Union nationale, led by Maurice Duplessis.[7] Duplessis was elected in 1936 on a program of provincial rights and opposition to the federal government and to English-owned business. With one exception, in 1939, this appeal led him to victory in every election until his death in 1959.

Under his leadership, conflict between the Quebec and federal governments often took the form of provincial protests against alleged federal encroachments on provincial jurisdiction, especially federal anti-Depression measures. The conflict thus became a more institutionalized one between governments, and this institutionalization was important in maintaining some restraint in French-English relations during most of the Duplessis period. With the exception of the 1944 conscription crisis, the most obvious expressions of the French-English cleavage were the arguments that broke out in federal-provincial conferences and in the "Ottawa-baiting" speeches of Duplessis.

Although this period could be characterized as one in which grievances for the future were stored up, the only sharp crisis in Canadian ethnic relations during the Duplessis years came during World War Two and again revolved around conscription. When Canada entered the war in 1939, the Mackenzie King government was understandably afraid of a recurrence of the bitter and divisive

---

[7] See: H.F. Quinn, *The Union Nationale: A Study in Quebec Nationalism* (Toronto: University of Toronto Press, 1963).

crisis of 1917 and hence promised not to institute conscription. But, just as in World War One, the demands of total war soon outran voluntary enlistment, and the Conservative Opposition, as well as other elements in English Canada and the military, began to demand compulsory military service. Mackenzie King, in the hope of avoiding a full-scale crisis, sought a national referendum to permit the government to back out of its promise to French Canada. The referendum was a disaster. French-Canadian groups such as La Ligue pour la défense du Canada, supported by much of the lower clergy, campaigned for a *non* vote. In the eight English-speaking provinces, the vote went 80% in favour of the referendum; in Quebec it was 72% against, and among French Canadians in Quebec the *non* vote rose to 85%. Opposition to the war in Quebec was polarized by the campaign and statements on each side grew more bitter. La Ligue grew stronger and became a political party, the Bloc populaire.

The government avoided imposing conscription until 1944, when it finally appeared that King could no longer walk a tightrope between the English and French sections of his party and of the country. In the final parliamentary vote on conscription, King lost the support of thirty-four French-Canadian Liberals, although they continued to support him as prime minister. His dismissal of his pro-conscription Defence Minister, J.L. Ralston, allayed some French-Canadian suspicion, but once again, as is so often the case in government, it was simply the passage of time that saved the day for, fortunately, the war was by then near conclusion, and it did not become necessary to use any of the conscripts in battle. In any event, most French-Canadian leaders appeared to realize that it was better to have limited conscription under King than full conscription under the English-dominated government that would replace him should he fall. King's political skill and the end of the war avoided a conscription crisis of anything like the magnitude of the earlier one, but again a residue of mistrust was left.

The Quiet Revolution and Separatism: 1960–1980

The immediate postwar period and the 1950s were a time of apparent calm in Quebec, and except for the occasional forays of Maurice Duplessis against the federal government, there was relatively little activity across the lines of French-Canadian cleavage in Canada. The calm was more apparent than real, however, for the rapid urbanization and industrialization of Quebec society combined with the economic hegemony of the English population both within and outside of Quebec, were sowing the seeds for the next crisis, that of separatism.

That crisis, which has proven to be more drawn-out and more threatening to the system than any of the earlier ones, really began with the death of Maurice Duplessis in 1959. His successors were unable to maintain the tight control he had had over Quebec politics, and in 1960 the Liberals, under the leadership of Jean Lesage, defeated the Union nationale using the slogan "*maître chez nous.*" It is difficult to know just how seriously many of the Lesage Liberals took their slogan, but it seems likely, in retrospect, that some, such as René Lévesque, took it very seriously indeed. It was in this period, often referred to as "the Quiet

Revolution,'' that a fair number of politically active Quebeckers began to agitate for a separate Quebec.

The Quiet Revolution in Quebec can be seen both as a reflection of the political will to leave behind the ''dark age of Duplessis'' and as the immediate forebearer of the separatist movement of the 1970s. Basically, Duplessis had left education, social services, and health care to the church, and economic development to the multinational corporations. The people of Quebec had become disgruntled with this state of affairs and demanded both a bigger role in the economy of the province and a higher level of social services, education, and health care. The Lesage government moved to provide all of these things.

In the area of education, for example, the new government very quickly took the responsibility for higher education out of the hands of the church and established the first secular department of education. The thrust of the educational system shifted from the very conservative emphasis on the old professions — law, medicine, and theology — to an emphasis on science, engineering, business administration, and the social sciences. This resulted in a large number of young French Canadians who were catapulted into the labour force with backgrounds in science, engineering, social sciences, etc., while the structure of the economy and of the labour market was not developed to the extent that these people could be absorbed. This circumstance, while immediately generating high levels of dissatisfaction among young educated Francophones, also helped to trigger rapid changes in the economy of the province.

Because the private sector either could not or would not adapt to this phenomenon quickly enough, the government was forced to move extensively into the private sector, and to stimulate and restructure the economy. The result was a rapid growth of government participation in the private sector, the most important symbol of this being the nationalization of Hydro-Quebec. This phenomenon and the consequent development of a new middle class in Quebec will be discussed further in a later section of this chapter.

While the economic components of the Quiet Revolution were perhaps the most significant, the new economic confidence of the province also helped to stimulate the new ethnic consciousness that was one of the triggers of the separatist movement of the following decade. A new awareness of the place of Quebec in the federation led the leaders of the Quiet Revolution to demand a level of social services equal to that of the other provinces. Part of this demand was that the federal government provide the revenue base upon which such services could be built. The implications of this for the financial structures of Canadian federalism are discussed at great length in Chapter 9, but again there was a spillover that affected, as well, the relationship between Quebec and the rest of Canada in other areas. For example, Quebec started to demand better treatment of Francophone minorities in other provinces, and began to take the necessary steps to protect the use of the French language in the schools and economic institutions in the province itself.

In sum, the Quiet Revolution began as an economic phenomenon — as a demand that Quebec become "*maîtres chez nous*" — but it became a state of mind among young Quebeckers. It was that new state of mind, a new ethnic consciousness, that was the intellectual trigger of the separatist movement.

Starting with a number of pamphlets such as one called *Pourquois je suis séparatiste* by Marcel Chaput, who was a disaffected scientist with the federal Defence Research Board, and escalating to a wave of terrorism under the *Front de libération du Québec* (FLQ), manifestations of separatist strength steadily grew in the province during the sixties and seventies. This growth culminated when René Lévesque left the Liberals, formally joined the Separatist cause and united the movement's various factions under the Parti Québécois banner.

From the time of its formation in 1968, the Parti Québécois gained steadily in popular vote. In the 1966 Quebec election, 8% of Quebec voters supported one of the PQ's predecessors, the RIN (*Rassemblement pour l'indépendance nationale*). In 1970 while the PQ won only seven seats, some 23% of Quebeckers supported the party; and of French-speaking Quebeckers, some 33% voted for it. Its representation in the National Assembly fell to six after the 1973 election, in spite of the fact that its share of the popular vote rose to 30%. Finally, in the provincial election of November 15, 1976, the Parti Québécois took power, gaining seventy-one of the seats in the Quebec National Assembly.[8]

It is difficult to evaluate what proportion of PQ voters was actually *séparatiste*, what proportion supported Lévesque the man or the democratic socialism that at least one faction of the party espoused, and what proportion was simply disgruntled with the Bourassa Liberals. However, the PQ came to power with 41% of the popular vote and with an overwhelming majority of seats. Surveys taken at the time of the election indicated that only 49% of PQ voters supported independence in 1976.[9] The level of popular support for independence fluctuated around 20% of Quebec voters throughout the 1970s, and did not change significantly after the PQ took power. On the basis of a detailed examination of public-opinion surveys prior to and at the same time as the 1976 election, Maurice Pinard and Richard Hamilton conclude:

> What made the difference between the PQ victory in 1976 and its previous defeats rests on factors other than independence. Very succinctly, these factors can be summarized as a set of very negative evaluations of the incumbent Liberal government as well as a set of positive evaluations of the PQ party, its leadership, and its platform on issues other that independence. The independence issue did not contribute much to the growth of the PQ in the election of 1976; actually, that option prevented a more decisive PQ victory (in terms of popular vote) by leading non-separatist voters to opt for third parties, despite their relative electoral weakness, or to opt for the Liberals, despite their political shortcomings.[10]

[8] For a general description of the rise of the Parti Québécois, see Vera Murray, *Le Parti Québécois: De la fondation du pouvoir* (Montreal: Editions Hurtubise, HMH, 1976). See also W.D. Coleman, *The Independence Movement in Quebec, 1945–1980*, (Toronto: University of Toronto Press, 1984).

[9] Maurice Pinard and Richard Hamilton, "The Parti Québécois Comes to Power," *CJPS*, XI: 4, December 1978, p. 745.

[10] Pinard, pp. 739–740.

The PQ victory in 1976, then, can be attributed to a feeling that it could provide a "good-government" alternative to what was widely viewed as a dishonest Liberal government, which had mismanaged the economy and was largely responsible for a spate of strikes that was crippling the public sector in Quebec. The Parti Québécois succeeded in maximizing its support by virtue of the strategy, adopted at its 1974 convention, of separating the election from the independence issue by declaring that, after the election, a referendum on the question of sovereignty association would be held.

Since support for sovereignty association did not seem to be growing, the referendum was put off for almost four years, but was finally held on May 20, 1980, after a fairly brief but intensive campaign. The wording of the referendum question itself was described as "soft." The Lévesque government did not want to scare off Quebeckers who wanted change but were not sure about how much change, so the referendum asked only for the right "to negotiate" sovereignty association, and promised that no action would be taken on the results of such negotiations until a further referendum was held. However, despite the cautious and conciliatory wording on the referendum ballot, the result was a rejection of the Parti Québécois proposal. Approximately 83% of Quebeckers turned out, and the final tally was 59.5% *non* and 40.5% *oui*. In fact, when we take into account that more than 90% of the non-French residents of Quebec supported the *non* side, the result indicates that French-Canadian Québécois split almost evenly on the question as posed.

Thus while it is tempting to cite the referendum decision as a victory for Canadian unity, we must be more realistic about the result. In fact there are a large number of Québécois who remain dissatisfied with their place in the federal system. Even many of those who voted against the Lévesque proposition still favour fairly radical change in the structure of the federal system, and the opposition Liberal Party of Quebec, headed by Claude Ryan at the time, was espousing some fairly radical constitutional reforms short of sovereignty association itself.

In summary, the "crisis" of the 1960s and 1970s in Quebec arose from demands for a revision of the constitution in the direction of greater provincial autonomy. The demands ran the gamut from those for the outright separation of Quebec, through recognition of a "special status" for Quebec, to relatively minor changes in the financial structure of Canadian federalism. Such differing ideas, said the Royal Commission on Bilingualism and Biculturalism somewhat prophetically, all have a common denominator: "They expressed *a wide and deep dissatisfaction with the present political position* and a manifest will to conduct a search for many possible roads, which almost all went in the direction of more or less radical reforms."[11] We must now turn to an examination of the causes of this wide and deep dissatisfaction.

---

[11] *The Preliminary Report of the Royal Commission on Bilingualism and Biculturalism* (Ottawa: Queen's Printer, 1967).

THE CAUSES OF ETHNIC CLEAVAGE IN CANADA

Perhaps the most appropriate starting point for attempting to explain the pre-eminence and the persistence of French-English conflict in Canadian political life is to locate the phenomenon within the broader context of ethnic conflict in general. To do this, we must first understand the nature of ethnicity itself, its component parts and its socio-cultural and economic correlates.

The Coincidence of Cleavage: Geography, Culture, and Economics

At the most elementary level of analysis, ethnicity is simply an accident of one's birth — if our parents happen to be German or Chinese or Irish, then our ethnic origin will be, by definition, the same as our parents'. However, what is most significant politically about ethnicity is not the simple genetic accident that links all of us to one or more national or cultural groups, but the various factors that are normally tied to ethnic origin. Hence, if an Anglo-Saxon child is adopted in infancy by a French-Canadian family, and brought up as a French Canadian, the genetic background will be virtually irrelevant in determining the patterns of behaviour, cultural values, and socioeconomic status of the individual at maturity. As we shall see in Chapters 4 and 5, the process of socialization, and not heredity, is what determines individual values. Thus the political relevance of ethnicity — the significance of ethnicity as a determinant of lines of cleavage in a society — is determined by the many non-hereditary factors that coincide with the inherited accident of birth. These each must be considered in more detail.

i) Geographical Concentration

As we have seen, for much of the period since the British conquest in 1760, the most obvious of Canada's cleavages has been that between Canadians of French origin and the rest of Canada — "English" Canada, so-called. French Canadians do form a most substantial minority. In 1981 Canadians claiming French as their mother tongue constituted 26.7% of the Canadian population. But the rest of Canada is not an undifferentiated "majority." As can be seen in Table 3-1, about 27% of Canadians are of neither British nor French ethnic background, and some 13% learned some language other than English or French in childhood.[12]

Hence, undoubtedly one of the main reasons that French-English cleavage has been pre-eminent throughout Canadian history and that other ethnic conflicts have tended to fade into merely local political significance is that no single one of the other groups is very large. Approximately 4.7% of the Canadian population is of German origin; native peoples constitute only 2%; and Ukrainians, Dutch, and Scandinavians each comprise between 1% and 3% of the total population.

---

[12] Census of Canada, 1981. See Table 3-1.

TABLE 3-1
POPULATION BY ETHNIC ORIGIN
1981 CENSUS

Total European	86.2[1]
U.K.	40.2
France	26.7
German	4.7
Italian	3.1
Ukranian	2.2
Other	9.3[2]
Total Non-European	4.4[3]
Aboriginal People	2.0[4]
Multiple Origins	7.3[5]
Total Population	

[1]Includes only those who cited single origin
[2]Includes those who cited other origin as Jewish
[3]Excluding native people
[4]Includes those who cited more than one origin, one of which was native
[5]Excludes Métis. The remaining multiple origins are overwhelmingly European, with the vast majority of those including French or English

However, while French Canadians are five times as numerous as the largest of the non-British ethnic groups, there are other factors, in addition to simple numbers, which have tended to exacerbate the English-French cleavage in Canada. One is simply the regional *concentration* of Francophones. In 1981, more than 83% of the residents of Quebec listed French as their mother tongue, while only 11% listed English as the language they had first learned.[13] Sixty per cent of the population of Quebec speaks *only* French. Outside of the Montreal area, the proportion of the population of Quebec claiming French ancestry rises to more than 90%, and of these about 80% are unilingual French. In the rest of Canada, of course, the position is reversed; French is the mother tongue of only about 4% of the people, and in British Columbia the proportion is only 1.7%.

The *concentration* of ethnic groups is significant in other cases as well. For example, Canada's Inuit are concentrated for the most part above the treeline in the Northwest Territories, in northern Quebec, and in Labrador, and Canadian Indians are concentrated in the northern regions of the provinces, the Northwest Territories and the Yukon. Similarly, although it is a manifestation of patterns of settlement and migration more than of historical residency, the phenomenon of "ghettoization," particularly of non-white immigrant groups, has also tended to exaggerate and reinforce social and ethnic differences in the urban context. Finally, we can also identify some tendency for non-French, non-English Canadians of European descent to concentrate in certain regions of the country and in distinct districts or neighbourhoods in the cities and larger towns. However, while these

[13] *Census of Canada*, 1981. Note that we are using "mother tongue" as an indicator of ethnic origin for French Canadians.

settlement patterns often persist for several generations, so that it is possible, for example, to identify communities in western Canada that have high concentrations of German or Ukrainian Canadians, or districts in eastern Canadian cities that have high concentrations of people of Italian origin, generally second- or third-generation European immigrants find little difficulty in integrating themselves into the Canadian social "mainstream."

ii) Cultural Diversity: Integration vs. Assimilation

But while we are making the point that the geographical concentration of various ethnic groups tends to reinforce existing ethnic cleavages, there is a positive side to this phenomenon as well: the survival of cultural diversity. For example, the concentration of French Canadians in the province of Quebec is significant because without it it is unlikely that French Canada could have persisted as a distinct cultural entity. As it is, the day-to-day contacts of most French Canadians are with their ethnic confrères, and while there is the occasional requirement to use English, especially in Montreal, it is quite possible for many French-speaking Quebeckers to get along without ever speaking English or seeing an English person. What is true for Quebeckers is true in reverse for many western Canadians: they have absolutely no need to use the French language in their home provinces.

Cultural diversity has been the hallmark of Canadian society, and while such diversity should not be allowed to manifest itself in the destruction of the federation, its existence enriches and stimulates Canadian political life. It has become almost a cliché to refer to Canadian society as an ethnic or cultural *mosaic*—this to distinguish it from the United States, which is often likened to a *melting pot*—but what is implicit in this superficial distinction is that there are at least two analytical models that can explain how the various ethnic components of immigrant societies are bonded together. These models are *assimilation* and *integration*, and each bears elaboration in the interest of clarifying the nature of ethnic cleavage in Canada.

Assimilation means essentially that the various ethnic components of a political community get absorbed or dissolved by the majority or mainstream ethnic *mélange* and ultimately the component parts cease to be distinguishable. What is gained in this form of "nation-building" is a reduction or elimination of ethnic cleavage, and a higher degree of consensus. But, because culture is such an important reflection of ethnicity, what is lost is the richness of a truly multicultural society — one opts for a seafood purée and forgoes bouillabaisse because the former is easier to concoct and much more manageable at the table.

By contrast to assimilation, an integrative model recognizes the fact that minority cultures are in a state of siege that is imposed unconsciously and, often, with no malice by the majority or mainstream culture. This model takes as its starting point the assumption that the many groups that make up a multi-ethnic or pluralist society have unique cultural characteristics that often can enhance and strengthen the national political community. The attractiveness of such a model of nation-building to the minority ethnic groups is that they are permitted to retain their cultural distinctiveness while simultaneously being able to participate fully in, enjoy the benefits of, and contribute to the shared experience of being Canadian.[14]

Generally the model that has been employed in the building of the Canadian nation is an integrative or pluralist one. Our constitution, as we shall see in a later chapter, has reflected this from the outset; more recently, policy outputs such as official bilingualism, multiculturalism, and the 1982 Charter of Rights and Freedoms[15] are indications of a continuing political will to foster cultural[16] and ethnic diversity.

iii) Religion and Culture in Canada

To return to the main focus of this chapter, it has to be recognized that in opting for cultural diversity rather than homogeneity, the price Canadians must pay is the almost constant phenomenon of ethnic conflict. As we have seen, the coincidence of geographic and ethnic cleavages has been important in heightening the intensity of such conflict, but there are other significant lines of cleavage as well that add to the difficulty of forging a national consensus.

Of particular importance is the coincidence of religious and ethnic lines. As can be seen in Table 3-2, some 47.3% of the population of Canada is Roman Catholic and 41.2% Protestant — and virtually all French Canadians are Roman Catholic. Granted that there is a difference between being nominally a member of a particular denomination and being a practising member, it can still be argued that certain cultural characteristics are transmitted via religion. In any case French Canadians were, up to the recent past, much more likely to attend church than English Canadians. In 1965, 85% of French-speaking Roman Catholics in Canada attended church at least weekly, compared with 31% of English-speaking Protestants.[17] The influence of the Roman Catholic church in Quebec has been directed towards the preservation of the cultural integrity of French Canada, partly because the church in Quebec has viewed the threat of cultural assimilation as a threat to its own position.[18] Furthermore, the parish churches formed the social centres of small Quebec communities, and traditionally provided the sort of gathering place that is essential to the establishment of that group cohesion that helps to maintain cultural independence.

Although the significance of religious factors has declined generally in the twentieth century, as we have seen, through long periods of Canada's early history the French-English ethnic and linguistic cleavage was often overshadowed

---

[14] See pp. 98–101 for a discussion of the *consociational* model of cultural integration. See also L. Driedger, "Conformity vs. Pluralism," in Nevitte and Kornberg, eds., *Minorities and the Canadian State* (Mosaic Press, 1985), p. 157.

[15] See also chapters 6 and 7 and Nevitte and Kornberg, *Minorities.*

[16] See chapter 4 *infra.*, for a more detailed discussion of cultural diversity.

[17] Data from a 1965 public opinion survey directed by Professor J. Meisel of Queen's University.

[18] On the role of the church in French Canada, see Jean Charles Falardeau, "The Role and Importance of the Church in French Canada," in Marcel Rioux and Yves Martin, *French Canadian Society* (Toronto: McClelland and Stewart, 1964). A more passionate separatist statement of somewhat the same ideas can be found in Marcel Rioux, *Quebec in Question* (Toronto: James Lewis and Samuel, 1971), pp. 27 ff.

TABLE 3-2
POPULATION BY RELIGION
(1981 CENSUS)

	%
Catholic	47.3
Protestant	41.2
Other denominations	4.1
No religion, agnostic, or atheist	7.4

by religious-based differences.[19] The Irish immigrants of the 1840s transplanted much of the Orange-Roman Catholic strife from Ireland, and for some fifty years afterwards the predominant cleavage in Canada was Protestant-Catholic rather than French-English. Schools were denominational, not ethnic, as were hospitals, welfare institutions, newspapers, and many of the other institutions that connect citizens to society.

Still, nineteenth-century Canadians, no less than some of their descendants today, had a tendency to equate religious and ethnic differences. Thus, Protestants in the nineteenth and early twentieth centuries often saw a close tie between "popery" and "knavery," and since the French Canadians were all papist, it followed that they must also be knaves. In 1889, Dalton McCarthy warned in the *Toronto Mail*:

> Ontario will not be safe. . . . Our eastern gate has already been opened. . . . Catholic invasion is already streaming through . . . to detach Eastern Ontario from the British and Protestant civilization of which it now forms a part and annex it to the territory of the French race which is also the dominion of the priest.

In speaking of the Jesuit Estates Bill, he added:

> This is a British country and the sooner we take in hand our French Canadians and make them British in sentiment and teach them the English language the less trouble we shall have to prevent. Now is the time when the ballot box will decide this great question; and if it does not supply the remedy in this generation, bayonets will supply it in the next.[20]

While we have, fortunately, never had recourse to bayonets for the settlement of Canada's religious disputes, and while generally the intensity of religious conflict has declined, there are still political issues that divide people along religious lines. As an example, the question of the extension of separate-school funding to grades eleven, twelve, and thirteen in Ontario became a major issue in the 1985 provincial election. While it is clear that the issue is a complex one, involving philosophical questions about, for instance, the appropriate relationships between

---

[19] K.D. McRae, "Consociationalism and the Canadian Political System," in K.D. McRae, ed., *Consociational Democracy: Political Accommodation in Segmented Societies* (Toronto: McClelland and Stewart, 1974), pp. 242 ff; see also the first section of this chapter.

[20] Both quoted in Schull, *Laurier*, p. 227.

church and state, it does lend credence to the view that religion is still a significant source of political conflict in this country.

As a second and more disturbing example, there have been increased incidents in Canada that would indicate a resurgence of anti-Semitism.[21] Again, while anti-Semitism is more than simply a reflection of religious cleavage, the fact that a schoolteacher in Alberta and a publisher in Toronto were convicted in 1985 on various charges stemming from their public expression of extreme anti-Jewish beliefs must stimulate grave concern in the minds of Canadians who have long felt that such ethno-religious issues were effectively dead. Thus, while it is still possible to conclude that religious cleavage is not the most important manifestation of ethnic conflict in Canada, and while Canadians can take some solace in the fact that religious factions in this country do not generally resort to physical violence or acts of terrorism to make their points, religion does remain a significant item on the agenda for political debate. Moreover, because lines of religious cleavage tend to coincide with ethnic ones, religious cleavage can help to reinforce and exacerbate ethnic conflict in general.

iv) Socio-Economic Deprivation and Ethnicity

The most important of the cleavages that coincide with ethnicity are the economic ones. As we have seen in Chapter 2, the distribution of wealth in Canada is extremely unequal, and the distribution of that wealth often reflects other demographic variables, such as geography and ethnicity. The fact that one ethnic group may be consistently short-changed relative to other ethnic groups in the work place can only serve to accentuate and reinforce existing ethnic conflicts. With respect to French-English relations in Canada, the relative economic deprivation of French-Canadians in the federation has been manifested in two ways. One of these has been and continues to be the economic disparity that exists between the province of Quebec and the "have" provinces of the federation, and the second, equally important, is the disparity that has existed within the province of Quebec between French and English citizens of that province.

Throughout Canadian history, French Canadians have generally received a proportionally smaller share of Canada's economic wealth than Canadians of English origin.[22] Even by 1961, the income of French-Canadian male members of the labour force was only 85.8% of the national average, whereas that of men who were of British origin was 110% of that average.[23] Within Quebec, French-Canadian incomes were 92% of the provincial average while English Canadians received 140% of the provincial average.[24] Among Canadian ethnic groups in 1961, only Italians had lower income levels than French Canadians. Moreover, in the province of Quebec, per-capita income in 1970 was 90% of the national average and only 78% of the Ontario average. Among French Canadians there

---

[21] See the Report of the Special Committee on Visible Minorities.

[22] See Table 3-3.

[23] Report of the Royal Commission on Bilingualism and Biculturalism, Book III, *The Work World*, vol. 3A (Ottawa: Department of Supplies and Services, 1969), pp. 18–19.

[24] *The Work World*, pp. 18–19.

TABLE 3-3
AVERAGE FAMILY INCOME
QUEBEC, ONTARIO, AND CANADA — SELECTED YEARS
CONSTANT (1971) DOLLARS

	61	71	75	77	79	81
Quebec	7,062	9,919	11,152	11,853	12,238	11,868
Ontario	7,701	11,483	13,030	13,435	13,231	13,576
Canada	7,093	10,368	11,994	12,503	12,680	12,846

Source: Statistics Canada, *Canada Yearbook, 1985.* Department of Supplies and Services, Ottawa, 1986.

TABLE 3-4
UNEMPLOYMENT RATE — QUEBEC, ONTARIO, AND CANADA
1979–1983

	79	80	81	82	83
Quebec	9.6	9.8	10.3	13.8	13.9
Canada	7.4	7.5	7.5	11.0	11.9
Ontario	6.5	6.8	6.6	9.8	10.4

Source: Statistics Canada, *Canada Yearbook, 1985.* Department of Supplies and Services, Ottawa, 1986.

was a larger proportion of poor families than among English Canadians, and there may also have been a larger disparity in incomes: for in 1961, 37% of the French-Canadian labour force received less than $3,000 per year and fully 78% were receiving less than $5,000, while the figures for the rest of Canada were 31% and 70% respectively.

While it is difficult to obtain unemployment figures by ethnic origin, it is clear that, next to the Atlantic provinces, Quebec consistently has the highest levels of unemployment in Canada. In Quebec, unemployment rates were an average of 3.3% in the period 1946–1951, where the corresponding figure for all of Canada was 2.9%. Since then, and even into the 1980s, Quebec unemployment rates average about 2% higher than the national average, with the rates in Quebec in 1983 at 13.9%, while the national rate stood at 11.9%.[25] The causes of these high unemployment figures are many and, while most of them have nothing to do with ethnicity *per se*, the effect has been to create fertile soil upon which ethnic conflict may grow.

This dissatisfaction of French Quebeckers was further fed historically by the fact that, both within and outside of Quebec, French Canadians have tended to hold jobs with lower status than those held by English Canadians. The "repatriation" of industry in Quebec (by which is meant the taking over of executive jobs by French Canadians) began in the early 1960s, but a disproportionate percentage of "boss" jobs, from foreman to company president, were still held by English Canadians through the 1970s.

If one looks at the Quebec economy in terms of sectoral distribution, it is clear

[25] See Table 3-4.

that Quebec has long been one of the most highly industrialized provinces in Canada. By the end of World War Two less than half the population of Quebec was rural: Quebec was ahead of Canada in this respect.[26] The annual rate of industrial growth in Quebec since then has been about equal to that of Ontario, although the gap between the provinces has not closed appreciably.

In 1971 Quebec was, next to Newfoundland and British Columbia, the least agricultural province in Canada, with only 4.5% of the labour force in agriculture, versus 6.5% for Canada as a whole.[27] Although considerable consolidation in Quebec farms has taken place since then, in 1963, a survey by the Agricultural and Rural Development Agency showed that more than half of Quebec's farm units were not properly profitable and that Quebec had the lowest farm incomes, the lowest educational levels of farmers, the largest per-capita debt among farmers, and the largest farm family size in Canada.

Despite this evidence, however, it is not accurate to describe the Quebec economy as backward. In fact, in terms of industrial development the province is quite advanced relative to many other parts of Canada, and accounts for about 25% of all Canadian manufacturing. However, it is clear that French Canadians did not share fully in the benefits of industrial development until the 1970s. The explanation for this unfortunate state of affairs likely lies in the economic history of French Canada and of the province of Quebec.

It is generally agreed that prior to the British conquest, French Canada was a feudal society with a mercantile bourgeoisie capable of operating business and industry. The conquest destroyed the commercial structure of French-Canadian society, and the British presence, plus the impoverishment of the colony by the war, induced most of the bourgeoisie to return to France. The loss of the entrepreneurial French élite was followed initially by a movement of French workers and small businessmen back to the soil and later to employee positions in industry. The proper ambition for a bright young French Canadian was not to enter business, but rather to become a member of the clergy, a doctor or a lawyer, or, failing that, a farmer or a worker. The élite left in the colony was that of the church, and it moved naturally, together with newly arrived English-speaking businessmen, to fill whatever power gap remained. The church took care of the spiritual and social needs of Quebec, and the English businessmen replaced the departed Francophone bourgeoisie and took care of its business needs.

Once the cycle had started, it was extremely difficult to break. The church and the English business élites naturally moved to perpetuate themselves, and a new élite, the governmental élite, arose to join the other two. Each of these élites developed vast bureaucratic structures and these structures had their own "maintenance needs," which conditioned their recruiting patterns. The church and governmental hierarchies were French-speaking, the business hierarchy English-speaking, and since recruitment in organizations is determined by the characteristics of those already there, the lack of Francophones in the private sector was exaggerated. To this was added a paucity of technically trained

---

[26] Raynauld, *The Canadian Economic System*, pp. 69–71.

[27] *Canada Year Book 1972*, p. 837.

Francophones, for the church, the largest of the hierarchies and the one that dominated Francophone education in the province, felt that technical or commercial employment was not an appropriate ambition for a young French Canadian.

For a cycle like this to be broken, one of the hierarchies had to gain ascendancy over the others and then respond to the emerging needs of the environment. This has been happening in Quebec at an accelerated rate since 1960, as the government hierarchy has displaced the church in such fields as education and social services. One of the results of the reformed education system has been an increasing number of technically trained French Canadians capable of handling many of the economic developmental needs of Quebec society. But an English-dominated business élite could not simply turf out its many settled English technocrats and managers, so there arose a situation of underemployment of large numbers of intelligent and qualified young French Canadians who could see that the English held the jobs to which they aspired — and in their own province, at that. Control of the Quebec economy hung tantalizingly just beyond the grasp of this rising class of French Canadians. Understandably, they grew impatient with "two hundred years of waiting" and turned in large numbers to support the separatist leanings of the Parti Québécois and its precursors. The changes in the distribution of income and the increasing availability of better job opportunities simply came too late and, indeed, it was the growing cadre of younger middle-class French Canadians able to pursue nationalist ends who played key roles in the separatist movement of the seventies.

Where French-English cleavages were accentuated and perpetuated throughout history by the coincidence of economic factors, and while French-English relations have certainly been the most dominant ethnic conflict area on the agenda of political debate in Canada, it must not be forgotten that there are other important ethnic cleavages. Most significant of these is the increasingly important cleavage between Canada's visible minorities and the Canadian mainstream. According to the report of the Special Committee on Visible Minorities in Canadian Society, non-whites comprise 7% of the total Canadian population.[28] Moreover, waves of immigration in recent years have tended to come disproportionately from Africa, Asia, and Central and South America as opposed to more traditional European sources of immigration.[29]

The evidence marshalled by the special committee indicates that the visible or non-white minorities in Canada generally suffer from a slower rate of social integration into Canadian society than do traditional immigrant groups from European countries. The reasons for this include the existence of racist attitudes on the part of many individual Canadians, as well as what the committee calls "systemic discrimination" (unintentional institutionalized discrimination).[30] Perhaps the most important manifestation of discrimination in Canada is in the employment markets, where many non-white ethnic groups are disproportionately

---

[28] Canada, House of Commons, *Equality Now!*, (Ottawa: Department of Supplies and Services, 1984), p. 2.

[29] Statistics Canada, *Canada Yearbook* (Ottawa: Department of Supplies and Services, 1985), p. 47.

[30] *Equality Now!*, p. 32.

excluded from participation in the labour force or, even more commonly, where such individuals are kept out of roles in sectors of the economy where these new Canadians would prefer to participate:

> The Committee recognizes that not all visible minority groups are unemployed to the same extent. It may be for example that Chinese Canadians or Canadians with origins in India are not disproportionately unemployed when compared with other groups, but they may be disproportionately *under-employed*.[31]

The committee points out, as well, that there are significant differences *among* the non-white ethnic groups. It was found, for instance, that West Indian blacks and South Asians particularly tend to have lower incomes and experience more unemployment than other Canadians,[32] and that in such groups the problem is exaggerated still more among young people in the fifteen- to twenty-four-year-old age groups.[33]

The committee also focused on aboriginal people in Canada. While in one sense the native people of Canada are racially "visible," they are significantly different from other non-white groups in that they are not an immigrant group. The native people were here first and in fact should perhaps be recognized more as the "*invisible* charter group" than as a visible minority. However, no matter how native people are classified, the fact remains that they continue to suffer from a wide range of discriminatory phenomena. The Indian Act itself, while intended to protect native people from exploitation by the majority and to provide them with a broad range of social programs, including health care and education, stands as a monument to the notion of unintentional or systemic discrimination.

As a vehicle for social integration, the Act has failed totally, and even in areas such as health, social services, and education, for which the Act was specifically designed to deliver programs to the natives, the record is fairly dismal. While the completion rate for high school today is around 75% nationally, the figure for native people is still only 20%. One of the results of this is a 50% rate of participation in the labour force, by contrast to 65% for non-natives, and an unemployment rate almost twice as high as the Canadian average. Even among native people who are employed, the average income is approximately two-thirds of the national average, and the proportion of aboriginal income in the form of transfers from government is twice that of non-native Canadians.[34]

When one moves to a comparison of general social conditions, the picture for aboriginal Canadians is still more bleak.[35] Native Canadians continue to suffer from extremely low standards of housing, with serious overcrowding and a disproportionately low level of facilities such as indoor plumbing, running water,

[31] *Equality Now!*, p. 32.

[32] *Equality Now!*, p. 33.

[33] *Equality Now!*, p. 36.

[34] See: Erik Nielsen, *New Management Initiatives* (Ottawa: Government of Canada, 1985), pp. 77–81; see also: *Indian Self-Government in Canada* (The Penner Report) (Ottawa: House of Commons, 1983), pp. 14–24.

[35] *Indian Self-Government in Canada.*

TABLE 3-5
NATIVE PEOPLES
(CENSUS OF CANADA, 1981)

Inuit	Status	Non-Status	Métis	Total
25,390	292,700	75,110	98,260	491,400

TABLE 3-6
DEATHS PER THOUSAND POPULATION BY AGE GROUP
(1973 TO 1976 AVERAGE)*

Age Group	Native	Non-Native
1– 4 years	3.1	0.8
5–19 years	1.9	0.7
20–44 years	6.0	1.5
49–64 years	15.7	9.0
65 and older	57.0	55.0

*Death rates for native people up to age sixty-five range from two to four times the Canadian average.

TABLE 3-7
NATIVE PEOPLES
(CENSUS OF CANADA, 1981)

Suicides per 100,000 population*

Age Group	Native	Non-Native
5–14 years	10.0	0.2
15–24 years	130.0	19.0
25–34 years	70.0	20.0
35–44 years	39.0	21.0

*For all age groups combined, the number of native suicides per 100,000 population is three times the Canadian average.

TABLE 3-8
JUVENILE DELINQUENCY RATE PER 100,000 POPULATION

Native	Non-Native
353	128

and electricity. Native people also have a higher crime rate than other Canadians. It has been estimated that 70% of status Indians can expect to be incarcerated in a provincial correctional centre by age twenty-five, as compared to an estimate of 8% for other Canadians; and that in western Canada and the north, native people currently comprise 40% of the prison population. Life expectancy, infant mortality, suicide rate, violent death, and rate of admission to hospital are all much worse for native people than for non-natives.[36] All in all, the standard of

[36] See Tables 3-6 to 3-10 for illustrations of these problems.

TABLE 3-9
NATIVE PEOPLES
(CENSUS OF CANADA, 1981)

Hospital admissions per 100,000 population

Illness	Native	Non-Native
Infectious and parasitic disease	3,700	400
Diseases of the nervous system	2,100	500
Diseases of the respiratory system	10,800	1,900
Diseases of the digestive system	2,600	1,800
Childbirth and complications of pregnancy	8,000	4,300
Accidents and violence	6,000	1,400

TABLE 3-10
VIOLENT DEATHS PER 100,000 POPULATION

Cause	Native	Non-Native
Motor vehicle	60.5	26.9
Burns and fire	23.6	3.5
Poisoning, overdose	14.9	3.0
Suicides	30.1	12.1
Other violent deaths	91.3	26.4

living and quality of life for Canada's aboriginal people is lower than for any other ethnic group, and there is little to indicate that this situation can be remedied in the near future.

To summarize our conclusions to this point: it is clear that the dominant ethnic cleavage in Canada has been and continues to be that between French and English, and this cleavage has manifested itself at least in part as conflict between the province of Quebec and the rest of Canada. The institutionalized conflict will be examined in more detail in the sections of the book on federalism and intergovernmental relations. However, in the case of the more general cleavage that exists between French and English Canadians, the causes of its pre-eminence are, first, the relatively large number of French Canadians and their concentration in one geographic area, and second, the coincidence of cultural factors, such as religion and language, and economic factors, such as lower income levels and higher unemployment for French Canadians and Quebec relative to English Canadians and the country.

Similarly, while we are dealing with much smaller ethnic minorities, it is clear that there is a serious, deepening cleavage between non-white immigrant groups and the white European majority, and between Canada's aboriginal peoples and other Canadians. In both cases these cleavages are to some extent accentuated by relative concentrations of the minorities; in the former instance, in certain urban areas or ghettos, and, in the latter, in the northern parts of the provinces and in the Northwest Territories and the Yukon. As well, relative economic and social deprivation has tended to reinforce the sense of alienation and injustice among non-white groups, and to deepen still more the conflict between the ethnic minorities and the majority.

The Psychological Dimension of Ethnic Conflict

The resolution of conflict between and among the various European ethnic groups that make up the Canadian mosaic has been, if admittedly difficult, at least possible. In the case of French-English cleavage, resolution came through institutional devices such as federalism, and cultural, linguistic, religious, and educational guarantees to the smaller charter group; and, in the case of other European groups, resolution came through policies of multiculturalism that permit integration without total assimilation of the immigrant groups. However, the conflicts between non-white immigrant groups or aboriginal peoples and the existing social system remain unresolved, if not unresolvable. It is likely that part of the explanation for the persistence and pervasiveness of conflict between non-white ethnic groups and the majority racial group is the psychological phenomenon of *ethnocentrism*, which in its uglier or more extreme manifestation is often referred to as *racism*.

At the root of ethnocentrism is a seemingly natural tendency for national or ethnic groups to perceive the world in we-they terms. This consciousness of ethnic differences has historically facilitated the global growth of nation states and has permitted cultural differentiation among the peoples of the world. While such differentiation may have benefits in organizing international politics, in helping national integration, and in enriching the global cultural mosaic, it can have negative consequences, too. On the international level, ethnocentrism can lead to interstate conflicts such as war, and within the context of a single national state it can be a serious disintegrative force.

However, while these broad systemic implications of ethnocentrism are important, perhaps the most serious result of this phenomenon within a political community is the hardship and injustice it imposes on the minority ethnic or racial group. At the individual level racism begins with prejudice, which is based on fear and suspicion and leads to the development of negative stereotypes of the minority ethnic groups. But racism is a two-way street. On the one hand what results is a kind of majority-culture chauvinism that justifies the discrimination against the minority group, and on the other hand the minority group tends to respond defensively by withdrawing still more from the mainstream society. As described by a witness before the Special Committee on Visible Minorities:

> the white Canadian . . . picks up on the fear and mistrust that the immigrant communicates — and communicates it right back.[37]

Similarly, with respect to white attitudes to native people in certain northern communities:

---

[37] *Equality Now!*, p. 10.

Rather than white racists creating the situation in Kenora, the situation there has created and is creating white racists . . . the oppressed condition of the Indians stirs prejudice in the white community, leading to treatment of Indians that worsens their condition, resulting in heightened prejudice among whites and so on.[38]

Racism, thus, is a vicious circle, which feeds on itself and becomes a self-perpetuating tragedy of human relationships.

As we shall see when we come to discuss the development of the franchise in the Canadian electoral system and when we discuss the machinery for the protection of civil liberties, Canada's record with respect to official racism is by no means unblemished. While Canada is no South Africa, federal and provincial legislation in the past has, by design, blatantly discriminated against sundry religious sects, non-white immigrant groups, native people, and even French Canadians. However, it is likely safe to state that, today, such deliberate and officially sanctioned discrimination is no longer tolerated, and is effectively barred by human-rights legislation and the Charter of Rights and Freedoms. On the other hand, there still remains the phenomenon of unintentional systemic discrimination, which, while gradually being eliminated in most jurisdictions in Canada as awareness of the problem increases among political leaders and in the public at large, is still reflected in many public policies. Time and the political will to do so can ultimately eliminate systemic discrimination in Canada, but the psychological root of such discrimination — racial intolerance on the part of average Canadians — still remains the most critical barrier to the fuller integration and participation of visible minorities in the Canadian community. As the Special Committee on Visible Minorities attests:

we are a flawed society. Research has shown that as many as 15 per cent of the population exhibit blatantly racist attitudes while another 20–25 per cent have some racist tendencies. Moreover even those individuals who are very tolerant can with the best of intentions, engage in racism without knowing it or meaning to do so. Similarly, institutions can unintentionally restrict the life chances of non-white individuals through a variety of seemingly neutral rules regulations and procedures.[39]

Thus, while it may be possible to eliminate systemic discrimination against Canada's visible minorities, and while it is also possible to find public policy solutions to problems such as discrimination in the work place, the ultimate means of reducing racial intolerance must be found with attitudinal changes on the part of individual Canadians. The integration of non-whites into the community can only be achieved if whites learn to accept the fact of ethnic and social differences without prejudice and only if our educational institutions, communications media, and public policies actively foster the goal of greater understanding among the various ethnic groups that make up the Canadian cultural mosaic.

---

[38] Gallagher and Gonick, "The Occupation of Anicinobe Park," *Canadian Dimension*, December 1985, p. 11.

[39] *Equality Now!*, p. 36.

Integration through Segmentation:
The Consociational Model

Before attempting to summarize the current state of ethnic relations in Canada it is necessary first to look at a distinctive model for the possible resolution of ethnic conflict in multicultural societies, *consociational democracy*.[40] In its barest form, consociational theory suggests that democratic politics in pluralist societies works best when its operating principles include at least partial segregation of the masses along either side of whatever cleavage lines are in question, together with a process of accommodation among the élites at the head of the various segments of society:

> The essential characteristic of consociational democracy is not so much any particular institutional arrangement as overarching cooperation at the elite level with the deliberate aim of concentrating disintegrative tendencies in the system.[41]

> Deep, mutually reinforcing social cleavages do not form an insuperable obstacle to viable democracy. The crucial factor in the establishment and preservation of democratic stability is the quality of leadership. The politics of accommodation open up the possibility of viable democracy even when the social condition appears unpromising.[42]

In order for consociationalism to work, it is not essential that subcultures be separated in a physical sense, but most consociational theorists at least imply that the work of the élites is made easier if there is considerable segregation. This will minimize tensions at the mass level and help maintain cohesion within each subculture, thus helping the élites to gain support for agreements they have made among themselves and to articulate adequately to each other the interests of their respective subcultures.[43]

If we apply these ideas to the study of French-English relations in Canada, some suggestions appear that have long been familiar to French-Canadian students of politics, but that often startle English Canadians. In theory, according to the assumptions of most English-speaking Canadians, if the two solitudes that are French and English Canada could be thrust together and the masses of the two groups partially integrated, then French-English tensions would disappear. In fact, the industrialization of Canada has partially achieved such a mixing of the

---

[40] The framework was originally developed by A. Lijphart and other European analysts. For a brief description, see A. Lijphart, "Consociational Democracy," *World Politics*, 21 (1969), pp. 207–225; "Cultural Diversity and Theories of Political Integration," *Canadian Journal of Political Science*, 4 (1971), pp. 1–14; and "Consociation and Federation: Conceptual and Empirical Links," *CJPS*, XII, 3, September 1977, p. 499–515. For Canadian applications, see S.J.R. Noel, "Consociational Democracy and Canadian Federalism," *CJPS*, 4 (1971), pp. 15–18; and *Democracy in Plural Societies: A Comparative Exploration* (New Haven: Yale University, 1977); and especially McRae, *Consociational Democracy*; and McRae, "Federation, Consociation, Corporatism — An Addendum to Arend Lijphart," *CJPS*, XII, 3, September 1979, pp. 517–522.

[41] A. Lijphart, "Typologies of Democratic Systems," *Comparative Political Studies*, 1 (1968), p. 21.

[42] A. Lijphart, *The Politics of Accommodation, Pluralism and Democracy in the Netherlands* (Berkeley, 1968), p. 211. Both these quotations may be found in McRae, "The Concept of Consociationalism."

[43] McRae, "Introduction," *Consociational Democracy*, pp. 1–28.

two populations. It could be argued, for instance, that if hard-rock miners from Chapais, P.Q. and Timmins, Ontario were put in the same tavern, they would very soon recognize that they have much more in common with each other than either group has with its provincial élites in Quebec City and Toronto. Yet why has ethnic conflict persisted, particularly when the scene of most unrest has been Montreal, where the two groups come together most closely?

Consociational analysis suggests that this worsening of relations may be caused indirectly by the very integration that was supposed to ameliorate the problem. The integration of the French and English solitudes may simply make it harder for the élites to establish the accommodations that produce inter-ethnic harmony, or it may reduce the significance of culture and ethnicity to both groups, and thus destroy the basis for the hegemony of the nationalist élites. The problem may be exacerbated by the fact that the French-Canadian élite sees its traditional clientele disappearing as more French people learn English and become part of the English-Canadian industrial tradition. Paradoxically, it is at least conceivable that the nearer cultural cleavage comes to disappearing at the mass level, the more desperately Canadian élites, both French and English, but particularly those whose main power base stems from the continued pre-eminence of cultural as opposed to economic issues, may fight to maintain or even escalate ethnic hostility.

For the French-Canadian political élites of the 1970s, the alternatives had become painfully clear: either the separation of Quebec, in which case they could continue to play a predominant role in the new state, or the amelioration of French-English cultural conflict, which would see the current French-Canadian élite replaced by one whose ideological *raison d'être* is economics and not ethnicity.

K.D. McRae has pointed out that there are both ideological and structural factors in the Canadian political tradition that may act to reinforce this apparently insoluble dilemma.[44] The factors are, paradoxically, the very ones that political scientists have thought held the country together. Structurally, Canada has lacked political parties that express and formulate the interests of English and French Canadians separately. In the politics of some ethnically plural European countries there are such parties, and the accommodations that must be made between various ethnic groups are then made among the parties themselves — often in the process of forming a coalition to govern. In Canada some accommodations have been worked out within the parties, but many are still being worked out on the federal-provincial stage. Here the rigidities introduced by the distribution of federal and provincial powers in the BNA Act and the existence of ponderous bureaucratic structures with their own maintenance needs may impede the process of cultural accommodation.

Perhaps equally important is that, despite all the "mosaic" rhetoric, a dominant but unstated premise of many English-Canadian political élites is that there is no particular need to accommodate ethnic minorities other than by encouraging them to do folk dances on July 1, because it is the political destiny (and indeed duty) of minorities either to become a majority or to be assimilated and

---

[44] McRae, "Consociationalism and the Canadian Political System," in *Consociational Democracy*, pp. 238–261.

disappear. This premise, reminiscent of the Durham Report but alive and well in many regions of the country today, is workable only if the minority is small and lacking in political clout. Moreover, it is a view unlikely to be appealing to French Canadians, who clearly will *never* become a majority as a whole, who certainly do *not* want to assimilate, and who *do* enjoy political and constitutional power.

According to the postulates of consociational theory, the implications of this English-Canadian "mind-set" for French Canada are clear: to be a majority, one must either separate or revert to the kind of "Quebec Reserve" politics that characterized the most tranquil periods during the years from 1867 to 1960. In that situation, French-Canadian politicians play a rather minor national role, while Quebec politics are left to them as their exclusive preserve. As long as Quebec life was controlled by the alliance of the church and the state, this "Fortress Quebec" option was viable. However, under the impact of modernization, its viability diminished to the point where, viewed from the perspective of many elements of the French Canadian élite, the *séparatiste* or sovereignty-association option was the only option. English Canadians have taken a long time to grasp the point that special accommodative devices are needed, and

> because they [the English] have not done so, French-Canadians have reacted in the only way open to them; by an instinctive attempt to build — either by themselves or in concert with others — stable majorities of their own. As long as English Canadians remain majority minded, many French Canadians will find their most effective response in an increasingly autonomous Quebec. . . . Any genuinely pluralist society must learn to do better.[45]

Thus, while the consociational model might serve as a helpful if only partial explanation of the tone and direction of French-English relations in the past, the theory may have less expository value as the French and English solitudes break down before economic and political forces of change. Before attempting to identify these forces of change, however, it is important to note a more recent attempt to apply the theory of consociationalism to ethnic conflict in Canada in the area of aboriginal rights and native self-government.

The consociational model was applied to French-English relations as an explanation or description of history; its application to the place of native peoples in the federation has been proposed in a more prescriptive mood. The notion of social segmentation coupled with political-élite accommodation is at least implicitly a cornerstone of the recommendations of the Report of the Special Committee on Indian Self Government (The Penner Report). Similarly, the constitutional proposals for native self-government that were presented to the federal-provincial constitutional conferences in 1985, which reflected in part the Penner recommendations, advocated a level of political autonomy for the various native constituencies in specific areas of jurisdiction. While these proposals failed to get the approval of a sufficient number of provinces at that conference, the movement towards aboriginal self-government appears likely to grow.

Finally, there are vestiges of what might be dubbed a "proto-consociational" approach at least implicit in some of the proposals of the native people of the

[45] From McRae, *Consociational Democracy*, p. 301.

Mackenzie Valley for a "Denendeh" government, and explicitly in recent work-ing papers commissioned by the Western Constitutional Forum (WCF).[46] The WCF includes representation from the legislative assembly of the Northwest Territo-ries and from the native organizations in the western territories, and is mandated to develop a constitutional framework for that region that would accommodate the interests of the natives and non-natives living there. The applicability of the consociational model would seem to be most promising in the western part of the territories, where the native population, including the Dene and Métis and possi-bly the Inuvialuit of the Mackenzie Delta-Beaufort region, form a significant minor-ity of the population and are concentrated in specific geographic areas. The segmentation of the white and native societies is thus a fact right now and any attempt to build political structures that might recognize and consolidate that fact might find a good fit with current political reality. Unfortunately, at the time of writing, the proposals have not been considered in any great detail, and the implementation of some modified form of the consociational model in the north may still be some time off.

Ethnic Conflict Today: The Changing Agenda

The current situation in French-English relations evokes a different and less extreme kind of ethnic hostility from that of past conflicts. The inflammatory declarations that characterized past conflicts such as those that accompanied the Riel, the Manitoba-schools, and the conscription crises are notably absent; reli-gion is no longer such a major and explosive component of the French–non-French cleavage in Canada; and the majority of Canadians avoid the recriminations of the past in seeking redress of current grievances. Even the separatist or *indépendantiste* sentiments that appeared to be gaining strength rapidly in the late seventies appear to be on the wane, if not on the verge of disappearing completely. The Parti Québécois reversed its decision to campaign in the 1985 election on the issue of sovereignty association and ultimately dropped indepen-dence from the party rhetoric entirely. Despite all of these efforts to reflect the growing lack of interest in independence, the PQ still lost the election by a land-slide to the solidly federalist Liberal party.

But perhaps the more peaceful face of French-Canadian nationalism in the 1980s should not surprise us. The conflict here became not French vs. English, but rather a conflict between differing opinions about what direction Quebec should take in the future among French Canadians. The referendum result of 1981, with French-speaking Québécois splitting virtually evenly, suggests that the debate was between two sets of attitudes in Quebec and not between Quebec and Canada. In fact all of the referendum rhetoric propounded by the leaders of the *oui* campaign, attempting to make the point that French Canadians should be given control over their own destiny, must have seemed puzzling to anybody outside of Canada. It does not take very sophisticated analysis to discover that, given the results of the 1980 federal election, French Canadians made up a

---

[46] See M. Asch, *Home and Native Land*, (Toronto: Methuen, 1984), for a discussion of the applicability of the consociational model in the Northwest Territories.

majority of the governing Liberal Party, while the prime minister and a significant percentage of the Cabinet were also from Quebec. Nor has this situation changed with the PC victory in the 1984 election, for the prime minister, a significant proportion of the Cabinet, and more than fifty of the members of the Tory caucus represent ridings in the province of Quebec. Finally, the outside observer might also be pardoned for asking whether the conduct of a referendum on separation did not itself constitute as complete a measure of control over one's destiny as that available to any people in the world.

As Reg Whitaker commented:

> The referendum was, in some ways, a moving example of a people undertaking a collective decision which would determine their destiny for the future. The debate penetrated into levels of society normally left untouched by party politics, and in some senses represented a moment of true democracy rarely witnessed in Quebec or elsewhere.[47]

Indépendantisme is "yesterday's issue"[48] both in Quebec and on the national political stage. But why has it changed from the central item on the national and political agenda to an item that is absent even on the agenda of political discourse in Quebec? One of the simplest answers to this question is that many of the goals of independence have been achieved without separation—many of the battles fought by French-Canadian nationalists for two centuries have in practical terms been won and other concerns dominate political debate:

> the generation which came of age at the time of the Quiet Revolution has moved through a historic alteration in the old pattern of unequal accommodation between the two language groups. The generation coming of age in the 1980s faces fewer of the blatant aggravations which galvanised an earlier generation into militant indépendantiste politics.[49]

Some of these "aggravations," such as unequal opportunity to seek jobs in the federal public service, the inability to feel confident that one could receive services from federal institutions in the language of choice, and, in general, the feeling that French Canadians could not feel at home in any part of Canada but Quebec, have been removed by a combination of federal policies, a new consciousness of the "French fact" in other parts of Canada, and, in the case of New Brunswick, the declaration of official bilingualism in the constitution. Ironically, although the then-separatist government of Quebec refused to ratify it, the constitutional reform passed in 1982, most notably the Charter of Rights and Freedoms, firmly entrenches French language and educational rights and affirms again the principle of bilingualism enunciated in the BNA Act.

Within Quebec, there have been many changes in the past decade that have served to redress the grievances and assuage the fears of Francophones. The French language is alive and well, and although it may turn out to be a pyrrhic

---

[47] R. Whitaker, "The Quebec Cauldron" in Whittington and Williams, eds., *Canadian Politics in the 1980s*, (Toronto: Methuen, 1984), p. 52.

[48] Ibid., p. 52.

[49] Ibid., p. 53.

victory to individuals in the new Quebec, the number of unilingual Francophones is actually on the increase, while the number of English Canadians in the province who do not speak French is declining. The problem here may turn out to be that in making it possible to get along in Quebec speaking only French but impossible speaking only English, the provincial language laws may have done English Quebeckers the biggest favour. French may well be the language of the work place in Quebec, but many of the higher-paying and higher-status jobs in government and in the private sector require personnel who can deal with English Canada and the United States. Any unilingual Francophones produced by the language legislation of the seventies may thus end up being disqualified from positions because they don't speak any English.[50]

In the area of education, too, provincial legislation has secured the provision that French is the language of instruction throughout the province. While Bill 101, the controversial Quebec Charter of the French Language, originally provided that only children with one parent educated in Quebec in English would be permitted to attend English-language schools, section 23 of the Canadian Charter of Rights and Freedoms effectively extends that right to all English-speaking Canadians. Nevertheless, despite this small reduction in the applicability of Bill 101, this legislation and subsequent reforms to the Quebec educational system do indeed guarantee the continued pre-eminence of the French language in the province's educational system.[51]

However, while such policy responses to the problem of French-English relations in Quebec and in Canada have contributed significantly to the cooling of ethnic conflict and to the decline in the efficacy of the independence movement in French Canada, it has been the relentless imperatives of economics that have most significantly altered the face of French-English conflict. At one level, this can be seen in terms of the global economic and fiscal crisis of the seventies and eighties. Quebec was affected by the recession of 1981–1983 as much or even more than many parts of Canada, and the preoccupation with nationalist issues simply became a luxury that politicians in both Canada and Quebec could no longer afford. Attention had to be turned to the more immediate and pressing concerns of the economy.

But economic variables affected the salience of ethnic conflict in a more positive way as well. The fact is that in the seventies the relative deprivation of Francophones *vis-à-vis* Anglophones within Quebec was either significantly reduced or eliminated. To a large extent, as a result of the rapid growth of the role of the Quebec state in the economy during the sixties and seventies,[52] and, as well,

---

[50] See: R. Gibbins, *Conflict and Unity* (Toronto: Methuen, 1985), pp. 38–80, for an excellent analysis of the language issue in Canada.

[51] For elaboration of the language and education issues in Quebec, see: H. Milner, *Politics in the New Quebec* (Toronto: McClelland and Stewart, 1978); H. Milner, "Quebec Educational Reform and the Protestant School Establishment," in Alain Gagnon, ed., *Quebec: State and Society*, (Toronto: Methuen, 1984), p. 410; W. Coleman, "The Class Basis of Language Policy in Quebec, 1949–1983," in Gagnon, *State and Society*, p. 388; and Coleman, *The Independence Movement*, chapters 6 and 7.

[52] See articles by Renaud, Niosi, and Fournier in Gagnon, *State and Society*, pp. 150–227, for a discussion of the phenomenon of the new middle class in Quebec. See also Coleman, in *State and Society*, chapter 4.

because of parallel changes in the education system in the province, French Canadians have been able to find good jobs. There is now solid evidence that French Canadians are paid as well or even better than English Canadians in the province,[53] and the end result of this phenomenon has been the development of a larger Francophone middle class in the province. Not only does the emergence of a bourgeoisie in French Canada reduce some of the economic aggravations that in the past fuelled Quebec *indépendantisme*, but, as well, this phenomenon may cause a turn towards more conservative policy goals. The new middle class inevitably will develop a vested interest in the status quo and will be still more hesitant to embark on nationalist adventures that might threaten the newly acquired affluence:

> some of the most flagrant abuses and injustices — which had sparked a generation of middle class Quebecois to lead a nationalist movement — have dissipated. The middle classes now turn their energies elsewhere.[54]

Nor should one assume that this new middle class in Quebec is made up only of employees of the state. There is growing evidence that French Canadians are increasingly successful as capitalists within Quebec, in Canada, and even in the multinational arena.[55] The traditional perspectives on Canadian capitalism that see the upper class as predominantly Anglo-Saxon are no longer accurate.

On the basis of such evidence, it is possible to conclude somewhat optimistically that the level and intensity of French-English conflict is declining. The material disparities that have traditionally existed between individuals from the two charter groups have been for the most part eliminated or reduced significantly. The aggravations that have traditionally fuelled the periodic explosions of French-Canadian nationalism, such as language rights, religious rights, and denominational schools, have been salved. The threat of separatism has faded from the agenda of both Quebec and national political discourse.

However, when one moves from a consideration of the strictly ethnic dimension of French-English conflict to the material status and economic potential of Quebec as a region within Canada and within the North American economy, it is more difficult to be optimistic. The fact remains that Quebec continues to be a have-not region. This is reflected in part by the fact that the successes of French-Canadian capitalists have been for the most part confined to what Jorge Niosi calls "the 'soft' sectors: finance, service and commerce"[56] and with a few exceptions such as Bombardier have not been able to move into the international or national markets in the manufacturing sector. The reason for this phenomenon is in part the fact that Quebec firms (as with most Canadian firms) lack the research and development capacity to move into the international markets and must either

---

[53] See: Whitaker in *Canadian Politics in the 80s*, pp. 52–53; and R. Lacrois and F. Vaillancourt, *Les Revenus et la langue au Québec* (Government of Quebec, 1981).

[54] J. Sher, "Québec and the Parti Québécois," *Canadian Dimension*, December 1985, p. 19.

[55] See J. Niosi, "The Rise of French Canadian Capitalism," and P. Fournier, "The New Parameters of the Quebec Bourgeoisie," in Gagnon, *State and Society*.

[56] Niosi, in *State and Society*, p. 196.

rely on imported technology or restrict their activities to the "softer" sectors, where either research or low-priced labour does not play as large a role. Another factor that has had an impact on the nature and rate of growth of the Quebec economy is the continued domination of the continental economy. The end result of these trends has been described as the "economic peripheralization" of Quebec as a region that has a disintegrative potential with or without the coincidence of traditional ethnic cleavages.[57]

However, even if the traditional ethnic and cultural patterns of conflict between Quebec and Canada have been superseded by economic ones, we still may not conclude that ethnicity has ceased to be an important determinant of cleavages in Canadian society. What can be perceived today and what will likely increase in the future is the salience of issues having to do with the rights of aboriginal people, the role of non-white immigrants in Canadian society, and the extent and nature of the integration of such groups into political, economic, and cultural life.

As we have seen, non-white immigrants often have difficulty finding employment; they face racial intolerance in social and community relations with individual Canadians of European extraction; and they are often discriminated against through insensitive (if well-intentioned) public policies. There is no indication that the trend towards more immigration from the non-traditional (non-European) areas of the world is about to change. It is essential, therefore, that governments in the next decade take measures to remove the obstacles that prevent non-whites from integrating into the mainstream of Canadian society. As well, obviously, racism at the individual, societal, and official levels must be eliminated before the economic plight of our visible minorities can be effectively tackled, and in the long run if all Canadians can learn a greater tolerance for peoples and cultures that are different their lives will have been enriched as much as those of the groups discriminated against.

The policy questions in the area of aboriginal rights that will have to be faced in the next decade may also serve to elevate the intensity of conflict between natives and non-natives. We may at present be seeing only the tip of the iceberg in the disputes involving the settlement of aboriginal land claims, the legitimacy of proposals for native self-government, and the constitutional development of the Northwest Territories and the Yukon. In all such cases the granting of special status to natives, or the affirmation of aboriginal title to land and resources, inevitably will have implications for the rights and privileges of non-natives. Justice demands that the settlement of such issues in a manner that is fair to our Indians, Métis, and Inuit should be achieved as soon as possible, but, ultimately, the resolution of conflicts between whites and natives can only be built on the understanding and goodwill of the non-native majority. Because the stakes in many cases are high, such accommodations will not be easy and definitely will be important items for political debate in national, provincial, and territorial forums in the next few years.

[57] See: Alain Gagnon and Marybeth Montcalm, "Economic Peripheralization and Quebec Unrest," in *State and Society*, pp. 15–30.

Conclusion

The reader may well wonder at this point whether the emphasis in these two chapters is not misplaced. By concentrating on cleavages and neglecting the sources of consensus in Canada, have we perhaps painted too bleak a picture of the problems with which the political system must deal?[58]

We think not. In these chapters, our emphasis on cleavages and problems is intentional. Politics is a process of conflict resolution, and in the end much of that conflict is generated by cleavages in society. There is a very broad area of consensus in Canada concerning politics. But the things Canadians *agree* about do not become political issues. Our intention here has been to emphasize the many extremely difficult problems with which the political system must cope. Much of the rest of the book is concerned with the institutional and procedural manifestations of consensus that allow it to do so.

Whatever the difficulties Canadians often have with the array of cleavages that cross our society, it must be said that, viewed in the context of a world where lesser differences often lead to bloody war, violent insurrection, or campaigns of terrorism, the Canadian political system copes with them very well indeed.

[58] A. Cairns, "Alternative Styles in the Study of Canadian Politics," *Canadian Journal of Political Science,* VII, 1 (March 1974), p. 15.

C H A P T E R 4

POLITICAL CULTURE AND IDEOLOGY: VALUES, ATTITUDES, AND OPINIONS

POLITICAL VALUES IN CANADA
- Popular Sovereignty - Political Equality - Majoritarianism
- Ideology: Liberalism and Canadian Democracy
- The Dilution of Canadian Liberalism - Corporatism in Canada
- Individual and Group Rights in Canada: The Communalist Streak
THE CANADIAN POLITICAL CULTURE: SUBCULTURAL VARIATIONS
CANADIAN POLITICAL ATTITUDES
- The Subjective Dimension - The Objective Dimension - Political Negativisim
PUBLIC OPINION AND OPINION FORMATION
- Opinion Formation and Change - Public Opinion — Informed and Uninformed
- The Measurement of Public Opinion

T he determinants of political behaviour can logically be reduced to two significant groups of variables: those that are external to the individual and those that are internal, or of the mind. Having discussed many of the former in chapters 2 and 3, we now seek to describe the latter, the basic values and attitudes that in the aggregate compose the Canadian political culture, and to elaborate upon their consequences for the Canadian political system.

We use the term "political culture" with some reservations, for there are nearly as many definitions of the term as there are political scientists. Most would agree, however, that it is composed of the political values, attitudes, and beliefs of the

107

citizens of a political system and that it is a determinant of political action or behaviour.[1] It is this sense of the term we shall use.

There are four major approaches to the study of political culture. First, it is possible to establish what attitudes and values make up a culture simply by asking a scientifically selected sample of individuals a set of carefully designed questions that plumb the basic question: "What are your values and attitudes?" A second approach is to speculate about the predominant attitudes of a political culture by observing the patterns of political behaviour that are typical of the political system. The researcher works backwards, deducing the likely attitudinal causes from the observed behavioural patterns. There are two broad styles of behavioural research commmonly employed here. One utilizes the qualitative tools and "hard data" of survey research[2] and the other employs the softer and more impressionistic techniques of historical analysis.[3]

The third of the approaches to political culture is institutional in its focus. Here the presumption is that we can discover something about the long-run value preferences of a society by investigating the legal and institutional framework within which politics occurs. For example, the existence of parliamentary institutions likely reflects a deep-seated commitment to the values of popular sovereignty and representative democracy in the Canadian political culture.

These three approaches to the study of political culture all focus on the need to discover the actual stuff of political culture — the attitudes and values that make it up. A fourth approach to political culture is to view it as the result of historical events and of the process called *political socialization*. Here it is assumed that, at the highest level, important clues to the nature of a political culture may lie in the particular pattern of development of a nation while, at a lower level, the nascent political values and attitudes of children may help us to understand the political culture by seeing it as a part of the process of individual development. These determinants or precursors of political culture will be examined in the next chapter.[4]

---

[1] See especially: Sydney Verba, "Comparative Political Culture," in Lucien Pye and Sydney Verba, eds., *Political Culture and Political Development* (Princeton, 1965), p. 513; and Samuel C. Patterson, "The Political Cultures of American States," in N.R. Luttbeg, *Public Opinion and Public Policy* (Homewood: Dorsey, 1968), p. 276. See also: Whittington, "Political Culture: The Attitudinal Matrix of Politics," in J. Redekop, ed., *Approaches to Canadian Politics* (Prentice-Hall, 1982).

[2] Examples of this approach to political culture in Canada are provided by R. Simeon and D. Elkins, "Regional Political Cultures in Canada," *CJPS*, September 1974.

[3] While Hartz, McRae, and Horowitz and Lipset are the best-known proponents of an historical approach to Canadian political culture, a 1977 article by Reg Whitaker breaks new ground, extending the usefulness of this approach. See "Images of the State in Canada," in Leo Panitch, ed., *The Canadian State: Political Economy and Political Power* (Toronto: University of Toronto Press, 1977). See also: D. Bell and L. Tepperman, *The Roots of Disunity: A Look at Canadian Political Culture* (Toronto: McClelland and Stewart, 1979).

[4] An additional approach to the study of political socialization, which unfortunately has been employed very little, is to focus on *immigrant political adaptation*. "Given that the study of immigrant learning involves largely *adult* learning and given that many scholars have begun to recognize that learning ought to be viewed as a more continuous process, far less determined by preadult learning, a focus on immigrant political learning may even be more compelling." See: J.H. Black, "Immigrant Political Adaption in Canada: Some Tentative Findings," *CJPS*, March 1982, p. 4.

In general, chapters 4 and 5 are concerned with the values, attitudes, opinions, and patterns of political participation of that large part of the Canadian population that is not engaged full-time in playing political roles. We are concerned here not so much with politicians, senior bureaucrats, or the leaders of the largest interest groups, but with the man on the street or the woman in the middle row of a community association meeting.[5] However, it is important to point out that most of the values and attitudes described here are shared by the players of more highly politicized roles. Indeed, it is this sharing of values that does a great deal to stabilize the Canadian political system and to insure that, in spite of the barriers the ordinary man or woman may encounter when trying to participate in politics, political decision makers do take account of many of the average person's attitudes. Their attitudes are very often the same.[6]

This view is not shared by those who prefer to use a class analysis of politics. In that approach, the élites of the political system are seen as manipulating the process of political socialization, so that the values inculcated in the masses are those that serve the interests of the dominant class. In this way the status quo is legitimized by creating false consciousness among the working class, so that they accept and even positively support a system that is contrary to their own interests. However, whether mass and élite values are congruent because of spontaneous social forces or because the élites are manipulating the masses (or both) is not as important, at this stage of our analysis, as the simple fact of that congruence.[7]

In the first of this pair of chapters, we will attempt to describe the basic values and attitudes that make up our political culture. We will also consider the formation of public opinion. In the second, we will look at both the causes and the effects of the patterns outlined in this chapter by studying political socialization, the historial roots of our political culture, and political participation.

POLITICAL VALUES IN CANADA

Political values underlie attitudes towards specific political objects and also set the broadest limits of political behaviour in a society. Because they are basic they are seldom articulated; but they form the guiding principles for the operation of the political system. Hence, they are usually reflected in its institutions as well as in the behaviour of citizens and governmental officials.

The most basic values held by Canadians are rooted in the western political tradition, in the Judaeo-Christian religious tradition, and in eighteenth- and nineteenth-century democratic theory modified to some extent by the traditions and events of the twentieth century. These basic values include a commitment to

[5] For a critical assessment of the significance of mass values for the political system, see J. Shiry, "Mass Values and System Outputs," in Pammett and Whittington, eds., *The Foundations of Political Culture: Political Socialization in Canada* (Toronto: Macmillan, 1976), pp. 36–58.

[6] On this point, see Luttbeg, *Public Opinion*, pp. 245–390.

[7] See Panitch, *The Canadian State*, articles by Leo Panitch and Reg Whitaker, for a full development of this argument. See also Zureik, "Major Issues in Political Socialization Research," in Zureik and Pike, eds., *Socialization and Values in Canadian Society, Vol. I: Political Socialization* (Toronto: McClelland and Stewart, 1975).

popular sovereignty, political equality, and majoritarianism. They form a set of unstated premises that underlie attitudes more directly related to the day-to-day workings of the political system, and are the bedrock of consensus in our political community.

Popular Sovereignty

Canadian political values are traditionally broadly described as *democratic*. Democracy may be viewed as a set of ultimate values, but we prefer to view it primarily as a set of operational procedures for realizing certain broad societal goals. Stated as a theoretical abstraction, the democratic aim or the ultimate democratic value is the common good or the common interest. Democracy, as a means of realizing the common good, is a system of government designed to reflect the will of the people as a whole rather than the will of an individual or of a small élite. The limitations of democracy, as stated in such ethereal terms as these, follow from the fact that there is likely to be imperfect agreement as to what the common good is. In many cases the common good will conflict directly with the particular short-run demands put forward by individuals and groups within the society. Therefore, democracy is perhaps best viewed as a form of government that attempts to maximize or optimize the common good by establishing operational rules that will satisfy the needs of as many people as possible. This attempt is expressed in the principal of popular control or *popular sovereignty*.

Direct democracy, or the actual involvement of all of the members of a society in the policy process, is not possible in a large nation state. The complex and technical policies being dealt with by governments today do not encourage direct participation in government by all the people. Indeed, the thought of passing even non-technical legislation in a legislature of twenty-five million is plainly ludicrous. Some indirect means must be found, therefore, to give effect to popular sovereignty, and the most common method of achieving this in a modern democracy is through elected representatives. Thus, in a modern democracy, the people do not govern; rather, they choose their governors.

Political Equality[8]

Popular sovereignty is usually institutionalized through a system of periodic elections, which fact, in turn, presumes certain secondary values. The secondary values have been referred to collectively as the principles of political equality: every adult should have the right to vote; each person should have one vote; no person's vote should be weighted differently from another person's vote; and representation should be at least roughly proportional to population.

Political equality, however, means more than "one man, one vote," for a further assumption behind democratic elections is that the voter has real alternatives from which to choose, and that the voter can make a choice freely. Thus,

---

[8] Note here that Robert Dahl views political equality as a goal of democracy and majority rule as a guiding principle for attaining it. The sociopolitical process for attaining the democratic goal he calls "polyarchy." See R.A. Dahl and C.E. Lindblom, *Politics, Economics and Welfare* (New York: Harper and Row, 1953), p. 41, and chapters 10 and 11.

the political freedoms — freedom of assembly, association, conscience, and expression — are fundamental values tied up inextricably with democracy as a governmental form. The institutional guarantees of these basic freedoms are to be found in devices such as the secret ballot, and in legal documents such as the federal and provincial elections acts and the 1982 Charter of Rights and Freedoms.

Majoritarianism

Majority rule is a key operational principle of democratic government. The term means two things. First, it applies to the electoral process itself, in that the candidate who gets the largest number of votes in an election becomes the representative for a societal unit. Second, it applies when the representatives make policy decisions. In cases where there is not unanimous agreement as to what should be done, the alternative preferred by the largest number of representatives is the one implemented. However, the majoritarian principle is not absolute; there are limits placed on the majority. For instance, if a majority decided to abolish one of the basic freedoms, such as freedom of association, the system would cease to be democratic. Such tampering with democratic values, even by the majority, is normally considered to be unacceptable in democratic political systems. Thus, while majority rule is a very important principle of democracy, it is seldom if ever deemed to be absolute.

A corollary of the limitation on the principle of majority rule is that the minority will accept decisions of the majority as long as the majority does not violate other democratic values, such as political equality. Should a dissident minority refuse to abide by a policy decision of the majority, or should the majority take an extreme measure to suppress the legitimate rights of the minority, the political system would be in danger either of breaking up or of ceasing to be democratic.

Ideology: Liberalism and Canadian Democracy

Many Canadians have come to identify democratic values with the somewhat more specific principles embodied in the "semi-ideology" of liberal democracy. In its most extreme incarnation, liberalism includes a commitment to individualism and to individual liberties, a closely related commitment to the principles of private-property and individual-property rights, and a commitment to economic free enterprise and capitalism. These may very well be important values held by a majority of people in the western democracies and particularly in the United States, but they are not necessary to a system of democratic politics.

In fact, it seems inarguable that liberal values in Canada have been gradually diluted by at least partial acceptance of such socialist principles as economic equality, social and economic planning, and increased intervention of government in our everyday lives.[9] More importantly, there is a school of thought (which we will describe below) that posits that the Canadian value system differs significantly from the American on just this point of commitment to liberal ideals, and that the differences spring from long-standing historical causes. However, the

---

[9] George Grant, *Technology and Empire* (Toronto: Anansi, 1968), pp. 43–44.

conflict between liberalism and socialism as sets of political values is a very central aspect of political life, not only in Canada but in other western democracies as well. To tie the fundamental principles of democracy, such as popular sovereignty, political equality, and majoritarianism, to either liberal or non-liberal values is to endanger the value consensus on which democracy rests. The commitment to democracy is far more important than the commitment to liberalism or to some non-liberal ideology such as socialism, for democracy can be made compatible with either.

We have already referred to liberalism as a "semi-ideology," largely because its principles, although widely held, are seldom made explicit by those who hold them. Values such as individualism, competition, private property, and a laissez-faire relationship of the state to the individual pervasively and persistently dominate the collective mind-set of Canadians. The pervasiveness can be seen in the extent to which liberal values are mouthed by our politicians, crusaded for by our media, and staunchly believed in by average Canadians. Even the "left" in Canada, while attempting to explicitly reject liberalism, never seems quite to succeed because bits and pieces of liberal values remain as part of their unconscious intellectual baggage. For example, Marxist intellectuals in Canada reject individualism at one level but embrace the fight for individual rights at another, and left-leaning political parties in Canada speak of controlling capitalism but not of replacing it with a different social and political order.

But the pervasiveness of liberalism in the Canadian political culture is only part of the mystery. The still more puzzling phenomenon of liberalism is the dogged persistence of liberal values, even in the face of factual evidence that sometimes contradicts them. Many of our cherished values are in fact myths or ideals, which bear little relationship to modern realities; yet even when confronted with evidence of the inappropriateness of these values we tend to explain away the contradictions and cling to the myths. For example, the notion of equal opportunity in the economic system — that every individual has the potential to become a millionaire or at least to be treated by the economic system in consonance with his or her contribution to it — is factually negated by the experiences of the vast majority of Canadians. There are relatively few Horatio Algers (or Roy Thompsons) today, and few of us seriously believe that we will ever actually get rich. There is widespread evidence of the persistent disadvantages faced by women and visible minority groups in the work place. But our political culture still nurtures the myth that is the liberal value of equal opportunity.

The persistence of this sort of false-consciousness can in part be explained through the blurring of the economic inequities in liberal societies and by the steps governments take to mitigate at least the worst evils of the untrammelled workings of the market-place. Even though there are wide disparities in the distribution of income, the better-off individuals in society are willing to inoculate themselves against radical change in the economic structure by providing welfare benefits, health care, etc. Moreover, average Canadians' hopes of "making it" are vainly boosted by the dream of winning a government-sponsored lottery. The lot of the have-nots in Canadian society is thus kept at a level far below that of the middle class but well above the level where material deprivation or psychological disgruntlement might be translated into working-class unrest or class revolution. The persistence of liberal values is also made easier because of the fact that liberalism is not codified as "Our Ideology" but rather remains a set of vague principles. As Elia Zureik has said: "What makes the process of legitimation so successful is the absence of an explicit, articulated set of abstract political principles which could be assessed and critically examined."[10] In this sense liberalism persists because it is too vague to be a clear target for criticism.

The overall point to be made here is that while liberalism is difficult to deal with as a true ideology, there is a set of political values we call liberal, and those values are so deep-rooted in our political culture that they colour the thinking even of explicitly anti-liberal critics of our system. We are presuming, then, that ours is basically a liberal society whose liberal values have been diluted (or polluted) by principles such as toryism, socialism, and corporatism. In the next section of this chapter we intend to analyze the influence of those non-liberal political values on the structure and content of Canadian liberalism.

The Dilution of Canadian Liberalism[11]

While all of the Anglo-Saxon democratic world has in common a commitment to the values of popular sovereignty, political equality, and majoritarianism, it is the relative purity of their commitment to liberalism that ultimately distinguishes their political cultures one from the other. Hence it can be generally concluded that the political culture of the United States of America is the most purely liberal, and that the political culture of the United Kingdom is the most diluted by strains of toryism. Canada, it seems, stands somewhere in the middle.

One of the best known of the various approaches to identifying Canadian patterns of political culture is the comparative historical approach known as the "fragment theory," which was introduced by Louis Hartz and modified and elaborated by K.D. McRae and Gad Horowitz. While McRae and Horowitz differ substantially on several points[12] concerning the differences between Canadian and American value systems, they essentially agree that the English-Canadian political culture is more conservative, or "tory," than that of the United States. They both conclude that the values of collectivism, corporatism, and an organic view of the state dilute Canadian liberalism far more than American liberalism:

Canadian political society has thus stressed order, loyalty, and deference to government more than popular assent. Rather than "life, liberty, and the pursuit of

[10] Zureik, *Socialization*, p. 49.

[11] In the writing of this section we are highly indebted to Professor David Falcone of Duke University, who synthesized much of the material in his Ph.D. dissertation. See "Legislative Change and Output Change: A Times Series Analysis of the Canadian System" (unpublished Ph.D. dissertation, Duke University, 1974). See also G. Horowitz, "Conservatism, Liberalism and Socialism in Canada: An Interpretation," *CJPS*, 32:2, May 1966, 144-171, and D. Bell and L. Tepperman, *The Roots of Disunity*.

[12] For more recent material on the difference between Horowitz and McRae, see: Horowitz, "Notes on 'Conservatism, Liberalism, and Socialism in Canada,'" *CJPS*, June 1978, p. 383; McRae, "Le Concept de la société fragmentaire de Louis Hartz: Son application à l'exemple Canadien," *Canadian Journal of Political and Social Theory*, Fall 1979, p. 69.

happiness," the need has been peace, order, and good government. Social equality is desired but with less fervour than in America. Hierarchy in all spheres of life is taken for granted.[13]

Paradoxically, it is pointed out by some authors, most notably Gad Horowitz,[14] that it is the "tory streak" in the Canadian political culture that supports collectivist tendencies. Because the tory tradition is rooted in feudalism, which is ultimately a system featuring an organic or collectivist relationship of the individual to the state, the Canadian political system has been far more willing to engage in egalitarian health and welfare programs than has that of the United States. In the same sense that the feudal landlord feels responsible for the well-being of his tenants or serfs and their families, the Canadian tory feels a "noblesse oblige" towards the less fortunate members of society. The liberal assumes all people are born free, but with different abilities and potential. The individual therefore must be freed to pursue the maximization of individual potential, and all the state must provide is equal opportunity and justice will be served. The tory, on the other hand, assumes that all people are not equal and never will be, so that the state must look after the genetically inferior members of society by providing redistributive social programs. This phenomenon, referred to as "red toryism," has meant that conservative politicians have often been willing to initiate economically egalitarian policies that one might expect to be more exclusively championed by socialists. Moreover, as Horowitz has argued, this red tory streak in our political culture has made possible the emergence and survival of "an influential and legitimate socialist movement in English Canada as contrasted with the illegitimacy and early death of American socialism."[15]

Thus, English Canadian liberal values have been diluted to the extent that Canada is inegalitarian socially and yet amenable to some of the norms of economic egalitarianism and to the use of state power to implement those norms. By contrast, the United States is committed to social equality, but more opposed to limits on the laissez-faire operation of the economy that would be necessary to achieve even modest steps in the direction of economic egalitarianism. This contrast is underscored by Seymour Martin Lipset, who used a broader framework, which includes Australia, Britain, Canada, and the United States, to make political cultural comparisons. Lipset used census data to show that Canadians generally evince more of a collective orientation than do Americans, albeit less than the British. Lipset also concludes, on the basis of his data, that Canadians are both more élitist and more ascriptive in their attitudes than Americans, but, again, less so than the British.[16]

The points Lipset makes are corroborated by many Canadian historical schol-

[13] Erwin Hargrove, "Popular Leadership in Anglo-American Democracies," in Lewis Edinger, ed., *Popular Leadership in Industrial Societies* (New York: John Wiley and Sons, 1966), p. 147.

[14] "Conservatism, Liberalism and Socialism in Canada: An Interpretation," *CJEPS* 32:2, May 1966. Note that "small-t toryism" and "small-l liberalism" cannot always be equated with the parties of the same names. As we point out frequently in this text, each of the two major Canadian parties contains the full spectrum of opinions.

[15] Horowitz, *Canadian Labour in Politics* (Toronto: University of Toronto Press, 1968), p. 9.

[16] For an updated version of Lipset's views, see "Canada and the United States: The Cultural Dimension," in C.F. Doran and J. Sigler, eds., *Canada and the United States*.

ars on the basis of more impressionistic material.[17] Moreover, Lipset and those same Canadian historians are also in agreement that another reason for Canadian-American differences revolves around the relatively tame style of Canada's westward expansion, the relative dominance of Anglican and Roman Catholic rather than Calvinist and fundamentalist religious traditions in Canada, and the non-revolutionary nature of Canada's achievement of nationhood.

Where liberal values do not form the dominant ideological dimension of the Canadian political culture is, perhaps, in Quebec. Here, as Ken McRae has pointed out in his adaptation of the Hartzian model to Canada, we have a "feudal fragment," which forms a stark contrast to the liberalism of English-Canadian society. Canada, according to McRae, is a "dual fragment," and although he tends to understate the tory dilution of English-Canadian liberalism emphasized by Horowitz, he is most astute in his description of the non-liberal value system of French Canada, which he sees as a legacy of the *ancien régime* in *La Nouvelle France*. To the extent that non-liberal components of the value system in French Canada are mirrored in similar values in English Canada, there may be a potential area of ideological congruence between the Anglophone and Francophone segments of the Canadian political culture. This area of potential congruence revolves around the political value system called *corporatism*. The questions here are: what is corporatism, does it provide a useful description of Canadian political values, and, if it does, then does a common acceptance of corporatist values provide any ground for consensus between French and English Canada?

Corporatism in Canada

A recent scholarly application of the term *corporatism* to the English Canadian scene was by Robert Presthus. In his book *Elite Accommodation in Canadian Politics*, Presthus provides a definition:

> Corporatism is essentially a conception of society in which government delegates many of its functions to private groups which in turn provide guidance regarding the social and economic legislation required in the modern national state. Corporatism rests upon an organic view of society in which collective aspirations are seen as prior to those of any discrete individual or group, including the state. In English Canada, corporatism has been widely celebrated by both the church and many leading intellectuals.[18]

Thus, the corporatist component of our political culture conceives of society as a collection of private groups, and hence it has an anti-individualistic bias. This means that unless an individual puts forward his or her claims on government as part of the claims of a large group, the individual's behaviour may be viewed as inappropriate, and political decision makers may dismiss him as a "crank" or

---

[17] See, for example, W.L. Morton, *The Canadian Identity* (Madison: University of Wisconsin Press, 1961), pp. 84–87; Chester P. Martin, *The Foundation of Canadian Nationhood* (Toronto: University of Toronto Press, 1955); A.R.M. Lower, *Colony to Nation: A History of Canada* (Toronto: Longmans Green, 1946); J. Porter, *The Vertical Mosaic*; Erwin C. Hargrove, "Notes on American and Canadian Political Culture," *CJEPS*, 33, February 1967, pp. 21–29; and George Grant, *Lament for a Nation* (Princeton, N.J.: Van Nostrand, 1967).

[18] Presthus, *Elite Accommodation in Canadian Politics*, pp. 25–26. There are also discussion of Presthus' work in our chapters on authorities and élites and on interest groups. Used with permission of Cambridge University Press.

otherwise ignore him. As a result, the corporate ideal may have major consequences for the way in which the Canadian political system operates. Presthus concludes:

> These components of Canadian political culture culminate, in turn, in a national political process that may be called one of elite accommodation. Essentially, . . . this is a system in which the major decisions regarding national socio-economic policy are worked out through interactions between governmental (i.e. legislative and bureaucratic) elites and interest group elites.[19]

However, all people would not agree with Presthus' understanding of corporatism. Leo Panitch argues that Presthus' definition "is cast at such a general level as to be virtually indistinguishable from pluralism and the long tradition of interest group theory that is intertwined with it."[20] We believe that the two terms should be distinguished, and we believe that the pluralist description provides a much more appropriate fit with the other values that dominate the Canadian political culture. The real difference between corporatism and pluralism is that the former tolerates fewer functional groups, features a more rigidly structured set of relationships both among the groups and between each of the groups and the state, and insists that all individuals "belong" to one of the groups so that the groups represent individuals' legitimate interests in the activities of the state. In contrast to this essentially organic view of society, interest-group pluralism is rooted in liberal individualism. Large numbers of groups compete with each other, and their relationships to each other and to the state are left to float according to the vagaries of group leadership, social and economic conditions, and widely disparate bargaining power. Individuals belong to as many groups as they choose, and multiple, overlapping memberships tend to be the rule rather than the exception. Individuals also have legitimate rights of their own, separate from their group identities.

But, while it may be difficult to analyze the Canadian polity, political economy, or public policy as corporatist, there is a clear corporatist streak in our political culture. Hartz, Horowitz, and McRae agree that corporatism was imported into Canada in part by the earliest French settlers, who brought with them a feudal concept of society not unlike modern corporatism, and in part as a component of the conservatism the loyalist element brought from the thirteen colonies after the American Revolution.[21] One of the strongest proponents of corporatism in Canada,

---

[19] Presthus, *Elite Accommodation*, pp. 20–21.

[20] Leo Panitch, "Corporatism in Canada," *Studies in Political Economy*, Spring 1979, p. 46. See also: Leo Panitch, "The Development of Corporatism in Liberal Democracies," *Comparative Political Studies*, April 1977, p. 61.

[21] Hartz, ed., *The Founding of New Societies*; K.D. McRae, in *The Founding of New Societies*, ch. 7; and G. Horowitz, "Conservatism, Liberalism, and Socialism." It might be worthwhile to suggest a reinterpretation of their views of French-Canadian society as a "feudal fragment" to take account of the prevailing view of French-Canadian sociologists and historians that the earliest French society in North America had a predominantly mercantile value system, and that it was only after the conquest that the mercantile elements of that value system disappeared, leaving the corporatist feudal fragment. Leo Panitch, who prefers to define corporatism as a "political form" and not as an ideology, admits that there is an "ideological basis for corporatism in Canada." He argues that while corporatist values were inherited from the Loyalist tory streak in English Canada, and from the pre-French revolutionary feudal streak in French Canada, and while these values have reappeared in the responses of Canadian liberalism, French-Canadian Catholicism, and agrarian populism, the values have never given birth to corporatist political forms.

although he didn't use the word, was Mackenzie King. In his *Industry and Humanity*, published first in 1918, King advocated that labour, capital, and government participate equally in the political decision-making processes, a scheme often touted today as "tripartism." As J.T. McLeod has put it, "King was not an orthodox liberal, not an advocate of individualistic, competitive laissez-faire. . . . His solution [to the problem of industrial conflict and class strife] was an advocacy of community interests as paramount over individual interests."[22] The fact that King's scheme was never acted upon, even though King was prime minister for most of thirty years of our history, is a compelling testimony to the persistence and resilience of Canadian liberal values!

In Quebec, as well, the corporatist strain has appeared from time to time, most prominently in the 1930s and 1940s when it was championed by *L'Action nationale* and reflected in the policies of the Catholic church and of the Union nationale governments.[23] As Jack McLeod has pointed out:

> In retrospect it seems fair to suggest that Quebec's strong corporatist strain, far from being an aberration in Canadian political thought, was well in tune with other theory and practise in Canada, emphasizing the primacy of community, but merely as a narrower linguistic community than liberals or English Canadians could contemplate. There can be no doubt, however, of the corporatist theme being indigenous to Quebec experience. Possibly this once prevalent Québécois view of the political economy of Canada is less atypical, or closer to the mainstream, than is generally aknowledged.[24]

However, advocacy of corporatism in Quebec was never coupled with implementation of the political forms. As Quebec entered its Quiet Revolution in the late fifties and sixties, the corporatist values were relegated to a minor place in the political culture of the province. In some ways the Quiet Revolution can be seen as a period when liberal values began to replace the pre-liberal thinking of the "feudal fragment" in the Canadian political culture. Finally, corporatist ideas can be seen in the political philosophy of the Progressive movement in Canada during the 1920s. Both the United Farmers of Alberta and the United Farmers of Ontario advocated "group government" and "functional representation," although once the farmers attained power there was virtually no attempt to actually implement these ideas. It would appear that, again, the indomitable values of liberalism prevailed over any effective experimentation with non-liberal (or pre-liberal) policies.

To return, then, to the question posed at the end of the last section, it would seem that English and French Canada do share a streak of corporatist ideology, but since it is only a small part of their respective political cultures, it is too weak to be a vehicle for ideological consensus between the two solitudes. The corporatist

---

22 J.T. McLeod, "The Free Enterprise Dodo is no Phoenix," *Canadian Forum*, August 1976, p. 12.

23 It is interesting to note that a young intellectual by the name of Trudeau launched a scathing critique of corporatism in his *The Asbestos Strike* (Toronto: James Lewis and Samuel, 1974), pp. 25–26. A translation: "Our thinkers saw corporatism . . . as a means to tame the democratic thrust of the trade union movement. . . . Our brand of corporatism was actually devised for an elite who saw it as a means to discipline popular movements."

24 McLeod, "The Free Enterprise Dodo," p. 12; see also R. Heintzman, "The Political Culture of Quebec 1840–1960," *CJPS*, March 1983, pp. 3–59; pp. 29–32.

strain is indeed there in our political culture; it appears and reappears in party platforms, government programs, and individual proposals for reform of the decision-making apparatus of the political system; but it very seldom is manifested by positive action. Only in Quebec, where liberal values are less compelling, have corporatist ideas been significant for policy outputs, and even there the persistence of such policies has been weak. Generally, as with conservatism and socialism, corporatism has been permitted only to tinge our political culture, to slightly qualify and to dilute the dominant liberal value system, but not to replace it.

Individual and Group Rights in Canada: The Communalist Streak

As we have seen, Quebec's political culture is different from that of the rest of Canada, and the existence of a culturally distinctive French-Canadian minority is a major influence on the overall nature of Canadian political life. But the "French fact" has had another and perhaps more subtle impact on the evolution of Canadian liberalism. It is an essential concomitant of the liberal ideology that rights and freedoms are vested in individuals rather than in collectivities, such as communities, groups, or classes. However, because of the way in which Canada was founded, the duality of the Canadian nation(s) is reflected both in our institutions and in our political values. Because the BNA Act recognizes and affirms the special place of French Canada in the federation, particularly through the sections dealing with language rights and minority religious education rights, Canadians are more willing than Americans or Britons to tolerate the vesting of special status or privileges in the hands of collectivities or minority groups.

Logically, within the liberal ideological context, the granting of special rights to a group of people on the basis of ethnic origin should be anathema — for by creating a group of citizens with rights that exceed those of the majority, we create a class of "citizens-plus." As Raymond Breton argues with respect to special rights for visible minorities, the extension of this conclusion may well be that the rest of us are "citizens-minus."

> Changes to accommodate visible minorities are sometimes interpreted by other groups as a decrease of their importance in the eyes of public authorities. Some feel resentment about being considered "invisible."[25]

The argument is made often that granting special educational rights to Roman Catholics and not to other religious minorities, and granting special status to the French language in Canada when other minority languages are given no protection at all, is unfair and discriminatory to other minority groups, if not to the English Protestant majorities. But the point is seldom pressed very hard. Neither politicians, nor, as it seems, the general public in Canada is willing to move from simple bitching to an out-and-out demand for the removal of such special-status provisions from the statute books and the constitution. The conclusion must be that, generally, Canadians are either willing to accept or are grudgingly resigned to such qualifications of the unitary nature of Canadian citizenship. This general

[25] R. Breton, "Multiculturalism and Canadian Nationbuilding," research paper prepared for the Royal Commission on the Economic Union (The MacDonald Commission), 1985, p. 50.

acceptance of the principle of majority rights and special status for collectivities in Canada has more recently been reflected in the provisions of the Charter of Rights and Freedoms, which entrenches the principles of minority language and education rights. Moreover, the Charter defines another group of Canadians, the aboriginal peoples, as having a special status, and subsequent proposals coming out of the federal government and out of federal-provincial conferences have advocated vesting special legislative power in native collectivities through a system of native self-government.

Thus, the Canadian political culture has always reflected a recognition of the rights of collectivities, which serves to moderate and adapt our basic liberal values. Moreover there are indications, since World War Two, of a growing significance of group or collective rights in the development of various public policies relating to, for instance, bilingualism, multiculturalism, affirmative action for visible minorities and women, and self-government for native people; and the Charter actually entrenches these principles in the Canadian constitution. This significant and growing collectivist streak in our basically individualist value set has been described by Bernard Blishen as "a form of communalism" whereby the society accepts the legitimacy of group rights along with those of the individual.[26]

The communalist or collectivist streak in our political culture is important in comparing Canada with its sister and neighbour democracies, the United States and Britain, for neither of those systems is reflective of such values in as visible a fashion. It might also be argued that the ideological shift towards "neo-conservative" relations between the state and society in both the United States and Britain during the latter part of the 1970s never really took hold in Canada, not only because of our socialist streak, but at least in part because of this growing communalist quirk in our basic political values. The commitment to a return to a more laissez-faire relationship between the state and the individual, a feature of both the Reagan and Thatcher programs, failed to blossom in Canada in the early 1980s, possibly because, during the same period, we were in the process of defining a new kind of relationship between the state and certain key social or cultural collectivities.

THE CANADIAN POLITICAL CULTURE: SUBCULTURAL VARIATIONS

Some people would challenge the assumption that it is possible to make generalizations about political culture at the level of the entire political community of Canada. The past decade has seen a spate of articles attempting to define regional or provincial political cultures,[27] and, while we do not dispute the fact that region or

---

[26] B. Blishen, "Continuity and Change in Canadian Values," research paper prepared for the Royal Commission on the Economic Union, 1985.

[27] See: Ullman, "Regional Political Culture in Canada, Part I: A Theoretical and Conceptual Introduction," *American Review of Canadian Studies*, Autumn 1977, pp. 1–22; and Ullman, "Regional Political Cultures in Canada, Part II"; *ARCS*, Autumn 1978, pp. 70–101; Bell and Tepperman, *op. cit.*, ch. 6; R. Simeon and D. Elkins, "Regional Political Cultures" and J. Wilson "The Canadian Political Cultures," both in *CJPS*, September 1974, pp. 397–484; A. Gregg and M. Whittington, "Regional Variation in Children's Political Attitudes," in Bellamy *et al.*, *The Provincial Political Systems* (Toronto: Methuen, 1976), p. 76.

province of residence are often good predictors of attitudinal variations, it is our contention that there is a need in Canada to try to look at the Canadian political culture as a single entity — albeit a single entity with many facets and attitudinal variations. The concept of political culture is an aggregate concept to begin with, for by definition one is talking about the sum of the attitudes and values of the individuals who comprise the selected unit of analysis. After all, it is not that much easier to generalize, for instance, about the political culture of Ontario, or to speak of the political culture of French Canada, than it is to simply generalize about a Canadian political culture. The problem is simply one of deciding arbitrarily the level of aggregation that is desired, with the realization that the more inclusive and the more sociologically complex the unit of analysis, the more general and more qualified will be the conclusions. Given that the focus of this volume is the Canadian political system, and that much of the book describes the factors that politically differentiate Canadians of different regions, classes, and ethnic groups, it is our intention ultimately to reiterate in general terms what we have discovered about the Canadian political culture as an aggregate concept.

However, before we proceed, it is important to look briefly at some of the "multiple political cultures" approaches, and to assess what they have discovered. In his article "The Canadian Political Cultures," John Wilson begins with the assumption that provinces are, in fact, separate political systems, with independent powers to make decisions for their citizens in fairly wide areas of jurisdiction:

> Each province is capable through the rules made by its government of giving expression to the particular goals which the society entertains without any external interference. It would be difficult to describe such a condition as anything other than political independence.[28]

Because he presumes that there must be one politial culture for every independent political system, Wilson concludes that, therefore, there are ten political cultures in Canada. The beauty of this distinction, although arbitrary in its own way, is that it precludes reducing the unit of analysis to the point where political scientists in Canada could be, for instance, writing articles on the political culture of middle-aged, lower-income, Eastern European female Jews in North Winnipeg. Wilson then proceeds to look at the ten provinces in terms of their respective levels of political development, as measured by the type of political party system that has evolved in each. On the basis of a very useful threefold classification of party systems, Wilson concludes that the four Atlantic provinces have *underdeveloped* political cultures; Quebec, Ontario, Manitoba, and British Columbia have *transitional* political cultures; and Alberta and Saskatchewan have *developed* political cultures.

The second of these influential articles, by Richard Simeon and David Elkins, selects nine provinces (they do not discuss Prince Edward Island), plus English-speaking Quebeckers, as the ten units of analysis. They look at variations in two attitudinal categories, efficacy and trust, and at one set of mainly behavioural indicators, dubbed "political involvement." Their conclusions in many ways contradict the findings of Wilson. They classify British Columbia, Manitoba, Ontario,

28 Wilson, *op. cit.*, p. 440–441.

and English Quebec as "citizen societies," Saskatchewan and Alberta as transitional, and Newfoundland, New Brunswick, and Nova Scotia as "disaffected societies." Thus, while both articles confirm that there are wide provincial and regional variations in political culture, they do not agree at all on how provinces and regions should be classified.

The fact that the conclusions of these two articles do not coincide could be due to a number of factors. In the first place, they attempt to simplify operationally the concept of political culture by reducing it to a few indicator variables. Political culture, however, includes all of the values and attitudes of Canadians towards politics and specific political objects. In using fairly exclusive indicators for a very inclusive phenomenon, they may have simply selected inappropriate indicators. Wilson, for instance, uses the level of development of the party system of a province as the indicator of its political culture, or, in other words, he uses structural and partly behavioural variables as proxy measures for a set of attitudinal variables. In this way, not only is the researcher forced to make the assumption that a few variables will reflect many, but also to assume that specific kinds of attitudinal variables underlie behavioural and structural ones. Moreover, with the specific selection of the nature of a provincial party system as an indicator, one is forgetting that political structures, like party systems, are often more reflective of the historical circumstances that prevailed at the time of their formation than they are of current realities. Reg Whitaker has made this point very convincingly in his book *The Government Party*:

> To understand the basis of party support it is not enough to understand contemporary issues and contemporary social structure. Parties in a sense represent frozen elements of earlier alignments. It is becoming increasingly obvious that only a longer historical perspective can begin to make sense of party systems [which] within a static framework raise more questions than answers.[29]

Thus, for instance, the party systems of Alberta and Saskatchewan might be more a reflection of the events and circumstances of the thirties than they are of the political culture of today.

Simeon and Elkins, too, labour under the difficulty of having to select a very few variables as indicators of many, but their research introduces a more serious question about the variations in political culture over time. The results of the 1974 election study find that, in direct contradiction to findings in the 1965 and 1968 data, Nova Scotian respondents moved from the lower section of the participation and efficacy scales to the top. We might argue, therefore, that Nova Scotia has moved from a "disaffected society" to a "citizen society" in only nine years. Perhaps it would be more realistic, however, to suggest that the sets of attitudes we are using as indicators are simply too fickle to be used as proxies for political culture.

This points to the question of how permanent an attitude must be for it to be sanctioned as part of the political culture. Obviously the moods and opinions of Canadians with respect to specific issues and political personalities would not be long-lasting enough to be called "political culture," but what about attitudinal

---

[29] Whitaker, *The Government Party* (Toronto: University of Toronto Press, 1977), pp. xiv–xv.

categories, such as trust and efficacy? In less than ten years the levels of efficacy and trust have varied widely in Canada, a fact that casts some doubt on the utility of such variables as indicators of political culture. Perhaps we should forget about the "hard" attitudinal data and the behavioural indicators and go back to old-fashioned analysis of history and institutions as the best indicators of what our political culture (or cultures) are all about — at least until our indicators and proxy measures get better than they would appear to be today.

It is important to make clear that our aim has not been to criticize these two pioneering articles on regional or provincial culture for failing to "prove" the existence of regional political cultures in Canada, but to take from them a lesson. First, it should be clear that it is almost as difficult to generalize about a province or region of Canada as it is to generalize about Canada itself. Second, political culture is an aggregate category, and empirical research can only proceed by selecting a few proxy indicators of the multiple values and attitudes that make up the aggregate. Third, because political culture is seen as having some permanence over time, one-shot surveys do not give the researcher a very strong basis for generalizations. Survey research can produce conclusive findings about political culture only if the research is conducted longitudinally.

And, finally, we must remember that the regional or provincial variations in political values represent but one dimension of the complexity of the Canadian political culture. As Ron Landes has pointed out, political subcultures "may be based on any of the major socioeconomic cleavages such as class, religion, race and ethnicity as well as around a particular ideology."[30] There is, for instance, evidence that social class in particular is a growing determinant of subcultural variations in the Canadian political culture:

> Regional effects are, however, less marked than differences among status groups and social classes in determining levels of political efficacy, participation, and most ideological preferences. Regional interests have not, therefore, superseded class interests in the Canadian political culture. . . .[31]

Similarly, while ethnicity has always been recognized as a significant determinant of political cultural variation with respect to French Canada, more recent research has begun to recognize the existence of other ethnically defined political subcultures. Recent immigrants,[32] the visible minorities,[33] and the aboriginal peoples[34] have all been singled out as reflecting patterns of values and attitudes that differ from those of the dominant groups in Canadian society.

---

[30] R.G. Landes, *The Canadian Polity* (Toronto: Prentice-Hall, 1983), p. 227.

[31] M. Ornstein, H.M. Stevenson and A.P. Williams, "Region, Class, and Political Culture in Canada," *CJPS*, June, 1980, p. 267.

[32] Jerome Black, "Immigrant Political Adaption in Canada: Some Tentative Findings," *CJPS*, March 1982, pp. 3–27.

[33] R. Breton, "Multiculturalism and Canadian Nationbuilding." See also: N. Nevitte and A. Kornberg, *Minorities and the Canadian State* (Oakville: Mosaic Press, 1985.)

[34] See F. Abele, in Nevitte and Kornberg, *op. cit.*, p. 239; G. Dacks, *A Choice of Futures* (Toronto: Methuen, 1983); Whittington, in Whittington, *The North* (Toronto: University of Toronto Press, 1985), and M. Asch, *Home and Native Land*, 1984.

CANADIAN POLITICAL ATTITUDES

Less fundamental than the basic values discussed in the preceding section are the attitudes or patterns of thought towards specific objects in the political world. Because they are more specific, our political attitudes may not be as universally accepted within the political community as our political values. On the other hand, because they are related directly to real-world objects, political attitudes are likely more important as immediate determinants of behaviour. Thus, for example, not only are individual attitudes to a particular political party likely to vary widely, but they are more likely to stimulate political action than would a basic value such as popular sovereignty. The latter is so widely accepted in Canada that most Canadians neither think about it nor have to act upon it.

The Subjective Dimension

Political attitudes can be classified according to two main sets of criteria or dimensions: a subjective one and an objective one.[35] Using the subjective criteria, we may classify an attitude as *cognitive*, *affective*, or *evaluative*, according to its psychological significance for the individual who holds it. Objective criteria classify attitudes according to the phenomenon on which they are based or focused. They will be discussed in the next section.

Cognitive attitudes involve simple knowledge of, or empirical beliefs about, real-world phenomena. If the manner in which we acquire cognitive attitudes is empirical or objective, we can communicate them by using "is" or "is not" statements. Affective attitudes, on the other hand, consist of the feelings and aesthetic preferences we have for things in the real world. While it is accepted that knowledge or awareness of a political object must logically precede any feelings towards it, in many cases we acquire positive or negative feelings simultaneously with simple awareness. Affective attitudes are a reflection of our likes and dislikes, and the mood in which we acquire them tends to be more emotional and aesthetic than empirical. Finally, evaluative attitudes are moral and ethical, and involve the conscious application of pre-existing values or standards to real-world phenomena. Evaluative attitudes are moral judgements about the goodness or badness of a political object, and are expressed as "should" or "ought" statements. These three subjective dimensions are summarized in Figure 4-1.[36] While it is helpful to make the analytical distinction among cognitive, affective, and evaluative attitudes, the distinction blurs somewhat in reality. Our values and emotions will colour our perceptions of political objects, our feelings towards them will depend upon how we perceive them, and our political evaluations will often tend to be rationalizations of our aesthetic or emotional preferences. Moreover, the *intensity* with which an attitude is held will have an important influence upon the extent to which it can effect our behaviour. Thus, the certainty with which we hold our beliefs, the strength of our likes and dislikes, and the

---

[35] For an elaboration of this framework, see the introductory article by Pammett and Whittington, *The Foundations of Political Culture.*

[36] *Ibid.*

FIGURE 4-1
THE SUBJECTIVE DIMENSION OF POLITICAL ATTITUDES

Type	Form	Mood	Mode of Expression
Cognitive	knowledge, beliefs, information	empirical, objective	is or is not statements
Affective	feelings, preferences	emotional, aesthetic	like or not like statements
Evaluative	values, judgements	moral, ethical	should or should not statements

FIGURE 4-2
THE OBJECTIVE DIMENSION OF POLITICAL ATTITUDES

Level of System	Objective Types		
	STRUCTURAL	SYMBOLIC	CONCEPTUAL
POLITICAL COMMUNITY (Canada)	Territorial factors: the geography of Canada, etc.,	Beavers, flags, maple leaves; also personalized symbols, such as national heroes	Nationhood or nationality — the Canadian way of life or the Canadian identity
REGIME (the framework of government)	The constitution, Parliament, the federal system, the public service, etc.	The Parliament Buildings, the Crown, the Charter of Rights and Freedoms; also: personalized symbols such as the Queen	Ideology: the principles of democracy liberalism, socialism, conservatism, etc.
AUTHORITIES (the government of the day, the political system)	Specific political roles and (rarely) the incumbents themselves	Images of political leaders, parties, politicians	Issues

firmness of our value commitments may be as significant as the substance of those attitudes.

The Objective Dimension

Using "objective criteria," we may classify political attitudes according to the phenomenon upon which they are focused. Naturally, the primary objects of political attitudes are those related to the political system. However, attitudes towards political participation or abstention, for instance, involve perceptions of a "self-to-system" relationship. The attitudes to that relationship are, in the first instance, affected by one's perceptions of the system, but can also be affected by one's perception of oneself. Thus, "self" as a political object must be considered when evaluating complex and behaviourally significant attitudes, such as efficacy and civic competence. For example, one's self-esteem can be an important factor in the level and intensity of political participation.

However, despite the fact that our political attitudes involve perceptions of self, the basic foci for our political attitudes are still objects in the political system. We can therefore categorize political attitudes as being related to the political community, the regime, or the authorities. By adding a second dimension, which views all political objects as "structural," "symbolic," or "conceptual" in form, we can classify the range of political objects in a still more detailed framework. Figure 4-2 is a nine-celled table showing the resulting objective dimensions of political attitudes, with examples from the Canadian political culture.

Figure 4-2 is fairly complex, and some of the categories require a bit of elaboration. Our attitudes to authorities, for instance, are based mainly on indirect contact; few of us know personally the people who "rule" us. What we know of them is based rather on our view of the roles they occupy, classified in Figure 4-2 as "structural objects"; stereotypes with which we can categorize them, such as their party affiliations or the images of them that are imparted to us through the media, classified as "symbolic objects"; and, finally, our view of how they handle the specific issues of the day, classified as "conceptual objects." Furthermore, political values can themselves become political objects. To the extent that our political values are conceptualized or articulated as ideology, it is possible for us to acquire attitudes towards them; thus, for example, Canadians learn cognitive, affective, and evaluative attitudes towards regime-related conceptual objects such as liberalism, capitalism, and welfare.

Political Negativism

Obviously the ultimate utility of the two-dimensional grid we have developed here depends upon massive attitudinal surveys that would give us the data to fill up the boxes with information about actual Canadian political attitudes. Then and only then could we have a comprehensive overview of the Canadian political culture. The only study that has tried explicitly to begin this process was undertaken by Clarke, Jenson, Leduc, and Pammett,[37] who, in a large sample survey

---

[37] H. Clarke *et al.*, *Political Choice in Canada* (Toronto: McGraw-Hill Ryerson, 1980).

TABLE 4-1

Objects of Attitudes	Positive	Neutral	Negative	N
	percentages			
Community structural	17	46	37	1764
Community symbolic	––	––	––	––
Community conceptual	42	18	41	566
Regime structural	18	23	59	580
Regime symbolic	––	100	––	44
Regime conceptual	33	17	50	987
Authorities structural	15	11	74	442
Authorities symbolic	23	40	37	585
Authorities conceptual	9	26	65	1660
Total	20%	30%	50%	6628

of the 1974 electorate, uncovered important facts about the overall orientations of Canadians to the various categories of political objects. As can be seen from Table 4-1, the general conclusion is that Canadians are extremely negative in their feelings towards the system.[38]

As can be seen from Table 4-1, Canadians have mixed feelings about political community-related objects, but their attitudes towards the regime objects are decidedly and emphatically negative in tone. This is explained by the authors of the study as "simply a feeling that 'government' as a vague, amorphous entity is remote from the people, spending too much money, and not providing adequate services."[39] Moreover, even when there is some positive response to "regime conceptual" objects, it is almost exclusively manifested in general feelings towards democracy and to the principles of the democratic process.[40] Finally, the most negative affect for political objects in Canada is at the level of the authorities. Canadians, it seems, are very cynical about their politicians and political parties.

While it is difficult to make accurate comparisons across time, it seems fair to say that this negativism described by Clarke *et al.*, is a fairly recent phenomenon in Canadian politics. It is a phenomenon of the seventies and can likely be explained, in part, in terms of the events, issues, and personalities of that period in Canadian history. In the first place, the decade of the seventies was dominated by major social and economic problems for which our political leaders were not able to provide solutions. Inflation ran at 8% to 10% per annum, unemployment rates steadily climbed, and resources were considered to be not only finite but also virtually depleted. On this latter point, according to the 1973 figures, the projected reserves of crude oil were to last us until the end of the twenty-first century, but in January 1980 a cryptic news item told us reassuringly that we would have enough fuel oil only to get us through the current winter! We

[38] Clarke, *Choice*, p. 29. Unfortunately, subsequent election studies conducted by these authors did not ask the questions that would have permitted an updating of Table 4-1.

[39] Clarke, *Choice*, p. 30.

[40] Clarke, *Choice*, p. 30.

certainly must have been extravagant to use up a century's worth of oil in seven years. It is no wonder that Canadians began to be a little cynical about politics, given the apparent failure of the system to solve the major problems facing it.

A second possible cause for this negativism might be related to a perceived general structural breakdown in our political system. The increased acrimony in federal-provincial debate, and the apparent failure of the federal government to "take charge" in the face of economic challenges in the seventies, might have generated a lack of confidence in government generally. Moreover, during the decade Canadians came to feel that we were not a very important power in international affairs and may never be more than a minor actor in a supporting role to the United States on the global stage. Rather than face the fact of being at best a "foremost" power and to deal with a significant but limited role in world affairs with dignity, most of our political leaders have persisted in making a pretense of having great influence on the superpowers and then decrying any rebuffs.

Linked closely to this is the third probable cause of negativism among the Canadian public, the general failure of our national leaders to live up to our expectations. The dominant figure in the decade was clearly Pierre Trudeau, who came in on a wave of support not paralleled since the Diefenbaker landslide of 1958. Trudeau was the new breed of leader, the man for the future; he combined personal charisma and "style" with intelligence and imagination. But while two of his three children were born on Christmas Day, he could neither walk on water nor turn it into wine. Our expectations of this man were so high that it would have been impossible for him to live up to them even in the absence of the economic malaise that descended upon the country during the decade. As it turned out, Trudeau could not solve our most serious economic problems, and we began to see a less attractive irascibility and arrogance in his forceful personality. He "failed" us — although no one could have succeeded — and the Opposition parties could offer us nothing that looked significantly better. The result: Canadians entered the decade of the eighties with a cynical and negative set of attitudes to the authorities and to system-related political objects, and the brief interregnum of the Clark government did not do much to restore confidence in our political leadership. In fact, the 1980s began in "an atmosphere of citizen disengagement from the political process and dissatisfaction with the political authorities."[41]

Nor is there any clear indication that the Progressive Conservative government of Brian Mulroney will fare much better. While the first few months — the honeymoon — after the Tory landslide in 1984 were characterized by favourable media reports and high public confidence in the opinion polls, after a year in office, the shiny new government had begun to develop some rust spots. Late-night trips to strip joints, rancid tuna fish, allegations of nepotism and of political interference in the justice system, and a multitude of Opposition claims of mismanagement and bungling have led to ministerial resignations and demotions, and to a public awakening to the fact that the new guys are not all necessarily very different from the ones we got rid of. Thus, given the difficulty of finding

[41] H. Clarke et al., *Absent Mandate: The Politics of Discontent in Canada* (Toronto: Gage, 1984), p. 183.

solutions to so many of our problems, and given the prevailing cynicsm with which all governments seem to be viewed throughout the western world in the 1980s, the negativism identified by the authors of the study — the "absent mandate" — is likely to be with us well into the next decade.[42]

PUBLIC OPINION AND OPINION FORMATION

An individual's political behaviour is determined partly by his or her environment, which includes the institutional channels of participation provided by the system itself, and partly by political attitudes. However, for this behaviour to be meaningful, it must be related to the specific political issues of the day; in other words, the individual must formulate a personal opinion about the various issues. The collectivity of private opinions about political issues is often called *public opinion*. It is, of course, possible to have opinions about a wide range of public affairs — such as sports or the sex lives of movie stars—that are certainly not political, but the term is used here in its explicitly political sense.[43]

It might logically be expected that public opinion would provide concrete guidance for the political system. However, considerable work by the Survey Research Center of the University of Michigan has shown that, in the United States, there is often relatively little correlation between public opinion and public policy. In some well-established areas of controversy there is a reasonably close correlation between constituency opinions and the representative's stand in the legislature, but in an area such as foreign policy, there is frequently none at all.[44]

In Canada there is less empirical evidence, but at least one source suggests that there is little significant correlation between the attitudes of legislative policy makers and the opinions of their constituents.[45] On some issues, such as capital punishment, there has been an easily visible gulf between public opinion (which favours capital punishment) and legislative decision. In general, we might expect even less correspondence between the views of Canadian MPs and their constituents than between U.S. members of Congress and theirs; after all, MPs are restricted in their voting by a more rigid party discipline.

As far as political stability is concerned, the important question is whether the opinions of Cabinet ministers, senior bureaucrats, and interest-group leaders approximate public opinion. Here we are in territory where there is very little research available in Canada or anywhere else. We do know that many social

---

[42] We were assisted in the preparation of this section by Jon Pammett and Jane Jenson, colleagues at Carleton University and coauthors of *Political Choice in Canada*. See also Clarke *et al.*, *Absent Mandate*.

[43] An old but convenient reference in this area is the excellent booklet by R.C. Lane and D.O. Sears, *Public Opinion* (Englewood Cliffs: Prentice-Hall, 1964). In addition, the student should be aware of V.O. Key, Jr., *Public Opinion and American Democracy* (New York: Knopf, 1961). An excellent collection of articles on the subject can be found in Norman R. Luttbeg, ed., *Public Opinion and Public Policy*. Each of the sources cited in this footnote is American, but the nature of the generic concept, public opinion, does not vary greatly from one western democracy to another.

[44] Lane and Sears, *Public Opinion*, pp. 3–4.

[45] See: A. Kornberg, Wm. Mishler, and Joel Smith, paper presented to the International Political Science Association, Montréal, August 1973.

values are shared by élite and mass, but as to opinion on specific issues we have little information.

For the individual, holding opinions about politics may fulfill certain psychic needs. These include the need to find meaningful contact with the world, or, more simply, to have something to talk about to other people. The opinions of most individuals about political matters are not usually sophisticated or complex, and they are often inconsistent with other views held by the same individual.[46] For the individual, the inconsistency is irrelevant but simplicity is important. To most people political questions are both difficult and of relatively low significance, and unless they can be simplified, the individual tends to ignore them. Therefore, the political opinions most people hold simplify complex issues to the point where the individual, however mistaken he or she may be, can take a stand and at least feel that he or she is participating in politics. This sense of participation, in addition to its importance for the individual (who may have been filled to the ears with public-school democratic ethics and the supposed obligations thereto), is vital to the system, for it is one of the bases of political legitimacy and consensus building.

Opinion Formation and Change

The formation of opinions is clearly affected by the political socialization process. The agents of opinion formation are the same as the agents of socialization in general, but in transmitting and helping to define opinions about issues and about the authorities who champion the issues, personal and group influences play perhaps the most significant role.

Group impact on opinions may occur through personal influence within the group, through mass persuasion by the group, or through the group providing reference points for the individual. Direct personal influence within a group will depend on the nature of the group itself. The likelihood of such influence is increased if the group is a primary one — that is, one where relationships are close and face-to-face, such as job cohorts at the work place or neighbourhood friendship networks. Influence is further enhanced if the group persists over long periods, if it meets frequently, and if it is relatively homogeneous. If the individual has participated in decision making in the group, and if the norms have not been externally imposed, the group's influence is heightened still further. The influence of the group will also depend on the salience of current issues for the group and for the individual members. Of secondary importance is the setting in which the group finds itself — the status of the group in the larger society, the presence or absence of external opposition, and the availability of alternative groups.

Between 50% and 60% of Canadians belong to some form of secondary group, such as a business organization or a trade union. Such organizations can be important in shaping an individual's opinions of public affairs.[47] Many of these

---

[46] R. Lane, *Political Ideology* (New York: The Free Press, 1982).

[47] In a 1965 survey of 2,100 Canadians, 55.5% belonged to some secondary organization. This particular definition excludes church membership, since almost all Canadians are at least nominally affiliated with some church. We have described churches as tertiary organizations.

organizations are used to represent their members' interests in politics, and, as part of their technique, they may try to shape their members' opinions in the "right" direction to support group aims.

There are also tertiary or categoric groups, and everyone is a member of a number of these. A person does not join such a group; one is in it because of one's socioeconomic class, one's religion, one's nationality or skin colour, or for any number of other reasons. Thus French Canadians form a categoric or tertiary group, as do blacks or Roman Catholics. The influence of a categoric group in defining a Canadian's opinions may be very great or it may be negligible, depending on whether the group has taken a stand on a particular issue, and whether a person actually identifies with the group in which he or she is categorized. For example, various segments of the Roman Catholic church have taken a negative stance towards abortion, homosexuality, and birth control. Whether an individual Catholic would agree with the church's stance would depend, among other things, on whether one identified oneself primarily as a Catholic rather than as something else, such as a feminist or a homosexual. Nevertheless, later on we will show that membership in a particular tertiary group is correlated with a person's political participation. Indeed, in practice there is virtually no difference between the limits of these categoric groups and some of the cleavages discussed in chapters 2 and 3. It should hardly be surprising, then, that being a member of such a group influences one's political opinions.

We have not yet examined, except incidentally, the direct influence of one individual over another in the formation of political opinions. Under what circumstances will an individual — a close friend or a political leader — be able to influence another individual, and under what circumstances will the influence not occur? To examine this question we may use the theory of cognitive dissonance.[48]

In any situation where a person is being influenced, that person will have three sets of "cognitions":

1. one's evaluation of the source seeking to exercise influence
2. one's judgement of what the source's position is
3. one's own opinion of the issue

Cognitive dissonance results if the three sets of cognitions are not consistent. Dissonance places a strain on the individual, the intensity of which will depend on the issue's salience. The person will try to resolve the strain by rationalizing the conflicting positions. The dissonance can be resolved in many ways, but generally, the weakest of the three cognitions is changed. For example, suppose you are the person being influenced and you have great respect for the leader, and perceive the leader's position on a certain issue to be very different from your own. If you do not hold your position on the issue strongly, then you will change your position, not your opinion of the leader.[49]

---

[48] For a fuller treatment, see Lane and Sears, *Public Opinion*, chapter 5. The most authoritative treatment is in Leon Festinger, *A Theory of Cognitive Dissonance* (Stanford: Stanford University Press, 1957).

[49] S. E. Asch, "Effects of Group Pressure upon the Modification and Distortion of Judgements," in D. Cartwright and Alvin Zander, eds., *Group Dynamics* (Evanston: Peterson, 1953); see also Lane and Sears, *Public Opinion*, pp. 34–39.

To take a concrete example: suppose that Prime Minister Mulroney found it necessary to go on nationwide television to attempt to justify a large increase in income tax. People who were not strongly against higher taxes and who were Mulroney fans would be convinced of the rightness of his point of view, whereas people who were great fans of the Prime Minister but are strongly against higher taxes might well misinterpret what he had said so that it would fit with their own policy predilections. Thus, a change of opinion will be impeded if the opinion has been tested and found to fit reality, if it is anchored somehow in group membership, if it serves some social or economic function or some psychic function for its holder, or if the holder has some public stake in it.

Public Opinion — Informed and Uninformed

Opinion may be expressed spontaneously or with little prompting and directed to relevant authorities by knowledgeable groups or individuals. The vast majority of people do not express opinions in this way but, few though they may be, such informed opinions are important inputs into the policy-making process.

A second type of opinion is drawn from people by opinion-sampling techniques or by less sophisticated methods. Such opinion is likely to be, at best, poorly informed. For example, three months after a general election in Canada, 25% of the population typically cannot identify their Member of Parliament, and 15% cannot name the party to which the member belongs; only about 60% claim ever to have heard or read anything about their MP. Yet 95% of the people interviewed after the 1965 election expressed an opinion about how good a job MPs from the major parties were doing, and only about 3.5% did not have opinions on the major issues of that campaign. Opinions are thus often held and expressed by large numbers of people in the virtual absence of information. In fact, opinions are often formed before information is gained, and then information is selected to fit the opinion already held. The French-Canadian separatist may simply not notice opinions that separatism would be detrimental to the Quebec economy, while the hater of all things French will not notice media reports of brilliant work by French-Canadian doctors.

The nature of public opinion also depends upon the type of issue involved. In their historic work on the influences behind electoral choice, Berelson, Lazarsfeld, and McPhee divide issues into *style* issues and *position* issues.[50] Position issues involve such questions as "Should taxes be raised or lowered?" or "Should Canada enter a free trade agreement with the United States?" They are more likely than style issues to evince a rational response, because they may be objectively rather than psychically important to the individual. Style issues, such as linguistic-rights issues or liquor laws, typically concern matters of taste, or "style of life," and may serve the ends of self-expression. Style issues, therefore, often evoke an irrational response and engage the attention of large numbers of people. The information content of such opinions is typically very low, and information is used mainly to buttress pre-existing opinions.

[50] Bernard Berelson, P.F. Lazarsfeld, and W. N. McPhee, *Voting* (Chicago: University of Chicago Press, 1966), p. 184.

The Measurement of Public Opinion

There are some problems with the way in which much of what we take to be public opinion is measured. Public opinion, as expressed in the many polls we see, is usually measured in terms of its direction; that is, its position with respect to a particular policy or personality. This is, however, incomplete information, for in order to evaluate it properly, we must also know something of the intensity with which an opinion is held. For instance, when 86% of Quebec's eligible voters went to the polls for the referendum on sovereignty association, the results were as follows:[51]

Response	Number	Percentage
Oui	1,485,761	40.4
Non	2,187,991	59.6

However, those who followed the campaign know that the results are in reality, very ambiguous. Some *oui* voters may have voted that way in order to give their Quebec government a strong bargaining position *vis-à-vis* Ottawa and the other provinces. For others, *oui* might have been an assertion of pride in being a Québécois, something many *oui* voters saw as consistent with remaining Canadians, too. Similarly, some *non* voters may have been satisfied with the status quo; some may have been demonstrating favour for the Quebec Liberal party's constitutional change proposal; some may have been supporting Trudeau or Claude Ryan; and some may simply have disliked the Parti Québécois.[52] While this issue was a particularly large and important one, almost any simple measure of public opinion will similarly hide a rich variety of shades of meaning.

To make matters even more difficult, public-opinion polls have to be based on appropriate sampling procedures. For example, if an MP mails out fifty thousand questionnaires to his constituents in an attempt to determine their opinion on several issues and receives seven thousand replies, the results are likely not going to be accurate. Despite the apparently large number of respondents, they were *self-selected*, i.e., not chosen at random, so they are bound to overrepresent heavily the fringes of the population that hold strong enough opinions to bother to write back. By contrast to CIPO (Gallup) polls, which sample only around twelve hundred respondents, but select them *randomly*, this type of survey has almost no scientific utility unless we want to deliberately overrepresent that group that will select itself. Hence, its results can in no way be taken as representative of public opinion at large. Large numbers of responses do not guarantee by themselves that the results will be valid. Thus, as guides to policy formulation, public-opinion polls are very tricky devices indeed. One, well done, can be very valuable, but one that is poorly done — and many still are — is worse than useless, for it may mislead policy makers as to the real nature of opinion.

[51] E. J. Feldman, ed., *The Quebec Referendum: What Happened and What Next?* (Harvard: 1980), p. 7.

[52] In fact, an article prepared for a conference at Duke University did indicate that the best single predictor of referendum voting was attitudes having to do with the support or lack of support for the political community. See: J. Pammett *et al.*, *Political Support and Voting Behaviour in the Quebec Referendum.*

There is little point in discussing the content of contemporary Canadian public opinion on specific issues.[53] Given the ephemeral nature of opinions and of many of the issues themselves, by the time a book can be set in type and published, the issues and the opinions are likely to have changed. What is more important for our concerns is the nature of the behaviour or political activity that results from the interaction of an individual's political values, attitudes, and opinions. And before we can discuss that, we must also examine the way in which political attitudes and values are acquired — the process of political socialization. We will turn to those questions in the next chapter.

---

[53] The most valuable sources of opinion on particular issues are the periodic soundings of the Gallup poll, conducted by the Canadian Institute of Public Opinion and the quarterly Decima surveys. Many universities maintain files of the raw data on which the newspaper reports are based, and there are also some valuable secondary analyses of the data. See, in particular, Mildred Schwartz, *Public Opinion and Canadian Identity* (Berkeley: University of California Press, 1967); and F. C. Engelmann and M. Schwartz, *Political Parties and the Canadian Social Structure* (Toronto: Prentice-Hall, 1967), chapter 10, pp. 204–221.

C H A P T E R 5

POLITICAL CULTURE: SOCIALIZATION AND PARTICIPATION

I n the preceding chapter, our focus was upon the values, attitudes, and opinions that make up the Canadian political culture. We viewed these "of-the-mind" phenomena within a basically static context: our concern was primarily with simply identifying and describing the component parts of our political culture at this time in history. However, in this chapter it is our intention to move from the passive description of the Canadian political culture to view Canadians' values and attitudes in a more dynamic context. First, we look at political culture as the result of complex processes that transmit values and attitudes both intergenerationally, over time, and interpersonally, within any given period in history. Generally these complex processes are referred to in the aggregate as *political socialization*. The second part of this chapter will focus upon political culture as a determinant of political behaviour. Here we will look at the patterns of *political participation* that characterize the Canadian political process as the result, in part, of the values and attitudes held by the individuals concerned.

134

POLITICAL SOCIALIZATION: THE LEARNING OF POLITICAL VALUES AND ATTITUDES

Before moving to a discussion of the process or processes of political socialization, it is necessary first to comment on the broader historical forces and factors that provide the political value "set" of our society. Too often, political socialization is viewed as an essentially conservative force that ensures value consistency over time in a political community — as a force that thwarts ideological change and development. On the contrary, political socialization can engender change as well as consistency over time, not only from one generation to the next, but as well through ongoing intellectual and moral development throughout the lifespan of an individual. As examples, attitudes towards racial discrimination in both the United States and Canada have, in the past fifty years, changed quite markedly. Policies that, for instance, provided for educational segregation, were not long ago either accepted as legitimate or even actively supported by a large number of North Americans. Today, however, such policies are held by the vast majority to be non-legitimate and have been replaced by policies that instead actively foster integration (such as integrated schools) and seek to redress past discrimination (such as affirmative action programs). Similarly, individuals who may grow up in an environment where, for instance, military service is viewed as a great honour and an important obligation of citizenship, may change in their later years and become pacifists or pro-disarmament. The phenomenon of individuals changing their minds during a lifetime, and the more macroscopic phenomenon of a generation taking on a set of values that differs from that of the previous one, testify to the fact that the process of socialization can give us clues to ideological change and development, as well as help us to explain the persistence of certain values over long historical periods.

However, having made the point that the political socialization process does facilitate change, we must still face up to the fact that, over long time periods, the political culture of one country will continue to differ from that of others. The reason that long-term consistency can be found in the political value differences between, for instance, Canada and the United States may have less to do with the process of socialization per se than it has to do with the sociohistorical matrix within which the politics of a nation occur. There are at least three schools of analysis that have attempted to explain the historical processes that set the broad context within which a nation's political values are formed and nurtured. Each of these bears a brief discussion before moving to our examination of political socialization in Canada.

The Sociohistorical Roots of Political Culture[1]

One of the most enduring interpretations of the origins of the Canadian political culture begins with the assumption that the earliest immigrants to this country

---

[1] This section is heavily influenced by the writings of David Bell, who provides the best synthesis of the historical interpretation of the origins of the Canadian political culture. See particularly: "Political Culture in Canada," in Whittington and Williams, eds., *op. cit.*, pp. 165-170. See also, Bell and Tepperman, *op. cit.*

imported with them, as part of their intellectual baggage, the values and attitudes of the mother country. As authors such as Louis Hartz, Ken McRae, and Gad Horowitz have concluded, North American society is composed of "fragments" of the European countries that provided the seventeenth- and eighteenth-century feedstock for the New World colonies. While these writers differ as to the exact nature of the fragment that was transported to the New World, and also as to the reasons Canada and the United States have ended up with similar but quite distinctive patterns of political values,[2] they would generally agree that the differences between French- and English-Canadian society are in large part reflective of the differences between seventeenth-century France and England. As well, it is now generally accepted that at least part of the difference and much of the similarity between the political culture of the United States and that of English Canada can be explained by the fact that the United Empire Loyalists (a counterrevolutionary element in American society) formed the largest portion of the earliest settlers to British North America.

Here, the "fragment" school has been challenged and enlarged upon by a second genre of interpretation of the origins of political culture. This approach, largely the creation of Seymour Martin Lipset, posits that the importation of cultural traits from the mother country is less significant than the "formative events" that shape its historical experience: "The variations between Canada and the United States stem from the founding event which gave birth to them both, the American Revolution."[3] Thus, the United States is seen as influenced by a liberal revolutionary tradition and Canada by the counterrevolutionary values of the Loyalists. Similarly, the formative-events approach can also help us to explain the political culture of French Canada, except that here the key event was not the American War of Independence, but the conquest of New France by the British. The sense of betrayal by France, coupled with the fear of assimilation by the English after the Loyalist migration, has obviously coloured French-Canadian political attitudes to the present time.

The fragment and the formative-events interpretations together help us to understand the historical roots of our political culture. They do, in fact, focus on the same phenomena, the Loyalist migration and the conquest, and in so doing have helped to focus the debate about the nature of ideology in Canada:

> Both Hartz's "fragment theory" and Lipset's "formative events" notion focus attention on the Loyalist experience as a major source of English Canada's political culture. Yet the cultural consequences of the Loyalist migration are a subject of considerable controversy among historians and social scientists. Much of the debate has turned on defining the ideological outlook of the Loyalists. The main issue has been to what extent the Loyalists presented an "organic conservative" alternative to the "liberal" world view of the revolutionaries who expelled them and shaped the political institutions and culture of the new United States.[4]

---

[2] These views are discussed in more detail in chapter 4.

[3] S. M. Lipset, "Canada and the United States: The Cultural Dimension," in C. F. Doran and J. H. Sigler, eds., *Canada and the United States: Enduring Friendship, Persistent Stress* (Englewood Cliffs: Prentice Hall, 1985), p. 110.

[4] Bell, *op. cit.*, p. 166.

However, despite the usefulness of the two approaches in better understanding the origins of the Canadian political culture, even in combination they offer only an incomplete picture. Their limitations lie in their failure to incorporate economic or structural variables in tracing the path of Canadian cultural development.[5] It is here that a third set of interpretations, based on what David Bell refers to as the "structural" or "material" bases of political culture,[6] can be employed as a complement to the more idealistic paradigms of Hartz and Lipset.

In fact, the materialistic or non-idealistic interpretations of the historical underpinnings of our political values are, in turn, rooted in two quite divergent intellectual traditions.The first of these, epitomized by the works of Harold Innes and Donald Creighton, argues that political culture is the product of economic factors such as the structure of the means of production and the technology of transportation and communication. According to this school, our political culture is a reflection of the fact that, as we have seen in chapter 2, our international economic role has been as a resource hinterland, supplying raw materials to the industrial heartland of, first, Britain and, more recently, the United States. This means, in the more macroscopic context, that we rest inextricably in a situation of economic dependency on the United States. On the sub-national level, it has meant that the Canadian economy is regionalized, with the resource hinterlands in the west, north, and the maritimes being dependent upon the Canadian industrial heartland in the St. Lawrence-Great Lakes basin, "central Canada." In terms of policy outcomes, it has meant that the process of nation building has been characterized by a series of "national dreams," each a reflection of the transportation and communications technologies of the times. Railways, canals, tariffs, pipelines, microwave systems, satellite communications, and programs fostering cultural nationalism have been the technological fixes both for cementing our independence from the United States and for healing the interregional rifts within the country. Thus, the long-standing debates about whether Canada has one or many political cultures and whether Canada has a political culture different from that of the United States have arisen at least in part as a product of the economic and technological circumstances of our cultural development.

The second type of non-idealistic approach to explaining the roots of the Canadian political culture finds its inspiration in Marxist and neo-Marxist paradigms. At the simplest level of analysis, one can assert that Canada is a capitalist country and as such there will exist a characteristic pattern of relationships among the various classes and class fragments in society. In other words, the structure of the economy differentially affects the material circumstances of individuals, and those differences in turn colour the way Canadians of various class groupings see the world. More specifically, the neo-Marxist interpretations of Canadian society argue that the role of the political system — of the state — in capitalist systems is to facilitate the accumulation of capital by the capitalist class, thus ensuring that the underdog classes remain as underdogs. To the extent that people are aware of this "favouritism" on the part of the political system, it will

[5] In fact, in his most recent work, Lipset has incorporated much of the political economy approach in his analysis. See Lipset, "Canada and the United States. . . ," *op. cit.* (1985).

[6] Bell, *op. cit.*, pp. 168-169.

colour their sense of efficacy and of the legitimacy of the political system as a whole.

Finally, the neo-Marxists also have an interpretation of the significance of economic dependency that differs from that of more traditional political economists such as Innes. One interpretation is that Canada's failure to develop a solid industrial base, compared to Britain and the United States, was in part deliberately fostered by the mercantile class fragment that made its fortunes not on the production of goods but on the *exchange* of raw materials for export and manufactured goods for import. Whether it was a deliberate conspiracy involving, variously, the mercantilists, the Canadian state, and foreign capitalists, the fact remains that the neo-Marxists conclude with the non-Marxist political economists that the Canadian economy is almost totally dependent upon that of the United States today,[7] and this has the potential of undermining indirectly our cultural and social uniqueness *vis-à-vis* our neighbour to the south. As an example of the impact of such material circumstances on attitudes and opinions in Canada, one need go no further than the growing debate over free trade with the United States in the middle years of the 1980s.

To conclude this section, we can say only that no one approach to explaining the historical roots of our political values, attitudes, and opinions can suffice. Rather, to effectively explain where our political culture comes from, we must look to the ideological DNA that our ancestors imported to North America, to the significant events that shaped our history, and to the economic and technological forces that formed the material matrix of nation building. We can now move to a more detailed discussion of the process of political socialization.

THE PROCESS OF POLITICAL SOCIALIZATION

Stated most generally, political socialization is the process whereby we acquire our political values, attitudes, and opinions. At root it is simply political learning, and must be seen as but one dimension of the total process of socialization. As political scientists, we may tend to assume that the political is as central to the day-to-day concerns of the average Canadian as it is to us; in fact, however, politics may be but a minor and intermittent concern in an average individual's life.[8] Moreover, political socialization and the more general process of socialization are in no way discrete processes. Political learning and non-political learning are profoundly related. Our manifestly political attitudes and values can be affected by our general attitudes and by aspects of our overall personalities, and it is possible, too, that political attitudes have an impact on personality development in general.

In this section we will first discuss political socialization, or how we learn about politics as an ongoing process. We will then examine the agents that teach us

---

[7] See particularly Glen Williams, *Not For Export: Toward a Political Economy of Canada's Arrested Industrialization* (Toronto: McClelland and Stewart, 1985).

[8] See: Weissberg, *Political Learning*, pp. 20-23; see also Pammett and Whittington, *The Foundations of Political Culture: Political Socialization in Canada* (Toronto: Macmillan, 1976).

TABLE 5-1
PERCENTAGE OF STUDENTS SCORING 50% OR BETTER ON TWELVE COGNITIVE
QUESTIONS, BY GRADE

| Score | Grade in School | | | | | |
	4	5	6	7	8	9
50% or better	20.7%	35.2%	56.1%	63.6%	81.5%	90.1%
Total number of respondents	816	869	884	845	896	172

about politics, and finally we will develop a profile of the early values, attitudes, and opinions of children as we discuss who learns what, and when.

Political Socialization as a Continuing Process

Political socialization is a lifelong process. While it is likely that the attitudes we acquire as children will have an important impact on our adult political attitudes, it is also the case that we will change our minds to varying degrees as we mature. We continue to learn new facts about politics, and such new information may either reinforce existing attitudes or cause us to revise our attitudes to various political objects.

That socialization is cumulative or developmental seems beyond dispute. Few would disagree that as we mature the amount of political information we possess increases (see Table 5-1).[9] Similarly, it is to be expected that the intensity with which we hold certain political facts to be true will vary as new information either reinforces or contradicts our existing beliefs.

However, cognitive development is but one aspect of the cumulative nature of the political socialization process; in the same way as our cognitive awareness of political objects increases over time, the sophistication of our political attitudes can also be expected to increase. While our earliest attitudes to politics may be vague perceptions of political symbols and personalities and possibly diffuse affection or dislike for the objects of which we are aware, with some degree of political sophistication we become more capable of evaluating political objects with respect to our individual political value systems. Thus, while cognitive and affective attitudes dominate our political make-up in the earliest years, as we grow older, evaluative attitudes will come to take an ever larger place. Tables 5-2 and 5-3 illustrate the development of sophistication in Canadian children's perceptions of political authority figures. In the early grades it appears that children's

[9] Tables 5-1 to 5-9 are taken from data collected in a cross-regional survey of children's political attitudes in Canada. The study was administered with the assistance of school boards and teachers through a questionnaire filled out by the children themselves. There were two versions of the questionnaire. One was filled out by children in grades two and three as the teacher read out the questions. The second version of the questionnaire was more elaborate and was filled out by the students in grades four to eight and was also administered to a small group of ninth graders. The completed study included almost six thousand children in Halifax, Trois Rivières, Ottawa, Peterborough, St. Boniface, Lethbridge, and Port Alberni. The principals in the survey were T. G. Carroll, of Brock University, D. J. Higgins, of St. Mary's University, and M. S. Whittington, of Carleton University. The research was furthered through grants from the Canada Council and Carleton University, and through the goodwill of involved school boards and officials. While the data base is by now quite "dated," it does still provide illustrations of many points made in this section.

TABLE 5-2
CHILDREN'S FAVOURITE AMONG HEAD-OF-STATE ROLES
(QUEEN, GOVERNOR GENERAL, PRIME MINISTER)

Role "Liked" Best	Grade				
	4	5	6	7	8
Queen	74.0%	73.3%	69.3%	65.9%	59.4%
Governor-General	9.2	12.8	16.3	20.4	29.3
Prime Minister	16.8	13.9	14.4	13.7	11.3
	100.0%	100.0%	100.0%	100.0%	100.00%
Total number of respondents	596	619	655	583	505

TABLE 5-3
CHILDREN'S EVALUATIONS OF MOST POWERFUL HEAD-OF-STATE ROLES
(QUEEN, GOVERNOR GENERAL, PRIME MINISTER)

Role Perceived as "Most Powerful"	Grade				
	4	5	6	7	8
Queen	60.5%	55.6%	46.6%	42.9%	35.3%
Governor-General	10.6	12.2	11.8	11.7	11.4
Prime Minister	29.0	32.2	41.7	45.4	53.2
	100.1%	100.0%	100.1%	100.0%	99.9%
Total number of respondents	559	590	629	557	481

affection for and objective assessment of the power of three head-of-state roles are closely interdependent. As they grow older, the children develop the ability to evaluate the power of an authority role in a more objective fashion. Thus, while relative affection for the prime minister declines slightly from grades four to eight, the likelihood that the prime minister will be judged the "most powerful" increases markedly; conversely, while affection for the Queen remains quite high, the likelihood that she will be judged "most powerful" declines significantly.

A further feature of the process of political socialization is that the earliest awareness of political objects occurs in the absence of any behavioural requirements. Children, while they may acquire knowledge of and feelings about political objects, are seldom, if ever, called upon to act upon those feelings. Thus, their perception of themselves as actors in the political process must be anticipatory or vicarious; their political attitudes are acquired in the anticipation that, at some future time, personal involvement will be permitted or even expected. An example of this anticipatory socialization is the development of partisan preferences in children, which follows a pattern similar to that of the acquisition of political knowledge. While there will be significant regional variations, and while the intensity of the preference for a party may be weak, children do begin to make such choices at an early stage in their personal development.[10]

[10] See Pammett and Whittington, op. cit., chapter 1.

The implications of the non-behavioural context of early socialization is that the pattern of socialization may be altered when an individual does become active in politics. One's perception of the voter's role or one's party preference, for instance, may be altered after some years of experience in the role. This *post-incumbency socialization* becomes particularly politically important with respect to highly political roles. The expectations that one might have of the role of MP, for instance, will likely alter considerably after a few years of experience in the job. In sum, not only do our attitudes shape our political behaviour, but our experiences, which result from our behaviour, shape our attitudes.

The Agents of Political Socialization

The acquisition of attitudes to objects in the world of politics is usually thought of as taking place through intermediary agents or media that transmit and interpret the real world to us. While it is clear that some of our information about political objects can be acquired directly through observation of a sitting of the House of Commons, attendance at an election meeting, or even a stroll around Parliament Hill, a far greater percentage of such information is transmitted to us through our parents, peers, schools, and the communications media. These four agents of socialization not only function as lines of communication connecting us to a reality with which we cannot have direct personal contact, but they also interpret, consciously or unconsciously, the information for us. Because in our younger years almost all of our contact with political objects occurs through such agents or interpreters, particularly our parents, the agents of socialization can have a deep-seated and lifelong impact on the substance and intensity of our political attitudes.

The family, since it gets to the child first, is virtually the only important socializing agency during the first few years. Like many learning processes, political socialization within the family does not usually proceed by direct parental teaching, but rather by the child's picking up what is in the air in the family environment. If no discussion of politics occurs in the child's home, then very early in life the child may decide that political stimuli are not worth attention. By contrast, if brought up in a home where politics are constantly under discussion, the child will begin to look for political information outside the home as well, so that he or she will be able to participate more actively in home life.

Time and again, politicians reminisce about how politics was a constant topic of discussion in their childhood homes, or about how politically active their parents were.[11] This process, of course, repeats itself, and leads to certain family names appearing over and over again in politics. This may, in effect, reduce the size of the population from which politicians are drawn.

The school is another agent of political socialization. The child can pick up political information through the curriculum, particularly through formal instruction about government in civics or social-studies courses. Several studies have indicated that there are wide variations in the interpretations of history, political events, and the functioning of political institutions. Of particular interest are the differences between French- and English-language history texts, which show radically different

---

[11] See, for example, C. G. Power, *A Party Politician* (Toronto: Macmillan, 1966), pp. 3–14.

TABLE 5-4
FORMAL CIVICS INSTRUCTION IN SCHOOL AND COGNITIVE AWARENESS

Cognitive Score	None	Some
75% or better	9.0%	14.4%
50% to 74%	44.3	45.7
Less than 50%	46.8	39.9
	100.1%	100.0%
Total number of respondents	4286	1110

explanations for the events in Canadian history.[12] Most of these studies, while they show that interpretive differences do exist in curricular materials, do not show the actual impact of these differences on Canadian children's political attitudes.[13] However, data from a 1971 national survey of Canadian elementary-school children's attitudes, shown in Table 5-4, indicate that while there is a relationship between formal instruction and cognitive awareness, it is fairly weak.

Perhaps more important than the impact of the school curriculum on the child's perception of politics is the structure of the school itself. While on the one hand it may pass on general attitudes towards authority that are necessary to the stability of the political system, an overly authoritarian school may serve to discourage the mass participation that is likely an important component of a healthy democratic system. A school environment that is overly permissive may have equally unhappy results. Also within the context of the school, children may be confronted with "significant others," authority figures to whom they can look for advice and for a personalized model on which to pattern their own political lives. Not only the teachers, but also informal leaders among peers and cohorts may emerge as important agents in moulding a child's attitudes to both authority in general and specific political objects.

The mass media can also be expected to have an impact during the period of transition from close adherence to the political views of parents to those of peer-group opinion leaders, teachers, etc. Tables 5-5 and 5-6 illustrate the impact of reading the newspaper on political cognitive awareness and partisanship. Only 3.7% of those children who seldom read newspapers achieve a high cognitive score, as opposed to 16.7% of those who read newspapers a lot. Of those who read newspapers seldom, almost 65% had not developed a party identification; the corresponding percentage of those reading newspapers a lot runs considerably lower, at 43.7%.

Perhaps surprisingly, no strong relationship appears to exist between exposure to television and political awareness. This finding, illustrated in Table 5-7, possibly reflects the tendency of the child to select programs that have little or no

[12] D. Pratt, "The Social Role of School Textbooks in Canada," in Zureik and Pike, eds., op. cit., p. 100; see also A. B. Hodgetts, What Culture? What Heritage? (Toronto: OISE, 1968).

[13] M. Trudel and G. Jain Canadian History Text Books: A Comparative Study (Ottawa: Queen's Printer, 1970). See also: David Bell, op. cit., p. 167.

TABLE 5-5
READING THE NEWSPAPER AND COGNITIVE AWARENESS

Cognitive Score	Reading		
	A Lot	Some	Seldom or Never
75% or better	16.7%	8.8%	3.7%
50% to 74%	50.0	42.9	32.2
Less than 50%	33.3	48.3	64.1
	100.0%	100.0%	100.0%
Total number of respondents	1343	1784	1143

TABLE 5-6
READING THE NEWSPAPER AND PARTISAN IDENTIFICATION

Partisanship	Reading		
	A Lot	Some	Seldom or Never
No party identification	43.7%	56.5%	64.9%
Party identification	56.3	43.5	35.1
	100.0%	100.0%	100.0%
Total number of respondents	1296	1305	1089

TABLE 5-7
HOURS OF TV WATCHING PER DAY AND COGNITIVE AWARENESS

Cognitive Score	2 Hours or Less	More than 2 Hours
75% or better	12.21%	12.19%
50% to 74%	44.04	46.81
Less than 50%	43.76	41.00
	100.01%	100.00%
Total number of respondents	1065	3339

political content. However, while children who watch a lot of television are marginally more aware of politics than are those who watch little, the difference is so small that it may call into question the long-held assumption that there is a direct causal connection between television and political attitudes. These findings may also serve to reinforce the suggestion that the relationship between the mass media and attitudes is a two-step or multi-step process, involving not only the media as the primary source of the information, but other, secondary agents who interpret or translate the political data for us.[14]

[14] E. Katz and P. Lazarsfeld, *Personal Influence* (Glencoe: Free Press, 1955), *passim.*

Political information appears to be picked out of the media by a fairly small portion of the population, whom we could call *political opinion leaders*. The majority of people pick relatively little political information directly out of the media. Instead, they receive it second-hand from opinion leaders who can be found in almost every formal or informal group. The information is further processed by the recipient in accordance with pre-existent beliefs and possibly even passed on to another group — perhaps the family — in which the individual functions as an opinion leader. One thing is certain: the role of the media as agents of socialization is a complex one.[15]

While most works on the subject of political socialization limit their discussion of agents to "family," "peers," "school," and "mass media," there are other socializing agents. Significantly, in a society that has come to be referred to as "organizational,"[16] and in which most adults spend many of their waking hours occupying an organizationally defined role, the organizations or institutions themselves must have a significant impact on the substance and intensity of our attitudes. To a large extent, people who operate within the context of organizations by necessity have to identify their personal best interests with those of the organization of which they are a part — what's good for General Motors may, in fact, be good for me, if I happen to work for that organization. Hence, some of the values of the organization either consciously or unconsciously will become internalized over time.

Voluntary associations, too, can come to influence our political attitudes through the use of in-house publications, by publicizing an organizational aim, and by providing an institutional vehicle through which opinion leaders can more efficiently reach a ready-to-be-convinced audience. Even children may feel the impact of such institutional socialization, not only through the school system, as mentioned above, but also through organizations such as the Boy Scouts, which foster and disseminate the values of worship, loyalty to Queen and country, and good citizenship.

Finally, institutional or organizational agents of socialization come to play a very significant role in our process of post-incumbency socialization. As discussed above, our political élites are socialized in part through the process of incumbency. Membership in the House of Commons, Cabinet, judicial system, or bureaucracy cannot help but have an impact, not only on the incumbent's perception of the institution of which he or she is a member, but on the importance of all related institutions. Because post-incumbency socialization affects only the élites and not the masses, and because it is the socialization of our political élites that in the long run will have a more pervasive effect on the kinds of policies our system produces, future studies of political socialization should address themselves more seriously to this aspect of the process.

Who Learns What, and When?

While it is not likely that politics has any great significance for very young children, we do know that they begin to learn about political objects at a fairly tender age.

[15] See also Pammett and Proudfoot, in Pammett and Whittington, *The Foundations of Political Culture, loc. cit.*
[16] Robert Presthus, *The Organizational Society* (New York: Knopf, 1962).

The first objects about which Canadian children become aware are ones that are primarily symbolic in content. The Canadian flag, for instance, is recognized by almost 90% of children in grades two and three, and the American flag was recognized by more than 70% of the same sample of Canadian children. Next to symbolic objects, it would appear that the more highly personalized roles in the political system, such as that of the prime minister, are the most likely to be identified by children.

Thus, it seems safe to conclude that the level of knowledge about political objects depends at least in part upon the nature of the object itself. Generally, it is the symbolic objects that are learned about first, with awareness of the more personalized structural objects coming next, and with an awareness of the conceptual objects coming quite a bit later. But there are variables other than the nature of the political object that can also have an impact on the level of cognition. Studies consistently indicate that male children acquire more political information than do female children; in a similar fashion, partisanship is higher and acquired sooner in boys than in girls. As might be expected, the socioeconomic status of parents,[17] the region of the country in which the child is living,[18] and even religion[19] are independent variables that correlate with the level and intensity of cognition and partisanship in Canadian children.

While it is clear that some awareness of political objects occurs early in the child's life, it was also found in the 1960s that one's earliest attitudes towards the political system reflect a positive affect. Young Canadian children—like their American counterparts—had a basically benevolent view of politics. Since it was suggested that one of the primary functions of political socialization is the inculcation of attitudes of support for the political system, this is obviously a vital point. Looking at some actual figures, it was discovered in Kingston in 1966 that among grade-four children, 52% thought the prime minister was doing a "very good" or "fairly good" job, and only 5.7% thought he was "not very good" or "bad." By grade eight, about 60% of school children evaluated the prime minister's work positively, while only 9.5% made a basically negative evaluation.[20]

This benevolent view of political life may be related to the subordinate and dependent position of the child in a multitude of life situations. With age and experience, the child becomes less dependent and less dominated, and thus more prone to cynicism about those in positions of authority. While it would be nice to think that such optimism and faith in our system is stimulated by inherent qualities of the Canadian system, the fact that other political systems enjoy similar loyalty from their children would indicate that the phenomenon is more a function of the nature of childhood than of the nature of the political system. Canadian children are also generally conservative, a fact that, again, is probably related to the subordination and dependency of most childhood situations.[21]

---

[17] See Richert, "Political Socialization in Quebec," *CJPS*, June 1973, p. 310.

[18] See Pammett and Whittington, *The Foundations of Political Culture, loc. cit.*

[19] *Ibid.*

[20] Pammett, *op. cit.* See also Greenstein, *Children and Politics* (New Haven, 1965).

[21] Taken from Whittington, "Political Socialization and the Canadian Political System," p. 214.

More recent studies, particularly in the United States, have indicated that the children of the seventies were likely to be more cynical about politics. Politicians in the age of the Vietnam war and Watergate did not look as trustworthy and as parental as they had in the previous decade. It would appear that American children have lost some of their idealism about politics,[22] and the same seems to be the case in Canada. Stephen Ullman[23] writes about the low levels of support for the Canadian political community among the Micmac subculture in Cape Breton; Grace Skogstad describes patterns of alienation in Alberta adolescents;[24] Donald Forbes points to significant and growing pro-separatist attitudes among French-Canadian high-school students; and J.P. Richert talks of the "non-idealistic conception of government" among both English- and French-speaking elementary-school children.[25] Simple observation tells us that the young of today are less benevolent and much more critical of and cynical about the political system than were their parents. The "negativism"[26] of adults in the seventies, which we have described, may well be a direct reflection of the declining benevolence of the youth of the sixties. The implications for our future political culture could be significant.

One idiosyncrasy of children's political attitudes in Canada is the fact that American political objects seem to play a significant role in their world. Table 5-8 indicates the relative awareness of Canadian children for selected Canadian and American political objects. They indicate that some Canadian children were more likely to recognize the U.S. flag than the Canadian flag, after grade four, and that their recognition of the U.S. president was nearly as high as that of the prime minister. There are any number of ways to interpret a table such as this, but one should probably avoid the temptation of inferring that Canadian children know *more* about the United States than they do about Canada. The differences in recognition of flags are very small and do not apply before grade four. In these data, the prime minister is consistently better known than the president.[27] By grade eight, nearly 25% of these Canadian schoolchildren could identify all four Canadian items in Table 5-8, whereas only 3.8% could identify all the U.S. items.

Table 5-9, which is taken from the same study as Table 5-8, indicates another facet of Canadian relations with the United States as seen through the eyes of schoolchildren. The term "affect" is used in that study to mean a positive feeling

[22] See particularly: H. Tolley, *Children and War* (New York: Teachers College Press, 1973); Jaros, Hirsch, and Fleron,"The Malevolent Leader: Political Socialization in an American Subculture," *APSR*, 1968, p. 564.

[23] See articles by Ullman and Forbes in Pammett and Whittington, *op. cit.*

[24] G. Skogstad, "Adolescent Political Alienation," in Zureik and Pike, *op. cit.*, p. 185.

[25] J. P. Richert, "Political Socialization in Quebec," *CJPS*, VI, 2, June 1973, p. 310.

[26] See: Clarke *et al.*, *op. cit.*, p. 26.

[27] These results disagree to some extent with a survey of some two hundred students in ten schools in Kingston, Ontario, in December 1966. In the Kingston survey, 17% of grade-eight students could give a reasonably accurate description of the Prime Minister, and 72% could name him, while more than 26% could describe the role of the U.S. president and 94% could name him. Jon Pammett,"Political Orientations in Public and Separate School Children," an unpublished M.A. thesis, Queen's University, 1967, pp. 41–42.

TABLE 5-8
RECOGNITION OF CANADIAN AND AMERICAN POLITICAL OBJECTS, BY GRADE[28]

Political Object	Per Cent of Correct Identification in Grade						
	2	3	4	5	6	7	8
Canadian flag	86.4%	91.8%	92.4%	92.0%	95.7%	95.5%	97.4%
American flag	71.7	87.7	95.8	96.7	98.2	97.1	98.8
Prime Minister	68.3	74.1	79.8	88.2	95.7	98.4	99.4
Governor-General	14.3	27.8	29.3	44.0	61.7	71.1	84.8
U.S. President	25.7	42.8	57.9	69.8	89.2	89.3	93.3
Canadian cabinet	NA*	NA	14.1	21.9	28.6	38.5	51.1
American cabinet	NA	NA	4.1	3.2	6.2	6.0	10.1
Canadian MPs	NA	NA	9.5	13.6	18.0	22.9	32.0
U.S. congressmen	NA	NA	3.3	5.2	5.2	6.0	6.8

* NA — question not asked of children in grades two and three.

TABLE 5-9
AMERICAN POLITICAL ROLES VERSUS CANADIAN POLITICAL ROLES

Political Role	Affect	Confidence
Queen	78.8	70.1
President of the United States	15.8	22.0
Don't know	5.4	7.9
President of the United States	28.8	34.3
Prime Minister of Canada	64.7	53.9
Don't know	6.5	11.8
President of the United States	22.4	37.8
Governor-General of Canada	70.6	50.7
Don't know	6.9	11.5

towards someone. Thus in the "affect" column of the table, we see that 78.8% of the children in this study chose the Queen over the president when asked, "Who is your favourite?" "Confidence" is used in the study to indicate who the respondent feels is more likely to be right if the leaders named disagreed. Thus, in the "confidence" column of the table, we see that 53.9% of these children felt that the prime minister was more likely to be right in a disagreement with the president. These are data gathered before the Watergate scandal of 1973, which severely damaged the credibility of the American president then in office, but they likely reflect the "normal" situation.

Again, the interpretation of Table 5-9 is to some extent up to the reader, but the consistently higher levels of affect for Canadian political leaders and the somewhat lower but still considerable edge that Canadian leaders hold in confidence

---

[28] The figures in Tables 5-8 and 5-9 are from Donald Higgins, "The Political Americanization of Canadian Children" in Pammett and Whittington, *The Foundations of Political Culture*, p. 251.

seem to suggest that, while significant, American cultural influence has not by any means obliterated the positive feelings Canadian children have for objects related to their own political system. On the other hand, it is perhaps alarming that such a sizeable percentage (ranging from 15.8% to 37.8%) of Canadian children do have higher regard for the American president than they do for significant Canadian authorities.

This concludes our discussion of political socialization. Although much of the data cited is by now almost fifteen years old, there has not been very much quantitative research in Canada with which to update the material. However, it seems likely that the same basic generalizations still apply, even where the substantive political objects might be different. Having dealt with the basic values and attitudes that characterize the Canadian political culture, and having discussed the process whereby values, attitudes, and opinions are transmitted from individual to individual and from generation to generation, we must turn to an analysis of political participation, to see how the attitudinal make-up of individuals affects their political behaviour.

POLITICAL PARTICIPATION IN CANADA: FROM ATTITUDE TO ACTION

Political opinions are significant for the political system only if they are translated into some kind of action by the opinion holder. The action may be voting, writing to an MP, or just talking to people at the factory; if the action is concerned with politics, we call it political participation. Obviously the participation of Canadians is a vital link — indeed, it is *the* link between the environment of politics and the political system. As such, it is a key part of the political process.[29] In addition, the ways in which Canadians participate in politics and the attitudes with which they do so provide a valuable additional indicator of the nature of the political culture.

We will be dealing with voting behaviour, and with the behaviour of Canadians within the contexts of political parties and interest groups later on in the book, but for the time being we wish to make some generalizations about categories of political participation and to outline a few of the social and attitudinal correlates of such behaviour.

The Categories of Political Participation

The most elementary categorization of political participation is a differentiation between electoral and non-electoral behaviour. The former, which has received the most attention in political science, we will deal with first. Electoral behaviour, or participation in the electoral process, includes a wide range of activities, from

---

[29] As pointed out earlier, political participation can occur at the input side and at the output side of the political system. In this section, when we speak of political participation we will be referring specifically to input participation. Output-side participation will be dealt with in the context of policy making.

FIGURE 5-1
A HIERARCHY OF ELECTORAL PARTICIPATION

Gladiatorial Level	Holding a public office
	Being a political candidate
	Holding an office within a party
	Soliciting party funds
	Attending a strategy meeting or planning a campaign
Transitional Level	Contributing money to a political party
	Being an active party member
	Contributing time in a campaign
	Attending a meeting or rally
	Contacting a public official or politician
	Attempting to convince people how to vote
Spectator Level	Initiating a political discussion
	Being interested in politics
	Exposing oneself to political stimuli
	Voting

Source: Adapted from Lester Milbrath, *Political Participation* (Chicago: Rand McNally, 1965), p. 18.

actually running for elected office to simply voting for a candidate. Figure 5-1 posits three broad levels of political activity, dividing participants into *gladiatorial*, *transitional*, and *spectator* roles in the political process. People who participate at any particular level of activity will likely participate in all or most of the activities below that level in a *hierarchy of participation*. Thus, virtually every person who holds a political office has also engaged in a variety of other political activities, including voting, campaigning either on one's own behalf or for someone else, and participating in political-strategy meetings. Similarly, a person who participates in strategy meetings will certainly vote and be an active party member as well. The hierarchy of political participation, as it applies to the electoral process in Canada, is summarized in Figure 5-1.

The higher up the hierarchy, the fewer participants there are. At the most, 5% of the Canadian people participate at the gladiatorial level, while up to 40% claim to participate in transitional-level activities.[30] The commonest of the transitional activities, according to the respondents of the 1974 election study, are: attending a political rally or all-candidates meeting, and attempting to convince friends and co-workers how to vote. The last category, however, is getting fairly close to the spectator form of participation. For in simply discussing politics casually with friends, one inevitably expresses a point of view and tries to sway the opinion of others, even if that isn't the main purpose of the exercise. Such discussion seems to be motivated more by *interest* than by deep commitment.

Finally, at the spectator level of activity, participation rates are generally quite a bit higher. Fewer than 5% of the respondents in the 1974 survey reported

[30] William Mishler, *Political Participation in Canada* (Toronto: Macmillan, 1979), p. 43; see also Kornberg, Smith, and Clarke, *Citizen Politicians — Canada* (Durham: Carolina Press, 1979), pp. 58–61.

never having voted in a federal election, and between 80% and 90% of the respondents indicated that they had followed the campaign to some extent through the media, and had discussed the election informally with friends. However, we have spoken so far only of participation rates at the federal level. Table 5-10 gives a breakdown of types of political participation comparing the federal and provincial arenas. As can be seen from the table, while both provincial and federal vote frequencies are high, Canadians are more likely to exercise their federal franchise than their provincial one. The only other type of political participation characterized by wide federal-provincial difference is attending political meetings, where federal meetings would seem to be better attended than provincial meetings. For the most part, however, the levels of political participation in provincial elections, as reported in the 1974, 1979, and 1980 surveys, do not appear to be very different from the levels of participation in federal elections.[31]

We will discuss the overall functions of elections in chapter 12, but it is important to recognize here that the electoral process is neither the only nor necessarily the most important forum within which to participate meaningfully in the political process. The hierarchical classification of participation in Figure 5-1 deals exclusively with *electoral* participation, and we must now turn to a consideration of non-electoral political participation.

Non-electoral participation in the Canadian political process is more difficult to substantiate than the political activity related to voting. We can glean hard data as to the actual turn-out of the electorate simply through the reports of the electoral office, and for the most part survey research in Canada has tended to focus far more on the activities related to elections than on other dimensions of political participation. Nevertheless, there have been a few studies that have made a start in attempting to uncover the nature and the extent of citizen involvement in non-electoral political activities,[33] and these have focused largely upon membership and activity in interest groups. In fact, 50 to 60% of Canadians report that they belong to at least one voluntary political association, which makes us a ''country of joiners'' when compared to almost any other country in the world except the United States. It would be nice to be able to conclude from this that, therefore, Canada is a very ''participant'' political culture in terms of non-electoral political activities, but unfortunately there is no necessary relationship between *belonging* to a group and being *active* in the political efforts of the group. In fact, the *intensity* of the involvement of most members of voluntary associations is likely extremely low. Very few of us will ever become the group ''gladiators'' and actually serve as elected officers of the organization, and even such involvement

[31] See: M. Burke, H. Clarke, and L. Leduc, ''Federal and Provincial Political Participation in Canada,'' *Canadian Review of Sociology and Anthropology*, February 1978, p. 61; William Mishler, ''Political Participation'' in *Political Culture*, p. 179; Clarke *et al.*, *Absent Mandate*, chapter 6, and J. Pammett, ''Elections,'' in *Political Culture*, pp. 271–286.

[32] From Clarke, *Absent Mandate*, p. 86.

[33] See Presthus, *Elite Accommodation in Canadian Politics* (Toronto 1973), pp. 22–63; and J. Curtis, ''Voluntary Association Joining: A Cross National Comparative Note,'' *American Sociological Review*, October 1971, p. 872.

TABLE 5-10
FEDERAL AND PROVINCIAL ELECTIONS[32]

		%[a]			
		Often	Sometimes	Seldom	Never
Vote frequency[b]	Federal	60%	28%	8%	5%
	Provincial	53	28	10	10
Read newspapers	Federal	41	29	18	13
	Provincial	42	29	16	13
Discuss politics	Federal	24	37	22	17
	Provincial	26	37	20	17
Convince friends	Federal	8	13	10	69
	Provincial	9	14	9	68
Work in community	Federal	5	15	12	67
	Provincial	6	15	11	68
Attend meetings	Federal	10	15	12	69
	Provincial	5	15	11	69
Contact officials	Federal	3	11	14	72
	Provincial	3	12	11	74
Sign, sticker	Federal	5	9	4	82
	Provincial	5	9	4	82
Campaign activity	Federal	4	7	6	83
	Provincial	4	7	6	84

[a] N = 1184
[b] For vote frequency only, the categories are: "voted in all elections," "most," "some," "none."
Source: From *Political Choice in Canada*, H. D. Clarke et al., McGraw-Hill Ryerson, Toronto, 1980, p. 66.

within an organization may not be in any way related to its political or interest-group functions. Bill Mishler concludes that "only a small number of citizens — probably fewer than 25% — can be classified as political activists on the basis of the level and content of their participation in voluntary organizations and interest groups."[34]

Another indicator of the extent of non-electoral participation in Canada has been the response to survey questions asking about individuals' attempts to contact MPs and government officials. In 1974, 16% of the respondents indicated that they had contacted public officials, and 24% said they had written or otherwise contacted their members of parliament. Such activities are clearly a form of political participation, but even here there are qualifications that must be entered. On the one hand, surveys of MPs themselves indicate that a great many of the letters from constituents do not address themselves to problems that can be classed as political. Personal problems, requests for jobs, or assistance in dealing with administrative agencies of government are far more frequent than genuine policy-related demands.[35] Hence, if fewer than one-quarter of our citizens choose to avail themselves of even this low-intensity form of involvement in the political process, and

[34] Mishler, *Political Participation*, p. 51.
[35] Kornberg and Mishler, *Influence in Parliament: Canada* (Durham, N.C., 1976).

if a large percentage of those who do are not concerned with political issues at all, we must conclude that such involvement is not a significant reflection of political participation in Canada.

Finally, it is important that, in our discussion of the patterns of political participation in Canada, we not forget that there are less conventional political activities, such as protests, demonstrations, sit-ins, boycotts, wildcat strikes, etc., all of which have become features of the political process in recent years. As well, when considering such unconventional tactics of exerting political influence over the authorities of the system, we must recognize that such activities range from the legitimate and peaceful forms of protest to the non-legitimate or even violent manifestations of political dissent, such as riots, the deliberate destruction of property, political assassination, and terrorism.

We generally think of Canada as "the peaceable kingdom," committed to the principles of "peace, order, and good government" and exhibiting a definite preference for change that is gradual, evolutionary, and according to the rules of the game of parliamentary democracy. However, the period of the 1960s was characterized by an increase in the amount of less-conventional and non-conventional political activity, particularly in the United States, and that trend spilled over to some extent to our peaceable, conservative, and law-abiding "kingdom." As indicated in Table 5-11, there is today generally a high rate of approval of mild forms of less-conventional political activity, such as signing petitions, but with a decreasing rate of approval for the more radical forms of protest, such as illegal strikes and marches. It is perhaps significant that a full 9% of those questioned in the survey even approved of demonstrations with a chance of violence at least in some circumstances.[36]

In fact, Canada has a long history of political violence, but such activity has never been widespread, nor has it ever been viewed as legitimate by most Canadians. The assassination of D'Arcy McGee shortly after Confederation was an early and rare example of political assassination in Canada. Similarly, there were a number of confrontations involving the labour movement in the period leading up to World War One, and the Winnipeg General Strike in 1919 stands as a distinct blot on our record as a perfectly peaceful land. The irony with the Winnipeg strike and with various confrontations during the Depression years (such as the so-called Regina Riots) is that it is a toss-up whether the ensuing violence was caused by the protesters or by the military and police authorities who were called upon by the governments of the day to "restore order."

In the 1950s there were few incidents of political violence, and the majority of those reported in that decade involved the Sons of Freedom Doukhobors in western Canada, and for the most part involved damage to property rather than injury or death. In the sixties, there was a definite turn in the direction of greater violence when a number of small French-Canadian nationalist groups such as the FLQ became involved in incidents ranging from demonstrations and defacing property to bombings and kidnappings. Several of these incidents resulted in personal injury

---

[36] See: H. D. Clarke, A. Kornberg, and M. C. Stewart, "Active Minorities: Political Participation in Canadian Democracy," in N. Nevitte and A. Kornberg, eds., *Minorities and the Canadian State* (Mosaic Press, 1985), pp. 280–281; see also Mishler in Whittington and Williams, pp. 178–179.

TABLE 5-11
CANADIAN ATTITUDES TO LESS-CONVENTIONAL AND UNCONVENTIONAL
POLITICAL ACTIVITY

(a)	Has signed petition	36%
(b)	Believe political studies are sometimes justified	80%
(c)	Believe boycotts sometimes justified	81%
(d)	Believe legal demonstrations sometimes justified	80%
(e)	Believe illegal but peaceful demonstrations sometimes justified	47%
(f)	Believe violent protests sometimes justified	9%

Source: Adapted from William Mishler, "Political Participation and Democracy," in Whittington and Williams, *op. cit.*, p. 179.

and loss of life. However, since the early 1970s the tendency in Quebec has been for the nationalist movement to use primarily conventional and legitimate forms of political participation. It is to be hoped that historians will be able to explain the brief, nasty period in the late sixties and early seventies as an aberration.

Into the 1980s, while there have been various protests, sit-ins, mass demonstrations, and marches (and a hunger strike by a Senator), the number and intensity of such activities, if anything, is on the decline, and the manner in which such events are staged has been well-organized, peaceful, and law-abiding for the most part. Where there is greater cause for concern in Canada today is in the increased incidents of extremely violent acts of terrorism and assassination by immigrant groups who have imported some of their historic political hatreds and grudges with them to Canada. While the most serious of these incidents, such as the bombing of commercial airlines or the assassination of foreign diplomats, are not usually directed at Canada, the Canadian government, or Canadians directly, the implications for the nature of political life in Canada are deeply disturbing. Whatever the legitimacy of the causes being espoused by groups such as the Armenians or the Sikhs living in Canada, acts of terrorism committed in Canada simply must not be tolerated. Sadly, too, one of the inevitable consequences of such imported violence is that it comes to reflect negatively upon the entire immigrant community involved, thus justifying and reinforcing whatever racist and discriminatory attitudes exist in the Canadian social mainstream.

While it is alarming to discover that our peaceable kingdom is not as orderly as our national myths would have it,[37] we are still significantly more peaceable than Britain and the United States, the countries with which Canadians most frequently seek to compare themselves. Moreover, very few individual Canadians ever actually participate in riots, demonstrations, political strikes, and other more violent forms of political protest. As Bill Mishler put it, "Despite the frequency of political protest in Canada, it is reasonable to estimate that the number of Canadians participating in the most extreme forms of political protest has never exceeded ten percent and probably has averaged less than one percent."[38]

[37] T. Mitchell, "Violence and Politics in Canada," a paper delivered at the ACSUS conference, Washington, D.C., 1979. See also M. Kelly, and T. Mitchell, "Post Referendum Quebec — The Potential for Conflict," *Conflict Quarterly*, Summer 1980, pp. 15–19.

[38] Mishler, *Political Participation*, p. 35.

The Determinants of Political Participation

We suggest that there are three basic determinants of a person's participation in politics. The first of these is the sum of the individual's socioeconomic resources: the amount of time and money one can "invest" in political activity. How much one invests will depend upon one's occupation and income, upon the other activities that compete for one's resources, and, of course, upon the nature of the political system itself. A second and vital determinant is the individual's personality resources. Political participation at most higher levels of the hierarchy is a sociable activity, and consequently has social costs and requires social resources. People who have more social aplomb and who find interaction with other people to be easy are therefore more likely to participate in politics. The third determinant is the political resources available to the citizen who wishes to participate in politics. If there are many institutions in which one can participate, or if the existing institutions, such as political parties, encourage participation, then one is more likely to become involved in politics. This last point can be examined further in two ways. First, we can look at Canadian institutions, such as political parties, to see whether they do, in fact, encourage participation. This we will do in Chapters 10 and 11. Second, we can determine whether Canadians feel that the political system responds to their efforts to influence it, and then determine whether their feelings in this respect correlate with participation. The feeling that one has a meaningful role in politics and one's confidence that the system will respond to the individual are termed a sense of *political efficacy*. Its role in Canada is summarized later in this chapter.

The next step, then, will be to outline who participates in the Canadian electoral process by examining, first, the socioeconomic correlates of participation, and second, the psychological determinants of participation.

Socioeconomic Factors and Political Participation   One of the most consistent correlates of political participation, not only in Canada but throughout the western democracies, is the socioeconomic status (SES) of the individual. Whether we utilize subjective criteria of class (self-classification through direct questions such as, "What class do you think of yourself belonging to?"), or objective criteria, such as personal income, occupation, or education, it is clear that lower SES correlates positively with lower levels of political participation. This finding was borne out by the data from a 1965 election survey, cited in previous editions of this text, and remains a significant finding in more recent studies.[39] The exceptions or qualifications that must be entered here are all with respect to the individual objective indicators of a social class. A 1974 election study, cited by Mishler, indicates that while high income is a good predictor of participation at the gladiatorial level in elections, and in non-electoral activities such as approaching government officials and MPs, wealthier people are "not appreciably more likely to vote or participate in political campaigns than even the poorest citizens."[40] Similarly, while occupation is a good predictor of gladiatorial participation, with members of the professions occupying a disproportionate percentage of elected

---

[39] See Mishler, *Political Participation*, pp. 88–95, especially p. 91.

[40] Mishler, *Political Participation*, p. 96.

offices in Canada, professional people are likely to be less concerned with participation in transitional activities such as campaigns, and are not significantly more likely to vote than members of lower-status occupations groups. This may be a reflection of the fact that higher-status groups perceive their opportunities to influence the political process to be greater if they deal directly with the elected officials of government, or if they actually become one themselves, than if they simply exercise their franchise or work in somebody's campaign.

If we look at the SES of participants in political protests, however, we get rather different impressions. While information about protestors is scarce, we can fairly safely say that much of the protest activity of the sixties and seventies was dominated by the university-age offspring of fairly high-status families, on the one hand, and by disaffected and alienated lower-status workers on the other.[41] The influence of education reflects a pattern similar to that of occupation. Levels of participation increase with education up to the high-school level, but university-educated people are no more likely to vote than high-school graduates. Similarly, people with a university education are more likely to attempt to influence the political process through direct involvement as gladiators, or in approaches to government officials, as individuals or as active members of interest groups. The fact that the distribution of participants is similar to that demonstrated by higher-status occupations is hardly startling, given that there is a direct connection between higher levels of education and the professional occupations. Again, because of the importance of the university in the sixties as a fertile milieu for political protest, there is a relationship between university-level education and participation in political protest.

Language, ethnicity, and religion are all fairly closely related variables, and as a combination of coincident cleavages they can affect both the opportunities for and the propensity towards political participation. However, if we expect a dramatic difference between ethnic groups, the findings demonstrated by Table 5-12 will be somewhat disappointing. What the data do indicate is that French Canadians are less likely than English Canadians to become involved in non-electoral activities such as contacting an MP, or belonging to a community association. Moreover, the French respondents were more likely to become involved in transitional activities, such as working in the campaign, but slightly less likely to vote in federal elections. Part of this discrepancy might be explained in terms of a more authoritarian or passive subject orientation to the system as a whole, coupled with the expectation that the way to get a share of the patronage goodies handed out after elections is to be involved as a volunteer during the election campaign. However, when we look to French Canadians' participation in provincial politics, we find that the discrepancy virtually disappears. Essentially it seems that, compared to Anglophones, French Canadians view themselves as relatively more efficacious at the provincial level than at the federal level. They are, therefore, more likely to vote in provincial elections, and more likely to approach provincial government officials than federal ones.[42]

---

[41] Michael Stein, *The Dynamics of Right Wing Protest* (Toronto: University of Toronto Press, 1973), pp. 173–175.

[42] Mishler, *Political Participation*, p. 99; Van Loon and Whittington, (1976), p. 113; Clarke *et al.*, *op. cit.*, p. 89.

TABLE 5-12
THE EXTENT OF POLITICAL PARTICIPATION BY ETHNIC ORIGIN[43]

Activity	British	French	Other European	Asian, Native, Other
Voting	88%	82%	85%	81%
Campaigning	38	43	43	41
Contacting MPs	26	19	26	25
Community activity	26	15	17	24
N* =	536	267	186	142

* Voting percentages are based on a total sample of 2,445. All other activities are based on a half-sample of 1,203. Ns are for the half-sample and vary slightly between activities because of differences in missing data.

As is also indicated by Table 5-12, the non-English and non-French respondents are much closer to the former than to the latter in the overall pattern of their participation in federal politics. The most significant difference is that the two "charter groups," the French and English, are disproportionally represented at the gladiatorial levels of the hierarchy of participation. The non-charter groups are only beginning to make inroads to elected office or even to candidacy in Canada, a point that will be explored more fully in the chapter on the authorities of the system.

It is difficult to generalize about the ethnic, religious, and linguistic composition of protest movements in Canada, partly because of the lack of hard information and partly because the pattern is only a very vague one. As Mishler has pointed out:

> Political protest is most prevalent among the least assimilated groups in society as is evident from the record of French-Canadian protest during the 1960s, from the activities of radical segments of groups such as the Doukhobors in B.C. and from the ethnic composition of labour protests over the first half of this century.[44]

Mishler's assertion, however, is tempered when viewed in historical context. We find, for instance, that English Canadians were a dominant force in the Rebellion of 1837 in Upper Canada, and that, in the 1960s and 1970s, the children of middle class WASPs were well-represented in campus unrest, anti-nuclear protest, and anti-Vietnam war demonstrations.

Much has been written in Canada about the influence of geography on patterns of political behaviour. While there are clear differences in partisan choice from one region to the next, attempts to demonstrate regional variations in the level and intensity of political participation have not been particularly successful. Overall differences in levels of participation by province are more likely affected by particular local political conditions than by regional cleavages. Any consistent differences that can be found are quite readily attributable to differing levels of education or income, with poorer and less well-educated regions show-

[43] From Mishler, *Political Participation*, p. 100.
[44] Mishler, *Political Participation*, p. 101.

ing slightly lower levels of most types of participation. The level of activity in a province, however, may be temporarily increased by a heightened level of political party competition, by a particularly exciting political leader, or by the emergence of a new political movement.[45] We will consider the significance of regionalism on patterns of political *attitudes* in the next section of this chapter, but for now we feel fairly safe in dismissing regional variations in the patterns of political participation as idiosyncratic and usually temporary.[46]

Urban and rural differences in political participation in Canada are fairly significant, although the patterns of variation are unlike those characteristic of the other socioeconomic and demographic determinants of participation. According to the 1974 election survey results, the relationship between urbanization and political participation is curvilinear.[47] The frequency of voting is highest in the large urban areas and in the rural or farm communities, and lowest in the medium-sized cities and towns. The same curvilinear pattern applies with respect to non-electoral participation, such as contacting MPs, etc., but participation in local or community activities increases linearly with the smaller size of community. Likely these differential patterns of political participation by community size can be explained in two ways.The higher levels of participation in the cities will generally be a reflection of higher SES, income, and education, coupled with the fact that cities simply afford more opportunities for participation. On the other side, the high participation in rural communities might be explained by the fact that involvement in community affairs is a result of a circumstance of more genuine community than prevails in larger urban centres. The involvement in local matters, of which politics is one aspect, is generally higher because people know each other, deal with each other regularly, and thus are more interested in being active in community affairs.

There are some sex and age differences in the Canadian population with respect to participation. In middle-class English Canada, there is not much difference in levels of participation between men and women, but in French Canada and among people with less than a high-school level of education, men have been generally much more likely to participate than women. The pattern in Canada in this respect is similar to that in other western democracies. In underdeveloped areas of a country, where educational levels are low, there are large differences between the sexes. Where educational levels are higher, sexual equality extends to political participation as well as to some other fields. An age profile of participation shows a peak in the middle years, with a trailing off at either end. Very old or very young voters appear particularly unlikely to be active participants in the electoral process, and this pattern prevails in Canada regardless of regional, cultural, or class differences.

---

[45] S. M. Lipset, in *Agrarian Socialism* (Berkeley: University of California Press, 1950), discusses in detail the effect of a new movement (the CCF) on patterns of participation in Saskatchewan.

[46] See also: Mishler, *Political Participation*, p. 58, who makes this point: "Although citizens of different provinces and regions develop distinctive political attitudes and perspectives, it appears that political participation is influenced less by regional or provincial factors than by characteristics of the individual or sub-group."

[47] Mishler, p. 105.

Any of the above facts can be explained without too much difficulty by keeping in mind what was said earlier about the individual's resources. The explanation can be further sharpened to apply to particular types of campaign activity if it is suggested that all activities have specific requirements that call more or less directly on specific resources.[48] For example, reading about a political campaign obviously requires the ability to read relatively easily. It is therefore not surprising to find a positive correlation between the level of education and reading about politics. On the other hand, belonging to a party or working for one takes time and requires social interaction. Thus, people with more time (retired people, housewives whose children are grown up), or with flexible time requirements for their jobs (lawyers, professors, or other professional people), could be expected to, and do, participate in this way more frequently than others.

Nonetheless, even a cursory glance is enough to indicate that socioeconomic factors alone are not sufficient to explain why people participate in politics. There are still many people who have all the necessary resources but pay no attention to politics. In some cases our predictions can be fairly clear. If the person in question is an older, poorly educated, rural French-Canadian woman, we can assert with a considerable degree of confidence that voting is likely to be her only political act. But much of the Canadian voting-age public is middle class or working class, with enough education to give it many of the necessary resources to participate; whether a member of this group will participate must depend upon some other factors, as well. We will turn now to a consideration of the psychological or attitudinal determinants of political participation.

Psychological Correlates of Participation   There are a number of psychological and attitudinal factors that might be supposed to underlie political participation. In other countries it has been found that such things as an absence of anxiety or an absence of authoritarian outlook on life are correlated with political participation. These findings have been replicated in enough different settings that we can probably expect they are true for Canada as well, though unfortunately there has been little specific research in Canada. The 1974 election survey does permit us to look at a few of these variables.

Interest in politics, as might be expected, is an important attitudinal trait distinguishing participants and non-participants in Canada. As Mishler has pointed out, there is a strong relationship between interest in politics and the level and intensity of political participation. This bears out the findings we reported in our second edition, based on the 1965 election survey. What is important to note is that, while there is a high correlation between interest and activity in politics, in general Canadians seem to be less interested in politics today than they were fifteen years ago.[49]

Closely related to interest is *knowledge* about the political system. The people who are the most interested also tend to know more about political objects, and, as might be expected, people who score high on political-information tests also tend to participate more frequently and at higher levels of the hierarchy of electoral

[48] L. Milbrath, in *Political Participation*, calls these requirements "dimensions"; see pp. 22ff.
[49] Mishler, p. 67.

participation. However, what is disturbing here is the apparently low level of cognitive sophistication among the Canadian electorate. The 1974 study showed that almost half of the respondents could not score 50% on a series of fairly straightforward questions about the powers of the federal and provincial governments. But on the more positive side, the level of knowledge about the system seems to be higher among individuals in the 1980s than it was in the 1960s and 1970s. Hence we would appear to have the unusual situation in Canada where the levels of cognitive political sophistication are increasing, at the same time as levels of interest in politics are declining. One possible explanation might be that political sophistication breeds boredom with politics. (We will discuss this later, in the context of the other psychological variables such as efficacy, ideological commitment, and partisanship.)

Partisan loyalty, or the psychological phenomenon of identifying with a political party, is a good predictor of higher levels and intensity of political participation. The findings of the 1965 election study showed a strong relationship, and the results of subsequent election studies mirror this finding. Clark *et al.* have pointed out that not only is there a strong relationship between partisanship and participation, but that the *intensity* of loyalty correlates positively with the intensity of political participation.[50] But while party loyalty generally correlates with higher levels of participation in politics, there are not significant differences among the supporters of different political parties in the Canadian scene. The exception here is that supporters of the NDP traditionally seem to be more likely to become involved at the gladiatorial and transitional levels than do supporters of the two traditional parties. This may be only a reflection of the intensity of NDP partisanship relative to PC or Liberal partisanship, but another explanation might be that partisanship is more intense if it is reflective of an ideological commitment. The literature in the United States indicates that very few citizens are genuinely ideological, and there have been no studies that might indicate that Canadians are any different. However, as Mishler has pointed out: "Little Canadian evidence exists on the subject, but what there is suggests that ideology encourages both voting and campaign participation provided that at least one of the political parties — even a minor one — shares the citizens' preferences."[51] Hence ideological commitment likely is related to the intensity of partisanship, and also to the level and frequency of political participation, but "ideologues" do not comprise a very large percentage of the Canadian citizenry.

It might be added here that, although there are not sufficient data to be certain, it seems likely that ideological commitment is an independent predictor of participation in the non-legitimate and less legitimate forms of political participation, such as demonstrations and violence. Further, it seems likely that ideologues with a strong partisan preference are less likely to seek political demonstrations and protests as a medium of expression than ideologically oriented people who cannot find a party whose stated principles conform to their own. In this sense, extremist political parties may serve the purpose of moderating the incidence of

---

[50] Clarke *et al.*, *op. cit.*, p. 306; see also, Mishler, *op. cit.*, pp. 72–74.

[51] Mishler, *op. cit.*, p. 72; see also Mishler, in Whittington and Williams, *op. cit.*, p. 188.

non-legitimate political behaviour by co-opting potential radicals into the conventional machinery of government, such as elections. As an example, it seems reasonable to hypothesize that the Parti Québécois offered a legitimate political medium for the expression of radical political views during the 1970s, and in so doing reduced the attractiveness of the non-legitimate political tactics of organizations such as the FLQ.

Political efficacy is the feeling or perception of one's ability to have an impact on the political process. While one of the determinants of participation in politics is the objective *opportunities* that the institutions of the system, socioeconomic factors, and attitudinal resources provide to the individual, the second set of determinants are those relating to our *motivation* to participate. Such motivation to be involved depends to a large extent on how much impact we believe we are capable of having, or our feelings of efficacy. Generally it can be stated that the levels of political efficacy in Canada are lower than those present in the other Anglo-American democracies.[52] Moreover, from 1965 until 1980, the levels of efficacy have generally declined in Canada, as have the general levels of *trust* in the authorities of the political system.[53]

Political efficacy is a good predictor of the levels and intensity of political participation. Although the relationship is not strong with respect to voting, for other levels of the hierarchy of electoral participation and for non-electoral categories of political participation, the propensity to participate declines with the level of political efficacy. A possible explanation of the fact that a relatively large percentage of respondents who believe that voting is important, despite general feelings of political inefficacy, *do* habitually exercise their franchise, is that the act of voting is seen as an important symbolic affirmation of the democratic process. In other words, people may vote out of a sense of civic duty rather than out of any faith that they can actually have an impact on policy outputs.[54] People may also become involved at the transitional levels of the political process, such as in election campaigns, because such activities are of social value to them. Thus, it is possible that the gregariousness of an individual generally, or the extent to which one is outgoing, may be an important correlate of political participation in group activities. Consistent with this is the finding, cited in the last edition of this text, that the non-political aspects of personality can have some impact on the motivation to become involved in politics. We return to this subject when we discuss Canadian political parties, in chapter 11.

Finally we must conclude this very brief discussion of the relationship between efficacy and participation in Canadian politics with a cautionary note. While we have been able to cite a strong correlation between the two sets of variables, we have not been able to determine the *direction* of the causal links. It is normally assumed that efficacy determines the level of participation, that the attitudes determine the behaviour. We would like to suggest that the reverse be considered as

---

[52] Mishler, *op. cit.*, p. 75.

[53] See section above where we noted the phenomenon of "political negativism." See also Clarke *et al.*, *op. cit.*

[54] See Clarke *et al.*, *op. cit.*, p. 33, and Mishler, *op. cit.*, p. 74.

a possible explanation of the empirical findings in this area; i.e., that people believe voting to be important because they have done it a lot and it has proven to be an easy, interesting, and psychologically satisfying experience. Similarly, people who do not get involved at higher levels of the hierarchy of participation may give, as an *excuse*, their conviction that such involvement is not worth their while, that it will not produce any positive results, and therefore that it is a waste of their valuable time. Thus, while a sense of civic duty motivates people to engage in activities such as voting, which do not take much time or effort, it is possible that out of laziness, complacency, ignorance, or even false consciousness, they are unwilling to invest the significantly greater time and effort required to participate in higher-order political activities. As a result, a sense of civic guilt may cause people to rationalize their non-participation in terms of cynicism, negativism, and inefficacious statements about the higher orders of political behaviour.

Political Participation and Political Culture

While it is difficult to generalize about any aspect of the Canadian political culture because of the socioeconomic, demographic, and attitudinal complexities of our political community, we feel that it is necessary to do so. It is important to at least make the attempt to find some common patterns that generally hold despite the wide regional, economic, ethno-linguistic, and ideological variations that qualify and elaborate our macro-level conclusions. In this spirit, we hypothesize that, at the highest level of generalization, the patterns of political participation in Canada can be described as *"spectator-participant."*[55] This seemingly self-contradictory phrase is used for a number of reasons. First, relative to most democratic countries, Canadians do have a very high level of political participation: only the United States shows one consistently higher.[56] Canada must therefore be described as a *participant* political culture. Not all Canadians, however, are participants. In particular, it was seen that lower socioeconomic groups do not participate beyond the lowest levels except in the fairly infrequent cases where people have picked up a high level of interest in politics. Indeed, with the exception of voting, those 20% or so of Canadians who are below or near the poverty line[57] are largely excluded from the input side of the political process, and consequently have to accept the outputs of the system with much less control over them than their middle-class fellow citizens. They are, then, the silent poor, although it might be a mistake to assume they will always remain so. With increasing levels of education, they may slowly become mobilized politically, and if they do not participate within the context of the legitimate political system in ways that have become traditional in Canadian politics, they may learn to participate in illegitimate ways.

[55] Robert Presthus uses a similar term, *quasi-participative*, to describe the Canadian political culture. See: *Elite Accommodation in Canadian Politics*, pp. 38ff.

[56] Comparative data can be found in L. Milbrath, *Political Participation*, R. Lane, *Political Life*, and G. Almond and S. Verba, *The Civil Culture* (Princeton: Princeton University Press, 1963).

[57] See chapter 2.

The term "spectator," in the phrase "spectator-participant," is used to describe the predominant motivational factors of people who do participate. To some extent, and for certain categories of political participation, they may be motivated by efficacy — a feeling that their efforts will be rewarded by the political system — but for the most part they appear to be motivated by a sort of spectator interest in what is going on in politics. They perceive little ideological difference between the parties, but they do feel that it does matter which leaders are in power. They will apparently participate in politics if they find the differences between political leaders and political parties to be interesting. Otherwise, aside from voting, they are unlikely to participate at all. Graphic illustration of this was provided during the 1968 election campaign, when electoral participation was higher than it had been since the 1958 halcyon days of John Diefenbaker, largely because of the emergence of a new and interesting personality, Pierre Elliott Trudeau. Similarly, the 1984 election sparked the interest and participation of large numbers of Canadians because of the appearance on the scene of new leaders, most prominently Brian Mulroney of the PCs.

Canadians appear to approach politics much as they would a sports event. If the game is good they will come out and cheer. On election day they may go to the game by voting and watching the returns on television, and if they are really interested they may participate at higher levels in the hierarchy. If their party wins they will be happy, and if it loses they may be sad, but not for long. Their involvement with the event has been motivated by interest and psychological identification with the principals, but is not based on well-defined objective concern or deep ideological commitment. When we study voting behaviour in chapter 12, we will see that this orientation to politics is also expressed in very ephemeral attachments to parties and by a very great propensity on the part of the Canadian voter to change his or her partisan stripes from election to election.

All of this has significant implications for the political system and, in particular, for its decision makers. One famous Canadian historian has described cabinet government as a system where the citizen "gives full power of attorney to a small committee each four years or so, well knowing that virtually nothing he can do in the interval will have much effect on the groups to whom he has given his blank cheque."[58] This means that, under normal circumstances, politics in Canada can be, if the authorities choose, about nothing. The system will appear to be retaining its legitimacy because the level of voting in elections, by which we typically measure that legitimacy, can remain high as long as politics are interesting. The level of interest can be kept high as long as colourful personalities are presented. Occasional infusions of new and interesting personalities or of "style issues" will serve to retain minimum democratic involvement in the system.

A further consequence of the spectator-participant nature of Canadian politics is a reinforcement of tendencies favouring the status quo. The people who most actively participate in the process are disproportionately drawn from the middle and upper-middle classes. They have reason to be satisfied with the status quo,

---

[58] A. R. M. Lower, *Canadians in the Making* (Toronto: Longman's, 1958), p. 281.

and they are organized into the types of group structure that allow them to promote their own interests in consonance with government élites. Thus:

> Government, to some extent, is pushed into the anomalous position of defending the strong against the weak. While the government elite plays an equilibrating role in welfare areas, much of its energy is also spent in reinforcing the security and growth of interests that already enjoy the largest shares of net social product.[59]

The spectator-participant orientation of the Canadian political culture may both allow and force political élites to behave in this way if they are to retain the legitimacy they require to maintain their hegemony.

The term *apolitical* is used by political scientists to denote a politics that is not concerned with genuine ideological or policy differences, but which is highly supportive of the status quo. It would occur, for example, if all the members of the political élite — that is, all the major actors inside the political system — were basically in agreement about policies and political objectives. The real differences between the actions of one group and those of another would be slight, and the real significance of elections or other changes of power would be small. Apolitical politics may or may not be dangerous; readers can make their own judgements on that. The main point here is that in such a system, the decisions of those in authority might not and probably would not represent the real cleavages in the environment, yet popular support for the decision makers could still be made to appear adequate.[60]

Apparent legitimacy can be disadvantageous for a political system. The system will remain stable as long as the outputs are at least marginally effective in satisfying active members of the political community, and the marginal level may be considerably depressed by the distraction of people's attention from issues to personalities. However, if there is an infusion into the system of people who were formerly politically inactive, as may occur when educational levels of the lower socioeconomic classes have been raised or when significant new issues arise, the system may become unstable unless its institutions can be adapted to accommodate the effective participation of many newly aroused citizens.

All of this may read like a denunciation of the Canadian political system. However, all that has been said so far is that the Canadian political culture is such that it may permit apolitical politics. It is too early in this book for us to finalize such an assessment. It must first be determined whether Canadian political institutions and the authorities occupying them behave in such a way as to make politics issue-less. Not only is it too early in this book; it may be too early in the history of Canadian political science. We are still only beginning to collect the quantitative data necessary to fully examine the hypotheses suggested here. While there have been many high-quality studies done in Canada since 1965, one must ask different types of questions of different people at many different times in order to verify what has been said here.

59 R. Presthus, *Elite Accommodation*, p. 347. Reprinted by permission of Cambridge University Press.

60 Ulf Himmelstrand, "A Theoretical and Empirical Approach to Depolitization and Political Involvement," *Acta Sociologica*, vol. 6, pp. 83–111, fasc. 1-2, 1962, provides a similar analysis in the Swedish setting and arrives at similar conclusions.

Canadian Political Culture: A Summary

With the material in these two chapters entered and noted,what *can* we say about the Canadian political culture by way of summary? First, from the evidence of history and from the study of Canadian political institutions, we can safely say that the Canadian political culture includes a commitment to democratic values such as popular sovereignty, majoritarianism, and the political rights and freedoms associated with representative government. Second, again, it is the evidence of history and of our political, economic, and legal institutions that tells us we have a political culture dominated by the pervasive and persistent ideological blend that is Canadian liberalism. While we have seen that our liberal values are qualified by streaks or strains of toryism, socialism, corporatism, and communalism, the fact remains that, for all regions, ethnic groups, and social classes in Canada, liberal values dominate. Third, when we come to look at Canadians' attitudes and orientations towards specific political objects, we do not have enough information to generalize effectively. On the basis of the few surveys there are, we do know that such attitudes vary quite widely with different regions, ethnic groups, and social classes, and that the only general impression is one of a growing cynicism or negativism towards politics that emerged in the late sixties and early seventies. This might prove to be the beginning of what will become a dominant strain in our political culture, or it might be a passing malady that will disappear as mysteriously as it appeared. Finally, on the basis of attitudinal, behavioural, institutional, and impressionistic information (not to mention a shot of introspection!), we can hypothesize that the patterns of political participation in Canada reflect *spectator*, *quasi-participative*, or *apolitical* attitudes towards direct personal involvement in the political process.

THE CONSTITUTIONAL AND LEGAL ENVIRONMENT

C H A P T E R 6

THE CONSTITUTIONAL CONTEXT

F rom the point of view of a political scientist, the constitution of a political system is significant for two reasons. First, the constitution can be viewed as a device that modifies human behaviour, for a constitution is one of the *independent variables* that influences the political process. Second, the constitution can be viewed as a reflection of the political culture; in this sense, it is a *dependent variable*, which is itself but a product of societal forces. In studying a constitution, therefore, we not only discover the formal institutional limits within which the policy process takes place, but we also find out more about the fundamental values of a political community.

THE FUNCTIONS OF THE CANADIAN CONSTITUTION

Paradoxically, all institutions of a political system must be both rigid and flexible.[1] On the one hand, rigidity is necessary if the regime is to acquire legitimacy; for, in order that the citizen may learn either positive or negative attitudes towards a political system, that system must to some extent be stable. The process of political socialization takes time, and it would be impossible to learn about the nature of our political system and its implicit values and norms if all of its institutions were constantly in a state of violent flux. On the other hand, because environmental conditions are continually changing, there is a necessity for considerable flexibility in the regime. If the system is to persist, it must be able to adapt relatively quickly to meet new problems and to relieve related stresses.

In the Canadian political system, flexibility is provided partly by political parties and pressure groups and partly by institutions such as the Cabinet and the bureaucracy. All of these institutions have at least some ability to react directly and immediately to rapid environmental changes. The constitution, because it cannot be changed as easily, provides the political system with some of its necessary rigidity. Thus, in the widest sense, the function of a constitution is to provide the system with a backbone — to give it the rigidity necessary for it to persist over time. But constitutions have more immediate and more specific functions to perform, which are often unique to the individual political system and to the particular form of government in operation. These we consider next.

The Rule of Law

The manifest function of any constitution is to define the relationship between the citizen and the state, and, to the extent that the relationship can be defined at all, every country can be said to have some form of constitution. However, this is too general an assertion to be of much value in the Canadian setting. What is implicit in the notion of constitutionalism, at least in the western democracies, is the basic principle of the *rule of law*. To put it simply, for Canada and other western nations, a constitution is one of the means of achieving the goal of a system where law is supreme.

The principle of rule of law in the British and Canadian tradition asserts that any interference with the freedom of any individual must be performed only according to the legal process and carried out by legitimate authorities. No one is exempt from the law, neither citizens nor officials of the government, and no one can interfere with the rights of any individual, except through the legal process. Finally, the principle of the rule of law means, as well, *equality* before the law for all members of a political community.

---

[1] Talcott Parsons refers to these requisites as "pattern maintenance" and "adaptation," each of which must be achieved if the system is to persist.

The rule of law is a doctrine we in Canada have inherited from the English constitution. It was transported to Canada during the colonial period and constitutionally implanted here through the BNA Act (or the Constitution Act, 1867), whose preamble states that Canada is to have a "Constitution similar in principle to that of the United Kingdom" — i.e., founded on the rule of law. In Britain, the doctrine of the rule of law dates from 1215, when the Magna Carta was signed (under some duress!) by King John, affirming that the king would henceforth rule *per legem terrae* — according to the law of the land. The principle has been expanded and refined since that auspicious occasion in history, and was explicitly entrenched in the constitution of Canada through the 1982 Charter of Rights and Freedoms, whose preamble states that Canada is founded upon (among other things) the rule of law.[2]

But if we grant that the constitution of Canada is built on the principle of the rule of law, we must also ask why the rule of law is so important. The function of the rule of law is, briefly, to protect us from the arbitrary interference of government, or of government officials, in our everyday lives. The law is knowable: in principle, one can become aware, through the law, of standards of behaviour that are expected of everyone. The relationship of the individual to the political system becomes, to some extent, fixed and impartial. By contrast, the rule of the most benevolent of dictators could conceivably deteriorate to rule by whim and caprice, for even benevolent dictators once in a while get out of bed on the wrong side, have quarrels with their spouses, or get cranky because of pressures at work. The law, on the other hand, is presumed to be impersonal, predictable, and coldly rational rather than emotional or moody.

Defining the Legitimate Role of Government

The rule of law is thus desirable in a society that values the principle of an impartial and predictable relationship between the citizen and the authorities of the political system. The principle of the rule of law, however, is not sufficient to secure in perpetuity such a set of values, for its inherent weakness is the fact that the law is made by people and applied and interpreted by them — and people are not always impersonal, predictable, and rational. Thus, in order to prevent unjust laws from being passed and to guard against the unjust or inequitable application of laws, a constitution must go beyond the mere recognition of the rule of law; it must also set limits on the kinds of laws that can be made.

Our constitution defines very broadly the area of legitimate lawmaking by giving us a body of fundamental principles to which all public policy must conform. These principles are the most elemental norms of the system and they define the boundary between legitimate interference of the state with the individual and those individual freedoms that are so important that even the authority of a democratically elected parliament must be restricted in such matters. Many of these basic limits on the legitimate role of the state are defined by constitutional conventions inherited from Britain and reflective of the dominant political values

---

[2] See F.L. Morton, ed., *Law, Politics, and the Judicial Process in Canada* (Calgary: University of Calgary Press, 1984), Chapter 1.

of our political culture. While their limits have been explicitly defined, set down, and entrenched in the 1982 Charter of Rights and Freedoms, their guarantee still rests most importantly in the continued commitment to them on the part of the government and the governed alike.

Defining the Regime: Political Structures and Processes

Not only does the Canadian constitution set the boundaries within which governments must operate — the legitimate *ends* of the state — but it also defines the form of government, or the *regime*. The Canadian constitution defines the operational structure of the political system, and it also defines the relationships among parts of the system. In J.A. Corry's words, "The constitution is the frame or chassis in which the working engine of government is set."[3] In this sense, for instance, the Constitution Act of 1867 gives us a federal system, representative democracy, a parliamentary system, an independent judiciary, etc. — the institutional features that characterize the Canadian political system.

Further, the Canadian constitution defines many of the rules of the game of politics. It broadly defines the tactics and the *means* that are acceptable within the Canadian political process, and describes formal procedures that must be followed in order to implement policy decisions. The Canadian constitution, in other words, sets formal limits beyond which the authorities may not go in performing the basic function of conflict resolution. It does not matter what the ends are, nor how popular the ends may be; the constitution sets limits on the means that can be legitimately employed to achieve them. An example of these rules of the game of politics in Canada is the principle that there should be ample time provided in the House of Commons for the Opposition to criticize government policy. No matter how urgent the government policy may seem at the time, the Opposition is always guaranteed at least some opportunity to debate any issue. Although the constitution does not specify exactly how much time, even in the cases where government has the power to limit debate, the Opposition must still be given a substantial opportunity to make its views known in Parliament.

Symbolic Functions

Finally, a constitution is, or should be, a source of pride and a unifying influence within a political community. Generally this is the case, and certainly it applies to the constitution of the United States and to the unwritten constitution of Britain. In each of these systems the constitution, for widely differing reasons, has become a symbol of the society's particular brand of democracy, and, indeed, an object of national pride. In Canada, however, our constitution has sometimes been maligned; and, rooted as it is in English law, it may even have been a disintegrative symbol for non-British Canadians.

---

[3] J.A. Corry and J.E. Hodgetts, *Democratic Government and Politics* (Toronto: University of Toronto Press, 1959), p. 85.

While it is still too early to come to a firm conclusion, it would appear that the 1982 "made-in-Canada" constitutional reforms have overcome some of the ambivalence Canadians have felt towards the BNA Act. We can only hope that our "new" constitution, with its Charter of Rights, can become a unifying symbol in the struggle to maintain a united Canada.[4] Moreover, as a formal, documentary codification of many constitutional principles heretofore "unwritten," the 1982 Charter can act as an important *educative* device in teaching new Canadians and young Canadians the basic values of our system.

COMPONENT PARTS OF THE CANADIAN CONSTITUTION

The British North America Act of 1867[5], as amended, forms the core of the Canadian constitution. Legally, the Act is a statute of the British parliament, the contents of which are based almost entirely on resolutions drawn up at two conferences, one in Quebec and one in London, by the representatives of the original four provinces. The legal-historical significance of the Act is that it created a federal union out of Upper and Lower Canada and the maritime provinces of New Brunswick and Nova Scotia. Because, at the time of Confederation, the Canadas were united, the BNA Act also created the provinces of Ontario and Quebec. The scope of the BNA Act is somewhat limited: it deals with certain broad topics like the federal distribution of powers and the general form of the central government. The farthest the BNA Act goes in defining the principles of government in Canada is in the preamble, where it states that Canada shall have a form of government "similar in principle to that of the United Kingdom." In other words, as a constitution, the BNA Act is rather restricted. It does not pretend to be the omnicompetent document that the constitution of the United States is, or was intended to be, and in fact much of what is described as "the constitution of Canada" is not found in the BNA Act.

The Constitution Act of 1982 has the effect of patriating the BNA Act and of providing an amending formula for the Canadian constitution. Schedule I of the 1982 document lists, and in most cases renames, the legislative components of the Canadian constitution; hence, for instance, the BNA Act itself is now formally called the "Constitution Act, 1867" and most of the subsequent amendments of that act, from 1867 to 1982, are also called Constitution Acts, and years are cited. The various acts of the British parliament and British orders in council that created the various provinces after 1867 are also renamed to reflect their purpose. Hence, for example, the order in council admitting Prince Edward Island into confederation is renamed the "Prince Edward Island Terms of Union." As well, the BNA Act of 1949 is renamed the "Newfoundland Act," etc.

---

[4] See R. Knopff and F.L. Morton, "Nation Building and the Charter," a research paper prepared for the Royal Commission on the Economic Union (Toronto: University of Toronto Press, 1985), for an excellent discussion of the National Unity Function of the Charter.

[5] While the BNA Act and its amendments have all been renamed the Constitution Act 1867, 1912, 1949, etc., we will generally refer to the Constitution Act of 1867 by its old name simply because it is pedagogically clearer and less confusing to the reader.

Schedule I of the 1982 Constitution Act also lists British statutes that apply to Canada, such as the Statute of Westminster, thus making it a formal documentary component of the constitution of Canada. Similarly, Schedule I also includes British orders-in-council, such as those ceding Rupert's Land and the Arctic Islands to the Dominion as part of the Canadian constitution. However, these British enactments all have to do with the gradual process of withdrawal of British authority over the Dominion and its territories, and were more significant at the time of their passage than they are now.

Some statutes passed by the Canadian parliament, such as the Alberta and Saskatchewan Acts of 1905, which created the provinces of Alberta and Saskatchewan out of the Northwest Territories, are also listed in Schedule I as constitutional components. These particular Canadian acts are unique, in that they are not amendable by the federal parliament. Since the Alberta and Saskatchewan acts form the constitutions of those provinces, once passed, they can be amended only by the provincial legislatures.

Other federal statutes that can be included in any inventory of the Canadian constitution, are classed by R. M. Dawson as "organic laws."[6] These laws, although legally amendable by a simple act of Parliament, involve fundamental principles of a constitutional nature. One such organic law, the Supreme Court Act, has been entrenched in its most important aspects by sections 41(d) and 42(d) of the Constitution Act of 1982. Still another, the Canadian Bill of Rights, has in part been superceded by the 1982 Charter of Rights and Freedoms. Thus, it may be that the amount of "organic" legislation has been reduced by the 1982 reforms although others such as the Canada Elections Act and the Citizenship Act allow us to continue to use the concept. While Parliament may from time to time change some of the provisions of such legislation, the fundamental principles remain, for practical purposes, entrenched.

Section 92(1) of the BNA Act originally and now s.45 of the Constitution Act of 1982 give the provinces the power to make laws with respect to their own constitutions, excepting the sections dealing with the office of the Lieutenant Governor. This means essentially that the provincial legislatures have the power unilaterally to amend the constitutions of their respective domains by an ordinary statute. Any provincial statutes that amend the provincial constitutions, therefore, must, like the British or Canadian federal statutes that originally set them up, be considered a part of the Canadian constitution.

Not all political scientists and constitutional experts would agree that provincial or state constitutions should be considered integral parts of the constitution of a particular federal political system. Perhaps there is some justification for separating the United States constitution from the constitutions of the various states, but in Canada such a separation would distort the realities of the Canadian political system. The provinces are given the power to legislate with regard to matters that directly affect the rights and freedoms of the individual in terms of the individual's relationship with the state. An example of this would be section 92(13)

---

[6] R. MacGregor Dawson, *The Government of Canada* (Toronto: University of Toronto Press, 1970), p. 63.

of the BNA Act, which gives the provinces the legislative competence to deal with "Property and Civil Rights in the Province." If the provinces possess the power to affect the property and civil rights of Canadian citizens, then surely the provincial constitutions that regulate the exercise of this power within the provinces must be considered a part of the Canadian constitution. At any rate, the Constitution Act of 1982 has affirmed the constitutional significance of the provincial constitutions by including them in Schedule I.

It has been asserted that constitutions are basically formal rather than informal, and are therefore basically static. But constitutions consist, in part, of laws or collections of laws, which means that they are general prescriptions that in practice must be applied to specific cases. The application of constitutional principles to specific cases involves the interpretation of the constitution, which, in our system, is performed by the judiciary.[7] As the courts apply the constitutional principles to many different cases, a body of judicial decisions is built up, which elaborates and fills out the constitution. The judicial decisions that interpret the constitution are an integral part of that constitution. In Canada, because our legal system is based on the English common-law tradition, and because the BNA Act states in the preamble that we are to have a form of government similar in principle to that of Britain, precedents established in British common law make up a part of our constitution. As well, the interpretation of the BNA Act itself by the Judicial Committee of the Privy Council, which was the final court of appeal for Canada until 1949, built a large body of decisions that elaborate and clarify the Act. These judicial decisions, plus those of the Supreme Court of Canada since 1949, are a most important component of the constitution of Canada, especially as they have helped to clarify the federal dimension of our constitution.

In addition, the Canadian constitution includes a number of clearly defined principles such as the conventions of Cabinet government and the firm, though unwritten, rule that the government must hold the support of a majority in the House of Commons or resign. These conventions are not found in the BNA Act, or in any constitutional document, yet they are as much a part of the Canadian constitution as the BNA Act itself. Because they have no documentary manifestation, however, their exact definition and their legal enforceability defies analysis. The only sanction that effectively enforces the principle of responsible government is the weight of public opinion that places value on it.[8] A few of the customary and conventional parts of our constitution have been written down in some form, and therefore have acquired the support of legal or quasi-legal sanction. For instance, the rules and privileges of Parliament are implicitly if not explicitly entrenched in the Standing Orders and the Rules of Procedure. Generally, however, while conventions and customs involve some of the most important principles of the Canadian constitution, they exist in an unwritten form rather than as documentary and legally enforceable instruments.[9]

---

[7] This subject is covered more extensively in chapter 7.

[8] As well, it can be argued that the prerogatives of the Crown in Canada as exercised by the Governor-General and the Lieutenant Governors of the provinces include the power to overrule the political executive (the prime minister and the Cabinet) in cases where there is a clear abrogation of these important conventions.

[9] See: *Attorney-General Manitoba v. Attorney-General Canada* (1981), also called "the Patriation Reference," for a judicial opinion as to the relative importance of *legality* and *constitutionality* with respect to convention.

Finally, a constitution can be considered to contain a number of principles or values that form the normative basis of the regime. These are difficult to pin down, for they exist largely as tacit assumptions in the minds of the members of the political community and they are passed on in very subtle ways through the process of political socialization. In Canada, they involve the whole complex of democratic political values. There is some argument whether such principles should be considered a part of the constitution itself or the principles that underlie it. However, within the context of this treatment of the Canadian political system, the important point is that these values are congruent with those reflected in the constitution. We have dealt with these values as part of the Canadian political culture in chapter 4.

Written and Unwritten Constitutions

It has become a tradition of political science, when making comparisons between the political systems of the United Kingdom and the United States, to state that the former has an unwritten constitution and the latter a written constitution. This distinction is a relative rather than a categoric one, which places constitutions, for the purposes of comparison, on a continuum ranging from the hypothetical extreme of "purely written" to that of "purely unwritten." Upon examination, it rapidly becomes apparent that the constitutions of the two largest English-speaking democracies are neither purely written nor purely unwritten. The American constitution, which started with the impressive document of 1789, has been filled out by conventions, judicial decisions, and statutes that express "fundamental" principles. Similarly, Britain's constitution, while consisting largely of principles embodied in the common law, has at its core written documents such as the Magna Carta and the Petition of Right. The Canadian constitution, which consists of a hodgepodge of written documents and unwritten conventions, falls on the continuum somewhere between the constitutions of Britain and the United States.[10]

With that said, there may be some further justification for discussing the relative merits of written and unwritten constitutions with respect to the function of political integration. Perhaps a written constitution may be more effective in creating a sense of national pride, but on the other hand, such a sense of national pride is not absent in Britain, where the constitution, by any criterion, is basically unwritten. Also, a written constitution may be more effective in inculcating the norms of the regime to children and newcomers, for through a written constitution the values of the society are given visible manifestation.

In summary, the Canadian constitution is a conglomeration of British, Canadian, and provincial statutes, the British common law, Canadian judicial decisions, and a number of real but invisible conventions, customs, values, and assumptions, all clustering rather loosely and haphazardly around the central kernel of the BNA Act and the more recent modifications in the Constitution Act, 1982.

---

[10] For a discussion of amendment of written and unwritten constitutions, see chapter 7.

THE OPERATIVE PRINCIPLES OF THE CANADIAN CONSTITUTION

It has already been established that all forms of constitutional government are rooted in the principle of the rule of law. But if law is to "rule" us, it is going to need a lot of help from the people who occupy positions of authority in the political system. Laws must be made by somebody, and they must be carried into effect by somebody. As a result, the substance of a constitution is fundamentally concerned with three political problems corresponding to the three functional classifications of allocative outputs of the political system: legislative outputs, executive outputs, and adjudicative outputs. In most political systems, it is possible to make at least some functional distinction among these three types of outputs, and usually it is possible to distinguish between the organs or branches of the political system to which the constitution delegates the performance of each function.[11] However, the constitutional relationship among these branches can vary a great deal from one political system to another.

Finally, it must be recognized that the three output functions of government in Canada are performed not by one but by several sovereign governments. The legislative, executive, and, to a certain extent, the adjudicative functions of government are performed by both federal and provincial governments in Canada. This operative principle of the constitution is *divided sovereignty*, which adds greatly to the complexity of the political process in Canada.

The Supremacy of Parliament and the Rule of Law: The Legislative Function in Canada

The constitution of the United States explicitly states not only that there is to be a functional distinction among the three branches of government, but also that each of these functions should be vested in separate persons or groups of people. This principle, which is known as the *separation of power*, originated with the writings of Montesquieu, and it means, in the American case, that no individual is permitted to hold office in more than one branch of government at the same time. Hence, for example, the president cannot be a member of the Senate or the House of Representatives during the term of office, nor can a member of Congress be a judge at the same time as being in the House or in the Senate. The logic behind the separation of powers is that the concentration of too much power in one person, or, for that matter, in one institution, is a corruptive influence. In an attempt to insure a good and just form of government, the drafters of the United States constitution tried to insure that no person would be tempted by the possession of too much governmental power. Just to make sure, the principle of the separation of powers was given an added twist: to prevent the abuse of any of the

---

[11] Later, when we discuss the policy process, it will be seen that it is very difficult to make realistic distinctions between different institutions such as Parliament, the civil service, etc., on the basis of these particular types of functions.

three powers by occupants of the respective branches, an elaborate system of *checks and balances* was woven into the relationship among branches. Thus, for instance, the president can veto any legislation passed by Congress, the Supreme Court can declare acts of Congress unconstitutional, the president appoints all members of the Supreme Court with the consent of the Senate, and Congress can impeach the president or override the president's veto by a two-thirds majority.

Starkly contrasting with this constitutional commitment to the principle of the separation of powers is the basic principle of the British constitution, the *supremacy of parliament*. In the British parliamentary system, not only is there no real separation of powers, but the legislative branch directly controls the executive branch, and is beyond interference by either the executive or the judiciary. No act of the British parliament can be declared unconstitutional by the courts. The executive branch (which is roughly equivalent to the U.S. cabinet) is made up of members of parliament; if a majority in the House of Commons fails to endorse the executive branch's policies, the executive must resign. Furthermore, no parliament may bind a future parliament by stating in a piece of legislation that the legislation is unamendable. Some parliaments have tried; the later parliament, which is supreme in its own time, merely passes another law, which takes precedence over the earlier one. Therefore, the principle of the supremacy of parliament vests awesome formal power in the legislative branch.

But we have already described the political system of Britain as being a constitutional form of government, and it has been pointed out that at the roots of the principle of constitutionalism is the principle of the rule of law. How can there be rule of law and parliamentary supremacy without contradiction? Is parliament bound by the principle of the rule of law, or is the rule of law subject to the supremacy of parliament? The only answer is that the concept of the rule of law must have two meanings. In the first sense, the rule of law means that any authoritative output of the political system can only be achieved by law. If this is all the concept of the rule of law means, then a contradiction does not exist between it and the supremacy of parliament, for any act of parliament *is* a law, or has the effect of law.

However, there is a second sense of the concept of the rule of law, which implies such things as the right to have access to the courts, the right not to be imprisoned without a trial, etc. If this definition is accepted, the rule of law and the supremacy of parliament are mutually exclusive principles. Parliament in Britain can, by "act of parliament," abolish such revered rights as *habeas corpus*, which would mean that parliament could, in effect, "abolish" the rule of law[12] in the second sense of the term. There is no way of settling this confusion in the terminology. It would be pointless to say that "henceforth the term shall mean such and such," for the term is so widely used in both senses that the confusion would remain. It must be kept in mind that, when speaking of constitutionalism generally, the first sense of the rule of law is usually what is intended, and when speaking

---

[12] See: Corry and Hodgetts, *Democratic Government*, p. 96. Note also that we are speaking here only in strict legal terms; in practice, because of the nature of the British political culture, there is a practical limitation on the extent to which Parliament can restrict the rule of law even in the narrower sense.

specifically of the British constitution, it is the broader sense that is intended. The significance of this distinction is that the narrower usage of the term is the purer form of the concept; the broader usage is the peculiarly British version of it.

As noted before, the preamble of the British North America Act (1867) states that Canada is to have "a Constitution similar in principle to that of the United Kingdom." This means, *prima facie*, that the supremacy of Parliament is a substantive principle of the Canadian constitution. The BNA Act, however, goes beyond this broad statement of intent of the preamble,[13] and the extent to which the Canadian parliament is really supreme must be examined in light of those provisions of the Act that limit the power of Parliament in Canada.

First of all, the Parliament of Canada is restricted by the provisions of the Constitution Act of 1982, which sets down formulae for amending the constitution. Those formulae require the participation of at least some or even all of the provincial legislatures for all matters except those having to do with federal government institutions.[14]

The second and perhaps the most important limitation on the supremacy of the Canadian parliament is found in the federal distribution of legislative powers, set out mainly in sections 91 to 95 of the BNA Act. Because of these sections of the Act, the courts in Canada, unlike the courts in Britain,[15] have the power to declare acts of the federal parliament unconstitutional if those actions are judged to be beyond the legislative jurisdiction assigned to the federal level by the BNA Act. Many pieces of legislation passed by the Canadian parliament have been declared invalid on these grounds, and in fact, the interpretation of the federal legislative competence by the judiciary has played a significant role in remodeling Canadian federalism since 1867.[16] The important point here is that the judicial branch in Canada has the power to declare laws passed by either the federal parliament or by the legislatures of the provinces to be *ultra vires*, and therefore invalid. In sum, legislative authority in Canada is divided among two separate types of legislative bodies: the parliament of Canada, and the legislatures of the ten provinces, with the judiciary deciding any jurisdictional disputes.

The final question concerning the extent to which the doctrine of the supremacy of Parliament obtains in Canada is whether the combination of these two levels of legislatures possesses legislative supremacy. In other words, is the legislative authority of ten provincial parliaments and the federal parliament *exhaustive*? In the United States, there clearly are matters that are beyond the legislative competence of all levels and branches of government. These are principles that are considered to be so fundamental that no government should be able to interfere with them, and that are therefore entrenched in the constitution.

---

[13] In fact, the preamble itself also specifies that Canada's constitution is *federal*, which implies a different form of parliamentary supremacy from the unitary form of Britain's parliament.

[14] See chapter 7 for a more detailed discussion of this situation. In fact there are small parts of the constitution — sections 44 and 45 — that can be amended by either the provinces or the federal government unilaterally.

[15] See chapter 7.

[16] See chapter 8.

Are any matters so entrenched in the Canadian constitution? Judicial opinion in this area has generally supported the doctrine of exhaustiveness, giving to the provinces and the federal parliament virtually complete authority.[17]

However, the 1982 Charter of Rights and Freedoms may have altered the situation by guaranteeing a wide range of rights and freedoms to Canadian citizens. The implication of the Charter is that it supersedes the enactments of both the federal parliament and the provincial legislatures. However, certain provisions of the Charter cast some doubt on the extent to which the *de facto* power of the eleven legislatures has really been limited.

In the first place, the Charter is filled with qualifiers that, depending upon subsequent judicial clarification, may take some force out of the guarantees. Most notably, the preamble to the Charter states that it operates "subject only to such reasonable limits prescribed by law as can be demonstrably justified in a free and democratic society." These "reasonable limits" likely include those made explicit in the War Measures Act, for instance, and in fact might include most legislation in Canada at the time of proclamation of the Charter if the courts should decide that we were a "free and democratic" society even before 1982.

Throughout the Charter there are specific qualifiers that could effectively leave the power of Parliament and the legislatures virtually unaffected, but more significant than these, perhaps, is the *non obstante* clause in section 33(i) that permits Parliament and the legislatures to declare that a given act should "operate notwithstanding a provision included in section 2 or sections 7 to 15 of this Charter." While such a "notwithstanding" clause must be limited to five-year (renewable) terms, its effect is to allow the legislative branch to override key sections of the Charter at will.

Despite these obvious restrictions on the clout of the Charter, however, there remain sections of it that are still clearly intended to be entrenched. Most significantly, these include the "democratic rights"; the right to vote; the five-year term of a legislature; the requirement of at least one session of the legislature per annum; and the complex official languages and "Minority Language Educational Rights" provisions. These important guarantees are not subject to the *non obstante* provision of the Charter, and while the actual limits they impose on the legislatures will depend upon judicial interpretation of the Charter, it is safe to say that there is at least a potential restriction on the exhaustive authority of the eleven legislatures.

> The supremacy of Parliament has been weakened in the sense that laws of Parliament may now be challenged in the courts by virtue of specific criteria set forth in the Charter. It remains unweakened, however, in the sense that the parliaments are still the bodies authorized to express the ultimate standards of the state in accordance with the constitution. Any dynamic law, the body of law that a society gradually creates for itself as its needs evolve, continues to flow, at the very highest level, from parliamentary legislation.[18]

---

[17] See: *Bank of Toronto v. Lambe* (1887), *Olmsted*, vol. 1; *Attorney-General for Ontario v. Attorney-General for Canada* ("Labour Convention Case") (1937), *Olmsted*, vol. 3.

[18] Henri Brun, "The Canadian Charter of Rights . . ." in C. Beckton and W. Mackay, *The Courts and the Charter* (Toronto: University of Toronto Press, 1985), p. 6.

There are some minor and technical restrictions on the doctrine of the supremacy of Parliament. One of these restrictions has come through a series of narrow
judicial interpretations of the ability of the provinces and the federal parliament
to delegate legislative authority to each other. The *Nova Scotia Interdelegation*
case of 1951 is a landmark in this regard, because the Supreme Court of Canada
found that interdelegation is incompatible with federalism.[19] While this imposes
a *de jure* limitation on the doctrine of the supremacy of Parliament in Canada, in
practical terms it would be possible for the federal government to secure an
amendment to the constitution specifically permitting interdelegation. Finally,
there are a few laws still in effect that were passed by the united legislature of
Upper and Lower Canada before Confederation. Legislation such as this cannot
be repealed or legally amended because it was the product of a legislative body
that no longer exists. Practically, however, it is possible for the legislatures of the
provinces of Ontario and Quebec to pass complementary laws, which would change
the effect of a pre-Confederation statute without actually altering it in law. Certainly,
limitations such as these on the legislative competence of Canadian legislatures
are of minimal importance in the total picture.

To conclude, then, while the principle of the supremacy of Parliament is definitely
still an integral part of the constitution of Canada, and, while the form it takes is
not as unambiguous as it is in Britain, its implications remain significant. Unlike
the constitution of the United States, which puts some matters beyond the grasp
of *all* legislative bodies, the constitution of Canada historically has vested exhaustive
legislative authority in the collectivity of federal and provincial legislatures, for
all practical purposes. While the Charter of Rights and Freedoms likely imposes
some *prima facie* limits on the legislative authority of both the legislatures of the
provinces and the parliament of Canada, these have to be seen in the limited
context within which they must operate. We have already spoken of the specific
qualifiers in the Charter itself, but at a more elemental level, the power of the
courts to override legislation is still only a *passive* power. The courts, in other
words, are limited to a sort of veto, and even then, they may exercise it only
when some other agency has brought the matter before the court.

> Although this new role for the courts is important it is essentially passive, since like
> a fire extinguisher, it operates only in an emergency. It can prevent the worst, but
> it is powerless to nourish the living law.[20]

Finally, the nature of the amending formulae set down in the Constitution Act
(1982) may give back the *de jure* supremacy of the eleven legislatures. This will
be discussed at greater length, but the fact remains, all parts of the constitution
are technically amendable through the combined intervention of the eleven (or
fewer) legislatures. Our constitution cannot be changed by referendum or by
any other form of direct public participation, nor can it be amended by executive
or judicial action. In this sense the *principle* of legislative supremacy can be

---

[19] *Attorney-General for Nova Scotia v. Attorney-General for Canada*, (1951) *SCR*, 31. See also: R.I. Cheffins
and R.N. Tucker, *The Constitutional Process in Canada*, pp. 33-34 for an excellent analysis of the legal
implications of this decision and its potential effect on the doctrine of the supremacy of Parliament.

[20] Brun, "The Canadian Charter," p. 6.

said to remain undiluted, although, as it will be seen when we discuss the process of amendment, our constitution places very important *practical* limits on its application.

The Crown and Cabinet Government: The Executive Function

The legislative function of a political system is to make laws. In Canada that function is performed, according to the constitution, by Parliament. The executive function of a political system is to put the laws into effect, to carry out or to execute acts of Parliament. In Canada, the executive power is defined by section 9 of the BNA Act: "the Executive Government and Authority of and over Canada is hereby declared to continue and be vested in the Queen." Formally, therefore, the executive function in Canada is performed by the Queen, and we can be said to have a monarchical form of government. The most significant implication of this fact is the consequent transferral of all prerogative rights of the Crown in Britain to the Crown in respect of Canada. This statement, however, requires some explanation, particularly the terms *the Crown* and *prerogative rights*.

The term "the Crown"[21] is used to describe the collectivity of executive powers that, in a monarchy, are exercised by or in the name of the sovereign. There is nothing mystical about the term. It does not imply the existence of an authority greater than that possessed constitutionally by the reigning monarch. These executive powers vested in the Queen flow from the historic common-law rights and privileges of the Crown in England that are referred to as the *royal prerogative*. Prerogative rights exist primarily because they always have, and not because they have been created at some point in time by statute. The prerogative rights and privileges of the Queen are the residue of authority left from an age when the power of the reigning monarch was absolute. This absolute power has been whittled away bit by bit, until today there are only a few remnants of it left to the Queen. It is important to emphasize here that prerogative rights cannot be created by statute. If a statute formally increases the power of the Crown, the effect is to delegate some of the authority of Parliament to the executive, but not to vest any new prerogative rights in the person of the monarch.

On the other hand, the prerogative can be limited by statute. An example of this is in the Crown Liability Act (1952), which took away the prerogative right of the Crown not to be held liable in tort for damages resulting from acts done by public servants or for acts done by the monarch personally. This prerogative can never be returned as a prerogative right, although a future parliament could return it as a statutory right. Hence, the royal prerogative is slowly shrinking, and in Canada it is being replaced by statutory provisions that define the real limits of executive power.

While the royal prerogative is not what it used to be, there are still some significant executive powers that are based on it. Among these are the right of the monarch to all ownerless property (Crown land); the right to priority as a creditor in the settlement of bankruptcies; and the right to summon, prorogue, and dissolve

---

[21] See F. MacKinnon, *The Crown in Canada* (Calgary: Glenbow-Alberta Institute, 1976), for an excellent analysis of a subject that has been to a large extent neglected in Canadian political science.

Parliament. Because of the convention that these powers are all exercised "on the advice" of the ministers of the Crown, in fact, they are almost all possessed in reality by the prime minister and the government of the day.

In Britain, the formal functions of the monarch are performed personally by the Queen. In Canada, while the Queen can still be called "Queen of Canada," most of the monarchical functions are performed in her name by the Governor-General at the national level and the Lieutenant Governors at the provincial level. The appointment of the Governor-General was originally the responsibility of the Queen acting on the advice of the government of Britain. This made the Governor-General effectively independent of the Canadian cabinet. Since the Imperial Conferences of 1926 and 1930, however, the Governor-General has been independent of the imperial government and is now removable by the Queen only on the advice of the government of Canada. While the appointment of the Governor-General is, formally, a function of the Queen, in fact it is always made today with the advice of the Canadian cabinet. Also, while the normal term of office of the Canadian Governor-General is five years, the term can be shortened or stretched according to the wishes of the government of the day.

While the BNA Act defines many of the powers of the Governor-General, the office itself is a creature of letters patent from the monarch. By the Letters Patent of 1947, the Governor-General is empowered to exercise "all powers and authorities" that belong to the Queen in right of Canada. This means that the exercise of the royal prerogative in Canada is a function of the Governor-General, to be carried out by the Governor-General, at personal discretion, with the advice of the Queen's Privy Council for Canada.[22] Among the powers specified by the letters patent are the use of the Great Seal of Canada, the appointment of judges, commissioners, diplomats, ministers of the Crown, etc., along with the power to dismiss or suspend them, and the power to summon, prorogue, and dissolve Parliament. In addition to the prerogative powers bestowed upon the Governor-General by the letters patent, there are certain other powers that are ceded to the Governor-General by the BNA Act. Among these are the authority to appoint senators and the Speaker of the Senate; the exclusive right to recommend legislation involving the spending of public money or the imposition of a tax; and the right, formally, to prevent a bill from becoming law by withholding assent or by reserving the bill "for the signification of the Queen's pleasure."[23] The Governor-General has the power, by section 56 of the BNA Act, to "disallow" any provincial legislation of which he or she disapproves. The real significance of the disallowance power is that it gives the federal government a potential veto power over all provincial acts. While it has not been used since 1943, the legal power to use it still remains as a reminder to the provinces that the Fathers of Confederation viewed the provincial legislatures as "second-class citizens."

The office of Lieutenant Governor was created by section 58 of the BNA Act. The holder of the office is appointed by the Governor-General in Council, and the salary is set by the Canadian parliament. Furthermore, the Lieutenant Governor

---

[22] See chapter 15 for a discussion of the Privy Council office.

[23] BNA Act, section 55.

is removable "for cause" by the Governor-General in Council. This means that, in some respects, the Lieutenant Governor is an officer of the federal government who is responsible to the Governor-General. On the other hand, the courts have decided that, in fact, the Lieutenant Governor is a representative of the Queen directly, despite the fact that the appointment and salary are controlled by the government of Canada, formally by the Governor-General in Council.

In an important constitutional case in 1892, the judicial committee of the Privy Council held that the Lieutenant Governor was a representative of the Queen in right of the province directly, and therefore could exercise all the prerogative powers that the monarch could.[24] The significance of this is that the Lieutenant Governor, while in some respects the subordinate of the Governor-General, is in other respects an equal and enjoys the same power in right of the province that the Governor-General enjoys in the right of Canada. In turn, this has the effect of making the provincial governments, which are personified in the Lieutenant Governors, more important than they would otherwise be. The BNA Act provides that the Lieutenant Governor of the province has the power to assent to or to refuse to assent to acts of the provincial legislature, and furthermore, by the BNA Act, is given the power to reserve a bill for the signification of the Governor-General's pleasure. In sum, the Lieutenant Governor in the province has powers that are analogous to and commensurate with the powers of the Governor-General at the level of the federal government.

Up until now we have been speaking in rather formal and legalistic terms about the powers of the Governor-General and the Lieutenant Governors. The intention has been to clarify the strict constitutional nature of the executive function in Canada. Now, however, it is necessary to bring the discussion of the executive function down from this rarefied atmosphere and to deal with the constitutional realities of the executive function in Canada.

The BNA Act provides for a body of advisors to assist the Governor-General in performing the onerous burden of executive responsibilities that come from the same Act, and from the letters patent of 1947. Section 11 of the BNA Act states that:

> There shall be a Council to aid and advise in the Government of Canada, to be styled the Queen's Privy Council for Canada; and the Persons who are to be Members of the Council shall be from time to time chosen and summoned by the Governor General and sworn in as Privy Councillors, and Members thereof may be from time to time removed by the Governor General.

The BNA Act states quite specifically that the Governor-General does not have to listen to advisors, but in fact even at the time of Confederation there was a well-established convention that the governor of the colony would, in almost all cases, act purely on the advice of the government of the day. The Queen's Privy Council for Canada includes a great number of people, such as ex-Cabinet ministers, who never function as advisors. The *Cabinet*, which is not mentioned at all in the BNA

---

[24] *The Liquidators of the Maritime Bank v. the Receiver General of New Brunswick* (1892), *Olmsted*, vol. l.

Act, is really a committee of privy councillors, chosen by the leader of the majority party in the House of Commons from among supporters in Parliament. Formally,
all executive acts are performed by the Governor-General in Council, but in reality,
executive decisions are made by the prime minister and Cabinet, and are rubber-
stamped by the Governor-General.

There is still a body of opinion among prominent experts that argues that one
should not dismiss the Governor-General as merely a rubber stamp for the prime
minister and Cabinet, for the simple reason that the Governor-General still does
possess a great deal of executive authority by virtue of the BNA Act and the
prerogatives. The argument is that if the government of the day attempted to
violate a basic principle of our political culture, for instance by abolishing free
speech, the Governor-General could step in and refuse assent to the bill, thus
thwarting the culprits. In doing so, however, the Governor-General would be
violating another fundamental norm of our system of government, by claiming to
represent the public interest better than the public's elected representatives. To
say that a Governor-General would never dare to oppose the will of the prime
minister is pure speculation, but the fact remains that the norm of popular sovereignty at the core of the Canadian constitution imposes severe political limitations on
the actual powers of the Queen's representative. The last time a Governor-General
went against the wishes of the prime minister was in 1926, when Lord Byng
refused Prime Minister Mackenzie King a dissolution of Parliament. The result
was a general outcry, led by Mackenzie King, against the unilateral action of the
Governor-General, and a subsequent electoral disaster for the man who had
immediately benefitted from Byng's decision.[25]

The relationship between the Lieutenant Governor of a province and the
provincial premier is almost identical to that between the prime minister of Canada
and the Governor-General, and the BNA Act provides that the Lieutenant Governor
may act with the advice of the executive council of the province. The executive
council is, in fact, the provincial cabinet, which is chosen by the premier. All
executive decisions are made by the premier and Cabinet, and the Lieutenant
Governor, like the federal counterpart, more or less rubber-stamps them. As
with the Governor-General, the one time a Lieutenant Governor might be called
upon to exercise some discretionary authority is in the case of the death in office
of the leader of the government, where the successor is not obvious. Clearly, the
Lieutenant Governor must seek the advice of the Cabinet ministers, but in some
cases their advice might not be unanimous. In such a situation, the Lieutenant
Governor must decide whose advice to take, on the basis of personal discretion
and political acumen, for above all else the Lieutenant Governor must insure
that there *is* a government. Such a situation appeared to develop at the death of
Quebec Premier Maurice Duplessis in 1959. Initially, the Cabinet was by no
means solidly united behind one candidate to succeed Duplessis. Apparently
the Cabinet managed eventually to achieve a consensus by itself, but the incident

[25] See E.A. Forsey, *The Royal Power of Dissolution of Parliament in the British Commonwealth* (Toronto: Oxford
University Press, 1968), chapter 5.

makes it clear that there is a potentially important political role to be played by the formal executive in such rare, but conceivable, circumstances.[26]

To conclude, the formal executive power in Canada is vested in the Crown and, in a very formal sense, Canada can be said to have a monarchical form of government. The Governor-General exercises all of the prerogative rights and privileges of the Queen in right of Canada, according to the BNA Act and the letters patent that define the office. The constitutional doctrine of popular sovereignty has, however, reduced the *de facto* role of the Governor-General to that of a figurehead. The real power is exercised by the prime minister and the Cabinet, who obtain their legitimacy from the fact that they possess a popular mandate.

The Judicial Function

The judicial function is the hardest to distinguish of the three basic output functions of the political system.[27] In fact, it can be argued that there are only two basic output functions — making law and applying it — and both the judiciary and the executive can be perceived as applying the law to specific cases, each doing it in a slightly different fashion. There are two reasons, however, for shying away, in this text, from that twofold method of classification. First, the core document of our constitution, the BNA Act, makes very definite distinctions among the "Executive Power," the "Legislative Power," and the "Judicature."[28] Second, even if a functional distinction is difficult, the judicial branch in Canada can be clearly distinguished through the principle of *judicial independence*, which insulates the judiciary from any direct responsibility to either of the other two branches. The independence of the judiciary is one of the essential principles of our system of government, and, as such, it merits a longer look.

The historical roots of the principle of judicial independence lie in the English common-law tradition, and it is from that source that Canada has inherited the doctrine. The principle was adopted formally in Britain through the Act of Settlement of 1701, where the security of tenure and salary and the independence from royal whim were legally guaranteed. British North American colonies were finally granted the privilege of an independent judiciary in the middle of the nineteenth century, and the doctrine was set down explicitly in the BNA Act in 1867.

In Canada, the constitutional source of judicial independence flows from sections 96 to 101 of the BNA Act. Section 99 states that superior court judges shall hold office during "good behaviour" up to the age of seventy-five, implying that a judge cannot be dismissed for incompetence or laziness but only for a criminal

---

[26] For a discussion of the role the Lieutenant Governor plays in finding a successor to a premier who dies in office, see J.R. Mallory, "The Royal Prerogative in Canada: The Selection of Successors to Mr. Duplessis and Mr. Sauve," *The Canadian Journal of Economics and Political Science*, 26 : 2, May 1960, pp. 314–319. See also G.F.G. Stanley, "A 'Constitutional Crisis' in British Columbia," *The Canadian Journal of Economics and Political Science*, 21 : 3, August 1955, pp. 281–292.

[27] W.R. Lederman, "The Independence of the Judiciary," *Canadian Bar Review*, 1956, p. 769ff.

[28] BNA Act, parts three, four, seven.

offence. Section 99 also provides that a judge is removable only by the Governor-General on a joint resolution by the Senate and the House of Commons. This means that the executive can remove a judge only at the request of both houses of the Canadian parliament, and the practice has evolved that even this is undertaken only after a judicial inquiry into the person's wrongdoings.

In 1971 the Canadian Judicial Council was created. This body, composed of the chief justices and the associate chief justices of all of the provincial superior courts, is chaired by the chief justice of the Supreme Court of Canada. The role of the Council is to investigate complaints about alleged judicial misconduct. If the Council concludes that there has indeed been serious misconduct, it has the power to remove county and district court judges directly, and to recommend such action to Parliament where the impugned judge is from a superior court.

The salary of a judge is set by statute, so that it is not possible for the judge to become involved in bargaining with the executive for salary increments, nor is it possible for the executive to pressure a judge by controlling the judge's livelihood. Every effort is made to ensure that the judge is protected from influences that might affect objectivity in the position. As R.M. Dawson has said,

> The judge is placed in a position where he has nothing to lose by doing what is right, and little to gain by doing what is wrong, and there is, therefore, every reason to hope that his best efforts will be devoted to the conscientious performance of his duty.[29]

Moreover, judicial independence is a two-way street. Judges are expected to act in a manner that is impartial and apolitical in all aspects of their lives, personal and professional. They are not even permitted to vote in elections, nor are they permitted to comment on general social or political issues.

The issue of the freedom of speech of a judge versus his or her obligation to remain totally above the fray of public discourse was tested in 1982, when Mr. Justice Thomas Berger spoke out against certain actions of the federal government. The matter was referred to the judicial council after a complaint by another superior court judge, and the council concluded that

> a judge's conscience is not an acceptable excuse for contravening a fundamental rule so important to the existence of parliamentary democracy and judicial independence.[30]

In commenting on the case, the chief justice of the Supreme Court of Canada, Bora Laskin, stated:

> It was said that the pursuit of the compaint against Justice Berger was an interference with his freedom of speech. Plain nonsense! A judge has no freedom of speech to address political issues which have nothing to do with his judicial duties. His abstention from political involvement is one of the guarantees of his impartiality, his integrity, his *independence*.[31]

---

[29] Dawson, *The Government of Canada*, p. 409.

[30] From the "Report of the Committee of Investigation to the Judicial Council," cited in Morton, *Law, Politics.*, p. 111.

[31] Cited in Morton, p. 118.

Further to the guarantees of the personal independence of the judge is the guarantee of jurisdictional integrity that is given to the superior courts in Canada. A common assumption is that any governmental official will attempt to widen the scope of jurisdiction, a practice often referred to as empire-building. Limits must be placed on this sort of activity, usually by the intervention of other officials. However, the independence of the judiciary is perceived as such an important value of our system that the danger of judicial empire-building is ignored. Instead, a remarkable faith in the honesty and level-headedness of our judges is indicated by allowing superior courts to decide not only their own jurisdiction, but the jurisdiction of other governmental offices as well.[32] In effect, this means that the legislative branch could not vest superior-court jurisdiction in a court other than a superior court without first securing amendments to the BNA Act (sections 96 to 101).[33]

Judicial review has been cited already as a possible limitation on the supremacy of Parliament in Canada. Now it is necessary to consider to what extent the principle of judicial review is itself a part of our constitution. Judicial review is essentially the power of superior courts to review the decisions or actions of governmental officials, administrative boards or tribunals, other courts,[34] and even Parliament itself. Its significance in *administrative law* is that no official of government, administrative agency, or executive body is above or outside the law of the land.[35]

Its significance in *constitutional law* is that the courts can declare acts of Parliament or of provincial legislatures unconstitutional, or *ultra vires*, and therefore void. In a broader sense, judicial review includes, as well, the ability of the courts to slow, or brake, the legislative branch by rigid interpretation of the law.[36] It is in this broader sense that constitutional judicial review might be said to exist even in political systems such as Britain, where, strictly speaking, no act of a *supreme* parliament can ever be *ultra vires*. Hence, when we speak of judicial review of legislation, we must keep in mind that there are two forms or levels at which the process operates.

J.E. McWhinney describes these two levels of judicial review as *direct* and *indirect* forms of judicial authority.[37] Direct judicial review is the kind exercised by, for example, the U.S. Supreme Court. In the United States, the Supreme Court

---

[32] See Lederman, "The Independence of the Judiciary," p. 1175.

[33] See E.A. Forsey, "Independence of the Judiciary," *Canadian Bar Review*, 1957, p. 240. He rejects Lederman's contention that 96-101 cannot be amended unilaterally by the federal government. See also B. L. Strayer, *Judicial Review of Legislation in Canada* (Toronto: University of Toronto Press, 1968), p. 37.

[34] Note that judicial review is to be distinguished from *appeal*. A judicial review includes an appeal. Review is a right of superior courts by virtue of the definition of a superior court as independent to determine its own jurisdiction. The right to hear appeals must be created by statute — it must be specifically vested in a court by legislation. Appeal is, today, virtually the only means whereby a court reviews the decision of lower courts in the same hierarchy.

[35] This will be discussed as one of the mechanisms of bureaucratic control in chapter 18. See also: *Roncarelli v. Duplessis*, Supreme Court of Canada, 1959.

[36] See Edward McWhinney, *Judicial Review* (Toronto: University of Toronto Press, 1969), p. 13; and J. Smith, "The Origins of Judicial Review in Canada," *CJPS*, March 1983, p. 115.

[37] *Ibid.*

has the power[38] to declare acts of Congress and acts of the state legislatures unconstitutional, and therefore void. This judicial power exists in Canada to the extent that the judiciary here has the authority to interpret the federal distribution of powers as laid out by the BNA Act, and to the extent that the Charter of Rights limits the powers of both the provincial and federal legislatures.

The constitutional origins of direct judicial review in Canada, however, are confused. The right to declare acts of parliament *ultra vires* certainly does not flow from the English common law, which recognizes the principle of parliamentary supremacy. On the other hand this judicial right is not specifically vested in the courts by the BNA Act, either. The historical origins of the practice of direct judicial review can likely be traced to the fact that the Privy Council traditionally had that power with respect to the colonial legislatures, which were subordinate to the imperial parliament. McWhinney argues that, although the Canadian parliament has long since ceased to be subordinate, the practice of judicial review has "ripened," through continued use, into a binding convention of our constitution.[39] Probably, too, the roots of direct judicial review in Canada can be traced to pragmatic considerations flowing implicitly from the principle of federalism, which is one of the critical dimensions entrenched in the BNA Act. To back up this hypothesis, it can be noted that, up until the proclamation of the Charter of Rights in 1982, direct judicial review of legislation in Canada occurred almost exclusively with respect to the distribution of powers between the federal parliament and the provincial legislatures as set out in the BNA Act, and never did it function to place matters beyond the legislative competence of government generally.

Indirect judicial review, as described by McWhinney,

> is where a court, either not having the power to annul or override enactments of the legislature as "unconstitutional" or else simply choosing not to exert that power in the instant case, says in effect in the process of interpretation of a statute, that the legislature may or may not have the claimed legislative power, but it has not in the language it has used in the enactment now in question employed that power.[40]

This form of judicial review will naturally be more significant in countries like Britain, where the constitution is extremely flexible and without clear boundaries, but such "judicial braking" will be used occasionally in countries like the United States and Canada, where direct judicial review is also an appropriate judicial alternative. The reason for a court's choosing indirect rather than direct review might be that the facts of the case are not clear enough to justify setting a precedent that may preclude legislative enactments in that area in the future. Or it may be a more practical reason: the court does not wish to become embroiled in the political hassle that could ensue if popular legislation were to be rendered void by a judicial decision.

---

[38] The predominant view, as set forth in *Marbury v. Madison* (1803), is that the power to review acts of Congress is "implicit" in the constitution.

[39] McWhinney, *Judicial Review*, p. 14.

[40] McWhinney, p. 13.

Indirect judicial review is achieved by a set of *presumptions*, which the courts make in the interpretation of a piece of legislation. For example, they will assume, unless the legislation states specifically to the contrary, that Parliament does not intend laws to have retroactive effect; and they will not interpret any statute in such a way as to take away a citizen's right to a fair hearing. The effect is to slow up, or to brake, the legislative branch when the judiciary feels it has overstepped the bounds of constitutional propriety, though perhaps keeping within the limits of *de jure* constitutionality.

The constitutional basis for the exercise of indirect judicial review in Canada is the English common law.[41] The limitation on this type of judicial review is that it is merely a stalling technique. Parliament can always, in theory, rework the legislation so that there is no ambiguity, and in this way bypass even the most rigorous and stringent application of the judiciary's power of indirect judicial review. However, as McWhinney points out, "at best this is likely to involve time-consuming delays and at worst, the corrective legislation may bog down completely."[42]

A further limitation on the power of judicial review may be imposed by the principle of *stare decisis*.[43] *Stare decisis* means that courts are bound by previous decisions when deciding current cases. While precedents established by earlier courts are usually adhered to by the Canadian judiciary, this is done by choice and not by constitutional proscription. Lower courts are bound by the decisions of higher courts, but this aspect of the principle of *stare decisis* does not affect the longer-term constitutional implications of judicial review.[44] (More will be said about the role of judicial review in the evolution of Canadian federalism in chapter 8.)

Divided Sovereignty: The Federal Principle

Divided sovereignty means basically that the legislative powers of government in Canada are divided between the federal Parliament and the legislatures of the ten provinces. While we often refer to the federal and provincial "levels" of government, within their specified spheres of jurisdiction there exists no superior-subordinate relationship. The legislatures of the provinces and the Parliament of Canada have constitutionally distinct functions, and neither can trench upon the constitutionally granted authority of the other. The term "orders of government" has increasingly come into use to express that fact.

The operative principle of divided sovereignty is ensconced in the British North America Act, and represents an intention on the part of the drafters of that act to establish a federal system of government in Canada. There have been many definitions of federalism, and many approaches to its study, and while the evolution

---

[41] McWhinney, p. 15.

[42] McWhinney, p. 15.

[43] See also chapter 7.

[44] See Morton, *Law, Politics*, p. 190; and P. Fitzgerald and K. McShane, *Looking at Law*, Bybooks, 1985, p. 78.

of the Canadian federal system will be discussed in subsequent chapters, a few words here on the concept itself will help to clarify the use of the term. The most important modern contribution to the study of federalism has been that of K.C. Wheare. Since the 1946 publication of Wheare's classic, *Federal Government*, theoretical writings on the concept of federalism have added relatively little except qualifications and interesting changes in emphasis. Wheare's analysis is institutional in the sense that he views federalism as a *form of government* that embodies what he calls the "federal principle":

> By the federal principle I mean the method of dividing powers so that the general and regional governments are each, within a sphere, coordinate and independent.[45]

He then draws a distinction between federal governments and federal constitutions, and states:

> It is not enough that the federal principle should be embodied predominantly in the written constitution of a country. . . . What determines the issue is the working of the system.[46]

The prerequisites of a federal system are two, according to Wheare:

> To begin with, the communities or states concerned must desire to be under a single independent government for some purposes. . . . They must desire at the same time to retain or establish independent regional governments in some matters at least.[47]

Thus, in functional terms, a federal system reconciles a desire for overall *unity* with a desire for local or regional *autonomy*. In structural terms, a federal system is seen as having independent national and regional governments, each operating in a hypothetically distinct jurisdictional compartment. The federal process — in Wheare's terms, "how federal government works" — will vary from federation to federation, but so long as the federal function is being performed and as long as the basic structural characteristics of federalism are present, the system can be called federal.

The major criticism of Wheare has come from people studying newer nations, many of which claim to be federal, and few of which conform perfectly to Wheare's definition. The result of this discontinuity between the term and the real world has been a redefinition of the term. Wheare's critics say that his concept of federal government is "institutional" and that his analysis is "legalistic." The most prominent of his detractors has been W.S. Livingstone, who argues that a legalistic definition of federalism is too narrow, and counters with a sociological one: "The essence of federalism lies not in the institutional or constitutional structure, but in society itself."[48] Livingstone goes on to state that a federal society is one whose diversity is reflected territorially, and that a federal government

---

[45] K.C. Wheare, *Federal Government* (Oxford University Press, 1961), p. 11.

[46] Wheare, p. 33.

[47] Wheare, pp. 35–36.

[48] W.S. Livingstone, "A Note on the Nature of Federalism," in J. Peter Meekison, ed., *Canadian Federalism: Myth or Reality* (Toronto: Methuen, 1971), p. 22.

is merely a "device by which the federal qualities of the society are articulated and protected."[49]

The great weakness of Livingstone's concept of federalism is that it is so inclusive that it is virtually useless for analyzing and categorizing real political systems. He defines a federal government as one that presides over a federal society, and he defines a federal society as one that has regional or territorial diversity. With such possible exceptions as Liechtenstein, Monaco, or San Marino, all modern states have varying degrees of regional diversity and therefore all modern governments could be classed as federal. Thus, where Wheare is too restrictive in his concept of federalism, Livingstone is far too broad in his.

W.H. Riker improves on Wheare without going as far as Livingstone. He describes federalism functionally as "the main alternative to empire as a technique of aggregating large areas under one government,"[50] and structurally as a system with a constitution having three basic characteristics; namely,

> (1) two levels of government rule the same land and people, (2) each level has at least one area of action in which it is autonomous, and (3) there is some guarantee (even though merely a statement in the constitution) of the autonomy of each government in its own sphere.[51]

Then Riker deals with the federal process as a continuous *bargaining relationship* that is carried on among the various leaders of the regional and national governments. Here, by viewing the origins and the operations of federal systems in terms of élite accommodation, Riker has added significantly to Wheare's rather mechanistic and admittedly legalistic analysis of federalism.

There are many tomes written on the subject of federalism, and most of them address themselves at some stage to the problem of definition. Riker, Livingstone, and Wheare represent the general range of approaches, and likely form the foundations for most other authors' conceptions of federal government.[52] The basic characteristics common to all federal systems can be derived from these authors. First, the origins and persistence of federal forms of government depend upon continuing general agreement among the various national and regional leaders that some form of union is desirable and that, because of differences in priorities among the member states or provinces, there should be at least some degree of independence guaranteed to them. (R.L. Watts speaks of this in terms of social integration, an equilibrium between integrating and disintegrating pressures within society.)[53] Second, in structural terms, federal systems are composed of two levels of government, each of which is permitted to function

---

[49] Livingstone, p. 22.

[50] W.H. Riker, *Federalism: Origin; Operation; Significance* (Boston: Little, Brown, 1964), p. 5.

[51] Riker, p. 11.

[52] The other significant source of inspiration for the development of the federal concept has been international-relations theory and the theories dealing with international political integration. For example, see: K.W. Deutsch *et al.*, *Political Community and the North Atlantic Area* (Princeton, 1957); E. Plischke, *Systems of Integrating the International Community* (Van Nostrand, 1964); and E.B. Haas, *The Uniting of Europe* (Stanford, 1958).

[53] R.L. Watts, *New Federations* (Oxford University Press, 1966), p. 111.

independently of the other in specified although probably changing areas of jurisdiction, and neither can destroy the other.[54]

Conceptual and definitional problems have arisen, moreover, only where political systems calling themselves federal have lacked these basic characteristics. In fact, most real governments can be very quickly and easily classified as either federal or non-federal; only a few stand on the effective borderline between federal and non-federal and thus challenge the governmental taxonomists' categories. Canada, although regionally diverse, has survived for one hundred and twenty years, and thus has the first basic federal characteristic. Also, the Canadian system does feature two levels or orders of government, each of which is independent of the other in constitutionally specified jurisdictional bailiwicks, and for that reason, too, Canada must be classified as federal. The evolution of the Canadian federal system and the idiosyncrasies of our particular brand of federalism will be discussed in later chapters. The fact that three separate chapters are to be devoted to federal aspects of the Canadian political system indicates the importance that must be attached to federalism as an operative principle of the constitution. (See chapters 8, 9 and 16.)

This concludes our discussion of the substance of the Canadian constitution. But this is only a snapshot at one point in time. To complete the picture, we must proceed to an analysis of the dynamic element of the Canadian constitution: its propensities and techniques for change.

---

[54] G. Stevenson, *Unfulfilled Union* (Gage, 1982). This is an important book on Canadian federalism. Not only is it fairly comprehensive, but it also takes a unique tack — first, it is written from a *political economy* perspective, and second, it is unabashedly *centralist* in its prescriptions.

THE DYNAMICS OF LAW AND THE CONSTITUTION IN CANADA

THE PROCESS OF CONSTITUTIONAL CHANGE
■ Revolution and Political Violence ■ Customary and Conventional Change
■ Judicial Change ■ Legislative Change ■ Constitutional Amendment: 1867–1982
THE ADMINISTRATION OF JUSTICE
■ The Nature of Law in Canada ■ The Judicial System
■ Federal Judiciary
CIVIL LIBERTIES IN CANADA
■ Rights, Freedoms, and Liberties ■ Civil Liberties: What Are They?
■ Civil Liberties: Pre-Charter Protections
■ The Charter of Rights and Freedoms

H aving looked at the component parts and substantive principles of the Canadian constitution, it is now necessary to put that information within a more dynamic setting. This chapter looks at the Canadian legal system and constitution from the perspectives of three different processes. The first section takes the broadest approach possible and looks at the process of constitutional change. We take the analytical position that the relationship between the individual and the state is reciprocal, for constitutional change not only *reflects* changes in a political culture, but also *induces* change in the individual behaviour patterns that characterize a political culture. In the second section, we look at the nature of the positive law and the judicial system in Canada. Here the analytical focus is narrower and the emphasis is on a process whereby the specific rules of behaviour set down in statutes are applied to individuals in society — the means by which a society protects itself from individual excesses. In the final section of the chapter, we analyse the process whereby civil liberties are protected in Canada; here, the analytical focus is on the means by which the individual is protected from the potential excesses of the state.

THE PROCESS OF CONSTITUTIONAL CHANGE

In the long run, the constitution of a political system must reflect the values of society if that political system is to persist. Hence, while it is true that the constitution provides the regime with necessary rigidity, the constitution must also have the capacity for change; it must not be so rigid that it cannot be adjusted to meet new needs and priorities in the environment of the political system. There are several ways in which the Canadian constitution can be changed. While we deal in some detail with the process of judicial review in our consideration of the history of Canadian federalism in chapter 8, at this point we wish to present an overview of the complete range of possibilities for constitutional change in Canada.

Revolution and Political Violence

The likelihood of a revolution[1] in Canada has always been fairly slim, for the simple reason that the social and political issues that divide us are usually moderated by a deep-seated consensus about basic values. In this sense, the perceived urgency of constitutional change has seldom been so great that people would feel the need to resort to violence to speed up the process. Even in instances where our political differences have become so severe that the *substantive consensus* about basic values has started to break down, there has remained a *procedural consensus* — an agreement as to the rules of the game of political and constitutional change, which effectively exclude most forms of political violence or revolution. Moreover, throughout most of our history, needed changes in the Canadian constitution have been attainable through legitimate, non-violent, and non-revolutionary means.

But although the Canadian political culture is relatively non-violent[2] when compared to other countries in the world, it must be recognized that violence, as a tactic of political change, is always a possibility. It takes but one deviant individual to assassinate a political leader, place an explosive device in a public place, or hijack an aircraft, so that, while the dominant values of a political system may be basically non-violent, isolated violent events may periodically occur. While, generally speaking, the evidence of our history has backed up the contention that Canada is a peaceable kingdom, isolated events, perhaps most significantly the FLQ terrorists' activities of October 1970, have lent some credence to the idea that perhaps even in Canada there is a tiny minority of deviant individuals always willing to engage in non-legitimate tactics to attempt to induce political

---

[1] The concept of revolution has two dimensions: One emphasizes the *means* of change that are extra-legal and normally violent, and the second emphasizes the *extent* of the changes that occur. Thus, on the one hand, extremely violent "revolutionary" upheavals may produce relatively minor changes in the regime or the political community; examples of this are *coups d'état*, which occur frequently in some military dictatorships. On the other hand, changes of "revolutionary" dimensions may occur in the regime or political community of a system through perfectly legal and non-violent means; an example of this might be the Indian Independence Act, which created the modern states of India and Pakistan out of what was previously British India.

[2] See also Chapter 4 for further references to violence and the Canadian political culture.

change[3] or to redress grievances. The virtual impossibility of achieving political change by this approach in Canada will not be a significant deterrent to such individuals.

The decade of the seventies did not witness an escalation of the kind of political violence that marred its first year, partly because of effective (and sometimes questionable) countermeasures by the police and the Canadian Security Service, but more importantly because the rapid ascension to power of the separatist Parti Québécois in the 1970s gave real hope for the possibility that Quebec could achieve independence legitimately and non-violently. It seems even the most extremist factions of the independence movement were willing to draw in their claws and wait to see if the PQ could succeed.

Thus, despite periodic and isolated incidents of a violent nature, we feel that it is still valid to conclude that violence has not been and is not likely to become a significant means of achieving constitutional change in Canada. The likelihood of political violence here would increase significantly only if the basic attitudes of Canadians towards the legitimacy of such tactics should change or if patterns of immigration allow new Canadians to import more violent political mores with them to their new homeland.[4] Widespread political violence could occur in Canada only if there were a radical alteration in the fabric of our political culture.

At the present time in Canada, a more likely form of non-legitimate constitutional change would appear to be that of a non-violent but extra-legal nature. A non-Canadian example of this form of constitutional change was the unilateral declaration of independence by the Smith regime in Rhodesia, where in an extra-legal but non-violent way a colony broke with the mother country. In a similar vein, if the province of Quebec were to seek separation through the device of unilateral secession of that province, such an action would be, strictly speaking, illegal, or *ultra vires* the provincial government. However, it could almost certainly be achieved non-violently, and in the long run the strict legality of such a move would be essentially irrelevant; for if such a change were brought about by the people of Quebec to provide a desired alteration in the regime or the political community, then the new regime would be, by its very nature, legitimate to its own citizens. Furthermore, the mere fact that the breakaway province would have gained its independence "illegally" might well be rapidly forgotten, or at least ignored, by Canadians, in the need to establish friendly diplomatic and economic relations with a neighbour. The distinction, therefore, between legal and illegal (or extra-legal) revolutionary constitutional change is in this context not particularly important. The more important question concerns the internal legitimacy of the change, and the measures, such as referenda or public opinion polls, which the rest of Canada would have accepted as indicators of support for

---

[3] See R.J. Jackson and M. Stein, *Issues in Comparative Politics* (Toronto: Macmillan, 1971), chapter 5, for a definition of revolution that combines both means and ends. Note here that violence may be considered a legitimate tactic of political change in some political cultures. Our referent in this text is the western democracies, and specifically Canada. Legitimacy, in other words, must be viewed in terms of the values of the existing regime.

[4] See chapter 4.

the change by the people of Quebec. Fortunately such conjecture is likely to remain in the abstract, given the apparent moderation of Quebec demands for independence in the 1980s.

Customary and Conventional Change

As pointed out in Chapter 6, conventions and customs[5] are important components of our constitution. These are rules and principles that, while important, are not written down anywhere. They are binding on governors and governed alike, but only insofar as people choose to adhere to them. If a convention or a custom ceases to be congruent with the basic values of the political culture, eventually the convention will be abrogated or ignored, and ultimately forgotten. In a sense, we can say simply that the customs and conventions of our constitution can be changed in the same way they originated; but where do they come from in the first place?

The origins of the customary and conventional components of the Canadian constitution lie in the misty labyrinths of English constitutional history, imported into our system as part of the ideological baggage of the earliest British settlers, and given a partial statutory sanction in the form of the preamble to the BNA Act, which grants Canada a "constitution similar in principle to that of the U.K." This means that if there is a dispute as to what the rule is in Canada, and if there is no act of either the Canadian or British parliaments that makes the rule explicit here, we must turn to the *practice*[6] in Britain as a precedent. Similarly, there are uniquely Canadian conventions whose existence and applicability can only be clarified by the citation of precedents here. The problem with constitutional principles that are manifested only in their practice (either here or in Britain) is that disputes frequently arise over which practice applies to the specific case, to what extent does it apply, and how binding is it in the current circumstance.

The arbiter of such disputes is sometimes the courts,[7] but more often, particularly when the dispute is over conventions such as those establishing the relationship of the House of Commons to the government of the day, the effective arbiter may be a constitutional expert who, while learned, may be totally outside the governmental process. It is not uncommon, in disputes over what the convention is in a given circumstance, for the parties to the dispute to quote Bagehot's or Jennings' writings on the English constitution, and in Canada, it might be said that our unwritten constitution is effectively what Eugene Forsey says it is! However, it must be reiterated that the interpretations of the accepted practice in the past, the citing of precedents, and the wisdom of the constitutional experts are still

---

[5] Dawson, *The Government of Canada*, p. 65n: "No attempt has been made to distinguish between custom, usage and convention. A common distinction is to treat custom and usage as synonymous terms, and convention as a usage which has acquired obligatory force." See also D.V. Smiley, *Constitutional Adaptation and Federalism Since 1945*, Royal Commission on Bilingualism and Biculturalism Study No. 4 (Ottawa: Queen's Printer, 1970).

[6] In fact, in some cases, the convention in Britain has been given clarification or elaboration in the form of statutes such as the Magna Carta, the Bill of Rights, the Act of Settlement, and the habeas corpus laws. This makes the convention easier to find in Britain, and easier to apply in Canada.

[7] See "The Patriation Reference," 1981, Reference re amendment of the Constitution of Canada [1981] 1 *SCR*, 754.

more *persuasive* than legally binding. If we wish a constitutional convention to change, all it takes ultimately is the will to change it, and, in most cases, the tacit acceptance or explicit approval (legislation) of the sovereign legislature or legislatures.

As a possible example of constitutional change made by altering a convention, we might consider an incident in 1968 in which a piece of federal financial legislation was defeated on third reading. The Liberal government of Lester Pearson was a minority government, which meant that on any division in the House of Commons the government had to scrape up some support from other parties in the House to gain a majority. Owing to a miscalculation by the party Whip and the acting prime minister, the Liberals allowed a vote on third reading at a time when there were not sufficient government supporters in the House, and the bill was defeated. Some constitutional experts (particularly in the Conservative party) thought the government should resign; as they said, it was a firm convention of the constitution that if a government were defeated on a piece of financial legislation, it had to resign. The Liberals, under the leadership of a rather cranky Lester Pearson, who had been called back from a southern vacation by this imbroglio, disagreed, and instead referred the question to the House of Commons in the form of a vote of confidence. As it turned out, the government was sustained easily, because while no Opposition party was very enthusiastic about the particular piece of legislation that had been defeated, at least one of the minor parties did not want an election at that time.[8]

In retrospect, we can see that this incident could have been interpreted in a number of different ways. It could have been viewed, by a majority of members of the House, as a betrayal of the basic conventions of our system, in which unlikely case, the government would have fallen on the confidence motion and the convention that the government must fall if defeated on a money bill would have been further ensconced. At the other extreme, the affirmation of the government's decision not to resign and to refer the matter to Parliament for a second opinion could have been viewed as a precedent. In this case, a new convention would have emerged whereby a particular piece of legislation could be defeated in the House without necessarily forcing the government's resignation. If this were to happen, the opposition in a minority situation would no longer have been handicapped by having to throw the baby out with the bath water if they don't like a piece of legislation, unless of course the government were to expressly choose to consider the matter an issue of confidence. This might have significantly enhanced the leverage of the Opposition in minority-government situations, for they would have acquired a real power to pick and choose among the government's policies without the threat of dissolution and a subsequent election constantly hanging over their heads.

However, the outcome in this particular case seems to have fallen somewhere between the two extremes. Subsequent minority Parliaments have not operated very differently than they always have in Canada, and the 1968 incident, far

---

[8] Note that although the government was sustained in office, the defeated legislation could not be reintroduced. A basic rule of Parliament is that the same bill cannot be introduced more than once in a single session.

from emerging as a key constitutional precedent, has faded into the category of exceptions and aberrations that don't quite fit the standing interpretations of the rule.

Another example where a convention of the constitution might have been changed occurred in 1981. Having failed to gain the support of a substantial number of the provinces, the Liberal government indicated its intention to patriate the constitution unilaterally. When the issue was referred to the Supreme Court,[9] the court concluded that the federal unilateral action was *legal* but *unconstitutional*, because, the Court said, there existed a convention that amendment of the constitution required the "substantial agreement" of the provinces.

As it turned out, the federal government and a "substantial" number of the provinces — nine — did arrive at an eleventh-hour agreement and the request for amendment went to Britain with provincial support. However, had the agreement not been forthcoming, the parliament of Canada could still have gone ahead with its unilateral request. In so doing, had Britain agreed to the federal request, as it likely could have, the convention would have been changed. The point of this illustration is that conventions are binding only as long as the legislators involved accept them as binding; conversely, conventional change occurs when a legislature sets a new precedent by ignoring heretofore accepted constitutional practice.

As mentioned earlier, conventional change can also be brought about by the *disuse* of a given constitutional provision. The best example of this is the disallowance power of the federal government, which has not been used since 1943 and appears now to be a dead letter. The reason it has ceased to be a viable constitutional device is related to the reality of power distribution in Canada today, which is, in turn, related to the coming of age of the provinces. However, it is also possible that if the federal government had continued to make a habit of disallowing provincial acts, the provinces might never have come of age. Desuetude, therefore, may indeed play a part in determining the fate of various constitutional devices in this country.

Customary and conventional change is occurring constantly through the use and desuetude of various constitutional practices. It is a difficult form of constitutional change to pinpoint, and that is why, throughout this section, we have used phrases such as "appears to have changed," but it does comprise a significant measure of the total of constitutional change in Canada.

Judicial Change

Judicial decisions fill out the bare bones of the constitution by interpreting it and by applying it to specific cases. In Chapter 8 we will consider such things as, for example, the way in which the federal power to regulate trade and commerce was interpreted by the Judicial Committee of the Privy Council. We will see that the judicial committee chose to interpret section 91(2) to mean the regulation of *interprovincial and international* trade and commerce, but not the regulation of purely intraprovincial trade. In that way, the judiciary effectively changed the

[9] Reference re Amendment of the Constitution of Canada [1981] 1 S.C.R. 754.

meaning of one of the provisions of the BNA Act in the process of interpreting it. Constitutional change through judicial review has certain built-in limitations, particularly because the courts do not review all legislation automatically. It is important to recognize that the courts can only interpret a law when its interpretation becomes central to deciding a case. In other words, the courts have to wait until, in the normal course of litigation, some citizen brings a case before them and questions the validity of a given statute before they can rule on its constitutionality. The only exception to this rule is a unique device available to Canadian governments known as a *constitutional reference*. A reference case occurs when the federal government submits a piece of legislation to the Supreme Court of Canada for a judgement regarding its constitutionality. The device was created by a section of the Supreme Court Act, and has the effect of allowing the federal government to test the constitutionality of a law in the highest court of the land before attempting to implement it. The provinces also have the right to submit reference cases to the highest court in the province and, ultimately, the decision on such a reference can be appealed to the Supreme Court of Canada. The problem with the constitutional reference as a method of judicial change is that the judges are forced to judge the legislation not merely within the context of the facts of a single case, but within all conceivable contexts in which it can be employed. Because we will discuss a number of specific constitutional references in the next chapter, at this time we merely wish to reiterate that the reference case is one way in which the judiciary can have the opportunity to change or shape the constitution through the interpretation of federal and provincial laws.[10]

Legislative Change

The forms of constitutional change that have been discussed thus far are all rather haphazard and incidental methods of producing change. Their end product is very difficult to plan for or to predict. This is not the case with *legislative* constitutional change, for its essence is that it is contrived, and existing regime mechanisms are employed to produce it. There are two broad types of legislative change in the Canadian political system, not including formal amendment, which will be discussed separately.

The first type of legislative constitutional change that has been employed in Canada involves the alteration of *organic laws* through acts of Parliament and orders-in-council.[11] An example of this kind of constitutional change would be the amendment of the Canadian Bill of Rights; while the subject matter can be considered constitutional, the method of altering it would be by a simple act of Parliament. In some cases, such as under the War Measures Act, the Governor-General in Council is given the power to alter fundamental legislation by executive fiat. Some of the changes that were introduced by order-in-council during World War Two significantly changed laws that could be considered constitutional.

---

[10] See Chapter 8 for a more detailed discussion of the role of the judiciary as an instrument of social and political change.

[11] Until we discuss Parliament and the policy process in chapter 19, we will speak of Parliament performing the functions that are formally its responsibility.

Although the achievement of change through this method is arbitrary, and not to be considered normal for Canada, the fact remains that it has happened in the past and could happen again in the future.

The second type of legislative change is the kind of amendment of the BNA Act that is authorized originally by the Act itself. Examples are provided by a whole class of clauses of the Act that are prefaced by the words "until the Parliament of Canada otherwise provides."[12] These provisions of the Act were intended to provide interim measures, at the time of Confederation, until Parliament could get around to setting up more permanent ones. Most of these clauses are now defunct, having been replaced by statutes soon after Confederation.

Constitutional Amendment: 1867–1982

Formal Amendment of the BNA Act: Joint Address   The most significant form of constitutional change in Canada for more than a century was formal *amendment* of the BNA Act. The Act had no general provision for its amendment when it was passed in 1867. Since it was a statute of the parliament of Britain, it seemed obvious at the time that it could and would be amended by ordinary British legislation. At Confederation, Canada was subordinate to the supreme British parliament, and her evolution to the independent status that she enjoys today was not foreseen by the British parliament or even by the Fathers of Confederation. The inability of the Dominion of Canada to amend the BNA Act soon became a problem for a young country growing rapidly, both in political autonomy and in population, and faced with a growing number of responsibilities due to the increasing involvement of government generally in matters such as education, welfare, and public works. In response to these demands for formal change of the BNA Act, a method, which involved various conventional procedures for amendment, was gradually developed.

At the core of this procedure for amendment of the BNA Act were three conventions or practices that defined, respectively, the roles of the provinces, the federal parliament, and the parliament of Britain. The earliest of these to evolve was that the parliament of Britain would not amend the BNA Act without an express request by Canada.[13] This convention, recognized before the turn of the century, was affirmed by the Statute of Westminster in 1931:

> 4. No act of Parliament of the United Kingdom passed after the commencement of this act shall extend or be deemed to extend, to a Dominion as part of the law of that Dominion, unless it is expressly declared in that act that the Dominion has requested, and consented to, the enactment thereof.

The standard means that emerged for requesting British legislative action was either a petition from the Canadian government or a joint address or "resolution" of the House of Commons and the Senate. The resolution is presented to the Queen

---

[12] See, for instance, sections 35, 40, 41, and 47 of the BNA Act, 1867.

[13] In fact, even the original BNA Act of 1867 was, with a few exceptions, entirely drafted on this side of the Atlantic. While it is *formally* an act of the British parliament, in reality it is and always has been a "made-in-Canada document.

in the form of a draft amendment with an attached request to place it on the agenda of Parliament. Executive petition by the government of the day was used in 1875 and 1895 to secure amendments to the BNA Act, and in these cases, the petition was approved by the federal parliament either explicitly or tacitly. In all other instances of amendment, however, the request has been made by a joint address of both houses of the Canadian parliament — and it has become a firm convention of the constitution that amendment today must be requested by the Canadian parliament and not directly by the government of the day.

The second convention is the positive aspect of the first: that is, that the British parliament *will always act* to amend the BNA Act if requested to do so by a joint address of the Canadian parliament. While this convention has never been given statutory expression, there has never been an occasion in Canadian constitutional history when the British parliament has refused to meet the request of the "Dominion" with regard to amendment of the BNA Act, and with the successful patriation of the constitution in 1982, there is no chance of this ever happening in the future.

The third convention or set of conventions was far more complicated than either of the first two, for it involved the extent to which the consultation and consent of the provinces should be sought by the federal government prior to petitioning Britain by a joint address. The rule here was complicated because the practice of amendment by joint address of the federal parliament was itself based on a constitutional convention. It is, of course, the particular procedure or practice that has been followed in the past that more or less defines the nature and limitations of this particular convention, but the situation was complicated not only by the fact that formal amendments of the BNA Act in areas logically requiring provincial compliance (because they involved provincial rights) have been rare, but also by the shift of much *de facto* political power to the provinces that has occurred during the past two decades of province building.

There are some facts that will guide us to a better understanding of the practice that evolved in this area. First, the British parliament never amended the BNA Act on the request of a province or of any number of the provinces, unless the provinces' wishes were expressed in a joint address by both Houses of the Canadian parliament. Secondly, the British parliament never turned down a request for amendment by the federal government because the amendment was opposed by the provinces or by any particular province.[14] Hence, in practice, the convention that emerged was that, as far as Britain is concerned, it would provide any amendment requested by the Canadian parliament, regardless of whether it might affect the rights of the provinces, and regardless of whether the provinces consented. This was logical historically, a recognition of the fact that Canada had come of age politically and should be given the power and responsibility to make the decisions and take the political consequences that might flow from an unpopular constitutional amendment.

---

[14] For details on past practice, see *The Canadian Constitution and Constitutional Amendment* (Ottawa, Federal Provincial Relations Office, 1978), p. 13. This paper comprises a useful survey of practice in four other federations, a historical summary, and a proposal for alternatives.

If, therefore, Britain would not step in to protect the provinces when the federal government requested an amendment by joint address, the entire question of the extent to which the provinces were to be consulted on amendments involves only the provinces directly concerned and the federal parliament. In order to understand the practice of provincial involvement in such amendments to the BNA Act, it is necessary to consider the provincial position with respect to consultation and consent of the provinces at some stage before the actual joint address. The original argument for the participation of the provinces in the amendment of the BNA Act stems from a theory of Confederation that has become known as the *compact theory*. The compact theory of the Canadian federal system states that the Act of 1867 was, in effect, a treaty or a *compact* among equal participants, who were the colonies extant at that time. It followed that any changes made in the original agreement must be made only with the consent of all the participants. This would mean that, for Canada to secure an amendment of the BNA Act, it would be necessary to canvass the views of the provinces, then prepare a draft amendment that took into account all of the provincial views and objections, and then secure the unanimous consent of the provinces, before securing a joint address of the Canadian parliament. Not only would this procedure have been time-consuming; it could also mean that any one province might veto an amendment that was agreed to by the rest of the provinces. To be sure, the state of affairs would protect provincial autonomy, but perhaps only at great cost in terms of other principles of our constitution, such as majority rule and representation by population. This version of the compact theory, however, has seldom been taken very seriously, even by those who favour a great deal of protection for the autonomy of the provinces. Aside from the fact that such a system of constitutional amendment might prove extremely costly in terms of time, and aside from the complications created by the fact that some provincial governments were the logical successors of the original colonial signatories while others represented colonies who came along later and still others (Alberta and Saskatchewan) were actually created by an act of the federal parliament, as R.M. Dawson points out, "The theory, while plausible, is constructed on sheer invention. It has no legal foundation; it has no historical foundation, and the precedents to support it are few."[15] Thus, not only is the compact theory impractical, it is apparently not based on either historical or legal fact.

Another version of the compact theory of Confederation has been fairly widely espoused since World War Two within the province of Quebec. This version claims that the original Confederation agreement was a compact between the two founding "races" or language groups. The implication here was that no amendment of the BNA Act could be carried out without the consent of both the English-speaking and the French-speaking partners in Confederation, with the latter represented by the province of Quebec. The basic premise of this version of the compact theory would appear to have some historical justification, in that the Confederation agreement did, in some respects, recognize cultural duality in

15 Dawson, *The Government of Canada*, p. 124. See also N.M. Rogers, "The Compact Theory of Confederation," in *Proceedings of the Canadian Political Science Association*, 1931, pp. 205–230; and G.F.G. Stanley, "Act or Pact? Another look at Confederation," C.H.A. *Annual Report* (Ottawa, 1956).

Canada. The BNA Act itself contains provisions such as language and religion guarantees, which are obviously intended to protect the rights of the French-Canadian minority. However, the argument that this should place any legal restrictions on the ability of the federal parliament to request amendments from Britain is unfounded in law. Thus, as a legal argument for the inclusion of the provinces or for the provision of a Quebec veto in the amendment process for the BNA Act, the compact theory in either of its forms was not very persuasive.

It is also worth noting that the form of sovereignty association espoused by the Parti Québécois in the 1970s was, in some respects, consistent with the compact-theory tradition.[16] According to the white paper on sovereignty association, a pact was to have been negotiated between a sovereign Quebec and "the rest of Canada" covering areas of joint jurisdiction such as tariffs and monetary policy with either party to the agreement retaining an effective veto power. The "compact" in this case would be between two new sovereign entities.

Despite the fact that the compact theory has little validity in law, the custom of consulting the provinces whenever an amendment under contemplation involves their rights has, in fact, developed slowly over the years. This fact was affirmed by the Supreme Court of Canada in its decision regarding the constitutionality of the federal move to unilaterally patriate the constitution in 1981. Here the judgement of a majority of the Court was that, while the joint address to the British parliament was *legal*, it was contrary to the constitutional convention.[17] Ironically, it was a successor to that joint address, buttressed by the support of nine provinces, that once and for all put an end to amendment by joint address to Westminster.

Formal Amendment of the BNA Act: Section 91(1) In 1949, by a joint address of the Canadian parliament, an amendment to the BNA Act was secured, which gave the federal parliament the power to amend, by simple act of Parliament, the "Constitution of Canada," with the exception of provisions that deal with the guarantees of minority-language and education rights, the rights of the provinces, the provision regarding the five-year limit on the life of a Parliament, and the requirement that the federal parliament meet at least once a year. The amendment was secured without consultation with or consent of the provinces, and although there were some objections to the unilateral action of the federal government at the time, they came to nothing in the end.

Ironically, in creating this amendment power in section 91(1) of the BNA Act, the federal government unintentionally limited its ability to amend federal "organic laws," such as the Supreme Court Act, because such legislation was viewed as part of "the Constitution of Canada," and because such federal laws guarantee certain provincial rights. The only test of the scope of 91(1) came in a 1980 reference case, when federal draft legislation to alter the structure and appointment procedure of the Senate was declared *ultra vires* the parliament of Canada. The basic reasoning was that the Senate provides for representation of provincial

[16] See Gouvernement du Québec, Conseil exécutif, *Quebec-Canada: A New Deal* (Quebec: Service des publications officielles, 1979).

[17] See: "Patriation Reference" cited above.

interests, and to alter the system of appointment or to abolish the Senate entirely would constitute an abrogation of provincial rights. Hence, it was a matter explicitly excluded from the scope of section 91(1).[18]

Thus, while we must assume that the intention of the 1949 "amendment amendment" was, in effect, to patriate a large portion of the BNA Act, because section 91(1) refers to the "constitution" and not to the BNA Act specifically, it actually narrowed the scope of unilateral federal amendment. In fact, the amending power of section 91(1) was only used five times before the 1982 amending formula replaced it, and three of these instances involved redistribution of seats in the House of Commons. The other two altered the rules of the Senate (compulsory retirement at age seventy-five, in 1965, and granting representatives to the Northwest Territories and the Yukon in 1974), but not in a manner that seriously affected the interests of the provinces.

The effect of the 1949 amendment, therefore, aside from transferring the amending power for much of the BNA Act from the British parliament to the parliament of Canada, was to explicitly preclude the federal government from directly tampering with minority rights and provincial rights without the consent of the provinces. When combined with the political limits on the federal use of "joint address" as an amending strategy, this meant that, by 1980, a large part of the constitution of Canada was, in practical terms, unamendable. The resolution of this stalemate lay only in securing federal-provincial agreement on a formal amending formula, or in a unilateral resolution by the parliament of Canada to Westminster requesting patriation.

In Search of an Amending Formula The question of how to deal with the amendment of those "entrenched" parts of the constitution of Canada, which were explicitly excluded from 91(1) and morally and politically precluded from change by joint address, was the subject of much debate in Canada and therefore deserves more detailed attention. Since 1927, there have been several federal-provincial conferences devoted almost entirely to discussions of ways in which the procedure for the amendment of the BNA Act could be completely "Canadianized"; that is, changed so that the Canadian parliament would no longer have to petition Britain's parliament in order to get the Act amended. Britain's parliament never did particularly cherish the function it was called upon from time to time to perform on our behalf, and, in fact, at the time of the passage of the Statute of Westminster, Britain attempted to give the parliament of Canada the unilateral power to amend the BNA Act in its entirety. Canada refused because of pressures from the provinces.

Hence, it was never the British parliament that stood in the way of handing over to authorities on this side of the Atlantic the power to amend the BNA Act. The problem in finding a satisfactory all-Canadian amending scheme was that we in Canada could not agree which authorities should have the power to amend the parts of the BNA Act that were excepted from the federal amendment power

[18] Reference re Legislative Authority of Parliament to Alter or Replace the Senate [1980] 1 S.C.R., 54. Note that while this indicated a willingness on the part of the Supreme Court to interpret the scope of section 91(1) narrowly, it did not deal expressly with the question of whether the Supreme Court Act should be considered a part of the "Constitution of Canada."

of section 91(1). Several schemes were proposed, the most promising of which involved a detailed breakdown of the various clauses of the BNA Act into categories, or "pigeon-holes,"[19] according to the extent of federal and provincial participation required.

At the 1964 federal-provincial conference, an agreement was actually reached on a formula: all of the provinces indicated that they were content with what clauses had been included in which pigeon-holes.[20] However, almost immediately after the conference, Jean Lesage, Premier of the province of Quebec, changed his mind and refused to give the proposal the support of his government. Quebec's sudden turnabout was probably in objection to the requirement for provincial unanimity for the amendment of matters such as language rights. If the government of the province of Quebec were to accept this part of the amending formula, it would have meant, for example, that she could no longer bargain bilaterally with the federal government for concessions in areas such as French language rights in provinces other than Quebec. In order to pry out concessions in such areas, it would have been necessary to gain the unanimous consent of the other provinces, as well as that of the federal parliament. The Quebec government seems to have felt, at that time, that there was no immediate threat to its constitutional position that would require the protection of the unanimity provision, and that it stood to gain considerable advantage by continuing the bilateral Quebec-Canada bargaining relationship. The province of Quebec, it seemed, had come full circle from the defensive and inward-looking nationalism of Duplessis to the aggressive and outward-looking nationalism of Jean Lesage, at precisely that period in Canadian constitutional history when we were attempting to write a defensive and rigid amending procedure into the consitution. Those who favour a relatively flexible constitution might well have been grateful that it had.

The successor to the Fulton-Favreau formula was the Victoria Charter of June 1971. This document, agreed to by all federal and provincial representatives at a constitutional conference in Victoria, British Columbia, proposed that all amendments to the Canadian constitution that affected significant provisions, such as the distribution of powers, required "a national consensus" expressed by the consent of Parliament and a majority of the provincial legislatures. The concurring provinces were to include: (1) every province that at any time has ever contained 25% of the population of Canada (the function of this provision was to give either Ontario or Quebec a veto power, in perpetuity, although, given current trends in population growth, British Columbia could also have entered this élite circle in the foreseeable future); (2) at least two Atlantic provinces (this gave some recognition of the fact that there are distinct *regional* interests in Canada that must be given a veto over decisions as fundamental as contitutional amendments); and (3) at least two western provinces, provided the two have a combined population equal to 50% of the total population of the west.

---

[19] See D.C. Rowat, "The 1949 Amendment and the Pigeon-Hole Method," in Paul Fox, ed., *Politics: Canada* (Toronto: McGraw-Hill, 1962), pp. 82–87.

[20] This version came to be known as the Fulton-Favreau formula after the two federal justice ministers who held office while it was being drafted. It required the consent of Parliament and all the provincial legislatures for amendments affecting the distribution of power, and the consent of Parliament and two-thirds of provincial legislatures in other areas of mutual concern.

All in all, the Victoria Charter's proposed amending formula was less rigid than the Fulton-Favreau formula, for it did not require the unanimous consent of the provinces for any matters at all. At the same time it provided protection for all major regional and ethnic interests in Canada. Unfortunately the Charter, as agreed to by the provincial representatives in Victoria, was never given the necessary ratification by the legislatures of the ten provinces and the federal parliament. As was the case with the Fulton-Favreau agreement, the legislature of Quebec was the major dissenter.

In June 1978, in response to the election of the Parti Québécois and other evidence that Canadians were not satisfied with the constitutional *status quo*, the federal government published two white papers: *A Time for Action* which set out general principles for "constitutional renewal," and *The Canadian Constitution and Constitutional Amendment*, which suggested alternative formal means for constitutional amendment, but did not choose among them. The tabling, in the House of Commons, of a constitutional-amendment bill completed a general statement of the federal position. On that occasion, the federal government proposed to proceed in two phases, first, to amend the constitution, including the Supreme Court Act, with regard to exclusively federal concerns as specified in section 91(1) of the BNA Act; and second, to reach agreement with the provinces on areas of joint concern including, particularly, the establishment of the formal amending process.

Concrete proposals were made only for the first of these phases. The Senate was to be abolished and replaced by a *House of the Federation*, with significantly increased powers, increased representation in the western and Atlantic provinces, and members chosen half by the federal government and half by the provinces. Representation among parties was to be determined on the basis of popular vote in the most recent election in each jurisdiction. The Supreme Court was to be expanded from nine members to eleven, and Quebec representation on the court was to rise from three to four. Provinces were to be consulted before judges were appointed, and appointments were to be approved by the House of the Federation. There was to be a constitutional requirement for an annual first-ministers' meeting, consultation between the federal and provincial governments before appointment of Lieutenant Governors, constitutional commitment for some federal transfer payments to provinces, and an obligation for the federal government to consult with the provinces before using its "declaratory" power to bring a work or project under federal jurisdiction (section 92[10]). Finally, a Charter of Rights and Freedoms was to be entrenched in the constitution.

As to the process of formal constitutional amendment with respect to provisions that touched upon the concerns of all or most provinces and the federal government, it was suggested that there were two possibilities in addition to the Fulton-Favreau and Victoria provisions. One was a combination of the Victoria formula with an appeal to the people via referendum. Here a referendum could be held in a region if the provincial governments in that region vetoed a proposal agreed to by the federal government and all other regions, or that a national referendum could be held if Parliament disagreed with a proposal agreed to by the provincial legislatures of all four regions. The second possibility was simply the automatic use of national referenda for all significant amendment proposals. It was also pointed out that there were several possible ways of proposing amendments, and that they, too, should be codified as part of a formal amending process. Suggestions included popular petition, a two-thirds vote of the new House of the Federation, a resolution of Parliament, resolutions from any four provincial legislatures, or from four legislatures or more, including one from each region. Again, no preference was expressed.

Like their predecessors, the constitutional talks of the late seventies did not come to fruition; indeed, the discussions never got far beyond early skirmishing over the proposals for changes to federal institutions. There was considerable disagreement, for example, about whether the federal government had any right to make unilateral changes to the Senate and Supreme Court, and whether these were not already joint institutions, exempted from the provisions of section 91(1), and therefore not changeable without provincial consent. Several provinces were suspicious that the more effective representation of regional interests in Ottawa would greatly strengthen the institutions of "intra-state federalism"[21] at their expense, and were therefore inclined to block any federal action. The federal Liberal government of Pierre Trudeau was widely believed to be nearing the end of its days, and its perceived imminent disappearance did nothing to make the seven provincial Conservative governments eager to cooperate. The Parti Québécois government of Quebec, still riding high on its initial wave of popularity, was hardly eager to cooperate in showing how federalism could be made more effective. The time was, once again, not very ripe politically for constitutional reform, even though there were many practical reasons to consider it urgent. The short-lived Conservative government of 1979–1980 was not inclined towards formal constitutional amendment, and, instead of making any concrete proposals, attempted to make the existing BNA Act work more smoothly. And so was dissipated another round in the continuing search for formal constitutional reform and amendment.

Success at Last: The 1982 Constitutional Amendment Procedure   In September 1980 Prime Minister Trudeau made one final attempt to reach a consensus with the premiers. Although some agreement was reached on a few issues, the sought-after consensus failed to materialize, and on October 2, 1980 the PM announced the intention of the federal government to go it alone and unilaterally seek patriation through a joint address. Although the federal initiative was strongly opposed by eight of the provinces (Ontario and New Brunswick supported the proposal), the federal government pressed on, and on November 6, 1980, a special joint committee of the House of Commons and the Senate commenced hearings on the constitutional resolution.

Finally, after a stormy passage of the resolution through both houses of Parliament, and after the Supreme Court of Canada declared that the unilateral action of the federal government was "legal" (but in violation of a convention that required "substantial provincial agreement"), the provinces agreed to one last-ditch effort to reach a consensus. A compromise constitutional accord between the federal

---

[21] See chapter 8 for a full discussion of the concept of "intra-state" federalism.

government and all of the provinces but Quebec was signed on November 4, 1981,[22] and the necessary amendments were passed by Parliament on December 8. The "Canada Bill" was given final approval by the British House of Lords in March 1982, and was proclaimed as the Constitution Act, 1982, on 17 April, 1982. As we noted in Chapter 7, the Constitution Act of 1982 does somewhat more than simply achieve the patriation of the BNA Act and its amendments. On the one hand, it provides an entrenched Charter of Rights and Freedoms, and on the other it provides for the amendment of the constitution of Canada.

The basic formula for the amendment of the Canadian constitution is set down in section 38(1) of the Constitution Act of 1982, and provides that changes to most parts of our constitution can be achieved with the agreement of both houses of parliament and the legislative assemblies of two-thirds of the provinces containing at least 50% of the population of Canada. Significantly, the formula does not give a veto to any specific province, but, through section 38(3), it provides any province that might disagree with such an amendment, the power to exclude itself from its provisions. This provision of dissent, while facilitating a system where no province has a veto over an amendment, was opposed by Prime Minister Trudeau at the time, on the grounds that it could result in a "checkerboard Canada." In the end, however, a federal acquiescence to the opting-out provision was likely essential to obtain the agreement of the nine provinces in November 1981. As well as permitting as many as three provinces to opt out of an amendment, the formula also provides that, where financial benefits would accrue to the provinces as a result of an amendment respecting education or culture, dissenting or opting-out provinces are to be awarded equivalent compensation (section 40).

There are also some types of amendment that are attainable through the general procedure but for which the right to dissent does not apply. These include such constitutional matters as changes to national institutions, the creation of new provinces, or the extension of existing provinces into the territories. Significantly, as well, there is no provision for obtaining the agreement of the legislative assemblies of the Northwest Territories or the Yukon, either on questions of provincehood or on the extension of existing provincial boundaries northward; a point the territorial governments, understandably, find alarming.

Certain constitutional matters, deemed especially important, cannot be amended by the basic formula, but require the *unanimous* consent of all provinces and the federal parliament. These matters include the following (from section 41):

(a) the office of the Queen, the Governor-General, and the Lieutenant Governor of a province;
(b) the right of a province to the number of members in the House of Commons not less than a number of senators by which the province is entitled to be represented at the time this part comes into force;
(c) subject to section 43, the use of the English or French language;
(d) the composition of the Supreme Court of Canada, and
(e) an amendment to this part.

[22] See R. Romanow, J. Whyte, H. Leeson, *Canada...Notwithstanding*, (Toronto: Methuen, 1984) for an excellent discussion of the process leading to the accord in November 1981.

Finally, the amending procedure also provides that constitutional matters such as the adjustment of interprovincial boundaries require only the consent of the provinces directly involved and the federal parliament; that the amendment of provincial constitutions remains in the hands of the individual provincial legislatures; and that, subject to other provisions of the Constitution Act, the parliament of Canada can, according to section 44, unilaterally make changes to federal institutions. However, because of the integrated nature of our system, and the manifestations of the federal principle even in national institutions, the unilateral amending power of the parliament of Canada may not include much:

> the illusion of section 44 is that it appears to offer the federal parliament much more control over its institutions in theory than it does upon closer examination of the details of the amending process.[23]

The conclusion here can only be very tentative because the new amending formula is as yet untested. Some would agree that the very fact that agreement on the amending formula itself took some fifty years (and that it required the threat of federal unilateral action and, even then, that agreement was not unanimous) likely indicates that unanimity, or even two-thirds assent of the provinces, will occur only rarely. The irony is that, having finally approved an amending formula for the constitution, it may, in practical terms, be virtually unamendable.[24]

In the long run, therefore, it would seem that the real significance of the "patriation" of the constitution lies in the satisfaction of psychic needs by giving Canadians the right to amend their own constitution. If this is important to Canadians in their search for an identity, and in the ongoing problem of cementing national unity, then that, in itself, is sufficient justification for having a mutually agreeable formula for constitutional amendment. It is likely, too, that people need certainty in their dealings with government, and our amending procedure will, for better or worse, lend a heretofore lacking constitutional certainty to Canadian political life.

THE ADMINISTRATION OF JUSTICE

In Chapter 6, the concept of the rule of law was introduced as a basic tenet of the Canadian constitution, but little was said about the nature of law in general or about the origins and characteristics of the Canadian judicial system. In this section, it is our intention to describe the structure of the Canadian judiciary and those aspects of the judicial process relevant to the political process as a whole. Because it is law that is the subject matter of judicial decision making, and because, formally, it is law that constitutes, regulates, or authorizes all allocative outputs

---

23 See Ron Cheffins, "The Constitution Act, 1982 and the Amending Formula . . .," *Supreme Court Law Review*, 4, 1982: p. 53.

24 For more detailed analysis of the implications of the new amending formula, see: S.A. Scott, "The Canadian Constitutional Amendment Process: Mechanisms and Prospects," a research paper prepared for the MacDonald Commission, 1985; S.V. La Selva, "Federalism and Unanimity . . .,"; and D.M. Kilgour, "A Formal Analysis of the Amending Formula" in *CJPS*, December 1983, pp. 757 and 771.

of the system, a brief discussion of the law, its nature, and origins is an appropriate introduction to this section.[25]

The Nature of Law in Canada

The function of law is to regulate human behaviour. In its broadest context, the law can be viewed as including all rules of human behaviour, whether customary, moral, ethical, or religious, which have application in a given society. However, when one speaks of the law in a modern society, what is usually implied is the positive embodiment of the customary, ethical, moral, and religious values of a society in the form of statutes and judicial decisions. In this more formal and positive sense, law is concrete and explicit in a way that a code of behaviour, implicit in customs or moral standards, can never be. Furthermore, as Professor J.A. Corry points out, in the more positive sense, law can be distinguished from custom and morality by the existence of explicit sanctions and positive means for enforcement: "What distinguishes law from customs and morality is the additional sanction of sheriffs, bailiffs, police, jails and armed forces to be called into operation if needed to coerce the stubborn."[26] For the purposes of this analysis, a narrow rather than broad definition of law has been chosen.

To perform effectively the function of providing guidelines for human behaviour in a society, the law must be *knowable*; people must be able to discover the standards of behaviour their society is imposing on them in order to be able to comply with those standards. The law must also be applied in a way that is *predictable* for the citizen. If we are to be capable of adjusting our behaviour so that it conforms to the requirements of the law, not only must we be aware of the broad principles embodied in the law, but we must also be able to predict the way in which the law will apply to us personally.[27]

The law in Canada can be said to consist primarily of statutes and judicial decisions or precedents. The former are enactments of the lawmaking institutions of the political system. They are the products of the legislatures — in the strictest sense of that word. But while there is a large annual output of legislation today, legislatures do no more than add to or make alterations to a vast body of law that is already in existence, and that is derived largely from other sources.[28] The bulk of the law is to be found not primarily in legislation, but in myriad judicial decisions that reflect a society's moral, ethical, religious, and customary foundations far better than the specific enactments of any legislature. In this sense, the law is incremental. It is a body of principles that have been accumulated over time and modified as the values of the society have changed — modified subtly through minute judicial reinterpretations, and from time to time modified more explicitly by legislation.

---

[25] See chapter 6 for a discussion of the principle of judicial independence and chapter 8 for a discussion of the role of the courts in interpreting the BNA Act. For discussion of the judicial system and the legal process in Canada, see especially F.L. Morton, *Law, Politics and the Judicial Process in Canada* (Calgary: University of Calgary, 1984), and P. Fitzgerald and King McShane, *Looking at Law: Canada's Legal System.* (Ottawa: Bybooks, 1985).

[26] Corry and Hodgetts, *Democratic Government and Politics*, p. 424.

[27] See chapter 6 for a discussion of the principle of the rule of law.

[28] Corry and Hodgetts, *Democratic Government*, p. 423.

While the law is a growing thing, its growth is controlled rather than random. The element of control in Canada is injected in part through the *rule of precedent*, the principle of *stare decisis*. The basic principle of the rule of precedent is that judges, when making a decision today, take into account the decisions of previous courts in similar cases in the past. Precedents can be of two types: *binding* or *persuasive*. W.R. Lederman points out that binding precedent exists where "within any particular system of judicature the lower courts in the hierarchy are bound to follow the rules previously used to decide sufficiently similar cases in the higher court or courts of the hierarchy."[29] Thus, in the Canadian system, decisions by higher courts are binding on lower courts in the same judicial hierarchy. However, the question as to whether a court is bound by its own precedents is dependent mainly on the court itself; a court can choose to consider itself bound by its own precedents, or it can choose not to be so bound. The Supreme Court of Canada and, before 1949, the Judicial Committee of the Privy Council have chosen not to be strictly bound by their own precedents. The practice of both these courts of final appeal, however, indicates that a previous decision has a great deal of persuasive force in helping them to decide current cases, and it is seldom indeed that the Supreme Court of Canada reverses the stand it took in a previous case: "Even though a court regards its own previous decisions as persuasive only, they turn out to be so highly persuasive that the distinction from a binding precedent becomes rather dim."[30]

The Canadian legal system stems from two quite distinct legal traditions, and is consequently a unique reflection of the duality of Canadian political culture. One tradition is rooted in the Roman law and the other in the English common law. Roman law is codified in the form of general rules and principles, which must be applied to each case individually. It is Roman law that was adopted in varying forms throughout western Europe at the time of the Renaissance. The settlers of New France naturally brought with them the laws of their mother country, so in the Province of Quebec the Roman legal tradition is still to some extent reflected. The English common law is based on "the common custom of the realm"[31] as interpreted by judges, and is derived from judicial precedents that build on earlier precedents and so on. It is not codified; rather, it is a set of principles merely implicit in the judicial decisions of England and of the courts in systems that have adopted the English legal system.[32] The common law came to Canada via the early English settlers, and was even partially introduced into Quebec through the Conquest. Today in Quebec, *private law* (or *civil law*) is based on the *Code civil du Québec*, which is derived from the French *Code Napoléon*, whereas in the other Canadian provinces, private law is based on the English common law. Criminal law in Canada is uniform across the country, being based on the Canadian Criminal Code, which, in turn, is derived almost exclusively from the principles of English criminal jurisprudence.

[29] W.R. Lederman, "The Common Law System in Canada," in E. McWhinney, ed., *Canadian Jurisprudence: The Civil Law and Common Law in Canada* (Toronto: Carswell, 1958), p. 36.

[30] Lederman, "The Common Law System," p. 37.

[31] Corry and Hodgetts, *Democratic Government*, p. 428.

[32] Note that parts of the common law are codified from time to time in various statutes such as the Criminal Code, the Landlord and Tenant Act, etc.

The Judicial System

Because Canada is a federal political system, it is only natural that the Canadian judicial system should reflect federalism in its basic structure. By contrast to the United States, however, where the federal and state courts exist separately from each other in vertically parallel hierarchies, each with its distinct jurisdiction, the Canadian system of courts divides provincial and federal court jurisdiction horizontally.[33] The course of litigation in the United States may begin in either a federal or a state court and can normally be appealed only to the top of the particular hierarchy. For example, in the United States, criminal law is primarily a state matter, and most criminal cases are tried only in state courts.[34] For such cases, the final court of appeal is normally the supreme court of the state. There is no appeal from the supreme court of the state to the Supreme Court of the United States in state criminal matters, except where the issue can be couched in constitutional terms. In Canada, by contrast, while there are separate provincial and federal courts, the eventual course of litigation may move from provincial courts to a final appeal at the level of the Supreme Court of Canada. However, this statement cannot be made without qualification, for most matters are not considered important enough to be appealable to the Supreme Court of Canada as of right, but only by leave. (The appellate jurisdiction of the Supreme Court of Canada will be discussed in more detail below.)

Not only are the various provincial and federal courts integrated in terms of jurisdiction; they are also integrated, to some extent, through the process of appointment set down in the BNA Act. Sections 96 to 100 provide for the appointment, removal, and salaries of all superior, county, and district court judges in the provinces. The judges of these provincial courts are all appointed and paid by the federal government. Federal court judges, naturally, are also appointed by the federal government, and it is only the lesser provincial court judges who are appointed and remunerated by the provincial governments. In describing the jurisdiction and functions of the various provincial courts, this discussion will focus primarily on the province of Ontario. While other provinces differ from Ontario in various ways, the judicial systems of all the Canadian provinces are similar, and there is not sufficient room to discuss each individually. Figure 7-1 provides an overall view of the system.

The Provincial Judicial System   The lowest level of the judicial hierarchy in most provinces is the *justice of the peace*. A justice of the peace is appointed by the province or territory — formally, by the Lieutenant Governor in Council or the Commissioner — and holds office "at pleasure." There are virtually no specific qualifications for the office, not even legal training. The jurisdiction of a justice of the peace is usually territorially limited to the municipality or judicial district where the appointment takes place. Within the territory, a justice of the peace is permitted to administer oaths, to take affirmations and declarations, and to try

---

[33] See sections 92(14) and 96 to 101 of the BNA Act, 1867.

[34] There are, as well, in the United States, "federal crimes," which are tried in federal courts.

FIGURE 7-1
THE JUDICIAL SYSTEM

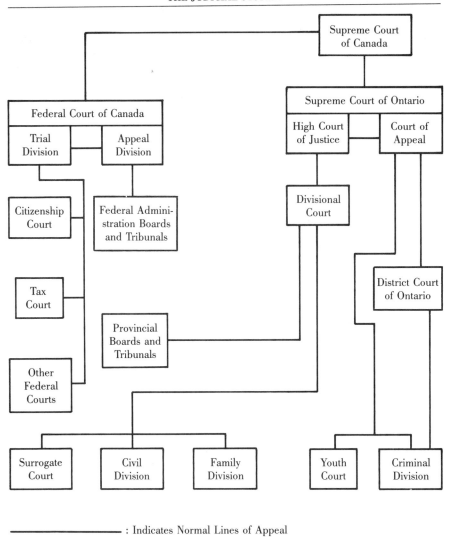

——————————— : Indicates Normal Lines of Appeal

prosecutions under municipal by-laws. Under the direction of a provincial or territorial judge, a justice of the peace in some jurisdictions may also try summary-conviction criminal offences. Other powers of a justice of the peace include the performing of civil marriages, the quelling of riots, and various procedural powers such as issuing warrants. Appeal from a decision of a justice of the peace usually goes to a justice of the Supreme Court of the province or territory, which sits alone. Justices of the peace in many jurisdictions are currently being phased out, and probably all of their functions will ultimately come to be performed by the more highly qualified provincial judges or magistrates, who possess all the powers of justices of the peace, *ex officio.*

It is interesting that the major exception to the decline in the role of JPs in Canada has been in the northern territories. In the 1970s, the commissioner of the Northwest Territories appointed more than a hundred new justices of the peace in an attempt to bring justice "closer to the people." Most of these appointees are local people in the remotest settlements of the Territories, and many of them are of native origins, so that, it is hoped, minor offenses can be dealt with by judicial officials who, while lacking in formal legal training, will have a sensitivity to local problems and to the cultural idiosyncrasies of the specific settlement.

In Ontario, which has a system broadly similar to those in other provinces, *provincial judges* have taken over all of the functions previously performed by justices of the peace, magistrates, and juvenile and family court judges. The judicial council was established in 1968, and is composed of representatives of the bench and of the bar. Its functions include consideration of the proposed appointment of provincial judges, advising the government, and conducting inquiries into complaints brought against judges in respect to their judicial capacity. A judge holds office during good behaviour until age sixty-five, with possible reappointment to age seventy-five, and can be removed by the Lieutenant Governor in Council, but only for misbehaviour or for inability to perform duties, and then only after a judicial inquiry. The jurisdiction of provincial judges includes presiding over the criminal, the civil, or the family divisions of the provincial courts, as well as presiding over the youth court in criminal matters under the Young Offenders Act.

The criminal jurisdiction of provincial judges includes summary-conviction trials under certain Ontario statutes and under certain federal statutes such as the Criminal Code and the Narcotics Control Act, as well as trial of indictable offences where the accused specifically selects trial by provincial judge. Provincial judges may also conduct preliminary hearings for indictable offences in which the accused has chosen a jury trial or trial by superior court judge. Appeal from decisions of the provincial judge is normally to the Supreme Court of Ontario, although some procedural matters are appealable to a District Court judge.

The *civil division* of the provincial court, formerly known as *small claims courts*, has been established under the Courts of Justice Act 1984 in various districts in the province. The judges of these courts are appointed by the Lieutenant Governor in Council, and their jurisdiction is territorially limited to the district for which they were appointed and is limited in subject matter to small civil claims. Procedure in the civil division is intended to be speedy, inexpensive, and informal, and specifically excludes certain tort actions such as libel, slander, breach of promise, and actions concerning estates of deceased persons. Appeal from civil division of the provincial court lies with the Divisional Court of the Supreme Court of Ontario.

There is also a *surrogate court* for each district of the province of Ontario, whose jurisdiction includes most testamentary matters, determination of minor financial claims against an estate, the appointment of guardians for the children of the deceased, and, generally, all such probate matters except interpretation of wills, administration of estates, and determination of actions for legacies. In most cases in Ontario, the judge acting as *surrogate court judge* is the district court judge, although the Lieutenant Governor in Council is not legally restricted in this regard. Appeal from the surrogate court lies normally to the Supreme Court of Ontario.

County court judges are appointed by the Governor General in Council, as provided for by section 96 of the BNA Act. The courts on which these judges sit, however, are set up by the provinces, who are empowered constitutionally to do so through section 92(14) of the BNA Act. Section 22 states that the provincial legislature can pass laws regarding

> The administration of justice in the province, including the constitution, mainte-nance and organization of provincial courts both of civil and criminal jurisdiction and including procedure in civil matters in those courts.

The county court system in Ontario was replaced in 1984 by an amalgamated *District Court of Ontario*. By this system, more than one county or parts of counties are designated as judicial districts in the province, and district court judges are assigned to these specific geographical jurisdictions. As with the old county court system in Ontario, the District Court is provincially administered and the judges are federally appointed and paid. The qualification of a district court judge is that he or she must be a barrister of at least ten years' standing, and tenure is during good behaviour until age seventy-five. A district court judge is removable by the Governor-General in Council for various statutory reasons, but only after an inquiry.

The jurisdiction of the district court judge includes civil matters, with or without a jury. Basically, the jurisdiction of the District Court of Ontario includes contract actions, most tort actions regarding land, partnership actions, certain actions for legacies, and equitable actions if the subject matter involved does not exceed $25,000. It is important to recognize here, however, that the jurisdiction of this court is held concurrently with that of the *Supreme Court of Ontario*, and as a result actions may be commenced at the higher level.

The district court judges also sit with a jury or alone to hear cases involving medium indictable offences. This court also hears certain appeals from sum-mary convictions by provincial judges. Appeals from decisions of the district court judge lie generally to the Ontario Court of Appeal, with the exception of procedural appeals, which can be heard by a single judge of the Supreme Court of Ontario.

The Supreme Court of Ontario has two divisions, the *High Court of Justice of Ontario*, which includes the chief justice of the high court and more than thirty puisne justices, and the *Court of Appeal of Ontario*, which includes the chief justice of Ontario and nine other justices of appeal. The appointment of all judges of the Supreme Court of Ontario is by the federal government, and while appointment is explicitly to either the high court or to the appeal court, judges may serve in the other division if required. Appointment, as with all superior court judges, is during good behaviour until age seventy-five, and removal is only possible by order-in-council after a joint address of the House of Commons and the Senate.

Salaries are set by federal statute and paid by the federal government, although the courts themselves are established and administered by the province.

The High Court of Justice of Ontario functions with judges sitting singly, with or without jury, and has general jurisdiction unlimited as to monetary value in all civil matters. The criminal jurisdiction of the High Court includes concurrent jurisdiction with lower courts for most indictable offences, and in the case of the most serious indictable offences, such as murder, the High Court has exclusive jurisdiction. The High Court of Justice has a separate division called the *Divisional Court*, which is composed of three High Court judges, and which performs the lesser appellate functions not vested in the Court of Appeal. Appeal from the High Court of Justice is to the Court of Appeal and, rarely, directly to the Supreme Court of Canada, through what is called an appeal *per saultern*.

The Court of Appeal of Ontario has a quorum of at least three judges. It functions as a general court of appeal for the province, hearing appeals from the lower courts and from certain provincial administrative tribunals, and delivering opinions on references by the Lieutenant Governor in Council. Appeal from the Ontario Court of Appeal is to the Supreme Court of Canada.

Federal Judiciary   Federal courts in Canada include the Supreme Court, the Federal Court, citizenship courts, the Tax Court, the Court-martial Appeal Court, and the superior courts in the Northwest Territories and the Yukon. The latter three types are very specialized in subject matter or geographically, but the Federal Court and the Supreme Court of Canada have more general jurisdiction and bear further discussion. *The Supreme Court of Canada* is a superior court of common law and equity in and for Canada, and was established by the Supreme Court Act in 1875. The Court is composed of a chief justice and eight puisne judges, all appointed by the Governor-General in Council. An appointee must be a judge of a provincial superior court or a barrister of at least ten years' experience, and must take up residence within five miles of Ottawa. Justices of the Supreme Court of Canada hold office during good behaviour until age seventy-five, and are removable by the Governor-General in Council on joint address of the Senate and the House of Commons. An additional requirement set down explicitly in the Supreme Court Act is that three of the nine judges must be appointed from the Quebec bench or bar.

The Supreme Court sits only in Ottawa and has three sessions per annum. Five judges normally constitute a quorum, except that on applications for leave to appeal, three is a quorum in civil matters. On appeal from the province of Quebec, it is mandatory that at least two of the sitting judges be from that province. Generally, the function of the Supreme Court of Canada is to be a general court of appeal, but the Supreme Court hears criminal appeals only in cases involving a capital offence or questions of constitutionality. There is an appeal by leave from the highest provincial court in civil matters, and from the highest provincial court on a constitutional reference. The Supreme Court of Canada is also required to give opinions on constitutional matters referred to it by the Governor-General in Council. In sum, the Supreme Court of Canada has all the powers of a superior court, and also, since the abolition of appeals to the Judicial Committee of the Privy Council in 1949, it functions as the final court of appeal for Canada.

The Federal Court, which has replaced the Exchequer Court, was set up by the Federal Court Act, 1970. The Federal Court consists of a court of original jurisdiction, known as the *Trial Division*, and a court of appeal, known as the *Appeals Division*. The Court is composed of a chief justice, who functions as the president of the appeals division, an associate chief justice, who functions as the president of the trial division, and up to ten puisne judges. At least three of the ten must be appeal judges, and the rest trial judges, and there is an additional requirement that at least four of the Federal Court judges must be appointed from among members of the bar or bench of the province of Quebec.

The basic requirements for appointment to the Federal Court are the same as for the Supreme Court of Canada, and tenure is during good behaviour until age seventy. While appointments are specifically to either the Trial or the Appeal Division, all judges are *ex officio* members of the division to which they were not appointed.

The original jurisdiction of the Federal Court includes matters involving claims against the Crown, intergovernmental actions involving interprovincial or federal-provincial disputes, citizenship appeals, and specific jurisdiction vested in the old Exchequer Court by federal statutes such as the Excise Act, the Customs Act, the Income Tax Act, the National Defence Act, the Patent Act, and the Shipping Act.

The jurisdiction of the Federal Court of Appeal includes hearing appeals from the Trial Division of the Federal Court, and reviewing the decisions of federal boards, commissions, and tribunals. This latter appellate jurisdiction of the Federal Court is limited, by section 28 of the Federal Court Act, to cases where administrative decisions are required by law to be judicial or quasi-judicial, or where the federal board or tribunal has failed to observe the principles of natural justice, has gone beyond its jurisdiction, has made an error in law, or has based its decision on erroneous findings of fact. Furthermore, the Act provides that there will be no such appeal if other legislation already provides for a statutory appeal to the Treasury Board, the Governor-General in Council, or the Supreme Court of Canada; nor are decisions of the Governor in Council or the Treasury Board reviewable by the Federal Court. These particular limitations on the appellate jurisdiction of the Federal Court were originally subjected to some criticism from the legal profession as being regressive and contrary to the generally liberalizing effect of the legislation as a whole. Despite these so-called "privative clauses" in the act, however, the Court has actually played a useful role in overseeing federal administrative boards and tribunals.

In fact, it can be argued that the Appeals Division of the Court has actually expanded its jurisdiction since its creation in 1971. The irony here is that the bulk of its expanded jurisdiction has been at the expense of the Trial Division of the same court. The trial side was originally given, by section 18 of the Act, supervisory jurisdiction to issue the traditional prerogative writs and remedies such as *mandamus, certiorari*, prohibition, etc., but not *habeas corpus*, against federal administrative authorities. However, instead of seeking these fairly simple remedies for abuses of administrative power, the tendency has been for litigants to seek redress of their legal grievances through the Appeals Division via the provisions of section 28. Thus, the jurisdiction and, hence, the workload of the appeals side of the Federal Court has expanded, and the trial side jurisdiction has effectively been reduced in administrative-law matters. This has stimulated demands for change in the Act to resolve this internal problem, but the overall verdict on the Federal Court has to be that it has proven successful.

Decisions of the Federal Court of Appeal are appealable to the Supreme Court of Canada as of right where the matter in controversy exceeds a set amount of money. Other than this general provision, an appeal to the Supreme Court of Canada lies by leave of the Supreme Court itself, or by the leave of the Federal Court of Appeal. Finally, an appeal lies automatically to the Supreme Court where the dispute is interprovincial or federal-provincial in nature.

Reform of the Supreme Court of Canada[35]   The Supreme Court of Canada has been subjected to much criticism since its creation in 1875, and has narrowly escaped abolition at several points in its history. However, since the abolition of appeals to the Judicial Committee of the Privy Council in 1949, when the Supreme Court of Canada became the final court of appeal for Canada, its position in the Canadian political system has been secure. The question now is not whether Canada needs a supreme court, but rather how the existing one can be improved. Much of the criticism of the Supreme Court (which applies equally to the higher provincial courts) has been levelled at the method of appointment of the judges, which is based, at times, on partisan considerations, and is done exclusively by the federal government. This does not usually mean that a Liberal government, for example, will appoint a bad lawyer to the bench just because he or she is a Liberal, but rather that the government will find a good lawyer who is also a Liberal and give that person the appointment. (We deal with this appointment process in Chapter 13.)

Basically, the argument against appointments to the bench that take into account party affiliation is that such a method of appointment is contrary to the principle of an independent judiciary, which is crucial to our legal system.[36] A few exploratory studies of judicial behaviour indicate that judges usually take characteristic and predictable stands when particular issues are involved,[37] and further, that no judge is ever really independent in an absolute way, for judges are human. Hence, the judge is influenced by all sorts of personal preferences and biases, and will tend to interpret the law in such a way that the decision made is congruent with personal values. On the other hand, none of these studies has indicated that there is a positive correlation in Canada between the stand a judge takes on issues and the tenets of the political party that appointed the judge to the bench.

---

[35] See Paul Weiler, *In the Last Resort: A Critical Study of the Supreme Court of Canada* (Toronto, Carswell 1974) for an excellent critical appraisal of the role of the Court.

[36] See chapter 6.

[37] D.E. Fouts, "Policy Making in the Supreme Court of Canada, 1950–60," and S.R. Peck, "A Scalogram Analysis of the Supreme Court of Canada, 1958-67," both in G. Schubert and D.J. Danelski, eds., *Comparative Behaviour* (Toronto: Oxford University Press, 1969), pp. 257–334. A study was also done for the MacDonald Commission entitled, "The Social Attitudes of Judges of the Supreme Court of Canada," by Robert Martin, 1985.

Suggestions for reform on the method of appointment of judges are two-fold. With respect to the Supreme Court, most legal experts feel that judges should be selected with some formal participation on the part of the existing bench, the Canadian Bar Association, the provinces, or all of these. The arguments in favour of participation by the existing bench or the Canadian Bar Association contend that in order to get the best judges, the selection should be made not so much by a non-partisan body as by, or with the advice of, a body of experts who have some knowledge about the requirements and qualifications of a good judge.[38] Such reform could be achieved informally, by simply co-opting the Canadian Bar Association into the selection process, while continuing to make the formal appointment as provided in sections 96 to 101 of the BNA Act.

The utility of provincial participation in the process of appointing justices to a court that so significantly affects their interests was recognized by the federal government in its 1978 Constitutional Amendment Bill. Here it was proposed to raise the size of the Court to eleven, and the principle of regional representation of justices was to be made explicit. When a justice was to be named from a province, the Attorney General of the province was to be informed of and agree to the appointment. If agreement proved impossible, a nominating council was to be formed consisting, at the province's option, of the federal and all provincial Attorneys General or their nominees, or of the specific federal and provincial Attorneys General concerned and a neutral chairman. A justice was to be chosen from among three names submitted by the federal government. For reasons discussed earlier in this chapter, the Bill was never passed, but it could be claimed to constitute significant recognition by the federal government of the day of the province's right to participate in the appointment process, and some such procedure may eventually be adopted. With respect to provincial courts, it is argued that vacancies in provincial superior, district, and county courts should be filled by the province and not by the federal government. In order to implement this type of reform, however, an amendment to sections 96 to 100 of the BNA Act would be required.[39] Amendment to the BNA Act, as we have seen, is a difficult business at best, and before altering these critical sections of the Act, it would be wise to consider very carefully how switching the locus of such appointments from the federal to the provincial level would affect both the principle of judicial independence and, at a more prosaic level, the balance of power in the federal system.

As outlined above, recent constitutional reform proposals have suggested changes in the structure of the Supreme Court of Canada. The key to the judicial reforms is a system of appointment to the Supreme Court that would require that

---

[38] Note that the Judicial Council in Ontario to some extent performs this function with respect to the appointment of provincial judges. See also A.W. MacKay and R.W. Bauman, "The Supreme Court of Canada: Reform Implications for an Emerging National Institution," in Beckton and MacKay, eds. *The Courts and the Charter* (Toronto: University of Toronto Press, 1985), pp. 37–131, for a thorough discussion of a proposed federal "appointing council."

[39] See G. Pepin, "The Problem of Section 96 of the Constitution Act, 1867," in Beckton and MacKay, p. 223, for an excellent discussion of this issue. See also P. Russell, "Constitutional Reform of the Judicial Branch, Symbolic vs. Operational Considerations," *C.J.P.S.*, June 1984, p. 227.

the justices be selected proportionally from the various regions of Canada. What is implicit in this proposal is the principle that the regions of Canada should be *represented* on the highest court of the land if that court is to have the final authority in settling constitutional disputes. The flaw in these proposals is that they effectively scuttle the constitutional principle of judicial independence, for there is no way that a *representative* judiciary can function independently — the justices will be expected, quite naturally, to reflect the interests of the region from which they were appointed.

It can be countered that the Supreme Court of Canada is already representative, in that three of the nine judges must be appointed from the bar or bench of the province of Quebec. However, the principle here is to insure that *expertise* in the codified civil-law system of Quebec — the *Code civil* — is present on the Court, along with judges trained in the English common-law system of other provinces. (The aim of the Supreme Court Act is not to represent Quebec in constitutional cases, but to ensure that there are judges sitting on the highest court of the land who have the legal training to be able to effectively cope with civil appeals from Quebec courts.)

Now, it *is* possible to make a case for a representative Supreme Court. In some democratic regimes, judges are even popularly elected. However, we must recognize that the constitutional implications of a change from an independent to a representative judiciary are significant. Through what, on the surface, is mere institutional "fiddling" with the Supreme Court, we could end up with a radically different judicial process. In some ways, the 1978 proposed reforms in the appointment procedures for Supreme Court justices would supplant judicial review with binding arbitration, replace the highest court of appeal with what is, in effect, an arbitration tribunal, and replace impartiality with advocacy as the *modus operandi* of judicial decision making.

Finally, the point can be made that, by custom, the Supreme Court of Canada is representative of the various regions of the country in terms of the province of origin of the nine judges. As we have seen, by the Supreme Court Act, 1949, three judges must be from Quebec. By convention, three are normally from Ontario, and there are one each from the Atlantic region, the prairie provinces, and British Columbia.[40] Moreover, the *practice* of filling vacancies by this sort of informal formula is born out by evidence marshalled by Peter Russell and by MacKay and Bauman.[41]

Other than the appointment procedure, the major criticism of the Canadian judicial system has focused on the jurisdiction of the Supreme Court of Canada. Particularly in the province of Quebec, it has been felt that appeals from the highest court in the province to the Supreme Court in matters involving the *Code civil du Québec* are unjust. The Supreme Court of Canada, although it includes three civil-code judges, functions predominantly as a common-law court, and as

---

[40] See F.L. Morton, *Law, Politics and the Judicial Process in Canada*, op. cit., p. 44. Note that the current composition of the Supreme Court of Canada is exactly as cited.

[41] P.H. Russell, *The Supreme Court of Canada as a Bilingual and Bicultural Institution* (Ottawa: Queen's Printer, 1969), p. 64; MacKay and Bauman, op. cit., p. 72; see Table 7-1.

TABLE 7-1
REGIONAL REPRESENTATION OF SUPREME COURT JUDGES AT SELECTED
DATES, 1875–1982

Date	Total Number of Judges	Quebec	Ontario	Atlantic	West
1875	6	2	2	2	0
1888	6	2	3	1	0
1893	6	2	2	2	0
1903	6	2	1	2	1
1905	6	2	2	2	0
1906	6	2	2	1	1
1924	6	2	3	0	1
1927	7	2	3	0	2
1932	7	2	2	1	2
1949	9	3	3	1	2
1979	9	3	2	1	3
1982	9	3	3	1	2
1986	9	3	3	1	2

Adapted from P.H. Russell, *The Supreme Court*, and from MacKay and Bauman, "Reform Implications."

such, it is felt that it should not have the power to overturn decisions of the highest court of Quebec in civil matters. The proposed constitutional amendment bill of 1978 tried to answer this criticism by appointing a fourth justice from Quebec, and by stipulating that *Code civil* cases were to be heard by panels including all four Quebec justices.

Finally, it is sometimes argued that the Supreme Court of Canada should not have both general appeal jurisdiction and jurisdiction to settle constitutional matters. The feeling here has been that the Supreme Court of Canada should become a final court of appeal only in constitutional matters or in matters within federal jurisdiction, and that either another court should be vested with final appeal jurisdiction in non-constitutional matters or that the final appeal in such matters should rest with the provinces. The argument against this latter suggestion is that, if there is to be uniformity of law throughout Canada, there should be a system whereby provincial supreme courts are all subjected to a common source of precedent flowing from a single higher court.

A partial solution was found in 1975, when changes were made to the procedures in the Supreme Court. At that time, the number of "appeals as of right" in civil cases was reduced significantly, and instead the Supreme Court grants "leave to appeal" in instances where cases of national concern are being addressed. The late Chief Justice Bora Laskin saw this altered role for the Court as important because it allowed the Court to have greater control over its own docket. At the same time, Laskin was pleased that the 1975 changes ". . . blunted the case that could be made for limiting the Supreme Court of Canada to federal and constitutional issues."[42]

Instead, the Court's role has changed, according to Laskin, from a "general appellate tribunal in the traditional sense" to a "*supervisory* tribunal,"[43] mandated to grant leave to appeal only where

> any question involved therein is, by reason of its public importance, or the importance of any issue of law, or any issue of mixed law and fact involved in such question, one that ought to be decided by the Supreme Court.

In conclusion, for our concerns, the most significant of the issues surrounding the Supreme Court are those that deal with its role in constitutional matters. The 1982 Constitution Act took an important step in the direction of recognizing the fundamental basis of that role by entrenching certain aspects of the nature and composition of the Supreme Court in the constitution.[44] But, as will become clear when we discuss the dynamics of federalism, no judicial arrangement can effectively supplant political compromise and conciliation in insuring the smooth functioning of the political system. However, the role of the Supreme Court is an essential one, and the increasing attention given to issues surrounding that body during recent constitutional discussions attests to a recognition of the increasingly important role of the judiciary not only as the arbiter of a federal system, but also as the arbiter of the relationship between the individual and the state as defined in the Charter of Rights of 1982.

CIVIL LIBERTIES IN CANADA

When the Queen proclaimed the Constitution Act on April 17, 1982, the Charter of Rights and Freedoms became part of our fundamental law. While the "entrenchment" of such rights and freedoms constituted a significant symbolic act, it must be recognized that these basic values of the Canadian political system have been a part of our constitution since 1867. Hence, before turning to a discussion of the Charter, we must look at the pre-existing guarantees of civil liberties in Canada, which form the base upon which the new charter will operate.

Rights, Freedoms, and Liberties[45]

For the purposes of this discussion, it will be assumed that the terms *liberties* and *freedoms* are synonymous. However, it is not as easy to dismiss distinctions between the terms *right* and *liberty*. In their broadest sense, the terms *civil rights* and *civil liberties* can viewed as meaning basically the same thing, the former term being more common in the United States and the latter more popular in Britain and Canada. In Canada, however, the term "civil rights," as used in section 92(13)

---

[43] *Ibid.*

[44] Sections 41 and 42, Constitution Act 1982. See also B.L. Strayer, "Comment on 'The Origins of Judicial Review in Canada'," *C.J.P.S.*, September 1983, pp. 595–596. Strayer argues, convincingly, that while certain aspects of the Supreme Court's role are entrenched,

"provisions concerning the composition and jurisdiction of the Court such as are now found in the Supreme Court Act would not, seemingly be entrenched until they are put into the constitution through the use of the new amendment process." (p. 596)

[45] See W.S. Tarnopolsky, *The Canadian Bill of Rights* (Toronto: McClelland and Stewart, 1975), pp. 1–3.

of the BNA Act and as modified through extensive judicial interpretation, is closely connected not only with the rights of individuals, but also with rights that accrue through property and through contract. It is better, therefore, to avoid the term "civil rights" when referring to fundamental political freedoms in the Canadian context.

In 1953, while delivering a judgement on a case involving the principle of religious freedom, Mr. Justice Ivan C. Rand attempted to clarify the distinction between civil rights and civil liberties. He assumed that every person, simply by virtue of being a person, has a total area of freedom, the limits of which are defined only by one's physical strength, mental capacity, etc. However, by virtue of being a member of a community that makes rules to which one must adhere, a person gives up a certain percentage of his or her absolute, or original, freedom. Each piece of positive law, therefore, limits the individual's freedom by creating some sort of obligation to obey the law. For example, a law prohibiting patricide creates an obligation in all sons not to kill their fathers, thus restricting the absolute freedom of sons. Conversely, however, such a law creates a right in all fathers not to be killed by their sons. The positive law thus creates *rights* and *obligations* out of the existing area of absolute freedom.[46]

To return to our definitions, then, *civil rights*, in the purest sense of the term, are created through the enactment of positive laws, while *civil liberties* are the residual area of freedom left to an individual after the totality of the positive law is subtracted from it. However, as W.S. Tarnopolsky has pointed out, most fundamental freedoms are, in fact, beefed up by the positive law.[47] By way of example, he cites religious freedom:

> In those terms, then, we speak of "freedom of worship," but only as defined by law, and not including such practices as human sacrifice, for example. Such freedoms can also be protected by law, for instance, by forbidding unlawful interference with the conduct of a religious service.[48]

A more current example of the evolution or development of a positive right out of an area of residual freedom might be occurring in the area of *privacy*. The foundation of a "right to privacy" likely lies in tradition and in the common law (a man's home is his castle). Violations of privacy on the part of private individuals are viewed as trespassing; and encroachments, even by governmental officials such as the police, require significant justification and some level of judicial involvement, such as a warrant. However, most of the original tenets of a common-law right to privacy involve only the physical or *territorial* dimension of privacy, which is related to the law of property.

Modern electronic technology has created a situation where *information* concerning an individual can be gathered, collated, and retrieved with frightening

---

[46] See *Saumur v. City of Quebec*, [1953] 2 S.C.R., p. 329.

[47] Note here that an entrenched and comprehensive Charter of Rights might be conceived of as replacing all residual freedoms with positive rights. Whatever the semantic difficulties with such a formulation of the terms, the effect would still be essentially to entrench certain freedoms once and for all behind a set of positive law barriers. In fact, the effect is to create a "right to a set of freedoms," whereby the existing residue of individual freedoms is protected from any further encroachment by the positive law.

[48] W.S. Tarnopolsky, *The Canadian Bill of Rights*, p. 2.

efficiency. It has been recognized that the common-law protections of the right to territorial privacy have to be backed up by legislation to protect the informational privacy of individuals from unscrupulous business enterprises and governmental agencies, as well. The positive legal response to this new threat to individual freedom has been legislation that limits the operation of consumer credit ratings, and that imposes strict limits on the use of electronic surveillance devices, by both public and private organizations. The result is that a previously unrecognized and seemingly, unnecessary "right to privacy" is being defined incrementally, through a series of positive law enactments.

The 1977 Canadian Human Rights Act provides for one of the members of the Human Rights Commission to act as a "privacy commissioner." The function of this official is to investigate complaints arising out of part four of the Human Rights Act. This part of the act requires the federal government to publicize the existence of the various information banks within the bureaucracy, to provide some access to this information on the part of the individual concerned, and to limit the use to which the information can be put. In the latter case, for instance, the federal government is restricted in the extent to which information gathered for one purpose and by one agency can be used by other agencies of the government or by other governments. While this legislation is a step in the right direction, it will likely be necessary for a future government to introduce separate and comprehensive legislation dealing with privacy, and structured in a way that its operation is complementary to recent legislation on freedom of information for full guarantees of individual privacy *vis-à-vis* federal institutions to be realized. Ultimately, as well, similar legislation will have to be introduced in each of the provinces, so that comprehensive protection of the right to privacy can be attained for all Canadians in dealings with all major information-gathering institutions.[49]

Finally, the point should be made here that an empirical distinction can be made between civil rights and civil liberties. The former tend to be concerned primarily with individual-to-individual relationships, whereas the latter tend to be concerned more with individual-to-state relationships. Civil liberties are thus viewed as freedom from interference or restriction by the state, and civil rights are viewed as protecting an individual from being discriminated against by another individual (as in the Civil Rights Bill in the United States).

Civil Liberties: What Are They?

Several implications derive from the fact that the BNA Act, 1867, gives Canada a constitution similar in principle to that of Britain. Because Britain's constitution reflects, or did reflect in 1867, primarily liberal democratic values, Canada also has a constitution that is democratic and predominantly liberal. Fundamental freedoms or civil liberties in Canada, therefore, can be related to either liberal values or democratic values.[50]

[49] For a detailed discussion of the protection of privacy in Canada, see G.B. Sharma, "The Protection of Personal Information by the Canadian Human Rights Act," in D.C. Rowat, ed., *The Right to Know* (Ottawa: Carleton University Press, 1980), p. 83.

[50] Note here that the constitution of Britain is also parliamentary in form. The implications of this in terms of supremacy of parliament were discussed in chapter 6.

Democratic Freedoms   These include both substantive freedoms and procedural rights, and are implicit in and necessary to a democratic system of goverment. The democratic freedoms are instrumental in realizing the basic democratic value of political equality, and they function by setting limits on governmental interference with the individual. The substantive democratic freedoms in Canada include freedom of association, freedom of assembly, freedom of expression, freedom of conscience, and freedom of the press. These are set down in section 2 of the Charter of Rights and Freedoms, under the heading "Fundamental Freedoms."

The procedural rights include freedom from arbitrary arrest, the right to a fair hearing, the right to counsel, and the right of *habeas corpus*. Moreover, they have come to include the rules of evidence that, in judicial proceedings, determine the admissibility of evidence and the determination of privileged information. As a "right to privacy" becomes more clearly articulated, the procedural right will likely be expanded to include further protection from invasions of informational privacy through electronic eavesdropping, etc. These procedural rights institutionalize the rule of law, insure "equality before the law" for all individuals, and prevent arbitrariness and discrimination on the part of governmental officials or the police. These procedural rights, or "legal rights," are enumerated in sections 7 to 14 of the Charter.

Liberal Freedoms   These are implicit in the values of liberalism, but not necessarily in the values of democracy. Where the democratic freedoms are negative, being freedom *from* government interference or hindrance, the liberal freedoms are positive, giving individuals freedom *to* do many things. In large part, these liberal freedoms deal with an individual's rights in regard to property and contract, including the right to own property, the right not to be deprived thereof except through due process of law, and the freedom of contract. While it is difficult to separate liberal freedoms from democratic freedoms in a country whose values are liberal-democratic, a possible distinction is that the former are very closely tied up with the economic system of capitalism. The liberal freedoms are therefore more important in achieving the liberal goal of a free economy than they are in achieving the democratic goals of popular sovereignty and political equality. Two aspects of these liberal rights, the freedom of movement and the right to earn a livelihood, are entrenched separately in the Charter as "mobility rights" (section 6).

Egalitarian Rights   These are the so-called "human rights," which are instrumental in achieving the goals of social and economic equality. Stated in the extreme, liberal and egalitarian values tend to conflict with each other, although, in fact, in Canada, there is gradual acceptance of limitations on the liberal freedoms to promote human rights. While the egalitarian freedoms would certainly limit governmental discrimination against classes of individuals, they also involve individual-to-individual relationships, and include freedom from discrimination in employment, accommodation, transportation, etc., by reason of race, religion, ethnic origin, or nationality.

Most Canadians would agree that these are indeed basic human rights, and egalitarianism and non-discrimination are becoming more and more important values in Canadian society. By now, all of the provinces and the federal government have human rights acts, which guarantee protection from discrimination by government agencies and private corporations alike. The Canadian Human Rights Commission, created in 1977, has as its mandate the investigation and resolution of claims of discrimination made against federal government agencies and federally incorporated companies. The Commission has been very active since its creation, and in fact has probably come a long way in discouraging would-be cases of discrimination. The Charter of Rights and Freedoms, as well, specifies equality of rights, although it does not directly protect individuals from discrimination in the private sector work place, etc. In fact, in the long run, the only effective way to eliminate discrimination is to eliminate the personal prejudices that underlie all acts of discrimination. In other words, legislation can only affect *acts* of discrimination, whereas it is the predisposition to discriminate or the discriminatory attitudes of Canadians that must ultimately be conquered if we are to eliminate the problem.[51]

Civil Liberties: Pre-Charter Protections

Before speaking of the specific legal guarantees of civil liberties in Canada, it is necessary to point out that such enactments may provide merely illusory protection. If the values reflected in the statutory and common-law statements defining our civil liberties are not congruent with the prevalent modes of thought and attitudes in the society at large, such laws will have little real effect on our substantive freedom. The best guarantee of fundamental freedom in society, therefore, is a consensus in the society as to what it is.

Federalism and Civil Liberties: 1867–1960 The principle of the supremacy of Parliament, which was discussed in some detail in Chapter 6, meant, until 1982, that nothing is beyond the legislative competence of Parliament. It meant that, at least in strictly legal terms, a majority of the members of Parliament could abrogate or abolish any civil liberties they wished to. Naturally, the normative limitations on this sort of legislative behaviour are very real, and because Canada is a federal system,[52] there are jurisdictional limitations as well. The BNA Act ostensibly divides up all legislative powers between the federal and provincial levels. The power to alter or to clarify the substance or extent of civil liberties is, therefore, also divided between the federal Parliament and the provincial legislatures.

Section 92(13) gives the provincial legislature the power to legislate upon matters dealing with "property and civil rights in the province," but because the exact scope of civil rights and liberties in this country was never clear to begin with, the exact limits of this "civil-rights power" had to be defined in piecemeal fashion as various civil-liberties cases arose. Some of the earliest of these involved

[51] See chapter 3 for a discussion of the problem of racial discrimination in Canada.

[52] See also chapter 8.

the discriminatory treatment of Orientals by certain laws in the province of British Columbia. In *Union Colliery Company of B.C. v. Bryden* (1899),[53] provincial legislation that prohibited Orientals from working in underground mines was declared invalid, not on the grounds that it was discriminatory, but because it interfered with the federal government's exclusive power to pass laws regarding "naturalization and aliens."[54] Four years later, British Columbia legislation denying naturalized Canadians of Japanese extraction the right to vote in provincial elections was upheld. The Judicial Committee of the Privy Council decided that it was quite within the rights of the provincial legislature, through section 92(1), "amendment of the provincial constitution," to pass laws, even discriminatory ones, relating to the provincial franchise: "The policy or impolicy of such an enactment as that which excludes a particular race from the franchise is not a topic which their lordships are entitled to consider."[55] Thus, early decisions relating to civil liberties were viewed entirely in terms of deciding *which* level of government had the power to interfere with them, and never whether *any* government should in fact have such power. This passivist or literalist approach to judicial interpretation has haunted Canadian constitutional development throughout our history,[56] and it has been particularly restrictive in the area of civil liberties. As J.R. Mallory has put it,

> This is not a very elevating way of looking at our much cherished liberties of speech, conscience and religion. . . . Before the enactment of the Charter, the dialogue — in constitutional terms — about basic political and civil rights was essentially confined to the narrow issue of jurisdiction.[57]

A partial breakthrough in this area was made by Chief Justice Duff in the Alberta Press Bill case (1938). The "Press Bill" was declared to be *ultra vires* the province because it was dependent upon the Alberta Social Credit Act, which had already been invalidated by Duff and his court. However, the bold lawmaking that emerged from this case was the by-product of a judicial "aside" (*obiter dictum*), which was not central to deciding the case and so could not become established as binding precedent until reinforced by further decisions. The substance of the "Duff Doctrine" established in this aside is based on the preamble to the BNA Act, which states that Canada shall have a system similar in principle to that of Great Britain. This, in turn, implies parliamentary democracy, which "contemplates a parliament working under the influence of public opinion, and public discussion,"[58] and, in effect, accepts as axiomatic that "the right to free

---

53 R.A. Olmsted, ed., *Judicial Committee Decisions Relating to the British North America Act, 1867*, vol. 1 (Ottawa: Queen's Printer, 1954), p. 443.

54 BNA Act, Section 91(25).

55 *Cunningham v. Tomey Homma* (1903), Olmsted, *op. cit.*, vol. 1, p. 484. See also *Quong Wing v. King* (1916), 49 S.C.R. 440.

56 See chapter 8.

57 See J.R. Mallory, "Evolving Canadian Constitutionalism," a research paper prepared for the MacDonald Commission (Toronto: University of Toronto Press, 1985), pp. 5–6.

58 *Reference Re Alberta Statutes*, [1939] S.C.R. 100 at. p. 133.

public discussion of public affairs, notwithstanding its incidental mischiefs, is the breath of life for parliamentary institutions."[59] Consequently, Chief Justice Duff held that:

> The parliament of Canada possesses authority to legislate for the protection of this right. . . . That authority rests upon the principle that the powers requisite for the protection of the constitution itself are, by necessity, implications from the BNA Act as a whole (Fort Frances Case, [1923] A.C. 695) and since the subject matter in relation to which the power is exercised is not exclusively a provincial matter, it is necessarily vested in Parliament.[60]

Thus, while Duff did not say that such interference with a fundamental democratic freedom was beyond the competence of *all* legislatures, in stating that it was beyond the power of the province, he definitely left the door open for future judges to view such matters as beyond the competence of the federal parliament, as well. Perhaps more important, Duff stated once and for all that any limitation on the democratic freedoms should not be applied *unequally* in different provinces.

The federal-provincial distribution of the legislative power to limit the extent of civil liberties was further developed in two important cases in the fifties. In the earlier of these, *Saumur v. City of Quebec*,[61] the validity of a city by-law that prohibited the distribution of religious pamphlets on the streets without a special permit was challenged. The legislation was declared to be valid in the lower courts and in the Supreme Court of the province, but the decision was ultimately overturned by a narrow five-to-four margin on appeal to the Supreme Court of Canada. In this judgement, four of the justices of the Supreme Court held that the Quebec by-law dealt merely with regulation and control of city streets, and therefore was valid. One judge, who had the deciding vote, as it turned out, held that the city by-law conflicted with existing provincial legislation (the Freedom of Worship Act), and was therefore invalid. He went on to declare, however, that the power to restrict freedom of religion was quite within the jurisdiction of the provincial government. The remaining four judges, among them Mr. Justice Ivan C. Rand, held that the city by-law was invalid because it interfered with the freedom of religious expression. Utilizing the preamble of the BNA Act and the "Duff Doctrine" to varying degrees in their judgements, these four judges went on to declare that legislation interfering with a freedom as fundamental as freedom of religion was beyond the competence of a provincial legislature.

In the second case, *Switzman v. Elbling* (the Padlock case),[62] legislation of the province of Quebec that banned the propagation of "Communism and Bolshevism" by closing up and padlocking any premises used for those purposes was declared invalid. While the province claimed that the legislation dealt with "property and civil rights in the province" and was therefore within its jurisdiction by section 92(13) of the BNA Act, the majority of the Supreme Court of Canada declared that the subject matter of the impugned legislation involved primarily criminal

[59] *Ibid.*
[60] *Ibid.*, p. 134.
[61] [1953] 2 S.C.R. 299.
[62] [1957] S.C.R. 356.

law, which is an exclusive federal area (section 91[27]). However, in a minority but concurring judgement, Rand, Abbott, and Kellock, three of the more liberal judges, held the act to be invalid because the provinces were not empowered to restrict the basic democratic freedom of opinion or conscience, which is implicit in the preamble to the BNA Act and in the "Duff Doctrine." They argued that such legislation could only be enacted by the federal parliament. Mr. Justice Abbott went further than this in an *obiter dictum*, stating that such fundamental freedoms were possibly even beyond encroachment by the federal parliament, although there is little indication that subsequent courts had any intention to follow his lead.[63]

Thus, through a number of cases dealing with restrictive provincial laws, the courts began to sort out the federal-provincial distribution of legislative power with regard to civil liberties. Through the federal power in the area of naturalization and aliens,[64] the criminal law power,[65] and the preamble to the BNA Act, the federal parliament was declared to have jurisdiction over many aspects of civil liberties. However, in the Tomey Homma case, the provinces were declared to have the power to discriminate against people on the basis of their racial origins, with respect to the right to vote; and in the Saumur case, a majority of the Supreme Court of Canada admitted that the provinces have the right to restrict freedom of religion. Thus, up until the passage of the Charter in 1982, the protection of these civil liberties lay almost entirely with the individual provinces. British Columbia has long since abolished its discriminatory practices and has guaranteed fundamental freedoms,[66] and while there is by no means complete uniformity from province to province, there was a general agreement in all provinces, even before the Charter, that certain rights and freedoms are too fundamental to be tampered with by any government.

Because of this vague consensus, legislative abrogation of substantive freedoms by the provinces has been rare in recent years. However, the record in terms of procedural rights and freedoms has not been as clean. There have been many specific cases, particularly in the province of Quebec, of violation of basic procedural rights, such as *habeas corpus* and freedom from arbitrary arrest,[67] and many provincial laws exist that provide for rather arbitrary search and seizure at the discretion of the police.[68] Nevertheless, with the press and the public ever more aware of their rights and freedoms, even before the Charter was proclaimed, such abuses occurred less and less frequently.

The Canadian Bill of Rights: 1960–1982 The focus of the discussion up until now has been on the distribution of legislative jurisdiction in the area of civil

---

[63] Note, however, that Mr. Justice Abbott reiterated his stand in a dissenting judgement in *Oil, Chemical and Atomic Workers International Ltd. v. Imperial Oil Ltd. and A-G. for B.C.*, [1963] S.C.R. 584.

[64] See also *Winner v. SMT*, [1951] S.C.R. 887.

[65] See also *Birks and Sons v. City of Montreal*, [1955] S.C.R. 799.

[66] For a list of federal and provincial legislation protecting human rights, see P.E. Trudeau, *A Canadian Charter of Human Rights* (Ottawa: Queen's Printers, 1968), Appendix IX.

[67] Ontario, Royal Commission Inquiry into Civil Rights, *Report*, vol. 1 (Toronto: Queen's Printer, 1968), *passim*.

[68] See, for instance, *Chaput v. Romain*, [1955] S.C.R. 834; *Lamb v. Benoit*, [1959] S.C.R. 321.

liberties, and on the civil-liberties records of the provinces. Now it is time to consider a specific federal statute that purported to protect many of our fundamental freedoms, the Canadian Bill of Rights, which was passed in 1960.

The *Canadian Bill of Rights* is divided into two parts. Part One begins with a list of "the human rights and fundamental freedoms" that exist in Canada, "without discrimination by reason of race, national origin, colour, religion or sex," and includes such things as property rights, equality before the law, freedom of religion, freedom of speech, freedom of assembly and association, and freedom of the press. The second section of Part One provides that "no law shall be construed or applied" so as to infringe on certain basic procedural rights such as freedom from arbitrary arrest, freedom from cruel punishment, the right to fair trial, the right to an interpreter, the right to be presumed innocent until proven guilty in criminal proceedings, the right to *habeas corpus* and to counsel, and the right to choose not to testify against oneself. The third section of Part One provides that the minister of justice must certify that each piece of draft legislation is consistent with the provisions of the Bill of Rights before it is introduced in the House of Commons.

Part Two of the bill states some limitations on the effect of the provisions in Part One. First, nothing in Part One can be interpreted so as to limit a right or freedom that existed before the Bill of Rights was passed. Second, Part One of the Bill is to apply to federal legislation only. It has no effect on legislation passed by a province that is within the competence of its legislature according to the BNA Act. Third, Part Two provides explicitly that

> Any act or thing done or authorized or any order or regulation made under the authority of [the War Measures Act] shall be deemed not to be an abrogation, abridgement, or infringement of any right or freedom recognized by the Canadian Bill of Rights.

The effect of this last is that the "human rights and fundamental freedoms" enumerated in the Bill of Rights become inoperative when the federal government decides that a state of national emergency exists and invokes the War Measures Act.

Whether such emergency procedures can ever be justified in a democratic political system is a question that can only be answered by trial and error. Great injustices were done to Canadians of Japanese origin during World War Two simply because Canada was at war with Japan.[69] In retrospect, this seems a shameful blot on the civil-liberties record of Canada, although at the time the government's action under the War Measures Act was probably condoned by nearly everyone except the Japanese Canadians themselves.[70] A similar interpretation appears to have developed with respect to the proclamation of the War Measures Act in the fall of 1970 because of an apparent crisis in the province of Quebec. While there was by no means unanimous agreement that the Quebec situation required such drastic measures, it would appear that a sizeable proportion of the Canadian population was, at the time, in agreement with the government's

---

[69] See [1946] S.C.R. 248 (the Japanese Canadians case).

[70] While many Canadians, particularly the CCF party, consistently opposed the treatment of the Japanese Canadians, they were definitely in the minority.

move. However, now that the "crisis" has faded, many Canadians, including many who, at the time, supported the actions of federal and Quebec authorities, look back on the FLQ emergency with something of the same sense of sheepishness or shame with which we regard the treatment of the Japanese Canadians in 1942. The only conclusion to which one can come in this regard is that if a comprehensive emergency power is to be vested in the government, and if that emergency power is to be exercised unilaterally at the discretion of the government, the public must be aware of the antidemocratic potential in such procedures.

The more fundamental question here, however, is whether a political system can permit legislation such as the War Measures Act and still remain a liberal democracy. If it is possible to conceive of circumstances when fundamental freedoms may be abrogated, then perhaps those freedoms are not so fundamental after all. Possibly, even in the most liberal societies, the stability and survival of the system becomes a more fundamental value than the substantive values implicit in the specific regime. Liberal-democratic systems are thus caught in a dilemma: on the one hand, if they do not take severe and arbitrary measures under certain circumstances, they might be taken over and replaced by an undemocratic regime; on the other hand, by taking such measures, they will be *ipso facto* less democratic themselves. There is no easy answer to this problem, but it is critical to an appraisal of the protection of civil liberties in Canada to ask the question. It is also significant that the 1982 charter does not go much further than the Bill of Rights with respect to the nature of emergency powers.

Another restriction on the effectiveness of the Bill of Rights is the implication in Part Two that the Bill can be bypassed if Parliament states explicitly that a law "shall operate notwithstanding the Bill of Rights." While Parliament seldom, if ever, actually used this power, the fact that it was written into the Bill of Rights significantly weakened its total impact.

Finally, perhaps the greatest weakness of the Bill of Rights has been the inconsistency of the Supreme Court's interpretation of it. Up until 1970, the Court took the general stand that legislation that existed prior to the Bill of Rights and that might, on the surface, appear to conflict with it must have been intended by Parliament to operate notwithstanding the Bill, or the offending legislation would have been repealed. In 1963, Mr. Justice Ritchie, in delivering the majority opinion of the Supreme Court, stated that the Bill of Rights "is not concerned with 'human rights and fundamental freedoms' as they existed in Canada immediately before the statute was enacted."[71] Furthermore, because the Bill of Rights is, in form, but another statute of the federal parliament, and because it is stated in very general terms, it was easy for the courts to interpret it in such a way that other more specific statutes are not repugnant to it.[72]

A single case in 1969 might have altered this conservative trend in interpretation to some extent. In *The Queen v. Drybones*,[73] the Supreme Court of Canada declared a section of the Indian Act invalid because it denied Indians the "equality before

---

[71] *Robertson and Rossetani v. The Queen*, [1963] S.C.R. 651, at p. 654. Note that Mr. Justice Cartwright dissented in the case and argued that all legislation of the parliament of Canada was meant to conform to the Bill of Rights.

[72] See Tarnopolsky, *The Canadian Bill of Rights*, chapter 24.

[73] *The Queen v. Drybones*, [1970] S.C.R. 282.

the law" that is guaranteed to all Canadians by the Bill of Rights. The rather timid interpretation of the Bill of Rights that the majority of the Court subscribed to in *Robertson and Rossetani* was qualified, and the Court agreed to view the Bill of Rights as having application to laws that existed before 1960. Mr. Justice Ritchie, in delivering the majority judgement, modified his conservative position in the earlier case and argued that:

> If a law of Canada cannot be sensibly construed and applied, so that it does not abrogate, abridge or infringe one of the rights and freedoms, recognized and declared by the Bill, then such law is inoperative "unless it is expressly declared by an Act of the Parliament of Canada that it shall operate notwithstanding the Canadian Bill of Rights." (p. 294)

The impugned section of the Indian Act was, therefore, declared to be inoperative because it created an offence that applied only to Indians and not to other classes of Canadian citizens.

However, some of the optimism about the applicability of the Bill of Rights that was generated by the *Drybones* decision was dashed by a 1974 decision of the Supreme Court. In *A-G. Canada v. Lavell*, the issue involved a section of the Indian Act that provides that an Indian woman who marries a white loses her status as an Indian, whereas an Indian male can marry a white woman and not only is his status unaffected but his wife acquires Indian status. Counsel for the respondent in the appeal held that the relevant sections of the Indian Act were invalid because they constituted discrimination by virtue of sex.

A majority of the Court held that the particular section of the Indian Act was indeed valid because it involved only "the internal regulation of the lives of Indians *on* reserves." The Indian Act does indeed discriminate against women, but the majority of the Court held that such discrimination did not constitute a denial of equality before the law as long as it was *applied* equally to everybody it affected (i.e., all Indians).

> The fundamental distinction between the present case and that of *Drybones*, however appears to me to be that the impugned section in the latter case could not be enforced without denying equality of treatment in the administration and enforcement of the law before the ordering courts of the land to a racial group, whereas no such inequality of treatment between Indian men and women flows as a *necessary* result of the application of s.12(1)(b) of the Indian Act.[74]

In sum, it would appear that the Supreme Court was ambivalent about the extent to which the Bill of Rights should be interpreted as rendering invalid existing federal legislation. In Lavell, the majority of the Court endorsed a retreat from the position taken in *Drybones*. The dilemma faced by the Court would seem to be a product of the various judges' perceptions of the legitimate role of the Court rather than their perceptions of the Bill of Rights itself. As Mr. Justice Abbott stated in a dissenting opinion, the Bill must have been intended as more than "rhetorical window dressing":

> The Canadian Bill of Rights has substantially affected the doctrine of the supremacy of Parliament. Like any other statute it can of course be repealed or amended,

74 [1974] S.C.R., 1354 (Mr. Justice Ritchie).

or a particular law declared to be applicable notwithstanding the provision of the Bill. In form the supremacy of Parliament is maintained but in practice I think that it has been substantially curtailed. In my opinion that result is undesirable, but that it is a matter for consideration by Parliament, not the courts. . . . Of one thing I am certain, the Bill will continue to supply ample grist to the judicial mills for some time to come.[75]

It did supply grist to the judicial mills throughout the 1970s, and although Mr. Justice (Chief Justice by 1975) Bora Laskin consistently presented articulate dissenting opinions, the Court essentially stuck to its fairly restrictive application of the Bill of Rights.[76]

Thus, the overall effect of the Bill of Rights and corresponding provincial enactments has been beneficial, in that such fundamental statements of our political values serve as symbolic objects of political socialization. Their function is as much to educate as it is to provide binding *de jure* protection of our civil liberties. In the long run, the most important sanction against repressive laws is a public opinion that is opposed to them. The danger lies in the public's ceasing to pay much attention to the government, thus letting repressive legislation slip by unnoticed, or in the majority's accepting laws that suppress the freedoms of minorities. Finally, the provision in the Bill of Rights that all federal legislation must be screened by the minister of justice before being introduced in Parliament is a sort of pre-audit, which may continue to deter the passage of new laws that are contrary to the basic values of the Canadian political culture.

The Charter of Rights and Freedoms

Perhaps the most significant aspect of the 1982 Constitution Act is the entrenchment in the Canadian constitution of a Charter of Rights and Freedoms. While the sorts of rights and freedoms so protected are not all that different from those listed in the Bill of Rights, the Charter is an improvement over the Bill because the charter applies equally to the provinces and the federal government, and is, in fact, entrenched in the sense that it can only be altered by the constitutional amendment process.

Section 2 of the Charter guarantees "fundamental freedoms," such as religion, conscience, thought, belief, expression, assembly, and association, and section 3 identifies the "democratic rights," such as the right to vote, and provides for a five-year limit on the life of a Parliament or legislature and at least one annual meeting of all legislatures. Where the Charter deviates a bit from the substance of pre-1982 rights is in the area of "mobility rights." The deviation is not, however, in the inclusion of the right of free movement of Canadian citizens, and of the corollary freedom to seek employment in any part of Canada — for such rights already existed both implicitly in the BNA Act and explicitly in common-law

---

[75] *A-G. Canada v. Lavell and Bedard.* For those interested in the detailed arguments presented in this case, both the majority judgement delivered by Mr. Justice Ritchie and a lengthy dissent delivered by Mr. Justice Bora Laskin bear careful reading. See Russell, *Leading Constitutional Decisions* (Ottawa: Carleton University Press, 1984), pp. 421–438.

[76] See, for instance: Burnshire Case [1975], 1 S.C.R. 693; Canard Case, [1976], 1 S.C.R. 170; Bliss Case [1979], 1 S.C.R., 183; and Prata Case [1976], 1 S.C.R. 376. See also Russell, *Leading Constitutional Decisions*, pp. 421–424.

jurisprudence — but in the qualifier that laws creating "local preferences" in hiring practices are exempt from this provision if unemployment in that province is above the national average.

Sections 7 to 14 guarantee "legal rights" most of which were already protected by the Bill of Rights, the Criminal Code and the British common-law precedents. The only distinctive provision with respect to legal rights is the "enforcement" section of the Charter, section 24(2), where the admissibility of evidence obtained illegally will depend upon whether "having regard to all circumstances, the admission of it in the proceedings would bring the administration of justice into disrepute." One can only expect that, before long, entire books will be able to be written about the judicial interpretation of that particular clause.

Section 15 provides for protection against racial, religious, sexual, and other kinds of discrimination, while still permitting affirmation-action programs where circumstances warrant. Official language rights are protected in sections 16 to 22, although there is little here that was not already in effect in Canada before 1982. Finally, section 23 provides for the rights of linguistic minorities to have their children educated in the language of choice, "out of public funds," "where numbers warrant."

While there are many qualifiers and exceptions written into the specific clauses of the Charter, two sections will be critical in determining the scope and impact of the Charter on Canadian society. The first of these is the *non obstante* provision in section 33, which permits Parliament or a provincial legislature to pass legislation that is to operate "notwithstanding a provision included in section 2 or sections 7-15." The impact of section 33 will ultimately depend upon the political will of legislators to utilize this power. In the first four years of the Charter's existence, there is little indication that it will be used frequently. The main use of this provision has been by the Parti Québécois government of Quebec, which passed blanket legislation exempting all of Quebec's laws from the relevant sections of the Charter. This was done, however, as a symbolic gesture disassociating the Quebec government from a constitutional evocation it did not agree to in the first place, and not as a way to bypass the explicit principles entrenched in the Charter. In fact, Quebec has its own charter, which essentially guarantees most of the rights and freedoms enumerated in the Canadian Charter.

The second clause of the Charter that will be extremely important in determining its scope is section 1, which states that the Canadian Charter of Rights and Freedoms guarantees these rights and freedoms set out in it "subject only to such reasonable limits, prescribed by law as can be demonstrably justified in a free and democratic society." By contrast to section 33 , which allows the legislature to affect the scope of the Charter, section 1 is an interpretation clause that allows the courts to endorse limits on the scope of the Charter so long as those limits are "reasonable," "prescribed by law," and "justified in a free and democratic society." Here the primary problem for the judiciary will be "to decide what is meant by reasonable, which is no mean feat, even in a specific context."[77] This

---

[77] Henri Brown, "The Canadian Charter of Rights and Freedoms as an Instrument of Social Development," in Beckton and MacKay, eds., *op. cit.*, p. 13.

doctrine of "reasonableness" has, in fact, been central to many of the Charter cases in the first four years of its operation.

One fact has emerged uncontested in the experience of the first few years of the Charter's existence, and that is that the Charter has been raised in a very large number of cases. Peter Russell estimates that "it is not far off the mark to estimate that the Charter has been raised in as many as fifteen hundred cases — forty to fifty a month — in its first three years of operation."[78] Most of these cases, naturally have been in the lower provincial courts, and most of them, as well, have involved criminal cases where the accused's lawyer has attempted to challenge the evidence on the basis of alleged procedural irregularities in the police conduct of the investigation.

Generally speaking, the Charter has not yet had a very great impact on either our system of government or the multitude of statutes currently on the books. One of the earlier cases where the Charter was involved, *Queen v. Operation Dismantle Inc.*,[79] featured the argument that the testing of the cruise missile in Canadian airspace violated our "security of the person." As such, the peace group held that the decision to allow the testing of the missile was unconstitutional. While the Supreme Court rejected this argument and dismissed the appeal, they did reject the contention that *all* such Cabinet decisions were immune to judicial review.

Early experiments with the judiciary's interpretation of the scope of the Charter indicate that "the courts will clearly put limits on the extent to which far fetched Charter claims can be used as a device to frustrate government programs."[80] But neither have they taken the approach that because something is enacted by a sovereign democratic legislature it is automatically reasonable in a free and democratic society:

> Generally Canadian judges have not taken the easy way out of giving the legislature the benefit of the doubt and presuming the legislation to be reasonable and there-fore constitutional. On the contrary they have, in effect, required the government to assume the burden of demonstrating the reasonableness of legislative limits on rights.[81]

One of the successful Charter challenges to legislation involved a new section of the Canada Elections Act, which made it an offence for private citizens and organizations to advertise independently for or against candidates or parties during a campaign. The Alberta Supreme Court held that such a restriction was not a "reasonable limit" because it could not be demonstrated that such independent participation in campaigns would damage the democratic election process.[82]

---

[78] Much of this section draws heavily on Professor Russell's excellent analysis of the first three years of the Charter. See P. Russell, "The First Three Years in Charterland," *CPA*, Fall 1985, p. 369. See also, F.L. Morton, "Chartering the Charter — Year One: A Statistical Analysis," a paper presented at CPSA Conference, 1984.

[79] [1985], 1 S.C.R.

[80] P. Russell, "The First Three Years," p. 374.

[81] *Russell*, p. 376.

[82] See *National Citizens' Coalition Inc. v. A-G. Canada*, [1984], 5 W.W.R. 436. The case was not appealed, and the impugned section was not reintroduced by the federal government with a *non obstante* clause, which would have been one way around the impasse.

A number of cases where the Charter was invoked involve a range of essentially moral issues, such as Sunday observance, abortion, and censorship. As a result of one of these cases, the *Big M Drug Mart* case,[83] the Alberta Lord's Day Act was declared to be in violation of the Charter, and therefore inoperative.[84] In an Ontario case, the parallel provincial legislation that provides for a day of rest each Sunday has also been challenged, but the decision of the Supreme Court has not yet been reported.[85]

In another case in Ontario, the powers of the Ontario Board of Censors were challenged, and the Ontario Court of Appeal upheld the decision of the lower court that the board, in fact, operated contrary to the provisions of the Charter. The case was never appealed to the Supreme Court of Canada because the provincial government changed the legislation, to bring the operation of the board in line with the provisions of the Charter.[86]

On the abortion issue, the courts have been reluctant to come down firmly on one side or the other. The Court of Queen's Bench in Saskatchewan held that a foetus is not included in the term "everyone" and therefore does not have the rights prescribed in section 7 of the Charter.[87] On the other side, a judge of the Ontario High Court of Justice rejected the claim that "liberty and security of the person" includes the right to have an abortion.[88] As Peter Russell wryly put it, "Canadian judges seem no more anxious than politicians to become involved in reforming abortion law."[89]

Perhaps the area where the affect of the Charter on legislation has been the most profound is that of language-education rights. Key sections of the Quebec Charter of the French Language were thrown out because they violated the rights of English Canadians under section 23 of the Charter of Rights.[90] In another case, the Ontario Court of Appeal upheld the rights of Franco-Ontarians to education in their own language.[91] Thus, the courts have given a clear signal in this area that they intend to take an active role in applying the Charter to language and education matters.

Finally, one of the fears of the critics of the Charter was that Canada could end up with a situation similar to the one in the United States, where obviously guilty criminals elude conviction because of technical violations of the rights of the accused. It would appear that, for the most part, these fears were unfounded, for while there have been some successful challenges of criminal procedure on the basis of the Charter, judges have generally taken a fairly generous view of what is reasonable in such cases. With respect to the admissibility of evidence, judges have tended to shift the burden of proof, so that the defence must show that to

---

[83] [1983] 5 D.L.R., 4th, 121.

[84] [1985] 1 S.C.R.

[85] See *R. v. Videoflicks Ltd.*, 12 W.C.B. 468 (cited in Russell, "The First Three Years," p. 380).

[86] *Ontario Film and Video Appreciation Society v. Ontario Board of Censors* [1983], 147 D.L.R. (3d) 58.

[87] *Borowski v. A-G. Canada* [1983], 4 D.L.R. (4th) 112.

[88] *R. v. Morgantaler* [1985], 12 D.L.R., 4, 502. All cited in Russell *op. cit.*

[89] Russell, "The First Three Years," p. 381.

[90] *A.G. Quebec v. Quebec Assoc. of Protestant School Boards* [1984], 10 D.L.R. (4th) 321.

[91] Reference Re Education Act of Ontario (1984) 10 D.L.R. (4th), p. 491.

admit the evidence would "bring the administration of justice into disrepute" to the accused.[92]

By way of summary, the first few years of the Charter indicate that "it has turned out to be not nearly as bad as opponents feared it might be nor nearly as great as its promoters promised it would be." [93] However, it is clear, as well, that "the court cases decided in the Charter's first three years clearly indicate that the Canadian Charter of Rights and Freedoms will have a greater influence on the way Canada is governed than did the Canadian Bill of Rights."[94] Moreover, while the direct impact of the Charter through its application by the courts may not be as extensive as expected, it has undoubtedly had an impact on the attitudes of the lawmakers themselves. All governments have been engaged in an ongoing process of auditing their existing laws with a view to bringing them in line with the provisions of the equality-rights section of the Charter when it came into effect in April 1985. As well, because the Charter is there and being applied by the courts, legislators screen all new policy proposals, to insure that the enactments fall within the boundaries defined by the Charter.

Finally, as a general conclusion to this discussion of the protection of civil liberties in Canada, it is necessary to qualify all that we have said about the formal, institutionalized, and entrenched devices for protecting the rights and freedoms of Canadians. While such institutional guarantees are important in that they may deter those who would try to abuse our freedoms, their more important role is as symbolic and educative devices. Legislation such as the Bill of Rights, the Canadian Human Rights Act, and the Charter of Rights and Freedoms is significant because it teaches Canadians about the value of civil liberties and about the importance of non-discrimination. In the final analysis, it is the values and attitudes of Canadians that determine the kind of society we are going to live in, and the symbolic role formal statements and guarantees of civil liberties play in the process of political socialization may be more important than the positive law remedies that are set down in such enactments.

Finally, it must also be emphasized that it is the values and attitudes of governmental officials, and particularly the police and national security investigators, that are most important in determining the extent of our freedoms and the quality of life in Canada. It is essential that we begin to pay more attention to the recruitment and training of police and security officials, to insure that people with deep prejudices, closed minds, or little tolerance are not given the sorts of wide discretionary powers that we have traditionally vested in members of the law-enforcement community. If it is desirable to reduce prejudice and intolerance in all Canadians, it is absolutely *imperative* that it be eliminated from the ranks of our law-enforcement officers, national security investigators, and those government officials who deal with the public directly. The noblest sentiments expressed in a charter of rights come to naught if the public officials implementing and enforcing our laws don't share those sentiments.

---

[92] Russell, "The First Three Years," p. 392.

[93] Russell, p. 368.

[94] Russell, p. 394.

PART 3

THE HISTORICAL ENVIRONMENT OF CANADIAN FEDERALISM

C H A P T E R 8

CONSTITUTIONAL DEVELOPMENT AND CANADIAN FEDERALISM

THE HISTORICAL ROOTS OF BRITISH NORTH AMERICAN UNION
- The Genesis of Federal Union
- The Distribution of Powers: Canadian Federalism in 1867
THE EVOLUTION OF CANADIAN FEDERALISM
- The Erosion of the Federal Power: The Judicial Committee and the BNA Act
- The Supreme Court of Canada and the BNA Act, 1949–1982
- The Supreme Court in the 1980s: A New Role?

T he Dominion of Canada came into existence with the passage of the British North America Act in 1867. Although this historic document is an act of the parliament of the United Kingdom, it was passed at the request of the British North American colonies themselves. The details of the legislation were largely based on resolutions that had been put forward jointly by the colonies, and which had been worked out over a number of years of bargaining and compromise at several colonial conferences.[1] Originally, the deliberations had included all of the British North American colonies, but Newfoundland and Prince Edward Island soon lost their enthusiasm, and it was left to the remaining colonies — Upper and Lower Canada, New Brunswick, and Nova Scotia — to come to an agreement on the terms of the union. Once the agreement had been thrashed out, it was a relatively simple matter for Britain's parliament to put it into the form of a statute, which came into effect on July 1, 1867.

---

[1] For an account of these conferences, see G.P. Browne, ed., *Documents on the Confederation of British North America* (Toronto McClelland and Stewart, 1969), p. 40.

THE HISTORICAL ROOTS OF
BRITISH NORTH AMERICAN UNION

In the mid-nineteenth century, as today, the most significant factor in the environment of the Canadian political system was the proximity of the United States. In the 1860s, awareness of this fact was heightened by a number of events that gave people in the British North American colonies cause to fear direct military invasion from the south. At the conclusion of the American Civil War, the Union Army was the most powerful and advanced fighting machine in the world.[2] Furthermore, incidents during the war — for example, the St. Alban's raid in 1864 and the activities of the British-built Confederate cruiser, the *Alabama* — had incurred the displeasure of the United States.[3] At the conclusion of the war, the American press was advocating the invasion of Canada, and there was a great fear in Canada that the newspapers would arouse sufficient public pressure to convince Congress and the president that invasion was, indeed, a good idea.[4]

The sense of danger was heightened by the militant activities of an American wing of an Irish nationalist organization called the Fenian Brotherhood. The Fenians attracted large numbers of Irish veterans of the Civil War who were happy to re-enlist in this unofficial army to free Ireland from "English tyranny."[5] One of the ways in which they hoped to achieve this was by conquering Canada. Their sundry pronouncements and the publicity they gained were received with trepidation in Canada. The subsequent "invasions" of British North America by the Fenians were, in retrospect, more comic opera than threatening, and all were repulsed by the Canadians without serious difficulty. But while the menace the Fenians presented to Canada was exaggerated, when it was added to the existing evidence of an American predisposition to continental imperialism, it did reinforce Canadian perceptions of a military threat from the south.[6]

While Canadians grew increasingly alarmed at the sabre rattling in the United States, the British, who had formerly taken much of the responsibility for defending their North American colonies, began to give every indication that they were no longer willing to go very far in that enterprise. Politicians in Britain began to speak of the necessity of shifting the responsibility for colonial defence to the colonies, and the British Cabinet was not overly generous in its budgeting for such things as the fortifications of Quebec. Thus, while the Canadians were looking apprehensively at the military might of the United States, "there was remarkably little evidence of a sense of acute peril, of desperate urgency, in Great Britain."[7]

---

[2] D. Creighton, *The Young Politician*, vol. 1 of *John A. Macdonald* (Toronto: Macmillan, 1952), pp. 409–410.

[3] See Creighton, *The Young Politician*, pp. 385–430, *passim*; Creighton, *The Road to Confederation* (Toronto: Macmillan, 1964), pp. 194–195; and W.L. Morton, *The Critical Years* (Toronto: McClelland and Stewart, 1964), p. 185.

[4] Creighton, *The Young Politician*, and Dawson, *The Government of Canada*, p. 21.

[5] Creighton, *The Young Politician*, pp. 405-406.

[6] The best source of information on this period in Canadian history is an article by C.P. Storey, "Fenianism and the Rise of National Feeling in Canada at the time of Confederation," *Canadian Historical Review*, vol. 12, September, 1931, pp. 238–261. See also Morton, *The Critical Years*, pp. 195–196.

[7] Creighton, *The Young Politician*, pp. 405–406.

Economic factors also helped in setting the stage for Confederation. Again, the United States played a starring role. The immediate economic problems of the British North American colonies actually dated back to 1846, when the navigation laws, which gave preferential treatment to colonial trade, were repealed by Britain. However, the negative effect of the repeal had been offset somewhat at the time by a reciprocity agreement with the United States that allowed Canadian primary products duty-free access to U.S. markets. In the 1860s, partly because of generally bad British-American relations and partly because of economic pressures at home, the United States served notice of its intention to terminate the reciprocity agreement. Reciprocity finally was terminated in 1866, at a time when Britain seemed more committed than ever to a policy of free trade. Thus, excluded from the American market and forced to compete with more advanced economies in the open British market, the British North American colonies looked at last to each other:

> If preferences in Britain and the United States were not to be had, the colonies could at least give preference to each other. Commercial union of the British American provinces would weld them into a single vast trading area within which products might be freely exchanged. If the markets of all the provinces could be opened to the industries of each, an economic system would be created, which, by lessening dependence on external markets,would offer greater stability than the economies of the separate provinces could hope for, and which, because of the diversity and complementarity of its resources, would have a potential for growth.[8]

Technological changes probably also helped to accelerate the movement towards Confederation, because the colonial economies were strained by the costs of taking full advantage of technology. The shift from sail to steam and from canals to railways, for instance, forced the colonies, especially the Maritimes, to incur large provincial debts:

> By incurring debts to build the railways which they so earnestly desired, the Maritime provinces had, as it were, given hostages to fortune. By increasing the burden of fixed charges on their revenues, they had curtailed their ability to withstand adversity.[9]

Thus, a commercial union offered Nova Scotia and New Brunswick not merely the hope of new markets in the Canadas, but also the promise of a share of national revenues, which would ease the burden of their debts. To insure that the Maritimes did, in fact, gain markets in central Canada, a very specific provision for the construction of the Intercolonial Railway was written into the BNA Act:

> It shall be the duty of the Parliament of Canada to provide for the commencement within six months after the Union of a railway connecting the River St. Lawrence with the city of Halifax in Nova Scotia and for the construction thereof without intermission, and the completion thereof with all practicable speed.[10]

---

[8] W. T. Easterbrook and H. G. J. Aitken, *Canadian Economic History* (Toronto: Macmillan, 1965), p. 251; see also D. Creighton, *British North America at Confederation* (Ottawa: Queen's Printer, 1963).

[9] Easterbrook and Aitken, *Canadian Economic History*, p. 250. Both quotes reprinted by permission of Macmillan of Canada, A Division of Canada Publishing Corporation.

[10] BNA Act, 1867, part X, section 145. This section was deleted from the act in 1893.

While the promise of the Intercolonial Railway looks very much like a simple bribe to entice the Maritimes into the Federation it can be argued that the Canadas also could anticipate certain advantages from the railway. As well as facilitating interprovincial trade, the Intercolonial Railway would provide exporters in Ontario and Quebec with an ice-free port in the winter months, when Quebec City and Montreal were normally closed.[11] This was an important consideration, for Canadian businessmen feared that the abrogation of the reciprocity agreement by the United States might close the winter ports on the U.S. eastern seaboard to Canadian exporters. The Maritimers certainly welcomed the opportunity to handle the trans-shipment of Canadian goods, in the winter months, through the ports of Halifax and Saint John.

Political factors also pushed the colonies towards Confederation. A union formed in 1841 had tied Upper and Lower Canada in an uneasy political marriage, but was no longer tolerable. The 1841 Act of Union had guaranteed equal representation in the colonial legislature to Canada East and Canada West, and by the 1860s, the population of Canada West (now Ontario), which was originally smaller than the population of Canada East (now Quebec), had been greatly increased by an influx of immigrants. Once the people of Canada West realized that the guarantee of equal representation was working against them, they began to agitate for "representation by population." The French Canadians of Canada East countered with demands for guarantees of their rights as a linguistic, religious, and ethnic minority. The colonial government was left in a virtually permanent stalemate. Impetus was added by the deadlock in the legislature of the United Canadas; for Confederation, whatever its faults, offered a viable solution by providing for the separation of the Canadas into two provinces within the larger union.

When we view the history of the Confederation period in Canada, it becomes clear that the section of North America that was to become the province of Ontario had more to gain from union than any other. In fact, as D.V. Smiley points out:

> The complicated compromise which was finally embodied in the British North America Act reflected in large part the aspirations and interests of that populous, prosperous and dynamic region, with such concessions to Lower Canada and the Maritimes as were necessary to gain the support of their leaders for union.[12]

The Maritimes saw certain economic advantages in Confederation, but a large proportion of the people living in New Brunswick and Nova Scotia were fervently opposed to any agreement that tied them to Canada. It can even be argued that the Maritimes were never really in favour of Confederation, and were railroaded into it by complicated political manoeuvring, the silver tongue of Sir John A. Macdonald, and the promise of a railway. French-Canadian politicians saw Confederation as a way of safeguarding their language and religious rights and, on the whole, as a lesser evil than the Union of 1841.

---

[11] Easterbrook and Aitken, *Canadian Economic History*, p. 249.

[12] D. V. Smiley, *The Canadian Political Nationality* (Toronto: Methuen, 1967), pp. 13–14.

Generally, it can be concluded that there was little common purpose, no vision of greatness, and no noble cause that united Canada initially. Perhaps, as Professor Smiley points out:

> The underlying agreement among colonial politicians which made Confederation possible was that the continuance of monarchial and parliamentary institutions and of the British connection was infinitely preferable to absorption into the U.S.[13]

But this is a very negative motivation for national unity, and it must be asked whether fear of invasion can ever produce any lasting unity among people. P.B. Waite makes this point when he refers to the Fenian raids:

> Fenianism could not itself create a British American national identity. . . . The effects of the Fenian invasion were direct and immediate, but like all negative effects, once removed, the elements in North America tended to revert to their original state.[14]

Thus, to return to the original query as to what motivated the British colonies in North America to seek a union of some kind, one finds a generally negative and unstable set of attitudes towards Confederation in 1867. Apparently abandoned by the mother country and left prey to the military and economic might of the war-torn but brawny United States, the British North American colonies turned, in desperation, to each other.

The Genesis of Federal Union

Having described the hesitant and uncertain way in which the colonies finally reached an agreement that *some* form of union was desirable for British North America, let us deal with the forces and events that influenced the decision that the union should be *federal* in form. The social, economic, and ethnic diversity of the colonies made a unitary form of government, or "legislative union," as it was then called, completely unacceptable to the Maritimes and Quebec, although evidence indicates that Macdonald and many of his Upper Canadian colleagues preferred this alternative.[15] Quebec wished to preserve its unique linguistic, religious, and cultural character, and the Maritimes wished to insure that the peculiar economic needs of their region be provided for. All provinces wished to retain control over matters that would allow them to preserve their local character and institutions. Provincial autonomy, therefore, had to be protected within any form of British North American union before the Maritimes and Quebec would agree to a union.

Given the obvious differences that existed among the founding provinces, the Fathers of Confederation realized that a legislative union was not a viable alternative for British North America. Furthermore, it was hoped that Prince Edward Island, British Columbia, Newfoundland, and the Northwest could subsequently

[13] Smiley, p. 2.

[14] P. B. Waite, *The Life and Times of Confederation* (Toronto University of Toronto Press, 1962), p. 281.

[15] Creighton, *The Young Politician*, chapters 14 and 15.

be lured into the union of 1867, in which case the regional and economic diversity of Canada would increase rather than diminish. Even Sir John A. Macdonald recognized that there could be no union *a mare usque ad mare* unless the provinces were left some degree of local autonomy:

> Macdonald argued the case for a legislative rather than a federal union, yet geography, provincial identities and Quebec separateness united to confound his principle. He was deftly persuaded from his folly.[16]

It was therefore incumbent upon the Fathers of Confederation to work out a distribution of powers between the provinces and the federal government.

The alternative of an economic and military *alliance* of the British North American colonies was initially considered as a form of union that would go a long way towards solving the immediate problems of the 1860s. At both the Charlottetown and Quebec conferences, a British North American customs union, or *Zollverein*, was suggested — an innocuous form of union that would leave the sovereignty of the members intact. Neither a customs union nor a military alliance, however, would have provided a permanent central decision-making body or a central enforcement mechanism. Since there would be no derogation of the sovereignty of the signatories of the treaty or alliance, the alliance itself would be powerless to enforce its own provisions. Furthermore, such a weak form of union would have been ineffectual in financing the joint defence or economic programs of the union. A project such as the Intercolonial Railway, for instance, would have been out of the question. Sir John A. Macdonald recognized the inadvisability of a customs union, and suggested that, because of the potential economic conflicts between the colonies, it would not be congenial to all its members: "It is impossible to have a *Zollverein*. We must continue to have hostile tariffs unless we have a political union."[17]

A second major disadvantage of any form of union less than political union is that it would lack permanence. Members would have the right to withdraw from it at any time if they felt that its terms were no longer advantageous. It was obvious that if the economic and military problems of British North America were to be solved, they would have to be dealt with continuously over a long period of time. It was not possible to find immediate cures for the ills of the colonies, and therefore a form of union that was not for keeps would not be acceptable.

The third drawback of a simple alliance of the British North American colonies was that an alliance is *functionally specific*. In other words, the terms of reference or functions of the alliance are set very specifically at the outset in such a way that new needs of the members of the alliance cannot be dealt with without renegotiating the original agreement. In a rapidly changing world, a form of union that could adapt itself quickly to the performance of new functions was viewed as imperative.

There were other objections to a non-political union, such as the fact that a mere alliance would not satisfy the need for Canada East and Canada West to be separated, and the legalistic point that colonies within the British empire were

---

[16] Rod Preece, "The Political Wisdom of Sir John A. Macdonald," *CJPS*, September 1984, p. 479.

[17] Browne, *Documents on the Confederation*, p. 96.

not sovereign and therefore could not enter into alliances unilaterally, even with sister colonies. These objections were secondary, however, and could have been overcome had the notion of an economic and military alliance been otherwise acceptable.

A *confederal* union was also an alternative for the British North American colonies, but when this form of union was subjected to scrutiny, it was recognized that a confederation[18] would provide only a slightly higher level of political integration than an alliance. A confederation is a union of sovereign states that features a permanent central decision-making body, or congress, to which the members of the confederation send delegates. In terms of the functions with which it deals, a confederation is considerably broader than an alliance, for the central congress is empowered to make decisions concerning a very wide range of subjects. The weakness of a confederation is that, as with an alliance, there is no transfer of sovereignty from the member states to the central congress. While empowered to make decisions, the congress is given no power to enforce them, and the members of the confederation can, if they choose, refuse to comply with any decision with which they disagree. The parties to a confederal agreement also have the right to secede from the union if they feel that its terms of reference no longer provide sufficient benefits. Thus, while the confederal form of union is functionally more diffuse than an alliance, it suffers from many of the same faults. Furthermore, the example of the United States under the Articles of Confederation in the 1780s, with the chaotic condition of government during that period, gave the Fathers of Confederation ample cause for avoiding that particular form of union.

A *federal* form of union was ultimately decided upon by the Fathers of Confederation because, unlike either an alliance or a confederal union, it vested real powers in the hands of a central decision-making body, the federal parliament. In a federal system, sovereignty is divided between the provinces and the federal parliament, and the exercise of legislative and executive powers of each is limited to subject matters allotted to them by the constitution. A federal system is also permanent, in the sense that the member states or provinces do not have the constitutional right to withdraw unilaterally from the union. This prohibition might, of course, be swept aside very quickly if the people of a member state or province were determined to secede from the union. In law, however, a federal union is indivisible.

The constitution of the federal system distributes the power and the responsibility for the authoritative allocation of resources between the provinces and the federal government, and that constitutional distribution of powers is exhaustive (with the possible exception today of basic rights and freedoms, which are entrenched in the Charter).[19] In a confederal union, on the other hand, it is simply assumed that the state or provincial governments have the responsibility for everything except

---

[18] "The term 'Confederation,' when applied to the Canadian union of 1867, is a misnomer, for the form of government set up by the BNA Act is definitely not 'confederal.' 'Confederation,' a word normally associated with the absence of a strong federal government, was deliberately misused by those who, in fact, intended to create one in an effort to confuse those who might find such a project alarming." (G. Stevenson, *Unfulfilled Union*, p. 9).

[19] See chapter 7.

a few matters that are specifically the responsibility of the confederation. In other words, in the case of a confederation, the *residual power* is always left with the states, and constitutes a very large area of jurisdiction; whereas in the case of a federal system, the residual power can be left with either the provinces or the federal government, and the residual area of jurisdiction is, in fact, very small. The advantage of such a comprehensive definition of the powers and responsibilities of government is that the element of uncertainty is eliminated. The federal government and the provincial or state governments are each in possession of exclusive and sovereign powers that cannot be encroached upon by the other level of government. Unlike the central congress in a confederal union, the national government in a federal union has the authority to make some decisions that are binding on the citizens of the member states, and furthermore, it is granted the power to enforce them.

Finally, a federal form of government was adopted by the Fathers of Confederation because they hoped to create a union that would eventually become more than a marriage of economic expedience and military convenience. People like Sir John A. Macdonald wished to create a new political community in North America, and it is largely to their credit that Canada has evolved as more than merely a temporary association of friendly but independent neighbours.

> That Canada exists today is probably the result of the effort and determination of Sir John A. Macdonald more than any other man. . . . It was he who provided the most determined leadership and who went on after the political framework of federation was accomplished to endow Canada with . . . nationhood.[20]

Thus, the fact that the form of union ultimately selected by the Fathers of Confederation was federal and not confederal was, to a large part, due to the political genius, vision, and ambition of Macdonald. The actual shape of our federal system and the idiosyncrasies that make Canadian federalism a genre apart also bear the stamp of Macdonald's personality, and of his view of the ideal relationship that should exist between the provinces and the national government in a federal system.

Having in mind the then-recent and tragic experiences of the Civil War in the United States, Macdonald wanted to see as centralized a federal system as the provinces would accept: "We should concentrate the power in the federal government and not adopt the decentralization of the United States."[21] In fact, there is some evidence that Macdonald viewed federalism as a temporary arrangement to secure initial unity, and that he fully expected provincial governments to wither away from lack of exercise, leaving a basically unitary system in Canada. Some aspects of the BNA Act, 1867 do indeed indicate that the intention of the drafters of the act was to leave the preponderance of legislative power with Ottawa.[22] But in spite of these biases, the British North America Act does vest

---

[20] Paul Martin, *Hansard*, Wednesday, January 11, 1967, pp. 11651.

[21] Browne, *Documents on the Confederation*, p. 124.

[22] W. L. Morton describes the union as ". . . a scheme of legislative union in a federal guise . . .": *The Critical Years* (McClelland and Stewart, 1964), p. 68, see also R. C. Vipond, "Constitutional Politics and the Legacy of the Provincial Rights Movement in Canada," *CJPS.*, June 1985, pp. 271–275.

some significant legislative power in the provinces. One eminent political scientist has asserted: "The provinces are of equal constitutional power and status, and they operate without any serious interference from the Dominion. . . . Provincial powers are as full and complete as those of the Dominion within the areas allotted by the BNA Act."[23]

The Distribution of Powers: Canadian Federalism in 1867

The legislative powers of the federal parliament are, for the most part, defined in section 91 of the BNA Act, 1867. Section 91 is in two parts. The first part is a broad and general grant of power, giving Parliament the authority to make laws for "the Peace, Order, and Good Government of Canada in relation to all Matters not coming within the Classes of Subjects by this Act assigned exclusively to the Legislatures of the Provinces." The second part of section 91 included twenty-nine (now thirty-one) enumerated matters such as "the Public Debt and Property," "the Regulation of Trade and Commerce," "the Raising of Money by any Mode or System of Taxation," etc., which were intended "for greater Certainty, but not so as to restrict the Generality of the foregoing Terms of this Section."

The legislative powers of the provinces are for the most part set out in section 92 of the Act, which has the appearance of being a far less complicated section than 91. Section 92 does not begin with any comprehensive grant of power to the provinces, but simply states that, "In each Province, the Legislature may exclusively make Laws in relation to Matters coming within the Classes of Subjects next herein-after enumerated," and then proceeds to list sixteen matters such as "Direct Taxation within the Province in order to the raising of a Revenue for Provincial Purposes," "the Solemnization of Marriage in the Province," "Property and Civil Rights in the Province," and "Generally all Matters of a merely local or private Nature in the Province." Thus, when sections 91 and 92 are read together, it is clear that the intention is to give the federal government a comprehensive power to make law and then to except from this general grant certain carefully specified powers, which are to be retained by provincial legislatures.[24]

Section 95 established concurrent federal-provincial powers in matters of agriculture and immigration, and amendments to the Act in 1951 and 1964 added a third concurrent power in the area of pensions. While establishing the right of both levels of government to make laws with regards to the specified subjects, the section establishes federal *paramountcy* in the case of conflicting legislation dealing with agriculture and immigration:

> Any Law of the Legislature of a Province relative to Agriculture or to Immigration shall have effect in and for the Province as long and as far only as it is not repugnant to any Act of the Parliament of Canada.

---

[23] Dawson, *The Government of Canada*, p. 78.

[24] The manner in which the Judicial Committee of the Privy Council interpreted these sections will be discussed in the next part of this chapter.

In the area of pensions, the federal government is given the power to

> make laws in relation to old age pensions and supplementary benefits including survivor's and disability benefits irrespective of age.

But in this case provincial legislation is to be paramount.

The subject of education is normally considered to rest within the exclusive jurisdiction of the provincial legislatures by section 93 of the Act. However, section 93 places certain limitations and conditions on the exercise of this power by the provinces. First, it states no provincial law shall "prejudicially affect any right or privilege with respect to denominational schools" that existed at the time of union. Second, it states that the rights of separate schools in Upper Canada shall continue after the union and shall apply equally to Protestant separate schools in Lower Canada. The third clause of section 93 establishes a right of appeal to the Governor-General in Council if the education rights of a Protestant or Catholic minority are abrogated by a provincial legislature. Finally, in the event that the province does not respond positively to an appeal that is allowed by the Governor-General in Council, provision is made for the parliament of Canada to "make remedial Laws for the due Execution of the Provisions of this Section."[25]

The significance of this section of the BNA Act is that it makes the federal government a policeman, with the power and the responsibility to protect the education rights of religious minorities from encroachment by the provinces. This has proved an awkward burden for the federal government to bear, from time to time, for in protecting the rights of a minority, the federal government is forced to interfere with the autonomy of the provinces. If the federal government doesn't act, it is damned by the minority concerned; if it does act, it is damned by the province concerned. We have already seen that one such dilemma, commonly referred to as the Manitoba Schools question, played a significant role in the downfall of the Conservative government in the election of 1896.[26] More recently, Bill 101 (1977), Quebec legislation restricting the access of non-French-speaking residents of Quebec to English-language education, posed a somewhat similar problem for the federal government, but the constitutional protection in section 93 is intended for *religious* education rights, rather than the *linguistic* rights most directly involved in the Bill 101 case.[27]

Finally, by section 109 the provinces are granted full title to "all Lands, Mines, Minerals, and Royalties" within their boundaries, a concession that was not viewed as very important in the pre-petroleum era. When the western provinces came into the federation, the title to Crown lands was retained by the federal Crown until provincial pressures forced Ottawa to give them up in 1930. This control over Crown land, and therefore over non-renewable natural resources, has proven to be one of the major foundations of province building in the twentieth century, and has been the major source of provincial power since World War Two.

---

[25] BNA Act, S. 93(4).

[26] See chapter 3.

[27] As we have seen in chapter 7, the offensive sections of Bill 101 were overturned by the Supreme Court of Canada in 1984.

A specific grant of federal legislative competence is specified by section 132, which states that the parliament of Canada

shall have all Powers necessary or proper for performing the Obligations of Canada or any Province thereof as Part of the British Empire towards Foreign Countries arising under Treaties between the Empire and such Foreign Countries.

This particular clause and the manner in which the courts have interpreted it will be discussed at greater length later.

Finally, to round out this snapshot of Canadian federalism at the time of Confederation, the federal government's power over the legislatures of the provinces contained in the *reservation* and *disallowance* provisions of the BNA Act must be mentioned. The power formally vested in the central government by these provisions amounts to a federal veto that may be applied to any act of the provincial legislatures. Through the Lieutenant Governor of the province, who was to function relative to the Governor-General as the pre-Confederation colonial governor functioned relative to the British government, it was intended that the federal government would be enabled to keep a tight rein on all provincial legislation. The Lieutenant Governor has the power to reserve a bill "for the pleasure of the Governor General in Council," after which, if no positive action is taken by the federal official, the bill is dead. In the case of the disallowance power, the federal government can unilaterally invalidate any provincial law within a year of its passage. These powers, the reservation and disallowance, were used extensively before the turn of the century, and then intermittently until the forties, when the last disallowance was recorded. Today, they have become vestigial appendages in a federal system that has evolved past the stage where such heavy handed devices are politically feasible.

Thus, the Canadian federal system at Confederation gave the lion's share of the legislative power to the federal government, established the principle of federal paramountcy in areas of concurrent jurisdiction, set up the federal government as a policeman in the area of the education rights of religious minorities, and, just to make sure nothing had been forgotten, gave the federal government a veto power over all provincial enactments.

Had the spirit of the BNA Act of 1867 been upheld in subsequent judicial decisions, our federal system would look very different than it does today. However, for a variety of reasons, that spirit was not upheld. To see the results, let us trace the development of Canadian federalism from its beginning as a highly centralized form of union to the form it takes today.

THE EVOLUTION OF CANADIAN FEDERALISM

The literature of Canadian constitutional law is replete with articles on the interpretation of sections 91 and 92 of the BNA Act by the Judicial Committee of the Privy Council. Some commentators approve and others strongly disapprove,[28]

---

[28] See, for instance, Kennedy, "Interpretation of the BNA Act," *Cambridge Law Journal*, vol. 8, p. 146; Macdonald, "The Constitution in a Changing World," *Canadian Bar Review*, vol. 26, 1948, p. 21; O'Connor, *Report to the Senate of Canada on the BNA Act*, annex 1, p. 25, 1939; Bora Laskin, "Peace, Order and Good Government Reexamined," in Lederman, *The Courts and the Canadian Constitution* (Toronto: McClelland and Stewart, 164), p. 66n. The best single article on the subject for political scientists is Alan

but virtually all are agreed that, in the process of interpreting the Act, the Judicial Committee significantly altered its effect. From the highly centralist document of 1867, the British North America Act was transformed, by the incremental process of judicial review, into a more truly federal constitution, which vests extensive legislative authority in the hands of the provinces. All of this was accomplished by a succession of British law lords, who took upon themselves the task of defending provincial autonomy, often at some cost to the English language, which had to be tortured until it met their requirements. In order to beef up the legislative competence of the provinces, the Judicial Committee developed certain principles of interpretation that explain the often puzzling construction placed on the crucial sections 91 and 92.

The Erosion of the Federal Power: The Judicial Committee and the BNA Act

The thin edge of the wedge that opened the way for a provincial-rights inter-pretation of sections 91 and 92 was the series of opinions that separated the peace, order, and good-government clause of section 91 from the twenty-nine enumerated subheadings of that section. This principle was initially conceived by Sir Montague Smith in the *Parsons* case in 1881,[29] and re-emphasized by Lord Watson in the *Local Prohibition* case (1896).[30] Lord Watson went a step further, placing the general part of section 91 in a position secondary and subor-dinate to the enumerated subheads of both sections 91 and 92:

> The exercise of legislative power by the parliament of Canada, in regard to all matters not enumerated in s. 91, ought to be strictly confined to such matters as are unquestionably of Canadian interest and importance, and ought not to trench upon provincial legislation with respect to any of the classes of subjects enumerated in s. 92. To attach any other construction to the general power which in supplement of its enumerated powers is conferred upon the parliament of Canada by s. 91 would, in their Lordships' opinion, not only be contrary to the intendment of the act but would practically destroy the autonomy of the provinces. If it were once conceded that the parliament of Canada has authority to make laws applicable to the whole Dominion in relation to matters which in each province are substantially of local or private interest, upon the assumption that these matters also concern the peace, order and good government of the Dominion, there is hardly a subject enumerated in s. 92 upon which it might not legislate to the exclusion of the provincial legislatures.[31]

Thus, by 1896, section 91 had been interpreted by the Judicial Committee of the Privy Council in such a way that the once proud peace, order, and good-government clause gave no exclusive jurisdiction to the federal parliament, but rather only a residual power, which permitted federal legislation with regard to a

Cairns, "The Judicial Committee and Its Critics," *Canadian Journal of Political Science,* IV, September 1971, pp. 301–345.

[29] *Citizens Insurance Company of Canada v. Parsons,* 7 *Appeal Cases* (A.C.) 96.

[30] *Attorney-General for Ontario v. Attorney-General of Canada* (1896) *A.C.* 348; also known as "the Local Prohibition case."

[31] *Ibid.,* p. 360.

few matters that could be found neither in the enumerated subheads of section 91 nor in section 92. The federal parliament now enjoyed exclusive jurisdiction only with regard to matters that came under the enumerated subheads of section 91, despite the fact that the drafters of the BNA Act had anticipated that the general grant of authority at the beginning of section 91 would put the largest part of the responsibilities of government in the hands of the central parliament.[32]

This narrow construction of the peace, order, and good-government clause evolved in spite of the fact that there were earlier decisions that upheld the more generous view of this clause. In the *Russell v. the Queen* decision in 1882, federal legislation that provided for local prohibition subject to local option was upheld by the Judicial Committee on the grounds that liquor control was a subject matter not enumerated in section 92, and therefore the federal parliament had jurisdiction through the peace, order, and good-government clause. Had the principles of interpretation that were employed in this case been followed in subsequent cases, the federal power to pass laws for the peace, order, and good government of Canada might have developed along the lines anticipated by the Fathers of Confederation. However, this was not to be.

In 1883, in a decision that involved the power of the provinces to regulate the liquor trade, their lordships invented another canon of interpretation, which has come to be known as the *aspect doctrine*.[33] In the case in point, the appellant was fined for an offence under an Ontario act that regulated liquor traffic in the province. He argued that the conviction was invalid because the regulation of the traffic of liquor was a federal matter, which concerned the peace, order, and good government of Canada, and he cited the *Russell* case as a precedent. In delivering the judgement of the Judicial Committee, Lord Fitzgerald held that the Ontario act was *intra vires* because it involved matters that are clearly enumerated in section 92. He went on to state that the *Russell* case did not apply because the federal legislation that was validated in that decision involved another aspect of the regulation of the liquor traffic: "Subjects which in one aspect and for one purpose fall within section 92, may in another purpose fall within section 91."[34] In this way, with the birth of the aspect doctrine, the tide was turned, and the decision in the *Russell* case never did gain the respectability as a precedent that would have ensured expansion of the federal power through the peace, order, and good-government clause.

The Judicial Committee of the Privy Council continued to whittle away at the introductory words of section 91 and to reduce further the significance of the *Russell* decision. In a 1916 case, Viscount Haldane, who was to become renowned for his championing of provincial rights and for his imaginative interpretation of

---

[32] The argument here is very complicated and it hinges on the way in which one construes the closing words of section 91: "and any matter coming within any of the classes of subjects enumerated in this section shall not be deemed to come within the class of matters of a local or private matter comprised in the enumeration of the classes of subjects by this act assigned exclusively to the legislatures of the Provinces." The best discussion can be found in Bora Laskin, *Canadian Constitutional Law*, (Toronto: Carswell, 1969), pp. 65–75.

[33] *Hodge v. the Queen* (1883), 9 A.C. 117.

[34] *Hodge.* See also Laskin, *Canadian Constitutional Law*, p. 79.

section 91, attempted to summarize the relevance of the peace, order, and good-government clause at that time:

> It must be taken to be now settled that the general authority to make laws for the peace, order and good government of Canada, which the initial part of Section 91 of the BNA Act confers, does not, unless the subject matter of legislation falls within some one of the enumerated heads which follow, enable the Dominion Parliament to trench on the subject matters entrusted to the provincial legislatures by the enumeration in s. 92. There is only one case outside the heads enumerated in s. 91 which the Dominion Parliament can legislate effectively as regards a province and that is where the subject matter lies outside all of the subject matters enumeratively entrusted to the province under s. 92. *Russell v. the Queen* is an instance of such a case.[35]

Not yet satisfied that peace, order, good-government and the *Russell* case were dead issues, Viscount Haldane continued to attack them in a series of cases in the 1920s. In the *Board of Commerce* case in 1922, he admitted that the peace, order, and good-government clause might be used as a justification for federal encroachments on matters enumerated in section 92, but only in extreme circumstances: "Circumstances are conceivable, such as those of war or famine, when the peace, order and good government of the Dominion might be imperilled."[36]

A year later, Haldane reinterpreted the peace, order, and good-government clause as purely an *emergency power*, to be used in times of national crisis: "In a sufficiently great emergency such as that arising out of war, there is implied the power to deal adequately with that emergency for the safety of the Dominion as a whole."[37]

Utilizing this fully developed interpretation of the peace, order, and good-government clause as an emergency power, Viscount Haldane went on to dispatch the precedent of the *Russell* case once and for all, in what is perhaps the most unusual judicial dictum in the history of Canadian constitutional law:

> Their Lordships think that the decision in *Russell v. the Queen* can only be supported today . . . on the assumption of the Board, apparently made at the time of deciding the case of *Russell v. the Queen*, that the evil of intemperance at that time amounted to one so great and so general that, at least for the period, it was a menace to the national life of Canada, so serious and pressing that the Parliament of Canada was called upon to intervene to protect the nation from disaster. An epidemic of pestilence might conceivably have been regarded as analogous.[38]

---

[35] *Attorney-General for Canada v. Attorney-General for Alberta*, (1916) *I.A.C.* 588; 26 *D.L.R.* 288.

[36] In *Re the Board of Commerce Act and the Combines and Fair Prices Act, 1919* (1922) *D.L.R.* 513.

[37] *Fort Frances Pulp and Power Co. Ltd. v. Manitoba Free Press Co. Ltd.*, (1923) 3 *D.L.R.* 629.

[38] *Toronto Electric Commissioners v. Sider*, (1925) 2 *D.L.R.5*; also in Laskin, *Canadian Constitutional Law*, p. 241. In defense of Haldane, it is possible that Canadian consumption of firewater in the 1870s was alarmingly high; O. J. Firestone, *Canadian Economic Development 1867–1953* (London: Bowes and Bowes) cites the per-capita consumption of spirits as 1.58 gallons in 1871 and only 0.59 gallons in abstemious 1951. See also J. Robinson, "Lord Haldane and the BNA Act," *University of Toronto Law Journal*, XX, 1970, pp. 55–69; XXI, 1971, pp. 175–251.

To summarize, having virtually emasculated the peace, order, and good-government clause in cases before the 1920s, the Judicial Committee then reinterpreted it as an emergency power. According to three decisions in the 1920s — the *Board of Commerce* case, the *Fort Frances* case, and the *Snider* case — the federal government could make laws for the peace, order, and good-government of Canada with regard to matters that would come *prima facie* within the powers of the provincial legislatures, but only if a national emergency required it.

In the *Fort Frances* case,[39] the Judicial Committee of the Privy Council allowed that the federal government should be given the full benefit of the doubt in determining when a national emergency existed and when the state of emergency had ceased to exist. This power was extended to the federal government during both world wars, when parliament vested significant powers in the federal executive through the War Measures Act. The privy council was not so generous, however, when the federal parliament attempted to implement a series of welfare measures, usually referred to as "the Bennett New Deal." In the reference case that tested the validity of these measures, their lordships refused to agree that the economic hardships of the Depression constituted a national emergency, largely because the federal government, for political reasons, had not formally declared in the legislation that one existed, and the entire legislative package was declared *ultra vires* the federal parliament.[40] Thus, after approximately fifty years of interpretation by the Judicial Committee of the Privy Council, the opening words of section 91 had been transformed from a general and comprehensive grant of legislative competence to the federal parliament, to a grant of temporary federal power in times of national emergency. Furthermore, in fifty years of judicial review, their lordships had construed only two events as national emergencies — World War One and an "epidemic of intemperance" in the 1870s.

At a very early point in the evolution of Canadian federalism, it became clear that the Judicial Committee of the Privy Council was willing to admit exclusive federal powers with regard only to subject matters *enumerated* in section 91. Accepting this setback, the federal authorities proceeded to try to find justification for federal legislation within the various subheads of that section. The one that seemed most comprehensive, and which the federal authorities hoped would replace the legislative competence lost with the narrowing of the peace, order, and good-government clause, was section 91(2), "the Regulation of Trade and Commerce." In two early judgements in the Supreme Court of Canada,[41] section 91(2) was interpreted not only as a very broad but also as an exclusive power of the Dominion. The Canadian judges, at least at the outset, seemed willing to view the regulation of trade and commerce as a comprehensive grant of power that might extend even to the regulation of trade carried on within the boundaries of one province. In *Citizen's Insurance Co. v. Parsons*, however, both the Supreme Court of Canada and the Judicial Committee of the Privy Council placed a far more limited construction on the federal trade and commerce power.

[39] (1923) 3 *D.L.R.* 1629.

[40] *Attorney-General for Canada v. Attorney-General for Ontario* (*Reference Re Unemployment and Social Insurance Act*), (1937) A.C. 355; (1937) 1 *D.L.R.* 684; Olmsted, vol. 3, p. 207.

[41] *Severn v. The Queen*, (1878) *S.C.R.* 70; *Fredericton v. The Queen*,(1880) 3 *S.C.R.* 505.

The words "regulation of trade and commerce" in their unlimited sense are suffi-ciently wide, if uncontrolled by the context and other parts of the act, to include every regulation of trade ranging from political arrangements in regard to trade with foreign governments, requiring the sanction of Parliament, down to minute rules for regulating particular trades. But a consideration of the act shows that the words were not used in this unlimited sense. In the first place the collocation of No. 2 with classes of subjects of national and general concern affords an indication that regulations relating to general trade and commerce were in the mind of the legislature when conferring this power on the Dominion Parliament. If the words had been intended to have the full scope of which in their literal meaning they are susceptible, the specific mention of several of the other classes of subjects enum-erated in Section 91 would have been unnecessary; as, 15, banking; 17, weights and measures; 18, bills of exchange and promissory notes; 19, interest; and even 21, bankruptcy and insolvency.[42]

Briefly, therefore, the federal trade and commerce power was construed so as not to interfere with the provinces' power to "regulate contracts of a particular business or trade such as the business of fire insurance in a single province."[43]

In *Montreal v. Montreal Street Railway* (1912), Lord Atkinson argued against broader interpretation of the federal trade and commerce power on the grounds that "taken in their widest sense, these words would authorize legislation by the Parliament of Canada in respect of several of the matters specifically enumerated in s. 92 and would seriously encroach upon the autonomy of the province."[44] This is notable partly because it is the same argument used by Lord Watson to justify his restrictive interpretation of the peace, order, and good-government clause in the *Local Prohibition* case. While both the "collocation argument" and the "provincial autonomy argument" produced inflexibility in determining the scope of the federal trade and commerce power,[45] it took the imagination of Viscount Haldane in the *Board of Commerce* case and the *Snider* case to defuse completely the federal power. In the former decision, Haldane queried:

> Must not it be taken that since the 1896 case, at all events, perhaps earlier, subs. 2 of s. 91 must be taken as containing merely ancillary powers? A power that can be exercised so as to interfere with a provincial right only if there is some paramount Dominion purpose as to which they are applicable.[46]

and, in the latter, he summed up the position of the trade and commerce power, concluding that:

> It must now be taken that the authority to legislate for the regulation of trade and commerce does not extend to the regulation, for instance, by a licensing system, of a particular trade in which Canadians would otherwise be free to engage in the provinces. It is, in their Lordships' opinion, now clear that, excepting as far as the power can be invoked in aid of capacity conferred independently under other

---

[42] Laskin, *Canadian Constitutional Law*, p. 303. All quotes from this publication are published with the permission of the Carswell Company Limited.

[43] Laskin, p. 302.

[44] *Montreal v. Montreal Street Railway*, (1912) 1 *D.L.R.* 681, at p. 687. See also Laskin, p. 306.

[45] Laskin, p. 314.

[46] Quoted in Laskin, pp. 312–313.

words in s. 91, the power to regulate trade and commerce cannot be relied on as enabling the Dominion Parliament to regulate civil rights in the province.[47]

In this fashion, Viscount Haldane reduced the federal trade and commerce power to a "merely ancillary" power that was only relevant "in aid of" some other subhead of section 91. Furthermore, it seems that the only aspect of trade and commerce that could be regulated by the federal government was international or interprovincial trade. As with the federal peace, order, and good-government power, the trade and commerce power had, courtesy of Viscount Haldane, been reduced to a mere shadow of what the Fathers of Confederation had intended it to be.

In the decade after the *Snider* case, there was a partial retreat from the restrictive view of both these parts of section 91. In *Proprietary Articles Trade Association v. Attorney-General for Canada* (the PATA case), Lord Atkin gave back some respectability to the trade and commerce clause by disassociating their lordships from the decision in the *Board of Commerce* case:

> Their Lordships merely propose to disassociate themselves from the construction suggested in argument from a passage in the Judgment of the Board of Commerce case, 1922 1 A.C. 191, 198, under which it was contended that the power to regulate trade and commerce could be invoked only in furtherance of a general power which Parliament possessed independently of it. No such restriction is properly to be inferred from that judgement.[48]

In 1946, an appellant asked Viscount Simon to find that the *Russell* case had been wrongly decided. Viscount Simon held that the decision in the *Russell* case should stand; he was also severely critical of the emergency power interpretation of the peace, order, and good-government clause in the *Board of Commerce, Fort Frances*, and *Snider* cases.[49] Despite these decisions, however, the damage had been done, and while, as we shall see later, other cases, particularly since the abolition of appeals to the Judicial Committee of the Privy Council in 1949,[50] may indicate the possibility of a slightly less restrictive interpretation of the federal power in the future,[51] the constitutional ground rules of Canadian federalism were likely fairly firmly established by 1925. If, therefore, much of the power that the Fathers of Confederation conceived as federal was taken away from the federal Parliament, it is time to consider where that power was transferred.

Section 92(13) reads "Property and Civil Rights in the Province," and it was intended as merely one of the sixteen subheads of section 92. The Judicial Committee of the Privy Council, however, chose to interpret the words of this subhead in their widest connotation. They were deemed to include such things as contracts, contractual rights, and civil rights in its broadest interpretation; that

---

[47] Laskin, pp. 313–314.

[48] Cited in Laskin, p. 314.

[49] *Attorney-General for Ontario v. Canada Temperance Federation*, (1946) 2 D.L.R. 1.

[50] *Attorney-General for Ontario v. Attorney-General for Canada (Reference Re Abolition of Appeals to the JCPC)*, (1947) A.C. 127.

[51] E.g., *Pronto Uranium Mine v. O.L.R.B. et al.* (1956), 5 D.L.R. (2d) 342.

is, including almost every aspect of all subject matters that are not specifically interprovincial or international in their scope. By construing section 92(13) in its widest sense, and by strictly limiting the interpretation of the more general sections of section 91, the Judicial Committee transformed the property and civil rights clause into the *de facto* residual clause of the BNA Act.[52] Thus, the general grant of power in the opening words of section 91 was transferred from the federal parliament to the provincial legislatures, with the result that, fifty years after Confederation, the face of Canadian federalism would have been unrecognizable to the men who created it.

One enumerated federal power that was permitted to encroach upon subject matters that are *prima facie* covered by this wide interpretation of section 92(13) is section 91(27), the *Dominion criminal law power*. The competence of the federal parliament to encroach upon the area of "Property and Civil Rights in the Province" when legislating with regard to criminal law was at first questioned, particularly by Viscount Haldane, who argued that the Dominion could not create a crime where the subject matter did not by its very nature belong to "the domain of criminal jurisprudence."[53] In the PATA case, mentioned above, the Judicial Committee of the Privy Council disassociated itself from Haldane's restrictive interpretation and admitted that the federal government could, in fact, declare an act to be criminal even if it had not in the past been considered so.[54] The only limitation on this federal power to declare a certain act or category of acts criminal is "the condition that parliament shall not in the guise of enacting criminal legislation in truth and in substance encroach on any of the classes of subjects enumerated in section 92."[55] Thus, the criminal law power of the federal parliament, while not to be used merely to secure entry into a field of legislation that is in pith and substance provincial, can properly encroach upon the powers of the provincial legislatures, if such an encroachment is truly incidental to the achievement of a genuine federal purpose.

Before concluding this section of the chapter, mention should be made of one section of the BNA Act that affects the federal-provincial distribution of powers, which became a bone of contention in the 1930s, and which arises at every occasion where the federal government attempts to negotiate a major international agreement affecting areas not strictly within federal jurisdiction. Free trade negotiations with the United States are the latest in a long line of such issues.

Section 132 defines the federal treaty-making power.[56] Essentially, this section means that, in the implementation of British empire treaties to which Canada is

[52] Royal Commission on Dominion-Provincial Relations, *Report* (Ottawa: Queen's Printer, 1954), Book 1, p. 247. (Also known as the Rowell-Sirois report.)

[53] The Board of Commerce Case, in Laskin, *Canadian Constitutional Law*, p. 282.

[54] *Proprietary Articles Trade Association v. Attorney-General for Canada*, (1931) 2 *D.L.R.1*; *A.C.* 310.

[55] *Attorney-General for British Columbia v. Attorney-General for Canada*, (1937) 1 *D.L.R.* 688, as quoted in Laskin, *Canadian Constitutional Law*, p. 284.

[56] See G. J. Szablowski, "Treaty-Making Power in the Context of Canadian Politics," a research paper prepared for the Macdonald Commission (Toronto: University of Toronto Press, 1985), for a recent analysis of the significance of the treaty power.

a signatory, the distribution of powers in sections 91 and 92 is inoperative, and the federal parliament possesses exclusive authority over all subject matters. In the *Aeronautics* case of 1932,[57] the Judicial Committee held that federal legislation dealing with the regulation and control of aeronautics was *intra vires* because it had been passed to implement the provisions of a treaty that Canada had signed as a member of the British empire. (While Lord Sankey went on to say that the legislation affected matters that "attained such dimensions as to affect the body politic of the nation," and that it therefore would have been *intra vires* the federal parliament through the peace, order, and good-government clause even if it had not been passed to implement a treaty, this part of the decision was an *obiter dictum.*)

The interpretation of this federal power did not come into question until Canada gained the right to enter into treaties with foreign countries, not as a member of the empire but as an independent signatory. The federal authorities felt that the evolution of Canada's independent role in foreign relations could not have been foreseen by the Fathers of Confederation, and that, as a result, the full power that the federal parliament had possessed with regard to the implementation of empire treaties should continue with regard to the implementation of treaties signed by Canada in her new international role.

The first real test of this came with the *Radio Reference* case of 1932. Here the decision of the Judicial Committee of the Privy Council, as delivered by Viscount Dunedin, basically supported the view of the federal government: namely, that although federal legislation to regulate and control radio communication was passed to implement a treaty that Canada had signed as an *independent* Dominion and not as a member of the empire, it amounted to the same thing: "In fine though agreeing that the convention was not a treaty as is defined in s. 132, their lordships think that it comes to the same thing."[58] The reasoning of the JCPC was that, because the matter of empire treaty implementation was dealt with as a separate subject and not included in either section 91 or 92, and because the notion of Canada functioning as an independent Dominion was not conceivable in 1867, therefore the federal parliament should have the jurisdiction over Dominion treaty implementation through the general power for the peace, order, and good-government of Canada. In other words, the peace, order, and good-government clause was operative as a "residuary" clause in the case of treaty implementation.

However, while the decisions of the *Radio* and *Aeronautics* cases seemed to augur well for a broad interpretation of the federal power in treaty implementation, and even gave a glimmer of hope for a restoration to respectability of the general power in section 91, such was not to be the case. In a 1937 case dealing with federal legislation purporting to implement labour conventions passed by the International Labour Organization, of which Canada was a member, Lord Atkin effectively reversed the judgement of Viscount Dunedin in the *Radio* case. That the federal executive possessed the full power to *make* treaties with foreign countries was never seriously questioned. However, their lordships held that the power to

---

[57] *Re Aerial Navigation*, (1932) A.C. 54.

[58] (1932) A.C. 304, p. 313.

sign such treaties does not give the federal parliament the unfettered right to pass laws implementing them in Canada:

> There is no existing constitutional ground for stretching the competence of the Dominion Parliament that it becomes enlarged to keep pace with enlarged functions of the Dominion executive. . . . The Dominion cannot, merely by making promises to foreign countries, clothe itself with legislative authority inconsistent with the constitution which gave it birth.[59]

The Judicial Committee went on to point out that "in totality of legislative powers," the provincial legislatures and the federal parliament can, together, pass laws implementing any treaty signed by the federal executive. The fact, however, that the legislation happens to be necessary to implement a treaty does not alter the constitutional distribution of powers in sections 91 and 92: "While the ship of state now sails on larger ventures and into foreign waters she still retains the watertight compartments which are an essential part of her original structure."[60]

It can be seen, from what has been said in the past several pages, that the interpretation of the BNA Act, specifically the interpretation of sections 91 and 92, had achieved a major alteration in the relationship of the provinces to the federal parliament, up to the time when appeals to the Judicial Committee were abolished in 1949. The clear intention of the Fathers of Confederation had been to leave the provinces as relatively insignificant entities, in the possession of relatively modest legislative powers. The Judicial Committee of the Privy Council, however, according to the tradition of the British legal system, took a passive attitude to the interpretation of the BNA Act. In short, they sought to construe the terms of the act literally, with little regard for either the intentions of the men who had drafted it or current political opinion. Based on this principle of a literal construction of the BNA Act, if a specific matter of a particular piece of legislation came *prima facie* under one of the subheads of section 91, then without question it was within the exclusive jurisdiction of the Dominion parliament. Second, if the subject matter came under one of the subheads of section 92, the federal parliament was still the paramount authority, as long as the subject was also covered by one of the enumerated subheads in section 91. If the jurisdiction was *shared*, either government could legislate, with the provision that if both levels of government occupied the *same* jurisdictional space, the federal laws would be unquestionably *paramount*. Third, the provincial authority to make laws with respect to property and civil rights in the province[61] was construed very broadly while the federal enumerated powers were, for the most part, construed narrowly, with the result that, in the case of any doubt as to the proper location of a particular subject matter, it was, more often than not, given to the provinces. The only exception to this rule was deemed to exist in times of national emergency, when the federal power to make laws for the peace, order, and good-government of Canada might permit federal encroachments on normally provincial matters.

---

[59] "The labour conventions case," 1937, is quoted in Laskin, *Canadian Constitutional Law*, p. 286.

[60] Cited in Laskin, p. 286.

[61] BNA Act, section 92(13).

Finally, if a subject matter could not be located either among the enumerated subheads of section 91 or within section 92, then it came within the jurisdiction of the federal parliament through the peace, order, and good-government clause as a *residuary power*.[62]

It is tempting, at this point in our analysis of the evolution of the federal-provincial distribution of powers, to pass judgement on the manner in which the Judicial Committee of the Privy Council rewrote our constitution. However, in order to come to any verdict as to the culpability of their lordships, it would be necessary to assume that the BNA Act, as drafted in 1867, was itself beyond criticism. Clearly this is not the case, for sections 91 and 92 contain especially ambiguous phrases that lend themselves to various and often conflicting constructions. Questions that come to mind are: if the Fathers of Confederation saw the peace, order, and good-government clause as a truly comprehensive grant of power, why did they confuse the issue be adding twenty-nine "examples"? If they viewed the trade and commerce power as a broad grant of authority to the federal parliament, why did they proceed to collocate other subheads that related to trade and commerce? If they wanted the provinces to have a modest role in the government of Canada, why did they give them the ambiguous and potentially vast power over property and civil rights in the province? Certainly, one can maintain that many of Viscount Haldane's judgements are puzzling, but it also must be admitted that the act itself is not exactly airtight. The purpose of this analysis is not to praise or blame the Judicial Committee of the Privy Council for altering the intention of the BNA Act, but to describe the shape into which our federal system has been moulded.

The Supreme Court of Canada and the BNA Act, 1949–1982

Two things must be remembered in looking at the interpretation of the BNA Act since the abolition of appeals to the Judicial Committee of the Privy Council. First, it is often held, mistakenly, that the Judicial Committee's decisions normally overturned the decisions of the Supreme Court of Canada; while that *did* happen, in many cases the decision of the former, in fact, merely confirmed that of the latter. Second, it must be recognized that it is more difficult to be a creative jurist in an area of law that has been picked over and poked at by judges for something approaching eighty years. There are a lot of givens, a lot of deeply entrenched canons of interpretation that severely hinder the lawmaking space of our more recent Supreme Court judges. Thus if anyone had expected the Supreme Court of Canada to immediately begin the dismantling of the house that Watson, Haldane, et al. built, they would have been doomed to disappointment. While there have been some changes since 1949 that bear elaboration, we could in no way have

---

[62] Cases such as this have been few and far between. The only example that comes to mind is the *Radio Reference* case in 1932. It is necessary to note, however, that even in this case there were other reasons cited for the decision. See *Reference Re Regulation and Control of Radio Communications*, (1932) 2 D.L.R. 81; and Laskin, *Canadian Constitutional Law*, pp. 267–269. In fact one of the reasons for upholding federal jurisdiction was that radio-communication devices could be viewed as analogous to "telegraphs," which are defined as "works or undertakings" *excluded* from provincial jurisdiction by section 92, 10(a).

expected radical reversals of the basic interpretive doctrines that are the heritage of the Judicial Committee of the Privy Council.

In a 1952 decision, the Supreme Court of Canada essentially reaffirmed the decision in the *Aeronautics Reference* case of thirty years earlier. In 1952, the issue was whether, in the course of zoning, a municipality might make regulations affecting airports.[63] The court decided that the subject matter involved was aeronautics and aerial navigation, and that the federal government has exclusive jurisdiction over such matters because the questions go beyond merely local or provincial concerns. As a precedent, a majority of the Supreme Court looked to Lord Sankey's *obiter dictum* in the *Aeronautics Reference*, that the subject of aeronautics and aerial navigation was of "national importance" and therefore within the exclusive domain of the federal parliament to make laws for the peace, order, and good-government of Canada, even if such legislation incidentally interfered with areas of provincial jurisdiction, such as civil rights and municipal institutions.

The same "national dimension" or "national concern" interpretation of the peace, order, and good-government clause of section 91 was used again in 1956 to give the federal parliament exclusive jurisdiction to make laws with respect to labour relations in the uranium industry.[64] The Supreme Court of Ontario was unanimous in affirming that the uranium industry is a matter that, by its very nature, went beyond matters of merely local concern, and therefore was within the exclusive domain of Parliament.

While the centralist cause was the victor in these cases of the fifties, there was little net gain in terms of federal jurisdiction, nor was there any indication that the opening words of section 91 were to be given a more liberal interpretation than they had received at the hands of the judicial committee. The "national dimension" test really goes back to Lord Watson in the *Local Prohibition* case of 1896, and was being applied in the post-war years in the *Johanesson* and *Pronto* cases in a fairly conservative manner. However some hope for a more liberal interpretation of the peace, order, and good-government clause as an effective *residuary* power may have been kindled by a couple of more recent decisions.

In *Munro v. National Capital Commission*,[65] in 1966, the right of the federally established NCC to expropriate land in the Ottawa area to create a "green belt" around the national capital was challenged on the grounds that the federal parliament did not have the legislative jurisdiction to grant the NCC the power to expropriate. The Supreme Court reasoned that the matter of national capital region was, in fact, a matter that went beyond local or provincial concerns; but, instead of relying on the national-dimension aspect of the general power to give the federal parliament the jurisdiction, the Court went on to state that the matter of a national capital was not enumerated within either section 91 or 92, and that, therefore, the subject came within the *residuary* power of the federal parliament to make laws for the peace, order, and good-government of Canada.

---

[63] *Johannesson v. West St. Paul*, (1952) 1 *S.C.R.* 292.

[64] *Pronto Uranium Mines v. OLRB* (156), 5 *D.L.R.* (2d) 342.

[65] (1966) *S.C.R.* 663.

Similarly, in a 1974 case that involved the validity of the Official Languages Act,[66] the Supreme Court held that all aspects of the subject of official languages *not* covered by section 91(1) and section 133 were within the federal parliament's jurisdiction because of the residuary power implied by the opening words of section 91. However, again, while the federal government clearly won these cases, the gains, either in net legislative authority or in freeing the peace, order, and good-government clause from the canons of interpretation of the JCPC, were still modest. The door had been opened slightly to a more liberal interpretation of the general words of section 91, but it was going to take a positive and radical stroke of jurisprudence to actually break out.

The opportunity to finally break out of the Watson-Haldane approach came in 1976. In what one author has called "probably the Court's most heralded decision since it became Canada's final court of appeal,"[67] the federal government's controversial Anti-Inflation Act was held to be *intra vires*.[68] According to Peter Russell, the AIB case was

> the first clear test of whether the Supreme Court would "liberate" the Federal Parliament's general power to make laws for the "peace, order, and good government of Canada" from the shackles placed upon it by the Privy Council's jurisprudence and thereby provide the constitutional underpinnings for a revolutionary readjustment of the balance of power in Canadian federalism.[69]

However, the court's verdict was, all in all, pretty tame. While the federal Anti-Inflation Act was upheld by a seven-to-two decision in the Supreme Court, the *rationale* of the case was Haldane's "emergency doctrine," and the jurisdiction of the federal parliament was seen as temporary — to last only as long as the economic crisis of inflation continued to plague us. While a minority of the Court felt that the legislation could be upheld permanently by utilizing the national-dimension interpretation of the peace, order, and good-government clause, a majority of the Court either rejected this view or declined to comment on the point at all.

The only substantive gain for the centralist perspective in the AIB case, therefore, was the admission of the court that the federal parliament does not have to *proclaim* the existence of a national emergency to justify legislation under the emergency doctrine. According to this test, Bennett's "New Deal" legislation of the 1930s, which was rejected by the courts at that time, might now be *intra vires* the federal parliament. As Peter Russell has put it:

> Temporary federal legislation may be upheld on emergency grounds if federal lawyers can persuade the Court that there is not enough evidence to conclude that it would have been unreasonable for parliament to have regarded a matter as an

---

[66] *Jones v. A.G. Canada* (1974), 45 *D.L.R.* (3d) 583.

[67] Peter Russell, "The Anti-Inflation Case: The Anatomy of a Constitutional Decision," *CPA*, Winter, 1977, p. 632.

[68] *Reference Re Anti-Inflation Act* (1976), 68 *D.L.R.* (3d) 452.

[69] Russell, p. 632.

urgent national crisis at the time it passed the legislation. Given the probable deference of most Supreme Court Justices to the judgment of Parliament, this is at least a small gain for federal authority.[70]

Thus, while we can conclude that the Supreme Court of Canada has generally been more sympathetic to the federal government since 1949, the justices themselves have not been willing to radically expand the scope of the general authority granted to the federal parliament by the opening words of section 91, beyond the narrow range of applicability established by the Judicial Committee.

The generally conservative approach of the courts with respect to the peace, order, and good-government clause has been maintained with respect to the federal trade and commerce power as well. The Judicial Committee had made the distinction between matters of interprovincial and international trade, on the one hand, and matters of intra-provincial trade, on the other. In the fifties, the Supreme Court of Canada clarified the distinction without significantly altering the balance of power between the federal government and the provinces. In *Reference Re: Farm Products Marketing Act (Ont.)*,[71] for instance, the Court reiterated the necessity for federal-provincial cooperation in marketing schemes because of the extent to which interprovincial and intra-provincial trade are intertwined. In this case, the Court recognized that even though a transaction is entirely intra-provincial, its regulation and control are not necessarily an exclusively provincial matter.

In Murphy v. CPR[72] the Canadian Wheat Board Act was declared to be *intra vires* the federal parliament because it concerned international and interprovincial trade; and in *R. v. Klassen*,[73] the court of appeal of Manitoba took the next step and affirmed the right of the Wheat Board to regulate intra-provincial transactions, as well, as being "necessarily incidental" to the regulation of the interprovincial and international aspects of marketing grain. However, these decisions have the effect of clarifying rather than expanding the federal power over trade and commerce, and they in no way have expanded the scope of section 91(2) beyond the limits set by the Judicial Committee of the Privy Council. In fact, in a 1968 case,[74] Quebec legislation aimed at regulating intra-provincial trade that affected interprovincial transactions was declared to be *intra vires* the province because the intention of the legislation was clearly intra-provincial and the interprovincial encroachments were only incidental. Thus because the *intent* was to do something within the province's jurisdiction, unless the law came into direct conflict with federal legislation, the Quebec law could stand.

The intent of the legislation or the aims of the legislators again became the critical variable in determining the scope of federal and provincial authority over marketing in *A.G. Manitoba v. Manitoba Egg and Poultry Association* (the *"Chicken*

---

[70] Russell, "Anti-Inflation," p. 662.

[71] (1957) *S.C.R.* 198.

[72] (1958) S.C.R. 626.

[73] (1959), 20 *D.L.R.* (2d) 406.

[74] *Carnation Co. Ltd. v. Quebec Agricultural Marketing Board*, (1968) *S.C.R.* 238.

and Egg case"),[75] *Burns Foods Ltd. v. A.G. Manitoba,*[76] and the 1978 *Agricultural Marketing Act Reference.*[77] Here provincial legislation was declared *ultra vires* because purportedly local marketing schemes had, as their primary object, the restriction of imports from other provinces. However, as if to consciously balance their pro-federal decisions, in a 1976 case, *Macdonald v. Vapour Canada,*[78] the Supreme Court found a section of the federal Trade Marks Act *ultra vires* because it was intended to regulate the conduct of local trades and to establish standards of fair competition in local business ventures. In deciding the case, the Supreme Court went right back to the *dicta* of the Judicial Committee in the *Parsons* case of 1881 to reaffirm the point that section 91(2) does not extend to the regulation of individual trades entirely within a single province. Their hesitancy about "opening up what sounds like the branch of trade and commerce with the greatest potential — 'general regulation of trade affecting the whole Dominion,' "[79] was confirmed by the Court's decision in the *Labatt* case[80] in 1980, where federal regulations that were not aimed explicitly at either interprovincial or international aspects of trade were declared *ultra vires.*

Finally, this apparent tendency to balance decisions favouring one level of government with decisions going the other way can be seen in a series of cases in the late 1970s and early 1980s. In the CIGOL case,[81] the Supreme Court placed limits on the provinces' power to tax natural resources; four years later, in the Exported Natural Gas Tax Reference,[82] it ruled that resources *owned* by the provinces could be exempted from federal taxation even if they were exported. Similarly, while the Supreme Court held that the British Columbia "nationalization" of auto insurance was *intra vires* even though that industry had an interprovincial aspect, it denied Saskatchewan's right to manage the international aspects of that province's important Potash industry.[83] To summarize, the scope of the federal power to regulate trade and commerce has not been expanded significantly by the Canadian courts since 1949, and, in fact, the canons of interpretation that apply to this section of the BNA Act remain virtually as they were at the time of the PATA case in 1931. As Peter Russell has stated, "Overall, the court's decisions affecting constitutional capacity for economic management have not tilted the balance of power decisively in one direction or the other."[84]

---

[75] (1971) *S.C.R.* 689.

[76] (1974), 40 *D.L.R.* (3d) 731.

[77] (1978) 2 *S.C.R.* 1198.

[78] (1976), 66 *D.L.R.* (3d) 1.

[79] P. H. Russell, "The Supreme Court and Federal Provincial Relations," *Canadian Public Policy,* June 1985, p. 163.

[80] *Labatt v. A. G. Canada,* (1980) 1 *S.C.R. 914.*

[81] *Canadian Industrial Gas and Oil Ltd. v. Government of Saskatchewan,* (1978) 2 *S.C.R.* 545.

[82] *Reference Re Exported Natural Gas Tax,* (1982) 1 *S.C.R.,* 1004.

[83] *Canadian Indemnity Co. v. A-G. B.C.* (1977) 2 *S.C.R.,* 504; *Central Canada Potash Co., Government of Saskatchewan,* (1979) 1 *S.C.R.,* 42.

[84] Russell, "The Supreme Court," p. 163.

The scope of the criminal-law power of the federal government, section 91(27), has not altered significantly either since 1949. In 1949,[85] in a case that involved a piece of legislation prohibiting the manufacture and sale of margarine and other butter substitutes, and which the federal government was trying to justify as being within the scope of its criminal law power, Mr. Justice Rand attempted to establish a test for the legitimate scope of criminal law:

> A crime is an act which the law, with appropriate penal sanctions, forbids; but as prohibitions are not enacted in a vacuum, we can properly look for some evil of injurious or undesirable effect upon the public against which the law is directed. That effect may be in relation to social, economic or political interests; and the legislature has in mind to suppress the evil or to safeguard the interest threatened.[86]

Then later in the same case Rand applied his test:

> Is the prohibition then enacted with a view to a public purpose which can support it as being in relation to criminal law? Public peace, order, security, health, morality: these are the ordinary though not exclusive ends served by that [criminal] law but they do not appear to be the object of the parliamentary action here. That object, as I must find it, is economic.[87]

Mr. Justice Rand concluded that the federal legislation, under the guise of creating a new crime, was, in fact, merely trying to protect the dairy producers from competition from the butter-substitute producers. The Supreme Court of Canada found the federal legislation to be *ultra vires*.

The *Birks* case[88] in 1955 and the *Padlock* case[89] in 1957 saw provincial legislation dealing with religious observance and freedom of expression, respectively, declared *ultra vires* on the grounds that these were matters relating to the criminal law, and therefore were within the exclusive purview of the federal parliament by virtue of section 91(27). The irony of provincial encroachments on fundamental freedoms being overturned only because they were deemed to be within the exclusive domain of the federal government in criminal matters is worth noting, but the net effect has not been to enhance the federal power significantly. Moreover, as we have seen in previous chapters, it may well be that the courts are in the process of reducing the federal jurisdiction over such matters as Sunday observance and freedom of expression through application of the Charter of Rights and Freedoms.

Finally, while the existing balance between federal and provincial powers in the area of criminal justice may not have altered, there have been a number of cases that may have changed the nature of that balance. On the one hand, the

---

[85] *Reference Re Validity of Section 5(a) of the Dairy Industry Act*, (1949) S.C.R. 1. (This is also known as the "Margarine Case.")

[86] The Margarine Case, p. 49.

[87] The Margarine Case, p. 50.

[88] *Birks v. Montreal and A.G. Quebec*, (1955) S.C.R. 799. See also the section on the protection of civil liberties in Canada in chapter 7.

[89] *Switzman v. Elbling*, (1957) S.C.R. 285. See also the section on civil liberties in Canada in chapter 7.

exclusiveness of the federal power under section 91(27) to determine the criminal law has been undermined to some extent by decisions in the late 1970s that allow a greater provincial role in determining the scope of what is "criminal."[90] On the other hand, the federal role with respect to the administration of justice appears to have been expanded significantly, reducing the once generally accepted exclusivity of the provincial authority in that area under section 92(14) of the BNA Act. In fact, two cases decided in 1983 may well have the result of transferring the exclusive power to prosecute federal offences from provincial to federal crown attorneys— i.e., reversing the practice that has been in effect since 1867.[91]

What, then, *can* be said, by way of conclusion, about the overall role of the Supreme Court in the evolution of Canadian federalism? In 1974, Peter Russell concluded:

> Throughout the 60s and 70s, constitutional cases have continued to reach the Supreme Court at the rate of three to four a year. On a purely box-score basis, the outcomes have been considerably more favourable to federal than to provincial interests. . . . Federal authorities have yet to lose a constitutional decision before an independent Supreme Court of Canada, whereas provincial claims have been defeated on numerous occasions.[92]

However, in 1985, Russell, the leading expert on the Supreme Court and the constitution, admitted that the federalist tendencies in the Court's decisions up to the mid 1970s were being "balanced" by decisions in the latter years of that decade and into the 1980s:

> I think this verdict of balance is correct so far as constitutional jurisprudence is concerned. Indeed, writing now, . . . I would add that the Supreme Court's record shows an uncanny balance. In so many areas, the net outcome of its decision-making is to strike a balance between federal and provincial powers.[93]

Thus, we can conclude that the Supreme Court of Canada has not put Viscount Haldane "away in mothballs."[94] Rather, since it became the final court of appeal for Canada, the Supreme Court has maintained a fairly conservative adherence to the precedents set by the Judicial Committee. But perhaps the Court was conservative, legalistic, and cautious simply because the constitutional questions being asked in the period up to the mid-1970s had been asked so many times

---

[90] See: *Nova Scotia Board of Censors v. McNeil* (1978) 2 *S.C.R.* 152; and *A-G Canada and Dupond v. Montreal* (1978) 2 *S.C.R.*, 152.

[91] See: Russell, *op. cit.*, pp. 166–167; *A-G Canada v. Canadian National Transportation Ltd.* (1983); and *R. v. Judge Wetmore et.al.* (1983), both cited in Russell, *ibid.*, p. 169. See also: *R. v. Hauser*, (1979), 1 *S.C.R.*, 984; *Cordes v. Queen* (1978) 1 *S.C.R.*, 1062; *A-G. Quebec and Keable v. A-G. Canada* (1979) 1 *S.C.R.*, 218; and *A-G. Alberta v. Putnam* (1981) 2 *S.C.R.*, 267.

[92] Peter Russell, "The Supreme Court's Interpretation of the Constitution," in Paul Fox ed., *Politics Canada*, (Toronto: McGraw-Hill Ryerson, 1982), p. 608.

[93] Russell, "The Supreme Court," pp. 162–163. See also: Russell, "The Political Role of the Supreme Court of Canada in its First Century," *Canadian Bar Review*, 1979, p. 721; and G. L'Ecuyer, *La Cour Suprême du Canada et la partage des compétences 1949–1978* (Government of Quebec, 1978.)

[94] Russell, "The Anti Inflation Case," p. 632.

before; there simply is not a very great opportunity for the judges to be particularly innovative as long as the issues are the scope of the peace, order, and good-government clause, sections 91(2) and 91(27), and section 92(13). However, we must now consider whether the constitutional issues of the 1980s will force the Supreme Court of Canada to play a more significant role as a policy maker in the process of social and political change.

The Supreme Court in the 1980s: A New Role?

While, as we have seen, it is difficult to find any dominant bias in the judicial pronouncements of the Supreme Court of Canada if one looks at the entire period of 1949 to the present, the fact remains that the *volume* of constitutional litigation increased dramatically from 1975 to 1982. (Since it became the final court of appeal, the Supreme Court has reported 158 constitutional decisions; 80 of these were reported in this recent period.)[95] Since the proclamation of the Canadian Charter of Rights and Freedom in 1982, there has been a sharp increase in the number of constitutional issues placed before the courts at all levels, and many of these are being heard by the highest court on appeal.

However, the role of the Supreme Court may be changing in ways other than simply a rapidly growing docket and a daunting backlog of cases yet to be decided and reported. On the one hand, in recent years, the Supreme Court has been called upon to decide issues that are simultaneously either the focus of heated partisan discourse or of federal-provincial conflict — or both. For example, the Canadian judiciary has been called upon to determine the validity of Quebec's Bill 101,[96] to settle the ownership of offshore resources,[97] to assess the jurisdiction of the Anti-Inflation Board,[98] and to judge the constitutionality of unilateral patriation of the BNA Act.[99] Clearly, in such important and current conflicts, it has been difficult for the Supreme Court to maintain the detached and passive literalist approach that characterized much judicial decision making since 1875. Moreover, the Charter of Rights has enhanced still more the political, social, and philosophical turmoil within which the judiciary must today operate:

> Even before the arrival of the Charter of Rights, the Supreme Court of Canada had begun to emerge from the mists of the Ottawa bureaucracy. The use of the reference mechanism to test such high profile political measures as the federal anti-inflation program and possible modifications of the Canadian Senate emphasized the political significance of rulings from the Supreme Court of Canada. Rulings under the Charter of Rights will further accentuate the impact of the Court on the social, political and economic life of Canadians.[100]

[95] Russell, "The Supreme Court," p. 162.

[96] *A-G. Quebec v. Blaikie* (1979) 2 *S.C.R.* 1016.

[97] Reference Re. Property in and Legislative Jurisdiction over the Seabed and Subsoil of the Continental Shelf Offshore Newfoundland, March 8, 1984.

[98] Reference Re: Anti-Inflation Act (1976) 2 *S.C.R.* 373.

[99] Re Objection to a Resolution to Amend the Constitution (1982) 2 *S.C.R.*, 793.

[100] MacKay and Bauman, "The Supreme Court of Canada . . .", in Beckton and MacKay (eds.), *The Courts and the Charter*, (Toronto: 1985), p. 39.

The question here is whether the Court will respond with a more activist role in deciding such cases, or struggle to maintain the more conservative "literal interpretation of legislation" role.

A number of observers and analysts of the Court have, in fact, begun to argue that the role of the Court was becoming more activist and more creative even before the advent of the Charter. Peter Russell states:

> While it is undoubtedly true that a constitutional Charter of Rights will expand the policy-making role of Canadian Courts, it is misleading to imply that the Canadian courts have had no significant policy-making role in the past.[101]

In a 1982 article, Russell scolded Van Loon and Whittington for contributing to the "blindness" of Canadians towards the "policy role" of the Canadian judiciary. He argued, convincingly, that a trend towards the admission of extrinsic evidence in deciding constitutional issues in the late 1970s and early 1980s formed a clear message, and that the Supreme Court is beginning to recognize that it has a social-policy responsibility as well as its more traditional responsibility, as a passive adjudicator of legal disputes.

The experiences of the first four years of the Charter of Rights indicate that the judiciary is willing to take a more activist role, particularly with respect to procedural rights in criminal matters and with respect to the determination of "reasonableness" under section 1. In its initial decisions, the Supreme Court of Canada certainly gave notice that

> They would interpret this constitutional Charter much more liberally and sympathetically than their predecessors had interpreted the statutory Bill of Rights.[102]

However, while there is clear evidence that the Charter has resulted in the transfer of some political decision making from the legislative and executive arena to the adjudicative, the extent of that transfer has been limited. One possible explanation of this residual hesitancy to move abruptly to a more American style of "activist-socially conscious" judicial decision making is that the judges of the Supreme Court are by no means in total agreement as to the wisdom of this shift in role.

In fact the battle lines in this debate were being drawn up several years ago, when the then Chief Justice Bora Laskin (dissenting) and the current chief justice, Brian Dickson, set down their different philosophies with respect to the role of the Court. Laskin chose the more activist role, decrying the "mechanical deference to *stare decisis.*" Dickson was hesitant about the Court being more "creative," and opts for a more conservative role for the Court. He thought the Court should "proceed in the discharge of its adjudicative functions in a reasoned way from principled decisions and established concepts."[103]

---

[101] Peter Russell, "The Effect of a Charter of Rights on the Policy-Making Role of Canadian Courts," *CPA*, Spring 1982, p. 2. See also Russell, "The Political Role of the Supreme Court of Canada in its First Century," *Canadian Bar Review*, 1975, p. 589; and Russell, "Judicial Power in Canada's Political Culture," in M.L. Friedland, ed. *Courts and Trials* (Toronto: 1975).

[102] Peter Russell, "The First Three Years in Charterland," *CPA*, Fall 1985, p. 385.

[103] *Harrison v. Carswell* (1976). Cited in F. L. Morton, *Law, Politics and the Judicial Process in Canada, op. cit.*, pp. 38–39.

As confirmation of the possibility of a philosophical split among members of the Supreme Court of Canada, we can cite some very candid observations by Justice Bertha Wilson, which were made in a series of lectures at the University of Toronto Law School. As reported by Southam News, Justice Wilson stated that

> You have judges who think it is more important to be consistent than to be correct, those who see caution as a virtue and denigrate "much speaking."[104]

According to the Southam report,

> Wilson used rhetorical devices to let her sophisticated audience know that a real intellectual donnybrook is raging in the inner chambers of the Supreme Court. Listeners winced when she described "pruning shears" taken to the decisions of activist judges.[105]

While the use of the term "donnybrook" may reflect a bit of journalistic license, it seems clear that there are differences among our Supreme Court justices as to the appropriate role of the Court. Certainly, if we may be permitted a bit of journalistic licence of our own, the jury is still out with respect to coming to a definite conclusion as to the future role of the Supreme Court in the Canadian political process — passive adjudicator or activist policy maker. Only time will tell, but there are clear indications that a combination of new issues in federal-provincial relations and the advent of the Charter of Rights have forced both the judges themselves and academic analysts of the judicial process to rethink the traditional model of Canadian judicial decision making.

---

[104] P. Calamai, "Justice Bertha Wilson: Odd Judge Out in Supreme Court," *Ottawa Citizen*, November 30, 1985, p. 137.

[105] Calamai, p. 137.

C   H   A   P   T   E   R   9

FEDERAL-PROVINCIAL FISCAL RELATIONS: 1867-1987

- The General Principles ■ The Move to Block Funding
THE EVOLUTION OF FISCAL FEDERALISM
- The Fiscal Balance in the Nineteenth Century
- The Statutory Subsidies ■ The Early Twentieth Century
- The Financial Structure in Crisis ■ The Postwar Period
- From Centralization to Decentralization: Federal-Provincial Fiscal
Arrangements, 1945–1987
- Conclusions: 1987 and Beyond

F ew subjects are as crucial to an understanding of the Canadian political system as the study of federal-provincial financial or fiscal relations. Unfortunately, however, few subjects are so poorly understood! Far from being uninteresting, it is an area capable of producing high drama as ministers of finance, premiers, and prime ministers confront each other in federal-provincial conferences, while their advisors shunt hurriedly back and forth behind the walls of the main conference chambers at the Conference Centre in Ottawa, seeking to find compromises that will permit the continuation of the financial arrangements that underpin Confederation. Will the first ministers be able to forge a compromise from the seemingly irreconcilable interests of eleven different governments? Will they be able to do it in time to avoid the unilateral imposition of a solution by the federal government, and a stormy exit by some of the provincial premiers? The press converges on the Conference Centre. The first ministers emerge to face a battery of cameras and microphones. Although some dissent is expressed, an agreement has been reached. The financial foundations of Confederation have once again been shored up — and just in time.

Whatever are they doing? Why is this exercise so important? Why must we be concerned with the arcane world of financial dealings among governments? We need not look far for the answer to that last question. At the core of most of the activities of government are the raising and spending of money. For the key decision makers in any political system, the essence of popularity and, hence, survival is to be able to spend money delivering popular programs without getting caught in the nasty business of raising it. This is a situation with significant implications for the real distribution of power among governments in Canada, for it means that a political decision maker wins if he or she can deliver a program while passing the costs of raising the money for the program onto another level of government. Winning, in this case, means not only augmenting one's own popularity; it also means increasing the general regard with which your level of government is viewed by the public, and hence increasing the real power of your level of government *vis-à-vis* the other. Thus, within a federation, the real distribution of power among governments is, in significant measure, determined by the complex processes of fiscal relations among governments.

The rules of the game of federal-provincial fiscal arrangements are established by three sets of factors. The first is the broad environment within which government is set: the demands imposed on the system by society, the demands the actors in the system succeed in creating in the society, and the economic and social context within which the system is set. The second is the set of rules about jurisdiction, and hence about the matters upon which government may spend money; these are imposed upon the system by its formal constitution. The third is the set of rules that determines the revenue sources available to governments, rules also imposed, at least in part, by the constitution.

At the root of federal-provincial fiscal relations is a mismatch built into the original Confederation settlement and increased by the passage of time and the changing nature of government. Through the intentions of the Fathers of Confederation, the pre-eminent ability to raise money resides with the federal government, while, through historical and jurisprudential evolution, the pre-eminent obligation to spend money resides with provincial governments, which are responsible for the delivery of costly services such as health care, education, and social programs. The dynamics of Canada's federal system have, to a significant degree, been created by the attempts of Canada's political decision makers to deal with this imbalance.

During the past half-century, attempts to deal with this situation have been spurred by two major sets of problems. The first was the fiscal crisis created by the Depression and subsequently altered by World War Two. The solution to that crisis was a significant centralization of the ability to control expenditures and an even further centralization of the ability to raise money. The second is what is sometimes referred to as the fiscal "crisis" of the 1980s — the extremely large and seemingly intractable federal deficit. Paradoxically, the centralizing response to the first crisis contained within it some of the seeds of the second problem. The excessive centralization of the period up to 1968, the response to the first crisis, crested like a wave and then collapsed, creating, together with other economic and social factors, a very rapid decentralization and, coincidentally, a huge fiscal problem for the federal government. The resolution of this second set of problems is likely to constitute the major issue of fiscal federalism for the 1980s.

Admittedly, fiscal federalism comprises a complex set of issues. However, if one wishes to comprehend the essence of Canadian politics, the case for understanding it is undeniable. To do so, we will look first at some of the general principles involved in the transfer of money from one level of government to another; then we will consider the evolution of these arrangements since Confederation.

The General Principles[1]

Over the years, we have developed in Canada a variety of different arrangements by which the governments transfer money among themselves. Intergovernmental transfers can be described according to several variables. The transfers may be

— with or without conditions,
— block-funded or cost-matching,
— in the form of cash or tax.

When the federal government transfers money to provincial governments, it may do so with or without conditions. In a *conditional* grant arrangement, federal legislation defines the general nature of the programs provinces must deliver if they are to receive the grant. Thus, for example, the Canada Health Act states that if provinces are to receive federal transfers to cover hospital and medical services, their programs must feature universal coverage of their population; must be available to everyone under equal terms and conditions, and, therefore, must be free of any barriers to access, such as extra-billing by doctors; must be portable from province to province; must be publicly administered; and must cover a comprehensive range of services. By contrast, transfers may also be made *unconditionally*. The receiving government may deliver its programs in whatever fashion it deems appropriate; it will still receive the money. The most important of these transfers in Canada is the fiscal equalization program, the principle of which is now entrenched in the constitution.

Some transfers are structured so that the amount transferred by the federal government depends upon the level of provincial government expenditures on particular programs. Such grants may be described as *cost-matching*. In order to qualify for them, a provincial government must spend money to deliver the program and then submit an account to the federal government, describing how the money was spent. The federal government then reimburses the provincial government for some fixed portion of the expenditures, usually 50%.

---

[1] A similar approach is followed in *The Report of the Royal Commission on the Economic Union* (Ottawa: Supply and Services, 1985), pp. 238–242. The reader should note that what is said here about transfers between the federal and provincial governments can also be said about transfers from provincial to municipal governments, except that the province can be much more directive towards the municipalities. Subsequent references to this source are indicated by *Economic Union*.

That kind of arrangement, used, for example, to cover social-assistance and social-services programs, may be contrasted with *block-funded* programs. In block-funding arrangements, the federal transfer is not directly related to current program costs. The Established Program Financing (EPF) arrangements, which are discussed in detail below and which cover post-secondary education and health-insurance programs, make grants based on the provincial population and the historical costs of those programs, escalated according to the rate of increase in nominal gross national product minus 2%.

Finally, transfers can be made in the form of cash or tax. *Cash transfers* are exactly what the term implies. *Tax transfers* involve one order of government reducing the amount of income tax it collects, thus allowing the other order of government room to collect more tax itself. For example, the EPF arrangements involve not only a cash transfer, but also a tax transfer, in which the federal government forgoes 13.5% of personal income tax and 1% of corporate income tax, allowing provincial governments the room to increase their own tax take. Tax transfers can go either way. During World War Two, provincial governments effectively vacated all major tax fields, thus making a tax transfer to the federal government. Since the 1950s, tax transfers have all moved the other way, with the federal government conceding tax room to provincial governments.

By now, the reader may have noted that any particular intergovernmental transfer may have several attributes. For example, EPF, the largest, most complex, and most recent of the major transfer programs, has a conditional component for health, with the conditions stated in the Canada Health Act, and an unconditional component for post-secondary education. The transfer is partly cash and partly tax. It is, however, pure in one sense — it is entirely block-funded; the amount of the federal transfer is unrelated to current provincial expenditures in the fields the transfer nominally covers.

With the exception of some tax transfers to Quebec and some modest block-funding elements in the transfers covering health-insurance programs, inter-governmental transfers in the years between 1913 and 1970, when most of the major programs were put in place, took the form of conditional cost-matching arrangements. The first conditional grants were for agricultural instruction and were offered for a ten-year period. A province received the money on the condition that it be spent for agricultural instruction that met certain standards.

In the early period, conditional transfer programs were often referred to as "grants-in-aid." They were initially viewed as either "experimental or . . . given under extraordinary circumstances",[2] and, as such, they were usually intended to be terminated after a specific time period. By the close of World War One, federal grants-in-aid were provided for such things as assistance for highways, technical education, the control of venereal disease, and the maintenance of employment offices.[3] At that time, two schools of thought regarding the utility

---

[2] *Report of the Royal Commission on Dominion-Provincial Relations* (Ottawa: King's Printer, 1940), Book I, p. 131. Subsequent references are to *The Rowell-Sirois Report*, or *Rowell-Sirois*.

[3] *Rowell-Sirois*, p. 131.

and the advisability of conditional cost-matching transfers first evolved. One group felt the transfers to be a handy device for pursuing vigorous policies of federal leadership, in spite of the strait-jacket of the BNA Act. The opponents of this particular form of subsidy agreed that it permitted the federal government to take vigorous initiatives in areas of provincial jurisdiction. They also agreed that the conditional, cost-matching form of grant was characterized by problems that could be alleviated if we moved in the direction of block funding.

Conditional grants do, in fact, permit the federal government to set spending priorities even in fields that are constitutionally beyond its legislative competence. The basic source of this federal influence is the "spending power" by which the central government is free to spend its tax dollars in any way it sees fit. By offering to make a transfer provided that provincial governments supply programs that meet certain standards, for example in the largely provincial jurisdictions of medical or welfare services, Ottawa can usually convince the province to implement programs that, constitutionally, the federal government could not undertake itself. The most extreme case occurs when transfers are both conditional and cost-matching. In these cases, the province will usually be forced, by economic expediency, to commit its limited resources to programs partially funded by the federal government, for the cost of such programs to the provincial treasury is only a part, usually one-half, that of programs the province must fund itself. Thus, by allowing the federal government to prejudice provincial priorities in predominantly provincial fields, shared-cost grants place the autonomy of the provinces in some jeopardy.[4] This intervention may be perfectly justified in public-policy terms. It may allow poorer provinces to implement programs they might otherwise be unable to provide, and it encourages service standards that might not be attained by provinces acting alone. There seems little doubt, however, that such grants can also be characterized as federal intervention in an area otherwise outside its jurisdiction.

All of this may be quite desirable from the public's point of view: whether it is good or bad from a provincial government perspective depends, to some degree, on where one stands in that government. Provincial program managers in areas that have cost-matching grants have some fondness for them, especially in the first few years after their inception, for it puts the program managers in a favoured bargaining position at budget time. If they operate programs in areas where the federal government agrees to match provincial expenditures, they can go to their provincial treasurers and make the point that a dollar given to their program will call forth a matching dollar from the federal government, whereas a dollar spent on a rival program will not call forth any matching grant. The programs are probably least appreciated by the provincial treasurers and premiers whose priorities are skewed by them, and who would prefer either more taxing power or unconditional grants.

---

[4] *Rowell-Sirois*, p. 131. See also: R.M. Dawson, *The Government of Canada* (Toronto: University of Toronto Press, 1968), p. 105; D. Smiley, "Conditional Grants and Canadian Federalism: The Issues," in Meekison, *Canadian Federalism* (first edition), (Toronto: Methuen, 1972) pp. 256–268; and *Economic Union*, vol. 3, pp. 237–247.

We should not exaggerate the current importance of this "expenditure" effect, however. The largest intergovernmental transfers are now made under terms that require that certain program standards be met, but that do not relate the amount of the federal transfer directly to provincial expenditures. Moreover, the largest of the older cost-matching grants are those provided under the Canada Assistance Plan for social assistance and services. These program areas have not, in recent years, been popular places for provincial governments to spend money, and thus the presence of the cost-matching formula does little to lever up the levels of expenditures for these programs. Much of the assumed initial expenditure effect may simply have been a result of the popularity of social programs in the 1960s, and our newness in managing in those sectors.

Another criticism, which can apply to virtually any form of intergovernmental transfer, is based on the old maxim of the English constitution, that the government that taxes to raise public revenues should be accountable for their expenditure.[5] Even with clearly conditional grants, once the money has been transferred to a province, there is no sure procedure by which the federal authorities can ensure that all of the funds transferred have been spent for the purposes specified, or that all conditions are being met. Accountability of a government to Parliament for expenditures is therefore diminished. Attached to all conditional grants are information requirements, but as time goes on, and as the rather high level of agreement as to the aims of a shared-cost program begins to deteriorate, there is an increasing tendency for provinces to attempt to maximize receipt of funds while minimizing compliance with the terms of the agreement. For example, a provincial government may forward an inordinate number of claims to the federal government, knowing that "the feds" will be unable to check them all, and hence will have to pay many of them. The only recourse for the federal government would be to refuse to support the province in future joint projects, a tactic that might prove politically unwise, since the people of the provinces also vote in federal elections.

There are other problems created by conditional programs. There is, for example, an incentive for provincial governments to spend money in ways that will ensure federal cost sharing, even if cost sharing is not the most efficient way to deliver the program. For example, early federal cost-sharing programs for hospital insurance provided direct support for treatment in expensive acute-care hospital beds, but not for many of the services necessary to support the types of home-care treatment that later proved to be both more effective and much less expensive. Provinces were thus encouraged to go on providing more acute-care beds than would have been the case had either level of government alone been funding and operating the entire program.

For the federal government, there is a further problem inherent in the basic cost-matching mechanism. Typically, under its terms, the federal treasury agrees to match, according to whatever proportion is specified in the agreement, the actual program costs incurred by provincial governments. This means that the size of

5 *Rowell-Sirois*, I, p. 131.

federal disbursements is actually under provincial control, a situation fraught with terror for federal finance ministers or treasury board presidents and their officials. The unpredictability of the federal expenditure budget caused by this situation is, by now, more apparent than real, since the federal officials who operate these programs are very good at predicting actual costs. However, disasters have happened, ranging from an additional $50 million obligation that resulted from an accounting error by British Columbia in 1974, to hospital insurance-cost increases, which approached 20% per year in 1974 and 1975.

The Move to Block Funding

The increasing recognition of the problems inherent in cost matching in conditional grant arrangements meant that no major new programs of this type were implemented after the Medicare Act of 1968 provided for federal sharing in the costs of medical services, primarily physicians' services. That recognition led, as well, to the development of a number of block-funding programs in areas such as health insurance and the support for provincial second-language education.

Block-funding arrangements are assumed to have three major advantages. They make total expenditures more knowable in advance to all involved. They assure a level of funding for provinces without imposing a requirement that provincial governments spend all the money on particular programs, a feature particularly appealing to provincial treasurers. Finally, they are simple to administrate, avoiding the complex auditing and reporting procedures inherent in cost-matching grants.

Block-funding programs are not, however, problem-free. They do encourage provincial governments to save money, but one way in which money may be saved is through reducing standards of service and accessibility — a problem that may be exacerbated during periods of financial restraint. Moreover, the programs often retain the rhetoric of conditionality: the transfers are made, according to the legislation that governs them, to assist the delivery of certain kinds of services. But they largely eliminate the financial terms that could permit the federal government to assure Parliament that the conditions are being met. Thus, they seem to promise an accountability they cannot deliver. The very nature of block grants means that accountability of the federal government to Parliament and the taxpayers for the expenditure of federal tax dollars is extremely difficult to achieve.

There is, thus, a conflict that has not been resolved by any of the current payment mechanisms. The conflict is between the need for accountability for expenditure within the federal government (in both the strict accounting sense, of assuring that the dollars are spent where they are intended to be spent, and in the broad policy sense, of assuring that the desired outcomes occur) and the problems created by federal interference in an area of provincial jurisdiction. Starkly stated, one cannot have accountability without interference. Neither can one have national program standards without interference. Yet interference negates the provincial jurisdiction in areas that are matters of "a local or private nature within the province.''[6] It may choke off innovation, and it makes a response to peculiar local or regional problems more difficult.

The situation is made all the more difficult by another set of conflicting factors. Political accountability could be assured by the complete transfer of sufficient taxing power to the provinces to allow them to raise all the money necessary to finance all the programs in their jurisdiction. In this way, the government levying the taxes would be spending the money. However, these programs comprise such a large portion of total government expenditure in Canada that, under such arrangements, the federal government would lose much of the revenue-raising clout it now possesses. Given that it is generally agreed in Canada that a pre-eminent role of the federal government must be management of the economy, and given that one of the two major tools available to it in accomplishing this task is the ability to tax and to spend the proceeds, such large-scale transfers of tax powers would emasculate the national government. Thus, not only are the concepts of a national standard and provincial autonomy in conflict, but so are the concepts of provincial fiscal accountability and national economic management. None of the mechanisms for intergovernmental transfers so far developed seem to solve the problems inherent in these conflicts, and so we can expect the arrangements to continue to shift.

THE EVOLUTION OF FISCAL FEDERALISM

The Fiscal Balance in the Nineteenth Century

The nature and content of any system of public finance depends largely upon the role government is expected to play in the lives of its citizens. In 1867, the role of government was perceived in terms of rugged individualism, and the best government was judged to be that which governed least. Government should confine itself mainly to the provision of national security, including defence, to the administration of justice, and to promoting national economic development through a few essential public works.

At the time of Confederation, these most important and costly of governmental functions were placed in the hands of the federal parliament, along with the burden of the provincial debts in existence at that time. The provinces, in turn, were given the responsibility for matters of a local nature. Among these were education, public welfare, and transportation within the province, all of which involved relatively modest expenditures when contrasted with the federal share in 1867. Expenditures for health, education, and welfare, for example, amounted only to 14% of total governmental outlays in 1866, compared to more than 60% in 1986.[7]

The largest revenue sources at Confederation were customs and excise duties, which accounted for approximately 80% of the revenues of the colonies of Nova

---

[6] BNA Act, section 92.

[7] 1867 figures are from *Rowell-Sirois*, I, p. 39. 1986 figures are consolidated from Statistics Canada.

Scotia and New Brunswick, and 66% of the revenues of Canada.[8] Provincial revenue at Confederation came from real property taxes, various types of fees and permits, and provincial licensing systems. Because the BNA Act vested the responsibility for the "great functions of government" in the federal parliament, and because the Dominion was to assume responsibility for the existing debts, the major sources of revenue at that time were given to the Dominion. The federal tax power, as specified in section 91(3), thus gives the parliament of Canada the authority over "the Raising of Money by any Mode or System of Taxation." The provinces, on the other hand, were limited by section 92(2) to direct taxation within the province for their revenue.

The Fathers of Confederation felt that the provinces' control over the public domain, with its incidental revenues and the power to impose systems of licensing, would provide adequate revenues to meet what were expected to be modest needs.[9] Provincial deficits that might occur from time to time were to be met by modest federal subsidies (described below). The area of direct taxation was viewed as a sort of residual source of provincial revenue, which was not intended to be used extensively: "Direct taxes were extremely unpopular: they had never been levied by the provinces and . . . the nature of the economy made the administration of direct taxation, except by the municipalities, very difficult."[10]

The terms *direct* and *indirect taxation* require some clarification. Sections 91 and 92 do not make any clear distinction between these two terms, and it was not until a decision of the Judicial Committee in 1887 that a working definition was set down. The distinction made then has stood the test of time, and remains even today the basic rule for determining the validity of provincial tax measures. The Judicial Committee took a definition from the writing of John Stuart Mill and stated:

> Taxes are either direct or indirect. A direct tax is one that is demanded from the very persons who it is intended or desired should pay it. Indirect taxes are those that are demanded from one person in the expectation and intention that he shall indemnify himself at the expense of another. Such are the excise or customs . . . . He shall recover the amount by means of an advance in price.[11]

Thus, direct taxes include such things as personal income tax, corporate income tax, real property tax, and succession duty, and indirect taxes include such levies as customs duties and excise taxes.

The courts have tended to emphasize the intention of a provincial tax measure as the crucial determinant of its validity, and have not too seriously limited the power of the provincial legislature to tax, merely because one of the effects of a measure may be indirect. In the case of corporation income taxes, for instance, it is quite likely that corporations do attempt to indemnify themselves at the expense of the consumer, but the courts have judged such a provincial tax valid because the intention is that it shall be paid directly by the corporation. In the case of

[8] *Rowell-Sirois*, I, p. 41.

[9] BNA Act, section 109. See also *Rowell-Sirois*, I, p. 44.

[10] *Rowell-Sirois*, I, p. 44.

[11] *Bank of Toronto v. Lambe* (1887). See also *Rowell-Sirois*, I, p. 59.

retail sales tax, the provinces have been enabled to collect from the retailer a tax that is levied on the customer because the retailer is assumed to be the agent of the government for the purposes of adminstering this tax. When store clerks punch up the cost of your purchase, they are functioning on behalf of the store. When the sales tax is calculated and added to the total, the clerks are functioning as agents of the province. By naming each retailer a sort of tax collector, and by requiring that the tax be calculated separately, the province ensures that the sales tax can pass as a direct tax on the consumer. If the sales tax were included in the prices of retail goods, and collected from the store, it would be indirect, because the retailer would be "indemnifying himself at the expense of the customer" by a rise in the retail price of the goods.

While the province is given the power to levy direct taxes, and the interpretation of the scope of "direct taxation within the province" has been very broad, this tax power has not been deemed to be exclusive. It has been felt, by the courts, that the terms of section 91(3) are general, and that they therefore give the federal parliament the power to impose both indirect and direct tax measures. Conversely, section 92(2) is very specific, and it therefore must be construed only to *limit* the provincial legislatures to the raising of revenues by direct taxation, and not to reserve the direct tax fields to the exclusive use of the provinces. The constitutional authority to levy indirect taxes therefore rests exclusively with the parliament of Canada, and the authority to levy direct taxes is shared by the provinces and the federal government.

In retrospect, the way in which sources of revenue were distributed between the provinces and the federal government could be considered short-sighted. The drafters of the BNA Act assumed that there would be no change in the distribution of the costs of government that each would bear. Furthermore, they assumed that the major revenue sources would remain the same after 1867. Both of these assumptions were to be proven incorrect.

It would be unfair, however, to criticize the Fathers of Confederation for such a lack of foresight. The changes in the environment of the Canadian political system, and the changing demands placed upon it since 1867, could not have been foreseen except through the gift of clairvoyance. One of the effects of these environmental changes was the enormous expansion of the revenue needs of the provinces. The federal share of the costs of government fell from more than two-thirds of the total, in 1867, to less than one-half of the total seventy years later, and to less than 40% in the 1980s.[12] Another effect was a major change in the tax base. Customs duties, for instance, which accounted for 63% of the total federal revenue in 1867–1868, accounted for less than 5% of the total by 1986. Thus, the balance between revenue-raising rights and expenditure responsibilities that had been struck by the Fathers of Confederation and enshrined in the BNA Act in 1867 eventually became a serious imbalance. While that imbalance has always created problems, it can also be claimed that it is one of the more appealing characteristics of Canadian federalism that governments had been able, though not always easily, to devise ways of circumventing it.

---

[12] *Rowell-Sirois*, I, p. 63; see also *Economic Union*, vol. 3, p. 224.

The Statutory Subsidies

It was clear even to the Fathers of Confederation that the provincial revenue sources provided in 1867 were not going to meet the expenditures of the provincial legislatures, at least for a transitional period. In recognition of this, provisions for federal subsidies to the provinces were written directly into the BNA Act. Section 118, which was subsequently repealed and replaced, gave the provinces three broad types of federal grants: annual grants to support provincial governments and legislatures; per-capita grants; and payments on debt allowances. The first of these was a subsidy based on the population of the province at the 1861 census, which was to be paid to the province to assist in the initial setting up and operation of the government and legislature in its first few years. This grant was to be given to the provinces annually and in perpetuity, and was not to be adjusted with population increase. When a general revision of the federal subsidies to the provinces took place in 1907, however, this grant was raised for all the provinces. Despite this, by comparison with total federal subsidies, the grants to support the provincial governments and legislatures amounted to a mere pittance, ranging from $100,000 for Prince Edward Island to $240,000 for Ontario.

The second subsidy, the per-capita grant, was intended to be the major assistance that the federal government would render to the provinces. Based on the 1861 census, the provinces were to be given eighty cents per capita per annum in perpetuity, although the per-capita grants to New Brunswick and Nova Scotia were to increase with population up to 400,000 people. The per-capita grant was manipulated, from time to time, through the device of estimating the population of the province generously in order to entice new provinces into the federation and to meet the special needs of one province or another. For instance, when British Columbia came into Confederation in 1871, her population was estimated at 60,000, when in fact it was only 34,000; Manitoba was given the fictitious population of 17,000 when it had only 12,200.[13] While these grants were to be fixed at the figure established at the time of Confederation, the 1907 revisions of the subsidies saw the eighty-cents-per-capita grant permitted to increase up to 2,500,000 people, and sixty cents a head was provided for any number over that figure.

Finally, while the federal government had accepted the responsibility for all of the debts of the provinces at Confederation, it was felt that the provinces with smaller debts should be rewarded, in order to equalize the benefits that each province would reap from the union. Each province was allowed a certain debt, based on approximately twenty-five dollars a head according to the 1861 census.[14] If the actual debt of a province amounted to less than this figure, that province was to receive 5% of the difference as a grant from the federal government, annually and in perpetuity. According to this scheme, while New Brunswick and Nova Scotia either broke even or gained a little from the Dominion, Ontario and Quebec had debts that were far in excess of the debt allowance. It was arranged that these provinces would pay the federal government a figure equal to 5% of

[13] R.M. Dawson, *The Government of Canada*, p. 102.

[14] Dawson, p. 100.

the difference between their actual debt and the amount allowed by the Confederation agreement. This arrangement was never implemented, partly because of the difficulty of assessing how much Ontario and Quebec should pay on a debt they incurred jointly as the colony of Canada. To get around this difficulty, and to further appease the province of Nova Scotia, the debt allowance was raised, so that Ontario and Quebec broke even and New Brunswick and Nova Scotia got an even larger payment from the Dominion. As the other provinces came into the federation, they also were given generous debt allowances. Even the provinces of Alberta and Saskatchewan, which had been federal territories before their coming of age and so obviously had no debt, received an annual payment based on the difference between their debt allowance and their non-existent debt.

In addition to these three basic subsidies, ever since Confederation there have been a number of special federal grants to various provinces and regions in order to meet special needs. New Brunswick, for example, received a grant for ten years after Confederation, and the province of Newfoundland received a healthy subsidy on entering Confederation in 1949. Special grants were given to the two western prairie provinces on entering Confederation in 1905, as compensation for the Dominion's retaining its rights to their natural resources. Even after the Dominion gave the natural resources of the prairies back to Saskatchewan and Alberta, the compensation grant was continued. Thus, while it was assumed that the arrangements concluded at Confederation would be permanent and unalterable, in fact the federal subsidies to the provinces began to undergo almost constant revision for the day of their inception. Despite these constant adjustments, the statutory subsidies today form a very tiny part of transfer payments to the provincial governments. Total federal cash transfers to the provinces in 1985–1986 amounted to $19.8 billion, and, of that, only $35.8 million was accounted for by statutory subsidies.[15]

The Early Twentieth Century

By the turn of the century, the federal-provincial financial structure had begun a startling metamorphosis. Following a period of economic stagnation when provincial expenditures did not increase markedly, the wheat boom stimulated an immense growth of overall government expenditures. The prosperity of the period generated the extra revenues, and all sectors of government — federal, provincial, and municipal — began to spend large sums of money on urban development, public works, and economic expansion. From 1896 to 1913, total expenditures by all governments quadrupled.[16] Initially, at least, the costs of this rapid expansion of the role and responsibilities of government had been matched by corresponding increases in federal revenue as customs and excise receipts, which at this time accounted for more than 90% of federal revenues, produced large budget surpluses during most of the years between 1900 and World War One.[17] Similarly,

---

[15] See Table 9-1.

[16] *Rowell-Sirois*, I, p. 80.

[17] *Rowell-Sirois*, I, p. 81.

provincial revenues from standard tax sources also increased, but provincial expenditures grew still more rapidly, so that the traditional tax bases of the provinces began to be squeezed dry. The inelasticity of federal subsidies and the inability of existing provincial revenue sources to cope with the rising costs of the government services forced the provinces to venture into the field of direct taxation, despite the unpopularity of such measures.[18]

From 1914 to 1920, the federal government was forced to impose special taxes, including a "temporary" income tax, in order to meet the costs of the war effort. During this period, under the provisions of the War Measures Act, the federal government virtually took over the control of the economy, and the question of federal-provincial financial relations was left in a state of suspended animation until the end of the war. During the immediate post-war period and through most of the 1920s, "in its whole fiscal policy, the Dominion was labouring for a return to prewar 'normalcy'."[19] In pursuit of this goal, the federal government tried to reduce or withdraw the special taxes that had been imposed at the time of war, but the economy had changed so much that it was difficult—or indeed impossible— to go back. Pre-war normalcy and post-war normalcy were completely different economic species.

Between 1921 and 1930, welfare expenditures increased by 130%, and three-quarters of this burden fell upon the provincial governments and the municipalities.[20] Federal outlays in this period were limited largely to grants to the provinces through the first of Canada's major shared-cost social programs, in support of provincial old-age pension schemes and unemployment relief. Meanwhile, the costs of the traditional provincial and municipal responsibilities for roads and highways grew rapidly. The coming of the automobile increased the need not only for interurban highways, but for better roads and road systems within the cities and in suburban areas.[21] Fortunately, during the 1920s, while the cost of the roads and relief soared, provincial revenues increased rapidly as well. The automobile, for instance, brought in large additional revenues through taxes on gasoline and motor-vehicle licences. Indeed, provincial revenues doubled from 1921 to 1930, and two-thirds of this increase was due to additional tax yields in the three fields of motor-vehicle licences, gasoline taxes, and liquor control. Thus, the growing responsibilities of the provinces and the fiscal instability of the provincial financial structure were disguised, to some extent, by a growing economy, which brought a high yield from direct taxation.

Revenues from the public domain, which had been expected to meet a large part of the costs of provincial programs, dropped to a mere 10% of the total provincial revenues in 1930. Succession duties and corporation taxes increased as sources of revenue during this period, but in 1930, of the total provincial revenue from these sources, 87% was collected in the provinces of Ontario and Quebec, which together accounted for only 60% of the population of Canada.

[18] *Rowell-Sirois*, I, p. 87.

[19] *Rowell-Sirois*, I, p. 127.

[20] *Rowell-Sirois*, I, p. 128.

[21] *Rowell-Sirois*, I, p. 129.

The reason for this disparity was the growing number of national companies with head offices in Toronto or Montreal. The imposition of provincial corporation taxes occurs at the head office of a corporation, with the result that profits the corporation makes elsewhere in Canada are taxed by the governments of Ontario or Quebec. This was to prove an important factor in producing serious regional disparities in per-capita revenues, as corporation taxes and succession duties came to play a larger and larger role in provincial finance during the 1930s.[22]

The Canadian federal system thus entered the hard years of the Depression with a seriously unbalanced revenue structure, which was already strained to the limit and was too inflexible to be able to meet any major new demands for expenditure, particularly in areas of provincial responsibility. The provinces relied heavily on revenue from tax fields such as liquor control and automobile licences, which tend to be very sensitive to economic fluctuations of a general nature. Similarly, the municipalities relied entirely on real property tax revenues, which declined when the value of real estate dropped during the Depression. Moreover, in relatively small provinces with homogeneous single-commodity economic bases, any major decline in that base could so diminish provincial revenues as to call the financial viability of the government into question. Without the spreading of risk inherent in the diversified economic base of larger units, single-industry provinces, such as the prairie provinces of that time, were extremely vulnerable, a situation that led to fiscal insolvency in the 1930s.

In addition, constitutional and practical considerations prevented the provinces from diversifying their tax bases. Indirect tax measures were constitutionally beyond the competence of the provincial legislature, and, given the low per-capita income of the Depression, direct tax measures such as personal income tax would have produced a very low yield, except perhaps in Ontario. Moreover, the federal government had already occupied the field of personal income tax, and any extra tax on the already hard-pressed individual income would have produced both further economic problems and political unrest.

Total government expenditures on relief grew nearly tenfold, from $18.4 million in 1930 to $172.9 million in 1935, and, since responsibility for such matters lies with the provinces, the federal government transferred large portions of its revenue to the provinces to help pay for them. Provincial and regional disparities were enhanced by the incidence of the Depression because:

> the larger the decline in the income and the larger the consequent rise in government expenditures in the most favourably situated provinces, the more rapidly did local revenues and credit become hopelessly inadequate and the larger was the support which had to be obtained from the Dominion.[23]

Thus, by the mid-thirties, Canadian federalism was faced with a financial crisis that was the product of several factors. First, traditional functions of government had grown far beyond the expectations of the Fathers of Confederation, and the bulk of this growth involved great increases in provincial expenditures. Second,

---

[22] *Rowell-Sirois*, I, p. 131.

[23] *Rowell-Sirois*, I, p. 160. Reproduced with the permission of the Minister of Supply and Services Canada.

new responsibilities of government had emerged, which had not even been conceived of in 1867, and the interpretation of the BNA Act by the judicial committee of the privy council had vested only the provincial legislatures with the constitutional power to deal with them. Third, the revenue structure of the Canadian federal system provided the provincial governments with inadequate tax fields to meet both new responsibilities and inflated traditional responsibilites. Fourth, the homogeneity and product specialization of many provincial economies meant that the decline of a single industry, such as agriculture, could virtually destroy the provincial financial base. Finally, the incidence of a worldwide Depression exaggerated all these factors, making worse the already serious disparities in wealth between the various regions of Canada, producing startling inequalities in the standard of governmental service from one province to the next, and creating a demand for still more expenditures in areas of provincial jurisdiction that could not be covered from existing provincial revenue sources.

The Financial Structure in Crisis

The combination of the asymmetrical distribution of tax powers and legislative jurisdiction and the economic crisis of the Depression conspired to challenge the Canadian federal system with a number of apparently insoluble problems. One major response was the appointment, in 1937, of the Royal Commission on Dominion-Provincial Relations, charged with undertaking "a reexamination of the economic and financial basis of Confederation and of the distribution of legislative powers in the light of the social and economic developments of the last seventy years."[24] The findings and recommendations were reported in May 1940.

The Rowell-Sirois Report focused on the two basic problems of federal-provincial finance in Canada: the distribution of responsibilities and revenues between the provinces and the Dominion; and the economic disparities that existed among the various provinces and regions of Canada. As a solution for the former, the Commission recommended an extensive shift of both governmental functions and tax powers, and as a solution for the latter, the Commission recommended unconditional "equalization payments"[25] from the federal treasury to the needy provinces.

Specifically, the Report stated in its recommendations that the Dominion should take over the debts of all of the provinces and responsibility for unemployment relief, and also pay a national adjustment grant to the less fortunate regions of Canada, to bring the standard of services in those regions up to the national average. In return for this, however, the Report recommended that the provinces give up all claim to the fields of income tax, corporation taxes, corporate income taxes, and succession duties, and that the original statutory subsidies be abolished.

The recommendations of the Rowell-Sirois Report were discussed in federal-provincial conferences in 1940 and 1941, and were not met with any great enthusiasm by the provinces. The "have" provinces, especially, were not willing to

---

[24] *Rowell-Sirois*, I, p. 9.

[25] Dawson, *The Government of Canada*, pp. 107–108.

give up their taxing powers in return for an allowance from the federal government, and even the "have-not" provinces were not very happy with being raised merely to the national average by the national adjustment grants. By 1940, too, Canada was involved in World War Two, and the focus of the national attention had shifted to matters other than federal-provincial relations. Besides, prosperity had returned, and it was easy for the provinces and the Dominion to postpone any serious consideration of the Commission's recommendations until after the war.

The Postwar Period

The outbreak of war had given the federal authorities the moral justification and the legal authority (under the "emergency power" in section 91 of the BNA Act) to take all of the remaining governmental spending and taxing initiatives from the provinces. The Dominion occupied, among other things, much of the field of direct taxation to the exclusion of the provinces, and paid the provinces a rent in lieu of the revenue that was lost to them, with the result that the federal government controlled the entire revenue structure of the federation, and the provinces were reduced to the state of receiving an allowance from the Dominion. In terms of the expectations and perceptions of the public, the federal government had become *the* government; the provinces were of secondary importance. Governmental initiative appeared to rest solely in the hands of the Dominion, and the provinces, particularly the have-not provinces, humbled as they were by the financial catastrophe of the Depression, seemed willing to accept the leadership of the Dominion.

Despite this apparent acceptance of the post-war leadership of the federal government, neither the have nor the have-not provinces were eager to adopt the terms of the Rowell-Sirois Report that would have permanently centralized both public finance and the responsibility for all major policy initiatives. The federal government countered with a new set of proposals for federal-provincial relations, which were produced in the "Green Book" of 1945. These proposals, in accord with the Rowell-Sirois Report, would have handed over to the federal government the exclusive power to levy income taxes, corporate income taxes, and succession duties. Unlike the Commission's report, the Green Book did not provide for unconditional equalization payments to the poorer provinces. Instead, the federal government proposed to subsidize the provinces through a series of cost-matching programs, which would provide services funded jointly by provincial revenues and federal conditional grants.[26] This alternative had been specifically singled out by the royal commission as undesirable:

> The conditional grant as it works under Canadian conditions is an inherently unsatisfactory device . . . We believe it to be more costly than if the service in question were financed by a single government. It unquestionably leads to delay and to periodic friction between Dominion and provincial governments.[27]

[26] D.V. Smiley, "Public Administration and Canadian Federalism," *Canadian Public Administration*, vol. VII, No. 3, September 1964, pp. 371–388.

[27] *Rowell-Sirois*, I, p. 259. Reproduced with permission of the Minister of Supply and Services Canada.

Because the Green Book proposals were presented as a package deal, and because the provinces would not give up their share of the key direct taxes, the Dominion-provincial conference of 1945 was unsuccessful in its attempts to secure a permanent arrangement. But as Donald Smiley points out, "Almost from the day the conference was finished, federal authorities began to seek limited and piecemeal agreements with the provinces in particular matters."[28]

It seems that, although provincial politicians were not willing to sell their birth-rights, some at least were willing to lease it, and to allow the federal government to continue setting the major policy priorities. The political pressure to equalize the standards of services in the various economic regions of Canada played a large part in securing this cooperation between the provinces and the federal government; and a faint blush of nationalism, the result of a common cause and shared hardships during the war, abetted the situation. Although there was some residual bitterness in Quebec as a result of the conscription issue, for a while at least, Canadians of all regions and walks of life became accustomed to thinking in national terms, rather than provincially or regionally. The goal of raising the standard of living of the less fortunate regions of Canada was politically popular in all provinces, and the natural vehicle for programs that would achieve this goal was the federal government. This was indeed the high tide of centralization in Canada, and the fiscal arrangements both reflected and reinforced this fact.

From Centralization to Decentralization: Federal-Provincial Fiscal Arrangements, 1945–1987

Through the Wartime Tax Agreements of 1941, the provinces had ceased to levy personal income taxes, corporation income taxes, and all other corporation taxes. While these fiscal arrangements are euphemistically referred to as "agree-ments," the fact was that, in 1941, because of the emergency conditions of wartime, the federal government possessed the constitutional power unilaterally to exclude the provinces from the field of direct taxation and, for that matter, to interfere with any of the matters reserved exclusively to the provinces by section 92 of the BNA Act.[29] Under the circumstances, all the provinces entered into tax agreements with the federal government for the period from 1941 to 1946. In return for the revenue that would be lost to them by giving up these fields of taxation to the Dominion, the provinces were to be paid a rent or a *tax rental payment*, based either on the revenue yields in the vacated fields in the year 1941, or on the total cost of servicing the provincial debt. The choice between these alternative formulae of compensation for lost revenue was left to the provinces themselves, and, as it turned out, Quebec, Ontario, Manitoba, and British Columbia opted for the former, and the rest of the provinces opted for the latter.

To discourage the provinces from increasing their succession duties, provincial succession duty collections were subtracted from the federal rental payment to

[28] Donald Smiley, "Public Administration and Canadian Federalism," p. 277.

[29] See *Fort Frances Pulp and Paper Company v. Winnipeg Free Press*, [1923] 3 *D.L.R.* 629; *Cooperative Committee on Japanese-Canadians v. Attorney General for Canada*, [1947] 1 *D.L.R.* 577; and *Reference Re Validity of Wartime Leasehold Regulations*, [1950] 2 *D.L.R.* 1.

those provinces that elected the formula based on the cost of servicing the provincial debt (i.e., New Brunswick, Nova Scotia, Prince Edward Island, Alberta, and Saskatchewan). Another provision that was unique to these wartime agreements was one guaranteeing the existing level of provincial revenue from liquor and gasoline taxes, regardless of the rental-payment formula selected by the province.[30]

1947–1957   By the time the 1941 tax-rental agreement had expired the war was over, and it was no longer possible for the Dominion to compel the provinces to enter into fiscal agreements. A second tax-rental agreement, which covered the period from 1947 to 1952, was signed by most provinces, but the federal government could not convince Quebec and Ontario that it would be to their advantage to participate; the two provinces did not sign. Upon entering Confederation in 1949, Newfoundland also agreed to the second tax-rental arrangements, which meant that eight provinces participated for most of the 1947 to 1952 period. During this period, the eight provinces agreed not to levy income taxes, corporation taxes, and succession duties; and, in return, the federal government paid them a rent based on either a per-capita payment or on the revenue yield from the vacated tax fields in the province — except in the case of Prince Edward Island, which was given a specified lump sum. The 1947–1952 tax agreement also permitted the participating provinces to levy their own 5% tax on corporation income in the province.

The real benefit the provinces gained by entering the tax-rental agreements was that the federal government, which had set up the machinery for collection of direct taxation on a national basis during the war years, could collect the taxes more cheaply than could the provinces. Most of the provinces could not afford to duplicate the federal machinery, and those that could afford it could see that the extensive administrative machinery required for the collection of personal income tax would render separate federal and provincial systems extremely inefficient. Moreover, since appearing to be the tax collector is something the vast majority of politicians seek to avoid, the offer by the federal government to act as the tax collector was not one most provincial governments wanted to turn down. Partly for these reasons, Ontario reconsidered its position during the negotiations for the next tax-rental, agreements, and Quebec alone refused to enter the federal-provincial tax agreements for the period from 1952 to 1957.

The 1952–1957 agreements were generally similar to the preceding two. The participating provinces refrained from imposing personal income taxes, corporation taxes, and succession duties. (Ontario continued to levy its own succession duties.) The most significant difference in the third arrangements was that the payments to the provinces were guaranteed at a certain minimum for each province, and the actual rent paid to each province was adjusted upwards according to a formula that related per-capita GNP and provincial population.[31] The have provinces received larger payments than the have-not provinces, but at the same time, the less fortunate provinces were guaranteed a certain amount regardless of the actual

[30] This was, in part, to compensate the provinces for revenue lost as a result of wartime rationing.

[31] Canadian Tax Foundation, *The National Finances, 1965–66* (Toronto; 1966), p. 126.

revenue yield of their vacated tax fields. This particular provision of the third tax-rental agreements is crucial, for it contained the germ of the principle of the unconditional equalization payments to the have-not provinces, which today form so significant a part of the federal-provincial fiscal arrangements.

1957–1962 The Tax Sharing Arrangements Act of 1956 set out the terms of the federal-provincial tax agreements for the period from 1957 to 1962. According to this act, the participating provinces agreed to vacate the *standard tax fields* of personal income tax, corporation taxes, and succession duties, as before. The federal government, in return, agreed to pay the provinces a rent based on the revenue yield in the vacated fields. The basic federal payment to the provinces, according to the agreement, amounted to 10% of federal personal income-tax collections in the province, 9% of corporation profits in the province, and 50% of the revenues of federal succession duties in the province, based on a three-year average of collections.

The 1957–1962 arrangements, however, also provided the first unconditional *equalization payment* to the poorer provinces. The federal government agreed to pay those provinces an amount sufficient to bring the potential per-capita yield of each province in the three standard taxes up to the average per-capita yield for those three years in the two wealthiest provinces. Finally, the Tax Sharing Arrangements Act also provided for a *stabilization grant*, which was calculated to raise the total yield for a province up to a set minimum, to prevent the revenue yield of the various provinces from fluctuating a great deal from one year to the next.

All of the provinces entered into these arrangements to some extent. However, Quebec accepted only the unconditional equalization payment, and Ontario chose not to vacate the fields of corporation tax and succession duties. For those provinces that did not participate fully, a *tax abatement* was granted, to provide tax room for the province. The federal government, to prevent the taxpayer from being doubly taxed, agreed to withdraw partially from any of the fields of income tax, corporation tax, or succession duties if a province continued to levy its own taxes. Thus, as the province of Ontario did not vacate corporation income-tax fields, the federal government abated its own corporation income tax by 9% of the corporation profits (an amount equal to what the province would have received as a rental payment had it chosen to rent that particular tax field). The province of Quebec was granted, in lieu of rental payments, a tax abatement in each of the three standard tax fields. The abatement was equal to the amount the province would have been paid by the federal government had it entered the agreement: 10% of federal personal income tax, 9% of the federal corporation tax, and 50% of the federal estate taxes.

In 1958, in response to demands by the provinces, the federal government raised the provincial share of personal income tax to 13% of the federal revenues collected, and provided an equivalent increase in the abatement in that tax field for the province of Quebec. In 1960, a new twist was added to the already confusing structure of federal-provincial relations: any province that wished to could opt out of the federal program of conditional per-capita grants to the provinces in aid of university education. If a province chose to opt out, it would receive, in lieu of the conditional grant, one per cent more of corporation profits in the province. It was provided that, if the revenue from one per cent of corporation profits was less than the province would have received in the form of per-capita conditional grants, the federal government would make good the difference. Conversely, if the one per cent happened to be greater than the per-capita grant would have been, the province had to refund some revenue to the federal government. Only the province of Quebec opted out of the university grants program, but the significance of this provision is that it set a precedent that led to a proliferation of opting-out formulae in federal-provincial programs.

Other provisions were included in the 1957–1962 agreements to meet the specific needs of the Atlantic provinces. Special Atlantic Provinces Adjustment Grants were added to the agreement in 1958, in order to meet specific economic problems that that region of Canada faced. These grants were unconditional, and they amounted to an extension of the principle of equalization to secure added assistance for a region that could not make ends meet with the standard equalized federal payments. The province of Newfoundland was also given additional annual grants by special legislation that was passed in 1959. The year 1957 saw the inception of the first of the huge post-war federal cost-matching conditional grant programs, in the form of the Hospital Insurance and Diagnostic Services Act (HIDS).[32] Paradoxically, given the drawbacks of conditional grant programs from the provincial point of view, HIDS was negotiated primarily at the behest of several provincial governments, including Ontario. Several provinces, led by Saskatchewan, already had hospital insurance, and most that did not were eager to implement it but could only afford to do so with federal assistance. That assistance was negotiated at a series of federal-provincial meetings in 1956 and 1957, and the new federal government of 1957 went ahead and implemented the program negotiated by its predecessor.

1962-1967 Until 1962, the federal-provincial tax agreements were based on the principle that the federal government should levy the taxes and collect the revenue, and then pass over a percentage of the take to the provinces participating in the agreement. The attitude of the federal government was that the ability to tax is crucial to the federal power, and that if the federal government could convince the provinces to give up at least some of this authority, it would enhance its own role in the management of the economy. However, the unfortunate consequence of this situation, from Ottawa's point of view, was that the federal government was perceived as the government that collected all the taxes, while the provinces were receiving credit as the governments that delivered the most popular programs. This made the provinces almost automatic winners in the game of fiscal federalism. If the provinces were to receive the praise from the public for spending money on popular programs, the federal authorities felt the provinces should also take some of the blame for high taxes.

For this reason, the Federal-Provincial Fiscal Arrangements Act (1961), which

---

[32] For details on HIDS and medicare, see Malcolm Taylor, *Health Insurance and Canadian Public Policy* (Montreal: McGill-Queen's Press, 1978). Taylor's work combines a thorough policy analysis with an excellent set of examples of the real workings of a fiscal federalism.

was to be in effect from 1962 to 1967, set out a tax-sharing plan that was different in form from anything that had existed before. According to the Act, the federal government would undertake to withdraw partially from the fields it had previously shared with the provinces, in much the same way that the federal government had agreed to grant tax abatements to non-participating provinces in the previous agreements. Thus, the federal government would actually withdraw from the corporation income-tax field to the extent of 9% of corporate profits, and from the personal income-tax field by 16% of the federal tax. The percentage withdrawal or abatement of the personal income-tax field was to increase from 16% in 1962 at a rate of one percent per annum, until it reached 20% by 1966. This arrangement was subsequently altered as a result of demands from the provinces so that the total withdrawal from the field of personal income tax was 24% in 1966. In the field of succession duties, the federal government agreed either to pay the province 50% of revenues from the federal tax or to grant an abatement to the extent of 50% of the federal tax in the provinces that wished to levy their own succession duties. In 1963, the federal payment-abatement of succession duties was increased to 75% of the federal tax.

Under the 1962–1967 arrangements, the equalization payment was based on the per-capita revenues from the three standard taxes, as before, but the equalization base was modified to include, as well, 50% of the three-year average yield from taxes on natural resources in the province. The provision was added because some provinces, particularly Alberta, with its vast revenues from oil and gas, were receiving healthy equalization payments under the old formula, and did not really need them. What Alberta lacked in income and corporation-tax revenue, she could easily make up with resource-tax revenue, whereas provinces like New Brunswick suffered from low revenue yields in all tax fields. A further change in the equalization formula was to base the calculation on the *national* average yield in the standard taxes, rather than on the average yield in the two wealthiest provinces. However, in 1963, this was changed once again, so that the equalization payment was calculated on the three standard taxes only, and was based on the average per-capita yield in the two wealthiest provinces, as it had been in 1957–1962. While natural-resources revenues thus, for the moment, did not figure directly in the equalization formula, it was provided that any province whose revenues from this field of taxation exceeded the national average would be faced with a deduction from its equalization grant.[33]

While the intention of the federal government in undertaking to withdraw from the shared tax fields was to distribute the political responsibility for taxes among the governments that were spending the revenues, it did not wish to penalize the provinces financially, and it did wish to maintain a uniform tax system throughout Canada. Hence, under the Fiscal Arrangements Act, the federal government offered to continue to collect the provincial share of income tax and corporation income tax, free of charge, provided the province utilized the same tax base. As a result, the provinces all began levying their own income taxes and corporation income taxes in 1962, and all except the province of Quebec, which had previously

---

[33] For a further explanation of this arrangement, see *The National Finances*, p. 128.

set up its own collection machinery, signed collection agreements with the federal government. In the field of corporation income tax, Ontario, like Quebec, chose to look after its own collections. From 1962 to 1967, six of the provinces set their tax rates equal to the amount of the federal withdrawal; Saskatchewan and Manitoba adopted higher rates, Quebec continued the rates already in existence in that province, and Ontario raised the corporation income-tax rate.

The stabilization grants continued from 1962 to 1967 much as they had in the previous period, with the federal government guaranteeing the provinces' yield from the standard taxes and equalization payments at the level equal to 95% of the average yield for the preceding two years. The Atlantic Provinces Adjustment Grants and the special grants to Newfoundland were continued for the period, with only slight changes. The one per cent abatement of corporation income tax in lieu of grants in aid to universities was continued as before, and the province of Quebec alone continued to exercise this option.

In 1965, the federal government passed the Established Programs (Interim Arrangements) Act, by which provinces were permitted to opt out of certain federal-provincial shared-cost programs without any financial penalty. For each program the province chose to opt out of, the federal government allowed either an additional abatement in the field of personal income tax or a direct cash payment in lieu of the federal share of the cost of the program. Provinces wishing to take advantage of the opting-out provisions were compelled by the federal legislation to continue the program along the same lines as the federal program for a certain specified interim period, during which they had to agree to a sort of audit by the federal authorities, to ensure provincial compliance with the terms. The Act also stated that the additional percentage points of income tax given up by the federal government would be equalized.

The programs to which the Established Programs (Interim Arrangements) Act applied were separated into two categories: those for which the province opting out would receive a certain number of equalized abatement points in personal income tax, and those for which the opting-out province would receive a straight cash compensation. The provinces were given until October 1965 to decide whether they wanted to exercise the option set down in the legislation. When the time limit expired, only the province of Quebec had accepted the opting-out formula; Quebec exercised the privilege in all of the category-one programs, and in the forestry program from category two. The effect was to give the province of Quebec an additional 20% of personal income tax. When this was added to the 24% abatement of personal income tax, which applied to all of the provinces by 1966, Quebec got a total abatement of 44% of personal income tax, 10% of the profits of corporations in the province, and 75% of succession duties. Quebec's choice was probably determined by the high level of nationalist feeling within the province, and by the desire of the provincial authorities to focus the loyalties of the Québécois on Quebec rather than on Canada. The rest of the provinces decided to stay in the joint programs for reasons of economic efficiency: it was less expensive for them to continue to use the federal machinery and procedures that existed at the time, rather than try to create completely new provincial ones.

The largest of the programs to which the opting-out formula was applied is the

Canada Assistance Plan (CAP), based on federal legislation passed in 1964. The Canada Assistance Plan, the second of the large post-war social programs to be covered by shared-cost arrangements, provides for 50% federal sharing in provincial social-assistance payments and in many of the personal social services, such as counselling, family services, and day care delivered by provincial and local governments. By 1985–1986, payments to provinces under CAP had grown to $4 billion.

1967–1977   By 1966, the renegotiation of the terms that would appear in the Federal-Provincial Fiscal Arrangements Act was well on the way to becoming an established five-yearly ritual of Canadian politics. These negotiations resemble nothing so much as an elaborate pantomime working its way up through various levels of the governmental hierarchy. Initial posturing requires that the provincial governments, usually in the person of the provincial treasurer, should anguish about their ability to pay for the vastly expensive programs into which they have been (allegedly) coerced or seduced via the mechanism of shared-cost programs, or to bemoan their inability to provide for the services necessary to put their citizens on an equal footing with other Canadians.

Federal authorities counter with concern over Ottawa's ability to manage the economy and absolute anguish about the huge federal deficit. Initial proposals, normally made by the federal government, emerge from this posturing about one year before the dreaded deadline imposed by the expiry of the legislation. Provincial governments attack the federal proposal as hopelessly inadequate. All dissolves in apparent disarray following a "final" meeting of finance ministers and treasurers just a few months before the critical deadline. In this Canadian political version of *The Perils of Pauline*, the stage is then set for the prime minister and premiers to meet and, at the last possible instant and after a certain amount of additional posturing both inside and outside the Conference Centre, to snatch an agreement from the jaws of fate, saving Canada from yet another crisis.

The Federal-Provincial Fiscal Arrangements Act that emerged from this process in 1966 defined the tax agreements and the various unconditional intergovernmental transfers for 1967–1972. Under it, the federal government increased its basic abatement of personal income tax from 24% to 28% of the federal tax payable in the provinces. The corporate income-tax abatement, which had been 9% of corporate profits in the provinces other than Quebec, was raised to 10% in all provinces for the 1967 tax year. The abatement of succession duties remained substantially the same as it had been under the previous arrangement: the abatement for provinces that levied their own estate taxes or the federal payment for provinces that did not levy their own taxes was 75% of the federal tax due in the provinces.

The formula for calculating equalization payments was altered radically by the 1967 arrangement. Instead of being calculated on the per-capita yield of the three standard taxes, the payment was figured on the revenue yield of sixteen different provincial revenue sources. Except for the fact that by 1977 the sixteen revenue sources had risen to twenty-nine, the formula remained basically unchanged from 1967 to the end of the 1977–1982 arrangements. Although the actual mathematical calculations are rather intricate, the principle is that a national-average per-capita provincial revenue is calculated for each of the agreed-upon number of revenue sources, and the potential per-capita yield in each is figured for a particular province, on the assumption that the province makes an average "tax effort" — that is, that it applies the national average rate of taxation for this tax field. Where the province's potential per-capita yield is lower than the national average for a given revenue source, the province is given a *positive entitlement*; where the province's per-capita yield is more than the national average for that field, the province is given a *negative entitlement*. If the total of all the entitlements for all of the revenue sources comes to a positive figure, the province receives that much in the form of a per-capita equalization payment. If, on the other hand, the total of all the entitlements of any province comes to a minus figure, the province does not get an equalization payment. This equalization formula was felt to be more equitable than older formulae because, being based on a "representative" tax system consisting of all major provincial revenue sources, it gave a more accurate reflection of provincial need.[34]

In order to prevent hardship being suffered by the provinces that were to receive smaller equalization payments under the new formula, the federal government agreed to make special interim equalization payments to such provinces. Saskatchewan was the only province that would have suffered under the new formula, so the federal government granted that province a five-year transitional equalization payment, based on the province's entitlement during the last year of the 1962–1967 arrangements. An additional equalization payment was also granted to the Atlantic provinces, to compensate them for revenue lost through the termination of the Atlantic Provinces Additional Grants. The amount of this additional equalization payment was exactly the same amount that they had been paid under the Additional Grants Act, so that the change here was only in the title given the specific unconditional transfer payment.

The stabilization grants were continued for the 1967–1972 period, and the formula used to calculate the actual payment was based on the same principle as the equalization formula; that is, the base was per-capita yield from the sixteen provincial revenue sources in the previous year. If the revenues of a province for the current year fell below 95% of the yield from the previous year, the province would get a stabilization grant. Partly because of growing provincial revenues, and partly because of the generosity of the federal government to Saskatchewan and the Atlantic provinces, no payments were ever made.

The 1972 *Federal-Provincial Fiscal Arrangements Act* established the basic tax agreements for the five-year period from 1972 to 1977. Under this agreement, the equalization formula remained basically the same as for the previous five years, although the revenue sources on which the payment was calculated were expanded from sixteen to nineteen. Stabilization grants were also provided for in the new act, but no province actually received any payments. The federal

---

[34] There is a particularly good description and analysis of equalization in *Economic Union*, vol. 3, pp. 181–197. See also *Federal Provincial Programs & Activities, 1983–1984* (1983–4) (Ottawa: Federal Provincial Relations Office, June 1984). Virtually all intergovernmental transfers are described in this source, which is updated periodically.

government had withdrawn completely from the estate-tax and gift-tax fields as a result of the 1971 federal income-tax reforms, and in many cases the provinces stepped in to occupy the vacated fields. The basic collection agreements that applied in the previous five years applied again. Other minor changes were incorporated in the legislation, but the system remained virtually identical in principle to its predecessor.

The opting-out provisions were increased, to provide an abatement of up to 24% of federal income tax. The percentage of the total income-tax field left to the provinces varied from province to province, under an arrangement whereby the revenues of the provinces were guaranteed not to fall below their 1971 level if they adopted income-tax acts modelled on the federal legislation.

This fiscal decade also saw the establishment of the last of the major federal shared-cost social programs — medicare. The *Medical Care Act*, passed by the federal government,[35] provided for 50% federal funding of the overall national costs of almost all physicians' services. The formula also provided for partial equalization among provinces, since provincial entitlements were actually the national-average per-capita costs of the services multiplied by the provincial population. The program has proven immensely popular with the public but, paradoxically, the provincial government most directly responsible for federal participation in hospital insurance in 1957, Ontario, was by 1967 vehemently opposed to any new federal shared-cost programs. Its opposition, plus the resentment of Quebec at this federal intrusion into an area of provincial jurisdiction, combined to ensure that medicare was the last of the major federal-provincial shared-cost programs. Continued opposition, combined with federal concern over the rapid increases in health-care costs in the early 1970s, led to the next major change in federal-provincial fiscal relations, the Established Programs Financing arrangements.

1977–1982   The 1977 version of the *Fiscal Arrangements Act* was given a new name, and to some extent a new purpose. Virtually all the features of the 1972 *Fiscal Arrangements Act* were kept in place. The number of revenue sources taken into account in the equalization formula rose to twenty-nine, but the method of calculation remained basically the same, as did the basic outlines of the tax-collection agreements and the opting-out formulae. The major change in the 1977 arrangements was the addition of a provision called *Established Programs Financing* (EPF). The result was a set of arrangements enshrined in legislation with a formidable title: *The Federal Provincial Fiscal Arrangements and Established Programs Financing Act* (1977). The EPF arrangements were intended to replace the older cost-sharing arrangements for medical and hospital-insurance programs with a combination of an abatement of tax points and a block-funding formula. As well, EPF provided for a continuing tax abatement and cash payment, nominally for the financing of post-secondary education. The formula is complex but, since the amounts involved (more than $16 billion in 1987–1988) are by far the

[35] For a complete description, see Malcolm Taylor, *op. cit.*, Richard Simeon, *Federal Provincial Diplomacy* (Toronto: University of Toronto Press, 1972), also contains a description of the negotiations surrounding medicare.

largest of the intergovernmental transfers, they merit some attention. Those with a love for complex formulae are referred to the legislation itself.

In essence, there were four parts to the EPF arrangement. First there was a per-capita block grant, amounting to about one-half of the former federal contribution for health insurance, based on 1975–1976 payments and escalated annually according to population and GNP increases. This block grant was payable only if provinces continued to meet the appropriate program conditions. Since it amounted to about one-quarter of the full program costs, and since the programs were very popular, the federal government felt that provinces would continue to meet those conditions. Second, the federal government agreed to vacate or abate 13.5 percentage points of personal income tax and one percentage point of corporate income tax, and to equalize the yield from these sources in the same way as other income-tax points. Third, a twenty-dollar per-capita annual payment was to be provided, escalated annually in the same way as the basic block payment; this payment was intended to provide funding "in respect of extended health care services," such as home nursing or ambulatory services. These presumably lower-cost alternatives were not covered by earlier cost-sharing legislation.

Finally, there was a "transitional adjustment payment," intended to ensure that provinces did not suffer financially as a result of the changes. The transitional adjustment payment was intended to guarantee that provinces would receive adequate funding even if something should happen to make the rate of increase in the revenue yield of tax points decline to less than the yield of the block fund. In that case, the federal government undertook to make up the difference, but federal officials never expected such payments to become very significant; the guarantee was expected to have a truly transitory impact. It was not to be so.

The result has been a boon to provincial treasuries and a difficult problem for the federal government. Several factors have conspired to produce this result. Because of a 1975 federal decision to index the value of personal exemptions to the rate of inflation, the yield of tax points has not risen as quickly as "nominal GNP" (the value of inflation plus real GNP increases), and the result is that the federal government has had to make good on its "transitional" guarantee, to the tune of $1 billion per year in the early 1980s. This was an unexpected turn of events for the federal government, and its impact was particularly onerous during the 1982–1983 recession, when even larger transitional payments had to be made from a very restricted federal tax take.

A further twist was added by the fact that provinces receive the cash grants pursuant only to rather vaguely defined program conditions for health services, such as portability from province to province and equal access to services, which was to be unimpeded by significant financial barriers. The grants for post-secondary education are made essentially without condition. These rather vague wordings provided provinces with an opportunity to reduce program costs in order to free up the money guaranteed by federal payments for other things, such as keeping a lid on provincial taxes and deficits, a practice the provincial governments could, quite rightly, say was encouraged and intended by all governments, including the federal government, at the time EPF was put in place. In the extreme, some provinces, given that opportunity, seemed inclined to reduce health-care and post-secondary-education expenditures as far as they possibly could without either forcing the federal government to suspend payment or inciting the wrath of their voters to the point where they might be turfed out of office. The result was that, by 1982, the federal government was providing enough funding to cover more than 60% of programs in respect of which it would have been liable for only 50% if it had continued the old arrangements. Moreover, in 1978, when the federal government wanted to reduce the rate of its expenditure growth to the equivalent of GNP growth minus 2%, it found itself locked into an $8 billion expenditure, for which the provincial governments received the credit, and which could not be touched without unanimous provincial agreement for a five-year period. Given the benefits of the EPF arrangement for provincial treasuries, that agreement was not forthcoming. Finally, to add insult to injury, provincial cost saving began to be associated with the passing on to the public of some of the hitherto insured costs of health care as doctors opted out and hospitals introduced various forms of user charges. And all provincial governments reduced the rate of increase of contributions to post-secondary education to less than the rate of increase of GNP. Not only was the federal government paying more, but the health-care and the post-secondary institutions appeared to be deteriorating.

The complications of fiscal federalism are such, however, that there are two sides to every story. Provincial authorities attest that the EPF payments were having exactly the effect intended, which we described in our discussion of block-funding versus cost-shared programs; they were resulting in lowered program costs and, in the economic circumstances of the early 1980s, that is just what the voter wanted. If the federal government was in a fiscal bind, provincial governments said too bad. That merely permits the appropriate decentralization of Canada by giving more money to the provinces, and, in any event, the tax system changes of 1972 have consistently cost the provinces money, and this is only a partial reimbursement.

1982–1987[36] While it is safe to say that provincial governments have generally been happy with the EPF arrangements, for the many reasons outlined above, the federal government generally has not. While there has not been a serious threat to terminate the agreements, the federal discontent has led, over the years, to a series of unilateral amendments to the federal legislation governing the transfers.[37] Technical changes have been made to eliminate an anomaly whereby the total amount of the transfer going to Alberta was larger than that to other

---

[36] As might be expected, given the importance of money to governments and the importance of federal-provincial fiscal arrangements in the money equation, there is ample material available on recent fiscal arrangements. The major journals covering this area are *Canadian Public Policy* and the *Canadian Tax Journal*. The Canadian Tax Foundation and the Economic Council of Canada also publish monographs on the subject. Recent articles include: T.J. Courchene, "Canada's New Equalization Program, *Canadian Public Policy*, vol. 9, December 1983, pp. 458–75; D.B. Perry, "Federal-Provincial Fiscal Arrangements for 1982–87," *Canadian Tax Journal*, vol. 31, January–February 1983, pp. 30–47; Richard Simeon, "Fiscal Federalism in Canada: A Review Essay," *Canadian Tax Journal*, vol. 30, January–February 1982, pp. 41–51; D.A.L. Auld, "Fiscal Federalism in Canada," *Canadian Public Policy*, vol. 8, pp. 278ff; and the spring 1982 edition of *Canadian Public Policy*, which contains a series of articles entitled "Financing Confederation."

[37] The EPF arrangements do not automatically expire with the expiry of the rest of the Fiscal Arrangements Act.

provinces.[38] The post-secondary-education portion of the transfer was subject to 6% and 5% ceilings on its escalator in 1983 and 1984. An appendage to the legislation called the "Revenue Guarantee" was eliminated in 1982, removing approximately $1 billion per year from the total transfer. There have been two other major changes as well.

The most important and contentious revision was not a change to the EPF legislation, but a change to the *Hospital Insurance and Medical Care Acts*, which set out the terms under which the EPF transfers for health programs are made. In 1984, in response to a considerable degree of public concern about extra billing by doctors and user fees in hospitals, the *Canada Health Act* was passed by Parliament. It stipulated that the EPF health transfer was to be reduced for any province allowing extra billing or user fees by an amount equal to the total value of extra billing or user fees in the province. The Act was the subject of very considerable federal-provincial controversy at the time it was passed and could be said to have been the most direct cause of the doctors' strike in Ontario in 1986. However, by 1986 most provinces either had complied or signalled their intention to comply with most of its provisions. Obviously, in spite of the move towards block funding inherent in the EPF arrangements, it was still possible for the federal government to influence the conditions under which provincial programs were delivered in areas covered by intergovernmental transfers.

Finally, in 1985, as part of a package of deficit-reduction measures, the federal minister of finance announced that intergovernmental transfers would be reduced by up to $2 billion per year by 1990–1991. In theory, the reductions could come from any intergovernmental transfer program. In reality, it seems the cost cannot be brought to bear on equalization, which supports poorer provinces, or on the *Canada Assistance Plan*, which supports poorer people. The reductions are therefore taken from EPF. After 1985–1986, EPF cash and tax transfers grow at two percentage points less than the rate of GNP growth. This produces reductions of $300 million in 1986–1987, a figure that grows by approximately $300 million per year for as long as that formula remains in place. Given rising health-care costs and a declining escalation of EPF, it seems certain that the federal share of health-insurance-program costs will be less than its historic 50% level by the late 1980s. At that point, while the federal government may be more satisfied with EPF, it is a safe bet that the provinces will be less satisfied. We can therefore look forward to continuing, sometimes heated discussion about our major block-funded transfer programs.

The major unconditional transfers are the equalization arrangements, amounting to nearly $5.1 billion in 1986–1987. We saw that equalization arrangements prior to 1982 were put into some disarray because of the rising oil prices of the 1970s. By 1980–1981, the equalization arrangements were, once again, being

---

[38] These "technical changes" involve changing EPF to a "total entitlement" program. The total entitlement of a province is equal to the sum of 50% of the national-average per-capita program costs in 1975–1976 for PSE operating costs and insured health programs, plus twenty dollars, all escalated, to 1985–1986 by the three years, moving average of nominal GNP increases and by GNP minus 2% thereafter, and all multiplied by the current provincial population. The value of the 13.5 percentage points of equalized personal income tax and the one percentage point of corporate income tax is then subtracted from the total entitlement, and the federal government makes up the remainder in cash.

put in a state of disarray by oil prices that were again rapidly on the rise. Since resource revenues were still considered an item for at least partial equalization, the very high royalty incomes received by Alberta were raising national average yields from resource taxation to such a level that, by 1982, Ontario could actually have qualified for equalization. Ontario did not ever receive equalization payments (because of a special agreement between Ontario and Ottawa), but clearly the formula had to be changed during the 1982 renegotiations of the *Fiscal Arrangements Act*.

In addition, Ottawa's precarious financial situation led it to want to reduce the total amount of the transfer. The result was a move from a national-average target level for equalization to a five-province standard. Instead of equalizing to the national tax yields, the formula was amended so that equalization was to the average of five provinces, excluding the richest and the four poorest provinces. In practice, this eliminated Alberta from the calculations, effectively doing away with the resource-revenue problem. It alone reduced the federal government's liability by some $560 million in the first year in which the new formula was in effect, although total payments still rose by 13% from the previous year. The number of tax fields equalized rose to thirty-three. An escalator cap was also put on the payments, so they could not increase by more than the rate of increase of gross national product, and transitional arrangements were again put in place, so provinces that were going to receive less than they would have under older formulae were eased into their new, poorer condition over a five-year period.

Equalization, like EPF, is a complex program in a complex world, and in a complex world, good intentions are not always easily converted to achievements. It is, nevertheless, viewed by Canadian governments as an essential building block of Confederation, so much so that section 36 of the Constitution Act of 1982 says that there must be an equalization program "to ensure that provincial governments have sufficient revenues to provide reasonably comparable levels of public service at reasonably comparable levels of taxation." As a result, we can expect to see continuing discussion and renegotiation of equalization arrangements every five years.

Conclusions: 1987 and Beyond

Tables 9-1 and 9-2 summarize the current situation with respect to intergovernmental transfer payments in Canada. In 1985–1986, total federal budgetary expenditures were $105 billion; the $19.8 billion in total cash transfers to the provinces accounted for more than 19% of total federal expenditures in that year. If the abated tax points in respect of EPF are excluded as an expenditure in the form of forgone income, such transfers account for some 24% of federal expenditures. The great bulk of these are provided through relatively inflexible agreements, which provide some guarantees to the provinces to ensure consistent levels of financing for the programs and the services they deliver. However, we have seen that these same guarantees have the effect of tying the hands of the federal government with respect to economic management, for the money has to be raised; that makes any lowering of the federal deficit more difficult.

TABLE 9-1

ESTIMATED FEDERAL TRANSFERS TO THE PROVINCES, TERRITORIES, AND MUNICIPALITIES

FISCAL YEAR 1986–1987

($ MILLIONS)

Program	Nfld.	P.E.I.	N.S.	N.B.	Que.	Ont.	Man.	Sask.	Alta.	B.C.	N.W.T.	Yukon	Total
A. GENERAL PURPOSE TRANSFERS													
Cash Transfers													
Fiscal Equalization	668.4	143.4	612.8	640.9	2,854.8	—	456.1	—	—	—	—	—	5,376.4
Supplementary Equalization	—	—	—	—	—	—	65.0	—	—	—	—	—	65.0
Statutory Subsidies	9.7	0.7	2.3	1.8	4.7	6.1	2.2	2.2	3.7	2.5	—	—	35.9
Reciprocal Taxation	15.2	4.8	25.6	25.0	62.0	88.7	17.1	—	—	24.9	—	—	263.3
Public Utilities Income Tax Transfer	13.0	3.3	—	—	4.3	35.0	4.2	0.1	225.0	4.7	0.2	0.2	290.0
Youth Allowances Recovery	—	—	—	—	-262.0	—	—	—	—	—	—	—	-262.0
Territorial Financial Agreements	—	—	—	—	—	—	—	—	—	—	477.0	160.0	637.0
Grants in Lieu of Property Taxes	5.1	1.3	15.8	11.1	58.4	130.3	16.3	8.6	17.6	27.6	2.1	1.9	296.1
Sub-total — Cash Transfers	711.4	153.5	656.5	678.8	2,722.2	260.1	560.9	10.9	246.3	59.7	479.3	162.1	6,701.7
Tax Transfers													
3.0 Personal Income Tax Points for Youth Allownaces	—	—	—	—	262.0	—	—	—	—	—	—	—	262.0
Sub-total — Tax Transfers	—	—	—	—	262.0	—	—	—	—	—	—	—	262.0
Total General Purpose Transfers	711.4	153.5	656.5	678.8	2,984.2	260.1	560.9	10.9	246.3	59.7	479.3	162.1	6,963.7

ESTIMATED FEDERAL TRANSFERS TO THE PROVINCES, TERRITORIES, AND MUNICIPALITIES (Continued)
FISCAL YEAR 1986–1987
($ Millions)

Program	Nfld.	P.E.I.	N.S.	N.B.	Que.	Ont.	Man.	Sask.	Alta.	B.C.	N.W.T.	Yukon	Total
B. GENERAL SUPPORT FOR HEALTH AND POST SECONDARY EDUCATION (PSE) UNDER ESTABLISHED PROGRAMS FINANCING (EPF) ARRANGEMENTS													
EPF Cash Transfers													
Insured Health Services	148.0	32.5	225.2	183.5	1,159.9	2,112.9	273.2	291.9	495.0	725.6	11.1	5.2	5,664.0
Extended Health Care Services (EHCS)	26.1	5.7	39.6	32.3	295.0	408.5	48.1	46.1	105.9	130.3	2.3	1.1	1,141.0
Post-Secondary Education	63.2	13.9	96.2	78.4	471.2	892.2	116.6	126.0	206.3	309.1	4.7	2.2	2,380.0
Sub-total — Cash Transfers	237.3	52.1	361.0	294.2	1,926.1	3,413.6	437.9	464.0	807.2	1,165.0	18.1	8.5	9,185.0
EPF Tax Transfers													
Insured Health Services	53.3	12.0	110.2	79.2	1,471.7	1,748.4	144.2	143.2	506.3	505.8	10.9	4.7	4,789.9
Post-Secondary Education	25.2	5.7	52.1	37.5	696.5	827.5	68.2	67.8	239.6	239.4	5.1	2.2	2,266.8
Sub-total — Tax Transfers	78.5	17.7	162.3	116.7	2,168.2	2,575.9	212.4	211.0	745.9	745.2	16.0	6.9	7,056.7
Associated Equalization*													
Insured Health Services	44.9	9.5	39.1	42.4	156.7	0	37.0	0	0	0	0	0	329.6
Post-Secondary Education	21.2	4.5	18.5	20.1	74.2	0	17.5	0	0	0	0	0	156.0
Sub-total — Associated Equalization	66.1	14.0	57.6	62.5	230.9	0	54.5	0	0	0	0	0	485.6
Insured Health Services	246.2	54.0	374.5	305.1	2,788.3	3,861.3	454.4	435.1	1,001.3	1,231.4	22.0	9.9	10,783.5
EHCS	26.1	5.7	39.6	32.3	295.0	408.5	48.1	46.1	105.9	130.3	2.3	1.1	1,141.0
Post-Secondary Education	109.6	24.1	166.8	136.0	1,241.9	1,719.7	202.3	193.8	445.9	548.5	9.8	4.4	4,802.8
Total General Support for Health and Post-Secondary Education under the EPF Arrangements*	381.9	83.8	580.9	473.4	4,325.2	5,989.5	704.8	675.0	1,553.1	1,910.2	34.1	15.4	16,727.3

*The equalization associated with the EPF tax transfer is paid and included under the fiscal equalization program (section A). To avoid double counting, the value of equalization associated with the tax transfer is excluded from the grand totals in section D.

C. SPECIFIC PURPOSE TRANSFERS

Cash Transfers

Canada Assistance Plan (CAP)	85.5	19.4	115.9	136.1	1,260.8	1,035.1	148.5	158.1	404.7	679.8	12.0	3.5	4,059.4
Other Health & Welfare	2.4	0.3	15.5	4.8	6.3	39.6	20.3	4.1	15.8	13.8	25.3	3.1	151.3
Official Languages in Education**	2.1	1.0	3.6	21.5	78.3	49.9	6.5	2.4	6.2	6.9	.6	.3	179.3
Services to Young Offenders	2.4	0.6	2.4	1.5	85.3	28.1	2.2	4.3	6.2	20.3	5.4	5.5	164.2
Crop Insurance	0.1	1.5	0.2	1.6	11.0	22.0	23.0	79.0	62.0	4.6	–	–	205.0
Transportation	11.7	1.8	5.9	6.9	11.9	12.9	2.7	0.4	1.0	21.5	4.8	0.9	82.4
Justice	1.2	0.1	2.2	1.2	16.2	27.8	2.6	2.1	5.7	6.0	0.8	0.5	66.4
Other Specific Purpose Cash Transfers**	10.6	1.6	10.5	0.4	81.1	6.0	1.3	6.8	-87.5	3.5	3.1	2.7	40.1
Sub-total – Cash Transfers	116.0	26.3	156.2	174.0	1,550.9	1,221.4	207.1	257.2	414.1	756.4	52.0	16.5	4,948.1

Tax Transfers

5.0 Personal Income Tax Points for CAP	–	–	–	–	408.5	–	–	–	–	–	–	–	408.5
Sub-total – Tax Transfers	–	–	–	–	408.5	–	–	–	–	–	–	–	408.5
Total Specific Purpose Transfers	116.0	26.3	156.2	174.0	1,959.4	1,221.4	207.1	257.2	414.1	756.4	52.0	16.5	5,356.6

D. GRAND TOTALS

Total Cash Transfers**	1,064.7	231.9	1,173.7	1,147.0	6,199.2	4,895.1	1,205.9	732.1	1,467.6	1,981.1	549.4	187.1	20,834.8
Total Tax Transfers	78.5	17.7	162.3	116.7	2,838.7	2,575.9	212.4	211.0	745.9	745.2	16.0	6.9	7,727.2
Total Cash And Tax Transfers*	1,143.2	249.6	1,336.0	1,263.7	9,037.9	7,471.0	1,418.3	943.1	2,213.5	2,726.3	565.4	194.0	28,562.0

*The equalization associated with the EPF tax transfer is paid and included under the fiscal equalization program (section A). To avoid double counting, the value of equalization associated with the tax transfer is excluded from the grand totals in section D.

**An additional $43.7 million of federal cash transfers has not been allocated by province. This includes $37.5 million for the Official Languages in Education program. When the undistributed amount is included, total federal cash transfers are $20,878.5 million and total cash plus tax transfers are $28,605.7 million.

Source: Treasury Board of Canada, Fact Sheet No. 4, 27 February, 1986. Reproduced with permission of the Minister of Supply and Services Canada.

TABLE 9-2
TOTAL FEDERAL TRANSFERS AS A PERCENTAGE OF GROSS GENERAL
PROVINCIAL REVENUES

	1980–1981	1984–1985
Newfoundland	47.7	47.2
Prince Edward Island	53.8	47.4
Nova Scotia	45.8	39.7
New Brunswick	43.9	42.4
Quebec	22.0	23.1
Ontario	17.3	16.1
Manitoba	37.6	30.3
Saskatchewan	16.9	14.9
Alberta	7.7	9.2
British Columbia	16.1	16.9
Canada	20.1	20.5[a]

Reproduced from the report of the *Royal Commission on the Economic Union and Development Prospects for Canada*, vol. 3, p. 229. Figures for 1980–1981 are based on data from *Provincial and Municipal Finances 1981* (Toronto: The Canadian Tax Foundation, 1981), p. 46. Figures for 1984–1985 are based on data from Karin F. Treff, "Provincial Estimates for 1984–85," *Canadian Tax Journal*, 32 (September–October 1984), pp. 1003–1012. Reproduced with permission of the Minister of Supply and Services Canada.

[a]Includes the Territories.

The very large size of these payments makes them a very large target in any effort by federal ministers of finance to reduce the deficit, and we have already seen, in the discussion of EPF, that it has been targetted for significant reductions in its rate of growth through the late 1980s. The other side of the equation can be seen in Table 9-2. The table indicates that, just as intergovernmental transfers account for more than 20% of federal expenditures, they also account for more than 20% of provincial revenues. Indeed, if the tax transfers are included, the total accounts for nearly 27% of provincial revenues. Table 9-2 also demonstrates that the dependence in some provinces is much greater than the national average would indicate. The governments of Newfoundland and Prince Edward Island receive nearly half their revenues in the form of federal cash transfers; New Brunswick receives more than 40% and Manitoba more than 30%. Thus, while the federal government has a very great desire to reduce the transfers, the provincial governments have at least as great a desire to keep them up; hardly a situation calculated to improve federal-provincial harmony.

All of this would seem to lead towards a fairly gloomy prognosis. However, we should not lose sight of the more optimistic side of the picture. First, the various forms of intergovernmental transfers have helped make possible the delivery of roughly comparable levels of government services in all provinces in Canada; hardly a mean feat, given the very great disparities in regional economies. Second, the tax-collection agreements have made possible a tax system that is quite well harmonized from coast to coast. A corporation or individual moving from one province to another will face different levels of taxation, but the base on which the tax is calculated is comparable throughout Canada, even in Quebec, which operates its own tax system.

Third, and perhaps most important, in spite of the considerable heat generated by intergovernmental fiscal discussions, the arrangements actually have been surprisingly flexible over the years. The centralization of government that followed World War Two was accompanied by conditional, cost-matching cash transfers. As the Canadian federation became more decentralized, in response to public opinion, economic changes, and world-wide trends, the transfer programs became less and less conditional and moved towards block funding and tax transfers. When the movement towards decentralization appeared to be going too far, the federal government was able to reduce the rate of escalation of transfers, and to make at least the health transfers more conditional through passage of the Canada Health Act. Thus, it seems likely that, in future, the structure of fiscal federalism will be able to adjust to prevailing trends in government. It should not surprise us that such large and important adjustments are not always placid, but we can continue to expect that they will be achieved.

PART 4

SYSTEM-ENVIRONMENT LINKAGES

POLITICAL PARTIES IN THE CANADIAN SYSTEM

THE ROLE OF CANADIAN POLITICAL PARTIES
■ Party Functions ■ Non-political Functions of Parties
PARTIES AND PARTY SYSTEMS
CANADIAN PARTY STRUCTURES
■ Typologies of Party Structures ■ Canadian Party Structure: Generalizations

F or many Canadians, politics *is* political parties. Media reports on politics concentrate on party and leader reactions to issues of the day. The best-selling books about politics in Canada are not, alas, textbooks, but rather those telling the inside stories about party politics. But what is the real role of parties in Canadian political life? Do they really determine what our governments will do? Who controls our political parties? The leaders? The members of parliament? The membership of the party? The fund raisers? And what do they control? Are parties strong organizations single-mindedly pursuing political goals? Or are they loose associations of people playing the political game for the sake of interest and the connections it brings? And what of elections, those grand contests of Canadian political life? How are they organized? What are the rules that govern them? What determines their outcome? What effect does their outcome have on Canadian government?

The three chapters that follow are intended to answer these questions. In this chapter, we will look at the functions and the general structures of Canadian political parties. In the next, we will consider how the Canadian parties have developed, and ask about the nature of the party system today. In the third chapter of this section we will look at the election process and at the ways in which the behaviour of Canadian voters determines the outcomes of elections.

THE ROLE OF CANADIAN POLITICAL PARTIES

Perhaps the simplest way to begin our examination of political parties in Canada is to look at their primary objective. That is, quite simply, to get people elected— preferably enough of them so that the party can formally control the government. Of course, party activists have other objectives, too. They may be eager to institute certain policies. They may even aim at a fundamental restructuring of Canadian society. Or they may just want to broaden their network of connections, or to be involved in something interesting during their spare hours. But, whatever their purpose, they have chosen to join an organization whose immediate operational goal is to gain and hold power through the electoral system.[1]

As by-products of their efforts to achieve power, political parties perform a number of other important functions for the system.[2] These are typically listed in the general literature on political parties as:

- the recruitment and training of political decision makers;
- the organization of the political decision process;
- the education, political socialization, and mobilization of the mass public;
- the articulation and aggregation of interests;
- national integration;
- the management of the flow of information into and out of the system;
- the generation of support for the political system of which the parties are a part; and
- the influencing of public policy.[3]

While these are often considered to be vital functions of parties or party systems, all can be performed more or less efficiently by other institutions, such as the bureaucracy or interest groups. Indeed, in Canada, as well as in other western democracies, most important functions are carried out simultaneously by various structures in the political system. It is important to make this point because there is a tendency among those who study political parties to assume that if the parties

---

[1] We refrain from giving a lengthy definition of the political party in this section, if only to avoid not very productive debates over whether organizations such as the Créditistes were really political parties. We prefer to adopt the same loose definition used by Leon D. Epstein in *Political Parties in Western Democracies* (New York: Praeger, 1976), pp. 9–10. Epstein suggests that "almost everything that is called a party in any western democracy can be so regarded for the present purpose. This means any group, however loosely organized, seeking to elect governmental office holders under a given label." We will see, in chapter 12, that it is necessary to be much more precise than this for some purposes, such as determining what organizations will receive public financial support for their campaign activities.

Epstein's work remains the classic comparative work on parties. Other comparative sources include Giovanni Sartori, *Parties and Party Systems; A Framework for Analysis* (London: Cambridge University Press, 1976), and Robert Harmel and Kenneth Janda, *Comparing Political Parties* (Washington: American Political Science Association, 1976).

[2] For an early succinct statement, see J.R. Mallory, "The Structure of Canadian Politics," in H.G. Thorburn, ed., *Party Politics in Canada* (Toronto: Prentice-Hall, 1967), pp. 22ff.

[3] For a typical comparative statement of party functions, see Anthony King, "Political Parties in Western Democracies: Some Skeptical Reflections," *Polity*, vol. 2, no. 2, 1969, pp. 111–141.

do not adequately perform some important function, the whole system must be at risk. This, we shall see, is not necessarily so. Parties are essential, and Canadian democracy would be very different without them. But they need not flawlessly perform every function ascribed to them all the time for the system to survive and prosper.[4] Indeed, it is worth noting that with a few minor exceptions, democracy thrives without political parties at the municipal level in Canada (sometimes in governments much larger than provincial governments) and in the legislature of the Northwest Territories.

Party Functions

The Staffing Function: Recruitment and Training Political parties are the major recruitment agencies that insure a steady flow of personnel to fill the political roles of prime minister, Cabinet members and members of the House of Commons and the Senate. This process of recruitment involves not only the selection of local candidates for elected office through constituency nominating meetings, but also the selection of party leaders through the national conventions. Similarly, the training for a career in politics is often provided through party organizations at the constituency, provincial, and national levels.

A secondary staffing function of parties in Canada is the selection and recruitment of people to fill appointed positions in the government. Although such patronage appointments are often vehemently criticized — usually by those out of office, and therefore without access to them — Canadian parties do continue to recruit people for a large number of positions, ranging from poll enumerators to the presidencies of large Crown corporations. We consider the issues surrounding patronage appointments when we discuss the public service, Parliament, and the judiciary elsewhere in this book. It may, however, be at least suggested here that, for some types of public positions, it is as appropriate to base selection on party service as on other types of past experience. We shall see, too, that patronage performs important functions for the party structures themselves. Meanwhile, we should note that nothing is more certain in Canadian politics than that parties will decry patronage when out of office, and then enthusiastically make use of it when in.

Because they are organizations themselves, parties must also recruit people to fill positions in their various constituency, provincial, and national wings. One incidental impact of this is that many Canadians get a closer look at their political system and learn about how it operates, and may thus be turned on to politics sufficiently that they will seek to become more involved in Canadian political life.

Political Education, Socialization, and Mobilization At election time (and, to a lesser extent, between elections), political parties provide stimuli to which people can respond. They provide publicity for the issues around which political

---

[4] Paul G. Thomas, "The Role of National Party Caucuses," in Peter Aucoin, ed., *Party Government and Regional Representation* (Ottawa: Royal Commission on the Economic Union, Research Studies, #36 [1985]) points out that Canadian parties have been particularly weak at integration of the political system, the aggregation of interests, and the making of public policy.

attitudes can be shaped, and they provide or popularize the symbols with which people can identify. It would be extremely difficult for the average citizen to make voting decisions on the basis of personal knowledge of all the issues. They can, however, use parties as convenient symbols to which they can attach their allegiance and with which they can simplify the complex realities of politics.

Political education and socialization are also remnants of a more basic and larger party function, that of mobilizing the mass electorate. By now virtually all citizens of developed nations are accustomed to the universal franchise, and we therefore tend to forget what a massive effort it must have taken to bring into the mainstream of political life the millions of electors enfranchised during the latter half of the nineteenth century and the early years of the twentieth. Political parties as we know them developed at that time, and their major early function was to bring the new voters into political life—on the side of the right political leaders, of course.[5]

Articulation, Aggregation, and Political Integration Political parties in Canada and elsewhere can mobilize enough of the electorate in their own support to win elections in three ways. First, they may seek to define or articulate issues in such a way that they mobilize support by differentiating themselves from other parties, and their supporters from other voters. When they do so they are usually described as performing *interest articulation*. At another level, however, they may seek to put together packages of positions, sometimes in the shape of formal electoral platforms, which, rather than seeking to maximize the differences among the voters, seek to maximize the common ground across the largest possible coalition of supporters. When they do this they are usually described as performing *interest aggregation*. Finally, parties may essentially avoid major issues and concentrate, instead, on the redress of grievances and on convincing voters that their leadership is the best suited to solve whatever immediate problems the voters may view as most important.

A moment's consideration will lead to the conclusion that all Canadian parties attempt to do all three. As we will see in the next chapter, however, different parties adopt different mixes. The two older parties concentrate more on aggregation and leadership. The NDP concentrates more on attempting to articulate the interests of the little guy against the prevailing élites. The Parti Québécois concentrates almost entirely on articulating the interests of Francophone Quebeckers.

What is more significant here, perhaps, is that the predominant modes of activity of political parties can have a significant impact on national integration or national unity. If parties seek to mobilize support by emphasizing or articulating interests that cut across regional cleavages (class cleavages being the pre-eminent example), then the threat of territorial divisions is likely to be reduced. If, by contrast, they seek to mobilize support by emphasizing regionally based differences, territorial integration is likely to be weakened, but class conflict will be reduced in importance. If they can succeed in putting together packages of positions acceptable

---

[5] Leon Epstein, "Political Parties: Organizations," in David Butler, et al., *Democracy at the Polls* (Washington: American Enterprise Institute, 1981), pp. 54–72.

across a wide spectrum of the community, that is, in performing interest aggregation, then national integration, not to mention the electoral success of whichever
party succeeds best in this approach, is also likely to be enhanced. The third
tactic, emphasis on leadership and short-term problems, may be either supportive of, or divisive for, national unity, depending on what stance the leader adopts
and on the universality of his personal appeal.

In Canada, the potential for territorial integration inherent in the articulation
of class interests has not been realized. Some analysts would claim that the
Canadian political culture has not yet attained a sufficient degree of maturity for
this to happen, but most are no longer awaiting that millenium.[6] Political scientists have therefore suggested that, in the absence of the regional and ethnic
political integration that could result from the articulation of class cleavages,
political parties could still play a major role in fostering national integration if
they were to succeed in aggregating the full range of non-class interests sufficiently across the whole nation. By doing so, political parties would be grand
brokers and mediators of Canadian society, and would play an essential part in
unifying a nation that otherwise is assumed to have a very great tendency to fly
apart at the seams. The suggestion that parties could, should, and frequently do
try to play this role is referred to as the *brokerage theory* of Canadian politics. The
examination and re-examination of that theory, and the decrying of the frequent
failure of Canadian parties to play that role, have been dominant themes in the
academic analysis of Canadian parties.[7] The characteristics of brokerage and
non-brokerage systems are summarized in Figure 10-1.

---

[6] This line of reasoning is described sympathetically, although not ultimately subscribed to, by John Wilson in
"On the Dangers of Bickering in a Federal State," in Alan Kornberg and H.D. Clark, eds., *Political Support
in Canada* (Durham, N.C.: Duke University Press, 1984), pp. 176–198. See also M. Janine Brody and
Jane Jenson, *Crisis, Challenge and Change: Class and Party in Canada* (Toronto: Methuen, 1980), and
"The Party System," in M.S. Whittington and Glen Williams, eds., *Canadian Politics in the 1980s*, and in
John Meisel, *Cleavages, Parties and Political Values in Canada* (London: Sage, 1974). The immaturity
view is still subscribed to by some Marxist scholars, although generally with qualifications.

[7] A. Cairns describes this as the prevalent mode of analysis in "The Electoral System and the Party System in
Canada 1921–1965," *Canadian Journal of Political Science*, vol. 1, no. 1, p. 63, March 1968. See also F.
Englemann and M. Schwartz, *Political Parties and the Canadian Social Structure* (Prentice-Hall, Toronto,
1975), pp. 222–239. The general interpretation of party politics in Canada in C. Winn and J. McMenemy,
Political Parties in Canada (McGraw-Hill Ryerson, Toronto, 1976) could also be called a brokerage
interpretation as could H.G. Thorburn's summary and interpretation in "Interpretations of the Canadian
Party System," in H.G. Thorburn (ed.) *Party Politics in Canada* (Prentice-Hall, Scarborough, 1979). The
original expressions of this "broker-mediator" function are found in H. Clokie, *Canadian Government and
Politics* (Longmans Green, Toronto, 1944), pp. 81–83; J.T. McLeod, "Party Structure and Party Reform"
in A. Rotstein (ed), *The Prospect of Change* (McGraw-Hill, Toronto, 1965) pp. 4–5, 9, 15; Alexander Brady,
Democracy in the Dominions; R.M. Dawson and N. Ward, *The Government of Canada*, 4th ed. (University of
Toronto Press, Toronto, 1963), pp. 468–470; J.A. Corry and J.E. Hodgetts, *Democratic Government and
Politics*, 3rd ed. (University of Toronto Press, Toronto, 1963), chs. 8–9; F.H. Underhill, *Canadian Political
Parties*, Canadian Historical Association pamphlet (Ottawa, 1957), pp. 4–5. For general critiques of this
theory, see Cairns, "The Electoral System and the Party System in Canada 1921–1965" and John Porter,
The Vertical Mosaic (University of Toronto Press, Toronto, 1965), pp. 373–377 and the specific sources
cited in the rest of this section. Cairns points out that "the necessity for inter-group collaboration in any
on-going political system makes it possible to claim of any party system compatible with the survival of the
polity that it acts as a nationalizing agency." (p. 63) By that interpretation, the brokerage theory of Canadian
politics has very limited utility since it is really tautological. We would not go that far. The issue is the extent
to which parties can, should, and do perform an integrating role by acting as brokers or aggregators of
political interests.

FIGURE 10-1
CHARACTERISTICS OF BROKERAGE AND NON-BROKERAGE PARTY SYSTEMS

Non-Brokerage Systems	Brokerage Systems
Well-defined, stable electoral support	Electoral coalitions recreated each election
Clear policy differences reflected in electoral support	Competition for same policy space and voters
Parties seek to minimize number of cleavages while maximizing political effects of them	Parties multiply cleavages but minimize effects of each
Voters presented with "world views"	Appeals to many narrow interests based on short-term views of specific issues
Fairly consistent follow-through on policies adopted in the past	Lack of consistency in policies caused by search for electorally successful positions
Organized around principles and ideologies	Organized around leaders

Material adapted from H. Clarke, Jane Jenson, Lawrence Leduc, and Jon Pammett, *Absent Mandate* (Toronto: Gage Publishing, 1984), p. 10.

The consensus of Canadian political scientists is that our political parties have generally tried to operate on brokerage principles, but that this has not been adequate to secure national integration. This putative failure is often held to account for much of what is viewed as the persistent weakness of national unity in Canada.[8] This failure of brokerage politics occurs either because the parties have failed as brokers or because, even if they succeeded, they could not be expected to provide political integration in a nation that has major territorial cleavages, provincial governments that reinforce those territorial cleavages, a parliamentary form of government, an electoral system that exaggerates the impact of regional voting patterns, and a lack of any overriding factors, such as a well-developed class consciousness.

Whatever its failures as an agent of national unity, there is little doubt that the brokerage approach can be an effective electoral tactic.[9] Canadian parties are hardly alone in the use of tactics such as leadership politics or concentration on short-term issues and grievances. Even in a class-based society such as Great Britain, the role of parties and party caucuses in the legislature tends to be confined to the expression of grievances, rather than to the development of grand integrating strategies, and the focus of national election contests seems more and more to be on leadership styles.[10] In Canada however, where there is not sufficient class

---

[8] See also chapters 4 and 8. While regional political cultures and attachments are very strong in Canada, there is also ample reason to believe that the attachment of Canadians to the whole nation is also very strong and persistent. Much of the apparent weakness of national integration particularly manifest in the late 1970s and early 1980s may have been a result of the types of issues that were to the fore, and of circumstances specific to that period. See Richard Johnson, *Questions of Confidence* (Ottawa: Royal Commission on the Economic Union, Research Report, 1986).

[9] H. Clarke et al *Absent Mandate* p. 9ff.

[10] Clarke, op. cit. and David Smith, "Party Government, Representation, and National Integration in Canada," in Peter Aucoin, ed., *Party Government and Regional Representation in Canada*, (Ottawa: Royal Commission on the Economic Union, Research Study, 1985).

consciousness to make the attempt to play upon it into a winning strategy for the parties, this electoral tactic becomes relatively even more effective. Indeed, only in the United States, which has the same low level of class consciousness as does Canada, do we see quite the same concentration on leaders and short-term issues during election campaigns.

The party structures themselves may constitute part of the explanation for the assumed failure of Canadian parties to provide significant national integration. We will see that the grass-roots level in Canadian political parties is very limited in its policy role, and that it tends to disappear between elections. According to this reasoning, the dominant party leadership in Parliament, therefore, has little connection with regional interests, and tends to ignore them in favour of an excessively centralist view, which damages national unity.[11]

A broader explanation for the failure of Canadian political parties to foster national unity through brokerage politics is that our first-past-the-post electoral system, combined with a parliamentary system of government, simply precludes their success. Since representation in the House of Commons is based upon single-member constituencies, a party may well obtain a very large proportion of the vote in a region yet harvest very few seats. They will therefore, perforce, fail to be effective as integrating agencies where it counts the most — in Parliament — and, hence, in government. In 1980, the Liberal Party won 22% of the vote in British Columbia, Alberta, and Saskatchewan without gaining a single seat. For the Conservatives, 13% of the vote in Quebec produced only one seat. Unless a party can foresee the possibility of gaining enough votes in an area for it to gain several seats (and that number of votes may be quite large), there is no incentive for it to attempt to aggregate the interests of that region into its electoral platform. If it wins the election, there is neither incentive nor opportunity to integrate those interests into its subsequent policies.[12] The result, notes William Irvine, is that:

> the regionalization of major party support . . . is badly exaggerated at the level of parliamentary seats . . . Canadian governments cannot find, in their own ranks, spokesmen for the various conflicts affecting Canada.[13]

Paul Thomas further describes the problem and its effects on the federal government:

> The skewed nature of party representation in the House of Commons diminished the capacity of national institutions to accommodate regional grievances. Party caucuses more closely resembled contending regional blocs than truly national bodies that could accommodate regional divergencies.
> Denied what they regarded as effective representation in national institutions,

---

[11] This theme is stated by Smith, *Party Government, Representation and National Integration in Canada* in his introduction, but is then rejected in his subsequent analysis.

[12] Smith, pp. 1–9. See also the *Report of the Royal Commission on the Economic Union*, vol. 3, pp. 77ff; and William Irvine, "The Canadian Voter," in H. Penniman, ed., *Canada at the Polls, 1979 and 1980* (Washington: American Enterprise Institute, 1982).

[13] Irvine, "The Canadian Voter," p. 389.

Canadians looked increasingly to their provincial governments, acting within the forum of intergovernmental relations to promote and defend their national interests.[14]

In the United States, the situation is greatly mitigated by the opportunity the congressional system affords individual senators and representatives, acting in the interests of their own constituents and regions, to have an impact on decisions at the centre. It is also mitigated by the weakness of state governments, compared to those of the Canadian provinces. These mitigating factors are absent in a parliamentary system with strong provincial governments.

This problem may be resolved, temporarily at least, by the massive Conservative electoral sweep of 1984. However, previous electoral sweeps, for example that by John Diefenbaker in 1958, did not fully resolve the problem, and in any case, the more enduring pattern of Canadian politics has been one of relatively small majorities or minorities with less than adequate regional representation in the governing party.

A final and most fundamental reason often posited for the failure of parties to provide national integration through the performance of brokerage roles is that the combination of federalism and a political culture that is fragmented by region is simply too strong for any party system to overcome. For example, John Wilson suggests:

> So far, therefore, from Canadian political behaviour representing the expression of a national electorate with merely idiosyncratic regional variations, it may be the case that the circumstances of provincial politics direct the fate of the country as a whole; and if it is true that these vary from one region to another in terms of different stages of political development, then no amount of compromise or conciliation through the medium of a national party system could be expected to foster the growth of greater Canadian unity. In other words our contemporary dilemma can hardly be blamed on the failure of the national party system. The problem is much deeper than that.[15]

By this construction, when the regionalized political cultures are added to the existence of provincial governments with jurisdiction over very major areas of government activitiy and to the lack of any well-developed class consciousness, the result is overwhelming. The national parties do not, most of the time, provide national integration, because the combination of the forces acting against them is just too great. It is this line of reasoning that has led some students of Canadian politics to become admirers of Mackenzie King, whose thirty-year tenure as leader of the Liberal Party is viewed as the period when brokerage politics did succeed, against all odds, in knitting together the Canadian polity.

All of this would seem to add up either to an overwhelming indictment of modern-day Canadian political parties or to a counsel of despair that nothing can overcome the fissiparous tendencies of the Canadian political community. However, there are a number of qualifications we should consider. First, it must be emphasized that other institutions, including the internal structures

---

[14] Paul Thomas, "The Role of National Party Caucuses," in Peter Aucoin, *Party Government and Regional Representation in Canada*, pp. 69–70.

[15] John Wilson in *Political Support in Canada: The Crisis Years* (Edited by Alan Kornberg and H.D. Clark), page 215. Copyright © 1984 Duke University Press.

of Cabinet and bureaucracy as well as the national media, can provide national integration, either by themselves engaging in brokerage activities or by defining symbols and issues that transcend regional divisions. Second, politicians may try, and sometimes will succeed, in overriding strong regional interests and provincial governments. Indeed, it is noted by some Canadian political scientists that Pierre Trudeau in particular, and before him John Diefenbaker, chose to attempt to create national integration by avoiding the brokerage approach almost entirely, and instead appealed over the heads of provincial premiers and regional interests directly to the Canadian people. Trudeau is claimed, in this respect, to have been the antithesis of Mackenzie King, the consummate brokerage politician of Canadian history. Since these two leaders, with apparently opposite approaches, rank first and third in political longevity in the history of the office of the prime minister, and since both of them successfully faced very great crises of national unity, the moral we should draw about the relative efficiency of the two contrasting approaches in fostering national integration is quite unclear. Third, the failure of national parties to provide national integration need not necessarily be a problem if one believes that the sum of regional interests, expressed by strong regional parties or strong provincial governments, can add up to the "national interest," and that the result is a sort of paradoxical national strength through regional and provincial power.[16]

It should also be noted that many of the more pessimistic analyses of the difficulties faced by Canada because of the assumed failure of all of her national institutions adequately to create national integration were written in the late 1970s and the early 1980s. Those years seem to have marked at least a cyclical high point in the apparent decentralization of Canadian government and in tendencies towards disintegration. As Richard Johnson has very eloquently demonstrated in a study for the Royal Commission on the Economic Union, those years were marked by a political agenda that focused attention on issues relevant to provincial governments and regional interests to the near exclusion of the federal government.[17] However, as the agenda shifted to economic issues with the deep recession of the early 1980s, and as Canadians again focused on issues that tended to put the federal government in the spotlight, the apparent tendency towards disintegration sharply diminished. The election of a new government with wide regional representation also helped significantly to allay regional discontent. Since these decentralizing tendencies seem to run in cycles in Canadian politics, we can anticipate that, in future, the same issues will arise again; but for the moment, at least, there is less concern with the ramifications of the assumed failure of Canadian political parties to perform the functions of national integration.

At the provincial level, aggregative behaviour may not be so valuable to either the party or to the provincial political system. In some cases, there is sufficient consensus within a province to allow a party based on a single overriding principle to attain power. For example, C.B. Macpherson has argued that, in the 1920s

[16] Wilson, "The Dangers of Bickering," p. 215.

[17] Richard Johnson, *Questions of Confidence: Public Opinion and Public Policy in Canada* (Toronto: University of Toronto Press, 1986). This work is a comprehensive and incisive study of the structure of Canadian public opinion and its influence on public policy.

and 1930s, Alberta was a homogeneous single-class society with a dominant interest in relieving the burdens of its "quasi-colonial status" *vis-à-vis* eastern Canada. It was therefore possible for dogmatic parties, which were not broker-mediators, to succeed in provincial elections. Both the United Farmers of Alberta and the Social Credit Party in that province were a far cry from the older national parties with their "omnibus" nature.[18]

In general, the larger and more diversified the province, the more difficult it becomes for a party of principle rather than a brokerage-oriented party to get into power. In Ontario, for example, only once did a party of principle gain power. The United Farmers of Ontario won office in 1919; they were defeated at the next election, and shortly thereafter disappeared from the political scene. In Quebec, the early Union Nationale could be considered to have been a party of principle, but the price of its survival seems to have been the adoption of classic patronage and brokerage behaviour soon after its accession to power. The Parti Québécois most certainly qualified as a party of principle in its pre-referendum days. It became less so after 1981 and, by the time of its electoral defeat in 1985, under the leadership of Pierre Marc Johnson, it appeared more and more like a party attempting to use the more classic brokerage and leadership oriented methods. Certainly the ideology of separatism played little part in its campaign rhetoric in 1985.

At the national level, the Progressive Party of the 1920s was a party of principle.[19] It won sixty-five seats in the 1921 federal election, but soon fell prey to internal dissension and was ultimately absorbed by the Liberals. The CCF was, of course, the most persistent of the non-brokerage parties at the national level. But, while the CCF competed electorally for some twenty-nine years, except for a brief period in 1944 and 1945, when its Gallup-poll popularity equalled that of the two older parties, it never seriously threatened the pre-eminence of the Liberals and Conservatives. Since the formation of the NDP from most of the elements of the old CCF in 1961, a conscious attempt on the part of most of its leaders has led that party in the direction of creating a more broadly based coalition with what they hope will be a correspondingly greater chance for electoral success.[20]

Communication Functions[21]   Canadian parties, like their counterparts throughout the world, act as communicators, transmitting messages back and forth between political decision makers (and their opponents) and the public. Between elections,

---

[18] C.B. Macpherson, *Democracy in Alberta* (Toronto: University of Toronto Press, 1953). See also S.M. Lipset, *Agrarian Socialism* (Berkeley: University of California Press, 1950), for an anlysis of the rise of the CCF in Saskatchewan. A more detailed analysis of all these parties is found in the next chapter.

[19] W.L. Morton, *The Progressive Party in Canada* (Toronto: University of Toronto Press, 1950).

[20] W. Baker and T. Price, "The New Democratic Party and Canadian Politics," in Thorburn, ed., *Party Politics in Canada*, pp. 168–179. A more complete analysis of the difficulties faced by the early NDP in making the transition is found in Desmond Morton, *NDP: Dream of Power* (Toronto: Hakkert, 1974).

[21] On the role of the media in Canadian politics, see Arthur Siegel, *Politics and the Media in Canada* (Toronto: McGraw-Hill Ryerson, 1983); see also Frederick Fletcher and Daphne Gottlieb Taras, "The Mass Media and Politics: An Overview," in M. Whittington and G. Williams, *Canadian Politics in the 1980s* pp. 193–228. Note, however, that these sources concentrate on the media rather than on parties.

the transmission of information is largely carried out through the media by elected members of the party, supported on the government side by bales of information produced by the bureaucracy and on the opposition side by opposition research offices and the small establishment that goes with leaders' offices. Since issues are what politicians must ostensibly concentrate upon in their struggle to present themselves in the best possible light, a good deal of information may be provided as a crucial by-product of the struggle for partisan advantage.

However, some types of issues are much more suited to discussion in the media than others. While the print media can handle complex issues, television, the dominant medium of today, is far better suited to simple — even simplistic — treatment of issues and to personalization of political information. Thus, odiferous tuna fish may appear to be more important than free trade simply because smelly tuna plays better on TV. This is a universal propensity in western democracies, and will account, in part, for the tendency of parties to concentrate on simple and even frivolous issues.[22]

Closely connected with the communication of political information to society is the feedback to decision makers of information about the effectiveness of their policies and about the general political climate. A party in power must have accurate information in order to assess public attitudes to its record, and the opposition parties must know the public's perception of the relative weaknesses of government, and of themselves, in order to launch a credible attack at the time of the next election. Like most of the functions described so far, this communication function is not performed either exclusively or particularly well by Canada's parties. The low level of involvement among the general membership of Canadian parties between elections, among other things, inhibits parties in this respect.

Support Functions Support for the Canadian political system or for specific aspects of it is often channelled through a political party. At the lowest level, this fostering of support can take the form of providing the opportunity for wider public involvement in the political process, through, for instance, working for a party or active campaigning in an election.

It was suggested in chapter 5 that many Canadians participate in electoral politics primarily because they find it an interesting social activity. It is parties that provide much of the campaign pyrotechnics, which, around election time, attract attention to politics. The party attempts to create support for its candidates by selling people on its policies, its leaders, and, on rarer occasions, its ideology. By creating support for itself, the party also incidentally creates support for the regime of which it is a part. This diffuse support, derived from general confidence and faith in the system, and simply from involvement in its processes, is important for the stability of the regime.

Diffuse or generalized support for the system can also be created directly through the process of political education, socialization, and through what is often referred to as party propaganda. People can be convinced that the system is good and

---

[22] For comparative data see Anthony Smith, "Mass Communications," in David Butler et al, *Democracy at the Polls*.

deserving of their support through symbolic outputs as well as through allocative ones. In the attempt to get their candidates elected, parties try to identify themselves with such values of the regime as justice, freedom, equality, opportunity, and democracy. An important incidental effect of this process is to make people aware of the values of the Canadian political system and to create in them a basically supportive orientation towards the regime embodying those values.

In other cases, however, support for a party may express a lack of support for the political system. Thus support for the Communist Party is hardly support for the liberal democratic regime, and support for the Parti Québécois, which has sought to take Quebec out of the federation, can be interpreted as a lack of support for the Canadian political community. However, the difficulty of any unambiguous interpretation of what kind of support is intended by a voter is highlighted by the fact that only a minority of Parti Québécois supporters have ever unequivocally supported the separatist option. In 1976, for example, since the PQ was the only effective opposition to a discredited Liberal government, the only way to express effective opposition was to vote PQ regardless of the separatist option. This appears to have been the intent of the majority of PQ voters, and was borne out by the *non* vote in the 1980 Quebec referendum.[23]

Paradoxically, even dissident parties such as the Communists or the Parti Québécois may be functional for the existing system in that they provide a legitimate channel for the expression of dissent. Were this dissent expressed entirely through rioting, bombing, and kidnapping, the effect would be devastating. Futhermore, by providing focal points for dissent, parties like the Parti Québécois make the system's authorities aware of the fact that certain segments of society have serious grievances, with which the political system must deal. Thus, oddly enough, even parties whose major goal is the overthrow of the existing political community may unintentionally perform useful support functions for the system to which they are opposed.

The Making of Public Policy Perhaps the most fundamental and also the most difficult of questions about modern government is the disarmingly simple query — where does policy come from? Much of this book is concerned with essentially that question, as is a very great portion of the literature of political science.[24] The mythical man or woman on the street might be able to provide a shorter answer — "political parties" — and it is traditional to list the policy function as one of the major roles of political parties. However, it is very difficult to differentiate between "government," in the form of the PM, his Cabinet, the government caucus, and their bureaucratic advisors, from "party" in this respect, and to identify what policies come from the party organization and what from government. Moreover, there are also fundamental characteristics of the Canadian

---

[23] M. Pinard and R. Hamilton, "The Parti Québécois Comes to Power: An Analysis of the 1976 Quebec Election," *Canadian Journal of Political Science*, XI, 4, December 1978, p. 739. See also the more extensive discussion of Parti Québécois support in chapter 3.

[24] We will spare afficionados of footnotes any attempt to reference so vast a body of literature, or even its Canadian branch. For a summary and extensive bibliography, see G.B. Doern and R.W. Phidd, *The Making of Public Policy in Canada* (Toronto: Prentice-Hall, 1985), and our own bibliographical section on parties.

electorate that militate against any attempt by parties to interpret electoral victories as policy mandates.

Certainly, under the long-lived Liberal regimes of the post-war period, it has often seemed as if, while the party structure outside government might "play at" policy making, in reality, policy was made at the executive level of government. Thus, the Liberals were referred to as the "Government Party," and several books developed the theme that there was no meaningful policy distinction between the Liberal party and government.[25] Towards the end of the Trudeau era, it was sometimes claimed that innovation had disappeared from the party system altogether, moving more and more into the public service and the federal-provincial arena. This ministerialist orientation meant a blurring of party-government lines and an increased reliance on the bureaucracy, both for innovation and as a feedstock for political recruitment. Executive federalism, described at length in chapter 16, also meant that the partisan identification of federal and provincial governments was almost irrelevant for policy formulation in intergovernmental forums. In summary, noted H.D. Clark, "these trends suggested rather strongly that the party system did not provide an arena for meaningful discussion of policy direction."[26]

The Conservative government, elected in 1984, came to office with some policies that were fairly well defined as a result of internal policy discussions. They also came determined to wrest power away from the public service (whom they did not know or trust) and return it to the party structure. We will see that, for the grass roots of the party, this approach was relatively short-lived. "Party" soon became defined as "elected politicians," primarily in the Cabinet, and, while the policy role of the bureaucracy had not, by 1986, returned to the pre-eminence it held under the Liberals, as time has gone on, the Conservative government has come to rely more and more on its non-elected officials. We will also note that the ties between Liberals and the bureaucracy were not as close as is often assumed — there always remained significant policy-making aspirations in the Liberal-party organization and caucus, and many Liberal ministers were as suspicious of their bureaucrats as were their Tory successors. Nonetheless, the fact remains that Canadian parties are not well-structured to develop sophisticated policies, although the NDP makes a considerably greater effort to do so than do the other parties. The parties' ephemeral extra-parliamentary structures and their relatively infrequent and mild-mannered policy conferences make it difficult to fulfil this role.

Non-political Functions of Parties

Political parties in Canada, like those in other Anglo-Saxon democracies, confine themselves almost entirely to electoral functions. In many other western democracies, such as Israel, Austria, and Sweden, however, parties perform an array of tasks for their members, including the provision of cooperative buying services,

[25] These books are cited in our discussion of the modern Liberal Party.

[26] H.D. Clarke et al., *Absent Mandate*, p. 12.

leisure-time activities, special educational programs, and even burial societies.[27] Canadian parties certainly provide a focus for a large number of Canadians' leisure-time activity. Involvement in the party process is, as we have seen in chapter 5, an important psychological variable in giving Canadians a club to belong to and a sense of camaraderie with like-minded cohorts.

However, while Canadian parties and the party system provide a vehicle for satisfying the sociability needs of individuals, and while party conventions and electoral campaigns are, for some, an entertaining spectator sport, generally our parties do not become involved in the provision of social services for their members. However, since nations where at least some political parties perform these functions outnumber those where they do not, Canada must be considered a sort of anomaly with respect to the rather limited social services performed by its parties.

PARTIES AND PARTY SYSTEMS

While so far we have considered the functions performed for the political system by the individual party, the *party system* also has important effects. The fact that, in the Canadian party system, several parties are competing for political office at election time means that the voter is presented with a choice. It matters little whether that choice is made according to perceived differences in the parties' leadership, policies, or campaign style; as long as the voter has some real choice, one basic requirement for the persistence of a democratic system is fulfilled.[28] A second result of party competition is that political leaders can be kept accountable. We can vote to throw the rascals out because we can draw a line, provided by parties, between rascals and non-rascals. As we shall see when we discuss the policy process, this accountability is of a very general nature only; yet it remains important to the workings of the Canadian system that the voter have this vehicle for expressing any disaffection, secure in the knowledge that another team is waiting on the bench to take over political leadership.

A further critical function of the party system is to provide the electorate with a definition of what politics is all about. The party system helps to set the agenda for political debate, for, as Janine Brodie and Jane Jenson state, it "shape[s] the interpretation of what aspects of politics should be considered political, how politics should be conducted, what the boundaries of political discussion most properly may be and what kinds of conflicts can be resolved through the political process.[29] Brodie and Jenson argue that it is through this process of defining "the political" that the Canadian party system has given us an agenda for political discourse that focuses on regionalism and ethnicity rather than on class.

---

[27] Leon D. Epstein, *Political Parties in Western Democracies* (New York: Praeger, 1969), pp. 119–120.

[28] How real are the alternatives with which we are presented at election time is a matter for discussion. The fact remains, though, that a Canadian's choice is still greater than the simple yes or no offered to the citizen of a one-party state.

[29] Janine Brodie and Jane Jenson, *Crisis Challenge and Change: Class and Party in Canada* (Toronto: Methuen, 1980), p. 67.

CANADIAN PARTY STRUCTURES

Typologies of Party Structures

The most durable typology of party structures is that first suggested by the French political scientist, Maurice Duverger. He suggested that political parties could be broadly typified as being *mass parties, cadre parties,* or *militia parties.*[30] *Mass parties* are characterized by extra-parliamentary origins and by the fact that the mass-party organization has a significant degree of control over the legislative branch of the party in policy making. The British Labour Party, continental Social Democratic parties and, perhaps, the NDP or Parti Québécois are occasionally adduced as examples of mass parties. The early CCF and the Social Credit movement in Alberta are other Canadian examples. However, an important qualification must be entered. Roberto Michels, writing early in the twentieth century, noticed that the Social Democratic parties in Europe showed a discouraging tendency to be controlled by small cliques within either the legislature or the party executive.[31] His "iron law of oligarchy" posits that large organizations — no matter how democratic their origins and ideology — will be controlled by a relatively small group of people at the top. This will limit the extent to which any political party can be controlled by its mass membership. At a certain point, the requirements of efficiency appear to override the requirements of democracy.

Militia parties are parties that have a tightly organized central core with highly dedicated supporters. In mass and cadre parties, the party is a relatively minor part of the life of most members, but in a militia party the party is virtually everything. The militia party is essentially an organizational weapon to be used to overthrow an existing political system or to maintain a totalitarian one. The Canadian Communist Party would like to be a militia party, but is too weak to be properly categorized as such. The *Front de libération du Québec* is the closest thing to a recent Canadian example, although it never took the step of running candidates in elections and so cannot be called a "party" at all. The Communist Party of the Soviet Union and the Chinese Communist Party are the classic examples of militia parties.

---

[30] M. Duverger, *Political Parties* (New York: John Wiley and Son, 1963), first published in 1951. Engleman and Schwartz have modified this typology to fit Canada. See *Political Parties and the Canadian Social Structure.* Other authorities posit different classifications. For example, Leon D. Epstein, *Political Parties in Western Democracies,* suggests a fourfold classification as follows:

> Rural — with a bare skeletal organization
> Urban — patronage-based
> Urban — middle-class mass-membership
> Urban — socialist working class

This classification seems to mix incentive and structural bases of classifications. Moreover, it is difficult to envisage just how to classify, accurately, Canadian parties in it. They are not patronage-based in the U.S. sense, yet it would be difficult to categorize the older parties as middle-class mass-membership, and they are certainly not urban-socialist or rural. Some other recent studies of political parties have made no real attempt to classify party structures. C. Winn and J. McMenemy have not used any classification in *Political Parties in Canada* nor did Jean Blondel in *Political Parties* (London: Wideworld House, 1978). We have returned to the standard Duverger typology with an elaboration of the cadre classification, as suggested below.

[31] Roberto Michels, *Political Parties* (Glencoe: Free Press, 1949).

Cadre parties are characterized by the fact that a relatively small group of leaders overtly holds power in the party. The small, well-organized élite that controls the party itself is usually to be found in the legislature. With the possible exception of the NDP, traditional Canadian parties are of this type, and, as we shall see, even the NDP likely should be considered basically a cadre party.

At one time it was widely assumed by political scientists engaged in the comparative study of political parties that the mass party with its large numbers of committed and highly active members would increasingly become archetypes of modern political parties. In part, at least, this view was supported by the high degree of success of European socialist parties in the twenty-five years after World War Two and by the apparent attempts by all western political parties to broaden their membership bases. However, the membership base of many European parties has declined over the years and, in fact, was always likely, overstated to some degree, because of the inclusion of large numbers of inactive members who only paid dues passively through their unions. Meanwhile, centrist parties have continued to achieve electoral success without greatly broadening their bases.[32] True, the major Canadian parties have launched periodic membership drives. These, however, are really fund-raising efforts rather than, heaven forbid, an attempt to elicit large-scale public participation in their core activities.

Within cadre parties, a further structural differentiation can be suggested. A cadre party may take the form of a hierarchy, a stratarchy, an alliance of sub-coalitions, or an open accordion.[33] *A hierarchical* structure is pyramidal, with a single leader at the top and direct and clear lines of authority running through successive levels to the bottom. A traditionally organized bureaucracy is typical of this organizational form. However, neither Canadian political parties nor most other large western political parties operate with this structure, for the lines of communication from top to bottom within a political party are generally very weak. Party members at large often do not know what the party managers are doing, and even when they do, they will not necessarily follow. The leaders of Canadian political parties have virtually no coercive powers over party members, and followers may consequently make statements and act in ways that are not at all what party leaders might like.

In recognition of this, it has been suggested that large political parties, especially in North America, more closely approximate a *stratarchy*.[34] A stratarchy is basically a hierarchical structure in which the lines of communication and authority between and within levels are rather weak. In Canada, constituency-association executives often have only the faintest idea of what the higher level is doing, and even when they do know they may take actions or suggest policies that actually run counter to national or provincial party policy. More important, the provincial organizations of Canadian parties can in no way be viewed as subordinate to the national organizations, as we might expect in a classical hierarchical structure.

As well, parties may take on a structural form, which could be described as an

---

[32] Leon Epstein, "Political Parties," in Butler, et al, *Democracy at the Polls*, pp. 60–61.

[33] This classification was first suggested by S. Eldersveld, *Political Parties* (Chicago: Rand McNally, 1964), pp. 47–178.

[34] Eldersveld, pp. 98–117.

alliance of sub-coalitions.[35] In its pure form, this type of structure consists of a miscellany of groups, each fairly cohesive in itself and bound loosely to the others in the organization. Party members are there by virtue of their attachment to the sub-coalitions rather than to the party itself. For example, this type of structure could occur if several religious groups, unions, trade associations, and community organizations came together in an attempt to gain power. Within Canadian parties this kind of structure occasionally occurs at the local level. In some local organizations of the NDP, for instance, union locals and labour councils may be allied with community associations. In Canada, however, the alliance of sub-coalitions is rare; Canadians join and work for political parties per se, rather than joining them as a result of belonging to some other organization.

Finally, a party structure may be described as an *open accordion.*[36] This term describes a party whose structure is extremely loose and flexible with respect to membership, expanding and contracting according to the party's needs and according to the potential for the agglomeration of new members, for instance, from among newly arrived immigrant groups. The open-accordion concept implies, as well, that the party can be used by its members as an avenue of upward mobility and social integration. Since the original development of the major parties in Canada occurred at a time of rapid growth of the electorate, both through expanding enfranchisement and through successive waves of immigration, all Canadian parties have from time to time performed this function. Open-accordion party structures can still be found in ethnically diverse areas such as metropolitan Toronto, where the parties have brought together new immigrants and older party loyalists in a number of constituencies.

While these typologies may help us to analyse party structures as a whole, they do not provide a full inside picture of how Canada's political parties actually operate. For that we must rely on party insiders themselves:

> Within all three of Canada's major political parties, there are a number of sayings that are regularly expressed by the various people who plan and execute campaigns. Of these maxims, none would have more Conservative heads nodding in agreement than the favourite of Norman Atkins, godfather of Ontario's Big Blue Machine: "Party politics is only about three things; friendship, loyalty and principles . . . in that order." Atkins' second favourite saying is "Remember who your friends are, Daddy." Both these mottoes make the same point: that no single factor better explains the functioning of the Conservative party than collegiality. The camaraderie generated by political campaigns forms a lasting bond among party workers that extends beyond politics into business and their social lives. To many outsiders, the intensity of that bond is difficult to understand; but for an insider, it is what politics is all about.
>
> That bond, in turn, creates a complex networking system among those who have fought in the political wars of the past. The enduring nature of partisan collegiality also goes far beyond mere card files and telephone calls. It shapes the lives and relationships of the key people who make up political parties. Joe Clark's chief strategist, Lowell Murray, shared an apartment with Clark and Michel Cogger of

35 Eldersveld, pp. 73–97.

36 Eldersveld, pp. 47–72.

the Mulroney campaign during the early Stanfield years. In addition to being godfather to Clark's daughter Catherine, he was also an usher at Brian Mulroney's wedding and shared a room with him and another Mulroney confidant, Pat MacAdam, at St. Francis Xavier University in Nova Scotia. Hugh Segal, a chief operative of Bill Davis, went out with Maureen McTeer before she married Clark. He now works with Norman Atkins who, besides chairing the 1981 PC campaign in Ontario, is Dalton Camp's brother-in-law. Joe Clark himself worked at Camp Advertising one summer and lived at Norman Atkins' house. He also managed Michael Meighen's successful bid for the party presidency in 1973. Meighen, in turn, was introduced to his wife Kelly by Hugh Segal, went to law school at Laval with Brian Mulroney, and ended up as Mulroney's Ontario campaign chairman during the leadership campaign.[37]

The Liberal and New Democratic parties are no different.[38] Whatever organizational chart we use to describe their structure, political parties, perhaps even more than most human organizations, operate on networks, contacts, friendships, enmities, and personal judgements about people. Canadian parties thus can be analytically described as stratarchical-cadre structures, with elements of alliances of sub-coalition and open accordions, but most of all they are networks of *people* scheming together — and sometimes separately — in pursuit of the Holy Grail of elected office.

Canadian Party Structure: Generalizations[39]

Figure 10-2 shows, in very general form, an organizational chart for Canadian political parties. Arrowheads have purposely been left off the connecting lines because in a stratarchical structure it is not always possible to say in what direction influence flows. For example, although it is normal on party-organization charts to show the national executive as subordinate to the national convention, in practice the relationship may be reversed. At levels below national or provincial offices, the party structures virtually cease to exist between elections. The local strategists and workers retire to their Rotary Clubs, neighbourhood committees, or union halls and the local voters return to whatever they were doing before they made their trip to the polls and watched the returns on television. Except for the local MP, small national and constituency offices, and a few hyperactive local strategists, the party disappears. This situation is more marked in the party that wins an election than in the party that loses. The phenomena noted by John Meisel in the period leading up to the 1979 election have been typical of other periods, too:

> Since the two old parties are chiefly electoral and not programmatic, their national extraparliamentary organizations tend to be inactive when the party holds office. The National Liberal Federation was therefore not much in the news in the interelection period. Among its routine events were a convention in the autumn of

---

[37] Peter Martin, Alan Gregg, and George Perlin, *Contenders: The Tory Quest for Power*, (Toronto: Prentice-Hall, 1984), pp. 125–126.

[38] See Christina McCall-Newman, *Grits* (Toronto: Macmillan, 1982).

[39] Detailed information on specific party organizations is also provided in chapter 11.

1975, a policy workshop in March 1977, a policy convention about a year later and a candidates' workshop in January 1979. For all practical purposes, these activities were of little electoral consequence. The program, strategy and personnel of the party were easily determined by the cabinet and particularly the PM.[40]

Leon Epstein notes that internationally, the relationship between the electoral apparatus and the part of the organization that participates in government is quite variable depending upon the origins of the party and its electoral success. Generally, parties originating outside parliaments show much more influence by the extra-parliamentary wing.[41]

This situation has many ramifications for Canadian politics. It means, first, that between elections, it is difficult to communicate with parties through channels other than the federal or provincial executives, or the members of parliament, or the provincial legislature. It is the well-organized representatives of the middle class or businesses who are most able to do that. Since 1973, MPs have been provided with a small budget to maintain local offices, and although virtually all of them try to be in their ridings frequently, the parties that did not win in a constituency generally do not maintain offices. The average person who might wish to contact the local Liberal Party in a constituency represented by a Conservative will have a hard time indeed. Moreover, the local machinery is not appropriate to articulate effectively the interests of the poverty-stricken, the poorly educated, and the unemployed. Because these people are, generally, reluctant to approach an organization as bourgeois as a Canadian political party, the party must approach them. However, except at election time, it does not have enough activists to do so.

We noted earlier that some of the traditional mass-membership parties in Europe have more recently become organizations more like their middle-class counterparts. However, they still do maintain, by North American standards, a very extensive local structure. In this respect, both Canadian and American parties stand in some contrast to their counterparts in other western democracies.[42] In Britain, Israel, the Scandinavian nations, Austria, and, to a somewhat lesser extent, other western nations, the political party is much more a continuing living presence in society, and hence is more able to act as an intermediary between citizen and state. This does not necessarily mean that the Canadian political system is deficient in some way. In part, Canadian parties may play a minor role in this process because other institutions, such as interest groups, the bureaucracy, the media, and party leaders, by direct contact, do it more effectively. Whether this is, in itself, undesirable is a question to which we will turn later.

Perhaps one of the most curious features of the picture shown in Figure 10-2

---

[40] John Meisel, "The Larger Context: The Period Preceding the 1979 Election," *Canada at the Polls, 1979 and 1980: A Study of the General Elections*, Howard R. Penniman, ed. (Washington, D.C.: American Enterprise Institute, 1981), p. 43.

[41] Leon Epstein, "Political Parties: Organization," in Butler, *Democracy at the Polls*, pp. 53–54.

[42] A more detailed account of the structure and activities of western political parties between elections can be found in Leon D. Epstein, *Political Parties in Western Democracies*, pp. 98–166. Political parties in developing countries typically play a much larger role between elections. For a summary, see Joseph Lapalombara and Myron Weiner, "The Origin and Development of Political Parties," in Lapalombara and Weiner, (eds.), *Political Parties and Political Development* (Princeton: Princeton University Press, 1966).

FIGURE 10-2
CANADIAN POLITICAL PARTIES: GENERAL PICTURE

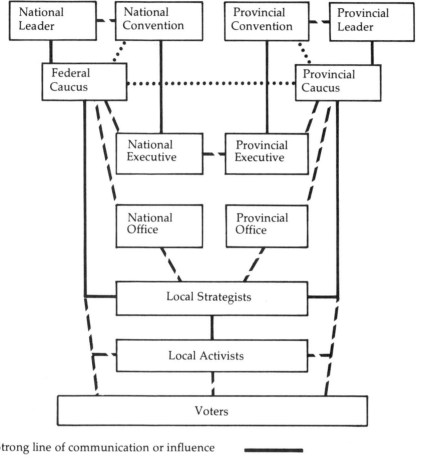

Strong line of communication or influence

Moderate line of communication or influence

Weak line of communication or influence

is the general absence of formal ties between federal and provincial party organizations down at least to the level of local strategists.[43] Federal and provincial leaders frequently disagree, or simply fail to communicate. The national and provincial executives and offices are often formally unconnected, and the national and provincial conventions, except for having some members in common, are also rather separate and independent entities. Since the major Canadian national parties are, in effect, *confederations* of provincial units, the provincial organiza-

[43] For an intensive examination of the relationship between party officials and party leadership, see Alan Kornberg, et al, *Citizen Politicians — Canada: Party Officials in a Democratic Society* (Durham: Carolina Academic Press, 1979).

tions and leaders may, at times, even dominate the national organizations and leaders, particularly when the national party is out of power.[44] Since there are only a limited number of local strategists and activists available, there is a great deal of overlap between federal and provincial parties at that level, and coordination of sorts may be achieved in that way. At the very bottom of the hierarchy of participation, however, there may again be considerable differentiation between federal and provincial parties, for Canadian voters frequently vote for different parties at the federal and provincial levels, and about one-third of Canadian voters show different long-term partisan loyalties at the federal and provincial levels of government.[45]

Lest we conclude that the structural differentiation between federal and provincial parties is always problematical for Canadian politics, we should note that it does leave provincial and federal governments free to agree or disagree regardless of the label of the party in power. This feature may be particularly appropriate in a federal system where intergovernmental bargaining is a critical dimension of policy making. In any event, this long-standing feature of the Canadian party system has stubbornly resisted sporadic efforts by federal-level parties to change it. Attempts to impose federal control over provincial parties inevitably cause a furor in the provinces, with the result that the federal party must either retreat or watch the provincial party sever its ties with the national party.[46] Thus, while the Canadian political system can be described as federal, its political parties are at most only confederal.

The most extreme example of the independence of a provincial party from its national counterpart is the Liberal Party of Quebec. Here, the federal and provincial organizations are completely separate formally, and very nearly so informally. There is frequent disagreement on fundamental issues between the federal and provincial Liberals, and yet the Liberal Party has been quite consistently successful in Quebec at both levels. The fact that parties with strong policy disagreements can share equal success on a common electoral base bears testimony to the benefits of the loose confederal structure adopted by the Canadian parties. Getting elected is their major concern, and by this measure the confederal arrangement used by the federal and provincial Liberal parties in Quebec would seem to be a very effective organizational form indeed.[47]

While the national and provincial executives and party head offices continue to exist between elections, the lines of communication between them and the parliamentary parties are often weak. The national executive committees meet at

---

[44] See Joseph Wearing, *The L-Shaped Party* (Toronto: McGraw Hill Ryerson, 1980), and John Wilson, "On the Dangers of Bickering."

[45] Clarke *et al., Political Choice in Canada*, p. 141, indicates that only 44% of Canadians studied in 1974 showed consistent patterns of identification (in both direction and intensity) across the two levels of government. For more recent data, see H.D. Clarke, *et al., Absent Mandate.* Consistency did not increase between the 1974 and the 1980 elections.

[46] For an example of this type of battle, see E.R. Black, "Federal Strains within a Canadian Party," *Dalhousie Review*, vol. 45, No. 3, 1965, pp. 226–240.

[47] Paul Andre Comeau, "La Transformation du parti libéral Québécois," *Canadian Journal of Economics and Political Science*, vol. 31, No. 3, August 1965, pp. 358–368. See also V. Lemieux, "Heaven is Blue, Hell is Red," in M. Robin, ed., *Canadian Provincial Politics* (Scarborough, Prentice-Hall, 1978), pp. 248–282.

least annually, and MPs are often also members of the executive; but the feeling persists, especially among the caucus and the parliamentary leadership, that the executive exists to administer the party electoral machinery, and the caucus or the leadership to determine party policy. Since members of legislatures are the most visible part of the party between elections, what they say or do is what the press reports and what the public picks up about the party. The extra-parliamentary executives are thus automatically relegated to second place in policy making. This situation is most marked when the party is in power. Then the tension between the Cabinet and appointees in the prime minister's office and the broader party organization may be quite intense. Joseph Wearing noted that, during the last years of the Trudeau government, "there has not been a single request from a single Cabinet Minister to test any question on the party membership and the public through them,"[48] a situation the non-parliamentary executive found to be too élitist and quite difficult to accept.

Attached to the executive of most provincial and national parties is a perma-nent party office under the direction of a national or provincial chief executive. Until the mid-1970s, a typical national party office might contain, between elections, a chief party organizer, an executive secretary for the party, two or three party researchers or administrative assistants, a public-relations person, and a typist or two. In the past decade there has been considerable expansion, made possible by the better financial situation in which the three national parties have found themselves as a result of the election-expense reforms of 1974 and the use of direct-mail fund-raising techniques. Now the typical national party office, described in more detail in the next chapter, numbers between forty and sixty-five full-time and part-time staff, and features a considerable elaboration and differentiation of functions. The party in power may considerably augment its organizational strength by appointing its organizers to the Senate. The Oppo-sition has no such recourse, but instead augments its organization through the caucus research office and the office of the party leaders.[49]

Another place in Figure 10-2 where lines of communication are unexpectedly weak is between the national or provincial offices and their local strategists and workers. The problem derives partly from the lack of work to do in a party organi-zation between elections. More suprising, however, is the fact that these lines of communication do not always become strong even during election campaigns. The torrent of directives, literature, and information that issues from provincial or national headquarters at election time is sometimes ignored by the local orga-nizations, which feel that the local issues, on which they are better informed than the party bureaucrats in the capital, are likely to determine the outcome in their riding.

The parliamentary structure of virtually all Canadian parties revolves around the *caucus*.[50] The Parliamentary caucus is essentially a regular meeting of the

[48] Wearing, *The L-Shaped Party*, p. 152.

[49] The structure of each party's national headquarters is discussed in greater detail in chapter 11.

[50] There is a thorough and excellent discussion of the structures and role of the parliamentary caucus in Paul G. Thomas, "The Role of National Party Caucuses," in Aucoin, *Party Government*. We also consider the role of caucus in chapter 19.

elected legislators of the party. While the legislature is in session, caucus meets at least once a week in plenary session. As well, there may be meetings of regional caucuses consisting of all the members from a particular region. In an Opposition party, caucus meetings can often be quite lively. Almost all MPs feel free to have their say, and consequently policy debates can become heated. In the caucus of a governing party, the situation may be different. There are clearly recognized party leaders—the prime minister and the Cabinet. The government back-benchers have the clearly defined role of supporting the policies put forward by the leaders. The Cabinet has access to considerable expertise from the public service and from its political technocrats in the Prime Minister's Office, and it is often more inclined to listen to these than to its own non-expert back-benchers on matters of policy. By the time the government caucus sees the policies, they have generally been approved by Cabinet and may even be in their final legislative form.

However, this is not to say that the government caucus has no influence on priority determination or policy formulation. Back-bench government MPs take their representational roles seriously, and while they virtually always will support their leaders in public, they may well disagree with them in private, particularly on issues that deeply affect their region. They may, in particular be able to influence the priority ordering that Cabinet assigns to issues, and in that way they may have a significant effect on the shape of policy. They may also, on occasion, succeed in forcing the government to withdraw proposed legislation they consider politically awkward, or they may convince the government to make major amendments to satisfy their view of what will be acceptable to the average voter in Wawa, Antigonish, or metropolitan Vancouver.

The general picture of Canadian political parties shown in Figure 10-2 places the *convention* near the top of the party structure, but in reality it is rather difficult to fit into the picture. Until recently, conventions were not a regular feature of Canadian politics. In the two older parties they were held whenever there was a need to elect a new leader, and only sporadically at other times.[51] Currently the Liberals, Conservatives, and New Democrats are all committed to holding a mass gathering of the party faithful every two years. For the two older parties, there are effectively three types of conventions — regular policy conventions, leadership review conventions, and leadership selection conventions.

As might be expected in organizations as heavily dependent for electoral success on their leaders as are Canadian parties, the real nature of the party convention will depend on its leadership-related activities. There is a leadership review at

---

[51] While there is considerable material available on leadership conventions in Canada, there is very little on regular policy conventions. For a more detailed discussion of the nature and role of leadership conventions, see D.V. Smiley, "The National Party Leadership Convention in Canada: A Preliminary Analysis," *Canadian Journal of Political Science*, vol. 1, no. 4, December 1968, pp. 373–397. See also J. Wearing, "Party Leadership and the 1966 Conventions," *Journal of Canadian Studies*, vol. 2, no. 1, February 1967, pp. 18–36, "A Convention for Professionals: The PCs in Toronto," *Journal of Canadian Studies*, vol. 2, no. 4, November 1967; "The Liberal Choice," *Journal of Canadian Studies*, vol. 3, no. 2, May 1968, and John Courtney, *The Selection of National Party Leaders in Canada* (Toronto: Prentice-Hall, 1974). Political memoirs of unsuccessful leadership candidates also contain material on conventions; the most recent is Jean Chretien, *Straight from the Heart* (Toronto: Deneau, 1985). For a particularly interesting description of the 1983 Conservative leadership convention, see Peter Martin, et al, *Contenders: The Tory Quest for Power* (Toronto: Prentice-Hall, 1984).

all NDP conventions, so they differ little in this respect from one time to the next. The Liberals and Conservatives hold a leadership review once between elections. The leadership review is accomplished by a vote on whether a leadership convention should be held — effectively a vote of confidence in the party leader. There is no firm rule about when a leader is assumed to have lost the confidence of the party, but considerably more than 50% support is required. (Joe Clark resigned the leadership of the Conservatives in 1983 after barely failing to carry a *two-thirds* majority.) Leadership-review conventions have a dramatic focal point, which general conventions do not, and are hence more intense, and, for the party, more important events than their regular policy counterparts. Of course, the greatest intensity is reserved for the leadership-selection conventions.

For all three parties, the routine policy convention performs similar functions, related more to improving levels of participation, maintaining group solidarity, and garnering free publicity via press and television coverage than to the establishment of party policy. The national NDP convention has considerably more influence over party policy than the Liberal and Conservative counterparts, although it is not as likely to have to "deliver" on its convention statements. The November 1969 NDP conference in Winnipeg, however, was more or less typical of all Canadian conventions. The only major difference was that the back-benchers' policy proposals discussed by the party leaders were somewhat more radical than those regularly handled (with similar disregard) by the leaders of the older parties.

That particular NDP convention was preceded by a great build-up of publicity surrounding the nationalist "Waffle Manifesto," drafted by a left-wing group of the extra-parliamentary party. The parliamentary wing of the party countered with a much less radical policy statement, which, supported by the rhetoric of the parliamentary party and the conservatism of the labour unions, was easily pushed through the convention. To no one's surprise, the party leader, Tommy Douglas, was given an overwhelming vote of confidence — something the voters had denied him in the previous election. Meanwhile, other potential leadership candidates, hoping desperately that Douglas would step down before too long, vowed undying support for their leader. The convention adjourned, the faithful went home, and the party carried on with little change in stated policy. In fact, some NDP MPs remained in Ottawa throughout the convention because, after all, Parliament *was* sitting!

The 1985 Liberal Party convention in Halifax might have been expected to have more dramatic ramifications. After all, the party had just incurred its worst electoral defeat of the twentieth century. Virtually all of the old-guard Trudeau phalanx had disappeared. The party was broke and searching for new policies, and the new leader, John Turner, appeared in a vulnerable position not only because of his recent defeat, but also because Jean Chrétien, his nearest rival at the previous leadership convention, retained considerable popularity, and perhaps a certain interest in the job.

The Halifax convention was not, however, a leadership-review convention. The policy discussions were discursive and, if occasionally heated on the issue of free trade with the United States, resulted in nothing the party-in-Parliament would be obliged to consider an unequivocal policy position. Since there was not a leadership review scheduled for this conference, Turner could not be deposed. Since he showed no sign of leaving of his own free will, the party faithful, including a rather reluctant-seeming Jean Chrétien, rallied around him, and the convention ended in a state of more peace and light than might have been anticipated given the party's circumstances. It also ended without even attempting to define major new policy directions.

By contrast, the 1983 Conservative Party convention in Winnipeg was fraught with drama. A leadership-review vote was scheduled, and for the three years since he was defeated in 1980, Joe Clark's hold on the Tory leadership had seemed very tenuous. Although these were policy discussions, in fact, the convention focused virtually exclusively on the dramatic vote scheduled for its last day, and media attention was rivetted on that event. Both the party faithful and the Canadian public were far more interested in the fate of Joe Clark than they ever were in the policy pronouncements from the more mundane policy conventions. The result, and the subsequent resignation of the leader, were the major Canadian political events of the year, once again underlining the heavy leadership orientation of Canadian party politics.[52]

A similar ambience overhangs most party policy conventions. Should they accord with what the parliamentary leaders want, the policy proposals are likely to be accepted. Should they be contrary to the leaders' thinking, then, even if the convention accepts the proposals, they will not appear in any legislative program proposed by the parliamentary wing.[53] Medicare, for example, was adopted by a Liberal convention in 1919, but was not enacted by the parliamentary party until almost half a century later. According to Joseph Wearing, the convention exerts a strong "moral force" on the leadership of the party,[54] but despite the formal accountability of the party to the convention on policy matters, a moral obligation is all that is really incurred.

Occasionally there will be considerably more interest in policy, particularly in parties more devoted to principle. Parti Québécois policy conventions, from 1976 to 1984, when the party governed Quebec, were always dramatic and generally fractious affairs. The active membership of the party—and hence the convention—tended to be considerably more radical than most of the elected leadership, particularly the leader, René Lévesque. Lévesque was thus occasionally put in the position of having to implicitly or even overtly threaten to resign rather than accept dogmatic policy positions on the separation of Quebec. Nor is the problem apparently confined to Canada. In other western democracies, too, "zealous party activists may be more interested in their programs than they are in winning current elections—hoping for lasting conversion of the electorate and indifferent to pragmatic victories that might be won in the short term."[55]

---

[52] See Martin, *Contenders*, for a full description of the event.

[53] After the 1966 convention, Prime Minister Lester Pearson said in the House of Commons that convention resolutions would be "taken very seriously as a guide to policy," but that they "did not establish policy." Even this was perhaps too generous an assessment of their significance. Joseph Wearing, "Party Leadership and the 1966 Convention," *Journal of Canadian Studies*, vol. 2, no. 1, p. 24.

[54] Wearing, p. 25.

[55] Epstein, "Political Parties: Organizations," p. 66.

A leadership convention is different in tone, but in its substantive effect on the party and its policies, it may not, after all, be so different.[56] It is bigger, noisier, and more exciting than a policy convention, and it gets the party vast amounts of free publicity, which helps in its attempts to get elected. However, the shifts in direction produced by a change in leadership have usually been small. The election of Pierre Trudeau as Liberal leader in 1968, while generating vast changes in style, probably made little long-term difference to the direction of the Liberal Party; the same can be said for the election of Ed Broadbent as leader of the NDP, of Joe Clark as Conservative leader, of Brian Mulroney as successor to Clark, and of John Turner as successor to Trudeau. The style and the face may change, but the policy orientations of the major Canadian parties are consistently middle-of-the-road.

But, whatever their impact on policy, for the party activists and the public alike, leadership races within parties carry much of the excitement of elections. They focus attention on the party, just as elections focus attention on the political system, and they provide a game activists can play and the public can watch — not unlike a spectator sport. While everyone would like to see the leader of his or her choice win, the contest has fun value in itself. Although there is little published data on the attitudes accompanying activity in leadership races, there is no reason to suppose that attitudes towards politics by most activists within parties should be greatly different from those towards the struggle between parties. They are exciting events in which participation is, to a considerable extent, its own reward.

What is true for the majority, however, is not always true for all party activists. Leadership races, after all, are, for some, high-stakes games, and the most active participants, particularly in the teams of the candidates who come close to winning, are not always quick to accept the outcome. This is particularly true if the party is not in power, and even more true if the chosen leader loses the next election. By tradition, Conservatives have been more likely to eat alive their defeated leaders than have the Liberals or the NDP, Joe Clark being only the latest in a long line of victims. As James Lightbody put it recently:

> [It is an] article of faith that Liberals support their leaders uncritically, unlike Conservatives who customarily initiate leaderly cannibalism (apparently a necessary party ritual spawned by the vernal equinox).[57]

While the more recent experiences of John Turner as Liberal leader seem to suggest that in Canadian intra-party politics, it is generally true that uneasy rests the head that wears the crown; when it came to the crunch in the 1986 Liberal leadership review, the party faithful held true to Lightbody's description and gave John Turner more than 80% support at the convention.

Another type of party activity that came into increasing use in the late 1960s was the "thinkers' conference." These were usually small conferences in out-of-the-way locations or at out-of-season vacation resorts, attended by those MPs and MLAs who liked to see themselves as policy thinkers; those party members who could afford to pay for their own transportation, accommodation, and registration

---

[56] See John Courtney, *The Selection of National Party Leaders in Canada.*

[57] James Lightbody, "Dancing with Dinosaurs: Alberta Politics in 1986," *Canadian Forum,* January 1986, p. 11.

fees; and a fair number of "resource people," or academics, who lent or rented themselves out for such occasions. The purposes of these meetings were to keep the party in touch with current trends in the intellectual community, and to provide policy initiatives. Conferences such as those at Niagara Falls (Conservatives) and Harrison Hot Springs (Liberals) in the autumn of 1969 may indeed have had some influence on party policy. Earlier thinkers' conferences — such as that of the Liberals at Kingston in 1960 and that of the Conservatives at Montmorency Falls in August 1967 — did produce discernible changes in party policy. The conference in Kingston helped push the Liberal Party some distance to the left in the early and mid-1960s, and laid the groundwork for the rapid growth in government spending in the late 1960s, while the conference in Montmorency Falls produced the Conservative Party's not overly successful flirtation with the *deux nations* theory.[58] The Niagara Falls conference in 1969 kept the Progressive Conservatives from moving fully in support of a guaranteed annual income, even though the leader espoused the concept. In spite of one policy meeting of Liberal "thinkers" during that party's brief vacation from power in 1979, and some internal discussion in the Liberal Party about conducting more sessions in the aftermath of the 1984 electoral defeat, such conferences seem to have fallen out of favour in the 1980s. This perhaps reflects a desire on the part of the parliamentary wing of the parties to maintain closer control over party policies, or perhaps there is a general anti-intellectual feeling in the 1980s.

The party structures discussed up to this point have been primarily at the national or the provincial level. In 1969, parties entered municipal politics in Toronto, and it is conceivable, if not highly probable, that the next few years will see further efforts by political parties in large urban areas.[59] The success of national parties in Toronto has been relatively limited, and both the Liberals and the NDP, after a fairly intensive effort in 1970, agreed to keep a low profile in 1972, and have abstained from conducting city-wide campaigns since then.[60] Even the specifically municipal Civic Party, which had considerable success in Toronto in 1970, disintegrated in 1972 as three of its leaders decided to run for mayor. In Montreal, Mayor Jean Drapeau led a political party of sorts, but it was really a personal machine rather than a real political party, and is unlikely to survive his disappearance from the scene for very long. Municipal politicians are very often known by their national or provincial party allegiance, and the people who knock on doors for them in municipal campaigns will often be predominantly from one or another political party. However, as far as overt activity by the parties is concerned, there is very little of it at the municipal level in Canada.

In the next chapter we will turn to a discussion of the specific features of Canada's political parties. When that has been done, we will be in a position to draw some further conclusions about the ways in which parties and the party system function within the Canadian political system.

---

[58] Dalton Camp, "Reflections on the Montmorency Conference," *Queen's Quarterly*, vol. 76, No. 2, summer, 1969, pp. 185–199.

[59] James Lightbody, "Party Politics and Local Elections," *Journal of Canadian Studies*, vol. 6, no. 1, February 1971, pp. 39–44.

[60] Stephen Clarkson, "Barriers to the Entry of Parties in Toronto Area Politics," in L. Axworthy and James M. Gillies, eds., *The City: Canada's Prospects, Canada's Problems* (Toronto: Butterworth, 1973).

C H A P T E R 1 1

THE PARTIES: A HISTORICAL PERSPECTIVE

THE RISE AND FALL OF THE TWO-PARTY SYSTEM, 1840–1917
■ The Evolution of the Party System: 1867–1896
■ The Two-Party System: 1896–1917
MODERN PARTY POLITICS: THE MAJOR PARTIES 1921–1986
■ The Liberals ■ The Conservatives
MODERN PARTY POLITICS: THE THIRD PARTIES 1921–1986
■ The Progressive Movement ■ Social Credit
■ The CCF-NDP: Socialism in Canada
■ Interpretations of Third-Party Movements in Canada
CONCLUSION: PARTIES AND THE PARTY SYSTEM

H aving discussed the overall role of political parties and the party system in the Canadian political system, we turn in this chaper to a more detailed examination of Canada's party system. First we will consider the early history of the system, then we will examine the two older parties, and finally we will discuss the more recent arrivals on the Canadian party scene.

THE RISE AND FALL OF THE TWO-PARTY SYSTEM, 1840–1917

The origins of the present-day party system in Canada can be traced to the legislature of the United Provinces of Upper and Lower Canada following the Act of Union of 1840.[1] The early years of the Union government were

---

[1] E.M. Reid, "The Rise of National Parties in Canada," in *Papers and Proceedings of the Canadian Political Science Association*, vol. 4, 1932. See also G.M. Hougham, "The Background and Development of National Parties," in H.G. Thornburn, ed., *Party Politics in Canada* (Scarborough: Prentice-Hall, 1972), pp. 2–14; and H.G. Thorburn, "The Development of Political Parties in Canada," in *Party Politics in Canada* (4th Edition), 1979, pp. 2–12. Peter Aucoin, "Regionalism, Party and National Government," in Peter Aucoin, ed., *Party Government and Regional Representation in Canada* (Ottawa: Royal Commission on the Economic Union and Development Prospects for Canada, Research Volume #36, 1985) David E. Smith, "Party Government, Representation and National Integration in Canada," and Paul G. Thomas, "The Role of National Party Caucuses," in Aucoin, *Party Government*, pp. 1–68 and 69–128.

characterized by a series of coalitions among various factions in the legislative assembly. The factions, formed around strong leaders, were quite stable. The coalitions of factions that constituted the "parties" were at first quite unstable, but they tended to become more constant as time went on, until Macdonald and Cartier managed to develop a Liberal-Conservative coalition, which not only promoted Confederation but survived after it. The basic dynamics of party government in a parliamentary system, then, were already understood at Confederation. "Party government would provide the legislative majority in the House of Commons to sustain effective executive power in the Cabinet and enable national and regional interests to be reconciled within the Cabinet at the apex of party government."[2]

The Evolution of the Party System: 1878–1896

The gradual evolution of firmer party lines, which had begun in the pre-Confederation era, continued after 1867. Between 1867 and 1873, the Canadian government still consisted of a loose collection of many of the Liberal and Conservative elements that had initially favoured Confederation. Their unity, such as it was, arose out of a common desire to build a nation, to keep it together, and, naturally, to stay in power.

John A. Macdonald may have been the leader, but several of his ministers had their own personal followings in both the House of Commons and the country. Building a government consisted of keeping enough of these factions together to form a voting bloc in Parliament.

Within the first House of Commons there were Tory and Grit factions, but there were, as well, other kinds of groupings. On the government side sat Cabinet members, their personal supporters, and assorted loose fish or ministerialists, who had been elected by their constituents for the express purpose of supporting the government in hopes of gaining favours for their constituencies. The existence of ministerialists was made possible by a system of non-simultaneous elections, whereby the party in power could call an election in safe seats first, and then gradually work to less favourable ridings. In addition to giving the party in power a great advantage by allowing it to create its own bandwagon, this system also removed any uncertainty on the part of ridings that wanted to ensure their share of patronage by electing a loose fish.

However, even by 1867 there were beginning to emerge some consistent patterns to the Liberal-Conservative governing coalition and to their Liberal opponents. The former comprised Cartier's *Bleus*, which consisted of the French-Canadian majority blessed by the Church establishment, Macdonald's Ontario Tories, big-business interests from Montreal arrayed around Alexander Galt, and various supporters of the Grand Trunk Railway. Their orientation was firmly protectionist, expansionist, and pro-business. The Liberal opposition consisted of Ontario Clear Grits — agrarian reformers loosely tied to George Brown and his newspaper, the *Globe* — plus the Parti rouge — radical reformers from Quebec. The Liberals' orientation was anti-railroad, anti-protectionist, and pro-agrarian. Maritime members, with the exception of a group of Nova Scotia MPs associated

2 Aucoin, "Regionalism, Party and National Government," p. 137.

with Joseph Howe and initially opposed to Confederation, made what alliances they could to ensure patronage for their area. For another ten years, individual MPs would move back and forth from one element of the coalition to another, or even from government to Opposition, but the positions of factional elements and the leaders were relatively stable.

> Patronage pervaded the political system. It was systematically followed and Macdonald played a central role in its conduct. The chief result of this development . . . was a party system both intensely local in its interests and profoundly personal in its management by the Party leader.[3]

In 1872, the group in power made the mistake of getting caught accepting rather large kickbacks (under the guise of "election-fund contributions") from the promoters of the Canadian Pacific Railway, and, although they won the election of 1872, Macdonald and his supporters were forced to resign shortly thereafter, when the dimensions of the "Pacific Scandal" became known.[4] The Liberals who replaced them, from 1873 to 1878, under Alexander Mackenzie, had little new or different to offer in the way of policy, and lacked a cohesive party organization. Indeed in 1873, it was not even absolutely certain who their leader was; Mackenzie had to fight a continual battle with Edward Blake, who was apparently unable to decide whether he really wanted to lead the party, but who nonetheless retained great personal popularity. After five years in power, the Liberals, perhaps because of their aversion to the patronage system so essential to early party government as much as because of their persisting leadership question, had developed virtually none of the organizational attributes necessary to retain office. In 1878, they were defeated by the better-organized Conservatives.

The first ten years of Confederation, then, were characterized by growing patronage-based party cohesion in the dominant coalition, with much slower development in the Opposition. The lack of simultaneous elections and of the secret ballot made party organization in the years before 1878 a rather different problem than it is today. Further, the process of functional differentiation of institutions—which accompanies industrialization and modernization in any society —takes time; and, in political parties no less than in other Canadian institutions, the process was just beginning in the last third of the nineteenth century.

By 1878, there were simultaneous elections by secret ballot in eastern Canada, so that it was necessary for candidates to choose party lines before, not during, an election. This alone produced much firmer party lines in Canada. From 1878 to 1891, there was a consolidation of Conservative party lines under Macdonald, and around his "National Policy," which included railway construction, westward expansion, and protective tariffs. The Liberal Party was characterized in this period by aimlessness and lack of organization, followed, after 1891, by consolidation and regrouping under the leadership of Wilfrid Laurier.

In the early years of the federation, the west was the particular home of non-partisan and ministerialist politics. The primary concern of the west was to ensure

3 Smith, "Party Government, Representation and National Integration in Canada," p. 17.

4 The "Pacific Scandal," as it was called, is described thoroughly by Pierre Berton in *The National Dream* (Toronto: McClelland and Stewart, 1970), pp. 90–134.

that the railway went through, and westerners would have supported any ministry that promised to build the railroad. In practice, that meant Macdonald's Conservatives, and the kindly Conservative government made it easy for westerners to support the government party by delaying the introduction of simultaneous elections in the west. This may account, in part, for the fact that strong two-party traditions never developed in the west. Early provincial governments in Manitoba and British Columbia, and later in Saskatchewan and Alberta, sometimes went under standard party labels, but the lack of strong bipartisan competition led to an administrative form of government that later lent itself to easy capture by third-party movements.

We should not, however, exaggerate the strength of our early parties. While parties existed and were used to organize both the House of Commons and the political life of the growing and expanding nation, the modern-day Canadian would have noticed some very considerable differences on stepping out of a time machine in 1880.

> In the first two or three decades after Confederation, the Canadian party system was not fully developed or truly national in scope. Individuals were recruited and supported in elections to the House of Commons by local elites and were more responsive to them than to the national party leadership.
>
> Party discipline was weak within the House of Commons. J.D. Edgar, who served during the 1870s as the informal whip in the House of Commons for the Liberal party, described the House as a contest of undisciplined factions, each laced through with a high proportion of members who did not take kindly to whipping.[5]

Thus, it is not surprising that during the first four sessions of the first parliament, Macdonald was defeated six times on minor bills, twice on resolutions preceding bills, and twice on supply votes. In that parliament, MPs failed to vote with their party 20% of the time, compared to 1.4% in 1963-1965.

The Two-Party System: 1896-1917

The post-Macdonald years from 1896 to 1917 could perhaps be characterized as the golden age of two-party politics in Canada. The Conservative and Liberal parties, led by Robert Borden and Wilfrid Laurier, had well-organized electoral machines and well-disciplined parliamentary parties. No other party movements of any significance existed. Regional discontent had not yet made a strong impression on Parliament and parties, ethnic cleavage was dormant for the time being, and the rural-urban cleavage that was to spawn the Progressive movement of the 1920s had not yet become important. Economic prosperity minimized dissent, and those who were discontented could move west to start again; the two-party system was able to successfully accommodate interests because the job was, for the first time, doable. The need for patronage and pork-barrel politics to cement the party organization faded, as the party leadership began to forge programmatic consensus among a wide range or interests. The new cement of party unity in this period was the successful accommodation of diversity and the

5 Thomas, "The Role of National Party Caucuses," pp. 61-62. Reproduced with permission of the Minister of Supply and Services Canada.

ability of Laurier and Borden to articulate alternative national visions of Canada. Although Laurier and the Liberal Party were defeated in 1911, the equilibrium of the two-party system persisted until 1917. World War One, the conscription crisis of 1917, and the formation of the Union Government ended those days. Some three years after the outbreak of World War One, it became necessary, in Prime Minister Borden's view, to institute conscription in order to keep up the size of Canada's forces in Europe. We have seen, in chapter 3, that French Canadians, particularly those living in Quebec, felt that the war had little relevance to their lives. This attitude, combined with evidence of inhospitable treatment received by any Francophone Canadians who did join the armed forces, ensured the opposition of French Canada, and particularly Quebeckers, to conscription. In an effort to unite Canadian opinion, the Conservative prime minister, Robert Borden, formed a Union government with most English-speaking Liberals supporting him; but practically all French-speaking Liberals opposed the coalition. The election that followed all but isolated French Canada, and temporarily destroyed the Liberal coalition Laurier had so carefully constructed. In addition, it spelled the end, for nearly forty years, of any strong support for the Conservative party in Quebec.

The brief emergence of a truly national party system may have been the result of a self-conscious effort by Laurier and Borden to overcome the local orientation of Canadian politics and to use parties as more than

> electoral instruments, consisting of individual political entrepreneurs held together for the purpose of electoral survival by the bond of patronage. In their opinion, parties should offer alternative definitions of the national interest and should bind their elected members to implement such broad programs once in office.[6]

In order to achieve this, a number of structural reforms were undertaken, including a move to separate party financing from the leader and to eliminate, or at least greatly reduce, patronage in civil-service appointments.[7] Laurier and Borden also sought to strengthen ties with the provincial wings of their parties, and to reflect regional interests in national party platforms. But the national party system that was the dream of Laurier and Borden did not survive World War One.

Although the immediate cause of the collapse of the two-party system was the conscription crisis and the formation of the Union Government, a number of more fundamental causes lay in the background. Despite the honest efforts of the party leaders to make their organization truly national, the Conservative Party structure had become overcentralized in eastern Canada, particularly in Ontario, while the Liberals had become too strongly identified with French Canada. Attempts to overcome these imbalances, which were recognized by both Laurier and Borden, had failed. The lack of any strong party tradition in the west was shortly to result in the election there of many Progressive MPs. Moreover, the parties had stopped trying to win elections by creating multi-dimensional consensus, and had turned instead to the tactic of playing exclusively on ethnic

---

[6] Thomas, p. 82. Reproduced with permission of The Minister of Supply and Services Canada.

[7] John English, *The Decline of Politics: The Conservatives and the Party System 1901–1920* (Toronto: University of Toronto Press, 1977), p. 15ff.

cleavages. Then as now, an excessive emphasis on ethnic cleavages was dangerous. By failing to take account of urban-rural, regional, and economic cleavages, both older parties moved out of touch with important elements of the electorate and lost the broadly based support needed to maintain a two-party system. Finally, both parties were entering periods of instability in leadership. The Liberals recovered quickly under Mackenzie King and were able to use brokerage methods to build enough of a national coalition to win elections; the Conservatives have been in a more or less perpetual leadership crisis since 1921.

MODERN PARTY POLITICS: THE MAJOR PARTIES, 1921–1986

The Liberals

In 1921 the Liberal Party of Canada elected as its leader a most unlikely man, William Lyon Mackenzie King. Historians have not always treated King kindly, and his biographers — even his official biographer — have made of him a less than heroic figure.[8] Yet in some ways King can be viewed as a hero, even if an unprepossessing one. He took over a party decimated by the events of the previous decade and rebuilt it into an organization that, for more than half a century, dominated Canadian electoral politics at the federal level. That he did so by equivocation, occasional deceit, large doses of compromise, and with the help of a spiritual medium, his departed mother, a dead dog, and the position of the hands on a clock is perhaps as much a measure of policy making in Canada as of the man himself.

Party Structure The party King and his advisors — dead and alive — constructed is a cadre party in many of the senses described by Maurice Duverger in his original analysis of party structures, but it has features of at least two of the other structural variants discussed earlier. First, it was, and remains, a stratarchy. There are nominal lines of authority and communication between the leader and the provincial and constituency levels, but in practice these lines of authority remain weak. In contrast to the early highly centralized Conservative Party under Bennett, the Liberals showed considerable decentralization both in financial structure — which King claimed not even to know about — and in policy matters.[9]

---

[8] There are a number of biographies of King. The best is undoubtedly the series of volumes begun by R. MacGregor Dawson and continued by Blair Neatby, *William Lyon Mackenzie King: A Political Biography* (Toronto: University of Toronto Press, 1958 and 1963). See also J.W. Pickersgill, *The Mackenzie King Record*, vol. 1, 1939–1944, and vol. 2, 1944–1948 (Toronto: University of Toronto Press, 1960 and 1970). Many of King's diaries became available in 1975, and they provide a fascinating picture of the man and his view of Canadian politics in his era. The diaries are in the National Archives in Ottawa.

[9] Reginald Whitaker, *The Government Party*, (Toronto: University of Toronto Press, 1977) is perhaps the definitive study of the Liberal Party during much of its period of dominance. Joseph Wearing, *The L-Shaped Party* (Toronto: McGraw-Hill Ryerson, 1980), provides a valuable source of information. Christina McCall Newman, in *Grits* (Toronto: MacMillan, 1982), provides a highly readable account of that part of the Liberal party in the 1970s represented by its Ottawa establishment. Because it focuses on Ottawa and on a few key personalities, it provides a somewhat less than complete picture of the Liberal Party of Canada.

Second, since 1921, the national Liberal Party has been an open accordion. It acted to swallow up, first, most of the agrarian discontent of the west in the 1920s and 1930s, many groups of new Canadians in the 1950s, and later, a portion of the unrest that characterized Quebec in the 1960s and 1970s. King and his party accommodated much of the western agrarian protest because they were primarily oriented towards electoral success and, unlike the somewhat more dogmatic Conservatives under Arthur Meighen and R.B. Bennett, they were willing to make room in their party leadership and on their platform for this discontent. Similarly, their lower-profile commitment to our British empire ties made the Liberals a more comfortable domicile for immigrants who were neither British nor French, and who came to Canada in the post-war period. Later, under Pearson, the party was also able to accommodate at least some of the Quebec unrest by allowing the Quebec provincial Liberal Party to become an almost completely separate entity, and by recruiting prominent spokesmen for reform in Quebec, such as Pierre Trudeau, Jean Marchand, and Gerard Pelletier.

The structure of the Liberal Party has changed surprisingly little and only very slowly since the days of Mackenzie King. The parliamentary organization and the Cabinet are undoubtedly the centre of power in the federal party, yet party control over the constituency and field organizations is far from complete, and there is no overt control over provincial organizations. West of Ontario, the provincial Liberals are a negligible political force. The Ontario Liberal Party is a separate organizational entity with fairly close organizational ties with the federal party. Ontario Liberals, in power, seem able to get along well enough with federal Tories, just as federal Liberals got along with Ontario Tories when the situation was reversed. While the Quebec Liberal Party is essentially a separate entity, at the level of campaign workers and local strategists, many of the same people work for both the federal and the provincial organizations. In the Maritimes, on the other hand, the ties between federal and provincial parties appear to be closer than in the rest of Canada.

There is some problem here in separating organizational myth from political reality. Except in Quebec, there is no separation, in the Liberal Party constitution, between the federal and the provincial parties; one provincial organization is supposed to subsume both federal and provincial constituency organizations. However, the concentration of real power within the federal and provincial cabinets or legislative caucuses, which are totally separate organizations, insures that there is a considerable split between the effective federal party and the effective provincial parties.

The national organization of the Liberal Party has a full-time president, who acts as the chief executive officer, and a secretary general, who acts as the chief operating officer of the party structure. Under the secretary general are a number of divisions concerned with such functions as communications, policy development, administration, organization, finance, and womens' activities. The largest of these divisions is organization, which includes a speakers' bureau; election planning; and a campaign college, which trains election workers and deals with the statutory requirements of the Elections Act. The full-time staff between elections numbers about thirty, and there is a large part-time staff. This is a large office by past standards of Canadian parties, but during the 1970s, when almost every office in the public service was expanding, the national office did not grow much. This might suggest something either about the importance of its role or about the financial state of the Liberal Party. It also may reflect the fact that much of the organization is actually contained in provincial offices. However, compared with the large and elaborate research establishments of British political parties, the office is small indeed.

Both the older parties have experienced innumerable problems keeping the extra-parliamentary wing of the party — which does much of the work in election campaigns—in touch with the elected politicians. This has been more of a problem for the Liberals than for the Conservatives, perhaps because the Liberals have been in power more often. The Cabinet ministers, who are at the centre of power both in government and in the party, are notoriously busy, and getting them to hold still long enough to communicate, even with their own power base in the party, has been difficult. More to the point, however, they may not wish to stay in active communication. A cadre party, after all, is built upon domination by the parliamentary wing.

In recent years, the extra-parliamentary wing of the Liberal Party has extracted from the elected members several structures intended to build better contact between the MPs and the executive of the party. These structures have a way of being launched with great expectations, but then they wither on the vine. One such structure was the "political cabinet."[10] Conceived by the National Liberal Federation (the formal name for the national party) as a way of politicizing a Cabinet perceived as being "dangerously apolitical," it consisted of the federal cabinet, the regional caucus chairmen, and the president and the national director (today's equivalent of the secretary general). The political cabinet met, with varying degrees of regularity, depending partly on the nearness of an election, at intervals of about one month. Its agenda, set by the party executive rather than by the prime minister, was designed to keep the party executive in touch with Cabinet thinking, and vice versa. The political cabinet was too big to be an effective forum for discussion, and it was later replaced by smaller structures, such as a political planning committee, which used only a few senior political ministers rather than the whole Cabinet. The party also has had provincial advisory groups, of varying degrees of vigour, consisting of the provincial president, one Cabinet minister from the province when the party controlled the government, and one caucus member from the legislative assembly, who nominally reported directly to the party leader. Similar structures come and go frequently as different people take on key roles in the process.

During election campaigns, the Liberal Party's extra-parliamentary structures expand, as the skeleton of full-time workers is fleshed out with hundreds of volunteers. The key national structure during a campaign is the National Campaign Committee, which has traditionally consisted of a national campaign chairman, a national organizer, a national treasurer (all appointed by the party leader), and representatives from each of the ten provincial campaign committees, chosen in

[10] Wearing, *The L-Shaped Party*, pp. 154–155.

consultation with the provincial Liberal associations. Since the 1974 campaign, the Liberals have used two co-chairmen, one for Quebec and one for the rest of Canada.

The National Campaign Committee plans and directs the general strategy of the campaign. It consults with advertising experts and pollsters, and draws up the national advertising campaign. In recent elections, instead of hiring one advertising agency, the Liberals have drawn together advertising experts from several agencies to form a "communications group" attached to the National Campaign Committee. This group not only advises the national committee on its advertising program, but also deals directly with each provincial campaign executive, to help adapt the national advertising campaign to that province's needs. Finally, for the 1980 campaign, the Liberals created the Platform Committee, composed of twenty members elected from the caucus and twenty extra-parliamentary party members, backed by the expertise of the party leader's staff. The committee looked at the 1979 campaign with a view to discovering what went wrong, and came up with a strategy to overcome the mistakes of the 1979 campaign with a better platform in 1980. It apparently worked in 1980, but not in 1984.

The national treasurer heads the Liberal Party of Canada Fund, which is the fund-raising arm of the party. In addition to the funding provided from the public purse under the Election Expenses Act of 1974, the party's sources are large corporations and, increasingly, individual Canadians. The fund-raising structure reflects this fact with continued attention to tracking down corporate donors, but with increased attention to direct-mail appeals to individuals. By 1984, the Liberal Party had not developed its direct-mail techniques to nearly the same degree of proficiency as had the Conservatives and the NDP. In consequence, they entered the 1984 campaign much poorer than their two rivals. Many of the corporate donors hedge their bets by giving money to both the older parties, 60% to the one in power, 40% to the one in opposition, or, if the race appears close, 50% to each. In 1979, for example, the Royal Bank, the Canadian Imperial Bank of Commerce, and Canadian Pacific gave $25,000 to each party.[11] The "bag-men," as the corporate fund raisers have come to be known, are generally well-to-do business people or lawyers who have good connections with corporation heads. The "first string bag-men" — to whom the many other collectors report — are located in the major cities of Canada, where business interests are concentrated. In 1974, the party's chief bag-man was Senator John Godfrey, a Toronto lawyer, while in 1980 another Toronto lawyer, Rob Brydon, took over the Liberals' top financial job.

It was, for years, traditional for Liberal Party leaders to disclaim all knowledge of the sources of their party's campaign funds, and hence to deny any temptation to reward the benevolent for their generosity.[12] To suspicious minds, such ignorance always seemed unlikely, and, pursuant to the 1974 election-expenses legislation, the names of all donors who have given more than $100 must be

---

[11] Toronto *Globe and Mail*, July 4, 1979, p. 1.

[12] K.Z. Paltiel, *Financing Political Parties in Canada* (Toronto: McGraw-Hill Ryerson, 1970), is the best single account of the process of election finance in Canada. We discuss election finance in more detail in the next chapter.

disclosed, so that not only the leader, but anyone else who is interested, will know.

Even while the funds are being raised, the campaign is underway. Indeed, payments for campaign costs are usually made on the instalment plan as donations are received. The National Campaign Committee arranges for national advertising, which includes radio and television productions, plans the leader's tour and big special events, and arranges for the extra staff needed at national headquarters. The provincial committees take charge of the leader's tour in their provinces, and supplement the national advertising if possible. They also provide advice and information to candidates. In most provinces, the "national" party simply takes over the "provincial" party office for the duration of the campaign. Since it is many of the same people who are involved, this is not too difficult to do. The Quebec Campaign Committee of the federal wing of the party has exercised considerable autonomy in both planning and fund-raising, and has run its own campaign, which was coordinated with the national committee. The appointment of Jean Marchand as co-chairman of the National Campaign Committee in 1974 indicated that this pattern had been formalized, and the arrangement was repeated in 1979 and 1980 with the appointment of Marc Lalonde and, in 1984, with André Ouellet. Locally, the party's structures and activities vary greatly from one constituency to another and often reflect the local candidate's own idiosyncracies. In chapter 12, which deals with elections in Canada, we give a general description of campaign activity at this level.

Party Support   No picture of a political party would be complete without some view of its supporters.[13] However, two cautionary comments are in order at the outset. First, only about 30% to 40% of Canadian voters can be described as strong, stable supporters of any party, and almost half of even these people will occasionally cross party lines. (We will consider this "flexible partisanship" in detail in the next chapter.) Second, there is relatively little difference in the socio-economic basis for support of different parties. While we can make statements of tendency, given the ephemeral nature of Canadian party support, virtually all of the correlations we express below are really rather weak.

Within this context, the Liberal base of support is paradoxically both broad and narrow. It is broad in the sense that no other Canadian party can claim to draw support consistently from such a broad social spectrum. It is narrow in some of its regional aspects, such as in its electoral dependency (with the notable exception of the 1958 and 1984 elections), on the French-Canadian and Quebec vote, and its major weakness in the west in 1979, 1980, and 1984.[14] There is

---

[13] We have not footnoted in detail this or subsequent sections on party support. We rely particularly on the following sources: John Meisel, *Working Papers on Canadian Politics* (Montreal: McGill-Queen's Press, 1972), pp. 34–51; Mildred Schwartz, "Canadian Voting Behaviour," prepared for R. Rose, ed., *Electoral Behaviour, A Comparative Handbook* (New York: Free Press, 1973); and H.D. Clarke, et al., *Political Choice in Canada* (Toronto: McGraw-Hill Ryerson, 1979), H.D. Clarke et al, *Absent Mandate* (Toronto: Gage, 1984), and William P. Irvine, "The Canadian Voter," in Howard R. Penniman, *Canada at the Polls, 1979 and 1980* (Washington: American Enterprise Institute, 1983). There is a discussion of the general nature of the Canadian voter in chapter 12.

[14] J. Meisel, *Working Papers*, p. 35. See also Pammett, et al., "Change in the Garden: The 1979 Federal Election," a paper presented to the Canadian Political Science Association conference 1980, pp. 7–17.

also strong support for the Liberals from French minorities outside of Quebec. Franco-Ontarians and Acadians have supported the federal (and provincial) Liberals in overwhelming proportions, and there was little evidence, even in the Conservative electoral sweep of 1984, that this support is evaporating.

Liberal voters have been drawn somewhat disproportionately from the upper socioeconomic stratum, while western farmers and small businesspeople have tended to avoid the party. The general lack of enthusiasm of western voters for the Liberal Party is well known, and is reflected in figures that show that rural, small-town, and farmer support for the Liberals is somewhat lower than the proportion of those groups in the population. In 1979, 1980, and 1984, this trend was even more pronounced than in previous elections.

In spite of strong efforts by all other parties, the Liberals have consistently held greater appeal for minority groups, ranging from the large English and French minorities in Quebec and Ontario to "new Canadians" — immigrants who have arrived since 1945. The party also has been better supported by younger voters than older ones. Liberal voters also have tended to be more satisfied with their economic situation, and more optimistic than Conservative or NDP supporters. Professor John Meisel has summed up this picture:

> The Liberal party can be thought of as being most progressive or "modern," in the sense of appealing most to those elements in society which feel at home in the so-called "advanced" urbanized and highly technological world usually associated with urban North America. This is not to say, of course, that the supporters of the other parties were all, or even predominantly, antique rustics dwelling in some sort of retarded psychological middle age but rather that the Liberals, on the whole, contained a larger proportion of "modern" electors . . . than the others.[15]

The Government Party   As Reginald Whitaker has suggested in his study of the Liberals, the essence of the structure and support of the party and the explanation of its long period of dominance over Canadian federal politics is that people have come to identify the Liberal party as the "government party."[16] In this situation, virtually all real power within the party will inhere in the leader and the Cabinet, and the party depends upon a compounding of the control over government to perpetuate its electoral advantage. Whereas European and British parties in the mid-twentieth century have built up extensive organizations outside the legislative wing of the party, for most purposes, the Liberals have utilized the apparatus of the federal government, and particularly the federal executive itself, as their proxy extra-parliamentary organization.

Under the Liberal version of this system, individual Cabinet ministers are essentially clients of the prime minister. They hold their positions of prestige and authority at his behest, and in return they are expected to provide loyalty and to use their departmental organizations not just to perform the functions of the modern state, but also to provide the rewards necessary to motivate party workers and to insure electoral support. The most powerful of them also operate as power

---

[15] Meisel, *Working Papers*, p. 38.

[16] The remainder of this discussion of the Liberal Party relies primarily on Whitaker, *The Government Party*, particularly pp. 401 ff. The same theme dominates in Joseph Wearing, *The L-Shaped Party*, and in Christina McCall-Newman, *Grits*.

brokers in order to consolidate support in the regions and, in turn, to represent those regional interests at the centre. The locus of power within the party, then, lies very obviously with the prime minister and the Cabinet. Instead of looking to the party structure at large for ideas, the élite of the party either formulates policy itself or relies upon its bureaucracy for innovation. The party outside the executive then tends to become almost entirely an electoral machine; its policy ideas are neither listened to nor appreciated. Joseph Wearing points out that this leads to particularly great tension between ministers and the party structure. Of the Trudeau government of the late 1970s, he noted, "there has not been a single request from a single cabinet minister to test any policy question on the party membership and the public through them."[17]

This arrangement will not automatically provide the troops necessary at election time. Voters still have to be canvassed and mobilized. Literature has to be distributed, and the myriad details of a local campaign have to be taken care of. For this, the party relies on a vast network of interpersonal connections running from Ottawa and provincial capitals down into constituency organizations. It also relies increasingly on the personal appeal of the leader, as projected on television, and on the potential satisfaction of being able to say "I was on the winning team." To some degree, it may also rely on patronage, but there are very few patronage plums relative to the thousands of campaign workers, so this is not a major incentive to the vast majority of party workers.

In general, all of this is a satisfactory situation as long as the party holds office. However, as Whitaker points out, the organizational structure of a cadre party operating in a federal system without firm class support and with heavy reliance on the public service as the source of many of its ideas is particularly vulnerable once it has lost office. In part, the problems result from the fact that the party's provincial bases are not really bases at all, but rather problematic elements in the overall structure of the national party. The provincial wings have different electorates, very different policy concerns (many of which compete head-on with those of the national party), and even different sources of party funding. A federal cadre party, out of office, cannot fall back on the provincial parties as a base of support in its hour of organizational need. Federal parties *do* realize this, and have attempted to deal with it by making Cabinet ministers responsible politically for the provinces they represent, as well as for their own portfolios. However, this system reached its zenith under Mackenzie King and today, when television has placed the focus on the national leader, the power of regional ministers has atrophied to a large extent.

Because of its lack of an organizational base outside the government structure, when the party loses office it is faced with the problem of rebuilding, out of nothing, an extra-parliamentary organization on which it can ride back to power. The Liberals had insufficient time to do this between 1957, when they narrowly lost an election, and 1958, when John Diefenbaker called a second election: the result was, for them, electoral disaster. Only the self-destructive tendencies of the federal Conservative Party in 1979 saved the Liberals from a similar fate in

17 Wearing, *The L-Shaped Party*, p. 152.

the elections of 1979 and 1980, but they were faced with precisely that problem again following the huge Conservative electoral victory in 1984.

Even in office, the maintenance of power for the dominant party in this system is a highly delicate exercise. The ministerialist, regional power-broker system requires that Cabinet ministers stay in close touch with their regions and with the interests of their constituencies. Yet the problems with which they grapple in office are highly complex, and the solutions are worked out and put into operation through giant bureaucracies. Hence, because they solve most major policy problems through the mobilization of bureaucracies, party leaders are in danger of losing touch with their voters. Traditional political patron-client relationships tend to be replaced with bureaucratic clientelism — farmers are represented by the Department of Agriculture, industry by Regional Industrial Expansion, ex-servicemen by the Department of Veterans Affairs, etc. Thus, in the extreme, ministerialism becomes administrative government, politics becomes bureaucracy, polling services replace the advice of individual MPs, and the party at large and the party in power becomes "the government party."

These problems are increased by the difficulty a party structure may have in recruiting and holding talent under this system. Because effective control over policy resides with ministers and public-sector bureaucracies, it is difficult to motivate people interested in policy change to become involved in the extra-parliamentary party, or even in Parliament, unless they are virtually guaranteed a Cabinet chair. Rather, the major reward that can be offered to those most interested in policy is recruitment into the federal public service, bypassing the party structure altogether. Thus people may be recruited to the public service after having served as the acolytes of a minister or a prime minister for a couple of years.

However, once in the public service, their support for the government party is, to a considerable extent, neutralized, the public service being proscribed by law and tradition from partisan activity. This situation becomes an acute problem at election time, when many of the party's previous supporters, now ensconced in non-partisan offices, back off from the party. It becomes all the more acute if there appears any possibility that the party might lose. The strict neutrality of erstwhile government supporters in the bureaucracy in Ottawa as the 1984 campaign wore on and a change of government appeared more and more possible was evidence of this problem. After all, they are at least as interested in policy as in Liberalism and, in many cases, simply interested in retaining their jobs. Thus, paradoxically, by attempting to perpetuate its hold on power through planting its supporters in the tenured ranks of the public service, the party had also placed its supporters above the requisite of continued partisan loyalty.[18] The danger is as great for any party that becomes the government party as it was for the Liberals of the early 1980s. However, as we shall see, the Conservatives face particular difficulties in achieving that long-term dominance of government that will attain for them the status of "the new government party."

---

[18] In *Grits*, Christina McCall Newman, presents an extensive picture of the network of connections that makes up the Liberal Party.

A change of leaders may also pose problems for a "government party," particularly if the former leader held office for a long period and the new leader is
anxious to distance himself from the old. These problems bore particularly heavily
on John Turner when he took over from Pierre Trudeau in 1984. If the Trudeau
regime, which had lasted sixteen years, was characterized by a strong mix of
ministerialist and government-party politics, and if it was viewed as being one
characterized by an excessive bureaucratization, then those things had to be
changed in order for the new leader to put a new face on government in the
hopes of winning his own mandate. But, of course, if that picture of the Liberal
Party was correct, then changing its face would destroy or seriously disrupt the
party organization itself, and greatly diminish the chances of electoral success.

Confronted with that dilemma, John Turner chose to break major elements of
the party-government connection and to appoint his own people to key party and
election posts. Probably the Liberal loss of power in 1984 was inevitable; a
four-year down trend in popular support is not easy to reverse, especially when
the Opposition has a new leader, too. However, Turner did discover, too late, that
his new levers were not connected to anything in the Liberal Party — partly
because the party machinery had atrophied under a leader little interested in
party organization, and partly because what connections there were operated
through the old government-party apparatus the new leader had eschewed. The
result, combined with a rusty campaign style by a new leader ten years out of
politics and a very smooth campaign by the Opposition, was at least the temporary end of liberal hegemony.

The Conservatives

While Mackenzie King set the tone of party structure for the Liberals from
1921 on, it may be a proper description of the Progressive Conservatives up to
the mid-1980s to suggest that no leader has succeeded in putting any very permanent stamp on the party. Since 1917, instability has been its most prominent
characteristic. If the Liberals have tended to become "the government party,"
the Conservatives have tended to suffer their own particular disease, the "Tory
Syndrome," a nearly perpetual opposition, interspersed with brief periods in
power during which the Opposition mentality of most members of the government
leads to an early defeat and a return to the Opposition role.

The Tory Syndrome: History   Arthur Meighen, Borden's successor as leader
of the Conservative Party, seemed unable to develop the common touch, and
this, combined with total lack of support in Quebec (in 1921 he won only 18% of
the vote there, and no seats), insured that he was a failure as a leader in that most
vital of tasks — getting elected.[19]

R.B. Bennett, who succeeded Meighen, did win an election, and from 1930 to
1935 definitely did set the tone of the party. This was made all the easier for

---

[19] Roger Graham, *Arthur Meighen* (Toronto: Clarke, Irwin, 1960). If the literature on the Liberals is thin, that
on the Progressive Conservatives is almost non-existent. The material presented here is pieced together
largely from news reports published during election campaigns, and from popular books referred to in other
footnotes.

Bennett, since he also "owned" the party, in that he was its largest financial backer. He completely dominated the party organization, "a benefit which his party scarcely survived."[20] The Conservative Party's misfortune in getting elected for a period that spanned most of the worst years of the Depression insured that it would fail electorally in 1935. It seems doubtful that any government or party could have successfully resolved the deep cleavages and crises caused by the Depression, but the Conservatives had developed an overcentralized structure that was singularly inappropriate for even attempting the task.

Bennett's departure from the leadership was followed by another of those periods in Conservative Party history that could most charitably be called a prolonged interregnum. One leader after another failed to lead the party out of the electoral wilderness. Between 1940 and 1956, the Conservative Party went through four leaders, and even supported an abortive comeback attempt by Arthur Meighen.[21] Finally, in 1957 and 1958, the perpetual leadership crisis seemed to be resolved when John Diefenbaker led the party to electoral victory. However, Diefenbaker's leadership ended in 1967 after electoral defeats in 1963 and 1965, leaving the party deeply and acrimoniously divided. His successor, Robert Stanfield, saddled with the vindictive former prime minister in his caucus, never did succeed in completely reuniting the party during the eight years he was leader. Moreover, his term of office coincided with the period of Pierre Trudeau's dominance of the federal stage as the absolute monarch of the Liberal Party. Stanfield's successor, Joe Clark, did initially succeed in getting the various warring factions within the party to work sufficiently in harness to enable the party to win a minority victory in the 1979 general election, but Clark's minority government was defeated after less than a year in office. Clark resigned in 1983 following his failure to gain at least two-thirds support for his leadership at the party convention that year.

Clark did run to succeed himself, just as Diefenbaker had, and, while he did not suffer the ignominious defeat incurred by his predecessor, he nonetheless lost on the last ballot to Brian Mulroney.

While Clark was somewhat identified with the left wing of the Tory party, Mulroney appealed initially directly to the centre and right. He came originally from a working-class background and had made an early reputation in labour law, but he was more generally identified, by the time of his victory, with the eastern establishment. Given his objective of holding together a party with most of its strength in the west, and given his conviction that electoral victory could only follow the garnering of support in the former Liberal bastion of Quebec, Mulroney generally avoided any very strong policy positions. Essentially, he presented himself as a popular, attractive, middle-of-the-road candidate who could give the Progressive Conservative Party what it wanted most — a solid victory at the polls. Particularly important to his appeal was the fact that he came from Quebec, was perfectly bilingual, and was, apparently, more marketable to the public than was his predecessor.

---

[20] Paltiel, *Financing Political Parties in Canada*, p. 17.

[21] See J.L. Granatstein, *The Politics of Survival 1939–1945* (Toronto: University of Toronto Press, 1967).

Electoral victory is what parties want most, and in that respect Mulroney delivered. In September 1984 his campaign led the party to the largest electoral sweep in Canadian history, taking 211 of the 282 seats in the House of Commons. At least as important as the absolute size was the breadth of the mandate obtained. The Conservatives won a plurality of votes in every province and an absolute majority in six. The most surprising and potentially significant aspect of this support was the Conservative sweep in Quebec. In that province, the Tories gained 58 of 75 seats (up from one seat in the previous parliament) and 50.2% of the popular vote (up from 12.6% in 1980).

Party Structure The basic structure of the Conservative Party in the past half-century has been, like that of the Liberals, essentially that of a stratarchical-cadre party. But the Conservative Party has shown few aspects of the open accordion. Only in the 1979, 1980, and 1984 elections was any very concerted effort made by most Conservatives to woo the Quebec voter or to understand French Canada, and it is, even now, by no means certain that the party is unanimously committed to this effort.

The Conservatives have occasionally tried to expand their organization by recruiting other groups. In the 1940s they attempted to co-opt Progressive support from the west by choosing as their leader the former Progressive premier of Manitoba, John Bracken, and by adding the name "Progressive" to their party masthead. Unfortunately for the Conservatives, Mackenzie King had already co-opted most western Progressive support some twenty years previously. Similarly, under Diefenbaker, the Conservatives tried to become the party of the "other" ethnic groups of Canada by emphasizing an "un-hyphenated" Canadianism. But, in attempting this, they alienated as many new Canadians as they attracted by calling attention to the differences in their cultural backgrounds. At any rate, the Tories were not successful in attracting much permanent allegiance from such groups: only about 15% of recent immigrants voted Conservative in 1968, as opposed to the 72% who supported the Liberals.[22] Even among longer established immigrant groups, the Conservatives have tended to do less well electorally than the Liberals, and for eastern Europeans, the figures are 58% Liberal and 27% Conservative.[23]

The formal structure of the Conservative Party is rather similar to that of the Liberals, and there are also many similarities in the two parties' informal structures.[24] Like the Liberals, the Conservatives have a permanent staff at a national party headquarters, and several regional offices with permanent staff. Like the Liberal structure, a vital component of Conservative party structure is the voluntary part that appears, magically, just before each election.

The permanent party organization consists of a national president, a national

---

[22] M. Schwartz, "Political Behaviour and Ethnic Origin," in John Meisel, ed., *Papers on the 1962 Election*, (Toronto: University of Toronto Press, 1964), pp. 253–272; John Meisel, *Working Papers on Canadian Politics*, pp. 37–38.

[23] Clarke, *Political Choice in Canada*, p. 104.

[24] See the organizational chart in C. Winn and J. McMenemy, *Political Parties in Canada*, (Toronto: McGraw-Hill Ryerson, 1976), pp. 170–1.

director and an associate, and seven full-time directors of party functions, such as tours and advance, information services, communications, and women's and youth bureaus. The Progressive Conservative national headquarters was, traditionally, slightly smaller than the Liberal Party headquarters, typically totalling about twenty people, but it has grown now to triple that size as the financial underpinnings of the Conservatives have become stronger than those of the Liberals. When the Conservative Party is in power, the Prime Minister's Office and the political, or "exempt," staff of ministers carry out many party functions, just as they did for the Liberals. During the Conservatives' years in opposition, the staff of the office of the leader of the official Opposition also played a crucial role in the party structure. The executive and special assistants and advisors in the Opposition leader's office, while formally House of Commons staff, were actually engaged in the overall direction and development of strategy for the party. For example, the national campaign director for 1979 and 1980, Lowell Murray, was employed in this office. In this sense, the Opposition leader's staff are performing functions analogous to those performed in the PMO for the party in power. In fact, after the Conservative election victories of 1979 and 1984, virtually all of the key staffers moved with the new prime minister into the PMO. Similarly, as the Liberals moved over to become the official Opposition, several of their key political staffers (those who were not already in the public service, the judiciary, or the Senate) moved into positions in the Opposition leader's office.

In 1969, Parliament voted funds for the establishment of small parliamentary research offices for the caucuses of the Opposition parties, and in 1970 similar funds were provided for the government caucus. The amount provided for each party is proportional to its strength in the House of Commons. The money is formally used to provide research services for MPs; most of the duties of the eight or nine researchers and the director and his or her assistant in the major parties' offices do involve the provision of research material for MPs. However, the research offices also provide broader policy research for the party as a whole, help out during annual meetings and conventions, and provide some auxiliary headquarters' support during campaigns.

At election time, the national president and national director of the party, both of whom hold part-time positions, are augmented by a national campaign chairman and a group of fund raisers, who begin the job of collecting money. The regional and provincial organizers (some of whom may be permanent employees of the party) suddenly spring to life, and constituency organizations, generally consisting of a campaign chairman and many helpers, together with poll captains, who work at the individual poll levels, appear where nothing was before. Candidates are nominated and the contest begins.

It takes little imagination to recognize that the Conservative Party is no less centralized and controlled by its parliamentary wing than is the Liberal Party; both are clear examples of a cadre party structure. In power, the lines of control available to a Conservative prime minister are identical to those of a Liberal prime minister. In opposition, the Conservative leader controls all the key appointments, including all members of the staff of the leader of the opposition, the membership of the treasury (money-spending) and finance (money-raising) committees, the shadow Cabinet, and the membership of various caucus committees. The sole exception, and this is as true for the Liberals as the Conservatives, is the national president. He or she is elected by the convention, and the convention does not always select the candidate favoured by the leader. Of course in a cadre party, any resulting tension redounds as much or more to the disadvantage of the extra-parliamentary party as to the parliamentary wing.

Party Support   With regard to popular support, up until 1984, the usual assertion was: "it is generally safe to assume that for practically every statement made about the Liberal party the reverse holds for the Conservative voters."[25] While that assertion seems quite categorical, the reader is cautioned to read the following figures bearing in mind that, over time, individual Canadian voters are very unstable in their partisanship. The generalizations about party support should not blind us to the fact that most Canadians vote for more than one party over their lifetimes.

In 1974, 53% of Liberal support came from Catholics, versus 20% of Conservative support. While only 6% of Liberal voters in 1968 were farmers, 15% of Conservatives were. Of those with thirteen or more years of education, 53% voted Liberal in 1974, whereas 30% voted Conservative. Of those of French origin, 72% voted Liberal whereas only 12% of them voted Conservative. Among those of British origin, the result was much more closely balanced, with 42% supporting the Liberals and 41% the Conservatives in 1974.

Conservative voters also were more likely than Liberals to be middle-aged or older and to come from small towns or rural areas. Only in the Atlantic provinces were these tendencies reversed; there, the PCs drew more heavily than the Liberals from upper-class urban voters. This pattern is perhaps attributable to the residual personal appeal of the former leader, Robert Stanfield, in his home base, the Atlantic region. Finally, of course, western support for the Conservatives derived in the 1970s and 1980s partly from the residual rural and western appeal of John Diefenbaker, but in large part from the particular antipathy Liberal Prime Minister Pierre Trudeau seemed to engender everywhere west of the Ontario border. Regional patterns of personal appeal or antipathy can be quite stable in Canadian politics, often persisting for decades, and the suggestion has sometimes been made that this pattern is the Canadian counterpart of the more strongly persistent party identification of United States voters.

With the exception of the ethnic composition of the vote, this situation began to change slowly in the later 1970s; by 1979, while the older patterns could still be detected, they were considerably attenuated.[26] The Conservative electoral victory of 1984 was so broadly based that it seems likely the patterns of support for the Tories in the mid-1980s are much like patterns of Liberal support in the mid-1970s.

Perhaps the most important overall point that emerges from an examination of Conservative Party support up to the time of the 1984 election is its relative lack

[25] Meisel, *Working Papers on Canadian Politics*, pp. 39–40.

[26] There is a large tabulation of party support by various socio-economic variables in William Irvine, "The Canadian Voter," in Howard R. Penniman, *Canada at the Polls: The General Elections of 1979 and 1980*, pp. 65–74.

of homogeneity. Liberal support was, with the partial exception of the west, more evenly distributed across the country and, as John Meisel has noted in all of his election studies since the late 1950s, shows less regional variation in the way supporters look at the party and the leader. This may produce problems and strains in the Conservative Party when it attempts to develop policies that will appeal to its supporters and also to broaden the base of party support. If the supporters themselves are a highly mixed bag, with highly divergent views of the world, reconciliation becomes difficult. Indeed, this divergent support is reflected among party activists as well. As Meisel notes,

> The task of reconciling the demands of the most active members from the Atlantic and Prairie regions and from Ontario (or, to put it slightly differently, those of the vestigial Drew men, the Stanfield admirers and the Diefenbakerites), imposes extremely awkward tensions on the leadership which, as a consequence, makes it difficult for the national party to appear forceful and consistent both inside and outside the House of Commons.[27]

This situation, combined with the massive electoral victory by the Progressive Conservatives in 1984, confronted the party with a real organizational dilemma equal in magnitude, if opposite in direction, to that faced by the outgoing Liberals. For the Liberals the problem was to develop a real extra-parliamentary structure outside the government, which they could use to return to power. For the Conservatives the problem was to learn to use the levers of government to perpetuate their hold on government.

The Tory Syndrome   In order to effectively use the levers of power, the party will have to overcome what George Perlin has referred to as the "Tory syndrome": a series of attributes that have, in the past, made it extremely difficult for the party to seize and to retain power.[28] Their difficulty in seizing power, hypothesizes Perlin, is caused by the fact that being out of government allows MPs and activists to express all kinds of divergent views, thereby making conflict resolution difficult. This, in turn, produces an appearance of factionalism, a perception that the party is not fit to govern, and ends inevitably in electoral defeat. Even out of power, suggests this hypothesis, Liberals have managed to keep their disagreements largely hidden; even in power, the Conservatives, due to their "opposition-party mentality," have not. Moreover, since the party is viewed as an opposition party, it attracts those more interested in opposing than in governing.

The Tory syndrome made Joe Clark's brief tenure as prime minister and party leader difficult. It was papered over by Brian Mulroney on his way to his huge electoral victory in 1984, but it is a still-present threat within the Conservative Party of the 1980s. Indeed, the huge electoral victory of 1984 may even exacerbate the party's difficulties in this regard. The Conservative Quebec caucus in Parliament is united primarily by its opposition to Liberals. Ideologically, the caucus ranges from left-wing erstwhile Parti Québécois supporters to right-wing centralist business interests to populist former supporters of the Créditistes. The national

---

[27] Meisel, *Working Papers*, p. 46.

[28] George Perlin, "The Progressive Conservative Party," in H.G. Thorburn, *Party Politics in Canada*, pp. 165ff; and *The Tory Syndrome* (Montreal: McGill-Queen's Press, 1980).

caucus combines these disparate Quebec interests with moderate Ontario and Atlantic Conservatives, a smattering of large business supporters, an array of small businessmen and supporting professionals, and a western caucus, some members of which mistrust the eastern establishment and all things Francophone. To weld this aggregation into a group capable of winning power required that the leader eschew much ideology and policy. The lack of a policy focus has left the Conservative government somewhat at the mercy of events during the first years in office, and the resultant decline in popularity, although normal for a party once it takes office, may leave the prime minister vulnerable to another attack of the Tory syndrome, made all the worse because there are so many MPs around to push that attack.

Obviously, the transition from a party in opposition to a government party, along the lines of the federal Liberals during their lengthy periods in office, requires massive organizational changes both within the party and in government itself. Perlin predicted in 1980 that the Conservative Party would not succeed. He argued that the Progressive Conservatives would win the occasional election:

> when there is serious social, economic or political strain or when the Liberal party falls victim to what John Meisel has argued is its disposition [as a result of its habitation to office] to become too arrogant in its exercise of power. However, both the historical evidence and the theory proposed to explain it suggests that even when the party wins it is likely to be subject to instability. In the long run, therefore, unless there is some dramatic change in the context of federal politics, the Conservative party may be expected to suffer from internal divisiveness and unstable leadership and to hold office only for brief intervals between extended periods of Liberal rule.[29]

George Perlin wrote and published these words well before the Progressive Conservatives' brief period in office in 1979 and its larger electoral victory in 1984. Given the party's behaviour in 1979, Perlin's analysis may well mark him as one of the great pundits of Canadian political analysis. It certainly will if the Conservative majority self-destructs in the federal election due in 1988 or 1989.

MODERN PARTY POLITICS: THE THIRD PARTIES, 1921–1986

The Progressive Movement

In November of 1919 there was a provincial election in Ontario and, when the smoke had cleared, the largest single group in the legislature and the backbone of the new coalition government was the United Farmers' Party of Ontario, the Ontario version of a movement whose political arm came to be known nationally as the Progressive Party.[30] The movement grew in strength in the ensuing years,

---

[29] Perlin, *The Tory Syndrome*, p. 167.

[30] The other party in the coalition was the small Independent Labour Party.

and in the 1921 federal election, any notion that Canada still had a two-party system was shattered when sixty-five Progressive MPs were elected. They were the second-largest group in the House of Commons, with fifteen more seats than the Conservative Party.[31] Where did they come from, and what was the structure of this newly emergent force in Canadian politics?

Compared to other Canadian parties, the Progressives relied upon relatively homogeneous electoral support. Aside from a few small-business interests from Manitoba, the group's support was almost entirely rural. They gained 28% of the vote in the federal election in Ontario in 1921 and won twenty-four seats, with virtually all their support coming from farming areas. In Manitoba they captured 44% of the vote and twelve seats, in Saskatchewan 61% and fifteen seats, and in Alberta 56% and eleven seats. In general, the more agricultural the economy of a province, the more likely it was to return Progressives. Even New Brunswick, which virtually never breaks with older party lines, returned a Progressive MP from a rural constituency in 1921, and Nova Scotia gave the Progressives 15% of the vote, although the group won no seats there.

What can explain this sudden outpouring of support for a new rural political movement? The first part of the answer to this question is that the rise of agrarian political consciousness was not quite as sudden as it appears. Party lines were always weak in the west. In Ontario there had been previous sporadic bursts of support for agrarian movements, with, for instance, the Patrons of Industry, an agrarian protest party, winning seventeen seats in the Ontario provincial election of 1894.

However, only in the period immediately following World War One did a number of factors coalesce to increase the support of the farmers' movement. The government in Ottawa was largely dominated by eastern urban and big-business interests, and these interests did use the traditional political parties as their means of control. Rural Ontario was being rapidly depopulated as farm families moved to the city and as the insecurity of farm life, combined with the feeling that the farmer was a dying species, led to cooperative action. Tariff structures had been hurting the farmers for years by keeping produce prices down and farm-equipment prices up. The problem was brought to a head by an over-supply of agricultural produce after World War One and by a recession following the war. The conscription of farmers' sons in 1917 after the government had specifically promised to exempt them, and the Union Government's ignoring of farmers' protest marches, helped to convince farmers that the older parties were not responsive to their needs.

To a significant degree, the farmers were right. Both their view of economic structures and their view of the parliamentary political system that supported these structures had considerable basis in fact. However, the attribution of pure malevolence or greed as the cause was more dubious: it may have been that

[31] The words "movement" and "party" are both used in political science literature to describe the Progressives. There are a number of excellent studies of the group. Two are: W.L. Morton, *The Progressive Party in Canada* (Minneapolis: University of Toronto Press, 1948); and C.B. Macpherson, *Democracy in Alberta* (Toronto: University of Toronto Press, 1954), pp. 62–92. Macpherson's book deals with the Alberta wing of the party.

national economic development at the turn of the century really was best accomplished by a mercantile system, and it may have been that calls for a shift westward in influence in Canada were premature.

Be that as it may, it has been seen that there are reasons the older parties were not then, and are not now, structurally adequate to accommodate genuine protest movements when they arise. Instead, they responded in 1921 much as they do now: only after the agrarian interests became politically mobilized and formed new social and political structures did the older parties adjust and attempt to assimilate them.

The farmers concentrated much of their criticism on the caucus-dominated structure of older parties because, as they pointed out, the agrarian-dominated western regional caucuses were inevitably out-voted by the parties' eastern interests. They therefore surmised that the only way to make themselves heard in Parliament was to get outside of caucus altogether and form a new movement; where conflict resolution within the older parties failed, they attempted to achieve their ends through the process of interparty competition.

The problem with their theories was that they had to be applied within a parliamentary system and, since the farmers had rejected the idea of a legislative caucus, there were no structural mechanisms for achieving integration among the Progressive MPs. Within four years, the movement had lost much of its impetus as the lack of internal cohesion produced a series of warring factions. The militant Alberta faction and the highly ideological "Ginger Group" could not work with the more moderate Ontario and Manitoba wings. Without cohesion they were not a credible alternative government, and the best they could hope for were the results they had already attained in 1921. Consequently, it became relatively easy for Mackenzie King to absorb some of the leaders of the movement into the Liberal Party.

Structurally, the Progressive Party was an alliance of sub-coalitions. Each of the sub-coalitions was a regionally based collection of farm organizations. The only acknowledged national leader in the movement was T.A. Crerar, a dissident Liberal, but he broke with the movement in 1922 and subsequently returned to the Liberal fold. What overall national cohesion existed was provided by adherence to a few common principles expressed in "The Farmers Platform." The most important of these was simply opposition to the old party system and to eastern business interests. There was considerable emphasis among Progressives on grass-roots democracy, but the means of achieving it varied from one regional sub-coalition to another. Thus, the Manitoba farmers' government and the United Farmers of Alberta experimented with legislation to provide for the recall of MPs to face their constituents in a by-election if a specified proportion of the voters in a riding requested it, and other wings of the Progressive Party toyed with various forms of the referendum. For the most part however these ideas were little acted upon.

In the Progressive Party, conventions were considerably more important in policy making than they had been in the older parties, although by 1923 yet another split was developing within the movement, between elected representatives, who were beginning to resent excessive interferences in their affairs by conventions, and the mass membership of the movement, which wanted to maintain its influential position. Most of the structural decentralization of the movement and its emphasis on constituency control derived from its anti-party ideology, for within the party, this ideology was extended into a form of syndicalism or corporatism, with a call for representation by occupational group rather than geographic constituency. This was combined with a call for cabinets that would not be overthrown if they lost a vote in Parliament. The concept of occupational-group representation was, however, quite antithetical to the Canadian parliamentary tradition of representation based on territorial constituencies. The notion that a government need not resign unless defeated on an explicit vote of confidence went against the then emerging trend towards consolidation and centralization of control within parliamentary parties (although, as will be seen when we come to discuss current ideas in parliamentary reform, that idea re-emerges frequently). But in the context of the times, the Progressives' ideology was unworkable without almost revolutionary action, and the farmers were much too conservative — and too weak politically — to espouse real revolution.

The Progressive movement perished of its own structural deficiencies. By the mid-1920s, the Progressive Party had lost most of its importance in Canadian national politics, although it continued to be important in provincial governments in the west; The United Farmers remained in power in Alberta until the Social Credit sweep in 1935, and in Manitoba, they held power in one form or another for some thirty years.

Social Credit

Strictly speaking, Social Credit is a financial theory developed by Major C.H. Douglas, a retired British army engineer, although it contains elements of a broader view of society as well. The root of the theory is the "A plus B theorem," where A is the flow of purchasing power to the people (i.e., wages, salaries, and dividends) and B is bank charges, overhead costs, taxes, and the cost of raw materials.

The discrepancy between purchasing power (A) and the costs of production (A plus B) was thought to be a permanent feature of modern capitalism that would always result in the people getting less than their share of the economic pie. The resulting deficiency in demand was assumed to be at the root of the Depression of the 1930s. The solution offered by Social Credit theory was to give people more purchasing power in the form of a bonus, or a direct transfer of "social credit" to the public.

> A functional financial system should be concerned with the issue of credit to the consumer up to the productive capacity of the producers so that the consumers' real demands may be satisfied and the productive capacity of the industrial system may be capitalized and developed to the fullest extent.[32]

As with the Progressive movement, Social Credit also featured a critique of parliamentary democracy, pointing out that control over members of parliament had escaped the little person and now rested with large financial interests. There

---

[32] J.A. Irving, *The Social Credit Movement in Alberta* (Toronto: University of Toronto Press, 1959), p. 6.

was also some anti-Semitism associated with the movement, since the large financial and banking interests were sometimes depicted as part of a purported Jewish conspiracy to control the world.

At first glance, Social Credit is a highly complex phenomenon. It held power in two provinces and has had a significant presence in the House of Commons. Yet the federal and provincial segments of the party were frequently scarcely on speaking terms, and the ties among the various branches of the party have never been strong. The Quebec-based wing of the party, the Ralliement des créditistes, was basically provincial in orientation, but its real presence was felt only in federal politics. In fact, Social Credit was not a single party at all, but rather a set of at least three separate parties operating largely independently of each other in quite different venues. While there are common threads, it is probably best to treat the three major segments, in Alberta, Quebec, and British Columbia, separately.

Alberta By the end of the third decade of this century, the Progressive movement no longer acted as an effective vehicle for protest in the west. Yet the Depression and the prolonged drought on the prairies in the early 1930s served, if anything, to emphasize still further the differences between eastern and western Canada. As a result, by 1935, a new protest movement had established itself in Alberta provincial politics. On August 22, 1935, Alberta voters eliminated all members of the government formed by the United Farmers of Alberta (the Alberta wing of the Progressives) and filled fifty-six of the sixty-three seats in their legislature with followers of Social Credit.[33]

While the peculiar ideology of Social Credit was certainly useful, the sudden ascendancy of Social Credit in Alberta was due primarily to the coincidence of the Depression of the 1930s with the organizational and histrionic abilities of William Aberhart. Aberhart began his working life as a school teacher and preacher. After moving to Alberta as a young man, he founded the Prophetic Bible Institute. Given his skill and the limited range of alternative Sunday-afternoon activities in Alberta in the early 1930s, Aberhart's religious radio broadcasts soon enjoyed tremendous popularity. John Irving describes him as combining,

> the functions of the prophet with the executive capacities of the great planner and organizer . . . . Aberhart's imposing physical presence, his performances as organizer and orator, his resolute and inflexible will, his infinite resourcefulness, his ability to hypnotize people by his voice, his contagious belief in himself—all these characteristics combined to produce in many people the attitude that here is the Leader.[34]

Aberhart began to use radio to present the ideas of Social Credit in 1932, and his broadcasts, together with an excellent grass-roots political organization, swept him into power in 1935. After a few attempts to apply Social Credit principles

---

[33] There are three major accounts of the Social Credit Movement in Alberta. These are C.B. Macpherson, *Democracy in Alberta*; J.A. Irving, *The Social Credit Movement in Alberta* (Toronto: University of Toronto Press, 1959); and J.R. Mallory, *Social Credit and the Federal Power in Canada* (Toronto: University of Toronto Press, 1954). On the politics of Alberta in general, see J.A. Long and F.W. Quo, "Alberta: The Politics of Consensus," in M. Robin, ed., *Canadian Provincial Politics* (Toronto: Prentice-Hall, 1978).

[34] Irving, *The Social Credit Movement in Alberta* p. 337.

through legislation, the Alberta Social Credit movement, thwarted by the realities of the constitution and the economic system, became a political party of more or less standard form. The prosperity of the province following the oil boom ensured the re-election of Social Credit governments in the province for thirty-six years, until 1971, when resurgent Alberta Conservatives captured the province.

In Alberta, Social Credit was "essentially a people's movement which sought to reform, but not to revolutionize the existing social order by changing the patterns of certain institutions."[35] As we have seen, it was born of the historical confluence of the social disruption of the Depression, the alienation of westerners from eastern institutions, the conservative entrepreneurial ethic of Alberta, and the particular genius of William Aberhart. It survived through the ability of his successor, E.C. Manning, to run a successful administration, and through the fortuitous prosperity ushered in by the discovery of oil in 1947. It perished, essentially, of old age and the voters' desire for change soon after Manning's retirement, and it has since largely faded from the scene in Alberta.

Quebec   Most similar to the Alberta party has been the Ralliement des créditistes, the Quebec-based wing of the party.[36] It was characterized by the same pragmatism and leadership orientation, which allowed it to exploit regional-cultural characteristics, and it has shown a similar vulnerability to decline once the strong leader disappears.[37] The Créditistes started life as a protest movement, and they were successful in Quebec largely because rural Quebeckers did not find the federal Conservative Party a credible alternative to the Liberals, and because the Liberals had, in the view of many voters, ceased to look after their interests. It has been suggested that, in situations where one party is dominant for long periods of time, like the Liberals in Quebec, the regular opposition party will lose its credibility and be replaced by a third party.[38]

The void left by the failure of the Conservatives in Quebec was filled by Réal Caouette, a Créditiste, who exploited the new medium of television in the 1960s as effectively as Aberhart had exploited radio in the thirties. In the 1962 federal election, the Créditistes won twenty-six seats in rural Quebec and captured 26% of the Quebec vote. Until 1974 they held more than 18% of the federal vote in Quebec and won never fewer than nine seats. For a time after the 1962 election, they were, outside of Montreal, the dominant federal electoral force in the province.[39]

[35] Irving, p. 334.

[36] The Ralliement des créditistes has also been extensively studied. See, particularly, Maurice Pinard, *The Rise of A Third Party* (Englewood Cliffs: Prentice-Hall, 1971), and Micheal Stein, *The Dynamics of Right Wing Protest: A Political Analysis of Social Credit in Quebec* (Toronto: University of Toronto Press, 1973); Graham White, "One Party Dominance and Third Parties," André Blais, "Third Parties in Canadian Provincial Politics," and Maurice Pinard, "Third Parties in Canada Re-Visited," all in *Canadian Journal of Political Science*, September 1973, vol. 6, pp. 439–60. Although the major success of the Ralliement has been in federal elections, it is realistic to treat it as a Quebec party, in accord with their electoral base.

[37] C. Winn and J. McMenemy, *Political Parties in Canada*, pp. 37–38.

[38] Pinard, *The Rise of A Third Party*. This is one basic theme of Pinard's book. The same situation may well have accounted, in part, for the rise of Social Credit in Alberta as well, although other explanations are more obvious there.

[39] M. Stein, "Quebec's Créditistes," in H.G. Thorburn, *Party Politics in Canada*, p. 255.

356 SYSTEM-ENVIRONMENT LINKAGES

Early in 1970 the Créditiste party also entered provincial politics. They entered hurriedly and were forced into action before they were ready, when the Union Nationale government called a snap election. Nonetheless, they did achieve considerable success. The region of Quebec that voted Créditiste in federal elections showed itself willing to support the party provincially, and the result was thirteen seats in the National Assembly. These seats were taken largely from the Union nationale and were important in the overthrow of that government. However, the Créditistes were unable to build their provincial strength into a permanent power base. In the 1973 provincial election the party's support declined and they were able to capture only two seats. They were crushed in the Parti Québécois victory of 1976.

The fortunes of the Ralliement des créditistes declined precipitously after 1974, and particularly after the death of Réal Caouette in 1976. Between then and the 1979 election, the party went through four leaders, including one from Manitoba, chosen in an ill-starred attempt to give the party a national identification outside Quebec. The leader for the 1979 federal election — chosen just six weeks before election day — was Fabien Roy. Roy was a populist deputy in the Quebec National Assembly with separatist leanings. He was supported in his federal campaign by the Parti Québécois leadership, but his impact was in no way comparable to Caouette's, and the separatist identification probably cost the party votes among its traditionally conservative electorate. In that election the party gained only five seats; it was completely eliminated in the 1980 election. With Caouette's death, it seems the Ralliement des créditistes had lost not only its founder and its leader, but its organizational base as well.

British Columbia   In British Columbia, the Social Credit Party (called "the Socreds") won a minority victory in the provincial election of 1952. Here again, the roots of the movement had some things in common with its origins in Quebec and Alberta.[40] Economic conditions in British Columbia were not nearly as bad as they were in Alberta in 1935 or in rural Quebec in 1962, but the British Columbia government in 1952 was a tired and disintegrating coalition of Conservatives and Liberals. Neither of the older parties had much in the way of provincial organization, and the CCF was too militant and too small to gain broad popular support. The only credible alternative that emerged was the Social Credit Party.

The 1952 Socred campaign was run with considerable help from Alberta, but without a leader; W.A.C. Bennett, a dissident former Conservative, did not become leader until after the election. Social Credit was helped in the election by the two older parties, who had enacted an "alternative-vote" electoral scheme, intended to shut out the socialist hordes of the CCF — a scheme that aided significantly in their own demise but left the CCF essentially as before.[41] Bennett, surmising that

[40] Martin Robin, "British Columbia, The Company Province," in M. Robin, ed., *Canadian Provincial Politics* (Toronto: Prentice-Hall, 1978); and E.R. Black, "British Columbia, The Politics of Exploitation," in Thorburn, *Party Politics in Canada.*

[41] Black, "British Columbia," p. 292.

a proportional-representation system rarely works to the advantage of parties in power, promptly eliminated it after the election.

In British Columbia, Social Credit fell rather than charged into power, but a prosperous economy and an ebullient, if not overly polished, party image kept it there for some twenty years, until its defeat by Dave Barrett's NDP in 1972. During that time, the various antics and policy peregrinations of W.A.C. Bennett, who defined social credit as simply "the opposite of socialism," served to create an image of British Columbia Politics as low-comedy. It would be hard, however, to dispute either his electoral success or his long-term impact on the British Columbia party system.

Unlike its namesakes in Quebec and Alberta, Social Credit in British Columbia was able to rejuvenate after its electoral defeat. Initially the accession to leadership by W.A.C. Bennett's son, Bill, was taken as further proof of the low-comedy aspect of British Columbia politics. However, the Social Credit under Bennett the younger did defeat the NDP in 1975, and retained power in 1979 and again in 1983. Under Bill Bennett, British Columbia's Social Credit Party effectively retained a base of middle-class and small-entrepreneur support. It also remained moderately right-wing in orientation. Following the 1983 election, the party moved somewhat further to the right, imposing a fairly Draconian (by Canadian standards) set of expenditure restraints. Any remnant of Social Credit theory has, however, long since disappeared from its repertoire and Bennett's successor, William VanderZalm returned the party to power in 1986 on a campaign based on middle-of-the-road policy proposals.

In two of three provinces, then, Social Credit caught on because a charismatic leader, skilled in using a new medium, arrived at a time when there were no other effective vehicles of protest. In all three provinces, effective political alternatives were lacking because the politics of the area were dominated by one party. The ideology of Social Credit was also helpful because it was easy to understand and because it blamed troubles on those convenient bugbears, absentee financial interests. Finally, like many Canadian protest or minor parties, Social Credit has generally done well in provincial politics and poorly in federal politics; the Créditiste wing is the exception to the rule.

There is a good explanation for the relative success of Social Credit provincially, one we will see again with the CCF-NDP. The impossibility of gaining national power with a regionally based protest group has made all protest movements conscious that their only real chance to gain power is in provincial elections. This has led to a concentration of the best party leaders and workers at the provincial level; the Alberta Social Credit party has taken only sporadic interest in federal politics, the British Columbia wing of the party little more. The federal orientation of the Créditistes can best be explained through Pinard's theory of one-party dominance and the consequent rise of a third party. That the third party used the Social Credit rhetoric was probably in large measure a coincidence; any other moderately conservative and relatively simple rhetoric would have served equally well. In fact, then, Social Credit is not a single phenomenon at all, but rather three very loosely related regional parties, and, with the exception of British Columbia, of increasingly historical, rather than current, significance.

The CCF-NDP: Socialism in Canada

We aim to replace the present capitalistic system, with its inherent injustice and inhumanity, by a social order from which the domination and exploitation of one class by another will be eliminated, in which economic planning will supersede unregulated private enterprise and competition and in which genuine democratic self-government based upon equality will be possible.

These words are from the Regina Manifesto, the declaration of principles passed at the first annual convention of the Cooperative Commonwealth Federation (CCF) in Regina in 1933. Since 1921, J.S. Woodsworth had led a tiny group of Socialist MPs in the federal parliament; by 1932, the Depression, Woodsworth's leadership, and the intense interest of many Canadian farm and labour leaders and academics led to the formation of a formal party structure oriented towards the principles outlined in the Regina Manifesto.

Ideological Evolution The CCF held to its doctrinaire socialist-party platform for the first twenty years of its life, but by 1956 it had begun to change its ideological face.[42] While it continued to call for an egalitarian and classless society, the party began to shift towards the ideological centre in Canadian politics, in response to the fact that its national electoral support appeared to have peaked in 1944–1945 without moving the party into national power or moving the electorate significantly to the left. No longer did the CCF consider it necessary to nationalize all industry, and no longer did it call for the eradication of capitalism. Its new ideology was expressed in the Winnipeg declaration of 1956 and called for

the application of social planning. Investment of available funds must be channeled into socially desirable projects; financial and credit resources must be used to help maintain full employment and to control inflation and deflation.

It was a set of principles either the Liberals or Progressive Conservatives could have happily endorsed. Support for the party, however, continued to run at only 14% to 16% of the popular vote.

Meanwhile, organized labour in Canada — particularly the Canadian Labour Congress — began to take an interest in openly supporting a political party, and the logical choice was the CCF. A change of name, however, seemed desirable, in order to expunge the western rural image that went with the old title. The result was a dissolution of the old Cooperative Commonwealth Federation and the formation of the New Democratic Party in 1961.[43] For the most part, NDP activists included the same people as had the CCF, by now sufficiently chastened to be willing to modify their principles somewhat in order to gain power. The years of watching policy making and trying to woo recalcitrant voters, it seems, had left

---

[42] Leo Zakuta, *A Protest Movement Becalmed: A Study of Change in the CCF* (Toronto: University of Toronto Press, 1964), pp. 169–173.

[43] The best study of the CCF is by W.D. Young, *The Anatomy of a Party: The National CCF 1932–61* (Toronto: University of Toronto Press, 1969). For the post-1961 period, see: Desmond Morton, *NDP: The Dream of Power* (Toronto: Hakkert, 1974), and N.H. Chi and George Perlin, "The NDP: A Party in Transition," in Thorburn, *Party Politics in Canada*, pp. 177–187. See also *Crisis, Challenge and Change.*

THE PARTIES: A HISTORICAL PERSPECTIVE   359

some scars. These changes, plus the influx of labour influences into the party
machinery, added a dash of pragmatism to the NDP, and the party leadership is
now moderately social-democratic, rather than doctrinaire in its ideological
stance.[44] And, as with most social-democratic parties, it has drifted closer to the
centre even as the structure of capitalist society as a whole has drifted to the left.
What has been said about ideological drift in the CCF-NDP, however, should
not be interpreted to mean that the party is identical to the older parties. For
example, the CCF-NDP has been more pacifist and is less likely to support the
Canadian military establishment or defence expenditures than are the Liberals
or Conservatives. The party itself has never been as extremely pacifist as its first
leader, J.S. Woodsworth, who voted against Canada's entry into World War Two,
but it has stood consistently some distance from the older parties in this regard,
particularly in the past, when the military aspect of foreign policy received much
more attention that it does today. As well, the CCF-NDP remains more committed
to economic equality than the older parties. The Liberals and Progressive
Conservatives will both express their allegiance to the concept of "equality of
opportunity," but the NDP has tended to be more favourable to the concept of
absolute equality in the here and now. While vast amounts of public ownership
are no longer part of its platform, it is a somewhat stronger advocate than the
Liberals and far to the left of the Conservatives on questions of public enterprise.
The NDP has also tended to be more nationalistic — and, in some cases, more
isolationist—than either of the major parties.[45] Thus, along with the union movement that supports it, the party has opposed the concept of free trade with the
United States and has, since 1969, opposed Canadian participation in military
alliances such as NATO and NORAD.
The range of ideological tendencies in the party has led to some severe organizational stresses. One of these was caused by the strongly nationalistic and more
radically left-wing "Waffle" group, which sought a return to more doctrinaire
socialist principles and greater domestic control of Canadian industry. In lines
reminiscent of the Regina Manifesto but also reflective of neo-Marxist paradigms,
the Waffle declared, "Capitalism must be replaced by socialism, by national
planning of investment and by public ownership of the means of production in
the interests of the Canadian people as a whole." The Waffle group became
sufficiently strong that, in the 1971 national leadership convention, their candidate
ran a fairly close second to the winner, David Lewis. However, the conservative
trade-union wing of the party and the almost equally conservative (for a socialist
party) parliamentary caucus were able to force the expulsion of the group from
the Ontario party in 1973. The group's direct influence has vanished since then,
although there can still be found strong traces of its views among many supporters of the party. The current national leader, Ed Broadbent, was associated with

[44] Robert Hackett, in "The Waffle Conflict in the NDP," in Thorburn, *Party Politics in Canada*, differentiates
between the democratic-socialism position and the social-democrat position. The former is much more
militantly left-wing, favouring broader government control and more public ownership than the latter. The
latter is the establishment position in the party.

[45] Garth Stevenson, "Foreign Policy," in Winn and McMenemy, *Political Parties in Canada*. See also George
Grant, *Lament for a Nation: The Defeat of Canadian Nationalism* (Toronto: McClelland and Stewart, 1965).
Grant sees many similarities between the positions of the NDP and the Diefenbaker Conservatives.

the original drafting of the Waffle manifesto, although his own positions since then have been in line with the much more conservative mainstream of the party. It has often been suggested that the CCF and NDP have been the parties of innovation in Canadian politics. The Liberals, especially, have often been accused of (or praised for) continually moving to adopt ideas that have been developed and popularized by the NDP or the CCF, thus taking the credit and the political kudos for putting them into play. This phenomenon, which is observed in some European party systems, is called "contagion from the left." William Chandler has found some empirical evidence for this in provinces where the NDP is a major factor in provincial politics.[46] The impact seems to be greatest with respect to health and social welfare—that is, in those social-policy areas where the CCF and NDP have traditionally been most active. However, the effects are not always very large and the relationship not always clear or simple. For example, in 1975 the Ontario Progressive Conservatives' reaction to a minority government situation in which the NDP was the leading Opposition party was in part a sharp turn to the right and severe restraint for health and social-service programs combined with more left leaning policies such as rent control and occupational health and safety regulations.

Party Structure   Structurally, the NDP is not so different from the older parties as its origins and ideology might lead one to expect. Its leader, like those of the two older parties, is elected at a convention and is subjected to a vote of confidence at biennial party conventions. An NDP convention is somewhat different in style from a convention of the Liberals or PCs, being more serious and more policy-oriented. As well, the presence of a large bloc of trade-union representatives from affiliated unions would be alien to either of the older parties. However, no CCF or NDP leader, once elected, has ever been seriously challenged by the convention, and the NDP caucus is likely to consider convention resolutions as advisory, not as compulsory positions to which they must hold. Certainly where the NDP has formed the government in some provinces, the objective and centralized tendencies identified in the major parties are just as pronounced.

The party is not formally a federation. However, like its older party counterpart, it is, in reality, very nearly federal in structure, with its provincial party organizations being fully autonomous, but represented both at the national convention and on the national council. The latter body is formally responsible for the operation of the party between elections and meets at least twice yearly at the call of the party executive. However, the council has more than one hundred members, and such large groups generally rule more in form than in substance. The real operation of the party machinery is directed by the executive members of the council and by the party caucus. The NDP leader's office is a smaller establishment than those of the leaders of the two older parties, but this is partially compensated for by the somewhat higher level of activity of constituency and provincial associations between elections. In sum, however, the locus of control for most matters

---

[46] William M. Chandler, "Canadian Socialism and Policy Impact: Contagion from the Left?" *Canadian Journal of Political Science*, x:4, December 1977, p. 755–780, and G. Caplan, *The Dilemma of Canadian Socialism: The CCF in Ontario* (Toronto: McClelland and Stewart, 1973).

in the NDP is not much different from the older parties, residing primarily in the leader and parliamentary caucus, the national executive, and the permanent officers of the party.[47]

The relationship between the NDP and organized labour in Canada has not been a consistent one. The party includes a bloc of union delegates from affiliated unions in its conventions, and the unions for years provided the bulk of financial support for the party. However, NDP governments have not been overly sympathetic to unions: in British Columbia, an NDP government allowed more union competition and ended a strike by legislation, as did the NDP government of Saskatchewan. When he was NDP premier of Manitoba, Ed Schreyer became an advocate of wage-and-price controls, a policy that is anathema to union leaders.[48] In federal politics, the Canadian Labour Congress historically vacillated between vociferous and direct support for the NDP and a more reserved position that would permit them to work as an interest group with whatever party is in power.

In 1979, the CLC made its biggest push to provide union support for the party, with direct participation by union activists in most aspects of the federal campaign that year. The result was a spectacular failure, with the NDP share of the vote actually declining in the Toronto and southern Ontario region, where Canadian Labour Congress efforts were concentrated; the CLC was conspicuous by its silence in the 1980 and 1984 federal elections.

There was, as well, a steady decline in the NDP share of the union vote, from 28% in 1968 to 22% in 1974, all of which has prompted Desmond Morton to conclude: "Big Labour is a lot smaller in Canada than either its friends or its enemies like to pretend."[49] In part, the problem is simply Canadian union members' tendency to relate unions only to their jobs, leaving politics to the specific agencies of the tradition parties. In part the problem lies with the Canadian Labour Congress itself, which is simply too weak *vis-à-vis* its affiliates to get them to do much, if anything, out of line with the standard bread-and-butter North American unionism, which concentrates on wages and working conditions.

Party Support: Class, NDP, and the Party System   There are some substantial differences between the base of support of the NDP and the support bases of the older parties. The religious distribution of NDP votes is broadly similar to that of the Conservatives, lacking the heavy Roman Catholic bias of the Liberals. This, however, is largely a reflection of the party's lack of support in Quebec. Some 45% of NDP votes in 1974 came from either skilled or unskilled labour, versus 40% for the Liberals and 33% for the PCs. NDP votes are more heavily concentrated in metropolitan areas than those of the older parties (in spite of the signal weakness in Montreal), and the age distribution of its voters is skewed

---

[47] There is an extensive description of the NDP party structure in Winn and McMenemy, *Political Parties in Canada*, pp. 167–190.

[48] Desmond Morton, "Labour's New Political Direction", in Thorburn, *Party Politics in Canada*, pp. 206–213. See also David Kwavnick, *Organized Labour and Pressure Politics* (Montreal: McGill-Queen's Press, 1972), and Gad Horowitz, *Canadian Labour in Politics* (Toronto: University of Toronto Press, 1968).

[49] Morton, "Labour's New Political Direction," p. 213.

towards youth. The NDP draws disproportionately from union voters; a union voter is about twice as likely to vote NDP as is a non-union voter. But for a party that appeals directly to the union vote, the other side of the story may be more revealing: 70% of union voters do not support the NDP.

The profile of NDP supporters suggests that, while Canadian politics in general is not class-based, support for the NDP to some extent is. Thus, we have the phenomenon of a somewhat class-based party in what is not a class-based voting system.[50] There is also a strong regional bias to NDP support. The CCF was born in Saskatchewan, had its first substantial victory there, and both the CCF and its successor, the NDP, have been strong there ever since in both federal and provincial elections. Another area of consistent support has been Winnipeg, and, more recently, support spread out across the province, producing NDP victories in the 1969, 1973, 1982 and 1986 Manitoba provincial elections. The same period has seen the NDP proportion of the popular vote in federal elections rise from 24% in 1965 to 32% in 1979, with the party gaining five of the twelve seats in the province in 1979. Moreover, support seems to have stabilized in that area, with 27% of the vote and four seats falling to the NDP in 1984.

There is also sufficient support centred in the powerful west-coast trade-union movement to have enabled the party to capture British Columbia's provincial government from 1972 to 1975, and to gain eight seats and 35% of the popular vote there in the 1984 federal election. However, the NDP remains largely without support in Quebec, most of the Atlantic region, and large sections of Ontario outside the metropolitan areas. It is conceivable that these holes may eventually be filled in, but, although the NDP made gains in the Atlantic provinces in 1979 and 1980, current movement in this direction is very slow. Until the NDP can increase its appeal east of Ontario, it is highly improbable that it will be a serious contender for national office.

The combination of an attempt to mobilize and hold labour support and a failure to articulate and sell a view of Canadian politics much different from that of the older parties has created difficulties for the NDP. Once the party became determined to pursue the essentially conservative union movement in Canada as its major organizational building block, it had to eschew much of the class-based rhetoric of its earlier years. After all, Canadian workers — blue- or white-collar, public- or private-sector — almost uniformly view themselves as middle class, not working class. The mainspring of NDP ideology after 1956 became, increasingly, the familiar Keynesian orthodoxy combined with large social safety nets, a position only slightly to the left of that espoused by the Liberals and Conservatives.

---

[50] Donald Blake, in "The Measurement of Regionalism in Canadian Voting Patterns," *Canadian Journal of Political Science*, 5, (1972), 55–81, suggests, on the basis of the results of several federal elections, that the class basis of overall Canadian voting patterns has not increased significantly, while the impact of ethnic, regional, and religious factors has remained strong. Again it should be emphasized that this does not mean that there is no class basis to NDP voting, but rather that the impact of class voting on the whole system is not strong. In examining the 1965, 1968, and 1974 elections, Clarke found a statistically significant correlate of NDP support only in 1974. More generally: "Several measures of social class all failed to yield strong correlations with voting behaviour in any of those national surveys" (*Political Choice in Canada*, p. 116).

The CCF's, and later the NDP's, failure to understand or explain the role of the state in the 1950s, which was a decade of relative economic prosperity, meant that the party did not constitute a clear alternative for the voters. With its liberal view of a basically neutral state, the NDP had only a single argument to rally support behind it — vote NDP for more honest and fair government. Moreover, the party's inability to recognize the contradictions inherent in the Keynesian state (that it benefited both capital and working people) was more debilitating in times of economic downturn, like those of the 1970s. The NDP had few policy alternatives to propose once full employment and investment policies came into conflict with each other. When the continued economic growth on which these policies were premised grew more and more difficult to achieve, the NDP was as confounded as the other parties.[51]

Not only did the attempt to mobilize organized labour (combined with a general lack of new ideas from the left, wherever it was in the western world) lead to ideological problems for the NDP, it also did not add much in the way of electoral support. As Brodie and Jenson explain, the NDP-CLC alliance was mainly "a marriage of notables."[52] The membership of the union movement displayed an active hostility to any idea of a radical transformation of a society that had delivered high wages and affluence to them. Even job insecurity, engendered by the 12% unemployment rates that followed the 1981–1983 recession, had no effect in convincing the mainstream membership of organized labour to support left-wing alternatives. Instead it, too, tended to support the "new" economic orthodoxy, which was that conservative, business-oriented solutions would provide the best hope of renewed economic and employment growth.

With no language of politics of its own, with no solid working-class support, and attached at the leadership level to a largely conservative labour movement, the NDP has had increasing difficulty offering any world-view that will clearly differentiate it from the Liberals. It has thus increasingly had to represent itself as essentially a more moral version of the Liberal party. Some 14% to 19% of Canadian voters seemingly continue to find that appealing, but it seems an unlikely base from which to move towards major-party status.

After the 1984 election, in which the NDP captured thirty seats and 18.8% of the vote to forty seats and 28% for a badly demoralized Liberal party, there was considerable talk that the NDP might provide "the real opposition" to the Conservative government. The NDP did not surpass the Liberals in share of popular vote but by 1987, to the surprise of almost everyone, they did surpass the Conservatives. Whether this constitutes a real breakthrough or is simply a temporary artifact of an extreme case of mid-term blues for the Conservatives, combined with limited appeal for the Liberals, must await the test of an election, which will occur after this publication.

However, for all its difficulties, the CCF-NDP is unique as a socialist movement that has had some electoral successes on this side of the Atlantic. Why has this

---

[51] M. Janine Brodie and James Jenson, "The Party System," in M. Whittington and G. Williams, *Canadian Politics in the 1980s*, p. 262.

[52] Brodie and Jenson, "The Party System," p. 264.

been possible in Canada and not in the United States? Gad Horowitz, developing the ideas of Louis Hartz, suggests one important reason.[53] Using a dialectical analysis, he posits that socialism, as an acceptable ideology in a society, can only grow out of confrontation of toryism with nineteenth-century liberalism.[54] If either of the two ingredients is missing, the essential dialogue cannot take place, and social-ism cannot develop. The United States can be looked at, ideologically, as a fragment thrown off from Europe — particularly from Britain — at a time when liberalism was ascendent. The tory streak is missing in the United States because, at the time of the American Revolution, counter-revolutionary conservatives left and came to Canada. Ideological dialogue is, therefore, less likely in the United States than in Canada, and nineteenth-century liberalism remains basically unchallenged in the United States because other ideologies are simply a bad fit with American political culture. In Canada, there is a predominance of the same liberal tradi-tion, but it is tempered with a tory touch, which has allowed Canadians both to see the state as something greater than the sum of its parts and to tolerate the socialist ideology, which is the dialectical synthesis of the two older ideologies.

The "socialism" of the Canadian NDP is a fairly tame form of that ideology, and, in many respects, does not diverge greatly from the Keynesian orthodoxy. That simple fact in itself may also go far in explaining why the NDP has survived as a movement in Canada.[55]

Interpretations of Third-Party Movements in Canada

By now it may very well be obvious to the reader that there is much in common among various third-party movements in Canadian politics, even when they have such widely disparate ideological stances as the Social Credit and the NDP. Virtually all of them originated elsewhere. Virtually all of them have expressed discontent with Canada's central political institutions. None of them has yet grown to be a major party, yet with the exception of the Progressives, all have survived in one form or another.

These common features have led several political scientists to suggest reasons that third parties have been such a persistent feature of the Canadian party sys-tem. The most frequent and probably the most convincing explanation revolves

---

[53] These ideas are expressed in Gad Horowitz, "Conservatism, Liberalism and Socialism in Canada: An Interpretation," *Canadian Journal of Economics and Political Science*, vol. 32, No. 2, May, 1966, pp. 143–171. Hartz's ideas are expounded in several places, most notably Louis Hartz, *The Liberal Tradition in America* (New York: Harcourt, Brace and World, 1955) and *The Founding of New Societies* (New York: Harcourt, Brace and World, 1964). See also K.D. McRae, "The Structure of Canadian History," in Hartz, *The Founding of New Societies* (New York: Harcourt Brace World, 1960). See also chapter 4 and 5.

[54] Horowitz' ideas have also engendered considerable controversy. Horowitz summarizes the arguments and replies to his critics in "Notes on Conservatism, Liberalism, and Socialism in Canada," *Canadian Journal of Political Science*, XI, 2, June 1978, pp. 383–399.

[55] We have ended this section of the chapter without discussing those political parties that operate exclusively on the Quebec stage, the Union Nationale and the Parti Québécois. It is our feeling that we cannot do justice to the details of the party system within any province, particularly Quebec, without going into more detail than we have space for here. As well, there is some discussion of the Quebec situation in chapter 3. In effect, each of the ten separate party systems deserves several pages of treatment. Since this text is not intended to cover provincial politics in detail, we have not provided it here. The interested reader is referred to M. Robin, ed., *Canadian Provincial Politics* (Scarborough: Prentice-Hall, 1978).

around the parliamentary system itself and the demands it makes on political parties. Hugh Thorburn sums up this point of view:

> Canadian parties, although vague in their policies, are disciplined parliamentary groups requiring of their members a high degree of conformity. The leader has great authority and there is little room for dissidence. Protest, then, must occur outside the old parties, and if it is to be effective must itself assume the form of a political party.[56]

Because of the necessity of maintaining cohesive parliamentary voting blocs, party discipline must be strict. In the United States, very loose party discipline allows protests to occur within parties, so the formation of third-party groups is seldom necessary. In Canada, by contrast, if radical dissent is to be heard at all, it must be heard outside the confines of the two older parties.

The Canadian federal system may also have provided some incentive to the formation of third parties, for even if a minor party cannot win a national election, it does have a fair chance of winning power in a province. Every province west of New Brunswick has, at some time, had a third-party government. At first glance, a similar potential for third-party power might appear to exist in the United States, but there are important differences between the Canadian and U.S. situations. First, state elections in the United States are held in conjunction with national elections. The ability of the national parties to dominate the media makes it very difficult for a smaller party to compete. Second, winning power in an American state is not as desirable as winning power in a Canadian province. Since American federalism is far more centralized than the Canadian variant, the winning of an American state is not nearly so attractive to an aspiring political party as a Canadian province.

The coincidence of social cleavage with some provincial or sectional boundaries, and the relative homogeneity of the provinces, have also been important in fostering third-party movements. It would be difficult to imagine much success for the Union Nationale or the Parti Québécois in a Quebec that was 50% English. C.B. MacPherson attributes much of the early success of third-party movements in Alberta to the relative social homogeneity of that province. The CCF may have succeeded in Saskatchewan partially because of a similar homogeneity.[57]

Another theory to account for the rise of third parties in Canada has been suggested by Maurice Pinard.[58] Canadian electoral politics is characterized by long periods of one-party dominance. Looking specifically at the rise of the Créditistes in Quebec, Pinard hypothesized that the long period of Liberal Party dominance in federal politics in rural Quebec led to a perception, on the part of Quebeckers, that the Conservative Party was not a legitimate alternative. They voted Progressive Conservative in 1958 so as not to be cut off politically from the party in power, but they shortly discovered that the Conservatives under Diefenbaker did not pay any attention to them. If they were still not satisfied

---

[56] *Party Politics in Canada*, p. 169.

[57] MacPherson, *Democracy in Alberta*; and S.M. Lipset, *Agrarian Socialism*, passim.

[58] Pinard, *The Rise of a Third Party*. See also the discussion of this theory in the *Canadian Journal of Political Science*, vol. VI, No. 3, September, 1973.

(and rural Quebec has had a great deal to be dissatisfied about), their only legitimate outlet for protest was through a third party, and the Ralliement des créditistes provided this. A similar situation prevailed in Alberta in 1935 — there was no effective opposition to the United Farmers government, and hence no place for voters to express their discontent, until Social Credit came along. One could apply this type of analysis fruitfully to others of Canada's third-party movements.

There were other reasons for the particular success of third parties in the west. C.B. MacPherson has suggested that the prairies constituted a quasi-colonial economy with respect to the east, and that they had, effectively, only one class of citizens; the result of this was a "quasi-party" system,[59] with one party or movement dominating for a long period, only to be replaced almost completely by another. Thus, the one-crop economy and lack of social cleavage on the prairies may well have made possible the type of mass-party political action represented by the CCF in Saskatchewan and the Social Credit and United Farmers in Alberta.

Finally, a suggestion about the genesis of the CCF victory in Saskatchewan in 1944 has been made by S.M. Lipset.[60] Given the one-crop economy of that province, and the antipathy western farmers felt for eastern grain-marketing organizations, the Saskatchewan farmers early organized a series of wheat pools and cooperatives. These organizations produced many active citizens, who later used the wheat-pool-cooperative structure to organize party opposition to the Liberal government then in power. Such a social infrastructure was not available in other provinces, and it did much to aid the organization of the CCF in Saskatchewan as a strong political force. The mass-membership nature of the NDP in Saskatchewan has persisted, with the average constituency membership for the NDP in Saskatchewan at 2,059 in the early 1970s. By contrast, in Manitoba and British Columbia, it was just more than 500, and in Ontario only 281.[61]

Undoubtedly, all these explanations have some validity. It is in the coincidence of two or more such factors that one finds the most fertile ground for third-party activity. Whatever the explanation, however, third parties at both the federal and provincial levels have done much to give the Canadian political system and the party system its distinctive complexion.

CONCLUSION: PARTIES AND THE PARTY SYSTEM

One of the favourite exercises of political scientists has been the attempt to characterize the party systems of various nations. The most widely accepted if not particularly imaginative taxonomy has been the number of parties. Thus, for instance, the United States and Britain are usually characterized as two-party systems, and the Scandinavian nations, France, and Israel are usually described as multi-party. There are obvious difficulties with this classification scheme; for

[59] MacPherson, *Democracy in Alberta*. See especially pp. 215–250.

[60] Lipset, *Agrarian Socialism*. This is a general theme running through Lipset's book.

[61] N.H. Chi and George Perlin, "The New Democratic Party," in Thorburn, *Party Politics in Canada*, p. 187.

THE PARTIES: A HISTORICAL PERSPECTIVE

example, lumping the party systems of France, Israel, and Norway together does relatively little to help us understand the political systems of those countries. Similarly, there are problems with the classical two-party systems: Britain found itself with a minority government in 1974 and with a very significant third party in the 1980s, and the third-party contender for the presidency of the United States in 1968 gathered 13.9% of the popular vote.

The numerical typing of party systems is also particularly difficult to apply to Canada. Does Canada have a one-party-dominant system because the Liberals held power in Ottawa for fifty-two of sixty-four years up to 1984? Do we have a two-party system because the Conservatives have proven capable of decisively defeating the Liberals? Do we have a three-party system because the CCF-NDP has received consistent support and has, in every federal election for forty years, won at least a few seats? Or is it a multi-party system? After all, the Créditistes and Social Credit have shown considerable staying power, and most provinces have had other than Liberal or Conservative governments.[62]

If a simple numerical typology is inadequate, H.G. Thorburn has identified a number of alternative ways of analysing the Canadian party system.[63] Several analysts prefer to disregard the impact of third parties (which were indeed insignificant until the past sixty years), preferring to view the party system simply as two alternative groups trying to exert a broad enough appeal to get elected, but devoid of ideological or policy differences. In these interpretations, much is made of the flexibility in ideology and policy orientations of the alternative parties. Thus: "No man in Canada has been more inconsistent than the man who has followed either political party for a generation."[64] And according to Lord Bryce: "In Canada ideas are not needed to make parties for they can live by heredity and, like the Guelfs and Ghibellines of medieval Italy, by memories of past combats."[65] A more modern variant of this theory is J.R. Mallory's "national mood" interpretation, which sees differences of mood and style between the two major parties as the significant determinants of success.[66] A party remains in power as long as it is in tune with "the national mood," i.e. until that mood changes and leaves it high and dry. Devotees of this approach would thus claim that in 1984 the Progressive Conservatives under Brian Mulroney were more in tune with the national mood than the Liberals under John Turner.

A similar point of view is espoused by C. Winn and J. McMenemy.[67] Their

---

[62] There is an extended discussion of the complications and difficulties of applying a numerical typology to party systems in Giovanni Sartori, *Parties and Party Systems*, vol. 1 (Cambridge: Cambridge University Press, 1976), pp. 119–129. "By now there is a nearly unanimous agreement that the distinction among one-party, two-party, and multiparty systems is highly inadequate. And we are even told that a judgement as to the number of major parties obscures more than it illuminates . . . . By now classifications of party systems are a plethora and confusion and profusion seems to be the rule" (p. 119).

[63] H.G. Thorburn, "Interpretations of the Canadian Party System," in *Party Politics in Canada*, pp. 34–51.

[64] Sir John Williston, cited in Alexander Brady, *Democracy in the Dominions* (Toronto: University of Toronto Press, 1947), p. 94; and in Thorburn, "Interpretations," p. 36.

[65] Cited in Brady, , *Democracy in the Dominions*, p. 103.

[66] J.R. Mallory, "The Structure of Canadian Politics" in H.G. Thorburn, ed., *Party Politics in Canada*, 2nd. ed., pp. 24–33.

[67] Winn and McMenemy, *Political Parties in Canada*.

general theme is that, while there are differences in style and electoral support, these "have a negligible effect on policy. Thus, implemented programs exhibit few systematic differences from one party government to another."[68] Again, they see the Canadian party struggle essentially as one between two groups whose real policy orientations are not much different from each other.

Still another variant of this interpretation is to paint the two major parties as tools of the dominant corporate élites. Thus, Frank Underhill asserts:

> The real function of the two-party system since the Laurier era has been to provide a screen behind which the controlling business interests pull the strings to manipulate Punch and Judy who engage in mock combat before the public. Both parties take for granted that their first duty in office is to assist the triumphant progress of big business in the exploitation of the country's resources.[69]

This interpretation remains a prevalent one, particularly in the neo-Marxian view of Canadian politics, which sees the function of the state in advanced capitalized societies as being to foster the accumulation of capital by the dominant classes.[70]

A second broad mode of analysis sees the party system as a one-party-dominant one. This theme relies on the fact that, both federally and in the provinces, one party tends to remain in power for a long period once it takes office. C.B. MacPherson's quasi-party theory of Alberta politics, described earlier, is one variant of this theme; another is Maurice Pinard's one-party-dominance theory of the rise of third parties. At the federal level, the title of Reginald Whitaker's *The Government Party* suggests the same view. Reinforcing this interpretation, George Perlin has, as described above, posited that the Progressive Conservatives are a permanent opposition, with an approach to governing that will cause them to self-destruct once in power.

H.G. Thorburn's synthesis of these various interpretations forms an appropriate conclusion. He suggests that, at the federal level, Canada has a persistent government party (the Liberals), a persistent opposition party (the PCs), and a persistent third party (the NDP). Recruitment patterns reinforce these positions. Those attracted to power opt for the Liberals and those inclined to opposition roles move to the PCs. Whether the Conservatives will be able to build their electoral victory of 1984 into a reversal of the Liberal and PC roles in this scenario remains to be seen. The NDP attracts more radical-opposition types, who are prepared to go slightly beyond ideological conformity. The Conservatives and Liberals are sufficiently close in their view of government that, when either becomes incompetent or loses touch with the nation, a safe alternative is readily available. Thus, overall, "The Canadian party system and therefore the political system for which it supplies the direction is both narrowly controlled by a fairly

---

[68] Winn and McMenemy, p. 1.

[69] Frank Underhill, *In Search of Canadian Liberalism* (Toronto: MacMillan, 1961), p. 168.

[70] F. Engelmann and M. Schwartz, *Canadian Political Parties* (Scarborough: Prentice-Hall, 1975). See also K.Z. Paltiel, "Canadian Election Expense Legislation," in Thorburn, pp. 100–110; and *Financing Political Parties in Canada* (Toronto: McGraw-Hill, 1970). The Marxian and neo-Marxian interpretations are expressed in various articles in Leo Panitch, *The Canadian State* (Toronto: University of Toronto Press, 1977).

closed elite of office holders and their associates and susceptible to influence from a broad spectrum of opinions."[71]

In conclusion: when we consider the functions of political parties identified in chapter 10, and then consider to what extent these may, in fact, be performed by other institutions, the overall significance of parties is cast in a clearer but not necessarily more flattering light. These functions included:

1) the recruitment and training of political decision makers;
2) the organization of the decision-making process;
3) the education, political socialization, and mobilization of the mass public;
4) the articulation and aggregation of interests and the creation of national integration;
5) the management of the flow of information;
6) the generation of support for the political system; and
7) the making of public policy.

John Meisel has suggested that parties are at a disadvantage in performing most of all of these tasks, and that there has been a substantial downgrading of the role of political parties over the past generation.[72] In particular, he would agree with the contention that very many of these functions have been lost to the executive — the Cabinet and the bureaucracy — and to organized interest groups, which operate at the boundary of the political system.

A number of reasons for the decline in the influence of parties can be suggested. The increasing complexity of issues and the rise of the executive-bureaucratic state are interconnected phenomena, but regardless of which came first, increasing technical complexity does tend to make issues extremely difficult for organizations, which are primarily electoral machines, to handle. The increasing role of many interest groups and the increasingly symbiotic relations between them and client-oriented departments that speak the same technical language they do has also been significant in diminishing both parliamentary and party influence. The increasing specialization and compartmentalization of government concerns means that "the general interest as aggregated by political parties tends to receive scant attention and parties are left with little choice but to approve what has already been decided by others.[73] The increasing number of issues that are dealt with in meetings between federal and provincial officials and ministers also tends to diminish the policy role of parties and of Parliament, for, increasingly, prior commitments made between the two orders of government preclude the making of significant changes by politicians who are not directly a part of that process.

---

[71] Thorburn, "Interpretations," p. 48.

[72] The case is made in many of Meisel's writings cited in the footnotes. A similar case is increasingly made about parties in other political systems. For example, Frank Sorauf writes, in the introduction to *Party Politics in America*, (third edition Boston: Little Brown, 1976): "In this book a strong case will be made for the proposition that the political parties have lost their pre-eminent position as political organizations and that competing organizations now perform many of the activities that have traditionally been regarded as the parties' exclusive prerogatives" (p. 5).

[73] Meisel, "The Decline of Party in Canada," p. 123.

The rise of the electronic media has stolen much of the political-communication role from parties, although it may have created a new role for them — the recruitment of media stars and the staging of "spectaculars" (leadership conventions) to launch those stars. In a related vein, the rise of investigative journalism may have usurped some of the party's opposition role and its job of uncovering government improprieties — although it can be countered that there has been investigative journalism, of one form or another, ever since there has been journalism at all.

The increasing use of public-opinion polling by Cabinet and by government departments has short-circuited another part of political parties' communication function. No longer do leaders have to rely on the time-consuming and potentially inaccurate practice of canvassing members of their party to find out where the public stands on an issue. The polls have replaced the pols as sources of information about public opinion. The only limitation of this technique has been cost of public-opinion polling, a significant limitation to parties in opposition but not to the party in power.

The apparent decline of parties in Canada is matched in other western democracies, and so would appear to be part of a general trend.[74] In view of this, Frank Sorauf has suggested that, in western democracies, we have, so far, seen three phases in the evolution of parties and party systems. In the first phase, parties began as loose organizations of limited access and narrow appeal. They were largely restricted to electioneering activities, and could perform these functions without highly complex organizations because of the limited franchise. In the second phase, parties expanded along with the electorate. North American parties expanded less rapidly than their European counterparts but, on both continents, the aggregation and mobilization of the new electorate was the primary concern, and parties dominated the political loyalties of the relatively unsophisticated citizenry. In the third and current phase, political interests become more complex and heterogeneous, with an increasing differentiation of politics. Political loyalties of the more sophisticated citizenry are given to other organizations, such as special-interest groups, as well as to parties. Parties lose their monopoly over many of their traditional functions and become, at best, first among equals among mass political organizations. The description would appear to fit well with the evolution of Canadian political parties.

---

[74] Sorauf, *Party Politics in America*, particularly p. 439; and Anthony King, "Political Parties in Western Democracies," in *Polity*, vol. 2, 1969, pp. 111–141.

C H A P T E R   1   2
ELECTIONS AND VOTING

THE FUNCTIONS OF THE ELECTORAL PROCESS
THE ELECTORAL SYSTEM IN CANADA
■ The Players ■ Election Officials ■ The Election Process
■ The Partisan Campaign ■ The Single Member Plurality System
THE DYNAMICS OF CANADIAN ELECTORAL BEHAVIOUR
CONCLUSION

F ederal general elections are the grand spectator events of Canadian politics. They are, to the majority of Canadians, the most visible and the most intrinsically interesting aspects of the political process. Moreover, voting is the commonest and in some ways the easiest form of political participation. Between 70% and 80% of the eligible population will show up at the polls on the day of a federal election, and the campaign leading to that election is, of all political phenomena in Canada, the most widely covered by the media and the most closely watched by the public.

THE FUNCTIONS OF THE ELECTORAL PROCESS

The primary function of the electoral system in Canada is to provide for an orderly and democratic succession from one set of political authorities to another.[1] It permits the citizens of Canada a periodic review of the performance of their political leaders and allows them to pass judgement as to whether the government of the day should be permitted to continue or should be replaced by a new set of authorities. While this may seem to be obvious and unremarkable, we must keep in mind that many political systems do not provide such procedures for review and peaceful change of the political leadership. Moreover, even in some systems that do provide an electoral system, we find that it is adhered to in form but not in spirit; people are called upon to vote from time to time, but informal restrictions on candidacy and rather unsubtle discouragement of those who would dare to oppose the existing regime insure that there is never a real choice on the ballot.

---

[1] See also the functions indicated by Jon Pammett in "Elections," M. Whittington and G. Williams, *Canadian Politics in the 1980s* (Toronto: Methuen, 1984), pp. 271–286.

In Canada, however, elections are real contests and the electors are faced with at least some choice when they go to the polls.

As a result, perhaps the most important function of the electoral process is the generation of support for the political system. It is obvious that elections elicit support for a group of candidates: the winners of the election! This electoral result becomes the mandate to govern, if not to implement a particular set of policies, and gives the government of the day the legitimacy to lead the country. However, elections also help to establish the legitimacy of the system as a whole, as well as that of the government of the day. This broader systemic support results from the fact that the election forces people to become interested and even directly involved in the democratic process. They learn about the rules of the game of politics and are faced with a very practical demonstration of the nature and extent of the power of the mass public in a democratic election. Because elections *do* produce change in the occupants of the elected offices of our political system, they serve to remind even the most cynical citizen that, while democracy sometimes works in strange ways, it still works.

A broad measure of support for the political community is also generated by the fact that, during the eight weeks of a campaign, all those Canadians who pay any attention to public affairs focus on one event. For a brief period, national issues supersede most local issues. In this manner, elections function as agents of national integration, reaffirming, at least for a day, that east and west, Francophone and Anglophone, we are ultimately all in the same boat.

Elections may also perform an input or policy-initiation function for the political system. During a campaign, parties search high and low for votes, and this search may lead them to articulate the interests of groups in the population that might otherwise remain in the background, for if enough non-voters can be motivated to cast a ballot, the outcome of a close election might possibly be altered. Since approximately half a million Canadians are working for the political parties during a national election campaign, if a relevant issue exists, it will likely be discovered by someone.

There are, however, a number of flaws in the image of political parties, ever vigilant for the vote, using the electoral process to form a vital link between the citizen and the policy-making apparatus of the modern state. The most important flaw is one we have already considered — many if not most political decisions in Canada are made with little input from the party organization. Thus, even if the articulation of policy needs does occur during a campaign, it is to some extent ineffectual; and anyway, once in power, parties seem to pay little attention to their election platforms. Politics in New Brunswick are not entirely typical of Canadian politics, but the following words will ring true to most people who have carefully observed parties in office:

> It is not unusual to find an item (expressed in different words) appearing on four election platforms of the same party in a row. The fact that the party was in power throughout the entire period and might presumably have enacted the required legislation during this time does not seem to occur to those who draw up the platform.[2]

[2] H.G. Thorburn, *Politics in New Brunswick* (Toronto: University of Toronto Press, 1961), p. 107.

Moreover, party platforms and the policies parties suggest during elections are, for the most part, highly nebulous: they usually contain a little bit for everyone but almost no detail that could facilitate their conversion to specific policy outputs. For example, the Liberal program for the 1963 election contained such items as:

PROSPERITY FOR CANADIANS
Fundamentals for a Sound Economy
Cure unemployment . . .
Manage the nation's finances well . . .
Expand Canada's foreign trade . . .
A new Liberal government will act positively. It will have a constructive plan for free trade with Britain, the United States, and the European Common Market, as a step towards the establishment of an Atlantic Community. Commonwealth nations, Japan, and other interested countries will be invited to join in progressively reducing the barriers to world trade.
Planning and Finance
Make monetary policy an instrument for steady economic growth. A new Liberal government will take clear responsibility for the money supply, credit policies, and the exchange rate of the Canadian dollar. It will improve the country's financial machinery, to make more Canadian capital available for industry and to safeguard the consumer against credit abuses.

If we now move the calendar forward to 1984 and change parties, we find that, with respect to economic development, the Progressive Conservative "commitment" is:

The main economic goal of a new PC Government will be to put unemployed Canadians back to work.

Prospects for our unemployed will improve only if lasting economic growth is assured, growth at a faster rate than the recent Liberal years.

Because one of the biggest obstacles to economic recovery and job creation is the federal debt, a new PC government will be dedicated to responsible deficit reduction.

Our second commitment is to genuine economic growth. Our priority is to re-establish Canada as a leading and powerful force in world trade, as the provider of quality goods and services at competitive prices.

The foundation of our economic policy is based upon four pillars:
•Lower interest rates achieved through new and realistic investment policies;
•Development and application of new technology in our farms, factories and offices;
•Effective and innovative training and retraining programs;
•Vast improvements to our international trade performance.

It would be difficult to find people anywhere in Canada who would not espouse these policies in 1963 *or* 1987. They have appeared in virtually every Liberal and Conservative party platform since at least 1945.

There are three other functions of the electoral process. First, elections have a "sociability function." In other words, participants in the electoral process are there simply because it is an enjoyable activity. Surveys of party activitists generally confirm this, and indeed, for many party workers, the election may be the high point of social and organizational life for a four-year period.

Secondly, elections provide "spectator interest." Whatever effect election campaigns have on the final outcome, they do make a fine national show, with leaders dashing to and fro trying to establish their images, followed by faithful retinues of weary and beery reporters. The latter daily fill television screens with carefully staged two-minute clips of leaders in action, and they fill newspapers with all manner of fact, fancy, and comment on the race.[3] Then there is the thrill of the race itself, with public-opinion polls and assorted pundits giving us a week-by-week picture of the positions of the various parties. At the local level, coffee parties and all-candidates' meetings abound and, for eight weeks at a stretch, local television producers are spared any anxiety about how to fill up prime time, and local newspapers are spared any anxiety about what to use to fill the space between advertisements.

Finally, in some parts of Canada elections are still a minor means of redistributing income or services. Middle-class metropolitan ridings see relatively little of this and it is, perhaps, a dying tradition even in much of the countryside. However, voters can still be swayed by promises of jobs, etc., and bridges can be built and roads paved, in regions that might otherwise lack them. The votes of local opinion leaders — not necessarily the upper class of a community — are particularly valuable. Although many party workers are volunteers, some are paid for their efforts and these are usually the less well-to-do. In Quebec, the "good old days" are now disappearing, but there, until recently, a provincial election in a marginal riding was always good for at least one road paving and a considerable number of farm electric installations, usually carried out by a local contractor who, incidentally, supported the governing party. Electoral patronage was not necessarily the most efficient redistribution system on earth, but it did have some advantages. Indeed, Hubert Guindon has pointed out that:

> The possibly unanticipated effect of the crackdown on patronage funds [by the Lesage government in Quebec], in actual fact, was to halt or substantially reduce the flow of provincial funds to the lower social strata. Holding up the new "bureaucratic" public morality was a hidden net reorienting of public expenditures to the other social classes.[4]

THE ELECTORAL SYSTEM IN CANADA[5]

While elections are held at all levels of government in Canada as well as in the selection of school boards, hospital boards, and other minor bodies with specific local responsibilities, the focus of this section will be primarily upon the federal

[3] For a thorough description of life on the campaign plans of both parties in the 1979 election, see Dalton Camp, *Points of Departure* (Toronto: Deneau & Greenberg, 1979).

[4] Hubert Guindon, "Social Unrest, Social Class and Québec's Bureaucratic Revolution," *Queen's Quarterly*, vol. 71, no. 2, 1964. The article is reprinted in Thornburn, *Party Politics in Canada*; the quotation is on p. 188.

[5] We were assisted in finding factual material for this section by the information services of Elections Canada. They should not be considered responsible for any errors of fact or omission. All interpretive material is our own or that of the authors cited.

level. The most important electoral event at the federal level is, of course, the general election, where all seats in the House of Commons are up for grabs. By-elections are held in specific constituencies to fill vacancies that may occur between general elections due to the death or resignation of the incumbent, and the rules that apply in elections for the most part apply equally for all by-elections. Because they are such complex events, elections cannot be understood if viewed from a single vantage point. Therefore, we will look at the Canadian electoral system as a number of separate but interrelated sub-processes with a wide variety of participants or actors. Before proceeding to an examination of these sub-processes, it is necessary to provide a brief sketch of the players who participate in the spectacle of a federal general election in Canada.

The Players

The Voters   The most numerous and, ultimately, the most important players in an election are the voters. Who votes and who does not is determined partly by the psychological and motivational characteristics of the Canadian electorate, and partly by the formal rules that set down the qualifications for voting, or the franchise. The former are the complex determinants of political participation, which have been discussed at length in chapter 5. It is the formal rules with which we are concerned here.

The franchise is defined by the *Canada Elections Act*. The basic rule today is that any Canadian citizen[6] eighteen years of age or older has the right to vote in a general election or in a by-election being held in the constituency in which the voter resides. Voters may cast one ballot and may vote only for a candidate whose name appears on the ballot. There are no write-in votes in the Canadian system, except for the very special cases of public service or armed-forces electors living abroad. A voter must vote in the constituency in which his or her name appears on the electoral list.[7] The Canada Elections Act, however, goes on to exclude certain classes of individuals. Those disqualified from voting are the chief electoral officer and assistant, the returning officers in each constituency (except that the returning officer has the deciding vote in the case of a tie), federally appointed judges (except citizenship court judges), inmates of penal institutions and mental institutions, and persons convicted of offences under the Canada Elections Act. In elections since the passage of the Charter of Rights and Freedoms, it has become common for prison inmates to challenge in the courts the restriction on their right to vote. In 1984 one such challenge came to the Supreme Court, which decided against the inmates, declaring that Parliament should address the problem of the relationship between the franchise and the Charter, something Parliament has not done at the time of this writing.

---

[6] The requirement here used to be "British subject" and not citizenship.

[7] Special provisions are made for members of the armed forces and public servants living abroad to vote in their "home" constituency even though they may not, at the time of the election, physically live there. Other Canadians living abroad do not vote, since they are not enumerated. The report of the House Standing Committee on Privileges and Elections has recommended that judges and all Canadians resident abroad be given the franchise.

The Canadian electoral system today features universal adult suffrage. However, what seems to be an obvious criterion for a liberal democratic regime has not always been accepted so fully in Canada. For much of the period between 1867 and 1920, when a major revision of the Dominion Elections Act was passed, the federal franchise was determined by the provincial elections acts. This meant that the qualifications and disqualifications of voters in federal elections varied with the whim and prejudice of provincial governments, and that the federal franchise was not consistent across the country. Many provinces originally had a property qualification for voting, a reflection of a basically élitist attitude to the responsibilities of choosing a government. The feeling was that people who owned property had a stake in the community and would be more responsible in casting a ballot. Women were generally excluded from voting until 1918, and could not stand as candidates until 1919; in Quebec, women remained disfranchised in provincial elections until 1940. Still more unusual and undemocratic were the provisions in the British Columbia Elections Act up to 1945 that disqualified Canadian citizens who were of Oriental or Hindu descent. Because provincial rules determined the federal franchise until 1920, Orientals in British Columbia were similarly disqualified from voting in federal elections. Some provinces also have had literacy requirements for voting. Nevertheless, despite the rather tarnished history of provincial franchises, all such disqualifications by now have been removed, and today the provincial elections acts define a voter in a manner close to identical to the Canada Elections Act.[8]

Neither has the federal franchise always been as universal as it is today. The most glaring exceptions have been in the treatment of native peoples. The Inuit ("Esquimau person" in the 1934 Dominion Franchise Act) were explicitly excluded until 1950, because there were no federal electoral districts in the territorial regions of Keewatin and Franklin, where most Inuit reside. It was not until the creation of the constituency of the Northwest Territories, after the 1961 census, that most Inuit were able to vote for the first time. Indians living on reserves were also explicitly excluded from the franchise until 1960, when such discriminatory provisions were removed from the elections act.

To be eligible to vote, a person must have his or her name appear on a voters' list. In Canada and in all provinces except British Columbia, lists are prepared anew for each election. This is done by a process of enumeration and appeal: prior to each election, enumerators visit each residence in the country and determine the names of all eligible voters residing there. Subsequent to the enumeration, preliminary voters' lists are prepared and everyone whose name appears on the list is notified by postcard. Simultaneously, advertisements appear in the media informing those who do not receive notices that, if they wish to vote, they must appeal, following the steps set out in the advertisements. The preliminary enumeration picks up 95% of those who should be eligible to vote, and revisions on appeal pick up 2% to 3% more. By contrast, in the United States, where voters must take active steps to register, the voters' lists pick up only 60% of those

---

[8] See: T.H. Qualter, *The Election Process in Canada* (Toronto: McGraw-Hill Ryerson, 1970). See also A. Anstett and T. Qualter, "Election Systems," in D. Bellamy, J. Pammett, and D. Rowat, *The Provincial Political Systems* (Toronto: Methuen, 1976), pp. 147–176.

who qualify for the franchise. Since only 50% of U.S. citizens on the voters' lists turn out to vote, in fact, U.S. presidents are typically elected by only about 30% of those technically qualified to vote. The comparable Canadian figure is much closer to 75%.

There is occasionally discussion of moving to a permanent voters' list in Canada. Such a system was tried from 1934 to 1938, but proved less satisfactory than our current, more active, enumeration system. The major drawbacks to the current system appear to be, first, that its self-policing nature could be open to abuse and, second, that it is very time-consuming. The enumeration system requires that campaigns last a minimum of fifty days compared to the thirty days required in Britain, where a permanent list is maintained. However, complaints of abuse of the self-policing mechanism are actually very rare. Moreover, we will see, when we consider the predisposition of Canadian voters affected by the campaign, that any change to a shorter campaign would not be trivial. Since a permanent-list system, which requires a bureaucracy to maintain it, would also be more costly, it seems unlikely that Canada will move in that direction. Of course, no system is perfect. In 1984, Elections Canada, the name currently used for the organization responsible for the conduct of federal elections, discovered that, among those Canadians enumerated, were two parakeets, Rubin and Robert. We were unable to discover how they voted.

The Candidates The qualifications and disqualifications for candidacy in a federal election are set down in the Canada Elections Act. The basic rule is that candidates must be eligible to vote in a Canadian election. Disqualifications include persons found guilty of corrupt election practices, persons involved in contractual relationships with the Crown, persons employed by the Crown (except public servants on leave of absence and Cabinet ministers), and members of a provincial legislature or a territorial assembly. Candidates must be nominated by twenty-five electors from within the constituency and they must make a deposit of $200. The deposit, which has been $200 since 1882, is lost if the candidate gets less than 15% of the total vote in a constituency. In 1984, 54% of candidates lost their deposit, including, alas, the Rhinoceros Party candidate in the riding of Guelph, a "broadcaster" by the name of Miss Suzy Mew-Catty.

In the past, candidates in federal elections were required to own a certain amount of property; but this stipulation was abolished soon after Confederation. To be a candidate in a federal election, the individual must reside in Canada. There is no legal requirement that candidates be residents of the constituencies in which they are running, although candidates who are parachuted into a riding by the party leadership are sometimes spurned at the polls by the local party faithful. In provincial elections acts, residence in the province is a requirement of being a candidate, although, as with the federal act, there is no requirement that the candidate be a resident of the constituency in which he or she runs.

The Political Parties We will discuss the party campaign machinery later in this chapter, but it is necessary at this juncture to deal briefly with the formal aspects of the role of political parties in the election system. Section 13 of the Canada Elections Act sets out the conditions and procedures for *registration* of a political party. Registration of a party gives its candidates the right to have the party name listed beside theirs on the ballot paper. Essentially, it is the responsibility of the chief electoral officer to maintain a registry of political parties and to determine which applications for registration meet the stipulations set down in the Act. To be registered, the party must field at least fifty candidates in an upcoming election; to maintain continuous registration and qualify for ongoing financial support, the party must have twelve seats in the House of Commons at dissolution. Restrictions on registration also include sundry formal requirements having to do with information about the party's address, the names of the party executive, chief party agent, and the party auditor; as well, the name of the party must not be the same or even too similar to the name of an already registered party. This latter requirement is to present a marginal group from calling itself, for instance, the Conservative Progressive Party or the NPD and thereby picking up gratuitous support from a careless minority, who thought they were voting for a major political party. Despite these provisions, in Canada's thirty-third general election, in 1984, there were eleven parties that had the party name on the ballot paper, one of which called itself the Libertarian Party. Although this label might have been deemed rather close to another, more prominent party in Canadian politics, the results of the election indicate that very few Liberal voters were fooled by the similarity in name. How many Libertarians voted Liberal by mistake is impossible to estimate.

Election Officials[9]

There are a number of offices created and defined by the Canada Elections Act, but the most important of these is that of the Chief Electoral Officer (CEO), who is appointed by special resolution of the House of Commons, with the effective rank of deputy minister. Because he or she is appointed directly by Parliament, because the costs of the office are provided directly from the consolidated revenue fund without approval of the Cabinet, and because he or she reports through the speaker to the House of Commons, the CEO has independence from the government of the day. The CEO can be removed only for "cause" (i.e., heinous crimes or failure to perform duties) following a joint address of both houses of parliament. There have been only four CEOs since the office was founded in 1920.

The responsibilities of this office are to "exercise general direction and supervision over the administrative conduct of elections" and generally to enforce all of the provisions of the Canada Elections Act. The CEO is also granted very broad discretionary powers to adapt the election process in the event of "unusual or unforeseen" circumstances. This power was exercised in the 1980 election to permit the voters' lists for the 1979 election (less than a year earlier) to suffice as the preliminary lists for 1980. This reduced the cost and administrative fuss of the second election in less than a year by forgoing the enumeration process. In 1984, discretionary powers were exercised on eight occasions, the most important of which was to extend the deadline for revisions of the voters' list by eleven

---

[9] A description of these roles and functions may be found in *The Office of the Chief Electoral Office of Canada Profile of an Institution* (Ottawa: Elections Canada, n.d.).

days, adding 82,300 electors to the voters' lists. The office of the representation commissioner, which was originally established in 1964, was intended to co-ordinate the process of electoral boundaries adjustments (redistribution). In effect, the federal representation commissioner was a member of each of the eleven electoral boundaries commissions, which make the recommendations to the House of Commons concerning federal constituency boundary adjustments in the provinces and the territories. However, in August 1979, the office of the repre-sentation commissioner was abolished and most of the responsibilities were trans-ferred to the CEO.

The office of the Chief Electoral Officer is now referred to as Elections Canada. Its role has changed very substantially over the past two decades. Prior to 1966, the primary responsibility of the office was to see that enumerations and vote counting took place according to the rules set forth by Parliament. Since 1966, a steady expansion of the office's functions has taken place, with the addition of responsibilities for representation and redistribution, the registration of political parties, and the administration of election-expenses legislation. Fortunately, the democratic values of Canadians make the job generally uncontentious, but it has become administratively very complex.

For each electoral district in Canada, the Governor-General in Council appoints a returning officer (RO). The RO, who actually reports to the CEO, is appointed permanently or until age sixty-five, and the requirements of tenure are that the RO remain a resident of the constituency for which the appointment is made, maintain a non-partisan stance in the performance of duties, and in general do the job defined by the elections act. The RO's responsibilities are to manage the election process in the electoral district, to appoint enumerators, to appoint an election clerk for the constituency, and to appoint a deputy returning officer (DRO) for each of the polls within the constituency. The RO must maintain an office in the constituency from the time the election writs are issued, and either the RO or the election clerk must be on duty in the office during the hours the polls are open throughout the election period. The job was once considered a patronage appointment, but it is now, more often than not, difficult to find any-one to perform the task, since it involves intense effort under considerable pressure for a fifty-day period and with rather little remuneration.

Deputy returning officers are minor officials who hold office at the pleasure of the RO in the electoral district and can be removed by the RO at any time. The roles of the DRO are to administer the election process at the level of the individual polling station and to oversee the balloting and unofficial count in the poll. To assist in these duties, the DRO is required by the Act to appoint a poll clerk.

As mentioned above, the returning officer of each constituency must appoint enumerators, who are charged with the responsibility for preparing the preliminary voters' lists in each polling division. Two enumerators are appointed for each urban poll, and the Canada Elections Act requires that the RO select them "so that they represent two different and opposed political interests." The procedure for achieving such bipartisan representation in each pair of urban enumerators is also set down in the Act. Essentially, the RO asks the successful candidate and the candidate who placed second to each nominate "a fit and proper person." "Fit and proper," in this instance, means an honest but faithful partisan. While the enumerators are supposed to travel in pairs to insure that there is no padding of the voters' list and no deliberate deletion of selected individuals, it is often the case that the enumerators split the work load between them and work individually, to save time. While no system is perfect, there are relatively few deliberate abuses of this system, and accidental omissions from the list can be caught on revision before the final lists are prepared.

A minor benefit of this system, from a partisan standpoint, is that the local candidates of the two most successful parties in the previous election may be able to dole out a bit of patronage in return for a little volunteer work later on in the campaign. However, with the ROs, it has become increasingly difficult to find people willing to do the work of enumerators for the small amount of money involved. In fact, one of the bigger administrative problems surrounding elections is to find, within ten days of an election, 110,000 enumerators who will work for seven days for $200. The quality of those applying is not always high; in 1984, applications were received for positions as "remunerators," "anomalies," and "eliminators."

The *Election Expenses Act* originally provided that the Chief Electoral Officer must appoint an official to serve as the commissioner of election expenses. The commissioner's job was to deal with complaints arising under the Election Expenses Act, and the original appointee was simply the assistant chief electoral officer, who was the second in command to the CEO. However, it soon became clear that the burdens of this office were such that it would be better performed by an entirely separate individual who could concentrate on the job full-time. Since then, the parliament of Canada passed legislation extending the jurisdiction of the commissioner to all provisions of the Canada Elections Act as well. His new role is to function as a sort of "elections ombudsman," to deal with all manner of complaints having to do with the conduct of elections and including, of course, campaign financing. The official title of this office was changed to "the commissioner of Canada elections," to reflect the expanded mandate; as well, the commissioner was given the power to prosecute offenders under the Canada Elections Act. This latter provision was intended to take the responsibility for such prosecutions away from the influence of the Attorney General for Canada who, being a member of the government, could be accused of partisanship.

There are other minor officials and functionaries who are bit players in the complex theatre that is a Canadian general election. These include the scrutineers, or "party agents," who are present in each polling station; the party auditors, who are required under the Election Expenses Act; and the staff of the CEO. They do not play a significant enough role in the election to bear closer study at this point. Their roles will become apparent as we move to a discussion of the election process itself.

The Election Process

Redistribution   The machinery of redistribution comes to life after each decennial census is reported. Its purpose is simply to insure that the structure of our constituencies is such that Canadians are more or less equally represented in the

House of Commons. The general rule is that the number of people represented by one member of parliament should be roughly equal from constituency to constituency. In the past, with some ridings in suburban regions growing very rapidly and others in rural areas, particularly in the Atlantic provinces, shrinking in population, we have seen pronounced disparities between the relative significance of people's votes in different regions.

However, even the principle of equal representation must be adjusted a bit in a country as vast and diverse as Canada. Thus, for instance, it has generally been agreed that, because a rural constituency is larger in physical size, it could be based on a smaller population size than a geographically compact but densely populated urban district. Furthermore, it has long been recognized that, because of our federal system, the House of Commons should be minimally reflective of all regions of the country. Hence, it is generally accepted that Prince Edward Island's four seats, while comprising far smaller constituencies than, for example, the Metro Toronto ridings, are a deviation from the norm of equal representation that can be tolerated.[10]

Nevertheless, it is accepted, as well, that the boundaries of the constituencies must from time to time be changed according to shifts in population, and the problem is how to achieve such boundary changes with a minimum of partisan strife or unfair partisan advantage. At one time, the changes in electoral boundaries were the prerogative of the House of Commons. This meant that the government of the day was always in a position to be able to adjust the ridings in such a way as to maximize its own electoral success. However, since 1964, Canada has had a system of electoral-boundary adjustments premised on the all-party acceptance of the need for impartiality.

The current system of federal redistribution in Canada is based on eleven impartial electoral-boundaries commissions, one for each province and one for the Yukon and the Northwest Territories. These are made up of a judge from the province, who is appointed by the chief justice of the provincial Supreme Court, and two other members, who are appointed by the Speaker of the House of Commons, one of whom is usually the speaker of the provincial legislature. The base from which these electoral-boundaries commissions begins is the number of seats assigned to their province by the Representation Act of 1986, which amends the BNA Act, which sets out the number of seats per province, and the Electoral Boundaries Readjustment Act, which determines how boundaries are drawn within each province.

The number of seats per province is established by a complicated formula, which, according to the House Committee on Privileges and Elections minutes of June 26, 1985, operates as follows:

1. Assign 2 seats to N.W.T. and one to Yukon (3 seats).
2. Use 279 seats and the census population (except N.W.T. and Yukon) to establish a "national electoral quotient," representing the average

---

[10] In fact, Prince Edward Island and New Brunswick are pegged at four and ten seats respectively by the BNA Act, which stipulated that no province should have fewer members of the House than it has senators.

number of voters per seat for Canada. After the 1981 census the quotient was 87,005.

3. Calculate number of seats per province based on the quotient.
4. Add seats to provinces pursuant to "senatorial clause" guarantee in the constitution and "grandfather clause" in the new formula.
5. Add seats to adjust for provincial population increases. In order to slow the rate of growth of seats in Parliament, a province only gets one-half the number of new seats to which its population growth would entitle it.

The "senatorial clause" guarantees that no province may have fewer Commons seats in the House of Commons than in the Senate. The "grandfather clause" guarantees that no province will lose seats by redistribution. The result will be a slow rise in the number of seats, over time, to 288, as a result of the 1981 census, and to an estimated 292 after 1991 and 296 after 2001.

It is the responsibility of the Chief Electoral Officer to calculate each province's entitlement of seats by applying the formula to the census data as soon as the chief statistician of Canada gives the CEO the required information. Having made these calculations, the CEO then instructs the electoral boundaries commissions to allocate the available seats within their provinces. The boundaries commissions have considerable leeway to set boundaries, in keeping with factors such as community borders or population concentrations, and it is thus very important that they be viewed as impartial. The Canada Elections Act specifies that in no case should the size of any electoral districts in a province deviate from the quotient by more than 25%, plus or minus.

The preliminary reports of the commissions are open to public scrutiny and comment within the province, and, after any changes brought about at this stage are completed, the completed report of the commission is sent on to the CEO. The Speaker then tables all of the reports of the electoral boundaries commissions in the House of Commons. The House has thirty days to examine the reports; objections signed by ten members can be filed with the Speaker. These are then debated, and the results of the debate, along with the appropriate copies of Hansard, are sent back to the relevant commission for reconsideration. The ultimate step in the process of redistribution is the approval of the reports of the electoral boundaries commissions by order-in-council.[11] Given the complicated nature of this process, not to mention the inevitable delays in getting census data out, the process is not a short one. The September 1984 election, for example, was carried out under the distributions determined by the 1971 census, and the redistribution for the 1981 census was finally passed by Parliament only in early 1986.

Timing of Elections Barring the defeat of a government in the legislature and with the exception of the constitutional provisions, that the life of a parliament is limited to five years, the timing of an election in Canada is wholly the prerogative

---

[11] The formal electoral machinery is described in greater detail in T. Qualter, *The Election Process in Canada* (Toronto: McGraw-Hill Ryerson, 1970).

of the prime minister or premier who decides, with advice from the Cabinet and personal advisors, not to mention the media, on the exact date. This has not always been so clearly the case. From 1876 to 1926, it seemed generally conceded that it was the right of the prime minister or premier to decide the occurrence and the timing of elections; at least, he always did so. However, in 1926, Lord Byng refused Mackenzie King a dissolution and asked Arthur Meighen to attempt to form a government in the existing House. Meighen did so, but was almost immediately defeated on a vote of confidence. King campaigned in the ensuing election largely on this issue, and won a clear majority of seats. In spite of some subsequent debate, King's victory seemed to establish the principle that not only does the prime minister alone have the right to control the timing of elections under normal circumstances, but also that even after a defeat in the House of Commons on a vote of non-confidence, the prime minister has the right to advise and very largely to control whether there should be a dissolution and election, or whether the Opposition leader should be called upon to try to form a government.

The issue could have risen again after the 1972 federal election, when the Liberals were returned with only two more seats than the Conservatives, the NDP holding the balance of power with thirty-one seats. If the Liberals had been defeated in a vote of confidence when they first met Parliament, would it have been Prime Minister Pierre Trudeau's right to ask for another election? Or would he have been obliged by constitutional convention merely to resign and let the Governor-General call upon the Leader of the Opposition to form a government? If the principle enunciated above stands, the Governor-General would have had to do whatever the prime minister suggested, but some constitutional experts did assert that, since the prime minister would not then have formed an effective government, even if Trudeau had requested dissolution, the Governor-General could have denied him that privilege and called instead on Robert Stanfield.

As it turned out, the issue blew over, leaving nothing more than residual ego satisfaction for the sundry academic constitutional experts who appeared on radio and television in the days following the election. The constitutional experts did seem to agree that once the Liberals had won one or two votes of confidence in the House and had their Throne Speech accepted, the normal rules would then apply; dissolution would be a prime-ministerial prerogative, or else would follow automatically from a major government defeat. Should the government have been defeated before that point, the burden of opinion was that the prime minister had no right to demand another election, but that he should merely resign, leaving the Governor-General to ask the Opposition leader to form a government. This procedure was followed in Ontario in 1985, paving the way for a government headed by the former Opposition leader, and it can probably now be taken to be a settled convention that, under similar circumstances, the same rule would apply federally. If a prime minister has formed an effective government and governed through several votes in the House, then his defeat in the House still leaves him the right to ask for dissolution. If he has not successfully survived even the debate on the Speech from the Throne, the Governor-General should call upon the Leader of the Opposition to attempt to form a government. One year and six months after the 1972 federal election, the government was in fact defeated, and dissolution did follow virtually automatically, as it did again when a minority conservative government was defeated in November 1979.

Customarily, if the government in power is in a majority, elections will occur at about four-year intervals, although the maximum allowable term under the Charter of Rights and Freedoms is five years. A government will not wait out the full five years unless it is in trouble, and then the results are not likely to be propitious — a fact discovered to their regret by Robert Bourassa in 1976 and Pierre Trudeau in 1979. A prime minister will usually make a decision about precise election timing on the basis of information from the party about its state of preparedness, from the Cabinet about how any policy initiatives undertaken by the party are progressing, and particularly from information obtained from public-opinion polls and interpreted by personal advisors about the party standing across the country. Depending on his temperament, the prime minister may also feel moved to look at horoscopes or tea leaves, or to consult his long-dead mother, for the timing of an election can be a tricky business.

Once a decision on timing has been made, the prime minister visits the Governor-General, who has the formal power to dissolve Parliament and call an election. (In the provinces, the premier visits the Lieutenant Governor, who has a similar formal power with regard to provincial elections.) The Governor-General then issues the writs, in the name of Her Majesty, declaring the election; the Chief Electoral Officer transmits the writs to his 282 returning officers; and the electoral machinery goes into motion. The world of politics has changed considerably since Stephen Leacock described the aftermath of the dissolution of parliament in Mariposa shortly after the turn of the century. But it has not changed with respect to the excitement general elections still generate:

> The whole town and country is a hive of politics, and people who have only witnessed gatherings such as the House of Commons at Westminster and the Senate at Washington and never seen a Conservative Convention at Tecumseh Corners or a Liberal Rally at the Concession Schoolhouse, don't know what politics means.
> So you may imagine the excitement in Mariposa when it became known that King George had dissolved the Parliament of Canada and had sent out a writ or command for Missinaba County to elect for him some other person than John Henry Bagshaw because he no longer had confidence in him.[12]

Polling the Electors Elections are generally held on Mondays, and the prime minister selects which Monday. Polling stations are occasionally located in the houses of supporters of the "right party," and the owners of the houses used are paid for the use of their premises. While this used to be a fairly significant bit of patronage, today, the remuneration is hardly worth the inconvenience of a stampede through one's house, so churches, schools, and other public buildings tend to be used more and more as polling stations.

The polling station contains tables or desks for the use of the poll clerk and the party scrutineers, and a polling booth where the voters can mark their ballots in privacy. The principle of the secret ballot is a long-standing requirement of truly

---

[12] From *Sunshine Sketches of a Little Town* by Stephen Leacock, reprinted by permission of The Canadian Publishers, McClelland and Stewart Limited.

free elections, and the Canada Elections Act very carefully specifies the procedures for protecting this right. There are also provisions in the act for proxy voting on behalf of an elector who is unable to get to the poll personally for reasons of illness, etc. Advance polls are established for those who must be out of town on voting day, and these are run on the ninth and seventh days before the election. Those who cannot vote on either election day or advance-polling day may vote in the office of the returning officer up to three weeks before polling day. The votes from advance polls are not counted until after the close of regular polls.

Ironically, while there is a provision in the Canada Elections Act that requires all drinking establishments and liquor outlets to be closed during the time that the polls are open on election day, this provision does not apply for advance polls. Perhaps the increased use of advance polls by electors in the last couple of elections reflects the Canadian voter's need for a drink before making a decision. At any rate, the Chief Electoral Officer's report on the 1979 election suggests that the pre-Confederation philosophy that booze and politics don't mix is no longer applicable, and that the parliament of Canada should soberly consider the deletion of such provisions from the Elections Act.[13] In 1986, however, the rule remains in force.

Counting the Vote   After the regular polls close on voting day, the deputy returning officers in charge of each poll count the ballots under the watchful eyes of the party agents or scrutineers. This is an entirely unofficial count, tabulated in newsrooms and party headquarters, but it is what produces the excitement on election night. The ballot boxes are delivered to the returning officer after the unofficial count, and the RO then has the responsibility of keeping them until the official count, which may not be sooner than seven days after the election. By this time, of course, the excitement is over in all but ridings that were very close.

In the case of close elections, or if irregularities are alleged in the conduct of the election, either the returning officer or one of the candidates may apply for a recount. A recount is automatic if the margin of victory is less than twenty-five votes. The recount is performed by a judge in the presence of the candidates or their agents. In the case of a tie even after a recount, the returning officer must cast the deciding vote in the constituency. When all of this is done, the returning officer then returns the election writ declaring the candidate with the most votes the winner to the Chief Electoral Officer.

The Partisan Campaign

National Campaign Headquarters   So far in our discussion of preparation for elections, we have mentioned parties only in passing, but parallel to the official activity during an election campaign, there is a great deal of unofficial activity. Indeed, by the time the prime minister visits the Governor-General to ask for a dissolution, political parties will already have undergone the long process of waking up from their deep sleep of the previous few years, oiling and polishing their

---

[13] Canada, Chief Electoral Officer, *Statutory Report 1979* (Ottawa: Supply and Services Canada, 1979), pp. 25–26.

electoral machines, nominating candidates, and reactivating their national and provincial organizations. The actual setting of the election date is rather like the firing of the starter's gun. Sometimes the runners trip over the starting blocks, but this has become less frequent through the 1970s, as the parties have become more professional.

At national campaign headquarters, a number of things will be happening. Schedules for speaking tours by the leaders will be set up for the whole campaign. An avalanche of party literature, speakers' handbooks, and so on will descend on the local constituency associations. Party fund-raising activities will redouble, and budgetary priorities will be set by a small, sometimes informal, campaign committee under the national chairman. New staff and volunteers will be taken on, and press releases and speeches ground out by the yard. National polls will be commissioned in order to divine the major issues — which are invariably inflation, unemployment, and the economy.

Significant changes have been taking place, through the 1970s and 1980s, in the structure of national campaigns. In particular, they have been becoming more decentralized.[14] In part, this is a response to the heightened ability of local and provincial party organizations to raise money; in part, it has been a deliberate choice by those responsible for operating the campaigns.

The changes have gone furthest in the Conservative Party.[15] There the provincial campaign chairmen are responsible for the maintenance of a structure parallel to that of the national campaign committee, with tour directors, communications directors, press-liaison officers, and other functionaries. Each provincial organization has its own team of workers and its own network in the province. The number of people directly involved at a managerial level in the campaign has grown from perhaps fifty to hundreds, and the increased numbers are associated with a new sense of professionalism.

> The people who were recruited into this structure might be volunteers but they were not amateurs. This was a sophisticated form of politics that relied on technical expertise and professional management. Those who participated in it were part of a new system of power and a new organization that demanded professional dedication.[16]

The new breed of "professional volunteers" expected that when their party won office they would receive some rewards for their efforts in the form of patronage or of direct influence over the activities of government. Since a government can never deliver sufficient patronage or influence to satisfy all of its highly committed workers, discontent seems inevitably to settle in not too long after the election.

While the Conservatives developed a strongly decentralized form of national organization, the Liberals have continued to operate somewhat more centralized national campaigns. The major exception is that the Quebec campaign is nor-

---

[14] Current descriptions of campaign organizations may be found in Joseph Wearing, *The L-Shaped Party*, P. Martin, Alan Gregg and George Perlin, *Contenders: The Tory Quest for Power*, Dalton Camp, *Points of Departure*, and Christina McCall Newman, *Grits*.

[15] See especially P. Martin et al., *Contenders*.

[16] Martin, *Contenders*, p. 38.

mally operated parallel to and largely independent of the rest of the national campaign, with the provincial campaign chairman essentially equal in status to the national chairman.

The NDP structure is somewhat different again. With a broader membership based on committed local activists, it depends more directly than do the older parties on constituency volunteers. NDP workers are well-known in Canadian electoral politics for their ability to mobilize supporters by direct door-to-door canvassing techniques. The large membership base of the NDP is, to some degree, a substitute for money, and the rather more ideological nature of the commitment of its organizers seems to act as a substitute for the patronage that organizers of the older parties come to anticipate.[17]

The Constituency Organizations　At the local level, events will be much more variable. Some local election machines are highly efficient; others are very much less so. Nominations of candidates will usually have taken place some time before the campaign begins, but in some ridings the announcement of the election date will find one or more parties so ill-prepared that no candidate is available; in others, parties may have delayed nomination meetings to take advantage of the publicity they generate. Nomination procedures vary from party to party and from riding to riding. At the one extreme are completely open conventions where anyone who has paid nominal party membership dues may vote, while at the other extreme are carefully controlled nominating conventions where all the delegates are hand-picked by the party executive to avoid any unfortunate "errors." In practice, most nominating conventions lie somewhere between the two extremes. In many ridings, parties are as likely to be embarrassed by a lack of potential nominees as by an excess, and at every election some constituency executives face the unpleasant task of searching frantically for someone to run as the party candidate. If all else fails, a member of the party executive will accept a draft, and carry the party's colours into the local campaign.

Ideally, the earliest stages of an election campaign will see the establishment of a careful schedule of activities, which peaks on election day. Local workers will be recruited and fund-raising efforts will be stepped up. Poll captains will be appointed to coordinate party efforts in given neighbourhoods. Some tentative door-to-door canvassing will begin, rising in intensity as the great day approaches, and mail and telephone campaigns will be conducted to reach as many voters as the party workers can find. On voting day the poll captain will arrange for the transportation of any known supporters who could not otherwise make it to the polls, and scrutineers will sit in the polling station to insure that irregularities do not occur, and, equally important, to chat with friends and neighbours.

In practice, it may be difficult to find willing party workers, and parties can always use more people. Canvassing itself is often a hit-and-miss affair, with large sections of the city, especially in lower-class areas, left untouched, and phone campaigns are also usually rather spotty. In many homes, the candidates'

---

[17] Leon Epstein, "Political Parties; Organizations" in David Butler et al., *Democracy at the Polls* notes that in all western party systems, a large membership base is a general substitute for dollars and makes patronage less important.

literature is filed in the garbage can. Meanwhile, communication is flowing back and forth between the constituencies and local, provincial, and national headquarters and, as befits a stratarchical structure, much of it gets lost or is grossly misinterpreted along the way. Leaders criss-cross the country, leaving enthusiasm — or sometimes black despair — in their wakes. The media give millions of dollars of free publicity to the parties, and the parties spend millions of dollars sponsoring events for the electorate to watch and the media to report.

Financing the Election   All this activity costs money, and the spending is often regarded with a jaundiced eye by the public. It is true that the total amounts spent are high. Norman Ward has estimated that the total costs of running the electoral machinery in 1972 amounted to about $47 million per year, an estimate made as "a trial run at the job by a political scientist who, it must be conceded, is not convinced that it can be done."[18] Inflation affects this area as it does others, and by the 1984 campaign, the total costs of the election, based on calculations by the Chief Electoral Officer, were $132 million, or $7.90 per elector.[19]

Elections Canada reported that total operating expenditures by parties in the 1984 election year was $36 million. Normal operating expenditures are about $20 million, so approximately $16 million were spent directly on the national campaign. In addition, of course, most of the $20 million in other annual costs are actually election related.[20]

At the national level alone, the Liberals, in 1984, raised more than 10.5 million, and spent more than $11 million, with the largest amounts being disbursed by provincial party organizations either for their own expenses or as partial reimbursement to candidates for local expenses. The Conservatives far outdid them, raising $21 million and spending more than $18 million, while the NDP raised $10 million and spent more than $6 million. These figures are for all national party operations in 1984, but in an election year it is safe to assume that most of the money found its way into activities directly related to the campaign. In the 1980 election, reported spending by the national parties specifically on the campaign was $4.4 million for the PCs, $3.8 million for the Liberals, and $3.1 million for the NDP.[21] In 1984, the figures were approximately 50%

---

[18] Norman Ward, "Money and Politics," *Canadian Journal of Political Science*, vol. 5, no. 3, September 1972, pp. 335–347. This article also gives a brief description of efforts at reform in the area of electoral finance.

[19] In *Contact*, no. 56, Elections Canada, July 1985, p. 9, the CEO reports *his* costs as $96.5 million, to which should be added another $36 million to cover non-reimbursed election expenses of the parties and candidates.

[20] Calculations for 1984 are based on *Contact*, no. 56. For material on earlier elections, see K.Z. Paltiel and F. Leslie Seidle, "Party Finance and Campaign Spending in 1979 and 1980," in H. Penniman, *Canada at the Polls: 1979 and 1980* and K.Z. Paltiel, "Some Aspects of Campaign Finance in Canada," a paper presented to the International Political Science Association, Montreal, in August 1973. For historical material, see K.Z. Paltiel, *Political Party Financing in Canada* and the Committee on Election Expenses, *Studies in Canadian Party Finance* (Ottawa: Queen's Printer, 1966). For a general overview, see K.Z. Paltiel, "Public Financing Abroad: Controls and Effects," in M. Malbin, ed., *Parties, Interest Groups, and Campaign Finance Laws* (Washington, 1979), p. 354; and Party Candidate and Election Finance, *Study No. 22*, (Ottawa: Royal Commission on Corporate Concentration, 1976).

[21] Very detailed expenditure accounts for the 1979 and 1980 elections are provided in F. Leslie Seidle and K.Z. Paltiel, "Party Finance, the Election Expenses Act, and Campaign Spending in 1979 and 1980," in Penniman, *Canada at the Polls, 1979 and 1980*.

higher. The largest expenditure item, by far, for the national parties is broadcast advertising. In 1980 the PCs spent 43% of their national budget on television and 15% on radio advertising. For the NDP and Liberal parties the proportion was approximately the same. By contrast, local candidates spend less than 10% of their budgets on the electronic media, but more than one-third of it on print advertising.[22]

Although new election-expenses legislation (which we describe later) has shifted the base of party finance strongly towards individual donors, the financing of the activities of Canadian parties has historically depended heavily on donations from corporations or large individual donors (or, in the case of the NDP, large labour unions). Even today, election activities, by contrast to the ongoing operating costs of the parties, are strongly dependent on large donors. Party bag-men have lists of corporations that have given in the past and can be expected to do so again. The calling of an election will see the bag-men knocking discreetly on the doors of company presidents or treasurers. It has already been noted that many corporations follow a sixty-forty policy, giving 60% of their donations to the party in power and 40% to the major Opposition party as an insurance gesture.[23] In situations where a change of government seems probable, corporations may reverse the proportions of donations going to government and Opposition. Others simply follow a fifty-fifty rule. In some cases, corporate giving is counted as a regular budgetary expenditure, although in other cases company donations may be highly personalized. In one such case a rookie bag-man was sent by the Ontario Provincial Liberal Association to a medium-sized southern Ontario firm and was firmly rebuffed by the president, who insisted that his company had never given money to the Liberal Party. A veteran bag-man was then called back into action and sent around to jog the president's memory. The happy ending for the Liberal Party was that the appearance of a familiar face was enough to revive the president's memory, and the party coffers were enriched by a tidy sum.

In addition to money, corporations often make substantial gifts of services. This is particularly true of public-relations and advertising agencies, which may donate the services of large staffs together with supporting supplies. Corporations that give money may often do so for relatively non-immediate reasons having to do with the preservation of the system or a good business climate. Advertising agencies, however, hope to benefit immediately from large governmental contracts for tourist advertising, the publicizing of new programs, and other governmental work, and if they have picked the winning party they are often suitably rewarded.

In non-election years, party operations are financed mainly by individual and corporate donations; many of the election expenses we have been discussing so far are additional to normal operating expenditures and are garnered by special financial campaigns. In 1983, total costs of day-to-day operations of the Liberal Party were $4.6 million. For the Conservatives it was more than $11 million, and for the NDP, $5.6 million. It is obvious that the Conservative electoral victory at

22 Seidle and Paltiel, p. 268.

23 It might be argued that the insurance is against an NDP victory. Corporations likely do not care much whether there is a Tory or Liberal government in power (although many of them did develop an antipathy towards the Trudeau Liberals), but they normally prefer to keep the more threatening socialists in the political wilderness.

the expense of the Liberals in 1984 was amply foreshadowed by the relative abilities of parties to raise money. In the late 1970s, the Liberals and Conservatives raised and spent approximately equal amounts of money. By 1984 the Conservative financial capacity was twice that of the Liberals and the NDP had also surpassed the Liberals, in part at least because the Conservatives and the NDP had mastered the techniques of raising money by direct-mail campaigns.

In addition to these sources of funds, there are assorted semi-institutionalized sources that come under the general heading of "kickbacks" or "rake-offs." For example, it is rumoured that in some provinces, distilleries are assessed a regular percentage of gross sales, which goes to the coffers of the party in power in the provincial government as an informal "tax" for listing their brands in liquor outlets. In at least one province, rumour has it that there are specialized lawyers who are very good at getting liquor licences. Their fees are high, but they don't get to keep quite all of them. A certain percentage goes to make the gears of the administrative machinery run more smoothly and, incidentally, tends to help the fortunes of the party in power. In total, however, these covert sources of money are probably very small compared to openly declared sources. Indeed, at the national level, surveillance by Elections Canada probably makes the risk attached to such sources far greater than the potential money to be gained and it is probably safe to assume that most, if not all, of the national party fund-raising takes place above the board.

Party finance can obviously be open to gross abuse, and the whole question of campaign finance in Canada has been a constant target for reformers. Early in 1974, Parliament passed a series of sweeping reforms, which have done much to change the face of campaign financing in Canada.[24] The legislation requires disclosure of the names of any donor and the amount of any donation of more than $100 to a party, while also allowing tax credits to the donors on a sliding scale, depending on the amount given. It requires that the public purse pay half the cost of television time for parties, and provides for the allocation among parties of a total of six and one-half hours of time on all television stations, according to a complex formula administered by an arbitration process and related to seats in the House of Commons and to popular vote. It limited total spending by national parties on the national campaign in 1984 to 39.5¢ per voter for the total number of voters registered in constituencies where the party has candidates. Since there were more than 16.7 million registered voters in Canada in 1984, the parties with candidates in every riding were allowed total expenditures of $6.4 million for their national campaigns.

The act also limits the amounts that can be spent by individual candidates in urban ridings to $1.32 for each of the first 15,000 voters on the list, 66¢ for each of the next 10,000 voters, and 33¢ for each voter after 25,000. The maximum allowable expenditures in an urban riding of 50,000 electors in 1984 were, therefore, $34,650. Any candidate who gets 15% of the vote will be reimbursed for part of his or her expenses — about half of them, in an average riding. The rest of local expenses are covered by local donors or by transfers from the national

---

[24] A detailed account is available in K.Z. Paltiel, "Some Aspects of Campaign Finance in Canada," and a more general account is available in the *Globe and Mail*, January 4, 1974, p. 1.

office. Parties and candidates, through their official agents, must provide full accounting of all money spent and received, and the gifts of services must be declared as part of overall expenditures. In 1984, parties were reimbursed $3.9 million, while individual candidates received $11.7 million, or 93¢ per eligible voter.[25]

While the legislation goes a long way to reducing abuses of the electoral system, there are still some problems. One was removed in 1983 when the levels of allowable expenditures were indexed to inflation. (Previously, they had been frozen at 1974 levels.) However, the proportion of costs paid out of the public purse is still quite low: 22.5% of election costs at the national level, provided that the party spends at least 10% of the maximum allowed. Therefore, parties still must engage in substantial outside money-raising activities. A tax-credit system has made it more attractive for individual donors to give money, while disclosure rules have made some corporations more reticent. The result has been an evening out of the amounts available to parties, with the NDP being the biggest relative winner. It has also meant that individual donors, especially those making contributions in the $100 to $1,000 range, are now a more important source of money for Canadian parties than are large corporate donors, particularly in non-election years.[26]

The tax-credit system has also made local and provincial organizations far less dependent on the national organization; in fact, the system often reverses the situation where most funds flowed into the national treasury and then were distributed across the country. Dalton Camp has given a picture of the great changes the 1974 Election Expenses Act has made in Canadian party structure and activity:

> Now that the taxpayer is helping to fund political parties and their election campaigns, the parties have become more like corporations. Politics is a multi-million dollar business, and raising money has become, to an increasing degree, the achievement of sure-fire techniques of direct mail; the computer has made the bag-man a lesser figure in the system. But more important, the new money enables the party to buy more people for the organization cadres, and, while voluntarism is still important, particularly at the constituency level, the central organization is becoming more professional, more numerous, more expensive and more important. . . .
>
> The old impoverishments that would drive a party to making-do, to feverish improvisation and to leaving much to chance, are gone, replaced by a rush of affluence which has produced a new world of modalities, structures, systems, printouts, flow-charts and cash on hand.[27]

Election-expense legislation is rigorously enforced by the Chief Electoral Officer, backed by the Commissioner of Canada Elections, and, with the exception of slowness in reporting on the part of some local candidates, non-reporting by

---

[25] *Contact*, no. 56 (Ottawa: Elections Canada, July 1985), p. 9.

[26] Joseph Wearing, *The L-Shaped Party*, pp. 58–64, provides a picture of the financing arrangements of the Liberal Party in the early 1980s.

[27] From *Points of Departure* by Dalton Camp, 1979. Reprinted by permission of Deneau Publishers and Company Ltd., Toronto. See pp. 140, 141.

some fringe candidates, and some difficulty in defining provisions with respect to the gratuitous provision of services to candidates, it is fairly well observed. One of the major enforcement problems has been in the area of individuals and corporations who do their own unsolicited advertising on behalf of candidates or political parties. In 1979 the CEO reported twenty-one complaints arising out of persons other than the gladiators themselves disseminating information that effectively supported or opposed policies clearly identifiable with one of the political parties.

In response to this, Bill C-169, passed in November 1983, prohibited organizations and individuals other than registered political parties from spending money at elections to promote or support a candidate or party. The legislation was promptly challenged as conflicting with provisions for freedom of expression in the Charter of Rights and Freedoms, and the appeal was upheld by the Alberta Supreme Court. The federal government did not contest that decision, and the CEO did not enforce the legislation in 1984. The issue of the extent to which and the manner in which private organizations or individuals may indirectly spend money to support parties during elections therefore remains an open one.

The other area of difficulty in enforcement has come with respect to the provisions of the Elections Expenses Act that prohibit campaign advertising on the day of the election and on the day immediately preceding polling day. However, the legislation does not prevent the media from dealing with public affairs, from reporting the activities of the party leaders, and even from interviewing the candidates during the blackout period. Forty-five such cases were brought to the attention of the Commissioner of Canada Elections in the 1979 campaign, but no prosecutions resulted. The CEO, in his report, points out the difficulty in interpreting the meaning of the Act in this respect, and suggests that the terms of the Act and its intentions be clarified in the future. Ultimately, it would seem, again, that the only real control possible here is the good faith and the cooperation of the media, the parties, and the candidates in insuring that the spirit of the legislation is maintained. Overall, the legislation does constitute a major reform in the electoral system in Canada. With such legislation as the Electoral Boundaries Readjustment Act and with a political culture that demands comparatively high standards of electoral morality, Canada is better served than most countries by the standards of behaviour in the electoral process.

The Single Member Plurality System

In spite of all the positive attributes of the Canadian electoral system, it has been widely argued that its basic structural feature, the single member plurality system of electing MPs, creates problems when viewed in the overall context of the political system. One of the traditional defences of the present electoral system in Canada has been that it provides the Canadian political system with electoral majorities, and consequently with government stability. However, the occurrence of five minority governments at the federal level in Canada between 1957 and 1979 set some scholars wondering about the validity of this assertion. In spite of the fact that minority government in Canada has been relatively effective when assessed in terms of policy outputs, many scholars, most notably Alan Cairns, have identified a number of anomalies and pointed out some potentially negative features of the electoral system.[28]

The present system does, to some degree, provide electoral stability by consistently giving the party gaining a plurality of votes a larger percentage of seats than its share of votes.[29] However, it has transformed a minority of votes into a stable majority of seats on only nine of seventeen occasions, and it has occasionally reduced an Opposition with a fair amount of public support to numerical ineffectiveness in the House of Commons. As Table 12-1 indicates, in fourteen of the last twenty-two elections, the electoral system has either not produced a majority government or has left the opposition ineffectually small. Moreover, the system encourages minor parties, such as the Social Credit or the Créditistes, with sectional bases of support while damaging minor national parties such as the NDP, whose support is spread evenly over the country. For example, in 1935 the Reconstruction Party got 9% of the vote and exactly one seat, while Social Credit, with less than half as many votes, got seventeen seats. In 1963, 13% of the vote garnered seventeen seats for the NDP, while 12% of the vote gained twenty-four seats for Social Credit and the Créditistes. Whatever the other merits of minor parties, they do not necessarily lead to more stability in parliament.

The results of the 1979 and 1984 elections constituted a demonstration of the potential for imbalance in representation. The Liberals, with 40% of the vote in 1979, did get 40% of the seats, but the PCs, with only 35.9% of the vote, got 48% of the seats, and the NDP, with 17.8% of the vote, held just 9% of the seats. Thus the NDP, with half the number of supporters of the Conservatives, got just one-fifth the number of seats, and the government of the day was supported by just a little more than one-third of the voters. Although the Liberals won in 1980, the regional imbalance between seats and votes was exaggerated still more, particularly in the west and in Quebec. In 1984 the Conservatives captured 50% of the national vote but 75% of the seats in the House of Commons. By contrast, the Liberals, with 28% of the vote, garnered just 14% of the seats, and the NDP, with 19% of the vote, gained 11% of the seats.

Cairns demonstrates that, within a given party, representation in the House of Commons by region has seldom been proportional to the party's votes by region. For example, in 1945 the CCF gained 260,000 votes in Ontario (32% of its total), yet won no seats, while the 167,000 votes the party received in Saskatchewan (21% of its total) resulted in 64% of its federal seats.[30] From 1921 to 1965, the Liberals had 752 electoral victories in Quebec, to the Conservatives'

[28] A.C. Cairns, "The Electoral and the Party System in Canada, 1921–65," *Canadian Journal of Political Science*, vol. 1, no. 1, March 1968. See also the critique of Cairns's ideas in J.A.A. Lovink, "On Analyzing the Impact of the Party System in Canada," *Canadian Journal of Political Science*, vol. 3, no. 4, pp. 497–516, and Cairns's reply, pp. 517–521 in the same issue. More generally, see Douglas Rae, *The Political Consequences of Electoral Laws* (New Haven: Yale Press, 1977); Edward Tufte, "The Relationship Between Seats and Votes in Two-Party Systems," *American Political Science Review*, vol. 67, 1973, pp. 540–554; and Duff Spafford, "The Electoral System of Canada," *American Political Science Review*, vol. 64, 1970, pp. 168–176.

[29] The 1972 election constitutes a minor exception to this rule, since it provided a better balance than usual between popular vote and seats won. We have updated some of the numbers in this section to take account of elections that took place after Cairns published his article.

[30] Cairns, "The Electoral and the Party System," p. 61.

TABLE 12-1
DISTRIBUTION OF THE VOTE IN ELEVEN FEDERAL ELECTIONS, 1945–1984 (PERCENTAGES)

Popular Vote	1945	1949	1953	1957	1958	1962	1963	1965	1968	1972	1974	1979	1980	1984
Liberal	41%	49%	49%	41%	34%	37%	41%	40%	46%	39%	43%	40%	44%	28%
PC	27	30	31	39	43	37	33	32	31	35	35	36	33	50
CCF-NDP	16	13	11	11	9	14	14	18	17	18	15	18	20	19
Social Credit	4	4	5	7	2	12	12	8	4	8	5	5	1.6	.13
Other	12	4	4	2	1	x	x	2	2	1	1	1.5	1.7	3.7
% Turnout	76	74	67	74	79	79	79	75	76	77	71	76	69%	75%

 # OF SEATS

	1945	1949	1953	1957	1958	1962	1963	1965	1968	1972	1974	1979	1980	1984
Liberal	125	190	171	105	49	99	129	131	155	109	141	114	147	40
PC	67	41	51	112	208	116	95	97	72	107	95	136	103	211
CCF-NDP	28	13	23	25	8	19	17	21	22	31	16	26	32	30
Social Credit	13	10	15	19	—	30	24	5	14	15	11	6	—	—
Other	7	3	2	2	—	1	—	10	—	1	—	—	—	—
*Independent	5	5	3	2	—	—	—	1	1	1	1	—	—	1
Total Common Seats	245	262	265	265	265	265	265	265	264	264	264	282	282	282

x = Less than 1%

Source: CEO Reports

135. Cairns continues, "The ratio of 5.6 Liberals to each Conservative in the House of Commons contrasts sharply with the 1.9 to 1 ratio of Liberals and Conservatives at the level of voters."[31]

As these results indicate, the peculiar arithmetic of the single-member constituency system works differently for large than for small parties. A large party will gain the maximum number of seats if its support is widely dispersed, while a small party will obtain the maximum number of seats if its support is concentrated in a few areas.[32] The popular wisdom that the Liberals have traditionally wasted support in Quebec and the Conservatives have wasted support on the prairies has some basis in fact. With the exception so far only of the 1984 election, such a system has made adequate representation from Quebec impossible in the Progressive Conservative Party. Thus, although the Progressive Conservatives won 13.4% of the popular vote in Quebec in 1979, Prime Minister Joe Clark was faced with forming a Cabinet with only two elected members from the seventy-five constituencies in that province. The mirror image of that problem exists for the Liberals, who had to create a 1980 Cabinet with just two MPs elected from west of Ontario and none from west of Manitoba. All of this, suggest Cairns and many other analysts ranging from academics to the Pépin-Robarts Task Force on National Unity to the Royal Commission on the Economic Union and Development Prospects for Canada, exaggerates the already deep sectional cleavages in Canadian society by insuring that any partisan discrepancy among regions will be magnified significantly by the electoral process.

Other difficulties may be created by the Canadian electoral system. We have already noted the difficulties faced by the two major parties in acting as unifying or nationalizing agencies. Cairns points out part of the problem:

> Sectionalism has been rendered highly visible because the electoral system makes it a fruitful basis on which to organize electoral support. Divisions cutting through sections, particularly those based on the class system, have been much less salient because the possibility of pay-offs in terms of representation has been minimal.[33]

There are several instances in Canadian history where parties have emphasized regional and, more particularly, ethnic differences in order to get elected. In Quebec in the 1920s and 1930s, Liberal campaigns were often directed towards stirring up the fears and animosities of French Canada in order to maximize electoral support. The "Gordon Churchill strategy," named after one of John Diefenbaker's major ministers and advisors, in 1957 was another example of the effects of sectionalism. Over the years, it had become clear to the Conservatives that money spent in Quebec was money lost because, although a substantial minority of Quebec voters might support them, they would get very few seats. So the decision was made in 1957 to forget about Quebec and to concentrate on the rest of the country. The result was a handsome pay-off in terms of seats. Perhaps, however, this analysis should not be pushed too far. Until 1957 and since

---

[31] Cairns, p. 62.

[32] Richard Johnston and Janet Ballantyne, "Geography and the Electoral System," *Canadian Journal of Political Science*, vol. 10, December 1977, p. 855.

[33] Cairns, p. 62.

1965, the Conservatives consistently did spend a large proportion of their campaign funds in Quebec, and all regions of the country have shown a propensity to swing their votes one way or another together.[34]

Indeed, given the different relationship between seats and votes for major and for minor parties, the proper seat-maximizing strategy for a major party is to attempt to disperse its votes, while the proper strategy for a minor party is to concentrate them. The persistent efforts by the Conservatives since 1963 to gain more votes in Quebec, and the persistent and even more frustrating effort by the Liberals to do the same in the west, attest to the parties' recognition of this. Indeed, one of the major reasons that the Progressive Conservatives selected Brian Mulroney as leader in 1983 was that he appeared to be the candidate most likely to make a breakthrough into Quebec for the Tories. He subsequently delivered handsomely in the aftermath of the departure of Pierre Trudeau and several of his strongest Quebec ministers, gaining 50.2% of the vote and fifty-eight out of seventy-five seats.

On balance, however, as Cairns concludes, the electoral system in Canada has a detrimental effect on national unity: "This is essentially because sectional politics (which are exacerbated by the electoral system) has an inherent tendency to call into question the very nature of the political system and its legitimacy. Classes, unlike sections, cannot secede from the political system and are consequently more prone to accept its legitimacy."[35] We need not agree entirely with this analysis, but it does force us to ask whether Canadian unity suffers from the divisive effects of an electoral system that highlights and exaggerates our regional cleavage. If the cleavages are exacerbated by the federal structure and only slightly counterbalanced by the brokerage activities of some of its national political actors, then we have a serious problem indeed.

The answer would appear to be that our electoral system *does* create some problems for us in this respect. However, that does not translate into an immediate requirement for fairly drastic institutional reform, such as full-scale proportional representation. As we have seen throughout this book, and as many other analysts have noted, there are other ways in which national unity can be affirmed, and other reforms, such as partial proportional representation, an elected Senate, or a revamped and regularized system of intergovernmental relations, which should also be considered.[36]

THE DYNAMICS OF CANADIAN ELECTORAL BEHAVIOUR

The target of all electoral activities is the Canadian voter. What effect does it all have on him or her? Is all of the campaign activity worthwhile, or do Canadian voters merely troop to the polls to cast their ballots on the basis of factors such as

---

[34] M. Beck, *Pendulum of Power*, pp. 422–423.

[35] Cairns, p. 75. Cairns has failed here to note that classes may question the legitimacy of the regime without questioning the political community.

[36] See, for example, the Report of the Royal Commission on the Economic Union, vol. 3, pp. 60–87, for a recent examination of the topic.

ethnic origin, religion, or their parents' party loyalties, factors that cannot be changed by the parties no matter what they do in the campaign? The answer, according to the most thorough studies of why Canadians vote the way they do, is that campaigns do, indeed, have a significant effect. Almost half the Canadian electorate claims to make up its mind during the campaign, and, in 1974, 19% claimed they decided in the last week.[37] In 1984, the Conservative Party began the campaign running well behind the federal Liberals in Quebec, yet at election day polled 50% of the vote to the Liberals' 35%. Sixteen months later, Conservative support in Quebec was back to 23%.

In *Absent Mandate*, their study of the 1980 election, Harold Clarke and his co-authors demonstrated that only 37% of Canadian voters could be categorized as "durable" partisans — voters who show consistent, stable, and strong patterns of support for a particular party.[38] The other 63% of Canadian voters are "flexible" partisans — "either unstable in their partisanship over time, inconsistent between the federal and provincial levels of the Canadian political system, or weak in their intensity of partisanship." These either do not hold an identity at the federal level or define themselves as independents.

Some further evidence of the flexibility of the Canadian voter and the change-ability of the Canadian electorate can be gained from the following figures, from 1968 to 1980:

- 33% of 1980 voters were not eligible to vote in 1968;
- 29% of 1980 voters did not vote in at least one election;
- 42% of 1980 voters had switched parties at least once;
- 22% of 1980 voters had supported the same party in all elections since 1968.[39]

Thus, given the high degree of flexibility of the Canadian voter, we should not be surprised at the kind of large electoral swing that allowed the Progressive Conservatives to go from a small Opposition party in 1956 to a landslide majority in 1958; the Liberals to climb more than 7% in popular support between the May 1979 and February 1980 elections; and the Conservatives to more from 33% of the popular vote and 103 seats in 1980 to 50% of the vote and 211 seats in 1984. It also makes possible the kind of situation described earlier, in which

[37] Jon Pammett, "Elections," in Whittington and Williams, *Canadian Politics in the 1980s*, p. 275.

[38] The discussion in this section is based largely on Clarke, et al., *Political Choice in Canada* (Toronto: McGraw-Hill Ryerson, 1979), and *Absent Mandate* (Toronto: Gage, 1984), as well as on William Irvine, "The Canadian Voter," in H. Penniman, *Canada at the Polls, 1979*) pp. 57ff. The typology of partisanship is found in *Political Choice*, pp. 303ff. In summarizing a great deal of material in the little space available in a textbook, a good deal of richness is inevitably lost, particularly when the original sources already summarize a great deal of material. The interested reader is therefore urged to consult the originals. There is considerable other literature on the Canadian voter and on electoral volatility. See, for example, Adam Przeworski, "Institutionalization of Voting Patterns, or, Mobilization the Source of Decay," *American Political Science Review*, 1975, pp. 49–67; P.M. Sniderman, H.D. Forbes, and Ian Melzer, "Party Loyalty and Electoral Volatility: A Study of the Canadian Party System," *Canadian Journal of Political Science*, 1974, pp. 266–288; Donald E. Blake, "1896 and All That: Critical Elections in Canada," *CJPS*, June 1979, pp. 259–279; Jane Jenson, "Party Loyalty in Canada: The Question of Party Identification," *CJPS*, 1975, pp. 543–553. David Elkins, "Party Identification, A Conceptual Analysis", *CJPS*, 1978, pp. 419–446; and Jane Jenson, "Comment: The Filling of Wine Bottles is Not Easy," in the same issue. The last three of these articles deal with the volatility of the individual voter, the first three with volatility of electoral results.

[39] Clarke, *Absent Mandate*, p. 179.

an apparently perpetual provincial dynasty in Alberta or Quebec can fall from pre-eminence to almost instant oblivion.

Earlier, in discussions of the individual parties, we indicated something of the socioeconomic and demographic composition of party voting. However, while the aggregate impact of these variables does add up to some seemingly consistent patterns of inter-party differences, the ability of these variables to predict the voting behaviour of individual Canadians is relatively limited. What appeared at first to be consistent patterns, and what struck pioneering political scientists in the field of election studies as constituting rather good explanations of the voting behaviour of individual Canadians, turn out, on closer examination, to constitute mere descriptions of overall bases of party support at a given moment. However, socioeconomic variables do not tell us much about how individual Canadians make their voting decisions, nor about the circumstances under which they change their minds.

For that portion of the electorate that shows stable, long-term partisan attachments, region, religion, father's party identification, and socioeconomic class accounted, in 1974, for about 37% of the variation in support for the older parties and 17% for the NDP. But these voters constitute only 37% of the electorate. For the flexible voters, the amount of variance explained by these standard variables drops to 5% for the Liberals and 11% for the Conservatives. Given, then, that 63% of the electorate fits the "flexible" category, it is obvious that we will have to look further than simple socioeconomic and demographic variables to get a proper picture of how Canadians make up their minds about how to vote.

Clarke found the most appropriate explanation in the short-term orientation of voters to issues and leaders. In 1974, these short-term factors, combined with attitudes towards local candidates, were crucial determinants for 62% of the voters. Studies of the 1979 and 1980 elections revealed the same degree of salience for short-term factors. They therefore deserve our attention here.

Leadership It is a truism of political analysis that Canadians are highly leadership-oriented when they come to make their voting decisions. Survey results indicate that orientations towards the leader *do* make a considerable difference, but even today party loyalty is of even greater significance. For example, the percentage of people voting Liberal varied much more markedly in 1974 according to whether evaluation of the party was positive, neutral, or negative than according to whether the attitude towards the leader was positive, neutral, or negative.[40] Similar results are seen not only for all parties but for all elections from 1968 to 1980.

It is important that the pattern, if not the intensity, is consistent in the 1968 election when Trudeaumania was afoot, in 1974, when leadership was not a crucial issue, in 1979, when there was considerable Trudeauphobia, and in 1980, when the incumbent, Conservative Prime Minister Joe Clark, was being widely characterized in very uncomplimentary terms. This suggests that even in highly leadership-oriented contests, independent perceptions of parties do exist and are important determinants of voting choice. Contrary to popular wisdom,

[40] Clarke, *Political Choice in Canada*, p. 328.

then, in Canada, the party and the leader are not synonymous to the voter. This is, perhaps, fortunate for the political system as a whole, since all leaders declined in esteem in the eyes of the public and the media through the 1970s.[41]

Leadership has its greatest impact among the 22% of the electorate characterized as "flexible, low-interest partisans." However, it is important to note that for no party and at no level of interest, does leadership orientation ever explain voter behaviour better than long-term party identification. This does not mean that the parties are wrong to place as much emphasis as they do on leadership. Because long-term party loyalties cannot be changed easily, leadership is the main variable that can be manipulated in a manner that will have the greatest net impact on voting in any given election. We will see that the net impact of issues washes out because of the large variety of issues and because of the failure of the parties to differentiate themselves very meaningfully on the most important of them. By contrast, if the tide is moving in the right direction on the leadership issue, large net gains are possible, something the federal Liberals realized to their delight in 1968 and to their chagrin in 1979, and which the Conservatives regretted in 1980 but appreciated in 1984.

Issues If the impact of leadership is concentrated on flexible, low-interest voters, the impact of issues is concentrated mainly among the 27% of the electorate characterized as flexible, *highly interested* voters.[42] The impact of issues is considerably lower among the durable partisans, no matter what their level of interest in politics.

The problem faced by parties with respect to issues is that, to have a significant net effect on electoral results, there must be a significant "skewness" — that is, one party must be perceived much more favourably than another with respect to some key issue. Because most issues lack this skewness, and because there are so many possible issues, their overall effect tends to wash out in aggregate electoral results. At times, of course, one issue can tend to dominate in an election. If this should happen and if one party can establish a unique and positive position with respect to that issue, it may win considerable support. As an example, after the election of the Parti Québécois, and intermittently though the 1970s, national unity was just such an issue for the federal Liberals.

In recent years, unemployment and inflation have been the major issues, and no party has been able to establish a unique or identifiable position in dealing with them. In 1974, for example, 33% of the national sample identified inflation as an important issue, whereas no other single issue was mentioned by more than 10% of the electorate. Similar results surfaced for the 1979 and 1980 election surveys, while in 1984, unemployment was the dominant concern. However, typically, among those identifying inflation as most important in 1974, 15.1% switched to the Liberals because of it, and 12.5% switched to the Conservatives. These results — a bit surprising, in view of the fact that the Liberals were already in power, and might therefore have been held culpable for inflation — indicate that no party gained much net benefit from the issue. With rare

[41] Clarke, *Absent Mandate*, pp. 100–126.
[42] Clarke, *Absent Mandate*, pp. 77–94.

exceptions such as the national unity question in 1980, this low salience of issues in determining election outcomes is to be expected. For once one party identifies an issue as important, the others are forced to do so as well and the voter is left with little in the way of issue choice on which to make a voting decision.[43]

In fact, then, even though issues can be identified as a determining factor for a highly significant group of Canadian voters, the net impact of election campaign issues on the ongoing business of government after the election tends to be negligible. This is because parties react to the fact that issues can be important in such a way that:

[There is] a marked predilection for the quick-fix approach. . . . In their scramble for immediate advantage, parties try to assess the state of the public mind at the moment and tailor their issue agendas accordingly. The result is that issues are presented and discarded with remarkable rapidity. What sells, and not what's needed remains the guiding principle.[44]

Thus, in spite of the fact that a significant group of voters does claim to be concerned with issues, and in spite of the fact that

part of political mythology is that elections are called in order to resolve policy differences and . . . an incoming government will have a mandate to implement specific policies . . . cases in which this actually happens are extremely rare. More often, elections turn on only the most general of issues (such as "the economy" or "inflation") on which no single party can stake out a unique position, or on a multiplicity of smaller issues which together provide only the fuzziest of electoral mandates. "Leadership" on the other hand, a factor of discernible importance in each of the last three elections, provides a mandate not for a set of policies, but only for a set of actors. The mandate given a political leader in an election is a potentially fleeting one, lacking any real substance.[45]

CONCLUSION

It is in the combination of the nature of Canadian voting behaviour and the characteristic brokerage pattern of political-party behaviour in Canada that we may find some answers to the question of why Canadian parties and politicians may play a smaller role in the determination of government policies than many Canadians might wish they did.

The first and foremost function of political parties is to contest and, the parties hope, to win elections. To do that, they must, of course, mobilize votes. In the absence of an electorate that exhibits stable partisanship based upon socioeconomic characteristics, particularly class, parties must concentrate on leaders or short-run issue packages as a way to sell themselves. But, as we have seen, this leads to no solid mandate on which to base policy activities after the election.

[43] Clarke, *Political Choice in Canada*, pp. 337–338.

[44] Clarke, *Absent Mandate*, p. 97.

[45] Clarke, *Absent Mandate*, pp. 171–172. Both quotes adapted from *Absent Mandate*, H. Clarke et al. Copyright © 1984 Gage Publishing Limited. Used by permission of the publisher.

Parties that do act as if they have such mandates seem to alienate voters very quickly; and, realizing this, leaders are left with little choice but to flow with broad tides of public opinion, or, when these, too, are lacking, to concentrate on smaller issues with direct local impact. It is in the chemistry created by the Canadian voters' lack of consistent allegiance and the electoral function of Canadian parties that we find an explanation of the lack of major policy role for Canadian political parties.

All of this could change, of course, if Canadians suddenly began to base party support on enduring socioeconomic differences. But, given the relatively non-ideological nature of the Canadian electorate and the tendency of Canadian activists to participate in politics out of interest rather than out of any clearly defined policy objectives, we should not anticipate this happening. Canadian parties will go on running election campaigns on the basis of shifting, ill-defined issues and leadership images. Canadian voters will respond by voting in large numbers, but on the basis of very flexible partisanship. Canadian governments will go on being dominated by ministerialist politics, in which policy decisions will be made by the executive ministers and their officials, MPs will play a relatively passive role in the policy process, and the rest of the party structure will continue to have rather little influence on the policy outputs of government. What is determined by the Canadian political culture cannot easily be changed by such ephemeral features as internal party reform. Meanwhile, elections and campaigns will continue to be highly interesting and popular events, for, given the flexible nature of Canadian partisanship, their outcomes are anything but predetermined or certain.

C H A P T E R 1 3

INTEREST GROUPS IN CANADA

THE POLITICAL FUNCTIONS OF INTEREST GROUPS
NON-POLITICAL ACTIVITIES OF INTEREST GROUPS
A TYPOLOGY OF INTEREST GROUPS
THE INPUT ACTIVITIES OF INTEREST GROUPS
■ The Focus of Activity ■ The Methods of Influence
■ The Determinants of Success ■ Summary: Group Impact on Government Policy
THE OUTPUT ACTIVITIES OF INTEREST GROUPS
■ Administrative Functions ■ Information Dissemination
CONCLUSIONS

Interest groups articulate political demands in the society, seek support for these demands among other groups by advocacy and bargaining and attempt to transform these demands into authoritative public policy by influencing the choice of political personnel and the various processes of public policy making and enforcements.[1]

Interest groups are active everywhere in Canadian politics. The industry-financed Canadian Tax Foundation examines and criticizes the whole of the financial structure and taxation policies of government in Canada. The Canadian Bar Association often works closely with the federal Department of Justice and various provincial Attorneys General. Ethnic associations are vital to the operation of federal citizenship and immigration programs, and to the delivery of government services to new Canadians. The commercial banks work hand in hand with the Bank of Canada. At times, the Canadian Federation of Agriculture appears to be almost an extension of various departments of agriculture. Federal and provincial departments of labour work very closely with labour unions. Provincial medical associations and provincial governments bargain over the fees to be paid doctors by government medical plans and argue

[1] Gabriel Almond, "Interest Groups and the Political Process," in R.C. Macridis and B.E. Brown, *Comparative Politics* (Homewood: Dorsey Press, 1964), pp. 132–133.

over the priority to be accorded to health-services funding. Anti- and pro-abortion advocates demonstrate and counter-demonstrate frequently and loudly at legislatures and hospitals. Native associations negotiate the constitution with first ministers in front of television cameras. The list could be continued endlessly. Wherever government turns its hand, it will find some kind of organized group operating — and wherever groups operate they find that government activities affect them.

THE POLITICAL FUNCTIONS OF INTEREST GROUPS

The quotation with which we began this chapter identifies the articulation of interests as the pre-eminent political function of interest groups. However, the hundreds of active interest groups in Canada perform other political functions as well, and they also perform an array of non-political functions, which are often more important to their members than the political activities.[2] First, among their political functions, they reinforce the legitimacy of government policies. They do so in part by moving political demands through peaceful and legitimate channels. They also do so by insuring that the various parties interested in a policy decision do have an input to the process. Governments will often actively solicit the participation of major interests for just those reasons.[3] More broadly, they also reinforce support for the political system by providing an integrative force in society that can connect the individual to the political system. As sociologist Emile Durkheim put it:

> Collective activity is always too complex to be able to be expressed through the single and unique organ of the state. Moreover, the state is too remote from individuals, its relations with them too external and intermittent to penetrate deeply within individual consciences and socialize them within. When the state is the only environment in which men can live communal lives, they inevitably lose contact, become detached and society disintegrates. A nation can be maintained only if, between the state and the individual, there is intercalated a whole series of secondary groups near enough to the individuals to attract them strongly to their sphere of action and drag them, in this way, into the general torrent of social life.[4]

[2] Isaiah A. Litvak, "National Trade Associations," *Business Quarterly*, vol. 47, October 1982, pp. 34–42, identifies more than seven hundred national trade associations, most of which are at least moderately active politically. The functions of interest groups are covered in Paul Pross, "Pressure Groups: Talking Chameleons," in M.S. Whittington and Glen Williams, *Canadian Politics in the 1980s*, pp. 288–292.

[3] Paul Pross, "Pressure Groups: Adaptive Instruments of Political Communication," in Paul Pross, ed., *Pressure Group Behaviour in Canadian Politics* (Toronto: McGraw-Hill Ryerson, 1975), p. 6 and Pross, "Pressure Groups: Talking Chameleons," p. 287.

[4] From Emile Durkheim, *The Division of Labour in Society*, translated by George Simpson. New York: The Free Press, 1964. Cited in R. Presthus, *Elite Accommodation in Canadian Politics* (Toronto: Macmillan, 1973). While we have alluded to Presthus at some length in this chapter, his work has not found universal acceptance among Canadian scholars. See, for example, R.E.B. Simeon's review (in *Canadian Journal of Political Science*, September 1974, pp. 567–571) and the review by John Meisel (in *Canadian Forum*, May–June 1974, p. 44). Critics such as Simeon have been more critical of Presthus' research and presentation than of the conclusions quoted in this text.

Second, interest groups communicate.[5] They communicate the demands of society to government, as we have already seen, and, perhaps equally important, they communicate messages from governments to their members. This outward communication function is a vital one for government, since laws, regulations, and other policy outputs can hardly be effective if no one is aware of them. It is another reason modern governments are very anxious to encourage and reinforce the activities of interest groups.

Third, interest groups administer programs for governments. In part they do this by the communication function just mentioned. If a program of subsidies for a particular industry is established, the industry's trade association is likely to communicate the details of the program, and may very well gather and coordinate applications from firms for support. They also perform more direct administrative functions. Medical associations determine the division of government-provided fees among various medical specialties, and hospital associations gather data governments use in allocating funds among medical institutions. Law societies determine who is qualified to become a lawyer, and provincial colleges of physicians are largely responsible for the regulation of the medical profession in each province. Again, it is scarcely surprising to find that the mutual dependency between interest groups and government makes them close bedfellows indeed.

There is by no means unanimity that the pervasiveness of interest groups and their close relationship to government is a desirable feature of modern society. In particular, the belief that older and more legitimate institutions of government, particularly parliament and political parties, are being supplemented or even supplanted by an alliance between the executive level of government and the constellation of interest groups that characterizes society is a very disquieting one for many political scientists.[6] The potential displacement of political parties by interest groups is of particular concern. Some decades ago, it seemed possible to suggest, as Harry Eckstein did in 1960, that there is a nice compatibility between interest groups and parties:

> In democratic systems, parties must perform simultaneously two functions which are, on the evidence, irreconcilable: to furnish effective decision makers and to represent, accurately, opinions. The best way to reconcile these functions in practice is to supplement the parties with an alternative set of representative organizations which can affect decisions without affecting the position of the decision makers. This is the pre-eminent function of pressure groups in effective democratic systems as the competition for power is the pre-eminent function of parties.[7]

More recently, however, the concern has become that, far from supplementing the policy role of political parties, interest groups have taken on such a major role in the policy process that they have supplanted the parties as policy actors.

---

[5] Paul Pross, in "Pressure Groups: Talking Chameleons," cites this communication function as the first use made of interest groups by the state.

[6] A wide sampling of such views is to be found in *Canadian Public Administration*, 25, 2, Summer 1982, a report on the IPAC 1981 annual seminars entitled "Governing Under Pressure." The most extreme version, in which the state is hypothesized to have created groups as a means by which to control and manipulate society, is in Dominique Clift, "L'état et les groups d'intérêts: perspectives d'avenir," pp. 265–278.

[7] Harry Eckstein, *Pressure Group Politics* (London: George Allen and Unwin, 1960), p. 163.

This view was encapsulated by K.Z. Paltiel in summarizing recent Canadian literature:

> The key feature of current Canadian politics is the replacement of spatial by sectoral politics and the emergence of the administrative and special interest state . . . a functionalist administrative structure has produced a parallel structure of interest groups which has subverted the role of parties in the policy communication area. As representative government is reduced to the merely symbolic and as policy outputs are seen to be largely the result of the interface between private and public sector elites, the legitimacy of the regime, as well as its decisions, has begun to wither.[8]

If this view is correct, it has alarming implications for the future of democracy, for it will mean that those who are not represented by one or more of the major interest groups that characterize Canadian society in the 1980s, and who lack the organizational skills to create associations, are effectively excluded from consideration when policies are being made.[9] It could also mean that the support accorded to the regime will diminish over time, eroding the legitimacy of the state. We will return to a consideration of the role and influence of interest groups in Canada in an attempt to assess this view in our conclusions to this chapter. Before that, however, we turn to a consideration of non-political functions of interest groups, and then to an examination of the structures and techniques of influence used by groups and governments in their mutual interactions.

NON-POLITICAL ACTIVITIES OF INTEREST GROUPS

Throughout most of this chapter, we will be focusing on the governmental role of interest groups. This, however, is not necessarily their primary activity. In fact, for many interest groups, "political activity — activity carried on within the political system — is a minor and unwelcome addition to more general concerns."[10] These more general concerns include a range of roles that groups play both for their own members and for society.[11] Thus, for example, the primary activity of the Canadian Construction Association — one of the most active interests in Ottawa — is the dissemination of information and the maintenance of communication among the various members of the Association; and the most important activities of the Alcoholism and Drug Addiction Research Foundation relate less

---

[8] K.Z. Paltiel, "The Changing Environment and the Role of Special Interest Groups," *Canadian Public Administration*, 25, 2, Summer 1982, p. 201. Paltiel is summarizing papers by Paul Pross, referred to elsewhere in this chapter. His own conclusions and those of Pross in later articles — such as "Pressure Groups: Talking Chameleons" — are not quite so iconoclastic.

[9] The classic statement of this point of view is found in T.J. Lowi, *The End of Liberalism* (New York: W.W. Norton, 1979). The central theme of Lowi's work is that the relationship between organized interests and the state serves to exclude a large portion of society that is not part of this association, and thereby eliminate it from any effective representation in government. We return to Lowi's themes in the conclusion to this chapter.

[10] Pross, "Talking Chameleons," p. 3.

[11] Lowi, *The End of Liberalism*, pp. 36–38. On page 38, Lowi points out that "all such interest groups possess political power but only occasionally are they politicized. The rest of the time they administer."

to the activities of government than to research and publicity about drug problems. Table 13-1, based on a survey of national trade associations, indicates that, while "government relations" is the activity most frequently cited by members of such organizations as their central concern, many non-political activities rate high among association work as well. For the most part, these are outward-looking activities, which help the associations' members to deal more effectively with their organizational, professional, and economic environment.

One of the major preoccupations of any organization is self-maintenance. The leaders of interest groups are, quite naturally, interested in keeping their jobs and in insuring the survival of the organization within which they work.[12] The organizational-maintenance imperative also occasionally leads to a situation where the greatest enemy of an interest group is another interest group pursuing the same goal, for both are competing for the allegiance of the same clientele and for the recognition of the same governmental agencies.[13] For example, the Consumers' Association of Canada and the Canadian Home Economics Association did not always get along well, and at times competed with each other, even though their goals were the same.[14] The Canadian Federation of Agriculture and the National Farmers Union often find themselves implacably opposed, even though one would expect their goals to be similar. The classic cases of this type of behaviour are to be found in the annals of labour-union relations. For example, David Kwavnick has hypothesized that one of the major incidents of labour unrest in Quebec in the 1970s — the Lapalme mail-truck drivers' strike — was exacerbated because it became the focal point for strife between the Quebec-based Confederation of National Trade Unions and the nationally based Canadian Labour Congress. Kwavnick goes on to contend that "the CNTU leadership risked, and ultimately sacrificed, the most vital interests of the Lapalme drivers in a dispute which ultimately concerned only those leaders' ambitions for organizational aggrandizement."[15] Thus, for interest groups no less than for other large organizations, the welfare of the organization itself may supersede the substantive interests of the membership as the primary organizational goal.

A TYPOLOGY OF INTEREST GROUPS

To make sense out of the political activities of the great number of interest groups in Canada, it may be useful to classify these groups in some way. One can then anticipate that groups that fall in the same category will tend to behave in similar

---

[12] For a series of examples, see David Kwavnick, "Pressure Group Demands and the Struggle for Organizational Status: The Case of Organized Labour in Canada," *Canadian Journal of Political Science*, vol. 3, no. 1, March 1970, pp. 56–72.

[13] David Kwavnick, "Pressure Group Demands," p. 58.

[14] H. Dawson, "The Consumers' Association of Canada," *Canadian Public Administration*, v. 6, 1963, pp. 92–118. Elsewhere, however, Dawson points out that one of the most successful tactics of the CAC is to harness other interest groups to pressure government. See pp. 111–112.

[15] David Kwavnick, "Pressure Group Demands and Organizational Objectives: The CNTU, the Lapalme Affair and National Bargaining Units," *Canadian Journal of Political Science*, VI, No. 4, December, 1973, p. 583. See also Kwavnick, *Organized Labour and Pressure Group Politics: The Canadian Labour Congress: 1956–1968* (Montreal: McGill-Queen's University Press, 1972).

TABLE 13-1
ASSOCIATION ACTIVITIES
RANKED ACCORDING TO OVERALL IMPORTANCE*

	Frequency
Government Relations	90
Industry or Market Information	60
Public Relations	54
Product or Service Standards	38
Inter-Industry Relations	36
Industry Promotion	36
Interest-Group Relations	29
Other	22
Education	14
Employment Standards	11

*Reported as among the associations' top four activities.
Source: Isaiah A. Litvak, "National Trade Associations," *Business Quarterly*, vol. 47, October 1982, p. 36.

ways. There are a number of bases on which such a typology could be constructed: the structure of groups, their origin, their activity, or their goals.

One typology divides interest groups into economic and non-economic groups. The economic groups are, in turn, subdivided into agriculture, labour, and business groups; the non-economic groups are divided into nine sub-types.[16] Such a scheme, however, tells us relatively little about the activities of a group or about its orientation towards government.

Another more useful taxonomy classifies groups according to a number of paired opposite categories.[17] The paired opposites suggested by Robert Presthus are:

compulsory vs. voluntary
temporary vs. permanent
economic vs. instrumental
mass vs. selective
producer vs. consumer
local-provincial vs. federal
federated vs. unitary
oligarchical vs. participative
private vs. public

A classification scheme developed by Paul Pross suggests that most groups can be easily classified as belonging to one of four categories: issue-oriented, fledgling, mature, or institutionalized. Their classification will depend on their objectives, their organizational features, their orientation towards the media, and the type of political access they enjoy.[18]

[16] Englemann and Schwartz, *Political Parties and the Canadian Social Structure* (Toronto: Prentice-Hall, 1975), pp. 95–96.
[17] Presthus, *Elite Accommodation in Canadian Politics*, p. 67.
[18] Pross, "Talking Chameleons," pp. 298–299.

While these categories are useful, and while we hesitate to add yet another classification scheme to a field that already has plenty, we prefer to categorize interest groups in Canada along four more or less independent continua, one referring to orientation, one to structure, a third to origin, and a fourth to degree of mobilization. Any particular interest group can be located towards one side or the other of each of these continua.

The first continuum refers to *orientation*. It can be suggested that the activities of interest groups can tend towards either the *self-interested* or the *promotional*.[19] Self-interested groups tend to look towards the economic advantage of their membership, whereas promotional groups are usually interested in doing things for some reason related to the good of the community. For example, the Canadian Manufacturers' Association is primarily concerned with securing an economic, political, and social environment that will be advantageous to its own members. It is thus identified as a self-interested group. So is the Canadian Federation of Agriculture, which, when it approaches government, is concerned basically with securing outputs advantageous to the interests of Canadian farmers. On the other hand, members of the John Howard Society, which is interested in penal reform and prisoner rehabilitation, do not expect ever to become prisoners. Thus, the John Howard Society is identified as a promotional interest group.

A second continuum, perhaps the most useful one for predicting the methods of operation of a group, is that between *issue-oriented* and *institutionalized* groups.[20] In essence, this continuum refers to structure. An institutionalized group is relatively well structured and has existed for a long time. It will possess continuity and cohesion and a stable membership willing to support the organization's leaders. It will have extensive knowledge of those sectors of government that affect its activities, and good access to important decision makers. While such groups have concrete operational objectives, generally the maintenance of the organization itself and of its privileged access to decision makers is more important than any single issue. Such groups are therefore reluctant to use heavy-handed tactics.

Issue-oriented groups, as the name implies, are more ephemeral. They are concerned only with one or two issues and they usually do not outlast the resolution of those issues. Their structural characteristics are almost completely opposite to those of institutionalized groups. Intermediate points on the continuum would see groups defined as "fledgling" or "mature" as they move from more purely issue-oriented to more purely institutionalized. Issue-oriented groups have become more prevalent over the past two decades as education levels have risen and organizational skills have become more widespread among Canadians. They can appear quickly. For example, when it seemed that the 1982 Constitution Act would be passed with no mention of women's rights, a women's lobby was quickly organized from among many women's organizations, and sufficient pressure was brought to bear on federal and provincial governments to get section 28, which guaranteed sexual equality, placed in the Charter of Rights and Freedoms.[21]

---

[19] S.E. Finer, *Anonymous Empire* (London: Pall Mall, 1958), p.3.

[20] Pross, "Talking Chameleons," provides an elaboration of this typology.

[21] Penney Kome, "Anatomy of a Lobby," *Saturday Night*, vol. 98, January 1983, pp. 9–11.

When the federal government proposed, in the 1985 budget, to partially de-index old-age-security payments, a powerful lobby of senior citizens quickly appeared and succeeded in forcing the government to back down.[22] Since some issues remain in the forefront of attention for long periods, some single-issue groups, such as women's-rights groups, actually achieve considerable permanence and develop many of the organizational characteristics of mature groups.

A third continuum is between groups that have been primarily responsible for their own creation and maintenance, and groups that have been either created or strongly encouraged by government itself. The former type we call *autonomous* pressure groups; the latter are called *reverse* groups. Reverse pressure groups may be created because political decision makers are anxious to have all the inputs they can get before they set out to make policy, because they wish to create generalized support for their approach or specific support for some important policies, or because they wish to counter some other organized interest running against the decision maker's own policy predilections. In addition to this function of creating or mobilizing a clientele, they may also be used for communication with an otherwise poorly organized portion of the public, or even to administer some aspects of an agency's program. If there is no existing organized interest to which they can turn, policy makers will often try to create a completely new interest group, which they can then use in this process. Alternatively, they may attempt to reinforce existing groups.

At one time or another, at least half of all federal government departments have created such groups.[23] The modern aboriginal peoples' associations were intially promoted by the federal government, and are still essentially dependent on it for "core" funding. The Eastern Fishermen's Federation was encouraged and supported by the federal and provincial governments, and now is a major source of communication to and from the fishermen.[24] As the groups used in our examples illustrate, reverse groups are not necessarily quiet, subordinate, and supportive tools of government.

As would be expected, it is not always simple to decide where a particular interest group fits. For example, although the John Howard Society was not created by the government, the departments of Justice and the Solicitor General provide support for the organization — speakers for meetings, information and other services, and even, in a sense, personnel, since many members of the society are employees of those departments. The Consumers' Association of Canada has been given government grants to continue expressing the viewpoint of the consumer, and might have difficulty surviving without its ties to government, although it would not likely admit to such dependence.[25] The Canadian Council on Social Development receives a substantial portion of its funds from National

---

[22] Don McGillivry, "Tories Listen to Groups with the Loudest Voices," *The Montreal Gazette*, June 26, 1985.

[23] Presthus, *Elite Accommodation*, p. 79.

[24] Pross, "Talking Chameleons," p. 289.

[25] Helen Jones Dawson, "The Consumers' Association of Canada," *Canadian Public Administration*, vol. 4, no. 1, March 1963, p. 96; W.T. Stanbury, *Business Interest and the Reform of Canadian Competition Policy* (Toronto: Methuen, 1977); and J. Goldstein, "Public Interest Groups and Public Policy: The Case of the Consumers' Institute of Canada," *Canadian Journal of Political Science*, 12 March, 1979, pp. 137–156.

Health and Welfare; the National Welfare Council, which, as an advisory committee to the federal Minister of Health and Welfare, probably comes as close as possible to the pure reverse interest group type, occupies space in the federal department's headquarters building and is funded entirely by the department, but does not hesitate to be very critical of government policy in its recommendations.

Finally, groups may be placed on a continuum defined by their degree of mobilization, according to whether they are *active* or *categoric* groups. This continuum assumes that there are latent interest groups in society that may become active only if a pressing issue presents itself. For example, practising Christians can hardly be viewed as a single cohesive interest group, yet if the political system threatened to outlaw religious practices, this categoric group would soon become active. Canadians older than sixty-five are a categoric group but, as we have seen, when governments threatened their pensions in 1985, they very quickly became an active special-interest group with very great political power. A categoric group, then, is one to which people belong by virtue of some classification into which they fall, and one that could coalesce if the right issue presented itself.[26]

THE INPUT ACTIVITIES OF INTEREST GROUPS

The input activities of interest groups involve the initiation of policy, attempts to influence the process of priority determination, and efforts to shape the details of policy development to their own ends or to block policy changes that the groups feel might be detrimental. With respect to these activities, three basic questions can be asked. First, where must the group apply pressure in order to have its demands recognized? Second, what methods are employed by the group? Third, what are the determinants of success of a group?

The Focus of Activity

The location at which pressure is applied and the channels of communication on which a group concentrates are related to the structure of the government and its decision-making processes, and to the structure of the pressure group itself.

The Structure of Government[27]   Interest groups in Canada face two essential facts about Canadian government: it is federal in structure and parliamentary in

---

[26] See D. Truman, *The Governmental Process* (New York: Alfred A. Knopf, 1965), pp. 23–26. Truman makes a distinction, similar to our own, between *categoric* and *institutionalized* groups.

[27] The reader is referred, for general information, to the articles by Paul Pross, Gabriel Almond and Harry Eckstein cited above, to Eckstein's *Pressure Group Politics* to Pross' *Pressure Group Behaviour in Canadian Politics*, and to Robert Presthus' *Elites in the Policy Process*. Specifically Canadian examples are also drawn from articles by Helen Jones Dawson (in addition to those cited above, see "Relations Between Farm Organizations and the Civil Services in Canada and Great Britain," *Canadian Public Administration*, vol. 10, no. 4, December 1967, p. 460; M.G. Taylor, "The Role of the Medical Profession in the Formulation and Execution of Public Policy," *Canadian Public Administration*, vol. 3, 1960, pp. 223–225; and *Health Insurance and Canadian Public Policy* (Montreal: McGill-Queens University Press, 1978); Ronald W. Lang, *The Politics of Drugs* (Lexington: Saxon House, 1974); from Englemann and Schwartz, *Political Parties and the Canadian Social Structure*; from some valuable journalistic accounts in "Pressure Groups in Canada," *Parliamentarian*, January 1970, prepared by the Research Branch of the Library of Parliament in Ottawa; from Hugh Winsor, "Lobbying: A Comprehensive Report on the Art and Its Practitioners," *The Globe*

nature. The former means that power is widely dispersed geographically. The latter means that, within each of the capital cities, real decision-making authority is found in the executive part of government — the Cabinet and the bureaucracy. Divided jurisdiction in the Canadian federal system frequently makes it necessary for a group to exert influence at both federal and provincial levels of government.[28] In his survey of national trade associations, Isaiah Litvak found that about 60% of their effort was focused on the federal government and 40% on the provinces.[29] For example, when the insurance companies were trying to block government-sponsored medical-care insurance, they were forced to operate at both governmental levels. At the federal level, they attempted to block enabling legislation that would permit the federal government to enter into cost-sharing arrangements with the provinces; and at the provincial level, they attempted to prevent the actual implementation of the plan. Medical associations, seeking to retain the right to extra bill patients for payments above those provided by medicare, sought to press their case both with the federal government, during development" and passage of the Canada Health Act in 1983, and with provincial governments, which actually control medicare in each province. On the other hand, when insurance companies have tried to block compulsory, government-sponsored auto insurance, they have had to operate exclusively at the provincial level, where the jurisdiction in such matters lies. Under the existing system of federalism, decisions are often taken at both levels of government simultaneously. Thus, if a group wants to achieve some end in Canada, it may find that it is necessary to insure that both levels of government pass parallel pieces of legislation. That can force a group to deal with eleven separate governments.

The federal system of government also creates opportunities for interest groups, for it allows groups to exercise influence at one level of government by using the other level to make its case. For example, as part of a successful fight against tax-reform proposals, mining companies found it an effective tactic to first convince provincial governments, in provinces where their major operations were located, of the alleged detrimental impact of the reforms on investment and employment opportunities in that province. Provincial treasurers then made the mining companies' point in discussions with Ottawa over the reform proposals.[30] In another area, David Kwavnick has found that labour unions will act so as to reinforce the

Magazine, February 27, 1971, pp. 2–7; Clive Baxter, "Familiars in the Corridors of Power," *Financial Post*, July 12, 1975, p. 6; Isaiah Litvak, "National Trade Associations," *Business Quarterly*, Special Supplement on Managing Business Government Relations in Canada, Summer, 1985; from Charlotte Gray, "Friendly Persuasion," *Saturday Night*, March, 1983; from Hubert Bauch, "Senators' Old-Fogey Image Obscures Links to Business," *Montreal Gazette*, January 15, 1983; and John Sawatsky, "Power Plays: How the Lobby System Works," *The Montreal Gazette*, May 28, 1985. Interest groups hold an eternal fascination for investigative reporters, so interested students are likely to find material in the feature pages of large newspapers and in the business press, as well as in more academic sources. Another useful source is William Stanbury, *Business-Government Relations in Canada* (Toronto: Methuen, 1986).

[28] For an exhaustive coverage of the federal-provincial aspects of interest-group activity, see H.G. Thorburn, *Interest Groups in the Canadian Federal System* (Ottawa: Royal Commission on the Economic Union, 1986).

[29] Litvak, "National Trade Associations," p. 37.

[30] M.W. Bucovetsky, "The Mining Industry and the Great Tax Reform Debate," in Pross, *Pressure Groups in Canadian Politics*.

position of one level of government *vis-à-vis* the other, to more effectively pursue their organizational goals, and to maximize their access to the national decision-making process.[31]

Since modern government in Canada concentrates the bulk of power in the Cabinet and the bureaucracy, Parliament is not the primary focus for interest-group activity. As one experienced lobbyist said, "When I see Members of Parliament being lobbied, it's a sure sign to me that the lobby lost its fight in the civil service and the cabinet,"[32] He might have added that, while the group lobbying MPs may occasionally win a temporary victory, its chances of success in the longer run are slight unless the group can convince some Cabinet ministers as well. This point is well borne out by Table 13-2. In another survey, interest-group leaders in Canada and the United States were asked about their primary focus of attention. As Table 13-3 indicates, Canadian group leaders are far more likely than their American counterparts to concentrate on Cabinet and the bureaucracy, a clear reflection of the differing locus of power in the two nations.

Yet it is surprising how much effort has occasionally gone into a pressure campaign when legislation is before Parliament. One of the most spectacular examples of a group's failure to recognize the difficulties faced by a group once a bill has reached Parliament was provided by the Pharmaceutical Manufacturers Association of Canada (PMAC).[33] The PMAC began to exert pressure in December 1967, when the government introduced Bill C-190, which would allow the importation of drugs, with the consequent lowering of drug prices in Canada. The PMAC organized many witnesses to go before the parliamentary committee studying the Bill, besieged reporters with propaganda, attempted to get suppliers of the pharmaceutical industry to write to MPs, and urged drug-company presidents to contact the one hundred top industrialists in Canada and request them to write to Cabinet ministers and to the prime minister.

The PMAC won an apparent victory and breathed a sigh of relief, for the Bill died on the order paper before the Liberal leadership convention. But the victory was short-lived. In the following session, the Bill was re-introduced and, notwithstanding the PMAC's earlier efforts, it was passed in March 1969. Obviously the PMAC was successful in delaying the legislation somewhat, but if a government is really committed to a piece of legislation, it will be a rare pressure campaign that will stop its passage after it has been tabled in Parliament. In fact, the PMAC had lost the fight long before the Bill was approved in Parliament; once the Cabinet had approved the establishment of a bureaucratic interdepartmental committee to investigate drug prices, it had already signalled an intention to do something about high drug prices. Had the PMAC learned of this committee in time, then contacted and worked with the appropriate officials, and had it reached the Cabinet ministers before the Cabinet ever decided to present legislation, its chances of success might have been much greater.

---

[31] David Kwavnick, "Interest Group Demands and the Federal Political System: Two Canadian Case Studies," in Pross, *Pressure Groups.*

[32] Quoted in Englemann and Schwartz, *Political Parties and the Canadian Social Structure,* p. 105. Similar quotes appear in many of the journal articles on interest groups.

[33] Described in "Pressure Groups in Canada," *Parliamentarian,* January 1970, pp. 15, 16.

TABLE 13-2
IMPORTANCE AS INFLUENCE ON GOVERNMENT*

	Frequency
Interaction with Senior-Level Civil Servants	75
Interaction with Cabinet Ministers	50
Favourable Media Coverage	36
Public Opinion	35
Participation on Joint Business-Government Committees	32
Support of other Trade Associations	28
Interaction with Junior or Mid-Level Civil Servants	22
Contact with Prime Minister's Office	22
Appearances before Parliamentary Committees	21
Support of Special Interest Groups	18
Union Support	12
Interaction with Government MPs	6
Interaction with Opposition MPs	4

*Defined according to number of associations who ranked category as "very important."

Source: T.A. Litvak, "National Trade Associations," *Business Quarterly*, Autumn 1982, p. 39.

TABLE 13-3
TARGET OF INTEREST-GROUP ACTIVITY IN THE UNITED STATES AND CANADA (FIGURES
ARE PERCENTAGES OF GROUPS USING EACH LOCATION AS A PRIMARY TARGET)

Location	United States	Canada
Bureaucracy	21	40
Legislators	41	10
Legislative Committees	19	7
Cabinet	4	19
Executive Assistants	3	5
Judiciary	3	3
Others	9	6

Source: Robert Presthus, *Elite Accommodations in Canadian Politics* (Toronto: Cambridge University Press, 1973) p. 218.

There are, of course, exceptions to the rule that the parliamentary arena is a bad one for interest groups to play in. In a minority government situation, the Cabinet has tended to pay a great deal more attention to Parliament than during majority governments. From 1972 to 1974, any group that could enlist NDP members to support its cause was in a very powerful position, since the government of the day was dependent upon the NDP for its survival. Too, in a minority situation, parliamentary committees do not have a majority of government members, so the possibility of achieving significant amendments in committee is increased.

Sometimes simply delaying a piece of legislation is worthwhile to a group, and some important pieces of legislation have been delayed, blocked, or radically altered after introduction to Parliament. Notable cases have been the Combines Investigation Act, several aspects of the tax-reform proposals of 1973, and legislation respecting beef marketing boards. The exceptions may well be evidence of limited government commitment or of successful behind-the-scenes lobbying directed at the Cabinet. Certainly in our three examples, a very considerable effort was also directed at the Cabinet and the bureaucracy.

Table 13-2 indicates that only 4% of national associations pay attention to Opposition MPs. The survey on which that table was based was taken relatively soon after an election, when the Opposition was obviously some years away from any opportunity to gain power. However, in 1983 and 1984, as an election loomed larger and as the government's popularity waned, interest groups began to pay more and more attention to Conservative MPs. It is impossible to trace the link between their attentions and Conservative policy when that party won election, but it seems at least possible that some enterprising associations found their efforts rewarded.

It may be that interest groups will pay rather more attention to Parliament in future. As we will see when we consider recent changes to parliamentary rules, parliamentary task forces, standing committees, and even individual back-benchers may have considerably more influence in the late 1980s than they did before. For example, as a result of rule changes made in 1983, governments must reply, within a hundred days, to the recommendations of special parliamentary committees. As a result, such committees will play a significant role in setting the public agenda. The Special Committee on Indian Self-Government, for instance, was the subject of great attention by native associations. It published recommendations favourable to their cause and its report has shaped much of subsequent policy in this area. Some back-benchers' private member's bills will actually come to vote in the House of Commons in future, making the bills a potential route for groups to use in forwarding a cause. It would be a careless interest group indeed that failed to pay close attention to the activities of special House committees working in areas of concern to them.

The Cabinet is a particularly fruitful pressure point and the relationship between individual ministers and interest groups may be quite close. For instance, when they entered the Cabinet during the Pearson years, both C.M. Drury and Mitchell Sharp were members of the Canadian Manufacturers' Association. James Gardiner, minister of agriculture for many years under Mackenzie King, developed a close personal relationship with the Canadian Federation of Agriculture, dating, oddly enough, from 1941, when the delegates to a London convention of the federation held him a virtual prisoner for several hours until he agreed to some concessions. C.D. Howe, of all people, seems to have gotten along particularly well with the Consumers' Association of Canada. However, Howe was particularly well known for his ties to the business community.

> Every day, over the phone, by letter and in person, Howe was informed of what was happening or what was about to happen everywhere in Canada. Howe was . . . the leader of a national business community as well as a party leader and a minister of the Crown who saw no contradictions in his role; it was his job to enforce the public interest and the public interest was, ultimately, business's interest.[34]

---

[34] Robert Bothwell and William Kilbourn, *C.D. Howe: A Biography*, cited in Charlotte Gray, "Friendly Persuasion," *Saturday Night*, March 1983, pp. 11–12.

Meetings between Cabinet ministers and interest-group leaders go on constantly, and it would be a rare week indeed when a minister's schedule did not provide for several such meetings. Ministers often use groups as a counterweight to the advice of their officials, and certainly if a group can succeed in convincing a strong minister of the rightness of its cause, its chances of success are greatly enhanced.

One technique of dealing with Cabinet that is well-publicized but probably not very effective is the annual briefing. Several large national groups, such as the Canadian Labour Congress, the Canadian Chamber of Commerce, and the Canadian Manufacturers' Association, present an annual brief to the whole Cabinet, with much attendant fanfare. Such briefs are generally filled with pious generalizations; they let the Cabinet know something about the mood of the country, but they are not usually important with respect to any specific policy issues. They may be significant in strengthening Cabinet's resolve in dealing with some general problems, such as the deficit or unemployment. They also may provide us with an opportunity to see ministers at their most human: being forced to sit, during a busy day, and listen to platitudes or badly researched policy proposals often brings out the testier side of the ministerial character, particularly if the group's orientation is at odds with the minister's.

Clearly, then, groups are not blind to the pivotal role of the Cabinet in the policy process. But neither are they blind to the fact that, while individual ministers come and go, the bureaucracy goes on forever and is more generally accessible than Cabinet ministers, whose schedules are too crowded to provide much time for interaction with groups. Thus, if they wish to maintain an ongoing influence, which is vital to them, groups must make their target a close relationship with the public service. The close ties between the Canadian Federation of Agriculture and officials in the Department of Agriculture, between veterans' groups and the Department of Veterans Affairs, between consumers' groups and several departments, between the hospital and medical associations and the various departments of health, have already been noted. To these one could add the close relationships of industry and trade associations with various branches of the Department of Regional Industrial Expansion and Supply and Services, of financial institutions with federal and provincial finance ministries, of mining associations with resource and mining ministries, or of the oil industry with the governments of the producing provinces. The list can be multiplied endlessly.

In dealing with the bureaucracy, probably the major problem for an interest group operating in Ottawa or in one of the larger provincial capitals is to determine who to talk to. Policy structures, the details of the policy process, and the influence of individuals in the policy process all shift rapidly in modern governments. To an insider the shifts can be dizzying, to an outsider they are nearly unfathomable. For example, the changes in Cabinet-committee structure from the Pearson to the Trudeau and the Trudeau to the Clark governments, and the creation of new agencies supporting those committees, changed the location of appropriate pressure points. Under the Pearson government, an industry association might be content that it had done its work well if it had good dealings with the branches of the federal Department of Regional Industrial Expansion and with a few regulatory agencies; but to maximize its influence in the later Trudeau era, it would have been well advised to develop contacts with central agencies, such as the Treasury Board or the Privy Council Office, and it would have been wise to be acquainted with officials in the Ministry of State for Economic and Regional Development, and all or most of the departments headed by some seventeen economic development ministers.

No sooner might a group have succeeded in cultivating its relationships with that new set of actors than John Turner revised the system again, eliminating some of the new agencies and potentially throwing power back to line departments. Two months later, Brian Mulroney was prime minister, the bureaucracy was at least temporarily largely left out of major decisions, and a whole new cast of characters appeared on the scene. It is little wonder that the past decade has seen a proliferation in Ottawa of executive and public-affairs consulting services, which, for a more than modest fee, will guide the bewildered outsider in determining who to see, and coach the client in what to say.

In general, the most important targets of interest-group attention within the bureaucracy are not at the very top. The deputy minister is almost as busy as the minister, and almost certainly will not have time for the type of detail that may be very important to a group. It is the middle-level officials — assistant deputy ministers, directors, and senior policy advisors, who are most likely to be influential in shaping the details of policy and, unless the group is interested only in lofty issues far removed from the day-to-day concerns of most of its membership, it will often be better advised to deal with the middle than the top.

For the sake of completeness, the role political parties play in this process should be mentioned, although in Canada it is generally not directly important. Much has been made of the interrelationship between parties and interest groups in other political systems. In Britain, most labour unions are directly affiliated with the Labour Party. In the United States, it has sometimes been suggested that the Democratic Party is little more than a coalition of interest groups. However, in both Britain and the United States, the groups that have been most successful — at least with respect to their political activities — tend to shy away from formal party affiliations. After all, the party might lose the election; and, even if it wins, as many British unions have found to their chagrin, it may be easier to affect policy from outside the party hierarchy than from within. Except for the direct affiliation of some union locals with the NDP, and the close ties between the NDP and the Canadian Labour Congress, Canadian interest groups have generally avoided formal connections with political parties. At election time, the parties themselves will attempt to incorporate the most important demands of the main groups in their platforms; but these platforms mean very little, and the more politically active members of interest groups know it. At other times, the interest group that wishes to approach a political party faces exactly the same problems as anyone else — it is nearly impossible to find a Canadian political party between elections. Even if a group succeeds in that enterprise, the party structures are of practically no value in directly influencing an output of the political system.

Even in the matter of campaign finance, the role of interest groups is not particularly significant. True, some groups and many corporations are major contributors to the parties, but, as we indicated when discussing party finance, they do not typically attempt to use donations to buy specific influence. The publication of the names of donors would now make this difficult, and even before the most recent series of election-expense reforms, party leaders attempted to isolate themselves from knowledge of major donors.

Interest-Group Structure   Most large Canadian interest groups are federations, and the provincial bodies that make up these federations are often, in turn, coalitions of locals. Frequently, the local and provincial organizations are more powerful than the national structure.[35]

The Canadian Hospital Association is typical. It has a national headquarters staff of about forty and has modest office quarters in Ottawa, whereas the Ontario Hospital Association has a far larger staff and owns a large office complex, which it shares with Blue Cross, in Toronto. In such organizations, it is sometimes difficult to arrive at any consistent national viewpoint, for that requires the finding of common ground among provincial organizations with widely disparate interests. The national director or president may find himself or herself contradicted by some provincial group whenever a point is being made, and this dilutes the group's strength in dealing with government. Moreover, very often there are no direct dues-paying members of the national organization. National headquarters thus exist on funds provided more or less reluctantly by the provincial associations, and since what they give to headquarters they lose for themselves, the central office is almost certain to find itself underfunded. Other groups, such as the National Farmers Union, have no effective central structure at all.

All these factors will have some influence on the ways groups make contact with governments. While the Canadian Hospital Association works with the federal government, its provincial affiliates are often relatively more influential in their own provinces. The Canadian Chamber of Commerce has a general role in Ottawa, as spokesman for a segment of the business community, but it is at the local level that the Chamber's power is greatest. For example, when the Alberta government was amending the Alberta Labour Act, both the provincial chamber and some local chambers were frequently consulted. The Calgary Chamber of Commerce presented its views in Edmonton, and when the legislation was drafted, the ministers of labour and industry and development arrived in Calgary to discuss the draft legislation with the local chamber.[36] A similar role for the Canadian Chamber of Commerce during amendments to the Canada Labour Code is most unlikely. That the national organization does not usually wield such direct power in Ottawa is partly a reflection of the decentralized structure of the group.

There are some exceptions: a few interest groups, some of them not formal federations, have become, in fact, highly centralized. The Consumers' Association of Canada does most of its governmental work from Ottawa, as does the Canadian Manufacturers' Association. In such cases, of course, contact between the federal government and the national organization is much stronger than that between the provincial government and provincial organizations.

---

[35] Helen Jones Dawson, "National Pressure Groups and the Federal Government," in Pross, *Pressure Groups*, p. 30.

[36] Engelmann and Schwartz, *Canadian Political Parties*, p. 104.

The Methods of Influence

The methods of influence used by interest groups may be broken down into several categories. Direct and continuous contact is probably the most effective technique, but the presentation of briefs and other sporadic contact may also be useful. The numerous advisory committees of the Canadian government may provide a convenient channel of access, and interlocking memberships between political structures and interest groups may be even more effective. Influencing public opinion in order to get through to the government is sometimes used, and its use may be increasing, although this is not a favourite technique in Canada.

David Kirk, known in the mid-1980s as the dean of Ottawa interest-group representatives, understood the key assets a group must have:

> an understanding of issues, reliable information, persistence and workable policy proposals that harmonize with government goals. Most important, a lobbyist must be able to deliver. When Kirk said he had the solid support of the farmers, successive agricultural ministers knew he wasn't exaggerating.[37]

Direct Contact and Briefing   Part of the secret of Kirk's success was the direct contacts he cultivated in Ottawa over more than thirty years with the Canadian Federation of Agriculture. "From the start he established the close cooperation with ministers and officials that resulted, for example, in national marketing plans for farm produce during the 1960s and 1970s."[38] Other successful groups, such as the Consumers' Association of Canada, spend much time and effort establishing a liaison with senior civil servants in many departments. The Consumers' Association has succeeded to the extent that it is now often consulted informally before action is taken. For example, Statistics Canada has informally consulted the association before revising its consumer price index.[39] As for the Canadian Manufacturers' Association: "The overwhelming bulk of CMA input is and will continue to be in the form of unpublicized, informal discussions with constant interchange of visits between government officials and CMA staff and committee personnel."[40] This process of consultation has virtually eliminated the need for formal submissions, except for those cases in which it is appropriate to provide rather full documentation of research in support of a particular policy proposal. Since the bulk of interest-group contacts concerns relatively mundane policy matters, this is seldom necessary.

The groups most successful in using these techniques have permanent offices in Ottawa and cultivate a wide range of contacts within the bureaucracy. For the most part, they create an image of reliability about the information they provide, and they are careful to guard confidences passed on to them by their contacts. They are able to keep their own members from excesses such as intemperate

[37] Gray, "Friendly Persuasion," p. 12.

[38] Gray, p. 12. See also H. Dawson, "Relations Between Farm Organizations and Civil Service in Canada and Great Britain," *Canadian Public Administrations*, v. 10, 1967, pp. 450–470.

[39] H. Dawson, "The Consumers' Association of Canada," p. 109.

[40] "Improve Business-Government Ties," *The Financial Post*, October 7, 1972, p. 39; quoted in W.T. Stanbury, *op. cit.*, pp. 2, 3. See also John Sawatsky, "Power Plays".

statements to the press or strident public speeches. Unless a change of government seems imminent, they shy away from dealing (publicly, at least) with the Opposition; their work is with the government. The representatives often hold office for long periods, for it is essential that they know their own sector and the major actors in it very well. In all ways they seek accommodation, not confrontation — at least so long as their vital interests are met.[41] One veteran Ottawa columnist has likened a successful lobbying effort to the perfect crime: "[If] it is done properly, no one knows it has been committed."[42] Another notes that successful lobbying is "sort of like adultery. It's not the sort of thing the successful ones will talk about."[43]

Continuing contacts may also be made at the Cabinet level. Indeed, it may be that:

> Consultation with politicians has become much more important today because even if you could understand the complex decision making process . . . you couldn't trust it to be the process where the final decisions on issues would be made.[44]

Canadian groups attempt to influence both the ministers who deal primarily with their subject area and, if the interest group has a well-defined regional focus to its activity, the minister responsible for representing their region. Generally, the technique is simple. The group leaders request a meeting. If the group is important enough in the minister's sector or region, they get it. A succinct briefing is then the best way to attempt to convince the minister of a point. Often the same officials with whom the group deals on a day-to-day basis will be present, and the minister will discuss the points made later with them — another reason the effective group keeps up its bureaucratic contacts.

Another form of direct contact is the presentation of briefs to the standing and special committees of the House of Commons. This tactic has, in the past, seldom proven very effective by itself. Indeed, it could not be expected to be very effective, since the committee stage follows second reading of a bill, which constitutes "approval in principle" of the bill's major measures. Instead, ministers and their officials tend to seize upon briefs favourable to their position as tangible evidence of wide support for their policies, and to ignore briefs that are against them. Again there are exceptions, such as the fight against anti-combines legislation cited above, but even in the exceptional cases where a bill is withdrawn or altered significantly during committee stage, the briefing of committees is but one part of a well-orchestrated campaign. We have seen, however, that there is reason to believe that this may change in the future.

Direct contact between groups and government may also be of a more sporadic nature. Sporadic contact at the executive level will occur when a group that normally is not active politically becomes so because of a particular issue. For example, before 1970, detergent manufacturers had not been noted for political

[41] See "The Lobbyists," a three-part series in the Toronto *Globe and Mail*, October 25, 27, 28, 1980.
[42] Don McGillivary, quoted in John Sawatsky, *op. cit.*
[43] David R. Hayes, "A Word from the Wise," Toronto *Globe and Mail*, February 12, 1983.
[44] Ernest Steele, of the Canadian Association of Broadcasters, cited in Gray, "Friendly Persuasion."

activity, and were quite unknown at the Department of Energy, Mines and Resources, but the formation of policy to limit the phosphate content of detergents brought them to the door of the minister. Contact between groups and political decision makers may also involve write-in campaigns by members, or deluges of telegrams may be organized and groups of delegates may attempt to see MPs or Cabinet ministers. However, sporadic contact is usually a last-ditch attempt to change policies that a better-organized interest group, which cultivates continuing contacts, would have known about long before hand.

The contact people in Ottawa, whose job it is to provide continuing representation of interests before government, range from local lawyers and relatively unheralded officers of small trade associations up to the superstars of the lobbying game. Some of the stars, such as Ross Tolmie of the Ottawa law firm bearing his name, have acted as representatives of just one company (in Tolmie's case, Trans-Canada Pipelines). Others, such as Ernest Steele and David Kirk (of the Canadian Association of Broadcasters and the Canadian Federation of Agriculture, respectively), have represented large economic groups. Still others, such as Bill Lee or Bill Neville, who are, respectively, the founders of Executive Consultants Limited and the president of Public Affairs International, work for different clients at different times.

The most successful people in the interest-group game have in common excellent connections with politicians and senior bureaucrats, and many of them have been in and out of top political and bureaucratic jobs. Ernest Steele was Under-secretary of State for broadcast policy. Bill Lee was executive assistant to Paul Hellyer, during Hellyer's sojourn as Minister of National Defence, managed the 1968 Liberal election campaign for Pierre Trudeau, and did the same for John Turner in 1984. Lee's partner for a time was William Neville, who began as an executive assistant to a Liberal Cabinet minister, later ran as a Conservative candidate, subsequently became principal secretary to Prime Minister Joe Clark, and then became a senior advisor on transition to power for Brian Mulroney. David Golden was Deputy Minister of Defence Production, then became head of the Air Industries Association.

The lesser lights of the direct-contact business are certainly more numerous. More than four hundred of the seven hundred national associations have Ottawa offices, a figure that has doubled over the last decade. It is not always necessary to retain a big-name lobbyist for an organization to have an input to the policy process. Bureaucrats often welcome contact with interest groups as alternative sources of information, and for alternative perspectives on the policy-related or administrative issues with which they may be concerned, while we have seen that a minister may welcome a group's views as alternatives to that of the minister's permanent officials. Moreover, the backing of a strong interest group can assist the bureaucrats in convincing the Treasury Board or the Cabinet that one of their programs should be given a bigger slice of the budgetary pie.

In summary, the most effective presentations of interest-group views are the kind the public never hears about: they involve direct and informal contact between the bureaucracy and interest groups during the process of policy formulation and, occasionally, between group leaders and Cabinet ministers. A formal brief is relatively rare in these circumstances, although the fortunate or diligent group that learns from friendly insiders that policy related to its interests is being drafted, and then manages to get a brief to the officials and ministers concerned, may be in a good position to influence the formulation process. This is more likely to occur if informal and continuing contacts are religiously maintained.

The Advisory Committee Advisory committees are committees of outside experts or representatives of various interest groups concerned with a particular issue area. They are formed to advise ministers or officials on policies, and virtually every federal department can boast several. Organizations like the Canadian Tax Foundation and the Canadian Bar Association act in many ways as advisory committees to the departments concerned with their areas of expertise. The Canadian Federation of Agriculture is asked to appoint representatives to advisory boards in the field of agricultural policy, and the head of the Alberta Wheat Pool holds a seat on the Canadian Wheat Board. At one time or another, the Canadian Manufacturers' Association has held positions on at least thirty-five different advisory boards and committees, and the Canadian Labour Congress must sometimes feel that its major *raison d'être* is to provide members for advisory committees.[45]

The importance of such committees in the policy process varies from department to department and from time to time. Helen Jones Dawson concludes that, in the field of agricultural policy making, group memberships on advisory committees are more important in Britain than in Canada.[46] On the other hand, Malcolm Taylor once concluded that, in the field of Canadian medical policy making, advisory groups are extremely powerful and the membership of medical associations on them is a valuable lever.[47] Taylor, however, wrote that article before the fight over government-sponsored health insurance came to a head in the mid-1960s. The members of the Canadian Medical Association lost this fight even though they put all their resources into it and their representatives on advisory committees consistently spoke out against the plan. Their representatives on such committees are currently less listened-to by senior Health and Welfare officials than they once were, although at the technical level they retain some importance.

Not all interest groups are anxious to serve on advisory committees. For one thing, they may realize that such committees are often set up by government not to consult but rather to explain policies on which the government has already settled, and to co-opt potential opponents. Interest groups may also feel that, if they are consulted about a policy, they then lose their right to criticize it, or at least that their credibility when they do so is compromised. This point of view has been particularly characteristic of organized labour, which resists strongly government blandishments to participate extensively in tripartite labour-business-government advisory committees. In labour's view, these exercises are, more often than not, merely ways for government and business to legitimize policies

---

[45] "Pressure Groups in Canada," *Parliamentarian*, January 1970, p. 19.

[46] Helen Dawson, "An Interest Group: The Canadian Federation of Agriculture," p. 147.

[47] M. Taylor, "The Role of the Medical Profession in the Formulation and Execution of Public Policy," *Canadian Public Administration*, v. 3, 1970, pp. 245ff.

that are unsatisfactory from organized labour's perspective. Rightly or wrongly, this view, combined with overt union support for the NDP, has often tended to make organized labour the odd man out among Canadian interest groups.

Interlocking Memberships One of the most effective routes of access to decision makers is the very direct one provided by the fact that political decision makers themselves are often members of the interest groups that seek to influence decisions. The membership of some Cabinet ministers in the Canadian Manufacturers' Association has already been mentioned, and a search through the biographies in the *Parliamentary Guide* will provide many similar examples.

A fairly powerful example, though far from a unique one, is that of Anthony Abbott, who was Minister of Consumer and Corporate Affairs and, later, minister of state for small business in the Trudeau cabinets of 1976 to 1979. Mr. Abbott was

> appointed President of the Retail Council of Canada in 1971. A few years later he became an MP, and in September 1976 he was appointed minister. Having participated in preparing the Council's brief in respect of the competition act, four years later Mr. Abbott, as an MP, was able to examine the representatives of the Council when they appeared before the House of Commons committee examining the Stage 1 amendments. It is fair to say that Mr. Abbott, on becoming the minister, was familiar with business views on competition policy legislation.[48]

In addition, many of the senators in Ottawa double as lobbyists, and particularly as industry representatives. Of 89 senators in 1983, 60 were businessmen or lawyers. It is again, perhaps, indicative of the difficulties faced by organized labour in representing its interests to government that at the same time, only 3 senators claimed a trade-union background. In 1978 the members of the 104-seat Senate collectively held 219 corporate positions. In 1973, Senator J.J. Connolly represented both IBM and Gulf Canada in Ottawa, and Gulf's president noted that the Senator "occasionally opens doors for us and provides the proper atmosphere" for discussions with officials. The fourteen members of the Senate Committee on Banking, Trade and Commerce held 116 corporate positions and directorships in 1975. The committee deals with such legislation as anti-combines law and the Bank Act. The chairman of the Senate Finance Committee in 1983 was Senator Douglas Everett, a Winnipeg businessman and Liberal fund raiser for Manitoba. He was also chairman of Royal Canadian Securities and a director of General Foods, the Canadian Indemnity Company, the Continental Bank of Canada, and Eaton-Bay Mutual funds.[49] Many of the doctors who have been health ministers or senior officials in federal-provincial departments of health have also been medical-association members. The suggestion that the Canadian or provincial medical associations are consulted whenever medical personnel are appointed to government positions is an exaggeration, but not a wild one.[50]

---

[48] W.T. Stanbury, *Business Interests and the Reform of Canadian Competition Policy 1971–5*, p. 209.

[49] Hubert Bauch, "Senators' Old-Fogey Image Obscures Links to Business," *Montreal Gazette*, January 15, 1983.

[50] Engelmann and Schwartz, *Political Parties and the Canadian Social Structure*, p. 100.

Many of Ottawa's higher-level bureaucrats or their spouses are members of the Consumers' Association of Canada — a fact that can hardly hurt that organization's political activities.

A peculiar but conceivably significant form of interlocking membership is that of part-time trade-association representatives in the parliamentary press gallery. Membership in the gallery does constitute an excellent entrée to ministers' offices; as ex-gallery president Charles Lynch put it, it is "a continuing problem. It's always been assumed over the years that the Gallery is used in this way by certain people, but it is very difficult to police."[51]

On occasion, an interest group will succeed in getting one of its members on a royal commission in which it is interested. The Hall Royal Commission on Health Services included two members nominated by the Canadian Medical Association.[52] In this case, however, it is interesting to note that the commissioners were true to their task rather than to the medical association, and were instrumental in the preparation of a report the medical association roundly condemned.

An even more important type of influence on political decisions occurs as people move from the private sector into a government department concerned with regulating the industry from which they come. The situation is further complicated when the same individual later moves back again to the private sector. When the Department of Industry, Trade and Commerce is recruiting employees to regulate the iron and steel industry, it naturally looks to people from that industry: after all, their experience is relevant. Later these same people may move back to a more or less grateful corporation. Such influence is not necessarily harmful, and it is officially encouraged through "executive-interchange" arrangements, but the close web that can be woven between those who regulate and those who are regulated, and between groups demanding certain policies and those who have the power to make the policies, does bear continuing scrutiny.

Public Relations   Because of the importance of Congress in the decision-making process in the United States, groups in that country frequently attempt to bolster their position by conducting large-scale public-relations campaigns intended to add general public support for their cause to the support of their own members. This, they hope, will, in turn, convince influential congressmen of the wisdom of supporting their cause. By contrast, because of the relatively minor policy role played by back-bench members of parliament, Canadian groups depend more on their access to bureaucratic decision makers and on the expertise they possess than on demonstrated public support. Nevertheless, because public support, or the appearance of it, can never be ignored by political decision makers, groups will from time to time launch large-scale public-relations offensives to supplement their other sources of influence.

Often it is groups that have been unsuccessful in establishing good lines of access to the decision makers, or groups that do not control a certain area of expertise, that are forced to utilize the public-relations campaigns as a tactic

---

51 *The Ottawa Citizen*, March 4, 1976, p. 33, cited in W.T. Stanbury, *op. cit.*, p. 37.

52 Engelmann and Schwartz, *Political Parties*, p. 100. See also Malcolm Taylor, *Health Insurance and Canadian Public Policy, passim.*

SYSTEM-ENVIRONMENT LINKAGES

of political influence. At other times it will be a group that stands to lose a good deal by a decision it has been unsuccessful at blocking at an earlier stage in the policy process. The Canadian Petroleum Association launched a $4 million advocacy advertising campaign against the National Energy Program in 1982. In 1981, the Auto Parts Manufacturers Association ran a full-page ad, complete with a "mail-to-Prime-Minister-Trudeau" coupon, to support an embargo against Japanese car imports.[53] Such instances, however, are not as common in Canada as they are in the United States. The lengthy series of newspaper advertisements for American fighter aircraft in the years before a final decision was made on what fighter aircraft to choose for Canada has been rather an anomaly in Canadian politics. Indeed, such campaigns are looked upon in Canada with some disdain — not only by the authorities in the system, but by other interest groups as well — for the recourse to these tactics is often taken to be indicative of weakness or of failure in more traditional tactics. However, given the success of such public-relations campaigns as that operated by the various manufacturing interests against anti-combines legislation or by the Canadian Mining Association, one might be tempted to attribute a little more efficacy than is usually credited to such tactics.[54]

Occasionally a public-relations campaign will backfire. In 1978, as part of its continuing struggle to gain higher fees within medicare, the Ontario Medical Association began to publicize the fact that many physicians were leaving Ontario to practise in the United States, where incomes were considerably higher. Presumably the intention was to create public pressure on the government to raise fee schedules, and hence to keep Ontario doctors at home. The result was rather different. The Ministry of Health had become convinced that a significant part of their difficulties in controlling health-care costs was created by too many physicians generating demand for extra services. The ministry estimated that every extra doctor in the province generated about $250,000 per year in extra demand for services in 1978. With no statistical indication that anyone's health was much improved by extra physicians, and with Ontario already having a population-to-physician ratio better than that recommended by any world authority, the health ministry was not particularly sorry to see doctors leaving. Moreover, the public reaction to physicians — whose earnings are, on average, more than four times that of the ordinary Canadian worker — wanting to leave to get more money in the United States tended to be something less than sympathetic. The medical association did not do particularly well in fee negotiations that year, and quickly dropped that campaign in favour of encouraging doctors to opt out of the medical plan in order to put upward pressure on fees. The denouement of the tactic was the Canadian Health Act and related provincial legislation intended to eliminate extra billing.

[53] Isaiah Litvak, "Lobbying Strategies and Business Interest Groups," p. 136.

[54] One point of view that dissents from the conventional wisdom is that of S.D. Clarke. Writing in 1938. Clarke suggested: "the major changes in government policy have been brought about through the mobilization of public opinion rather than through the application of technical counsel." In "The Canadian Manufacturers' Association." Clarke is quoted in *CJEPS*, 4, 1983, p. 522. For a more disparaging view of public-relations lobbying, see "Lobbying in Ottawa Still in Stone Age," *Calgary Herald*, October 18, 1985.

In any event, successful groups seldom employ only one tactic at a time. A full-scale campaign will involve several techniques used simultaneously to back up continuing close contact with decision makers. For example, when the Consumers' Association of Canada began its campaign against trading stamps, it requested that all its members write to MPs and ministers; it made submissions to local authorities and to federal and provincial Attorneys General; it made submissions to the prime minister and the Minister of Justice; it obtained the full support of many other groups, including the Retail Merchants Federation, the Canadian Federation of Agriculture, the Canadian Labour Congress, and various women's groups; and, simultaneously, it provided material for the media so that they, too, could become involved in the issue. In spite of this impressive effort, the Association was not totally successful, although market forces eventually completed their work. Speculation about why they weren't successful leads directly to the next consideration of this chapter: what determines the effectiveness of interest groups influencing the policy process?

The Determinants of Success

Some groups are much more successful in influencing government than are others. Yet even the highly successful groups occasionally suffer significant reversals in their attempts to influence policy. Our look at the determinants of the success or failure of a group will examine the group's own structure and that of government, the existing policy orientations of the government, and the extent of conformity of the group's interest to the needs of the environment.

The Structure and Resources of the Group   Plainly enough, one of the most important resources any group can have is money, and most interest groups, even those we might usually consider well-to-do, are chronically short of it. The Canadian Federation of Agriculture is probably fairly typical: it receives widely varying amounts of money from year to year, as farm fortunes rise and fall. Many industry associations suffer the same problem, for they are vulnerable to cutbacks whenever their industry hits a cyclical downturn. Promotional interest groups seem to suffer even more difficulty in finding money than self-interest groups, while single-issue groups, particularly when they are also promotional in nature, are the most vulnerable of all.

Not all interest groups are perpetually short of funds; indeed, some of the most powerful are very well-financed. In a 1982 survey of national trade associations, Litvak found that 64% of his ninety-three respondents had annual budgets of less than $600,000, but 26% had budgets larger than $1 million, and two reported budgets greater than $10 million.[55] The Canadian Manufacturers' Association is probably one of the last groups. It had an annual budget of nearly $1 million in the late 1960s. By 1973, its annual salary bill alone for its full-time staff was greater than $1 million, and, presumably, current dollar figures would at least quadruple that figure. Overall, the CMA budget is greater than that of our national

---

[55] I.A. Litvak, "National Trade Associations," p. 36.

political parties.[56] Its main source of funds is membership dues from more than nine thousand firms, which represent more than 80% of Canada's manufacturing capacity. For its money, the CMA is able to buy, among other things, a permanent staff of more than 190 people, with at least 70 experts in various fields related to the promotion of interests of Canadian industry. Thus, CMA briefs to governments are invariably well-prepared, and often influential in the formulation of regulations or the creation of new legislation.

With its budget, the CMA is able to carry on a wide array of activities.[57] Its most effective activities are almost certainly related to its efforts to influence the implementation of legislation. The CMA studies all regulations made under the Customs Act, the Excise Tax Act, the Income Tax Act, and the various sales tax acts, and makes representations to the bureaucracy in those areas where the departments have wide discretionary powers. The CMA is concerned with the formulation and application of all regulations dealing with restrictive trade practices, monopolies, combines, and mergers. It cooperates with provincial departments of education and with federal manpower authorities to provide information about what employee skills are required and what training programs would be useful. Such pervasive contracts with governments are made possible by the large financial resources available to the CMA. With its impressive organization and solid financing, it is hardly surprising that the Association is so successful.

The number of members an interest group can boast is a less important determinant of success than one might expect. Decision makers know that a person's membership in a group does not guarantee agreement with the group's views on a particular issue. If sheer numbers were the determining factor, labour organizations would be Canada's most important interest groups. In fact, a more important attribute of a group may be its organizational cohesiveness. If an organization's executive really does speak for its members, and if the members might be mobilized en masse in support of the group's ideas, any threats the group makes or implies will have considerable credibility.

The prestige of a group is important. Decision makers may be impressed by the group's ideas in direct proportion to how impressed they are by its members as individuals. Almost everyone will at least listen to the medical associations, and the Business Council on National Issues makes much of the fact that its members include the chief executive officers of Canada's 150 largest corporations. By contrast, the Canadian Piranha Breeders' Association or the Canadian Institute of Motorcycle Buffs might have more difficulty getting a hearing. Monopoly over a certain area of expertise is a potent factor in determining the prestige of a group. The Canadian Bar Association, for instance, is always listened to with respect by authorities both because it is the only national outlet for the legal profession in Canada and because it has established a reputation for reason in its recommendations. The power of knowledge was recognized early on by John Bulloch in his

---

[56] "Pressure Groups in Canada." *Parliamentarian*, January, 1970, pp. 13–14; and W.T. Stanbury, *op. cit.*, pp. 208ff.

[57] "Pressure Groups in Canada," p. 18.

struggle to make the Canadian Federation of Independent Businessmen into a significant political force. Said Bulloch:

> I began to see how the system is stacked in favour of those who own all the lawyers. I found out that the big corporations, without being conspiratorial, control the knowledge factory in the country, all the positions that government takes are the product of conversation, the chinwags, that go on between the experts who are owned by the major corporations and the trade unions and the experts who work for government. It's a mandarin to mandarin process.[58]

Prestige may also depend on how much the government needs the expert resources of the group, on the past record of the group in its relationship with the government, and on the socioeconomic status of group members.

Given all these factors, it is not surprising that many of the promotional and issue-oriented interest groups have great difficulty playing in the same arena with their institutionalized and self-interested counterparts. They lack funds; their leaders come and go and are mostly volunteers; and the leaders can never be sure that members will follow them. The techniques used by the groups are often distasteful to élite policy makers, and the groups are seldom able to keep up their activities long enough to seriously disrupt the policy process and seldom able to insure that members will turn out for demonstrations. Those few that can (women's organizations are examples) have considerable success in garnering concessions. Issue-oriented and promotional groups also suffer from difficulties in defining their own priorities, since no clear economic self-interest defines it for them. The job of influencing policy is thus quite different and much more difficult for most of the issue-oriented and promotional groups than it is for members of well-institutionalized and well-connected groups.

The Structure of Government   Among those who write about interest groups, there is some disagreement concerning just what influence the structure of government has on group effectiveness. It is often suggested that interest groups are more successful in the United States than in Canada because the congressional system, with its many centres of decision making, is much more open to group activity than the parliamentary system. In the United States, if a group is not successful at the presidential level, it may still influence congress or the bureaucracy, each of which is a separate centre of power. In Canada, if a group fails with the bureaucracy and Cabinet, which are closely tied together, it is in considerable trouble.

Such suggestions oversimplify the situation. Britain, with a system more centralized than Canada's, has a very high level of interest-group activity, so a parliamentary form of government need not mitigate against such activity. Interest-group activity has, in any event, proliferated in Canada over the past decade. Moreover, because Canadian groups tend to deal with the bureaucracy, much of their activity is hidden from public view. These quiet dealings with anonymous bureaucrats certainly create an *appearance* of lesser activity than prevails in the

---

[58] Quoted in Alexander Ross, "How to Join the March to New Politics," *Quest*, February 1977, p. 47: cited in W.T. Stanbury, *Business Interests*, p. 212.

United States, but perhaps the actual level of influence may be as great or even greater in Canada.[59] There has as yet been very little investigation of interest-group activity in the provinces, and that, too, may lead to a consistent under-estimation of the strength of interest-group activity in Canada. We saw earlier that national trade associations direct 40% of their activity to the provincial level.

It is also difficult to determine whether Canada's federal system aids or hinders interest-group activity. On the one hand, we have suggested that it does provide more access points at which change undesirable to a group can be blocked. On the other hand, it imposes on groups, most of which are perpetually short of money, the necessity to cover several capital cities simultaneously, and it often forces a federalized structure upon the groups, which is no less onerous for the groups than for the nation. Thus, most groups are forced to concentrate on only a few issues that affect them, and on immediate goals.

There is probably a mutually reinforcing effect between the distribution of power within the federal system and the activities of interest groups. The distribution of power influences the structure, cohesion, and even the existence of groups, while the groups, in turn, will attempt to influence the distribution of powers so as to enhance the strength of the governments with which they are most closely affiliated.[60] Thus, for example, in the 1960s and 1970s, national student organizations in Canada, the National Federation of Canadian University Students (NFCUS) and its successor, the Canadian Union of Students (CUS), waxed and waned in strength in direct proportion to the level of involvement of the federal government in university education. The Canadian Labour Congress tends to make demands (such as a stronger federal involvement in health-insurance plans) that will result in a strengthening of the federal role, and the Confederation of National Trade Unions tends to make demands that will reinforce the strength of "their" government in Quebec. "Strong governments give rise to strong interest groups which can realistically make demands when satisfaction would necessitate an expansion of the role of the government upon which the demands are made."[61]

But whatever the overall impact of federalism, it does provide a larger number of points of access than the interest group would have in a unitary system. Given that the ultimate minimum requirement for the political success of any interest group is *access*, we can conclude that groups in Canada have a wide range of opportunities for political influence. On the other hand, rapid changes within federal and provincial government structures and constant shifts in the balance of power between the various levels of government conspire to impose upon interest groups a requirement for nimbleness and constant attention to the question of who is doing what in areas of interest to the group.

Overall Government Policy   Failure to recognize the overall direction of government policy and to work with it, and with the public opinion that lies behind

---

[59] See particularly Robert Presthus' *Elites in the Policy Process.*

[60] David Kwavnick, "Interest Group Demands and the Federal Political System."

[61] P. Pross, *Pressure Group Behaviour in Canadian Politics*, p. 83.

it, can be disastrous. The Canadian Petroleum Association and the multi-national oil firms made such a mistake in 1980. The returning Liberal government, buttressed by public opinion that was both mildly nationalistic and strongly against big oil companies stated clearly that it was the federal government's intention to intervene in a major way in all aspects of the oil industry. The industry, misreading the state, public opinion, and the direction of government policy, didn't believe it was going to happen. It did, however, in the form of the National Energy Program, which cut far more deeply into the petroleum sector than it might have done had the oil companies correctly interpreted the prevailing policy directions of government and ridden with them in an attempt to mold them. Bill Neville, now president of Ottawa's largest executive consulting company, is quoted as saying:

> This was a classic example of what can happen when you misread the political climate. The key to successful lobbying is realizing when a general objective has widespread public support, associating yourself with that objective, then trying to alter how it is eventually expressed as public policy.[62]

As concern with the government deficit rose in the mid-1980s, and as expenditure reductions increasingly took hold in government programs, it became more and more difficult for groups demanding new or increased government expenditures to be successful. Conversely, groups such as business associations could claim greater success, since their view—that governments should reduce their activities—was much more in keeping with the prevailing direction of government policies.

The Nature of the Environment An interest group will succeed best if its overall aims are in keeping with the prevailing values of the society in which it operates. In Canada, the activities of interest groups are generally perceived, at least by government decision makers and other élites, to be legitimate and worthwhile: because the environment is supportive of their activities. For instance, 93% of the MPs interviewed in the early 1970s agreed that "most legislators do not regard the activities of lobbyists as a form of improper pressure," and 85% agreed that "interest groups are necessary to make government aware of the needs of all the people."[63] Donald MacDonald, former federal Minister of Finance and later chairman of the Royal Commission on the Economic Union, is quoted by columnist Donald MacGillivry as saying:

> What is of greatest value is for the minister to be apprised of the impact of the legislation from the particular viewpoint of the group concerned. Legislation must of necessity speak generally but there may be special cases which persons in a particular industry or group might recognize more easily than can someone in government surveying industry or the community generally.[64]

The supportive nature of the environment for interest-group activity in Canada appears to apply more to business-oriented than to consumer-oriented and labour

---

[62] Cited in David Hayes, "A Word to the Wise," Toronto *Globe and Mail*, February 12, 1983.

[63] Presthus, "Interest Groups and the Canadian Parliament," p. 455.

[64] Cited in J.E. Anderson, "Pressure Groups and the Canadian Bureaucracy," in W.D. Kernaghan, *Bureaucracy in Canadian Government*, p. 102.

groups. W.T. Stanbury sums the situation up by pointing out that "the socially approved pursuit of a living profit together with large-scale intervention by government in the nation's economic life has resulted in a combination of economic affairs unequally suited to ensure the dominance of producer interests over consumer interests."[65]

Summary: Group Impact on Government Policy

Access to the decision makers of government is the *sine qua non* of interest-group influence on public policy, but in a way, that is *all* it is, for, having convinced decision makers to listen to the group's case, the group must still be convincing about the merits of its argument. Because a minister must ultimately seek re-election, he or she will not always meet the demands of big business or single-issue groups at the cost of broader, if less articulate or less organized, interests; the group must make its case on both technical grounds and on the grounds of some wider appeal to public support. Similarly, because the bureaucrat must ultimately sell a policy idea to the minister, he or she must not automatically accede to the demands of a close friend or client, unless those demands have at least some broad support in Canadian society, and unless they are well-researched and documented. Tommy Shoyama, a former deputy minister of finance, notes: "The person with documentary information to back up his cause is far more effective than one who pounds you on the back and says you are a wonderful fellow."[66]

By way of illustration, we can return to the example of the Canadian Medical Association at the height of its power in the late 1950s and early 1960s. Having analyzed that group's activities, one writer attributed its relatively high degree of success not only to its privileged access to the focal point of decision making in its field, but also to the Association's prestige; the identification of the medical profession with the public interest; the cohesiveness of the group's membership; the lack of articulation of an opposing point of view; and general agreement among key policy makers on the group's high level of responsibility and public interest.[67] Whether the medical associations will retain quite such a high level of influence after the extra-billing wars of the 1980s remains to be seen; but two decades ago, they provided a classic picture of a powerful group.

THE OUTPUT ACTIVITIES OF INTEREST GROUPS

Many organizations are deeply involved in the administration of government policy. For example, even though they might shudder to think so, doctors are acting as public employees when they make out birth and death certificates or process hospital admissions or health-insurance claims. When they sit on hospital boards or workers' compensation boards, and when they administer public-health programs, they are acting as agents for important executive outputs of the political system.

---

[65] W.T. Stanbury, *Business Interest and the Reform of Canadian Competition Policy 1971–5*, p. 45.

[66] Cited in John Sawatsky, "Power Plays; How the Lobby System Works," *Montreal Gazette*, May 28, 1983.

[67] M. Taylor, "The Role of the Medical Profession in the Formulation and Execution of Public Policy," p. 254.

And many argue that, in practising under medicare, they are really employees of the state, something that is anathema to many of them. Indeed, "no other group is as deeply involved in public administration . . . despite the fundamental antipathy between the healing arts and the bureaucracy."[68] Similarly, the Canadian Legion is vital in the administration of veterans' pensions through close cooperation with the Department of Veterans Affairs; and provincial hospital associations are generally important in their management of hospital programs in their province. The output activities of interest groups can be divided into those of an *administrative* nature, where the group or its members are a direct part of the output process, and those of an *informational* nature, where the group is acting as an indirect agent of the political system. Each of these output roles bears more elaboration.

Administrative Functions

One of the most important administrative functions of many groups, and certainly the most cherished by the group itself, is self-regulation. For example, society assumes it would be undesirable to have a large number of unqualified people claiming to be doctors or dentists or lawyers, or perhaps even teachers. Accordingly, governments delegate self-policing powers to the medical profession, to law societies, and to some teachers' groups, which allow them to define who is qualified to practise their profession. This self-regulatory mechanism extends far in Canadian society, for not only are professions controlled in this way, but so also are trades and crafts. The function extends beyond the mere definition of who is qualified to practise, and includes a definition of ethical or fair practices and appropriate fee structures. In this form, such mechanisms have also evolved in the business community, through Better Business Bureaus and other self-explanatory business associations. Were it not for the self-regulatory functions of many interest groups in society, the governmental structure in Canada would have to be considerably larger than it is now. The self-regulatory function is particularly valuable to groups because of the monopoly position it gives group members in the provision of services — and, of course, in receiving the rewards therefrom. The right to restrict numbers of practitioners of a trade is crucial in maintaining the incomes of the members of the trade, and so it is guarded jealously by the association holding that right.[69]

The actual administration of government programs is also an important function of many groups. The administrative tasks many doctors carry out under government medical-insurance programs have already been mentioned. In a similar way, grain-elevator cooperatives and farmers' associations administer many aspects of government farm price-support programs; groups interested in fighting pollution provide inspection services and warn government agencies of sources of pollution; and universities administer student-aid programs subject to advice, in some cases, by student associations. As well, voluntary associations, such as

[68] Taylor, p. 108.

[69] Carolyn Touhy, "Private Government, Property and Professionalism," *CJPS*, IX, 4. December 1976, p. 668.

children's aid societies, are essential to the administration of many social services. In sum, these activities cannot be viewed as anything but an integral part of government activity; the interest groups in such cases become an extension of the output side of the political system.

Information Dissemination

Probably the most important of output activities of interest groups is the dissemination of information about government policies. People cannot obey the law unless they know what the law is, and they cannot take advantage of government programs unless they know about them. Interest groups often provide the required communications. Endless examples can be provided. Virtually every trade association, union, or promotional group at least publishes a newsletter, and much of the work of the head offices of interest groups consists of determining which government activities are pertinent to the group's interests and then informing members about those activities.

The factors that affect the usefulness of interest groups as output communicators for the political system are broadly similar to those that affect their value as input communicators. Of particular importance are group cohesiveness or dedication to a single set of aims and the possession of good internal communications. Obviously, the strength of the offices in the capital cities is important — especially the effectiveness of their communication with the governmental structures with which they are concerned.

Scholars who have studied interest groups have tended to concentrate almost exclusively on the input side of their activities. While this aspect is vital, the failure to look seriously at the output activities of groups can result in a substantial underestimation of their importance in modern society. The political system in Canada and in other developed countries has become highly dependent on these activities, and wise group leadership will try to take advantage of this fact when making demands upon political decision makers.

CONCLUSIONS

One of the greatest difficulties in writing about interest groups in Canada — indeed, in any industrialized western society — is the problem of determining where to place them in any conceptual scheme of the political system. Interest groups pervade the whole of the policy process in Canada, so much so that at least one analyst has been led to characterize the Canadian political process as a process of élite accommodation between interest group and governmental élites,[70] and a whole school of analysis, called "consociationalism," has been erected on a very similar foundation and applied widely in Canadian political science.[71] Although we have continually indicated the difficulty of assessing the relative strength of groups in various nations, Canada is scarcely unique in respect to the

[70] Presthus, *Elite Accommodation in Canadian Politics.*

[71] Consociationalism is described in detail in chapter 3, where there is an extensive discussion of the themes raised here.

significance of its organized interests. The "group approach" to politics, in which all of politics was described in terms of group interactions, was one early recognition of this significance, and a latter-day recognition of the all-pervasive role of interest groups in the United States is found in Theodore Lowi's description of the American system as one of "interest-group liberalism."

Interest groups provide undoubted benefits in Canadian society. Since there are far more Canadians who participate in interest-group activities than in political parties, we might be tempted to define such groups as the pre-eminent representative structures in Canadian society. There is no doubt that, if one wishes to influence the political process, the channels afforded by interest groups are the most effective ones to use. We have seen, too, that groups provide information to government and to their own members, that they are prominent in the administration of government policy, and that they create a support structure for the political system upon which much of its legitimacy depends.

However, one must be careful not to go too far in eulogizing the interest-group system. And, as Theodore Lowi is at great pains to point out with respect to the United States, one must recognize the dangers inherent in too heavy a reliance upon interest groups as the real and only representative structures of society. We pointed out, in an earlier chapter, that about 40% of Canadians are not integrated in any way into the interest-group structure of Canada, and that this 40% is generally within the lower strata of society. Thus, if the influence of interest groups is as significant as we have suggested, such groups may act to reinforce the disparity of power. If political leaders react only to organized interests and disregard the needs of the relatively inarticulate members of our society, then the consequences for unorganized Canadians will continue to be disastrous.[72]

Because there is no shortage of recognition of the importance of interest groups and of lobbying in the Canadian political process, there is no shortage of proposals for reform. One proposal frequently put forward has been the recommendation that all those engaged in "representative" activities be required to register as lobbyists and to name the people or corporations on whose behalf they act. The federal government proposed such a system in a white paper tabled in 1985.[73] The proposals, modelled on a not overly successful American attempt to bring lobbying out into the open, met a mixed reaction. Trade associations, whose clients are, in any case, quite obvious, scarcely objected, and some were even supportive. Executive-consultant groups, which have proliferated over the past decade, objected mightily, since their stock-in-trade is the provision of confidential advice to corporate clients who would prefer not to be seen to be reliant on such services. Umbrella groups such as the Business Council on National Issues claimed that they should not be referred to as members of a vaguely tainted group called "lobbyists."

> There's nothing absolutely *wrong* with being a lobbyist. Its just that I prefer to
> think that, since the Council was founded in 1976, we've demonstrated that we're

---

[72] This line of reasoning is carried much further in Lowi's classic, *The End of Liberalism* (Chicago: Norton, 1979).

[73] *Lobbying and the Registration of Paid Lobbyists* (Ottawa: Consumer and Corporate Affairs Canada, 1985). Similar limitations have been described for Britain by R.M. Punnett, *British Government and Politics* (New York: W.W. Norton, 1971), pp. 152–156.

above bottom line preoccupations. Our members are all chief executive officers of large companies who are invited to join because they can rise above day-to-day concerns and contribute to national issues. We are, I like to think, the board of directors of last resort, exercising our responsibility to help determine the national interest.[74]

The registration legislation has not been passed at the time of this writing, and there is no evidence that the government feels it to be urgent. In any case, such changes would constitute only a very modest and perhaps even unnecessary reform to the existing system.

There are, of course, already limits to the power of interest groups. The Cabinet has a collective policy role, which may effectively counter pressure on individual ministers, and the requirements of party unity in the parliamentary system limit the legislature as an arena for lobbyists. The public service is by no means always sympathetic to interest-group demands, and while it may, at times, encourage the activities of groups, it does on occasion also act as an effective counterpoise and as a representative of less articulate interests. Even the largest and wealthiest interest group can in no way approach the research resources available to even smaller federal departments. One should not underestimate the tenacity of the public servant in pursuing either the public good as he or she sees it or the aggrandizement of his or her own power, and both of these may be inimical to interest-group desires. For example, W.T. Stanbury suggests that the survival of any vestige of anti-combines legislation in Canada, in spite of the massive attack by business,

> is not the result of the counter-pressure of consumer interest groups such as the Consumers' Association of Canada but rather of the efforts of a handful of senior officials in the Bureau of Competition policy in the Department of Consumer and Corporate Affairs. They kept the flame burning. It is hard to overestimate their importance to the maintenance of any form of competition policy in this country. Both within the bureaucracy and in the wider policy arena they operate in an environment almost unflaggingly hostile to the virtues of competition and the consumer interest.[75]

This is hardly a unique case, but it and ones like it lead us not to agree fully with those political scientists cited in the introduction to this chapter who fear that an alliance of the executive level of government and interest groups will usurp a vast share of the political power in our society. Indeed, it would have potentially disastrous consequences for many millions of Canadians, and perhaps even for the political system as a whole if the round of government and bureaucrat-bashing so prevalent in western democracies in the 1980s were to obliterate even this counterpoise to organized interests. Such interests are a legitimate and vital component of the Canadian political system, but if no effective counterweight is provided to them, they could dominate the system to such an extent that any pretense to equality of opportunity or to any form of just society will scarcely merit even the moniker of empty rhetoric.

[74] Thomas D'Aquino, cited in Charlotte Gray, "Friendly Persuasion," p. 11.
[75] W.T. Stanbury, *Business Interests*, p. 222.

PART 5

INSIDE THE SYSTEM

AUTHORITIES AND ELITES IN THE CANADIAN POLITICAL SYSTEM

PROBLEMS OF DEFINITION
ELITE STUDIES AND APPROACHES
THE CABINET IN CANADA
■ The Provincial and Ethnic Distribution of Cabinet Ministers
■ The Socioeconomic Background of Cabinet Ministers
■ The Career Patterns of Cabinet Ministers
■ The Business Connections of Cabinet Ministers
THE BUREAUCRACY IN CANADA
■ The Ethnic Distribution of Bureaucrats
■ The Socioeconomic Background of Bureaucrats ■ The Career Bureaucrat
MEMBERS OF PARLIAMENT
■ The Socioeconomic Background of MPs ■ The Career Patterns of MPs
THE JUDICIAL ELITE IN CANADA
CONCLUSIONS

N ot everyone shares equally in the making of political decisions; time after time, we are confronted with the fact that effective political power rests in the hands of relatively few people in Canadian society. These people are variously identified as the political decision makers, the authorities, or the political élite. This chapter looks at some of them in more detail.

PROBLEMS OF DEFINITION[1]

There are nearly as many definitions of the term "political élite" as there are people who have studied the subject. Part of the confusion stems from the highly

---

[1] For a broader consideration of the general questions of definition and approach in Canada, see Dennis Forcese, "Elites and Power in Canada," see Dennis Forcese, "Elites and Power in Canada," in John Redekop, ed., *Approaches to Canadian Politics* (Toronto: Prentice-Hall, 1978), and the more complete treatment in Dennis Forcese, *The Canadian Class Structure*, 2nd edition (Toronto: McGraw-Hill Ryerson, 1980).

value-laden nature of the term "élite." Elites can be seen as benevolent, as they are in Plato's *Republic* — philosopher kings, whose mandate stems from the fact that they are an aristocracy of knowledge and wisdom; or they may be seen as purely malevolent — a ruling class that governs in its own selfish interest. Between these extremes there are interpretations of both the morality and instrumentality of political élites ranging along the entire continuum.

In our own definition, we attempt to avoid these normative interpretations. Ideally we would define the political élite as a relatively small group of people who share a relatively large amount of the power to influence policy decisions in Canada. The problem presented by this functional definition, however, is how to actually identify the members of the élite and distinguish them from non-élites. To solve this very practical problem, we define the Canadian political élite in structural or *positional* terms,[2] i.e., as those men and women who occupy roles, offices, or positions in the political system that vest formal decision-making power in their incumbents.[3] In these terms, the Canadian political élite is comprised of Cabinet ministers, members of parliament, upper-level bureaucrats, and superior court judges.[4] This positional definition provides a manageable number of actors with whom to deal, and it does encompass positions that bestow on their holders a disproportionate amount of political power. Moreover, because most Canadian analysts of the political élites have used a similar definition, it is possible to find the data that will help us identify and describe the incumbents.

The reader is cautioned, however, that our chosen definition might be too restrictive. Every government has advisors who are important in the decision-making process but who do not occupy formal positions of authority. Sometimes it might be the wife of the premier, sometimes a trusted friend of top Cabinet members or bureaucrats, or some anonymous middle-level technocrat whose influence may stem from his or her expertise in a narrow but important policy field. We cannot include all such people in our definition, nor can we hope to describe them, for the members of an élite who are not there by right of a formal position may move in and out faster than those who are, and, in any event, they are, by their very nature, difficult to trace. The influence of such people may be great, but in ideological and socioeconomic background, they are not likely to differ much from the positional élite through whom they must communicate their ideas. In spite of the power often credited to the proverbial Toronto cab driver or the bartender at the press club, very few of the upper-middle-class

---

[2] John Porter, in *The Vertical Mosaic*, adopts this approach. He attempts to differentiate between the political and the bureaucratic élite, but we suggest that, in terms of the actual making of decisions, such a differentiation is not necessarily appropriate. Porter's work has recently been extended and updated by Wallace Clement in *The Canadian Corporate Elite* (Toronto: McClelland and Stewart, 1975), and by Dennis Olsen, *The State Elite* (Toronto: McClelland and Stewart, 1980).

[3] Suzanne Keller, in *Beyond the Ruling Class* (New York: Random House, 1963), on p. 4 describes élites in general as "a minority of individuals designated to serve a collectivity in a socially valued way. . . . Socially significant elites are ultimately responsible for the realization of major social goals and for the continuity of the social order."

[4] The description of the élite that follows refers almost exclusively to the federal level of government. Our positional definition would not change for provincial élites, but the socioeconomic composition of the élite could be expected to vary slightly from province to province.

professional men and women who make up most of the Canadian political élite would choose people much different from themselves for their confidants.

ELITE STUDIES AND APPROACHES

In truth, virtually any realistic approach to the study of politics is an élite approach, for in no political system are the critical decisions of state actually taken by the masses. The most critical of the élite theorists assert that the political and economic systems of modern capitalist societies are controlled by a coherent industrial-military-political ruling class, which attempts to insure that in policy making, its own interests supersede those of the masses.[5] Pluralists, on the other hand, as we pointed out earlier, hold that there are multiple competing élites rather than a single cohesive ruling class, and that the competition among these élites insures that mass interests are reflected in policy decisions.[6] John Porter and Robert Presthus, who have both addressed themselves specifically to the Canadian scene, assert that, while there may, indeed, be some competition among élites and some differentiation of élites, depending upon the issue involved, most of them have been drawn disproportionately from the upper class. Having shared the same basic socialization, our élites thus tend to bring a common set of biases to bear upon their decisions.[7]

In the middle of the pluralist and élite approaches stand authors such as Dye and Zeigler. While critical of the pluralist assumptions about the distribution of power in the modern industrialized nations, Dye and Zeigler go on to argue that the "irony of democracy" is that it is only the élites who are committed to democratic values. Speaking of the United States, they say that:

> Democratic values have survived because elites not masses govern. Elites in America — leaders in government, industry, education, and civic affairs; the well educated, prestigiously employed, and politically active — give greater support to basic democratic values and "rules of the game" than do the masses . . . . In

---

[5] The writer most usually cited as the original proponent of this view is C. Wright Mills, *The Power Elite* (New York: Oxford University Press, 1959). Many others use this perspective—for example, most of the community power studies of the 1950s do so, and the term "military-industrial complex" was first used publicly by President Dwight Eisenhower in 1959. It is also a common component of popular or semipopular writings on politics. In general, the pure élite model has been more the province of sociologists than of political scientists. There is relatively little pure class analysis in Canadian political science, although the neo-Marxian mode of analysis can be construed as being in this vein. See, for example, Leo Panitch, ed., *The Canadian State* (Toronto: University of Toronto Press, 1978). See also Leo Panitch, "Elites, Classes and Power in Canada," in Whittington and Williams, *Canadian Politics in the 1980s.* pp. 229–250. Panitch distinguishes between élite analysis and class analysis. Our consideration of the nature of Canadian political culture deals with closely related issues, and we touch on this issue in our intoductory chapter as well.

[6] See, for example, the classic examples of this approach in Robert Dahl, *Who Governs?* (New Haven: Yale University Press, 1961); Edward Banfield, *Political Influence* (Chicago: University of Chicago Press, 1961); or Nelson Polsby, *Community Power Studies* (New Haven: Yale University Press, 1964). The pluralist approach is more often utilized by political scientists than by sociologists, and probably was the most commonly accepted approach in Canadian political science in the fifties, sixties, and early seventies.

[7] Robert Presthus, *Elite Accommodation in Canadian Politics* and *Elites in the Policy Process*; John Porter, *The Vertical Mosaic.* See also Dennis Olsen, *The State Elite.* Most academic analysts stand on the middle ground in this controversy.

short, it is the common man not the elite who is most likely to be swayed by anti-democratic ideology; and it is the elite and not the common man who is the chief guardian of democratic values.[8]

Our assumptions are also in the middle ground. As we have already indicated, we do not assume that there is a single cohesive ruling class that controls the Canadian political system, either nationally or in any of the larger provincial jurisdictions. But, at the same time, we do assume that there is a good deal of ideological congruence among the various élites. As Robert Presthus writes,

> We assume that these three elites [interest group leaders, M.P.s and high level bureaucrats] play the major role in shaping and carrying out public policy, through a sustained process of mutual accommodation encouraged by a battery of compatible social, experiential and ideological ties.[9]

This does not imply that there is complete harmony among the élites. In fact, evidence of serious schisms appears in the newspapers every day. We are accustomed to often acriminious partisan conflict among members of the political élite, profound differences between, for instance, the primary and secondary sectors of the economic élite, and competition among regional élites for the relative benefits of national policy. Within government itself, representatives of different parts of the élite often contest strongly to sway policy towards the groups they, in some sense, represent. However, some form of accommodation based on a shared view of the state and their role in it is usually worked out. The small size of the Canadian national élite compared to what might be found in the United States or Britain has made possible a situation where considerable interaction is probable, and where a high degree of self-consciousness of élite status could be expected to develop.[10]

> Interaction between the governmental elite and the one-quarter of interest groups who are most active politically, the shared socio-economic properties, their strategic political roles and . . . the pervasive cohesion among them on selected ideological and cognitive dimensions all tend to provide behavioural and affective commonalities that enable them to interact effectively.[11]

It is this fact that leads Presthus to characterize Canadian politics primarily in terms of a system of *élite accommodation*. John Porter, and Wallace Clement and Dennis Olsen, who have continued Porter's work, focus more on the sociological determinants of élite behaviour than on its role in the policy process, but their conclusions are not much different than Presthus'. While Canadian political scientists may use different terms, most of them form similar interpretations to those of Porter and Presthus.[12]

---

[8] Dye and Zeigler, *op. cit.*, pp. 14–15. See also P. Backrach, *The Theory of Democratic Elitism* (Boston: Houghton Mifflin, 1967).

[9] Presthus, *Elite Accommodation*, p. 268.

[10] Presthus, p. 174. See also our discussion of consociational democracy in chapter 3.

[11] Presthus, p. 332. Both quotes are copyrighted by Cambridge University Press and are reprinted with their permission.

[12] Neither is the position of Presthus' major critics — Richard Simeon and John Meisel — greatly different. They take issue more with the details of Presthus' analysis and with his data manipulations than with his ideological stance.

In the remainder of this chapter, we will look at the socioeconomic backgrounds of our major policy makers and the manner in which they approach the allocation of resources in Canada.[13] We can then attempt to determine whether there is a common set of attitudes among these élites, and what this might mean to an interpretation of Canadian politics.[14] Given that we have already considered interest-group leaders and their political connections (in the previous chapter), we will concentrate (in this chapter) primarily upon élites *within* the political system. However, the links and common attitudes among élites within the political system and those in the linkage institutions at the boundary of the system are important determinants of political decision making.

THE CABINET IN CANADA

In describing the people who make up the Cabinet in Canada, there are two possible approaches. One can examine the process through which a prime minister constructs a Cabinet, in order to see what constraints exist and what groups the prime minister seeks to represent in the structure of the Cabinet. Alternatively, one can examine the *results* of Cabinet formation — the types of people who end up in the Cabinet when the selection process has been completed. This section will concentrate on the latter, but it would be artificial to discuss the results of Cabinet making without saying something in passing about the actual process of selecting a Cabinet.

One can look at the people who have become Canadian ministers from a number of perspectives: their geographical distribution, their ethnic and social backgrounds, and their career patterns can all be examined. When that is done, one can take a fresh look at the well-worn question of how Canada's various social cleavages are represented in the Cabinet; for, as will be seen, this highest forum of decision making in Canada is consciously designed to be representative of some of the country's major cleavages.

The Provincial and Ethnic Distribution of Cabinet Ministers[15]

I think I may defy them to show that the cabinet can be formed on any other principle than that of a representation of the several provinces in that cabinet. Your federal problem will have to be worked out around the table of the Executive Council.[16]

This prediction was made in 1865 by Christopher Dunkin, one of the most perceptive critics of the original Confederation settlement. From the very first

---

[13] Interest-group leaders and behaviour are dealt with primarily in chapter 13.

[14] Canadians, no less than other people, have an ongoing fascination about their élite, which gives rise to an array of popular literature on the subject. See, as examples, Peter Newman, *The Canadian Establishment* (Toronto: McClelland and Stewart, 1975) or Newman's *The Bronfman Dynasty* (Toronto: McClelland and Stewart, 1978); or Peter Foster, *The Blue-Eyed Sheiks* (Toronto: Collins, 1979). Such accounts provide interesting detail to complement broad-brush or primariy statistical academic approaches.

[15] The major data sources for material on Cabinet ministers are Parliamentary Guides and biographies published by the Prime Minister's Office at the time appointments are made.

[16] Christopher Dunkin, *Confederation Debates* (Ottawa: Queen's Printer, 1951), pp. 496, 513.

days of Confederation, it was obvious that the Senate, which was intended to represent regions or provinces in Ottawa, would not suffice as an arbiter of the regional cleavages of the federation. The Senate had little power, and representation there was only very imperfectly based on federal principles. Yet four very different colonies had been brought together, and each was anxious to retain some substantial degree of control over federal political decision making. In the first Cabinet, Sir Georges Etienne Cartier would accept no fewer than four positions for Quebec, of which three were to be held by French Canadians. Ontario, which was larger than Quebec, had to demand one more seat, and if Nova Scotia and New Brunswick were to have any say in the councils of Confederation, they should have two posts each. The federal principle of Cabinet composition was thus immediately established as the most important determinant of Cabinet structure, and there has been no substantial change since.

Table 14-1 compares the 1966 Cabinet of Lester Pearson with Pierre Trudeau's Cabinet of early 1974 and that appointed by Brian Mulroney in 1984. While we have not added the figures on the 1980 Trudeau Cabinet, it differs relatively little from earlier Trudeau cabinets. With respect to the 1974 Trudeau Cabinet, with the temporary exception of New Brunswick, each province had at least one minister. And once again, the prairie provinces made the prime minister's task of selection unappealingly simple by returning so few Liberals, a favour they again bestowed upon him in 1980.[17] This favour Trudeau bequeathed to John Turner, whose short-lived Cabinet also had but one minister from west of Ontario. The first edition of the Trudeau Cabinet, in 1968, was the only one in history to have more Quebeckers than Ontarians; by 1984, though, Trudeau had an equal number of Quebeckers and Ontarians in his Cabinet. John Turner had thirteen Ontarians and ten Quebeckers, while Brian Mulroney returned to equal representation for the central provinces, in spite of the fact that his contingent of Quebec MPs was considerably less experienced in federal office than his Ontario caucus.

The Clark Cabinet of 1979 attempted to retain the same principles of provincial representation but, again, some distortions were introduced by the whims of the electorate. Clark could muster only two Quebec MPs and, although he appointed both to the Cabinet, it was still necessary to appoint two senators from Quebec in order to avoid too great an under-representation of that province. Even so, he was left with a considerable imbalance between his four Quebeckers and his twelve Ontarians. Significant efforts to recruit other Quebeckers had not met with success by the time his government fell after six and a half somewhat harried months in office.

In his brief period as prime minister, John Turner was supported by a Cabinet considerably smaller in size (twenty-nine members) than those of either his predecessor or his successor. Given that he inherited his parliamentary contingent

---

[17] The omission of New Brunswick was rectified immediately after the 1974 election. Alberta again failed to give the Prime Minister a chance to represent it in the Cabinet, so a Senator from Alberta was appointed to the ministry, in a partial attempt to compensate for Alberta's unrepentent Conservatism. When Jack Horner crossed the floor in 1977, he was immediately welcomed into the Cabinet as the Alberta representative, a move he regretted at the next election. In 1980, Trudeau was forced to go to the Senate for Cabinet representation in Saskatchewan, Alberta, and British Columbia.

TABLE 14-1
PROVINCIAL REPRESENTATION IN THE CABINET UNDER LESTER PEARSON,
PIERRE TRUDEAU, AND JOE CLARK

	Pearson (December 1966)		Trudeau (February 1974)		Mulroney (September 1984)	
	Liberal MPs		Liberal MPs		PC MPs	
Province	Cabinet	Elected	Cabinet	Elected	Cabinet	Elected
Newfoundland	1	7	1	3	1	4
Prince Edward Island	0	0	1	1	1	3
Nova Scotia	2	2	1	1	2	9
New Brunswick	3	6	0	5	1	9
Quebec	7	56	11	56	11	58
Ontario	10	51	12	36	11	67
Manitoba	1	1	1	2	4	9
Saskatchewan	0	0	1	1	2	9
Alberta	0	0	0	0	3	21
British Columbia	2	7	2	4	3	19
Yukon	—	—	—	—	1	1

from Pierre Trudeau, the heavy Ontario-Quebec representation in Turner's Cabinet is not surprising. Turner did include representatives of all other provinces where the Liberal Party had seats.

Brian Mulroney had far more opportunity than his predecessors to provide adequate provincial representation in his Cabinet, since his parliamentary legions included an ample supply of MPs from every province. He responded by producing a Cabinet that, at forty members, was the largest in Canadian history. It was also roughly representative of the provinces on a basis proportional to their population. We have already remarked that he chose to represent Ontario and Quebec equally, as had Trudeau, and we might begin to view this as a precedent in Cabinet construction. His over-representation of Manitoba resulted in part from the fact that his one Senate Cabinet member (Duff Roblin, the government leader in the Senate) came from there, but it seems quite clear that, once again, in Cabinet building, the imperative to represent provinces on a basis roughly proportional to their population has been served.

Clark also appointed an *inner Cabinet* (described in more detail in chapter 15), and there was considerable grumbling in provinces such as Nova Scotia, Saskatchewan, and New Brunswick, which were not represented in it. The grumblings from British Columbia were sufficiently loud that a minister from that province was added to the inner Cabinet. Pierre Trudeau may not have felt the need to take explicit account of regional representation in his *Committee on Priorities and Planning* (his version of an inner Cabinet), but then he could not have done so in any case, given the geographical distribution of his parliamentary caucus. Brian Mulroney expanded his Priorities and Planning Committee to fourteen ministers. We do not know to what extent he made a conscious attempt at provincial representation, but all provinces were represented except Prince Edward Island

TABLE 14-2
THE DISTRIBUTION OF CABINET MINISTERS BY PROVINCE, 1867–1965

Province	Per Cent of Ministers	Corrected Per Cent*	Per Cent of National Population, 1971
Newfoundland	0.9	4.6	2.4
Prince Edward Island	2.4	2.4	0.5
Nova Scotia	8.9	8.4	3.7
New Brunswick	8.0	7.6	3.0
Quebec	32.0	30.4	27.9
Ontario	30.8	29.2	35.7
Manitoba	5.3	5.2	4.6
Saskatchewan	2.4	3.7	4.3
Alberta	2.7	4.2	7.5
British Columbia	4.4	4.3	10.1

* To take account of the different lengths of time various provinces have been in Confederation, the figures in the first column have been multiplied by the numbers of years between when a province joined Confederation and 1965. The figures so derived were totalled, and new percentage distribution within that total was calculated.

and New Brunswick. Moreover, if provincial representation had been vital to him, he did have ministers from both of those provinces whom he could, presumably, have appointed to the committee.

Historically, the pattern of regional representation in Cabinet has been evident. Table 14-2 summarizes the historical data up to 1965. The reader should concentrate on the corrected per cent column rather than the simple per cent column. For comparative purposes, the provincial distribution of population by provinces for 1971 is also shown in the table. It can be seen that the distribution of cabinet ministers and of population by province was roughly parallel up to 1965, and Table 14-1 confirms that this rough parallelism has persisted. However, the provinces of Saskatchewan and Alberta appear to have had rather fewer than their share of ministers, and the Maritimes rather more than their share. Perhaps some explanation of this can be found in the fact that, during the long post-war period of Liberal dominance, the western provinces have often returned only MPs from minor parties or from the Progressive Conservative party; these MPs could not be considered for the Cabinet. The Maritimes, on the other hand, have supplied a constant flow of Liberals.

The number of ministers shown from Quebec may be somewhat misleading, for, relative to English Canadians, French Canadians have tended to stay in the Cabinet for shorter periods. When the distribution is examined by person-years, the parallel with provincial populations in every period since Confederation is almost exact, although the shorter period of service of French Canadians in the Cabinet may have acted to diminish their real power. Alternatively, such a rapid turnover may be a reflection of a more profound disgruntlement with their role in federal decision making.

The ethnic distribution of Cabinet ministers shows similar patterns. In 1966, Lester Pearson's Cabinet contained nine French-Canadian ministers and eighteen

English-Canadian ministers, including the prime minister, in a Cabinet of thirty members. The 1974 composition of 30% French ministers is very close to the average since Confederation, and, once again, the proportion of French-Canadian ministers very closely paralleled the proportion of French Canadians in the population. We have already described the difficulties Joe Clark faced in striking a proper ethnic balance in his 1979 Cabinet, for he had but one Francophone MP. The important point is that he considered this an extremely serious problem, as would any prime minister anxious to strike a proper linguistic balance in his government. Pierre Trudeau and John Turner both had more than 40% Francophone ministers, partially, again, a reflection of their lack of Anglophone MPs from outside Ontario. Brian Mulroney appointed ten Francophones, or one-quarter of the total, to his first Cabinet in 1984. By comparison, the Canadian population was approximately 30% Francophone in 1984.

At one time there was a type of hidden under-representation in the French-English distribution in the Cabinet, which becomes apparent when one examines the distribution of portfolios by ethnic groups. Until 1968, no French Canadian had ever led the Department of Industry, Trade and Commerce (or its organizational ancestors) and, up to 1978, none had been Minister of Finance. This situation pertained no less under Canada's first two French-Canadian prime ministers as well, but it was corrected by Pierre Trudeau as part of his policy of ensuring French-Canadian representation at the highest levels in Ottawa. Under Trudeau, virtually all of the heaviest portfolios, including finance, were held by Francophones at one time or another.

There may be some reasons for the historical under-representation of Francophones in the most important financial portfolios of the Cabinet. The great majority of Cabinet ministers from Quebec have been lawyers; most of them have known relatively little about business or finance, and were unknown to Bay Street or St. James Street. Consequently, French-Canadian ministers were usually not considered for the portfolios of finance or industry. But whatever the reason, the tendency, until recently, to assign French Canadians to portfolios such as Public Works, Postmaster General, or Veterans' Affairs, with the hope that at Cabinet meetings they would not speak unless spoken to, did lead to an under-representation of French Canadians in the more significant positions in the executive decision-making process.

One caveat must be entered to the general assumption that it is possible to equate portfolio with power. Sometimes portfolios that have very little departmental responsibility can be very powerful, depending upon the person who occupies the portfolio. Occasionally, "light" or less visible portfolios are given to vital ministers, in order to free them to consider broader questions of national policy. Thus some of the less visible portfolios, such as the presidency of the Treasury Board (occupied in 1974 by C.M. Drury and subsequently by Jean Chrétien), or Communications (once occupied by Gerard Pelletier), or Minister of State for Federal-Provincial Relations (occupied in 1977 and 1978 by Marc Lalonde) may be held by ministers with a considerable amount of personal influence in cabinet decision making.

As with provincial representation, the attempt to provide proportional representation by ethnic group, at least between the French and English segments of the population, has been intentional. On the other hand, there is less evidence of a conscious effort on the part of prime ministers to represent "other Canadians" in the Cabinet. Occasionally, prior to 1960, someone such as J.T. Thorson, a man of Icelandic descent who was Minister of National War Services in 1941 and 1942, did enter the Cabinet; and Trudeau's short-lived appointment of Stanley Haidasz as Minister of State for Multiculturalism could certainly have been construed as an attempt at representing other ethnic groups. Joe Clark's Cabinet contained more ministers with non-charter ethnic-group backgrounds, including Ray Hnatyshyn, Steve Paproski, Jake Epp, and Don Mazankowski. However, with the exception of Paproski, who was Minister of Multiculturalism, it is doubtful that there was any conscious attempt to represent ethnic diversity; Hnatyshyn, Epp, and Mazankowski were almost certainly appointed on the basis of regional representation and merit, with no attention paid to their ethnic origins at all. They all reappeared in Brian Mulroney's Cabinet in 1984, as did several other ministers of non-charter-group background, such as Otto Jelinek and James Kelleher. All, or most, of these people are likely in Cabinet for reasons unrelated to their sometimes remote ethnic backgrounds, and it seems most unlikely that prime ministers lose much sleep at Cabinet-building (or shuffling) time trying to ensure that non-charter ethnic groups are represented.

In the nineteenth and early twentieth centuries there was also an attempt to provide balanced representation of sub-groups within the portion of the Cabinet having its roots in the British Isles. Thus, under John A. Macdonald or Wilfrid Laurier, the well-balanced Cabinet would have perhaps one-quarter of its members of English descent, one-quarter Scottish, and about one-fifth Irish. Each of these nationalities formed a powerful and cohesive voting group in Canada, and a prime minister could offend them only at his peril. There is no such attempt made today.

The Socioeconomic Background of Cabinet Ministers

The Cabinet is clearly intended to be representative of provinces and charter groups in Canada, but is it representative in other ways? If so, one would expect to find it in a social cross-section of Canadians. A reader who has even a passing knowledge of Canadian politics will realize that this is simply not the case. The poor are not represented in the Cabinet by any of their number, nor are Canadian Indians or Inuit, nor are unskilled labourers. Women are vastly under-represented. But how far does the discrepancy go? How socially and economically unrepresentative is the Cabinet?

Both by education and by occupation, Cabinet ministers have been distinctly unrepresentative of the general population. Between 1867 and 1965, fully 52% of Canada's Cabinet ministers were lawyers, whereas the proportion of lawyers in the population is far less than one per cent. Lately, the preponderance of lawyers in Cabinet has declined even as their numbers in the general population have risen. Table 14-3 indicates that, in Lester Pearson's Cabinet in 1966, only nine of twenty-seven members were lawyers. In Pierre Trudeau's Cabinet, in 1974, the proportion was up again to fifteen out of thirty, and exactly the same number and proportion of lawyers were present in Joe Clark's 1979 Cabinet.

TABLE 14-3
OCCUPATIONS OF CABINET MINISTERS

Occupation before entering politics	Pearson Cabinet (1966)	Trudeau Cabinet (1974)	Mulroney Cabinet (1984)
Law	9	15	8
Other professions	7	6	14
Civil service	5	2	0
Business	5	4	11
Farm	0	0	0
Labourer	0	0	0
Politician (no other experience)	0	0	3
Other	1	1	0

Brian Mulroney's first Cabinet had considerably fewer lawyers: less than 20% of his ministers were from the legal profession. Some 22% of ministers since Confederation have been from the business world. Again, the Mulroney Cabinet marked a modest departure in this respect, with thirteen members—one-third of the total number—coming from the business world. Since Confederation, 6% of ministers have been farmers, and 4% have come from the public service. Only six ministers since Confederation have had a labour background or a close connection with labour, and none since the mid 1970s.

A similar bias pertains if one looks at the educational background of Canada's ministers. Only two of the more than four hundred since Confederation have had no formal education, and only 17% stopped at elementary school. Only one minister since World War Two has not had at least high-school education. In the fairly typical 1970s Cabinet, there were two members with only high-school education, one who had attended technical college, seven who stopped after one university degree, ten lawyers, and nine members with a post-graduate degree or some post-graduate studies. The 1984 PC Cabinet had five members (13%) with only a secondary level of education, fifteen members (38%) with one post-secondary degree, and nineteen members (49%) with some post-graduate training, including law. By contrast, in 1981, Statistics Canada reported that 28% of the Canadian population older than twenty-five had some post-secondary education, and 9.6% had a post-secondary degree. In terms of education, then, the Cabinet has been far from a microcosm of the Canadian social structure.

The family backgrounds of the members of the political élite have been examined by John Porter in 1960 and by Dennis Olsen, a student of Porter's who replicated a portion of Porter's study for a period up to 1973. Both conclude that the socio-economic origins of Cabinet ministers are basically middle class, with Olsen noting that the only change from Porter's findings was that both the upper-class and the working-class segments of Canadian society lost ground to the middle class. Fully 69% of Olsen's 1961 to 1973 population of Cabinet ministers have middle-class origins, and there is no indication that the trends have been altering during the 1970s and the 1980s.[18]

[18] See Olsen, The State Elite, pp. 29–32.

One more aspect of the "representative" nature of the Canadian Cabinet should be mentioned, and that is its religious composition. In the 1970 Cabinet, there were fourteen Roman Catholics, four members from the United Church and the Anglican Church, one Baptist, two Presbyterians, and three "others." Between Confederation and 1965, there were almost equal numbers of Anglican, Presbyterian, and United Church or Methodist Cabinet ministers, while about 35% of Cabinet ministers were Catholics. However, in an age when religious differences no longer stir people's deepest passions in Canada, the religious affiliation of Cabinet ministers is of no great consequence. Indeed, since 1970, it has become quite difficult to trace the religious background of Cabinet ministers. In the biographical sketches distributed at the time of their appointment, no member of Brian Mulroney's Cabinet listed his or her religious affiliation, and it can be concluded that religion is now irrelevant as a selection criterion for Cabinet. Yet, as we demonstrated in chapter 3, there was a time when religious differences in Canada were taken more seriously, and in that era a proper balance of religions within the Cabinet was vital. While it may seem ludicrous today, Alexander Mackenzie, Prime Minister during the 1870s, remarked: "I may, with feelings of pride, refer to the standing of the members of the Cabinet. . . . In the matter of religious faith there are five Catholics, three members of the Church of England, three Presbyterians, two Methodists, one Congregationalist and one Baptist."[19] It is possible that, if a modern prime minister discovered he had appointed twenty-seven Roman Catholics in a thirty-five member Cabinet, he might feel a bit embarrassed, but much beyond that the question of religious distribution does not go.[20]

It bears emphasis that the federal Cabinet, like virtually all other aspects of Canadian government and business life, greatly under-represents women. In 1981, 50.4% of the Canadian population was female, and by 1986, approximately 55% of Canadian women of working age were in the paid labour force. By contrast, the 1980 Trudeau Cabinet had three women members (8%) and the 1984 Turner Cabinet only two (7%). The 1984 Mulroney Cabinet was somewhat better, with six female members, but that is still just 15% of the total. Yet, the proportion of women in Cabinet is greater than that in the House of Commons, for the 1980–1984 parliament had less than 5% of its seats filled by women, and the House elected in 1984 had 9.6% women. There were no women at all in the Cabinet until 1957, when Ellen Fairclough was appointed to the Cabinet by John Diefenbaker.

Aside from geographical and French-English cleavages, then, the Cabinet is anything but representative. In part, this is a reflection of what cleavages are the most important in Canadian politics, but it is also a reflection of other factors. The vast preponderance of male lawyers, especially in our earlier Cabinets, was

---

[19] Cited in William Buckingham and George W. Ross, *The Honourable Alexander Mackenzie: His Life and Times* (New York: Greenwood, 1969), p. 354.

[20] But see Paul Fox, "The Representative Nature of the Canadian Cabinet," in Paul Fox, ed., *Politics: Canada*, 3rd edition (Toronto: McGraw-Hill Ryerson, 1970), especially p. 341. Later in his career, even Mackenzie asserted, "I have no sympathy personally with the feeling that appears to be growing . . . that every available place should be filled in accordance with the religious views of certain portions of our population." Mackenzie, *Papers*, Vol. I. p. 121.

partly due to the fact that a law career was considered the appropriate one for a young man to follow if he wanted to go into politics, and, of course, it was well understood that no right-thinking young lady would consider a political career at all. The élite nature of present Cabinets also results, to some extent, from the facts that middle-class and upper-middle-class socialization patterns are more likely to give a person the skills and attitudes essential to the effective performance of political roles, and that upper-middle-class occupations are more likely to provide the flexibility of hours and careers necessary to politicians. While universities and law firms will cheerfully provide leaves of absence so their faculty or partners can go into politics, and will generally welcome them back later, we are a long way yet from a situation where blue-collar workers are accorded the same privileges. Which brings us to the issue of the nature of political careers.

The Career Patterns of Cabinet Ministers

What do people do to point their careers towards a Cabinet post? There is a wide variety of possible ways into the cabinet, but some career paths are more common than others. Some ministers, particularly in Liberal Cabinets since World War Two, have been welcomed into the Cabinet more or less directly from outside Parliament, especially from the public service. The most prominent example was Lester Pearson, but others such as Marc Lalonde, Bud Drury, and Mitchell Sharp have also been taken directly into the Cabinet from government posts, or very shortly after leaving such positions. A similar attempt was made in 1975 by Pierre Juneau, who was appointed Minister of Communications, after serving as head of the Canadian Radio-Television Commission. He was, however, defeated in his attempt to get elected in Hochelaga, resigned from the Cabinet, and reappeared in the bureacracy. It is not uncommon to arrange beforehand that a political candidate will join the Cabinet if both the candidate and the party are successful in a general election.[21]

The practice of taking people from the public service directly into the Cabinet has not been attempted since Juneau's abortive bid for election. The inclination to utilize people with public-service experience at more distant points in their backgrounds may also be diminishing. In 1980, Trudeau had seven ministers with some public-service background. Turner had only five, and Brian Mulroney had none.

In the early years of Confederation, it was usual for ministers to serve a fairly long apprenticeship in Parliament before being appointed to the Cabinet. The relative importance of Parliament in a minister's activities has decreased steadily over the years, while the importance of administrative, departmental, federal-provincial, and general priority-setting duties has steadily increased. For this reason it has become increasingly the norm to choose ministers not on the basis of parliamentary experience but rather on the basis of policy-making skills, administrative capabilities, or, occasionally, tactical skills in electioneering. This has occa-

---

[21] The Clark Cabinet of 1979 contained no ministers with civil-service backgrounds. In part, this is related to the "government party" syndrome of the Liberals (described in chapter 11), and in part to the evident mistrust with which the Progressive Conservative Party viewed the public service before it took office.

sionally led to the spectacle of a Cabinet that is administratively quite competent but that cannot defend its activities effectively under the scrutiny of the Opposition in Parliament. This point requires some qualification.

The Pearson Cabinets of 1963 to 1968 seemed particularly prone to parliamentary pratfalls caused by legislative inexperience. However, by the late 1970s, many members of those early Pearson Cabinets were still in office, well-experienced in the parliamentary game, and hence less liable to make the spectacular goofs that characterized Liberal Cabinets in the 1960s. Most of the holders of major portfolios in the Clark Cabinet had previous parliamentary experience, and therefore faced little difficulty in defending most of their policies in the House. Their collective tragic flaw was that none of them had any experience in government. In attempting to apply the lessons they had learned in opposition to the problems of governing, they soon ended up back in opposition. Some of the well-publicized problems of the first years of the Mulroney government have also undoubtedly resulted from such inexperience. Issues that could have been handled relatively easily by experienced ministers and staff were fumbled by political neophytes. The problem was particularly acute with respect to Quebec ministers, who, on average, had less than two years of experience in the House; one of the most inexperienced, it must be remembered, was the prime minister himself.

Cabinets have also been tending to get younger since World War Two. Prior to 1945, the average age on entering the Cabinet was 50 years. Pearson's 1965 cabinet had an average age of 47.7 years at appointment, nearly the same as that of the Clark Conservatives, while Trudeau's 1970 Cabinet ministers averaged only 44.4 years of age at the time of their appointment. The Mulroney cabinet of 1984 was, again, a moderate exception to the trend, with an average age at appointment of 48.6 years — the oldest Cabinet in the last quarter-century.

It has occasionally been suggested that, in Canadian politics, there is no place in public life for a person to go after leaving the Cabinet. Thus, a defeated minister must go back to private industry in order to earn a living. The result of this, it is alleged, is that ministers are never free of the necessity to look over their shoulders to be certain that they are not offending industry, with the result that they are psychologically (if not ideologically) limited as articulators of other interests in society.[22] Evidence, however, does not really support this suggestion. Only 26% of the Cabinet ministers who left their portfolios for any reason from 1867 to 1965 returned to private life. Olsen cites a slight increase in the number of Cabinet ministers who exited directly to business from 1961 to 1977, from 9% to 19%.[23] But there are far more jobs in politics or public life for former Cabinet members than is popularly supposed, and Olsen's data show that more than one-third of the ministers who left the Cabinet from 1961 to 1973 took "patronage" opportunities in the Senate, the judiciary, and other order-in-council positions. Another 25% stayed active in politics after they left the Cabinet.[24]

[22] Porter, *The Vertical Mosaic*, especially pp. 405–411. See also our chapter 16.

[23] Olsen, *The State Elite*, pp. 38–39.

[24] Olsen, pp. 38–39.

Indeed, current conflict-of-interest guidelines, which make it unacceptable for a minister to be employed for one year after leaving the Cabinet with a firm or industry with which he or she was dealing directly in Cabinet, serve to make it very difficult for some ex-ministers to obtain private-sector employment.

The Senate, which has little direct involvement in the policy process, has at least one vital indirect role; since Confederation, it has provided a convenient pasture for more than 20% of retired Cabinet ministers. Provided that the party does not go out of power before he or she leaves office, a minister can be fairly well assured of appointment to the Senate. The importance of this role of the Senate must not be underestimated, for it means that ministers need not depend on the goodwill of the private sector for employment when they retire from office.

As we pointed out, a lot of ex-ministers simply return to being ordinary MPs before eventually retiring. This happens most commonly when a government is defeated, but Pierre Trudeau did demote several of his former Cabinet ministers to the back benches in 1974, perhaps establishing, for Canada, a precedent often followed in Great Britain. Another 12% of ex-ministers went into the judiciary, 10% became Lieutenant Governors, and 10% went into some form of public service, usually on a board or commission. Thus, contrary to some analyses, the ex-Cabinet minister does have available places in public life when the days in power are over.

The Business Connections of Cabinet Ministers

There have frequently been close connections between Cabinet ministers and the Canadian business community. The politics of the immediate post-Confederation era were largely concerned with railways, and Cabinet ministers were deeply involved. Thus, six of the original directors of the Grand Trunk Railway were Cabinet ministers. In 1885, while he was a Cabinet minister, Sir Charles Tupper had no qualms about accepting $100,000 of CPR stock—a gift given in grateful appreciation of his help in selling CPR bonds.[25] Earlier, while acting as secretary of state, Sir Charles had simultaneously held three paid directorships; yet none of these activities precluded his serving as prime minister for a brief stretch in 1896, nor were they held against him at any time.

Wilfrid Laurier continued to be a director of Mutual Life Assurance during his term as prime minister,[26] and one of his ministers, Allen Bristol Aylesworth, carried on a private law practice at the same time as he held the justice portfolio. Sir Robert Borden refused to permit his ministers to maintain outside business connections, but Mackenzie King had no such compunctions. His Minister of Justice, Lomer Gouin, was simultaneously a director of the Bank of Montreal, the Cockshutt Plough Company, Montreal City and District Savings Bank, Royal Trust, and the Mount Royal and Mutual Life Assurance Companies.

[25] E.M. Saunders, *The Life and Letters of the Rt. Hon. Sir Charles Tupper*, vol. 2 (Toronto: Carswell, 1916), pp. 60–61. See William A. Matheson, "The Canadian Cabinet and the Prime Minister: A Structural Study," an unpublished Ph.D. dissertation, Carleton University, April, 1973, pp. 249–258.

[26] Matheson, "The Canadian Cabinet," p. 252.

In 1922, King stated, "In the long run we will gain more in virility in our public life by leaving some matters to conscience and honour rather than by seeking to enforce prohibitions that may be too severe and too drastic."[27] One of the major pillars of King's and Louis St. Laurent's Cabinets was C.D. Howe, who had been, prior to his appointment in 1935, a highly successful construction engineer. The C.D. Howe Company, of which he "disposed" before taking office, continued to receive government business and to employ Howe's son and son-in-law. St. Laurent's Cabinets also contained two ministers who retained private business practices after entering the Cabinet; George Prudham was one, and the other was J.J. McCann, who retained a directorship in Guaranty Trust even though his department, National Revenue, often engaged in negotiation with that company. St. Laurent may have been embarrassed, but the ministers remained unrepentant even under an Opposition barrage. In more recent years, however, convention and conflict-of-interest guidelines have required ministers to divest themselves of directorships and holdings before taking office, a practice followed, for example, by Eric Kierans and Robert Winters in Liberal Cabinets of the 1960s and by all ministers with such connections in more recent Cabinets.

The three federal Cabinets that held office in 1984 as the government moved from the Liberal hands of Pierre Trudeau, through John Turner, and to the Conservatives under Brian Mulroney present an interesting contrast in business representation. Trudeau had only two ministers with significant business experience. Turner, who, no doubt, would have liked to have more, had only the same two, but Brian Mulroney had thirteen ministers whose primary occupational background was business. This change alone may account in considerable part for the quite different orientation towards the processes and policies of government evidenced by the Liberal and Conservative governments.

The relationship between the private vocational and the public lives of ministers always raises the question of conflicts of interest. In 1973, the issue was broached directly by the prime minister in the House of Commons, but no legislation was introduced. Instead, Trudeau said:

> Guidelines are preferable to additional legislation. . . . An element of discretion, to be exercised by a minister on the basis of discussion with the Prime Minister of the day, seems the best solution. . . . A minister will be expected in the future, as is the policy today, to resign any directorships in commercial or other profit-making corporations that he may have held before becoming a minister.[28]

Cabinet ministers are also covered by the provisions of the Independence of Parliament Act, which would require disclosure of any pecuniary interest or benefit the member might have in any matter upon which he or she wished to speak in parliament.[29]

Under the Trudeau administrations, ministers were required to place their assets in a trust that would either maintain them exactly as they were at the time

[27] Matheson, p. 253.

[28] Pierre Trudeau, *Statement on Conflict of Interest*, House of Commons, July 18, 1973.

[29] *Members of Parliament and Conflict of Interest* (Ottawa: Information Canada, July, 1973), p. 34.

the minister was appointed or administer them on a blind basis, so that the minister could not know what transactions were taking place. Prime Minister Joe Clark issued similar but more stringent guidelines, which applied not just to ministers but to their immediate families.[30] Assets could be placed only in blind trusts. A minister's activities were sharply curtailed after he or she left the Cabinet. For a period of two years, ex-ministers could not serve on boards of directors of corporations with which they dealt as ministers; nor could they act on behalf of any such people or corporations, or act as lobbyists. For a period of one year, they could not accept jobs with companies with which they formerly dealt, nor act as a consultant for those companies. These guidelines were maintained when the Trudeau government returned to office in 1980, and were applied as well to the Mulroney government, which took office in 1984. The post-employment guidelines were significant innovations, since several of Trudeau's ministers, most notably John Turner and Donald Macdonald, both ex-Ministers of Finance, had gone almost directly from Cabinet onto the boards of various corporations and had immediately taken up legal practices, some aspects of which might have contravened the Clark guidelines.

Overall, there may be some dangers inherent in the heavily middle-class professional-male bias of the Cabinet, the highest decision-making body in the country. It is difficult to make equitable and sympathetic decisions affecting welfare, poverty, abortion, or discrimination if few of the decision makers have ever been welfare cases, or been poor, or pregnant, or suffered discrimination. However, it must also be pointed out that it is not necessary for a person to be the mirror image of the people he or she represents to be a good representative. It is at least possible that ministers can represent people quite unlike themselves, because being a good representative is a learned skill, which, in theory at least, may be unconnected with social background. We will return to this issue after we have discussed the representative nature of the bureaucracy.

THE BUREAUCRACY IN CANADA

We have made the point frequently in this book that the Canadian public service is a vital cog in the policy-making machinery of government. Together with the cabinet and the various constellations of interest groups that revolve around any given issue, Canada's senior bureaucrats must be viewed as largely responsible for the shape of public policy in Canada. Who are these people, and where do they come from? What are their career patterns and their socioeconomic backgrounds?

The Ethnic Distribution of Bureaucrats

No one will disagree, I am sure, with the notion that the execution of public policy in Canada deserves the best minds and the highest executive, administrative and

---

[30] "Conflict of Interest Guidelines for Ministers of the Crown" (Ottawa: Privy Council Office, August 1, 1979), mimeo.

professional skills available in the land. The Civil Service Act recognizes this requirement and makes provision for its fulfillment. However it is an unfortunate fact that the Public Service of Canada has, up to now, been unable to attract and retain its fair share of competent persons reflecting the two cultures of Canada. We have not succeeded in recruiting, particularly for intermediate and junior positions, a sufficient number of well qualified citizens from French Canada, and it is the Commission's view that this vacuum is detrimental to the public interest.[31]

This statement, made by a former chairman of the Public Service Commission, is a reflection of the concern federal leaders felt in the 1960s and 1970s, and still feel, to a smaller degree, in the 1980s. The situation has undergone some rather sharp fluctuations in the past. For example, the proportion of French Canadians in highly responsible positions in the public service declined steadily from some 25% in 1918 to 8.1% in 1949.[32] Paradoxically, the cause of the decline during this period, and the reason for many subsequent problems, was a rationalization of recruiting methods and the introduction of a merit system of recruitment and promotion in 1918. Under the old patronage system, French-Canadian Cabinet ministers and members of parliament were allowed to appoint their ethnic confrères to civil-service positions. Under the merit system, largely English-speaking boards tended to equate merit with facility in the English language, and French representation in the federal bureaucracy fell drastically. Nathan Keyfitz has pointed out:

> There is a tendency for the English to judge the French not by the breadth of their vision, nor by their ability to communicate, but by their mastery of the intricacies of English usage and vocabulary and even by their pronunciation of English. Since the French, in judging one another, attach very little weight to speaking English at all and none whatsoever to whether it is spoken with a good accent, they will, as far as this element is concerned, arrange one another in a different order of merit from that in which English speakers make the choices. [The English] not only choose too few French but they also do not choose the right ones.[33]

The general response of the federal government has been to redefine "merit" somewhat, to make ability in both of Canada's official languages a component of the concept. Thus many of the lower- and middle-rank jobs in the public service, and all of the upper-rank jobs, have been classified as requiring some level of capability in both official languages. The level of capability varies according to the job itself, but no one can be brought in or moved to fill any of the two thousand or so top jobs unless he or she is either already bilingual or willing to undergo continuous training to become so.

---

[31] J.J. Carson, "The New Role of the Civil Service Commission," an outline of remarks to the Federal Institute of Management, Ottawa, February 1966. Quoted in V.S. Wilson, "Staffing in the Canadian Federal Bureaucracy," an unpublished Ph.D. dissertation, Queen's University, 1970.

[32] Chambre de commerce du District de Montreal, *Memoire soumis à la commission royale d'enquête sur le service civil fédéral*, avril, 1946.

[33] Nathan Keyfitz, "Canadians and Canadiens," *Queen's Quarterly*, vol. 77, no. 2, 1963, p. 174. The presence of Francophones on the selection boards has improved the situation somewhat since 1963, but there is still some tendency for the English to rate the French by the ability of the latter to speak English, a tendency that is probably reciprocated, but to a lesser degree, by Francophones when rating Anglophones.

The problem of insuring adequate high-level Francophone participation, then, has proven quite difficult. In part, it stems from the fact that Ottawa is still primarily an English-speaking milieu, hardly calculated to make a Francophone feel at home. In part, it stems from the attachment many young, highly educated Francophone Quebeckers have felt at one time in their lives for the *séparatiste* cause or for working for "their" government in Quebec. In part, it is simply a reflection of salary differences, since public-service salaries in Quebec at the executive level are generally higher than elsewhere in Canada.

Despite all this, however, it is significant that the distribution by ethnic origin of members of the Canadian bureaucratic élite is not as bad as it has been.[34] In 1953, John Porter found that 84% of federal senior bureaucrats were English and 13% were French. By contrast, in 1973 Olsen discovered that the percentage of federal senior bureaucrats of British origin had declined to 65% and the percentage of French had risen to 24%. The Public Service Commission reports that, in 1985, 20% of the management category in the federal public service was Francophone, a proportion that has been fairly constant for some years.[35] While Francophones make up 28% of the population (as of 1981), so that their representation in the senior bureaucracy is slightly less than proportional, the fact remains that in thirty years the situation has improved considerably.

The Socioeconomic Background of Bureaucrats

While there have been few Cabinet ministers with less than middle-class background, a significant proportion of the middle levels of the federal bureaucracy has either a farming or a working-class background. Indeed, the public service appears to be an important path of upward mobility in Canada — provided that somewhere along the way our potential Horatio Alger manages to obtain a university degree. However, Olsen's data indicate that the bureaucratic élite of 1980 is more middle class than was the comparable élite studied by John Porter in 1953.[36] Today, nearly 75% of that élite can be characterized as having middle-class origins.

As we mentioned, a university education is extremely important in climbing to higher decision-making levels in the federal service. In 1967, some 81% of the people at "senior-officer" levels (director, director-general, and assistant deputy minister) had obtained at least one degree.[37] Olsen shows that, in 1973, 92% of officers in these positions were in this category,[38] and in 1986, only about three hundred out of four thousand senior managers whose educational background

[34] Olsen, *The State Elite*, p. 79. See also C. Beattie, J. Desey, and S. Longstaff, "Bureaucratic Careers: Anglophones and Francophones in the Canadian Public Service," an internal report for the Royal Commission on Bilingualism and Biculturalism p. 211.

[35] *Annual Report 1985* (Ottawa: Public Service Comission of Canada, 1986. Data are from galley proofs.

[36] Olsen, *The State Elite*, p. 79.

[37] P.J. Chartrand and K.L. Pond, "A Study of Executive Career Paths in the Public Service of Canada," *Public Personnel Association*, Chicago, 1970.

[38] Olsen, *The State Elite*, p. 79.

was known did not have at least one university degree.[39] Olsen reports that in 1973, 61.2% of senior bureaucrats had training beyond the undergraduate level.[40] By 1986, that percentage had risen to sixty-eight.[41] The particular university attended is not of much significance: some 18% of top-level public servants attended the University of Toronto, 8% went to McGill, and 7% to Queen's University; these figures are close to the proportional size of these universities in the 1940s and 1950s, when the public servants were students. Among the educational specializations, the largest groups of senior public servants in 1986 have backgrounds in commerce or business, engineering, economics, political science, and public administration.[42]

There has been a great deal of discussion about whether the Canadian public service, like the Cabinet, should mirror fairly accurately the regional cleavages in Canada. Whatever the theoretical merits of representative bureaucracy, the fact is that the federal bureaucracy has traditionally exhibited a strong bias, in its middle levels, towards those who were born in Ontario, particularly those born in Ottawa. Some 36% of Canadians lived in Ontario in 1971; yet 48.3% of the middle- and upper-rank civil servants in 1965 were born in Ontario, and 23% grew up in the Ottawa-Hull region, which contained only 2% of the nation's population.[43] Among French-Canadian, middle-rank civil servants, 43% grew up in Ottawa-Hull. This bias is explicable. People tend to stay where they are brought up. Moreover, in the Ottawa-Hull area, a civil-service job is looked upon as a legitimate form of work, whereas this is not always true in other areas of the country. Nonetheless, this heavy centralist bias is regrettable, and may, in fact, lead to a lack of sympathy towards Canadians in other regions when decisions are being made. It is perhaps difficult to create policies appropriate for the west or the maritimes if the policy maker knows these regions only from an airplane window or a hotel room.

One of the most important biases in the make-up of the senior levels of the public service is the under-representation of women. Table 14-4 indicates that the proportion of women diminishes drastically as one moves up the salary (and responsibility) scale in the federal public service. Thus, while women make up more than 60% of the lowest-paid workers in the public service, they make up less than 5.5% of the two highest categories. Since the educational level of women in the public service is not vastly different from that of men, one would have to infer a significant bias against the recruitment of women into the most important bureaucratic positions. The suspicion is increased when one notes that, in 1984, among the management-category positions in the federal bureaucracy, only 7%

---

[39] Data supplied by the Public Service Commission.

[40] Olsen, *The State Elite*, p. 79.

[41] Data supplied by Public Service Commission.

[42] Data supplied by Public Service Commission.

[43] More recent data are not available in published sources, although the Public Service Commission does keep a record of such information.

TABLE 14-4
SEX AND LINGUISTIC DISTRIBUTIONS OF FEDERAL PUBLIC SERVICE
POSITIONS BY SALARY, 1985.

Salary in 1985 in Current Dollars	Men	Women	Percentage Who Are Women 1985	Francophones	Percentage Who Are Francophones 1985
Less than 15,000	225	506	69.2	204	27.9
15,000–19,000	10,900	23,264	68.1	10,648	31.2
20,000–24,999	18,941	26,102	57.9	13,326	29.6
25,000–29,999	25,136	12,641	33.5	9,994	26.5
30,000–34,999	24,360	9,709	28.5	9,195	27.0
35,000–44,999	21,888	5,509	20.1	7,494	27.4
45,000–54,999	12,965	1,524	10.5	3,038	21.0
55,000–69,999	6,834	401	5.5	1,207	16.7
70,000–79,999	869	40	4.4	166	18.3
80,000 & more	255	8	3.0	59	22.8
Totals	122,373	79,704	39.4	55,331	27.4

Source: *Annual Report 1985* (Ottawa: Public Service Commission of Canada, 1986). Reproduced with permission of the Minister of Supply and Services Canada.

are occupied by women; and at the top of the category, among assistant deputy ministers, only 14 of 295 positions were held by women.[44]

The Career Bureaucrat

There is a great deal of switching between private and public careers among top-level bureaucrats. Among public servants at the deputy-minister level, 80% followed a private-public career pattern, working first outside the public service.[45]

The overall picture that emerges of the typical senior executive in the federal government is one of a thoroughly upper-middle-class male. In 1986, his salary was likely about $80,000. He was forty-five to fifty years old, and had at least a BA, most likely in a social or management science. He was bilingual—at least by the standards of the federal government. That is to say that if he were Francophone he would be truly bilingual and if Anglophone, he likely would read French very well, understand some of what was said in French (provided one spoke slowly), and could, at the cost of some offense to his listeners' ears and French syntax, make himself understood. There would be about one chance in five that he be Francophone. He is more likely to have come from central Canada than from the periphery.

[44] *Annual Report 1984* (Ottawa: Public Service Commission of Canada, 1984), p. 77.

[45] Wilson, "Staffing in the Canadian Federal Bureaucracy" chapter 8 of Professor Wilson's thesis has been very helpful in the writing of this section. See also P.J. Chartrand and K.L. Pond, "Executive Career Paths," pp. 47–75. Data has been updated by referring to the annual report of the Public Service Commission in Ottawa.

What motivates a person to go into a civil-service career? At the middle levels, such a career can be attractive. Salaries are competitive with salaries in industry. The work is varied, and, while a restrained public service has limited the opportunities for advancement, there is still opportunity for upward mobility. At the top level, however, motivations may well be different. Salaries, while hardly at starvation level, are far lower than those of top executives in the private sector.[46] The responsibilities are often huge and the work load crushing. At such levels, other compensations — such as the opportunity to actually do something for the public welfare, the chance to work on huge programs of nation-wide importance, and love of the power that derives from this opportunity — may well be the primary motivators.

Even at that, the motivation is sometimes difficult to comprehend. The ability to exert much control over policy is constrained by the large number of actors involved, and even the ability to manage one's own department is severely constrained by the impositions of central agencies and of public-sector unions and hiring and firing procedures. The reductions in the size of the bureaucracy set in place in the mid-1980s have severely curtailed promotion opportunities, and have given managers the unpleasant task, familiar to the private but not to the public sector, of actually firing people. Salaries are sometimes frozen by the government, which is eager to show a restraint face to the public, and the Conservative government seems much less inclined to listen to its bureaucrats than was its Liberal predecessor. Given all these factors, coupled with the fact that the public holds the public service in relatively low esteem, it often requires a strong sense of public duty, or maybe an inability to find another job, to ignore opportunities elsewhere.

There are no comprehensive data on provincial public servants.[47] In the larger provinces, public-service posts are well paid, and the higher-level civil servants in Quebec and Ontario may be no less involved in national decision making than their federal counterparts. On the other hand, holding a deputy-minister post in a maritime province may give relatively little real power to the incumbent, when viewed in national perspective, and the financial rewards may also be smaller. Provincial civil services differ quite markedly from one another in their make-up, and, as yet, research has not gone much farther than to point out that these differences exist.[48] It is unlikely, however, that their socioeconomic make-up differs very greatly from that of the federal bureaucracy.[49]

Just as it was appropriate to raise the question of the extent to which a Cabinet that is not truly socially representative can be responsive to social needs, so, too,

[46] It may seem strange to rate the salaries of deputy ministers, who in 1986 could earn up to $120,000 per year, as relatively low. However, when compared to corporation presidents, who usually head organizations that are smaller than government departments but who frequently earn much larger salaries, they are indeed low. The comparison with the salaries paid professional athletes is even more discrepant.

[47] For data that include a sample of provincial bureaucrats, see Olsen, *The State Elite*. However, his data do not isolate provincial élites for specific analysis.

[48] Porter, *The Vertical Mosaic*, pp. 417–457. See also Presthus, *Elite Accommodation*.

[49] There is some information on backgrounds to be gleaned from the pages of D. Belamy, J.H. Pammett, and D.C. Rowat, *The Provincial Political Systems* (Toronto: Methuen, 1976). On provincial MPs, see H.D. Clarke, Richard Price, and Robert Krause, "Backbenchers," in *op. cit.*, pp. 214–236.

it is appropriate to raise that question with respect to the bureaucracy. There is a large body of literature on this issue.[50] Its conclusions are tentative and sometimes even contradictory. Indeed, there are two quite opposed themes that run through the literature on representative bureaucracy. One suggests that bureaucracies are far from capable of acting representatively and that major administrative controls are therefore essential; while the other suggests that bureaucracies can, indeed, be responsive to the needs of their clientele, and that the "administrative culture" is, in fact, a quite faithful reproduction of the broader political culture.[51] In Canada, the evidence suggests that the socioeconomic backgrounds of the most senior bureaucrats would make this latter interpretation unlikely to apply, but there is also more concrete evidence based upon attitude and behaviour. Lee Sigelman and William Vanderbok suggest: "[Our] findings provide precious little empirical support for the notion that careerist civil servants in Canada are more broadly responsive than legislators. . . . Almost invariably it was the legislators, not the bureaucrats who were more favourably disposed to the needs of the less favoured and advantaged."[52] Sigelman and Vanderbok also find that the senior bureaucracy is less representative of the Canadian social fabric than are the legislators, so it is possible that their lesser responsiveness is caused, in part, by this factor.

MEMBERS OF PARLIAMENT

Among the most visible of Canada's political élites are the members of parliament. While their role in deciding what policies the government will promulgate is sometimes marginal, they are nonetheless the most visible link between the public and the rest of Canada's political élites. Because they have important symbolic significance in addition to whatever policy role they may play, it is important to ask ourselves what they look like with respect to ethnicity, socioeconomic status, career patterns, and the like.

The Socioeconomic Background of MPs[53]

Since Canadian MPs are elected from geographically based constituencies that are apportioned among the provinces roughly in accordance with population,

---

[50] For Canadian literature, see Lee Singleman and W.G. Vanderbok, "Legislators, Bureaucrats, and Canadian Democracy," *CJPS*, x, 3, September 1977, pp. 615–623; and Kenneth Kernaghan, "Representative Bureaucracy," *CPA*, 21, 4, Winter 1978, p. 489ff. Singleman and Vanderbok also provide a valuable succinct review of the literature.

[51] The first point of view derives from Herman Finer, "Administrative Responsibility in Democratic Government," *Public Administration Review*, 1, 1940–1941, pp. 335–350. The second derives from Carl Friedrich, "Public Policy and the Nature of Administrative Responsibility," in Friedrich and E.G. Mason, eds., *Public Policy* (Cambridge: Harvard Press, 1940), pp. 3–24.

[52] Singleman and Vanderbok, "Legislators," pp. 621, 619.

[53] We have drawn heavily, in this section, on D.J. Falcone, unpublished Ph.D. dissertation, Duke University, 1974. See also D. Hoffman and N. Ward, *Bilingualism and Biculturalism in the Canadian House of Commons*, Royal Commission on Bilingualism and Biculturalism, Document No. 3 (Ottawa: Queen's Printer, 1970),

there is no point in describing the provincial distribution of MPs. Nor is there as much point now as there once was in discussing the rural-urban distribution of federal MPs, since decennial redistributions of seats by impartial electoral-boundaries commissions has, for the most part, rectified the huge rural over-representation that persisted until the late 1950s. In any case, many consti-tuencies mix rural and urban voters.

The ethnic distribution of MPs shows a heavy bias towards the two charter ethnic groups. Of all MPs since 1940, 94% have been of either British or French descent, while only 78% of the general population is British or French. The distribution between the English and French groups has been quite equitable, since French MPs normally represent French ridings. It is unfortunate that, in the past, there have not been included within the ranks of MPs more "other" Canadians. In a body as symbolically important as the House of Commons, that sort of representation would be valuable. Elections since 1970, however, have shown some increase in the number of non-charter group candidates and MPs. The religious distribution of MPs parallels fairly closely that of the general public. Thus, from 1940 to 1972, some 56% of MPs were Protestant, 41% Catholic, and 3% "other." The corresponding population percentages were fifty, forty-five and five. In common with Cabinet ministers, it is becoming increasingly difficult to determine the religious backgrounds of MPs; many no longer report that information.

It is when we turn to the class backgrounds of MPs that we find the greatest discrepancies between the public and their representatives. Table 14-5 indicates that the occupational status of MPs, though not as high as that of Cabinet minis-ters, is nonetheless quite high. Only about 16% of the general public hold occu-pations that could be classified high-status, but 75% of the MPs and 85% of the Cabinet ministers elected in 1984 belonged to this group before entering poli-tics. Although lawyers make up much less than one per cent of the Canadian population, 41% of all new MPs elected between World War Two and 1965 were lawyers.[54] The 1980 and 1984 parliaments saw a reversal of this trend, with the proportion of lawyers in the House declining to 25.5% in 1980 and to less than 20% in 1984.[55] Indeed, the 1980s may be characterized as the heyday of the business-oriented MP. In 1980, 18.4% of MPs had a business background, and more than 28% of those elected in 1984 came from business. The other signifi-cant occupational background for MPs is education. Of MPs elected in 1984, 17% listed education as their primary occupational background.

As one might expect, the educational level of MPs is correspondingly much higher than that of the public. Since 1940, some 70% of MPs have been to

especially chapter 2; Dennis Forcese and John DeVries, "Occupational and Electoral Success in Canada; the 1974 Election," *CRSA*, 14, (3), 1977, pp. 331–340; and Dennis Forcese, *The Canadian Class Struc-ture*. Material is updated from annual *Parliamentary Guides*, and from part four of the report of the Chief Electoral Officer, 33rd general edition, 1984.

54 Norman Ward, *The Canadian House of Commons: Representation* (Toronto: University of Toronto Press, 1950), p. 132. A. Kornberg, *Canadian Legislative Behaviour* (New York: Holt, Rinehart and Winston, 1967), p. 43, and data supplied by Professor R.R. March.

55 1980 and 1984 data are from *Contact*, No. 55, March 1, 1985, Elections Canada, Ottawa, p. 8.

TABLE 14-5
**OCCUPATIONAL STATUS OF CABINET MINISTERS, MPs, AND THE
PUBLIC, SHOWING THE PERCENTAGE OF EACH GROUP IN
HIGH-STATUS OCCUPATIONS PRIOR TO ENTERING POLITICS**

Period	Cabinet Ministers	MPs	Public
1867–1904	80.4%	71.8%	8.6%
1905–1939	83.0	73.8	11.0
1940–1979	81.0	65.0	15.0
1980–1987	85.0	75.0	16.0

Source: 1867–1968 D.J. Falcone, Ph.D. dissertation, Duke University, 1974;
1968–1979 Dennis Forcese and J. Devries, "Occupational and Electoral Success in
Canada," and *Parliamentary Guides* and biographical data from the Prime Minister's
Office. The classifications are somewhat arbitrary in some categories, such as
"business," where it is assumed that one-half of those naming that category come
from relatively low-status positions.

university, compared with a general population figure of less than 10%.[56] In the
thirty-third Parliament, elected in 1984, 82% of MPs had at least some post-
secondary education.[57] Moreover, MPs have tended to come disproportionately
from homes with a relatively high socioeconomic status. Some 16% of MPs elected
in 1962 had fathers who were professionals, whereas in 1921 (when most of
these fathers would have been working), only 6% of the labour force could have
been classified as professional.

Thus, Canadian MPs, like their legislative counterparts in the United States
and Britain, are territorially but not socially representative. Table 14-6 summarizes the occupational and educational backgrounds of MPs in 1978, and compares
them to American senators and to candidates for the British House of Commons.
It will be seen that U.S. senators appear to be an even more élite group than
Canadian MPs, but that the British House of Commons comes somewhat closer
in occupational structure to mirroring its name. At least one-third of its members
have less than a post-secondary education, and about one-fifth come from blue-
collar or farming occupations.

The Career Patterns of MPs

Aside from what has already been said about the occupational backgrounds of
MPs, what can one assert about their political careers? Are most of them rank
amateurs in politics? Or do they have significant amounts of political experience
before coming to the House of Commons?

Both Kornberg and Ward have found that a large proportion of MPs did have
considerable political experience before they were elected to the House of
Commons. In the period between 1921 and 1954, 31% had been members of
various provincial legislative assemblies, and 5% had been in a provincial Cabinet.

[56] D.J. Falcone, *op. cit.*

[57] *Contact*, No. 55, March 1, 1985, p. 8.

TABLE 14-6
OCCUPATION AND LEVEL OF EDUCATION OF CANADIAN MPs, UNITED STATES SENATORS,
AND CANDIDATES FOR THE BRITISH HOUSE OF COMMONS

Occupation and Education	Canadian MPs	American Senators	Candidates for British House of Commons
Professional	60%	70%	55%
Proprietor-Manager	26	26	28
Farmer	7	4	6
Blue-collar or clerical	7	—	12
College or University	72	85	63
Less than College	28	15	37

Source: Canada: *Parliamentary Guide* 1978; United States: *Congressional Quarterly*, 96th Congress, vol. 37, no. 3, p. 81; Britain: Colin Mellors, *The British* MP (London: Saxon House, 1978), pp. 43–44, p. 65.

However, since Confederation, the proportion of MPs with prior experience in provincial or municipal politics has been steadily declining. In the Parliament elected in 1887, which was fairly typical of parliaments of that time, only 34% of MPs had no prior experience in provincial or municipal politics. By 1945, the proportion of MPs without prior experience had risen to 60%.[58] In the House elected in 1980, only 34% of MPs had prior political experience (27.3% in municipal and 6.7% in provincial politics). In 1984, the proportions declined again, to 20.2% with municipal experience and 6.4% with provincial experience.[59] The federal House of Commons no longer seems to be considered the summit of a political career. Indeed, at least since the turn of the century, the concept of a hierarchy of political careers in Canada with the House of Commons at the top has not pertained. A lack of experience in other legislative bodies cannot necessarily be equated with a complete lack of political experience. Many Canadian MPs have served a political apprenticeship in their own party organizations, but this does not provide the same type of experience as formal elected office.[60]

Not least among the disincentives of political life in Canada is the difficulty many MPs find in returning to private life.[61] A few MPs trickle into the Senate or the judiciary or to the various commissions and boards of the public service. However, most defeated MPs return to private life or retire. In the absence of professional qualifications, it may be quite difficult for an ex-MP to find private-sector employment, since it is difficult to suggest for what private-sector jobs a parliamentary career provides pertinent experience. Stories of MPs requiring two years to find employment are not uncommon, and this problem suggests

[58] Ward, *The Canadian House of Commons: Representation*, p. 123. Current data is from *Parliamentary Guides*.

[59] *Contact*, No. 55, March 1, 1985, p. 8.

[60] Kornberg, *Canadian Legislative Behaviour*, pp. 54–55.

[61] Ward, *The Canadian House of Commons: Representation*, p. 145, has a tabulation of the careers of ex-MPs up to 1935. His data, however, must be interpreted carefully, for he has apparently not separated ex-ministers from other MPs. The ex-ministers, of course, get a disproportionate share of the plums.

another reason for the heavy concentration of professionals not only in Canada, but presumably in the U.S. and British legislatures as well.

In spite of this problem, and in spite of more or less constant grumbling about their role in the scheme of things, members of parliament seem to have a relatively high level of satisfaction with their jobs:

> 75 percent of members of the 25th Parliament (in the mid 1960s) said there were not other public offices in which they were interested; 9 percent were interested in judgeships or appointments to the Senate; 7 percent wanted to return to provincial politics; 6 percent said they would like to be the mayors of cities in which they resided and an additional 3 percent said they were interested in other public offices but they would not reveal what these were.[62]

Allen Kornberg attributes this satisfaction to a number of factors, but it is possible that the major one was that he was interviewing just after an election. Whether legislators would feel the same way halfway through a Parliament, or with an election approaching, is doubtful. Back-bench MPs are frequently quoted as expressing considerable dissatisfaction with their jobs, and, in particular, with the amount of influence they can exert over the making of policy.[63]

It is perhaps paradoxical, in view of the highly public nature of their jobs and the need to gain support from a broad spectrum of voters, that MPs can be so unlike the people they represent. They are representative of the French and English divisions in Canadian society, and they are quite representative with respect to religion and geography, but there the resemblance ends. MPs are not at all representative of whatever class differences exist in Canadian society. Some writers have suggested that this may be caused by the deferential nature of Canadian society compared to, for example, the United States or Australia.[64] However, the "deferential" British regularly elect approximately 15% union leaders and working-class people to their parliament, while, as Table 14-6 indicates, our allegedly non-deferential southern neighbours elect senators almost exclusively from upper socioeconomic groups. Perhaps the easiest explanation of the non-representative nature of our parliamentary élite is simply the lack of a working-class party in Canada comparable in size to the British or Australian Labour Parties.

THE JUDICIAL ELITE IN CANADA

As we noted in our earlier discussion of the Charter of Rights and Freedoms, the potential importance of the judiciary in shaping the nature of Canadian life is greatly enhanced by the constitutional settlement of 1982. In chapters 6 and 7, we considered the issue of how likely the Canadian judiciary is to adopt an activist political stance akin to its U.S. counterparts. While that approach is certainly

---

[62] Kornberg, *Canadian Legislative Behaviour*, p. 35.

[63] See M. Atkinson, unpublished Ph.D. dissertation, Carleton University, 1976, and R. Jackson and M. Atkinson, *The Canadian Legislative System* (Toronto: Macmillan, 1975).

[64] R. Alford, *Party and Society*.

not settled at the time of this writing, it is important to recognize the possibility that the judiciary as a policy élite may become more important in the future than it now is. It is, therefore, important to consider the nature of this group.

Judges are naturally an élite group, because of the relatively few judgeships that are available in Canada, and because of the special qualifications one must have to become a judge. Moreover, because of the principle of judicial independence that dominates our entire legal process, the mode of appointment of judges and the operation of the judicial process may serve to exacerbate the élitist nature of our courts.

The qualifications to become a superior or county-court judge, appointed by the Governor-General in Council according to section 96 of the BNA Act, are basically to have been a member of the bar of one of the provinces for at least ten years. To be a member of the bar of a province, an individual must have a law degree from a recognized institution, must have undergone a period of articling, must have taken the provincial bar-admission course, which is usually approximately of six months' duration, and must have passed the bar-admission examinations, which are set, administered, and marked by the provincial law society. In other words, in the same manner that the senior bureaucrats are an élite by virtue of educational level, so the judiciary in Canada is an élite by virtue of the fact that explicit educational qualifications are a prerequisite for a sanctioned place in the professional pool from which judges are exclusively selected.

When we move a step further, to consider the sorts of people who get to law school in the first place, as one might expect, the recruitment for these institutions is disproportionately from the upper and middle classes of Canadian society. As Dennis Olsen points out, "Lawyers in Canada are certainly not drawn from a representative cross section of the population. . . . The class and ethnic biases that will ultimately find their expression in the composition of the high courts have their beginning in the selection for law school".[65] Although there has been a tendency on the part of many law schools in recent years to attempt to include people from non-charter ethnic groups, people from working class or farm backgrounds, and people other than the sons and daughters of lawyers, Olsen points out that the subsequent career patterns of lawyers still reflect ethnic and socioeconomic biases. He finds that the plum legal positions, such as partnerships in large firms and specialization in the more lucrative sub-disciplines of the profession, tend to be dominated by charter-group and upper-middle-class Canadians. The only significant exceptions to these generalizations would seem to be women and Jews, who are making definite inroads into the legal profession in Canada.[66]

Reinforcing the heavily selective process of recruitment to the legal profession in Canada is the even more selective process that fills the approximately six hundred federally appointed judgeships. Because of the principle of judicial independence, judges are appointed until age seventy-five, are given a fixed salary by Parliament, and are placed in a position where they are expected to be above the temptations that face mere mortals. For the most part, judges cannot

---

[65] Olsen, *The State Elite*, p. 44.

[66] Olsen, p. 44.

be fired, except for gross crimes or misdemeanors. Even blatantly biased judgements or incompetence are not sufficient cause for dismissal, although our system of appeals does provide a litigant (who has sufficient cash) with the opportunity of overturning biased or incompetent judgements in a higher court. Because judges hold office "for the duration," therefore, the process of appointing them in the first place is very important, and the responsibility for such appointments lies *de facto* with the federal Cabinet, particularly the Prime Minister and the Minister of Justice.[67]

Considering the fact that it is members of the political élite who select the members of the judicial élite, and that it seems likely that even the best-intentioned Minister of Justice will lean towards a personal view of what constitutes a good judge, in the long run, the appointments to the bench will tend to reflect the same class and ethnic biases as the political élite. As Olsen states, "the political elites are looking for someone very much like ourselves" when they select judges.[68]

The largest amount of criticism has been levelled at the judicial-appointment process in the area of the political affiliation of the appointees. Historically, the members of the bench have been selected unabashedly from the ranks of the party faithful. Certainly there has been a consistent attempt to select good legal minds for the judgeships, but, all things being equal, a Liberal government will select a good Liberal legal mind over a good Conservative legal mind almost all the time. While there is some indication that the patronage dimension of judicial selection and appointment is declining — Porter found in 1960 that 57% of appointments[69] had a previous party affiliation and Olsen found that figure had slipped to 42% in 1973[70] — a judgeship is still a handy reward to be doled out by grateful prime ministers to defeated or worn-out Cabinet ministers or to deserving supporters.

Since the late 1960s, the practice has been for the federal justice minister to submit the names of potential judicial appointees to a committee of the Canadian Bar Association. The aim of this practice was to insure that legal rather than political qualifications would be the critical determinants of who might become a judge in the Canadian courts. This procedure has likely worked fairly well, for in fact there has been an increasing number of non-partisan or even "wrong-party" appointments to the bench since that time, but it is not always followed faithfully. The critics of the procedure, however, argue that the political élites and the élite of the legal profession, which dominates the Canadian Bar Association, are virtually identical in terms of their class and ethnic origins, and the end result of the procedure is simply that "some degree of control over judicial appointments has now shifted from politicians to the legal profession; that is, in reality, from lawyers wearing political garb to lawyers wearing legal garb."[71] Without judging the overall impact of the involvement of the profession in the appointment of judges, however, it is clear that such a procedure has already reduced, and may well prove to reduce

[67] See chapter 7.

[68] Olsen, *The State Elite*, p. 44.

[69] Porter, *op. cit.*, p. 415.

[70] Olsen, *The State Elite*, p. 45.

[71] Olsen, p. 47.

quite drastically in the future, the extent to which the power of judicial appointment is to be used simply as a partisan patronage power.

Beyond the claims of partisanship in the appointment process, what the critics of the élitism of the Canadian judiciary can claim is that the class and ethnic origins of the judges are reflective of the biases in the legal profession itself; the judiciary in Canada is, indeed, dominated by ethnic charter-group and middle-class Canadians. Moreover, the gains that have been made by women in the legal profession generally in the past few years are not reflected as prominently in the appointments to the bench; judgeships in Canada, except for rare exceptions, have always been a male preserve.

Finally, while the focus of this chapter is more on *who* the élites in Canada are than how the Canadian system helps them to maintain their hegemony, we must say a few words about the élitist nature of the legal process itself. The problem here is, in part, that it costs money to use our court systems. Lawyers' fees alone are beyond the means of many Canadians, and the legal process, especially in higher-level courts, is dominated exclusively by members of the legal profession. This means that lower-class Canadians and the non-charter ethnic-group Canadians tend to dominate the docket in the lower courts, and middle-class Canadians tend to dominate the business of the higher courts.

This stratification exists, in part, because the jurisdiction in civil matters is determined by the amount of money involved.[72] It is therefore natural, in some respects, for middle-class Canadians to appear before the higher courts simply because they, by definition, have more money. Similarly, there are definite correlations between minor criminal offences, which are dealt with by lower courts, and variables such as non-charter ethnicity (particularly native people), lower socioeconomic status, and place of residence. Thus, while we could see the legal system as *reflective* of serious social, economic, and ethnic inequities in Canadian society, it is difficult to lay the blame for these problems at the feet of the judiciary.

On the other hand, when we turn to *appeal* cases, we find that such use of the courts, except in serious criminal offences, is almost exclusively restricted to more privileged Canadians. Here the legal system *can* be blamed, for the access to the avenues of appeal in our system are virtually closed to all but middle-class Canadians by reasons of cost. Even legal-aid programs, which are in operation in all provinces, and which are aimed at providing free access to legal advice to those who cannot afford it, only begin to solve the problem. As studies cited by Dennis Olsen show, many potential users of the legal aid system don't even know of its existence,[73] and those that have discovered the program often find that they end up being represented by a green (if earnest and well-meaning) recent graduate of the bar-admissions course. Legal aid, therefore, is a step in the right direction, but it is only a step. Ultimately, we have to develop better devices for insuring that all Canadians of all ethnic and socioeconomic groups have equivalent access to the courts.

---

[72] See chapter 7.

[73] Olsen, *The State Elite*, p. 47.

The verdict on the élite nature of our judicial system is very difficult to arrive at. The involvement of the legal profession in the appointment of section-96 judges has helped to reduce the amount of partisan bias in the selection process, and any further evolution in this direction can only improve the credibility, if not the operational effectiveness, of the courts. However, it is also argued that the judiciary in Canada is an education élite. This point is incontrovertible, but on the other hand, to have a non-élite judiciary in a system built on the premise of judicial independence is likely impossible. Most Canadians would agree that it is better to be judged by a well-trained professional who is paid to be an *objective* arbiter of disputes and not an advocate of any particular point of view. This means that judgements will continue to be limited to members of the legal profession, and that any significant improvement in the ethnic and class representativeness of the Canadian judiciary will depend upon democratizing the law schools and the legal profession in general, and not upon making structural changes to the legal system.

CONCLUSIONS

There is no such thing as a "politically irrelevant" élite, for élites are normally defined as those who have a disproportionate share of power in society, and such people will naturally be involved in the authoritative allocation of a society's resources. John Porter has suggested that many of Canada's élites are interconnected; many are members of more than one sub-élite, and they cannot help but carry ideas from one to another. Thus, for example, Robert Winters, who finished a fairly close second to Pierre Trudeau in the Liberal Party leadership race of 1968, moved back and forth freely between the political world and the business world, where he was president of such corporations as Rio Algom and Brascan. In a different vein, Jean Marchand moved from being president of the Confederation of National Trade Unions, Quebec's largest grouping of labour unions, to being a powerful member of the federal Cabinet. Pierre Trudeau provides an excellent example of inter-élite connections. His father was a millionaire, which by most reckoning puts Trudeau in the economic élite; he edited the small but influential periodical *Cité libre*, which puts him in the communications élite; he lectured at the University of Montreal Law School, edited a seminal book entitled *La grève de l'amiante*, and wrote many articles, which qualify him as part of the intellectual élite; and he has certainly managed to get into the political élite. Brian Mulroney did not come from an élite family background, but prior to his career as leader of the Progressive Conservatives and Prime Minister, he was president of the Iron Ore Company of Canada, and he started his career as a lawyer. John Turner came from a middle-class background, but early in his career developed an array of élite connections, not least of which was marriage into an old moneyed family.

In *The Vertical Mosaic*, John Porter identified not only political and bureaucratic élites, which were approximately the same ones as those discussed here, but also labour, communications, and religious élites. Porter was able to show that

the political and economic élites, and to a lesser extent the religious and communications élites, shared common backgrounds such as those described in this
chapter. Wallace Clement in the *Canadian Corporate Elite* has more recently
found that the social background of élites in the mid-1970s was not greatly different
from what Porter found in the 1960s, although the proportion of United States
citizens in what he defined as the Canadian corporate élite had increased greatly.
This material did not show, although it implied, that those common backgrounds
led to common attitudes and values, which would lead to similar policy predilections. Thus, Porter was not able to show directly whether the élites at the top
of each segment of Canadian society were likely to agree among themselves because
they were élite, or whether they were likely to disagree because they represented
different segments of Canadian society.

The evidence suggests at least the possibility of a shared overall value consensus
among élites, combined with a certain amount of inter-élite conflict over specific
issues. Robert Presthus has demonstrated that the common factors in the social
backgrounds of various élites have led at least the political, bureaucratic, and
industrial élites to have many attitudes in common.[74] The members of Presthus'
élites were hardly intensely ideological creatures; their most cherished common
ethic was perhaps best characterized as "managerial" or "pragmatic." The process
of accommodation among them was lubricated primarily by agreement on this
managerial ethic.[75] But commitment to the managerial ethic — that the problem
is not to provide sweeping social changes but rather to maintain and operate
more efficiently the system we already have — is certainly enough to provide a
basis for interaction, and, above all, provides a decision-making atmosphere
that will most often favour the status quo over social change. When that interaction
is further facilitated by common backgrounds and overlapping membership in
clubs, on boards of directors, boards of governors, or Cabinets, we find in Canada,
no less than in any other developed nation, the framework for the politics Presthus
characterizes as "elite accommodation." Other analysts have other names to
describe, in more or less critical terms, the same phenomenon. Thus, for example,
some speak of "consociational democracy," others define the system as based
upon "class injustice," and still others refer to "interest group liberalism."

There are elements of both heterogeneity and homogeneity among Canada's
politically relevant élites. Regional, French-English, and religious cleavages are,
on the whole, quite faithfully reflected in the composition of élites; occupational,
educational, and general class differences are not. The upper-socioeconomic
class bias is most marked in the family backgrounds of Cabinet ministers, and
perhaps least marked among bureaucrats, although even there the educational
requirements eliminate the vast majority of Canadians from contention, and insure
that whatever the background, the senior bureaucracy is thoroughly upper-
middle-class by the time it takes office.

The temptation is to conclude, from this analysis, that the political process
in Canada is bound to favour middle- and upper-class Canadians. When one

[74] Presthus, *Elite Accommodation*, chapter 11.

[75] Presthus, p. 344.

adds the evidence presented earlier concerning political participation and political socialization, and the information on interest-group activity, and when one looks at the distributional impact of most Canadian public policy, that evidence begins to appear overwhelming. A very large body of Canadians may be placed, by the combination of these circumstances and by the nature of the political system, in a situation where they can react to the political system only as objects of its policies without having any real ability to influence them. Cut off by their lack of education, money, membership in interest groups, or representation among decision makers, they have little real control at all over what emerges from "their" political system, and less possibility of achieving the lion's share of benefits from it.

On the other hand, there are some small cracks in the élite monolith, which tough-minded critics of the system, such as Olsen and Clement, dismiss as "exceptions," as conscious attempts on the part of the dominant class to renew itself, or as cynical gestures to legitimize the status quo.[76] If we choose to be more optimistic, we can point to the fact that a few non-charter group Canadians are making the team of the state élite — Haidasz, Hnatyshyn, Mazankowski, Paproski, Jelinek, Danson, Gray, and Kaplan have made it to the cabinet; Reisman, Gottlieb, Ostry, Shoyama and Rasminsky among others have made it to the highest levels of the mandarinate; the last chief justice of the Supreme Court of Canada was Jewish; Edward Schreyer, the Governor-General of much of the Trudeau era was of German descent; the Lieutenant Governor of Ontario, Lincoln Alexander, is black; Dave Barrett in British Columbia, Joe Ghiz in Prince Edward Island, and Edward Schreyer were or are non-charter-group provincial premiers; and we now have both Inuit and Indian MPs and Senators. In terms of the class composition of our state élite, the fact is that 15% of the top bureaucrats, at least one Supreme Court judge, and a number of Cabinet ministers have family backgrounds *outside* the upper and middle strata of society. It is to be hoped that these cases indicate a growing openness and accessibility of the élite ranks in our political system, and perhaps in the next decade, we will see still more significant lower-class and non-charter ethnic encroachments on the Canadian state élite.

Perhaps, too, the real signifiance of these success stories is symbolic; they may function to encourage non-élite Canadians to pursue avenues of upward mobility, such as higher education. In fact, when we consider that high level of education is the only élite characteristic that has actually been reinforced since John Porter's path-breaking 1953 study, it is not difficult to conclude that the problem with Canadian democracy is not that the ranks of the state élite are inaccessible, but that our institutions of higher learning are too exclusively the preserves of the well-born. The solutions to élite dominance in the Canadian system may therefore lie in improving access to higher education, so that more of the children of working-class Canadians can acquire the qualification that open the doors to careers in politics, the bureaucracy, and the judicial system.

[76] Olsen, *The State Elite*, p. 22.

C H A P T E R   1   5
CABINET AND EXECUTIVE SUPPORT AGENCIES

A complex society generates an almost infinite array of demands on government. Unfortunately, the resources available to meet those demands are all too finite. Moreover, the demands of one group will usually conflict with those of others, which means that to satisfy one interest will often mean thwarting others. Thus, with multiple and conflicting demands, and with scarce resources, it is not surprising that the central concern of modern political decision makers is to sort out which problems deserve to be considered, and which of those should be considered first. This process we refer to as *priority determination*. The most important institutions for the determination of priorities in the Canadian political system are cabinets and their arrays of supporting agencies.

While the determination of priorities is centred in the Cabinet, the sorting process begins in the environment of the political system. There, political parties and interest groups reduce and combine policy demands in such a way as to maximize the likelihood of electoral success or the benefits flowing to their members. By determining which policy options to ask for and when, these agencies help to define the range of choices with which the Cabinet is ultimately confronted.

Cabinet receives considerable support in the determination of priorities. This support is provided by the organizations most often referred to as *central agencies*. In the federal government, these include, most notably, the Privy Council Office (PCO), the Department of Finance, and the Treasury Board Secretariat. The Prime Minister's Office (PMO), members of ministerial staffs and individual ministerial contacts within the party structure also provide advice and support. The various supporting agencies often begin to consider priorities well before their political masters are required to come to any conclusions. They do so because a major problem in the consideration of priorities is to bring adequate supporting information to the table. This task may mean finding or generating data or, at least equally often, filtering and selecting from what would be, for already overloaded ministers, an undigestible mass of data. This so-called "briefing function" (for much of the work involves the preparation of briefing notes or the provision of oral briefings for ministers) is at the heart of the influence of the central agencies.

It has been a characteristic of the past decade that the federal and some provincial governments have experimented with a series of realignments among central agencies. Such changes have been made more complex by independent changes in the structures of the Cabinet.[1] These changes in the executive arena have generally been intended to increase the extent of central coordination and control within government; to assist the political executive in producing reasonably consistent — or at least not blatantly self-contradictory — policies in a complex society. In part, they are a reaction to the recognition that under straitened financial circumstances, program initiatives cannot grow like Topsy, but rather must be balanced by program reductions. The complex trade offs involved require a more sophisticated set of support mechanisms than needed when the only real question about a policy proposal was, "How will it sell in Moose Jaw?"

COLLECTIVE AND INDIVIDUAL RESPONSIBILITY

Many of these changes seek to resolve what is one of the oldest problems in parliamentary governments: the tension between individual ministerial and collective governmental responsibility. One of the major conventions of Parliamentary government is that ministers are *individually* accountable to Parliament for the management of their departments. In the extreme, this means that a minister must resign if he or she can be shown to have been negligent or irresponsible in the expenditure of the taxpayer's money. A second major convention of parliamentary government is that the government is *collectively* responsible to Parliament for the conduct of the affairs of the state. As the political executive of the government, the Cabinet may hold office only for so long as it retains the confidence of Parliament. The collective principle means

[1] In fact, a similar process can be seen to have occurred in many other industrialized countries, but not as rapidly or extensively as in Canada. See Colin Campbell, *Governments Under Stress* (Toronto: Macmillan, 1984).

that "all ministers should have the opportunity to express an informed view within the cabinet process on a proposal for which they will bear collective responsibility."[2] In the extreme, this convention means that a minister must resign if he or she disagrees fundamentally with a policy collectively determined by cabinet. In practice, the extreme application of the collective principle is impractical. Some decisions involve security matters, which are better not shared with forty ministers and hordes of advisors. Some are too small to merit the time of many ministers. Some are too big, and require too rapid a decision, to be shared so widely. Finally, Cabinet ministers are, like most people, quite attached to their jobs, and the principle at stake must be a mighty one indeed before they will resign.

These two conventions, of collective and of individual responsibility, carry, in combination, the makings of a paradox. Obviously, if Cabinet decisions bearing on individual departments are made collectively, it is difficult to hold an individual minister accountable before Parliament for those decisions. If the issue is one of personal rectitude, the individual ministers may well be held responsible, but if it is a question of government policy, that would be difficult. Conversely, if the individual minister is deemed to be fully responsible for policy and expenditures, then Cabinet cannot be viewed as collectively responsible. There is always, therefore, some inherent conflict in practice between the dictates of individual and collective responsibility.[3]

There is also a power paradox, which must be dealt with in Cabinet-level decision making. For virtually all ministers, a seat in cabinet is the fulfilment of a lifetime spent chasing the holy grail of political power. Yet power, exercised collectively, cuts two ways. On the one hand, it expands a minister's role, since ministers will have the potential to influence decisions in portfolios other than their own; on the other hand, it gives fellow ministers a say in one's own departmental decisions, thus reducing power. This is not a problem for the Prime Minister or the Minister of Finance, who generally can influence any other minister's priorities while precluding any unwanted interference in their own affairs, but for other ministers, collective decision making is very much a two-edged sword, and many of them view it as a transgression on their turf.

Finally, to add one more complication to an already complex picture, in Canadian Cabinets we have seen that ministers also represent regional interests. Thus, when the ministers sit down together to determine policy priorities and to choose among different policy alternatives, each one of them speaks from the point of view of a department, as the representative of a region, and from a conception of collective responsibility.

Given the tensions involved in Cabinet-level decision making, it is hardly surprising that there is no universally correct balance and no one set of structures and processes that can be guaranteed to work. Instead, the nature of Cabinet decision making very much reflects the way in which a prime minister wants to

---

[2] Ian Clark, "Recent Changes in the Cabinet Decision-Making System," *Canadian Public Administration*, vol. 28, no. 2, Summer 1985, p. 198. Clark updated this article in mimeograph form in December, 1986.

[3] *Bureaucracy in Canada: Control and Reform*, Research Study no. 43, (Ottawa: Royal Commission on the Economic Union), p. 164.

operate the Cabinet, and the balance of power among ministers. Although there are some seemingly eternal principles, the details of the process will change fairly frequently. Whatever the reasons, the rapid creation, deletion, and realignment of the details of the process and the agencies surrounding the Cabinet means problems for the intrepid textbook writer, whose work faces the danger of instant obsolescence. The reader is therefore urged to be alert to changes in the Cabinet and central agencies, for it is a reasonable prediction that change will continue to take place.[4]

The following sections of this chapter will comprise a more detailed consideration of the priority-determining activities of the Canadian cabinet in the late 1980s. We will describe the structure of both the Cabinet and of the key political and financial advisory bodies operating in the federal executive arena, and we will consider the dynamics of the decision-making process in this complex arena.

THE CABINET: STRUCTURE AND PROCESS

The Standing-Committee Structure of Cabinet

The Cabinet is formally a committee of the Queen's Privy Council for Canada, but since that august body has met only twice since 1867, it has no consequence beyond providing the names of its members with the prefix "the Honourable." The Cabinet, which is the *de facto* executive instrument in Canadian government, in turn delegates the responsibility for priority determination among a number of committees of its own.

The Evolution of the Cabinet Committee System The creation of a permanent committee structure for Cabinet is generally considered to have begun under Lester Pearson in the mid-1960s. However, well before that time, committees were used to expedite Cabinet business. John Macdonald and Wilfrid Laurier both used *ad hoc* committees. During World War One, most of Cabinet business

---

[4] Aided by the fact that structural changes among executive-support agencies may appear greater than the real changes in the process, and by the fact that there are certain verities introduced into these activities by virtue of the nature and socialization processes of the people who are recruited into the agencies, several authors have produced work that retains its value in spite of the changes. See, for example, G.B. Doern and Peter Aucoin, *Public Policy in Canada* (Toronto: Macmillan, 1979); articles by Doern, Aucoin, J.J. Rice, H. Kroeker, V.S. Wilson, J. Langford, and M. Prince; R.M. Punnett, *The Prime Minister in Canadian Government and Politics* (Toronto: Macmillan, 1978), particularly chapters 1 to 5; Punnett, *Canadian Public Policy* (Toronto: Methuen, 1983); Thomas Hockin, *Apex of Power*, second edition, (Toronto: Prentice-Hall, 1978); Richard French, *How Ottawa Decides*, second edition (Toronto: James Lorimer, 1984); Terrence J. Downey, "Representation Versus Efficiency: Confronting the Size-of-Cabinet Dilemma in Canada," a paper presented to the 1985 annual conference of the Institue of Public Administration; Audrey Doerr, *The Machinery of Government in Canada* (Toronto: Methuen, 1981); Ian Clark, "Recent Changes in the Cabinet Decision-Making System," *Canadian Public Administration*, vol. 28, no. 2, spring, 1985; James C. Simeon, "Prime Minister Brian Mulroney and Cabinet Decision Making," a paper presented to the annual meeting of the Canadian Political Science Association, Montreal, May 1985. R.J. Van Loon has produced an excessive number of articles on policy- and expenditure-management systems and Ottawa decision-making processes in the 1980s. These can be found in G.B. Doern, ed. *How Ottawa Spends, 1983*; Richard French, *How Ottawa Decides*. M.S. Whittington and G. Williams, *Canadian Politics in the 1980s*, 1st and 2nd edns. and *Canadian Public Administration*, Summer, 1981; Summer 1983; and Summer, 1984. See also the exchange of open letters in *CPA* Summer, 1984, 1985 with Colin Campbell. Probably the best source for immediate updates on changes among these agencies is *The Financial Post* or *The Globe and Mail*.

was carried out by two committees: a war committee and a reconstruction committee.[5] While there were as many as ten standing committees of Cabinet during World War Two, one of them, the War Committee, "to all intents and purposes displaced the parent body."[6] After the war, Mackenzie King, Louis St. Laurent, and, to a lesser extent, John Diefenbaker continued to use *ad hoc* committees. Under Pearson, the rather chaotic non-procedures of the Diefenbaker era were replaced by eleven special committees and ten standing committees, which made "recommendations" to full Cabinet. Cabinet, in turn, after discussion, converted the "recommendations" to decisions.

This structure was slowly developed and formalized during the pre-1979 Trudeau governments. The Cabinet under Pierre Trudeau's first government had nine standing committees, including the Cabinet Committee on Priorities and Planning, which was chaired by the prime minister and was occasionally likened to a sort of inner Cabinet. Its smaller size, the eminence of its chairman, and the fact that the most powerful Cabinet ministers were its members made it a better forum for important decisions than a full-scale Cabinet meeting, where thirty-five or more ministers might be present. Compared to a mandate of the Committee on Priorities and Planning, the mandate of the Social and Native Affairs Committee (now called the Cabinet Committee on Social Development), for example, was considerably more restricted, as the committee dealt only with matters arising from the policy concerns of departments falling within its own subject area.

In 1979, the new government of Joe Clark reduced the size of the Committee on Priorities and Planning, renamed it the "inner Cabinet," gave it formal executive responsibility to act in Cabinet's name, and reduced the total number of standing committees to seven. The 1980 Trudeau government kept the reduced number of committees, but went back to calling the inner Cabinet the Committee on Priorities and Planning. John Turner, in his brief stint in office, eliminated one committee, and Brian Mulroney originally reduced the number by one more, but subsequently returned to the same formal committee structure as Turner. The 1986 version of the Cabinet committee structure is shown in Figure 15-1.

The Committee Systems in Operation   Each of the standing committees meets regularly, usually once a week. Ministers normally are members of two or three committees, although any minister may attend any committee meeting except Priorities and Planning, Security and Intelligence, or the Treasury Board. Each committee, with the exception of the Treasury Board, has a small permanent secretariat, provided by the PCO. These secretariats assist the ministers with committee paperwork, help to set committee agendas, brief the chairmen, write the committee decisions, and generally facilitate the flow of information from departments of government to the Cabinet. The Treasury Board has a much larger secretariat, which performs all the functions of the other secretariats but which is also responsible for much of the day-to-day management of government and for the annual-expenditure estimates.

[5] See Terence J. Downey, "Representation Versus Efficiency," pp. 11 and 12; and W.A. Matheson, *The Prime Minister and the Cabinet* (Toronto: Methuen, 1976) and Ian Clark, op. cit., 1986 version, pp. 3–8.

[6] A.D.P. Heeney, "Cabinet Government in Canada," cited in Matheson, p. 84.

FIGURE 15-1
CABINET COMMITTEE STRUCTURE

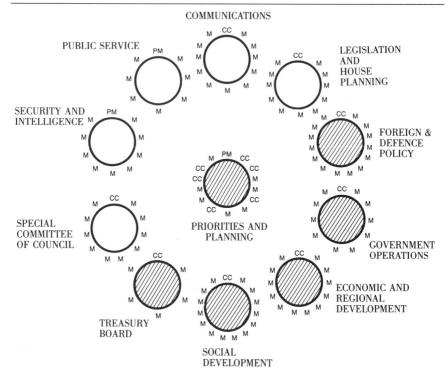

PM PRIME MINISTER

CC COMMITTEE CHAIRMAN

M MINISTER

ENVELOPE/POLICY
COMMITTEE

Source: Adapted from Ian Clark, "Recent Changes in the Cabinet Decision Making System", Privy Council Office, Mimeo, 1986.

Most items are dealt with by standing committees. However, special committees of the cabinet are established from time to time to deal with specific policy problems. For example, there has at times been a Labour Relations Committee, which deals with particularly serious national strikes, and there have been special committees on western issues and on tax reform — the latter working on the white paper on taxation and its implementation in 1969 and the early 1970s. The Conservative government after 1984 has made particularly extensive use of *ad hoc* committees and "ministerial task forces." For example, a Ministerial Task Force on Program Review, under Eric Neilsen, was made responsible for reviewing the majority of federal programs during the first two years of that government.

In the Trudeau Cabinets of the mid 1970s, the normal flow of Cabinet business was from the sponsoring minister to the appropriate PCO secretariat, to be placed on the agenda of the appropriate Cabinet committee. Committee discussion produced a "Committee Recommendation." The item then went to the Treasury Board, for consideration of the financial and personnel implications. The Treasury Board recommendation, together with the Committee Recommendation, then went to plenary cabinet, where decisions were usually confirmed, although major debates could take place there and decisions could be overturned, particularly when the Treasury Board and the subject committee deferred.

The structure and operations of Cabinet were changed considerably after the election of the Progressive Conservative government in May 1979. The major structural innovations were the creation of an inner Cabinet and of two Ministries of State, one for social development and one for economic development, while the major innovation in process was the creation of what came to be known as the "envelope" system of financial and policy management. The whole system is known formally as the *Policy and Expenditure Management System*, or PEMS. John Turner eliminated the two Ministries of State in 1984, but maintained the general outlines of the PEMS system. Until 1984, the formal flow of Cabinet business was from the sponsoring ministry to the Ministry of State responsible for the policy sector in question. The Ministry of State ensured that the proposal was discussed by a committee of the deputy ministers of departments in that sector, and that all necessary interdepartmental discussion had taken place. The Ministry then prepared an assessment of the proposal, which was forwarded to the appropriate Cabinet committee along with the original proposal.

The Ministries of State and the deputy minister committees were eliminated in 1984, but the rest of the process remains essentially intact. Following Cabinet-committee discussion, a decision, called a "Committee Recommendation" (CR), is prepared and forwarded to the Committee on Priorities and Planning (P & P). The CRs are generally approved by P & P, for an important principle of the system is the delegation of real decision-making authority to the committees of Cabinet. If the policy under consideration requires major reallocations of resources (human or monetary), the Treasury Board is required to look at detailed proposals for the implementation of the policy. If the proposal requires new legislation, the Committee on Legislation and House Planning is required to examine the proposed legislation. Otherwise, a department may implement proposed changes as soon as P & P has put its imprimatur on the proposal. The full Cabinet meets weekly, but was not generally used as a decision-making body, being devoted, instead, largely to political discussions.

The Committee on Priorities and Planning obviously sits at the centre of this system. In addition to the prime minister, who chairs it, the committee includes the chairman of the standing committees, the Minister of Finance, and some other ministers personally close to the prime minister. P & P performs five major roles. First, it establishes the overall priorities for the government and thereby sets the context within which the other committees operate. Second, it allocates budgets to the standing committees. These are, in effect, spending targets in the "envelopes" of the PEMS system. Third, it reviews all committee decisions. Fourth, it deals directly with particularly big or particularly important issues, or issues that cut across the lines of responsibility of other committees. And, finally, it has some program responsibilities of its own, such as equalization payments to the provinces and general responsibilities for fiscal transfer payments.

Memoranda to Cabinet In both the Liberal and Conservative versions of the Cabinet structure, the normal input to a Cabinet committee has been a "Memorandum to the Cabinet." The memorandum is now fronted by "Ministerial Recommendations" and sometimes backed up by a more detailed "Discussion Paper." The memoranda and Ministerial Recommendations are not made public, but the discussion papers, which contain most of the information of the memoranda, often amplified with considerable technical detail, are publicly available under the Freedom of Information Act. The Auditor General, as an agent of Parliament, has access to all parts of the memoranda except the Ministerial Recommendations.

By far the largest number of these documents are written within the bureaucracy. They may express demands arising within the bureaucracy (for example, when officials ask for change in departmental terms of reference or programs); they may result from demands from client groups, which have been communicated through bureaucratic channels; or they may represent departmental responses to ministerial requests generated by political communication channels such as caucus, the party organization, the PMO, or the minister's own contacts. Items appearing before Cabinet committees may also be written by individual ministers or by the Privy Council Office, but documents from these sources are relatively rare. Memoranda produced personally by a minister may appear when ministers want to deal with sensitive topics. Those produced by the PCO normally deal with procedural matters or matters of overall government priorities.

The former Ministries of State also produced memoranda when officials, supported by the committee chairman, felt that they had seen policy needs that departments missed because of the fragmented nature of departmental responsibilities; when the subject was a major policy change cutting across the interests of several departments; when a major statement of priorities was required; or when financial issues dealing with a whole sector required Cabinet consideration. All memoranda to Cabinet bear the signature of a minister or a group of ministers, who then become responsible for piloting the document through Cabinet with the aid of their departmental officials.

The Cabinet Committee System in the 1980s The creation of an inner Cabinet, the development of the "envelope" system, and the delegation of much effective final decision-making power to committees, together with the virtual elimination of full Cabinet as a decision-making body under the 1979 Progressive Conservative government, marked a quantum leap in the elaboration of Cabinet structure. This new machinery has been, to a large extent, retained under subsequent Liberal and Conservative governments.

Under the system in place in 1987, the framework for decision making is set by the Committee on Priorities and Planning.[7] The cycle begins with the pre-

[7] See Ian Clark, *op. cit.* for a description of the system put in place by Brian Mulroney.

paration, by the Department of Finance, of four-year projections of economic conditions, and hence of government revenues, and the parallel preparation of expenditure forecasts by the Treasury Board Secretariat. Basing the system on forecasts is always risky, because the making of economic projections one month ahead is difficult; the making of four-year projections is somewhere between a black art and blind luck—sanctified, of course by computer printouts. Expenditure projections, which themselves depend on economic assumptions, such as rate of inflation and unemployment, are equally difficult to make with any accuracy. Nonetheless, the projections can still contribute to an effective planning framework, as long as common assumptions are adhered to throughout the system.

On the basis of these projections, P & P determines the total amount of money that will be available over the planning period to each of the Cabinet committees with expenditure envelopes. The amounts made available to the government operations committee determine how much can be spent on the actual administration of government programs. The amounts made available to other committees determine what benefits are available to be delivered in the form of government programs.

The Committee on Priorities and Planning may opt to provide a policy committee with some money in excess of its requirements, to cover the needs of ongoing programs. This money, called a "policy reserve," is then available to the committee, to be allocated to new programs within its area of jurisdiction. Alternatively, a *policy reserve* may be created by the committee itself, when its members agree to cut programs.

Creating a policy reserve by cutting old programs is not easy. The bulk—more than 90% — of expenditures remains part of the "A-Budget" or "A-Base," and there is a certain sanctity to the A-Base. Once a program is created, it is extremely difficult to eliminate it, for every program has both a clientele and a bureaucratic agency to deliver it, each of which will lose significantly if the program vanishes. By contrast, the savings in eliminating the program are usually so widely distributed among taxpayers as to be virtually negligible to any one of them. Those who benefit from the program will have an incentive to fight hard to keep it; those who benefit from its elimination have no such strong incentive, and hence are relatively indifferent. For the political priority setter, concerned with avoiding the kind of conflict that can result in electoral defeat, the A-Base that finances existing programs therefore takes on the kind of sanctity that requires extraordinary courage, extraordinary stubbornness, or extraordinary tendencies to self-destruction to violate. The result, in a time of rising revenues, need not necessarily be a major problem, but in a time of declining revenues it can produce virtual paralysis.

Various special attempts, such as the Ministerial Task Force on Program Review (also called the Nielsen Task Force) of 1984 to 1986, which is described in more detail later, have been not much more successful than the ordinary machinations of the policy committees. Large cuts are therefore typically made by P & P, or by the Minister of Finance and the PM acting in concert. The process of cutting was somewhat easier in the early 1980s, when there was still some "fat" left in the system, but policy reserves, which were typically $200 to $300 million per year in the early 1980s, have dwindled to much less than $100 million in the late 1980s.

Policy proposals for new programs are forwarded to Cabinet committees through the PCO by the individual minister or ministers responsible for the program area in question. There are inevitably many more proposals on which to spend money than there is money to spend. Ministers must therefore determine their priorities. This they do in two ways. First, they may discuss among themselves periodically what their priorities should be, issue a general statement, and hope that departments will forward proposals in accord with these priorities. In general, this approach has not been successful; departments have an intrinsic urge to submit what *they* want, while making more or less strained attempts to have their proposals appear to be in accordance with the collective priorities.

The second approach has been more successful. Ministers, acting in committee, may simply decide to fund some of the proposals that come forward but not others, thus letting their real priorities emerge simply by virtue of their concrete decisions. This process generally succeeds because it forces a sorting out of the wheat from the chaff, using whatever criteria ministers believe to be appropriate.

Once the policy committees have reached their decisions, they forward these as Committee Recommendations to P & P, which, for the most part, will ratify them. A minister who has lost at the policy-committee meeting may attempt to have the decision revised at P & P, and P & P always may reopen a discussion, but in general the policy-committee recommendations survive. Before money can actually be spent on new programs, it is often necessary, as well, to obtain Treasury Board confirmation that the expenditures accord with the estimates voted by parliament, and with the procedures set out in the Financial Administration Act.

Ministers may increase their chances of success by finding ways to fund new expenditures through reallocations within their own department. A decision will still have to be taken by the policy committee if a significant policy issue is at stake, but the committee is much more likely to say yes if the minister merely seeks permission to divert departmental funds rather than going after the policy reserve to which fellow ministers also feel entitled. Reallocation is obviously much easier for large departments than for small, and it is obviously easier if there is a bit of financial fat in the system. That financial fat has become less and less evident through the 1980s, as restraints and cuts have removed whatever potential surpluses departments may have. Restraint thus means less flexible government as well as smaller government.

Some policy issues do not go through this process. If the issues are very large or politically very contentious, then it is likely that the prime minister and the most senior ministers who sit on P & P will wish to become involved early in the process, and may even wish to exclude the lesser lights among their ministerial colleagues altogether. Thus the largest issues are typically not dealt with by the policy committees at all. This may, naturally, lead to some resentment on the part of excluded ministers, but it should hardly surprise us that the prime minister would wish to have the most important decisions taken by a small group of his most trusted advisors. It is not otherwise in any human decision-making forum.

The prime minister, of course, sits at the centre of this system. It is generally true that the Minister of Finance is second only to the prime minister in influence. The major discipline in the system is a financial one, and the realm of the possible for most ministers most of the time is, therefore, established by the budgetary framework set by the Minister of Finance. It is the minister's right, in consultation only with the prime minister, to bring down the budget, and while he is obviously greatly constrained in his actions by the programs already in place, the economic climate, and the political situation, he still retains broad latitude to propose such things as the level at which policy reserves should be set. His influence is further enhanced by the budget speech. The speech is normally used as the vehicle for announcing major new initiatives in both tax and expenditure policy. Since it is prepared in secret, kept even from the Cabinet itself, and is controlled by the Minister of Finance himself, it constitutes a further source of power for him. It is scarcely any wonder, then, that most ministers await the budget speech with at least the same degree of anticipation and trepidation as all other Canadians, and that they sometimes view the Minister of Finance with nearly the same awe with which they regard the prime minister or Wayne Gretzky.[8]

The changes made in Cabinet decision-making processes in 1979 and elaborated in the early 1980s tended to emphasize the convention of collective decision making at the expense of individual ministerial responsibility. The amendments made by John Turner appeared to go part way back towards an emphasis on the role of the individual minister and department. Brian Mulroney appeared, initially at least, to move in the direction of centralizing authority again, but this time in the hands of the prime minister himself rather than in the Cabinet. He did so by strengthening the role of agencies that reported directly to him, particularly the PMO, and he was initially reluctant to delegate much real authority to the committees: indeed, they did not even meet regularly for the first six months of his term. As time passed, as ministers became more experienced, and as new government became more comfortable with the task of operating a government, the balance appeared to shift again, to a situation in which the collective nature of Cabinet decision making is increasingly emphasized. It seems doubtful if, without the Ministries of State that supported the collective responsibilities of ministers under Clark and Trudeau, the collective convention can be as strongly emphasized as it was in the early 1980s. However, with the great limitations on the individual ministers' discretionary policy-making power, which are implicit in the virtual disappearance of all excess financial resources in departments, and with the consequent need for ministers with policy ideas to slug it out in committee with their colleagues for every penny that will be devoted to new initiatives, it is difficult to see that individual ministers can hope to have greatly expanded discretionary policy authority.

Inside the Cabinet: Prime-Ministerial Power and Collective Responsibility It should already be evident that, in Canadian politics, the prime minister is much more than "first among equals." Since he appoints and dismisses ministers and distributes responsibilities among them, and since he is the person whom most

---

8 Well, maybe not in as much awe as they hold Wayne Gretzky.

Canadians view as epitomizing the government of the day, the prime minister sets the tone and style of the government and can establish the broad outlines of its most important policies. A Trudeau or a Mulroney stamps his era of Canadian politics unmistakably with his style and his ideals. But the power of a prime minister is very far from being absolute, for there are also many checks on what a prime minister can do to influence either the determination of priorities or the details of policy of the government.[9]

Undoubtedly, the most important of these checks is simply the domestic and international environment of the political system. By this we mean no more — and no less — than that the prime minister is subject to the same limitations as other politicians. For example, no matter how much he might personally want to do so, there is no way that a prime minister could institute a real guaranteed annual income of $20,000 per capita. The environment of the political system is simply not productive enough to provide the goods and services involved. A related environmental constraint derives from the vast number of inputs that would face a modern prime minister were there any attempt to exercise absolute power in the executive-policy process. Even with expanded central agencies, there is, realistically, no way in which a prime minister or any one person could ever hope to deal personally with more than a tiny fraction of the myriad issues facing government.

Cabinet colleagues also place restraints on the prime minister's power to set priorities. While, the prime minister as their leader, can likely force them to accept any single policy initiative he chooses, he will choose not to force the point on most issues. The reason is that, like any person, the prime minister only has so much power; and, in many ways, that power is very much like currency. Invested judiciously, it multiplies; spent too widely, on too many separate items and against the interests of too many colleagues, it diminishes and may vanish. Thus, except for a few concerns to which there is a great personal attachment, the prime minister is always somewhat amenable to being convinced by colleagues. No one would resign from the Cabinet in a huff if the prime minister pushed a few items down its collective throat; but a Cabinet must, in the parliamentary system, at least appear to work as a team, and too many such incidents could be damaging to the image of Cabinet solidarity. A prime minister must walk a narrow line between allowing ministers too much leeway — creating disarray, disunity, and bickering on the team, and allowing them too little — thus bringing himself to ruin through defections. The problems of the Pearson cabinets are amply illustrative for the former fault, while the breakup of the Diefenbaker cabinet in 1963 illustrates the latter.[10]

---

[9] See also the discussion in R.M. Punnett, *The Prime Minister in Canadian Government and Politics*, and in Thomas Hockin, "The Prime Minister and Political Leadership: An Introduction to Some Restraints and Imperatives," in Hockin, *Apex of Power*, pp. 1–22, and "Two Canadian Prime Ministers Discuss the Office," *ibid.*, pp. 184–199. The three volumes of *Memoirs* of Lester Pearson published by the University of Toronto Press from 1972 to 1975 also constitute a valuable picture of the constraints faced by a prime minister.

[10] The results of too much personal exercise of power during the last days of the Diefenbaker Cabinet are particularly well covered in Patrick Nicholson, *Vision and Indecision* (Toronto: Longmans, 1968), particularly pp. 227–266. On the assorted fiascos of the Pearson era, see Peter C. Newman, *The Distemper of Our Times* (Toronto: McClelland and Stewart, 1969); and Judy LaMarsh, *Memoirs of a Bird in a Gilded Cage*

In addition, the Cabinet has some control over the prime minister by virtue of its numbers, the personal strength of its members, the access and contact ministers have to information and sources in the bureaucracy, and the personal followings some ministers have managed to establish either in caucus or in the country at large. On the other hand, the prime minister has power over their jobs. He can reorganize the Cabinet at any time, and remove troublesome ministers to lower-status portfolios, to the back benches, to the Senate, or to the judiciary.

Perhaps the greatest source of control a prime minister has over the Cabinet is simply his personal popularity. Highly popular or freshly elected prime ministers, or those who have established a solid tradition of getting themselves and their parties re-elected, have rarely had much trouble with their cabinets. This prime-ministerial asset will, of course, vary a great deal from time to time, as well as from leader to leader. The Pierre Elliott Trudeau of March 1980, fresh from a major electoral victory, was more powerful *vis-à-vis* his Cabinet colleagues than was the personally unpopular and about to be defeated Pierre Elliott Trudeau of March 1979. Lester Pearson, who never succeeded in getting a parliamentary majority, always had problems controlling his ministers, while Brian Mulroney, with 211 seats out of 282, faced no difficulty in the aftermath of his victory in controlling his Cabinet.

The Limits to Cabinet Supremacy in Priority Determination

If there are constraints on the prime minister when dealing with the Cabinet, there are equal constraints on the Cabinet and prime minister when they are acting together to determine priorities. In the first place, there are the environmental constraints, which one should by now expect. Another significant restriction on the activities of both federal and provincial governments derives from the division of powers under the British North America Act. It will do the federal government little good to establish elementary education as a high priority unless the provinces can somehow be induced to go along. Nor will it be very useful for the provinces to establish the revision of the Criminal Code as a high priority unless the federal government cooperates and begins the venture. The role of the federal-provincial process in the determination of priorities as well as in the more detailed formulation of policies is so vital that we devote the whole of the

---

(Toronto: McClelland and Stewart, 1969); as well as the last two volumes of Pearson's *Memoirs*. Peter C. Newman, *Renegade in Power, The Diefenbaker Years* (Toronto: McClelland and Stewart, 1963) is also highly instructive and useful. See also the volumes of the Mackenzie King biography, *William Lyon Mackenzie King*, by R.M. Dawson and Blair Neatby. There are, as of 1986, not yet many analytical treatments of the Trudeau style of leadership, although there are certainly enough treatments to form a basis for discussion. See, for example, Christina McCall-Newman, *Grits* (Toronto: Macmillan, 1985); Jean Chrétien, *Straight from the Heart* (Toronto: Deneau, 1985); and Donald Johnson, *Up the Hill* (Montreal: Optimum Publishing, 1986). For many examples of prime-ministerial management style combined with a more objective assessment, see R.M. Punnett, *The Prime Minister in Canadian Politics*. With the exception of Punnett and the Mackenzie King biographies, the books mentioned are examples of inside books about politics in Ottawa, and they provide valuable insight into the workings of politics in Ottawa. However, when dealing with them, the reader should try to maintain a broader perspective. Politics is not simply the activities of a few people in Ottawa or in the provincial capitals. It is an extremely complex process set in an extremely complex environment. Its actors in capital cities are only transient figures who shape some events, and are, in turn, shaped by them.

next chapter to it. For the moment, it is necessary only to keep in mind that it forms the greatest of the formal contstraints on priority determination in Canada.

Paradoxically, the regular departments of government—by far the largest source of information for the Cabinet—can also be viewed as one of its greatest constraints. Although the situation may be slowly changing in the late 1980s, the bureaucracy's near monopoly over many types of information has often served to insure that the Cabinet is highly dependent upon it when most priority decisions are made. Despite attempts to alleviate this dependency somewhat—via task forces (themselves usually composed of bureaucrats), royal commissions, and the expansion of the PMO, the PCO, ministries of state, and ministers' personal staffs, and sometimes simply just trying to ignore the bureaucrats—Canadian cabinets are still highly dependent on their bureaucracies. We have already seen that, unlike many of their counterparts in Britain and Continental Europe, Canadian party structures are not really adequate as alternative information sources. Canadian legislatures have not generally formed an effective counterweight to bureaucratic power, although the increasing use of parliamentary task forces and standing committees and the more substantial resources available to Parliament may be changing that, at least at the federal level. Interest groups can provide an effective counterweight to bureaucratic advice, and we have seen that, at the federal level in Canada, they are increasingly doing so by dealing directly with ministers or their political advisors. However, most of the time most interest groups still work through the bureaucracy, hoping to influence decisions through the departmental advisors. The "Yes, Minister" image of the well-intentioned but slightly naive Cabinet minister on his or her own against a sea of plotting, scheming, power-grabbing bureaucrats is a far-overstated caricature of reality. But reality still is that bureaucracies are, among other things, large information-gathering networks that will, if counterweights are not provided, dominate priority determination no less than they do other stages of the political process.

EXECUTIVE SUPPORT AGENCIES: THE CABINET'S ADVISORS

Figure 15-2 presents a taxonomy of the various agencies that provide support to Cabinet in its priority-determination role. The agencies are classified by the primary and formal roles, but in practice, all of them are concerned, to a greater or lesser degree, with all the functions.

In particular, political considerations colour all of the deliberations of these agencies; since their function is to provide support for political leaders, it could hardly be otherwise. It is important, however, to differentiate between political considerations and partisan considerations. The Prime Minister's Office, ministerial staff, the party structure, and the caucus provide support to ministers because those ministers are of a particular partisan stripe. If the government changes, these people lose their jobs. Indeed, even if the incumbent of a position changes without a change of government, they may well be jobless. Their support is thus for a very particular set of people. By contrast, all of the other support agencies

FIGURE 15-2
EXECUTIVE-SUPPORT AGENCIES FOR PRIORITY DETERMINATION

Partisan Political Advisors	Prime Minister's Office (PMO)
	Parliamentary Caucus
	Party Structures
	Individual Ministerial Staff
Process and Procedure Advisors	Privy Council Office (PCO)
Policy Design and Integration Advisors	Treasury Board
	Department of Finance
	Federal-Provincial Relations Office (FPRO)
Financial Advisors	Department of Finance
	Treasury Board Secretariat
	Office of the Controller-General
Ad Hoc Advisors	Royal Commissions
	Task Forces, Advisory Committees

provide support for the elected government of the day regardless of its partisan stripe for as long as it is in office. When it is defeated, they provide support for the next government. Being human, they have their preferences as to parties and incumbents, but they will generally serve regardless of their personal feelings, for they are both professionals and career public servants.

Aside from the partisan advisors, then, very few holders of positions in executive-support agencies change with a change in government. The change from a sixteen-year-old Liberal government to a Progressive Conservative government under Joe Clark in 1979 was accompanied by a change of the head of the Privy Council Office (his successor, though, came from within the ranks), by the "resignation" of one other top PCO official who was near retirement age, and by the removal of the Deputy Minister of Finance. The return of the Liberals in 1980 saw the reinstatement of the former head of the PCO, the transfer of that position's temporary incumbent to another top public-service job, and the "resignation" of the

Tory-appointed Deputy Minister of Finance. All other changes that occurred were nothing more than would have happened in any event. The transition from Pierre Trudeau to John Turner to Brian Mulroney in 1984 saw the disappearance of the two Ministries of State, but no other major personnel changes in executive-support agencies. Any impression that most of the central agencies are hives of partisanship is quite unfounded — not necessarily because ministers would not like to make them so, but because they are staffed by officials originally recruited under the merit system, which makes use of overt partisan appointments difficult, and because the successful heads of these agencies jealously guard their partisan neutrality. Moreover, a new government usually needs the experience of the old hands in these agencies to ease them through the transition period.

Partisan Political Advisors

The PMO   Since the prime minister bears the pre-eminent responsibility for the political fortunes of the government, it is the Prime Minister's Office that bears the largest responsibility among support agencies for the provision of partisan political advice.[11] The PMO is always staffed at the senior levels by close partisan advisors and people whose advice is valued by the prime minister. The office staff itself has grown rapidly over the past twenty years, and currently has more than two hundred members. By contrast, R.B. Bennett had a staff of about twelve during the 1930s, while Mackenzie King, Louis St. Laurent, and John Diefenbaker had about thirty staff members, and Lester Pearson about forty.[12] However, it is not so evident that the number of top policy advisors has increased. Nearly one-half of the staff of the PMO handles the vastly increased volume of prime-ministerial mail.

The uses a prime minister will make of the PMO will vary from time to time. In the early Trudeau years, the PMO was avowedly a source of many major policy initiatives. Later, as an election approached and then a minority government and another election followed, the PMO became much more a political machine devoted to electoral politics, providing advice to the prime minister on the political pros and cons of various policy options. Brian Mulroney, who sought, like all new prime ministers, to move power close to the political level and who also had a Cabinet in which many ministers were new and inexperienced, expanded the PMO in both numbers and influence.

In spite of these variations, it remains generally true that major changes in policy directly involve the PMO. In August 1978, for example, the PMO and the

---

[11] See the description of the PMO in Marc Lalonde, "The Changing Role of the Prime Minister's Office," *Canadian Public Administration*, vol. 14, no. 4, Winter 1971, pp. 487–537. For a much more controversial point of view, see Denis Smith, "President and Parliament: The Transformation of Parliamentary Government in Canada," and the different point of view expressed by Joseph Wearing in "President or Prime Minister," both in Thomas Hockin, ed., *Apex of Power*. Somewhat more recently, see Thomas D'Acquino, "The Prime Minister's Office: Catalyst or Cabal," and Denis Smith, "Comments on the 'Prime Minister's Office: Catalyst or Cabal'," both in *Canadian Public Administration*, vol. 17, no. 1, Spring 1974. The role, structures, and personalities within the PMO form an endless source of material for newspaper columnists, who love to speculate on who is "in" around Ottawa. Since insiders become outsiders, and vice versa, with great frequency, the role of individual personalities should not be overemphasized.

[12] R.M. Punnett, *The Prime Minister in Canadian Government and Politics*, p. 77.

prime minister almost alone produced a major series of restraint proposals and established the first national refundable tax-credit program.[13] Indeed, it has been argued that the creation of major policy changes in Canada requires a sudden centralization of authority of the sort that can only occur in the federal government when the prime minister and the PMO suddenly take power into their own hands, acting before the web of opposition, which can form rapidly in Ottawa, has had time to mobilize.

Partisan political advice is also provided by parliamentary caucus and individual MPs.[14] The caucuses of all major parties meet at least weekly, and there are numerous regional caucus and caucus-committee meetings as well. Ministers are members of caucus, and generally try to attend meetings, so they have considerable exposure to the ideas of their fellow members. Individual MPs will also try to get ideas to ministers, either by buttonholing them or through office appointments. Ministers, although not always enthusiastic about it, are generally willing to see them. Since ministers and back-benchers share at least a common interest in being re-elected, and since that can depend on highly visible priority decisions, there is some tendency to listen to parliamentary advice. We will say more about the role of caucus committees and the government back-benchers in Chapter 19.

The Extra-Parliamentary Party We have already discussed at length the structures and lines of communication (or, more often, the lack of them) that link the party outside Parliament with the government. Although a few highly influential party functionaries may have a considerable impact on policy, the weakness of these links makes that a relatively rare phenomenon. Indeed, those party functionaries who are powerful usually exert their influence from a formal position somewhere else in the political system, perhaps the PMO or the Senate.

Beyond this, the recommendations of the extra-parliamentary party, developed, for instance, through the annual policy convention, are more persuasive than binding. The major limitation on the power of the party organization is ultimately the fact that the PMO has more information upon which to base its political advice while the line ministers, supported by their departments, have more technical expertise.

The Ministers' Staff Finally, the personal staff of the ministers, the chiefs of staff, and the special assistants who work directly for the minister can be influential in partisan political decisions. Cabinet ministers are busy people, and they require considerable administrative and advisory support. These functions are performed by the departmental staff, and also by the many gentlemen in dark suits and striped ties and women in beige skirts who stalk the corridors and antechambers adjacent to ministerial lairs, politely fending off most would-be visitors, quietly ushering in those deemed worthy of audience, controlling the flow of paper to their minister and acting as the minister's confidant when there are important

---

[13] R. Van Loon, "Reforming Welfare in Canada," *Public Policy*, Fall, 1979.

[14] See Paul Thomas, "The Role of National Party Concensus," in Peter Aucoin, ed., *Party Government and Regional Representation* (Ottawa: Royal Commission on the Economic Union, 1985).

issues to be chewed over. By determining who is important enough to get a personal hearing with the minister, which memoranda and briefing notes the minister needs to see and by often having the last word with the minister, these people can have a major impact on what policy options ultimately get to the Cabinet level.

In a somewhat similar way, correspondence units must filter the tons of incoming mail, bringing the most important correspondence (as they see it) to the minister's attention, and insuring that appropriate replies are drafted for all letters. Press secretaries also must help to interpret and, they hope, to shape the opinions expressed by daily newspapers all across Canada, and must inform decision makers of trends in public opinion as reflected by the press. Thus, while there is no doubt that priority decisions must ultimately be made by the political executive, the nature and number of the policy options from which it chooses, and the information upon which choice is based, are to a large extent defined by the gatekeepers who choreograph the political chorus line of information, ministerial appointments, correspondence, and daily media exposure.

Process Advisors: The Privy Council Office

The Structure of the PCO   The PMO and its non-partisan first cousin, the Privy Council Office, share office space in the immediate vicinity of Parliament Hill, space that symbolizes both the role of serving the Cabinet committees that meet there and the proximity to power. Since the late 1960s, the role of the PCO has evolved from that of an agency almost entirely concerned with moving paper through Cabinet, through a somewhat abortive attempt to coordinate all aspects of government policy, to a position as architect of much of the machinery and process of government in Ottawa; a task that is now combined with the function of providing major logistical and decision-making support for the Cabinet.

The current organizational structure of the PCO is largely dictated by the Cabinet-committee structure itself. The secretariat of each Cabinet committee normally has eight to twelve officers and is headed by an Assistant Secretary to the Cabinet; these Secretariats are grouped under two or three Deputy Secretaries. There are also Secretariats or Directors responsible for the machinery of government and for senior personnel. The whole structure is headed by Canada's highest-ranking public servant, the Secretary to the Cabinet and Clerk of the Privy Council. Paradoxically, the President of the Privy Council has no direct responsibility for the Privy Council Office. That post is at present used to give a position in the Cabinet to the Deputy Prime Minister and the Government House leader, while not tying him to any specific departmental responsibility that might impede his efforts in supporting the prime minister and in manoeuvring the overall government program through the House of Commons.

The PCO and the Senior Bureaucracy   Since 1968, there have been continual changes in the structure and functions of the Privy Council Office and in its relations with other central agencies. To understand this evolution, we will have to go back to the years prior to 1968, when (with the possible exception of the Diefenbaker era) not only did the bureaucratic establishment dominate the process of policy formation, but the senior bureaucratic mandarins played a major role in the process of priority determination as well.[15]

> The pre-eminent positions that senior bureaucrats occupied for a number of years in Ottawa is humorously illustrated in the story of the ambitious young man who wrote the Prime Minister asking that he be given a position in the cabinet. The Prime Minister replied to the effect that he did not feel that the member had the depth of experience, the breadth of knowledge, and the intellectual vigour required for such an exalted position. Undaunted, the young MP wrote back: "My dear Prime Minister, I believe you misunderstood the nature of my request: high as my ambition can aspire, I do not expect to become a Deputy Minister; I merely want to be a Minister."[16]

The influence of the mandarins over the determination of priorities was based on a number of factors, some related to structural features of the system and others to the personal characteristics of the individuals involved. The most important of the structural factors was the deputy ministers' control over the flow of information upwards from the departmental technocracy and downwards from the Cabinet. A large vestige of this particular source of policy influence still resides with the senior bureaucrats.

The most important personal factor contributing to the hegemony of the mandarins was the combination of expertise in a substantive field and long experience as a participant in the policy process. Because the mandarin's experience extended over a number of years, and frequently through a series of different governments, the senior bureaucrat often possessed a perspective that was much broader than that of the political boss. The result was that the deputy minister could have a profound influence on the minister not only because the deputy possessed a higher level of technical competence in the field, but also because, over the years, a feel for the political market-place had been acquired; the deputy had a political acumen that had significance in the roles of political and technical advisor. While the influence of the mandarins would naturally also be related to the willingness of the individual ministers and the government of the day to take their advice, for the most part they either became trusted, and therefore influential, or they simply ceased to be mandarins. It was apparently the intention of the 1968 Trudeau government to temper this influence through the obvious solutions of providing alternative sources of policy advice and of moving deputy ministers about more rapidly, so that they were not in one position long enough to monopolize the field and therefore control their minister.

During the Diefenbaker era, alternative information had been derived from the Conservative Party, from the personal acquaintances of the prime minister and the Cabinet, from the press, and from the mind of the leader himself. The somewhat strained relations between the leader and the bureaucracy during the

---

[15] See F. Schindeler, "The Prime Minister and Cabinet: History and Development," pp. 27–28; Maurice Lamontagne, "The Influence of the Politician, *Canadian Public Administration*, vol. 40, no. 3, fall 1968, p. 265; as well as R.M. Punnett, *The Prime Minister in Canadian Government and Politics*, and J.L. Granatstein, *The Mandarins*.

[16] "The Prime Minister and Cabinet: History and Development," in Thomas Hockin, ed., *Apex of Power* (Toronto: Prentice-Hall, 1971).

Diefenbaker years insured that there was less chance of priorities being determined by the bureaucracy, and that more than normal attention was paid to these alternate sources. Similar alternatives had been available during the Liberal years before 1957, and again under Lester Pearson, from 1963 to 1968, but Liberal prime ministers had shown little propensity to use them. Prime Minister Trudeau and his advisors, on the other hand, appear to have believed that the most effective counter for one bureaucratic institution was another bureaucratic institution with parallel responsibilities. The political-advisory power of the mandarins was to be attenuated through the increase in size and influence of the PMO, and their technical advice was to be placed in competition with that coming from a revamped and expanded PCO.

The PCO in the Seventies and Eighties The Privy Council Office never has quite succeeded in fulfilling the hopes (or fears) expressed for it in the 1970s. While composed of regular public-service personnel, the Trudeau version of the PCO was initially viewed by many old-style senior bureaucrats as an organization of upstarts and outsiders. This was probably inevitable; any new or newly expanded agency will be viewed in that light, and it is a problem that is overcome only by time. The larger problems were internal. The initial head of the PCO under this new system declined to add much in the way of technical expertise to the organization, and the PCO's ability to conduct independent analyses and critiques of policy proposals emanating from departments remained very limited.[17] His successor, Michael Pitfield, followed a somewhat similar course, and although he strengthened the agency considerably by the quality of his senior appointments, the PCO did not achieve the critical mass necessary to perform major independent policy analysis.

The causes of the problem may well have lain in good intentions. The other central agencies of the 1970s, the Treasury Board Secretariat and the Department of Finance, did conduct independent appraisals of most major policy proposals. The dictates of efficiency would seem to have argued against duplicating their work in another agency, and thereby producing a debilitating degree of central-agency warfare. However, the other agencies did primarily financial and economic impact analyses, with the result that no one, in spite of desultory efforts from time to time on the part of all the agencies involved, ever succeeded in getting an established set of priorities from the Cabinet and examining the diverse proposals emanating from departments in the light of these priorities. The result was a predictable dispersal of government activities and a lack of coherent strategies in fields such as industrial development or social or cultural policy. In retrospect, it seems unlikely that the PCO could have forced such coherence, since it had no means of effecting control over government expenditures. The agencies that did have such control (Treasury Board and Finance) had no way of determining priorities and no way of forcing ministers to make trade-offs. We will look at more recent attempts to solve these problems in the next section.

---

[17] See Gordon Robertson, "The Changing Role of the Privy Council Office," *Canadian Public Administration*, vol. 14, no. 4, Winter 1971, for a description of changes by the first head of the revamped agency.

In the meantime, it must be pointed out that the procedural and organizational mandate that the PCO continues to possess, and the somewhat enhanced briefing role it picked up after the elimination of the Ministries of State, give it very considerable power within the federal government, a power that is also retained by Cabinet Secretariats in most provincial governments. Since Cabinet committees are the key decision points for priority decisions, control over the agendas of committees and over the working of their decisions is a significant source of power. In the case of the two major spending committees, these powers were shared from 1980 to 1984 with the Ministries of State for Social Development and for Economic and Regional Development, but the ultimate control over agendas always resided in the PCO secretariats. The writing of committee recommendations to the Committee on Priorities and Planning is done by PCO officials after Cabinet committee discussions. A decision is circulated in draft format before it is finalized, but there is always some latitude to interpret what the ministers really decided and, while a PCO officer cannot produce a committee recommendation that flies in the face of all discussion, there is always the possibility of a bit of shaping.

Further influence accrues to the PCO because of its overall responsibility for the organization of the bureaucracy and because of its power to tender advice to the prime minister via the Secretary to the Cabinet on all senior personnel matters and order-in-council appointments. However, the final, and perhaps the most significant, source of PCO influence is the briefing of the prime minister. Formally, these briefings are a joint FPRO, PCO, and PMO function, with the PCO having primary responsibility for all but the political aspects of the briefing notes. In reality, the relative influence of the three agencies, and the subject matter on which they tender advice, will depend on the relative degree of confidence the prime minister has in the personnel of each group. The source of material for PCO notes is most often within operating departments, but it will also be gleaned from other central agencies and outside sources, and the responsible officer will often have had sufficient years of experience with the subject matter to add considerable shape to the material. As we have seen, these briefing notes are far from the only source of prime-ministerial information, but they are seen by the leader and they are significant.

Policy Design and Integration Advisors

We have seen that among the problems faced by the PCO in the 1970s in its attempts to help rationalize and integrate government policy were the lack of statements of government priorities operationalized by reference to accompanying financial statements, and the lack of ability to do much in the way of detailed analysis of ongoing programs and of possible changes in such programs. To this should be added lack of any mechanism other than full Cabinet meetings to permit, or force, ministers to trade off one program or policy against another, and thus to make their real priorities manifest.

Ministries of State and the PEMS System   One early attempt to solve the problem of lack of analysis and knowledge and the lack of priorities was the creation, in the early 1970s, of Ministries of State for the relatively confined subject areas of Urban Affairs and of Science and Technology. These ministries had no direct control over departmental budgets, no large budgets of their own, and no dedicated cabinet committee through which to report. They were to collect and, if necessary, conduct research into their subject areas, and they were to use the power of superior knowledge and persuasion to provide program integration. However, contrary to the old adage, in this case it turned out that knowledge is not power — at least not sufficient power to move a large department or a minister set on having his or her way. At the time of this writing, one such ministry, for Science and Technology, remains alive. It has added some new program responsibilities for the management of the government's research effort to keep it viable.

A later but similar attempt to deal with this problem was made on the economic-development front.[18] By 1978 it seemed obvious that, if Canada were to compete successfully in international trade, some coherent industrial strategy was required. Consequently, a Board of Economic Development Ministers was created under the chairmanship of Robert Andras, one of the strongest Cabinet ministers of his day. The Board met regularly for several months, but faced persistent problems because, while it discussed policy and while its deliberations were informed by a strong deputy minister and secretariat, there was no way to force the integration of policies and no way to force trade-offs of one expenditure versus another. The solution was a relatively simple one — give the Board (soon to be reconstituted as the Cabinet Committee on Economic Development) responsibility for control of the entire economic-development budget. The arrival on the scene of an inner Cabinet under Joe Clark was originally unrelated to this evolution, but, with its arrival, the final piece was in place. The inner Cabinet constituted a source of authority that could set the economic-development budget. As well, by setting the social-development, foreign and defence, and government-operations budgets, the inner Cabinet could assign the relative priority each area was to receive. These budgetary envelopes had to be administered, and, more importantly, Cabinet committees had to be given technical backup in the determination of priorities within the envelopes. Because this job would be most difficult on the economic-development and social-policy fronts, two new central agencies — the Ministries of State for Social Development (MSSD) and for Economic Development (MSED) — were created.

We have already seen that the return of a Liberal government in March 1980 did not change the trend of this evolution, except that the allocation of envelope figures was to be carried out by the reincarnated Cabinet Committee on Priorities and Planning, rather than by the now defunct inner Cabinet. As we have seen, John Turner eliminated two new ministries of state, but maintained the essentials of the envelope system of budgetting, with policy committees retaining responsibility for the policies of their sector within a defined budgetary ceiling.

These Ministries of State were relatively small, as Ottawa bureaucracies go, with the social-development ministry ultimately containing approximately one

---

18 See R.W. Phidd and G.B. Doern, *The Politics and Management of Canadian Economic Policies* for a much more detailed description of the early steps of this evolution.

hundred staff members and the economic-development ministry approximately twice that size. They carried out several functions for the political system, some of which have disappeared with their demise. Each engaged in long-range planning activities for its sector. Each administered the forecast expenditures for new programs within its envelope, with the finances for existing programs being managed by the Treasury Board. Each attempted to insure policy coordination throughout its sector. Each gained its power primarily by acting as a gatekeeper in the policy and financial-management systems: before proposals went to the appropriate Cabinet committee, they were normally discussed with ministry officials and considered by a committee of deputy ministers chaired by the secretary (deputy minister) of the ministry. The Cabinet committee was provided with written advice on the basis of these deliberations, and, in addition, the ministry briefed the chairman of the Cabinet committee before the committee meeting on the substance of proposals. Coordination and integration within the sector were to be achieved through the policy review functions of these agencies and because proposals did not normally proceed to Cabinet committees before a thorough examination by the ministries themselves. In addition, the ministries from time to time actually initiated their own proposals and took some responsibility for coordinating events such as national sectoral conferences or federal-provincial negotiations in their policy sector.

While earlier versions of Ministries of State were, for a variety of reasons, too weak to have any significant influence on the policy and expenditure-management processes in Ottawa, the latter-day ministries were in some senses too strong, particularly in an environment already heavily cluttered with other central agencies. Their main clients were their own Cabinet committees, but, while ministers may have appreciated the ministries' critiques of other ministers' proposals, they generally did not appreciate critiques of their own ideas. The ministries, therefore, were not necessarily very popular with the ministers they were intended to support. This situation was exacerbated by the frustrations inevitably felt by ministers in the dying days of the Trudeau government, as they watched poll results steadily come to favour the Opposition. It was made worse, too, by the fact that the plethora of central agencies associated with the high tide of rationality in the early 1980s made any management of programs in Ottawa extraordinarily difficult, and by inevitable competition for power among central agencies.[19]

A broad commentary on the whole array of new political and bureaucratic support and control mechanisms of the Trudeau era is made by Sharon Sutherland and Bruce Doern. They remark that:

Within the executive in the Trudeau Liberal era there was an array of central agencies, that is, new or expanded bureaucratic agencies to help control the civil service proper. Within the ambit of parliament, there was erected a new parliamentary civil service, an array of devices that included more research support for the opposition parties, more staff for committees, more rights commissioners and

---

[19] Several of the articles cited in footnote 3 are critical of some aspects of ministry and PEMS operations. A particularly critical account is to be found in Colin Campbell, *Governments Under Stress* (Toronto: Macmillan, 1984). See also the exchange of letters between Campbell and Van Loon in *Canadian Public Administration*, Summer, 1985.

watchdogs and their staff and advisory bodies. Some of these were, no doubt, useful. Still, the cumulative judgement that emerged is that none fundamentally assisted the elemental focal points of democratic life, such as ministers themselves, MPs and the caucus, political parties and parliament as an assembly of elected politicians rather than just a team of disciplined troops. It was as if the Liberal view was to trust the managerial/organizational trappings of democracy, but not its essential elected and representative underpinnings.

[But] the practical conundrum is a real one: the ambivalence we have about delegating powers to the bureaucracy on one hand and the need to maintain the pace of the overall policy agenda on the other, which makes increased delegation inevitable.[20]

When John Turner took over from Pierre Trudeau in 1984, he was anxious to develop some distance between his government and its predecessor — to put a new face on his Ottawa government. One way in which he sought to do what was by making changes to the policy process, and the easiest change was to eliminate some of the complexities of the envelope-management system, by eliminating Ministries of State. This he accomplished as his first (and nearly his last) executive act.

It will not have escaped the attention of some readers that, in many respects, the functions conducted by the latter-day Ministries of State could have been carried out in the Privy Council Office. Indeed, around Ottawa, the ministries were often viewed as PCO extensions by another name. It was therefore anticipated that the demise of the ministries would be accompanied by an expansion of the Privy Council Office, particularly in the secretariats of committees formerly served by ministries. While some of the ministry functions have devolved to the PCO, many have not. It may be that some of the coordination problems of the early years of the Mulroney government have resulted from that oversight.

FPRO Overall policy integration with respect to federal-provincial concerns was, in the late 1970s, to be the responsibility of the Federal-Provincial Relations Office (FPRO) and its Minister of State. The genealogy of the FPRO can be traced to the original reorganization of the Cabinet-committee system by the newly elected Trudeau government of 1968. The plan at that time was for a Committee of Cabinet on Federal-Provincial Relations to coordinate the federal side in all dealings with the provinces, and the staff support for this committee was to be a branch of the PCO, under a deputy secretary to the Cabinet. The coordinative role of the Cabinet committee, however, never really blossomed, for the simple reason that relations with the provinces were either so all-encompassing in their scope that the prime minister himself and the Committee on Priorities and Planning had to carry the ball, or so narrow and portfolio-specific that the individual federal departments would organize things through their own federal-provincial relations branches. The end result was that, while the committee remained officially in existence until the defeat of the Liberals in 1979, it seldom met after 1974, and completely ceased to function after 1977. It has been revived since

[20] Sharon Sutherland and G. Bruce Doern, *Bureaucracy in Canada: Control and Reform:* Royal Commission on the Economic Union, Research Study 43, Privy Council of Canada (Toronto: University of Toronto Press, 1985). Reproduced with permission of the Minister of Supply and Services Canada.

1986 under the chairmanship of a Minister of State for Federal-Provincial Relations.

In the meantime, the federal-provincial relations secretariat in the PCO had evolved into the FPRO by 1975, when it was given a separate existence under a full secretary to the Cabinet. The FPRO went through a growth spurt, aided by the fact that the Canadian Unity Information Office was domiciled within it, and remained a separate bureaucratic agency presided over by a full secretary to the Cabinet under the administration of Joe Clark, Pierre Trudeau, John Turner, and Brian Mulroney. The influence of the FPRO has waxed and waned. It reached a recent zenith in the early 1980s when, with Michael Kirby as its Secretary, it was the major centre of bureaucratic action for the constitutional patriation and reform process. At other times, it has had difficulty performing its coordinating role. Since it does not have an expenditure envelope of its own, the FRPO is not in a position to play a financial gatekeeper role in the bureaucracy. To counter this difficulty, it does retain a significant role in briefing the PM on the federal-provincial aspects of issues, it acts as the Secretariat for the Federal-Provincial Relations Committee of Cabinet, and it is the central coordinator for First Ministers' Conferences, where many of the priorities for joint federal-provincial action are established. However, the line departments and the other central agencies have sometimes still found it rather easy to ignore or overlook FPRO in their day-to-day affairs.

Finance and Treasury Board Secretariat   The Department of Finance and the Treasury Board secretariat also have policy-integration roles. More and more, the Treasury Board is coming to function as the board of management for the government.[21] It retains responsibility for current-year budgets and, along with the Department of Finance, is charged with advising Cabinet on the size of future-year allocations to various envelopes. More important, in this context, the Treasury Board Secretariat is in a unique position to effect control and coordination through its responsibilities for government labour relations, for many aspects of personnel policy, for administrative policy, for most aspects of administrative procedures, for personnel allocations, and for the details of the administration of the government's recurrent bouts of restraint.

The Department of Finance retains primary responsibility for advising the government on overall aspects of economic policy, for the bulk of transfer payments to the provinces, and for the effect of government policies on the economy. It is the inner Cabinet's primary advisor at the time when future-year expenditure allocations are made. Finally, it is responsible for all aspects of the raising of revenues and, hence, all aspects of the taxation system, including those devices intended to provide financial inducements to people and corporations to behave in certain ways—the so-called "tax expenditures." If any policy proposal is to be carried out through the tax system, or if it will have a significant effect on the economy or government revenues, the role of the Department of Finance becomes paramount. If any other department's policy designs would appear to clash with

---

[21] The concept is most fully outlined in the *Report of the Royal Commission on Financial Accountability* (Ottawa: Queen's Printer, 1979).

those of the Department of Finance, the other department tends to emerge the loser.

The New Mandarins?

By now, the astute reader may be moved to ask — with so many agencies having a role in the coordination and integration of policy, who coordinates the coordinators? In part, this is achieved through the Committee on Priorities and Planning, where all of the ministerial heads of the integrating agencies sit and where the financial envelopes are established. In part, it is achieved through various meetings and committees of deputy ministers. The broadest coordination is achieved through regular gatherings of all of the deputy ministers. Deputies gather weekly for a relatively informal breakfast meeting, and usually once per month for more formal luncheons. At these meetings, hosted by the Clerk of the Privy Council, one or more deputies will often speak about the broad policy approaches and priorities bearing on his or her area. The Clerk, and often some other very senior deputy, such as the Deputy Minister of Finance, may also speak of overall government approaches, and deputies are afforded a chance to mingle and discuss common problems. Occasionally the prime minister himself may speak. Some coordination is also achieved through the Committee on Senior Officers (COSO). COSO was originally formed to advise the Clerk of the Privy Council on the evaluation and appointment of deputy ministers. It has continued to perform this service, but clerks have also occasionally used COSO to try out new policy ideas and to attempt to achieve better integration of approaches. COSO still exists, and still may be used for both purposes, although it is primarily a personnel management committee. A parallel committee, called the Senior Personnel Advisory Committee, chaired by the chairman of the Public Service Commission, advises on appointments of Assistant Deputy Ministers. The Secretary of the Treasury Board chairs another deputy-ministerial-level committee called the Treasury Board Senior Advisory Committee, which provides advice on management issues.

The most senior of the committees providing senior coordination is called the Coordinating Committee of Deputy Ministers (CCDM). It meets almost weekly and includes the Deputy Minister of Finance, the Secretary of the Treasury Board, the Secretary to the Cabinet for Federal-Provincial Relations, the Undersecretary of State for External Affairs, and, from time to time, other deputies whose departments have become hot areas. The CCDM is chaired by the Clerk of the Privy Council. This group discusses both policy and management issues of major concern to the government, and, since it consists of the deputy heads of all the major integrating and coordination agencies, it could itself be viewed, along with the Committee on Priorities and Planning, as the major centre of coordination in the government of Canada.

One further source of coordination among senior bureaucrats was lost when the Ministries of State and the "mirror committees" of deputy ministers, which went with them, were abolished. Since the mirror committees met weekly, they afforded a regular opportunity for all the deputies in each sector to get together and discuss common problems. A major reason for the abolition of these committees was the fear that they were the cutting edge of a new "neo-man-darinate," which would usurp power from ministers. Whatever the merits of that argument, their loss did make the achievement of common priorities in each sector more difficult.

Financial Advisors Figure 15-2 indicated that three agencies play the major roles in advising Cabinet on financial issues. We have already seen some indication of the interrelationships among them. The Department of Finance is responsible for overall economic management, for the raising of revenues, and for the economic forecasts and fiscal framework on which expenditure allocations are based. The Treasury Board with its secretariat is responsible for the management of current-year expenditures, for the provision of advice on the allocation of funds between one broad area and another, for general management of the public service, and for keeping the financial accounts of the Cabinet policy committees. The Office of the Controller General is responsible for insuring that proper financial-control procedures are in place and for insuring that all government programs are evaluated regularly. The financial-control procedures have little bearing on the determination of priorities. Evaluation procedures *could*, in theory, be more influential, but since most ministers ignore routine evaluations most of the time, their impact on priority determination is minimal.

We have already pointed out the pre-eminence of the minister and the Department of Finance in this system, and we need only underscore it here. The department has as one of its duties the responsibilities for preparing economic forecasts and projections for the whole economy and for government revenues. This information will become a vital part of the data required to make a priority decision on all substantive policy issues. If the Department of Finance is forecasting declining government revenues, then the Cabinet will be extremely reluctant to take on a big new program, however desirable it may otherwise be. Similarly, if the Department of Finance opines that a new program will create critical economic problems in the country, the Cabinet will very likely be reluctant to assign a high priority to the program. Since Cabinet ministers are not normally economists, and since they are too busy to be able to engage in extensive searches for alternative information, they are rather at the mercy of the Department of Finance when large economic questions are at issue.

The Treasury Board and its secretariat has a unique status in the system.[22] The Board is a statutory committee of the Privy Council, and is composed of five Cabinet members whose portfolios affect the financial affairs of the government of Canada, the Minister of Finance, *ex officio*, and the President of the Treasury Board, who is its chairman and is also the minister in charge of the secretariat and of the Office of the Controller General. We have seen that the Treasury

---

[22] For a description of the older budgetary system, see A.W. Johnson, "The Treasury Board of Canada and the Machinery of Government in the 1970s," *Canadian Journal of Political Science*, vol. 4, no. 3, September 1971, pp. 354–356. When Johnson wrote the article, he was Secretary of the Treasury Board. For a more extensive critique of the older system, see Douglas Hartle, *The Expenditure Budget Process in the Government of Canada* (Toronto: Canadian Tax Foundation, 1978). Some comments on the evolutionary process described here are provided in D. Hartle, "The Report of the Royal Commission on Financial Management and Accountability: A Review," *Canadian Public Policy*, Summer 1979, pp. 366–382.

Board has two broad sets of responsibilities. The first of these relates to the management of the public service. In this regard, it attempts to improve the public service as an administrative system, offers more or less welcome advice to the line managers of government as to how they might improve their individual operations, acts as the employer for purposes of collective bargaining, and issues guidelines for administrative and financial procedures; the guidelines have the effect of law. In part these functions are carried out within the secretariat, but many of the financial-management issues are handled in the Office of the Controller General. This management function is a vital one; we will discuss it when we consider bureaucratic processes.

The second set of responsibilities of the Treasury Board relates to the budgetary process. The Financial Administration Act, which is the legislation governing the expenditure process, delegates to the Treasury Board responsibility as the overseer of the budgetary process. In support of this role, the Treasury Board Secretariat keeps track of current and projected expenditures within envelopes according to a common set of rules, and it also approves current expenditures and allocates personnel resources.

The Treasury Board's financial-administration responsibilities are carried out primarily through control of a sharply focused eighteen-to twenty-four-month expenditure-management cycle that is embedded within the four-year overall planning cycle. In practice, this is a very complex process and it is accompanied by procedures for supplementary estimates and for the audit and evaluation of expenditures (the details of this are considered in Chapter 16). It is made further complicated by the fact that the whole system is properly described as a "rolling cycle." Each year, the four-year revenue and expenditure projections are rolled forward one year; the intermediate years are updated; new program forecasts are prepared; new policy reserves are created and spent; and new priority determinations are made. The control of this complex control mechanism gives the Treasury Board and its secretariat a major role in the determination of priorities.

Ad Hoc Executive Support Agencies: Royal Commissions, Task Forces, and Study Teams

Frequently, areas of special concern to the Cabinet are dealt with by special task forces, study teams, or royal commissions, which are set up by Cabinet decree. The use of task forces, and, to a lesser extent, royal commissions, has in recent years become increasingly popular at both federal and provincial levels of government as a way of combining external and governmental expertise in a particular area.[23] Royal commissions of inquiry have a long history in Canadian politics.[24] At first, they were usually set up to investigate particularly sensitive areas where some wrong-doing in the governmental structure was suspected,

---

[23] M. Lamontagne, "The Influence of the Politician," pp. 271–366, especially p. 286ff.

[24] John C. Courtney, "In Defense of Royal Commissions," *Canadian Public Administration*, vol. 12, no. 2, Summer, 1969, pp. 198–212. See also H.R. Hanson, "Inside Royal Commissions," *Canadian Public Administration*, vol. 2, no. 3, Fall, 1969, pp. 356–364; and C.E.S. Walls, "Royal Commissions: Their Influence on Public Policy," *Canadian Public Administration*, vol. 12, no. 3, Fall, 1969, pp. 365–371.

and they were usually headed by a superior court judge. They had little real importance in the policy-making process.

By the mid 1960s, however, royal commissions were used increasingly to investigate areas of policy concern, such as taxation, health services, or bilingualism and biculturalism. Today's typical royal commission is still small, with a relatively confined mandate, and headed by one to three commissioners and has a staff of some ten or twelve. But there are exceptions. The Carter Commission on Taxation and the Hall Commission on Health Services both had considerably larger staffs of experts. The Royal Commission on Bilingualism and Biculturalism featured nine commissioners with a staff of hundreds, and managed, for a few brief years, to eliminate, almost completely, unemployment among Canadian social scientists. The Royal Commission on the Economic Union and Development Prospects for Canada (the MacDonald Commission), which had the incidental benefit of providing lots of research for this text, was a worthy successor to the bilingualism and biculturalism commission. It featured thirteen commissioners, about the same size staff as the bilingualism and biculturalism commission, and research contracts for a very substantial portion of Canada's social scientists. A government is not formally bound by a royal commission report, but by the very act of appointing the royal commission, it indicates substantial concern about a problem. Since most royal commissions publish most of their findings, and since there has, presumably, been considerable public interest in the issue under study, governments often move to implement at least a part of what is suggested in the reports.

It has often been suggested that governments will appoint a royal commission when they want to defuse an issue or to bury it in studies. No doubt this is the intention behind the appointment of many commissions, but in following this route, a government must be aware that it is creating a ticking time bomb. Eventually the commission will report, and the report will usually be made public and be widely read or reported. Since the commission is quite independent, the government cannot control its output, and since it is viewed by the public as being expert, independent, and impartial, there may be very considerable pressure to implement its proposals. The Hall Commission almost certainly sped up the provision of public health insurance in Canada. The Carter Commission helped create a demand for tax reform even if the reform was considerably different than what the commission proposed.

Perhaps for these reasons governments frequently make use of task forces rather than royal commissions to provide input and advice on priorities. Task forces vary widely in formality, size, and structure; but, frequently, they have one overall director and a small staff of professionals, and typically, they farm out many of their research responsibilities in the form of contracts. Many of them, including those that are most important at the priority-setting stage of the policy process, report directly to a Cabinet committee through some responsible minister, but the term "task force" is not a precisely defined one and is therefore increasingly used to describe both lower-level working groups set up to investigate some area of concern within a department, as well as groups of ministers engaged in a major study. As far as governments are concerned, the great advantage of the task force is that its work can often be kept secret. Consequently, if a government does not like what it is told, it simply fails to publish the task force's report and makes policy choices in another way.

The most recent and perhaps most famous task force in Canadian political history had some of the characteristics described above, but went considerably beyond what we normally think of when we use the term "task force." The Ministerial Task Force on Program Review (the Nielsen Task Force) was actually a group of senior ministers, active during 1984, 1985, and early 1986, under the chairmanship of the deputy prime minister, Erik Nielsen. It was intended to review the need for and the efficiency and effectiveness of delivery of a vast array of programs covering nearly all aspects of government activity. The review work was actually conducted by study teams of public-sector and private-sector people who held hearings across the country and delved, more or less deeply and with more or less competence, into a broad range of programs. There were nineteen study teams in all. Each produced a large report. The reports were boiled down to standard memoranda to Cabinet, then considered by the Ministerial Task Force and the Committee on Priorities and Planning. Unlike most task-force activities, the study-team reports were published in March 1986.

The Ministerial Task Force was created because of recognition on the part of the new Conservative government that it was difficult for government departments or the ministers directly responsible for them to propose cuts in their own programs. It was thus another in the long line of attempts to attack the sanctity of the A-base. Its success cannot be easily assessed. Under the Conservative government, after 1984, and particularly after 1985, restraint did seem to hit quite hard and federal expenditures grew at a rate much less than GNP growth. However, most of the reductions could be traced to decisions made outside the framework of the Nielsen exercise and within the preserve of the normal operations of the Department of Finance and the Treasury Board. In some cases, the results may have been quite the opposite of what was expected. For example, the leak of the report on Indian programs mobilized very substantial opposition and in the end, the prime minister was forced to promise there would be no cuts to Indian programs, and any viable suggestions which the study team made were lost.

CONCLUSIONS

The image that emerges from this description of the Cabinet and its related agencies is one of considerable complexity. It is one of a priority-management system in a state of considerable flux as governments attempt to grapple with the problem of maintaining enough flexibility in an era when social and financial pressures appear to preclude any substantial increase in expenditures. The restraint-and-reduction ethic has been particularly dominant in the mid 1980s, but the other objectives of the system have been quite consistent since at least the early 1970s. For example, the emphasis on relating priority choices and expenditures decisions can be seen in the Treasury Board manual, *Planning Programming Budget Guide* from 1974. It says the new expenditure and priority management system will involve the following concepts:

a) the setting of specific objectives;
b) systematic analysis to clarify objectives and to assess alternative ways of meeting them;
c) the framing of budgetary proposals in terms of programs directed towards the achievement of the objectives;
d) the projection of the costs of these programs a number of years in the future;
e) the formulation of plans of achievement year by year for each program; and
f) an information system for each program to supply data for the monitoring of achievement of program objectives and the appropriateness of the program itself.

The manual goes on to emphasize that this is a process for determining priorities through resource allocation:

> The elements of the Canadian government PPB system have been developed . . . within the context of total resource allocation. By the latter phrase is meant that there is an explicit recognition that the total resources are limited in terms of the individual and collective demands of departments and there has to be a setting of priorities by the government itself in light of which departments can plan and budget. . . . Program budgeting is primarily concerned with resource allocation within the department.[25]

With the important exception of an emphasis upon sector-wide rather than departmental reallocation, and of more emphasis on expenditure reduction, the same concepts underlie expenditure management in the 1980s.[26]

The internal dynamics of priority determination and expenditure-management systems constitute another constant, for they always involve sets of bargaining relationships. Since resources are scarce, they must be rationed, and as soon as people begin to feel any sort of shortage, they will begin to bargain to maximize their satisfactions.[27] Thus, when decision makers discover that not all the demands they consider important can be satisfied, they will begin to trade off one project

---

[25] Treasury Board, *Planning, Programming, Budgeting Guide* (Ottawa: Queen's Printer, 1968), p. 4. Much has been written about PPBS. On the general system, see F.J. Lyden and E.G. Miller, eds., *Planning Programming, Budgeting: A Systems Approach to Management* (Cambridge: Harvard University Press, 1965); J. Burkehead, *Government Budgeting* (New York: John Wiley and Son, 1966); H.A. Hovey, *The Planning-Programming-Budgeting Approach to Government Decision-Making* (New York: Praeger, 1968). On Canadian applications, see Treasury Board, *Planning, Programming, Budgeting Guide* (Ottawa: Queen's Printer, 1968); *Statement to the Senate Committee on Science Policy*, by S.S. Reisman, Feb. 2, 1969; G. Guruprasad, "Planning for Tax Administration in Canada: The PPB System in National Revenue and Taxation," *Canadian Public Administration*, vol. 16, no. 3, Autumn 1973, pp. 399–421; A.W. Johnson, *The Treasury Board and the Machinery of Government in the 1970s*," Michael Hicks, "The Treasury Board of Canada and its Clients, Five Years of Administrative Reform 1966–1971," *Canadian Public Administration*, vol. 16, no. 2, Summer 1973; and Douglas Hartle, *The Expenditure Budget Process in the Government of Canada*. The second edition of this text also contains an extensive section on PPBS (See pp. 347–350.)

[26] The system is similar in many respects to attempts to introduce a long-term planning cycle in Britain. There, the system has run into several of the problems we outlined. See M. Wright, "Public Expenditure in Britain: The Crisis of Control," *Public Administration*, vol. 55, summer 1977.

[27] See, for example, Thomas C. Schelling, "An Essay on Bargaining," *The American Economic Review*, vol. 66, no. 3, June 1956, pp. 281–306. The classic statement of this approach, developed in the United States, but, we suggest, also very applicable to Canada, is Aaron Wildavsky, *The Politics of the Budgetary Process* (Boston: Little, Brown, 1974). See also Ira Shaskansky, *The Politics of Taxing and Spending* (Indianapolis: Bobbs Merrill, 1969); H. Heclo and A. Wildavsky, *The Private Government of Public Money* (Berkeley: University of California Press, 1974); and G.T. Allison, *Essence of Decision* (Boston: Little Brown, 1970), particularly "model 3".

against another in an attempt to insure that those they consider to be most important can be satisfied. Officials who are well down the line are concerned with only one or two programs or parts of programs that directly affect them, and it is usually up to them to administer these projects, not bargain for them in the first instance. The higher officials in departments and agencies bargain within their own departments to insure that their own spheres of influence survive and expand. In the game of interdepartmental politics, departments themselves are engaged in a continuous process of bargaining and building coalitions to maximize their own departmental power and to optimize their own program mix.

At the Cabinet and intergovernmental levels, this bargaining process is particularly evident. Cabinet ministers must frequently trade their support on one issue for the support of a colleague on another, and federal-provincial conferences at the ministerial level—or, more particularly, the back rooms and dinner parties at ministerial conferences—tend to be the arenas for a great deal of intergovernmental bargaining. Thus, while the structures for priority determination tend to look somewhat different at various levels within the political system, and sometimes within each level, there do tend to be underlying similarities of process that shape the nature of priority determination.

Before we leave the subject of priority determination, there are two particularly important points that need to be emphasized, especially since they draw attention to dangers and problems in the Canadian political system. The less important of these is the problem of blockages caused by breakdown in the bargaining process among bureaucratic agencies. These blockages are caused by the normal desire of departments or agencies to expand or to avoid contraction, and the necessity — in view of the scarcity of resources — of doing so partially at the expense of other departments and agencies. Blockages developed in this way introduce major inefficiencies and delays into priority determination, but they are to some degree inevitable in complex multidepartment systems.

There is, however, a larger problem revolving around the establishment of new priorities for Canada. In the end, such priorities are normally set by elected politicians. No matter how important the bureaucracy may be in priority determination, the final gatekeepers are and must continue to be, the Cabinet ministers. Their motivation is, at least partially, to get votes for what is being done, and that is perfectly appropriate in a democracy. But one result is that the determination of new priorities may be largely induced by immediate demands, for only if a politician is acting directly in response to a demand is he or she likely to get much immediate recognition for those actions. No one gets much political credit for planning ahead and thus solving a problem if the problem has not yet become serious enough to be perceived by the public. Hence, political systems often tend to respond to crises rather than to anticipate them. Those who must formulate new policies are often thrust into the middle of a problem with no time to develop long-range strategy, rational goals, or activities and processes that will get them to those goals.

This point cannot be taken too far, however, for politicians have to do two things to keep themselves in power. They must, of course, win elections, but at an even more fundamental level, they must maintain support for the system of government within which they work. A regime that is constantly faced with crises may eventually lose public support and collapse. Therefore, in addition to responding to demand inputs, a Cabinet must plan ahead to some extent to avoid too many crises, and to avoid giving the appearance of merely stumbling from one crisis to another.

We shall leave this chapter as we began it, by warning the reader that, although there are underlying commonalities in the process, the relationships among agencies, the occupants of positions, and many of the surface rules of the game can change very quickly. What remains constant is the necessity to select priorities, the need to do it in the context of restricted resources, and the consequent requirement that bargaining and trade-offs lie at the root of the whole process.

PRIORITY DETERMINATION: INTERGOVERNMENTAL RELATIONS IN THE POLICY PROCESS

W│ e have seen in Chapters 8 and 9 that the responsibility for policy making in Canada is divided between the provinces and the federal government, each of which is sovereign in its own jurisdictional sphere and each of which possesses at least some of the financial resources necessary for carrying into effect its own policies. We have also looked at the manner in which the Supreme Court of Canada, and, before it, the Judicial Committee of the Privy Council, were called upon to resolve the jurisdictional disputes that arose between the federal government and the provinces. It is our intention, in this chapter, to provide an overview of the structures and processes of intergovernmental coordination and to consider the impact of divided jurisdiction on the policy process.[1]

Before we move to an overview of the process whereby federal and provincial governments interact in Canada, it is necessary to say a few words about the extent to which the various institutions at the level of the national government reflect the federal principle, or what Donald Smiley and Ron Watts call *"intra state federalism."* The point is made by the current analysts of intrastate federalism that such regional and provincial accommodation occurs in virtually *all* institutions of the national government. Thus, the nature and distribution of seats in the House of Commons is based in part upon federal principles. The Senate was originally established, among other reasons, to reflect regional interests in the national parliament, and, by convention, the structure and the operation of the political executive features many regional and provincial accommodative measures.

In recent years there have been several proposals put forward to reform our national institutions so that they might be better equipped to represent the interests of the regions and of provincial governments. There have been proposals to base membership on the Supreme Court of Canada explicitly on provincial representation, and even to give the provincial governments a direct role in the appointment of judges. As well, there have been proposals, many of which have their origins before the turn of the century, to reform the Senate, giving the provincial governments the power over some or all of the appointments to that house and giving the Senate, as a "House of the Provinces" or a "House of the Federation," a much more powerful legislative role with respect to issues that potentially affect provincial rights. While none of these reform proposals has met with success, the fact remains that there has been an ongoing effort to complement the essentially *ad hoc* machinery of intergovernmental relations with institutionalized protection of provincial rights within the national political system itself. This process, and the perception of the necessity to enhance the federal component of national institutions, have been given recent impetus by trends in intergovernmental relations in the late 1970s and 1980s. We will return to a consideration of these trends and their relationship to the current status of reform proposals affecting intrastate federalism in the conclusion to this chapter. Now we must turn to an evaluation of intergovernmental relations in Canada, its historical roots, institutional framework, and current status.

THE PROBLEM:
INTERJURISDICTIONAL POLICY COORDINATION

That there is a need for intergovernmental coordination in Canada is not difficult to establish. The very existence of a federal system is predicated on the existence of

---

[1] "Intrastate Federalism in Canada," research paper prepared for the MacDonald Commission, (Toronto: University of Toronto Press, 1985).

regional diversity. The cultural and economic variance among the regions of our federation produces wide differences in policy priorities not only among the provinces, but between the provinces and the federation. If all policy issues docilely conformed to the rigid jurisdictional boundaries established by the BNA Act and its judicial interpreters, the conflicting priorities of the various governments in Canada would not be a serious problem. However, there are, in fact, very few subject areas of public policy today that do not in some way fall into the juris-dictional bailiwicks of more than one government — what Richard Simeon has referred to as "the contradictory pressures of political independence and policy interdependence."[2] Thus, if government in Canada is to meet the problems of a modern society with policies that are both appropriate and effective, there must be coordination of the efforts of eleven governments.

Elsewhere in this volume, we discuss the process of *interdepartmental* com-petition and coordination in terms of bargaining; similarly, the process of intergovernmental competition and coordination is also one of bargaining. However, intergovernmental bargaining is substantially different from inter-departmental bargaining for the simple reason that the latter occurs among legally *subordinate* agencies. While the *de facto* decision-making power usually rests within the complex maze of interdepartmental coordination, any log-jams that might crop up in the negotiations can ultimately be settled by Cabinet-level or central-agency intervention. This not only encourages the bureaucrats to com-promise in the interest of avoiding an imposed settlement that might please nobody, but it also means that stalemates will generally not be permitted to stand in the way of needed action to solve pressing problems. While we cannot underestimate the primacy of the bureaucratic-level bargaining process, in the final analysis, hierarchical processes of control do exist, and these can be utilized where interdepartmental bargaining has broken down.

By contrast to interdepartmental bargaining within a single government, intergovernmental bargaining occurs between legally equal and sovereign entities. There is no superior authority empowered to intervene and force a settlement when the negotiations have broken down. The judicial system can, to some extent, play the role of arbitrator in intergovernmental disputes, but only if the stale-mate involves jurisdictional issues, and then only if the courts are asked to intervene. As we have seen in Chapter 7, the Canadian judiciary cannot initiate litigation; it can act only when legal action is initiated by parties to a real dispute, or when a government refers a piece of legislation for judicial opinion. Thus, in the arena of federal-provincial relations, the basic sociopolitical mechanism of control known as hierarchy is absent. The federal-provincial dimension of policy making is therefore a purer form of bargaining than either the process of interdepartmental bargaining, which occurs within a single government, or the process of intergroup and group-system bargaining, which was discussed in Chapter 13.

The implications of the fact that federal-provincial relations in Canada involve a process of bargaining among constitutionally equal parties is that intergovern-

---

2 "Intergovernmental Relations and the Challenges to Canadian Federalism," *CPA*, Spring 1980, p. 21.

mental conflict can only be resolved if the active process of self-interested horse trading is tempered with some fundamental consensus. There must be some mutual feelings of good will, a basic agreement on very fundamental values, and, most importantly, the shared acceptance of Canada as a legitimate political community; these attitudes form the pedestal upon which the machinery of intergovernmental conflict resolution is mounted.

Such attitudes do appear to be generally encouraged by the matrix of public opinion. The empirical evidence on the national unity question has shown us that even in the tempestuous years of the 1970s, while provinces were an important focus for Canadians, in fact people tend, on the average, to feel more warmly towards Canada than they do towards their province. However, the authors of *Political Choice in Canada*[3] also discovered that affection for Canada relative to the province is weaker in the peripheral provinces than it is in the central provinces. Newfoundlanders, likely because their province was the last into Confederation, actually feel more warmly about their province, and Prince Edward Island and Alberta respondents, in 1974, rated the country and the province about equally in their hearts.

The feeling of warmth towards Canada is tempered by the fact that when respondents in the same national survey were asked which government they feel closest to, in every province except Ontario they picked the provinces. As one might expect, the farther the respondent lives from Ottawa, the stronger the attachment to the provincial government. Finally, when asked which level of government is more important in their lives, "Canadians give equal weight to each, a judgement which matches that of most impartial observers."[4]

The conclusion to be taken from this is that "the two levels of government are perceived by the population as jointly important and having positive characteristics."[5] While this does not provide us with a complete explanation for the legitimacy or persistence of the Canadian political community, it does indicate that the existence of a governmental system featuring divided jurisdiction, with the provinces and the federal government resolving conflict through a process of bargaining, political conciliation, and compromise, is accepted by Canadians. As Clarke put it, intergovernmental conflict resolution

> works best in a situation where the population is not polarized into opposing camps, as federalists or provincial rightists, but rather where for some purposes they look to the federal actors and for others they turn to their provincial governments.
>
> Our examination of attitudes toward the federal system and behaviour within it has led to the conclusion that such a polarization has not taken place in Canada.[6]

Thus, while it is difficult to find a unifying philosophy, dominant myth, or glowing symbol of our Canadianness, it may be that the processes we have created for settling disputes help unite us. In this way, like boxers who have gone the distance in the ring as opponents and in the end find a common bond that unites them, so

---

[3] Clarke *et al.*, *Absent Mandate*, ch. 3.

[4] *Ibid.*, p. 81.

[5] *Ibid.*

[6] *Op. cit.*, p. 90.

Canadians have been united by their political differences. Thus, somewhat ironically, perhaps we can be defined by our conflicts, and by our uniquely Canadian way of resolving them. Certainly at the élite level this would seem to be the case. Olsen argues that, while the public performances of politicians at federal-provincial conferences show us a picture of constant bickering and profound disagreement:

> more candid views show Canadians a smiling group of chattering politicians and bureaucrats enjoying each others' company while basking in the afterglow of their common public performance. Thus, the conflicts between and among members of the state elite are real, while at the same time they are simply an expectation associated with their role . . . a hard driving negotiator fighting for a jurisdictional interest [as well as] a convivial colleague.[7]

Moreover, as we will see later, there is evidence that, at the level of officials and technocrats, who are not required to posture for the television cameras or motivated to win popular support from a fickle electorate, intergovernmental relations are still more cordial.

Our conclusion about the legitimacy of the Canadian political community is, thus, that Canadian unity is *sui generis*. The national unifying myths, economic interdependencies, and cultural homogeneity that form the basis of political community in other countries are not present — or else are weak — in Canada. In fact, most Canadians see ethnic and regional conflict as a constant; what makes us unique and what provides the basis of political community is that, with rare exceptions, such as the separatist threat of the late 1970s, we never doubt that the conflicts will be resolved. Thus, by contrast to countries such as the United States and Britain, where the existence of political community was a prerequisite for a political system, in Canada we did it backwards. We started with a set of political institutions and processes, and it may be our common faith in these institutions and processes that now forms the basis of political community, and is, thus, the glue that holds the pieces of the Canadian mosaic together.

THE EVOLUTION OF INTERJURISDICTIONAL COORDINATION: 1867–1970

In the earliest days of the federation, the dominant medium of federal-provincial coordination was the political hegemony of the Dominion rather than any true process of bargaining. Despite the anti-federal sentiments in the maritimes, the leadership of the federal government in matters of public policy was virtually unchallenged. This is likely a partial reflection of the ultimate capture, by the Dominion, of most of the prominent political figures of the colonial era, in the 1860s and 1870s. Canadian politicians expected that the major functions of government would be performed by the Dominion, and for a brief time the provincial politicians were either convinced as well, or too timid and insecure to complain.

[7] Denis Olsen, pp. 18–19.

While this quasi-hierarchical process of coordination, expressed formally in devices such as the reservation and disallowance powers, never became firmly established, an analogous situation does occur even today when the War Measures Act is proclaimed; during such times, the federal distribution of powers is effectively suspended and the federal government can achieve the necessary policy coordination by fiat. Needless to say, this is rare and has only passing relevance for the practical problems of intergovernmental coordination.

It did not take long after 1867 for the provinces to begin to assert their sovereign right to establish their own priorities in public policy. They quickly matured during the 1870s and 1880s and became capable of recruiting committed and capable politicians and public servants. The provinces very rapidly acquired the confidence and the political legitimacy to challenge the policy priorities of the federal government when those touched upon matters within the legislative jurisdiction of the provinces. The dominant mechanism of interjurisdictional coordination during this period of *classical federalism* was the arbitration of jurisdictional disputes by the judiciary. In fact, it can be argued that this period was characterized by an almost total lack of interest in face-to-face consultation, prompted in part by the lack of modern means of travel and communication and in part by a presumption on the part of both the federal government and the provinces that all matters of concern to policy makers could be parcelled out once and for all to one or the other of the various governments in Canada. Thus any apparent overlap in jurisdiction was simply a cue to ask the courts to refine their interpretations with a new pronouncement.

That this combative attitude to federal-provincial relations continued well into the twentieth century was due to the essentially uncomplicated nature of the issues facing the policy makers of the day, to the continuing difficulties of communication, and to the competing goals of nation building and province building.[8] That the sovereign governments in Canada had different policy priorities was beyond question, but fortunately the kinds of policy alternatives being considered were usually straightforward enough that they lent themselves more readily to being introduced and administered unilaterally, by either the federal government or one of the provinces.

The settlement of jurisdictional disputes through judicial arbitration is used somewhat less now than it was in the first fifty years of the federation.[9] The decline of this mode of conflict resolution in Canada was precipitated in large part by social and economic forces in the 1930s. In the first place, where power

[8] For a discussion of the process of "province building" and of its significance for the structure of Canadian federalism, see: Garth Stevenson, *Unfulfilled Union* (Toronto: Macmillan, 1979), chapter 5; J. Richards and L. Pratt, *Capitalism: Power and Influence in the New West* (Toronto: McClelland and Stewart, 1979); Sheilagh M. Dunn, "Unity and Diversity? Nation Building in an Historical Perspective," a paper prepared for the MacDonald Commission, August 1984; R.C. Vipond, "Constitutional Politics and the Legacy of the Provincial Rights Movement in Canada," *CJPS*, June 1985, p. 267; and R.A. Young, P. Faucher, and A. Blais, "The Concept of Province-Building: A Critique," *CJPS*, December 1984, p. 783.

[9] In fact, as we have seen in chapters 7 and 8, there was, in the late 1970s and 1980s, an increase in the number of jurisdictional disputes where the Supreme Court has been called upon to act as arbiter. However even with the increase, the generalization that the importance of judicial review as a factor in intergovernmental relations is less today than in the period of 1880 to 1930 still stands.

to make policy had once depended primarily upon the constitutional jurisdiction to do so, the expanding scope and complexity of the problems facing government in the twenties and thirties dictated that the costs of implementing the programs would become an even more serious constraint. Often it was the case that the provinces, while possessing the full jurisdiction to initiate policies, lacked the money to finish the job. The federal government, on the other hand, seemed to possess the necessary resources, but all too often lacked the jurisdiction.

The second factor precipitating the decline of the combative style of federal-provincial relations was the untidiness of contemporary problems. Policy makers began to recognize that most issues facing them were interrelated, and that it was impossible for a single level of government to produce a policy that would deal comprehensively with major problems that crossed jurisdictional boundaries. It was a combination of the growing financial crisis facing the provinces and the realization that one government acting alone lacked the full jurisdiction to deal adequately with most contemporary policy matters that led to the adoption of a coordinative mechanism based on true interjurisdictional bargaining.

Through the thirties, the mood of federal-provincial relations remained basically combative; however, the desperate circumstances of the period forced genuine federal-provincial coordination. Differences in priorities among the various governments were resolved through consultation and the negotiation of piecemeal agreements to meet specific problems. The emphasis was on specific problem solving and not on the consummation of a new federal marriage. The attitude was that federal-provincial collaboration and the coordination of federal and provincial programs were only necessary evils, and the most common policy manifestations of these bargains were shared-cost programs or federal conditional grants to the nearly bankrupt provinces. While not a highly integrated system of conflict resolution, the piecemeal coordinative efforts of the thirties flowed from a genuine bargaining situation; the bargaining "capital" (or "currency") used in the negotiations was jurisdiction and tax revenues. The provinces, for the most part, could promise to implement necessary social legislation that met federally established standards, in return for which the federal government would pay all or a percentage of the operating costs of the programs. While, naturally, some provinces were financially better off than others, and hence could afford to hold out for better offers from the feds, by and large, because the provinces possessed equal jurisdictional clout, all nine could take an active part in periodic negotiations.

But the process of Canadian federalism changed somewhat during the war years. At the termination of hostilities the provinces were initially resigned to the fact that, for a while at least, the federal government would be in the driver's seat; having provided both substantive and psychic leadership during the war, the federal government would continue to assume that role in the public eye for the period of post-war economic reconstruction. The federal government maintained this initiative in policy making into the fifties, setting many of the priorities for the provinces through the traditional instrument of conditional grants and subsidies, which the provinces could not politically afford to reject. The provincial role, in the meantime, a role dominated by Ontario and Quebec primarily, was to act as a brake on the activities of Ottawa.

However, as the war became merely tragic history, and as the Canadian economy continued to grow despite minor setbacks, the federal government began to fade in the eyes of the public as the government that necessarily could and should set our national political goals. The initiative began to shift again to the provinces, who could now afford to get back to the business of province building.[10] Moreover, the public focus and public expectations turned to social programs and highway construction, both of which lie in provincial spheres of jurisdiction. Also, towards the end of this period, Quebec was involved in what has loosely been referred to as the "Quiet Revolution," with the result that the erstwhile passive and defensive nationalism that had characterized the province's posture towards federalism became aggressive and assertive. The government of the province of Quebec began to demand a sufficient share of the tax dollar and to run its own programs, instead of merely sharing the costs and administrative responsibilities for those that were federally sponsored. Taking the lead from Quebec, the other provinces also began to assert themselves, reflecting the new confidence inspired by an economic and administrative coming of age and a patent dissatisfaction with the inherent paternalism of the grant-in-aid device.

But the rejuvenated political muscles of the provinces did not precipitate a return to the federalism of the thirties. Not only had the mood of federal-provincial relations become more cooperative and less combative, but the interjurisdictional bargaining ceased to be purely piecemeal, pragmatic, and problem-oriented. There was by now a tendency to seek more completely integrated programs, such as the comprehensive tax-sharing system.[11] Moreover, the provinces were growing very important with respect to their effect on the Canadian economy as a whole, and it was becoming clear that any meaningful control over economic fluctuations would have to be exercised through joint federal and provincial action. An example of this is the ongoing effort to stem the tide of inflation in Canada through policies of fiscal restraint. In order to restrain or stimulate the Canadian economy, it is no longer sufficient for the federal government to undertake an austerity program or to grant tax incentives to certain industries. Unilateral action by the federal government will only make a dent in the economic status quo; the provinces themselves control directly, or through their municipalities, more than half the public-sector expenditures, and are therefore in a position to strongly affect the working of the economy through fiscal measures that are constitutionally within their exclusive jurisdiction. The regulation of the Canadian economy, which had traditionally been considered one of the prerogatives of the central government, had to be achieved through federal-provincial cooperation. Thus, where cooperative federalism was characterized at one time by the federal government's sharing the responsibility for provincial matters with the provinces, the tables were turned, and, by 1975, cooperative federalism included the additional sharing of federal matters with the provinces.

As intergovernmental policy coordination became broader in focus, the bargaining process became a regular, indeed a constant, activity for the eleven

---

[10] See Dunn "Unity and Diversity," for a provocative analysis of province building in the post-war period.

[11] See Chapter 9.

governments. It is obvious that this could tax the resources of the smaller provinces more than those of the big ones; but the introduction, in the 1960s, of unconditional federal subsidies for the poorer provinces, in the form of equalization grants, has helped them to cover the growing costs of government in the modern era of intergovernmental relations. Hence, despite the new administrative burdens of cooperative federalism, possession of the basic bargaining capital of jurisdiction over social programs permitted all the provinces to participate actively if not equally in the negotiations. Coordination was ultimately achieved where it was necessary to integrate federal and provincial programs; and mutual compromise, in the interest of solving Canada's problems, was made easier by a basic mood of cooperation. Before moving to a consideration of the current trends in federalism in Canada, it is necessary to describe the institutional devices that have evolved to facilitate the almost constant process of interjurisdictional bargaining.

THE STRUCTURES OF INTERJURISDICTIONAL COORDINATION

In the early years of federal-provincial relations, meetings of federal and provincial officials occurred in an *ad hoc* manner, and at fairly senior levels in the governmental hierarchies. Meetings of the premiers and the prime minister would be called at irregular intervals, usually at the initiative of the federal government, to discuss specific problems of concern to all jursidictions. In recent times, however, these conferences have become institutionalized to the extent that the ministers now meet on a regular basis and the meetings include bureaucratic as well as political decision makers. While *ad hoc* meetings still occur, the necessity for such informal talks is reduced by the existence of many formal bodies, which meet at least annually if not more often.

In an article published in 1965, Edgar Gallant (then a deputy secretary to the Cabinet) remarked that "the number of [federal-provincial] conferences and committees doubled over eight years."[12] In absolute terms, the number of such committees had risen from 64, in 1957, to 125, in 1965, which by most standards is indeed a remarkable rate of growth. However, based on information sifted from an *Inventory of Federal Provincial Committees* compiled in 1972, the number of inter-jurisdictional institutions in existence at the time could be established at more than 400.[13] While growth of such institutions seems to have stabilized since the mid-1970s, it is still safe to conclude, even from the imperfect

---

[12] Edgar Gallant, "The Machinery of Federal Provincial Relations," *CPA*, December 1965, p. 515.

[13] *Inventory of Federal Provincial Committees* (Ottawa: PCO, 1972), two volumes. The inventory listed 482 committees, but there is considerable duplication in the list, because committees attended by more than one federal department were sometimes listed twice. On the other hand, there are many subcommittees, which went completely unlisted, so that while no exact figures can be stated, the general trends indicated by this inventory can still be very helpful in making some generalizations about the nature of such committees in Canada. A more recent study uses a different set of classifications and arrives at a lower total figure of 158 "mécanismes de liaison intergouvernementale." The lower figure is a result of a data base that does not include the many bilateral operational committees, which existed, for instance, under the Canada Water Act. See G. Veilleux, "L'évolution des Mécanismes de liaison intergouvernementale," in R. Simeon, ed., *Confrontation and Collaboration* (Toronto: IPAC, 1979), p. 35.

data available to us, that more is happening in the federal-provincial arena every day. For example, the Federal Provincial Relations Office (FPRO) identifies 239 federal-provincial programs in a 1984 report.[14] and many of these programs would require a bilateral liaison body or coordinating committee for each participating province. Moreover, there are a great many areas of joint federal-provincial concern where there are no explicit programs, but where ongoing liaison is required.

The number and frequency of federal-provincial meetings is another indicator of the extent of intergovernmental activity in Canada. Veilleux identified only 158 interjurisdictional bodies in 1977, but cites 335 recorded meetings of those joint bodies.[15] In the same volume that contains Veilleux' report, Gordon Robertson states that 500 is likely a more realistic number of actual meetings,[16] and this does not take into account the countless informal meetings among federal and provincial officials that happen as a day-to-day part of their jobs.

However, while the volume and frequency of intergovernmental meetings and the number of formally constituted intergovernmental bodies is very large; and while it is indisputable that less formal contacts, meetings, lunch dates, telephone calls, and documentary correspondence, are almost constant, what is ultimately more interesting is the distribution of this activity by policy area, decision-making level, and institutional form.

The Distribution of Interjurisdictional Bodies by Policy Area

The largest number of committees has traditionally been in the policy areas of the environment, health and social assistance, and regional development. The reasons for this concentration of federal-provincial institutions in these broad areas is related in part to the contemporary political relevance of such issues in Canadian society, and in part to the degree of jurisdictional untidiness, or overlap, which characterizes the fields. These suggestions are borne out by the fact that, as the federal government has moved out of a number of shared-cost programs in the health and welfare field, as the political importance of environmental issues has been overshadowed by energy-related problems,[17] and as the decentralized General Development Agreements were replaced by the Economic and Regional Development Agreements (ERDA),[18] the amount and intensity of intergovernmental activity in these fields has declined sharply.

However it does not always follow, that where the jurisdiction is clear and settled there will be less intergovernmental contact. In fact, where the matter is clearly within the legislative jurisdiction of the federal government, such as veterans affairs or national defence, it holds true that there is little federal-provincial

---

[14] Veilleux, "L'évolution," p. 37.

[15] Veilleux, p. 37.

[16] "The Role of Interministerial Conferences in the Decision-Making Process," in Simeon, *Confrontation and Collaboration*, p. 79.

[17] See M. Whittington, "The Department of the Environment," in G.B. Doern, ed., *Spending Tax Dollars* (Ottawa: 1980).

[18] J.S. Dupré, "Reflections on the Workability of Executive Federalism," in R. Simeon, ed., *Intergovernmental Relations* (Toronto: 1985), pp. 13–14.

interaction. On the other hand, in areas such as housing, highways, education, and urban affairs, which are fairly clearly provincial matters, it is not rare to see a number of interjurisdictional bodies in existence to coordinate the activities of the several governments involved and to negotiate the amount and disposition of federal transfer payments. Thus, it would seem plausible to hypothesize that the federal government's "spending power,"[19] combined with its relative wealth and the pragmatic need for national coordination of policies, give it a potential if fragile and sporadic bargaining lever even in policy areas totally within the jurisdiction of the provinces. Unfortunately for those of a centralist bent, however, the federal spending power is far more significant when dealing with the have-not provinces than it is when dealing with the wealthier provinces. The bargaining process at the root of cooperative federalism is, thus, not only one-sided in favour of the federal level but it is also quite asymmetrical in its effect on the various provinces.[20]

The Distribution of Interjurisdictional Bodies by Decision-Making Level

Another important dimension in the analysis of interjurisdictional institutions is the level of government at which the institutions operate. The level is determined first by whether the personnel on the committee are political or bureaucratic, and second, if they are bureaucrats, by their organizational rank in governmental hierarchy. For clarity and ease of discussion, we have defined four decision-making levels at which interjurisdictional committees operate in Canada: the *political*, the *senior bureaucratic* (including deputy ministers and assistant deputy ministers), the *technical* or professional, and the *operational*. It must be noted that operational and technical committees (while functionally quite distinct) may, in fact, include personnel at approximately the same level. The former tend to be involved directly in the implementation of joint federal-provincial programs, while the latter tend to act more as policy-analysis and research groups. Similarly, at the political level, we must distinguish between *specialized* ministerial conferences, (such as those held by ministers of agriculture, ministers of finance, provincial treasurers, and health ministers) and the First Ministers' Conferences, which have a more *generalist* role over time.

The actual distribution of committees among these decision-making levels in Canada is uneven. For the most part, there will be but one political-level committee in each policy area, composed of appropriate federal and provincial Cabinet ministers. On the other hand, more than two-thirds of all the committees in any given policy area will be at the technical and operational levels. One can thus conclude that the most common form of federal-provincial interaction occurs below the ministerial level meetings, which we read about in the newspapers, and in fact most are even *below* the senior bureaucratic level.

---

[19] Simply, the power of the federal government to spend money on any matter it chooses, provided it does not pass legislation that is *ultra vires*.

[20] See K. McRoberts, "Unilateralism, Bilateralism, and Multilateralism," in Simeon, *Intergovernmental Relations*, pp. 120–121.

The problem with analyzing federal-provincial committees in the context of their numerical distribution by decision-making level is that this does not take into account comparative measures of their impact on policy outputs. For instance, perhaps the most important interjurisdictional committee in operation in Canada today (with the possible exception of the First Ministers' Conference) is the Continuing Committee on Fiscal and Economic Matters. This is a senior bureaucratic-level committee composed mainly of the deputy ministers of finance or the deputy provincial treasurers. Its responsibility is to provide technical support for the Conference of the Ministers of Finance and, to a large extent, for the Conference of the First Ministers. The fact that this body meets more frequently than its political-level parent committee, the fact that it is composed mainly of highly skilled professionals in key administrative roles, and the fact that the committee membership is more constant than that of the political-level bodies, mean that this committee is in a position of great potential influence over the country's broad fiscal priorities, and over the coordination of measures designed to cope with economic difficulties.

Finally, in terms of the actual frequency of meetings, perhaps the greatest increase was witnessed by the First Ministers' Conferences (FMCs), which proliferated through the 1970s and early 1980s.[21] While some of this increase in first ministerial interaction can be explained by the special circumstances of the period, such as the constitutional reform process, it may also be reflective of a new style of federal-provincial summitry, which is extremely visible to the public and also highly combative or conflictual.[22] The Mulroney government has indicated its intention to regularize the powers of federal-provincial summitry by holding at least one FMC annually at a fixed time of the year.

The Distribution of Interjurisdictional Committees by Inclusiveness

Federal-provincial committees can also be classified according to the number of governments included. Because of the amount of attention paid to the political-level conferences by the media, one might get the impression that interjurisdictional committees are for the most part *omnilateral*, or composed of representatives of all eleven governments. This is far from the case, for, in fact, at least half the bodies listed in the 1972 PCO inventory are *bilateral*, composed of representatives of the federal government and one province only. Less exclusive than the bilateral committees, and yet more inclusive than the omnilateral committees, are the *multilateral* committees, composed of the federal government and at least two but not all of the provinces. Major exceptions to the general rule about the predominance of bilateral committees are in the areas of finance, fiscal relations, and constitutional reform, where almost all of the active committees are omnilateral.

One further development in intergovernmental relations that has emerged in

---

21 Brooke Jeffrey, "A New Era in Intergovernmental Relations," in *Machinery of Government in Transition* (Research Branch, Library of Parliament, December 1984), p. 141.

22 See Smiley in R. Simeon, *op. cit.*, 1979; D. Savoie, "Les Conférences des Premiers Ministres," *Policy Options*, September 1983; and Dupré, *op. cit.*, p. 15.

514 INSIDE THE SYSTEM

the 1980s is the increased participation of the Yukon and the Northwest Territories in federal-provincial deliberations. Partly this is because of provisions of the Constitution Act that recognize, at least implicitly, a role for those governments in matters relating to aboriginal rights. However, there is also a growing recognition (albeit grudgingly on the part of some of the western provinces, who would prefer to see their own boundaries extended north to the Arctic Ocean) that the territorial governments are coming of age. While not sovereign, they have fully elected legislatures, responsible government, and delegated responsibility for most of the matters under provincial jurisdiction in the south. As such, while they are not provinces, they are being included in many intergovernmental forums where they had once been excluded.[23]

The overall distribution of interjurisdictional committees by decision-making level and by inclusiveness is illustrated graphically with examples in Figure 16-1. As illustrated by this chart, the political-level committees tend to be omnilateral or multilateral. The reason for this is threefold. First, the ministers are less likely than their bureaucratic and technical staff to be able to deal with the nitty-gritty negotiations that often occur at the bilateral level. Second, it is at the political level that the final agreement on priorities affecting the federation as a whole must be reached. While often the political-level meetings only confirm agreements hacked out by lower-level officials, formal agreements must ultimately come at the ministerial level. Finally, the ministers at the federal level tend to be too busy to devote the time needed to haggle individually with the provinces. They prefer to meet only after some general agreement has been worked out at lower levels through bilateral and multilateral talks.

By contrast, almost all of the technical-level and operational-level committees are either bilateral or multilateral. While some of the technical-level committees in the area of finance involve representatives of all of the provinces and the federal government, for the most part the role of the technical people is more specific — not only in terms of subject matter but in terms of geography as well. Finally, and again this is specific to the emerging political systems in the north, there are a large number of federal-territorial committees at the technical and operational levels. Most of these are bilateral, but a few are trilateral, including representatives of the two territories and the federal government.

Structural Variations

Up until now we have spoken only of federal-provincial committees. While such committees make up by far the largest percentage of interjurisdictional bodies in Canada, it must be pointed out that there are other organizational forms. The *interprovincial* committees are bodies that exclude the federal government, although in many cases the feds are permitted to send an observer.

As with the federal-provincial bodies, the interprovincial ones can be classified as omnilateral (including all provinces), multilateral, or bilateral (including two provinces). They also vary as to the decision-making level in the same way the

[23] *National Goals and National Policy: Interprovincial Relations and Interprovincial Mechanisms*, a paper prepared for the MacDonald Commission, 1985, p. 108.

FIGURE 16-1
INCLUSIVENESS OF COMMITTEES

Decision-Making Level of Committees	Omnilateral	Multilateral	Bilateral
Technical and Operational	Few — e.g., some technical level financial committees	Some — e.g., Prairie Provinces Water Board, Atlantic Tidal Power Programming Board	Most — e.g., Coordinating Committee on Northern Ontario Water Resources
Senior Bureaucratic	Most — e.g., Continuing Committee on Fiscal and Economic Matters	Some — e.g., Federal-Provincial Atlantic Fisheries Conference	Some — e.g., Joint Planning Committees of DREE, Consultative Committees under Canada Water Act, Manpower Needs Committees
Political	Most — e.g., Plenary Conference of First Ministers, Conference of Ministers of Finance	Very few — e.g., Forestry Minister's Conference, (because P.E.I. has very little forestry)	Few formally — Ministers are too busy for the most part — frequent *ad hoc* meetings such as between Alberta and Ottawa over oil pricing

federal-provincial committees do, and, for the most part, the generalizations about the distribution of such bodies by level and inclusiveness apply to the inter-provincial arena as well. While it has been suggested that some political-level, multilateral interprovincial committees — such as the Council of the Maritime Premiers and the Prairie Provinces Economic Council — are "proto-coalitions," which will ultimately strengthen the federal-provincial bargaining power of individual regions, there has been little hard evidence that this trend is evolving very rapidly. For the most part, the provinces will squabble among themselves as much as or more than they currently do with the federal government, and more-over, informal and *ad hoc* collusion among groups of provinces tends to be a better way of maximizing the provincial bargaining position on any particular issue. As Howard Leeson has pointed out,

> despite a mushrooming of interprovincial contact, and, in part, because of the political ambivalence toward this activity, there is a disturbing lack of coherence to such contact. Most is *ad hoc* in nature, and though formal or structured, is usually uncoordinated.[24]

Thus, we can likely conclude that there is a great latent potential in interprovincial relations, particularly in the rare instances where most or many of the provinces find themselves together in their opposition to a federal proposal. However:

> it is unlikely that interprovincial institutions can be used consistently for the development of national policy. . . . They lack the authoritative structures neces-sary to take hard decisions.[25]

A third structural variation in intergovernmental bodies is the tri-level conference. This type of committee features representatives of the federal government, the provinces, and municipalities. While the federal government has very little constitutional authority in the area of urban affairs, its vast financial resources and its access to the multitude of experts in federal agencies gave the federal government an entrée to such negotiations in the 1970s. The provinces were very jealous of their primacy in the urban area, but they agreed to permit the federal government to invest its money in urban projects that have the joint approval of the provinces and the municipalities concerned. Such federal contributions to municipal development were negotiated in conferences where all three govern-ments were represented, but where municipal officials attended formally as part of the provincial delegation.[26] While it is still difficult to assess the impact of tri-level conferences on intergovernmental relations in Canada, the combination of growing deficits and the new mood of provincial self-assertiveness has led to the virtual disappearance of tri-level meetings in the 1980s.

Another organizational form often included in compilations of intergovernmental institutions is the *federal advisory council*. While organizations of this sort are formally unilateral (they are established under federal statute to advise a federal

---

[24] Howard Leeson, *ibid.*

[25] *National Goals*, p. 109.

[26] The province of Manitoba is an exception in this regard, for, during the 1970s, the city of Winnipeg was permitted to attend tri-level conferences as a *de facto* independent party to the negotiations.

minister) and are usually located within the organizational labyrinth of a federal department, they often feature representatives from provincial governments. Edgar Gallant points out that "their composition, with representation from all provincial governments, is such that they do, in effect, function as federal-provincial committees to a large extent."[27] Gallant, however, goes on to cite examples of these advisory committees, most of which seem to have disappeared since his article was first published in 1965. On the basis of this admittedly flimsy evidence of the attrition of such federal advisory councils, and with the knowledge that "true" federal-provincial committees have proliferated in the same period of time, it seems reasonable to hypothesize that the unilateral advisory council is of little importance in federal-provincial relations in the 1980s.

Until now, our focus has been on interjurisdictional coordinative bodies, which are purely governmental in composition. We must note that there are some committees that operate in the intergovernmental arena but that have non-governmental members as well. Perhaps the best traditional examples of this genre of interjurisdictional body are the subcommittees of the Atlantic Fisheries Committee, which deal with sport fish, and which are composed of relevant governmental representatives as well as local anglers' associations and commercial fishermen. More recently, the inclusion of non-governmental actors in federal-provincial bodies became fairly common in the area of aboriginal rights and the constitution. Here, even at the level of first ministers, the leaders of major native organizations participated as full members of conferences convened to deal with issues of direct concern to their constituents.

At still another level, this "mixed" composition type of committee could become more commonplace with the growing incidence of joint government/private-sector enterprises,[28] and with an increased tendency to directly involve the private sector in national economic conferences. There are advantages to such organizational forms. On the one hand, intergovernmental bargaining must occur with representatives of the private sector looking on, thus keeping government honest. On the other hand, by including members of public-interest groups in the early stages of policy development, policy ideas can be presold or legitimized before they enter the political arena through co-opting of non-governmental organizations.

Finally, it is becoming more commonplace for federal and provincial governments to become directly involved in enterprises along with private-sector corporate actors. The Syncrude project was an early example of this trend, where the federal, Alberta, and Ontario governments launched an oil-sands recovery venture along with private-sector partners such as Esso Resources, Gulf Canada, and Canada Cities Service.[29] A more recent example is Fishery Products International Ltd., which involves the Federal and Newfoundland governments and Forintek Canada Corporation, which involves the governments and forest-products corporations.[30]

[27] Gallant, "Machinery," p. 515.

[28] Gallant, "Machinery."

[29] See Larry Pratt, *The Tar Sands: Syncrude and the Politics of Oil* (Edmonton: Hurtig, 1976). See also P. Foster, *The Blue-Eyed Sheiks* (Toronto: 1979).

[30] See K.J. Huffman, J.W. Langford, and W.A.W. Neilson, "Public Enterprise and Federalism in Canada," in Simeon, *Intergovernmental Relations*, pp. 131–178, for an insightful discussion of such enterprises.

The motivation for moving into such ventures is usually either to bail out a failing industry (as with Fishery Products or Massey-Ferguson), to subsidize research and development activities (as with Forintek), or to defray the start-up costs of large capital projects (such as Syncrude). However, an important latent function of this style of intergovernmental interaction is that:

> joint ventures tend to reduce rather than exacerbate "turf" disputes between levels of government. A joint venture makes it clear that the problem is being dealt with in a cooperative way, because all the parties share a common interest or concern. . . . Symbolically the joint venture makes it clear that all parties are "onside."[31]

More will be said about such ventures and their overall significance for the political process later in this book. At this point it is sufficient to conclude that the boards of these enterprises comprise an important and growing mechanism among the many institutional devices of interjurisdictional coordination.

Support Staff: Intergovernmental Bureaucracy

While we have indicated that interjurisdictional coordination has become institutionalized and less *ad hoc* than it once was, the same is less true of the support staff for the committees. Generally, the provision of secretariat services to intergovernmental committees, even today, is still primarily *ad hoc*, worked out informally by the members of the committee. The most common arrangement seems to be for the necessary support staff to be provided by the government whose representative chairs the particular committee. This has meant, in the past, that federal departments often provided support services for federal-provincial committees, a convenient arrangement, since the feds had the financial and personnel resources to be able to afford it. This was reversed to some extent during the seventies, in part because it became normal practice for provincial ministers to co-chair federal-provincial committees. This latter trend was reinforced by the fact that a number of the provinces also possessed the resources to provide support staff, and, in fact, became increasingly suspicious of support services domiciled in the federal bureaucracy. In the case of interprovincial committees, the secretariat is normally part-time, composed of temporarily seconded officials of the government that chairs the meetings. As the chairing of interprovincial committees often rotates, this means that the secretariat to the committee is located in a different provincial capital each year.

While permanent support staff is the exception rather than the rule for interjurisdictional committees in Canada, there have been significant exceptions, and the current trend is, if anything, away from *ad hoc* or rotating secretariats. The most common form of permanent secretariat is a staff paid by and located in Ottawa. This is the case with the important Continuing Committee on Fiscal and Economic Matters, whose secretariat is a division of the Department of Finance, and with the Canadian Intergovernmental Conference Secretariat, which provides the logistical support and documentation for a range of senior intergovernmental committees. The latter is nominally supported by both the federal and provincial governments, although the feds have tended to foot most of the bill.

---

[31] Hoffman *et. al.*, pp. 159–160.

The strengths of permanent secretariats are that they provide continuity and a level of expert advice that the committee could not achieve with rotating secondments from year to year. However, the great potential weakness of the examples we cited is obviously that the host government may come to dominate the setting of committee agenda, the briefing of conferees, and, to an extent, the conduct of the meetings themselves. While the provincial members have the opportunity to bring their own advisors to meetings, some smaller provinces can either ill afford the expense or do not have expert advisors in the same numbers and quality as the federal government. In addition to the fairly obvious advantage to the federal government of having the committee on payroll, the legitimacy of the secretariat may be doubted by provincial officials who come to feel that the support staff is in Ottawa's pocket.

An experiment aimed at overcoming the weakness of the federally domiciled style of permanent secretariat in the intergovernmental affairs was tried with the Canadian Council of Resource and Environment Ministers (CCREM) in the 1970s. This interjurisdictional body has the status of a private corporation, although its members and its board of directors consist of federal and provincial Cabinet ministers. The presidency of the council rotates annually among the member governments, and the secretariat is permanent, composed of staff who are employees of the corporation but not of any of the member governments. The effectiveness of CCREM, in the ten years from 1963 to 1973 was related largely to its secretariat, which operated as a clearing house for information, as a direct non-governmental link with the public through its publications, and as the administrative and support component of a number of major omnilateral conferences at political, senior bureaucratic, and technical levels. Perhaps the greatest strength of this secretariat was that it never carried the brand of any government; its explicit mandate was to serve all eleven governments equally.

The fatal flaw of such a body was the difficulty in exercising political control over it. The fact that it was permanent and independent of any single government gave it the potential to become an intergovernmental bureaucracy within the federation, analogous, perhaps, to the permanent staff of international organizations such as the EEC or the UN. The fear of losing control of the secretariat caused some of the CCREM's member governments to become increasingly suspicious of it. Some of the provincial ministers on the Council came to view the CCREM, and particularly its permanent secretariat, as dangerous competitors in the process of wooing public support for environmental policy reforms. Because of this, and because of a general decline in the political sexiness of environmental causes, since 1973 we have seen a drastically reduced role for the Council itself, and a reduction of the secretariat to a very small caretaker operation. Whatever its ultimate fate, the secretariat of the CCREM is an organizational form, which could still be used as a prototype for future forays into interjurisdictional coordination.

Finally, in the seventies, there was a rapid evolution of very specialized bureaucratic structures designed to deal with intergovernmental matters. The Quebec Department of Federal-Provincial Relations was the prototype of this kind of agency, and was set up originally in 1961 by the Lesage government. (In 1967 it was reconstituted as Intergovernmental Affairs.) In the 1970s the wealthier provinces, Ontario, Alberta, and Saskatchewan, and the federal government[32] followed Quebec's example, and most of the rest have followed suit in the current decade.

While this trend is significant as an indication of the growing importance of the intergovernmental arena to all governments in Canada, it also has implications for bureaucratic politics. What has happened is that a new breed of specialized official, analogous to the foreign-service officers who represent Canada in international dealings, has emerged. These public servants are not directly involved with specific programs, but rather have influence over a wide range of policy areas that have an intergovernmental component. These intergovernmental diplomats have evolved as important power brokers within both federal and provincial bureaucracies during the 1980s, and can perhaps be seen as part of the emergent "neo-mandarinate" discussed in chapters 15 and 18.[33]

TRENDS IN CANADIAN FEDERALISM

Executive Federalism

As the need for continual federal-provincial consultation and cooperation increases in response to the growing interdependence of all social and economic problems, the institutions of interjurisdictional cooperation that we have described will continue to grow in terms of their political significance. These bodies will increasingly be entrusted with the responsibility for making policy decisions that affect the allocation of resources in Canada. The critical political decisions will more frequently be referred to the federal and provincial representatives who meet at federal-provincial conferences, and there is little to indicate that existing institutions are capable of countering the trend.

There is a startling lack of attention paid to federal-provincial relations in either Parliament or the provincial legislatures. There is virtually no contact between legislators of the eleven senior governments, and there are no federal-provincial committees composed of legislators other than Cabinet ministers; certainly members of the opposition parties in the legislature are completely locked out of the process.[34] While there is no question that the phenomenon of *executive federalism*[35] has contributed to the continued shrinking of the role of Parliament and the provincial legislatures in the policy process, the causal links are likely in the reverse direction; that is, the evolution of executive federalism is a symptom of the general impotence of legislative institutions *vis-à-vis* the executive branch. As Garth Stevenson has pointed out: "Executive federalism may be as much a consequence as a cause of the weakness of legislatures in a system of responsible

---

[32] We have already discussed the role of the FPRO in our section on central agencies (see chapter 15).

[33] See Dupré, *op. cit.*

[34] See John Meisel, "The Decline of Party in Canada," in H.G. Thorburn, ed., *Party Politics in Canada* (Toronto: Prentice-Hall, 1979), pp. 119–136. Note that the offer by Prime Minister Trudeau in 1980 to permit the opposition parties to participate in constitutional reform negotiations is an exception.

[35] See Smiley, *Canada in Question*, ch. 4.

government where a single, disciplined party normally holds a majority of the seats."[36] While it could be suggested that the representatives at intergovernmental conferences continue to feel a responsibility to their home governments, that responsibility is not direct. The legislature back home does not exercise day-to-day control on its delegates; rather, it functions as an electoral college, which goes no further than making the initial choice of who will represent the government in the particular interjurisdictional arena.

Similarly, the party system does not appear to play a very significant role in the resolution of intergovernmental conflict. Even where governments at the provincial and federal levels share the same party label, there does not appear to be a significantly greater propensity to get along. While some authors, such as Stevenson, suggest that there is still a residual role for the party system in this regard — "The importance of party ties in resolving or avoiding federal-provincial conflict can not yet be completely dismissed, particularly in the Atlantic provinces where the federal and provincial parties remain fairly integrated"[37] — unless there are some fairly radical changes in either the party system or the process of intergovernmental relations, we must conclude, with Donald Smiley, that "political parties are . . . of decreasing importance in the Canadian federal system. Partisan politics have relatively limited capabilities for effecting the resolution of federal-provincial conflicts either through intraparty relations or general elections."[38]

The irony of the trend towards "executive federalism" is that, while it fosters decentralization and exaggerates the centrifugal forces in the federation, it is manifested in a heavy concentration of decision-making power in the hands of a very tiny political élite. Certainly, where the key priority decisions are made by committees of eleven at federal-provincial conferences, democratic control is more difficult than in a system where such decisions are approved by a parliament of 282 men and women from all parts of Canada, and by provincial legislatures comprising hundreds more.

Thus, while the dominance of any one government is being reduced as power is dispersed among several, the power of the state in general becomes more concentrated through the phenomenon of executive federalism. The problem is, in part, a lack of accountability, for the process not only reflects but contributes to the general phenomenon of increasing executive domination in the political system:

> How ironic it would be if federalism, the noble form of government lauded by Madison as a means of extending freedom over larger geographic areas should now be exposed in its Canadian variation as a means of extending unaccountable processes of government over larger geographic areas. . . . The exigencies of *responsiveness* in Canada as a *federal* polity have long since carried the day over the demands of *accountability* in Canada as a *democratic* polity.[39]

[36] *Unfulfilled Union*, p. 203.

[37] Stevenson, *op. cit.*, p. 191.

[38] Smiley, *op. cit.*, p. 146.

[39] M. Paul Brown, "Responsiveness versus Accountability in Collaborative Federalism: The Canadian Experience," *CPA*, Winter 1983, p. 639.

Bureaucratic Federalism

Executive federalism, therefore, may have helped to precipitate a new trend towards a concentration of power in the Canadian system. However, in earlier chapters, we have spoken of the general tendency for policy making to depend heavily upon technical inputs from various non-elected officers of government residing in the federal and provincial bureaucracies. When these two trends are viewed with the fact of the increased number of interjurisdictional committees operating at the senior bureaucratic, technical, and operational levels of government, one cannot avoid the suspicion that bureaucratic executives are at least as dominant as political executives in the practice of contemporary Canadian federalism.

Undoubtedly, the bureaucratic executives play an increasingly dominant role in the interjurisdictional coordination at the stages of policy formulation and implementation. It is more difficult to maintain that bureaucratic committees dominate interjurisdictional *priority determination*, for the policies under consideration must ultimately be justified to eleven electorates by the ministers concerned. Nevertheless, given that there is more constant interaction among the non-elected officials, and given that politically successful programs will often be contingent upon technical feasibility, it is likely that ideas will often be generated by senior bureaucratic and technical committees, and adopted with only formal consideration as priority items by the ministerial committees. While it is impossible to conclusively show that this tendency is a fact, we do know, from even the most casual observation, that little real bargaining goes on in the public portions of ministerial meetings; to the extent that intergovernmental priorities are determined by the politicians, therefore, the process is *in camera* and not in front of camera.

One result of bureaucratic federalism is that intergovernmental coordination is probably improved. In the first place, as the frequency of interaction has increased at the non-elected levels of government, the people involved in the bargaining process actually come to know each other. They often supplement formal exchanges at committee meetings with informal contact through telephone calls and correspondence.[40] Second, because the personnel involved are not constrained directly by a critical public, they do not have to be as concerned as the politician with faithfully advocating the interests of a particular region; there is greater freedom for compromise. For instance, if forestry officials are meeting to set up a program for combatting a spruce-budworm epidemic, they are usually more concerned with solving the real-world problem in forestry than they are with defending provincial priorities. The combination of shared professional interests, personal ties, such as friendships, which grow through long-standing formal and informal contact, and a non-partisan milieu thus tends to facilitate coordination at the bureaucratic level. As advisors to the ministers, the bureaucrats

---

[40] Note that the original evidence for that hypothesis was uncovered in a series of thirty-four interviews with members of federal-provincial committees from all ten provinces and with the federal government, which were conducted in the summer of 1972. While most of those interviewed were in the resources field, it does seem likely that they were fairly typical of the sorts of people involved in interjurisdictional coordinative activities, and, in fact, they represented a good mix of senior bureaucrats and technical personnel. Subsequent discussions with federal and provincial officials indicate that the trend is still intact in 1980.

can, in turn, help to ease the more public and political dimension of federal-provincial bargaining, and contribute to an overall environment within which interjurisdictional compromise and cooperation is possible. In this sense, executive federalism can be said to operate because of networks or trust relationships among senior officials, program officers, and functional ministers at both levels of government, who work together to solve common problems and achieve common program goals.[41]

There may be, however, additional trends within bureaucratic federalism that run counter to the accommodative and integrative role we have already described. On the one hand, there has been a tendency recently for more and more of the responsibility for intergovernmental affairs to be transferred to the central agencies of the participating governments. Thus, federal-provincial relations offices, Cabinet secretariats, and the political technocracies of the federal and provincial executives may be taking over some of the functions heretofore performed by the functional or program departments. Coincident with this trend towards greater centralization of the intergovernmental role within the participating governments is a more "institutionalized" Cabinet structure,[42] which both encourages the hegemony of central agencies and breaks down the functional autonomy of the individual ministers in dealing with their counterparts in other governments. Thus, while federal-provincial relations can still be deemed "bureaucratic," it is, increasingly, central agencies rather than program departments that are interacting; similarly, at the political level, it is collectivities or governments dealing with other governments rather than individual functional ministers dealing with each other in a long-established relationship of mutual trust and understanding.

A further effect of this change in the intra-governmental balance of bureaucratic power is that the process may tend to reward conflict rather than the resolution of it. As Richard Simeon has put it,

> the process, far from being an effective mechanism for the resolution of conflict, in fact, exacerbates it. Indeed, it is even suggested that the emergence of larger ministries of intergovernmental affairs — an internal diplomatic corps — creates a group whose sole *raison d'être* is to look out for and promote their government's interest and for whom the federal-provincial game is an end in itself. The process engages institutional rivalries, not real policy disputes.[43]

Thus, not only does intra-governmental centralization attenuate the positive trust relationships among federal and provincial program officials; it actually can foster more combative relations between and among the governments involved.

Finally, partly as a result of the institutionalization of Cabinet government and partly because of broader trends towards leadership politics in Canada generally, more intergovernmental activity is occurring at the very top. This federal-provincial

---

[41] See Dupré, *op. cit.*, p. 5. See also A. Breton and R. Wintrobe, *The Logic of Bureaucratic Conduct* (Cambridge: 1982).

[42] Dupré, *ibid.*, p. 4. Dupré refers to the increased complexity of the Cabinet-committee structure and the need for greater central-agency support that rivals the more specialized technical advice flowing from the line departments.

[43] "Intergovernmental Relations and Challenges," *op. cit.*, p. 23.

summitry, because it occurs in the highly visible and highly political forum of the First Ministers' Conference, is a mechanism ill-suited to resolving conflict. It is, by its very nature, suited to adversarial posturing on the part of ministers who are pitching for votes back home by bearding the federal lion in its own den, and on national television at that. The painstaking accommodations worked out by program officials, while technically appealing as policy solutions, can sometimes be bypassed, in the short run, in favour of what are seen to be more immediate political advantages.

Bilateral Federalism: "Divide and Conquer"

Coupled with the related trends of bureaucratization and executive federalism is the apparent tendency for intergovernmental relations in Canada to be carried on in bilateral rather than multilateral or omnilateral committees. This tendency towards bilateral committees can be explained, in part, by the need for federal-provincial coordination in the *implementation* of many joint programs; a large percentage of the bilateral committees are, in fact, at the operational level, and are exclusive in their composition simply because the particular program being administered involves only two governments.

However, this tendency towards bilateral rather than multilateral or omnilateral interaction may reflect more complex trends in the nature of federal-provincial bargaining. The multilateral meetings, particularly at the ministerial level, do not appear to be particularly effective as forums for intergovernmental bargaining; at the First Ministers' Conference, for instance, it is not uncommon for eleven separate sets of policy priorities to be presented as bargaining positions. The number of combinations of positions possible as compromise solutions in an eleven-person situation is so great that negotiation becomes very difficult. The individuals doing the bargaining have difficulty recognizing all options open to them, let alone choosing the one that maximizes the benefits to their government. The result is that the provincial representatives are often hesitant about making a deal in a multilateral or omnilateral situation, for fear of missing something; they instead do what is safest, and simply state and restate the position they started with. Moreover, in bilateral relations, the "extensive media coverage which inevitably surrounds and, some say, undermines multilateral conferences may be avoided".[44] The federal government particularly feels this way, given the tendency, in recent years, for omnilateral ministerial conferences to simply provide opportunities for "fed bashing."[45]

Given the difficulty of bargaining in a highly complex omnilateral conference, and given the evidence of much bilateral interaction in operational and technical committees, one might hypothesize that there is, in fact, a lot of bilateral interaction at the more senior levels, as well. This, however, will not be manifested by the existence of many formal or permanent bilateral committees; the ministers and

[44] Ken McRoberts, "Unilateralism, Bilateralism and Multilateralism," in Simeon, *Intergovernmental Relations*, p. 79.

[45] McRoberts, p. 79.

senior bureaucrats are simply too busy to be involved in regular meetings. However, informal bilateral meetings or telephone conversations between a federal minister and a provincial counterpart occur frequently so the ministers can discuss specific policy questions. In such a setting, with only two governments "present," and only two sets of priorities to deal with, bargaining is a much simpler process. Moreover, as such sessions are informal and *ad hoc*, they will not be publicized to any great extent (although the meetings between Alberta and Ottawa on the question of oil pricing have tended to go against this rule). However, the more important point is that the bilateral meetings are held behind closed doors, so that the horse trading can go on in a fairly honest and candid manner, with little need for governmental representatives to engage in symbolic combat or to posture for their electorates.

Not only is compromise facilitated through informal bilateral bargaining; it may also be that the federal government can use this type of negotiation to control the bargaining process at omnilateral meetings. On a one-to-one basis, the federal government can often dominate a bargaining situation; on a one-to-ten basis, the provinces hold sway. By consummating deals in several bilateral situations before going to the multilateral conferences, the federal government may be able to divide and conquer. One counter to this trend may be the increased amount of bilateral interaction among the provinces. By making deals among themselves, the provinces can establish united bargaining positions before facing the feds in a bilateral situation; such temporary coalitions may offset the potential domination by the national government, but, to be truly effective, the tactic will have to be used more frequently and more consistently than it is at present.

Finally, the wealthier provinces and those provinces that are influential in the intergovernmental arena have actually reached a level of sophistication where they do not fear the bilateral bargaining process. Provinces such as Alberta, which has real clout because of its oil reserves, prefer to bargain with the feds one-to-one, for the simple reason that, in an omnilateral meeting, Ottawa will have strong allies in the ranks of the energy-consuming provinces such as Ontario. Similarly, Quebec has had enormous success in negotiating its special status with respect to a wide range of federally sponsored shared-cost programs throughout the 1960s and 1970s. None of these deals could have been struck in any but a bilateral forum. The "divide-and-conquer" strategy thus is a two-edged sword.

Asymmetrical Federalism

In the first part of this chapter, we determined that federal-provincial coordination was essentially a process of bargaining. In the trends discussed thus far, we have simply presumed that the traditional capital goods used for bargaining in the Canadian system have remained unchanged; that the provinces, for the most part, will bargain from their position of jurisdictional strength in key policy areas such as welfare and education, and that the federal government will bargain with its large revenues and spending power. It becomes clear, however, that the bargaining levers of the federal partners have changed.

It is true that there have always been asymmetrical aspects to the system of intergovernmental relations in Canada. The BNA Act established principles that necessitated different kinds of relationships among the various governmental actors. Quebec is the most obvious example, because, as the homeland to most of Canada's second charter group, it enjoys a special constitutional status in areas such as the use of the French language and denominational schools. Moreover, the special constitutional status of the province of Quebec has given its claims for special privileges *vis-à-vis* the other provinces a higher order of legitimacy than similar demands from other provinces or regions would ever enjoy. In another way, special bargaining relationships have evolved with, for instance, the maritime provinces. Because of the federal jurisdiction over fisheries, and because the fishery has been a principal economic concern of the Atlantic region since Confederation, continual coordination among the governments involved is required to develop joint programs in that industry. Finally, the luck of the draw has determined that certain provinces and regions will be much wealthier than others. For instance, Alberta, with its gas and oil, Quebec, with its hydroelectric potential, and Ontario, with its large population and stable industrial sector, have sources of economic wealth that enhance their bargaining strength at intergovernmental meetings.

However, while a province such as Alberta has extraordinary bargaining power because its natural resources are so important to the economic health of the federation as a whole, the secondary bargaining strength of wealthier provinces flows from their fiscal potential and the uses to which their considerable tax revenues can be put. One of the objects of provincial expenditure that can directly alter the bargaining clout of the participants in the intergovernmental arena is human resources. The ability to hire professional and technical help in large numbers, and of the highest quality, can enhance the power of a given province enormously when governmental decisions depend more and more upon the input of technical advice.

A general trend in policy making we have noted before is the increasing use of policy planning. No longer is it considered adequate for policy makers to make decisions about what we should do in future on the basis of what we are doing now. In rejecting this erstwhile acceptable incremental mode of setting new policies, the advocates of planning argue that decisions we make today should be more than linear extensions of past ones. Instead, policy decisions should be made on the basis of full knowledge of present public demands, projections identifying future needs, a full awareness of all present policy options, and a careful analysis of the relative costs and benefits of each policy option. The determination of the policies that should be implemented must then be made, with a view to maximizing long-range benefits and minimizing political and financial costs. This approach is normally referred to as *rationalist* (as opposed to *incrementalist*), and rests on two pillars — systems analysis and cost-benefit analysis. Systems analysis assumes the interrelationship of all policies and posits the necessity to consider all options before coming to a decision; cost-benefit analysis assumes that relative costs and benefits of policy options can be measured quantitatively, and that choices among alternatives should be based on such information. While the success of such techniques in real decision-making situations may be limited, the principles of policy planning have been adopted to some extent by almost all governments in Canada.

The impacts of this new emphasis on policy planning, and that of rationalist policy analysis on interjurisdictional relations, are still not clear. However, one apparent change is that the ability to bargain effectively in the intergovernmental arena is linked to whether a government's policy priorities are articulated in rationalist terms. The ability to bargain in this fashion is, in turn, linked to the number and quality of human resources available to the particular government. That the federal government and the wealthier provinces can afford to buy the commitment of high-priced policy planners is beyond question. However, the poorer provinces are less able to pay for sufficient high-priced help, and may be reduced to accepting, on faith, the kinds of policy alternatives articulated by the have provinces and the federal government. In this sense, a new lever or capital with which to bargain successfully in the interjurisdictional sphere is the possession of expert human resources; governments lacking this resource may be functionally disenfranchised from taking a full part in federal-provincial relations.

One possible way to offset the tendency in interjurisdictional relations towards a virtually permanent oligarchy of the have provinces and the federal government is for the federal government to increase unconditional grants to the poor provinces in absolute rather than per-capita terms. Although it is unlikely that the larger provinces would ever accept this measure, it would, if adopted, perhaps increase the financial ability of the have-not provinces to hire the necessary people. Another possible solution (although one that has never been tried) is to establish an intergovernmental secretariat, patterned after the secretariat of the CCREM but composed of planners and policy analysts. This would provide the provinces with access to a bank of experts responsible to all governments equally, and, while it would only partially offset the advantage of the bigger governments, it might be a step in the right direction. However, in the absence of a remedy, the implication of *rationalist federalism* is that intergovernmental relations will continue to be asymmetrical, with a select few provinces and the federal government dominating centre stage and determining the major policy priorities into the 1990s.

Finally, the Canadian federal system is also asymmetrical in terms of the *results* of the intergovernmental bargaining process:

> In our use of the term, asymmetrical federalism involves variation among provinces in the respective roles assumed by the federal and provincial governments. In some provinces a function may be discharged through close federal provincial collaboration; in others it is assumed wholly by one level or another.[46]

As examples, we can cite the fact that all provinces and territories except Ontario and Quebec contract their policing responsibilities out to the RCMP; Ontario, Alberta, and Quebec collect their own corporation income tax; Quebec has opted out of most shared-cost programs; and Quebec alone entered into an agreement with the federal government having to do with federal assistance to municipalities.[47] However, where the other manifestations of asymmetrical federalism can

---

[46] McRoberts, p. 120.

[47] McRoberts, p. 120. The Institute of Public Administration of Canada has granted permission to use this material.

be viewed as negative factors, enhancing the gap between the have and have-not provinces, here we have an instance where the asymmetry is useful. As Ken McRoberts points out:

> Asymmetrical federalism would seem to be tailor made for a political system such as Canada's in which the accommodation of societal diversity has been an endemic problem. It should not be surprising then that asymmetry has emerged in so many areas as governments have sought to reconcile competing objectives and concerns.[48]

CONCLUSION:
CANADIAN FEDERALISM INTO THE 1990s

When the Liberal government was returned to power in 1980 after the short-lived Clark interregnum, it served notice very quickly that it was going to assert the federal presence in the federation to a much greater extent than before. This was a reaction to the "community-of-communities" notion of Canada that had been espoused by Joe Clark, and to a sense that Canadians had to decide whether we were going to have a country here or not. Prime Minister Pierre Trudeau declared in 1981 that:

> [it is] time to reassert in our national policies that Canada is one country which must be capable of moving with unity of spirit and purpose towards shared goals. If Canada is, indeed, to be a nation, there must be a national will which is something more than the lowest common denominator among the desires of the provincial governments.[49]

The Liberal government then embarked on a period of fairly remarkable unilateral initiatives that challenged the right of the provincial governments to speak (even collectively) for Canada as a whole. Trudeau, never famed for his understatement, declared that cooperative federalism was effectively dead:

> The old type of federalism where they [the provinces] kick us in the teeth because they didn't get enough . . . is finished. The pendulum would keep swinging until we end up with a community of communities . . . a confederation of shopping centres . . . and that is not my view of Canada. I thought we could build a strong Canada through cooperation. I have been disillusioned.[50]

The Liberals were true to their word from 1980 to 1984. The 1982 constitutional accord was achieved largely because of the unilateral initiative of the federal government; the National Energy Program, which included a lot of measures deeply resented by the oil-producing provinces, was imposed without consultation with the provinces; and the Canada Health Act used to force provinces to outlaw extra billing and amendments to certain parts of the Established Programs Financing legislation that directly affected provincial income from transfer pay-

[48] McRoberts, p. 121. The Institute of Public Administration of Canada has granted permission to use this material.
[49] Cited in S. Dunn, "Federalism, Constitutional Reform and the economy," *Publius*, Winter 1984, p. 134.
[50] Cited in Jeffrey, "A New Era," p. 131.

ments went through with very little consultation, and over the unanimous objections of the provinces.

However, whether related to their flirtation with unilateralism or not, the Liberals saw themselves humiliated in the 1984 election at the hands of the Progressive Conservatives, led by Brian Mulroney. Buoyed by his enormous national mandate and reassured by the presence of so many Conservative governments at the provincial level, Mulroney served notice that we were about to embark on a new era of cooperation in intergovernmental relations. True to *his* word, the new prime minister quickly worked out essentially bilateral accords with Newfoundland and Alberta with respect to the roles of the two levels of government in matters of exploration, development, production, and taxing of petroleum resources. While on the surface these accords appear to be very generous to the provinces, in fact the federal government was forced to give up very little. In all cases, the constitutional powers of the federal government are intact, unchanged from the previous government, and the agreements are clear that there is a federal override in the instance of a demonstrated national interest. Since then, things have not gone quite so well. The 1985 First Ministers' Conference on aboriginal self-government failed substantially, and the prime minister found himself to be at odds with the premiers in important policy areas such as the question of free trade with the United States and Quebec's appropriate role in a proposed Francophone commonwealth. Significant unilateral reductions by the federal government of intergovernmental transfers reduced more than one federal-provincial finance ministers' meeting to near shouting matches.

By mid-1985, the honeymoon was over for the federal Tories, and this, coupled with the gradual reduction in the number of Conservative governments at the provincial level and the natural regional interests that conflict with national ones, has seen the federal system move back to what seems to be its more natural combative and adversarial mode. The end result may well be a new resurgence of federal unilateralism in the late 1980s.

Finally, another indicator of the continued assertiveness of the federal government in national policy matters is the ongoing discussion of changes in the nature and role of the various institutions of that government. Most of these proposals, such as Senate reform, redistribution of the House of Commons, and changes in the composition and appointment mechanisms of the Supreme Court of Canada, seek to strengthen the machinery of *intra-state* federalism. While these proposals are all put forward in the name of enhancing the power of the provinces, in fact, the end result will be to increase the legitimacy, and hence the power, of the national government to act as the spokesman for national interests. While improved machinery of intra-state federalism may well increase the ability of the Canadian political system as a whole to respond to the diverse interests of the various regions of our federation, such improvements will all inevitably achieve their purposes at the expense of the *governments* of those same regions.

This concludes the discussion of trends in modern federal-provincial relations in Canada. Much of this final section has been speculative. All that can be said in conclusion is that, whatever constitutional settlements may come, Canadian federalism is today, and always has been, in a state of flux; it has evolved from what it was in 1867 to what it is today through constant adaptation to new environmental circumstances. It is today a very tightly integrated network of federal-provincial consultative bodies at various governmental levels. There is a constantly changing relationship among the actors in the federal system, as each of the provinces and the federal government attempt to maximize their bargaining advantages *vis-à-vis* the others. However, for the most part, and despite the evidence of a new assertiveness of the national government, there remains, under the coverlet of constant conflict, a willingness to seek agreement, to compromise, and to continue to bargain.

THE CANADIAN BUREAUCRACY: FUNCTIONS AND STRUCTURES

THE FUNCTIONS OF THE CANADIAN BUREAUCRACY
■ The Policy Function ■ The Output Functions
THE STRUCTURE OF THE CANADIAN BUREAUCRACY
■ The Government Department ■ Non-Departmental Agencies

L ong used as a term of contempt by the media, the word "bureaucracy" has come to be associated, by the public, with qualities such as inefficiency, "red tape," depersonalization, and slowness of execution. There is, however, a more proper use of the term, which is derived from the literature of organization theory and which refers only to the objective structural characteristics of a certain type of organization. In this sense, bureaucracy is a purely descriptive rather than a pejorative term. We use the word in its descriptive sense, and do not mean to imply inefficiency, red tape, or depersonalization, all of which result, in fact, from perversions of bureaucracies or maladies in bureaucratic structures.

The classic description of the pure bureaucracy derives from the work of Max Weber, but R.K. Merton has provided us with perhaps the most complete brief description:

> There is integrated a series of offices, of hierarchized statuses, in which inhere a number of obligations and privileges closely defined by limited and specific rules. Each of these offices contains an area of imputed competence and responsibility. Authority, the power of control which derives from an acknowledged status, inheres in the office and not in the particular person who performs the official role. Official action ordinarily occurs within the framework of preexisting rules of the organization. The system of prescribed relations between the various offices involves a

considerable degree of formality and clearly defined social distance between the occupants of these positions. Formality is manifested by means of a more or less complicated social ritual which symbolizes and supports the "pecking order" of the various offices. Such formality, which is integrated with the distribution of authority within the system, serves to minimize friction by largely restricting [official] contact to modes which are previously defined by the rules of the organization. Ready calculability of others' behaviour and a stable set of mutual expectations is thus built up. Moreover, formality facilitates the interaction of the occupants of offices despite their [possibly hostile] private attitudes towards one another. In this way, the subordinate is protected from the arbitrary action of his superior, since the actions of both are constrained by a mutually recognized set of rules. Specific procedural devices foster objectivity and restrain the "quick passage of impulse into action."[1]

Thus, a bureaucracy is simply a form of organization, with precise structural characteristics. While the term "bureaucracy" can be used to apply to governmental and non-governmental organizations alike, in common usage in the discipline of political science the term refers specifically to the *public service* or to the *administrative branch* of government. The focus of this chapter is on the role of the non-elective officials of government, the bureaucrats, who work within the Canadian public service, the public services of the various provinces, municipalities and territorial governments, and within the multitude of public-sector agencies and corporations that are not formally a part of the public service.

We will see that Canadian bureaucratic structures, like their counterparts elsewhere in the world, do not perfectly mirror the ideal type as set out in the statements of Weber and Merton. There is considerably more flexibility and variability in bureaucratic structures than is implied in the classical descriptions. This is a desirable attribute of real-world bureaucracies, since it enables them to react more effectively to the multifaceted strains imposed on them by the modern world. However, the ideal type presented here provides us with a benchmark against which to measure real bureaucracies and is, as a first approximation, still a reliable guide to much of the internal form of administrative structures in Canada. We will return to a more detailed classification and description of bureaucratic structures after we have examined the functions of the Canadian bureaucracy.

THE FUNCTIONS OF THE CANADIAN BUREAUCRACY

The Policy Function

That the public service[2] in Canada has a significant role in the policy process is now accepted as fact, a point that is decried more than disputed. As we have

---

[1] R.K. Merton, "Bureaucratic Structure and Personality," *Social Forces*, 18 (1940), pp. 561–568. Weber's classic statement is in H.H. Gerth and C. Wright Mills, eds., *From Max Weber: Essays in Sociology* (New York: Oxford University Press, 1946), pp. 196–244.

[2] We use the term "public service" to refer to the entire bureaucracy, including Crown agencies as well as the "public service" as defined in the Public Service Employment Act.

indicated, this role is based largely on the concentration of expertise within the public service, making the bureaucracy the major source of information concerning the technical and financial feasibility of policy alternatives faced by the politicians. As the complexity of our society increases, the reliance of political decision makers on bureaucratic or technocratic specialists tends to increase commensurately.

It has already been mentioned that the bureaucracy performs important functions both as an initiator of policy and as a channel of policy initiation to be used by other institutions and actors in the political process. Beyond this first-stage policy role, the bureaucracy becomes more and more deeply involved in the business of policy making. When priorities are being established, bureaucratic institutions such as the Treasury Board Secretariat and the Department of Finance have a great deal of control over policy planning because of their expertise in the area of public finance, the public purse, and macro-economics. It is in this particular area that the increasing application of rationalist principles to the budgetary process tends to regularize, to consolidate, and perhaps even to further aggrandize the position of the bureaucrat in the Canadian policy process.

Federal-provincial committees at the bureaucratic level also play an important role in the setting of policy priorities in Canada. Specifically, these intergovernmental bodies are usually concerned with coordination of federal-provincial programs; but, for example in the process of considering the problems of fiscal relations, the intergovernmental meetings of finance and treasury officials have great influence on the spending priorities of both levels of government. However, while intergovernmental bureaucratic committees can and do affect the setting of governmental priorities in Canada, their greatest impact is felt at the *formulation* stage of policy making.

As we pointed out in Chapter 1, the bureaucracy is the core institution at the formulation stage of policy making in Canada. Although it is often interdepartmental committees or the cabinet that decide which department will be responsible for policy formulation in a certain area, and although several departments (under the aegis of the interdepartmental committee) look at most major policy decisions, the actual detailed formulation of specific policies is normally accomplished by the policy branches of the individual departments of the public service. Through briefing notes, discussion papers, reports, and memoranda to Cabinet — "Cabinet documents" — the departments set out the policy alternatives that are most feasible in technical, administrative, financial, and even political terms. The practical options for government action are most frequently defined[3] in this way although ministers will not hesitate to come to a decision that runs counter to departmental advice if they feel that political considerations outweigh the advice of their officials.

While policy formulation has been described here as a stage in the policy process that follows priority determination, it is, in fact, often the case that the bureaucracy's formulation activity has begun long before any clear priority has

---

[3] See M.J. Prince, "Policy Advisory Groups in Government Departments," in Doern and Aucoin, eds., *Public Policy in Canada* (Toronto: Macmillan, 1979), pp. 275–300.

been established. Indeed, the Cabinet often finds it impossible to make a clear priority decision in the absence of a good deal of detailed advice on policy formulation. The bureaucratic institutions are ever alert to indicators of future government priorities, and the officials within the various government departments attempt to anticipate Cabinet-level decisions and begin working on policy areas that are likely to be given priority, or areas they feel should be pushed forward to Cabinet.

One reason for this anticipatory activity by the institutions of the Canadian bureaucracy is that a department that has already prepared preliminary proposals is more likely to be given the responsibility for policy formulation and ultimate implementation than one that arrives on the scene later. Another reason is that the department may have already been asked to comment on the feasibility of the proposal at the earliest priority stage. And, of course, the department may have played a role in the initiation of the policy in the first place. Thus, bureaucratic involvement at the initiation and priority-determination stages of the process may not only determine which department wins the responsibility for formulation and implementation, but may also result in many of the formulation decisions having been made at earlier stages in the process. We will deal with the policy role of the bureaucracy in greater detail in Chapter 18, when we discuss the bureaucratic process.

The Output Functions

Rule Making While the policy role of the Canadian bureaucracy may seem to place significant power in the hands of the bureaucrats and technocrats, this power is merely advisory, and is subject to the ultimate approval of the elected officials of our government. However, in many areas, even the formal power to directly convert policy to legislative output has been delegated to various administrative, regulatory, and supervisory agencies of the government of Canada.

The delegation of legislative power to the executive is not a new phenomenon in Canada; for instance, in time of national emergency, Canadian legislation has, for many years, granted very broad powers to the executive to make law by order-in-council. While this delegation of legislative power achieves a short-circuiting of the normal procedures of lawmaking by the sovereign Parliament, the concerned citizen might take some solace in the fact that the *de facto* executive in this country is the Cabinet, which is ultimately responsible to Parliament. However, two factors must be taken into account when assessing the total affect of such legislation on the democratic process. First, since the Cabinet is not an expert body, it often must *redelegate* the power to make law to non-elected officials in government departments, in police forces, and in a multitude of regulatory boards and commissions. Moreover, as legislation becomes more technical and more complex, this function of executive lawmaking will tend to rest increasingly with non-elected officials.

A second point is that legislation today requires such detail that the elected actors in the policy process do not have time to go much beyond debating the broad principles of the policy either before or after the non-elected officials have made their decisions. Hence, the legislation setting up the Canadian Transportation Commission, for instance, sets down certain broad objectives, creates the Commission, and then delegates to it the power to make detailed regulations as to air traffic and so on. To take another example, Canada Post makes regulations regarding postal rates, contents of packages, the use of mails, and so on, which directly affect our postal privileges and the quality of service we receive. In each case, elected officials may discuss broad policy issues, but they seldom discuss the details of regulations made by bureaucrats pursuant to the legislation. The point here is that the power to make regulations that have the effect of law and that directly affect the rights and privileges of citizens frequently rests directly with bureaucrats, and not with the constitutionally supreme lawmaker — Parliament — or with the political executive — the Cabinet. A most important bureaucratic function, therefore, is the power to make decisions that constitute legislative outputs of the political system.[4]

Another important rule-making function of the bureaucracy is the internalized making of regulations regarding the administrative process itself. For instance, an agency such as the Public Service Commission is concerned directly and constantly with service-wide problems of staffing. The Commission was created precisely to take matters of promotion, recruitment, and discipline out of the hands of the politicians. It was felt that public-service appointments should be based not on patronage but rather on the merits of the individual job applicant and the requirements of the position to be filled; the logical way of doing this was to create a central agency that was independent of political control, and to give it the power to make regulations necessary for bringing into effect a career public service based on the *merit principle*. Similarly, each department or agency must produce sets of rules outlining internal procedures and practices. The decisions as to what these rules should be are all made directly by administrative officials, and are subject to little practical control by politicians. Although it is perhaps difficult to characterize these rules as outputs of the political system, such administrative regulations are very important because of their potential effect on the administration side of the administrator-to-public relationship.

Rule Application   It has been seen that the Canadian constitution distinguishes between executive and judicial functions. However, under closer scrutiny, one finds that the executive function and the judicial function are broadly similar,

---

[4] See E.A. Driedger, "Subordinate Legislation," *Canadian Bar Review*, vol. 38, no. 1, March, 1980, pp. 1–34. See also: Driedger "Delegated Legislation in Canada," in Kernaghan and Willms, *Public Administration in Canada: Selected Readings* (Toronto: Methuen, 1971), p. 406. There is also a burgeoning literature dealing with regulation as one of the broad functions of government generally, and then focusing on the specific structures and processes of regulation, most of which are bureaucratic. See especially G.B. Doern, *The Regulatory Process in Canada* (Toronto, 1978); Doern, "Regulatory Process and Regulatory Agencies," in Doern and Aucoin, *Public Policy*, pp. 158–189; and Doern, "Rationalizing the Regulatory Decision Making Process; The Prospects for Reform," ECC Working Paper no. 2 (Ottawa: 1979). See also: D.C. Hartle, *Public Policy Decision Making and Regulations* (Toronto: IRPP, 1979); and I. Bernier and A. Lajoie, *Regulations, Crown Corporations, and Administrative Tribunals* (Toronto: University of Toronto Press, 1985), especially pp. 81–154. Many of the research reports of the Royal Commission on Economic Development Prospects for Canada deal in one way or another with regulatory policy. See, in particular, volume 42, Richard Schultz and Alan Alexandroff, *Economic Regulation and the Federal System*. Schultz has a large body of perceptive writings on both general and specific aspects of regulatory policy in Canada.

in that they both require the application of general rules to specific cases. Viewed in this way, the rule-application function of the bureaucracy includes both executive and judicial decision making, and with respect to time, resources, and immediate impact on the public, it constitutes the central function of the Canadian bureaucracy.

While in theory the role of the administrator is simply to passively implement the laws of the land, the application of general laws to specific situations always involves some interpretive and judgemental decisions on the part of the public servant. Hence, in applying the law, administrators are called upon to make discretionary decisions all the time. As an example, public servants or committees set up by the public service have to make decisions as to which students are eligible for financial support, scholarships, etc., and administrative boards and inspectors under public-health acts are called upon to decide who gets a restaurant licence and under what circumstances a licence should be revoked for non-compliance with the conditions established by the legislation.[5] In cases such as this, the act itself does not provide very clear guidelines as to the practical application of the principles involved. These sorts of decisions are left to the discretion of the administrative officers charged with carrying the act into effect. In the extreme case, peace officers charged with the responsibility for enforcing the law possess discretionary powers up to and including the right to use force, and even in some circumstances to shoot to kill. The law cannot specify when the use of such extreme force is necessary, and the decision is left to the discretion of the officer, who must make a judgement call in the field and on the spur of the moment. As we shall see in the next chapter, there are judicial controls over the abuse of discretionary powers by officials of the state; but the only practical safeguards of our rights lie in the training, experience, and good faith of the individuals involved.

Moreover, in many areas of administrative decision making, the distinctions among the legislative, administrative, and judicial functions become blurred. A decision, for instance, that involves the granting or revoking of a licence, or the imposition of a fine in lieu of revocation of a licence is not only administrative: because it can have a punitive or compensatory effect on individuals, it is also judicial. At the same time, because such judgement calls can become precedents that form guidelines for future applications of the legislation in future cases, the administrative decision can also have the effect of altering the long-run impact of the law. Part of this blurring of the distinctions between the three functions of government occurs because the role of government generally has become positive. Thus, as government moved from a thou-shalt-not, or punitive, orientation to a more positive or preventive orientation, much of the responsibility for applying the law has moved from the judiciary to the administrative branches of government.

A sort of hybrid function of some bureaucratic agencies in Canada combines the roles of policy advisor and adjudicator. This is the *investigative function*, which is distinguishable from the policy-advisory function because the focus of

---

[5] Corry and Hodgetts, *Democratic Government and Politics*, p. 528. In this and similar cases, the law usually states that the ultimate decision rests with the responsible minister, but in fact the vast majority of cases never reach the minister's notice, so the real power resides in the inspector.

the investigation is a specific case or situation; the investigative function can be differentiated from the adjudicative function because the findings of the board or commission are only recommendatory to the minister. For example, many regulatory agencies in Canada such as the Atomic Energy Control Board (AECB) or the National Energy Board (NEB) are required by law to investigate accidents that occur in the industries they are regulating, and to report the findings to the minister. In the case of the NEB, the regulatory agency is vested with the powers of a superior court of record when conducting hearings, which implies the right to subpoena witnesses, to require the presentation of documents and to convict people for contempt of court.

Symbolic Outputs There is a class of governmental outputs that cannot be called legislative, executive, or judicial.[6] Frequently today, one can see the political system producing outputs that take the form of information, and the basic agencies for the dissemination of information from the political system are found predominantly within the bureaucracy.[7] For example, it is necessary to inform the public of changes in the law. Some years ago, amendments to the Criminal Code made it an offence to drive while one's blood alcohol was in excess of .08%. In order to insure that the public is aware of this new legislation, the Department of Justice publicized the changes widely on radio, and television, and in the newspapers. All new legislation is, in fact, published in the *Canada Gazette*, and the onus in law is on the individual citizen to find out what the law is and to obey it. However, it is also recognized by the government that a piece of legislation such as the "breathalizer" law is designed to act as a deterrent, and will only be effective if everyone is aware of it. Furthermore, laws such as this affect so many people that it pays the government politically to widely publicize the fact that they are in effect.

Information outputs — such as the campaign to inform the public about the "breathalizer" law — are produced by the bureaucracy, possibly at the urging and certainly with the acquiescence of the Cabinet. Outputs of such information are purely informative; what they say is, in effect: "Here is a new law. You must, as with all laws, obey it." However, other outputs of information are not so neutral as this one. Consider, for example, campaigns by the Department of Employment and Immigration and provincial employment departments to increase the number of summer jobs for students. Here a bureaucratic agency is not stating that there is any law in existence; instead, it is actively campaigning to convince businesspeople to hire a certain class of worker. What is implicit in this piece of government advertising is the proposition that students should be hired instead of other classes of workers in the society. Perhaps this is not purely the brainchild of a group of public servants in a government department, but rather of some political advisor to the Cabinet, who feels that university and college students or their parents are politically a more important force than are other types of unemployed people. That is not really important to our discussion; the point is that somebody

---

6 See Chapter 1, where we discuss "symbolic outputs."

7 See also Chapter 13, where we point out that interest groups also may play an important part in the dissemination of information.

has decided that an output of information should be made, which appears to be completely neutral and yet which is very definitely favourable to one class of person and not another.

Another interesting illustration of symbolic outputs that have an allocative impact is the federal Department of Health and Welfare's campaign against smoking. While pointing out to Canadians that smoking is injurious to one's health is a legitimate role for that department to play, it can be seen as running counter to parallel efforts in the Department of Agriculture to develop programs that will alleviate the plight of the tobacco farmers in southern Ontario. Thus the more successful the campaign in one department, the less successful will be the programs of another. Without taking sides — Whittington smokes a pipe and Van Loon is a marathoner — it is clear that there must be a Cabinet-level decision as to which goal is to have priority, so that the activities of sister departments of the federal bureaucracy do not work at cross purposes.

Whether, in the examples cited above, the decision to disseminate information was bureaucratic or political does not matter as much as the fact that the bureaucracy *can* make such decisions almost unilaterally, subject to only the most cursory ministerial supervision. Most government departments publish information in the form of brochures, pamphlets, and even quarterly magazines, all aimed at informing a segment of the public; and yet most of these publications impart sets of values and points of view. This is not necessarily a result of public servants consciously attempting to propagandize, but rather it is often simply a function of the nature of information. It is impossible to publish information without some editing; and in the process of editing, the values of the editor are served, either consciously or unconsciously.

Most departments have information-services branches,[8] and some agencies, such as Statistics Canada, are concerned primarily with the collection, compilation, and publication of information. While the people in these bureaucratic roles likely try very hard to be impartial, they are only human, with biases, prejudices, and misconceptions of reality. Thus, what is virtually unavoidable is that the bureaucrats who are charged with the responsibility for producing information packages will inevitably colour the outputs with their own values. It can be hoped that the values that are pushed will be congruent with those of society at large; but more important, if one recognizes that the potential for bias, intentional or not, is very real, one will be able to evaluate all outputs in a critical light.

In the 1970s, an attempt was made to rationalize and coordinate the educative function of the Canadian bureaucracy, by creating a semi-independent administrative agency known as Information Canada. The role of this agency was to provide information about the policies of the government, and its goal was to create a more informed public, which would be then more capable of participating in the policy process. Whether it is possible to inform the public to that extent is another question, but what concerns us here is the nature of Information Canada. Most critical comment originally zeroed in on the potential for political propaganda

---

[8] See the Report of the Royal Commission on Government Organization, vol. 3 (Ottawa: Queen's Printer, 1962), pp. 63–72.

from such an agency. While fear was expressed that the government in power would be enabled to promote its own particular programs at the expense of the Canadian taxpayer, this did not seem to happen to a significantly greater extent that it did before InfoCan was created. The fairly rapid demise of Information Canada likely came about because the departmental information offices resisted the centralization of the "information-out" function that InfoCan implied. The departmental officials resented, and denounced as ineffective, the attempt to centralize functions they felt should remain decentralized, and this made InfoCan a ready target during one of the federal government's periodic bouts of austerity.

Despite the failure of the InfoCan experiment, the symbolic, educative, or informative function of the Canadian bureaucracy is, even in 1987, a rapidly expanding and important one. While this type of output is not itself an "allocation," it is, nonetheless, a vital ancillary to the allocation process, for it insures that citizens know what rules have been made, and it supplies active citizens with information through which they can interact with the political system. The constant output of information from within the bureaucracy will be a beneficial development if the public can avoid being brainwashed by seemingly neutral (but in reality coloured) facts emanating from "impartial" bureaucratic editors. Since most of the public will pay no attention whatever to these outputs, and since those who do will be among the better-educated or more actively concerned citizens, it seems at least plausible to hope that such an effect will be minimized.

Finally, the movement to a more open bureaucracy with a Freedom of Information Act has gone some of the way to insuring that the public can get information directly, instead of waiting to see what the public servants are willing to give up. The only negative result has been the increased person-years required to provide assistance to the members of the public who seek information — the immediate beneficiaries may well turn out to be the information-services branches of departments and agencies, whose share of the budgetary pie can be expected to grow handsomely!

Systemic Functions Beyond the operational functions we have described, the Canadian bureaucracy also performs a number of ancillary or latent functions for the political system as a whole. First, and in some ways an extension of its role in the generation of symbolic outputs, the bureaucracy likely plays a part in the fundamental process of creating diffuse support for the political system. The accomplishments of Canadian government agencies in world affairs, in scientific research, and in the effective delivery of services to Canadian citizens can have a legitimizing effect for the system. When a career diplomat gains worldwide recognition and praise for efforts in a faraway embassy, or when a foreign government decides to buy one of our Canadian developed CANDU reactors, it may help to generate a pride in Canadians about Canadian accomplishments, and, in so doing, help to create support for our political community. Similarly, when it is publicized that, for instance, Air Canada has maintained an excellent air-safety record, or when a film produced by the National Film Board receives wide acclaim (or even an Oscar!) it may help to legitimize the role of government in those sorts of enterprises, and to foster support for the regime. Thus, while there may be a lot of public cynicism and disgruntlement with the evils and inefficiencies of "bureaucracy," the fact remains that bureaucracy is so pervasive in our society that, without a certain amount of praise for and faith in our more successful public enterprises, the system would likely fail rapidly.

Another systemic role played by bureaucracy, and here we need not even be specific to Canada in our generalization, is that of maintaining stability and continuity over time. For those who are committed to radical and rapid social change, this may well be viewed as a dysfunction of bureaucracy, but any system must have a static or conservative element, which enables it to persist over time. The constitution, a stable-party system, or a stable economy may perform this function to varying degrees in different political systems, but because, as we have seen, bureacracies are by definition predictable and, by empirical observation, sometimes pathologically inert, they provide continuity and stability even in a regime where other stabilizing institutions are failing.

Finally, it may be that the bureaucracy in Canada is performing a representative function in policy making.[9] Ironically, the normal line of argument regarding the role of the technocrats in the formulation of public policy is that, because the elected representatives of the people in Parliament have little say in technical decisions, democracy is being slain by technocracy. The counter to this is that if, in fact, the technocrats are becoming more influential than Parliament in the policy process, we must look to the composition of the technocracy before we judge the trend to be undemocratic. In Chapter 14 we considered this issue and concluded, unfortunately, that the evidence is inconclusive. The bureaucracy overrepresents males, central Canada, and high-status Canadians, as do Parliament, Cabinet, and other élite institutions, so there may be little to choose among our various political institutions, including the bureaucracy, on this score.

At another and more important level, however, it may be that the bureaucracy is an important representative institution in Canada, not because bureaucrats and technocrats reflect a broad cross-section of our society, but because of structural factors. In Canada, most departments of government can identify a clientele group in the political community at large. The function of the department, in the administrative process, is to implement programs designed to benefit that clientele and, in the policy process, to represent the interests of that clientele in policy initiation and priority determination. Thus, policy-advisory units within clientele-oriented departments press their political masters to adopt new policies or new programs, which will serve the interests of their clients. We cannot pretend that the department fosters the interests of its clients for purely altruistic motives; rather, the motivation is that, if the department can invent and sell fancy new programs to the Cabinet, the department's share of the budgetary pie and the size of its manpower establishment will grow accordingly. Thus, serving the interests of a clientele is merely good business — a device for building or expanding a departmental empire. But whatever the motives, the fact remains that the clientele-oriented departments of government may well represent the larger interests in

[9] See K. Bryden, "Public Input into Policy-Making and Administration", *CPA*, Spring 1982, pp. 81–107.

Canadian society better and more consistently than the MPs, and perhaps even better than interest groups.

To conclude what is as yet a fairly speculative set of comments about the representative functions of the Canadian bureaucracy, we must enter an important qualification. While structural factors may encourage bureaucrats to act as representatives of their clientele, officials are still an élite by virtue of the level of education required in their jobs. This means that, in the long run, the technocratic élites will only be as representative as the educational and other institutions that incubate, hatch, and nurture their career aspirations.

Far from being the passive instrument of the era of the negative state, then, the modern bureaucracy has a very active role to play in government. Bureaucratic agencies not only implement law, but they make law; they adjudicate; they make policy; and they control the outflow of masses of information to the general public. Moreover, because bureaucracy is such a pervasive force in the operation of the political system, it may well be performing broader systemic functions, which heretofore have been considered the exclusive domain of other state institutions. It is necessary to proceed to a discussion of the structures and the organizational forms that have evolved to perform these functions.

THE STRUCTURE OF THE CANADIAN BUREAUCRACY

It has already been explained that the term "bureaucracy" refers to a kind of organization with certain structural characteristics. We asserted that prime among its characteristics is its large size; most of the other factors of bureaucratic structure have evolved to accommodate the pre-eminent problem of "bigness." Bureaucratic structures feature a well-developed division of labour, whereby the officials occupying roles within the organization perform clearly defined functions. Ideally, there is no duplication of effort and no overlapping of roles within a bureaucracy, although this is more difficult to achieve in practice than in the abstract.[10]

Furthermore, it was noted that a bureaucratic role is defined by the office itself, and not by the incumbent of the office. This is essential if bureaucratic behaviour is to be predictable in the short run, and if there is to be continuity over time in the performance of the duties of that office. Continuity over time is also facilitated by the keeping of detailed written records of all actions taken by the bureaucratic officers. In this way, every decision can be backed up by precedents established in the past, and in turn, itself becomes part of the body of precedents for future decisions. There is no legal rule of precedent in bureaucratic decision making, but the fact is that if someone else has made a certain decision in the past and has gotten away with it, the chances are that a similar decision today can be justified by the officer responsible. Also contributing to the continuity

---

[10] See the Task Force on Program Review (the Nielsen Task Force), *An Introduction to the Process of Program Review* (Ottawa: Supply and Services, 1986), p. 26.

of bureaucratic decision making is the fact that the holding of a bureaucratic office is a full-time occupation. In recent years, bureaucratic officers have been tenured; they do not hold office merely at the pleasure of their employer. Finally, although it is not unique to bureaucratic organizations, the basic mechanism of control within a bureaucracy is hierarchical. This means that authority flows downward through the organization, with each level of the organization being responsible to the level above.

Before describing the bureaucratic structures in the Canadian government, we shall look briefly at the reasons for adopting a bureaucratic type of organization. Given all of its real or imagined malfunctions, what is good about the bureaucratic form? First, because equality is a value of our system of government, it is necessary, when applying the law to specific cases, to treat similar cases in a similar fashion. Bureaucratic organization permits a maximum of impartiality in dealing with the public by *routinizing* the decision-making process. Second, the application of the law must be predictable to be fair, and a bureaucratic system can be made highly predictable. The problem here is that, in applying the law equally and impartially, the person with the special case, who requires an equitable decision instead of an impartial one, is frequently penalized. How many times have we met with the standard bureaucratic answer: "If we do that for you we will have to do it for everyone else as well"; or, "We are sorry but our regulations do not permit any exceptions." Thus, while bureaucratic procedures are valid for, perhaps, 90% of the cases, for the 10% that may be exceptional, the system imposes difficulties. The justification for such a system is that it is the only way we have of dealing fairly and at reasonable cost with the majority of the vast number of cases that come up.

Modern bureaucracies have, of course, developed some mechanisms for dealing with special cases. Many large programs dealing directly with the public have some form of appeal procedure, and, as we have seen, individual bureaucrats at the operating levels do have discretion in dealing with special cases. We will note, too, in our discussions of the functions of Parliament, that one of the most important parts of the MP's role is helping constituents who have not been adequately dealt with by the bureaucracy. More and more Canadian governments are utilizing ombudsmen to insure that special cases are fairly dealt with. Nonetheless, in conclusion, we must return to the rather unsatisfactory comment that bureaucratic organization is the best-known way of dealing with bigness in government, and that some problems inevitably arise.

The basic organizational form found in the Canadian bureaucracy is the *department*, accounting for almost two-thirds of the employees of the federal government. Most of the non-departmental agencies are classed as *Crown corporations*, although there are a number of federal government agencies — such as the Bank of Canada, the Canada Council, the Canadian Wheat Board, and the National Arts Centre — that operate in a manner similar to Crown corporations but that are not formally classified as such. Moreover, since the 1970s, we have seen a rapid increase in the use of "mixed" public-private agencies and "joint" federal-provincial or Canadian-American corporations. Finally, there are the central control agencies, such as the Treasury Board Secretariat, the Privy Council Office, and the Public Service Commission, which are dealt with elsewhere in the text.

The Government Department

Characteristics Several characteristics distinguish the departmental form of organization from other types within the Canadian bureaucracy. First, a government department is answerable directly to a Cabinet minister, who functions as its formal head and who, conversely, is responsible for the actions of both the department and the departmental officials. The practical effectiveness of the minister in heading a department will depend, to a large extent, upon his or her competence and personality, but while there is a lot of room for the minister to provide encouragement and to generate excitement within the department, generally the administrative decisions will be left to the permanent officials. There is even a theory that the best minister is one who has ideas and influential stature in the Cabinet, but who knows relatively little about the line functions of the department itself. The minister can then represent the broad interests of the department in Cabinet meetings, but is not motivated to meddle in the internal affairs of the department. Perhaps this theory is just the wishful thinking of public servants, who would prefer to keep the political head of the department involved in "political" priority decisions and out of their hair. On the other hand, this situation may occur in reality simply because the minister is too busy with other things to become very involved in the administrative process.

The overall result of the growing complexity of departmental administrative affairs and of the increased overall workload of Cabinet ministers is that the once-sacred principle of *ministerial responsibility* has come to be watered down in practice. There is no question that a minister is still directly and personally responsible, in a formal constitutional sense, for what happens in his or her department. However, more and more, ministers are getting away with the simple plea of ignorance — "I didn't know" — and are rarely forced to resign or to face the music politically. This was demonstrated particularly well in the testimony of Solicitors General who were in charge of the RCMP when its security service committed illegal acts during the 1970s. In this case, as in many cases in other departments in recent years, senior public servants are fingered and become the scapegoats for departmental errors and indiscretions.

One of the partial remedies to the practical limitations on the minister's direct involvement in and responsibility for departmental affairs has been the rapid growth in the size and complexity of the ministers' personal staffs. In a 1983 study, Donald Savoie states that the ministerial staffs of the government ranged in size from nine to sixty full-time personnel.[11] While many of these people will be political, bearing responsibility for constituency affairs, for the writing of speeches, and for ministerial briefings on a range of political issues, the growing trend has been for ministerial staff to bear the main burden of liaison between

[11] D.J. Savoie, "The Minister's Staff: The Need for Reform," *CPA*, Winter 1983, p. 512.

the minister and the department. To better perform this liaison and coordination role, Don Savoie recommended that:

> To assist their outside experts in working with the bureaucracy, ministers should be allowed to bring to their office, for a two or three year assignment, senior officials from their department or from other departments and central agencies. Preferably they would be chosen from the multitude of policy planning, policy coordination and policy and program evaluation units in the federal government.[12]

It is not clear whether the Mulroney government read Savoie's article, but it is clear that the practice of seconding officials from the bureaucracy to the ministers' offices has become more common since 1984. Moreover, the PC government has also instituted the position of *chief of staff* in ministers' offices. This individual functions as the senior advisor to the minister, and, as well, acts as a sort of deputy minister of the ministerial office, overseeing and coordinating all the people and responsibilities involved.

The second distinguishing characteristic of the government department is the fact that it is subject to the *estimates system* of budgeting, which means simply that the money appropriated to the department by Parliament must be spent in the manner directed by Parliament. The coming of the system of Planning Programming Budgeting (PPB) in the 1960s, and the more recent adoption of a more centralized *envelope* or PEMS system of budgetary apportionment,[13] have not changed this basic fact of departmental finance, although such systems permit planning of departmental programs over longer than one-year periods, subject to the approval of the Treasury Board and relevant Cabinet committees.

The third characteristic of the government department is that it recruits departmental officials under the supervision of the Public Service Commission. With the exception of deputy ministers and some temporary and part-time help, all the personnel of government departments are public servants under the Public Service Employment Act, and are recruited according to the principle of merit.

The Deputy Minister The administrative head of the department is a deputy minister (DM). This appointment is a prerogative not of the minister of a department but of the prime minister, usually advised by a senior mandarin, normally the secretary to the cabinet. This process of appointment gives the prime minister some measure of control over individual departments, even if a minister becomes recalcitrant or remiss, but since the deputy minister usually works in very close contact with the minister and at arm's length from the prime minister, this power is more formal than real. The deputy minister, unlike a public servant, holds office "at the pleasure" of the government. As we saw in Chapter 15, the appointment of senior officials is done through the PMO, but recent changes in the procedures of the House of Commons allow standing-committee involvement in such appointments as well.[14]

---

[12] Savoie, p. 522.

[13] See chapter 15.

[14] See J. Chenier, "Why Shouldn't MPs Question the PM's Choice?" in *Policy Options*, March 1986, pp. 9–11; and D.J. Savoie, "Putting Deputies Through Hoops," *Policy Options*, January 1986, p. 3.

FIGURE 17-1
FUNCTIONS OF THE DEPUTY MINISTER

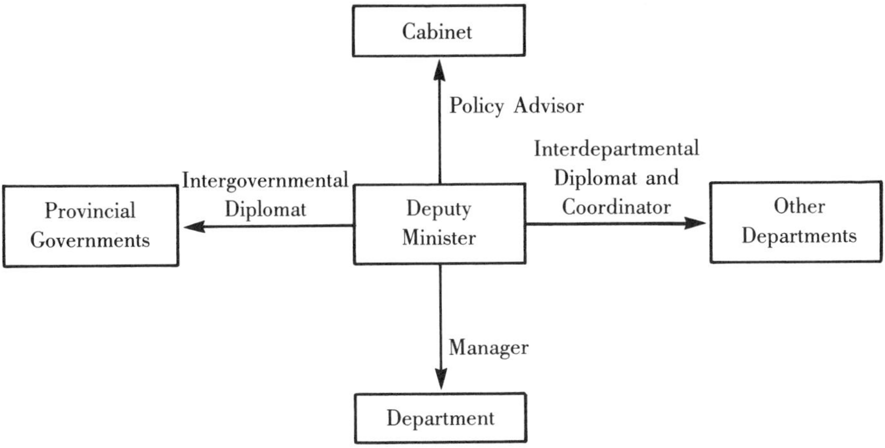

Perhaps the major function of the deputy minister is a *managerial* one; i.e., he or she must function as the manager of an organization called a department, and must therefore plan, direct, and control the department. Like all managers in large organizations, the deputy minister must set intra-departmental policy, participate in the selection of officers for senior positions within the department (subject to the merit principle), and coordinate departmental activities through executive leadership. The function of coordination is usually facilitated through the delegation of some managerial functions to subordinates, and in many departments through a *central management committee* or *executive committee*, which consists of the deputy minister, as chairman, and all the assistant deputies, as members. The management committee sets the broad objectives and priorities of the department, examines any new proposals that may emerge from the bowels of the organization, and deals as well with such vital management questions as the date of the departmental picnic. However, properly operated, the committee can do much, together with the budget process, to rationalize intra-departmental priorities, and can be used effectively by the deputy minister as a tool of internal planning and liaison.

The deputy minister does not have permanent tenure, and it is considered quite proper for a new government to occasionally ask that the DMs in certain key departments resign. Similarly, the DM, in a department such as Finance, may offer to resign without being asked if a different political party takes over after an election. It is essential that the minister have confidence in the permanent head of the department (and vice versa) if he or she is able to function effectively as its political head; if there are suspicions that the existing DM is still friendly to the old government and has forgotten that it is his or her duty to serve whatever government the people have elected, it is best that there be a replacement. However, it must be emphasized that, in most cases, a change in government does not necessitate their removal. Usually the incoming government is glad to have the help of such senior bureaucrats in learning the ropes, and the DMs are willing to adapt to the needs and programs of their new political masters.

The deputy minister is responsible for the maintenance of liaison with people in other departments as well. This is necessary partially because each department must depend, to some extent, on other departments, whose function is to provide services for the rest. The most important example of such a service department is the Department of Supply and Services, which was created by a 1969 governmental reorganization. This type of liaison is not usually difficult and does not normally require much of the deputy's personal time, but, in addition, liaison must be maintained with other departments that have similar or overlapping responsibilities. All of this is achieved through a semi-institutionalized process of protocol and interdepartmental diplomacy, which has evolved to meet at least some of the needs of interdepartmental coordination and overall public-service efficiency. DMs also act as intergovernmental diplomats, a function that has already been discussed when we looked at federal-provincial relations.

In terms of the policy process in Canada, the most important function of the deputy minister is to act as the senior departmental advisor to the government. The DM has the key role in the transmission of policy information from administrative underlings with many types of expertise to the minister and, through the minister, to the Cabinet. Because of their positions in the departments, and in most cases because of their many years of administrative experience, deputy ministers must go beyond merely transmitting neutral information to their superiors. They are expected to interpret and explain the advice flowing from the departments; and, where political decisions are required by the minister and the Cabinet, they must, to the best of their abilities, tender political or quasi-political advice when asked. While the DM is but one person and incapable of total understanding of the specialist decisions made by his or her administrative underlings, as a professional manager the DM is in a good position to decide which of several departmental technical advisors the government should put its faith in. It has been mentioned before that one of the important aspects of Cabinet decisions at the policy-formulation stage of the policy process is deciding which policy advice to convert into formal outputs. In this respect, the deputy minister, as a manager of expertise, is invaluable to the government. Not just because the DM understands the substance of their advice, but because he or she knows the advisors, the DM can decide which advice is likely to be better.

In summary, the deputy minister of a Canadian government department plays the role of a manager of a very large organization. However, as we will see in the next chapter, the nature of government organization, with its emphasis on political accountability and control, places unique powers and restrictions on the management function, and the extent to which the DM can exercise those unique powers and cope with those unique restrictions ultimately rests on personal ability. Deputy ministers, both in Ottawa and in the provinces, hold some of the most difficult and important jobs in Canada, and play a very central role in the entire working of the Canadian political system.

The Internal Structure of Departments   The internal functions of an organization can broadly be classed as *line* or *staff*. In Canada, this distinction is based on the type of relationship between various intra-departmental administrative structures and the goals of the department as a whole. To use the example of a specific department, the goal of the Department of National Revenue, simply stated, is tax collection. Those branches of the department involved directly in collecting tax revenues are said to be performing *line functions*. On the other hand, there are branches or divisions of the same department involved in matters such as personnel, administration, finance, and legal advice, none of which directly involves the performance of the line function. These branches of the department are said to perform a *staff function*, and they exist to assist the line managers, in an advisory capacity or through the performance of a service.[15]

The basic structure of a government department is hierarchical, with the deputy minister at the top of the pyramid. Under the DM, there are a number of subordinate levels. Each of these is itself hierarchical in structure, and each is directly accountable to the level above. The staff role carries no direct authority over the line officers, and the branches of the department involved in the performance of staff functions are often organized more simply than those of the line.

When we come to look at some departments (such as Finance), which have a constant and very direct connection with policy, and other departments (such as Employment and Immigration or Energy, Mines, and Resources), which are deeply involved in the contemporary policy process because of current public interest and political priorities in the areas of immigration, employment and unemployment, or energy policy, the line and staff distinction becomes somewhat confused. If there is a policy-and-planning branch in a government department, the officers in that branch will have a purely advisory relationship with the officers in the various operations or line branches. In other words, the relationship of the policy branch to the line branches of the organization will be a staff relationship. On the other hand, one of the major goals of many modern government departments is to formulate policy for the Cabinet. Thus, policy formulation becomes a line function of that department. A manager in the policy-and-planning branch will therefore have a staff relationship with the managers in the operations branches, and a line relationship with other officers in his or her own branch and with the deputy minister. This same line and staff confusion occurs when we look at, for instance, information services in a department. As has already been seen, an important function of a modern bureaucracy is to disseminate information; this is, in one context, a line function. However, the information-services division of a department also performs a service, and therefore has a staff relationship with the other branches and divisions. Thus, while it is important to recognize the distinction between line and staff functions within a department, the attempt to

---

[15] Professor Willms makes a distinction between three kinds of functions: line, staff, and service. We have retained the more traditional classification here because, for purposes of explaining the workings of a government department, the important point is to set the line function off from the rest. Service functions are very close, conceptually, to staff functions, and hence the distinction is more important for public administration than it is for an introductory text in Canadian politics.

TABLE 1
FEDERAL DEPARTMENTS

Department of Agriculture
Department of Communications
Department of Consumer and Corporate Affairs
Department of Employment and Immigration
Department of Energy, Mines and Resources
Department of the Environment
Department of External Affairs
Department of Finance
Department of Fisheries and Oceans
Department of Indian Affairs and Northern Development
Department of Insurance
Department of Justice
Department of Labour
Department of National Defence
Department of National Health and Welfare
Department of National Revenue
Department of Public Works
Department of Regional Industrial Expansion
Department of the Secretary of State of Canada
Department of Supply and Services
Department of the Solicitor General
Department of Transport
Treasury Board
Department of Veterans Affairs

classify on the basis of this distinction must fail if we carry it too far. Modern bureaucratic organizations are far too complicated structurally to permit anything but the broadest of generalizations. The aim of this section is to set out some of the principles and terms that can be employed when looking at any specific department. To understand the structure of the Canadian bureaucracy today, however, one must analyze each government department separately, for they are all different, displaying their own organizational quirks and idiosyncracies. The reader will be relieved to know that a department-by-department analysis is beyond the scope of this text, so we must be satisfied with the few generalizations and specific examples above.

Non-Departmental Agencies

The *Crown corporation* is a non-departmental bureaucratic institution with a corporate form created by the government to perform a public function. Such institutions aim at combining the need for some degree of public accountability with the freedom of initiative usually associated (rightly or wrongly) with private enterprise.[16] While Crown corporations must report through a minister to Parlia-

[16] See J. Langford, "The Identification and Classification of Federal Public Corporations," *CPA*, Spring 1980, p. 76.

ment, particularly in budgetary matters, they are not subject to either the estimates system of budgeting or the direct control of a minister in the same way that a government department is. Personnel administration in Crown corporations, furthermore, differs from that within a government department in the extent to which the Public Service Commission regulates recruitment, promotion, and transfer procedures. In the case of the departmental corporation, the employees are public servants. In Crown corporations, however, employees generally are not affected by the terms of the Public Service Employment Act, because personnel matters are dealt with internally and independently. Similarly, most Crown corporations are not subject to the Public Service Staff Relations Act with respect to collective bargaining, and, in fact, proprietary corporations are governed by the Industrial Relations Disputes Investigation Act, as are private companies.

Basically, Crown corporations differ from government departments in the degree of political control exercised over them. As we noted above, the minister is the formal head of a department, and a deputy minister is the administrative head. However, because the Crown corporation is designed to give a measure of freedom of action, it is usually headed by an independent board, which is appointed by the government for a set period of time. The members of this board usually include a full-time chairman or president, who functions as the administrative head and chief executive of the corporation, and part-time members, who meet as a board only a few times each year. In the case of some Crown corporations, members of the board include public servants from other governmental agencies. The relationship of the chief executive of the corporation to the board will differ, depending on the nature of the corporation and the personalities involved.[17]

The activities of Crown corporations, unlike those of government departments, are not supervised directly by a Cabinet minister. Indeed, independence from direct ministerial control is one of the major reasons for creating a Crown corporation. Despite this, and mainly because it is felt that public enterprise financed by public money should be subjected to at least some parliamentary control, each Crown corporation is assigned to a minister of the Crown, through which it must report to Parliament.[18] The minister, however, does not in any way direct the activities of the corporation, and, conversely, is in no way personally responsible for the activities of the corporation. Rather, the minister acts as a communication link between Parliament and the corporation, which is engaged in public enterprise and which, in most cases, is spending public money. The bulk of the work on behalf of a Crown corporation for which the minister reports will entail piloting the corporation's estimates through the House of Commons. Naturally, it is possible for a minister to influence corporation policy informally, but this is difficult to document. All that can be said is that informal ministerial control over a Crown corporation will depend largely on the personalities involved and on the political circumstances of the times.

The greatest restriction on the activities of a Crown corporation occurs through its financial relationship with the government of Canada, particularly in the case

---

[17] See T. Mitchell, *The Role of the Board of Directors in Crown Corporation Accountability* (Ottawa: Conference Board, 1985).

[18] P. Garant, "Crown Corporations," in Bernier and Lajoie, *Regulations, Crown Corporations and Administrative Tribunals* (Toronto: University of Toronto Press, 1985).

of corporations whose activities are totally financed by parliamentary appropriations of the Consolidated Revenue Fund. While the estimates for most Crown corporations are voted in far less detailed form than departmental estimates, the fact remains that most of their expenditures do have to be annually and publicly justified. Furthermore, with the exception of a few specified Crown corporations, the accounts of Canadian Crown corporations are subject to audit by the Auditor General. While this is a post-audit control, somewhat analogous to closing the barn door after the horse has run off, the executive of a Crown corporation must still be aware that careless expenditure of public money one time may result in a less generous appropriation next time.

Finally, Crown corporations are controlled by the legislation that creates them. The terms of reference of a Crown corporation are set down in a statute, which is subject to amendment or repeal by act of Parliament. While this does not in any way approach the directness of control exercised over a government department, it does define jurisdictional limits beyond which the corporation is not competent to act. The Financial Administration Act defines the basic types of Crown corporations as departmental corporations and parent Crown corporations. We will deal with each of these in turn, and then move to a consideration of other non-departmental forms of organization.

Departmental Corporations   A departmental corporation is an agency of the government of Canada that is engaged in "administrative, supervisory, or regulatory services," in much the same way a department is. Schedule B of the Financial Administration Act lists the departmental corporations:

SCHEDULE B
Agriculture Stabilization Board
Atomic Energy Control Board
Canada Employment and Immigration Commission
Canada Aviation Safety Board
Canadian Centre for Occupational Health and Safety
Crown Assets Disposal Corporation
Director of Soldier Settlement
The Director, The Veterans' Land Act
Economic Council of Canada
Fisheries Prices Support Board
Medical Research Council
The National Battlefields Commission
National Museums of Canada
National Research Council of Canada
Natural Sciences and Engineering Research Council
Science Council of Canada
Social Sciences and Humanities Research Council

For purposes of the Financial Administration Act, these corporations are exactly the same as regular government departments. For instance, a departmental corporation does not buy, sell, or own any assets in its own name, but only in the name of the Crown in right of Canada. Similarly, all the financial affairs of this type of corporation are carried out through the Consolidated Revenue Fund and are subject to the control of the Treasury Board, Auditor General, etc. However, while the money spent by a departmental corporation must be appropriated by Parliament and encumbered from the Consolidated Revenue Fund, as with a government department, there is a much greater degree of independence in how the appropriated funds are actually spent. The estimates for a departmental corporation are usually put through Parliament in the form of one vote in the estimates of the department through whose minister the corporation must report to Parliament. Hence, the National Museums of Canada, which is a departmental corporation reporting to Parliament through the Secretary of State, gets its money, for any given budgetary year, in the form of one item in the main estimates of the department of the Secretary of State. A government department must be able to justify, through the minister, every item of expenditure for the upcoming year to a skeptical Parliament, but the entire budget for a Crown corporation is debated (if at all) as one item. The limitation on this independence is that the Treasury Board must examine and approve the estimates for a departmental corporation before they are included in the departmental estimates. Hence, independence from parliamentary control may not mean very much when we consider that the Treasury Board, which exercises much of the real financial control over government expenditure, has as close a look at a Schedule-B corporation's financial needs as it has at a department's.

The boards of departmental corporations and their chairmen are generally appointed by the Governor-General in Council. The tenure of these positions varies from set ten-year periods to "the pleasure of Her Majesty in right of Canada," as with other boards. The employees of departmental corporations are often appointed by the Public Service Commission and hold office during good behaviour. Thus, most of the employees of the National Museums of Canada are public servants, as are the employees of the Director of Soldier Settlement or the Director of the Veterans' Land Act. On the other hand, the employees of some departmental corporations are not public servants; their remuneration and terms of employment are set by the board itself. This is the case with corporations such as the Agricultural Stabilization Board. The employment practices of other departmental corporations come somewhere between these two extremes.

Finally, all the departmental corporations must submit, to the minister responsible, an annual report, which must be tabled in the House of Commons within fifteen days of the minister receiving it. This report is provided for in most of the legislation setting up the various departmental corporations, and its function is essentially to provide publicity for the activities of the organization, acting, perhaps, as a sort of deterrent to abuses of power or squandering of public funds. The effectiveness of the annual report as a control measure is very difficult to assess, and likely varies with the political sensitivity of the subject matter dealt with by the particular Crown corporation.

Parent Crown Corporations A parent Crown corporation is defined, in the Financial Administration Act, as a corporation that is wholly owned directly by the Crown, but is not a departmental corporation. These are all listed in Parts I and II of the Financial Administration Act. Part-I corporations are generally responsible for the management of trading or service operations on a quasi-commercial basis, or for the management of procurement, construction, or disposal activities on behalf of Her Majesty in right of Canada.

Part I of Schedule C of the Financial Administration Act lists the following corporations:

SCHEDULE C
Part 1

Atlantic Pilotage Authority
Atomic Energy of Canada Limited
Canada Deposit Insurance Corporation
Canada Harbour Place Corporation
Canada Lands Company Limited
Canada Mortgage and Housing Corporation
Canada Museums Construction Corporation Inc.
Canada Post Corporation
Canadian Arsenals Limited
Canadian Commercial Corporation
Canadian Dairy Commission
Canadian Institute for International Peace and Security
Canadian Livestock Feed Board
Canadian National (West Indies) Steamships, Limited
Canadian Patents and Development Limited
Canadian Saltfish Corporation
Canadian Sports Pool Corporation
Canagrex
Cape Breton Development Corporation
Defence Construction (1951) Limited
Export Development Corporation
Farm Credit Corporation
Federal Business Development Bank
Freshwater Fish Marketing Corporation
Great Lakes Pilotage Authority, Ltd.
Harbourfront Corporation
Laurentian Pilotage Authority
Loto Canada Inc.
Mingan Associates, Ltd.
National Capital Commission
Northern Canada Power Commission
Pacific Pilotage Authority
Pecheries Canada Inc.
Royal Canadian Mint
St. Anthony Fisheries Limited
The St. Lawrence Seaway Authority
Societa a responsibilita limitata Immobiliare San Sebastiano
Standards Council of Canada
Uranium Canada, Limited
VIA Rail Canada Inc.

Part-I parent corporations that have the word "Limited" after their names were set up under the Companies Act, and the rest were set up by separate acts.

The boards of directors of the limited corporations are formally appointed by the shareholders; but, because the shares are held in trust for the Crown, in fact, the Governor-General in Council makes the appointments. Most of the other corporations are headed by a board of directors, which is appointed for a set term by the Governor-General in Council.

The employees of the Part-I corporations are all appointed by the management of the corporation itself, and the salaries and conditions of work are also determined in a manner similar to private industry. While there are exceptions, generally these corporations are empowered to maintain accounts in their own names in any bank that is formally approved by the Minister of Finance. The operating budget of the corporation is scrutinized by the minister through which the corporation reports to Parliament, but the actual estimates for operating costs are placed before Parliament in the form of one item in departmental estimates. Capital budgets of Part-I parent corporations are subject to more detailed scrutiny by Parliament, and, as with departmental corporations, an annual report, including financial statements, must be presented to the minister responsible at the end of the financial year. These reports are then tabled in Parliament. All the financial statements of Part-I Crown corporations are subject to the scrutiny of the Auditor General.

The Part-I corporations display a great diversity in terms of their real financial status. Some operate at a profit; others, such as the Canada Museum Construction Corp., operate entirely on parliamentary appropriations. Some, like the Northern Canada Power Commission, hold large capital assets; others, like Canadian Arsenals Limited, hold very little in the way of capital assets. Many of these agencies are also subsidized, in part, through the provision of office facilities and furniture, by the Department of Public Works in the same way a government department is.

The legal position of such corporations is much the same as any corporation created under the Corporations Act. Most Part-I corporations can be sued in any court just as if they were not agents of the Crown. This is important in that it places them in much the same legal position *vis-à-vis* their clientele as any firm operating in the private sphere. By making them legally directly responsible for their activities, the government can also afford to grant them a great deal of independence from financial and political control.

The second category of parent corporation essentially includes those corporations that used to be called *proprietary*. These are responsible either for the management of lending or financial operations, or for the management of commercial or industrial operations involving the producing of or dealing in goods and the supplying of services to the public. These corporations are, furthermore, expected to function without the aid of parliamentary appropriations. The following corporations are listed as proprietary corporations in Part II of Schedule C of the Financial Administration Act:

SCHEDULE C
Part II

Air Canada
Canada Development Investment Corporation

Canada Ports Corporation
Canadian National Railway Company
Halifax Port Corporation
Montreal Port Corporation
Northern Transportation Company Limited
Petro-Canada
Prince Rupert Port Corporation
Port of Quebec Corporation
Teleglobe Canada
Vancouver Port Corporation

Many of the Part-II corporations in Canada not only have a direct commercial relationship with the public, but also are in competition with private corporations that perform the same functions or provide the same services. The best examples of this kind of competitive Crown corporation are Air Canada and Petro Canada, each of which must compete with other firms in the private sphere. Because these proprietary corporations must compete with private industry, they have been guaranteed a great deal of protection from both parliamentary and public scrutiny. The principle has been established, for instance, that information regarding salaries of individuals will not be released to Parliament, and the annual reports of these corporations, unlike those listed in Part I, are only required to include the sort of information required from a private firm under the Companies Act. As with all Schedule-C corporations, these are subject to the Financial Administration Act, except where the terms of that act conflict with another act — in which case, the latter legislation applies. Similarly, Part-II corporations are legally liable in the same way any non-government corporation is.

The directors of this type of corporation are appointed by the Governor-General in Council. Each of these corporations is required to submit a capital budget to the minister through whom it reports to Parliament. This capital budget is subsequently approved by the Cabinet and submitted to Parliament by the minister. Some corporations, such as Air Canada, are also required by their individual legislation to submit an operating budget, although this is not the case with the corporations set up under the provisions of the Companies Act. A form of financial control is also exercised over the activities of these Crown corporations through the power of Parliament to vote special financial assistance to make up deficits. While it is stated in the Financial Administration Act that Part-II corporations are normally expected to operate without appropriations, in fact, most of them, from time to time (and some of them all the time), require help from Parliament to balance their budgets. However, none of these corporations gets free accommodation or furniture from the Department of Public Works, and, like private firms, they have to pay corporate income taxes. Many of these corporations are subject to the scrutiny of the Auditor General, although others, such as Air Canada, are not. This fact has frequently been a bone of contention, introduced in parliamentary debates, although recent developments in the government's attitude of the office of the Auditor General indicate there will likely not be any change in this regard.

"Para"-Crown Corporations There are many corporations wholly owned and operated by the government of Canada that are not listed in Schedules B and C of the Financial Administration Act. While these are not classed as departmental, or parent corporations, they perform mostly the same kinds of functions as those corporations listed in the Financial Administration Act, and therefore should be considered briefly at this point.

Most of these unclassified Crown corporations are set up by separate federal legislation to perform functions that require a degree of independence of action but, often for unstated reasons, they have not been included in the Financial Administration Act. The best examples of this sort of bureaucratic agency are the Bank of Canada and the Canadian Wheat Board, each of which has been set up by its own special legislation. These corporations display as many varieties of internal organization and procedures for control as there are acts. Because of their structural diversity, that is all that can be said about them here. It should also be mentioned, at this point, that there are many government corporations at the provincial level that function in approximately the same way their federal counterparts do. Because of their organizational diversity and great numbers, we can do no more in this study than mention the fact of their existence.

Finally, it must be pointed out that there are a number of intra-departmental agencies that have a position of relative independence within the department, but that are not strictly Crown corporations. These independent boards and commissions are usually set up by special legislation to perform functions that require a degree of independence from direct political or ministerial control, and that come within the organizational boundaries of one of the departments. Basically, these independent boards and commissions function in the same way as departmental corporations. Examples of this type of bureaucratic agency are the National Energy Board, the Canadian Pension Commission, the Fisheries Research Board, the Board of Grain Commissioners, and the Canada Labour Relations Board. There are many more such organizations, and there are also other important agencies of the government of Canada that function in much the same way as departmental corporations but that have varying relationships with the Cabinet, Parliament, and the departments. Again, unfortunately (some might say "fortunately"), the scope of this text does not permit a more detailed analysis of these structurally diverse and multi-functional bureaucratic agencies.

Joint Corporations There are a number of government corporations and commissions in existence that are unique not because of their line functions but because their structure, composition, and legislative mandates are intergovernmental. Examples of these are federal-provincial agencies, such as the interprovincial and territorial boundary commissions, the only active ones today being the Manitoba-Saskatchewan Boundary Commission and the Alberta-British Columbia Boundary Commission. Each consists of a commissioner from the provinces concerned and the Surveyor-General of Canada as the federal representative. Another example of joint federal-provincial enterprise is provided by Syncrude, where federal and provincial governments as well as the private sector are joint participants.

In the international sphere, there are also joint Canadian-U.S. corporations and commissions in existence. Some of these, such as the International Joint Commission and the International Boundary Commission, have been in existence for a long time and are concerned more with the settlement of international disputes than with the management of some genuinely joint enterprise. However, a more current trend is for such joint bodies to have operational responsibilities for managing or developing a shared resource. Perhaps the earliest such body is the Columbia River Permanent Engineering Board, which was set up in 1964; more recent examples include the Roosevelt Campobello International Park Commission, where a Canada-U.S. board actually administers an international park jointly. While such bodies are still the exception, it seems likely, particularly in the areas of conservation and recreation, that there will be greater need for them in the future, both in the federal-provincial and in the international context.

Mixed Corporations   A prominent phenomenon of the late 1960s and the 1970s is the mixed public-private enterprise, and by 1980 the federal government was the majority shareholder in about fifteen such corporations. One of these mixed corporations, which is now defunct, the Canada Development Corporation (CDC), had more than seventy subsidiaries located not only in Canada but around the world. Because these mixed-enterprise corporations have a major responsibility to their private-sector partners and shareholders, a major corporate goal is to make money. However, because these are at least partly "public enterprises," there are policy-related goals as well, which likely complicate and qualify the single-minded search for profits.

Some of the larger of these mixed corporations besides CDC and its successor, CDIC, are Telesat Canada and Panarctic Oils Limited, which differ from Crown corporations and other wholly owned government enterprises in that they are not subject to any of the provisions of the Financial Administration Act; their corporate budgets are in no way subject to the approval of the government; and, for the most part, the role of the government is reduced to that defined for a shareholder under company law. Needless to say, one of the major problems government will face in the 1990s is to find ways of accommodating the unique requirements of mixed enterprise with the traditional imperatives of political accountability, which characterizes all government activity in a liberal democracy.

This concludes our analysis of the various institutional forms found within the Canadian bureaucracy. Although it has been sketchy, it has pointed to a few of the tentative generalizations that can be made about the structures that dominate the formulation stage of the policy process in Canada. We now turn to a discussion of the bureaucratic process, and attempt to explain how these bureaucratic institutions actually fit into the political process.

C H A P T E R   1   8

THE BUREAUCRATIC PROCESS: MANAGEMENT, POLICY MAKING, AND CONTROL

MANAGEMENT IN THE CANADIAN BUREAUCRACY
■ Planning ■ Organizing ■ Staffing ■ Directing
THE MANAGEMENT OF POLICY MAKING
■ Policy Initiation ■ Policy Formulation
THE PROCESS OF CONTROL
■ Control by Cabinet ■ Financial Control: The Budgetary Process
■ Judicial Safeguards ■ Collective Bargaining
■ Management and Control: A Conclusion

T his chapter is concerned with how the bureaucracy goes about attaining its goals.[1] As with any organization, the essence of that process is *management*, defined simply as *the coordination of individual effort to accomplish group or organizational goals*. While management essentially involves coordination of individual effort, that coordination, in either the public or the private sector, can be broken down into a number of sub-processes or activities, including planning, organizing, staffing, directing, and controlling. Each of these activities will be discussed separately, but before we do so it is important to elaborate the characteristics that differentiate management in the private sector from management in the public sector — if only because so many analysts fail to

---

[1] The subject matter of this chapter is a constant preoccupation of journals devoted to public-sector management in parliamentary democracies. An excellent summary and analysis is provided in Sharon L. Sutherland and G. Bruce Doern, *Bureaucracy in Canada: Control and Reform* (Ottawa: Royal Commission on the Economic Union, Research Report 43, University of Toronto Press, Toronto 1985).

note the differences, and hence prescribe "cures" for various presumed ills of public-sector management that have no hope whatever of success.

The first and major difference is simply that private management is analytically less complex. That is because the basic organizational goals in the private sector can, for the most part, be reduced to one — making a profit.[2] This means that secondary criteria of evaluating management systems, such as efficiency and economy, can be employed in their literal sense. The organization that survives and makes a profit for its shareholders is obviously blessed with "good management," and one that goes bankrupt or fails to make money is not. By contrast, for public management the criteria for being successful are not so clear. How, for instance, can one reduce the administration of a welfare program, the enforcement of the law, or the funding of medical research to profit? The goals of government are regulatory, distributive, redistributive, and punitive, but seldom accumulative, as they are for most private-sector organizations. The ultimate measure of the worth of government is how effectively it has contributed to the happiness of most of its citizenry, and not how frugally it has managed to run its operation, nor how much wealth it has been able to accumulate for its "owners." Thus, public management is different in part because the ultimate goals of the organization are so diffuse and so very difficult to define in concrete and measurable terms.

In September 1984, the newly elected Mulroney government initiated a Ministerial Task Force on Program Review (the Nielsen Task Force), whose mandate it was to evaluate a wide range of government programs with a view to improving the overall performance of the federal government. While the basic philosophy applied was instructed by the experience of the private sector, the task force and its various sectoral working groups explicitly recognized from the start that government is indeed different from private enterprise. Thus the task force took the position that:

> Government should be as efficient as possible while providing all essential programs and services. In this context, outdated regulations, waste, duplication, and conflicting program objectives can add to federal spending without meeting national goals. In fact, by rendering the economy more rigid and unadaptive, they can, and do, hinder the achievement of both economic and social goals.[3]

Thus, while the Ministerial Task Force addressed the problem of inefficiency and ineffectiveness in government, the study teams involved did not necessarily attempt to apply the oft-cited panacea of making government more like business. Government is simply different, and must be evaluated according to a separate set of criteria.

The public manager faces a second problem his or her counterpart in a private corporation is able to avoid: the goals of government are sometimes mutually

---

[2] Note that while survival through profitability is the fundamental goal of private-sector organizations, many organizations do not behave in such a way as to maximize profits. Most organization theorists treat such behaviour as dysfunctional, thus maintaining the proposition that such organizations *should* be profit-maximizing; that is, that profit maximization is the highest private-sector goal. See Charles Perrow, *Complex Organizations* (Glenview: Scott Foresman, 1972).

[3] Task Force on Program Review. *An Introduction to the Process of Program Review* (Ottawa: Supply and Services Canada, 1986), p. 1.

exclusive. Redistributive policies, for instance, take money from those who have more and give it to those who have less. The latter will inevitably find this arrangement more pleasing than the former who will demand compensating measures — which they often get! Indeed, it is almost axiomatic that all government policies will please some people and displease others. In the overall attempt to satisfy as many Canadians as possible, managers in one part of the bureaucracy may be pursuing goals that directly conflict with the goals of those in another part of the government, with obvious consequences for interagency or interdepartmental coordination.

Third, management in the public sector is distinguished by the extent to which one of the sub-processes, *control*, is emphasized. The need for accountability of bureaucrats to the elected branches of the government is a given in a democratic political system, and the consequence of this for the bureaucratic process is that the systems of financial and personnel administration are oriented more towards controlling the line managers than they are towards the facilitation of the managerial role. Indeed, this emphasis on control in public management is so pronounced that we will discuss control in a separate section of the chapter.

Finally, the bureaucratic process in the government of Canada is, as we have seen, distinguished by the extent to which public servants are called upon to tender policy advice to the political arm of the government when it is determining priorities and choosing modes of policy implementation. Much has been said about this function in previous sections of the book. But because it is a major theme of this text that the bureaucracy is a central actor in this most central activity of the political process, it is necessary now to look specifically at how the bureaucrats and technocrats actually go about the business of generating and disseminating the information on which their political masters depend in their work.

To elaborate on the bureaucratic process in the public sector in Canada, we will break down the rest of this chapter into three parts, addressed to each of the three broad sets of activities in which the bureaucracy is involved: management, policy making, and control.

MANAGEMENT IN THE CANADIAN BUREAUCRACY

We have already remarked that the core processes of management involve planning, organizing, staffing, directing, and controlling. In this section we consider the first four of these, leaving the issue of control to a separate section because of its particular complications in the Canadian public sector.

Planning

Planning is at the core of any system of management, whether in the private or the public sector. Essentially, all this means is that it is necessary to decide what to do and how best to do it before actually launching into the task. In other words, it is necessary to define operational goals and to develop the means of accomplishing those goals before actually trying to do anything. In the private sector, because goals are fairly well agreed upon, the manager's task is to plan the most effective and efficient means of attaining these goals. In government, however, the task is not so simple. Not only are the goals less clearly defined and less agreed upon, but the means of accomplishing them must fit within the particular norms of a liberal democratic polity and must comply with the particular rationale of a set of decision makers in Cabinet whose main and quite legitimate motivation is to get themselves re-elected. These constraints on the process of goal determination and on the choice of means have two important implications for the planning process in the public sector, each of which deserves further discussion.

The Bifurcation of Planning First, because one of the requirements of a democratic system is that the goals of government must reflect the will of the public, those goals are inevitably set by the politically accountable executive, namely the Cabinet. Indeed, the Cabinet and its executive-support agencies take the major role not only in the determining of policy priorities, but also in approving the general means to be employed by the bureaucracy in implementing those priorities. The permanent officials of the government, those entrusted with the task of managing policy implementation, on the other hand, do not have much control over goal determination. If the politicians, as they sometimes are prone to do, set goals that are not implementable and are perhaps adopted contrary to the advice of the bureaucrats or, if they approve means of implementation which the bureaucrats feel are unworkable, the public-service managers are nevertheless faced with trying to do their best in accomplishing those goals. In this sense the ultimate responsibility for setting goals is separated from the ultimate responsibility for accomplishing them, a situation all senior managers in the public service have found extremely frustrating at some point in their careers. This is what we mean by the bifurcation of planning in government.

Similarly, the public managers often do not have a free hand in working out the techniques and procedures for accomplishing the goals that have been set for them. Rather, the public manager, while perhaps highly influential in determining the means of policy implementation, must still develop procedures that meet the requirements of the political arm of the government. Thus politically significant but administratively difficult procedures may be forced upon the public-service manager.

Thus, the bifurcation of the planning function in government reduces the ability of the public-service manager to plan in the same way a private-sector manager would. Basically, the infusion of politics into the planning process means that there is not only a derationalization of the process of goal determination, but that there is also a situation where, because means are as significant as ends in a democratic system, efficiency becomes a negotiable criterion of managerial effectiveness.

Planning as Evaluation The second implication of a governmental context for the planning function is that there is an almost paranoid concern with keeping the bureaucracy *accountable* to the political branches of government. This has meant that managerial tools such as the expenditure budget, which in the private sector are employed as planning mechanisms, in the public service have been geared almost single-mindedly to maintaining the accountability of the department to Parliament and the Cabinet. Even budgetary devices such as the Planning Programming Budgeting System (PPBS), which is distinguishable from other budgetary systems precisely because of its emphasis on planning, failed in the Canadian public service in large part because it was converted from a tool to help managers to a system of central control *over* the managers. As some public managers have commented whimsically, "They took away the first *P* (planning) and left only a little *p* and some BS."

With the bifurcation of the planning function and the extreme concern with control and accountability in the public service of Canada, what has been left to managers is the ability to assess their performance over time, given the constraints imposed by their public-sector context. While the managers in the public sector cannot plan very systematically, they can at least set baseline targets for themselves, which take into account the givens imposed on them by the politicians, and try to improve their own procedures over time. They are thus often left in the position of trying to measure the extent to which they have made the most of a difficult managerial situation.

The result of this attitude among responsible managers in the federal bureaucracy has been an attempt to emphasize the evaluative dimension of the planning process. Many systems of evaluation of managerial performance have been tried, such as the Operational Performance Measurement System (OPMS). These tools of evaluation were developed to permit managers to set realistic performance targets that take into account the ultimate goals their programs are expected to achieve, the relationship of their programs to complementary programs in other agencies, and the constraints imposed on them by the political environment within which they must operate. In this way, managers are permitted to see how well they have done in reaching a predetermined goal, to evaluate the branch's effectiveness in hitting the target, and to experiment with new procedures that might prove more efficient.

One major problem with many of these systems of performance evaluation, however, has been that, once in place, despite the best intentions of their creators, they inevitably become highly centralized in the manner in which they are enforced. The pervasive concern with control means that the system of evaluation is not regarded by managers as a tool for assessing the performance of their units. Instead, the system comes to be viewed as a mechanism of centralized surveillance and control, and ultimately as a threat to managers' personal security. Whether this conversion of systems of evaluation from tools of line management to contrivances of central control is a deliberate plot of the central agencies is a moot point; the fact remains that it happens consistently in the federal bureaucracy. It remains to be seen whether the still-evolving Office of the Comptroller General, which is charged with developing procedures for evaluation, can escape this role of central-agency villain in the eyes of the line managers. Up to now it has, but perhaps that is in part because it is viewed as a toothless tiger. To this particular problem we can add the equally vexing problems of ill-defined methodology for evaluation and the general diffuseness of goals; thus the prognosis is not very encouraging.

Overall, then, the planning function of public-sector management is very seriously constrained by the givens of a democratic political system. Because of the bifurcation of the planning function and because of the dominance of the mechanisms of control, the only aspect of the planning process that thrives in the federal government is performance evaluation; and, as we have seen, even that dimension of the planning process tends to face problems of over-centralization, inadequate methodology, and unstated or unmeasurable goals.

Planning as Coordination: Interdepartmental Committees One major device for advising on priorities and integrating policy designs among the various departments and agencies of the Canadian government that are not a part of the central agency mafia is the interdepartmental coordinating committee. Typically, an interdepartmental committee will be created wherever more than one department is responsible for a single subject area. In some cases, the committees may be quite formalized. For example, because many departments within the federal government have responsibility for programs that bear upon northern development, there is an Advisory Committee on Northern Development (ACND), on which the departments of Transport, Environment, National Health and Welfare, Energy, Mines and Resources, and Indian Affairs and Northern Development are each represented. Similarly, there have been formal interdepartmental committees within the federal government on water and resources, on pesticides, and on many other subjects. Far more often, ad hoc committees are struck to deal with issues of shorter duration. Frequently, the formal membership of interdepartmental committees will consist of deputy ministers or assistant deputies, but the meetings are generally attended by the middle-ranking delegates of the formal members. This is perhaps fortunate since the bulk of professional expertise is concentrated at these middle levels, and, if any detailed policy work is to be done, these delegates are perhaps the most appropriate people to do it.

The manifest function of interdepartmental committees is to ensure the coordination of policies in some issue area. However, their effectiveness is often negated by a latent function — the pursuit of departmental interests. Interdepartmental "coordination" often becomes a competitive process through which departments bargain for aggrandizement or where they defend their own spheres of authority. This is a necessary reflection of the fact that the members of these committees spend most of their time taking care of their own departmental responsibilities, and only a relatively small part of their time in interdepartmental coordination. Moreover, it may be inevitable, given the segregated hierarchical structures of the Canadian bureaucracy. People naturally tend to view matters in the light of the interests of the department in which they spend so much of their working day, and on whose growth and prosperity their own careers may depend.

This defensive posture of committee members may have severe repercussions for the policy-making process, as it tends to preclude a truly problem-oriented approach to issues. For example, if both the Department of Environment and the Department of Energy, Mines, and Resources are eager to expand their influence over the uses of energy resources, it means that each may view the other's quite legitimate actions as a "power grab" and either act to block them or provide a counter-offensive of its own. The institutional forums of interdepartmental coordination often become the arena for these battles, and the result may be committee deadlock, or much bureaucratic redundancy with no clear policy decision. The problem is compounded by the fact that the Cabinet may often choose to delay its own decisions if there is lack of consensus among its bureaucratic advisors. In cases like this, the Cabinet may simply wait until one group or the other has gained ascendancy and a clear-cut policy alternative has been articulated.

There are partial solutions to such blockages. First, the prime minister can move to break up such deadlocks by a pre-emptive reallocation of departmental responsibility. Second, and more important, perhaps, is the fact that the interdepartmental priority-setting process is not purely a conflict situation: in fact, not all departments are imperialistic, and indeed most individual bureaucrats are genuinely interested in solving substantive problems, even if they sometimes get in one another's way. Because many of the middle-level specialists in a given subject area get to know each other personally, there are many channels of informal communication, which can help to ease the process of interdepartmental coordinations. Furthermore, department heads are not always anxious to expand their own departmental work-loads, and are often willing to share the burden. This tendency may be reinforced because, where senior bureaucrats have difficulty delegating authority, they quickly find themselves in a position where they cannot imagine their organization undertaking greater responsibilities, even when there may be considerable spare capacity lower down in the department.

A third partial solution is to be found in another aspect of the activities of the central agencies. The major central agencies are represented on virtually all the formal interdepartmental coordinating committees, sub-committees, working groups, and so on. They are there not because they have programs in these particular areas but rather because of their coordinative and supervisory responsibilities. Thus, attached to these agencies are people whose job it is to stay on top of interdepartmental coordination, mainly by attending an endless round of meetings. These people then report back to the appropriate division of their own agency, thus producing a check on all facets of interdepartmental activity.

The overall verdict on interdepartmental committees, however, must be that they do not achieve many great coordinative successes. In fact, some participants have dubbed the interdepartmental committee system "institutionalized discord" — the coordinative mechanism, in other words, has itself become, in several respects, one of the battlegrounds where interdepartmental combat occurs.

As we move, now, to a discussion of the managerial activities of organizing, staffing, and directing, we must keep in mind the operational primacy of planning in all decision-making activity. Even within the other analytically discrete sub-processes that make up the process of management, it must be remembered that planning must occur as well. Hence, while the public-service manager may be denied a central role in the setting of policy goals and in determining the overall means of goal attainment in the federal bureaucracy, there remains a responsibility, on a smaller scale, for the manager to plan strategies for organizing, staffing, and directing the department. Hence as we discuss organizing, staffing, and directing, keep in mind that planning must be seen as part of each activity, as well as a sub-function in its own right.

Organizing

In order for individuals to work effectively towards the attainment of organizational goals, a contrived structure of roles — an organization — must be designed and maintained. The student must recognize, however, that bureaucracies have both formal and informal organizational structures. The latter reflect unplanned patterns of personal interaction that develop within any group of people. Informal leaders will inevitably emerge in any working place, and these people sometimes rival the authority of the formal leaders or the bosses by virtue of their personal charisma, job competence, or long-time experience in the particular work place. While the phenomenon of informal organization, which occurs in all formal social structures, has implications for the managerial function of "directing," we want to concentrate here upon the formal and not the informal aspects of bureaucracy. We must keep in mind, however, that parallel to the contrived formal structure of government there is an invisible informal network, which can have an impact on the effectiveness of the organization.

The rest of this section will focus on the managers' role in defining the intradepartmental *span of control* and unified *chain of command* within government agencies and in outlining the principles that determine the interdepartmental distribution of responsibilities in the federal bureaucracy.

Span of Control and Chain of Command   The span of control in hierarchical organizations is defined by the number of individuals at any level who must report directly to a supervisor, senior manager, or boss. Thus, if a government department has six assistant deputy ministers (ADMs) who report directly to the deputy minister (DM), the DM's span of control is six. Different textbooks on management have tried to define the optimum span of control, but without success, because the appropriate span of control will vary with the nature of the organization, the personalities of the people involved, and the significance of informal organizational structures in either facilitating or short-circuiting the vertical communication links. Generally, however, a span of control exceeding eight is thought to be too wide — one is incapable of effectively directing the operation if one has to ride herd on more than eight immediate subordinates.

Where span of control defines the breadth of an organizational hierarchy, the concept of *chain of command* has to do with the length of the hierarchy. The length of the chain of command is the number of levels from top to bottom in the organization. Obviously, if the span of control is to remain less than, for example, eight, as organizations become larger, the chain of command lengthens. While it is not possible to state that there is any universal optimum length of chain of command, generally, as the chain of command lengthens, the senior manager will be called upon increasingly to delegate responsibilities to subordinates. Thus, an important part of the managerial activity of organizing is to structure the formal organization in such a way that the span of control and the chain of command permit effective delegation of responsibilities without losing control over the extremities of the operation.

Finally, closely related to the concept of chain of command is the concept of *unity of command*. What this means is that, in a hierarchical organization, there should be only one boss at the top. According to this principle, subordinate managers in a government department, for instance, must not have more than one superior; the chain of command must lead directly from top to bottom in the organization and it must be clear to managers at every level to whom they are responsible. It is impossible for a middle-level manager to function effectively if there is more than one boss giving orders.

To apply these concepts to the process of management in the federal public service in Canada, we can begin by stating that in some ways the activity of organizing is the one least affected by the fact that the manager is in the public sector. The questions of length of chain of command and span of control tend to be left pretty well to the line managers, and there is a minimum of meddling by the political branches of the government. Because of the rapid growth of most government departments in Canada in the past twenty years, the senior managers, in attempting to delegate responsibility while at the same time maintaining control, have generally opted to lengthen the chain of command and narrow the span of control at the top of the organization. Thus, a typical organization chart of a federal department in 1956 might have had six or seven *directors* reporting directly to the DM; a typical department in the 1980s might have as many as three or four levels of management between the DM and the directors, and a span of control of four or five. The increase in the senior management positions in the federal public service has been remarkable in the past two decades; where DMs and directors were the first- and second-line managers in government organizations twenty years ago, today we can see a proliferation of associate deputy ministers, assistant deputy ministers, and directors-general — all inserted *between* the DM and director levels of the department.

Limits to the Unity of Command It is hard to evaluate the effectiveness of this trend in maintaining the unity of command in the federal bureaucracy because the workability of the various organizational forms depends upon the people involved and upon the idiosyncrasies of the informal organizational features of the department. In the latter case, one of the factors that can affect the unity of command in the organization is the extent to which the minister and personal staff can bypass the DM (and personal staff) in influencing directly the activities at lower levels of the department. It is by now commonplace for ministers who fear they will be kept in the dark by their DMs or who wish to remain informed about the actual operation of the department to have bright young men and women from within the bowels of their department seconded to them as "special assistants." Besides functioning as technical advisors to the minister, the special assistants are also often called upon to maintain informal communication links with their friends and colleagues in the department, thus giving the minister a network, which serves to keep the deputy minister honest in any dealings with his or her superior. However, while such informal communications systems might be used by a minister to actually subvert the chain of command or to permit direct ministerial influence on the operational activities of the department, for the most part the uses to which they have been put by the political executive has not been manipulative.

The other way in which the chain of command can be subverted in the federal government is through the activities of the central agencies, particularly the Treasury Board Secretariat. While formally mandated only to provide assistance and advice for the line managers in the departments, the advisory branches of the TBS have been able to do some arm twisting in getting senior managers to adopt "recommended" procedures. However, here the problem is one of interagency conflict, and it does not often subvert the internal chain of command within the department.

Where the TBS does sometimes subvert the chain of command within a department is in its role in scrutinizing the departmental estimates and in the program-review stage of the budgetary cycle, for in this process the TBS does have the authority unilaterally to alter the department's priorities. However, the staff officers in the financial branch of the department will usually have established prior informal contact with the personnel in the TBS who will ultimately be dealing with the department's forecasts, as will middle managers responsible for particular programs. This informal communication network between departmental program officers or financial administrators and TBS people helps to ease the way for departmental spending proposals by working out the deals and bargains before the formal package of departmental estimates is submitted to the Board. In this way, the informal communications system facilitates the budgetary process and likely improves upon the formal machinery of the estimates.

On the negative side, however, such informal processes can occasionally subvert the chain of command within the department. Because it is the friendly folks in the Financial Administration Branch of the department or in the middle depths of program operations, and not the senior managers, who maintain many of the links with the TBS, the former can become small-time power brokers within the department. Their influence with a key central agency makes them informal leaders, and they can nibble away at the formal authority defined by the departmental chain of command. Thus while it is not the intention of the TBS to subvert the formal power structure of the department, the Secretariat can sometimes have that effect by becoming part of the informal interagency bargaining networks, which play a growing role in the preparation of the estimates.

Informal organization is therefore one of the variables that affects the effectiveness of the formal command and control mechanisms of the federal bureaucracy. However, depending upon the skill of the senior manager of the government in directing and staffing the department, the informal organizational structures can become benign implements, to be used to improve the overall effectiveness of the formal organization the manager has helped design and maintain.

The Principles of Departmentalization Where formal organization is virtually imposed on the senior managers of the Government of Canada is in the interdepartmental structure of the bureaucracy. The interdepartmental distribution of responsibilities and jurisdiction is based on the closely related principles of *function* and *clientele*. The Department of Labour and the Department of Agriculture, for instance, exist to perform administrative and policy-making functions in certain specific areas relating to labour and farmers respectively. Basically, the name of a department will give some indication of the function it is intended to perform and the clientele to which it is expected to cater. However, while the distribution of functions between the various departments is intended to eliminate interdepartmental confusion and conflict over who is to do what, there is much overlapping of departmental jurisdiction. The result of this jurisdictional conflict is a process whereby bureaucratic agencies compete with each other for jurisdiction in areas of potential overlap. Thus, the departments of Energy, Mines, and Resources; Indian Affairs and Northern Development; Environment; Transport; National Health and Welfare; Fisheries and Oceans; and Agriculture, all have some responsibility for water-pollution control. Which of these departments ultimately emerges supreme in the various aspects of this policy area will depend on a process of interdepartmental bargaining, Cabinet decisions, and the political influence of each department's clientele.

As time passes and conditions change, new departments spring up and other departments disappear. Sometimes the functions of one department are absorbed into another; at other times, two departments will be amalgamated administratively even though the functions are not very closely related. Often it is apparent that the demands of a certain clientele perpetuate the existence of archaic departments long after their functions should have been absorbed into newer departments. For instance, the Department of Veterans' Affairs continues to exist, though it is difficult at first glance to see why such matters are not merely placed under the jurisdiction of the Department of Health and Welfare. The politician knows better — there are still several hundred thousand veterans and their dependants in age categories where voter turnout is high.

Some government departments, for example the Secretary of State, have a sort of catch-all jurisdiction; any matters that are not important enough or large enough to be placed in a separate department are administratively lumped together here. Still other departments, such as Supply and Services or Public Works, perform a number of services for all the other departments. On the other hand, some of the more traditional departments of government, such as National Defence and External Affairs, have responsibilities that are only secondarily concerned with any specific clientele in Canada.

Hence, the rationale for the interdepartmental distribution of responsibilities in Canada is very difficult to state in any succinct fashion. Departments exist for a number of reasons, and most of them justify their existence through some specific function they perform or some clientele they serve. Because government reorganizations are usually reflective of political trends in the world at large, more than of considerations of administrative efficiency, the role of the public manager in this process is usually small.

Staffing

The managerial activity referred to as *staffing* essentially involves manning the organization — by recruiting candidates for positions in the organization, by selecting the best people from those recruited, by training the ones selected so they can do the job required of them, and by facilitating the development of their careers in the organization. In the private sector, the senior manager has control over virtually all aspects of the process of staffing and usually is assisted in this process by a fairly sizeable personnel branch. However, ultimate decisions as to hiring and firing of employees, and decisions as to promotion, transfer, and discipline rest with senior management within the organization. In the public service, however, the authority of the senior manager is not as comprehensive. In the federal bureaucracy, the senior manager must share the staffing function with central agencies, such as the Treasury Board and particularly the Public Service Commission.

Legislation passed in 1967 has as one of its major aims the implementation of the Glassco Commission's admonition to "let the managers manage." As a result, the legislation purports to give the deputy minister and his or her delegates a great deal of flexibility in dealing with the management of human resources within the department, and at the same time to ensure uniform standards and procedures across the public service through the Treasury Board and the Public Service Commission. For practical purposes, however, the DM is forced to operate within very tightly defined procedures and guidelines set by the central agencies, and the DM's independent authority over the staffing process within the department is very restricted.

According to the Financial Administration Act, the Treasury Board, as the central management agency of the government, has the responsibility for the management of all personnel functions in the public service. Most significant among the Board's personnel-administration functions is the responsibility to act as the "employer" in all collective negotiations with employee unions. This is a very serious limit to the deputy's authority, for if there is a dispute within the department between management and employee, the DM does not have the power to act as management independently of the Board.

The Public Service Commission The creation of the first Civil Service Commission in Canada in 1908 was precipitated by changes that occurred in the functions of the bureaucracy and in the attitudes of Canadians concerning the nature of the public service. At one time there was a general acceptance that appointment to bureaucratic office should be based not on the qualifications of the applicant and the requirements of the job but on partisan considerations. Liberal governments rewarded the party faithful by granting them jobs in the public service, and Conservative governments did the same.[4] The short-run effect of this practice was to aid the political parties in building strong party organizations in most of the country's constituencies. As the parties built up bases of support, however, they no longer needed the promise of patronage appointments to entice people into working for the party; by then, the administrative problem of distributing the patronage had become a great headache to the party leader.

As well, people began to consider such tactics morally and ethically improper, and movements sprang up to reform the civil service. Finally, as the role of gov-

---

[4] Political biographies give many of the details of the development of patronage in Canada. See especially Donald Creighton, *John A. Macdonald, Vol. 2: The Old Chieftain, passim.*

ernment expanded, the jobs to be done in the public service began to require a degree of expertise that was often sadly lacking in a person who was appointed for reasons of political preference. The upshot of all of these changes was that the recruitment practices of the public service were changed from the principle of patronage to the principle of *merit*. In other words, applicants for public-service positions were now to be chosen on the basis of their qualifications and the requirements of the position, and if more than one person fit the same position, the choice between them was to be made on the basis of a competitive examination. The original Civil Service Commission was set up to supervise the implementation of the merit system of recruitment in the public service.

Today, the Public Service Commission is made up of three commissioners — all of whom are appointed for a set term by the Governor in Council, with salaries set by Parliament — and a large permanent staff. The functions of the PSC include the overseeing of the merit system and other responsibilities related to staffing the public service of Canada, as well as certain types of appeals concerned with staffing. In short, because of its large measure of control over the people who get into the Canadian public service, the Public Service Commission is an important independent agency in the staffing process. In practice, however, while the PSC controls the rules within which the process of staffing must be carried on, the central agencies have delegated the responsibility for staffing, with the exception of the most senior levels of the bureaucracy, to the department.

Training and Development The staffing function, however, does not cease with recruitment. As with any organization, it is necessary to train the people who are part of it, not only with respect to the technical skills of the specific occupation, but also with respect to the goals of the organization. The employee who has been thoroughly socialized into a bureaucratic organization will likely function more enthusiastically, and even more efficiently, than the person who looks on his or her occupation as just a living. Hence there is an almost constant process of training and development[5] within the Canadian bureaucracy, which, by moulding the attitudes of public servants, very subtly affects bureaucratic decision making. The formal responsibility for training and development is shared by the senior managers in the departments and the Treasury Board. However, the Board has, for the most part, delegated its responsibility in this area to the Public Service Commission. Thus training and development programs within the federal bureaucracy are run by the managers in the departments, by the Public Service Commission, and often through the cooperation of both.

Thus the DM does not have as much control over staffing activity as his or her counterpart in the private sector. Because, as was pointed out elsewhere, the kinds of decisions being made in an organization and the type of managerial system that is to prevail will depend largely on the kinds of people within the organization, the restrictions placed on the role of management in matters of staffing reduce the overall impact of the senior bureaucrats.

[5] The Glassco Commission distinguishes between *training*, which teaches people specific skills and techniques, and *development*, which provides periodic exposure to broad courses on subjects related only tangentially to the job itself. Each can be important in the process of socializing an employee to the organizational norms.

The Obligations of Public Employment Having discussed the nature of the recruitment, selection, and training process in the public service, this is perhaps an appropriate juncture to say something of the nature of employment in the federal bureaucracy and to outline some of the rights, obligations, and restrictions attached to the role of public servant.

Public servants have traditionally been viewed as different from employees in the private sector. In part, this is because they are "servants of the public" and should therefore take a highly responsible attitude to their jobs; but by far the greatest justification for treating public servants differently from their counterparts in private industry is simply their proximity to politics. Because they have access to information that the general public does not, and because they are involved in the process of policy formulation, public servants could potentially do a great deal of damage to the government of the day. By leaking information to the Opposition parties or by sabotaging government projects, the public servant could potentially bring down the government. Thus a tradition has evolved: while the public servant must be cognizant of personal responsibility to the public, if duty to the public conflicts with the interests of the government, the public servant must look to the government first, since it is the government—not the bureaucracy—which must ultimately face the public. For instance, one public servant felt that it was his responsibility to the public to tell them, through the media, that the government's metrification program was unwise; that public servant was dismissed.

To protect the government from this kind of betrayal, there are clauses in the Official Secrets Act providing for severe penalties for public servants who make unauthorized statements based on official information. Furthermore, upon entering the federal public service, public servants must take an oath of office in which each swears not to "disclose or make known any matter that comes to my knowledge by reason of such employment." Violation of this principle can mean immediate dismissal, as it did to a senior executive in the Central Mortgage and Housing Corporation who leaked a secret Cabinet document to some native groups.

There are also restrictions on the extent to which a public servant can become involved in politics. He or she can vote, contribute money to parties, and attend political meetings while a public servant, but cannot actively campaign on behalf of a candidate or run for elected office. Since the passage of the most recent Public Service Employment Act, public servants have been permitted to request a leave of absence without pay from their jobs to seek election at the federal, provincial, or municipal levels.[6] The restrictions on the political activities of provincial public servants are generally similar to those at the federal level.

Directing

The key to the managerial activity of directing is the motivation of human resources within an organization so that the individuals will be willing to put the goals of the group before their individual goals, at least while on the job. For the most part, this can be achieved if the goals of the organization happen to be congruent

---

[6] See E. Gallant, "Service Above Party," *Policy Options*, March 1986, p. 8; and T.D. Aquino, "The Public Service of Canada: The Case For Political Neutrality," *CPA*, Spring 1984, p. 14.

with those of the individual or if the organization can offer inducements that benefit the individual in some material fashion. The former rarely occurs except in voluntary associations, but in the case of bureaucratic organizations, the inducement to employees is almost always a monetary reward in the form of salary or wages.

In the private sector, the manager has considerable control over the relative financial rewards (and penalties) to be allotted to his or her personnel. By influencing the processes of promotion, by parcelling out the opportunities for advancement through training programs, and by having the power to impose disciplinary sanctions, the manager in the private sector has the tools, the material sanctions, and the inducements to motivate human resources. By stark contrast, the manager in the federal bureaucracy has very little direct control over the salary, benefits, and career-development opportunities of employees. Because it is the Treasury Board and not the deputy minister that functions as the employer in collective bargaining, the DM is severely limited in the extent to which the managerial prerogatives, which are used as motivators in the private sector, can be exercised. Thus while the ability to manipulate sanctions and inducements as motivators in the process of directing exists, it must be shared by the DM and the central officers in the PSC and the TBS.

Lacking personal control over the material factors of motivation, the public-service manager must therefore resort to the more ethereal leadership skills in attempting to get the most out of subordinates. It is the qualities of the individual manager *per se*, such as charisma, professional expertise, and overall job competence, and not what the manager can do for the employee, which must be employed as motivators. If the manager is liked and respected by the employees, or if the employees believe in the kinds of goals the manager is trying to accomplish, they will work harder and more enthusiastically at their jobs; on the other hand, if they hold the manager in low regard and spend a lot of time figuring out how to avoid work, the manager has only limited options with which to discipline them.

The other problem is that, lacking the formal authority to reward and punish subordinates, a manager in the public service may find it difficult to compete with informal leaders in the organization. The one edge the manager in the private sector has when dealing with informal organization is possession of full authority within the formal organization. In the government, however, the ability of the manager to motivate underlings may hinge on the ability to become part of, or at least to figure out how to use, the informal authority patterns in the organization. Thus, managerial leadership in government is not command, as it tends to be in most hierarchical organizations, but a complex of personality resources, social and political skills, and a full awareness of the informal alliances, friendships, and personal animosities among the people employed. Directing in this sort of an organizational environment resembles more an art form than a professional skill.

This concludes our discussion of the process of management in the Canadian bureaucracy. While the overall conclusion has to be that the manager in the public sector generally works within extremely severe constraints imposed by the overall environment of government, by the central agencies, and by the requirements for political accountability, the Canadian bureaucracy does get managed somehow. It is easy to be critical of management in the bureaucracy, but before attempting any overall verdict, it is necessary first to look at the role of the bureaucracy and of senior managers in the policy process. Here the manager must function as a facilitator and coordinator of expert knowledge, a role that involves a set of managerial skills almost unique to government.

THE MANAGEMENT OF POLICY MAKING

Elsewhere in the text we touched upon the role of the Canadian bureaucracy in the policy process. We analyzed its place in the process of priority determination within the context of our discussion of the Cabinet and the central agencies, but we have not said very much at all about policy formulation or policy initiation as sets of activities within the federal departments. It is the aim of this section of the chapter to describe these activities and to explain the responsibilities of the senior bureaucrats as managers of policy-relevant information.

Policy Initiation

At the policy-initiation stage, we see the bureaucracy acting both as a channel of input and as a *gatekeeper* in filtering demands from the environment, and as an *advocate* for the interests of a specific clientele. In the advocacy role, the government department enters into a sort of symbiotic relationship with the relevant interest groups in jointly attempting to convince the priority setters in the Cabinet and the central agencies to meet the policy demands of their shared clientele. The interest group-department relationship is symbiotic because a successful campaign that influences the priority setters to embrace the desired policy or program benefits both the department and the interest group. The latter benefits directly in that the clientele group it represents gets an immediate payoff from the new program. The former benefits through the increased budget and human resources it gets to implement the new policy.

To act as an effective channel of input, the departmental manager is required simply to maintain open lines of communication and to establish a close working relationship with the key interest groups in the appropriate policy sector. This means that the department is functioning as a representative institution, often directly in competition with other institutions, such as Parliament, the political parties, and the electoral system. However, the most effective bureaucratic agencies in the process of channeling policy ideas into the system are those that take more than a passive role in the process. It is not uncommon for government officials today to become involved as social animators. It is not necessary to simply wait for demands to emerge: the department may anticipate the needs of a clientele group before the group itself has felt those needs. Hence, since the 1970s, the departmental policy managers have become increasingly involved in the process of education of their clients and in assisting the groups whose interests they serve to better organize and to more effectively articulate their demands to government. In effect, modern clientele-oriented agencies of government, at both federal and provincial levels, not only help to articulate the policy demands of their clients but they also may help to create and organize the interest groups with which they must deal.

In sum, government departments, in functioning as channels of input for demands from interest groups, often go far beyond the passive gatekeeper role and become active advocates of client interests. Moreover, in some cases the department will actually enter into a sort of collusion with the interest groups in the environment, in attempting to generate and articulate policy demands to the priority setters in the Cabinet and in the central agencies.

Policy Innovation   Thus, in its role as a channel for input from the environment, the bureaucracy functions not only as a facilitator but also as an active manipulator of the flow of information from the environment to the system. However, a further mode of bureaucratic involvement in the process of policy initiation is still more active and direct. Here the government agency actually creates its own policy demands internally, and triggers the mechanisms of priority determination.

The basic problem for the senior bureaucratic manager in organizing the department to act as an agency of innovation stems from the very nature of bureaucratic organization. The *raison d'être* of bureaucracy is to make administrative behaviour predictable, and this is accomplished largely through the *routinization* of decision making. In an organization geared to predictability and routinization, creativity and innovativeness become negative or dysfunctional traits. Hence the challenge of the public service manager is to find organizational devices that will permit innovative activity and at the same time not compromise the basic organizational goal of routinization — to integrate creativity and predictability.

Ghettoization of Innovation   Two managerial devices have been employed in an attempt to resolve the inherent contradiction between the goals of innovation and routinization in federal bureaucratic structures. The first device is the *ghettoization* of innovation. This is achieved through organizing the department so that the policy branch or policy-planning branch is encapsulated and insulated from the line operators. The aim here is to foster creative thinking and experimentation within the ghetto and at the same time to prevent the mood in the policy branch from infecting the line administration and hampering the normal routine.

One problem with the ghettoization of innovation is that, after a period of time, even these very carefully designed policy structures tend to routinize their operations. If this routine is allowed to develop to its logical extreme, we end up with the somewhat paradoxical situation where the creativity and imagination within these units becomes routinized. "Routinized innovation" is, of course, not very innovative at all, and to offset this tendency a second managerial device, which might be dubbed "personnel transfusion," has been developed in the government of Canada. The aim of these personnel transfusions is to ensure a constant supply of new blood to the policy ghetto, which works against the relentless forces of routinization. Thus it is rare for an individual to serve more than a few years in one of the policy branches of government. People simply get rotated out, and either find a transfer to another government agency or move back to the line operations of the same department.

The operational results of these managerial tactics for facilitating innovation within the federal bureaucracy, while not cataclysmic, are worth note. The most prominent result has been a high output of *procedural* innovations. A large number of improvements in the managerial process itself have been spawned as a direct product of the brainstorming that goes on in these policy units. Much of the experimentation with new systems of performance evaluation, operational planning, and different organizational modes that has been witnessed in the past decade in the federal public service has been at least partly the result of the activities of the planning and policy branches in the various departments. Unfortunately, little of it has been overwhelmingly successful.

In the process of substantive policy development, the success rate has been somewhat better. The focus here has been in thinking up "neat new things" the department might do for its clients, and in developing novel strategies for trying to sell the ideas to the Cabinet and to the sombre superbureaucrats in the central agencies. While the batting average for getting such new policy ideas adopted is not high, where the policy innovators can define a new clientele and help to mobilize them in support of a new program, there is usually a possibility of at least partial success.[7]

Innovation and Crisis Management   Finally, the innovative ghettos have had some impact in the business of *crisis management*. We have already spoken of the evolution of "crisis government" within the context of the process of priority determination. This mode of decision making may have become a discrete style of governance in the 1970s. However, here we wish to say something about the role of crisis management in the policy-initiation stage of policy making.

In essence, a crisis approach to policy initiation involves the departmental policy branches in a process of anticipatory innovation or of policy contingency planning. Here the policy innovator uses a combination of vigilance, achieved through maintaining good lines of communication with clientele groups, and intelligence operations, designed to uncover, through research, public needs or clientele demands before they become manifest. Often this means anticipating what the clientele will need in the near future, before the clientele or its representative interest group become aware of the need themselves.

Obviously, as we have stated it above, the process of crisis management must be seen as simply an important implement of good government. However, it is the ends to which such innovative activities are put that determine their ultimate outcome. In its purest form, crisis management is a rationalist device, which utilizes the ideas of bureaucratic innovators to prevent crises by foretelling them and nipping them in the bud. The most common adulteration of rationalist crisis management in the Canadian system is characterized by a Machiavellian use of the imminent crisis for political gain. Here the policy innovators anticipate the crisis and set up the contingency responses, but then wait for the crisis to develop before acting. In this way the government will gain political kudos for having risen to the occasion and saved the day. The extreme perversion of crisis

---

[7] For a slightly different perspective on departmental policy branches see: M.J. Prince and John Chenier, "The Rise and Fall of Policy Planning and Research Units: An Organizational Perspective," *CPA*, Winter 1980, p. 519.

management, however, is where the policy innovators, possibly in cahoots with the political leadership, actively precipitate crises so that they will have a justification for implementing policy responses that might otherwise be unacceptable to the public. This sort of Orwellian manipulation of the public by the government, while clearly a potential tactic, is likely not used very much in Canada. Such deliberate and cynical manipulation of the public will for political (or bureaucratic) gain is simply unacceptable to people socialized to the values of our political culture. Besides, they might get caught!

Innovation and Incrementalism Despite attempts to make the bureaucratic dimensions of the policy process innovative and to permit the effective management of crises, there remain severe limitations on the effectiveness of these devices. In fact, most new policies that come to the surface at the priority-determination phase of the policy process are simply linear extensions of existing policies — logical outgrowths of current practice, rather than genuinely new policy initiatives. But why, then, does innovation in government meet with only limited success? And why does the process of new-policy development remain so relentlessly incremental?

Incrementalism prevails because it is safe. In a decision-making environment characterized by *uncertainty*—the inability to predict the future accurately—it is always easier for the policy makers either to decide to do nothing or to opt for small adjustments to the status quo. In a situation of incomplete information, it is risky to attempt great leaps forward with radical policy options, for the great leap may precipitate unforeseen consequences more serious than the problem the policy is designed to solve in the first place.[8] Finally, the persistence of incrementalism in the policy process may reflect the fact that the kinds of real-world changes the policy makers are faced with are themselves incremental: perhaps less is unexpected than in the past. Although we are faced with serious problems such as an economic malaise, energy shortfalls or excesses, and ethnic conflict, these are chronic and not acute ills. Developments in these problem areas are neither sudden nor totally unexpected, and perhaps the most appropriate policy responses are of constant but incremental adjustments as new information becomes available.

Policy Formulation

As we have explained elsewhere, policy formulation involves developing a policy idea into a detailed set of proposals for implementation. While analytically this part of the process occurs after a priority has been established, in fact the proposals for implementation are being developed at the initiation and priority stages. What distinguishes the formulation stage is that the process is more exclusively internal to the department. At the stage of policy initiation, the focus is upon generating new policy ideas that can be sold to the priority setters; but once a priority has been established, the department must concern itself with developing the means of achieving the desired goals.

---

[8] On this point, the classic statements remain Herbert Simon's *Administrative Behaviour* and James March and Herbert Simon, *Organisations*.

The stuff of policy formulation is ultimately specialized information and technical data, which must be brought to bear on the problems of how to achieve the policy goals defined by the priority setters. The activity of policy formulation is basically problem solving, and the role of the manager in this process is to coordinate the efforts of the technical staff of the department. As with the process of policy initiation, the policy branch of the department often plays the central role in formulation. Here, however, the goal is not so much to define policy problems and to attempt to convince the Cabinet and central agencies that they are deserving of a policy response, but rather to develop the most practical and effective procedures for achieving agreed-upon goals. Because "implementability" is a concern at this stage, there is a much greater need to integrate the efforts of the technocrats in the innovation ghettos with the operational expertise that resides in the line managers, who, ultimately, will actually have to get the job done. This is a major challenge to the senior managers in the department, and it can prove to be a difficult task.

The problem of integrating policy considerations and operational considerations is made difficult by the isolation of the policy branch from the line functions in the department. While the isolation or ghettoization of the policy advisors is essential if innovation is to be reconciled with routine, even the most brilliant policy ideas must be ultimately reformulated so they can be put into effect. Beyond the problems of blending the creative juices of the policy advisory branch with the more pedestrian concerns of the line administrators, the senior manager must also ensure that the policy proposal, once formulated, is acceptable to the central agencies and to the Cabinet. This means that the central agencies must be in on the process almost from the start, to ensure that the means being developed are financially feasible and practically acceptable.

In terms of time and numbers of people directly involved, policy formulation is not the largest role played by the Canadian bureaucracy, but it is certainly the largest *policy* role. And because policy formulation involves greater utilization of technical expertise than do other stages of policy making, this function of the bureaucracy is the most difficult to control. Usually the department will offer alternative proposals for accomplishing the policy goals defined by the priority setters. Superficially, this means that the Cabinet and its advisors must choose from the options developed by the department. However, in some cases the choice will be an illusion, for inevitably one alternative, the one preferred by the department, will be painted with far more attractive colours than its competition. Furthermore, by the time a large team of highly specialized economists has spent seven hours a day for eighteen months putting together material such as might be found in a white paper on taxation, it is unlikely that their political masters in the Cabinet will be able to mount an effective criticism of the detailed substance of their recommendations.

At another level of analysis, it can be argued that one of the important results of the increased use of white papers is the enhancement of the participation of Parliament and parliamentary committees in policy deliberations. Audrey Doerr has pointed out that, through the white paper,

Parliament is linked to the policy activities of the government and is given the opportunity to scrutinize and review government intentions and actions. To the extent that parliamentary committee hearings can encourage and facilitate the participation of interest groups and individuals in the discussion of policy issues contained in the papers, the representative role of parliament is also enhanced. Thus the accountability of the government to parliament may be strengthened.[9]

More will be said about the role of Parliament in the policy process in the next chapter.

Sometimes, to weaken any potential criticism in central agencies, Cabinet, or Parliament in advance, the team of experts might cook up and include a few throwaway items in its proposals. Obviously, red herrings can be carefully integrated into the policy paper to draw the fire of the Opposition, whether it be the media, interest groups, or potential dissenters in Cabinet. Then, after a period of debate, the technical advisors can graciously accede to the wishes of their political critics and excise the troublesome proposals. In this way, it is possible to retain intact the basic structure of a policy option (as recommended by the technical people) while giving the critics a feeling of efficacy. While the actual use of this tactic is difficult to document, and while it is clearly devious on the part of the technical advisors, its use is sometimes apparent in the formulation process. Perhaps the greatest impediment to this type of behaviour, particularly when bureaucrats attempt to use it in dealing with the Cabinet, is that the technical experts themselves, in various departments, are rarely sufficiently agreed to mount this sort of attack on the Cabinet's supremacy.

In fact, it may be an irony of technocracy that the degree of specialization of technical policy advisors is at once their source of strength and their greatest weakness. In this sense, the specialized policy advisor can become so expert in a narrow field that the substance of the advice given is virtually unassailable by the non-expert Cabinet, and difficult to challenge even for the generalist-manager senior bureaucrat to whom the advisor reports. However, on the other side of the coin, the technocrats become so specialized that they lack perspective on the overall policy implications of their advice, and end up being erudite but irrelevant. At the broadest level of speculation, we can hypothesize that this phenomenon may be symptomatic of a fundamental weakness in the policy-formulation process in many modern industrialized systems. If the experts are too specialized to see or understand the significance of their knowledge in relationship to the input of their equally specialized peers in different areas of expertise, and if the senior bureaucratic generalists in the government in whom we vest the responsibility for integrating and coordinating the process of policy formulation cannot deal meaningfully with the substance of the highly technical information being generated from within their policy-advisory groups, is there anybody with the philosopher-king-like combination of skills to actually pilot the ship of state?

This situation (which is admittedly painted in the extreme here to make the point) goes a long way to explain the apparent failure or limited success of many

[9] Audrey Doerr, "The Role of Coloured Papers," *CPA*, Fall 1982, p. 377.

of the rationalist experiments in the 1970s, such as PPBS and Management by Objectives (MBO). A partial remedy to the problem may lie in fostering a different view or ethos of management in both federal and provincial bureaucracies. Where the function of management in traditional bureaucratic structures is viewed as the coordination of personnel and materials towards the attainment of organizational goals, in bureaucratic agencies mandated to produce policy advice, the function of the manager is to organize expertise in such a way that it can be directed not only to the attainment of predetermined political goals, but to the determination of the goals as well. While there are clear indications in the government of Canada that there is a new breed of senior bureaucrats who possess these policy skills as well as the perspective to use them effectively in the process of managing the technical information generated from within their departments, there is still too wide a variation from agency to agency in the performance of this critical policy-formulation function.

Finally, to return to our discussion of the bureaucracy and the policy process, astute, policy-wise managers will also be looking even further down the road than Cabinet approval, to the parliamentary stage of the process. In recognition of the fact that getting legislation through the House quickly and with a minimum of fuss requires some trade-offs between government and the Opposition, it is sometimes prudent to include some expendable proposals even after the conclusion of the formulation stage. By judiciously retaining a few red-herring clauses in the draft legislation, the formulators can draw the fire of the ever-vigilant Opposition. In this way the government has some items upon which to yield to Opposition pressure (after an appropriate struggle), in return for a speedy passage of the remainder of the package through the House of Commons.

This concludes what is admittedly a fairly cursory look at the process of bureaucratic policy making. We have not dealt with the role of the line departments in the *budgetary process*; that will be discussed within the context of processes of control, in the next section.

THE PROCESS OF CONTROL

The concern in this section is with the modes of control or the constraints placed on bureaucratic decision making by other governmental institutions. We will look at political control of bureaucracy in terms of the relationship between the Cabinet and the line managers, at the financial control established by the budgetary system, at judicial review of administrative decisions, and finally at one of the most significant constraints on the public-sector manager today: the system of collective bargaining.

Control by Cabinet[10]

Bureaucratic power flows from the concentration of various kinds of expertise within the bureaucracy and from the degree of control over the flow of informa-

[10] For a series of articles dealing with this overall question of public-service responsibility see *CPA*, Winter, 1984 (entire issue).

tion to the Cabinet. The bureaucracy influences priority determination and largely dominates policy formulation because it is expected to advise the Cabinet on the basis of the information it possesses. However, while the bureaucracy occupies a position of great importance in the policy process, ultimate political power still rests with the Cabinet and the prime minister. Whether on whim or political exigency, whether wisely or unwisely, the Cabinet and the prime minister can and do periodically choose to disregard bureaucratic advice, even when that advice was requested by the government in the first place.

The actual exercise of this ultimate control by the Cabinet is usually limited to situations where the action demanded by political expedience is not congruent with the course of action indicated by technical or administrative considerations. When this happens, the political advisors to the Cabinet (such as those in the prime minister's office), the party structure, the Cabinet ministers, and the prime minister tend to be in a position of competition *vis-à-vis* the bureaucracy proper. If the prime minister or the Cabinet as a whole should become convinced that the political considerations are more important than the technical, financial, or administrative ones, the regular bureaucrats will, at least for the moment, lose out. This situation of competing advice from the political advisors and the bureaucratic advisors can exist at all stages of the decision-making process, although in many cases it is likely that political and other considerations will in fact coincide. The point that must be emphasized in this regard is simply that the political advisors, particularly in the PMO or among the staff of Cabinet ministers, may function as an alternate source of information, which can place major restrictions on the power of the bureaucracy.

When it comes to the process of management in the public service, the presence of political control is more difficult to demonstrate. Naturally, in the case of policy decisions relating to organization and reorganization of the departmental structure of the bureaucracy, the planning apparatus that includes the Cabinet and the central agencies will supersede the line managers, and political considerations will tend to hold more weight than administrative ones. Nevertheless, the mechanisms of control here tend to be dominated by central-agency types rather than the politicians themselves, so for the most part what appears to be "political" control over the bureaucracy is in fact central-agency control over the line managers in the departments.

Financial Control: The Budgetary Process

Further mechanisms of control over the policy-making role of the Canadian bureaucracy and over the line managers are to be found in the budgetary process.[11] With gradual implementation of a system called Planning, Programming, and Budgeting in the 1960s, the role of the Treasury Board in the determination of spending priorities was greatly enhanced. To the extent that the Treasury Board Secretariat bears much of the responsibility for controlling government spending, this situation can be viewed as an aggrandizement of bureaucratic power, for the Secretariat is, after all, a part of the bureaucracy. On the other hand, if one views the Treasury Board in terms of its formal composition as a committee of the

---

[11] See also chapter 15 for a discussion of the budgetary process and priority determination.

Privy Council, Treasury-Board control over spending priorities can be viewed as placing new restrictions on the priority-setting role of the bureaucracy. Certainly, the power of the individual department and the line manager in some ways has been decreased through the placing of new power in the hands of the more centralized Treasury Board Secretariat, whose role has been further enhanced as the board has taken on more of the aspects of a *board of management.*

The "Public Purse" Additional control over the bureaucracy is exercised through the traditional processes of public finance. According to Norman Ward, there are two basic principles of public finance in Canada. First, the executive should have no money that is not granted to it or otherwise sanctioned by Parliament; and second, that the executive should make no expenditures except those authorized specifically by Parliament.[12] In brief, therefore, the executive branch and its operational arm, the bureaucracy, can only get funds through parliamentary appropriation, and they can only spend those funds for purposes specified by Parliament. The implementation of these two basic principles is facilitated by a complicated set of practices and procedures. First, there must be a budget, which is a clear enunciation of the present financial needs of the government, the plans for the upcoming year, and a general statement of the financial state of the nation. Following reforms made in 1985, the budget statement is provided annually in February or March. (More will be said about the budget and the budget debate in chapter 19.)

The basic premise of the entire system of public finance in Canada is that the public purse strings are held by Parliament. We will discuss the *de facto* limitations on the power of Parliament to control public spending later, when we discuss Parliament and the legislative process. Here it is necessary to describe only the formal process of appropriating public money through the system of *estimates.* Basically, this is a system of appropriation of funds by Parliament to meet the estimated costs of the various governmental programs in the next year.

The Estimates Since the program-review[13] stage of preparing the departmental estimates has been mentioned at several points in our analysis already, the discussion here commences when the program review has been completed and the Treasury Board has set *spending targets* based on expenditure *guidelines* issued by the Cabinet. At this time — usually in late summer — a letter is issued asking the departments to prepare their estimates for the upcoming year. In fact, the various branches and divisions of the department have already been preparing information since the spring in anticipation of the Treasury Board's letter, and by late September the deputy minister (and in some cases the departmental policy committee) reviews the total estimates of the department. In late fall, the minister reviews the departmental estimates and gives them formal approval, usually without making many significant changes. It must be noted that in discussing this process as a series of distinct stages, we distort the true picture; in fact, the deputy minister, the ADMs, the various branch directors and division chiefs, and officials in the treasury-

---

[12] N. Ward, *The Public Purse* (Toronto: University of Toronto Press, 1955), *passim.*

[13] See P.L. Little and C.L. Mitchel, "The Program Budget: Planning and Control for the Public Sector," in Kernaghan and Willms, *Public Administration in Canada: Selected Readings,* pp. 188–195.

board staff are in continuous contact. Often this contact is informal, characterized by a phone call from one person to another, but its effect is to keep the
people involved in the preparation of the estimates aware of what to expect from
the next stage of the process.

Once the estimates have been approved by the minister, they are sent to the
Treasury Board Secretariat, which goes over them in great detail, with an eye to
cutting down on expenses. The concern of the TBS at this point is with economy
and frugality — not with the overall advisability of the various departmental programs that have already been approved in principle. Once again, there will be
considerable interaction between the TBS and individual departments at this stage,
much of it of a bargaining nature.

Having passed the meticulous and penny-pinching staff of the Treasury Board
Secretariat, the estimates are then handed to the Treasury Board itself, whose
responsibility it is to put all the estimates of all the departments in some kind of
perspective. If the spending priorities set at the program-review stage have been
reasonably accurate, and if, in preparing the estimates, the departments have
adhered to the original targets and programs, there should be relatively few
significant changes at this stage. Such changes inevitably produce hurt feelings
and bitterness on the part of the ministers and bureaucrats whose estimates have
been reduced or eliminated. However, because of the almost constant informal
contact among senior bureaucrats in the TBS, the Department of Finance, and
the various other government departments, these changes are almost never completely unanticipated.

Having survived the scrutiny of the Treasury Board, the formal approval of the
Cabinet as a whole is not usually difficult, or of any interest. It is possible at this
stage for a minister whose department has been seriously affected by the Treasury Board's frugality to die in flames before colleagues, although it is unlikely
that they should be very impressed for they are likely to have been equally hard
done by.

After Cabinet approval, the *main estimates* are printed up in a form usually
referred to as *Mains* or the *blue book*, and tabled in the House of Commons. The
mains list the actual votes that ultimately will be passed in Parliament, and also
include supporting details, which give an even more specific breakdown of the
department's estimated expenses for the coming year. In fact, there is no longer
just one blue book; rather, there is a whole series of them, including one for each
major department or agency and two summary volumes in the form of a general
expenditure plan and a detailed summary. The main estimates ultimately become
the *Appropriation Act*; the supporting details are stated merely for the information of
the members of parliament and the general public, and as more detailed guidelines
for the spending of funds by the department.

The estimates for the various departments are then given to an appropriate
standing committee of the House of Commons to be considered in detail. These
committees go over the estimates item by item, calling upon officials of the department whose estimates are being discussed to defend its programs and estimated
expenditures. The committees then report back to the House of Commons, and
the estimates of all the departments are passed through Parliament as one bill

like any other piece of legislation. When this *Supply Bill* has passed through Parliament and has been assented to by the Governor-General, it becomes the Appropriation Act, part of the law of the land.[14]

Spending the Appropriations Once the money has been appropriated by Parliament, it can be spent only by the executive. Parliament does not spend money, it merely appropriates it. The actual spending of money requires an *encumbrance* of funds from the revenue pool of the government of Canada, the *Consolidated Revenue Fund*. The money is encumbered by the Treasury Board to the departments as they need it for specific purposes. The Deputy Minister of Services and Deputy Receiver General for Canada acts as a gatekeeper for the Consolidated Revenue Fund, ensuring that the expenditure for which the money is being encumbered is within the terms of the Appropriation Act, that there are sufficient funds in the fund to meet the cost, and that appropriate vouchers for the goods and services purchased are forthcoming. The function of the Deputy Minister of Services is, in effect, a pre-audit function. He or she is assisted by officers located throughout the public service who are responsible not only for operational audit of the financial affairs of the department to which they are attached, but also for the preparation of the accounts of the departments. While to an increasing extent (because of the recommendations of the Glassco Commission) the internal-audit or operational-audit function is being performed not by treasury officers seconded to the department but by departmental officials themselves, in the case of the smaller departments and agencies of the government of Canada, the Department of Supply and Services still supplies these financial officers on request to perform operational-audit functions. Finally, the Office of the Comptroller General is responsible for developing and overseeing the implementation of sound accounting and operational audit procedures.

When it comes time for the department to spend the money encumbered to it, it must spend it for the exact purposes stated in the Appropriation Act; although, with the approval of the Treasury Board, the department is permitted to deviate somewhat from the more detailed presentation of the estimates in the main estimates. Normally, however, it is expected that the department will closely adhere even to the supporting details of the mains as well as to the votes of the Appropriation Act itself. Of course, all departments are bound by the Appropriation Act and are not permitted to use funds appropriated for one purpose for something else. Furthermore, money voted for a certain purpose is voted for one year only. If the money is not spent by the end of the fiscal year, it reverts or lapses to the Consolidated Revenue Fund.

Additional Supply The discussion up until now has centred on the preparation of the main estimates and the main supply bill, which indeed involves the most important and the most substantial appropriation of public funds. However, there are a few additional kinds of supply that must be mentioned briefly here.

The *supplementary estimates* or *"sups,"* which are intended to meet contingencies unforeseen at the time of the preparation of the main estimates, are voted late in

---

[14] See chapter 19.

the parliamentary session. It is expected that these will not be large, although they seem to increase in amount annually. Further supplementary estimates are introduced just before the close of the fiscal year to look after any additional items not covered by the main or supplementary estimates. These are sometimes voted near the end of the parliamentary session, and as a result they are passed without too much fuss by MPs who want to get on with the summer recess.

Interim supply is passed after the current fiscal year has begun, but before the main estimates are approved. A vote of interim supply merely assumes that the main supply bill will pass successfully, and approves expenditures in amounts such as one-twelfth or one-sixth of the main estimates. This permits the departments to continue to carry out their programs even while Parliament is considering whether to give them the money to do so. An interesting problem would arise if a main supply bill were actually defeated; for, with the longer parliamentary sessions that are frequent today, it is not unusual for the departments to have been voted a significant percentage of the main estimates by the time the main supply bill is actually passed. Such a defeat, however, is highly unlikely, and supply is granted virtually automatically by June 30.

Finally, when Parliament is not in session the government can spend money through the use of *Governor-General's warrants*. These are expected to be used only for emergencies, and are subsequently approved by Parliament in the formal way as part of the next supplementary estimates.

Post Audit   The Auditor General also performs a significant control function. He is an officer of Parliament, not of the government, and is responsible only to Parliament. His salary is set by statute and he can be removed from office only through a joint address by the House of Commons and the Senate. The office was created in 1878, and its functions today are defined in the Financial Administration Act. Basically, the role of the Auditor General is to check up on all expenditures in the public service, to ensure that money has been spent efficiently and according to law, and to bring any matter involving the financial affairs of the government deemed to be relevant to the attention of Parliament. In short, he performs the function of the post-audit of the public accounts.

The basic strength of the Auditor General flows from his power to access of all the government's financial books, and his ability to make public any indiscretions found therein. The report of the Auditor General comes out annually, and is tabled in the House of Commons. The normal procedure at this stage is for the Auditor's report to be handed over immediately to the House of Commons Public Accounts Committee for more detailed study (see Chapter 19.) The basic weakness inherent in the office of the Auditor General is that his staff consists of public servants and not parliamentary officials, like himself. This means that the establishment of the Office of the Auditor General depends on recommendations of the Cabinet and the TBS. There is nothing in law to prevent the government of the day from cutting back on the staff of the Auditor General and in this way weakening his effectiveness as a financial watchdog for Parliament. In fact, however, no government can politically afford to go too far in this regard, for the Auditor General to some extent symbolizes the financial authority of Parliament. Any attempt to limit his independence from the government of the day, although quite legal, might do political damage to the party that so dared. Indeed, over the past several years, the Office of the Auditor General has actually expanded more rapidly than most of the rest of the bureaucracy.

In recent years, following the passage of new legislation in 1977, Auditors General have attempted, with considerable success, to expand their role from a purely financial-audit function to include responsibility for *comprehensive* or *value-for-money* auditing. Comprehensive auditing means, to the Auditor General, the right to consider not merely whether Parliament's appropriations have been spent prudently and in accordance with the estimates, but also to consider whether the executive arm of government has been prudent in the policies it has adopted and whether tax policy is solidly conceived as well as executed.[15] This definition of the Auditor General's watchdog role can be wide-ranging indeed, and has been extended, in recent years, to include such matters as whether the National Energy Policy was well founded and whether the government's oil company, Petro Canada, in acquiring Petrofina gave due regard to the effect of the purchase on the country's balance of payments, the value of the dollar, tax revenues and future capital spending requirements.[16]

Such issues are not merely issues of financial rectitude, but of the wisdom of government policy as well. It is hardly surprising, therefore, that each of the last two governments has been distinctly unenthusiastic about the Auditor General's proclivity to snoop beyond what the government has considered his proper mandate. The government argues that it has been elected to govern, and that its accountability for policy is directly to Parliament and ultimately to the voters of Canada. The Auditor General, by contrast, is unelected, and not directly responsible to the people. The Auditors General argue that they are officers of parliament, appointed to be guardians of the rectitude of public expenditures. This, they argue, must include not merely the efficiency with which funds are spent but also the appropriateness of what they are spent on. The disagreements have become sufficiently rancorous that the courts have been asked to determine the nature of material to which the Auditor shall have access, and have ruled that the Auditor has the right to see documents providing policy advice to Cabinet, but not actual recommendations made to Cabinets by ministers. This presumption of a policy role by the auditor may have very considerable consequences. Sharon Sutherland and Bruce Doern argue, in their study for the Macdonald Commission:

> The new OAG [Office of the Auditor General] is, in essence, an entrenched autonomously led force at the heart of both policy and management in the federal public sector. . . . For, while the OAG has no share in ongoing executive decision-making . . . the new scope of its activity (the inclusion of a review of policy advice and of the revenue budget in its self-ascribed mandate) creates an environment where the parameters for action by a cabinet may be seriously limited.[17]

[15] Sharon L. Sutherland, "On the Audit Trail of the Auditor General: Parliament's Servant 1973–1980," *Canadian Public Administration*, Vol. 23, No. 4 (Winter, 1980); and Sharon Sutherland and Bruce Doern, *Bureaucracy in Canada: Control and Reform* (Ottawa: Royal Commission on the Economic Union, Research Study #43, 1985), particularly pp. 49–51.

[16] See Doern and Sutherland, *op cit*, for further elaboration.

[17] *Ibid.* p. 50

We can anticipate continued tension between the government of the day and Auditors General, since, by its very nature, the watchdog role is bound to be contentious, and since modern Auditors General have adopted a very aggressive approach to the job.

Judicial Safeguards

Judicial control over the Canadian bureaucracy is exercised not with respect to policy decisions or advice from public servants, but rather with respect to administrative jurisdiction and procedures. In the case of most administrative functions, public officials are granted fairly wide discretionary powers with which to carry out their responsibilities. Within the area of discretion granted them by law, public servants enjoy a significant degree of independence from judicial control. However, the courts will review the administrative decisions of public officials to determine whether these decisions were within the jurisdiction granted to the official by law. If the public official has made a discretionary decision that is lacking in good judgement but that is within the jurisdiction granted by law, the courts will take no action.[18] However, if an official makes a decision or takes administrative action beyond his or her competence, or *ultra vires* his or her discretionary powers, the courts will step in to quash the decision. Note that this can occur only with respect to administrative decisions — actual outputs of the political system that originate in the bureaucracy. In the case of policy decisions or advice, the bureaucratic official is formally only making a recommendation to the political decision makers in the process. A policy recommendation has no immediate or necessary impact on citizens, for it does not become a system output, except at a much later stage.

If administrative decisions are judicial or quasi-judicial in nature, the courts will act to control the bureaucracy in another way. Here the courts question not only the jurisdiction of the administrative official or board, but the procedures followed in coming to the decision. Basically, a judicial control over bureaucratic decisions exists if an individual is affected by that decision and if the administrative official or board, in making the decision, has not adhered to the principles of *natural justice*. The principles of natural justice define the standards for fair procedures in coming to decisions that affect the rights and privileges of individuals. The first principle is that no one should be a judge in his or her own cause. In other words, the administrative officials on the board or tribunal making the decision must be impartial and not directly affected themselves by the outcome of the hearing. The second principle is that the individual affected by the decision has a right to be heard. His or her side must be aired and considered by the board before a decision is made. If either of these principles has been ignored by a bureaucratic agency or by an individual bureaucrat in coming to a judicial or quasi-judicial decision, the court will order that the decision be quashed.[19]

It is important to emphasize the nature of judicial remedies as mechanisms of control over the bureaucracy. In the case of many decisions by bureaucratic

[18] See: P.G. Thomas, "Administrative Law Reform: Legal vs Political Controls on Administrative Discretion," *CPA*, Spring 1984.

[19] See chapter 7 for a discussion of the federal court.

agencies or officers, the decisions are not appealable. However, they are *reviewable*, which means that the court, while not empowered to reconsider the case on its substantive merits, is empowered to look at the procedures of the bureaucratic decision. If the court decides that the board, tribunal, or administrative officer either acted *ultra vires* or acted *intra vires* but improperly, the result is that the original decision is nullified or quashed. The problem, particularly where the court quashes a decision because it was taken improperly, is that the tribunal of first instance can go back, implement the correct procedures, and bring down exactly the same decision. Thus judicial review, while ensuring fairness in administrative decisions, does not permit the court actually to *replace* the administrative decision with its own decision in the manner of appeal.

Dissatisfaction with the effectiveness of judicial remedies in curbing abuses of bureaucratic power is growing. Not only are the courts unable to deal with misuses of discretionary power unless the administrative act is also *ultra vires*, but, even in cases where judicial action is appropriate, the backlog of cases means that litigants must often wait years for satisfaction. One solution at the federal level has been to create an explicitly administrative court, the *federal court*, which has jurisdiction to hear appeals from federal boards and tribunals. A partial solution in some of the provinces has been to appoint an *ombudsman*,[20] whose function is to investigate complaints by individuals who feel they have been wronged by a bureaucratic decision. As an independent official of the legislature whose salary is set by statute, the ombudsman has broad powers of access to most public files and a modest staff to aid in investigations. Unlike the courts, the ombudsman can investigate cases where the bureaucratic decision has been *intra vires*, but, in terms of equity, a bad decision. However, the ombudsman has the power only to investigate, to publicize abuses of bureaucratic power, and, in some cases, to initiate legal action, much as a private citizen would. The ombudsman alone cannot order a decision to be quashed. In the final analysis, the ombudsman can only be an effective check on bureaucratic excesses if the bureaucrats themselves respect or fear the office. Much of the work has to be done by phone calls to the official about whom there has been a complaint. The official might agree to reconsider the decision, to change it somewhat, or to rehear the case, and will, at least, offer reasons for the decision. There are ombudsmen in a majority of provinces, but, although the concept was actively considered by the federal government in the 1970s, it is not currently under consideration in Ottawa.

Collective Bargaining

Some amount of control over the decisions of bureaucrats is exercised by agencies and procedures that are themselves a part of the bureaucratic process. This is, of course, a different kind of control from that exercised by the courts, which are institutions outside the bureaucracy itself. Perhaps the subtlest form of this control from within is imposed through recruitment and training, which we discussed earlier with respect to the process of management. However, one of the newer and potentially more important mechanisms of intra-bureaucratic control

[20] See Donald Rowat, *The Ombudsman* (Toronto: University of Toronto Press, 1965).

is the system of collective bargaining, which has continued to evolve in the federal public service.

The Evolution of Collective Bargaining in the Public Service Until 1966, the public servant, as an employee, had very little in the way of true bargaining rights *vis-à-vis* the government-as-employer. The attitude was that the government, being a sovereign employer, could not constitutionally or morally be coerced in any way by the public service unions, or "staff associations" as they were then euphemistically called. This meant essentially that public servants could organize in much the same way that any union in the private sector could, but that their relationship with the government employer was a consultative one, and in no way a bargaining one. In a bargaining relationship, after all, the parties involved each have certain inducements and sanctions with which to threaten or entice the other side into meeting their demands. In private industry, the employer holds the power to raise wages or alter working conditions, and, in the last resort, to lock out the employees. The employees, on the other hand, have the threat of strike action as an ultimate bargaining weapon. In such a situation, each side holds certain powers that enable it to bargain with the other. Up until 1966, therefore, while there were joint councils that facilitated the consultation of the government-as-employer with the staff associations, and while the relationship was filled with good intentions, there was no collective-bargaining relationship because the staff side had no bargaining power.

Because of the unique situation of staff relations in the public service before the current collective-bargaining legislation, a very special kind of quasi-collective bargaining relationship emerged. Given the fact that they had no economic sanctions to bring to bear against the sovereign employer, the staff associations very slowly began to realize that politically — in terms of the number of votes they represented in certain constituencies — they did have a real bargaining power. It was not the direct economic sanction of the labour union, but the subtler political sanction of the pressure group. The demand of the public-service "union" was not "meet our demands or we will strike," but "meet our demands or our members will vote against you in the next election." While this sort of a bargaining relationship is hardly overwhelming, and while it did not in any way give the staff associations the power of labour unions in the private sector, it did permit them to speak with greater authority when making wage demands on the government. Members of parliament in constituencies with large numbers of public servants, particularly in the Ottawa area, were forced to speak for the staff associations; and a failure to adequately support their demands could very well spell a defeat at the polls.

The Current System With the collective-bargaining legislation, the public-service staff associations were given a genuine system of collective bargaining. In 1967, the Public Service Staff Relations Act (PSSRA) established a system of collective bargaining for federal public servants that includes the right to strike. The Act also sets up a Public Service Staff Relations Board (PSSRB), which is responsible for certification of the bargaining agents on the staff side. Excluded from the collective-bargaining system are employees in managerial positions, those acting in confidential, policy-related capacities, part-time and casual workers, and those declared by the government to be "essential workers." Any disputes over exclusionary decisions are settled by the PSSRB, and its decisions are final and binding.

There are at present approximately ninety certified bargaining units in the federal public service, and most of them are affiliated with either the Public Service Alliance of Canada (PSAC) or the Professional Institute of the Public Service (PIPS). As we pointed out earlier in this chapter, the Treasury Board is the bargaining agent for the government in all of its negotiations with the employee associations, although in a few cases the senior managers in the department are given a larger role in the bargaining process.

While generally "terms and conditions of employment and related matters" can be the subject of a collective agreement, there are several matters explicitly excluded from the process by the PSSRA. For instance, because the PSSRA cannot be interpreted so as to interfere with the supremacy of Parliament, any matter that requires legislative implementation is not bargainable, nor are matters dealt with in legislation such as the Public Service Employment Act, the Superannuation Act, the Government Vessels Discipline Act, etc. Perhaps the most objectionable exclusions to the unions are the matters of the "merit system," under the jurisdiction of the Public Service Commission, and matters having to do with the organization of the Government. The former include such things as recruitment, promotions, transfers, discharge for incompetence, layoffs, and pension benefits, and the latter include subjects such as job evaluation and classification, all of which are normally bargainable in the private sector.

As with any collective bargaining system, there is a provision for settlement of disputes. In the case of disputes that arise in the negotiation of a collective agreement, or *interest disputes*, the PSSRA provides for two distinct methods of settlement: *compulsory arbitration* and *conciliation* (with the right to strike). The bargaining agent has the right to decide which route to take, but the decision must be made before bargaining begins, and the union is bound to stick to the method chosen until the settlement is reached.

In the first years of the PSSRA, the tendency was for bargaining agents to opt for the arbitration method of settlement. By this system, either a single arbitrator or a three-person arbitration tribunal is set up by the PSSRB. Both sides present their cases and the arbitrator reaches a decision that is binding on both sides. In recent years, however, the trend has been for more and more of the bargaining units to opt for the conciliation route. Here the PSSRB names a conciliation board or a single conciliator who attempts to assist the parties to come to an agreement that is mutually acceptable. The recommendations of a conciliation board are not binding, however, and if the union is not satisfied, its next step is to strike. It is perhaps a weakness of the system that the bargaining unit is not permitted to switch to compulsory arbitration if conciliation fails. Instead, the employee side must either accept the unsatisfactory conciliation-board finding or go out on strike.

The PSSRA provides for the settlement of grievances as well. Unlike in the private sector, the right to grieve under the PSSRA is extended not only to employees who are excluded by the Act, but also to many matters that do not come within the collective agreement. There are two methods of grievance settlement, each of which applies in a different set of circumstances. In the case of grievances arising out of the interpretation of a collective agreement or out of disciplinary actions that involve severe penalties such as dismissal or financial penalty, the procedure involves four internal hearings up to the deputy-minister level and thence, if no settlement is reached, to adjudication. Adjudicators are appointed from within the PSSRB and their decisions are final and binding. The second type of grievance is that involving the job-evaluation system. This is one of the matters generally excluded from the collective-bargaining system and is generally viewed as a prerogative of the employer in the federal public service. As a result, the grievance is heard by *classification officers* only, and their decisions are not adjudicable.

The *National Joint Council*, which was the major institution of staff relations before the PSSRA, exists today and has become a useful forum for discussion of matters that are not formally bargainable. The NJC is also useful for consultations between the employer and the employee organizations where a service-wide approach is more useful than piecemeal bargaining.

We must now return to our first assumption: that the collective-bargaining relationship in the public service is a form of intra-bureaucratic control. This control exists to the extent that the government employer (the management side) and the government employee (the staff side) have power over each other. Each limits the other's freedom of action because each holds inducements and sanctions with which to convince the other to at least partially meet its demands. The employer in the modern public-service collective-bargaining relationship is the Treasury Board. It is the agency that actually does the horse trading with the staff associations that ends in a compromise collective agreement. The effect of this rather new power relationship is certainly to reduce the power of the line managers. It hinders their ability to motivate their subordinates because the employer authority is vested in the Treasury Board. Let it suffice to say here that the staff associations, which include among their members people who, in the aggregate, are involved in policy making, which still retain the residual political power of a pressure group, and which now possess the right to strike, have gained significant power in the Canadian system.

Management and Control: A Conclusion

We have seen that the most effective mechanisms of control over the bureaucracy as a whole are those related to the budget and financial accountability. While the goal of making the bureaucracy accountable to the political arm of government is noble and an ideal to be sought after with fervour, too much attention to accountability can severely tie the hands of the senior managers and hamper their ability to get the job done. Thus, reforms in this area must proceed on the middle ground. It is necessary to try to develop controls that make the bureaucracy as a whole accountable to the Cabinet, and which at the same time recognize the need to let the managers do their jobs without excessive meddling on the part of the central agencies. To make line bureaucrats more accountable to central-agency bureaucrats does not make the bureaucracy writ large more accountable, and it certainly handcuffs the managers in the departments.

Control over the policy role of the bureaucracy is more problematical. With the exception of certain broad powers exercised by the Cabinet (which may decide to disregard its advisors) or by a vigilant press (which may criticize policy formulation on those occasions when it can penetrate the veil of secrecy), there are very few direct checks over the policy advice provided by bureaucrats. The press, academics, interest groups, the parliamentary Opposition, and even the provincial governments are, to a large extent, prevented from evaluating the policies formulated by federal bureaucrats by the strong control over information and technical expertise possessed by the large numbers of federal policy advisors; moreover, outsiders can only rarely find out what that advice has been. The situation is exacerbated by strong Canadian traditions of administrative secrecy and by the Official Secrets Act. It is clear that the Canadian public is not always well served by this situation; one of the more important reforms in recent years has been the passage of the Freedom of Information Act, which guarantees freer access for the public to the information necessary to criticize the bureaucratic policy makers.

Finally, given the role of the senior bureaucrats as managers of the information generating and disseminating machinery that produces policy advice in Canada, it is possible that one medium of control over the technocrats is a skilled corps of policy managers who possess the standard managerial skills the public sector shares with industry, understanding the ins and outs of the adversarial process of bureaucratic politics, and, finally and most importantly, trained to manage technical information.

We would like to conclude with a note on the general quality of management in the Canadian public service. While public-service managers in both federal and provincial bureaucracies perform all the same functions as private-sector managers, they must do so within the awkward constraints placed upon them by an organization whose *raison d'être* is difficult to define and whose dominant concern turns out to be accountability and control. On top of this, public sector managers must also function as coordinators of expertise in the process of initiation and formulation of public policy — roles largely alien to their counterparts in the private sector.

It is all too easy to decry the lack of efficiency in the public service and to lay the blame at the feet of senior management. Similarly, the media and the management wizards from industry repeatedly offer as a solution the adoption, holus bolus, of the managerial techniques and philosophy of the private sector. We demur! Given the situational constraints, the quality of management in public life in Canada is pretty damn good, and the facile application of private-sector nostrums is no more likely to improve it than would the application of public-sector precepts improve the performance of private-sector managers.[21]

This concludes our discussion of the Canadian bureaucracy. The reader will have to look further into other sources listed in the bibliography for more detailed information about the structures and processes of this country's public service. We have attempted to give a perspective on the bureaucracy in the political process and to demonstrate that, while the bureaucracy is crucial to the process of policy formulation, it is also an important actor in every other aspect of the political process in Canada.

[21] The authors, both of whom will be serving in managerial roles in the public sector at the time this edition is published, must admit to just a teensy weensy conflict of interest in making this statement.

C H A P T E R   1   9

PARLIAMENT

P arliament, the legislative branch of government in Canada, is legally the supreme authority for all matters falling within federal jurisdiction. The legal implications of the constitutional principle of parliamentary supremacy have already been discussed at great length, and there is no need to reiterate them here. In this chapter, our concern is with Parliament's role in the policy process. It will be seen that, while Parliament is legally supreme, it is functionally subordinate in the making of public policy to the executive, consisting of Cabinet and its supporting bureaucracy. Moreover, as we have seen in earlier chapters, the Charter of Rights and Freedoms may place still more legal limitations on the supremacy of Parliament. Thus, today, parliamentary supremacy is in many respects a symbolic expression of the belief that, in our system of government, ultimate political power *should* reside in the elected representatives of the people. But it is also a reflection of the continued commitment of Canadians to the basic value of popular sovereignty, and despite the very real functional limitations on Parliament's ability to be truly "supreme," the institution remains significant both as a symbol and as an important part of the working of democratic government.

The structure of the Canadian legislature is *bicameral*: that is, Parliament consists of two separate legislative bodies, the House of Commons and the Senate. The House of Commons is the elected branch of Parliament and is therefore more important than the Senate, which is an appointed body. The bulk of our analysis of the role of Parliament in the policy process will therefore focus on the House of Commons.

THE FUNCTIONS OF PARLIAMENT
The Policy Function

In chapter 1, we set up a linear descriptive model of the policy process in Canada, which posits policy making as a four-stage process. Generally speaking, Parliament dominates only at the fourth (refinement and legitimation) stage of that process. However, it can and does have some impact at all stages of policy making, and we must comment briefly on that before proceeding to the more detailed discussion of Parliament as a core institution at the policy-refining and formal-output stage.

As an initiator of policy ideas, Parliament has ample opportunity to influence policy decisions. As was pointed out in chapter 1, the basic problem of policy initiation is one of communication. It is necessary to communicate one's policy idea to the Cabinet, which functions as the main priority-setting institution in Canadian government. Parliament functions as a communication link between the public at large and the Cabinet. When people make demands on the political system, they often do so by writing letters or by speaking to a Member of Parliament. This particular input channel was especially important at an early period in Canadian political history, when other channels of access to the political decision makers were not as well developed as they are now. As an input channel today, however, Parliament is in competition with many other institutions, such as interest groups, parties, the media, and the bureaucracy, and most of these other institutions can communicate policy ideas to the Cabinet as well as, if not better than, Parliament. Furthermore, some of the modern techniques, such as survey research, and institutions, such as large departmental field organizations, have permitted the Cabinet and the bureaucracy to go out into the environment of the system and actively seek out or promote new policy ideas. Hence, Parliament's role as a communicator of new policy ideas to the system's priority setters has been much diluted. Parliament can still convey demands to the Cabinet, but there are many other institutions and many other techniques that achieve the same end and can possibly achieve it more effectively.

The MP can also function as policy initiator in a very immediate way by communicating a personal idea directly to the Cabinet. One example of policy initiation by an individual MP was the abolition of capital punishment. The idea was introduced in Parliament originally as a private member's bill, and was subsequently picked up by the Cabinet and re-introduced as government policy. Perhaps the classic example is the inception of an old-age security scheme in Canada. The introduction of that idea in 1927 was largely the work of the Independent Labour Member of Parliament, W. S. Woodsworth. Indeed, in the 1920s and 1930s, Woodsworth used Parliament as an effective platform to prompt Liberal governments into much of the social-welfare legislation that we have today. Occurrences such as these are not frequent. However, a Cabinet decision in 1973 to have all private members' bills examined by the bureaucracy with a view to allowing some that are in line with government priorities to pass may have gone some way to returning at least the potential for influencing policy initiation. Still more recently, procedures introduced by the Mulroney government in response to recommendations of the McGrath Committee on Parliamentary Reform have regularized a system of allowing a limited number of private members' bills to be fully debated and brought to a vote.

In practical terms, an MP's influence on the Cabinet often will depend on the prestige, knowledge, and constituency of the individual involved. For instance, where a course of action being considered by the Cabinet is likely to affect a particular geographic region of Canada, there is some chance that concerted opposition or support by that region's members will influence the Cabinet in setting its priorities. However, the Cabinet will probably have independent sources of information about the attitudes of the people in the affected region, and if the independent information contradicts the position of the MPs, the Cabinet is just as likely to heed the former. Thus, the role of Parliament at the priority-setting stage of policy making depends on the willingness of the Cabinet to be influenced by the MPs, on the availability and substance of competing advice, on the ability of the MPs or groups of MPs to sell their ideas, and on factors, such as regional coalitions formed in caucus.

Policy formulation is the business of the bureaucracy, subject to the control of the cabinet. Parliament's role at this stage is very limited, because of the generally technical and complex nature of the problem of formulating policy alternatives. In terms of expertise and available time, the MP is ill-equipped to contribute much at this stage of policy making.

However, Parliament is the core institution at the refinement stage of the policy process. While it is the legislative drafting branch of the Department of Justice that converts the raw policy, as formulated by the Cabinet and bureaucracy, into a bill, and while the Cabinet Committee on Legislation and House Planning conducts a clause-by-clause review of pending legislation, parliament cleans up and polishes the draft so that it is a workable piece of legislation without unintended and perverse consequences. In the House of Commons, and more specifically in committees, the MPs go over government legislative proposals, tightening up the wording, criticizing any weaknesses, suggesting amendments, and, through public debate, publicizing the inherent advantages and disadvantages of the bill.

Finally, Parliament is one of the institutions involved in the ultimate conversion of government policy to system output. While the formal votes in the House of Commons and the Senate may appear to be merely *pro forma* steps akin to executive proclamation and the Governor-General's assent, this final ratification or rejection of government policy proposals may, in fact, be the most significant function of Parliament. It is true that the number of government proposals actually defeated in Parliament is very small, but this is partially the result of Parliamentary watchfulness, which may have discouraged governments from introducing intemperate legislation in the first place, and of the fact that many a controversial piece of legislation is simply allowed to die on the order paper in the face of significant parliamentary or outside opposition without any government attempt to bring it forward for second or subsequent readings. So it is the ultimate power to reject a government's legislative proposals in a formal vote that is significant as a deterrent, even though its formal exercise has been extremely rare.

Functional Limitations on Parliamentary Supremacy

The functional subordination of Parliament to the Cabinet in policy making has been mentioned previously, but we have yet to say why this is the case. To examine this point, it is necessary to look first at the control exercised by the Cabinet over its own back-benchers, and then consider the Cabinet control exercised over the Opposition MPs, particularly in a minority-government situation.

Party Discipline: Government Control over Government Back-benchers

The control by the prime minister and Cabinet over the government back-benchers is one aspect of what is usually known as party discipline. It is maintained by threat of various sanctions and by various inducements, although it is seldom indeed that the government is forced overtly to impose a sanction or withhold a promise in order to enforce discipline. Usually these powers of the parliamentary leadership are tacitly recognized and accepted by the government MPs so that party discipline is maintained without resort to specific sanctions.

Perhaps the most important single factor facilitating the Cabinet's control over its own back-benchers in the House of Commons is the simple fact that the Cabinet ministers are the parliamentary leaders of the party. There is a natural tendency and willingness in a government MP to accept the control of a prime minister who has been selected as party leader at a convention and who is responsible, to a large extent in this era of leadership politics, for the party's success at the polls. Besides this, the very fact that back-benchers and Cabinet ministers are members of the same political party provides at least limited grounds for a consensus. This point should not be overemphasized, for, as has been pointed out in an earlier chapter, the major Canadian political parties tend not to be heavily ideological and are omnibus or brokerage parties, which attempt to aggregate large numbers of interests, and a fairly wide range of political views. However, while Canadian parties are often fraught with internal disagreements, the obvious fact remains that the government of the day will more likely be able to find agreement among its own back-benchers than among the Opposition members. And, where a majority of MPs are from the government party, the ability to control the government side of the House is, naturally, all that is needed to control Parliament.

The power of dissolution is the basic constitutional control the prime minister possesses over the back-bench MP. According to this constitutional convention, the prime minister has the sole power to advise the Governor General to dissolve Parliament and call an election. In a general election, MPs must put their jobs on the line, and, for most members, this means a tough struggle. Not very many MPs have seats so safe that they can afford to campaign without great energy and large outlays of money, and the typical Canadian federal election will see some 30 to 40 per cent of MPs losing their jobs. Thus, although Parliament has never been dissolved in order to force dissident government back-benchers into line, the fact that most MPs do not enjoy fighting for their jobs probably has some effect on their attitudes to the government's policies. While it would be unwise for a government to call an election to whip its own back-benchers into line — it would show the public that there was a split in the party's ranks, and members of the Cabinet have even more to lose than back-benchers — the threat of dissolution can be very important in controlling the House of Commons in a minority government situation.[1]

A more subtle but very real power of the government to control its own members flows from the control over the party purse strings. Fighting elections today, in the era of television campaigns and Madison Avenue techniques, is an expensive proposition, and an individual candidate who is not a representative of one of the official political parties will be unable to afford the kind of campaign that will ensure a high probability of success, for the public funds that flow to support campaigns waged by individual candidates depend on the candidate having the nomination of a recognized political party. Thus, the prime minister, the Cabinet, and, to a certain extent, the leaders of the opposition parties, can control maverick back-benchers through either explicit or implicit threat of withdrawal of party identification and financial assistance in the next election campaign.

There are non-financial elements of party support in an election that can be almost as important to the MP as assistance from the party treasurer. MPs who "have been good" and supported the government in Parliament will be assured of a visit to their constituencies by one of the party's notables to assist them in their campaigns. In an election campaign the visit to a constituency of the party leader might well enhance the prestige of the local candidate, and hence have an effect on the outcome of that riding's contest. Furthermore, while the party leaders must beware of overtly meddling with the autonomy of the constituency nominating process, if it is known that a sitting member is unlikely to get support from the national level of the party, or if it is made clear that the candidate is not in the good graces of the party leader, the local people might be influenced to ditch the member. Finally, if all else fails, the Canada Elections Act gives to the leader of a political party the right to refuse a candidate the privilege of having the name of the party appear beside his or her name on the ballot. While a constituency association could still choose to nominate such an individual, they would clearly be dissuaded from doing so if their candidate had to be listed as an independent on the ballot. This technique was employed by Robert Stanfield, the leader of the Progressive Conservative Party, in the 1974 election, when he refused to sanction the candidacy of Leonard Jones in Moncton. The local party organization, although split on the issue, selected a new candidate, and Jones, a popular ex-mayor of the city, ran as an independent. In that case, the sanction was not wholly effective, since Jones still won the seat, but, deprived of caucus membership, his power in Ottawa was virtually non-existent and he did not run in the subsequent election.

Expulsion from the party caucus is another technique of control that can be exercised by the leadership of a parliamentary party if a maverick MP gives trouble. The case of Ralph Cowan, a Liberal member from Toronto during the 1960s, is a good example. By constantly levelling bitter criticisms at the Liberal government, Cowan became such an embarrassment to the party that he was finally expelled from the caucus. This meant that he was not informed of the party's plans and policies, and thus had to sit as a virtual independent in the House of Commons.

---

[1] We will provide a more detailed description of minority government later.

When the next election was called, Cowan tried to get the Liberal nomination in his constituency again and failed. (Mr. Cowan ran instead as an independent and was defeated.) However, while it is possible to use the rather drastic measure of expulsion from caucus in the case of a single MP, this technique cannot be used to control the opposition of large numbers of government MPs, for the simple reason that it publicizes the party's internal disunity and could, if party standings are close in the House, result in the government's defeat.

The major inducement available to a government to control its back-benchers is the promise that the well-behaved and efficient member may be promoted to the Cabinet, or at least to a temporary sojourn as parliamentary assistant to a minister. Since these positions bestow both income and prestige, potential dissidents may consider them sufficiently desirable incentives for toeing the line. The converse of this, however, is that the offer of a Cabinet post or other favours controlled by the party leader can sometimes induce a disgruntled back-bencher to switch parties. Not surprisingly, members who have been induced into crossing the floor of the House are usually rejected by their constituents in the next general election.

Party discipline is similarly applied in the relationship of the Opposition leaders to their back-benchers. The situation varies from party to party, but, with the exception of the power of dissolution, the sanctions and inducements available to the government to control its back-benchers are also available to the leaders of Opposition parties. For instance, the hope for a Cabinet post if and when the Opposition party comes to power can keep dissident Opposition back-benchers in line. But, while party discipline is a factor in the relationship of the leaders of the Opposition parties to their back-benchers, it is not as important here as it is for the government party. The leaders of the Opposition party can afford to tolerate a higher degree of dissension and disagreement among their MPs because the fate of a government does not hang in the balance; if a few Opposition back-benchers split with the leaders of the party "on division" (a formal vote in the House of Commons), the result will be little more than embarrassment for the Opposition leader. Furthermore, when criticizing the government, an Opposition MP can oppose in a number of ways. As long as the MP is against the policy of the government, the leaders of the Opposition will generally permit some deviation from the party line.

The primary focus of the analysis thus far has been on the relationship of the government to the government back-benchers, for in a majority government situation, the basic problem of maintaining control over the House of Commons is co-extensive with the problem of government party discipline. If the Cabinet in a majority-government situation can control its own back-benchers, it can stay in power. In fact, there has never been a case of a majority government's defeat in Canada by a vote in the House of Commons, and the likelihood of that eventuality in the future is virtually nil. As a Liberal back-bencher from Toronto was quoted as saying, "We're on call sometimes fourteen or sixteen hours a day just to support legislation that usually we didn't have any part in framing and sometimes don't even particularly like."

Government Control over the Parliamentary Opposition   In a majority-government situation, the basic strengths and weaknesses of the Opposition parties in Parliament are determined primarily by the procedures of the House of Commons. Since they are never going to be able to outvote the government on any policy proposal, the Opposition parties must content themselves with using more subtle techniques to attempt to influence policy.

The basic power of the Opposition in the House of Commons stems from its ability to control time through debate. The House rules of procedure are founded on a balance between two conflicting principles of parliamentary democracy. The first is that the government should be able to get on with the business of governing in an efficient and expeditious fashion, and the second is that the Opposition should have ample time to criticize the government's proposals. In other words, the Opposition should be able to oppose, but not to the extreme of obstructionism, and the government should be able to get its programs through the House of Commons efficiently, but not without permitting thorough and often tiresome debate.

Current House of Commons procedures are such that if every Opposition member were to speak as long as the rules permitted on every stage of the debate, most legislation would be debated almost endlessly. Given this situation, the Opposition, although unable to vote down the government's legislation, could achieve the same end by the technique of filibuster, or endless debate. However, in order to prevent filibustering, the procedures of the House of Commons have always provided for closure, which is a counter-technique whereby the government party, with the aid of the Speaker, can unilaterally terminate a debate. While these techniques have long been a part of the rules of debate in the House, they have not often been used; it is bad politically for the Opposition to filibuster and be branded obstructionist, or for the government to apply closure and be branded dictatorial or heavy-handed. In practice, the government will usually make deals with the Opposition regarding the specifics of the legislation being debated. In return for a minor change in the legislation, the Opposition parties will often agree to limit their criticism to a few spokespeople for the party, and thus speed up the passage of the bill in question. The government will seldom agree to a change in the substance of legislation in return for this kind of agreement, and this fact is generally respected by the Opposition parties.

In the spring of 1969, a fundamental change in the Standing Orders (SO) of the House of Commons was passed after long debate, and, ultimately, only after the government was forced to invoke closure. The point of contention at that time was SO 75(c), which provides for unilateral limitation of debate at each stage of the passage of a bill through the house. If the government cannot achieve the agreement of all parties or at least of a majority of the parties in setting time limits for debate, it is permitted unilaterally to impose the desired time limits. Initially it was feared that this would take away the fundamental source of opposition influence in the House of Commons, the control of time. However, the extensive use of SO 75(c) by a government would be a very unpopular tactic with the public, for its effect is to gag the Opposition almost as effectively as closure. It is still far better for both the government and the Opposition to seek some sort of mutually acceptable agreement on the limitation of debate. Hence, while procedurally the balance may have shifted from the Opposition to the government, actual practice indicates that the government-Opposition relationship has not substantially altered as a result of the passage of SO 75(c).

The great flaw in the argument that the Opposition can influence policy through control over parliamentary time is that this power is a negative one. It is indeed possible to stall the government, and it is possible even to influence the government to make minor changes in its legislation, but if the government is committed to a piece of legislation, the substance of that legislation is non-negotiable. Furthermore, the government can usually stand firm even on the minor demands of the Opposition if it chooses, and the Opposition can merely balk temporarily.

The other technique of government that can be employed to enhance its bargaining power *vis-à-vis* control of time in the House is the legislative red herring. Here the government puts contentious legislation, to which it is only mildy committed, on the order paper, along with less contentious legislation, to which it is committed, so that the government House leader has something to give away to the Opposition. The theory is that the contentious legislation draws the fire of the Opposition parties, and the government can agree to withdraw it in return for a promise of easy passage for other government proposals, which, while less contentious, are more important to the prime minister and the Cabinet. This tactic can also be used at later stages of the legislative process, where clever drafting can see to it that there are attackable but also non-essential red-herring clauses deliberately written into government bills. This allows the Opposition, or, conceivably, government back-benchers, to feel they are having an impact without compromising the overall integrity of a piece of legislation. The only limit to this sort of tactic is the savvy of the Opposition House leaders, who should be aware that their opposite numbers are not above such puckish pranks.

Other than its control over the time to be used in the passage of government legislation, the Opposition has only one fundamental strength in attempting to influence the government. This is the traditional power to criticize publicly the government's policy proposals. In debates in the House of Commons, and increasingly in the lobby of Parliament before the television cameras,[2] the Opposition MPs do their very best to make the government's policies appear foolhardy, irresponsible, dangerous, opportunistic, or just plain silly. The arguments they present to back this up are designed to convince the voting public that a new government should be put in power at the earliest opportunity. Unfortunately, the great weakness of the Opposition parties in endeavouring to convince the public that the government policy is bad is — once again — their lack of information and expertise. By the time the Opposition parties are involved in the policy

---

[2] Although the debates in the House are now televised in their entirety, very few television stations are willing to bump their own programming to pick up the Commons broadcasts. In fact, a few stations broadcast taped versions of the Oral Question Period, and special events such as the budget speech, while cable services often devote one channel to House of Commons debates. But for the most part, very few Canadians actually watch Parliament on television. While of interest to political scientists and the relatives or friends of the MPs, for the most part the goings-on of the Canadian House of Commons cannot match the ratings of *Hockey Night in Canada* or the latest sitcom or cops-and-robbers show.

process, the legislation they are considering has usually been the object of intensive research by innumerable experts in task forces, royal commissions, interdepartmental committees, government departments, and central agencies — all of which have probably taken into account the recommendations of interest groups and other private institutions. While the Freedom of Information Act has increased the amount of technical information available to Opposition MPs, the multiple demands on MPs' time, make it very unlikely that they will be able effectively to analyze a greatly increased amount of technical information. Thus, the likelihood is still slim that a handful of MPs, with little time to spare for even cursory research, will ever be able to add much substantial criticism to such heavily studied proposals.

Finally, in the context of what we said in chapter 16 about executive federalism, the MP is effectively excluded from one of the key arenas of policy making in Canada, federal-provincial relations. So many of the critical priority decisions in our system are taken behind closed doors by senior Cabinet ministers and their top hired hands from the bureaucracy that the MP is almost completely shut out of this level of the process. As Robert Stanfield has said: "The frustrations of Members of Parliament are increased by federal-provincial deals, agreements and resulting legislation which confront Parliament as *faits accomplis.* There may be no way to avoid this in contemporary Canada, but federal-provincial arrangements have significantly reduced the role of Parliament."[3]

Thus, while the Opposition can criticize government policy both publicly and in the House, the impact of this criticism is not likely to be great. Empowered and expected to criticize the government, the Opposition in the House of Commons is functionally disqualified from doing so through its lack of information and expertise and through its exclusion from the strategic forums of policy decision making in the cabinet and in the intergovernmental committees. The really significant arguments will have been made and met already by competing experts in the various institutions vested with the responsibility for advising the government, and these arguments may never see the light of day.

Minority Government   The relationship of the Cabinet to Parliament is significantly altered when there is a minority-government situation in the House of Commons. Minority government occurs when the government party does not have a majority of the seats in the House of Commons; to stay in power, it must at all times be able to secure the support of some members of other parties. The government, in this case, is usually formed by whichever of the major parties holds a plurality of seats, although it is conceivable that a party standing second in number of seats could form the government, as happened in Ontario in 1985. The third party or parties hold the balance of power in the House, and can choose either to defeat the government by voting against it, or to maintain the government by siding with it. The government can often be sustained at length in this situation.

---

[3] Robert Stanfield, "The Legislative Process: Myths and Realities," in W.A.W. Neilson and J.C. MacPherson, eds., *The Legislative Process in Canada: The Need for Reform* (Toronto: Butterworths, 1978), pp. 44–45.

The Liberals have been particularly successful in maintaining minority governments, most notably from 1963 to 1968 and again from 1972 to 1974, when they managed to stay in power with little difficulty. From 1963 to 1968, the minority Liberal government needed only a few Opposition votes to retain control of the House of Commons, and, with thirty to fifty seats in the hands of the NDP, Ralliement créditiste, and Social Credit, it was usually a simple matter to find them. The real strength of the Liberal government during this period was that it stood pretty much in the middle on most issues, with the NDP and Créditistes taking positions to the left and right of the government respectively. Virtually all of the government's policy proposals were opposed by the Conservative official Opposition "on principle," and by one or the other of the Créditistes or the NDP. However, the two minor parties were never able to vote on the same side because of their radically different points of view, and also because, through much of that period, the third-party MPs feared an election at least as much as the Liberals did.

In the period from 1972 to 1974, the Liberals again formed a minority government and successfully stayed in power by consistently acquiring support from the NDP. They were eventually defeated in a vote of confidence when the NDP finally abandoned them, but, in the subsequent election, the Liberals were swept to power with a majority, and the ranks of the NDP were seriously depleted, confirming a fear of third-party MPs that the forcing of elections in such circumstances could well cost them their seats.

The lesson of these two examples is not only that the problem of controlling the House of Commons in a minority-government situation is much more complicated and difficult than it is in the majority situation, but that it is still quite possible to govern if some adjustments are made. From 1972 to 1974, for example, it was common practice for Cabinet ministers to consult Opposition spokespeople before bringing bills forward, and ministers could be certain that they would have great difficulty in getting their bills on the Order Paper at all if they could not convince their Cabinet colleagues and the prime minister that sufficient discussions had taken place with the Opposition to assure passage of the legislation. Meetings between government and opposition House leaders, weekly events in any case, became much more frequent, and the views of the opposition House leaders were given much more weight both in House scheduling and in Cabinet deliberations. With such efforts, a minority government can be made to work very successfully.

If the 1972–1974 parliament provides us with an example of a successful minority government, the 1979–1980 one demonstrates how fragile a minority can be if not properly managed. Prime Minister Joe Clark took the approach that he would govern "as though he had a majority," likely in the belief that, if defeated, his party would be returned with a majority, and likely in the belief that the Liberals, preoccupied with the initial labour pains of a leadership convention to replace Pierre Trudeau, would not permit the Tory government to fall. The result was that the Tories introduced a stringent budget, refused to accede to any of the demands of the other parties, and were defeated on an NDP non-confidence motion. Trudeau rose from the ashes, withdrew his resignation as leader of the party, and received a majority government from the same electorate that had turfed him out less than a year previously. The lesson of the Clark interlude is that minority government can work *only* if the prime minister is willing to seek compromise with the Opposition parties. Moreover, with the demise of the Ralliement créditiste in the 1980 election, another problem has been added for the plurality party in the minority situation, for we have returned to a basic three-party system, which means that the opportunities for government-Opposition deals to hold off defeat in the House are somewhat reduced for minority governments in the future.

In the spring of 1968, a constitutional issue arose and was settled in a manner that has at least the potential of altering the status of minority governments. The Liberal government was defeated, quite by accident, because of a very high rate of absenteeism on the part of the government back-benchers. The vote had been on the third reading of an important piece of financial legislation, and such a defeat of an important government bill would normally have meant the resignation of the government and an immediate election. At this time, the Liberals were embroiled in a leadership campaign, and the Opposition parties were not prepared to fight an election either. The solution was for the government to introduce a motion of confidence in itself at the next sitting of the House, essentially asking the House of Commons if it really wanted an immediate election. The government was given a vote of confidence by a majority of the House and was permitted to stay in power. The significance of this is that, whereas previously a minority government could force unpalatable legislation on the Opposition by threat of election, now it is at least possible to argue that the legislation can be defeated without forcing the resignation of the government.

In fact, during the 1972–1974 minority-government period, the Liberal government lost a total of eight recorded votes, and only the vote in May 1974, which precipitated the election, was viewed as indicating a want of confidence in the government. In assessing the historical evolution of the confidence convention, the Special Committee on the Reform of the House of Commons (the McGrath Committee) concluded that clearly not every vote involves confidence, and that governments in future should specify explicitly which votes are to be considered confidence matters.[4]

To conclude this section, it can be re-emphasized that, while there is a potential for greater policy-making power in the hands of the Opposition in the situation of minority government, there still remain severe limitations on the ability of the opposition to exercise this power. First, the fact remains that the Opposition does not have the same access to expert advice as does the Cabinet, and cannot therefore deal as meaningfully with policy issues. Second, procedure in the House of Commons is such that any control exercised by the Opposition is largely negative in nature. Third, as we pointed out, the existing alignment of political parties in Canada militates against concerted Opposition effort. The Opposition parties are often too divided among themselves to unite to defeat the government

---

[4] *Report of the Special Committee on Reform of the House of Commons* (hereafter referred to as the McGrath Committee) (Ottawa: June 1985), pp. 5–10.

in a minority situation. Finally, majority government has become a norm in our system of government, and, in spite of its prevalence, a minority situation is always viewed as atypical and merely temporary. In fact, the 1965 election called by the Liberal minority government was fought in part on the issue of a return to majority government, although in that case the electorate was not convinced.

Government Party Caucus[5] It has been seen that party discipline prevents the government MP from either voting against the government on division or from actively criticizing government policy in debates in the House of Commons. The government MP is alleged to have a say in the policies of the government in the caucus, where, it is traditionally held, the MP can influence policy through concerted criticism and articulate dissent. Caucus consists of all the supporters of a political party in the House of Commons, and is intended to establish a communication link between the party leaders and the rank and file. While all parties have a caucus, the one that is most potentially significant in the policy process is that of the government. The meetings of government caucus occur weekly while the House is sitting; they are attended by the Cabinet ministers, and they are held in camera. The tradition of caucus procedure is that decisions are not made by a formal vote, but rather that a consensus is achieved through dialogue and a willingness to seek mutually satisfactory agreement. Because the meetings are held in camera, the MPs can speak their minds freely, with no fear of endangering the image of party unity.

When there is back-bench solidarity in caucus, it is possible for the members to stall or even completely arrest legislative proposals put forward by the Cabinet, but this happens very seldom. The odds that a group as diverse in its interests as the caucus will ever be unanimous in opposition to the Cabinet are very slight. For the most part, the Cabinet can bank on divergencies of opinion among the back-benchers in caucus being at least as wide as the gulf between the Cabinet and the rank and file. The basic weakness of the caucus, however, stems from its relative lack of information. The minister who is proposing and defending a given policy in caucus has a fund of facts and figures from which to draw, while the MP with limited research facilities and limited personal expertise cannot compete with the vast array of expert advice of the minister.

A secondary argument about the caucus' utility as a policy organ of the party posits the role of the MP as a representative of interests. The argument is that the Cabinet can test its legislative proposals by submitting them for the consideration of a representative body. In most cases today, however, the MP is not as well equipped as the prime minister and the political advisors to speak authoritatively about the wishes of Canadians and the feasibility, in political terms, of any particular policy proposal. Again, the problem is not so much that the articulation of interests has been avowedly taken away from Parliament or, more specifically, from

---

[5] A thorough analysis of the role of caucus, with particular emphasis on regional representation, may be found in Paul G. Thomas, "The Role of National Party Caucuses," in Peter Aucoin, ed., *Party Government and Regional Representation in Canada* (Ottawa: Royal Commission on the Economic Union, Research Report #36, Toronto: University of Toronto Press, 1985).

the caucus, but that other institutions, such as the bureaucracy and the central-ized political advisory bodies, are competing with the MP in the performance of this function.

After a great deal of criticism from back-benchers, a new set of ground rules for caucus procedure and a major reorganization of the federal Liberal caucus itself was approved by the Cabinet and introduced in the fall of 1969. Basically, those rules bound the ministers to introduce all legislative proposals in caucus before introducing them in the House. Previously, it had been a fairly common practice to discuss the policy proposals in caucus after the legislation had actu-ally been introduced and the government had already been publicly committed to it. The Mulroney government, with its enormous majority, has also had to institute procedures to ensure that back-benchers do not become too discontent. As with the previous administration, the Conservative government has instituted a system of caucus committees that attempts to regularize the role of the back-bench MP in the policy process. While there has been little to suggest that the new set-up has made the caucus any more effective as an organ for changing the government's mind about policy proposals, at least the government back-benchers are now the first to know when the Cabinet is about to introduce a policy.

In an attempt to permit a degree of specialization in caucus deliberations, the same 1969 reorganization also divided the Liberal caucus into functional sub-committees roughly paralleling the standing committees of the house itself. A similar system was subsequently adopted by the other parties, although, in the case of the NDP, because of smaller numbers, the procedure does not have to be as formalized. Each of these sub-committees of the caucus is given some research assistance to enable it to develop a measure of expertise in a particular area of concern. While this is generally a good idea, the fact remains that one or two researchers working on a given policy area will not enable a caucus sub-committee to compete with a minister who has an entire government department to provide research assistance. While these changes will make the discussion in caucus marginally more meaningful, they do not alter fundamentally the relationship between the caucus and the Cabinet in the policy process.

Basically, then, the caucus is neither sufficiently united nor sufficiently equipped with expertise and research personnel to effectively intitiate substantive changes in government policy proposals. New freedom-of-information legislation might be expected to result in a somewhat stronger policy role for caucus, for back-bench MPs are hampered by the same problems as the public in access to relevant data. However, even the most liberal of freedom-of-information provisions will not ensure that caucus or the public gets information as early as does the Cabinet. Since the timeliness of data has as much to do with its utility in the policy process as have its quality and quantity, the relative power of caucus and Cabinet is unlikely to be changed by any freedom-of-information stipulations. More and more, then, the function of the caucus is to assist the government in scheduling the parliamentary speeches of its members, and to inform them what to expect in the upcoming parliamentary week.

The General Audit Function[6]

Perhaps, because of the functional limitations on the role of the Parliament in the policy process, the most important function of Parliament today is what we might call the general audit function. This is not a financial audit, although, through the Public Accounts Committee, Parliament does, in a sense, audit the financial affairs of the government. Rather, the general audit function of the Canadian parliament involves broadly based public criticism of the total record of the government. This process goes on almost constantly, and brings to the attention of the press and the public many of the shortcomings and potential shortcomings of the government of the day. Because of party discipline and loyalty, the general audit of the overall record of the government is performed primarily by the Opposition parties and not by the government back-benchers. Furthermore, the focus of this kind of criticism is not specific policy proposals but the state of the nation. While the general audit of the government's record goes on at all stages of government legislation, the bulk of such criticism comes out through various procedural devices and special debates, which occur intermittently during each parliamentary session. Each of these deserves more detailed mention.

The Throne Speech Debate   The Standing Orders of the House of Commons provide for a debate on the Address in Reply to Her Excellency's Speech. The Speech from the Throne is prepared by the closest advisors to the prime minister and read by the Governor General to a joint sitting of the House of Commons and the Senate. In this speech, which is delivered at the opening of Parliament, there is a review of the state of the nation and a statement of the legislative program of the government in the coming session. Eight days are set aside for Opposition criticism and comment on the record of the government, and on these days the normal rules of relevance that apply in debates in the House are suspended. Back-bench members have the opportunity to speak their minds on anything that has been bothering them or any matter of special concern to their constituents, while government front-benchers may use the occasion to defend aspects of government policy. The tendency is for the back-benchers to make special pleas for local needs and interests, and for the Opposition front-benchers to use the debate to introduce motions of non-confidence in the government. The subject matter of the Throne Speech Debate, while varied, does not usually involve specific policy proposals of the government, but tends, rather, to be devoted to broad criticisms and defences of the record. To the extent that the speeches of the various MPs are reported in their home newspapers, this debate is helpful in showing the voters that their MP in Ottawa is working on their behalf. Similarly, to the extent that the front-bench speeches of the Opposition parties are reported in the news media, the throne speech debate functions to publicize the real and imagined shortcomings of the government as seen through Opposition eyes.

Opposition Days   A total of twenty-five days, spread over three separate supply periods, is allotted to the Opposition. On these allotted days, called "Opposition days,'' Opposition motions take precedence over government business, and debates on the motions are limited to twenty minutes per speaker, with the exception of the mover and seconder. The function of these allotted days was traditionally to permit the Opposition ample opportunity to criticize the government's spending policy. However today the debates on these days cover a wide range of issues and constitute an important part of the general audit function of Parliament. These debates force the government to defend publicly its policies against tough Opposition criticism, and in fact, normally, six of these Opposition days actually end in votes of non-confidence.

The Budget Debate This is the second free-for-all debate that occurs during the parliamentary year (the first is the Throne Speech Debate). During the budget debate, the back-benchers are permitted to put on the record their own comments on the government's overall financial policy for the benefit of their constituents and the nation. The budget debate begins after the Minister of Finance has brought down the budget in the House of Commons, and it lasts for six days. As with the Throne Speech Debate, the relevancy rule for speeches is relaxed and MPs can wander fairly far afield in seeking to embarrass the government or to make themselves look good, although they are encouraged to speak to the ways-and-means proposals set down in the budget.

Urgent Business Standing Order 30 of the House of Commons provides for a motion to adjourn the House ''for the purpose of discussing a specific and important matter requiring urgent consideration.'' If a matter has arisen suddenly and is not likely to be brought before the House of Commons in any other way, and if it is not a purely administrative matter, this standing order permits a special debate to consider it immediately. The Speaker is given final say as to whether the matter is urgent and whether it is a matter for consideration under SO 30. If the speaker decides that the matter is deserving of further consideration, the motion to adjourn is held over until the evening sitting of the House, at which time the matter is debated. There is no formal time limit on this form of debate, although the Speaker can declare the motion to adjourn carried when he or she ''is satisfied that the debate has been concluded,'' and can forthwith adjourn the House until the next day.

A time limit of twenty minutes is placed on speeches in an SO 30 debate. While such debates are not granted frequently, we have had more and more of them since the 1969 rules revisions. Basically, these debates permit the Opposition to raise issues with which the government is not dealing in the House, and to make public their opinion that the government should be doing something. While an SO 30 debate will not be granted to discuss something the government has already done but with which the Opposition disagrees, it is an important means for pointing out something the government should be doing but is not. Moreover, it is not necessary that the Speaker grant the request for a debate in order for SO 30 to serve its purpose. Simply by requesting a debate, the Opposition can suggest that something is amiss and requires attention.

Another procedural device that has been inserted in the standing orders recently is a provision, SO 21, which allows members to make a 60-second statement immediately before question period. As with SO 30 motions, this device functions to allow back-bench MPs to put a point of view on the record or get something off their chest with a minimum of disruption to the routine business of the House of Commons.

The Question Period   The question period provides the most interesting and lively interchange between ministers and Opposition members in the daily routine of the House of Commons. The question period is covered most closely by the press gallery and in nightly television news clips. In the public eye, it is likely that the question period is viewed as the most important opportunity for the Opposition to attack the government. Any back-bencher, including those on the government side of the House, can ask a question of a minister, but, because of party discipline, because the government back-bencher can usually get the information wanted without a formal question, and because the Speaker traditionally recognizes Opposition members more often than government members, the question period has become a time almost exclusively for Opposition questions.

Questions simply seeking information from a minister of the Crown are normally written down and placed on the Order Paper. The answers to such written questions are, in turn, handed to the Clerk of the House, and subsequently printed in Hansard. The function of this form of question is to assist MPs in gathering information relevant to their interests and those of their constituents. However, in some cases the Opposition will ask questions simply to get on the record information that might be embarrassing to the government in the future. Sometimes, if the answer is potentially embarrassing, an Opposition member will ask for an oral answer. Oral answers are requested by placing an asterisk beside the written question. No member may have more than three such questions on the Order Paper at the same time.

More important, however, than either the written question or the starred questions, are those asked during the daily forty-five minute oral question period. Its purpose is to permit a member to ask a minister questions on matters of urgency, or questions that should be answered immediately rather than placed on the Order Paper. The Speaker is formally empowered to direct that an oral question is not urgent and therefore should be placed on the Order Paper, although, in practice, this stipulation is seldom invoked. Generally, the Oral Question Period, particularly since it is that part of the parliamentary day that is usually seen on our television sets and reported in the press, is an opportunity for the Opposition to ask questions that could potentially embarrass the government. The question must be very carefully phrased, in order to force the minister to answer it on the Opposition's terms, for there is no debate permitted during the question period. Sometimes a member will receive the permission of the Speaker to ask a "supplementary" question if the minister has evaded the point of the main question, although even then it is difficult to pin down the minister if that minister is determined to be evasive. One of the interesting features of the Oral Question Period is the seemingly random banter that is carried on by members who have not been recognized by the speaker. Such heckling and wisecracking, which is often reported verbatim in Hansard, provides some opportunity for back-benchers on both sides of the House to put a few comments on the record on behalf of their side. What usually ensues is a verbal fencing match, with Opposition members sparring with the ministers, attempting to bait them into saying something that will embarrass the government. The minister must keep cool and not be goaded into saying anything more than is necessary to provide factual information or, as is often the case, to gracefully evade the question.

A member who is not satisfied with the answer to a question may serve notice of an intention to raise the matter "on the adjournment" of the House. This procedure, often referred to as the "late show," provides for a thirty-minute debate at the termination of the daily sitting, wherein up to three members are recognized by the Speaker and are given seven minutes each to speak. Questions asked on the adjournment are more important in Britain than in Canada, but they provide an opportunity to debate a question that would not be debatable in the Oral Question Period. Generally, adjournment debates are simply another opportunity for the Opposition members to attempt to embarrass the government, and for all members to raise questions involving the interests of their particular constituencies or regions.

Questions in the House thus perform two functions. First, they can provide the MP with information. Second, they can give the Opposition MPs an opportunity to expose the shortcomings of the government. However, the limitations on questions as a device for parliamentary criticism of the government are many. In the first place, the minister may refuse to answer the question on the grounds that a government policy statement is forthcoming, or that to answer would be a breach of national security. Second, in the case of questions on the Order Paper, the minister can take a long time to answer the question, or may even choose not to answer at all. At the end of each session of Parliament, there is always a long list of questions on the Order Paper that have not been answered, and that probably never will be answered. Finally, the minister can simply refuse to answer the question, even in the Oral Question Period. There is nothing that compels a minister to answer parliamentary questions, although for political reasons a minister cannot afford to treat Parliament with indifference or disdain. Furthermore, unanswered questions get asked over and over again, until either an answer is obtained or the public is made aware of the fact that a minister is covering up, withholding information from the Canadian people.

Perhaps the most important limitation of the Question Period as a tool to facilitate the general audit function of Parliament is the simple fact that most of the exchanges that occur between Opposition members and ministers deteriorate to mere banter. Often this is a relatively friendly session of wisecracks and in jokes, which does not become elevated to the discussion of any matters of substance. The questions asked are loaded, and the answers given are usually evasive and designed to defuse the question rather than to answer it. Once in a while the question period provides truly bitter exchanges between members, with much name-calling by the principals and jeering by the rest. Sometimes such an exchange causes a minister to blurt out information the government would have preferred to keep quiet or to appear in a bad light because he or she is angry.

Thus, while at times the Question Period does not accomplish anything of substance, it functions to keep the government alert. Corruption in high places is sometimes uncovered through the Opposition's use of the Question Period, and the threat of such public exposure perhaps serves as a conscience for the government. Despite its limitations, therefore, the Question Period remains one of parliament's most important procedural devices for criticizing the Cabinet and for auditing the record of the government.

Opportunity for broad criticism of government policy comes up during the proceedings on public bills and at almost all stages of parliamentary debate, but on these occasions the debate is usually restricted to the specific legislation being considered. In other words, the Speaker will enforce the relevancy requirement for all speeches at all stages in the normal process of passing public bills. Thus, the best opportunity for broadly criticizing the Cabinet and publicly auditing the government's record occurs in the various special debates and in the Question Period. The effectiveness of the Opposition in Parliament as an auditor of the record of the government is lessened by that lack of information and expertise that is the fundamental weakness of the MP in the policy process. Nevertheless, there is still an important function to be performed here, and it is hoped that, with the addition of research assistants in the caucus research offices of the various parties, through other means such as the "Parliamentary Internship" program, whereby young university graduates serve for one year as assistants to individual MPs, and with the much-broadened forum provided by the televising of Parliament, the MP can remain an effective political auditor even though he or she cannot be a particularly effective policy maker.

The Representative Function: The MP and the Constituency

It has been seen that Parliament as an institution and individual MPs as actors in that institution are functionally disqualified from having a substantive impact on government policy decisions. The primary policy role of Parliament is to refine and polish government policy and not to set priorities or formulate policy outputs. Because of this limitation on Parliament's policy role, we hypothesize that the most important aspects of the MP's representative role must be limited to non-policy matters. The MP today is acting more and more as a channel through which the individual constituent can register and seek redress for grievances. The types of problems being dealt with by MPs do not require large-scale policy decisions in order to effect a remedy; they involve inequities in the application of existing policies to individual cases, which can be remedied by specific administrative action. The redress of many individual grievances can be achieved through simple means such as a telephone call to the minister or public official involved, or, if that should fail, through a question in the House of Commons, which has the effect of publicizing an injustice or inequity being perpetrated by the administration. This function of the MP is like that of an ombudsman. Because the MP has some official status in Ottawa, and because of the power to publicly assert the case in Parliament, the MP is in a good position to act as an ombudsman for individual constituents, or at least for those constituents who have the initiative to request assistance. The ombudsman function of the MP is carried out in a non-partisan context. MPs, in other words, represent all their constituents, and not just those who voted for them or for their parties.

This same concern with the inequities and injustices inevitably committed by large government administrations probably also affects the individual MP's role in the policy-refining stage of the policy process, where Parliament can and does take a positive and active role. At this stage, administrative consequences missed by the Cabinet and the bureaucracy are sometimes seen by Parliament. Because of a familiarity with the sorts of problems created by carelessly drafted legislation, the MP can attempt to minimize the number of grievances likely to arise from the administration of an act while it is at the refining stage of the policy process. Thus, the MP represents the interests of individual constituents not only in seeking to redress grievances, but also in attempting to prevent their occurrence.

The ombudsman function of the MP is important to the system, for it creates support for the system among people who might otherwise feel that they have no access to the authorities. While many MPs still feel that their most important role is to represent the interests of their constituencies, their regions, or the country as a whole in the policy process, it is unlikely that back-bench MPs will ever again be able to take a very positive policy role. However, as long as the MP remains alert to the injustices and inadequacies in the implementation of public policy, particularly as they affect individual Canadians, such unfortunate concomitants of big government can perhaps be minimized.

Summary and Conclusions: The Functions of Parliament

The functions of Parliament include the positive functions of refining policy and converting it into legislative outputs of the system. However, in relation to the political system as a whole, Parliament's more "negative" ratification or rejection and general audit functions are of much greater importance. In the extreme case, if it is clear that the prime minister is losing his marbles—if he should grow a little moustache, comb his hair down over one eye, and start wearing a uniform to work—it is still open to Parliament to say, "Party discipline be damned," and to reject his proposals. More routinely, it is through day-by-day criticism and comment by the Opposition parties in the House of Commons and the publicizing of that criticism through the press and the televising of debates that the government is kept on its toes. Cabinet ministers are constantly called upon publicly to justify the government's record through procedural devices, such as the Question Period and a number of special debates. Finally, what may be a very important aspect of the role of the individual MP, but one that has not been extensively studied, is the ombudsman function. The MP, in this regard, is both an elected watchdog and a communication link between the anonymous bureaucrat and the individual citizen.

More could be said here about secondary functions of Parliament in the Canadian political system. For instance, Parliament is a symbol of some of the things we believe in, like representative democracy and responsible government. It could be argued that this symbolic function of Parliament is as important as the policy, audit, and ombudsman functions, if not more so; after all, Parliament and the provincial legislature are the symbols around which most Canadians centre their perceptions of politics. On the other hand, a more cynical argument suggests that Parliament is no longer of any significance in the Canadian political process, and that it functions purely as an "electoral college" through which we indirectly elect a prime minister on the pattern of a presidential election in the United States. This, however, is a textbook and not a polemic. There are many points of view about the function and importance of Parliament in our political system today; we have tried to state some of them and to take a middle ground in describing them. The reader must decide, personally, just how important Parliament is in the process.

THE ORGANIZATION OF PARLIAMENT

The House of Commons

Officers of the House   The most important office of the House of Commons is the Speakership.[7] The office of Speaker of the House was created by the BNA Act, Section 44, which states that

> The House of Commons on its first assembling after a General Election shall proceed with all practicable speed to elect one of its members to be speaker.

The main function of the Speaker, to preside over the debates in the House of Commons, is also defined by the BNA Act, although the elaboration of the duties of this role is left to the Standing Orders. Constitutionally, it is clear that the Speaker is an officer of the House who is selected by the House itself and not by the Cabinet. In practice, however, because of the functional supremacy of the Cabinet in the parliamentary process, the Speaker was, until 1986, nominated by the Prime Minister and was usually elected without opposition. In 1986 House Speaker John Bosley resigned, and in September members of the House elected a new Speaker. All members' names were on the ballot unless a member withdrew his or her name from the nominations. The member elected, John Fraser, was apparently not the choice of Prime Minister Brian Mulroney. Almost invariably, the Speaker is a member from the government side of the House, although it is expected that he or she will function in a non-partisan and impartial manner. More recently, the tradition of impartiality has become more firmly established. From 1963 to 1986, the Speaker was nominated by the Prime Minister with the Leader of the Opposition as the seconder. In 1968, the Conservatives went one step further by indicating that they were willing to permit Mr. Lamoureux to continue as the Speaker even if they won the election, despite the fact that he had originally been elected as a Liberal. To facilitate this, the Speaker ran as an independent and the Conservatives did not run a candidate against him in his own riding. This paved the way for procedural changes that have streamlined

---

[7] See W.F. Dawson, *Procedure in the Canadian House of Commons* (Toronto: University of Toronto Press, 1962), chapter 2, for a detailed description of the office of the Speaker of the Canadian House of Commons. See also D.S. Macdonald, "Changes in the House of Commons — New Rules," *Canadian Public Administration*, Vol. 12, Spring 1970.

debate in the House by making most procedural rulings by the Speaker not subject to appeal to the House. The response of the first Speaker to possess this grant of final authority in procedural matters was to take an extremely fair and impartial stand, often in opposition to the wishes of the government. Although Lamoureux did not contest the 1974 election, his replacement was James Jerome, a Liberal back-bencher who proved to be so impartial and fair in his dealings with all parties in the House that the Conservatives agreed to leave him in that post when they came to power in 1979. Jerome, in turn, did not run in 1980, and since then, the Speakership has been filled by a government-party supporter. The Speaker does not participate in debates except where necessary to defend the internal estimates of the House of Commons. Furthermore, Standing Orders explicitly state that the Speaker cannot vote except to break a tie.

Thus far, all that has been discussed is the Speaker's function as a presiding officer of the House. A secondary function of the office is to act as the administrative head of the House of Commons. The Speaker is responsible for the internal economy of the House, for the staffing of the House with permanent employees, such as secretaries, and for preparing the estimates of internal costs and piloting them through the House of Commons. Thus, in some ways, the Speaker is like a minister of a small department who is responsible in a formal way for the administrative policies of that department.

The *Deputy Speaker* of the House is elected at the same time as the Speaker. The functions of this position are: to take the place of the Speaker when the Speaker is not able to be present, and to act as the chairman of Committee of the Whole. Like the Speaker, the Deputy Speaker is elected for the duration of a parliament and is expected to be proficient in whichever of the official languages is not the language of the Speaker. The general practice is that the Deputy Speaker is selected from among the members of the government party, although, with the office of the Speaker becoming less partisan than in the past, there is some possibility that the office of the Deputy Speaker will be affected as well.

In the absence of the Deputy Speaker, standing orders provide for the temporary appointment, by the Speaker, of any member to chair the Committee of the Whole. However, it is more common today for a *Deputy Chairman of Committees* (appointed for the duration of the session) to function as the chairman of the Committee of the Whole in the absence of the Deputy Speaker. This person also can take over as Speaker in the unlikely case that both the Speaker and the Deputy Speaker are absent. This appointment is made by the House and is invariably a member of the government party.

The *Clerk of the House* is the permanent head of the House of Commons staff. The function of this position is to supervise all permanent officers and staff of the House of Commons, to ensure that the Order Paper for the day is prepared and delivered to the Speaker, to print up certain documents for the distribution to all members of the House, and to ensure that two copies of every bill presented in the House are forwarded to the Minister of Justice.[8] In short, the Clerk of the

---

[8] This latter provision was originally created to comply with the provision of the Canadian Bill of Rights; now the minister makes sure that legislation is not repugnant to the Charter of Rights and Freedoms.

House is a "deputy minister" of the House of Commons. His or her "department" is the permanent staff of the House, and the "minister" is the speaker. The Clerk of the House is the most important permanent officer of the House of Commons.

It is interesting to note here that the House of Commons staff of approximately three thousand persons, including the Library of Parliament, are not public servants according to the Public Service Employment Act, but are the employees of Parliament directly. They have a separate pension system, a separate system of employee-employer relations, and they are not subject to the regulations of the Public Service Commission. While this situation is merely a reflection of the need for Parliament to be independent from the whims of the government of the day in managing its own internal affairs, there is growing discontent among many of the employees themselves, who would like to have the benefits and the collective-bargaining rights of public servants. The coming two years will likely see a settlement of this problem, although the nature of the agreement is impossible to speculate upon.

In this discussion of the officers of the House of Commons, we must also say a word about the *Party Whips*.[9] While they are not strictly officers of the House, but rather officers of the various political parties represented there, they must be included in this section because of the important role they play in the organization of the business of the House. They are appointed by the parties to represent their respective interests in the *Striking Committee* (which assigns individual MPs to committees), and to maintain party discipline. They ensure that the members are all present when there is to be a recorded vote in the House, and they check to see that the members vote the right way on division. Finally, arrangements between parties, for instance concerning the limitation of debate and the agenda for the sitting day, are sometimes worked out through the Whips. Thus, while the Whips are in no way official House of Commons officers, they do have an integral part to play in the day-to-day workings of the House, and particularly in enforcing party discipline.

The *House Leaders* of the various parties are responsible for the overall in-House conduct of their own MPs, and consequently for the overall flow of business through the House. The Government House Leader is a member of the Cabinet, and is responsible for seeing that the business of the government gets through the House as quickly as possible. Each Opposition House Leader acts as formal spokesman of his or her caucus to negotiate with the government House Leader the apportioning of the scarce time of the House. The high prestige of House Leaders, and the fact that they are really chosen by the party leaders to take much of the legislative load off their own backs, ensure that they can usually direct the caucus to do what they think is necessary to expedite the legislative process.

The Committee of the Whole   Standing Order 75(3) states that "any Bill based on a supply or ways and means motion after second reading thereof shall stand

---

[9] A. Herbert Morrison, *Government and Parliament: A Survey From the Inside* (New York: Oxford University Press, 1964); Robert J. Jackson, *Rebels and Whips: An Analysis of Discipline and Cohesion in British Political Parties* (New York: St. Martin's Press, 1968). The best recent work on procedural aspects of the House of Commons is J. Stewart, *The Canadian House of Commons: Procedure and Reform* (Montreal: McGill-Queens, 1977).

referred to Committee of the Whole." The Committee of the Whole is composed of all the members of the House sitting as a committee, with the Speaker out of the Chair and the Deputy Speaker presiding. Standing Orders generally apply when the House is sitting as a Committee of the Whole, with the exception that speeches have a shorter time limit, relevancy criteria are more strictly enforced, and debate is less formalized. Today, the function of the Committee of the Whole is primarily symbolic, with the exception of Ways and Means (taxation) bills, which are still given detailed clause-by-clause consideration in the Committee of the Whole after second reading. Traditionally, all legislation was considered clause by clause in the Committee of the Whole after second reading or approval in principle. Now, however, the clause-by-clause consideration of non-money bills is given in specialized legislative committees, thus making the Committee-of-the-Whole stage unnecessary. Similarly, special Committees of the Whole — the Committee of Supply and the Committee of Ways and Means — were once required to give clause-by-clause consideration to all financial legislation. The Committee of Supply was responsible for the detailed consideration of the Estimates before a Supply Bill could be introduced, a task now left to the Standing Committees.[10] The Committee of Ways and Means was required to deal separately with taxation proposals before introducing the actual bills in the House; but now this is achieved through a blanket motion by the Minister of Finance that "the House approve in general the budgetary policy of the Government." In 1969, the Committee of Supply and the Committee of Ways and Means were abolished. Thus, the function of the Committee of the Whole is today mostly symbolic, as its main substantive functions have been taken over by the Standing Committees.

Division   Debates in the House of Commons that have been commenced by a specific motion inevitably end in a vote. The basic rule in a parliamentary system is that a majority of those present in the House decide the outcome of a motion. When debate on a question has been concluded, the Speaker puts the question to the House by reading the main motion and any amendments. Those in agreement say "yea" and those against say "nay," and the Speaker announces which side has won — according to personal interpretation. If at least five members rise to demand a recorded vote or a "division," the division bells are rung, to inform members not sitting in the House at the time that a division is about to occur. Sometimes the division bells are rung for more than twenty minutes, to allow the Party Whips to round up as many votes as they can, although, in most cases, ten minutes is sufficient to summon members from offices and other places within the Parliament buildings. When the Whips of the various parties are content that they have as many as possible of their members present, the doors of the House are closed and the vote is taken. Members register their votes by standing in their places in the House of Commons to be counted by the Clerk of the House. When the vote is counted and recorded, the Speaker announces the outcome.[11]

---

10 Macdonald, "Changes in the House of Commons — New Rules," p. 33.

11 The second report of the McGrath Committee recommended the adoption of an electronic voting system to streamline the process of recorded votes.

Recorded votes in the House are very time-consuming, but fortunately many votes in the House are settled without a formal division; in most circumstances, it is obvious to all members that the government has a majority of the members in the House, so that there is never any real question that the government will be able to carry any motion. In recognition of this, the Opposition parties force a recorded vote only on non-confidence motions, second reading of important bills, etc. For the most part, the question is decided by a voice vote, with the Speaker declaring the government side to have carried the motion.

A member who is going to be absent from the House for a time will often arrange to "pair" with a member of the Opposition party. This means that both members agree not to vote on division if one is absent from the House. This practice, while based only on gentleman's agreement, means that even if many members are absent from the House, there is no danger that the government will fall by mistake. The practice of pairing is obviously more important in the situation of a minority government than when the government has a healthy majority. Frequently, after a division, a member who abstained from voting will rise in his place and state the way he would have voted had he not been paired. The supervision of pairing in the House is usually left to the Whips, who organize pairs for members and who ensure that their own members who are paired do not vote on division. It is interesting to note that on one occasion in 1926, the government was defeated in the House by one vote because of a broken pair, and although everyone was embarrassed, the vote stood and the government was forced to resign.

Rules of Debate   Some discussion has already been devoted to the basic functions of the Canadian parliament. However, what has been left unsaid until now is the fact that the general method or technique whereby Parliament performs all of these functions is debate. Above all else, the House of Commons would appear, to an uninitiated observer, primarily as a forum of debate, for it is debate that occupies the bulk of time in the parliamentary day. The rules of debate are consequently an important aspect of the parliamentary process.

The rules of debate, as already pointed out, are enforced by the Speaker, Deputy Speaker, or Deputy Chairman of Committees. The Chair does not exercise control over debate in an arbitrary fashion; there are definite rules and procedures, which the Speaker is called upon to apply from time to time in the course of debate. It is a basic principle that every member who wishes to speak to a question should be permitted to do so. The problem faced by the Speaker is, therefore, not *who* should be permitted to speak, but who should be permitted to speak first. The procedure for being recognized by the Speaker, or for catching the Speaker's eye, is for the member wishing to speak to rise in his or her place in the House. The Speaker attempts to switch attention from the Government side of the House to the opposition side, to permit a fair alternation of speakers by party. The Speaker's job has been greatly simplified through the practice of the Party Whips supplying the speaker with a daily list of members who wish to speak on that day. In the Question Period, it is traditional that the Speaker first recognizes the Official Opposition Leader and then turns to the leader of one of the minor

Opposition parties. In debates, however, the basic rule is that the parties themselves have worked out which of their members they wish to have heard and in which order, and the Speaker merely rotates from one party to another. If the Whips have done their job, there will be only one person from a given party rising to address the House at any given time.

Speeches in the House have a time limit of forty minutes when the Speaker is in the chair, and no member may speak more than once on any question. The exceptions to this rule are the Prime Minister, the Leader of the Official Opposition, any minister moving a government order, and any member making a motion of non-confidence in the government, all of whom may speak more than once, and for longer than forty minutes. A twenty-minute time limit applies to speeches during Private Members' Hour and during various extraordinary types of debates, such as those under Standing Order 30.

It is a convention of parliamentary debate that members should not read their speeches but should deliver them *extemporaneously*. This is not a written rule, however, and cannot be enforced by the Speaker. The result is that any member who so desires will read the speech, with some kidding and heckling from other members who observe the practice. The stock reply by a member who is chided for reading a speech is that he or she is merely following extensive notes very closely. There is a similar rule that the member may not repeat a point in a speech and that arguments made previously by other members may not be repeated. The former is applied infrequently by the Speaker, and the latter never; it defies enforcement. There are also rules requiring relevance in debate, which are similarly difficult to apply. The major impetus for relevance in speeches comes from the Party Whips, who try to ensure that time is not wasted during important debates. As already seen, there are certain debates, such as the Throne Speech Debate and the Budget Debate, to which the requirement of relevance does not apply at all.

In addition to the more explicit rules of debate, there is a general rule that members should not use what is euphemistically called "unparliamentary language." What this means is that the members should treat each other with politeness and should not revert to name-calling or *ad hominem* arguments in debate. Generally the members do abide by this rule, and it is seldom that the Speaker is called upon to rebuke a member for the use of unparliamentary language. Unparliamentary comments by members other than the member who has the floor usually go unrecognized formally, and appear in Hansard as "Some Hon. Members: Oh, Oh!" The phrase "Oh, Oh!" is a cryptic euphemism for earthy comments ranging from those that cast aspersions on the honourable member's ancestry to harmless but quaint colloquialisms such as "yer mother wears army boots," "fuddle-duddle," "horsefeathers," or "bulltwaddle."

Privilege   Parliamentary privilege is the sum of the rights and privileges of both Houses of the Canadian parliament, which function to place Parliament in a position above all other institutions and individuals in the land. These rights are held by Parliament as a whole and by each individual MP. They include such rights as freedom from arrest arising out of civil action while the House is in session, exemption from jury duty or from subpoena as a witness, and the protection from libel actions for the content of speeches in the House and publications of the House. Another part of parliamentary privilege in Canada is the right of parliamentary committees to hear witnesses under oath. Breaches of privilege are considered to be analogous to contempt of court, and are punishable by imprisonment, fine, or censure by the House itself. For matters of privilege, the House can act as court, calling witnesses "before the Bar of the House of Commons."

The real importance of parliamentary privilege has waned. Its significance today is primarily as a symbolic reminder of the principles of freedom of speech and freedom from arrest, which were at one time not so widely accepted as they are today. Occasionally today, a member will rise in the House on a question of privilege to complain about statements made about him or her in the press, or to complain about the conduct of another member, but in most cases the question raised has very little to do with privilege as such, and sometimes is merely a stalling technique. As Professor W. F. Dawson has pointed out:

> At the root of the problem is the ignorance of the Canadian House of the true meaning of privilege, which is essentially the defensive weapon of a legislature which has been used to protect itself against interference. The Canadian House has never had to fear such trouble and has never bothered to develop a defence.[12]

Sporadic attempts to raise questions of privilege in the Canadian House of Commons have been motivated by purely partisan needs and not by genuine threats to the security and freedom of the House. Parliamentary privilege, therefore, while important for its historical meaning, is not an important aspect of the modern parliamentary process in Canada.[13]

Committees in the House of Commons

One of the first responsibilities of the House of Commons at the beginning of the first session of each parliament is to appoint a Committee of Selection, or, as it is usually known, a Striking Committee. The Striking Committee is made up of seven MPs, and usually includes the Chief Whips of the Opposition Parties, a representative of the ministry, and the Chief Government Whip, who acts as the chair. The function of the Striking Committee is to select the members of the Standing Committees of the House within ten days of the commencement of the session, and to ensure that all committees have a full complement of members throughout the session.

At the present time, there are twenty Standing Committees of the Canadian House of Commons, thirteen of which are specialist committees in various substantive areas of government policy. Specialist committees have between seven and fifteen members. The Committees are:

[12] Dawson, *Procedure in the House*, p. 54.

[13] See Dawson, *Procedure in the House*, chapter 3, for a general discussion of privilege in Canada.

STANDING COMMITTEES	No. of Members
Aboriginal Affairs and Northern Development	7
Agriculture	11
Communications and Culture	7
Consumer and Corporate Affairs	7
Elections, Privileges and Procedure	7
Energy, Mines and Resources	7
Environment and Forestry	7
External Affairs and International Trade	13
Finance and Economic Affairs	13
Fisheries and Oceans	7
Government Operations	7
Human Rights	7
Justice and Solicitor General	11
Labour, Employment and Immigration	11
Management and Members' Services	8
Multiculturalism	7
National Defence	7
National Health and Welfare	7
Private Members' Business	7
Public Accounts	8
Regional Industrial Expansion	7
Research, Science and Technology	7
Secretary of State	7
Transport	11
Veterans' Affairs	8

In addition to these specialist committees, there are two Special Committees of the House responsible for acid rain and child care respectively. The Striking Committee is also responsible for appointing the House members of the *Joint Standing Committees* of the Senate and House of Commons, on Parliament, Official Languages and Regulations and other Statutory Instruments.

Special Committees, or Parliamentary Sub-committees, such as the Committee on Indian Self-Government, the Committee on Visible Minorities, or the Committee on the Handicapped, and Special Joint Committees, such as the Committee on Employer-Employee Relations in the Public Services, or the Joint Committee on the Constitution, are set up from time to time to deal with specific problems in specific policy areas. The Striking Committee is also responsible for assigning members to these committees. But, given their importance, ministers and party leaders may also become involved in selecting members.

Membership on the Standing Committees is now limited to fifteen. The guiding principle for selection of committee members by the Striking Committee is that the parties should have representation proportional to their membership in the House. In the case of the Liberals and Conservatives, Party Whips assign their party's allotment of members to the various committees according to the membership on the party caucus committees that correspond roughly to the Standing Committees of the House. Thus, a Conservative MP who is a member of the Caucus Committee on Agriculture is likely also to be a member of the House Committee on Agriculture. The NDP usually determines its members in a less formal way, depending largely upon which committees the MP wishes to sit on and upon seniority in the party caucus. It is generally accepted that the Striking Committee bases its selection of committee membership entirely on the recommendation of the Party Whips, and does not interfere with a party's wishes except with regard to the number of members allocated to each party for each committee.

One of the changes introduced by the Mulroney Government that came to power in 1984 was to create a new type of committee of the House of Commons. These are called *Legislative Committees* because their role is limited to the consideration of bills after second reading. They are appointed for a period of time coinciding with the consideration of the specific legislation, are appointed pretty much in the same manner and format as the Standing Committees, and they are normally restricted in size to a maximum of seven members. The strength of this system of legislative committees is that the composition of the committees doing clause-by-clause review of legislation can be based on the experience and specialisation of the members — a "match" between the subject matter of the legislation and the specific aptitudes and interests of the MPs.

Membership on committees used to be subject to change simply through notification of the Clerk of the House by the Chief Government Whip. However, since rule changes in 1982, the practice of frequent rotation of committee members has been limited. To maintain continuity and to accentuate the specialist role of the committees, only pre-selected alternates are allowed to fill in for committee members who are absent. Neither Cabinet ministers nor parliamentary secretaries are selected as members of the House committees.

The Chair and Vice Chair of Standing Committees are elected by the committees themselves, and, because the government has a majority of the members of the committees, these officers are normally government MPs. The single exception to this rule is the Public Accounts Committee, which, in recent years, has been chaired by a member of the Opposition. From time to time, an Opposition committee member with unique interest or expertise in the area of the committee's responsibility might be elected Vice Chair, but such occurrences are, as yet, relatively rare in Canada. The function of the Chair in Canadian committees is primarily to preside over the hearings of the committee, and not to assume the aggressive and dominant role of the Chairs of U.S. congressional committees. While this is a general rule, the practice of committees in this regard varies widely from committee to committee and from chair to chair.

Procedure in the Standing Committees of the Canadian House of Commons is basically the same as that for the House itself, except that Standing Orders restricting the length of speeches and the number of times of speaking do not apply, in order to ensure a less formal discussion of the issues. The Committees hear witnesses, mainly from the public service but frequently from the private sector and the academic community, and they report back to the House of Commons. All committee hearings are public in Canada, although neither the press nor the general public seems to give very much attention to the proceedings of most committees.

Committees of the House are all staffed by Clerks who are permanent employees of the House of Commons, and the research staff of the Library of Parliament can also give specialized assistance to the members. While there is a potential, in the case of the former, for these people to acquire some degree of power *vis-à-vis* their committees simply by virtue of their possible continuance in the same roles for a number of parliaments, they tend to be rather junior people with purely clerical responsibilities. The library research staff, while tending to be fairly senior professional personnel, cannot have a long-term influence on committees because they are moved from committee to committee, depending upon where the maximum work load is.

Special Committees and Parliamentary Task Forces have become particularly important since procedural reforms in 1982. These committees are established by the House, under the aegis of the government of the day, which will refer a subject for detailed study and for public hearings. Such committees are ad hoc, and their members remain with the committee for the duration of its work — usually about six months. The committees travel and hear witnesses; they may hire expert research support. Eventually, they table a report complete with recommendations.

We considered the impact of these committees on the policy process when we looked at the priority-setting stage of the policy process, but it bears emphasis here that they can be very influential. The major sources of their influence lie in the experience they develop, the research they conduct, the broad hearings they hold, and the fact that, in general, committee members from all parties tend to develop a common view and may file a unanimous report. Most of all, the committees are influential because the government is obliged to table a reply to their recommendations within sixty sitting days of receipt of the report. They therefore cannot be merely ignored by government, and they often serve to set the agenda in a particular policy area in a way quite uncharacteristic of other parliamentary institutions.

However, Special Committees and Task Forces may come to be used less in the future. The rules changes introduced in 1986 have given the Standing Committees greater freedom to investigate various policy aspects of the departments for which they are responsible. While the Standing Committees always played this role with respect to the detailed scrutiny of departmental estimates, they now have more leeway to determine *what* they are going to investigate. This freeing up of the committees to set their own agenda to a greater extent, coupled with the onerous responsibility for dealing with legislation after second reading being transferred to the newly created Legislative Committees, allows them to perform some of the investigative tasks previously assigned to Special Committees, Task Forces, or Sub-committees.

The Functions of the House Committees[14]

The committees of the House of Commons have at least four major functions to perform in the legislative process. First, they are expected to take the major role in the detailed consideration and refinement of public bills; second, they are delegated the responsibility for detailed scrutiny of the Estimates before the Supply Bills are introduced formally and given first reading; third, both Standing Committees and Special Committees or their sub-committees sometimes conduct pre-legislative investigation of policy proposals, much in the same way that a royal commission or task force would; and fourth, the Public Accounts Committee is responsible for performing a parliamentary "post audit" of the public accounts and the report of the Auditor General. Beyond these four major functions, the committees of the House also undertake a number of sundry tasks assigned to them specifically or to joint House of Commons-Senate committees. These all must be considered in detail.

Refining Government Policy: The Legislative Function   The most important function of committees of the House of Commons as regards the policy process is the detailed scrutiny and polishing of government bills. After a bill has been given second reading, it is normally referred to a legislative committee. The committee studies the legislative proposal, hears witnesses from the public service and experts from other sectors, and proposes changes it feels would improve the quality of the final legislative output. The committees can perform this function much more effectively than the House itself, because their pattern of debate is more open and procedurally less restrictive. It is possible for the committee members simply to discuss the issues involved, rather than debate them, as is the case in the House. Legislative committees are also generally more specialized.

Furthermore, the principle of the legislation has already been accepted by the House at second reading, and, consequently, the focus of the committee's deliberations is genuinely focused on improving the end product, although the Opposition parties may still try to sneak substantive changes into an act under the guise of improving the wording. In the House debate, on second reading, the Opposition parties perform the negative role of opposition, but in committee they can concentrate on more positive criticism of the form of the legislation, and they often propose useful amendments to the bills before them. The argument that committees are, to a lesser extent, partisan forums for debate than the House of Commons must be qualified by the fact that the matters they discuss — the details — are less likely to lend themselves to partisan divisions. However, it must be remembered that partisanship runs deep in the House of Commons. Most disagreements, even in committees, tend to go along party lines, and party discipline in committees is enforced by the government much in the same way it

[14] For a more detailed discussion of the committee system and of possible reforms, see: C.E.S. Franks, "The Reform of Parliament," *Queen's Quarterly*, Spring 1969, pp. 113–117; "The Dilemma of the Standing Committees of the Canadian House of Commons," *CJPS*, December 1971, pp. 461–476; "Procedural Reform in the Legislative Process," in Neilson and MacPherson, *The Legislative Process in Canada*, p. 256; J. Stewart, *The Canadian House*, passim; and R.J. Jackson, Doreen Jackson, and Nicolas Baxter-Moore, *Politics in Canada* (Scarborough: Prentice Hall, 1986), chapter 8.

is in House debates. If an Opposition member proposes in committee an amendment with which the government does not agree, the amendment will be defeated on division in the committee. Nevertheless, it is not uncommon for an Opposition proposal in committee to be accepted by the government, if it is agreed that the suggestion would genuinely improve the bill.

There are some limitations and weaknesses in the committee system that must be considered to clarify its role in the policy process. The first and most obvious is that a committee considering a government bill reports back to the House of Commons; all decisions made in committee are merely decisions to recommend something to the House, and have no final or binding effect by themselves. At the report stage, a recommendation of the committee can be simply reversed by a vote of the whole House. Paradoxically, a further limitation on the effectiveness of committees is the fact that, although they are intended to be specialist bodies that apply some expertise to the legislation, members of parliament tend to be generalists and not specialists. While the majority of MPs will remain on a Standing Committee for a full session, quite a number will have multiple and overlapping committee responsibilities, which also inhibits the development of real expertise in a single policy area.

The basic tasks of committees in dealing with government bills, then, are to refine the legislation, to attempt to foresee difficulties that might arise in the administration of the legislation, and to make such amendments as are necessary to achieve the desired improvements. Committees dealing with bills that have already passed second reading are precluded, by the rules of procedure, from making substantive changes in the legislation, and are precluded, by party discipline and the recommendatory nature of their decisions, from making even small changes with which the government does not agree.

Detailed Scrutiny of Estimates: The Business of Supply   Before the procedural changes of 1969 abolished the Committee of Supply, it was that committee's responsibility to go over the departmental estimates in detail. Now the estimates for a particular department go instead to the appropriate Standing Committee for detailed consideration. Thus, for instance, the Estimates of the Department of National Health and Welfare are reviewed by the Committee on Health, Welfare, and Social Affairs; the Department of National Defence Estimates are reviewed by the Committee on External Affairs and National Defence; and so forth. This has meant a large saving of time for the House of Commons, but it has increased commensurately the amount of time each member must spend in committee. Currently, by far the largest part of time spent in committees is devoted to a consideration of departmental Estimates.[15]

The ability of a standing committee to effectively criticize the spending plans of a given department is limited, once again, by the lack of independent expertise in the committee. The witnesses called to back up the Estimates of the department are departmental officials, and, furthermore, by the time the Estimates reach

---

[15] In fact, there is never enough time to consider the Estimates thoroughly in committee. Standing Order 58(14) states that the Estimates "shall be deemed to have been reported" by May 31 whether the committee is through with them or not.

Parliament, they have already run the gauntlet of criticism from the Cabinet, Cabinet committees, the Treasury Board, the Treasury Board Secretariat, and departmental financial experts. It is unlikely that the Standing Committee will be able to improve substantially or reduce the Estimates. Of course, the fact that the minister of each department must publicly justify estimated expenditures in committees probably prevents carelessness in the preparation of the Estimates in the first place but, in fact, getting the Estimates passed by Treasury Board is far more difficult than getting them passed by the Standing Committee.

Finally, it must be mentioned that the Opposition parties can, to some extent, use the consideration of the Estimates in committee as an additional forum for criticism of the government's programs and policy priorities. In this sense, the committee stage of the Estimates is at least as important for the general-audit function of Parliament as it is for improving the detailed estimates.

Pre-Legislative Functions: Policy Committees It is becoming more common in Canada for House committees to be used as investigatory bodies to examine policy proposals before the legislative stage. In this way, the committees can play a role at both the priority-setting and the formulation stages of the policy process. In the priority-setting stage, the House committee may travel across the country hearing briefs submitted by interested parties, apparently to gather information that ultimately can be used by the Cabinet in setting priorities. The recommendations that the committee comes up with are often less important than the data it gathers about the attitudes of the public towards a particular problem. At the policy-formulation stage, the committees again act as information gatherers, but usually with respect to a specific set of policy alternatives, such as those set down in a government white or "coloured" paper. In this case, the priority has already been set, and the problem faced by the committee is to discover public attitudes to the various alternatives.

There are Standing Committees capable of taking on investigatory duties in most policy areas[16] and perhaps the most significant contribution that committees of the House of Commons can bring to the policy process at the pre-legislative stages is the ability to conduct hearings and listen sympathetically to the submissions of the public. Here the committees can augment the government-sponsored task forces and royal commissions, and the bureaucratic political advisory bodies, in sounding public attitudes before any concrete policy commitments have been made.

In the pre-legislative role, committees, although they report back to the House of Commons, can afford to be less partisan than committees involved in the refining of government legislation. At the pre-legislative phase, the government is not firmly committed to any policy, and if the findings of the committee differ

---

[16] See: B.J. Creamer, "Parliamentary Task Forces in the First Session of the Thirty Second Parliament (MA Thesis, Carleton University, 1985); Commonwealth Parliamentary Association, "The Role of Parliamentary Committees and Task Forces," *Ninth Canadian Regional Seminar* (Regina, 1983); Nora Lever, *et al,* "The Parliamentary Task Forces: Committees of the Future?" *Canadian Parliamentary Review*, Spring 1981, Audrey O'Brien, "Parliamentary Task Forces in the Canadian House of Commons, *Parliamentarian*, January 1985, Paul Thomas, "The Influence of Standing Committees of Parliament on Government Legislation," *Legislative Studies Quarterly*, November 1978, p. 683.

from the government's attitudes to the problem being studied, the government can still back down without losing face. Furthermore, whereas a legislative committee's report on a government bill is subject to debate in the House at the report stage, the reports of committee investigations need not be debated at all.

An obvious latent function of the pre-legislative use of House committees is the stimulation of wider participation in the policy process and the creation of feelings of efficacy among the public and the MPs. The extent to which investigatory committees will actually affect policy will depend entirely on the quality of the information they gather and the consistency of that information with information gathered through other agencies. In short, there is a definite potential for additional input to the policy process through the use of parliamentary committees at the earlier stages of the process. The development of that potential will depend on the willingness of the government to utilize it fully, and on the recognition by the public and the committees themselves that such inputs can seldom be accepted without the additional input of other sources of advice. There must be a realistic understanding that simple committee recommendation of a policy alternative does not necessarily ensure its implementation, particularly if there exists a mass of technical advice that contradicts the committee findings.

The Public Accounts Committee: The Post-Audit Function The Canadian Public Accounts Committee is perhaps the most specialized of the Standing Committees of the House of Commons, and it is in some ways the most effective. It consists of eight members, and, like other committees, is controlled numerically by the government party. However, unlike the other Standing Committees, Public Accounts has had, since 1957, an Opposition member as its chair. Furthermore, the Auditor General, who is an independent officer of parliament, makes the job of the committee easier by providing it with expert assistance in scrutinizing the accounts of the government's expenditures. The functions of the Public Accounts Committee are to investigate the financial shortcomings of the government—as pointed out by the Auditor General, and as discovered through independent examination of the Public Accounts by the committee members themselves — and to make recommendations to the government as to how it should improve its spending practices.

The basic weakness of this procedure as a meaningful exercise of control over the financial affairs of the government is that the government usually chooses not to heed the recommendations. Each year, the Auditor General lists a number of recommendations, made over the past years by the Public Accounts Committee, which have never been implemented by the government. Furthermore, the government frequently releases the Public Accounts to the committee only very late in the session, and this has the effect of making the recommendations of the committee seem out of date by the time they are presented. This situation could be improved by making automatic the referral of the Public Accounts to the committee, instead of waiting for a specific referral by the government. As it stands today, it is not uncommon for the committee to fail to make any inquiries at all before the prorogation of Parliament.

To summarize, the Public Accounts Committee has considerable potential for investigating and publicizing the financial bungling and sleight-of-hand of the government and of government officials, but as yet it has not been very successful. The committee reports directly to the House, as do all Standing Committees, but the report does not produce any debate; it is simply received by the House and forgotten or ignored by the government. This committee could be made more effective by making debate of its report mandatory, and by creating a public consciousness of the importance of its role and the relevance to the citizen of its recommendations.

Miscellaneous Committee Functions   Finally, mention must be made of the fact that there are a number of Standing Committees whose functions are basically outside the realm of government policy. The Striking Committee, for instance, exists primarily to insure that the other committees are all staffed. The Committee on Elections, Privileges and Procedure is concerned primarily with the internal affairs of the House of Commons. It is relatively inactive most of the time, and becomes active only when specific circumstances necessitate. The Joint Committee on Parliament is mainly concerned with mundane business such as running the parliamentary restaurant, the Library of Parliament, and the printing services; while some such committees are actually quite active, their role is not critical to the working of the Canadian political system, and hence does not require more than this cursory mention.

   The exception to this rule is the Joint Standing Committee on Regulations and other Statutory Instruments, which was set up in 1972 pursuant to the Statutory Instruments Act of 1971. The function of this committee is to scrutinize all *subordinate legislation*[17] in much the same way that the "Scrutiny Committee" in Britain does. Given the amount of subordinate legislation and the general extent of delegation of legislative functions to executive and bureaucratic officers, such a committee could come to perform an invaluable control function *vis-à-vis* the bureaucracy. Moreover, it could in some ways aggrandize the general audit function of Parliament and give to the Senate a new and genuine responsibility. The success or failure of this committee, however, will depend on the way in which its mandate is carried out, and not on the principles stated in its charter. No final assessment of the role of the Committee on Regulations and Statutory Instruments can be made until it has had a few more years of operation. So far, however, it has not lived up to the potential indicated above.

   This concludes the discussion of the functions of parliamentary committees. The verdict, briefly, is that they are necessary to streamline the parliamentary process, and that they are central actors in the refining of government legislation. They have some positive role to play in assessing government policy proposals through the investigation of the public's attitudes via public hearings, etc. However, for most of the same reasons that Parliament as a whole has a restricted role in the policy process, the committees of the House of Commons do not occupy a very important place at the most critical stages of policy making.

---

[17] This is legislation that is passed by executive or administrative officials, pursuant to "enabling legislation," which is passed by Parliament, and which vests wide discretionary authority to make subordinate regulations that have the effect of law in officials and agencies *other than* the supreme lawmaking agency, Parliament.

THE SENATE

The Canadian parliament is bicameral in structure, consisting of the House of Commons and the Senate. The House of Commons (or "Lower House") functions virtually exclusively as the effective legislative branch of the Canadian political system, while the Senate (or "Upper House") plays a relatively insignificant role in the legislative process. While it is likely that the Senate was always intended to be a minor partner in the business of passing legislation, its legislative role was once seen as more significant than it is today. The Senate was originally viewed as the representative of various regions of the federation, with the maritimes, Quebec, Ontario, and the west alloted twenty-four Senators each. The entry of Newfoundland in 1949 added six more Senators, and two more seats were added in 1975 to give representation to the Northwest Territories and the Yukon. This makes up today's total of 104. The importance of the Senate today as a regional and provincial representative is not significant, because other institutions, such as the Cabinet and the federal-provincial conferences, which are more deeply involved in the policy process, are much better equipped to perform this function. The 1979 and 1980 House of Commons elections underrepresented the government parties in certain regions of the country, and one response to this was to appoint Senators to the Cabinet to give Quebec, in the case of the short-lived Clark government, and the west, in the case of the 1980 Trudeau government, some representation. Although this considerably enlivened the daily question period in the Senate, it likely did not enhance the role of the Senate in the policy process as much as it simply reduced the credibility of the governments forced to employ Senators as policy-related ministers. The 1984 Conservative landslide gave the government a large number of potential Cabinet ministers from all regions to choose from in the House of Commons, and there are only two senators in the Cabinet in 1987.

The second function of the Senate as perceived by the Fathers of Confederation was to act as a conservative restraint on the young, the impressionable, and the impulsive in the House of Commons. To secure this more sober voice in the legislative process, Senators are required to be at least thirty years of age and to own property valued at a minimum of four thousand dollars in the province they represent. Unlike the members of the Lower House, who are elected, Senators are appointed by the Governor-General-in-Council, and enjoy permanent tenure until age seventy-five.[18]

Most of the factors that function to restrict the role of the House of Commons in the policy process apply also to the Senate. Specifically, the Senate cannot compete with the Cabinet as a priority setter, and it lacks the expertise to become deeply involved in policy formulation. There are, however, even more handicaps placed on the policy role of the Senate than on that of the House of Commons. First, a Senator is not elected to office, as is an MP, but is appointed by the

[18] Until 1965, tenure was for life. Senators appointed before that date have the option today of staying on or retiring at age seventy-five. Any Senator appointed since 1965 must retire at seventy-five.

government when a vacancy occurs. This has meant traditionally that the party in power appoints people who have shown themselves to be faithful: Liberal governments have appointed Liberals and Conservative governments have appointed Conservatives, much to the annoyance of the NDP, which is virtually unrepresented in the Upper House. The effect of this partisan pattern of Senate appointments has been to deny the Senate both the legitimacy enjoyed by the House by virtue of popular election and the respect that would accrue to a body that is independent of partisanship. In recent times, there has been less reluctance to appoint Senators from non-government parties and from among people who have been basically non-partisan in their politics, but this has not been done often enough to give us a standard for evaluating its effect on the role or effectiveness of the upper chamber.

Another weakness of the Senate has been the tendency to offer Senate posts largely to people whose useful political lives have been terminated. As a reward for many years of faithful service to the party, an old politician is "retired" by being put in the Senate. Because of this tendency, the image of the Senate is that of an old-folks home for tired and retired party faithfuls, an image that severely restricts the prestige of the Upper House. Again, more recent trends may somewhat counter this opinion. First, the appointment to the Senate of people such as Michael Pitfield, Lowell Murray, Michael Kirby, Lorna Marsden, and Jean Bazin, whose useful lives are hardly at an end, has enhanced the prestige of the Upper House in the eyes of the public and in the eyes of public officials. Second, the Senate has been used several times in recent years to provide a home base in Ottawa, an office on Parliament Hill, and a secure, if modest, income for important party backroom people. Senators Keith Davey and Norman Atkins, the leading political strategists for the Liberal and Conservative parties, are the foremost examples. Another way in which a younger group was being introduced into the Senate will likely not take hold in Canada. This was the appointment to the Senate of "front-bench losers," potential Cabinet ministers who could not get elected to the House of Commons, as a device for getting them into the Cabinet. Although it had the effect, in 1979 and 1980, of bringing younger people into the Senate, this ploy was seen as impugning the electoral process and as spurning the will of the public, because the practice saw people appointed to high political office who had been rejected explicitly in a democratic election.

The Senate is not permitted by the constitution to introduce money bills, and in practice it cannot amend or defeat money bills either. (There is still some question as to the constitutionality of Senate amendments of money bills, but in practical terms the Senate does not even attempt to amend them today.) Because of the lack of government ministers in the Senate, virtually all government bills are, by convention, introduced in the House of Commons. It is increasingly rare for the Senate even to attempt to amend a government bill that has been passed by the Lower House, let alone to defeat it. While the Senate is legally empowered to make substantive amendments to or even to defeat government legislation passed by the House of Commons, and although senators ocasionally brandish this threat as a way to get ministerial attention or minor amendments, the legitimacy of any significant interference by the Senate in the policy process is questionable in a system that values popular sovereignty. The important exception to this is the practice of having Senate committees study the subject matter of all government bills (including money bills) before they are introduced in the Senate, and while they are being considered in the House. Through this procedure, the Senate can suggest amendments to the government, which, if accepted, can then be presented to the House of Commons for approval before the bill actually reaches the Senate. In this way, the wisdom to be found among the Senators can be brought to bear profitably on government proposals without raising the spectre of an appointed body amending the wishes of the elected representatives of the people who sit in the Lower House.

Despite the fact that the Senate is not a very active institution in the Canadian policy process today, there are a few items on the positive side of the ledger. Most important, the Senate does most of the parliamentary work involved in private bills, giving the overworked House of Commons more time for dealing with government legislation. Secondly, committees of the Senate are becoming more involved in investigations of political problems that might otherwise be left to royal commissions. An example of the use of a Senate committee in a pre-legislative investigatory role is the 1970 study done on the mass media in Canada. Moreover, Senators played a prominent role in the Joint Committee on the Constitution in 1981, and a Senate report on legislation to create the Canadian Security Intelligence Service (the Pitfield Report) was extremely influential in securing an acceptable draft of the act. Because the Senate is less involved in the politics of the day, it can conduct such studies without the danger of sensationalism and grandstanding on the part of the committee people that might occur if the same investigation were undertaken by the more "political" House of Commons. Also, of course, the House of Commons simply does not have the time to conduct hearings in the leisurely fashion typical of the Senate. Thus, through Senate committees, the Canadian Upper House can contribute some meaningful inputs to the policy process, and simultaneously relieve some of the pressure on the House of Commons.

The Senate also performs an important function for the Canadian party system, in that it permits the party in power to retire party faithfuls without too seriously alienating them, or imposing on them financial disaster. The Senate is, in this sense, a convenient place for stacking "over-age pols" who might cause political embarrassment if permitted to continue in the House of Commons, or who might be forced back into the private sector at a rather advanced age. The importance of this function of the Senate should not be minimized, for it provides some slight security for the politician. A politician, particularly a cabinet minister, who manages to retire while his or her party is in office is likely to get either a Senate seat or some other patronage position. As a consequence, the politician need not constantly pander to private interests in the hope that they might be future employers when his or her days in politics are done.

By way of conclusion to these brief remarks about the Senate, it should be mentioned that reform or abolition of the Upper House has been considered continually since 1967. Some reforms have been tried, such as compulsory retirement at age seventy-five but, functionally, the Senate has not changed significantly since Confederation. Basically, however, there is little that can be done in the way of incremental structural or procedural reform to improve the Senate.

If it is made elective, the House of Commons will be duplicated. We have an elected House already, and although the American system has a bicameral elective legislature, there is no reason to assume that one is needed here. If the Senate were abolished, some functions it performs today would have to be taken over by the already overworked House of Commons.

We have seen earlier that there have been a number of proposals for reform of the Upper House, which see it being converted to a "House of Federation" or a "House of the Provinces." By giving all or part of the power to appoint the members of the upper chamber to the provincial governments, it is felt by some that the Senate can be made more representative of regional interests within the central government, thus revitalizing both the moribund Upper House and the ailing federal system in one fell swoop! The problem, however, is that a more powerful Senate would have to take power away from the elected House of Commons, provincial governments, or the unseen labyrinth of interjurisdictional institutions. While some diminution of the influence of the latter might be desirable, the transfer of power from the House of Commons—which is, after all, representative of all parts of Canada, even if the government of the day is not—to a less directly elected body is a proposition that would require very careful scrutiny. On the other hand, if a "House of the Provinces" were to remain a minor legislative partner in the federal parliament, the provinces would catch on to the fact that their regions were simply being given more extensive representation in a relatively powerless institution, and, under these circumstances, their participation would be lukewarm at best.

Aside from such a radical restructuring, the major hope for improvement, therefore, seems to rest in functional changes. If, instead of proliferating commissions and bureaucratic task forces to undertake investigations that should be non-partisan in focus and visible to the public, the government would delegate still more investigatory powers to the Senate and appoint more Senators who are capable of taking a vigorous role in this respect, the Upper House might be given a more meaningful role in the policy process.[19]

THE LEGISLATIVE PROCESS: PARLIAMENT AND GOVERNMENT POLICY

Before discussing the steps a bill must pass in order to become law, some terminological clarification is necessary. Once a policy has been formulated and a draft of the proposed legislation has been completed by the Department of Justice, it is then introduced in the House of Commons by the minister responsible for that particular policy area. At this stage, the policy proposal takes the form of a *bill*. When a bill has been passed by Parliament it becomes an *act*, and after formal assent by the Governor General and after proclamation, an act becomes

---

[19] For further enlightenment on the role of the Senate, see F.A. Kunz, *The Modern Senate of Canada 1925–1963* (Toronto: University of Toronto Press, 1965); R.A. MacKay, *The Unreformed Senate of Canada* (Toronto: McClelland and Stewart, 1963); Dawson, *The Government of Canada*, chapter 15; and C. Campbell, *The Canadian Senate: A Lobby from Within* (Toronto: Macmillan, 1978).

law. Thus, although Parliament may have some impact at any of several stages of the policy process, the *formal* involvement of Parliament in the policy process is limited to converting bills introduced by the government into acts. This process naturally includes the refining of government policies and their ultimate conversion to formal outputs of the political system.

All bills introduced in Parliament can be classed as either *public* or *private*, depending on whether their effect is intended to be general or specific. Private bills are aimed at altering the law only insofar as it affects an individual or a corporate individual. Examples of this kind of legislation are laws altering the charters of companies or incorporating companies. Most such private bills are introduced in the Senate, where they are discussed and revised in detail by committees. Passage by the House of Commons is usually more or less perfunctory, with first, second, and third readings being virtually simultaneous. Private bills that have been passed by the Senate are frequently passed by the House of Commons in packages rather than individually, a practice that speeds up the process considerably.

Public bills, on the other hand, are intended to have a general effect and to alter the law as it affects all Canadians. Public bills take up by far the largest amount of parliamentary time, for it is by such measures that government policies are converted to outputs of the system. Most of the legislation passed by Parliament can be classed as public; for example, the Official Languages Act, the Income Tax Act, the Canada Pension Act, the Canadian Grain Act, etc. Because they generally involve the implementation of government policy, public bills are introduced in the House of Commons by the minister concerned. In contrast with private bills, public bills provide the focal points for heated partisan debate in the House of Commons.

As we noted, most public bills originate with the government and hence are referred to as *government bills*. There are, however, provisions in the rules and procedures of the House of Commons for the introduction of public bills by individual MPs. This type of public bill is a *private member's bill*, signifying that it is the creation of an individual MP and has nothing to do with the government or government policy. (Note here that *private member's bills* are completely different from *private bills*; the former term signifies the originators of the legislative proposals, and the latter signifies their intended applications.) Private member's bills, although procedurally a part of the parliamentary process, seldom go very far in the House of Commons; in fact, it is rare indeed for a private member's bill to go beyond first reading, unless the government likes the idea and adopts it as its own. New rules, adopted in 1985, provide that a few private member's bills per session will be debated fully and brought to a vote. While this may improve somewhat the chance that such non-government legislation will be passed, it is still possible to say with confidence that consideration of private member's bills does not constitute an important part of the policy role of Parliament.

The high mortality rate of private member's bills results from the fact that very little time is set aside for private member's business. There is usually a long list of private members who wish to introduce their pet bills, and they all must take turns in spending the allotted one-hour units of private members' time debating their proposals. Once a member has used a private members' hour to introduce a bill, the member's name drops to the bottom of the long list, and he or she doesn't get another chance until everyone else has had a turn. The result is that most private member's bills are introduced, debated for one hour, and never dealt with again. Bills accorded this treatment are said to have been "talked out." At the end of the parliamentary session, any government or private member's bills that are not completely passed by Parliament lapse and must be reintroduced at the next session. The new provision for allowing certain private member's bills some "government time" in the House is aimed at alleviating this problem, but only time will tell how much substantive impact the new rules will have.

It would be misleading, however, to limit our assessment of private member's bills to their function in the policy process. The more important function of the private member's bill is that it permits the MP to state publicly the policy proposals he or she considers important and feels the government is ignoring. Such bills are often passed down the line for consideration by bureaucrats, who may eventually incorporate the ideas in government bills. The MP can, in other words, put on the record a point of view on a certain policy area. Furthermore, by introducing a bill that favours a certain constituency's interests, the MP can publicize problems that exist there and are, perhaps, unique. In this way, the MP can use the private member's bill as a device to assist in the performance of the representative, or ombudsman, function, which we discussed earlier. In the past, Opposition members have often utilized the private member's hours to perform the general audit function of Parliament. By raising contentious issues through the introduction of a private member's bill, an Opposition member can attempt to embarrass the government without committing the Opposition as a whole to a firm stand on the issue. Thus it can be concluded that, although the private member's bill is not important as a category of legislative proposals to be considered by Parliament, it is a useful device for criticizing the government's policy priorities and for publicizing special problems and needs within certain regions and constituencies of the country.[20]

Government bills occupy the lion's share of the time available in the Canadian House of Commons, and the passage of these bills must be considered at greater length as part of the policy process. The procedures for dealing with government bills differ slightly, depending on whether the legislation in question involves the spending or raising of public money. We have seen that money bills, such as the Main Supply Bill or tax amendments, cannot be introduced in the Senate, and while there is no similar restriction on *non-money bills*, virtually all government bills are introduced in the House of Commons simply because most of the Cabinet members sit there. With these few points by way of introduction, let us now follow the passage of a government bill through Parliament. (See Fig. 19–1.)

Government bills are introduced by a minister in the House of Commons upon a *Motion for Leave*, which specifies the title of the bill and which may include a brief explanation of the provisions of the proposed legislation. After forty-eight

---

[20] For an excellent discussion of the significance of private member's bills, see Stewart Hyson, "The Role of the Backbencher—an Analysis of Private Member's Bills in the Canadian House of Commons," *Parliamentary Affairs*, vol. 27, no. 3, Summer 1974, pp. 262–272.

FIGURE 19-1
BILL BECOMES A LAW

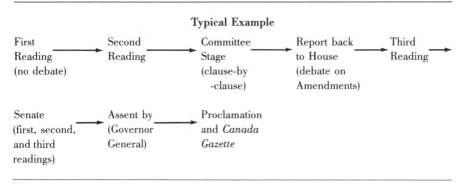

Typical Example

First Reading (no debate) → Second Reading → Committee Stage (clause-by-clause) → Report back to House (debate on Amendments) → Third Reading →

Senate (first, second, and third readings) → Assent by (Governor General) → Proclamation and *Canada Gazette*

hours, the bill may then be given *first reading*; this occurs in a non-debatable and non-amendable motion, "that this bill be read a first time and be printed."[21] First reading is very much a *pro forma* stage in the process, and simply serves to get the legislation before the House. The bill is then printed in both languages and made available to the members of the House.

Second reading of the bill takes place on a motion by the minister that it be granted second reading and referred to a legislative committee. The motion is debatable but not amendable, and the focus of second reading is upon the *principle* of the legislation. When the debate is concluded, the motion is voted on and the bill stands as referred to the committee. (Ways and Means and Supply bills are referred to the Committee of the Whole after second reading.)

The committee stage involves a clause-by-clause consideration of the legislation, and when its deliberations are concluded, the bill, as amended, is reported back to the House of Commons. The *report stage* provides the members with the opportunity to move amendments to the bill. After giving twenty-four hours' notice of intentions to move an amendment, any MP may "amend, delete, insert or restore any clause"[22] of the bill. These amendments are debatable and each member has the opportunity to speak once for twenty minutes; the Prime Minister, the Leader of the Opposition, the sponsoring minister of the bill, and the member moving the amendment may speak for forty minutes.

The report stage potentially gives the greatest opportunity to stall for time in an attempt to pressure the government to make changes. If there are a lot of amendments and if all Opposition MPs were to speak their allotted twenty minutes on the amendment, the House could be tied up for a long period of time indeed. The only defence against this sort of filibuster is for the government to invoke closure, or to secure time limits on the debate by the use of Standing Order 75(c). (Both procedures are so heavy-handed that the government is loath to use them.) The Speaker has the power to combine amendments that are similar in intent in an effort to streamline the procedures at the report stage, but even this does not

---

[21] Standing Order 74(5).

[22] Standing Order 74(12).

very effectively restrict the power of the Opposition to use up valuable time in an effort to force concessions on the government.

Under Standing Order 79(10), the Speaker has the power to *select* or *combine* amendments at the report stage in order to speed up the debate, but, in the past, Speakers have been reluctant to exercise the power to select. As stated in the McGrath report, the problem is that

> the practice of using the report stage as an obstructive tactic has developed because of the frustration of the opposition parties with the manner in which controversial bills are frequently dealt with at the committee stage. The report stage has become, in the words of one member, a vehicle for vengeance.[23]

While one solution is for the government to take a more sympathetic approach to the attitudes of the Opposition in committee, the McGrath report recommends that the Speaker use the power to select under Standing Order 79(10) to streamline the report stage in the future.

When the report stage is concluded, the minister moves "that the bill as amended be concurred in."[24] This motion is not amendable or debatable. Third reading is moved, usually at the next sitting of the House, and, while the motion to read the bill for a third time is debatable, and while general amendments are allowed, this stage of the process is normally perfunctory.

After third reading, the bill then goes to the Senate, where it is also given three readings and committee hearings. If the Senate amends the legislation, it must come back to the House for approval or rejection of its changes, although, if there were a stalemate between the Senate and the House, the legislation would end up dying on the Order Paper. When the Senate is finished with the bill, it is presented to the Governor General for Royal Assent. Depending upon what is provided for in the bill itself, the legislation may stand *proclaimed* immediately, or it may take effect at a later date.

This concludes our discussion of the role of Parliament in the Canadian political system. Parliament performs an important function in refining and legitimizing legislation that was usually dreamed up elsewhere and given priority by the Cabinet. As we have seen, the role of Parliament at other stages of the policy process is a sharply circumscribed one. Parliament is important as an ombudsman, as an electoral college, and as an auditor of the government's record. Its symbolic position as the focus — around which revolve the more active parts of the policy-making process — is vital to the way Canadians relate to their political system, but one must be careful not to base the evaluation of Parliament as an institution on a misapprehension about its role in the political process. Parliament plays a central role in Canadian politics, but it is not the role usually ascribed to it at service-club luncheons.

---

[23] Special Committee on Reform of the House of Commons, p. 39.

[24] Standing Order 74(12).

A P P E N D I X

Constitution Acts,
1867 to 1982

FOREWORD

This consolidation contains the text of the *Constitution Act, 1867* (formerly the *British North America Act, 1867*), together with amendments made to it since its enactment, and the text of the *Constitution Act, 1982,* as amended by the *Constitution Amendment Proclamation, 1983.* The *Constitution Act, 1982* contains the *Canadian Charter of Rights and Freedoms* and other new provisions, including the procedure for amending the Constitution of Canada.

The *Constitution Act, 1982* also contains a Schedule of repeals of certain constitutional enactments and provides for the renaming of others. The *British North America Act, 1949,* for example, is renamed in the Schedule, the *Newfoundland Act.* The new names of these enactments are used in this consolidation, but their former names may be found in the Schedule.

The *Constitution Act, 1982,* was enacted as Schedule B to the *Canada Act 1982* (U.K.) 1982, c. 11. It is set out in this consolidation as a separate Act after the *Constitution Act, 1867,* and the *Canada Act 1982* is contained in the first footnote thereto.

The law embodied in the *Constitution Act, 1867* has been altered many times otherwise than by direct amendment, not only by the Parliament of the United Kingdom, but also by the Parliament of Canada and the legislatures of the provinces in those cases where provisions of that Act are expressed to be subject to alteration by Parliament or the legislatures. A consolidation of the Constitution Acts with only such subsequent enactments as directly alter the text of the Act would therefore not produce a true statement of the law. In preparing this consolidation an attempt has been made to reflect accurately the substance of the law contained in enactments modifying the provisions of the *Constitution Act, 1867.*

The various classes of enactments modifying the text of the *Constitution Act, 1867,* have been dealt with as follows:

I. DIRECT AMENDMENTS

1. Repeals

Repealed provisions (e.g. section 2) have been deleted from the text and quoted in a footnote.

Amended provisions (e.g. section 4) are reproduced in the text in their amended form and the original provisions are quoted in a footnote.

3. *Additions*

Added provisions (e.g. section 51A) are included in the text.

4. *Substitutions*

Substituted provisions (e.g. section 18) are included in the text, and the former provision is quoted in a footnote.

II. INDIRECT AMENDMENTS

1. *Alterations by United Kingdom Parliament*

Provisions altered by the United Kingdom Parliament otherwise than by direct amendment (e.g. section 21) are included in the text in their altered form, and the original provision is quoted in a footnote.

2. *Additions by United Kingdom Parliament*

Constitutional provisions added otherwise than by the insertion of additional provisions in the *Constitution Act, 1867* (e.g. provisions of the *Constitution Act, 1871* authorizing Parliament to legislate for any territory not included in a province) are not incorporated in the text, but the additional provisions are quoted in an appropriate footnote.

3. *Alterations by Parliament of Canada*

Provisions subject to alteration by the Parliament of Canada (e.g. section 37) have been included in the text in their altered form, wherever possible, but where this was not feasible (e.g. section 40) the original section has been retained in the text and a footnote reference made to the Act of the Parliament of Canada effecting the alteration.

4. *Alterations by the Legislatures*

Provisions subject to alteration by legislatures of the provinces, either by virtue of specific authority (e.g. sections 83, 84) or by virtue of head 1 of section 92 (e.g. sections 70, 72), have been included in the text in their original form, but the footnotes refer to the provincial enactments effecting the alteration. Amendments to provincial enactments are not referred to; these may be readily found by consulting the indexes to provincial statutes. The enactments of the original provinces only are referred to; there are corresponding enactments by the provinces created at a later date.

III. Spent Provisions

Footnote references are made to those sections that are spent or are probably spent. For example, section 119 became spent by lapse of time and the footnote reference so indicates; on the other hand, section 140 is probably spent, but short of examining all statutes passed before Confederation there would be no way of ascertaining definitely whether or not the section is spent; the footnote reference therefore indicates the section as being probably spent.

The enactments of the United Kingdom Parliament or the Parliament of Canada, and Orders in Council admitting territories, referred to in the footnotes, may be found in Appendix II to the Revised Statutes of Canada, 1970, and in the subsequent sessional volumes of the statutes of Canada.

The reader will notice inconsistencies in the capitalization of nouns. It was originally the practice to capitalize the first letter of all nouns in British statutes and the *Constitution Act, 1867*, was so written, but this practice was discontinued and was never followed in Canadian statutes. In the original provisions included in this consolidation nouns are written as they were enacted.

* * * * * * * * *

This consolidation contains material prepared by the late Dr. E. A. Driedger, Q.C., which was last published by the Department of Justice in 1982 under the title *The Constitution Acts, 1867 to 1982*. The material has been updated where necessary but the Department gratefully acknowledges Dr. Driedger's earlier work.

THE CONSTITUTION ACT, 1867

30 & 31 Victoria, c. 3.

(Consolidated with amendments)

An Act for the Union of Canada, Nova Scotia, and New Brunswick, and the Government thereof; and for Purposes connected therewith.

(29th March, 1867.)

WHEREAS the Provinces of Canada, Nova Scotia and New Brunswick have expressed their Desire to be federally united into One Dominion under the Crown of the United Kingdom of Great Britain and Ireland, with a Constitution similar in Principle to that of the United Kingdom:

And whereas such a Union would conduce to the Welfare of the Provinces and promote the Interests of the British Empire:

And whereas on the Establishment of the Union by Authority of Parliament it is expedient, not only that the Constitution of the Legislative Authority in the Dominion be provided for, but also that the Nature of the Executive Government therein be declared:

And whereas it is expedient that Provision be made for the eventual Admission into the Union of other Parts of British North America: (1)

1.—PRELIMINARY.

1. This Act may be cited as the *Constitution Act, 1867*.(2) Short title.

---

(1) The enacting clause was repealed by the *Statute Law Revision Act, 1893*, 56-57 Vict., c. 14 (U.K.). It read as follows:

Be it therefore enacted and declared by the Queen's Most Excellent Majesty, by and with the Advice and Consent of the Lords Spiritual and Temporal, and Commons, in this present Parliament assembled, and by the Authority of the same, as follows:

(2) As enacted by the *Constitution Act, 1982*, which came into force on April 17, 1982. The section, as originally enacted, read as follows:

1. This Act may be cited as The British North America Act, 1867.

2. Repealed.(3)

II.—UNION.

Declaration
of Union.

3. It shall be lawful for the Queen, by and with the Advice of Her Majesty's Most Honourable Privy Council, to declare by Proclamation that, on and after a Day therein appointed, not being more than Six Months after the passing of this Act, the Provinces of Canada, Nova Scotia, and New Brunswick shall form and be One Dominion under the Name of Canada; and on and after that Day those Three Provinces shall form and be One Dominion under that Name accordingly.(4)

Construction
of subsequent
Provisions of
Act.

4. Unless it is otherwise expressed or implied, the Name Canada shall be taken to mean Canada as constituted under this Act.(5)

Four
Provinces.

5. Canada shall be divided into Four Provinces, named Ontario, Quebec, Nova Scotia, and New Brunswick.(6)

---

(3) Section 2, repealed by the *Statute Law Revision Act, 1893*, 56-57 Vict., c. 14 (U.K.), read as follows:

> **2.** The Provisions of this Act referring to Her Majesty the Queen extend also to the Heirs and Successors of Her Majesty, Kings and Queens of the United Kingdom of Great Britain and Ireland.

(4) The first day of July, 1867, was fixed by proclamation dated May 22, 1867.

(5) Partially repealed by the *Statute Law Revision Act, 1893*, 56-57 Vict., c. 14 (U.K.). As originally enacted the section read as follows:

> **4.** The subsequent Provisions of this Act, shall, unless it is otherwise expressed or implied, commence and have effect on and after the Union, that is to say, on and after the Day appointed for the Union taking effect in the Queen's Proclamation; and in the same Provisions, unless it is otherwise expressed or implied, the Name Canada shall be taken to mean Canada as constituted under this Act.

(6) Canada now consists of ten provinces (Ontario, Quebec, Nova Scotia, New Brunswick, Manitoba, British Columbia, Prince Edward Island, Alberta, Saskatchewan and Newfoundland) and two territories (the Yukon Territory and the Northwest Territories).

The first territories added to the Union were Rupert's Land and the North-Western Territory, (subsequently designated the Northwest Territories), which were admitted pursuant to section 146 of the *Constitution Act, 1867* and the *Rupert's Land Act, 1868*, 31-32 Vict., c. 105 (U.K.), by the *Rupert's Land and North-Western Territory Order* of June 23, 1870, effective July 15, 1870. Prior to the admission of those territories the Parliament of Canada enacted *An Act for the temporary Government of Rupert's Land and the North-Western Territory when united with Canada* (32-33 Vict., c. 3), and the *Manitoba Act, 1870*, (33 Vict., c. 3), which provided for the formation of the Province of Manitoba.

British Columbia was admitted into the Union pursuant to section 146 of the *Constitution Act, 1867*, by the *British Columbia Terms of Union*, being Order in Council of May 16, 1871, effective July 20, 1871.

6. The Parts of the Province of Canada (as it exists at the passing of this Act) which formerly constituted respectively the Provinces of Upper Canada and Lower Canada shall be deemed to be severed, and shall form Two separate Provinces. The Part which formerly constituted the Province of Upper Canada shall constitute the Province of Ontario; and the Part which formerly constituted the Province of Lower Canada shall constitute the Province of Quebec.

Provinces of Ontario and Quebec.

7. The Provinces of Nova Scotia and New Brunswick shall have the same Limits as at the passing of this Act.

Provinces of Nova Scotia and New Brunswick.

8. In the general Census of the Population of Canada which is hereby required to be taken in the Year One thousand eight hundred and seventy-one, and in every Tenth Year thereafter, the respective Populations of the Four Provinces shall be distinguished.

Decennial Census.

III.—EXECUTIVE POWER.

9. The Executive Government and Authority of and over Canada is hereby declared to continue and be vested in the Queen.

Declaration of Executive Power in the Queen.

Prince Edward Island was admitted pursuant to section 146 of the *Constitution Act, 1867*, by the *Prince Edward Island Terms of Union*, being Order in Council of June 26, 1873, effective July 1, 1873.

On June 29, 1871, the United Kingdom Parliament enacted the *Constitution Act, 1871* (34-35 Vict., c. 28) authorizing the creation of additional provinces out of territories not included in any province. Pursuant to this statute, the Parliament of Canada enacted the *Alberta Act*, (July 20, 1905, 4-5 Edw. VII, c. 3) and the *Saskatchewan Act*, (July 20, 1905, 4-5 Edw. VII, c. 42), providing for the creation of the provinces of Alberta and Saskatchewan, respectively. Both these Acts came into force on Sept. 1, 1905.

Meanwhile, all remaining British possessions and territories in North America and the islands adjacent thereto, except the colony of Newfoundland and its dependencies, were admitted into the Canadian Confederation by the *Adjacent Territories Order*, dated July 31, 1880.

The Parliament of Canada added portions of the Northwest Territories to the adjoining provinces in 1912 by *The Ontario Boundaries Extension Act, 1912*, 2 Geo. V, c. 40, *The Quebec Boundaries Extension Act, 1912*, 2 Geo. V, c. 45 and *The Manitoba Boundaries Extension Act, 1912*, 2 Geo. V, c. 32, and further additions were made to Manitoba by *The Manitoba Boundaries Extension Act, 1930*, 20-21 Geo. V, c. 28.

The Yukon Territory was created out of the Northwest Territories in 1898 by *The Yukon Territory Act*, 61 Vict., c. 6, (Canada).

Newfoundland was added on March 31, 1949, by the *Newfoundland Act*, (U.K.), 12-13 Geo. VI, c. 22, which ratified the Terms of Union between Canada and Newfoundland.

Application of Provisions referring to Governor General.

10. The Provisions of this Act referring to the Governor General extend and apply to the Governor General for the Time being of Canada, or other the Chief Executive Officer or Administrator for the Time being carrying on the Government of Canada on behalf and in the Name of the Queen, by whatever Title he is designated.

Constitution of Privy Council for Canada.

11. There shall be a Council to aid and advise in the Government of Canada, to be styled the Queen's Privy Council for Canada; and the Persons who are to be Members of that Council shall be from Time to Time chosen and summoned by the Governor General and sworn in as Privy Councillors, and Members thereof may be from Time to Time removed by the Governor General.

All Powers under Acts to be exercised by Governor General with Advice of Privy Council, or alone.

12. All Powers, Authorities, and Functions which under any Act of the Parliament of Great Britain, or of the Parliament of the United Kingdom of Great Britain and Ireland, or of the Legislature of Upper Canada, Lower Canada, Canada, Nova Scotia, or New Brunswick, are at the Union vested in or exerciseable by the respective Governors or Lieutenant Governors of those Provinces, with the Advice, or with the Advice and Consent, of the respective Executive Councils thereof, or in conjunction with those Councils, or with any Number of Members thereof, or by those Governors or Lieutenant Governors individually, shall, as far as the same continue in existence and capable of being exercised after the Union in relation to the Government of Canada, be vested in and exerciseable by the Governor General, with the Advice or with the Advice and Consent of or in conjunction with the Queen's Privy Council for Canada, or any Member thereof, or by the Governor General individually, as the Case requires, subject nevertheless (except with respect to such as exist under Acts of the Parliament of Great Britain or of the Parliament of the United Kingdom of Great Britain and Ireland) to be abolished or altered by the Parliament of Canada.(7)

Application of Provisions referring to Governor General in Council.

13. The Provisions of this Act referring to the Governor General in Council shall be construed as referring to the Governor General acting by and with the Advice of the Queen's Privy Council for Canada.

---

(7) See the notes to section 129, *infra.*

14. It shall be lawful for the Queen, if Her Majesty thinks fit, to authorize the Governor General from Time to Time to appoint any Person or any Persons jointly or severally to be his Deputy or Deputies within any Part or Parts of Canada, and in that Capacity to exercise during the Pleasure of the Governor General such of the Powers, Authorities, and Functions of the Governor General as the Governor General deems it necessary or expedient to assign to him or them, subject to any Limitations or Directions expressed or given by the Queen; but the Appointment of such a Deputy or Deputies shall not affect the Exercise by the Governor General himself of any Power, Authority or Function.

Power to Her Majesty to authorize Governor General to appoint Deputies.

15. The Command-in-Chief of the Land and Naval Militia, and of all Naval and Military Forces, of and in Canada, is hereby declared to continue and be vested in the Queen.

Command of armed Forces to continue to be vested in the Queen.

16. Until the Queen otherwise directs, the Seat of Government of Canada shall be Ottawa.

Seat of Government of Canada.

IV.—LEGISLATIVE POWER.

17. There shall be One Parliament for Canada, consisting of the Queen, an Upper House styled the Senate, and the House of Commons.

Constitution of Parliament of Canada.

18. The privileges, immunities, and powers to be held, enjoyed, and exercised by the Senate and by the House of Commons, and by the Members thereof respectively, shall be such as are from time to time defined by Act of the Parliament of Canada, but so that any Act of the Parliament of Canada defining such privileges, immunities, and powers shall not confer any privileges, immunities, or powers exceeding those at the passing of such Act held, enjoyed, and exercised by the Commons House of Parliament of the United Kingdom of Great Britain and Ireland, and by the Members thereof.(8)

Privileges, etc. of Houses.

---

(8) Repealed and re-enacted by the *Parliament of Canada Act, 1875*, 38-39 Vict., c. 38 (U.K.). The original section read as follows:

> **18.** The Privileges, Immunities, and Powers to be held, enjoyed, and exercised by the Senate and by the House of Commons and by the Members thereof respectively shall be such as are from Time to Time defined by Act of the Parliament of Canada, but so that the same shall never exceed those at the passing of this Act held, enjoyed, and exercised by the Commons House of Parliament of the United Kingdom of Great Britain and Ireland and by the Members thereof.

First Session
of the Parlia-
ment of
Canada.

19. The Parliament of Canada shall be called together not later than Six Months after the Union.(9)

20. Repealed.(10)

The Senate.

Number of
Senators.

21. The Senate shall, subject to the Provisions of this Act, consist of One Hundred and four Members, who shall be styled Senators.(11)

Representa-
tion of Prov-
inces in
Senate.

22. In relation to the Constitution of the Senate Canada shall be deemed to consist of Four Divisions:—

1. Ontario;
2. Quebec;
3. The Maritime Provinces, Nova Scotia and New Brunswick, and Prince Edward Island;
4. The Western Provinces of Manitoba, British Columbia, Saskatchewan, and Alberta;

which Four Divisions shall (subject to the Provisions of this Act) be equally represented in the Senate as follows: Ontario by twenty-four senators; Quebec by twenty-four senators; the Maritime Provinces and Prince Edward Island by twenty-four senators, ten thereof representing Nova Scotia, ten thereof

---

(9) Spent. The first session of the first Parliament began on November 6, 1867.

(10) Section 20, repealed by the Schedule to the *Constitution Act, 1982,* read as follows:

> **20.** There shall be a Session of the Parliament of Canada once at least in every Year, so that Twelve Months shall not intervene between the last Sitting of the Parliament in one Session and its first Sitting in the next Session.
>
> Section 20 has been replaced by section 5 of the *Constitution Act, 1982,* which provides that there shall be a sitting of Parliament at least once every twelve months.

(11) As amended by the *Constitution Act, 1915,* 5-6 Geo. V, c. 45 (U.K.) and modified by the *Newfoundland Act,* 12-13 Geo. VI, c. 22 (U.K.), and the *Constitution Act (No. 2), 1975,* S.C. 1974-75-76, c. 53.

The original section read as follows:

> **21.** The Senate shall, subject to the Provisions of this Act, consist of Seventy-two Members, who shall be styled Senators.

The *Manitoba Act, 1870,* added two for Manitoba; the *British Columbia Terms of Union* added three; upon admission of Prince Edward Island four more were provided by section 147 of the *Constitution Act, 1867;* the *Alberta Act* and the *Saskatchewan Act* each added four. The Senate was reconstituted at 96 by the *Constitution Act, 1915.* Six more Senators were added upon union with Newfoundland, and one Senator each was added for the Yukon Territory and the Northwest Territories by the *Constitution Act (No. 2), 1975.*

representing New Brunswick, and four thereof representing Prince Edward Island; the Western Provinces by twenty-four senators, six thereof representing Manitoba, six thereof representing British Columbia, six thereof representing Saskatchewan, and six thereof representing Alberta; Newfoundland shall be entitled to be represented in the Senate by six members; the Yukon Territory and the Northwest Territories shall be entitled to be represented in the Senate by one member each.

In the Case of Quebec each of the Twenty-four Senators representing that Province shall be appointed for One of the Twenty-four Electoral Divisions of Lower Canada specified in Schedule A. to Chapter One of the Consolidated Statutes of Canada.(12).

23. The Qualification of a Senator shall be as follows: Qualifications of Senator.

(1) He shall be of the full age of Thirty Years:

(2) He shall be either a natural-born Subject of the Queen, or a Subject of the Queen naturalized by an Act of the Parliament of Great Britain, or of the Parliament of the United Kingdom of Great Britain and Ireland, or of the Legislature of One of the Provinces of Upper Canada, Lower Canada, Canada, Nova Scotia, or New Brunswick, before the Union, or of the Parliament of Canada, after the Union:

(3) He shall be legally or equitably seised as of Freehold for his own Use and Benefit of Lands or Tenements held in Free and Common Socage, or seised or possessed for his own Use and Benefit of Lands or Tenements held in Franc-alleu or in Roture, within the

(12) As amended by the *Constitution Act, 1915*, the *Newfoundland Act*, 12-13 Geo. VI, c. 22 (U.K.), and the *Constitution Act (No. 2), 1975*, S.C. 1974-75-76, c. 53. The original section read as follows:

> **22.** In relation to the Constitution of the Senate, Canada shall be deemed to consist of Three Divisions:
>
> 1. Ontario;
>
> 2. Quebec;
>
> 3. The Maritime Provinces, Nova Scotia and New Brunswick;
> which Three Divisions shall (subject to the Provisions of this Act) be equally represented in the Senate as follows: Ontario by Twenty-four Senators; Quebec by Twenty-four Senators; and the Maritime Provinces by Twenty-four Senators, Twelve thereof representing Nova Scotia, and Twelve thereof representing New Brunswick.
>
> In the case of Quebec each of the Twenty-four Senators representing that Province shall be appointed for One of the Twenty-four Electoral Divisions of Lower Canada specified in Schedule A. to Chapter One of the Consolidated Statutes of Canada.

Province for which he is appointed, of the Value of Four thousand Dollars, over and above all Rents, Dues, Debts, Charges, Mortgages, and Incumbrances due or payable out of or charged on or affecting the same:

(4) His Real and Personal Property shall be together worth Four thousand Dollars over and above his Debts and Liabilities:

(5) He shall be resident in the Province for which he is appointed:

(6) In the Case of Quebec he shall have his Real Property Qualification in the Electoral Division for which he is appointed, or shall be resident in that Division.(13)

Summons of Senator.

24. The Governor General shall from Time to Time, in the Queen's Name, by Instrument under the Great Seal of Canada, summon qualified Persons to the Senate; and, subject to the Provisions of this Act, every Person so summoned shall become and be a Member of the Senate and a Senator.

25. Repealed.(14)

Addition of Senators in certain cases.

26. If at any Time on the Recommendation of the Governor General the Queen thinks fit to direct that Four or Eight Members be added to the Senate, the Governor General may by Summons to Four or Eight qualified Persons (as the Case may be), representing equally the Four Divisions of Canada, add to the Senate accordingly.(15)

---

(13) Section 2 of the *Constitution Act (No. 2), 1975*, S.C. 1974-75-76, c. 53 provided that for the purposes of that Act (which added one Senator each for the Yukon Territory and the Northwest Territories) the term "Province" in section 23 of the *Constitution Act, 1867*, has the same meaning as is assigned to the term "province" by section 28 of the *Interpretation Act*, R.S.C. 1970, c. I-23, which provides that the term "province" means "a province of Canada, and includes the Yukon Territory and the Northwest Territories."

(14) Repealed by the *Statute Law Revision Act, 1893*, 56-57 Vict., c. 14 (U.K.). The section read as follows:

25. Such Persons shall be first summoned to the Senate as the Queen by Warrant under Her Majesty's Royal Sign Manual thinks fit to approve, and their Names shall be inserted in the Queen's Proclamation of Union.

(15) As amended by the *Constitution Act, 1915*, 5-6 Geo. V, c. 45 (U.K.). The original section read as follows:

26. If at any Time on the Recommendation of the Governor General the Queen thinks fit to direct that Three or Six Members be added to the Senate, the Governor General may by Summons to Three or Six qualified Persons (as the Case may be), representing equally the Three Divisions of Canada, add to the Senate accordingly.

27. In case of such Addition being at any Time made, the Governor General shall not summon any Person to the Senate, except upon a further like Direction by the Queen on the like Recommendation, to represent one of the Four Divisions until such Division is represented by Twenty-four Senators and no more.(16)

Reduction of Senate to normal Number.

28. The Number of Senators shall not at any Time exceed One Hundred and twelve.(17)

Maximum Number of Senators.

29. (1) Subject to subsection (2), a Senator shall, subject to the provisions of this Act, hold his place in the Senate for life.

Tenure of Place in Senate.

(2) A Senator who is summoned to the Senate after the coming into force of this subsection shall, subject to this Act, hold his place in the Senate until he attains the age of seventy-five years.(18)

Retirement upon attaining age of seventy-five years.

30. A Senator may by Writing under his Hand addressed to the Governor General resign his Place in the Senate, and thereupon the same shall be vacant.

Resignation of Place in Senate.

31. The Place of a Senator shall become vacant in any of the following Cases:

Disqualification of Senators.

(1) If for Two consecutive Sessions of the Parliament he fails to give his Attendance in the Senate:

(2) If he takes an Oath or makes a Declaration or Acknowledgement of Allegiance, Obedience, or Adherence to a Foreign Power, or does an Act whereby he becomes a Subject or Citizen, or entitled to the Rights or Privileges of a Subject or Citizen, of a Foreign Power:

---

(16) As amended by the *Constitution Act, 1915*, 5-6 Geo. V, c. 45 (U.K.). The original section read as follows:

> **27.** In case of such Addition being at any Time made the Governor General shall not summon any Person to the Senate except on a further like Direction by the Queen on the like Recommendation, until each of the Three Divisions of Canada is represented by Twenty-four Senators and no more.

(17) As amended by the *Constitution Act, 1915*, 5-6 Geo. V, c. 45 (U.K.), and the *Constitution Act (No. 2), 1975*, S.C. 1974-75-76, c. 53. The original section read as follows:

> **28.** The Number of Senators shall not at any Time exceed Seventy-eight.

(18) As enacted by the *Constitution Act, 1965*, Statutes of Canada, 1965, c. 4 which came into force on the 1st of June, 1965. The original section read as follows:

> **29.** A Senator shall, subject to the Provisions of this Act, hold his Place in the Senate for Life.

(3) If he is adjudged Bankrupt or Insolvent, or applies for the Benefit of any Law relating to Insolvent Debtors, or becomes a public Defaulter:

(4) If he is attainted of Treason or convicted of Felony or of any infamous Crime:

(5) If he ceases to be qualified in respect of Property or of Residence; provided, that a Senator shall not be deemed to have ceased to be qualified in respect of Residence by reason only of his residing at the Seat of the Government of Canada while holding an Office under that Government requiring his Presence there.

Summons on Vacancy in Senate.

32. When a Vacancy happens in the Senate by Resignation, Death or otherwise, the Governor General shall by Summons to a fit and qualified Person fill the Vacancy.

Questions as to Qualifications and Vacancies in Senate.

33. If any Question arises respecting the Qualification of a Senator or a Vacancy in the Senate the same shall be heard and determined by the Senate.

Appointment of Speaker of Senate.

34. The Governor General may from Time to Time, by Instrument under the Great Seal of Canada, appoint a Senator to be Speaker of the Senate, and may remove him and appoint another in his Stead. (19)

Quorum of Senate.

35. Until the Parliament of Canada otherwise provides, the Presence of at least Fifteen Senators, including the Speaker, shall be necessary to constitute a Meeting of the Senate for the Exercise of its Powers.

Voting in Senate.

36. Questions arising in the Senate shall be decided by a Majority of Voices, and the Speaker shall in all Cases have a Vote, and when the Voices are equal the Decision shall be deemed to be in the Negative.

The House of Commons.

Constitution of House of Commons in Canada.

37. The House of Commons shall, subject to the Provisions of this Act, consist of two hundred and eighty-two members of whom ninety-five shall be elected for Ontario,

---

(19) Provision for exercising the functions of Speaker during his absence is made by the *Speaker of the Senate Act*, R.S.C. 1970, c. S-14. Doubts as to the power of Parliament to enact such an Act were removed by the *Canadian Speaker (Appointment of Deputy) Act, 1895*, 59 Vict., c. 3 (U.K.) which was repealed by the *Constitution Act, 1982.*

seventy-five for Quebec, eleven for Nova Scotia, ten for New Brunswick, fourteen for Manitoba, twenty-eight for British Columbia, four for Prince Edward Island, twenty-one for Alberta, fourteen for Saskatchewan, seven for Newfoundland, one for the Yukon Territory and two for the Northwest Territories.(20)

38. The Governor General shall from Time to Time, in the Queen's Name, by Instrument under the Great Seal of Canada, summon and call together the House of Commons.

Summoning of House of Commons.

39. A Senator shall not be capable of being elected or of sitting or voting as a Member of the House of Commons.

Senators not to sit in House of Commons.

40. Until the Parliament of Canada otherwise provides, Ontario, Quebec, Nova Scotia and New Brunswick shall, for the Purposes of the Election of Members to serve in the House of Commons, be divided into Electoral districts as follows:

Electoral districts of the four Provinces.

1.—ONTARIO.

Ontario shall be divided into the Counties, Ridings of Counties, Cities, Parts of Cities, and Towns enumerated in the First Schedule to this Act, each whereof shall be an Electoral District, each such District as numbered in that Schedule being entitled to return One Member.

2.—QUEBEC.

Quebec shall be divided into Sixty-five Electoral Districts, composed of the Sixty-five Electoral Divisions into which Lower Canada is at the passing of this Act divided under Chapter Two of the Consolidated Statutes of Canada, Chapter Seventy-five of the Consolidated Statutes for Lower Canada, and the Act of the Province of Canada of the Twenty-third Year of the Queen, Chapter One, or any other Act amending the same in force at the Union, so that each such Electoral Division shall be for the Purposes of this Act an Electoral District entitled to return One Member.

(20) The figures given here result from the application of section 51, as enacted by the *Constitution Act, 1974*, S.C. 1974-75-76, c. 13, amended by the *Constitution Act (No. 1), 1975*, S.C. 1974-75-76, c. 28 and readjusted pursuant to the *Electoral Boundaries Readjustment Act*, R.S.C. 1970, c. E-2. The original section (which was altered from time to time as the result of the addition of new provinces and changes in population) read as follows:

37. The House of Commons shall, subject to the Provisions of this Act, consist of one hundred and eighty-one members, of whom Eighty-two shall be elected for Ontario, Sixty-five for Quebec, Nineteen for Nova Scotia, and Fifteen for New Brunswick.

3.—NOVA SCOTIA.

Each of the Eighteen Counties of Nova Scotia shall be an Electoral District. The County of Halifax shall be entitled to return Two Members, and each of the other Counties One Member.

4.—NEW BRUNSWICK.

Each of the Fourteen Counties into which New Brunswick is divided, including the City and County of St. John, shall be an Electoral District. The City of St. John shall also be a separate Electoral District. Each of those Fifteen Electoral Districts shall be entitled to return One Member.(21)

Continuance
of existing
Election Laws
until Parliament of
Canada
otherwise
provides.

41. Until the Parliament of Canada otherwise provides, all Laws in force in the several Provinces at the Union relative to the following Matters or any of them, namely,—the Qualifications and Disqualifications of Persons to be elected or to sit or vote as Members of the House of Assembly or Legislative Assembly in the several Provinces, the Voters at Elections of such Members, the Oaths to be taken by Voters, the Returning Officers, their Powers and Duties, the Proceedings at Elections, the Periods during which Elections may be continued, the Trial of controverted Elections, and Proceedings incident thereto, the vacating of Seats of Members, and the Execution of new Writs in case of Seats vacated otherwise than by Dissolution,—shall respectively apply to Elections of Members to serve in the House of Commons for the same several Provinces.

Provided that, until the Parliament of Canada otherwise provides, at any Election for a Member of the House of Commons for the District of Algoma, in addition to Persons qualified by the Law of the Province of Canada to vote, every Male British Subject, aged Twenty-one Years or upwards, being a Householder, shall have a Vote.(22)

---

(21) Spent. The electoral districts are now established by Proclamations issued from time to time under the *Electoral Boundaries Readjustment Act*, R.S.C. 1970, c. E-2, as amended for particular districts by Acts of Parliament, for which see the most recent Table of Public Statutes.

(22) Spent. Elections are now provided for by the *Canada Elections Act*, R.S.C. 1970 (1st Supp.), c. 14; controverted elections by the *Dominion Controverted Elections Act*, R.S.C. 1970, c. C-28; qualifications and disqualifications of members by the *House of Commons Act*, R.S.C. 1970, c. H-9 and the *Senate and House of Commons Act*, R.S.C. 1970, c. S-8. The right of citizens to vote and hold office is provided for in section 3 of the *Constitution Act, 1982*.

42. Repealed.(23)

43. Repealed.(24)

44. The House of Commons on its first assembling after a General Election shall proceed with all practicable Speed to elect One of its Members to be Speaker.

As to Election of Speaker of House of Commons.

45. In case of a Vacancy happening in the Office of Speaker by Death, Resignation, or otherwise, the House of Commons shall with all practicable Speed proceed to elect another of its Members to be Speaker.

As to filling up Vacancy in Office of Speaker.

46. The Speaker shall preside at all Meetings of the House of Commons.

Speaker to preside.

47. Until the Parliament of Canada otherwise provides, in case of the Absence for any Reason of the Speaker from the Chair of the House of Commons for a Period of Forty-eight consecutive Hours, the House may elect another of its Members to act as Speaker, and the Member so elected shall during the Continuance of such Absence of the Speaker have and execute all the Powers, Privileges, and Duties of Speaker.(25)

Provision in case of Absence of Speaker.

48. The Presence of at least Twenty Members of the House of Commons shall be necessary to constitute a Meeting of the House for the Exercise of its Powers, and for that Purpose the Speaker shall be reckoned as a Member.

Quorum of House of Commons.

---

(23) Repealed by the *Statute Law Revision Act, 1893*, 56-57 Vict., c. 14 (U.K.). The section read as follows:

> **42.** For the First Election of Members to serve in the House of Commons the Governor General shall cause Writs to be issued by such Person, in such Form, and addressed to such Returning Officers as he thinks fit.
>
> The Person issuing Writs under this Section shall have the like Powers as are possessed at the Union by the Officers charged with the issuing of Writs for the Election of Members to serve in the respective House of Assembly or Legislative Assembly of the Province of Canada, Nova Scotia, or New Brunswick; and the Returning Officers to whom Writs are directed under this Section shall have the like Powers as are possessed at the Union by the Officers charged with the returning of Writs for the Election of Members to serve in the same respective House of Assembly or Legislative Assembly.

(24) Repealed by the *Statute Law Revision Act, 1893*, 56-57 Vict., c. 14 (U.K.). The section read as follows:

> **43.** In case a Vacancy in the Representation in the House of Commons of any Electoral District happens before the Meeting of the Parliament, or after the Meeting of the Parliament before Provision is made by the Parliament in this Behalf, the Provisions of the last foregoing Section of this Act shall extend and apply to the issuing and returning of a Writ in respect of such vacant District.

(25) Provision for exercising the functions of Speaker during his absence is now made by the *Speaker of the House of Commons Act*, R.S.C. 1970, c. S-13.

Voting in
House of
Commons.

49. Questions arising in the House of Commons shall be decided by a Majority of Voices other than that of the Speaker, and when the Voices are equal, but not otherwise, the Speaker shall have a Vote.

Duration of
House of
Commons.

50. Every House of Commons shall continue for Five Years from the Day of the Return of the Writs for choosing the House (subject to be sooner dissolved by the Governor General), and no longer.(26)

Readjustment
of represent-
ation in
Commons.

51. (1) The number of members of the House of Commons and the representation of the provinces therein shall upon the coming into force of this subsection and thereafter on the completion of each decennial census be readjusted by such authority, in such manner, and from such time as the Parliament of Canada from time to time provides, subject and according to the following Rules:

Rules.

1. There shall be assigned to Quebec seventy-five members in the readjustment following the completion of the decennial census taken in the year 1971, and thereafter four additional members in each subsequent readjustment.

2. Subject to Rules 5(2) and (3), there shall be assigned to a large province a number of members equal to the number obtained by dividing the population of the large province by the electoral quotient of Quebec.

3. Subject to Rules 5(2) and (3), there shall be assigned to a small province a number of members equal to the number obtained by dividing

(*a*) the sum of the populations, determined according to the results of the penultimate decennial census, of the provinces (other than Quebec) having populations of less than one and a half million, determined according to the results of that census, by the sum of the numbers of members assigned to those provinces in the readjustment following the completion of that census; and

---

(26) The term of the twelfth Parliament was extended by the *British North America Act, 1916*, 6-7 Geo. V, c. 19 (U.K.), which Act was repealed by the *Statute Law Revision Act, 1927*, 17-18 Geo. V, c. 42 (U.K.). See also subsection 4(1) of the *Constitution Act, 1982*, which provides that no House of Commons shall continue for longer than five years from the date fixed for the return of the writs at a general election of its members, and subsection 4(2) thereof, which provides for continuation of the House of Commons in special circumstances.

(*b*) the population of the small province by the quotient obtained under paragraph (*a*).

4. Subject to Rules 5(1)(*a*), (2) and (3), there shall be assigned to an intermediate province a number of members equal to the number obtained

(*a*) by dividing the sum of the populations of the provinces (other than Quebec) having populations of less than one and a half million by the sum of the number of members assigned to those provinces under any of Rules 3,5(1)(*b*), (2) and (3);

(*b*) by dividing the population of the intermediate province by the quotient obtained under paragraph (*a*); and

(*c*) by adding to the number of members assigned to the intermediate province in the readjustment following the completion of the penultimate decennial census one-half of the difference resulting from the subtraction of that number from the quotient obtained under paragraph (*b*).

5. (1) On any readjustment,

(*a*) if no province (other than Quebec) has a population of less than one and a half million, Rule 4 shall not be applied and, subject to Rules 5(2) and (3), there shall be assigned to an intermediate province a number of members equal to the number obtained by dividing

(i) the sum of the populations, determined according to the results of the penultimate decennial census, of the provinces (other than Quebec) having populations of not less than one and a half million and not more than two and a half million, determined according to the results of that census, by the sum of the numbers of members assigned to those provinces in the readjustment following the completion of that census, and

(ii) the population of the intermediate province by the quotient obtained under subparagraph (i);

(*b*) if a province (other than Quebec) having a population of

(i) less than one and a half million, or

(ii) not less than one and a half million and not more than two and a half million does not have a population greater than its population determined according to the results of the penultimate decennial census, it shall, subject to Rules 5(2) and (3), be assigned the number of members assigned to it in the readjustment following the completion of that census.

(2) On any readjustment,

(a) if, under any of Rules 2 to 5(1), the number of members to be assigned to a province (in this paragraph referred to as "the first province") is smaller than the number of members to be assigned to any other province not having a population greater than that of the first province, those Rules shall not be applied to the first province and it shall be assigned a number of members equal to the largest number of members to be assigned to any other province not having a population greater than that of the first province;

(b) if, under any of Rules 2 to 5 (1)(a), the number of members to be assigned to a province is smaller than the number of members assigned to it in the readjustment following the completion of the penultimate decennial census, those Rules shall not be applied to it and it shall be assigned the latter number of members;

(c) if both paragraphs (a) and (b) apply to a province, it shall be assigned a number of members equal to the greater of the numbers produced under those paragraphs.

(3) On any readjustment,

(a) if the electoral quotient of a province (in this paragraph referred to as "the first province") obtained by dividing its population by the number of members to be assigned to it under any of Rules 2 to 5(2) is greater than the electoral quotient of Quebec, those Rules shall not be applied to the first province and it shall be assigned a number of members equal to the number obtained by dividing its population by the electoral quotient of Quebec;

(b) if, as a result of the application of Rule 6(2)(a), the number of members assigned to a province under paragraph (a) equals the number of members to be assigned to it under any of Rules 2 to 5(2), it shall be assigned that number of members and paragraph (a) shall cease to apply to that province.

6. (1) In these Rules,

"electoral quotient" means, in respect of a province, the quotient obtained by dividing its population, determined according to the results of the then most recent decennial census, by the number of members to be assigned to it under any of Rules 1 to 5(3) in the readjustment following the completion of that census;

"intermediate province" means a province (other than Quebec) having a population greater than its population determined according to the results of the penultimate decennial census but not more than two and a half million and not less than one and a half million;

"large province" means a province (other than Quebec) having a population greater than two and a half million;

"penultimate decennial census" means the decennial census that preceded the then most recent decennial census;

"population" means, except where otherwise specified, the population determined according to the results of the then most recent decennial census;

"small province" means a province (other than Quebec) having a population greater than its population determined according to the results of the penultimate decennial census and less than one and half million.

(2) For the purposes of these Rules,

(*a*) if any fraction less than one remains upon completion of the final calculation that produces the number of members to be assigned to a province, that number of members shall equal the number so produced disregarding the fraction;

(*b*) if more than one readjustment follows the completion of a decennial census, the most recent of those readjustments shall, upon taking effect, be deemed to be the only readjustment following the completion of that census;

(*c*) a readjustment shall not take effect until the termination of the then existing Parliament.(27)

---

(27) As enacted by the *Constitution Act, 1974*, S.C. 1974-75-76, c. 13, which came into force on December 31, 1974. The section, as originally enacted, read as follows:

51. On the Completion of the Census in the Year One Thousand eight hundred and seventy-one, and of each subsequent decennial Census, the Representation of the Four Provinces shall be readjusted by such Authority, in such Manner, and from such Time, as the Parliament of Canada from Time to Time provides, subject and according to the following Rules:

(1) Quebec shall have the fixed Number of Sixty-five Members:

(2) There shall be assigned to each of the other Provinces such a Number of Members as will bear the same Proportion to the Number of its Population (ascertained at such Census) as the Number Sixty-five bears to the Number of the Population of Quebec (so ascertained):

(3) In the Computation of the Number of Members for a Province a fractional Part not exceeding One Half of the whole Number requisite for entitling the Province to a Member shall be disregarded; but a fractional Part exceeding One Half of that Number shall be equivalent to the whole Number:

(4) On any such Re-adjustment the Number of Members for a Province shall not be reduced unless the Proportion which the Number of the Population of the Province bore to the Number of the aggregate Population of Canada at the then last preceding Re-adjustment of the Number of Members for the Province is ascertained at the then latest Census to be diminished by One Twentieth Part or upwards:

(5) Such Re-adjustment shall not take effect until the Termination of the then existing Parliament.

The section was amended by the *Statute Law Revision Act, 1893*, 56-57 Vict., c. 14 (U.K.) by repealing the words from "of the census" to "seventy-one and" and the word "subsequent".

By the *British North America Act, 1943*, 6-7 Geo. VI, c. 30 (U.K.), which Act was repealed by the *Constitution Act, 1982*, redistribution of seats following the 1941 census was postponed until the first session of Parliament after the war. The section was re-enacted by the *British North America Act, 1946*, 9-10 Geo. VI, c. 63 (U.K.), which Act was also repealed by the *Constitution Act, 1982*, to read as follows:

51. (1) The number of members of the House of Commons shall be two hundred and fifty-five and the representation of the provinces therein shall forthwith upon the coming into force of this section and thereafter on the completion of each decennial census be readjusted by such authority, in such manner, and from such time as the Parliament of Canada from time to time provides, subject and according to the following rules:

(1) Subject as hereinafter provided, there shall be assigned to each of the provinces a number of members computed by dividing the total population of the provinces by two hundred and fifty-four and by dividing the population of each province by the quotient so obtained, disregarding, except as hereinafter in this section provided, the remainder, if any, after the said process of division.

(2) If the total number of members assigned to all the provinces pursuant to rule one is less than two hundred and fifty-four, additional members shall be assigned to the provinces (one to a province) having remainders in the computation under rule one commencing with the province having the largest remainder and continuing with the other provinces in the order of the magnitude of their respective remainders until the total number of members assigned is two hundred and fifty-four.

(3) Notwithstanding anything in this section, if upon completion of a computation under rules one and two, the number of members to be assigned to a province is less than the number of senators representing the said province, rules one and two shall cease to apply in respect of the said province, and there shall be assigned to the said province a number of members equal to the said number of senators.

(4) In the event that rules one and two cease to apply in respect of a province then, for the purpose of computing the number of members to be assigned to the provinces in respect of which rules one and two continue to apply, the total population of the provinces shall be reduced by the number of the popu-

lation of the province in respect of which rules one and two have ceased to apply and the number two hundred and fifty-four shall be reduced by the number of members assigned to such province pursuant to rule three.

(5) Such readjustment shall not take effect until the termination of the then existing Parliament.

(2) The Yukon Territory as constituted by Chapter forty-one of the Statutes of Canada, 1901, together with any Part of Canada not comprised within a province which may from time to time be included therein by the Parliament of Canada for the purposes of representation in Parliament, shall be entitled to one member.

The section was re-enacted by the *British North America Act, 1952*, S.C. 1952, c. 15, which Act was also repealed by the *Constitution Act, 1982*, as follows:

51. (1) Subject as hereinafter provided, the number of members of the House of Commons shall be two hundred and sixty-three and the representation of the provinces therein shall forthwith upon the coming into force of this section and thereafter on the completion of each decennial census be readjusted by such authority, in such manner, and from such time as the Parliament of Canada from time to time provides, subject and according to the following rules:

1. There shall be assigned to each of the provinces a number of members computed by dividing the total population of the provinces by two hundred and sixty-one and by dividing the population of each province by the quotient so obtained, disregarding, except as hereinafter in this section provided, the remainder, if any, after the said process of division.

2. If the total number of members assigned to all the provinces pursuant to rule one is less than two hundred and sixty-one, additional members shall be assigned to the provinces (one to a province) having remainders in the computation under rule one commencing with the province having the largest remainder and continuing with the other provinces in the order of the magnitude of their respective remainders until the total number of members assigned is two hundred and sixty-one.

3. Notwithstanding anything in this section, if upon completion of a computation under rules one and two the number of members to be assigned to a province is less than the number of senators representing the said province, rules one and two shall cease to apply in respect of the said province, and there shall be assigned to the said province a number of members equal to the said number of senators.

4. In the event that rules one and two cease to apply in respect of a province then, for the purposes of computing the number of members to be assigned to the provinces in respect of which rules one and two continue to apply, the total population of the provinces shall be reduced by the number of the population of the province in respect of which rules one and two have ceased to apply and the number two hundred and sixty-one shall be reduced by the number of members assigned to such province pursuant to rule three.

5. On any such readjustment the number of members for any province shall not be reduced by more than fifteen per cent below the representation to which such province was entitled under rules one to four of the subsection at the last preceding readjustment of the representation of that province, and there shall be no reduction in the representation of any province as a result of which that province would have a smaller number of members than any other province that according to the results of the then last decennial census did not have a larger population; but for the purposes of any subsequent readjustment of representation under this section any increase in the number of members of the House of Commons resulting from the application of this rule shall not be included in the divisor mentioned in rules one to four of this subsection.

6. Such readjustment shall not take effect until the termination of the then existing Parliament.

Yukon Territory and Northwest Territories.

(2) The Yukon Territory as bounded and described in the schedule to chapter Y-2 of the Revised Statutes of Canada, 1970, shall be entitled to one member, and the Northwest Territories as bounded and described in section 2 of chapter N-22 of the Revised Statutes of Canada, 1970, shall be entitled to two members.(28)

Constitution of House of Commons.

51A. Notwithstanding anything in this Act a province shall always be entitled to a number of members in the House of Commons not less than the number of senators representing such province.(29)

Increase of Number of House of Commons.

52. The Number of Members of the House of Commons may be from Time to Time increased by the Parliament of Canada, provided the proportionate Representation of the Provinces prescribed by this Act is not thereby disturbed.

Money Votes; Royal Assent.

Appropriation and Tax Bills.

53. Bills for appropriating any Part of the Public Revenue, or for imposing any Tax or Impost, shall originate in the House of Commons.

Recommendation of Money Votes.

54. It shall not be lawful for the House of Commons to adopt or pass any Vote, Resolution, Address, or Bill for the Appropriation of any Part of the Public Revenue, or of any Tax or Impost, to any Purpose that has not been first recommended to that House by Message of the Governor General in the Session in which such Vote, Resolution, Address, or Bill is proposed.

Royal Assent to Bills, etc.

55. Where a Bill passed by the Houses of the Parliament is presented to the Governor General for the Queen's Assent, he shall declare, according to his Discretion, but subject to the Provisions of this Act and to Her Majesty's Instructions, either that he assents thereto in the Queen's Name, or that he

---

(2) The Yukon Territory as constituted by chapter forty-one of the statutes of Canada, 1901, shall be entitled to one member, and such other part of Canada not comprised within a province as may from time to time be defined by the Parliament of Canada shall be entitled to one member.

(28) As enacted by the *Constitution Act (No. 1), 1975*, S.C. 1974-75-76, c. 28.

(29) As enacted by the *Constitution Act, 1915*, 5-6 Geo. V, c. 45 (U.K.).

withholds the Queen's Assent, or that he reserves the Bill for the Signification of the Queen's Pleasure.

56. Where the Governor General assents to a Bill in the Queen's Name, he shall by the first convenient Opportunity send an authentic Copy of the Act to one of Her Majesty's Principal Secretaries of State, and if the Queen in Council within Two Years after Receipt thereof by the Secretary of State thinks fit to disallow the Act, such Disallowance (with a Certificate of the Secretary of State of the Day on which the Act was received by him) being signified by the Governor General, by Speech or Message to each of the Houses of the Parliament or by Proclamation, shall annul the Act from and after the Day of such Signification.

Disallowance by Order in Council of Act assented to by Governor General.

57. A Bill reserved for the Signification of the Queen's Pleasure shall not have any Force unless and until, within Two Years from the Day on which it was presented to the Governor General for the Queen's Assent, the Governor General signifies, by Speech or Message to each of the Houses of the Parliament or by Proclamation, that it has received the Assent of the Queen in Council.

Signification of Queen's Pleasure on Bill reserved.

An Entry of every such Speech, Message, or Proclamation shall be made in the Journal of each House, and a Duplicate thereof duly attested shall be delivered to the proper Officer to be kept among the Records of Canada.

V.—PROVINCIAL CONSTITUTIONS.

Executive Power.

58. For each Province there shall be an Officer, styled the Lieutenant Governor, appointed by the Governor General in Council by Instrument under the Great Seal of Canada.

Appointment of Lieutenant Governors of Provinces.

59. A Lieutenant Governor shall hold Office during the Pleasure of the Governor General; but any Lieutenant Governor appointed after the Commencement of the First Session of the Parliament of Canada shall not be removeable within Five Years from his Appointment, except for Cause assigned, which shall be communicated to him in Writing within One Month after the Order for his Removal is made, and shall be communicated by Message to the Senate and to the House of Commons within One Week thereafter if the Parliament is then sitting, and if not then within One Week after the Commencement of the next Session of the Parliament.

Tenure of Office of Lieutenant Governor.

Salaries of
Lieutenant
Governors.

60. The Salaries of the Lieutenant Governors shall be fixed and provided by the Parliament of Canada. (30)

Oaths, etc., of
Lieutenant
Governor.

61. Every Lieutenant Governor shall, before assuming the Duties of his Office, make and subscribe before the Governor General or some Person authorized by him Oaths of Allegiance and Office similar to those taken by the Governor General.

Application
of provisions
referring to
Lieutenant
Governor.

62. The Provisions of this Act referring to the Lieutenant Governor extend and apply to the Lieutenant Governor for the Time being of each Province, or other the Chief Executive Officer or Administrator for the Time being carrying on the Government of the Province, by whatever Title he is designated.

Appointment
of Executive
Officers for
Ontario and
Quebec.

63. The Executive Council of Ontario and of Quebec shall be composed of such Persons as the Lieutenant Governor from Time to Time thinks fit, and in the first instance of the following Officers, namely,—the Attorney General, the Secretary and Registrar of the Province, the Treasurer of the Province, the Commissioner of Crown Lands, and the Commissioner of Agriculture and Public Works, with in Quebec, the Speaker of the Legislative Council and the Solicitor General. (31)

Executive
Government
of Nova
Scotia and
New Bruns-
wick.

64. The Constitution of the Executive Authority in each of the Provinces of Nova Scotia and New Brunswick shall, subject to the Provisions of this Act, continue as it exists at the Union until altered under the Authority of this Act. (32)

Powers to be
exercised by
Lieutenant
Governor of
Ontario or
Quebec with
Advice, or
alone.

65. All Powers, Authorities, and Functions which under any Act of the Parliament of Great Britain, or of the Parliament of the United Kingdom of Great Britain and Ireland, or of the Legislature of Upper Canada, Lower Canada, or Canada, were or are before or at the Union vested in or exerciseable by the respective Governors or Lieutenant Governors of those Provinces, with the Advice or with the Advice and Consent of the respective Executive Councils thereof, or in

---

(30) Provided for by the *Salaries Act,* R.S.C. 1970, c. S-2.

(31) Now provided for in Ontario by the *Executive Council Act,* R.S.O. 1980, c. 147, and in Quebec by the *Executive Power Act,* R.S.Q. 1977, c. E-18.

(32) A similar provision was included in each of the instruments admitting British Columbia, Prince Edward Island, and Newfoundland. The Executive Authorities for Manitoba, Alberta and Saskatchewan were established by the statutes creating those provinces. See the notes to section 5, *supra.*

conjunction with those Councils, or with any Number of Members thereof, or by those Governors or Lieutenant Governors individually, shall, as far as the same are capable of being exercised after the Union in relation to the Government of Ontario and Quebec respectively, be vested in and shall or may be exercised by the Lieutenant Governor of Ontario and Quebec respectively, with the Advice or with the Advice and consent of or in conjunction with the respective Executive Councils, or any Members thereof, or by the Lieutenant Governor individually, as the Case requires, subject nevertheless (except with respect to such as exist under Acts of the Parliament of Great Britain, or of the Parliament of the United Kingdom of Great Britain and Ireland,) to be abolished or altered by the respective Legislatures of Ontario and Quebec.(33)

66. The Provisions of this Act referring to the Lieutenant Governor in Council shall be construed as referring to the Lieutenant Governor of the Province acting by and with the Advice of the Executive Council thereof.

Application of Provisions referring to Lieutenant Governor in Council.

67. The Governor General in Council may from Time to Time appoint an Administrator to execute the office and Functions of Lieutenant Governor during his Absence, Illness, or other Inability.

Administration in Absence, etc., of Lieutenant Governor.

68. Unless and until the Executive Government of any Province otherwise directs with respect to that Province, the Seats of Government of the Provinces shall be as follows, namely,—of Ontario, the City of Toronto; of Quebec, the City of Quebec; of Nova Scotia, the City of Halifax; and of New Brunswick, the City of Fredericton.

Seats of Provincial Governments.

Legislative Power.

1.—ONTARIO.

69. There shall be a Legislature for Ontario consisting of the Lieutenant Governor and of One House, styled the Legislative Assembly of Ontario.

Legislature for Ontario.

70. The Legislative Assembly of Ontario shall be composed of Eighty-two Members, to be elected to represent the Eighty-two Electoral Districts set forth in the First Schedule to this Act. (34)

Electoral districts.

---

(33) See the notes to section 129, *infra*.

(34) Spent. Now covered by the *Representation Act*, R.S.O. 1980, c. 450.

2.—QUEBEC.

Legislature
for Quebec.

71. There shall be a Legislature for Quebec consisting of the Lieutenant Governor and of Two Houses, styled the Legislative Council of Quebec and the Legislative Assembly of Quebec. (35)

Constitution
of Legislative
Council.

72. The Legislative Council of Quebec shall be composed of Twenty-four Members, to be appointed by the Lieutenant Governor, in the Queen's Name, by Instrument under the Great Seal of Quebec, One being appointed to represent each of the Twenty-four Electoral Divisions of Lower Canada in this Act referred to, and each holding Office for the Term of his Life, unless the Legislature of Quebec otherwise provides under the Provisions of this Act.

Qualification
of Legislative
Councillors.

73. The Qualifications of the Legislative Councillors of Quebec shall be the same as those of the Senators for Quebec.

Resignation,
Disqualifi-
cation etc.

74. The Place of a Legislative Councillor of Quebec shall become vacant in the Cases, *mutatis mutandis*, in which the Place of Senator becomes vacant.

Vacancies.

75. When a Vacancy happens in the Legislative Council of Quebec by Resignation, Death, or otherwise, the Lieutenant Governor, in the Queen's Name, by Instrument under the Great Seal of Quebec, shall appoint a fit and qualified Person to fill the Vacancy.

Questions as
to Vacancies,
etc.

76. If any Question arises respecting the Qualification of a Legislative Councillor of Quebec, or a Vacancy in the Legislative Council of Quebec, the same shall be heard and determined by the Legislative Council.

Speaker of
Legislative
Council.

77. The Lieutenant Governor may from Time to Time, by Instrument under the Great Seal of Quebec, appoint a Member of the Legislative Council of Quebec to be Speaker thereof, and may remove him and appoint another in his Stead.

Quorum of
Legislative
Council.

78. Until the Legislature of Quebec otherwise provides, the Presence of at least Ten Members of the Legislative Council, including the Speaker, shall be necessary to constitute a Meeting for the Exercise of its Powers.

---

(35) The Act respecting the Legislative Council of Quebec, S.Q. 1968, c. 9, provided that the Legislature for Quebec shall consist of the Lieutenant Governor and the National Assembly of Quebec, and repealed the provisions of the *Legislature Act*, R.S.Q. 1964, c. 6, relating to the Legislative Council of Quebec. Sections 72 to 79 following are therefore completely spent.

79. Questions arising in the Legislative Council of Quebec shall be decided by a Majority of Voices, and the Speaker shall in all Cases have a Vote, and when the Voices are equal the Decision shall be deemed to be in the Negative.

Voting in Legislative Council.

80. The Legislative Assembly of Quebec shall be composed of Sixty-five Members, to be elected to represent the Sixty-five Electoral Divisions or Districts of Lower Canada in this Act referred to, subject to Alteration thereof by the Legislature of Quebec: Provided that it shall not be lawful to present to the Lieutenant Governor of Quebec for Assent any Bill for altering the Limits of any of the Electoral Divisions or Districts mentioned in the Second Schedule to this Act, unless the Second and Third Readings of such Bill have been passed in the Legislative Assembly with the Concurrence of the Majority of the Members representing all those Electoral Divisions or Districts, and the Assent shall not be given to such Bill unless an Address has been presented by the Legislative Assembly to the Lieutenant Governor stating that it has been so passed. (36)

Constitution of Legislative Assembly of Quebec.

3.—ONTARIO AND QUEBEC.

81. Repealed. (37)

82. The Lieutenant Governor of Ontario and of Quebec shall from Time to Time, in the Queen's Name, by Instrument under the Great Seal of the Province, summon and call together the Legislative Assembly of the Province.

Summoning of Legislative Assemblies.

83. Until the Legislature of Ontario or of Quebec otherwise provides, a Person accepting or holding in Ontario or in Quebec any Office, Commission, or Employment, permanent or temporary, at the Nomination of the Lieutenant Governor, to which an annual Salary, or any Fee, Allowance, Emolument, or Profit of any Kind or Amount whatever from the Province is attached, shall not be eligible as a Member of the Legislative Assembly of the respective Province, nor shall he sit or vote as such; but nothing in this Section shall make

Restriction on election of Holders of offices.

---

(36) The Act respecting electoral districts, S.Q. 1970, c. 7, s. 1, provides that this section no longer has effect.

(37) Repealed by the *Statute Law Revision Act, 1893*, 56-57 Vict., c. 14 (U.K.). The section read as follows:

> **81.** The Legislatures of Ontario and Quebec respectively shall be called together not later than Six Months after the Union.

ineligible any Person being a member of the Executive Council of the respective Province, or holding any of the following Offices, that is to say, the Offices of Attorney General, Secretary and Registrar of the Province, Treasurer of the Province, Commissioner of Crown Lands, and Commissioner of Agriculture and Public Works, and in Quebec Solicitor General, or shall disqualify him to sit or vote in the House for which he is elected, provided he is elected while holding such Office. (38)

Continuance
of existing
Election
Laws.

84. Until the legislatures of Ontario and Quebec respectively otherwise provide, all Laws which at the Union are in force in those Provinces respectively, relative to the following Matters, or any of them, namely, — the Qualifications and Disqualifications of Persons to be elected or to sit or vote as Members of the Assembly of Canada, the Qualifications or Disqualifications of Voters, the Oaths to be taken by Voters, the Returning Officers, their Powers and Duties, the Proceedings at Elections, the Periods during which such Elections may be continued, and the Trial of controverted Elections and the Proceedings incident thereto, the vacating of the Seats of Members and the issuing and execution of new Writs in case of Seats vacated otherwise than by Dissolution, — shall respectively apply to Elections of Members to serve in the respective Legislative Assemblies of Ontario and Quebec.

Provided that, until the Legislature of Ontario otherwise provides, at any Election for a Member of the Legislative Assembly of Ontario for the District of Algoma, in addition to Persons qualified by the Law of the Province of Canada to vote, every male British Subject, aged Twenty-one Years or upwards, being a Householder, shall have a vote. (39)

Duration of
Legislative
Assemblies.

85. Every Legislative Assembly of Ontario and every Legislative Assembly of Quebec shall continue for Four Years from the Day of the Return of the Writs for choosing the same (subject nevertheless to either the Legislative Assembly of Ontario or the Legislative Assembly of Quebec

(38) Probably spent. The subject-matter of this section is now covered in Ontario by the *Legislative Assembly Act*, R.S.O. 1980, c. 235, and in Quebec by the *Legislature Act*, R.S.Q. 1977, c. L-1.

(39) Probably spent. The subject-matter of this section is now covered in Ontario by the *Election Act*, R.S.O. 1980, c. 133, and the *Legislative Assembly Act*, R.S.O. 1980, c. 235, in Quebec by the *Elections Act*, R.S.Q. 1977, c. E-3, the *Provincial Controverted Elections Act*, R.S.Q. 1977, c. C-65, and the *Legislature Act*, R.S.Q. 1977, c. L-1.

being sooner dissolved by the Lieutenant Governor of the Province), and no longer. (40)

86. There shall be a Session of the Legislature of Ontario and of that of Quebec once at least in every Year, so that Twelve Months shall not intervene between the last Sitting of the Legislature in each Province in one Session and its first Sitting in the next Session. (41)

Yearly Session of Legislature.

87. The following Provisions of this Act respecting the House of Commons of Canada shall extend and apply to the Legislative Assemblies of Ontario and Quebec, that is to say, — the Provisions relating to the Election of a Speaker originally and on Vacancies, the Duties of the Speaker, the Absence of the Speaker, the Quorum, and the Mode of voting, as if those Provisions were here re-enacted and made applicable in Terms to each such Legislative Assembly.

Speaker, Quorum, etc.

4.—NOVA SCOTIA AND NEW BRUNSWICK.

88. The Constitution of the Legislature of each of the Provinces of Nova Scotia and New Brunswick shall, subject to the Provisions of this Act, continue as it exists at the Union until altered under the Authority of this Act. (42)

Constitutions of Legislatures of Nova Scotia and New Brunswick.

---

(40) The maximum duration of the Legislative Assemblies of Ontario and Quebec has been changed to five years. See the *Legislative Assembly Act*, R.S.O. 1980, c. 235, and the *Legislature Act*, R.S.Q. 1977, c. L-1, respectively. See also section 4 of the *Constitution Act, 1982*, which provides a maximum duration for a legislative assembly of five years but also authorizes continuation in special circumstances.

(41) See also section 5 of the *Constitution Act, 1982*, which provides that there shall be a sitting of each legislature at least once every twelve months.

(42) Partially repealed by the *Statute Law Revision Act, 1893*, 56-57 Vict., c. 14 (U.K.), which deleted the following concluding words of the original enactment:

> and the House of Assembly of New Brunswick existing at the passing of this Act shall, unless sooner dissolved, continue for the Period for which it was elected.

A similar provision was included in each of the instruments admitting British Columbia, Prince Edward Island and Newfoundland. The Legislatures of Manitoba, Alberta and Saskatchewan were established by the statutes creating those provinces. See the footnotes to section 5, *supra.*

See also sections 3 to 5 of the *Constitution Act, 1982*, which prescribe democratic rights applicable to all provinces, and subitem 2(2) of the Schedule to that Act, which sets out the repeal of section 20 of the *Manitoba Act, 1870*. Section 20 of the *Manitoba Act, 1870*, has been replaced by section 5 of the *Constitution Act, 1982*.

Section 20 reads as follows:

> **20.** There shall be a Session of the Legislature once at least in every year, so that twelve months shall not intervene between the last sitting of the Legislature in one Session and its first sitting in the next Session.

89. Repealed. (43)

6.—THE FOUR PROVINCES.

Application
to Legisla-
tures of
Provisions
respecting
Money Votes,
etc.

90. The following Provisions of this Act respecting the Parliament of Canada, namely,—the Provisions relating to Appropriation and Tax Bills, the Recommendation of Money Votes, the Assent to Bills, the Disallowance of Acts, and the Signification of Pleasure on Bills reserved,—shall extend and apply to the Legislatures of the several Provinces as if those Provisions were here re-enacted and made applicable in Terms to the respective Provinces and the Legislatures thereof, with the Substitution of the Lieutenant Governor of the Province for the Governor General, of the Governor General for the Queen and for a Secretary of State, of One Year for Two Years, and of the Province for Canada.

VI.—DISTRIBUTION OF LEGISLATIVE POWERS.

Powers of the Parliament.

Legislative
Authority of
Parliament of
Canada.

91. It shall be lawful for the Queen, by and with the Advice and Consent of the Senate and House of Commons, to make Laws for the Peace, Order, and good Government of Canada, in relation to all Matters not coming within the Classes of Subjects by this Act assigned exclusively to the Legislatures of the Provinces; and for greater Certainty, but not so as to restrict the Generality of the foregoing Terms of this Section, it is hereby declared that (notwithstanding anything in this Act) the exclusive Legislative Authority of the Parliament of Canada extends to all Matters coming within the Classes of Subjects next hereinafter enumerated; that is to say,—

---

(43) Repealed by the *Statute Law Revision Act, 1893*, 56-57 Vict., c. 14 (U.K.). The section read as follows:

5.—Ontario, Quebec, and Nova Scotia.

89. Each of the Lieutenant Governors of Ontario, Quebec and Nova Scotia shall cause Writs to be issued for the First Election of Members of the Legislative Assembly thereof in such Form and by such Person as he thinks fit, and at such Time and addressed to such Returning Officer as the Governor General directs, and so that the First Election of Member of Assembly for any Electoral District or any Subdivision thereof shall be held at the same Time and at the same Places as the Election for a Member to serve in the House of Commons of Canada for the Electoral District.

1. Repealed. (44)

1A. The Public Debt and Property. (45)

2. The Regulation of Trade and Commerce.

2A. Unemployment insurance. (46)

3. The raising of Money by any Mode or System of Taxation.

4. The borrowing of Money on the Public Credit.

5. Postal Service.

6. The Census and Statistics.

7. Militia, Military and Naval Service, and Defence.

8. The fixing of and providing for the Salaries and Allowances of Civil and other Officers of the Government of Canada.

9. Beacons, Buoys, Lighthouses, and Sable Island.

10. Navigation and Shipping.

11. Quarantine and the Establishment and Maintenance of Marine Hospitals.

12. Sea Coast and Inland Fisheries.

13. Ferries between a Province and any British or Foreign Country or between Two Provinces.

14. Currency and Coinage.

15. Banking, Incorporation of Banks, and the Issue of Paper Money.

16. Savings Banks.

---

(44) Class 1 was added by the *British North America (No. 2) Act, 1949*, 13 Geo. VI, c. 8 (U.K.). That Act and class 1 were repealed by the *Constitution Act, 1982*. The matters referred to in class 1 are provided for in subsection 4(2) and Part V of the *Constitution Act, 1982*. As enacted, class 1 read as follows:

> 1. The amendment from time to time of the Constitution of Canada, except as regards matters coming within the classes of subjects by this Act assigned exclusively to the Legislatures of the provinces, or as regards rights or privileges by this or any other Constitutional Act granted or secured to the Legislature or the Government of a province, or to any class of persons with respect to schools or as regards the use of the English or the French language or as regards the requirements that there shall be a session of the Parliament of Canada at least once each year, and that no House of Commons shall continue for more than five years from the day of the return of the Writs for choosing the House: provided, however, that a House of Commons may in time of real or apprehended war, invasion or insurrection be continued by the Parliament of Canada if such continuation is not opposed by the votes of more than one-third of the members of such House.

(45) Re-numbered by the *British North America (No. 2) Act, 1949*.

(46) Added by the *Constitution Act, 1940*, 3-4 Geo. VI, c. 36 (U.K.).

17. Weights and Measures.

18. Bills of Exchange and Promissory Notes.

19. Interest.

20. Legal Tender.

21. Bankruptcy and Insolvency.

22. Patents of Invention and Discovery.

23. Copyrights.

24. Indians, and Lands reserved for the Indians.

25. Naturalization and Aliens.

26. Marriage and Divorce.

27. The Criminal Law, except the Constitution of Courts of Criminal Jurisdiction, but including the Procedure in Criminal Matters.

28. The Establishment, Maintenance, and Management of Penitentiaries.

29. Such Classes of Subjects as are expressly excepted in the Enumeration of the Classes of Subjects by this Act assigned exclusively to the Legislatures of the Provinces.

And any Matter coming within any of the Classes of Subjects enumerated in this Section shall not be deemed to come within the Class of Matters of a local or private Nature comprised in the Enumeration of the Classes of Subjects by this Act assigned exclusively to the Legislatures of the Provinces.(47)

Exclusive Powers of Provincial Legislatures.

Subjects of exclusive Provincial Legislation.   **92.** In each Province the Legislature may exclusively make Laws in relation to Matters coming within the Classes of Subject next hereinafter enumerated; that is to say,—

---

(47) Legislative authority has been conferred on Parliament by other Acts as follows:

1. The *Constitution Act, 1871*, 34-35 Vict., c. 28 (U.K.).

   2. The Parliament of Canada may from time to time establish new Provinces in any territories forming for the time being part of the Dominion of Canada, but not included in any Province thereof, and may, at the time of such establishment, make provision for the constitution and administration of any such Province, and for the passing of laws for the peace, order, and good government of such Province, and for its representation in the said Parliament.

1. Repealed. (48)

2. Direct Taxation within the Province in order to the raising of a Revenue for Provincial Purposes.

3. The borrowing of Money on the sole Credit of the Province.

4. The Establishment and Tenure of Provincial Offices and the Appointment and Payment of Provincial Officers.

---

3. The Parliament of Canada may from time to time, with the consent of the Legislature of any province of the said Dominion, increase, diminish, or otherwise alter the limits of such Province, upon such terms and conditions as may be agreed to by the said Legislature, and may, with the like consent, make provision respecting the effect and operation of any such increase or diminution or alteration of territory in relation to any Province affected thereby.

4. The Parliament of Canada may from time to time make provision for the administration, peace, order, and good government of any territory not for the time being included in any Province.

5. The following Acts passed by the said Parliament of Canada, and intituled respectively, — "An Act for the temporary government of Rupert's Land and the North Western Territory when united with Canada"; and "An Act to amend and continue the Act thirty-two and thirty-three Victoria, chapter three, and to establish and provide for the government of "the Province of Manitoba", shall be and be deemed to have been valid and effectual for all purposes whatsoever from the date at which they respectively received the assent, in the Queen's name, of the Governor General of the said Dominion of Canada.

6. Except as provided by the third section of this Act, it shall not be competent for the Parliament of Canada to alter the provisions of the last-mentioned Act of the said Parliament in so far as it relates to the Province of Manitoba, or of any other Act hereafter establishing new Provinces in the said Dominion, subject always to the right of the Legislature of the Province of Manitoba to alter from time to time the provisions of any law respecting the qualification of electors and members of the Legislative Assembly, and to make laws respecting elections in the said Province.

The *Rupert's Land Act, 1868*, 31-32 Vict., c. 105 (U.K.) (repealed by the *Statute Law Revision Act, 1893*, 56-57 Vict., c. 14 (U.K.) had previously conferred similar authority in relation to Rupert's Land and the North Western Territory upon admission of those areas.

2. The *Constitution Act, 1886*, 49-50 Vict., c. 35, (U.K.).

1. The Parliament of Canada may from time to time make provision for the representation in the Senate and House of Commons of Canada, or in either of them, of any territories which for the time being form part of the Dominion of Canada, but are not included in any province thereof.

3. The *Statute of Westminster, 1931*, 22 Geo. V, c. 4 (U.K.).

3. It is hereby declared and enacted that the Parliament of a Dominion has full power to make laws having extra-territorial operation.

4. Section 44 of the *Constitution Act, 1982*, authorizes Parliament to amend the Constitution of Canada in relation to the executive government of Canada or the Senate and House of Commons. Sections 38, 41, 42, and 43 of that Act authorize the Senate and House of Commons to give their approval to certain other constitutional amendments by resolution.

(48) Class I was repealed by the *Constitution Act, 1982*. As enacted, it read as follows:

1. The Amendment from Time to Time, notwithstanding anything in this Act, of the Constitution of the province, except as regards the Office of Lieutenant Governor.

5. The Management and Sale of the Public Lands belonging to the Province and of the Timber and Wood thereon.

6. The Establishment, Maintenance, and Management of Public and Reformatory Prisons in and for the Province.

7. The Establishment, Maintenance, and Management of Hospitals, Asylums, Charities, and Eleemosynary Institutions in and for the Province, other than Marine Hospitals.

8. Municipal Institutions in the Province.

9. Shop, Saloon, Tavern, Auctioneer, and other Licences in order to the raising of a Revenue for Provincial, Local, or Municipal Purposes.

10. Local Works and Undertakings other than such as are of the following Classes:—

    (*a*) Lines of Steam or other Ships, Railways, Canals, Telegraphs, and other Works and Undertakings connecting the Province with any other or others of the Provinces, or extending beyond the Limits of the Province;

    (*b*) Lines of Steam Ships between the Province and any British or Foreign Country;

    (*c*) Such Works as, although wholly situate within the Province, are before or after their Execution declared by the Parliament of Canada to be for the general Advantage of Canada or for the Advantage of Two or more of the Provinces.

11. The Incorporation of Companies with Provincial Objects.

12. The Solemnization of Marriage in the Province.

13. Property and Civil Rights in the Province.

14. The Administration of Justice in the Province, including the Constitution, Maintenance, and Organization of Provincial Courts, both of Civil and of Criminal Jurisdiction, and including Procedure in Civil Matters in those Courts.

15. The Imposition of Punishment by Fine, Penalty, or Imprisonment for enforcing any Law of the Province made in relation to any Matter coming within any of the Classes of Subjects enumerated in this Section.

16. Generally all Matters of a merely local or private Nature in the Province.

Non-Renewable Natural Resources, Forestry Resources and Electrical Energy.

92A. (1) In each province, the legislature may exclusively make laws in relation to

(*a*) exploration for non-renewable natural resources in the province;

(*b*) development, conservation and management of non-renewable natural resources and forestry resources in the province, including laws in relation to the rate of primary production therefrom; and

(*c*) development, conservation and management of sites and facilities in the province for the generation and production of electrical energy.

(2) In each province, the legislature may make laws in relation to the export from the province to another part of Canada of the primary production from non-renewable natural resources and forestry resources in the province and the production from facilities in the province for the generation of electrical energy, but such laws may not authorize or provide for discrimination in prices or in supplies exported to another part of Canada.

(3) Nothing in subsection (2) derogates from the authority of Parliament to enact laws in relation to the matters referred to in that subsection and, where such a law of Parliament and a law of a province conflict, the law of Parliament prevails to the extent of the conflict.

(4) In each province, the legislature may make laws in relation to the raising of money by any mode or system of taxation in respect of

(*a*) non-renewable natural resources and forestry resources in the province and the primary production therefrom, and

(*b*) sites and facilities in the province for the generation of electrical energy and the production therefrom,

Section 45 of the *Constitution Act, 1982,* now authorizes legislatures to make laws amending the constitution of the province. Sections 38, 41, 42, and 43 of that Act authorize legislative assemblies to give their approval by resolution to certain other amendments to the Constitution of Canada.

whether or not such production is exported in whole or in part from the province, but such laws may not authorize or provide for taxation that differentiates between production exported to another part of Canada and production not exported from the province.

"Primary
production"

(5) The expression "primary production" has the meaning assigned by the Sixth Schedule.

Existing powers or rights.

(6) Nothing in subsections (1) to (5) derogates from any powers or rights that a legislature or government of a province had immediately before the coming into force of this section.(49)

Education.

Legislation
respecting
Education.

93. In and for each Province the Legislature may exclusively make Laws in relation to Education, subject and according to the following Provisions:—

(1) Nothing in any such Law shall prejudicially affect any Right or Privilege with respect to Denominational Schools which any Class of Persons have by Law in the Province at the Union:

(2) All the Powers, Privileges, and Duties at the Union by Law conferred and imposed in Upper Canada on the Separate Schools and School Trustees of the Queen's Roman Catholic Subjects shall be and the same are hereby extended to the Dissentient Schools of the Queen's Protestant and Roman Catholic Subjects in Quebec:

(3) Where in any Province a System of Separate or Dissentient Schools exists by Law at the Union or is thereafter established by the Legislature of the Province, an Appeal shall lie to the Governor General in Council from any Act or Decision of any Provincial Authority affecting any Right or Privilege of the Protestant or Roman Catholic Minority of the Queen's Subjects in relation to Education:

(4) In case any such Provincial Law as from Time to Time seems to the Governor General in Council requisite for the due Execution of the Provisions of this Section is not made, or in case any Decision of

(49) Added by the *Constitution Act, 1982.*

the Governor General in Council on any Appeal under this Section is not duly executed by the proper Provincial Authority in that Behalf, then and in every such Case, and as far only as the Circumstances of each Case require, the Parliament of Canada may make remedial Laws for the due Execution of the Provisions of this Section and of any Decision of the Governor General in Council under this Section.(50)

Uniformity of Laws in Ontario, Nova Scotia and New Brunswick.

94. Notwithstanding anything in this Act, the Parliament of Canada may make Provision for the Uniformity of all or any of the Laws relative to Property and Civil Rights in Ontario, Nova Scotia, and New Brunswick, and of the Proce-

Legislation for Uniformity of Laws in Three Provinces.

---

(50) Altered for Manitoba by section 22 of the *Manitoba Act, 1870*, 33 Vict., c. 3 (Canada), (confirmed by the *Constitution Act, 1871*), which reads as follows:

22. In and for the Province, the said Legislature may exclusively make Laws in relation to Education, subject and according to the following provisions:—

(1) Nothing in any such Law shall prejudicially affect any right or privilege with respect to Denominational Schools which any class of persons have by Law or practice in the Province at the Union:

(2) An appeal shall lie to the Governor General in Council from any Act or decision of the Legislature of the Province, or of any Provincial Authority, affecting any right or privilege, of the Protestant or Roman Catholic minority of the Queen's subjects in relation to Education:

(3) In case any such Provincial Law, as from time to time seems to the Governor General in Council requisite for the due execution of the provisions of this section, is not made, or in case any decision of the Governor General in Council on any appeal under this section is not duly executed by the proper Provincial Authority in that behalf, then, and in every such case, and as far only as the circumstances of each case require, the Parliament of Canada may make remedial Laws for the due execution of the provisions of this section, and of any decision of the Governor General in Council under this section.

Altered for Alberta by section 17 of the *Alberta Act*, 4-5 Edw. VII, c. 3, 1905 (Canada), which reads as follows:

17. Section 93 of the *Constitution Act, 1867*, shall apply to the said province, with the substitution for paragraph (1) of the said section 93 of the following paragraph:—

(1) Nothing in any such law shall prejudicially affect any right or privilege with respect to separate schools which any class of persons have at the date of the passing of this Act, under the terms of chapters 29 and 30 of the Ordinances of the Northwest Territories, passed in the year 1901, or with respect to religious instruction in any public or separate school as provided for in the said ordinances.

2. In the appropriation by the Legislature or distribution by the Government of the province of any moneys for the support of schools organized and carried on in accordance with the said chapter 29 or any Act passed in amendment thereof, or in substitution therefor, there shall be no discrimination against schools of any class described in the said chapter 29.

dure of all or any of the Courts in Those Three Provinces, and from and after the passing of any Act in that Behalf the Power of the Parliament of Canada to make Laws in relation to any Matter comprised in any such Act shall, notwithstanding anything in this Act, be unrestricted; but any Act of the Parliament of Canada making Provision for such Uniformity shall not have effect in any Province unless and until it is adopted and enacted as Law by the Legislature thereof.

> **3.** Where the expression "by law" is employed in paragraph 3 of the said section 93, it shall be held to mean the law as set out in the said chapters 29 and 30, and where the expression "at the Union" is employed, in the said paragraph 3, it shall be held to mean the date at which this Act comes into force.

Altered for Saskatchewan by section 17 of the *Saskatchewan Act*, 4-5 Edw. VII, c. 42, 1905 (Canada), which reads as follows:

> **17.** Section 93 of the *Constitution Act, 1867*, shall apply to the said province, with the substitution for paragraph (1) of the said section 93, of the following paragraph:—
>
> (1) Nothing in any such law shall prejudicially affect any right or privilege with respect to separate schools which any class of persons have at the date of the passing of this Act, under the terms of chapters 29 and 30 of the Ordinances of the North-west Territories, passed in the year 1901, or with respect to religious instruction in any public or separate school as proviced for in the said ordinances.
>
> **2.** In the appropriation by the Legislature or distribution by the Government of the province of any moneys for the support of schools organized and carried on in accordance with the said chapter 29, or any Act passed in amendment thereof or in substitution therefor, there shall be no discrimination against schools of any class described in the said chapter 29.
>
> **3.** Where the expression "by law" is employed in paragraph (3) of the said section 93, it shall be held to mean the law as set out in the said chapters 29 and 30; and where the expression "at the Union" is employed in the said paragraph (3), it shall be held to mean the date at which this Act comes into force.

Altered by Term 17 of the Terms of Union of Newfoundland with Canada (confirmed by the *Newfoundland Act*, 12-13 Geo. VI, c. 22 (U.K.)), which reads as follows:

> **17.** In lieu of section ninety-three of the *Constitution Act, 1867*, the following term shall apply in respect of the Province of Newfoundland:
>
> In and for the Province of Newfoundland the Legislature shall have exclusive authority to make laws in relation to education, but the Legislature will not have authority to make laws prejudicially affecting any right or privilege with respect to denominational schools, common (amalgamated) schools, or denominational colleges, that any class or classes of persons have by law in Newfoundland at the date of Union, and out of public funds of the Province of Newfoundland, provided for education,
>
> (*a*) all such schools shall receive their share of such funds in accordance with scales determined on a non-discriminatory basis from time to time by the Legislature for all schools then being conducted under authority of the Legislature; and
>
> (*b*) all such colleges shall receive their share of any grant from time to time voted for all colleges then being conducted under authority of the Legislature, such grant being distributed on a non-discriminatory basis.

See also sections 23, 29, and 59 of the *Constitution Act, 1982*. Section 23 provides for new minority language educational rights and section 59 permits a delay in respect of the coming into force in Quebec of one aspect of those rights. Section 29 provides that nothing in the *Canadian Charter of Rights and Freedoms* abrogates or derogates from any rights or privileges guaranteed by or under the Constitution of Canada in respect of denominational, separate or dissentient schools.

Old Age Pensions.

94A. The Parliament of Canada may make laws in relation to old age pensions and supplementary benefits, including survivors, and disability benefits irrespective of age, but no such law shall affect the operation of any law present or future of a provincial legislature in relation to any such matter.(51)

Legislation respecting old age pensions and supplementary benefits.

Agriculture and Immigration.

95. In each Province the Legislature may make Laws in relation to Agriculture in the Province, and to Immigration into the Province; and it is hereby declared that the Parliament of Canada may from Time to Time make Laws in relation to Agriculture in all or any of the Provinces, and to Immigration into all or any of the Provinces; and any Law of the Legislature of a Province relative to Agriculture or to Immigration shall have effect in and for the Province as long and as far only as it is not repugnant to any Act of the Parliament of Canada.

Concurrent Powers of Legislation respecting Agriculture, etc.

VII.—JUDICATURE.

96. The Governor General shall appoint the Judges of the Superior, District, and County Courts in each Province, except those of the Courts of Probate in Nova Scotia and New Brunswick.

Appointment of Judges.

97. Until the laws relative to Property and Civil Rights in Ontario, Nova Scotia, and New Brunswick, and the Procedure of the Courts in those Provinces, are made uniform, the Judges of the Courts of those Provinces appointed by the Governor General shall be selected from the respective Bars of those Provinces.

Selection of Judges in Ontario, etc.

98. The Judges of the Courts of Quebec shall be selected from the Bar of that Province.

Selection of Judges in Quebec.

99. (1) Subject to subsection two of this section, the Judges of the Superior Courts shall hold office during good

Tenure of office of Judges.

---

(51) Added by the *Constitution Act, 1964*, 12-13 Eliz. II, c. 73 (U.K.). As originally enacted by the *British North America Act, 1951*, 14-15 Geo. VI, c. 32 (U.K.), which was repealed by the *Constitution Act, 1982*, section 94A read as follows:

> **94A.** It is hereby declared that the Parliament of Canada may from time to time make laws in relation to old age pensions in Canada, but no law made by the Parliament of Canada in relation to old age pensions shall affect the operation of any law present or future of a Provincial Legislature in relation to old age pensions.

behaviour, but shall be removable by the Governor General on Address of the Senate and House of Commons.

Termination at age 75.

(2) A Judge of a Superior Court, whether appointed before or after the coming into force of this section, shall cease to hold office upon attaining the age of seventy-five years, or upon the coming into force of this section if at that time he has already attained that age. (52)

Salaries etc., of Judges.

100. The Salaries, Allowances, and Pensions of the Judges of the Superior, District, and County Courts (except the Courts of Probate in Nova Scotia and New Brunswick), and of the Admiralty Courts in Cases where the Judges thereof are for the Time being being paid by Salary, shall be fixed and provided by the Parliament of Canada. (53)

General Court of Appeal, etc.

101. The Parliament of Canada may, notwithstanding anything in this Act, from Time to Time provide for the Constitution, Maintenance, and Organization of a General Court of Appeal for Canada, and for the Establishment of any additional Courts for the better Administration of the Laws of Canada. (54)

VIII.—REVENUES; DEBTS; ASSETS; TAXATION.

Creation of Consolidated Revenue Fund.

102. All Duties and Revenues over which the respective Legislatures of Canada, Nova Scotia, and New Brunswick before and at the Union had and have Power of Appropriation, except such Portions thereof as are by this Act reserved to the respective Legislatures of the Provinces, or are raised by them in accordance with the special Powers conferred on them by this Act, shall form One Consolidated Revenue Fund, to be appropriated for the Public Service of Canada in the Manner and subject to the Charges of this Act provided.

Expenses of Collection, etc.

103. The Consolidated Revenue Fund of Canada shall be permanently charged with the Costs, Charges, and Expenses incident to the Collection, Management, and Receipt thereof, and the same shall form the First Charge thereon, subject to

---

(52) Repealed and re-enacted by the *Constitution Act, 1960*, 9 Eliz. II, c. 2 (U.K.), which came into force on the 1st day of March, 1961. The original section read as follows:

> **99.** The Judges of the Superior Courts shall hold Office during good Behaviour, but shall be removable by the Governor General on Address of the Senate and House of Commons.

(53) Now provided for in the *Judges Act*, R.S.C. 1970, c. J-1.

(54) See the *Supreme Court Act*, R.S.C. 1970, c. S-19, and the *Federal Court Act*, R.S.C. 1970, (2nd Supp.) c. 10.

be reviewed and audited in such Manner as shall be ordered by the Governor General in Council until the Parliament otherwise provides.

104. The annual Interest of the Public Debts of the several Provinces of Canada, Nova Scotia, and New Brunswick at the Union shall form the Second Charge on the Consolidated Revenue Fund of Canada. *Interest of Provincial Public Debts.*

105. Unless altered by the Parliament of Canada, the Salary of the Governor General shall be Ten thousand Pounds Sterling Money of the United Kingdom of Great Britain and Ireland, payable out of the Consolidated Revenue Fund of Canada, and the same shall form the Third Charge thereon. (55) *Salary of Governor General.*

106. Subject to the several Payments by this Act charged on the Consolidated Revenue Fund of Canada, the same shall be appropriated by the Parliament of Canada for the Public Service. *Appropriation from Time to Time.*

107. All Stocks, Cash, Banker's Balances, and Securities for Money belonging to each Province at the Time of the Union, except as in this Act mentioned, shall be the Property of Canada, and shall be taken in Reduction of the Amount of the respective Debts of the Provinces at the Union. *Transfer of Stocks, etc.*

108. The Public Works and Property of each Province, enumerated in the Third Schedule to this Act, shall be the Property of Canada. *Transfer of Property in Schedule.*

109. All Lands, Mines, Minerals, and Royalties belonging to the several Provinces of Canada, Nova Scotia, and New Brunswick at the Union, and all Sums then due or payable for such Lands, Mines, Minerals, or Royalties, shall belong to the several Provinces of Ontario, Quebec, Nova Scotia, and New Brunswick in which the same are situate or arise, subject to any Trusts existing in respect thereof, and to any Interest other than that of the Province in the same. (56) *Property in Lands, Mines, etc.*

110. All Assets connected with such Portions of the Public Debt of each Province as are assumed by that Province shall belong to that Province. *Assets connected with Provincial Debts.*

111. Canada shall be liable for the Debts and Liabilities of each Province existing at the Union. *Canada to be liable for Provincial Debts.*

---

(55) Now covered by the *Governor General's Act*, R.S.C. 1970, c. G-14.

(56) The three prairie provinces were placed in the same position as the original provinces by the *Constitution Act, 1930*, 21 Geo. V, c. 26 (U.K.).

Debts of
Ontario and
Quebec.

112. Ontario and Quebec conjointly shall be liable to Canada for the Amount (if any) by which the Debt of the Province of Canada exceeds at the Union Sixty-two million five hundred thousand Dollars, and shall be charged with Interest at the Rate of Five Per Centum per Annum thereon.

Assets of
Ontario and
Quebec.

113. The Assets enumerated in the Fourth Schedule to this Act belonging at the Union to the Province of Canada shall be the Property of Ontario and Quebec conjointly.

Debt of Nova
Scotia.

114. Nova Scotia shall be liable to Canada for the Amount (if any) by which its Public Debt exceeds at the Union Eight million Dollars, and shall be charged with Interest at the Rate of Five per Centum per Annum thereon. (57)

Debt of New
Brunswick.

115. New Brunswick shall be liable to Canada for the Amount (if any) by which its Public Debt exceeds at the Union Seven million Dollars, and shall be charged with Interest at the Rate of Five per Centum per Annum thereon.

Payment of
Interest to
Nova Scotia
and New
Brunswick.

116. In case the Public Debts of Nova Scotia and New Brunswick do not at the Union amount to Eight million and Seven million Dollars respectively, they shall respectively receive by half-yearly Payments in advance from the Government of Canada Interest at Five per Centum per Annum on the Difference between the actual Amounts of their respective Debts and such stipulated Amounts.

Provincial
Public Property.

117. The several Provinces shall retain all their respective Public Property not otherwise disposed of in this Act, subject to the Right of Canada to assume any Lands or Public Property required for Fortifications or for the Defence of the Country.

118. Repealed. (58)

---

(57) The obligations imposed by this section, sections 115 and 116, and similar obligations under the instruments creating or admitting other provinces, have been carried into legislation of the Parliament of Canada and are now to be found in the *Provincial Subsidies Act*, R.S.C. 1970, c. P-26.

(58) Repealed by the *Statute Law Revision Act, 1950,* 14 Geo. VI, c. 6 (U.K.). As originally enacted the section read as follows:

> **118.** The following Sums shall be paid yearly by Canada to the several Provinces for the Support of their Governments and Legislatures:
>
> | | Dollars |
> |---|---|
> | Ontario | Eighty thousand. |
> | Quebec | Seventy thousand. |
> | Nova Scotia | Sixty thousand. |
> | New Brunswick | Fifty thousand. |
>
> Two hundred and sixty thousand;

and an annual Grant in aid of each Province shall be made, equal to Eighty Cents per Head of the Population as ascertained by the Census of One thousand eight hundred and sixty-one, and in the Case of Nova Scotia and New Brunswick, by each subsequent Decennial Census until the Population of each of those two Provinces amounts to Four hundred thousand Souls, at which Rate such Grant shall thereafter remain. Such Grants shall be in full Settlement of all future Demands on Canada, and shall be paid half-yearly in advance to each Province; but the Government of Canada shall deduct from such Grants, as against any Province, all Sums chargeable as Interest on the Public Debt of that Province in excess of the several Amounts stipulated in this Act.

The section was made obsolete by the *Constitution Act, 1907*, 7 Edw. VII, c. 11 (U.K.) which provided:

1. (1) The following grants shall be made yearly by Canada to every province, which at the commencement of this Act is a province of the Dominion, for its local purposes and the support of its Government and Legislature:—

(*a*) A fixed grant—

where the population of the province is under one hundred and fifty thousand, of one hundred thousand dollars;

where the population of the province is one hundred and fifty thousand, but does not exceed two hundred thousand, of one hundred and fifty thousand dollars;

where the population of the province is two hundred thousand, but does not exceed four hundred thousand, of one hundred and eighty thousand dollars;

where the population of the province is four hundred thousand, but does not exceed eight hundred thousand, of one hundred and ninety thousand dollars;

where the population of the province is eight hundred thousand, but does not exceed one million five hundred thousand, of two hundred and twenty thousand dollars;

where the population of the province exceeds one million five hundred thousand, of two hundred and forty thousand dollars; and

(*b*) Subject to the special provisions of this Act as to the provinces of British Columbia and Prince Edward Island, a grant at the rate of eighty cents per head of the population of the province up to the number of two million five hundred thousand, and at the rate of sixty cents per head of so much of the population as exceeds that number.

(2) An additional grant of one hundred thousand dollars shall be made yearly to the province of British Columbia for a period of ten years from the commencement of this Act.

(3) The population of a province shall be ascertained from time to time in the case of the provinces of Manitoba, Saskatchewan, and Alberta respectively by the last quinquennial census or statutory estimate of population made under the Acts establishing those provinces or any other Act of the Parliament of Canada making provision for the purpose, and in the case of any other province by the last decennial census for the time being.

(4) The grants payable under this Act shall be paid half-yearly in advance to each province.

(5) The grants payable under this Act shall be substituted for the grants or subsidies (in this Act referred to as existing grants) payable for the like purposes at the commencement of this Act to the several provinces of the Dominion under the provisions of section one hundred and eighteen of the *Constitution Act, 1867*, or of any Order in Council establishing a province, or of any Act of the Parliament of Canada containing directions for the payment of any such grant or subsidy, and those provisions shall cease to have effect.

(6) The Government of Canada shall have the same power of deducting sums charged against a province on account of the interest on public debt in the case of the grant payable under this Act to the province as they have in the case of the existing grant.

Further
Grant to New
Brunswick.

119. New Brunswick shall receive by half-yearly Payments in advance from Canada for the period of Ten years from the Union an additional Allowance of Sixty-three thousand Dollars per Annum; but as long as the Public Debt of that Province remains under Seven million Dollars, a Deduction equal to the Interest at Five per Centum per Annum on such Deficiency shall be made from that Allowance of Sixty-three thousand Dollars. (59)

Form of Payments.

120. All Payments to be made under this Act, or in discharge of Liabilities created under any Act of the Provinces of Canada, Nova Scotia, and New Brunswick respectively, and assumed by Canada, shall, until the Parliament of Canada otherwise directs, be made in such Form and Manner as may from Time to Time be ordered by the Governor General in Council.

Canadian
Manufactures, etc.

121. All Articles of the Growth, Produce, or Manufacture of any one of the Provinces shall, from and after the Union, be admitted free into each of the other Provinces.

Continuance
of Customs
and Excise
Laws.

122. The Customs and Excise Laws of each Province shall, subject to the Provisions of this Act, continue in force until altered by the Parliament of Canada. (60)

(7) Nothing in this Act shall affect the obligation of the Government of Canada to pay to any province any grant which is payable to that province, other than the existing grant for which the grant under this Act is substituted.

(8) In the case of the provinces of British Columbia and Prince Edward Island, the amount paid on account of the grant payable per head of the population to the provinces under this Act shall not at any time be less than the amount of the corresponding grant payable at the commencement of this Act, and if it is found on any decennial census that the population of the province has decreased since the last decennial census, the amount paid on account of the grant shall not be decreased below the amount then payable, notwithstanding the decrease of the population.

See the *Provincial Subsidies Act*, R.S.C. 1970, c. P-26, *The Maritime Provinces Additional Subsidies Act*, 1942-43, c. 14, and the Terms of Union of Newfoundland with Canada, appended to the *Newfoundland Act*, and also to *An Act to approve the Terms of Union of Newfoundland with Canada*, chapter 1 of the Statutes of Canada, 1949.

See also Part III of the *Constitution Act, 1982*, which sets out commitments by Parliament and the provincial legislatures respecting equal opportunities, economic development and the provision of essential public services and a commitment by Parliament and the government of Canada to the principle of making equalization payments.

(59) Spent.

(60) Spent. Now covered by the *Customs Act*, R.S.C. 1970, c. C-40, the *Customs Tariff*, R.S.C. 1970, c. C-41, the *Excise Act*, R.S.C. 1970, c. E-12 and the *Excise Tax Act*, R.S.C. 1970, c. E-13.

123. Where Customs Duties are, at the Union, leviable on any Goods, Wares, or Merchandises in any Two Provinces, those Goods, Wares, and Merchandises may, from and after the Union, be imported from one of those Provinces into the other of them on Proof of Payment of the Customs Duty leviable thereon in the Province of Exportation, and on Payment of such further Amount (if any) of Customs Duty as is leviable thereon in the Province of Importation. (61)

Exportation and Importation as between Two Provinces.

124. Nothing in this Act shall affect the Right of New Brunswick to levy the Lumber Dues provided in Chapter Fifteen of Title Three of the Revised Statutes of New Brunswick, or in any Act amending that Act before or after the Union, and not increasing the Amount of such Dues; but the Lumber of any of the Provinces other than New Brunswick shall not be subject to such Dues. (62)

Lumber Dues in New Brunswick.

125. No Lands or Property belonging to Canada or any Province shall be liable to Taxation.

Exemption of Public Lands, etc.

126. Such Portions of the Duties and Revenues over which the respective Legislatures of Canada, Nova Scotia, and New Brunswick had before the Union Power of Appropriation as are by this Act reserved to the respective Governments or Legislatures of the Provinces, and all Duties and Revenues raised by them in accordance with the special Powers conferred upon them by this Act, shall in each Province form One Consolidated Revenue Fund to be appropriated for the Public Service of the Province.

Provincial Consolidated Revenue Fund.

IX.—MISCELLANEOUS PROVISIONS.

General.

127. Repealed. (63)

---

(61) Spent.

(62) These dues were repealed in 1873 by 36 Vict., c. 16 (N.B.). And see *An Act respecting the Export Duties imposed on Lumber,* etc. (1873) 36 Vict., c. 41 (Canada), and section 2 of the *Provincial Subsidies Act,* R.S.C. 1970, c. P-26.

(63) Repealed by the *Statute Law Revision Act, 1893,* 56-57 Vict., c. 14 (U.K.). The section read as follows:

> **127.** If any Person being at the passing of this Act a Member of the Legislature Council of Canada, Nova Scotia, or New Brunswick to whom a Place in the Senate is offered, does not within Thirty Days thereafter, by Writing under his Hand addressed to the Governor General of the Province of Canada or to the Lieutenant Governor of Nova Scotia or New Brunswick (as the Case may be), accept the same, he shall be deemed to have declined the same; and any Person who, being at the passing of this Act a Member of the Legislative Council of Nova Scotia or New Brunswick, accepts a Place in the Senate, shall thereby vacate his Seat in such Legislative Council.

Oath of Allegiance, etc.

128. Every Member of the Senate or House of Commons of Canada shall before taking his Seat therein take and subscribe before the Governor General or some Person authorized by him, and every Member of a Legislative Council or Legislative Assembly of any Province shall before taking his Seat therein take and subscribe before the Lieutenant Governor of the Province or some Person authorized by him, the Oath of Allegiance contained in the Fifth Schedule to this Act; and every Member of the Senate of Canada and every Member of the Legislative Council of Quebec shall also, before taking his Seat therein, take and subscribe before the Governor General, or some Person authorized by him, the Declaration of Qualification contained in the same Schedule.

Continuance of existing Laws, Courts, Officers, etc.

129. Except as otherwise provided by this Act, all Laws in force in Canada, Nova Scotia, or New Brunswick at the Union, and all Courts of Civil and Criminal Jurisdiction, and all legal Commissions, Powers, and Authorities, and all Officers, Judicial, Administrative, and Ministerial, existing therein at the Union, shall continue in Ontario, Quebec, Nova Scotia, and New Brunswick respectively, as if the Union had not been made; subject nevertheless (except with respect to such as are enacted by or exist under Acts of the Parliament of Great Britain or of the Parliament of the United Kingdom of Great Britain and Ireland), to be repealed, abolished, or altered by the Parliament of Canada, or by the Legislature of the respective Province, according to the Authority of the Parliament or of that Legislature under this Act. (64)

Transfer of Officers to Canada.

130. Until the Parliament of Canada otherwise provides, all Officers of the several Provinces having Duties to discharge in relation to Matters other than those coming within the Classes of Subjects by this Act assigned exclusively to the Legislature of the Provinces shall be Officers of Canada, and shall continue to discharge the Duties of their respective Offices under the same Liabilities, Responsibilities, and Penalties as if the Union had not been made. (65)

Appointment of new Officers.

131. Until the Parliament of Canada otherwise provides, the Governor General in Council may from Time to Time

---

(64) The restriction against altering or repealing laws enacted by or existing under statutes of the United Kingdom was removed by the *Statute of Westminster, 1931*, 22 Geo. V, c. 4 (U.K.) except in respect of certain constitutional documents. Comprehensive procedures for amending enactments forming part of the Constitution of Canada were provided by Part V of the *Constitution Act, 1982*, (U.K.) 1982, c. 11.

(65) Spent.

appoint such Officers as the Governor General in Council deems necessary or proper for the effectual Execution of this Act.

132. The Parliament and Government of Canada shall have all Powers necessary or proper for performing the Obligations of Canada or of any Province thereof, as Part of the British Empire, towards Foreign Countries, arising under Treaties between the Empire and such Foreign Countries. *Treaty Obligations.*

133. Either the English or the French Language may be used by any Person in the Debates of the Houses of the Parliament of Canada and of the Houses of the Legislature of Quebec; and both those Languages shall be used in the respective Records and Journals of those Houses; and either of those Languages may be used by any Person or in any Pleading or Process in or issuing from any Court of Canada established under this Act, and in or from all or any of the Courts of Quebec. *Use of English and French Languages.*

The Acts of the Parliament of Canada and of the Legislature of Quebec shall be printed and published in both those Languages. (66)

Ontario and Quebec.

134. Until the Legislature of Ontario or of Quebec otherwise provides, the Lieutenant Governors of Ontario and Quebec may each appoint under the Great Seal of the Province the following Officers, to hold Office during Pleasure, that is to say, — the Attorney General, the Secretary and Registrar of the Province, the Treasurer of the Province, the Commis- *Appointment of Executive Officers for Ontario and Quebec.*

---

(66) A similar provision was enacted for Manitoba by Section 23 of the *Manitoba Act, 1870, 33 Vict., c. 3 (Canada), (confirmed by the Constitution Act, 1871)*. Section 23 read as follows:

> **23.** Either the English or the French language may be used by any person in the debates of the Houses of the Legislature, and both these languages shall be used in the respective Records and Journals of those Houses; and either of those languages may be used by any person, or in any Pleading or Process, in or issuing from any Court of Canada established under the British North America Act, 1867, or in or from all or any of the Courts of the Province. The Acts of the Legislature shall be printed and published in both those languages.

Sections 17 to 19 of the *Constitution Act, 1982*, restate the language rights set out in section 133 in respect of Parliament and the courts established under the *Constitution Act, 1867*, and also guarantees those rights in respect of the legislature of New Brunswick and the courts of that province.

Section 16 and sections 20, 21 and 23 of the *Constitution Act, 1982*, recognize additional language rights in respect of the English and French languages. Section 22 preserves language rights and privileges of languages other than English and French.

sioner of Crown Lands, and the Commissioner of Agriculture and Public Works, and in the Case of Quebec the Solicitor General, and may, by Order of the Lieutenant Governor in Council, from Time to Time prescribe the Duties of those Officers, and of the several Departments over which they shall preside or to which they shall belong, and of the Officers and Clerks thereof, and may also appoint other and additional Officers to hold Office during Pleasure, and may from Time to Time prescribe the Duties of those Officers, and of the several Departments over which they shall preside or to which they shall belong, and of the Officers and Clerks thereof. (67)

Powers, Duties, etc. of Executive Officers.

135. Until the Legislature of Ontario or Quebec otherwise provides, all Rights, Powers, Duties, Functions, Responsibilities, or Authorities at the passing of this Act vested in or imposed on the Attorney General, Solicitor General, Secretary and Registrar of the Province of Canada, Minister of Finance, Commissioner of Crown Lands, Commissioner of Public Works, and Minister of Agriculture and Receiver General, by any Law, Statute, or Ordinance of Upper Canada, Lower Canada, or Canada, and not repugnant to this Act, shall be vested in or imposed on any Officer to be appointed by the Lieutenant Governor for the discharge of the same or any of them; and the Commissioner of Agriculture and Public Works shall perform the Duties and Functions of the Office of Minister of Agriculture at the passing of this Act imposed by the Law of the Province of Canada, as well as those of the Commissioner of Public Works. (68)

Great Seals.

136. Until altered by the Lieutenant Governor in Council, the Great Seals of Ontario and Quebec respectively shall be the same, or of the same Design, as those used in the Provinces of Upper Canada and Lower Canada respectively before their Union as the Province of Canada.

Construction of temporary Acts.

137. The words "and from thence to the End of the then next ensuing Session of the Legislature," or Words to the same Effect, used in any temporary Act of the Province of Canada not expired before the Union, shall be construed to extend and apply to the next Session of the Parliament of

---

(67) Spent. Now covered in Ontario by the *Executive Council Act*, R.S.O. 1980, c. 147 and in Quebec by the *Executive Power Act*, R.S.Q. 1977, c. E-18.

(68) Probably spent.

Canada if the Subject Matter of the Act is within the Powers of the same as defined by this Act, or to the next Sessions of the Legislatures of Ontario and Quebec respectively if the Subject Matter of the Act is within the Powers of the same as defined by this Act.

138. From and after the Union the Use of the Words Upper Canada", instead of "Ontario," or "Lower Canada" instead of "Quebec," in any Deed, Writ, Process, Pleading, Document, Matter, or Thing shall not invalidate the same. _{As to Errors in Names.}

As to Errors in Names.

139. Any Proclamation under the Great Seal of the Province of Canada issued before the Union to take effect at a Time which is subsequent to the Union, whether relating to that Province, or to Upper Canada, or to Lower Canada, and the several Matters and Things therein proclaimed, shall be and continue of like Force and Effect as if the Union had not been made. (69)

As to issue of Proclamations before Union, to commence after Union.

140. Any Proclamation which is authorized by any Act of the Legislature of the Province of Canada to be issued under the Great Seal of the Province of Canada, whether relating to that Province, or to Upper Canada, or to Lower Canada, and which is not issued before the Union, may be issued by the Lieutenant Governor of Ontario or Quebec, as its Subject Matter requires, under the Great Seal thereof; and from and after the Issue of such Proclamation the same and the several Matters and Things therein proclaimed shall be and continue of the like Force and Effect in Ontario or Quebec as if the Union had not been made. (70)

As to issue of Proclamations after Union.

141. The Penitentiary of the Province of Canada shall, until the Parliament of Canada otherwise provides, be and continue the Penitentiary of Ontario and of Quebec. (71)

Penitentiary.

142. The Division and Adjustment of the Debts, Credits, Liabilities, Properties, and Assets of Upper Canada and Lower Canada shall be referred to the Arbitrament of Three Arbitrators, One chosen by the Government of Ontario, One by the Government of Quebec, and One by the Government of Canada; and the Selection of the Arbitrators shall not be made until the Parliament of Canada and the Legislatures of

Arbitration respecting Debts, etc.

---

(69) Probably spent.

(70) Probably spent.

(71) Spent. Penitentiaries are now provided for by the *Penitentiary Act*, R.S.C. 1970, c. P-6.

Ontario and Quebec have met; and the Arbitrator chosen by the Government of Canada shall not be a Resident either in Ontario or in Quebec. (72)

Division of Records.

143. The Governor General in Council may from Time to Time order that such and so many of the Records, Books, and Documents of the Province of Canada as he thinks fit shall be appropriated and delivered either to Ontario or to Quebec, and the same shall thenceforth be the Property of that Province; and any Copy thereof or Extract therefrom, duly certified by the Officer having charge of the Original thereof, shall be admitted as Evidence. (73)

Constitution of Townships in Quebec.

144. The Lieutenant Governor of Quebec may from Time to Time, by Proclamation under the Great Seal of the Province, to take effect from a Day to be appointed therein, constitute Townships in those Parts of the Province of Quebec in which Townships are not then already constituted, and fix the Metes and Bounds thereof.

145. Repealed. (74)

XI.—ADMISSION OF OTHER COLONIES.

Power to admit Newfoundland etc., into the Union.

146. It shall be lawful for the Queen, by and with the Advice of Her Majesty's Most Honourable Privy Council, on Addresses from the Houses of the Parliament of Canada, and from the Houses of the respective Legislatures of the Colonies or Provinces of Newfoundland, Prince Edward Island, and British Columbia, to admit those Colonies or Provinces, or any of them, into the Union, and on Address from the Houses of the Parliament of Canada to admit Rupert's Land and the

---

(72) Spent. See pages (xi) and (xii) of the Public Accounts, 1902-03.

(73) Probably spent. Two orders were made under this section on the 24th of January, 1868.

(74) Repealed by the *Statute Law Revision Act, 1893*, 56-57 Vict., c. 14, (U.K.). The section read as follows:

X.—Intercolonial Railway.

145. Inasmuch as the Provinces of Canada, Nova Scotia, and New Brunswick have joined in a Declaration that the Construction of the Intercolonial Railway is essential to the Consolidation of the Union of British North America, and to the Assent thereto of Nova Scotia and New Brunswick, and have consequently agreed that Provision should be made for its immediate Construction by the Government of Canada; Therefore, in order to give effect to that Agreement, it shall be the Duty of the Government and Parliament of Canada to provide for the Commencement, within Six Months after the Union, of a Railway connecting the River St. Lawrence with the City of Halifax in Nova Scotia, and for the Construction thereof without Intermission, and the Completion thereof with all practicable Speed.

North-western Territory, or either of them, into the Union, on such Terms and Conditions in each Case as are in the Addresses expressed and as the Queen thinks fit to approve, subject to the Provisions of this Act; and the Provisions of any Order in Council in that Behalf shall have effect as if they had been enacted by the Parliament of the United Kingdom of Great Britain and Ireland. (75)

147. In case of the Admission of Newfoundland and Prince Edward Island, or either of them, each shall be entitled to a Representation in the Senate of Canada of Four Members, and (notwithstanding anything in this Act) in case of the Admission of Newfoundland the normal Number of Senators shall be Seventy-six and their maximum Number shall be Eighty-two; but Prince Edward Island when admitted shall be deemed to be comprised in the Third of Three Divisions into which Canada is, in relation to the Constitution of the Senate, divided by this Act, and accordingly, after the Admission of Prince Edward Island, whether Newfoundland is admitted or not, the Representation of Nova Scotia and New Brunswick in the Senate shall, as Vacancies occur, be reduced from Twelve to Ten Members respectively, and the Representation of each of those Provinces shall not be increased at any Time beyond Ten, except under the Provisions of this Act for the Appointment of Three or Six additional Senators under the Direction of the Queen. (76)

As to Representation of Newfoundland and Prince Edward Island in Senate.

---

(75) All territories mentioned in this section are now part of Canada. See the notes to section 5, *supra*.

(76) Spent. See the notes to sections 21, 22, 26, 27 and 28, *supra*.

SCHEDULES

THE FIRST SCHEDULE. (77)

Electoral Districts of Ontario.

A.

EXISTING ELECTORAL DIVISIONS.

COUNTIES.

1. Prescott.	6. Carleton.
2. Glengarry.	7. Prince Edward.
3. Stormont.	8. Halton.
4. Dundas.	9. Essex.
5. Russell.	

RIDINGS OF COUNTIES.

10. North Riding of Lanark.
11. South Riding of Lanark.
12. North Riding of Leeds and North Riding of Grenville.
13. South Riding of Leeds.
14. South Riding of Grenville.
15. East Riding of Northumberland.
16. West Riding of Northumberland (excepting therefrom the Township of South Monaghan).
17. East Riding of Durham.
18. West Riding of Durham.
19. North Riding of Ontario.
20. South Riding of Ontario.
21. East Riding of York.
22. West Riding of York.
23. North Riding of York.
24. North Riding of Wentworth.
25. South Riding of Wentworth.

---

(77) Spent. *Representation Act*, R.S.O. 1970, c. 413.

26. East Riding of Elgin.
27. West Riding of Elgin.
28. North Riding of Waterloo.
29. South Riding of Waterloo.
30. North Riding of Brant.
31. South Riding of Brant.
32. North Riding of Oxford.
33. South Riding of Oxford.
34. East Riding of Middlesex.

CITIES, PARTS OF CITIES, AND TOWNS.

35. West Toronto.
36. East Toronto.
37. Hamilton.
38. Ottawa.
39. Kingston.
40. London.
41. Town of Brockville, with the Township of Elizabethtown thereto attached.
42. Town of Niagara, with the Township of Niagara thereto attached.
43. Town of Cornwall, with the Township of Cornwall thereto attached.

B.

NEW ELECTORAL DISTRICTS.

44. The Provisional Judicial District of ALGOMA.

The County of BRUCE, divided into Two Ridings, to be called respectively the North and South Ridings:—

45. The North Riding of Bruce to consist of the Townships of Bury, Lindsay, Eastnor, Albermarle, Amable, Arran, Bruce, Elderslie, and Saugeen, and the Village of Southampton.

46. The South Riding of Bruce to consist of the Townships of Kincardine (including the Village of Kincardine), Greenock, Brant, Huron, Kinloss, Culross, and Carrick.

The County of HURON, divided into Two Ridings, to be called respectively the North and South Ridings:—

47. The North Riding to consist of the Townships of Ashfield, Wawanosh, Turnberry, Howick, Morris, Grey, Colborne, Hullett, including the Village of Clinton, and McKillop.

48. The South Riding to consist of the Town of Goderich and the Townships of Goderich, Tuckersmith, Stanley, Hay, Usborne, and Stephen.

The County of MIDDLESEX, divided into Three Ridings, to be called respectively the North, West, and East Ridings:—

49. The North Riding to consist of the Townships of McGillivray and Biddulph (taken from the County of Huron), and Williams East, Williams West, Adelaide, and Lobo.

50. The West Riding to consist of the Townships of Delaware, Carradoc, Metcalfe, Mosa and Ekfrid, and the Village of Strathroy.

[The East Riding to consist of the Townships now embraced therein, and be bounded as it is at present.]

51. The County of LAMBTON to consist of the Townships of Bosanquet, Warwick, Plympton, Sarnia, Moore, Enniskillen, and Brooke, and the Town of Sarnia.

52. The County of KENT to consist of the Townships of Chatham, Dover, East Tilbury, Romney, Raleigh, and Harwich, and the town of Chatham.

53. The County of BOTHWELL to consist of the Townships of Sombra, Dawn, and Euphemia (taken from the County of Lambton), and the Townships of Zone, Camden with the Gore thereof, Orford, and Howard (taken from the County of Kent).

The County of GREY divided into Two Ridings to be called respectively the South and North Ridings:—

54. The South Riding to consist of the Townships of Bentinck, Glenelg, Artemesia, Osprey, Normanby, Egremont, Proton, and Melancthon.

55. The North Riding to consist of the Townships of Collingwood, Euphrasia, Holland, Saint-Vincent, Sydenham,

Sullivan, Derby, and Keppel, Sarawak and Brooke, and the Town of Owen Sound.

The County of PERTH divided into Two Ridings, to be called respectively the South and North Ridings:—

56. The North Riding to consist of the Townships of Wallace, Elma, Logan, Ellice, Mornington, and North Easthope, and the Town of Stratford.

57. The South Riding to consist of the Townships of Blanchard, Downie, South Easthope, Fullarton, Hibbert, and the Villages of Mitchell and Ste. Marys.

The County of WELLINGTON divided into Three Ridings to be called respectively North, South and Centre Ridings:—

58. The North Riding to consist of the Townships of Amaranth, Arthur, Luther, Minto, Maryborough, Peel, and the Village of Mount Forest.

59. The Centre Riding to consist of the Townships of Garafraxa, Erin, Eramosa, Nichol, and Pilkington, and the Villages of Fergus and Elora.

60. The South Riding to consist of the Town of Guelph, and the Townships of Guelph and Puslinch.

The County of NORFOLK, divided into Two Ridings, to be called respectively the South and North Ridings:—

61. The South Riding to consist of the Townships of Charlotteville, Houghton, Walsingham, and Woodhouse, and with the Gore thereof.

62. The North Riding to consist of the Townships of Middleton, Townsend, and Windham, and the Town of Simcoe.

63. The County of HALDIMAND to consist of the Townships of Oneida, Seneca, Cayuga North, Cayuga South, Rainham, Walpole, and Dunn.

64. The County of MONCK to consist of the Townships of Canborough and Moulton, and Sherbrooke, and the Village of Dunnville (taken from the County of Haldimand), the Townships of Caister and Gainsborough (taken from the County of Lincoln), and the Townships

of Pelham and Wainfleet (taken from the County of Welland).

65. The County of LINCOLN to consist of the Townships of Clinton, Grantham, Grimsby, and Louth, and the Town of St. Catherines.

66. The County of WELLAND to consist of the Townships of Bertie, Crowland, Humberstone, Stamford, Thorold, and Willoughby, and the Villages of Chippewa, Clifton, Fort Erie, Thorold, and Welland.

67. The County of PEEL to consist of the Townships of Chinguacousy, Toronto, and the Gore of Toronto, and the Villages of Brampton and Streetsville.

68. The County of CARDWELL to consist of the Townships of Albion and Caledon (taken from the County of Peel), and the Townships of Adjala and Mono (taken from the County of Simcoe).

The County of SIMCOE, divided into Two Ridings, to be called respectively the South and North Ridings:—

69. The South Riding to consist of the Townships of West Gwillimbury, Tecumseth, Innisfil, Essa, Tossorontio, Mulmur, and the Village of Bradford.

70. The North Riding to consist of the Townships of Nottawasaga, Sunnidale, Vespra, Flos, Oro, Medonte, Orillia and Matchedash, Tiny and Tay, Balaklava and Robinson, and the Towns of Barrie and Collingwood.

The County of VICTORIA, divided into Two Ridings, to be called respectively the South and North Ridings:—

71. The South Riding to consist of the Townships of Ops, Mariposa, Emily, Verulam, and the Town of Lindsay.

72. The North Riding to consist of the Townships of Anson, Bexley, Carden, Dalton, Digby, Eldon, Fenelon, Hindon, Laxton, Lutterworth, Macaulay and Draper, Sommerville, and Morrison, Muskoka, Monck and Watt (taken from the County of Simcoe), and any other surveyed Townships lying to the North of the said North Riding.

The County of PETERBOROUGH, divided into Two Ridings, to be called respectively the West and East Ridings:—

73. The West Riding to consist of the Townships of South Monaghan (taken from the County of Northumberland), North Monaghan, Smith, and Ennismore, and the Town of Peterborough.

74. The East Riding to consist of the Townships of Asphodel, Belmont and Methuen, Douro, Dummer, Galway, Harvey, Minden, Stanhope and Dysart, Otonabee, and Snowden, and the Village of Ashburnham, and any other surveyed Townships lying to the North of the said East Riding.

The County of HASTINGS, divided into Three Ridings, to be called respectively the West, East, and North Ridings:—

75. The West Riding to consist of the Town of Belleville, the Township of Sydney, and the Village of Trenton.

76. The East Riding to consist of the Townships of Thurlow, Tyendinaga, and Hungerford.

77. The North Riding to consist of the Townships of Rawdon, Huntingdon, Madoc, Elzevir, Tudor, Marmora, and Lake, and the Village of Stirling, and any other surveyed Townships lying to the North of the said North Riding.

78. The County of LENNOX, to consist of the Townships of Richmond, Adolphustown, North Fredericksburgh, South Fredericksburgh, Ernest Town, and Amherst Island, and the Village of Napanee.

79. The County of ADDINGTON to consist of the Townships of Camden, Portland, Sheffield, Hinchinbrooke, Kaladar, Kennebec, Olden, Oso, Anglesea, Barrie, Clarendon, Palmerston, Effingham, Abinger, Miller, Canonto, Denbigh, Loughborough, and Bedford.

80. The County of FRONTENAC to consist of the Townships of Kingston, Wolfe Island, Pittsburgh and Howe Island, and Storrington.

The County of RENFREW, divided into Two Ridings, to be called respectively the South and North Ridings:—

81. The South Riding to consist of the Townships of McNab, Bagot, Blithfield, Brougham, Horton, Admaston, Grattan, Matawatchan, Griffith, Lyndoch, Raglan, Radcliffe,

Brudenell, Sebastopol, and the Villages of Arnprior and Renfrew.

82. The North Riding to consist of the Townships of Ross, Bromley, Westmeath, Stafford, Pembroke, Wilberforce, Alice, Petawawa, Buchanan, South Algoma, North Algoma, Fraser, McKay, Wylie, Rolph, Head, Maria, Clara, Haggerty, Sherwood, Burns, and Richards, and any other surveyed Townships lying Northwesterly of the said North Riding.

———————

Every Town and incorporated Village existing at the Union, not specially mentioned in this Schedule, is to be taken as Part of the County or Riding within which it is locally situate.

———————
———————

THE SECOND SCHEDULE.

———————

Electoral Districts of Quebec specially fixed.

COUNTIES OF—

Pontiac.	Missisquoi.	Compton.
Ottawa.	Brome.	Wolfe and
Argenteuil.	Shefford.	Richmond.
Huntingdon.	Stanstead.	Megantic.

Town of Sherbrooke.

———————
———————

THE THIRD SCHEDULE.

———————

Provincial Public Works and Property to be the Property of Canada.

1. Canals, with Lands and Water Power connected therewith.
2. Public Harbours.

3. Lighthouses and Piers, and Sable Island.
4. Steamboats, Dredges, and public Vessels.
5. Rivers and Lake Improvements.
6. Railways and Railway Stocks, Mortgages, and other Debts due by Railway Companies.
7. Military Roads.
8. Custom Houses, Post Offices, and all other Public Buildings, except such as the Government of Canada appropriate for the Use of the Provincial Legislature and Governments.
9. Property transferred by the Imperial Government, and known as Ordinance Property.
10. Armouries, Drill Sheds, Military Clothing, and Munitions of War, and Lands set apart for general Public Purposes.

_____

_____

THE FOURTH SCHEDULE.

_____

Assets to be the Property of Ontario and Quebec conjointly.

Upper Canada Building Fund.
Lunatic Asylums.
Normal School.
Court Houses, ⎫
   in   ⎪
Aylmer.   ⎬ Lower Canada
Montreal.   ⎪
Kamouraska. ⎭
Law Society, Upper Canada.
Montreal Turnpike Trust.
University Permanent Fund.
Royal Institution.
Consolidated Municipal Loan Fund, Upper Canada.
Consolidated Municipal Loan Fund, Lower Canada.
Agricultural Society, Upper Canada.
Lower Canada Legislative Grant.
Quebec Fire Loan.
Temiscouata Advance Account.
Quebec Turnpike Trust.
Education—East.
Building and Jury Fund, Lower Canada.
Municipalities Fund.

Lower Canada Superior Education Income Fund.

THE FIFTH SCHEDULE.

OATH OF ALLEGIANCE.

I, *A.B.* do swear, That I will be faithful and bear true Allegiance to Her Majesty Queen Victoria.

Note.—The Name of the King or Queen of the United Kingdom of Great Britain and Ireland for the Time being is to be substituted from Time to Time, with Proper Terms of Reference thereto.

DECLARATION OF QUALIFICATION.

I, *A.B.* do declare and testify, That I am by Law duly qualified to be appointed a Member of the Senate of Canada [*or as the Case may be*], and that I am legally or equitably seised as of Freehold for my own Use and Benefit of Lands or Tenements held in Free and Common Socage [*or seised or possessed for my own Use and Benefit of Lands or Tenements held in Franc-alleu or in Roture (as the Case may be),*] in the Province of Nova Scotia [*or as the Case may be*] of the Value of Four thousand Dollars over and above all Rents, Dues, Debts, Mortgages, Charges, and Incumbrances due or payable out of or charged on or affecting the same, and that I have not collusively or colourably obtained a Title to or become possessed of the said Lands and Tenements or any Part thereof for the Purpose of enabling me to become a Member of the Senate of Canada [*or as the Case may be,*] and that my Real and Personal Property are together worth Four thousand Dollars over and above my Debts and Liabilities.

THE SIXTH SCHEDULE. (78)

Primary Production from Non-Renewable Natural Resources and Forestry Resources

1. For the purposes of section 92A of this Act,

(*a*) production from a non-renewable natural resource is primary production therefrom if

(i) it is in the form in which it exists upon its recovery or severance from its natural state, or

(ii) it is a product resulting from processing or refining the resource, and is not a manufactured product or a product resulting from refining crude oil, refining upgraded heavy crude oil, refining gases or liquids derived from coal or refining a synthetic equivalent or crude oil; and

(*b*) production from a forestry resource is primary production therefrom if it consists of sawlogs, poles, lumber, wood chips, sawdust or any other primary wood product, or wood pulp, and is not a product manufactured from wood.

---

(78) As enacted by the *Constitution Act, 1982.*

CONSTITUTION ACT, 1982 (79)

SCHEDULE B

CONSTITUTION ACT, 1982

PART I

CANADIAN CHARTER OF RIGHTS AND FREEDOMS

Whereas Canada is founded upon principles that recognize the supremacy of God and the rule of law:

Guarantee of Rights and Freedoms

1. The *Canadian Charter of Rights and Freedoms* guarantees the rights and freedoms set out in it subject only to such reasonable limits prescribed by law as can be demonstrably justified in a free and democratic society. Rights and freedoms in Canada

Fundamental Freedoms

2. Everyone has the following fundamental freedoms: Fundamental freedoms

(*a*) freedom of conscience and religion;

(*b*) freedom of thought, belief, opinion and expression, including freedom of the press and other media of communication;

---

(79) Enacted as Schedule B to the *Canada Act 1982*, (U.K.) 1982, c. 11, which came into force on April 17, 1982. The *Canada Act 1982*, other than Schedules A and B thereto, reads as follows:

An Act to give effect to a request by the Senate and House of Commons of Canada

Whereas Canada has requested and consented to the enactment of an Act of the Parliament of the United Kingdom to give effect to the provisions hereinafter set forth and the Senate and the House of Commons of Canada in Parliament assembled have submitted an address to Her Majesty requesting that Her Majesty may graciously be pleased to cause a Bill to be laid before the Parliament of the United Kingdom for that purpose.

Be it therefore enacted by the Queen's Most Excellent Majesty, by and with the advice and consent of the Lords Spiritual and Temporal, and Commons, in this present Parliament assembled, and by the authority of the same, as follows:

1. The *Constitution Act, 1982* set out in Schedule B to this Act is hereby enacted for and shall have the force of law in Canada and shall come into force as provided in that Act.

2. No Act of the Parliament of the United Kingdom passed after the *Constitution Act, 1982* comes into force shall extend to Canada as part of its law.

3. So far as it is not contained in Schedule B, the French version of this Act is set out in Schedule A to this Act and has the same authority in Canada as the English version thereof.

4. This Act may be cited as the *Canada Act 1982*.

(*c*) freedom of peaceful assembly; and

(*d*) freedom of association.

Democratic Rights

Democratic rights of citizens

3. Every citizen of Canada has the right to vote in an election of members of the House of Commons or of a legislative assembly and to be qualified for membership therein.

Maximum duration of legislative bodies

4. (1) No House of Commons and no legislative assembly shall continue for longer than five years from the date fixed for the return of the writs of a general election of its members. (80)

Continuation in special circumstances

(2) In time of real or apprehended war, invasion or insurrection, a House of Commons may be continued by Parliament and a legislative assembly may be continued by the legislature beyond five years if such continuation is not opposed by the votes of more than one-third of the members of the House of Commons or the legislative assembly, as the case may be. (81)

Annual sitting of legislative bodies

5. There shall be a sitting of Parliament and of each legislature at least once every twelve months. (82)

Mobility Rights

Mobility of citizens

6. (1) Every citizen of Canada has the right to enter, remain in and leave Canada.

Rights to move and gain livelihood

(2) Every citizen of Canada and every person who has the status of a permanent resident of Canada has the right

(*a*) to move to and take up residence in any province; and

(*b*) to pursue the gaining of a livelihood in any province.

Limitation

(3) The rights specified in subsection (2) are subject to

(*a*) any laws or practices of general application in force in a province other than those that discriminate among persons primarily on the basis of province of present or previous residence; and

---

(80) See section 50 and the footnotes to sections 85 and 88 of the *Constitution Act, 1867.*

(81) Replaces part of Class 1 of section 91 of the *Constitution Act, 1867*, which was repealed as set out in subitem 1(3) of the Schedule to this Act.

(82) See the footnotes to sections 20, 86 and 88 of the *Constitution Act, 1867.*

(*b*) any laws providing for reasonable residency requirements as a qualification for the receipt of publicly provided social services.

(4) Subsections (2) and (3) do not preclude any law, program or activity that has as its object the amelioration in a province of conditions of individuals in that province who are socially or economically disadvantaged if the rate of employment in that province is below the rate of employment in Canada.

Affirmative action programs

Legal Rights

7. Everyone has the right to life, liberty and security of the person and the right not to be deprived thereof except in accordance with the principles of fundamental justice.

Life, liberty and security of person

8. Everyone has the right to be secure against unreasonable search or seizure.

Search or seizure

9. Everyone has the right not to be arbitrarily detained or imprisoned.

Detention or imprisonment

10. Everyone has the right on arrest or detention

Arrest or detention

(*a*) to be informed promptly of the reasons therefor;

(*b*) to retain and instruct counsel without delay and to be informed of that right; and

(*c*) to have the validity of the detention determined by way of *habeas corpus* and to be released if the detention is not lawful.

11. Any person charged with an offence has the right

Proceedings in criminal and penal matters

(*a*) to be informed without unreasonable delay of the specific offence;

(*b*) to be tried within a reasonable time;

(*c*) not to be compelled to be a witness in proceedings against that person in respect of the offence;

(*d*) to be presumed innocent until proven guilty according to law in a fair and public hearing by an independent and impartial tribunal;

(*e*) not to be denied reasonable bail without just cause;

(*f*) except in the case of an offence under military law tried before a military tribunal, to the benefit of trial by jury where the maximum punishment for the offence is imprisonment for five years or a more severe punishment;

(*g*) not to be found guilty on account of any act or omission unless, at the time of the act or omission, it constituted an offence under Canadian or international law or was criminal according to the general principles of law recognized by the community of nations;

(*h*) if finally acquitted of the offence, not to be tried for it again and, if finally found guilty and punished for the offence, not to be tried or punished for it again; and

(*i*) if found guilty of the offence and if the punishment for the offence has been varied between the time of commission and the time of sentencing, to the benefit of the lesser punishment.

Treatment or punishment

12. Everyone has the right not to be subjected to any cruel and unusual treatment or punishment.

Self-crimination

13. A witness who testifies in any proceedings has the right not to have any incriminating evidence so given used to incriminate that witness in any other proceedings, except in a prosecution for perjury or for the giving of contradictory evidence.

Interpreter

14. A party or witness in any proceedings who does not understand or speak the language in which the proceedings are conducted or who is deaf has the right to the assistance of an interpreter.

Equality Rights

Equality before and under law and equal protection and benefit of law

15. (1) Every individual is equal before and under the law and has the right to the equal protection and equal benefit of the law without discrimination and, in particular, without discrimination based on race, national or ethnic origin, colour, religion, sex, age or mental or physical disability.

Affirmative action programs

(2) Subsection (1) does not preclude any law, program or activity that has as its object the amelioration of conditions of disadvantaged individuals or groups including those that are disadvantaged because of race, national or ethnic origin, colour, religion, sex, age or mental or physical disability. (83)

Official Languages of Canada

Official languages of Canada

16. (1) English and French are the official languages of Canada and have equality of status and equal rights and

---

(83) Subsection 32(2) provides that section 15 shall not have effect until three years after section 32 comes into force.

Section 32 came into force on April 17, 1982; therefore, section 15 had effect on April 17, 1985.

privileges as to their use in all institutions of the Parliament and government of Canada.

(2) English and French are the official languages of New Brunswick and have equality of status and equal rights and privileges as to their use in all institutions of the legislature and government of New Brunswick.

Official languages of New Brunswick

(3) Nothing in this Charter limits the authority of Parliament or a legislature to advance the equality of status or use of English and French.

Advancement of status and use

17. (1) Everyone has the right to use English or French in any debates and other proceedings of Parliament. (84)

Proceedings of Parliament

(2) Everyone has the right to use English or French in any debates and other proceedings of the legislature of New Brunswick. (85)

Proceedings of New Brunswick legislature

18. (1) The statutes, records and journals of Parliament shall be printed and published in English and French and both language versions are equally authoritative. (86)

Parliamentary statutes and records

(2) The statutes, records and journals of the legislature of New Brunswick shall be printed and published in English and French and both language versions are equally authoritative. (87)

New Brunswick statutes and records

19. (1) Either English or French may be used by any person in, or in any pleading in or process issuing from, any court established by Parliament. (88)

Proceedings in courts established by Parliament

(2) Either English or French may be used by any person in, or in any pleading in or process issuing from, any court of New Brunswick. (89)

Proceedings in New Brunswick courts

20. (1) Any member of the public in Canada has the right to communicate with, and to receive available services from, any head or central office of an institution of the Parliament or government of Canada in English or French, and has the

Communications by public with federal institutions

---

(84) See section 133 of the *Constitution Act, 1867*, and the footnote thereto.

(85) *Id.*

(86) *Id.*

(87) *Id.*

(88) *Id.*

(89) *Id.*

same right with respect to any other office of any such institution where

(*a*) there is a significant demand for communications with and services from that office in such language; or

(*b*) due to the nature of the office, it is reasonable that communications with and services from that office be available in both English and French.

Communications by public with New Brunswick institutions

(2) Any member of the public in New Brunswick has the right to communicate with, and to receive available services from, any office of an institution of the legislature or government of New Brunswick in English or French.

Continuation of existing constitutional provisions

21. Nothing in sections 16 to 20 abrogates or derogates from any right, privilege or obligation with respect to the English and French languages, or either of them, that exists or is continued by virtue of any other provision of the Constitution of Canada. (90)

Rights and privileges preserved

22. Nothing in sections 16 to 20 abrogates or derogates from any legal or customary right or privilege acquired or enjoyed either before or after the coming into force of this Charter with respect to any language that is not English or French.

Minority Language Educational Rights

Language of instruction

23. (1) Citizens of Canada

(*a*) whose first language learned and still understood is that of the English or French linguistic minority population of the province in which they reside, or

(*b*) who have received their primary school instruction in Canada in English or French and reside in a province where the language in which they received that instruction is the language of the English or French linguistic minority population of the province,

have the right to have their children receive primary and secondary school instruction in that language in that province. (91)

---

(90) See, for example, section 133 of the *Constitution Act, 1867,* and the reference to the *Manitoba Act, 1870,* in the footnote thereto.

(91) Paragraph 23(1)(*a*) is not in force in respect of Quebec. See section 59 *infra.*

(2) Citizens of Canada of whom any child has received or is receiving primary or secondary school instruction in English or French in Canada, have the right to have all their children receive primary and secondary school instruction in the same language.

Continuity of language instruction

(3) The right of citizens of Canada under subsections (1) and (2) to have their children receive primary and secondary school instruction in the language of the English or French linguistic minority population of a province

Application where numbers warrant

(*a*) applies wherever in the province the number of children of citizens who have such a right is sufficient to warrant the provision to them out of public funds of minority language instruction; and

(*b*) includes, where the number of those children so warrants, the right to have them receive that instruction in minority language educational facilities provided out of public funds.

Enforcement

24. (1) Anyone whose rights or freedoms, as guaranteed by this Charter, have been infringed or denied may apply to a court of competent jurisdiction to obtain such remedy as the court considers appropriate and just in the circumstances.

Enforcement of guaranteed rights and freedoms

(2) Where, in proceedings under subsection (1), a court concludes that evidence was obtained in a manner that infringed or denied any rights or freedoms guaranteed by this Charter, the evidence shall be excluded if it is established that, having regard to all the circumstances, the admission of it in the proceedings would bring the administration of justice into disrepute.

Exclusion of evidence bringing administration of justice into disrepute

General

25. The guarantee in this Charter of certain rights and freedoms shall not be construed so as to abrogate or derogate from any aboriginal, treaty or other rights or freedoms that pertain to the aboriginal peoples of Canada including

Aboriginal rights and freedoms not affected by Charter

(*a*) any rights or freedoms that have been recognized by the Royal Proclamation of October 7, 1763; and

(b) any rights or freedoms that now exist by way of land claims agreements or may be so acquired. (92)

Other rights and freedoms not affected by Charter

26. The guarantee in this Charter of certain rights and freedoms shall not be construed as denying the existence of any other rights or freedoms that exist in Canada.

Multicultural heritage

27. This Charter shall be interpreted in a manner consistent with the preservation and enhancement of the multicultural heritage of Canadians.

Rights guaranteed equally to both sexes

28. Notwithstanding anything in this Charter, the rights and freedoms referred to in it are guaranteed equally to male and female persons.

Rights respecting certain schools preserved

29. Nothing in this Charter abrogates or derogates from any rights or privileges guaranteed by or under the Constitution of Canada in respect of denominational, separate or dissentient schools. (93)

Application to territories and territorial authorities

30. A reference in this Charter to a Province or to the legislative assembly or legislature of a province shall be deemed to include a reference to the Yukon Territory and the Northwest Territories, or to the appropriate legislative authority thereof, as the case may be.

Legislative powers not extended

31. Nothing in this Charter extends the legislative powers of any body or authority.

Application of Charter

Application of Charter

32. (1) This Charter applies

(a) to the Parliament and government of Canada in respect of all matters within the authority of Parliament including all matters relating to the Yukon Territory and Northwest Territories; and

(b) to the legislature and government of each province in respect of all matters within the authority of the legislature of each province.

Exception

(2) Notwithstanding subsection (1), section 15 shall not have effect until three years after this section comes into force.

---

(92) Paragraph 25(b) was repealed and re-enacted by the *Constitution Amendment Proclamation, 1983. See* SI/84-102.

Paragraph 25(b) as originally enacted read as follows:

"(b) any rights or freedoms that may be acquired by the aboriginal peoples of Canada by way of land claims settlement."

(93) See section 93 of the *Constitution Act, 1867*, and the footnote thereto.

33. (1) Parliament or the legislature of a province may expressly declare in an Act of Parliament or of the legislature, as the case may be, that the Act or a provision thereof shall operate notwithstanding a provision included in section 2 or sections 7 to 15 of this Charter. *(margin: Exception where express declaration)*

(2) An Act or a provision of an Act in respect of which a declaration made under this section is in effect shall have such operation as it would have but for the provision of this Charter referred to in the declaration. *(margin: Operation of exception)*

(3) A declaration made under subsection (1) shall cease to have effect five years after it comes into force or on such earlier date as may be specified in the declaration. *(margin: Five year limitation)*

(4) Parliament or the legislature of a province may re-enact a declaration made under subsection (1). *(margin: Re-enactment)*

(5) Subsection (3) applies in respect of a re-enactment made under subsection (4). *(margin: Five year limitation)*

Citation

34. This Part may be cited as the *Canadian Charter of Rights and Freedoms.* *(margin: Citation)*

PART II

RIGHTS OF THE ABORIGINAL PEOPLES OF CANADA

35. (1) The existing aboriginal and treaty rights of the aboriginal peoples of Canada are hereby recognized and affirmed. *(margin: Recognition of existing aboriginal and treaty rights)*

(2) In this Act, "aboriginal peoples of Canada" includes the Indian, Inuit and Métis peoples of Canada. *(margin: Definition of "aboriginal peoples of Canada")*

(3) For greater certainty, in subsection (1) "treaty rights" includes rights that now exist by way of land claims agreements or may be so acquired. *(margin: Land claims agreements)*

(4) Notwithstanding any other provision of this Act, the aboriginal and treaty rights referred to in subsection (1) are guaranteed equally to male and female persons. (94) *(margin: Aboriginal and treaty rights are guaranteed equally to both sexes)*

35.1 The government of Canada and the provincial governments are committed to the principal that, before any amendment is made to Class 24 of section 91 of the "*Constitution Act, 1867*", to section 25 of this Act or to this Part, *(margin: Commitment to participation in constitutional conference)*

---

(94) Subsections 35(3) and (4) were added by the *Constitution Amendment Proclamation, 1983.* *See* SI/84-102.

(*a*) a constitutional conference that includes in its agenda an item relating to the proposed amendment, composed of the Prime Minister of Canada and the first ministers of the provinces, will be convened by the Prime Minister of Canada; and

(*b*) the Prime Minister of Canada will invite representatives of the aboriginal peoples of Canada to participate in the discussions on that item. (95)

PART III

EQUALIZATION AND REGIONAL DISPARITIES

Commitment to promote equal opportunities

36. (1) Without altering the legislative authority of Parliament or of the provincial legislatures, or the rights of any of them with respect to the exercise of their legislative authority, Parliament and the legislatures, together with the government of Canada and the provincial governments, are committed to

(*a*) promoting equal opportunities for the well-being of Canadians;

(*b*) furthering economic development to reduce disparity in opportunities; and

(*c*) providing essential public services of reasonable quality to all Canadians.

Commitment respecting public services

(2) Parliament and the government of Canada are committed to the principle of making equalization payments to ensure that provincial governments have sufficient revenues to provide reasonably comparable levels of public services at reasonably comparable levels of taxation. (96)

(95) Section 35.1 was added by the *Constitution Amendment Proclamation, 1983. See* SI/84-102.

(96) See the footnotes to sections 114 and 118 of the *Constitution Act, 1867.*

PART IV

CONSTITUTIONAL CONFERENCE

37. (97)

PART IV.1

CONSTITUTIONAL CONFERENCES

37.1 (1) In addition to the conference convened in March 1983, at least two constitutional conferences composed of the Prime Minister of Canada and the first ministers of the provinces shall be convened by the Prime Minister of Canada, the first within three years after April 17, 1982 and the second within five years after that date. Constitutional conferences

(2) Each conference convened under subsection (1) shall have included in its agenda constitutional matters that directly affect the aboriginal peoples of Canada, and the Prime Minister of Canada shall invite representatives of those peoples to participate in the discussions on those matters. Participation of aboriginal peoples

(3) The Prime Minister of Canada shall invite elected representatives of the governments of the Yukon Territory and the Northwest Territories to participate in the discussions on any item on the agenda of a conference convened under subsection (1) that, in the opinion of the Prime Minister, directly affects the Yukon Territory and the Northwest Territories. Participation of territories

---

(97) Section 54 provided for the repeal of Part IV one year after Part VII came into force. Part VII came into force on April 17, 1982 thereby repealing Part IV on April 17, 1983.

Part IV, as originally enacted, read as follows:

"**37.** (1) A constitutional conference composed of the Prime Minister of Canada and the first ministers of the provinces shall be convened by the Prime Minister of Canada within one year after this Part comes into force. Constitutional conference

(2) The conference convened under subsection (1) shall have included in its agenda an item respecting constitutional matters that directly affect the aboriginal peoples of Canada, including the identification and definition of the rights of those peoples to be included in the Constitution of Canada, and the Prime Minister of Canada shall invite representatives of those peoples to participate in the discussions on that item. Participation of aboriginal peoples

(3) The Prime Minister of Canada shall invite elected representatives of the governments of the Yukon Territory and the Northwest Territories to participate in the discussions on any item on the agenda of the conference convened under subsection (1) that, in the opinion of the Prime Minister, directly affects the Yukon Territory and the Northwest Territories." Participation of territories

Subsection
35(1) not
affected

(4) Nothing in this section shall be construed so as to derogate from subsection 35(1). (98)

PART V

PROCEDURE FOR AMENDING CONSTITUTION OF CANADA
(99)

General
procedure for
amending
Constitution
of Canada

38. (1) An amendment to the Constitution of Canada may be made by proclamation issued by the Governor General under the Great Seal of Canada where so authorized by

(*a*) resolutions of the Senate and House of Commons; and

(*b*) resolutions of the legislative assemblies of at least two-thirds of the provinces that have, in the aggregate, according to the then latest general census, at least fifty per cent of the population of all the provinces.

Majority of
members

(2) An amendment made under subsection (1) that derogates from the legislative powers, the proprietary rights or any other rights or privileges of the legislature or government of a province shall require a resolution supported by a majority of the members of each of the Senate, the House of Commons and the legislative assemblies required under subsection (1).

Expression of
dissent

(3) An amendment referred to in subsection (2) shall not have effect in a province the legislative assembly of which has expressed its dissent thereto by resolution supported by a majority of its members prior to the issue of the proclamation to which the amendment relates unless that legislative assembly, subsequently, by resolution supported by a majority of its members, revokes its dissent and authorizes the amendment.

Revocation of
dissent

(4) A resolution of dissent made for the purposes of subsection (3) may be revoked at any time before or after the issue of the proclamation to which it relates.

---

(98) Part IV.1 was added by the *Constitution Amendment Proclamation, 1983. See* SI/84-102.

(99) Prior to the enactment of Part V certain provisions of the Constitution of Canada and the provincial constitutions could be amended pursuant to the *Constitution Act, 1867. See* the footnotes to section 91, Class 1 and section 92, Class 1 thereof, *supra.* Other amendments to the Constitution could only be made by enactment of the Parliament of the United Kingdom.

39. (1) A proclamation shall not be issued under subsection 38(1) before the expiration of one year from the adoption of the resolution initiating the amendment procedure thereunder, unless the legislative assembly of each province has previously adopted a resolution of assent or dissent.

Restriction on proclamation

(2) A proclamation shall not be issued under subsection 38(1) after the expiration of three years from the adoption of the resolution initiating the amendment procedure thereunder.

Idem

40. Where an amendment is made under subsection 38(1) that transfers provincial legislative powers relating to education or other cultural matters from provincial legislatures to Parliament, Canada shall provide reasonable compensation to any province to which the amendment does not apply.

Compensation

41. An amendment to the Constitution of Canada in relation to the following matters may be made by proclamation issued by the Governor General under the Great Seal of Canada only where authorized by resolutions of the Senate and House of Commons and of the legislative assembly of each province:

Amendment by unanimous consent

(*a*) the office of the Queen, the Governor General and the Lieutenant Governor of a province;

(*b*) the right of a province to a number of members in the House of Commons not less than the number of Senators by which the province is entitled to be represented at the time this Part comes into force;

(*c*) subject to section 43, the use of the English or the French language;

(*d*) the composition of the Supreme Court of Canada; and

(*e*) an amendment to this Part.

42. (1) An amendment to the Constitution of Canada in relation to the following matters may be made only in accordance with subsection 38(1):

Amendment by general procedure

(*a*) the principle of proportionate representation of the provinces in the House of Commons prescribed by the Constitution of Canada;

(*b*) the powers of the Senate and the method of selecting Senators;

(c) the number of members by which a province is entitled to be represented in the Senate and the residence qualifications of Senators;

(d) subject to paragraph 41(d), the Supreme Court of Canada;

(e) the extension of existing provinces into the territories; and

(f) notwithstanding any other law or practice, the establishment of new provinces.

Exception (2) Subsections 38(2) to (4) do not apply in respect of amendments in relation to matters referred to in subsection (1).

Amendment of provisions relating to some but not all provinces **43.** An amendment to the Constitution of Canada in relation to any provision that applies to one or more, but not all, provinces, including

(a) any alteration to boundaries between provinces, and

(b) any amendment to any provision that relates to the use of the English or the French language within a province,

may be made by proclamation issued by the Governor General under the Great Seal of Canada only where so authorized by resolutions of the Senate and House of Commons and of the legislative assembly of each province to which the amendment applies.

Amendments by Parliament **44.** Subject to sections 41 and 42, Parliament may exclusively make laws amending the Constitution of Canada in relation to the executive government of Canada or the Senate and House of Commons.

Amendments by provincial legislatures **45.** Subject to section 41, the legislature of each province may exclusively make laws amending the constitution of the province.

Initiation of amendment procedures **46.** (1) The procedures for amendment under sections 38, 41, 42 and 43 may be initiated either by the Senate or the House of Commons or by the legislative assembly of a province.

Revocation of authorization (2) A resolution of assent made for the purposes of this Part may be revoked at any time before the issue of a proclamation authorized by it.

Amendments without Senate resolution **47.** (1) An amendment to the Constitution of Canada made by proclamation under section 38, 41, 42 or 43 may be made without a resolution of the Senate authorizing the issue of the proclamation if, within one hundred and eighty days after the adoption by the House of Commons of a resolution authorizing its issue, the Senate has not adopted such a resolution and if, at any time after the expiration of that period, the House of Commons again adopts the resolution.

(2) Any period when Parliament is prorogued or dissolved shall not be counted in computing the one hundred and eighty day period referred to in subsection (1). *Computation of period*

48. The Queen's Privy Council for Canada shall advise the Governor General to issue a proclamation under this Part forthwith on the adoption of the resolutions required for an amendment made by proclamation under this Part. *Advice to issue proclamation*

49. A constitutional conference composed of the Prime Minister of Canada and the first ministers of the provinces shall be convened by the Prime Minister of Canada within fifteen years after this Part comes into force to review the provisions of this Part. *Constitutional conference*

PART VI

AMENDMENT TO THE CONSTITUTION ACT, 1867

50. (100)

51. (101)

PART VII

GENERAL

52. (1) The Constitution of Canada is the supreme law of Canada, and any law that is inconsistent with the provisions of the Constitution is, to the extent of the inconsistency, of no force or effect. *Primacy of Constitution of Canada*

(2) The Constitution of Canada includes *Constitution of Canada*

(*a*) the *Canada Act 1982*, including this Act;

(*b*) the Acts and orders referred to in the schedule; and

(*c*) any amendment to any Act or order referred to in paragraph (*a*) or (*b*).

---

(100) The amendment is set out in the Consolidation of the *Constitution Act, 1867*, as section 92A thereof.

(101) The amendment is set out in the Consolidation of the *Constitution Act, 1867*, as the Sixth Schedule thereof.

Amendments
to Consti-
tution of
Canada

(3) Amendments to the Constitution of Canada shall be made only in accordance with the authority contained in the Constitution of Canada.

Repeals and
new names

53. (1) The enactments referred to in Column I of the schedule are hereby repealed or amended to the extent indicated in Column II thereof and, unless repealed, shall continue as law in Canada under the names set out in Column III thereof.

Conse-
quential
amendments

(2) Every enactment, except the *Canada Act 1982*, that refers to an enactment referred to in the schedule by the name in Column I thereof is hereby amended by substituting for that name the corresponding name in Column III thereof, and any British North America Act not referred to in the schedule may be cited as the *Constitution Act* followed by the year and number, if any, of its enactment.

Repeal and
consequential
amendments

54. Part IV is repealed on the day that is one year after this Part comes into force and this section may be repealed and this Act renumbered, consequentially upon the repeal of Part IV and this section, by proclamation issued by the Governor General under the Great Seal of Canada. (102)

Repeal of
Part IV.1 and
this section

54.1 Part IV.1 and this section are repealed on April 18, 1987. (103)

French ver-
sion of Con-
stitution of
Canada

55. A French version of the portions of the Constitution of Canada referred to in the schedule shall be prepared by the Minister of Justice of Canada as expeditiously as possible and, when any portion thereof sufficient to warrant action being taken has been so prepared, it shall be put forward for enactment by proclamation issued by the Governor General under the Great Seal of Canada pursuant to the procedure then applicable to an amendment of the same provisions of the Constitution of Canada.

English and
French ver-
sions of cer-
tain constitu-
tional texts

56. Where any portion of the Constitution of Canada has been or is enacted in English and French or where a French version of any portion of the Constitution is enacted pursuant to section 55, the English and French versions of that portion of the Constitution are equally authoritative.

---

(102) Part VII came into force on April 17, 1982. *See* SI/82-97.

(103) Section 54.1 was added by the *Constitution Amendment Proclamation, 1983. See* SI/84-102.

57. The English and French versions of this Act are equally authoritative. English and French versions of this Act

58. Subject to section 59, this Act shall come into force on a day to be fixed by proclamation issued by the Queen or the Governor General under the Great Seal of Canada. (104) Commencement

59. (1) Paragraph 23(1)(*a*) shall come into force in respect of Quebec on a day to be fixed by proclamation issued by the Queen or the Governor General under the Great Seal of Canada. Commencement of paragraph 23(1)(*a*) in respect of Quebec

(2) A proclamation under subsection (1) shall be issued only where authorized by the legislative assembly or government of Quebec. (105) Authorization of Quebec

(3) This section may be repealed on the day paragraph 23(1)(*a*) comes into force in respect of Quebec and this Act amended and renumbered, consequentially upon the repeal of this section, by proclamation issued by the Queen or the Governor General under the Great Seal of Canada. Repeal of this section

60. This Act may be cited as the *Constitution Act, 1982*, and the Constitution Acts 1867 to 1975 (No. 2) and this Act may be cited together as the *Constitution Acts, 1867 to 1982*. Short title and citations

61. A reference to the *"Constitution Acts, 1867 to 1982"* shall be deemed to include a reference to the *"Constitution Amendment Proclamation, 1983"*. (106) References

---

(104) The Act, with the exception of paragraph 23(1)(*a*) in respect of Quebec, came into force on April 17, 1982 by proclamation issued by the Queen. *See* SI/82-97.

(105) No proclamation has been issued under section 59.

(106) Section 61 was added by the *Constitution Amendment Proclamation, 1983. See* SI/84-102.

SCHEDULE

to the

CONSTITUTION ACT, 1982

MODERNIZATION OF THE CONSTITUTION

Item	Column I Act Affected	Column II Amendment	Column III New Name
1.	British North America Act, 1867, 30-31 Vict., c. 3 (U.K.)	(1) Section 1 is repealed and the following substituted therefor: "1. This Act may be cited as the *Constitution Act, 1867*." (2) Section 20 is repealed. (3) Class 1 of section 91 is repealed. (4) Class 1 of section 92 is repealed.	Constitution Act, 1867
2.	An Act to amend and continue the Act 32-33 Victoria chapter 3; and to establish and provide for the Government of the Province of Manitoba, 1870, 33 Vict., c. 3 (Can.)	(1) The long title is repealed and the following substituted therefor: "*Manitoba Act, 1870*." (2) Section 20 is repealed.	Manitoba Act, 1870
3.	Order of Her Majesty in Council admitting Rupert's Land and the North-Western Territory into the union, dated the 23rd day of June, 1870		Rupert's Land and North-Western Territory Order

SCHEDULE

to the

CONSTITUTION ACT, 1982—*Continued*

Item	Column I Act Affected	Column II Amendment	Column III New Name
4.	Order of Her Majesty in Council admitting British Columbia into the Union, dated the 16th day of May, 1871.		British Columbia Terms of Union
5.	British North America Act, 1871, 34-35 Vict., c. 28 (U.K.)	Section 1 is repealed and the following substituted therefor: "1. This Act may be cited as the *Constitution Act, 1871.*"	Constitution Act, 1871
6.	Order of Her Majesty in Council admitting Prince Edward Island into the Union, dated the 26th day of June, 1873.		Prince Edward Island Terms of Union
7.	Parliament of Canada Act, 1875, 38-39 Vict., c. 38 (U.K.)		Parliament of Canada Act, 1875
8.	Order of Her Majesty in Council admitting all British possessions and Territories in North America and islands adjacent thereto into the Union, dated the 31st day of July, 1880.		Adjacent Territories Order

SCHEDULE

to the

CONSTITUTION ACT, 1982—*Continued*

Item	Column I Act Affected	Column II Amendment	Column III New Name
9.	British North America Act, 1886, 49-50 Vict., c. 35 (U.K.)	Section 3 is repealed and the following substituted therefor: "3. This Act may be cited as the *Constitution Act, 1886.*"	Constitution Act, 1886
10.	Canada (Ontario Boundary) Act, 1889, 52-53 Vict., c. 28 (U.K.)		Canada (Ontario Boundary) Act, 1889
11.	Canadian Speaker (Appointment of Deputy) Act, 1895, 2nd Sess., 59 Vict., c. 3 (U.K.)	The Act is repealed.	
12.	The Alberta Act, 1905, 4-5 Edw. VII, c. 3 (Can.)		Alberta Act
13.	The Saskatchewan Act, 1905, 4-5 Edw. VII, c. 42 (Can.)		Saskatchewan Act
14.	British North America Act, 1907, 7 Edw. VII, c. 11 (U.K.)	Section 2 is repealed and the following substituted therefor: "2. This Act may be cited as the *Constitution Act, 1907.*"	Constitution Act, 1907

SCHEDULE

to the

CONSTITUTION ACT, 1982—*Continued*

Item	Column I Act Affected	Column II Amendment	Column III New Name
15.	British North America Act, 1915, 5-6 Geo. V, c. 45 (U.K.)	Section 3 is repealed and the following substituted therefor: "3. This Act may be cited as the *Constitution Act, 1915*."	Constitution Act, 1915
16.	British North America Act, 1930, 20-21 Geo. V, c. 26 (U.K.)	Section 3 is repealed and the following substituted therefor: "3. This Act may be cited as the *Constitution Act, 1930*."	Constitution Act, 1930
17.	Statute of Westminster, 1931, 22 Geo. V, c. 4 (U.K.)	In so far as they apply to Canada, (*a*) section 4 is repealed; and (*b*) subsection 7(1) is repealed.	Statute of Westminster, 1931
18.	British North America Act, 1940, 3-4 Geo. VI, c. 36 (U.K.)	Section 2 is repealed and the following substituted therefor: "2. This Act may be cited as the *Constitution Act, 1940*."	Constitution Act, 1940
19.	British North America Act, 1943, 6-7 Geo. VI, c. 30 (U.K.)	The Act is repealed.	

SCHEDULE

to the

CONSTITUTION ACT, 1982— *Continued*

Item	Column I Act Affected	Column II Amendment	Column III New Name
20.	British North America Act, 1946, 9-10 Geo. VI, c. 63 (U.K.)	The Act is repealed.	
21.	British North America Act, 1949, 12-13 Geo. VI, c. 22 (U.K.)	Section 3 is repealed and the following substituted therefor: "3. This Act may be cited as the *Newfoundland Act*."	Newfoundland Act
22.	British North America (No. 2) Act, 1949, 13 Geo. VI, c. 81 (U.K.)	The Act is repealed.	
23.	British North America Act, 1951, 14-15 Geo. VI, c. 32 (U.K.)	The Act is repealed.	
24.	British North America Act, 1952, 1 Eliz. II, c. 15 (Can.)	The Act is repealed.	
25.	British North America Act, 1960, 9 Eliz. II, c. 2 (U.K.)	Section 2 is repealed and the following substituted therefor: "2. This Act may be cited as the *Constitution Act, 1960*."	Constitution Act, 1960

SCHEDULE

to the

CONSTITUTION ACT, 1982—*Continued*

Item	Column I Act Affected	Column II Amendment	Column III New Name
26.	British North America Act, 1964, 12-13 Eliz. II, c. 73 (U.K.)	Section 2 is repealed and the following substituted therefor: "2. This Act may be cited as the *Constitution Act, 1964.*"	Constitution Act, 1964
27.	British North America Act, 1965, 14 Eliz. II, c. 4, Part I (Can.)	Section 2 is repealed and the following substituted therefor: "2. This Part may be cited as the *Constitution Act, 1965.*"	Constitution Act, 1965
28.	British North America Act, 1974, 23 Eliz. II, c. 13, Part I (Can.)	Section 3, as amended by 25-26 Eliz. II, c. 28, s. 38(1) (Can.), is repealed and the following substituted therefor: "3. This Part may be cited as the *Constitution Act, 1974.*"	Constitution Act, 1974
29.	British North America Act, 1975, 23-24 Eliz. II, c. 28, Part I (Can.)	Section 3, as amended by 25-26 Eliz. II, c. 28, s. 31 (Can.), is repealed and the following substituted therefor: "3. This Part may be cited as the *Constitution Act (No. 1), 1975.*"	Constitution Act (No. 1), 1975

SCHEDULE

to the

CONSTITUTION ACT, 1982—*Concluded*

Item	Column I Act Affected	Column II Amendment	Column III New Name
30.	British North America Act (No. 2), 1975, 23-24 Eliz. II, c. 53 (Can.)	Section 3 is repealed and the following substituted therefor: "3. This Act may be cited as the *Constitution Act (No. 2), 1975*."	Constitution Act (No. 2), 1975

BIBLIOGRAPHY

GENERAL REFERENCE WORKS

A. *Frameworks for the Study of Political Systems*

Almond, G.A. and G.B. Powell, Jr.: *Comparative Politics: A Developmental Approach* (Little, Brown, Boston, 1978).

Dahl, R. A.: *Modern Political Analysis* (Prentice-Hall, Englewood Cliffs, 1970).

—— and C. E. Lindblom: *Politics, Economics and Welfare* (Harper and Row, New York, 1963).

Deutsch, K. W.: *The Nerves of Government* (The Free Press, New York, 1966).

Easton, David: *A Framework for Political Analysis* (Prentice-Hall, Englewood Cliffs, 1965).

—— : *A Systems Analysis of Political Life* (John Wiley and Sons, New York, 1965).

Lasswell, H.: *Politics: Who Gets What, When, How?* (Meridian, Cleveland, 1958).

Lemieux, V.: *Les Cheminements de l'influence: systèmes, stratégies et structures du politique* (Les Presses de l'Université Laval, Montreal, 1980).

Parsons, T. and E. A. Shills (eds.): *Toward a General Theory of Action* (Harper and Row, New York, 1962).

Young, R. (ed.): *Approaches to the Study of Politics* (Northwestern University Press, Evanston, 1958).

B. *General Works on Canada*

Baldwin, Douglas and Emily Odynak: *Canada's Political Heritage: Conflict or Compromise?* (Weigh Educational Divisions, Regina, 1985).

Banting, K. (ed.): *State and Society: Canada in Comparative Perspective*, study prepared for the Royal Commission on the Economic Development Prospects for Canada, vol. 31 (University of Toronto Press, Toronto, 1986).

Bashevkin, Sylvia (ed.): *Canadian Political Behaviour: Introductory Readings* (Methuen, Toronto, 1985).

Bellan, R.C. and W.H. Pope (eds.): *The Canadian Economy: Problems and Options* (McGraw-Hill Ryerson, Scarborough, 1981).

Bennett, Paul, Cornelius Jaenen, Jacques Manet, and Richard Jones: *Emerging Identities: Selected Problems and Interpretations in Canadian History* (Prentice-Hall, Toronto, 1986).

Bernard, A.: *Politics in Canada and Quebec*, adapted by J. Driefelds (Methuen, Toronto, 1981).

Black, Derek: *Winners and Losers: The Book of Canadian Political Lists* (Methuen, Toronto, 1984).

Blishen, B.R. *et al.* (eds.): *Canadian Society: Sociological Perspectives*, 3rd ed. (Macmillan, Toronto, 1968).

Bothwell, Robert, Ian Drummond, and John English: *Canada since 1945: Power, Politics and Provincialism* (University of Toronto Press, Toronto, 1981).

Byers, R.B. (ed.): *Canadian Annual Review of Politics and Public Affairs* (University of Toronto Press with York University, Toronto, 1982, 1983, 1984, 1985).

Carty, R. Kenneth and W. Peter Ward (eds.): *Entering the Eighties: Canada in Crisis* (Oxford University Press, Toronto, 1980).

Cassidy, Carla, Phyllis Clarke, and Wayne Petruzzi (eds.): *Authority and Influence: Institutions, Issues and Concepts in Canadian Politics* (Mosaic Press, Oakville, 1985).

Cheal, D.: "Models of Mass Politics in Canada," *Canadian Review of Sociology and Anthropology*, vol. 15, no. 3, 1978, pp. 325–338.

Chorney, H. *et al.*: "The State and Political Economy," *Canadian Journal of Political and Social Theory*, vol. 1, 1977, pp. 71–86.

Christian, William: "Harold Innis as Political Theorist," *Canadian Journal of Political Science*, vol. 10, no. 1, 1977, pp. 21–42.

Clarke, Harold D., Jane Jenson, Lawrence LeDuc, and Jon H. Pammett: *Absent Mandate: The Politics of Discontent in Canada* (Gage, Toronto, 1984).

Clarkson, Stephen: *Canada and the Reagan Challenge* (Canadian Institute for Economic Policy, Ottawa, 1982).

Corry, J. A. and J. E. Hodgetts: *Democratic Government and Politics* (University of Toronto Press, Toronto, 1959).

Couchiching Institute on Public Affairs: *Free Enterprise and the State: What's Right? What's Left? What's Next?* (CBC Enterprises, Montreal, 1985).

Dauphin, R. L.: "Une Nouvelle Politique économique canadienne," *Journal of Canadian Studies*, vol. 14, no. 3, 1979, pp. 118–125.

Dawson, R. M.: *The Government of Canada*, rev. N. Ward (University of Toronto Press, Toronto, 1970).

Dickerson, Mark O. and Thomas Flanagan: *An Introduction to Government and Politics: A Conceptual Approach*, 2nd ed. (Methuen, Toronto, 1986).

——— , Thomas Flanagan, and Neil Nevitte: *Introductory Readings in Government and Politics* (Methuen, Toronto, 1984).

Djwa, Sandra and R. St. J. Macdonald: *On F. R. Scott: Essays on His Contributions to Law, Literature and Politics* (McGill-Queen's University Press, Montreal, 1983).

Doran, Charles F.: *Economic Interdependence, Autonomy and Canadian/American Relations* (Institute for Research on Public Policy, Montreal, 1983).

Drache, Daniel and Wallace Clement: *The New Practical Guide to Canadian Political Economy* (James Lorimer, Toronto, 1986).

Flaherty, D. H.: "Access to Historic Census Data in Canada: A Comparative Analysis," *Canadian Public Administration*, vol. 20, no. 3, 1977, pp. 481–498.

Fortin, P.: "La Dimension économique de la crise politique canadienne," *Canadian Public Policy*, vol. 4, no. 3, 1978, pp. 309–324.

Fox, Paul (ed.): *Politics: Canada*, 5th ed. (McGraw-Hill Ryerson, Toronto, 1982).

Fox, Paul W.: "Psychology, Politics and Hegetology," *Canadian Journal of Political Science*, vol. 13, no. 4, Dec. 1980, pp. 675–690.

French, Richard and André Beliveau: *The RCMP and the Management of National Security* (Butterworths for Institute for Research on Public Policy, Toronto, 1979).

Gibbins, Roger: *Conflict and Unity: An Introduction to Canadian Political Life* (Methuen, Toronto, 1985).

Glazebrook, G. P. de T.: *A History of Canadian Political Thought* (McClelland and Stewart, Toronto, 1966).

Granatstein, J. L.: *Canada 1957–1967; Volume XIX: The Years of Uncertainty and Innovation* (McClelland and Stewart, Toronto, 1986).

—— et al.: *Twentieth Century Canada*, 2nd ed. (McGraw-Hill Ryerson, Toronto, 1986).

——, Irving Abella, David J. Bercuson, R. Craig Brown, and H. Blair Neatby: *Twentieth Century Canada: A Reader* (McGraw-Hill Ryerson, Toronto, 1986).

—— and Paul Stevens: *A Reader's Guide to Canadian History; 2: Confederation to the Present* (University of Toronto Press, Toronto, 1982).

Guinsberg, T. N. and A. L. Renber: *Perspectives on the Social Sciences in Canada* (University of Toronto Press, Toronto, 1974).

Gwyn, Richard: *The 49th Paradox: Canada in North America* (McClelland and Stewart, Toronto, 1985).

Higgins, D. J. H.: *Urban Canada: Its Government and Politics* (Macmillan, Toronto, 1977).

Hockin, T. W.: *Government in Canada* (McGraw-Hill Ryerson, Toronto, 1976).

Jackson, Robert J., Doreen Jackson, and Nicholas Baxter-Moore: *Politics in Canada: Culture, Institutions, Behaviour and Public Policy* (Prentice-Hall, Scarborough, 1986).

Jenson, J. and B. Tomlin: *Canadian Politics: An Introduction to Systematic Analysis* (McGraw-Hill Ryerson, Toronto, 1977).

Khan, R. A., S. A. MacKown, and J. D. McNiven: *An Introduction to Political Science* (Irwin-Dorsey, Ltd., Georgetown, Ont., 1972).

Landes, Robert G.: *The Canadian Polity: A Comparative Introduction* (Prentice-Hall, Scarborough, 1983).

—— : *Canadian Politics: A Comparative Reader* (Prentice-Hall, Scarborough, 1985).

Landry, R. (ed.): *Introduction à l'analyse des politiques* (Les Presses de l'Université Laval, Quebec, 1980).

Laxer, J.: *Liberal Idea of Canada* (Lorimer, Toronto, 1977).

Levitt, Joseph: *A Vision beyond Reach: A Century of Images of Canadian Destiny* (Deneau, Ottawa, 1982).

McGrath, W. T. and M. P. Mitchell: *The Police Function in Canada* (Methuen, Toronto, 1981).

McMenemy, J.: *The Language of Canadian Politics: A Guide to Important Terms and Concepts* (Wiley, Toronto, 1980).

McNally, David: "Staple Theory as Commodity Fetishism: Marx, Innis and Canadian Political Economy," *Studies in Political Economy*, vol. 6, Autumn 1981, pp. 35–64.

MacPherson, C. B.: *The Rise and Fall of Economic Justice and Other Essays* (Oxford University Press, London, 1985).

Mallory, James R.: *The Structure of Canadian Government*, rev. ed. (Gage, Toronto, 1984).

Mann, W. E. (ed.): *Canada: A Sociological Profile* (Copp Clark, Toronto, 1968).

Marr, W. and D. Paterson: *Canada: An Economic History* (Macmillan, Toronto, 1980).

Marritt, Allen S. and George W. Brown: *Canadians and Their Government*, rev. ed. (Fitzhenry and Whiteside, Toronto, 1983).

Minogue, K. R.: "Humanist Democracy: The Political Thought of C. B. Macpherson," *Canadian Journal of Political Science*, vol. 9, no. 3, 1976, pp. 377–422.

Morton, Desmond: *Canada at War: A Military and Political History* (Butterworths, Scarborough, 1981).

Naylor, R. T.: "The Canadian State: The Accumulation of Capital and the Great War," *Journal of Canadian Studies*, vol. 16, nos. 3–4, 1981, pp. 26–55.

Neatby, H. Blair: *The Politics of Chaos: Canada in the Thirties* (Copp Clark Pitman, Toronto, 1985).

O'Donovan, Joan E.: *George Grant and the Twilight of Justice* (University of Toronto Press, Toronto, 1984).

Offe, C.: "The Separation of Form and Content in Liberal Democratic Politics," *Studies in Political Economy: A Socialist Review*, Spring, vol. 3, 1980, pp. 5–16.

Panitch, L. V. (ed.): *The Canadian State: Political Economy and Political Power* (University of Toronto Press, Toronto, 1977).

Parker, I.: "Harold Innis, Karl Marx and Canadian Political Economy," *Queen's Quarterly*, vol. 84, no. 4, 1977, pp. 60–90.

Pearson, L. B.: "Canada's Role as a Middle Power," in J. King Gordon (ed.), *Canada's Role as a Middle Power* (Canadian Institute of International Affairs, Toronto, 1966).

Phillips, P.: "The Hinterland Perspective: The Political Economy of Vernon C. Fowke," *Canadian Journal of Political and Social Theory*, vol. 2, no. 2, 1974, pp. 35–46.

Pocklington, T. C. (ed.): *Liberal Democracy in Canada and the United States: An Introduction to Politics and Government* (Holt Rinehart and Winston, Toronto, 1985).

Porter, J.: *The Vertical Mosaic* (University of Toronto Press, Toronto, 1978).

Qualter, Terence H.: *Conflicting Political Ideas in Liberal Democracies* (Methuen, Toronto, 1986).

Redekop, J. H.: *Approaches to Canadian Politics* (Prentice-Hall, Toronto, 1978).

Reilly, W. G.: *Encounter with Canada: Essays in the Social Sciences* (Center for International Studies, Duke University, Durham, N.C., 1980).

Reuber, Grant: *Canada's Political Economy: Current Issues* (McGraw-Hill Ryerson, Toronto, 1980).

Roald, Bruce (ed.): *Political Life in Canada* (Prentice-Hall, Toronto, 1983).

Roussopoulos, D.: "Beyond Reformism: The Ambiguity of the Urban Question," *Our Generation*, vol. 11, no. 2, 1977, pp. 46–58.

Rowat, D. C.: *Your Local Government*, 2nd ed. (Macmillan, Toronto, 1975).

Sabourin, M. Louis (ed.): *Le Système politique du Canada* (Editions de l'Université d'Ottawa, Ottawa, 1969).

Schmidt, Ray: "Canadian Political Economy: A Critique," *Studies in Political Economy*, vol. 6, Autumn 1981, pp. 65–92.

Schultz, R. and O. M. Kruhlak: *The Canadian Political Process*, 3rd ed. (Holt Rinehart & Winston, Toronto, 1979).

Schwartz, M. A.: "The Social Make-up of Canada and Strains in Confederation," *Canadian Public Policy*, vol. 3, no. 4, 1977, pp. 458–470.

Simeon, R. E. B.: "The 'Overload Thesis' and Canadian Government," *Canadian Public Policy*, vol. 2, no. 4, 1976, pp. 541–552.

Smiley, D.: "Must Canadian Political Science Be a Miniature Replica?" *Journal of Canadian Studies*, vol. 9, no. 1, 1974, pp. 31–41.

Sodurlund, N. C. *et al.*: "A Critique of the Hartz Theory of Political Development as Applied to Canada," *Comparative Politics*, vol. 12, no. 1, 1979, pp. 63–67.

Stairs, D. and G. R. Winnam: *The Politics of Canada's Economic Relationship with the United States*, study prepared for the Royal Commission on the Economic Union and Development Prospects for Canada, vol. 29 (University of Toronto Press, Toronto, 1986).

Svacek, Victor: "The Elusive Marxism of C. B. Macpherson," *Canadian Journal of Political Science*, vol. 9, no. 3, 1976, pp. 359–422.

Taylor, Charles: *The Pattern of Politics* (McClelland and Stewart, Toronto, 1970).

Thorburn, H.: "Canadian Pluralist Democracy in Crisis," *Canadian Journal of Political Science*, vol. 11, no. 4, 1978, pp. 723–738.

Tindal, C. R. and S. Nobes: *Local Government in Canada*, 2nd ed. (McGraw-Hill Ryerson, Toronto, 1984).

Urquhart, M. G. (ed.) and K. A. H. Buckley (ass. ed.): *Historical Statistics of Canada* (Macmillan, Toronto, 1965).

Van Loon, R. J. and Michael S. Whittington: "Alternative Styles in the Study of Canadian Politics: A Brief Rejoinder," *Canadian Journal of Political Science*, vol. 7, no. 1, 1974, pp. 132–134.

Vaughan, F., J. P. Kyba, and O. P. Dwivedi (eds.): *Contemporary Issues in Canadian Politics* (Prentice-Hall, Toronto, 1970).

Wand, Bernard: "C. B. Macpherson's Conceptual Apparatus," *Canadian Journal of Political Science*, vol. 4, no. 4, 1971, pp. 526–540.

Ward, Norman: "Money and Politics: The Costs of Democracy in Canada," *Canadian Journal of Political Science*, vol. 5, no. 1973, p. 335.

—— : "Alternative Styles: A Comment," *Canadian Journal of Political Science*, vol. 7, no. 1, 1974, pp. 128–129.

Warkentin, John (ed.): *Canada: A Geographical Interpretation* (Methuen, Toronto, 1968).

White, W. L., R. H. Wagenberg, and R. C. Nelson: *Introduction to Canadian Politics and Government*, 4th ed. (Holt Rinehart and Winston, Toronto, 1985).

Whittington, Michael and Glen Williams (eds.): *Canadian Politics in the 1980s*, 2nd ed. (Methuen, Toronto, 1984).

C. The Policy Process in Canada

Abdel-Malek, T. and A. K. Sarkar: "An Analysis of the Effects of Phase II Guidelines of the Foreign Investment Review Act," *Canadian Public Policy*, vol. 3, no. 1, 1977, pp. 36–49.

Adamson, A.: "We Were Here Before: The Referendum in Canadian Experience," *Policy Options*, vol. 1, no. 1, Mar. 1980, pp. 50–54.

Adie, Robert F. and Paul G. Thomas: *Canadian Public Administration: Problematic Perspectives* (Prentice-Hall, Scarborough, 1982).

Andrew, Caroline, André Blais, Rachel DesRosiers: "Le Logement public à Hull," *Canadian Journal of Political Science*, vol. 8, no. 1975, pp. 403–430.

Armstrong, C.: "Federalism and Government Regulation: The Case of the Canadian Insurance Industry, 1927–1934," *Canadian Public Administration*, vol. 19, no. 1, 1976, pp. 88–101.

Atkinson, Michael M.: "Parliamentary Government in Canada," in Michael S. Whittington and Glen Williams (eds.), *Canadian Politics in the 1980s*, 2nd ed. (Methuen, Toronto, 1980), pp. 331–350.

—— and Marsha A. Chandler (eds.): *The Politics of Canadian Public Policy* (University of Toronto Press, Toronto, 1983).

—— and William D. Coleman: "Bureaucrats and Politicians in Canada: An Examination of the Political Administration Model," *Comparative Political Studies*, vol. 18, no. 1, 1985, pp. 58–80.

—— and K.R. Nossal: "Bureaucratic Politics and the New Fighter Aircraft Decisions," *Canadian Public Administration*, vol. 24, no. 4, 1981, pp. 531–562.

Aucoin, Peter and Herman Bakvis: "Organizational Differentiation and Integration: The Case of Regional Economic Development Policy in Canada," *Canadian Public Administration*, vol. 27, no. 3, 1984, pp. 348–371.

Aucoin, P. and R. French: "The Ministry of State for Science and Technology," *Canadian Public Administration*, vol. 17, no. 3, 1974, pp. 461–481.

Baccigalupo, A.: "L'Informatique dans les administrations publiques et para-publiques Québécoises," *Canadian Public Administration*, vol. 17, no. 4, 1974, pp. 542–562.

Baetz, Mark and Donald Thain: *Canadian Cases in Business-Government Relations* (Methuen, Toronto, 1985).

Baldwin, J. R.: "The Evolution of Transportation Policy in Canada," *Canadian Public Administration*, vol. 20, no. 4, 1977, pp. 600–631.

Banting, K. (ed.): *The State and Economic Interests*, a study prepared for the Royal Commission on the Economic Union and Development Prospects for Canada, vol. 32 (University of Toronto Press, Toronto, 1986).

Beckman, M. Dale: "The Problem of Communicating Public Policy Effectively: Bill C–256 and Winnipeg Businessmen," *Canadian Journal of Political Science*, vol. 8, no. 1, 1975, pp. 138–143.

Berkes, F.: "Management of Recreational Fisheries in Northern Quebec: Policies versus Tools," *Canadian Public Policy*, vol. 4, no. 4, 1978, pp. 460–473.

Bernier, I. and A. Lajoie (eds.): *Consumer Protection and Environmental Law and Corporate Power*, a study prepared for the Royal Commission on the Economic Union and Development Prospects for Canada, vol. 50 (University of Toronto Press, Toronto, 1986).

Blais, A. (ed.): *Canadian Industrial Policy*, study prepared for the Royal Commission on the Economic Union and Development Prospects for Canada, vol. 44 (University of Toronto Press, Toronto, 1986).

Blais, André: "Le *Public Choice* et la croissance de l'état," *Canadian Journal of Political Science*, vol. 14, no. 4, 1982, pp. 783–808.

Borins, Sandford F.: *The Language of the Skies: The Bilingual Air Traffic Control Conflict* (McGill-Queen's University Press for IPAC, Montreal, 1983).

Bregha, F.: "The Mackenzie Valley Pipeline and Canadian Natural Gas Policy," *Canadian Public Policy*, vol. 3, no. 1, 1977, pp. 63–75.

Bryden, K.: *Old Age Pensions and Policy-making in Canada* (McGill-Queen's University Press, Montreal, 1974).

Bulmer, Martin: *The Uses of Social Research: Social Investigation in Public Policy-making* (Allen and Unwin, Toronto, 1982).

Burke, D. P.: "Hellyer and Landymore: The Unification of the Canadian Armed Forces and an Admiral's Revolt," *American Review of Canadian Studies*, vol. 7, 1978, pp. 3–27.

Campbell, H. F.: "A Benefit/Cost Rule for Evaluating Public Projects in Canada," *Canadian Public Policy*, vol. 1, 1975, pp. 171–275.

Carrothers, A. W. R.: "Collective Bargaining as Public Policy: Let Us Not Pre-empt Disaster," *Canadian Public Administration*, vol. 18, no. 4, 1975, pp. 527–540.

Castonguay, C.: "An Analysis of the Canadian Bilingual Districts Policy," *American Review of Canadian Studies*, vol. 6, no. 2, 1976, pp. 57–73.

Chamber, E. J. *et al.*: "Bill C-20: An Evaluation from the Perspective of Current Transportation Policy and Regulatory Performance," *Canadian Public Policy*, vol. 4, no. 1, 1980, pp. 47–62.

Chapman, I. and M. Gibbons: "Innovation and the Senate: Report on Science Policy," *Journal of Canadian Studies*, vol. 13, no. 1, 1978, pp. 30–37.

Clarkson, Stephen (ed.): *An Independent Foreign Policy for Canada?* (The University League for Social Reform, McClelland and Stewart, Toronto, 1968).

Conference Board of Canada: *Consultation and Consensus: A New Era in Policy Formulation?* (Conference Board of Canada, Ottawa, 1978).

Contandriopoulos, A. P.: "Changer l'organisation du système de santé plutôt que limiter le nombre de médecins: un commentaire de l'article d'Evans," *Canadian Public Policy*, vol. 2, no. 1976, pp. 161–168.

Copes, P.: "Canada's Atlantic Coast Fisheries: Policy Development and the Impact of Extended Jurisdiction," *Canadian Public Policy*, vol. 4, no. 2, 1978, pp. 155–271.

Corry, J. A.: "Changes in the Functions of Government," in *The Canadian Historical Association: Report of Annual Meeting 1945* (University of Toronto Press, Toronto, 1945), pp. 15–24.

Crenna, C. D.: "Ghost Writers in the Sky: On Explaining What You Do as a Policy Advisor," *Optimum*, vol. 12, no. 2, 1981, pp. 60–63.

Crispo, John H.: *International Unionism: A Study in Canadian-American Relations* (McGraw-Hill, Toronto, 1967).

Darling, H.: "What Belongs in Transportation Policy," *Canadian Public Administration*, vol. 18, no. 4, 1975, pp. 659–669.

Davies, G. W.: "Macroeconomic Effects of Immigration: Evidence from CANDIDE, TRACE, and RDX," *Canadian Public Policy*, vol. 3, no. 1977, pp. 299–306.

Denton, F. T. and B. G. Spencer: "On the Prospect of a Labour Shortage," *Canadian Public Policy*, vol. 4, 1978, pp. 101–118.

Dewees, D. N. and L. Waverman: "Energy Conservation: Policies for the Transport," *Canadian Public Policy*, vol. 1, 1975, pp. 536–545.

Dobell, Rob: "How Ottawa Decides Economic Policy," *Policy Options*, vol. 1, Sept./Oct. 1980, p. 14.

Doern, G. Bruce: *How Ottawa Spends* (James Lorimer, Toronto, 1981).

—— (ed.): *How Ottawa Spends Your Tax Dollars 1982* (James Lorimer, Toronto, 1982).

—— (ed.): *How Ottawa Spends: The Liberals, the Opposition and National Priorities* (James Lorimer, Toronto, 1983).

—— : "The Mega-project Episode and One Formulation of Canadian Economic Development Policy," Canadian Public Administration, vol. 26, no. 2, 1983, pp. 219–238.

—— : *Political Policy-making: A Commentary on the Economic Council's Eighth Annual Review and the Ritchie Report* (The Private Planning Association of Canada, Montreal, 1972).

—— (ed.): *The Politics of Economic Policy*, study prepared for the Royal Commission on the Economic Union and Development Prospects for Canada, vol 40 (University of Toronto Press, Toronto, 1986).

—— : "Recent Changes in the Philosophy of Policy-making in Canada," *Canadian Journal of Political Science*, vol. 4, no. 2, 1976, pp. 243–264.

—— : *The Regulatory Process in Canada* (Macmillan, Toronto, 1978).

—— : *The Role of Interdepartmental Committees in the Policy Process*, unpublished M.A. thesis (Carleton University, Ottawa, 1966).

—— : *Spending Tax Dollars: Federal Expenditures 1980–81* (School of Public Administration, Carleton University, Ottawa, 1980).

—— and Peter Aucoin: *The Structures of Policy Making in Canada* (Macmillan, Toronto, 1971).

—— and A. M. Maslove (eds.): *The Public Evaluation of Government Spending* (Institute for Research on Public Policy, Montreal, 1978).

—— and R. W. Morrison (eds.): *Canadian Nuclear Policies* (Institute for Research on Public Policy, Montreal, 1980).

—— and R. W. Phidd: *Canadian Public Policy: Ideas, Structures and Processes* (Methuen, Toronto, 1983).

—— and R. W. Phidd: *The Politics and Management of Canadian Economic Policy* (Macmillan, Toronto, 1978).

—— and Glen Toner: *The Politics of Energy* (Methuen, Toronto, 1985).

Doran, Charles F. and John H. Sigler (eds.): *Canada and the United States: Enduring Friendship, Persistent Stress* (Prentice-Hall, Englewood Cliffs, 1985).

Drury, C. M.: "Quantitative Analysis and Public Policy Making," *Canadian Public Policy*, vol. 1, no. 1975, pp. 89–96.

Eayrs, James George: *The Art of the Possible: Government and Foreign Policy in Canada* (University of Toronto Press, Toronto, 1961).

Evans, R. G.: "Does Canada Have Too Many Doctors? — Why Nobody Loves an Immigrant Physician," *Canadian Public Policy*, vol. 2, 1976, pp. 147–160.

Forget, C. E.: "Développement et implantation de l'idée de régionalisation des services de santé et des services sociaux au Québec," *Canadian Public Policy*, vol. 1, 1975, pp. 402–414.

Freeman, M. M. R. and L. M. Hackman: "Bathurst Island, N.W.T.: A Test Case of Canada's Northern Policy," *Canadian Public Policy*, vol. 1, 1975, pp. 402–414.

Friedmann, K. A.: "Controlling Bureaucracy: Attitudes in the Alberta Public Service towards the Ombudsman," *Canadian Public Administration*, vol. 19, no. 1, 1976, pp. 51–87.

——— and A. G. Milne: "The Federal Ombudsman Legislation: A Critique of Bill C–43," *Canadian Public Policy*, vol. 6, no. 1, 1980, pp. 63–77.

Gillespie, W. Irwin: "Tax Reform: The Battlefield, the Strategies, the Spoils," *Canadian Public Administration*, vol. 26, no. 2, 1983, pp. 182–202.

Gillies, James: *Where Business Fails* (Institute for Research on Public Policy, Montreal, 1981).

Globerman, S.: "Canadian Science Policy and Technological Sovereignty," *Canadian Public Policy*, vol. 4, 1978, pp. 34–35.

——— and S. H. Book: "Formulating Cost and Output Policies in the Performing Arts," *Canadian Public Policy*, vol. 2, 1976, pp. 33–41.

Gwyn, Richard: *The 49th Paradox: Canada in North America* (McClelland and Stewart, Toronto, 1985).

Hart, M. M.: *Canadian Economic Development and the International Trading System*, study prepared for the Royal Commission on the Economic Union and Development Prospects for Canada, vol. 53, (University of Toronto Press, Toronto, 1986).

Hartle, D. G.: "The Public Servant as Advisor: The Choice of Policy Evaluation Criteria," *Canadian Public Policy*, vol. 2, 1976, pp. 424–438.

——— : *Public Policy Decision Making and Regulation* (Institute for Research on Public Policy, Montreal, 1979).

Hawkins, F.: "Immigration and Population: The Canadian Approach," *Canadian Public Policy*, vol. 1, 1975, pp. 285–295.

Helliwell, J.: "The National Energy Board's 1974–1975 Natural Gas Supply Hearings," *Canadian Public Policy*, vol. 1, 1975, pp. 415–425.

——— : *Arctic Pipelines in the Context of Canadian Energy Requirements, Canadian Public Policy*, vol. 3, 1977, pp. 344–354.

Hickson, David J., Richard J. Butler, David Cray, Geoffrey R. Mallory, and David C. Wilson: *Top Decisions: Strategic Decision-making in Organizations* (Jossey-Bass, London, 1986).

Hockin, Thomas A. (ed.): *Apex of Power: The Prime Minister and Political Leadership in Canada* (Prentice-Hall, Toronto, 1971).

Hodgetts, J. E.: "The Civil Service and Policy Formation," in J. E. Hodgetts and D. C. Corbett (eds.), *Canadian Public Administration* (Macmillan, Toronto, 1960).

Islam, Nasir and Sadrudin A. Ahmed: "Business Influence on Government: A Comparison of Public and Private Sector Perceptions," *Canadian Public Administration*, vol. 27, no. 1, 1984, pp. 87–101.

Jenkin, Michael: *The Challenge of Diversity: Industrial Policy in the Canadian Federation* (Science Council of Canada, Ottawa, 1983).

Johnson, A. N.: "Public Policy: Creativity and Bureaucracy," *Canadian Public Administration*, vol. 21, no. 1, 1978, pp. 1–15.

Johnston, D. M.: "Coastal Zone Management in Canada: Purposes and Prospects," *Canadian Public Administration*, vol. 20, no. 1, 1977, pp. 140–151.

Johnston, B.: *Public Opinion and Public Policy in Canada*, study prepared for the Royal Commission on the Economic Union and Development Prospects for Canada, vol. 35, (University of Toronto Press, Toronto, 1986).

Jones, J. C. A.: "The Bureaucracy and Public Policy: Canadian Merger Policy and the Combines Branch, 1965–1971," *Canadian Public Administration*, vol. 18, no. 1, 1975, pp. 269–296.

Kernaghan, K.: "Representative Bureaucracy: The Canadian Perspective," *Canadian Public Administration*, vol. 21, no. 4, 1978, pp. 489–512.

Kierans, E.: "Notes on the Energy Aspects of the 1974 Budget," *Canadian Public Policy*, vol. 1, 1975, pp. 426–432.

Kirby, M. J. L. *et al.*: "The Impact of Public Policy-making Structures and Processes in Canada, *Canadian Public Administration*, vol. 21, no. 3, 1978, pp. 407–417.

Kliman, M. L.: "The Setting of Domestic Air Fares: A Review of the 1975 Hearings," *Canadian Public Policy*, vol. 3, 1977, pp. 186–198.

Lacroix, R. and C. Montmarquette: "Inflation et indexation: perspective canadienne et considérations théoriques," *Canadian Public Policy*, vol. 1, 1975, pp. 185–195.

Lamontagne, Maurice: *Business Cycles in Canada* (James Lorimer, Toronto, 1984).

Laxer, James: *Canada's Economic Strategy* (McClelland and Stewart, Toronto, 1981).

Laxer, James: *Rethinking the Economy: The Laxer Report on Canadian Economy, Problems and Policies* (N.C. Press, Toronto, 1984).

Leiss, W.: "The Social Consequences of Technological Progress: Critical Comments on Recent Theories," *Canadian Public Administration*, vol. 13, no. 3, 1970, pp. 246–262.

Lepore, G.: "Effluent Charges and Pollution Control: A Case Study," *Canadian Public Policy*, vol. 2, 1976, pp. 482–491.

Lerner, George (ed.): *Probing Leviathan: An Investigation of Government in the Economy* (Fraser Institute, Vancouver, 1985).

LeSage, E. C., Jr.: "A Hitch-hiker's Guide to Ottawa Public Policy," *Canadian Public Administration*, vol. 28, no. 3, 1985, pp. 463–476.

Levitt, Kari: *Silent Surrender: The Multi-national Corporation in Canada* (Macmillan, Toronto, 1970).

Lindblom, Charles E.: *The Policy-making Process* (Prentice-Hall, Englewood Cliffs, 1968).

—— : "The Science of Muddling Through," in A. Etzioni (ed.), *Readings on Modern Organizations* (Prentice-Hall, Englewood Cliffs, 1969), pp. 154–165.

—— : "Still Muddling, Not Yet Through," *Public Administration Review*, vol. 39, 1979, pp. 517–526.

Lowi, T.: "Decision Making vs. Policy Making: Toward an Antidote For Technocracy," *Public Administration Review*, vol. 30, 1970, pp. 314–325.

—— : *The End of Liberalism*, 2nd ed. (W. W. Norton, New York, 1979).

Lukasiewicz, J.: "Public Policy and Technology: Passenger Rail in Canada as an Issue in Modernization," *Canadian Public Policy*, vol. 5, no. 4, 1979, pp. 518–532.

Lundquist, L. J.: "Do Political Structures Matter in Environmental Politics? The Case of Air Pollution Control in Canada, Sweden, and the United States," *Canadian Public Administration*, vol. 17, no. 1, 1974, pp. 119–141.

McCready, Douglas J.: *The Canadian Public Sector* (Butterworths, Toronto, 1984).

McFadyen, S.: "The Control of Foreign Ownership of Canadian Real Estate," *Canadian Public Policy*, vol. 2, 1976, pp. 65–77.

Mahon, Rianne: *The Politics of Industrial Strategy in Canada: Textiles* (University of Toronto Press, Toronto, 1983).

Manzer, Ronald: "Social Policy and Political Paradigms," *Canadian Public Administration*, vol. 24, no. 4, 1981, pp. 641–648.

—— : "Public Policy-making as Practical Reasoning," *Canadian Journal of Political Science*, vol. 17, 1984, pp. 577–594.

—— : *Public Policies and Political Development in Canada* (University of Toronto Press, Toronto, 1985).

Martin, D'Arcy: "Public Policy Debate: A View from the 'Union Culture,' " *Optimum*, vol. 16, no. 2, 1985, pp. 92–108.

Maslove, Allan M. (ed.): *How Ottawa Spends, 1984: The New Agenda* (Methuen, Toronto, 1984).

—— (ed.): *How Ottawa Spends, 1985: Sharing the Pie* (Methuen, Toronto, 1985).

Matthews, R.: "Ethical Issues in Policy Research: The Investigation of Community Resettlement in Newfoundland," *Canadian Public Policy*, vol. 1, 1975, pp. 204–216.

Matthews, R. L. (ed.): *Public Policies in Two Federal Countries: Canada and Australia* (Australian National University, Canberra, 1982).

Meisel, John: *Bureaucrats and Reformers*, Allan B. Plaunt Memorial Lecture, (Carleton University, Ottawa, 1983).

Meyboom, P.: "In-house vs. Contractual Research: The Federal Make or Buy Policy," *Canadian Public Administration*, vol. 17, no. 4, 1974, pp. 563–585.

Mills, C. W.: *The Power Elite* (Oxford University Press, New York, 1956).

Mishler, N. and D. B. Campbell: "The Health State: Legislative Responsiveness to Public Health Care Needs in Canada, 1920–1970," *Comparative Politics*, vol. 10, no. 4, 1978, pp. 479–498.

Mitchell, C. L.: "The 200-Mile Limit: New Issues, Old Problems for Canada's East Coast Fisheries," *Canadian Public Policy*, vol. 4, 1978, pp. 172–183.

Moffat, M. J. and T. E. Reid: "Comment on Indicators and Policy Formation," *Canadian Public Administration*, vol. 19, no. 4, 1976, pp. 633–637.

Molot, Maureen Appel and Brian W. Tomlin: *Canada among Nations 1985: The Conservative Agenda* (James Lorimer, Toronto, 1986).

Muller, F. G.: "Distribution of Air Pollution in the Montreal Region," *Canadian Public Policy*, vol. 3, 1977, pp. 199–204.

Muller, R. A.: "A Simulation of the Effect of Pollution Control on the Pulp and Paper Industry," *Canadian Public Policy*, vol. 2, 1976, pp. 91–102.

Nord, D. C.: "The 'Problem' of Immigration: The Continuing Presence of the Stranger within our Gates," *American Review of Canadian Studies*, vol. 7, no. 2, 1978, pp. 116–133.

Osberg, L.: "Unemployment Insurance in Canada: A Review of the Recent Amendments," *Canadian Public Policy*, vol. 2, no. 2, 1979, pp. 223–235.

Pal, Leslie A.: *Public Policy Analysis: An Introduction* (Methuen, Toronto, 1987).

Palda, Kristian S.: *Industrial Innovation: Its Place in the Public Policy Agenda* (The Fraser Institute, Vancouver, 1985).

Palumbo, Dennis J. and Marvin A. Harder: *Implementing Public Policy* (D. C. Heath, Toronto, 1981).

Paquin, M. and R. A. Hurtubise: "L'Utilisation de la méthode des cas et des jeux de simulation dans l'enseignement de l'administration publique," *Canadian Public Administration*, vol. 17, no. 2, 1978, pp. 242–258.

Paul, Ellen F. and Philip A. Russo, Jr.: *Public Policy: Issues, Analysis and Ideology* (Chatham House, Chatham, N. S., 1982).

Pitfield, M.: "The Shape of Government in the 1980s: Techniques and Instruments for Policy Formulation at the Federal Level," *Canadian Public Administration*, vol. 19, no. 1, 1976, pp. 8–20.

—— : *Politics and Policy Making*, address to the Alma Mater Society, Queen's University, Feb. 10, 1983.

Pratt, L.: *Tar Sands: Syncrude and the Politics of Oil* (Hurtig, Edmonton, 1976).

Pratt, Larry: "Energy: The Roots of National Policy," *Studies in Political Economy*, vol. 7, Winter 1982, pp. 27–59.

Prince, Michael J.: *How Ottawa Spends, 1986–87: Tracking the Tories* (Methuen, Toronto, 1986).

Pross, A. Paul: "From System to Serendipity: The Practice and Study of Public Policy in the Trudeau Years," *Canadian Public Administration*, vol. 25, no. 4, 1982, pp. 520–544.

Purvis, Douglas D. (ed.): *Issues in Canadian Public Policy*, 2 vols. (Institute for Economic Research, Kingston, 1980).

Raynauld, A.: "Social Indicators: The Need for a Broader Socio-Economic Framework," *Canadian Public Administration*, vol. 18, no. 1, 1975, pp. 91–103.

Relyea, H. C.: "The Provision of Government Information: The Federal Freedom of Information Act Experience," *Canadian Public Administration*, vol. 20, no. 2, 1977, pp. 317–341.

Renaud, François and Brigitte Von Schoenberg: "L'Implantation des conseils régionaux de la santé et des services sociaux: analyse d'un processus politique," *Canadian Journal of Political Science*, vol. 7, no. 1, 1974, pp. 52–69.

Rickover, R. M.: "The 1977 Bank Act: Emerging Issues and Policy Choices," *Canadian Public Policy*, vol. 1, 1975, pp. 66–79.

Ritchie, R. S.: "Public Policies affecting Petroleum Development in Canada," *Canadian Public Policy*, vol. 1, 1975, pp. 66–79.

Roberts, L. U.: "Some Unanticipated Consequences of Affirmative Action Policies," *Canadian Public Policy*, vol. 1, 1975, pp. 66–79.

Rowan, M.: "A Conceptual Framework for Government Policy-making," *Canadian Public Administration*, vol. 13, no. 3, 1970, pp. 277–296.

Royal Commission on the Economic Union and Development Prospects for Canada: *Report*, vols. 1–3 (Canadian Government Printing Office, Ottawa, 1985).

Ruppenthal, K. M. and W. T. Stanbury (eds.): *Transportation Policy: Regulation Competition and the Public Interest* (The Centre for Transportation Studies, University of British Columbia, Vancouver, 1976).

Sayeed, K. B.: "Public Policy Analysis in Washington and Ottawa," *Policy Sciences*, vol. 4, no. 1, 1973, pp. 85–101.

Schultz, Richard: "Regulatory Agencies," in Michael S. Whittington and Glen Williams (eds.), *Canadian Politics in the 1980s*, 2nd ed. (Methuen, Toronto, 1984), pp. 434–448.

Sharman, G. C.: "The Police and the Implementation of Public Law," *Canadian Public Administration*, vol. 21, no. 2, 1977, pp. 291–304.

Sharp, M.: "Decision-making in the Federal Cabinet," *Canadian Public Administration*, vol. 19, no. 1, 1976, pp. 1–7.

Skogstad, G.: "The Farm Products Marketing Agencies Act: A Case Study of Agricultural Policy," *Canadian Public Policy*, vol. 6, no. 1, 1980, pp. 89–100.

Smith, L. B.: *Anatomy of a Crisis: Canadian Housing Policy* (Fraser Institute, Vancouver, 1977).

Sokolsky, J. J.: "The Canada-U.S. Alaska Highway Pipeline: A Study in Environmental Decision-making," *American Review of Canadian Studies*, vol. 9, no. 2, 1979, pp. 84–112.

Solomon, Peter H., Jr.: "Government Officials and the Study of Policy-making," *Canadian Public Administration*, vol. 26, no. 3, 1983, pp. 420–440.

Spragge, G. L.: "Canadian Planners' Goals: Deep Roots and Fuzzy Thinking," *Canadian Public Administration*, vol. 18, no. 2, 1975, pp. 216–234.

Sproule-Jones, Mark: "Public Choice Theory and Natural Resources: A Methodological Explication and Critique," *American Political Science Review*, vol. 76, no. 4, 1982, pp. 790–804.

Stairs, Denis: "Myth-making for Canada," *Policy Options*, vol. 4, no. 1, Jan./Feb. 1983, pp. 59–60.

Stanbury, W. T.: *Business Interest and Reform of Canadian Competition Policy, 1971–75* (Methuen, Toronto, 1977).

——— : *Business-Government Relations in Canada* (Methuen, Toronto, 1986).

Star, S.: "In Search of a Rational Policy," *Canadian Public Policy*, vol. 1, 1975, pp. 328–342.

Slayton, Philip and Michael J. Trebilcock: *The Professions and Public Policy* (University of Toronto, Toronto, 1979).

Steele, G. G. E.: " 'Needed — A Sense of Proportion!' Notes on the History of Expenditure Control," *Canadian Public Administration*, vol. 21, no. 3, 1977, pp. 433–443.

Suleiman, Ezra N. (ed.): *Bureaucrats and Policy Making: A Comparative Overview* (Holmes and Meier Publishers, New York, 1984).

Swartz, Michael: *The Environment for Policy Making in Canada and the United States* (National Planning Institute and C. D. Howe Research Institute, Washington, D. C., 1981).

Tassé, R.: "The Role of Social Science in Crime and Delinquency Policy," *Canadian Public Administration*, vol. 19, no. 2, 1976, pp. 267–278.

Taylor, M. G.: "Quebec Medicare: Policy Formulation in Conflict and Crisis," *Canadian Public Administration*, vol. 15, no. 2, 1972, pp. 211–250.

——— : *Health Insurance and Canadian Public Policy* (McGill-Queen's University Press, Montreal, 1978).

Trebilcock, M. J., R. S. Prichard, D. G. Hartle, and D. N. Dewees: *The Choice of Governing Instruments* (Ministry of Supply and Services, Ottawa, 1982).

Van Loon, Richard: "A Revisionist History of Planning Processes in Ottawa? An Open Letter to Colin Campbell S. J.," *Canadian Public Administration*, vol. 28, no. 2, 1985, pp. 307–318 and the reply by Colin Campbell, pp. 319–328.

——— : "Kaleidoscope in Grey: The Policy Process in Ottawa," in Michael S. Whittington and Glen Williams (eds.), *Canadian Politics in the 1980s*, 2nd ed. (Methuen, Toronto, 1984), pp. 412–433.

Villanueva, A. B.: "Nuclear Power, Private Attorneys-General, and the Regulatory Process," *Canadian Public Administration*, vol. 18, no. 3, 1975, pp. 399–408.

Waters, W. G.: "Investment Criteria and the Expansion of Major Airports in Canada," *Canadian Public Policy*, vol. 3, 1977, pp. 23–35.

Williams, Glen: *Not for Export: A Political Economy of Canada's Arrested Industrialization* (McClelland and Stewart, Toronto, 1983).

Wilson, V. S.: *Canadian Public Policy and Administration: Theory and Environment* (McGraw-Hill Ryerson, Toronto, 1981).

Wolfe, D. A.: "Economic Growth and Foreign Investment: A Perspective on Canadian Economic Policy, 1945–1957," *Journal of Canadian Studies*, vol. 13, no. 1, 1978, pp. 3–20.

Wood, J. R.: "East Indians and Canada's New Immigration Policy," *Canadian Public Policy*, vol. 4, 1978, pp. 547–567.

THE ENVIRONMENT

A. *Geographical and Economic Cleavages*

Alford, R. R.: "The Social Bases of Political Cleavage in 1962," in John Meisel (ed.), *Papers on the 1962 Election* (University of Toronto Press, Toronto, 1965), pp. 203–234.

Armstrong, D. E. *et al.*: "Income Distribution in Canada: A Reply to Needleman and Shed," *Canadian Public Policy*, vol. 5, no. 4, 1979, pp. 510–517.

Armstrong, Muriel: *The Canadian Economy and Its Problems* (Prentice-Hall, Toronto, 1970).

Black, Errol: "One Too Many Reports on Poverty in Canada" (review article), *Canadian Journal of Political Science*, vol. 5, 1972, pp. 439–443.

Blackman, W. J.: "A Western Canadian Perspective on the Economy of Confederation," *Canadian Public Policy*, vol. 3, 1977, pp. 414–430.

Blake, D. E.: "LIP and Partisanship: An Analysis of the Local Initiatives Program," *Canadian Public Policy*, vol. 2, 1976, pp. 17–32.

Breton, Albert and Raymond Breton: *Why Disunity? An Analysis of Linguistic and Regional Cleavages in Canada* (Institute for Research on Public Policy, Montreal, 1980).

Brewis, Thomas Newton: *Regional Economic Policies in Canada* (Macmillan, Toronto, 1969).

——— , H.E. English, Anthony Scott, and Pauline Jewett: *Canadian Economic Policy*, rev. ed. (Macmillan, Toronto, 1965).

——— and G. Paquet: "Regional Development in Canada: An Exploratory Essay," *Canadian Public Administration*, vol. 11, no. 2, 1968.

Brym, R. J.: "Regional Social Structure and Agrarian Radicalism in Canada: Alberta, Saskatchewan and New Brunswick," *Canadian Review of Sociology and Anthropology*, vol. 15, no. 3, 1978, pp. 339–351.

Brym, Robert and James Sacouman: *Underdevelopment and Social Movements in Atlantic Canada* (Hogtown Press, Toronto, 1979).

Buckley, Helen and Eva Tihan: *Canadian Policies for Rural Adjustment* (Queen's Printer, Ottawa, 1967).

Cameron, David M.: "Regional Integration in the Maritime Provinces," *Canadian Journal of Political Science*, vol. 4, 1971, pp. 24–25.

Cameron, D. (ed.): *Regionalism and Supranationalism* (Institute for Research on Public Policy, Toronto, 1980).

Classen, H. B.: "The Chimera of the Homogeneous State," *Queen's Quarterly*, vol. 79, no. 4, 1972, pp. 458–469.

Clow, Michael: "Politics and Uneven Capitalist Development: The Maritime Challenge to the Study of Canadian Provincial Economy," *Studies in Political Economy*, vol. 14, Summer 1984, pp. 117–140.

Coburn, David and Virginia L. Edwards: "Objective and Subjective Socioeconomic Status: Intercorrelations and Consequences," *Canadian Review of Sociology and Anthropology*, vol. 13, 1976, pp. 178–188.

Copithorne, L.: "Natural Resources and Regional Disparities: A Skeptical View," *Canadian Public Policy*, vol. 5, no. 2, 1979, pp. 181–194.

Cuneo, Carl J. and James E. Curtis: "Quebec Separatism: An Analysis of Determinants within Social-Class Levels," *Canadian Review of Sociology and Anthropology*, vol. 11, 1974, pp. 1–29.

Curtis, James E. "Educational Status and Reactions to Social and Political Heterogeneity," *Canadian Review of Sociology and Anthropology*, vol. 11, 1976, pp. 189–203.

——— : and Ronald D. Lambert: "Status Dissatisfaction and Out-group Rejections: Cross-cultural Comparisons within Canada," *Canadian Review of Sociology and Anthropology*, vol. 12, 1975, pp. 178–192.

Daniels, N.: "The Birth and Shaping of Regional Policies," *Policy Options*, vol. 2, no. 2, May 1981, pp. 55–61.

Dehem, R. *et al.*: "Concepts of Regional Planning," *Canadian Public Administration*, vol. 9, 1966, pp. 158–176.

Easterbrook, William Thomas and Hugh G. J. Aitkin: *Canadian Economic History* (Macmillan, Toronto, 1956).

Easterbrook, W. T. and M. H. Watkins: *Approaches to Canadian Economic History* (McClelland and Stewart, Toronto, 1967).

Economic Council of Canada: *Living Together: A Study of Regional Disparities* (Supply and Services, Ottawa, 1977).

Ferguson, C. B.: "Maritime Union," *Queen's Quarterly*, vol. 77, no. 2, 1970, pp. 167–179.

Flanaghan, Thomas: "Political Theory of the Red River Resistance: The Declaration of December 8, 1869" (note), *Canadian Journal of Political Science*, vol. 11, 1978, pp. 153–164.

Gibbins, R.: *Regionalism: Territorial Politics in Canada and the United States — A Comparative Analysis* (Butterworths, Toronto, 1981).

Grayson, J. Paul and L. M. Grayson: "The Social Base of Interwar Political Unrest in Urban Alberta," *Canadian Journal of Political Science*, vol. 7, 1974, pp. 289–313.

Guindon, Hubert: "Two Cultures: An Essay on Nationalism, Class and Ethnic Tension," in Richard H. Leach (ed.), *Contemporary Canada* (Duke University Press, Durham, 1968), pp. 33–59.

Hanson, E. J.: "The Future of Western Canada: Economic, Social and Political," *Canadian Public Administration*, vol. 18, no. 1, 1975, pp. 104–120.

Howland, R. D.: *Some Regional Aspects of Canada's Economic Development* (Queen's Printer, Ottawa, 1957).

Innis, H.: *Essays in Canadian Economic History* (University of Toronto Press, Toronto, 1956).

Kalbach, W. E.: "Demographic Concerns and the Control of Immigration," *Canadian Public Policy*, vol. 1, 1975, pp. 302–310.

Krueger, R., F. Sargent, A. de Vos, and N. Pearson (eds.): *Regional and Resource Planning in Canada* (Holt Rinehart and Winston, Toronto, 1963).

Levitt, Kari: *Silent Surrender: The Multi-national Corporation in Canada* (Macmillan, Toronto, 1970).

Lipset, S. M.: "Social Structure and Political Activity," in B. R. Blishen *et al.* (eds.), *Canadian Society: Sociological Perspectives*, 3rd ed. (Macmillan, Toronto, 1968), pp. 396–409.

MacPherson, C. Brough: *Democracy in Alberta: Social Credit and the Party System*, 2nd ed. (University of Toronto Press, Toronto, 1962).

Martin, F.: "Incidence de la crise de l'énergie sur le développement régional canadien," *Canadian Public Policy*, vol. 1, 1975, pp. 39–46.

Matthews, Ralph: "Two Alternative Explanations of the Problem of Regional Dependency in Canada," *Canadian Public Policy*, vol.7, no. 2, 1981, pp. 268–283.

———: *The Creation of Regional Dependency* (University of Toronto Press, Toronto, 1983).

Myers, Gustavus: *A History of Canadian Wealth* (Argosy-Antiquarian, New York, 1968).

Needleman, L.: "Income Distribution in Canada: Policy Implications," *Canadian Public Policy*, vol. 5, no. 3, 1979, pp. 497–505.

Nelson, J. G. and M. J. Chambers: *Process and Method in Canadian Geography*, 4 vols. (Methuen, Toronto, 1969, 1970).

Newman, Peter: *The Canadian Establishment* (McClelland and Stewart, Toronto, 1975 and 1976).

Norrie, K. H.: "Some Comments on Prairie Economic Alienation," *Canadian Public Policy*, vol. 2, 1976, pp. 211–224.

Officer, L. H. and L. B. Smith (eds.): *Canadian Economic Problems and Policies* (McGraw-Hill, Toronto, 1970).

Pesando, J. E.: "The Indexing of Private Pensions: An Economist's Perspective on the Current Debate," *Canadian Public Policy*, vol. 5, no. 1, 1979, pp. 80–89.

Proulx, Pierre-Paul: "Industrial Redeployment and Regional Development: Diagnosis and Policy Approaches," *Optimum*, vol. 14, no. 4, 1983, pp. 49–66.

Raynault, André: *The Canadian Economic System* (Macmillan, Toronto, 1967).

Rea, K. J. and J. T. McLeod (eds.): *Business and Government in Canada* (Methuen, Toronto, 1969).

"Regionalism/Le Régionalisme": *Journal of Canadian Studies*, vol. 15, no. 2, 1980 (special issue).

Reid, T. E. (ed.): *Contemporary Canada: Readings in Economics* (Holt Rinehart and Winston, Toronto, 1969).

Rinehart, James W. and Ishmael O. Okraku: "A Study of Class Consciousness," *Canadian Review of Sociology and Anthropology*, vol. 11, 1974, pp. 197–213.

Rutan, Gerard F.: "Western Canada: The Winds of Alienation," *American Review of Canadian Studies*, vol. 12, no. 1, 1982, pp. 74–97.

Sacouman, R. James: "The 'peripheral' Maritimes and Canada-wide Marxist Political Economy," *Studies in Political Economy*, vol. 6, Autumn 1981, pp. 135–150.

Safarian, A. E.: *Foreign Ownership of Canadian Industry* (McGraw-Hill, Toronto, 1966).

Savoie, Donald J.: *The Canadian Economy. A Regional Perspective* (Methuen, Toronto, 1986).

———: "The Toppling of DREE and Prospects for Regional Economic Development," *Canadian Public Policy*, vol. 10, no. 3, 1984, pp. 328–337.

Schwartz, Mildred A.: *Politics and Territory* (McGill-Queen's University Press, Montreal, 1974).

Schweitzer, Thomas T.: *Old Myths and New Choices: Railway Freight Rates and Western Economic Development* (Economic Council of Canada, Ottawa, 1984).

Shedd, M. S.: "The Measurement of Income and Distribution in Canada: Policy Implications," *Canadian Public Policy*, vol. 5, no. 4, 1979, pp. 506–509.

Sinclair, P. R.: "Political Powerlessness and Sociodemographic Status in Canada," *Canadian Review of Sociology and Anthropology*, vol. 16, no. 2, 1979, pp. 125–135.

Sitwell, O. F. G. and N. M. R. Seifried: *The Regional Structure of the Canadian Economy* (Methuen, Toronto, 1984).

Smith, D. E.: "The Third Canada (An Alienated West)," *Policy Options*, vol. 2, no. 2, May/June 1981, pp. 27–29.

Stevenson, P.: "Class and Left-wing Radicalism," *Canadian Review of Sociology and Anthropology*, vol. 14, pp. 269–284.

Tepperman, L. J.: *Social Mobility in Canada* (McGraw-Hill Ryerson, Toronto, 1975).

Thorburn, Hugh G.: "The Politics of Economic Development in Canada," *Queen's Quarterly*, vol. 90, no. 1, Spring 1983, pp. 138–150.

Usher, D.: "Some Questions about the Regional Development Incentives Act," *Canadian Public Policy*, vol. 1, 1975, pp. 557–575.

Vano, Gerard S.: *Neo-feudalism: The Canadian Dilemma* (House of Anansi Press, Toronto, 1981).

Veltman, C. J.: "Demographic Components of the Francisation of Rural Quebec: The Case of Rawdon," *American Review of Canadian Studies*, vol. 6, no. 2, 1976, pp. 22–41.

Warkentin, John (ed.): *Canada: A Geographic Interpretation* (Methuen, Toronto, 1968).

Weller, G. R.: "Hinterland Politics: The Case of Northwestern Ontario," *Canadian Journal of Political Science*, vol. 10, no. 4, 1977, pp. 727–754.

Whalley, J.: *Regional Aspects of Confederation*, study prepared for the Royal Commission on the Economic Union and Development Prospects for Canada, vol. 68 (University of Toronto Press, Toronto, 1986).

Woodward, R. S.: "The Effectiveness of DREE's New Location Subsidies," *Canadian Public Policy*, vol. 1, 1975, pp. 217–230.

Wyman, Ken, Robin Matthews, and G. Lermer: "The Task Force on Foreign Ownership," *Canadian Dimension*, vol. 5, April/May 1968, pp. 15–20.

B. Ethnic, Religious, Gender, and Class Cleavages

Abella, Irving (ed.): *On Strike: Six Key Labour Struggles in Canada, 1919–1949* (James, Lewis & Samuel, Toronto, 1974).

—— and Harold Troper: *None Is Too Many: Canada and the Jews of Europe, 1933–1948* (Lester and Orphen Dennys, Toronto, 1982).

Adams, Ian: *The Poverty Wall* (McClelland and Stewart, Toronto, 1970).

—— : *The Real Poverty Report* (McClelland and Stewart, Toronto, 1970).

Allan, Richard: *The Social Passion: Religion and Social Reform in Canada, 1914–28* (University of Toronto Press, Toronto, 1971).

Anderson, A. B. and J. S. Frideres: *Ethnicity in Canada: The Theoretical Perspectives* (Butterworths, Toronto, 1981).

Andrews, M. N. "Attitudes in Canadian Women's History, 1945–1975," *Journal of Canadian Studies*, vol. 12, no. 4, 1977, pp. 69–78.

Armstrong, D. E., P. H. Friesen, and D. Miller: "The Measurement of Income Distribution in Canada: Some Problems and Some Tentative Data," *Canadian Public Policy*, vol. 3, 1977, pp. 479–488.

Armstrong, Hugh and Pat Armstrong: "The Segregated Participation of Women in the Canadian Labour Force, 1941–1971," *Canadian Review of Sociology and Anthropology*, vol. 12, 1975, pp. 370–384.

Asch, Michael: *Home and Native Land: Aboriginal Rights and the Canadian Constitution* (Methuen, Toronto, 1984).

Atcheson, M. Elizabeth, Mary Eberts, and Beth Symes with Jennifer Stoddart: *Women and Legal Action: Precedents, Resources and Strategies for the Future* (Canadian Advisory Council on the Status of Women, Ottawa, 1984).

Avery, Donald: "Continental European Immigrant Workers in Canada, 1896–1919: From 'Stalwart Peasants' to Radical Proletariat," *Canadian Review of Sociology and Anthropology*, vol. 12, 1975, pp. 53–64.

Baetz, R. C. and K. Collins: "Equity Aspects of Income Security Programs," *Canadian Public Policy*, vol. 1, 1975, pp. 487–498.

Banting, K.: "The Radical Interpretation of Social Security: A Critique, *Canadian Public Policy*, vol. 1, 1975, pp. 520–526.

Bercuson, David J.: *Fools and Wise Men: The Rise and Fall of the One Big Union* (McGraw-Hill Ryerson, Toronto, 1978).

——— : "Western Labour Radicalism and the One Big Union: Myths and Reality," *Journal of Canadian Studies*, vol. 9, no. 2, 1974, pp. 3–11.

Berkowitz, S. D.: *Models and Myths in Canadian Society* (Butterworths, Toronto, 1981).

Blishen, B. R. *et al.* (eds.): *Canadian Society: Sociological Perspectives*, 3rd ed. (Macmillan, Toronto, 1968).

Bolaria, B. C.: *Oppressed Minorities in Canada* (Butterworths, Toronto, 1980).

Boldt, Menno: "Enlightenment Values, Romanticism and Attitudes towards Political Status: A Study of Native Leaders in Canada," *Canadian Review of Sociology and Anthropology*, vol. 18, no. 4, 1981, pp. 545–565.

——— : "Social Correlates of Nationalism: A Study of Native Indian Leaders in a Canadian Internal Colony," *Comparative Political Studies*, vol. 4, no. 2, 1981, pp. 205–232.

——— : "Tribal Traditions and European-Western Political Ideologies: The Dilemma of Canada's Native Indians," *Canadian Journal of Political Science*, vol. 17, 1984, pp. 537–553.

——— and Anthony Long (eds.): *The Quest for Justice: Aboriginal Peoples and Aboriginal Rights* (University of Toronto Press, Toronto, 1985).

Briskin, Linda and Lynda Yanz: *Union Sisters: Women in the Labour Movement* (Women's Press, Toronto, 1983).

Brotz, H.: "Multiculturalism in Canada: A Muddle," *Canadian Public Policy*, vol. 6, no. 1, 1980, pp. 41–46.

Cairns, A. and C. Williams (eds.): *The Politics of Gender, Ethnicity and Language in Canada*, study prepared for the Royal Commission on the Economic Union and Development Prospects for Canada, vol. 34 (University of Toronto Press, Toronto, 1986).

Canada, DIAND: *In All Fairness: A Native Claims Policy* (Supply and Services Canada, Ottawa, 1981).

——— : *Outstanding Business: A Native Claims Policy* (Supply and Services Canada, Ottawa, 1982).

Canada, Privy Council Office, Special Planning Secretariat: *Meeting Poverty* (Ottawa, 1965). (Hereafter referred to as "MP" issues.)

——— : "Profile of Poverty in Canada" (MP–6).

——— : "Statistical Profile and Graphic Presentation of Urban Poverty" (MP–15).

——— : "The Nature of Poverty in Canada," by D.R. Richmond (MP–26).

——— : "Social Aspects of Poverty," by Daniel Thursz (MP–30).

Chi, N. H.: "Class Voting in Canadian Politics," in O. Kruhlak, R. Schultz, and S. Pobihushchy, *The Canadian Political Process: A Reader*, rev. ed. (Holt Rinehart and Winston, Toronto, 1973).

Chiasson, Beatrice *et al.*: *The History of the Trade Union Movement in Quebec* (Black Rose Books, Montreal, 1986).

Clark, S. D.: *Church and Sect in Canada* (University of Toronto Press, Toronto, 1948).

Clement, Wallace: *Class, Power and Property: Essays on Canadian Society* (Methuen, Toronto, 1983).

Craven, Paul: *An Impartial Umpire: Industrial Relations and the Canadian State, 1910–1911* (University of Toronto Press, Toronto, 1980).

Cuneo, C. J. "Class Exploitation in Canada," *Canadian Review of Sociology and Anthropology*, vol. 15, 1978, pp. 284–300.

—— : "Has the Traditional Petite Bourgeoisie Persisted?" *Canadian Journal of Sociology*, vol. 9, no. 2, 1984, pp. 269–301.

—— and James E. Curtis: "Social Aspiration in the Educational and Occupational Status Attainment of Urban Canadians," *Canadian Review of Sociology and Anthropology*, vol. 12, 1975, pp. 6–24.

Curtis, James E.: *Social Stratification in Canada* (Prentice-Hall, Toronto, 1973).

Dahlie, Jorgen and Tissa Fernada (eds.): *Ethnicity, Power and Politics in Canada* (Methuen, Toronto, 1981).

Drache, Daniel: "The Formation and Fragmentation of the Canadian Working Class 1820–1920," *Studies in Political Economy*, vol. 15, Fall 1984, pp. 43–90.

Federal-Provincial Conference on Poverty and Opportunity: "Profile of Poverty in Canada" (digest of papers prepared for the Conference), *Labour Gazette*, vol. 66, May 1966.

Finkel, A.: "The 'Beautiful People' of Winnipeg," *Canadian Dimension*, vol. 7, no. 4, 1970, pp. 10–18.

Flanagan, Thomas: "The Sovereignty and Nationhood of Canadian Indians: A Comment on Boldt and Long," *Canadian Journal of Political Science*, vol. 18, no. 2, 1985, pp. 367–374.

—— : "The Case against Metis Aboriginal Rights," *Canadian Public Policy*, vol. 9, no. 3, 1983, pp. 314–325.

Forcese, Dennis: *The Canadian Class Structure*, 3rd ed. (McGraw-Hill Ryerson, Toronto, 1986).

Forsey, Eugene: *Trade Unions in Canada 1812–1902* (University of Toronto, Toronto, 1982).

Frankel, J. A. and Michael Kelly: "Etude préliminaire sur la violence collective en Ontario et au Québec, 1963–1973" (note), *Canadian Journal of Political Science*, vol. 10, 1977, pp. 145–157.

French, D. C.: *Faith, Sweat and Politics: The Early Trade Union Years in Canada* (McClelland and Stewart, Toronto, 1962).

Gibbins, Roger and J. Rick Ponting: "The Paradoxical Nature of the Penner Report," *Canadian Public Policy*, vol. 10, no. 2, 1984, pp. 221–224.

Glasbeek, H. J.: "Labour, Politics and Economics," *Canadian Forum*, vol. 63, no. 732, October 1983, pp. 16–17.

Goffman, I. J.: "Canadian Social Welfare Policy," in Richard H. Leach (ed.), *Contemporary Canada* (Duke University Press, Durham, 1968).

Goldstein, J. E. and R. M. Bienvenue (eds.): *Ethnicity and Ethnic Relations in Canada* (Butterworths, Toronto, 1980).

Grabb, Edward G.: "Class Conformity and Political Powerlessness," *Canadian Review of Sociology and Anthropology*, vol. 18, no. 3, 1981, pp. 362–369.

Grayson, J. (ed.): *Class, State Ideology and Change* (Holt Rinehart and Winston, Toronto, 1980).

—— and L. M. Grayson: "Class and Ideologies of Class in the English-Canadian Novel,"

Canadian Review of Sociology and Anthropology, vol. 15, no. 3, 1979, pp. 165–283.

—— and L.M. Grayson: "The Social Base of Interwar Political Unrest in Urban Alberta," *Canadian Journal of Political Science*, vol.7, no. 2, 1974, pp. 289–313.

Guindon, Hubert: "Social Unrest, Social Class and Quebec's Bureaucratic Revolution," *Queen's Quarterly*, vol. 71, 1964, pp. 150–162.

Heron, Craig and Robert Storey (eds.): *On the Job: Confronting the Labour Process in Canada* (McGill-Queen's University Press, Kingston and Montreal, 1985).

Horowitz, Gad: *Canadian Labour in Politics* (University of Toronto Press, Toronto, 1968).

House of Commons: *Equality Now!*, report of the Special Committee on Visible Minorities in Canadian Society (Supply and Services, Ottawa, 1984).

Hughes, Patricia: "Indians and Lands Reserved for the Indians: Off-limits to the Provinces?" *Osgoode Hall Law Journal*, vol. 22, no. 1, 1983, pp. 82–112.

Hull, B.: "Equity Aspects of Income Security Programs: A Comment," *Canadian Public Policy*, vol. 1, 1975, pp. 498–502.

Hunter, Alfred A.: *Class Tells: On Social Inequality in Canada* (Butterworths, Toronto, 1981).

—— : "On Class, Status and Voting in Canada," *Canadian Journal of Sociology*, vol. 7, no. 1, 1982, pp. 19–39.

Hutcheson, J.: *Dominance and Dependency* (McClelland and Stewart, Toronto, 1978).

Irvine, William P.: "Comment on 'The Reproduction of the Religious Cleavage in Canadian Elections,' " *Canadian Journal of Political Science*, vol. 18, 1985, pp. 115–117.

Ismael, Jacqueline S.: *Canadian Social Welfare Policy, Federal and Provincial Dimensions* (University of Toronto Press, Toronto, 1985).

Johnson, A. W.: "Canada's Social Security Review 1973–1975: The Central Issues," *Canadian Public Policy*, vol. 1, 1975, pp. 456–472.

Johnston, Richard and Janet Ballantyne: "The Reproduction of the Religious Cleavage in Canadian Elections," *Canadian Journal of Political Science*, vol. 18, 1985, pp. 99–113.

Johnston, William and Michael D. Ornstein: "Class, Work and Politics," *Canadian Review of Sociology and Anthropology*, vol. 19, no. 2, 1982, pp. 196–214.

—— : "Social Class and Political Ideology in Canada," *Canadian Review of Sociology and Anthopology*, vol. 22, no. 3, 1985, pp. 369–393.

Kalin, Rudolf and J. W. Berry: "Canadian Ethnic Attitudes and Identity in the Context of National Unity," *Journal of Canadian Studies*, vol. 17, no. 11, 1982, pp. 103–110.

Kallen, E.: *Ethnicity and Human Rights in Canada* (Gage, Toronto, 1982).

Kent, Thomas Worrall: *Social Policy for Canada: Towards a Philosophy of Social Security* (Policy Press, Ottawa, 1962).

Knight, David B.: "Territory and People or People and Territory? Thoughts on Postcolonial Self-determination," *International Political Science Review*, vol. 6, no. 2, 1985, pp. 248–272.

Lachapelle, R. and J. Henripin: *La Situation démolinguistique au Canada* (Institute for Research on Public Policy, Toronto, 1980).

Langdon, G.: "The Emergence of the Canadian Working Class," *Journal of Canadian Studies*, May/Aug. 1973, pp. 22–34.

Laxer, R. M.: *Canada's Unions* (Lorimer, Toronto, 1975).

Laycock, J. E.: "New Directions for Social Welfare Policy," in A. Rotstein (ed.), *The Prospect of Change: Proposals for Canada's Future* (McGraw-Hill, Toronto, 1965), pp. 308–327.

Leman, Christopher: *The Collapse of Welfare Reform: Political Institutions, Policy, and the Poor in Canada and the United States* (MIT Press, Cambridge, 1980).

Li, P. S.: "A Historical Approach to Ethnic Stratification: The Case of the Chinese in Canada, 1858–1930," *Candian Review of Sociology and Anthropology*, vol. 16, no. 3, 1979, pp. 320–332.

———— : "The Stratification of Ethnic Immigrants: The Case of Toronto," *Canadian Review of Sociology and Anthropology*, vol. 15, no. 1, 1978, pp. 31–40.

Lijphart, Arend: "Cultural Diversity and Theories of Political Integration," *Canadian Journal of Political Science*, vol. 4, no. 1, 1971, pp. 1–14.

Lindsey, J. K.: "The Conceptualization of Social Class," *Studies in Political Economy: A Socialist Revew*, vol. 3, Spring 1980, pp. 17–36.

Lipton, C.: *The Trade Union Movement in Canada, 1827–1959* (Canadian Social Publications, Montreal, 1967).

Little Bear, Leroy, Menno Boldt, and J. Anthony Long: *Pathways to Self-determination: Canadian Indians and the Canadian State* (University of Toronto Press, Toronto, 1984).

Logan, Harold Amos: *Trade Unions in Canada* (Macmillan, Toronto, 1948).

Lorimer, James and Myfanwy Phillips: *Working People* (James, Lewis & Samuel, Toronto, 1971).

McInnes, Simon: "The Inuit and the Constitutional Process: 1978–81," *Journal of Canadian Studies*, vol. 16, no. 2, 1981, pp. 53–68.

Mahon, Rianne: "Canadian Labour in the Battle of the Eighties," *Studies in Political Economy*, vol. 11, Summer 1983, pp. 149–175.

———— : "Canadian Public Policy: The Unequal Structure of Representation," in Leo Panitch (ed.), *The Canadian State: Political Economy and Political Power* (University of Toronto Press, Toronto, 1977), pp. 164–198.

Mann, W. E.: *Poverty and Social Policy in Canada* (Copp Clark, Toronto, 1970).

Marchak, P.: "Labour in a Staple Economy," *Studies in Political Economy: A Socialist Review*, vol. 2, Autumn 1979, pp. 7–36.

Mealing, S. R.: "The Concept of Social Class in the Interpretation of Canadian History," *Canadian Historical Review*, vol. 46, no. 3, 1965, pp. 30–49.

Meisel, J.: "Religious Affiliation and Electoral Behaviour: A Case Study," in John Courtney (ed.), *Voting in Canada* (Prentice-Hall, Toronto, 1967), pp. 144–161.

Miles, Angela and Geraldine Finn: *Feminism in Canada: From Pressure to Politics* (Black Rose Books, Montreal, 1982).

Milling, G. B.: "Immigration and Labour: Critic or Catalyst?" *Canadian Public Policy*, vol. 1, 1975, pp. 311–316.

Morse, Bradford W. (ed.): *Aboriginal Peoples and the Law: Indian, Metis and Inuit Rights in Canada* (Carleton University Press and Oxford University Press, Toronto, 1985).

Morton, Desmond with Terry Copp: *Working People: An Illustrated History of the Canadian Labour Movement*, rev. ed. (Deneau, Ottawa, 1984).

Nevitte, Neil and Allan Kornberg (eds.): *Minorities and the Canadian State* (Mosaic Press, Oakville, 1985).

Niosi, J.: *La Bourgeoise canadienne: la formation et le développement d'une classe dominante* (Editions Boréal express, Montreal, 1980).

Noel, S. J. R.: "Consociational Democracy and Canadian Federalism," *Canadian Journal of Political Science*, vol. 4, no. 1, 1971, pp. 15–18.

Osberg, L.: *Economic Inequality in Canada* (Butterworths, Toronto, 1981).

Palmer, B. D.: *Working Class Culture in Canada* (Butterworths, Toronto, 1981).

Palmer, Howard: "Canadian Immigration and Ethnic History in the 1970s and 1980s," *Journal of Canadian Studies*, vol. 17, no. 1, 1982, pp. 35–50.

Paltiel, Freda L.: *Poverty: An Annotated Bibliography and Reference* (Canadian Welfare Council, Ottawa, 1966). Supplement I: Mar. 1967. Supplement II: Oct. 1967.

Panitch, Leo (ed.): *The Canadian State: Political Economy and Political Power* (University of Toronto Press, Toronto, 1977).

——: "Dependency and Class in Canadian Political Economy," *Studies in Political Economy*, vol. 6, Autumn 1981, pp. 7–34.

——: "Elites, Class and Power in Canada," in Michael S. Whittington and Glen Williams (eds.), *Canadian Politics in the 1980s*, 2nd ed. (Methuen, Toronto, 1984), pp. 229–251.

——: "Trade Unions and the Capitalist State," *New Left Review*, no. 25, Jan./Feb. 1981, pp. 21–43.

Parker, Ian: " 'Commodity Fetishism' and 'Vulgar Marxism': On 'Rethinking Canadian Political Economy,' " *Studies in Political Economy*, vol. 10, Spring 1983, pp. 143–172,

Pelletier, M.: "Le Revenu minimum garanti: une stratégie de bien-être social ou un instrument de politique économique?" *Canadian Public Policy*, vol. 1, 1975, pp. 503–510.

Pinard, M.: "Poverty and Political Movements," in B.R. Blishen *et al.* (eds.): *Canadian Society: Sociological Perspectives*, 3rd ed. (Macmillan, Toronto, 1968), p. 462.

Plunkett, T. J. and W. Hooson: "Municipal Structure and Services (Graham Commission)," *Canadian Public Policy*, vol. 1, no. 1975, pp. 367–375.

Ponting, J. Rick and Roger Gibbins: *Out of Irrelevance: A Socio-political Introduction to Indian Affairs in Canada* (Butterworths, Toronto, 1980).

Porter, John: "The Economic Elite and the Social Structure in Canada," in B.R. Blishen *et al.* (eds.), *Canadian Society: Sociological Perspectives*, 3rd ed. (Macmillan, Toronto, 1968), p. 754.

Reuber, G.: "The Impact of Government Policies on the Distribution of Income in Canada: A Review," *Canadian Public Policy*, vol. 4, 1978, pp. 505–529.

Rich, H. "The Vertical Mosaic Revisited: Towards a Macro-sociology of Canada," *Journal of Canadian Studies*, vol. 11, no. 1, 1976, pp. 14–31.

Richmond, A.H.: "Immigrant Adaptation: A Critical Review of 'Three Years in Canada,' " *Canadian Public Policy*, vol. 1, no. 1975, pp. 317–327.

Rouland, N.: "L'Acculturation judiciaire chez les Inuits du Canada," *Recherches amérindiennes*, vol. 13, 1983, p. 179.

Rubinoff, Lionel: "Multiculturalism and the Metaphysics of Pluralism," *Journal of Canadian Studies*, vol. 17, no. 1, 1982, pp. 122–130.

Schlesinger, Benjamin: *Poverty in Canada and the United States: Overview and Annotated Bibliography* (University of Toronto Press, Toronto, 1966).

Schwartz, M.: "Political Behaviour and Ethnic Origin," in John Meisel (ed.), *Papers on the 1962 Election* (University of Toronto Press, Toronto, 1965), pp. 253–271.

Smith, Allan: "National Images and National Maintenance: The Ascendancy of the Ethnic Idea in North America," *Canadian Journal of Political Science*, vol. 14, 1981, pp. 227–257.

Smith, David, C.: *Incomes Policies: Some Foreign Experiences and Their Relevance for Canada*, Economic Council of Canada Special Study 4 (Queen's Printer, Ottawa, 1966).

Steinberg, C.: "The Welfare Rip-off and All That: A Comment," *Canadian Public Policy*, vol. 1, 1975, pp. 480–486.

Teeple, Gary (ed.): *Capitalism and the National Question in Canada* (University of Toronto Press, Toronto, 1972).

Van Ober, Hadley: "Canadian Approaches to Rural Poverty," *Journal of Farm Economics*, vol. 49, no. 5, 1967, pp. 1209–1224.

Vogler, Carolyn M.: *The Nation State: The Neglected Dimension of Class* (Gower Publishing, Aldershot, England, 1985).

Watson, Graham: "The Reification of Ethnicity and Its Political Consequences in the North," *Canadian Review of Sociology and Anthropology*, vol. 18, no. 4, 1981, pp. 453–469.

Weaver, Sally: *Making Canadian Indian Policy* (University of Toronto Press, Toronto, 1981).

Wilson, J.: "Politics and Social Class in Canada," *Canadian Journal of Political Science*, vol. 1, 1968, pp. 288–308.

—— : "Sociological Aspects of Poverty: A Conceptual Analysis," *Canadian Review of Sociology and Anthropology*, vol. 2, no. 4, 1965, pp. 175–189.

Wilson, V. S. and W. A. Mullins: "Representative Bureaucracy: Linguistic/Ethnic Aspects in Canadian Public Policy," *Canadian Public Administration*, vol. 21, no. 4, 1978, pp. 513–538.

Winn, C.: "Affirmative Action and Visible Minorities: Eight Premises in Quest of Evidence," *Canadian Public Policy*, vol. 11, no. 4, 1985, pp. 684–700.

C. Quebec and "The French-Canadian Question"

Note: There is a large bibliography on French Canada in vol. 1, 1968, pp. 107–118 of the *Canadian Journal of Political Science*. It is a useful source of references for the period up to 1978. See also Chapters 11 and 12 for additional listings.

Abley, Mark: "The Lévesque Effect," *Saturday Night*, June 1985, pp. 13–25.

Adamson, Christopher R., Peter C. Findlay, Michael K. Oliver, and Janet Solberg: "The Unpublished Research of the Royal Commission on Bilingualism and Biculturalism" (review article), *Canadian Journal of Political Science*, vol. 7, no. 4, 1974, pp. 709–720.

Allard, M.: *The Last Chance: The Canadian Constitution and French Canadians* (Editions Ferland, Quebec, 1964).

Archibald, Clinton: *Un Québec corporatiste* (Editions Asticou, Hull, 1984).

Ares, Richard: *Les Positions—éthniques, linguistiques et religieuses des canadiens français la suite du recensement de 1971* (Les Editions Bellarmin, Montreal, 1975).

Armstrong, Robert: *Structure and Change: An Economic History of Quebec* (Gage, Toronto, 1984).

Arnopoulos, Sheila McLeod: *Voices from French Ontario* (McGill-Queen's University Press, Kingston and Montreal, 1982).

—— and Dominique Clift: *The English Fact in Quebec* (McGill-Queen's University Press, Montreal, 1980).

Aubery, P.: "Nationalisme et lutte des classes au Quebec," *American Review of Canadian Studies*, vol. 5, no. 1975, pp. 130–145.

Bakvis, H.: "French Canada and the Bureaucratic Phenomenon," *Canadian Public Administration*, vol. 21, no. 1, 1978, pp. 103–124.

Barbeau, R.: *Le Québec, est-il une colonie?* (Editions de l'homme, Montreal, 1962).

Barberis, Robert: *Les Illusions du pouvoir* (Editions select, Montreal, 1980).

Bauer, Julien: "Patrons et patronat au Québec," *Canadian Journal of Political Science*, vol. 9, no. 3, 1976, pp. 473–491.

Beaujot, R. P.: "A Demographic View on Canadian Language Policy," *Canadian Public Policy*, vol. 5, 1979, pp. 16–29.

Behiels, Michael D.: "The Bloc populaire canadien and the Origins of French-Canadian Neo-nationalism 1942–48," *Canadian Historical Review*, vol. 4, 1982, pp. 487–512.

—— : *Prelude to Quebec's Quiet Revolution: Liberalism versus Neo-nationalism, 1945–1960* (University of Toronto Press, Toronto, 1985).

Belanger, Gerard: *L'Economique du secteur public* (Morin, Chicoutimi, 1981).

Bélanger, M.: "Le Rapport Bélanger: dix ans après," *Canadian Public Administration*, vol. 19, no. 3, 1976, pp. 457–465.

Benjamin, Jacques: "La Minorité en état bicommunautaire: quatre études de cas," *Canadian Journal of Political Science*, vol. 4, no. 4, 1971, pp. 447–496.

—— : "La Rationalisation des choix budgétaires: les cas québécois et canadien," *Canadian Journal of Political Science*, vol. 5, no. 3, 1972, pp. 348–364.

Bergeron, Gérard: *Le Canada français après deux siècles de patience* (Sévil, Paris, 1967).

—— : *Ce Jour-là . . . le referendum* (Les Editions quinze, Montreal, 1978).

—— : *L'Indépendance oui, mais . . .* (Les Editions quinze, Montreal, 1977).

—— : *Notre Miroir a deux faces* (Québec-Amérique, Montreal, 1985).

—— : *Pratique de l'état au Québec* (Québec-Amérique, Montreal, 1984).

—— and Réjean Pelletier (eds.): *L'Etat du Québec en devenir* (Boréal express, Montreal, 1980).

Bergeron, Marie-Hélène, D. Brown, and R. Simeon (eds.): *The Debate on the Referendum Question, Quebec National Assembly, March 4–20, 1980* (Institute of Intergovernmental Relations, Queen's University, Kingston, 1980).

Bernard, André: *Quebec: Elections 1981* (Hurtubise, Montreal, 1981).

—— : *La Politique au Canada et au Québec*, 2nd ed. (Les Presses de l'Université du Québec, Montreal, 1977; English version: Methuen, Toronto, 1981).

—— : *What Does Quebec Want?* (James Lorimer, Toronto, 1978).

Bernier, Bernard: "The Penetration of Capitalism in Quebec," *Canadian Review of Sociology and Anthropology*, vol. 13, 1976, pp. 422–434.

Boismenu, Gérard: *Le Duplessisme: politique économique et rapports de force 1944–1960* (Les Presses de l'Université de Montreal, 1981).

—— et al.: *Espace régional et nation: pour un nouveau débat sur le Québec* (Boréal express, Montreal, 1983).

Boisvert, M. A.: *Les Implications économiques de la souveraineté association* (Les Presses de l'Université de Montréal, Montréal, 1980).

Bonefant, Jean-Charles: "Le Bicaméralisme dans le Québec," *Canadian Journal of Economics and Political Science*, vol. 29, 1963, pp. 495–504.

—— : "Les Etudes de la Commission royale d'enquête sur le bilinguisme et le biculturalisme" (bibliographical note), *Canadian Journal of Political Science*, vol. 4, 1971, pp. 406–416.

Borgeat, Louis, René Dussault, and Lionel Ouellet with Patrick Moran and Marcel Proulx: *L'Administration Québécoise: organisation et fonctionnement* (Presses de l'Université du Québec, Québec, 1982).

Bourdreau, Ernest: *Le Rêve inachevé: le PQ, l'indépendance et la crise* (Nouvelle optique, Montreal, 1983).

—— and J. C. Falardeau: "Cultural and Political Implications of French-Canadian Nationalism," *Canadian Historical Annual Report* (Ottawa, 1946).

Bourgault, P.: *Québec quitte ou double* (Ferron, Montreal, 1970).

Bourgue, G.: "Class Nation and the Parti Québécois," *Studies in Political Economy: A Socialist Review*, vol. 2, Autumn 1979, pp. 129–158.

Bourhis, Richard Y. (ed.): *Conflict and Language Planning in Quebec* (Multilingual Matters Ltd., Clevedon, England, 1984).

Bourque, G. and G. Destaler: *Socialisme et indépendance* (Editions Boréal express, Montreal, 1980).

—— and N. Laurin-Frenette: "Classes sociales et idéologies nationalistes au Québec 1960–1970," in *L'Homme et la sociéte* (Paris, 1972).

Brachet, B.: "La Crise du fédéralisme canadien et le problème québécois," *Revue du Droit publique et de la Science politique*, vol. 88, no. 2, 1972, pp. 303–324.

Breton, R.: "The Socio-political Dynamics of the October Events," *Canadian Review of Sociology and Anthropology*, vol. 9, no. 1, 1972, pp. 33–56.

Brichant, A.: *Option Canada: The Economic Implications of Separatism for the Province of Quebec* (The Canada Committee, Montreal, 1968).

Brière, M. and J. Grandmaison: *Un Nouveau Contrat social* (Les Editions Leméac, Ottawa, 1980).

Brossand, Jacques: *L'Accession: la souveraineté et le cas du Québec* (Les Presses de l'Université de Montreal, Montreal, 1976).

Brunet, Michel: *Québec-Canada anglais: deux intinéraires un affrontement* (Editions H.M.H., Montreal, 1978).

Caldwell, G.: "English-speaking Quebec in the Light of Its Reaction to Bill 22," *American Review of Canadian Studies*, vol. 6, 1976, pp. 42–56.

Canada: *Royal Commission on Bilingualism and Biculturalism Report* (Queen's Printer, Ottawa, 1965).

Canadian Broadcasting Corporation: *Québec: Year Eight* (Glendon College Forum, Toronto, 1968).

Caron, André H., Chantal Mayrand, and David E. Payne: "L'Imagerie politique à la télévision: les derniers jours de la campagne référendaire," *Canadian Journal of Political Science*, vol. 16, 1983, pp. 473–488.

Carson, J. J.: "Bilingualism Revisited; Or, the Confessions of a Middle-aged and Belated Francophile," *Canadian Public Administration*, vol. 21, no. 4, 1978, pp. 539–547.

Castonguay, C.: "Why Hide the Facts? The Federalist Approach to the Language Crisis in Canada," *Canadian Public Policy*, vol. 5, no. 1, 1979, pp. 4–15.

Chamberland, Paul: *Un Parti pris anthropologique* (Editions Parti pris, Montreal, 1983).

Champagne-Gilbert, Maurice: *Batir ou Détruire le Québec* (Les Editions primeur, Montreal, 1983).

Chaput, M.: *Why I Am a Separatist* (Ryerson, Toronto, 1962).

Chaput-Rolland, S.: *De l'unité à la réalité* (Tisseyre, Montreal, 1981).

—— : *My Country: Canada or Québec* (Macmillan, Toronto, 1966).

Charbonneau, M.: "La Commission des valeurs mobilières du Québec, *Canadian Public Administration*, vol. 20, no. 1, 1977, pp. 87–139.

Chodos, Robert and Nick auf der Maur (eds.): *Quebec: A Chronicle, 1968–1972* (James, Lewis & Samuel, Toronto, 1972).

Clift, Dominique: *Le Déclin du nationalisme au Québec* (Libre expression, Montreal, 1981).

—— : *Quebec Nationalism in Crisis* (McGill-Queen's University Press, Montreal, 1982).

Cody, H.: "The Ontario Response to Quebec's Separatist Challenge," *American Review of Canadian Studies*, vol. 7, no. 1, 1978, pp. 43–55.

Cohen, R. I.: *Quebec Votes* (Saje Publications, Montreal, 1965).

Coleman, N.: "The Class Bases of Language Policy in Quebec 1949–1975," *Studies in Political Economy: A Socialist Review*, vol. 13, Spring 1980, pp. 93–118.

Coleman, William D.: *The Independence Movement in Quebec 1945–1980* (University of Toronto Press, Toronto, 1984).

—— : "From Bill 22 to Bill 101: The Politics of Language under the Parti Québécois," *Canadian Journal of Political Science*, vol. 14, 1981, pp. 459–485.

Comeau, P. A.: "Acculturation ou assimilation: technique d'analyse et tentative de mesure chez les franco-ontariens," *Canadian Journal of Political Science*, vol. 2, no. 2, 1969, pp. 158–172.

Cook, Ramsay: *Canada and the French-Canadian Question* (Macmillan of Canada, Toronto, 1976).

—— (ed.): *French-Canadian Nationalism: An Anthology* (Macmillan, Toronto, 1969).

—— : "Has the Quiet Revolution Ended?" *Queen's Quarterly*, vol. 90, no. 2, Summer 1983, pp. 330–342.

Corbett, E. M.: *Quebec Confronts Canada* (Copp Clark, Toronto, 1967).

Crean, Susan and Marcel Rioux: *Two Nations* (James Lorimer, Toronto, 1983).

Dagnais, André: *Libérer, renverser* (Etat du Québec, Montreal, 1981).

d'Allemagne, A.: *Le Colonialisme au Québec* (Editions Renaud et Bray, Montreal, 1966).

Dawson, Robert MacGregor: *The Conscription Crisis of 1944* (University of Toronto Press, Toronto, 1961).

Desbarat, P.: *The State of Quebec* (McClelland and Stewart, Toronto, 1965).

Dion, G.: "Securalisation in Quebec," *Journal of Canadian Studies*, vol. 3, no. 1, 1968, pp. 35–44.

Dion, Léon: *Le Bill 60 et la société québécoise* (Editions H.M.H., Montreal, 1967).

—— : *Le Québec et le Canada: les voies de l'avenir* (Les Editions Québecor, Montreal, 1980).

—— : *Quebec: The Unfinished Revolution* (McGill-Queen's University Press, Montreal, 1976).

Doern, Russell: *The Battle over Bilingualism in the Manitoba Language Question 1983–85* (Cambridge Publishers, Winnipeg, 1985).

Dofny, Jacques and Nicole Arnaud: *Nationalism and the National Question* (Black Rose Books, Montreal, 1977).

Dooley, D. J.: "Quebec and the Future of Canada," *The Review of Politics*, vol. 27, no. 2, Jan. 1965.

Drache, Daniel (ed.): *Quebec—Only the Beginning: The Manifestos of the Common Front* (New Press, Toronto, 1972).

Dumont, F. and Y. Martin: *Situation de la recherche sur le Canada français* (Les Presses de l'Université Laval, Quebec, 1962).

—— and Jean-Paul Montminy (eds.): *Le Pouvoir dans la société canadienne-francaise* (Les Presses de l'Université Laval, Quebec, 1966).

Elkin, F.: "Ethnic Revolutions and Occupational Dilemmas," *The International Journal of Comparative Sociology*, vol. 13, no. 1, 1972, pp. 48–54.

Even, A.: "Domination et développement au Nouveau-Brunswick," *Recherches socio-graphiques*, vol. 12, no. 3, 1971, pp. 271–318.

Feldman, Elliot J. and Neil Nevitte: *The Future of North America: Canada, the United States, and Quebec Nationalism* (Institute for Research on Public Policy, Montreal, 1979).

Forsey, E. A.: "The British North America Act and Biculturalism," *Queen's Quarterly*, vol. 71, no. 2, 1964, pp. 141–149.

—— : "Canada: Two Nations or One?" *Canadian Journal of Economics and Political Science*, vol. 28, no. 4, 1962, pp. 485–501.

Fortin, P. *et al.*: "Quebec in the Canadian Federation: A Provisional Evaluative Framework," *Canadian Public Administration*, vol. 21, no. 4, 1978, pp. 558–578.

Fournier, P. (ed.): *Capitalisme et politique au Québec* (Coll. Recherches et documents, Editions coopératives Albert Saint-Martin, Montreal, 1981).

—— : "The New Parameters of the Quebec Bourgeoisie," *Studies in Political Economy: A Socialist Review*, vol. 3, Spring 1980, pp. 67–92.

—— : *The Quebec Establishment: The Ruling Class and the State* (Black Rose Books, Montreal, 1976).

Fraser, Graham: *PQ, René Lévesque and the Parti Québécois in Power* (Macmillan, Toronto, 1984).

Frechette, P.: "L'Economie de la Confédération: un point de vue québécois," *Canadian Public Policy*, vol. 3, 1977, pp. 431–440.

Gagnon, Alain G.: *Les Opérations dignité: naissance d'un mouvement social dans l'est du Québec* (Carleton University, Ottawa, 1981).

—— (ed.): *Quebec: State and Society* (Methuen, Toronto, 1984).

—— and Mary Beth Montcalm: "Economic Peripheralization and Quebec Unrest," *Journal of Canadian Studies*, vol. 17, no. 2, 1982, pp. 32–43.

Gagnon, Serge: *Quebec and Its Historians: The Twentieth Century* (Harvest House, Montreal, 1985).

Garigue, P.: *Bibliographie du Québec, 1955–1965* (Les Presses de l'Université de Montréal, Montreal, 1967).

—— : *L'Option politique du Canada francais* (Editions du lévrier, Montreal, 1963).

Garnier, G.: "Les Enterprises multi-nationales et l'indépendance éventuelle du Québec," *Canadian Public Policy*, vol. 5, no. 1, 1979, pp. 59–69.

Gélina, A.: "Les Parlementaires et l'administration publique au Québec," *Canadian Journal of Political Science*, vol. 1, no. 2, 1968, pp. 164–179.

George, Pierre: *Le Québec* (Presses universitaires de France, Paris, 1979).

Gérin-Lajoie, P.: *Pourquoi le bill 60* (Editions du jour, Montréal, 1963).

Gow, J. I.: "Histoire administrative du Québec et théorie administrative," *Canadian Journal of Political Science*, vol. 4, no. 1, 1971, pp. 141–145.

—— : "One Hundred Years of Quebec Administrative History 1867–1970," *Canadian Public Administration*, vol. 28, no. 2, 1985, pp. 244–268.

—— : "Les Québécois, la guerre et la paix, 1945–60," *Canadian Journal of Political Science*, vol. 3, no. 1, 1970, pp. 88–122.

Grant, D. (ed.): *Quebec Today* (University of Toronto Press, Toronto, 1960).

Griffin, Anne: *Quebec: The Challenge of Independence* (Fairleigh Dickinson University Press, Rutherford, N.Y., 1984).

Groupe des recherches sociales: *Les Electeurs québécois* (Montreal, 1960).

Guindon, Hubert : "The Church in French-Canadian Society," *Canadian Dimension*, vol. 4, no. 3, Mar./April 1967, pp. 29–31.

—— : "Two Cultures: An Essay on Nationalism, Class and Ethnic Tension in Contemporary Canada," in O. Kruhlak, R. Schultz and S. Pobihushchy, *The Canadian Political Process: A Reader* (Holt Rinehart and Winston, Toronto, 1970).

—— : "The Modernization of Quebec and the Legitimacy of the Canadian State," *Canadian Review of Sociology and Anthropology,* vol. 15, no. 2, 1978, pp. 227–245.

—— : "Social Unrest, Social Class, and Quebec's Bureaucratic Revolution," *Queen's Quarterly*, vol. 71, no. 2, 1964, pp. 150–162. See also correction in vol. 71, no. 3, 1964, p. xiii.

Heintzman, Ralph: "The Political Culture of Québec, 1840–1960," *Canadian Journal of Political Science*, vol. 16, no. 1, 1983, pp. 3–60.

Hero, Alfred O., Jr. and Marcel Daneau (eds.): *Problems and Opportunities in U.S.-Quebec Relations* (Westview Press, Boulder and London, 1984).

Herzeg, Lynn: "The New Quiet Revolution," *Canadian Forum*, vol. 64, no. 741, Aug./Sept. 1984, pp. 6–11.

Hughes, Everett Cherrington: *French Canada in Transition* (University of Chicago Press, Chicago, 1943).

Jacobs, Jane: "The Question of Separatism: III, Excellence in Diversity," *Canadian Forum*, vol. 60, no. 698, April 1980, pp. 22–24.

Jones R.: *Community in Crisis: French-Canadian Nationalism in Perspective* (McClelland and Stewart, Toronto, 1967).

———— : "French Canada and the American Peril in the Twentieth Century," *American Review of Canadian Studies*, vol. 14, no. 3, 1984, pp. 333–350.

Joy, R. J.: "Languages in Conflict: Canada, 1976," *American Review of Canadian Studies*, vol. 6, no. 2, 1976, pp. 7–21.

Jutreas, R.: *Québec libre* (Les Editions actualité, Montreal, 1965).

Kanungo, R. N.: *Biculturalism and Management* (Butterworths, Toronto, 1980).

Keyfitz, N.: "Canadians and Canadiens," *Queen's Quarterly*. vol. 70, no. 2, 1963, pp. 163–182.

Kwavnick, D.: "The Roots of French-Canadian Discontent," *Canadian Journal of Economics and Political Science*, vol. 31, no. 4, 1965, pp. 509–523.

———— (ed.): *The Tremblay Report* (Carleton Library, McClelland and Stewart, Toronto, 1972).

Lamontagne, L.: *Le Canada francais d'aujourd'hui* (University of Toronto Press, Toronto, 1970).

Lamontagne, Maurice: *The Double Deal: A Response to the Parti Quebecois White Paper and Referendum Question* (Optimum, Montreal, 1980).

Lanphier, C. Michael and Raymond N. Morris: *Three Scales of Inequality: Perspectives on French-English Relations* (Longman Canada, Don Mills, 1977).

Laponce, Jean A.: *Langue et territoire* (Les Presses de l'Université Laval, Quebec, 1984).

Larochelle, Louis: *En Flagrant Délit de pouvoir* (Boréal express, Montreal, 1982).

Latouche, Daniel: "Anti-séparatisme et messianisme au Québec depuis 1960," *Canadian Journal of Political Science*, vol. 3, no. 4, 1970, pp. 559–578.

———— : *Canada and Quebec, Past and Future: An Essay*, study prepared for the Royal Commission on the Economic Union and Development Prospects for Canada, vol. 70 (University of Toronto Press, Toronto, 1986).

———— : "La Vrai Nature de . . . la révolution tranquille" (note), *Canadian Journal of Political Science*, vol. 7, no. 3, 1974, pp. 525–536.

———— and E. Cloutier (eds.): *Le Système politique québécois* (Hurtubise HMH, Montreal, 1980).

Laurendeau, André: *La Crise de la conscription, 1942* (Les Editions du jour, Montreal, 1962).

Laurin, C.: *Ma Traversée du Québec* (Les Editions du jour, Montreal, 1970)

Laurin-Frenette, Nicole: *L'Impasse: en jeux et perspectives de l'après-référendum* (Nouvelle optique, Montreal, 1980).

LeDuc, Lawrence, Harold D. Clarke, Jane Jenson, and Jon H. Pammett: "Sovereignty-Association 'Non' — Parti Québécois 'Oui': Trends in Political Support in Quebec," *American Review of Canadian Studies*, vol. 12, no. 3, 1982, pp. 61–71.

Legare, A.: "Les Classes sociaux et le gouvernement PQ à Québec," *Canadian Review of Sociology and Anthropology*, vol. 15, no. 1, 1978, pp. 218–226.

Lescop, René: *Le Parti québécois du Général de Gaulle* (Boréal express, Montreal, 1981).

Lévesque, René: *My Quebec* (Totem Books, Toronto, 1979).

———— : *Option Quebec* (Les Editions de l'homme, Montreal, 1968; English edition: McClelland and Stewart, Toronto, 1968).

———— : *Oui* (Editions de l'homme, Montreal, 1980).

———— : *La Solution: programme du Parti québécois* (Les Editions du jour, Montreal, 1970).

———— : *La Souveraineté et l'économie* (Les Editions du jour, Montreal, 1970).

—— : "For an Independent Quebec," *Foreign Affairs* (Toronto), vol. 34, July 1976, pp. 733–744.

Levitt, J. (ed.): *Henri Bourassa on Imperialism and Biculturalism, 1900–1918* (Copp Clark, Toronto, 1970).

Lieberson, Stanley: *Language and Ethnic Relations in Canada* (John Wiley and Sons, New York, 1970).

Lipsig, Munné, C.: "Quebec Unions and the State: Conflict and Dependence," *Studies in Political Economy: A Socialist Review*, vol. 3, Spring 1980, pp. 119–146,

Loomis, Dan G.: *Not Much Glory: Quelling the FLQ* (Deneau, Ottawa, 1984).

Macdonald, L.: *From Bourassa to Bourassa: A Pivotal Decade in Canadian History* (Harvest House, Montreal, 1984).

Mackay, Jacques: *Le Courage de se choisir* (Hexagone, Montreal, 1983).

MacMillan, C. Michael: "The Character of Henry Bourassa's Political Philosophy," *American Review of Canadian Studies*, vol. 12, no. 1, 1982, pp. 10–29.

—— : "Henri Bourassa on the Defence of Language Rights," *Dalhousie Review*, vol. 62, no. 3, Autumn 1982, pp. 413–430.

—— : "Language Rights and Bill 101," *Queen's Quarterly*, vol. 90, no. 2, Summer 1983, pp. 343–361.

MacRae, C. F. (ed.): *French Canada Today*, report of the Mount Allison 1961 Summer Institute (Sackville, 1961).

McRae, K. D.: "Bilingual Language Districts in Finland and Canada: Adventures in the Transplanting of an Institution," *Canadian Public Policy*, vol. 4, no. 3, 1978, pp. 331–351.

—— : "The Structure of Canadian History," in L. Hartz, *The Founding of New Societies* (Longmans, Toronto, 1964).

McRoberts, Kenneth and Dale Posgate: *Quebec: Social Change and Political Crisis*, rev. ed. (McClelland and Stewart, Toronto, 1980).

Maheu, Pierre: *Un Parti pris revolutionnaire* (Parti pris, Montreal, 1983).

Maheux, A.: "French Canadians and Democracy," *University of Toronto Quarterly*, vol. 27, 1958, pp. 341–351.

Mallory, J. E.: "The Canadian Dilemma: French and English," *Political Quarterly*, vol. 41, no. 3, 1970, pp. 281–297.

Marier, R.: "Les Objectifs sociaux du Québec," *Canadian Public Administration*, vol. 12, no. 2, 1969, pp. 181–197.

Meyers, H. B.: *The Quebec Revolution* (Harvest House, Montreal, 1964).

Milner, Henry: *Politics in the New Quebec* (McClelland and Stewart, Toronto, 1978).

—— and Sheilagh Hodgins Milner: *The Decolonization of Quebec: An Analysis of Left-wing Nationalism* (McClelland and Stewart, Toronto, 1973).

Moniere, Denis: *Ideologies in Quebec* (University of Toronto Press, Toronto, 1981).

—— : *Pour la suite de l'histoire: essai sur la conjoncture politique au Québec* (Québec-Amérique, Montreal, 1982).

Morchain, Janet: *Search for a Nation: Canada's Crises in French-English Relations 1759–1980* (Fitzhenry and Whiteside, Markham, 1984).

Murray, Vera and Don Murray: *De Bourassa à Lévesque* (Editions quinze, Montreal, 1978).

Neatby, H. B.: *Laurier and a Liberal Quebec: A Study in Political Management* (McClelland and Stewart, Toronto, 1973).

—— : "Mackenzie King and French Canada," *Journal of Canadian Studies*, vol. 11, no. 1, 1976, pp. 3–13.

O'Grady, William: *The Quebec Problem: An Inquiry into the Ethics of Sovereignty and Secession* (Borealis Press, Ottawa, 1980).

Oliver, M: "Quebec and Canadian Democracy," *Canadian Journal of Economics and Political Science*, vol. 23, no. 5, 1957, pp. 504–515.

Orban, E.: *Le Conseil législatif du Québec* (Bellarmin, Montreal, 1967).

—— : "La Fin du bicaméralisme au Québec," *Canadian Journal of Political Science*, vol. 2, no. 3, 1969, pp. 312–326.

Ornstein, Michael D. and H. Michael Stevenson: "Elite and Public Opinion before the Quebec Referendum: A Commentary on the State in Canada," *Canadian Journal of Political Science*, vol. 14, 1981, pp. 745–774.

Paquette, Gilbert and Jean-Pierre Charbonneau: *L'Option* (Les Editions de l'homme, Montreal, 1978).

Pare, G.: *Au-delà du séparatisme* (Collection Les idées du jour, Montreal, 1966).

Parti pris: *Les Québécois* (Maspero, Paris, 1967).

Payette, Lise: *Le Pouvoir? Connaie pas!* (Québec-Amérique, Montreal, 1982).

Pelletier, Gerard: *Years of Impatience 1950–1960* (Stanké, Montreal, 1983).

Pelletier, Jean: "The Resurrection of Bourassa," *Saturday Night*, Feb. 1984, pp. 13–16.

Pelletier, R.: "Le Militant du R.I.N. et son parti," *Recherches sociographiques*, vol. 13, no. 1, 1972, pp. 41–72.

Pinard, Maurice: "Working Class Politics: An Interpretation of the Quebec Case," *Canadian Review of Sociology and Anthropology*, vol. 7, no. 2, 1970, pp. 87–109.

Piotte, Jean-Marc and Bela Egyed: "A Morose Quebec," *Canadian Forum*, vol. 62, no. 726, Mar. 1983, pp. 12–13.

Pontaut, Alain: *René Lévesque; ou, l'idéalisme pratique* (Leméac, Ottawa, 1983).

Premier congrès des affaires canadiennes: *The Canadian Experiment: Success or Failure?* (Les Presses de l'Université Laval, Québec, 1962).

Quebec: *Report of Royal Commission of Inquiry on Constitutional Problems* (Tremblay Report), 4 vols. (Queen's Printer, Quebec, 1956).

—— : *Le Rapport de la Commission royale d'enquête sur l'enseignment* (le Rapport Parent), 3 vols. (L'Imprimeur de la reine, Quebec, 1963–1966).

—— : *Le Rapport de la Commission royal d'enquête sur la fiscalité* (le Rapport Bélanger) (L'Imprimeur de la reine, Québec, 1966).

Quesnel-Ouellet, Louise: "Régionalisation et urbaine conscience politique régionale: la communauté du Québec," *Canadian Journal of Political Science*, vol. 4, no. 2, 1971, pp. 191–205.

—— : "Situations et attitudes face au changement dans les structures municipales," *Canadian Journal of Political Science*, vol. 6, no. 2, 1973, pp. 195–218.

Quinn, Herbert Furlong: "Political Resurrection in Quebec: The Re-election of Robert Bourassa as Liberal Leader," *Dalhousie Review*, vol. 64, no. 1, Spring 1984, pp. 115–124.

—— : *The Union Nationale: A Study in Quebec Nationalism* (University of Toronto Press, Toronto, 1963).

—— : *The Union Nationale: Quebec Nationalism from Duplessis to Lévesque* (University of Toronto Press, Toronto, 1979).

Raabe, C.: "Business Images of the PQ: Investment and the Political Economy," *American Review of Canadian Studies*, vol. 9, no. 2, 1979, pp. 130–147.

Raboy, Marc: *Movements and Messages: Media and Radical Politics in Quebec* (Between the Lines, Toronto, 1984).

Raynauld, A.: "Les Implications économiques de l'option Québec," *Le Devoir*, 24 avril 1970, p. 5, col. 1.

Reid, Malcolm: *The Shouting Signpainters: A Literary and Political Account of Quebec Revolutionary Nationalism* (McClelland and Stewart, Toronto, 1972).

Rioux, Marcel: "Conscience ethnique et conscience de classe au Québec," *Recherches sociographiques*, vol. 6, no. 1, 1965, pp. 23–32.

—— (ed.): *L'Eglise et le Québec*, minutes of a meeting of l'Institut canadien des affaires publiques, 1961 (Les Editions du jour, Montreal, 1961).

—— : *Pour prendre publiquement congé de quelques salauds* (Hexagone, Montreal, 1981).

—— and Y. Martin: *French-Canadian Society* (McClelland and Stewart, Toronto, 1964).

Rotstein, A. (ed.): *Power Corrupted: The October Crisis and the Repression of Quebec* (New Press, 1971).

Rutan, G. F.: "Two Views of the Concept of Sovereignty: Canadian-Canadien," *Western Political Quarterly*, vol. 24, no. 3, 1971, pp. 456–466.

Ryan, C.: "Un Cas pertinent: le Québec," *Canadian Public Policy*, vol. 2, 1976, pp. 587–595.

—— : "La Dualité canadienne," *Policy Options*, vol. 3, July/Aug. 1982, pp. 17–23.

San Roman, Pilar: *Deux Cultures et un amour . . . le Canada* (University of Ottawa Press, Ottawa, 1983).

Savard, Pierre *et al.*: *Québec et Ontario francais: mythes et réalités* (University of Ottawa Press, Ottawa, 1985).

Schabas, Bill: "The PQ and the Socialists," *Canadian Forum*, vol. 62, no. 726, Mar. 1983, pp. 14–15, 35.

Scott, F.R. and M. Oliver (eds.): *Quebec States Her Case* (Macmillan, Toronto, 1964).

Seguin, M.: "Genèse et historique de l'idée séparatiste au Canada français," *Laurentie*, no. 119, 1962.

Shaw, W. and L. Albert: *Partition: The Price of Quebec's Independence* (Thornhill Publishing, Montreal, 1980).

Siegried, A.: *The Race Question in Canada* (McClelland and Stewart, Toronto, 1966).

Silver, A. L.: *The French-Canadian Idea of Confederation 1864–1900* (University of Toronto Press, Toronto, 1982).

Simeon, R.: "Quebec 1970: The Dilemma of Power," *Queen's Quarterly*, vol. 79, no. 1, 1972, pp. 100–107.

Singer, Howard L.: "Internal Conflicts within a Quebec Separatist Organization: The Case of the RIN," *American Review of Canadian Studies*, vol. 11, no. 1, 1981, pp. 1–14.

Sloane, T.: *Quebec: The Not-so-quiet Revolution* (Ryerson, Toronto, 1965).

Smiley, D. V.: *The Association Dimension of Sovereignty-Association: A Response to the Quebec White Paper* (Discussion Paper 8) (Intergovernmental Relations, Queen's University, Kingston, 1980).

Smith, Denis: *Bleeding Hearts — Bleeding Country: Canada and the Quebec Crisis* (Hurtig, Edmonton, 1971).

Société Saint-Jean Baptiste de Montréal: *Le Fédéralisme: l'Amérique du nord britannique et les Canadiens francais* (report to Comité parlementaire de la constitution du gouvernement du Québec (Les Editions de l'agence Duvernay, Montreal, 1964).

Stein, Michael B.: *The Dynamics of Right-wing Protest: A Political Analysis of Social Credit in Quebec* (University of Toronto Press, Toronto, 1973).

Thomson, Dale: *Jean Lesage and the Quiet Revolution* (Macmillan, Toronto, 1984).

—— : *Quebec Society and Politics: Views from the Inside* (McClelland and Stewart, Toronto, 1973).

Tremblay, Marc-Alélard: *L'Identité québécoise en péril* (Les Editions Saint-Yves, Sainte-Foy, 1983).

Tremblay, Rodrique: *Le Quebec en crise* (Editions select, Montreal, 1981).

Trofimenkoff, S. M.: *The Dream of Nation: A Social and Intellectual History of Quebec* (Macmillan, Toronto, 1982).

Troisième congrès des affaires canadiennes: *Les Nouveaux Québécois* (Les Presses de l'Université Laval, Québec, 1964).

Trudeau, P. E.: (ed.): *The Asbestos Strike* (James, Lewis & Samuel, Toronto, 1974).

——— : *Federalism and the French Canadians* (Macmillan, Toronto, 1968).

——— "Some Obstacles to Democracy in Quebec," *Canadian Journal of Political Science*, vol. 24, no. 3, 1958.

Ullman, Stephen H.: "Political Development and Party Change in Quebec, 1980–1983," *American Review of Canadian Studies*, vol. 13, no. 2, 1983, pp. 29–41.

Usher, D.: "The English Response to the Prospect of the Separation of Quebec," *Canadian Public Policy*, vol. 4, no. 1, 1978, pp. 57–87.

Vaillancourt, F.: "La Charte de la langue francaise du Québec: un essai d'analyse," *Canadian Public Policy*, vol. 4, no. 3, 1978, pp. 284–308.

——— : "La Situation démographique et socio-économique des francophones du Québec: une revue," *Canadian Public Policy*, vol. 5, no. 4, 1979, pp. 542–558.

Vaillancourt, Yves: *Le PQ et le social: éléments de bilan des politiques sociales du gouvernement du Parti québécois 1976–1982* (Editions cooperatives Albert-Martin, Montreal, 1985).

Vallières, Pierre: *Choose!* (New Press, Toronto, 1972).

——— : *The Impossible Quebec* (Black Rose Books, Montreal, 1980).

——— : *Nègres blancs d'Amérique* (Editions Parti pris, Montreal, 1968).

——— : *White Niggers of America*, trans. Joan Pinkham (McClelland and Stewart, Toronto, 1971).

Vanasse, Diane: *L'Evolution de la population scolaire du Québec* (Institut de recherches politiques, Montreal, 1981).

Veltman, C. J.: "Ethnic Assimilation in Quebec: A Statistical Analysis," *American Review of Canadian Studies*, vol. 5, no. 2, 1975, pp. 104–129.

Wade, M. (ed.): *Canadian Dualism: Studies of French-English Relations* (University of Toronto Press, Toronto, 1960).

——— : *The French-Canadian Outlook: A Brief Account of the Unknown North Americans* (McClelland and Stewart, Toronto, 1964).

——— : *The French Canadians*: vol. 1, 1760–1911; vol. 2, 1912–1967 (Macmillan, Toronto, 1968).

Wardhaugh, Ronald: *Language and Nationhood: The Canadian Experience* (New Star Books, Vancouver, 1983).

Whitaker, Reginald: "The Competition for Power: Hobbes and the Quebec Question," *Canadian Forum*, vol. 58, Feb. 1979, pp. 6–10.

——— : "The Quebec Cauldron," in Michael S. Whittington and Glen Williams (eds.), *Canadian Politics in the 1980s*, 2nd ed. (Methuen, Toronto, 1984), pp. 33–57.

Woolfson, P.: "The French Fact: Linguistic Challenge, Demographic Reality, Political Distortion," *American Review of Canadian Studies*, vol. 6, no. 2, 1976, pp. 1–6.

——— : "Language in Quebec: Legal and Societal Issues," *American Review of Canadian Studies*, vol. 13, no. 2, 1983, pp. 42–51.

POLITICAL CULTURE

A. *Political Culture and Ideology*

Alford, R. R.: "The Social Bases of Political Cleavage in 1962," in J. Meisel (ed.), *Papers on the 1962 Election* (University of Toronto Press, Toronto, 1964).

Almond, G. and S. Verba: *The Civic Culture* (Princeton University Press, Princeton, 1963).

Armour, Leslie: *The Idea of Canada and the Crisis of Community* (Steel Rail Publishing, Ottawa, 1981).

—— and Elizabeth Trott: *The Faces of Reason: An Essay on Philosophy and Culture in English Canada 1850–1950* (Wilfrid Laurier University Press, Waterloo, 1981).

Armstrong, J.: "Canadians in Crisis: The Nature and Source of Support for Leadership in a National Emergency," *Canadian Review of Sociology and Anthropology*, vol. 9, no. 4, 1972, pp. 299–324.

Bélanger, André J.: *A Framework for Political Sociology* (University of Toronto Press, Toronto, 1985).

Bell, David V. J.: "Political Culture in Canada," in Michael S. Whittington and Glen Williams (eds.), *Canadian Politics in the 1980s*, 2nd ed. (Methuen, Toronto, 1984), pp. 155–174.

—— and Lorne Tepperman: *The Roots of Disunity* (McClelland and Stewart, Toronto, 1979).

Berton, Pierre: *Why We Act Like Canadians: A Personal Exploration of our National Character* (McClelland and Stewart, Toronto, 1982).

Brooks, Stephen (ed.): *Political Thought in Canada* (Irwin, Toronto, 1984).

Christian, William: *The Idea File of Harold Adams Innis* (University of Toronto Press, Toronto, 1980).

Converse, Philip E.: "The Nature of Belief Systems in Mass Publics," in D. Apter (ed.), *Ideology and Discontent* (The Free Press, New York, 1964), pp. 206–262.

——, Georges Dupeux, and John Meisel: "Continuities in Popular Political Culture: French and Anglo-Saxon Contrasts in Canada," paper prepared for the International Conference on Comparative Electoral Behaviour (Ann Arbor, Michigan, April 1967).

Cook, R.: *The Maple Leaf Forever: Essays on Nationalism and Politics in Canada* (Macmillan, Toronto, 1971).

Cunningham, R. B.: "Attitudes on Pollution and Growth in Hamilton; or, There's an Awful Lot of Talk These Days about Ecology," *Canadian Journal of Political Science*, vol. 5, no. 3, 1972, pp. 389–401.

Devall, W. B.: "Support for Civil Liberties among English-speaking Canadian University Students," *Canadian Journal of Political Science*, vol. 3, no. 3, 1970, pp. 433–449.

Dion, L.: "Régimes d'opinions publiques et systèmes idéologiques," *Ecrits du Canada français*, vol. 12, 1962.

Elkins, David J. and Richard Simeon: *Small Worlds: Provinces and Parties in Canadian Political Life* (Methuen, Toronto, 1980).

Forbes, H. D. (ed.): *Canadian Political Thought* (Oxford University Press, Toronto, 1985).

Friedenberg, E. Z.: *Deference to Authority: The Case of Canada* (M. E. Sharpe, White Plains, N.Y., 1980).

Gibbins, Roger: "Models of Nationalism: A Case Study of Political Ideologies in the Canadian West," *Canadian Journal of Political Science*, vol. 10, 1977, pp. 341–373.

—— and Neil Nevitte: "Canadian Political Ideology: A Comparative Analysis," *Canadian Journal of Political Science*, vol. 18, 1985, pp. 577–598.

Gordon, Walter Lockhart: *A Choice for Canada* (McClelland and Stewart, Toronto, 1966).

Grant, G. P.: *Lament for a Nation: The Defeat of Canadian Nationalism* (McClelland and Stewart, Toronto, 1970).

—— : *Technology and Empire* (House of Anansi, Toronto, 1969).

Johnson, H. G.: *The Canadian Quandary* (McGraw-Hill, Toronto, 1963).

———: "The Economics of the 'Brain Drain': The Canadian Case," *Minerva*, vol. 3, 1965, pp. 299–311.

———: "Problems of Canadian Nationalism," *International Journal*, vol. 16, 1961, pp. 238–249.

———: "The Watkins Report: Towards a New National Policy," *International Journal*, vol. 23, 1968, pp. 615–622.

Katz, D. *et al.* (eds.): *Public Opinion and Propaganda* (Holt Rinehart and Winston, New York, 1960).

Key, V. O.: *Public Opinion and American Democracy* (Alfred A. Knopf, New York, 1961).

Kierans, Eric W.: *Challenge of Confidence: Kierans on Canada* (McClelland and Stewart, Toronto, 1967).

Kim, Y. C.: "The Concept of Political Culture in Comparative Politics," *Journal of Politics*, vol. 26, 1964, pp. 313–336.

Kroker, Arthur: *Technology and the Canadian Mind: Innis/McLuhan/Grant* (New World Perspectives, Montreal, 1984).

Laczko, L.: "English Canadian and Québécois Nationalism," *Canadian Review of Sociology and Anthropology*, vol. 5, 1978, pp. 206–217.

Lane, R. E.: *Political Ideology* (The Free Press, New York, 1962).

——— and D. O. Sears: *Public Opinion* (Prentice-Hall, Englewood Cliffs, 1964).

Laponce, Jean: *Left and Right: The Topography of Political Perceptions* (University of Toronto Press, Toronto, 1981).

Lippman, W.: *Public Opinion* (Macmillan, New York, 1960).

Lipset, S. M.: *Political Man* (Anchor-Doubleday, Garden City, 1969).

———, Paul Lazarsfeld, Allen Barton, and Juan Linz: "The Psychology of Voting," in Lindzey Gardner (ed.), *Handbook of Social Psychology, II* (Addison-Wesley, Cambridge, 1965), pp. 1124–1175.

Lumsden, Ian (ed.): *Close the 49th Parallel: The Americanization of Canada* (University of Toronto Press, Toronto, 1970).

Luttbeg, Norman R. (ed.): *Public Opinion and Public Policy: Models of Political Influence* (The Dorsey Press, Homewood, Ill., 1968).

McDonald, L.: "Attitude Organization and Voting Behaviour in Canada," *Canadian Review of Sociology and Anthropology*, vol. 8, no. 3, 1971, pp. 164–184.

McInnis, Edgar: *Canada: A Political and Social History* (Holt Rinehart and Winston, New York, 1959).

Malcolm, Andrew H.: *The Canadians* (Paperjacks, Toronto, 1985).

Marchak, M. Patricia: *Ideological Perspectives on Canada* (McGraw-Hill Ryerson, Scarborough, 1981).

Mascotto, Jacques: *Démocratie et nation: neo-nationalisme, crise et formes du pouvoir* (Editions cooperatives Albert-Saint-Martin, Laval, 1980).

Melody, William H., Liora Salter, and Paul Heyer (eds.): *Culture, Communication and Dependency: The Tradition of H. A. Innis* (Ablex Publishing, Norwood, N.J., 1981).

Mitchell, Thomas: "Review Essay: Violence and Politics in Canada," *American Review of Canadian Studies*, vol. 12, no. 2, 1982, pp. 87–96.

Morton, W. L.: *The Canadian Identity* (University of Toronto Press, Toronto, 1972).

Nevitte, Neil and Roger Gibbins: "Neo-conservatism: Canadian Variations on an Ideological Theme?" *Canadian Public Policy*, vol. 10, no. 4, 1984, pp. 384–394.

Ontario Legislative Assembly: *Final Report on Economic Nationalism of the Select Committee on Economic and Cultural Nationalism* (Queen's Printer, Toronto, 1975).

Ornstein, M. D. *et al.*: "Public Opinion and the Canadian Political Crisis," *Canadian Review of Sociology and Anthropology*, vol. 15, no. 2, 1978, pp. 58–105.

Ornstein, M. D., H. Michael Stevenson, and A. Paul Williams: "Region, Class and Political Culture in Canada," *Canadian Journal of Political Science*, vol. 13, 1980, pp. 227–271.

Qualter, T. H.: Conflicting *Political Ideas in Liberal Democracies* (Methuen, Toronto, 1986).

—— : "The Manipulation of Popular Impulse: Graham Wallas Revisited," *Canadian Journal of Economics and Political Science*, vol. 25, no. 2, 1969, pp. 165–173.

Reilly, W. G.: "Political Attitudes among Law Students in Quebec," *Canadian Journal of Political Science*, vol. 4, no. 1, 1971, pp. 122–131.

Resnick, P.: *Land of Cain: Class and Nationalism in English Canada* (New Star Books, Vancouver, 1972).

—— : *Parliament vs. People: An Essay on Democracy and Canadian Political Culture* (New Star Books, Vancouver, 1984).

Richards, John: "Populism: A Qualified Defence," *Studies in Political Economy: A Socialist Review*, vol. 5, Spring 1981, pp. 5–28.

Rosenberg, Shaim: "Sociology, Psychology, and the Study of Political Behavior: The Case of the Research on Political Socialization," *Journal of Politics*, vol. 47, no. 2, 1985, pp. 715–735.

Rutman, G.: "Doctrinal Folly in the Name of Canadianism: Doctrine of the 'New' Nationalism in Canada," *American Review of Canadian Studies*, vol. 4, 1974, pp. 37–53.

Schwartz, M.: *Public Opinion and Canadian Identity* (Fitzhenry and Whiteside, Toronto, 1967).

Simeon, Richard and D. J. Elkins: "Regional Political Cultures in Canada," *Canadian Journal of Political Science*, vol. 7, 1974, pp. 397–437.

Smiley, Donald V.: *The Canadian Political Nationality* (Methuen, Toronto, 1967).

—— : "The Challenge of Canadian Ambivalence," *Queen's Quarterly*, vol. 88, no. 1, Spring 1981, pp. 1–12.

—— : "Political Metaphysicians," *Canadian Forum*, vol. 60, no. 703, October 1980, pp. 13–14.

Sproule-Jones, Mark: "The Enduring Colony," *Publius*, vol. 14, no. 1, 1984 (special issue "Crisis and Continuity in Canadian Federalism"), pp. 93–108.

Taylor, Charles: *Radical Tories* (Anansi, Toronto, 1982).

Ullman, S. H.: "Regional Political Cultures in Canada. Part I: A Theoretical and Conceptual Introduction," *American Review of Canadian Studies*, vol. 7, no. 2, 1977, pp. 1–22.

—— : "Regional Political Cultures in Canada. Part II," *American Review of Canadian Studies*, vol. 7, no. 2, 1978, pp. 70–101.

Underhill, Frank H.: *In Search of Canadian Liberalism* (Macmillan, Toronto, 1960).

Whitaker, Reginald: "The Political Ideas of Harold Innis," *Queen's Quarterly*, vol. 90, no. 3, Autumn 1983, pp. 818–831.

Wilson, John: "The Canadian Political Cultures: Towards a Redefinition of the Nature of the Canadian Political System," *Canadian Journal of Political Science*, vol. 7, no. 3, 1974, pp. 438–483.

B. Political Socialization

Abramson, Paul: "The Differential Political Socialization of English Secondary School Students," *Sociology of Education*, vol. 40, 1967, pp. 246–269.

Atherton, P. J.: "Education: Radical Reform in Nova Scotia," *Canadian Public Policy*, vol. 1, 1975, pp. 384–392.

Baldus, B. and V. Tribe: "The Development of Perceptions and Evaluations of Social Inequality among Public School Children," *Canadian Review of Sociology and Anthropology*, vol. 15, no. 1, 1978, pp. 50–60.

Bender, Gerald J.: "Political Socialization and Political Change," *The Western Political Quarterly*, vol. 20, part 1, 1967, pp. 390–407.

Briggs, J. L.: "The Creation of Value in Canadian Inuit Society," *International Social Science Journal*, vol. 31, no. 3, 1979, pp. 393–403.

Cameron, David R. and Laura Summers: "Non-family Agents of Political Socialization: A Reassessment of Converse and Depeux," *Canadian Journal of Political Science*, vol. 5, no. 3, 1972, pp. 418–432.

Chalmers, J. N.: "Strategy for Native Education, 1960–1970," *Journal of Canadian Studies*, vol. 11, no. 3, 1976, pp. 37–49.

Clausen, John A.: "Recent Developments in Socialization Theory and Research," *The Annals of the American Academy of Political and Social Science*, vol. 377, 1968, pp. 139–155.

Cuneo, Carl, J.: "The Social Basis of Political Continentalism in Canada," *Canadian Review of Sociology and Anthropology*, vol. 13, no. 1, 1976, pp. 50–70.

Dawson, Richard and Kenneth Prewitt: *Political Socialization* (Little, Brown, Boston, 1968).

Easton, David: "The Theoretical Relevance of Political Socialization," *Canadian Journal of Political Science*, vol. 1, 1968, pp. 125–146.

Froman, Lewis A., Jr.: "Learning Political Attitudes," *Western Political Quarterly*, vol. 15, 1962, pp. 304–313.

Greenstein, Fred I.: "The Benevolent Leader: Children's Images of Political Authority," *American Political Science Review*, vol. 54, 1960, pp. 934–943.

——— : *Children and Politics* (Yale University Press, New Haven, 1965).

Hess, Robert D. and Judith V. Torney: *The Development of Political Attitudes in Children* (Aldine Publishing Co., Chicago, 1967).

Hill, John L. A.: "Political Socialization of Children in a Rural Environment," unpublished M.A. thesis) (Queen's University, 1969).

Hodgetts, A.: *What Culture, What Heritage? A Study of Civic Education in Canada* (Ontario Institute for Studies in Education, Toronto, 1970).

Hyman, Herbert H.: *Political Socialization* (The Free Press, Glencoe, 1959).

Jabbra, J. G. and R. G. Landes: "Political Orientation among Adolescents in Nova Scotia: An Exploratory Analysis of a Regional Political Culture in Canada," *Indian Journal of Political Science*, vol. 37, no. 4, 1976, pp. 75–96.

Jaros, Dean: *Socialization to Politics* (Praeger, New York, 1973).

Jennings, M. Kent: "Pre-adult Orientations to Multiple Systems of Government," *Midwest Journal of Political Science*, vol. 11, 1967, pp. 291–317.

Johnstone, John C.: *Young People's Images of Canadian Society* (Queen's Printer, Ottawa, 1969).

Kendall, J.: "A Canadian Construction of Reality: Northern Images of the United States," *American Review of Canadian Studies*, vol. 4, no. 1, 1974, pp. 20–36.

Kornberg, Allan and Joel Smith: "Self-concepts of American and Canadian Party Officials," *Polity*, vol. 3, no. 1, 1970, pp. 70–99.

——— , Joel Smith, and David Bromley: "Some Differences in the Political Socialization Patterns of Canadian and American Party Officials: A Preliminary Report," *Canadian Journal of Political Science*, vol. 2, no. 1, 1969, pp. 64–88.

—— and Norman Thomas: "The Political Socialization of National Legislative Elites in the United States and Canada," *Journal of Politics*, vol. 27, 1965, pp. 761–775.

Lane, Robert E.: *Political Life* (Free Press, Glencoe, 1959).

Langton, K. P.: *Political Socialization* (Oxford University Press, New York, 1969).

Mathews, R.: "Susanna Moodie, Pink Toryism, and Nineteenth Century Ideas of Canadian Identity," *Journal of Canadian Studies*, vol. 10, no. 3, 1975, pp. 3–14.

Pammett, J. H.: "The Development of Political Orientations in Canadian School Children," *Canadian Journal of Political Science*, vol. 4, no. 1, 1971, pp. 132–141.

—— and M. S. Whittington (eds.): *Foundations of Political Culture: Readings on Political Socialization in Canada* (Macmillan, Toronto, 1976).

Pross, A. P. and V. S. Wilson: "Graduate Education in Canadian Public Administration: Antecedents, Present Trends and Portents," *Canadian Public Administration*, vol. 19, no. 4, 1976, pp. 515–541.

Redekop, John H.: "Authors and Publishers: An Analysis of Textbook Selection in Canadian Departments of Political Science and Sociology" (note), *Canadian Journal of Political Science*, vol. 9, no. 1, 1976, pp. 107–120.

Reilly, Wayne G.: "Political Attitudes among Law Students in Quebec," *Canadian Journal of Political Science*, vol. 4, no. 1, 1971, pp. 122–131.

Richert, J. P.: "Canadian National Identity: An Empirical Study," *American Review of Canadian Studies*, vol. 4, no. 1, 1974, pp. 89–98.

—— : "English and French-Canadian Children's Perception of the October Crisis," *Journal of Social Psychology*, vol. 89, no. 1, 1973, pp. 3–13.

—— : "Political Socialization in Quebec: Young People's Attitudes toward Government" (note), *Canadian Journal of Political Science*, vol. 6, no. 2, 1973, pp. 303–313.

Schonfeld, N. R.: "Political Attitudes, Expressed Views and the Centrality of Politics: A Case Study of French Secondary School Students," *Canadian Journal of Political Science*, vol. 12, no. 1, 1979, pp. 21–54.

Smith, J. and A. Kornberg: "Self Concepts of American and Canadian Party Officials: Their Development and Consequences," *Social Forces*, vol. 3, no. 2, 1970, pp. 210–226.

—— , A. Kornberg, and D. Bromley: "Patterns of Early Political Socialization and Adult Party Affiliation," *Canadian Review of Sociology and Anthropology*, vol. 5, no. 3, 1968, pp. 123–155.

Solberg, Patricia Anne: "Attitudes of Canadian Veterans to Political Economic Issues," *Journal of Social Psychology*, vol. 38, 1953, pp. 73–86.

Trudel, Marcel and Genevieve Jain: *Canadian History Textbooks* (Queen's Printer, Ottawa, 1970).

Ullman, S. H.: "Nationalism and Regionalism in the Political Socialization of Cape Breton Whites and Indians," *American Review of Canadian Studies*, vol. 5, no. 1, 1975, pp. 66–97.

Williams, T. R.: "Some Facts and Fantasies concerning Local Autonomy in the Metropolitan Toronto School System," *Canadian Public Administration*, vol. 17, no. 2, 1974, pp. 274–288.

Woolfson, P.: "Value Orientation of Anglo-Canadian and French-Canadian School Children in a Quebec Community near the Vermont Border," *American Review of Canadian Studies*, vol. 4, no. 1, 1974, pp. 75–88.

Zeligs, Rose: "Children's Concepts and Stereotypes of Turk, Portuguese, Roumanian, Arab, Chinese, French-Canadian, Mulatto, South American, Hawaiian and Australian," *Journal of Genetic Psychology*, vol. 83, 1953, pp. 171–178.

C. Political Participation

Note: Much of the literature on women in politics is listed below; see also the section "A. Geographical and Economic Cleavages" under the heading "The Environment" in this bibliography.

Alford, R. R.: *Party and Society* (Rand McNally, Chicago, 1963).
Bashevkin, Sylvia, B.: "Women's Participation in the Ontario Political Parties 1971–1981," *Journal of Canadian Studies*, vol. 17, no. 2, 1982, pp. 44–54.
——— : "Political Participation, Ambition and Feminism: Women in the Ontario Party Elites," *American Review of Canadian Studies*, vol. 15, no. 4, 1985, pp. 405–420.
——— : "Social Change and Political Partisanship: The Development of Women's Attitudes in Quebec, 1965–1979," *Comparative Political Studies*, vol. 16, no. 2, July 1983, pp. 147–172.
——— : *Toeing the Lines: Women and Party Politics in English Canada* (University of Toronto Press, Toronto, 1985).
——— : "In a Man's World? Women and the Ontario NDP," *Canadian Forum*, vol. 61, no. 715, February 1982, pp. 34–35.
Black, J. H.: "Immigrant Political Adaptation in Canada: Some Tentative Findings," *Canadian Journal of Political Science*, vol. 15, no. 1, 1982, pp. 3–27.
——— and N. E. McGlen: "Male-Female Political Involvement Differentials in Canada, 1969–1974," *Canadian Journal of Political Science*, vol. 12, 1979, pp. 471–498.
——— and Nancy E. McGlen: "Revisiting the Effects of Canvassing on Voting Behaviour," *Canadian Journal of Political Science*, vol. 17, 1984, pp. 351–374.
Brodie, M. Janine: "Canada," in Joni Lovenduski and Jill Hills (eds.), *The Politics of the Second Electorate* (Routledge and Kegan Paul, London, 1981), pp. 52–82.
——— : *Women and Politics in Canada* (McGraw-Hill Ryerson, Toronto, 1985).
——— and Jill McCalla Vickers: *Canadian Women in Politics: An Overview* (Canadian Research Institute for the Advancement of Women, Ottawa, 1981).
Burke, M. *et al.*: "Federal and Provincial Political Participation in Canada: Some Methodological and Substantive Considerations," *Canadian Review of Sociology and Anthropology*, vol. 15, 1978, pp. 61–75.
Campbell, Angus: "The Passive Citizen," *Acta Sociologica*, vol. 6, fasc. 1–2, pp. 9–21.
——— *et al.*: *Elections and Political Order* (John Wiley and Sons, New York, 1966).
Clarke, H. *et al.*: *Political Choice in Canada* (McGraw-Hill Ryerson, Toronto, 1978).
Cohen, Yolande: "Stratégies feministes: le pouvoir dérivé du centre-pouvoir," *International Political Science Review*, vol. 6, no. 3, 1985, pp. 382–392.
Conley, Marshall W. and Patrick J. Smith: "Political Recruitment and Party Activists: British and Canadian Comparisons," *International Political Science Review*, vol. 4, no. 1, 1983, pp. 48–56.
Eulau, Heinz and Peter Schneider: "Dimensions of Political Involvement," *Public Opinion Quarterly*, vol. 20, Spring 1956, pp. 128–142.
Eyzenck, H. J.: *The Psychology of Politics* (Routledge and Kegan Paul, London, 1954).
Frenkel-Brunswick, Else: "The Interaction of Psychological and Sociological Factors in Political Behaviour," *American Political Science Review*, vol. 46, 1952, pp. 44–65.
Hunter, Alfred A. and Margaret A. Denton: "Do Female Candidates 'Lose Votes'? The Experience of Female Candidates in the 1979 and 1980 Canadian General Elections," *Canadian Review of Sociology and Anthropology*, vol. 21, no. 4, 1984, pp. 395–406.
Katz, Elihu and Paul Lazarsfeld: *Personal Influence* (The Free Press, Glencoe, 1955).

Kome, Penny: *Women of Influence: Canadian Women and Politics* (Doubleday Canada, Toronto, 1985).

Kopinak, Kathryn M.: "Women in Canadian Municipal Politics: Two Steps Forward, One Step Back," *Canadian Review of Sociology and Anthropology*, vol. 22, no. 3, 1985, pp. 394–410.

Kornberg, A.: "Public Support for Community and Regime in the Regions of Contemporary Canada," *American Review of Canadian Studies*, vol. 10, 1980, pp. 75–93.

—— et al.: "Federalism and Fragmentation: Political Support in Canada," *Journal of Politics*, vol. 4, no. 1979, pp. 889–906.

—— and Harold D. Clarke (eds.): *Political Support in Canada: The Crisis Years* (Duke University Press, Durham, N. C., 1983).

Lane, R. E.: *Political Life* (The Free Press, Glencoe, 1959).

Levin, Murray B.: *The Alienated Voter* (Holt Rinehart and Winston, New York, 1960).

Lipset, S.M.: *Agrarian Socialism* (University of California Press, Berkeley, 1950).

MacInnis, Grace: "Women in Politics," *The Parliamentarian*, vol. 53, 1972, pp. 8–12.

MacKinnon, Frank: *Posture and Politics: Some Observations on Participatory Democracy* (University of Toronto Press, Toronto, 1973).

Meisel, John: "Citizen Demands and Government Response," *Canadian Public Policy*, vol. 2, 1976, pp. 564–572.

Milbrath, L.: *Political Participation* (Rand McNally, Chicago, 1965).

Miller, W.: *Political Participation in Canada* (Macmillan, Toronto, 1979).

Mishler, William: "Political Participation and Democracy," in Michael S. Whittington and Glen Williams, *Canadian Politics in the 1980s*, 2nd ed. (Methuen, Toronto, 1984), pp. 175–192.

Nie, Norman H., G. Bingham Powell, Jr., and Kenneth Prewitt: "Social Structure and Political Participation: Developmental Relationship, I and II," *American Political Science Review*, vol. 63, 1969, pp. 301–378, 808–872.

Polsby, Nelson, W.: *Community Power and Political Theory* (Yale University Press, New Haven, 1963).

Presthus, Robert: *Men at the Top: A Study in Community Power* (Oxford Press, London, 1968).

Richards, John: "Populism: A Qualified Defence," *Studies in Political Economy*, vol. 5, Spring 1981, pp. 23–25.

Scarrow, Howard A.: "Patterns of Voter Turnout in Canada," *Midwest Journal of Political Science*, vol. 5, 1961, pp. 351–365.

Sewell, John: *Up against City Hall* (James, Lewis & Samuel, Toronto, 1972).

Sproule-Jones, Mark and Kenneth D. Hart: "A Public-Choice Model of Political Participation," *Canadian Journal of Political Science*, vol. 6, 1973, pp. 175–194.

Templeton, Frederick: "Alienation and Political Participation," *Public Opinion Quarterly*, vol. 30, 1966, pp. 249–261.

Van Loon, R. J.: "Political Participation in Canada: The 1965 Election," *Canadian Journal of Political Science*, vol. 3, 1970, pp. 376–399.

Welch, Susan: "Dimensions of Political Participation in a Canadian Sample," *Canadian Journal of Political Science*, vol. 8, 1975, pp. 553–559.

D. The Mass Media

Babe, R. E.: "Regulation of Private Television Broadcasting by the Canadian Radio-Television Commission: A Critique of Ends and Means," *Canadian Public Administration*, vol. 19, no. 4, 1976, pp. 552–586.

Beckton, C. F.: *Law and the Media* (Carswell, Toronto, 1982).

Black, Edwin R.: *Politics and the News* (Butterworths, Toronto, 1982).

Breed, W.: "Social Control in the Newsroom: A Functional Analysis," *Social Forces*, vol. 33, no. 4, 1955, pp. 326–335.

Bruce, C.: *News and the Southams* (Macmillan, Toronto, 1968).

Cabatoff, Kenneth: "Radio-Québec: une institution publique à la recherche d'un mission," *Canadian Public Administration*, vol. 19, no. 4, 1976, pp. 542–551.

Canada, Committee on Broadcasting: *Report* (Queen's Printer, Ottawa, 1965).

—— , Royal Commission on Broadcasting: *Report*, 2 vols. (Queen's Printer, Ottawa, 1957).

—— , Royal Commission on Newspapers (Kent Commission): *Report* (Supply and Services Canada, Ottawa, 1981).

—— , Royal Commission on Publications: *Report*, (The O'Leary Report), 2 vols. (Queen's Printer, Ottawa, 1961).

—— , Senate: *Report of the Senate Committee on the Mass Media*, 3 vols., esp. vol. III, *The Uncertain Mirror* (Queen's Printer, Ottawa, 1971).

Compton, Neil: "The Mass Media," in Michael Oliver (ed.), *Social Purpose for Canada* (University of Toronto Press, Toronto, 1961), pp. 50–87.

Cook, R.: *The Politics of John W. Dafoe and the Free Press* (University of Toronto Press, Toronto, 1963).

Dahrin, R.: "The Media and the Rise of P. E. Trudeau," *Canadian Dimension*, vol. 5, June/July 1968, pp. 5–6.

Dexter, Lewis Anthony and David Manning White (eds.): *People, Society and Mass Communication* (The Free Press, New York, 1964).

Donnelly, M.: *Dafoe of the Free Press* (Macmillan, Toronto, 1968).

Eggleston, W.: "The Press in Canada," in Royal Commission on National Development in the Arts, Letters and Science, Massey Report (King's Printer, Ottawa, 1951).

Ferguson, George Victor: *Press and Party in Canada: Issues of Freedom* (Ryerson, Toronto, 1955).

Fletcher, Frederick J.: *The Newspaper and Public Affairs*, vol. 7, research publication of Royal Commission on Newspapers (Supply and Services Canada, Ottawa, 1981).

—— and Daphne Gottlieb Taras: "The Mass Media and Politics: An Overview," in Michael S. Whittington and Glen Williams (eds.), *Canadian Politics in the 1980s*, 2nd ed. (Methuen, Toronto, 1984), pp. 193–228.

Gordon, D. R.: *Language, Logic and the Mass Media* (Holt Rinehart and Winston, Toronto, 1966).

Hamilton, D. L. B. (ed.): *The Press and the Public* (University of Toronto Press, Toronto, 1962).

Harkness, R.: *J. E. Atkinson of "The Star"* (University of Toronto Press, Toronto, 1963).

Hornby, Robert: *The Press in Modern Society* (Muller, London, 1965).

Irving, John Allan (ed.): *Mass Media in Canada* (Ryerson, Toronto, 1962).

Kesterton, Wilfred H.: *A History of Journalism in Canada* (McClelland and Stewart, Toronto, 1967).

—— : *The Law and the Press in Canada* (Carleton University Press, Ottawa, 1984).

Lloyd, Trevor Owen and Jack McLeod (eds.): *Agenda 1970* (University of Toronto Press, Toronto, 1968).

McCormack, Thelma: "The Political Culture and the Press of Canada," *Canadian Journal of Political Science*, vol. 16, 1983, pp. 451–472.

Morton, Desmond: "Democracy and the Mass Media," *The Canadian Forum*, vol. 49, July 1969, pp. 82–84.

Ostman, R. E.: "CBC's 'The World at Six' Looks at the U.S.: Content Analysis as an Aid to Understanding the Media," *American Review of Canadian Studies*, vol. 7, 1977, pp. 33–50.

Peers, R.: *The Politics of Canadian Broadcasting, 1920–1951* (University of Toronto Press, Toronto, 1969).

Qualter, T. H. and K. A. MacKirdy: "The Press of Ontario and the Election," in John Meisel, *Papers on the 1962 Election* (University of Toronto Press, Toronto, 1964), pp. 145–168.

Reader's Digest Foundation and Erindale College: *Politics and the Media* (Reader's Digest Foundation, Montreal, 1981).

Salter, L.: *Dimensions of the Message: Communication Studies in Canada* (Butterworths, Toronto, 1981).

Schultz, J.: "Whose News? The Struggle for Wire Distribution 1900–1920," *American Review of Canadian Studies*, vol. 10, 1980, pp. 27–62.

Seymour-Ure, Colin: "The Parliamentary Press Gallery in Ottawa," *Parliamentary Affairs*, vol. 16, 1962–63, pp. 36–41.

Siegel, Arthur: *Politics and the Media in Canada* (McGraw-Hill Ryerson, Toronto, 1983).

Singer, B. D.: "Violence, Protest, and War in Television News: The U.S. and Canada," in *Public Opinion Quarterly*, vol. 34, 1970–71, pp. 611–616.

Stewart, N. B.: "The CBC: Canadian? Regional? Popular? An Examination of Program Objectives for English Television," *Canadian Public Administration*, vol. 18, 1975, pp. 337–365.

Stursberg, Peter: *Mr. Broadcasting: The Ernie Bushnell Story* (Peter Martin Associates, Toronto, 1971).

Tataryn, Lloyd: *Power, Politics and the Press: the Pundits* (Deneau, Ottawa, 1985).

United Nations Educational Scientific and Cultural Organization: *Communication in the Space Age: The Use of Satellites by the Mass Media* (Paris, UNESCO, 1968).

Wagenberg, Ronald H. and Walter C. Soderlund: "The Effects of Chain Ownership on Editorial Coverage: The Case of the 1974 Canadian Federal Election," *Canadian Journal of Political Science*, vol. 9, 1976, pp. 682–689.

Wallace, Donald C. and Frederick J. Fletcher (eds.): *Canadian Politics through Press Reports* (Oxford University Press, Toronto, 1984).

Weir, E. A.: *The Struggle for National Broadcasting in Canada* (McClelland and Stewart, Toronto, 1965).

Wilson, H. H.: "Techniques of Pressure: Anti-nationalization Propaganda in Britain," *Public Opinion Quarterly*, vol. 15, Summer 1951, pp. 225–242.

Wilson, R. Jeremy: "The Impact of Communications Developments on British Columbia Electoral Patterns 1903–1975," *Canadian Journal of Political Science*, vol. 13, 1980, pp. 509–535.

Windlesham, David J. G. H.: *Communication and Political Power* (Cape, London, 1966).

Young, Walter D.: "The Voices of Democracy: Politics and Communication in Canada," *Canadian Journal of Political Science*, vol. 14, 1981, pp. 683–700.

THE CANADIAN CONSTITUTION

A. General Materials

Bernier, I. and A. Lajoie (eds.): *Law, Society and the Economy*, study prepared for the Royal Commission on the Economic Union and Development Prospects for Canada, vol. 46, (University of Toronto Press, Toronto, 1986).

Cairns, A. C.: "The Living Canadian Constitution," *Queen's Quarterly*, vol. 77, no. 4, Winter 1970.

—— and C. Williams (eds.): *Constitutionalism, Citizenship and Society in Canada*, study prepared for the Royal Commission on the Economic Union and Development Prospects for Canada, vol. 33, (University of Toronto, Toronto, 1986).

Canada: *Constitution 1982* (Supply and Services, Ottawa, 1983).

Cheffins, R. I.: *The Constitutional Process in Canada*, 2nd ed. (McGraw-Hill Ryerson, Toronto, 1976).

—— and Patricia A. Johnson: *The Revised Canadian Constitution: Politics as Law* (McGraw-Hill Ryerson, Toronto, 1986).

Clokie, H. M.: "Basic Problems of the Canadian Constitution," *Canadian Journal of Economics and Political Science*, vol. 8, 1942.

Corry, J. A.: "The Prospects for the Rule of Law," *Canadian Journal of Economics and Political Science*, vol. 21, 1955, pp. 405–415.

—— and J. E. Hodgetts: *Democratic Government and Politics* (University of Toronto Press, Toronto, 1959).

Dawson, R. M.: *The Government of Canada*, rev. N. Ward (University of Toronto Press, Toronto, 1970).

Dicey, A. V.: *Introduction to the Study of the Law of the Constitution* (Macmillan, London, 1966).

Flaherty, David H. (ed.): *Essays in the History of Canadian Law* (University of Toronto Press for the Osgoode Society, Toronto): vol. I, 1981; vol. II, 1983).

Gibson, Dale and Janet K. Baldwin (eds.): *Law in a Cynical Society? Opinion and Law in the 1980s* (Carswell Legal Publications, Toronto, 1985).

Hodgins, Barbara: *Where the Economy and the Constitution Meet in Canada* (C. D. Howe Research Institute, Montreal, 1981).

Jennings, W. I.: The British Constitution (Cambridge University Press, London, 1966).

—— : The Law and the Constitution (University of London Press, London, 1959).

Keith, A. B.: *The Governments of the British Empire* (Macmillan, London, 1935).

Kennedy, W. P. M.: *The Constitution of Canada, 1534–1937* (Oxford University Press, London, 1938).

Lederman, W. R.: *Continuing Canadian Constitutional Dilemmas: Essays on the Constitutional History, Public Law and Federal System of Canada* (Butterworths, Toronto, 1981).

McWhinney, Edward: *Constitution-making: Principles, Processes, Practice* (University of Toronto Press, Toronto, 1981).

Morton, F. L. (ed.): *Law, Politics and the Judicial Process in Canada* (University of Calgary Press, Calgary, 1984).

Quinn, J. (ed.): *The International Legal Environment*, study prepared for the Royal Commission on the Economic Union and Development Prospects for Canada, vol. 52 (University of Toronto Press, Toronto, 1986).

Robinette, J. J., Q.C.: "The Future of Our Constitution," *University of British Columbia Law Review*, vol. 18, no. 2, 1984, pp. 335–349.

B. Democratic Values

Boyd, Neil: *The Social Dimensions of Law* (Prentice-Hall Canada, Scarborough, 1986).

Clarke, S. D.: "The Frontier and Democratic Theory," in Royal Society of Canada, *Proceedings and Transactions*, June 1954, p. 65.

Cnudde, C. F. and D. E. Neubaur (eds.): *Empirical Democratic Theory* (Markham, Chicago, 1969).

Corry, J. A. and J. E. Hodgetts: *Democratic Government and Politics* (University of Toronto Press, Toronto, 1959).

Grant, George P.: *English-speaking Justice* (University of Notre Dame Press, Notre Dame, Indiana, 1985).

Dahl, R. A.: *A Preface to Democratic Theory* (University of Chicago Press, Chicago, 1963).

MacIver, R. M.: *The Web of Government* (The Free Press, New York, 1965).

Macpherson, C. B.: *The Real World of Democracy* (CBC, Toronto, 1965).

Mayo, H. B.: *An Introduction to Democratic Theory* (Oxford University Press, New York, 1960).

Sartori, G.: *Democratic Theory* (Praeger, New York, 1965).

Schumpeter, J. A.: *Capitalism, Socialism and Democracy* (Harper and Row, New York, 1950).

Underhill, F. H.: "Some Reflections on the Liberal Tradition," in F. H. Underhill, *In Search of Canadian Liberalism* (Macmillan, Toronto, 1960).

UNESCO: *Democracy in a World of Tension* (Paris, 1951).

C. Civil Liberties and the Charter of Rights and Freedoms

Abella, Judge Rosalie: *Canada's Judges and Public Policy: Implications of the Charter of Rights and Freedoms* (John Porter Memorial Lecture) (Carleton University, Ottawa, 1985).

Applebaum, Isaac: "The Keegstra Case," *Canadian Forum*, vol. 65, no. 749, May 1985, pp. 7–15.

Arbess, Daniel J.: "Limitations on Legislative Override under the Canadian Charter of Rights and Freedoms: A Matter of Balancing Values," *Osgoode Hall Law Journal*, vol. 22, no. 1, 1983, pp. 113–141.

Archambault, Jean-Denis: "La Liberté d'expression des avocats garantie par les chartes: récents développements judiciaires," *La Revue du barreau*, vol. 45, no. 3, 1985, pp. 329–345.

Atcheson, M. Elizabeth, Mary Eberts, and Beth Symes: *Women and Legal Action* (Canadian Advisory Council on the Status of Women, Ottawa, 1984).

Barry, Leo D.: "Law, Policy and Statutory Interpretation under a Constitutionally Entrenched Canadian Charter of Rights and Freedoms," *Canadian Bar Review*, vol. 60, no. 2, 1982, pp. 237–264.

Batshaw, H.: "A Landmark Decision against Discrimination in Canada," *Revue des droits de l'homme*, vol. 4, 1971, pp. 207–211.

Bayefsky, Anne and Mary Eberts (eds.): *Equality Rights and the Canadian Charter of Rights and Freedoms* (Carswell, Toronto, 1985).

Beckton, Clare F. and A. Wayne MacKay: *The Courts and the Charter*, study prepared for the Royal Commission on the Eonomic Union and Development Prospects for Canada, vol. 58 (University of Toronto Press Toronto, 1985).

—— : "Obscenity and Censorship Re-examined under the Charter of Rights," *Manitoba Law Journal*, vol. 13, 1983, p. 351.

—— : "The Impact on Women of Entrenchment of Property Rights in the Canadian Charter of Rights and Freedoms," *Dalhousie Law Journal*, vol. 9, no. 2, 1985, pp. 288–312.

Belobaba, E. P. and E. Gertner (eds.): "The New Constitution and the Charter of Rights: Fundamental Issues and Strategies," *Supreme Court Law Review*, vol. 4, 1982 (special issue).

Bender, Paul: "The Canadian Charter of Rights and Freedoms and the United States Bill of Rights: A Comparison," *McGill Law Journal*, vol. 28, no. 4, 1983, pp. 811–866.

Bercuson, David and Douglas Wertheimer: *A Trust Betrayed: The Keegstra Affair* (Doubleday Canada, Toronto, 1985).

Berger, Thomas R.: "The Constitution, the Charter and 'Fragile Freedoms,' " *Canadian Forum*, vol. 62, no. 719, June/July 1982, pp. 8–14.

────── : *Fragile Freedoms: Human Rights and Dissent in Canada* (Clarke Irwin, Toronto, 1981).

Berlin, Mark L.: *New Proscribed Grounds of Discrimination and Emerging Human Rights in Canada* (Department of the Secretary of State, Ottawa, 1983).

Bilodeau, R.: "La Langue, l'éducation et les minorités: avant et depuis la Charte canadienne des droits et libertés," *Manitoba Law Journal*, vol. 13, 1983, p. 371.

────── (ed.): *Human Rights and Affirmative Action* (Canadian Human Rights Foundation, Montreal, 1985).

Bilson, R. E.: "A Workers' Charter: What Do We Mean by Right?" *Canadian Public Policy*, vol. 11, no. 4, 1985, pp. 749–755.

Binavince, Emilio S.: "The Impact of Mobility Rights: The Canadian Economic Union — A Boom or a Bust," *Ottawa Law Review*, vol. 14, 1982, pp. 340–365.

Blair, Justice D. G.: "The Charter and the Judges: A View from the Bench," paper delivered at the Canadian Institute for the Administration of Justice Symposium, Oct. 1983.

Block, W. E. and M. A. Walker (eds.): *Discrimination, Affirmative Action, and Equal Opportunity* (Fraser Institute, Vancouver, 1982).

Brun, Henri: "Quelques notes sur les articles 1, 2, 7 et 15 de la Charte canadienne des droits et libertés," *Les Cahiers de droit*, vol. 23, no. 4, 1982, pp. 781–794.

Canada, Parliament: *Minutes of Proceedings and Evidence* (Special Joint Committee on Human Rights and Fundamental Freedoms), nos. 1–7 and nos., 1–11 (King's Printer, Ottawa, 1947).

────── : *Proceedings*, nos. 1–10 (King's Printer, Ottawa, 1950).

────── : *Minutes of Proceedings and Evidence concerning Bill C–79* (Queen's Printer, Ottawa, 1960).

────── : *Royal Commission on Security* (abridged) (Queen's Printer, Ottawa, June 1969), *passim*.

────── : *Protection of Privacy Act*, 1973.

────── : *Equality Issues in Federal Law* (Communications and Public Affairs, Department of Justice Canada, Ottawa, 1985).

Canadian Bar Review, vol. 37, 1959: Bowker, W. F.: "Basic Rights and Freedoms: What Are They?" pp. 43–65; Laskin, Bora: "An Inquiry into the Diefenbaker Bill of Rights," pp. 77–134; Leaderman, W. R.: "The Nature and Problems of a Bill of Rights," pp. 4–15; Pigeon, L. P.: "The Bill of Rights and the British North America Act," pp. 66–76; Scott, F. R.: "The Bill of Rights and Quebec Law," pp. 135–146.

────── : "The Canadian Charter of Rights and Freedoms,"vol. 61, no. 1, March 1983 (entire issue).

"The Charter: Initial Experience, Emerging Issues and Future Action," (*Manitoba Law Journal*), vol. 13, no. 4 (special issue), 1983.

Choquette, Marie: "Les Articles 8, 9, et 10 de la Charte canadienne des droits et libertés," *Les Cahiers de droit*, vol. 25, no. 3, 1984, pp. 677–698.

Christian, Timothy J.: "Section 7 of the Charter of Rights and Freedoms: Constraints on State Action," *Alberta Law Review*, vol. 22, no. 2, 1984, pp. 222–246.

Clokie, H. M.: "Basic Problems of the Canadian Constitution," *Canadian Bar Review*, vol. 20: May 1942, pp. 395–429; Dec. 1942, pp. 817–840.

Cohen, Stanley A.: "Controversies in Need of Resolution: Some Threshold Questions affecting Individual Rights and Police Power under the Charter," *Ottawa Law Review*, vol. 16, no. 1, 1984, pp. 97–116.

Commission of Inquiry concerning Certain Activites of the Royal Canadian Mounted Police: *Report*, vols. I–III (Supply and Services, Ottawa, 1981).

de Montigny, Yves: "La Charte des droits et libertés, la prérogative royale et les 'questions politiques,' " *Revue du barreau*, vol. 44, 1984, pp. 156–172.

Deudney, S. J.: "The Data Bank Society," *Canadian Chartered Accountant*, vol. 98, Mar. 1971, pp. 175–179.

Devall, W. B.: "Support for Civil Liberties among English-speaking Canadian University Students," *Canadian Journal of Political Science*, vol. 3, 1970, pp. 433–449.

Doherty, A.: "What's Done Is Done: An Argument in Support of a Purely Prospective Application of the Charter of Rights," *Criminal Reports*, vol. 26, no. 3, 1982, p. 131.

Driedger, Elmer A.: "The Canadian Charter of Rights and Freedoms," *Ottawa Law Review*, vol. 14, 1982, pp. 366–378.

Duplé, N.: "L'Art. 7 de la Charte canadienne des droits et libertés et les principes de justice fondamentale," *Les Cahiers de droit*, vol. 25, 1984, p. 99.

Dworkin, R.: *Taking Rights Seriously* (Duckword, London, 1977).

Ely, John Hart: *Democracy and Distrust* (Harvard University Press, Cambridge, 1980).

Ericson, Richard V.: *The Constitution of Legal Inequality* (John Porter Memorial Lecture, Carleton University, Ottawa, 1983).

Fichaud, Joel: "Analysis of the Charter and Its Application to Labour Law," *Dalhousie Law Journal*, vol. 8, no. 2, 1984, pp. 402–434.

Fitzgerald, P.: "Canadian Rights and Freedoms — First Class or Charter?" *Manitoba Law Journal*, vol. 13, 1983, p. 277.

Flanagan, Tom: "Insurance, Human Rights and Equality Rights in Canada: When Is Discrimination 'Reasonable'?" *Canadian Journal of Political Science*, vol. 18, no. 4, 1985, pp. 715–737.

—— : "Policy-making by Exegesis: The Abolition of 'Mandatory Retirement' in Manitoba," *Canadian Public Policy*, vol. 11, Mar., 1985, pp. 40–53.

Forsey, Eugene: *Freedom and Order: Collected Essays* (McClelland and Stewart, Toronto, 1974).

Foucher, Pierre: "Les Droits scolaires des acadiens et la Charte," *University of New Brunswick Law Journal*, vol. 33, 1984, pp. 97–154.

Friedland, M. L.: "Legal Rights under the Charter," *Criminal Law Quarterly*, vol. 24, 1981–82, p. 430.

—— : "Criminal Justice and the Charter," *Manitoba Law Journal*, vol. 13, 1983 (special issue), pp. 549–572.

—— : *National Security: The Legal Dimensions*, study prepared for the Commission of Inquiry concerning Certain Activities of the RCMP (Supply and Services Canada, Ottawa, 1980).

Frum, David: "Equal Opportunity," *Saturday Night*, Jan. 1984, pp. 9–11.

Gall, Gerald L.: *Civil Liberties in Canada: Entering the 1980s* (Butterworths, Toronto, 1982).

Garant, Louis: "La Charte de la langue francaise et la langue du travail," *Les Cahiers de droit*, vol. 23, no. 2, 1982, pp. 263–276.

Gibson, D.: "The Charter of Rights and the Private Sector," *Manitoba Law Journal*, vol. 12, 1982, p. 213.

——— : "Determining Disrepute: Opinion Polls and the Canadian Charter of Rights and Freedoms," *Canadian Bar Review*, vol. 61, 1983, pp. 377–396.

——— : "Reasonable Limits under the Canadian Charter of Rights and Freedoms," *Manitoba Law Journal*, vol. 15, no. 1, 1985, pp. 27–53.

——— : "Shocking the Public: Early Indications of the Meaning of Disrepute in Sec. 24(2) of the Charter," *Manitoba Law Journal*, vol. 13, 1983, p. 495.

Gill, Penny: "The Entrenchment of Rights and Liberties," *Saskatchewan Law Review*, vol. 46, no. 2, 1981–82, pp. 213–234.

Gold, Marc E.: "Equality before the Law in the Supreme Court of Canada: A Case Study," *Osgoode Hall Law Journal*, vol. 18, no. 3, 1980, pp. 336–427.

Gopalakrishna, K. C.: "The Canadian Bill of Rights," *Journal of Constitutional and Parliamentary Studies*, vol. 5, 1971, pp. 24–226.

Green, Philip: "Affirmative Action and the Individualist Principle," *Social Policy*, vol. 2, no. 5, Mar./Apr., 1981, pp. 14–20.

Hayward, Ann: "R. v. Jack and Charlie and the Constitution Act, 1982: Religious Freedom and Aboriginal Rights in Canada," *Queen's Law Journal*, vol. 10, no. 1, 1984, pp. 165–182.

Hogg, P. W.: "Supremacy of the Canadian Charter of Rights and Freedoms," *Canadian Bar Review*, vol. 61, 1983, p. 69.

Hovius, Berend: "The Legacy of the Supreme Court of Canada's Approach to the Canadian Bill of Rights: Prospects for the Charter," *McGill Law Journal*, vol. 28, no. 1, 1982, pp. 31–58.

——— and R. Martin: "The Canadian Charter of Rights and Freedoms in the Supreme Court of Canada," *Canadian Bar Review*, vol. 61, 1983, p. 354.

How, W. G.: "The Case for a Canadian Bill of Rights," *Canadian Bar Review*, vol. 36, 1958, pp. 750–796.

Jaconelli, J.: *Enacting a Bill of Rights: The Legal Problems* (Clarendon, Oxford, 1980).

Janisch, Hudson N.: "Judicial Review and the Charter of Rights," *La Revue du barreau*, vol. 43, no. 2, 1983, pp. 401–408.

Johnson, H. R.: "Antoine: A Too Cautious Approach to Interpreting Unreasonable Delay," *Criminal Reports*, vol. 84, 1983, p. 154.

Johnston, Stephen, Stephen Marshall, and Eugene Bhattacharya: "Supreme Court Charter Decisions, 1984: An Analysis," *University of New Brunswick Law Journal*, vol. 34, 1985, pp. 145–157.

Kinsella, N. A.: "The Canadian Model for the Protection from Discrimination," *Revue des droits de l'homme*, vol. 4, no. July 1971, pp. 270–277.

Kushner, Howard: "Constitutional Law — Standing — Canadian Bill of Rights — Minister of Justice *et al.* v. Borowski," *University of British Columbia Law Review*, vol. 17, no. 1, 1983, pp. 143–162.

——— : "Election Polls, Freedom of Speech and the Constitution," *Ottawa Law Review*, vol. 15, 1983, pp. 515–552.

Laforest, G.: "The Canadian Charter of Rights and Freedoms: An Overview," *Canadian Bar Review*, vol. 61, 1983, p. 19.

Laselva, Samuel V.: "Only in Canada: Reflections on the Charter's Notwithstanding Clause," *Dalhousie Review*, vol. 63, no. 3, 1983, pp. 383–398.

Laskin, J. B., E. L. Greenspan, G. B. Dunlop, and M. Rosenberg: *The Canadian Charter of Rights* (Canada Law Book, Aurora, 1982).

Law Reform Commission of Canada: *Police Powers — Search and Seizure in Criminal Law Enforcement*, Working Paper 30 (Law Reform Commission, Ottawa, 1983).

Law Society of Upper Canada: *Charter of Rights and Administrative Law* (Carswell, Toronto, 1983).

Lawford, Hugh: "Privacy versus Freedom of Information," *Queen's Quarterly*, vol. 78, 1971, pp. 365–371.

Lederman, W. R.: "The Power of the Judges and the New Canadian Charter of Rights and Freedoms," *University of British Columbia Law Review*, vol. 16, 1982 (entire issue).

Lee, John A.: "The RCMP's Real Dilemma," *Canadian Journal of Sociology*, vol. 6, no. 1, 1981, pp. 33–52.

Low, D. Martin: "The Canadian Charter of Rights and Freedoms and the Role of the Courts: An Initial Survey," *University of British Columbia Law Review*, vol. 18, no. 1, 1984, pp. 69–94.

Lyon, Noel: "The Charter as a Mandate for New Ways of Thinking about Law," *Queen's Law Journal*, vol. 9, no. 2, 1984, pp. 241–262.

McCloskey, Herbert and Brill Alida: *Dimensions of Tolerance: What Americans Think about Civil Liberties* (Russell Sage Foundation, New York, 1983).

McDonald, Hon. David C.: *Legal Rights in the Canadian Charter of Rights and Freedoms: A Manual of Issues and Sources* (Carswell, Toronto, 1982).

McDonald, Lynn: "The Charter of Rights and the Subjection of Women," *Canadian Forum*, vol. 61, no. 710, June 1981, pp. 17–18.

MacDonald, P. J. and J. P. Humphrey: *The Practice of Freedom* (Butterworths, Toronto, 1979).

McGinn, Frances: "The Canadian Charter of Rights and Freedoms: Its Impact on Law Enforcement," *University of New Brunwick Law Journal*, vol. 31, 1982, pp. 177–204.

MacGuigan, Mark R.: "The Development of Civil Liberties in Canada," *Queen's Quarterly*, vol. 72, 1965, pp. 270–288.

Mackay, A. Wayne: "Fairness after the Charter: A Rose by Any Other Name?" *Queen's Law Journal*, vol. 10, no. 2, 1985, pp. 263–335.

—— et al. (eds.): *The Canadian Charter of Rights: Law Practice Revolutionized* (Dalhousie Continuing Legal Education, Halifax, 1982).

McKercher, William R. (ed.): *The U.S. Bill of Rights and the Canadian Charter of Rights and Freedoms* (Ontario Economic Council, Toronto, 1983).

Macklem, Patrick: "Freedom of Conscience and Religion in Canada," *University of Toronto Faculty of Law Review*, vol. 42, no. 1, 1984, p. 78.

McLellan, A. Anne and Bruce P. Elman: "The Enforcement of the Canadian Charter of Rights and Freedoms: An Analysis of Section 24," *Alberta Law Review*, vol. 21, no. 2, 1983, pp. 205–250.

McLeod, R. M., J. D. Takach, H. F. Morton, and M. D. Segal: *The Canadian Charter of Rights* (Carswell, Toronto, 1983).

McWhinney, Edward: "The Canadian Charter of Rights and Freedoms: The Lessons of Comparative Jurisprudence," *Canadian Bar Review*, vol. 61, 1983, p. 55.

McWilliams, P.: "Safeguard against False Police Records," Globe and Mail *(Toronto), May 3, 1974, p. 7.*

Magnet, J. E.: "The Charter's Official Languages Provisions: The Implications of Entrenched Bilingualism," *Supreme Court Law Review*, vol. 4, 1982, p. 163.

Manitoba: *Personal Investigations Act*, 1971.

Manning, Morris: *Rights, Freedoms and the Courts: A Practical Analysis of the Constitution Act, 1982* (Emond-Montgomery, Toronto, 1983).

Menezes, J. (ed.): *Decade of Adjustment: Legal Perspectives on Contemporary Social Issues* (Butterworths, Toronto, 1980).

Mertl, Steve and John Ward: *Keegstra: The Issues, The Trial, The Consequences* (Western Producer Prairie Books, Saskatoon, 1985).

Morton, F.L.: "Charting the Charter, Year One: A Statistical Analysis," paper delivered at the annual meeting of the Canadian Political Science Association, Guelph, 1984.

—— and Leslie A. Pal: "The Impact of the Charter of Rights on Public Administration," *Canadian Public Administration*, vol. 28, no. 2, 1983, pp. 221–243.

Murphy, Brian F. D.: "Operation Dismantle, Inc. *et al.* v. Her Majesty the Queen: The Application of the Charter of Rights and Freedoms to Prerogative Powers," *University of New Brunswick Law Journal*, vol. 33, 1984, pp.354–362.

Ontario, Royal Commission on Civil Rights, *Report Number One*, 3 vols. (Queen's Printer, 1968).

—— : *Report Number Two* (Queen's Printer, Toronto, 1968).

—— : "A Democratic Approach to Civil Liberties," *University of Toronto Law Journal*, vol. 119, 1969, pp. 109–131.

Pentney, William and Daniel Proulx (eds.): *Canadian Human Rights Yearbook 1984–85* (Carswell, Toronto, 1985).

Pratt, A.: "The Charter and How to Approach It: A Guide for the Civil Practitioner," *Advocate's Quarterly*, vol. 4, 1983, p. 425.

Proulx, D.: "La Précarité des droits linguistiques scolaires ou les singulières difficultés de la mise en oeuvre de l'article 23 de la Charte canadienne des droits et libertés," *Revue générale de droit*, vol. 14, 1983, p. 335.

—— : "La Suprématie des droits et libertés de la personne et la question constitutionnelle au Canada," *Revue générale de droit*, vol. 12, 1981, p. 413.

Queen's Law Journal: "The New Constitution and the Charter: Background, Analysis and Commentary," vol. 8, nos. 1–2, 1982 (special issue in honour of Professor William R. Lederman).

Robinson, R. E., S. C. Coval, and J.-C. Smith: "The Logic of Rights," *University of Toronto Law Journal*, vol. 33, 1983, p. 267.

Robinson, Svend: "The NDP, the Charter and the Constitution," *Canadian Forum*, vol. 61, no. 710, June 1981, pp. 14–16.

Rowan, Andrew J.: "The Charter of Rights: Renewing the Social Contract?" *Queen's Law Journal*, vol. 8, Fall 1982, Spring 1983.

—— : "The Possible Impact of the Canadian Charter of Rights and Freedoms on Administrative Law," *Les Cahiers de droit*, vol. 26, no. 2, 1985, pp. 339–360.

Russell, J. Stuart: "Discrimination on the Basis of Political Convictions or Beliefs," *la Revue du barreau*, vol. 45, no. 3, 1985, pp. 377–423.

Russell, Peter H.: "The Effect of a Charter of Rights on the Policy-making Role of Canadian Courts," *Canadian Public Administration*, vol. 25, no. 1, 1982, pp. 1–33.

—— : "The First Three Years in Charterland," *Canadian Public Administration*, vol. 28, no. 3, 1985, pp. 367–396.

—— : "The Political Purposes of the Canadian Charter of Rights and Freedoms," *Canadian Bar Review*, vol. 61, 1983, p. 30.

—— : "The Proposed Charter for a Civilian Intelligence Agency: An Appraisal," *Canadian Public Policy*, vol. 9, no. 3, 1983, pp. 326–337.

—— : "Mr. Trudeau's Bill of Rights: Disadvantages," *The Canadian Forum*, vol. 49, Mar. 1969, pp. 274–276.

—— (ed.): *Leading Constitutional Decisions*, 3rd ed. (Carleton Library, Ottawa, 1982).

Ryan, S.: "Charting Our Liberties," *Queen's Quarterly*, vol. 55, 1959, pp. 389–404.

Samek, Robert A.: "Untrenching Fundamental Rights," *McGill Law Journal*, vol. 27, no. 4, 1982, pp. 755–787.

Schmeiser, Douglas, A.: *Civil Liberties in Canada* (Oxford University Press, London, 1964).

—— : "The Entrenchment of a Bill of Rights," *Alberta Law Review*, vol. 19, no. 3, 1981, pp. 375–383.

Scott, Francis Reginald: *Civil Liberties and Canadian Federalism* (University of Toronto Press, Toronto, 1959).

Sharp, J. M.: "Consumers and the Laws of Privacy," *Canadian Consumer*, vol. 3, April 1973, pp. 17–19.

Sharpe, R. J.: "Bora Laskin and Civil Liberties," *University of Toronto Law Journal*, vol. 35, no. 4, Fall 1985, pp. 632–672.

—— : "Injunctions and the Charter," *Osgoode Hall Law Journal*, vol. 22, no. 3, Fall 1984, pp. 473–486.

Shearing, C. D. and P. C. Stenning: *Private Security and Private Justice: The Challenge of the 80s: A Review of Policy Issues* (Institute for Research on Public Policy, Montreal, 1982).

Skogstad, Grace: "Affirmative Action: A Palliative Condemned for the Wrong Reasons," *Canadian Public Administration*, vol. 26, no. 1, 1983, pp. 105–112.

Smiley, D.: *Canadian Charter of Rights and Freedoms* (Ontario Economic Council, Toronto, 1981).

Smith, Lynn: "Charter Equality Rights: Some General Issues and Specific Applications in British Columbia to Elections, Juries and Illegitimacy," *University of British Columbia Law Review*, vol. 18, no. 1, 1984, pp. 351–406.

Stevenson, Colin P.: "A New Perspective on Environmental Rights after the Charter," *Osgoode Hall Law Journal*, vol. 22, no. 3, 1983, pp. 390–421.

Tarnopolsky, Walter Surma: *The Canadian Bill of Rights* (Carswell, Toronto, 1963).

—— : "Comparison between the Canadian Charter of Rights and Freedoms and the International Covenant on Civil and Political Rights," *Queen's Law Journal*, vol. 18, 1982–83, p. 211.

—— : *Discrimination and the Law in Canada* (Richard DeBoo Ltd., Don Mills, 1982).

—— : "The Historical and Constitutional Context of the Proposed C.C.R.F.," *Law and Contemporary Problems*, vol. 44, 1981, p. 169.

—— : "The New Canadian Charter of Rights and Freedoms as Compared and Contrasted with the American Bill of Rights," *Human Rights Quarterly*, vol. 5, 1983, p. 227.

—— and Gerald A. Beaudoin (eds.): *The Canadian Charter of Rights and Freedoms: Commentary* (Carswell, Toronto, 1982).

Tremblay, Luc: "Section 7 of the Charter: Substantive Due Process?" *University of British Columbia Law Review*, vol. 18, no. 2, 1984, pp. 201–254.

Trudeau, Pierre Elliott: *A Canadian Charter of Human Rights* (Queen's Printer, Ottawa, 1968).

Weiler, P. C.: "Of Judges and Rights; or, Should Canada have a Constitutional Bill of Rights?" *Dalhousie Review*, vol. 60, 1980/81, p. 205.

Whyte, John D.: "Fundamental Justice: The Scope and Application of Section 7 of the Charter," *Manitoba Law Journal*, vol. 13, 1983 (special issue), pp. 455–476.

Winn, Conrad: "Affirmative Action for Women: More than a Case of Simple Justice," *Canadian Public Administration*, vol. 28, no. 1, 1985, pp. 24–46.

Woehrling, José: "L'Article 15(1) de la Charte canadienne des droits et libertés et la langue," *McGill Law Journal*, vol. 30, no. 2, 1985, pp. 266–292.

D. *Operative Principles of the Constitution*

Amyot, Bernard: "De la notion de jurisdiction en droit administratif canadien," *Les Cahiers de droit*, vol. 24, no. 3, 1983, pp. 605–642.

Ballem, John Bishop: "Oil and Gas under the New Constitution," *Canadian Bar Review*, vol. 61, no. 2, 1983, pp. 547–558.

Beaudoin, G.: "Les Aspects constitutionnels du référendum," *Etudes internationales*, vol. 8, no. 2, 1977, pp. 197–207.

—— : *Essais sur la Constitution* (Université d'Ottawa, Ottawa, 1979).

Beaupré, R. Michael: "Vers l'interprétation d'une constitution bilingue," *Les Cahiers de droit*, vol. 25, no. 4, 1984, pp. 939–958.

Beck, Stanley M. and Ivan Bernier (eds.): *Canada and the New Constitution: The Unfinished Agenda*, vols. 1–2 (Institute for Research on Public Policy, Montreal, 1983).

Bernier, Ivan (ed.): "Egalité juridique des langues," *Les Cahiers de droit*, vol. 24, no. 1, 1983 (devoted issue), pp. 9–176.

Bronaugh, Richard N. *et al.*: *Readings in the Philosophy of Constitutional Law* (Kendall-Hunt, Dubuque, 1983).

Brun, H. and G. Tremblay: *Droit constitutionnel* (Editions Yvon Blais, Montreal, 1982).

Cairns, Robert D.: "The Constitution as Regulation: The Case of Natural Resources," *Canadian Public Policy*, vol. 7, no. 1, 1981, pp. 66–74.

Canada: *The Constitution and You* (Supply and Services Canada, Ottawa, 1982).

"Canadian Constitution, 1982": *Law and Contemporary Problems*, 45, 1982 (entire issue).

Cheffins, R. I.: *Constitutional Process in Canada*, 2nd ed. (McGraw-Hill Ryerson, Toronto, 1976).

Chester, S. "Holy Joe and the Most Vexed Question: Standing to Sue in the Supreme Court of Canada," *Supreme Court Law Review*, vol. 5, 1983, pp. 289–308.

Cloutier, Edouard: "Les Conceptions américaine, canadienne-anglaise et canadienne-française de l'idée d'égalité," *Canadian Journal of Political Science*, vol. 9, no. 1974, p. 581.

Cobham, Viscount: "The Governor General's Constitutional Role," *Political Science*, vol. 15, no. 2, Sept. 1963.

Colvin, Eric: "Constitutional Law — Paramountcy — Duplication and Express Contradiction — Multiple Access Ltd. v. McCutcheon," *University of British Columbia Law Review*, vol. 17, no. 2, 1983, pp. 347–359.

Corry, J. A.: "The Prospects for the Rule of Law," *Canadian Journal of Economics and Political Science*, vol. 21, 1955, pp. 405–415.

—— and J. E. Hodgetts: *Democratic Government and Politics* (University of Toronto Press, Toronto, 1959).

Cumming, R. (ed.): *Perspectives on the Harmonization of Law in Canada*, study prepared for the Royal Commission on the Economic Union and Development Prospects for Canada, vol. 56 (University of Toronto Press, Toronto, 1986).

Dawson, R. M.: *The Government of Canada*, rev. by N. Ward (University of Toronto Press, Toronto, 1970).

—— (ed.): *Constitutional Issues in Canada, 1900–1931* (Oxford University Press, London, 1933).

Dawson, W. F.: *Procedure in the Canadian House of Commons* (University of Toronto Press, Toronto, 1962).

"Documents relating to the Constitution Act, 1982:" *McGill Law Journal*: vol. 30, no. 4, 1985, pp. 645–752.

Driedger, E. A.: "The Spending Power," *Queen's Law Journal*, vol. 7, no. 1, 1981, pp. 124–134.

Esberey, J. E.: "Personality and Politics; A New Look at the King-Byng Dispute," *Canadian Journal of Political Science*, vol. 6, 1973, pp. 37–55.

Evans, J. M.: "Federal Jurisdiction: A Lamentable Situation," *Canadian Bar Review*, vol. 59, 1981, p. 124.

Evatt, H. V.: "The Discretionary Authority of Dominion Governors," *Canadian Bar Review*, vol. 28, 1940, pp. 1–9.

——— : *The King of the Dominion Governors: A Study of the Reserve Powers of the Crown in Great Britain and the Dominions* (Cass, London, 1967).

Forsey, E. A.: *The Royal Power of Dissolution of Parliament in the British Commonwealth* (Oxford University Press, Toronto, 1943).

——— : "The Courts and the Conventions of the Constitution," *University of New Brunswick Law Journal*, vol. 33, 1984, pp. 11–42.

——— : *Essays on Freedom and Order* (McClelland and Stewart, Toronto, 1973).

——— : "The Extension of the Life of Legislatures," *Canadian Journal of Economics and Political Science*, vol. 26, 1960, pp. 604–616.

——— : "Independence of the Judiciary," *Canadian Bar Review*, vol. 35, 1957, p. 240.

Franck, T.: "The Governor General and the Head of State Functions," *Canadian Bar Review*, vol. 32, 1954, pp. 1084–1099.

Gold, Marc: "The Rhetoric of Constitutional Argument," *University of Toronto Law Journal*, vol. 35, no. 2, 1985, pp. 154–182.

Graham, Roger (ed.): *The King-Byng Affair, 1926: A Question of Responsible Government* (Copp Clark, Toronto, 1967).

Hendry, J. McL.: *Memorandum on the Office of Lieutenant-Governor of a Province: Its Constitutional Character and Functions* (Department of Justice, Ottawa, 1955).

Hogg, Peter: *The Canada Act 1982 Annotated* (Carswell, Toronto, 1982).

——— : *Constitutional Law of Canada*, 2nd ed. (Carswell, Toronto, 1985).

Huband, Charles: *Rights and Remedies: New Developments 1983* (Law Society of Manitoba, Winnipeg, 1983).

Jackson, Michael: "The Articulation of Native Rights in Canadian Law," *University of British Columbia Law Review*, vol. 18, no. 2, 1984, pp. 255–288.

Kennedy, W. P. M.: "The Office of Governor General of Canada," *Canadian Bar Review*, vol. 3, 1953, pp. 994–999.

LaForest, G. V.: *The Allocation of Taxing Powers under the Canadian Constitution* (Canadian Tax Foundation, Toronto, 1981).

——— : *Disallowance and Reservation of Provincial Legislation* (Department of Justice, Ottawa, 1955.

Laskin, B.: *Canadian Constitutional Law* (Carswell, Toronto, 1969).

Lederman, W. R.: "The Independence of the Judiciary," *Canadian Bar Review*, vol. 3, no. 4, 1956, pp. 769–809, 1139–1179.

"Legislative Texts relating to the Constitution Act, 1982": *McGill Law Journal*, vol. 30, no. 4, 1985, pp. 753–897.

Lysyk, K: "Developments in Constitutional Law: The 1980–81 Term," *Supreme Court Law Review*, vol. 3, 1982, pp. 65–113.

MacDonald, R. A.: "Absence of Jurisdiction: A Perspective," *Revue du barreau*, vol. 43, 1983, p. 307.

——— : "Constitutional Law — Validity of Legislation — Privative Clause Ousting Judicial Review — Crevier v. Attorney General for Quebec *et al.*," *University of British Columbia Law Review*, vol. 17, no. 1, 1983, pp. 111–142.

—— : "The Proposed Section 96B: An Ill-Conceived Reform Destined to Failure," *Les Cahiers de droit*, vol. 26, no. 1, 1985, pp. 251–298.

McGregor, D. A.: *They Gave Royal Assent: The Lieutenant-Governors of British Columbia* (Mitchell Press, Vancouver, 1967).

Macpherson, James D.: *Developments in Constitutional Law* (University of British Columbia, Vancouver, 1978).

—— : "Developments in Constitutional Law: The 1979–80 Term," *Supreme Court Law Review*, vol. 2, 1981, pp. 49–123.

—— : "Economic Regulation and the British North America Act: Labatt Breweries and Other Constitutional Imbroglios," *Canadian Business Law Journal*, vol. 5, 1980–81, p. 172.

McWhinney, E.: *Judicial Review in the English Speaking World* (University of Toronto Press, Toronto, 1969).

—— , J. R. Mallory, and E. A. Forsey: "Prerogative Powers of the Head of State (The Queen or the Governor General)," *Canadian Bar Review*, vol. 35, nos. 1–3, Jan./Feb./Mar. 1957, pp. 92–96, 242–244, 368–369, 369–371.

Mallory, J.R.: "The Appointment of the Governor-General: Responsible Government, Autonomy and the Royal Prerogative," *Canadian Journal of Economics and Political Science*, vol. 26, 1960, pp. 96–107.

—— : "Disallowance and the National Interest: The Alberta Social Credit Legislation of 1937," *Canadian Journal of Economics and Political Science*, vol. 14, 1948, pp. 342–357.

—— : "The Election and the Constitution," *Queen's Quarterly*, vol. 64, 1957–58, pp. 465–483.

—— : "The Lieutenant-Governor as a Dominion Officer: The Reservation of the Three Alberta Bills in 1937," *Canadian Journal of Economics and Political Science*, vol. 14, 1948, pp. 502–507.

—— : "The 'New' Canadian Constitution: Will the Old Answers Do for New Questions?" *Canadian Public Adminstration*, vol. 27, no. 1, 1984, pp. 110–119.

—— : "The Royal Prerogative in Canada: The Selection of Successors to Mr. Duplessis and Mr. Sauve," *Canadian Journal of Economics and Political Science*, vol. 26, 1960, pp. 314–325.

—— : "Seals and Symbols: From Substance to Form in Commonwealth Equality," *Canadian Journal of Economics and Political Science*, vol. 22, 1956, pp. 281–291.

—— : *Social Credit and the Federal Power in Canada* (University of Toronto Press, Toronto, 1954).

Marshall, Geoffrey: "What Are Constitutional Conventions?" *Parliamentary Affairs*, vol. 38, no. 1, 1985, pp. 33–39.

Meekison, J. Peter, Roy J. Romanow, and William D. Moull: *Origins and Meaning of Section 92A: The 1982 Constitutional Amendment on Resources* (Institute for Research on Public Policy, Montreal, 1985).

Milne, David: *The New Canadian Constitution* (James Lorimer, Toronto, 1982).

Morton, W. L.: "The Meaning of Monarchy in Confederation," in Royal Society of Canada, *Transactions*, Fourth Series, vol. 1, 1963, pp. 271–282.

Moull, William D.: "Natural Resources: Provincial Proprietary Rights, the Supreme Court of Canada and the Resource Amendment to the Constitution," *Alberta Law Review*, vol. 21, no. 3, 1983, pp. 472–487.

—— : "Section 92A of the Constitution Act, 1867," *Canadian Bar Review*, vol. 61, no. 2, 1983, pp. 715–734.

Rémillard, Gil: "Le Contrôle de la constitutionnalité des lois au lendemain de la loi constitutionnele de 1982," *La Revue du barreau*, vol. 42, no. 4, 1982, pp. 565–596.

—— (ed.): "La Loi constitutionnelle de 1982: un premier bilan," *Les Cahiers de droit*, vol. 25, no. 1, 1984 (entire issue).

Russell, P. H.: "The Anti-inflation Case: The Anatomy of a Constitutional Question," *Canadian Public Administration*, vol. 20, 1977, pp. 632–665.

—— (ed.): *Leading Constitutional Decisions*, rev. ed. (Carleton Library Series, Ottawa, 1982).

Sanders, Douglas E.: "Aboriginal Peoples and the Constitution," *Alberta Law Review*, vol. 19, no. 3, 1981, pp. 410–427.

Saywell, J. T.: "The Crown and the Politicans: The Canadian Succession Question, 1891–1896," *Canadian Historical Review*, vol. 37, 1956, pp. 309–337.

—— : *The Office of Lieutenant-Governor* (University of Toronto Press, Toronto, 1957).

Scott, A.: *Divided Jurisdiction over Natural Resources*, Discussion Paper 10 (Institute of Intergovernmental Relations, Queen's University, Kingston, 1980).

Scott, F. R.: *Essays on the Constitution* (University of Toronto Press, Toronto, 1977).

Semkow, Brian W.: "Energy and the New Constitution," *Alberta Law Review*, vol. 23, no. 1, 1985, pp. 101–134.

Stanley, G. F. G.: "A 'Constitutional Crisis' in British Columbia," *Canadian Journal of Economics and Political Science*, vol. 21, 1955, pp. 281–292.

Strayer, B.: *The Canadian Constitution and the Courts*, 2nd ed. (Butterworths, Toronto, 1983).

—— : *Judicial Review of Legislation in Canada* (University of Toronto Press, Toronto, 1969).

Swan, John: "The Canadian Constitution, Federalism and the Conflict of Laws," *Canadian Bar Review*, vol. 63, no. 2, 1985, pp. 271–321.

Swinton, Katherine: "Bora Laskin and Federalism," *University of Toronto Law Journal*, vol. 35, no. 4, 1985, pp. 353–391.

Vaughan, F.: "Precedent and Nationalism in the Supreme Court of Canada," *American Review of Canadian Studies*, vol. 6, 1976, pp. 3–31.

Vipond, Robert C.: "Constitutional Politics and the Legacy of the Provincial Rights Movement in Canada," *Canadian Journal of Political Science*, vol. 18, no. 2, 1985, pp. 267–294.

Ward, N.: *The Canadian House of Commons: Representation* (University of Toronto Press, Toronto, 1963).

—— : *The Public Purse: A Study in Canadian Democracy* (University of Toronto Press, Toronto, 1962).

Whyte, J. D.: "Developments in Constitutional Law: The 1982–83 Term," *Supreme Court Law Review*, vol. 6, 1984, pp. 49–94.

—— : "Developments in Constitutional Law: The 1981–82 Term," *Supreme Court Law Review*, vol. 5, 1983, pp. 77–137.

Willis-O'Connor, H.: *Inside Government House* (Ryerson, Toronto, 1954).

CONSTITUTIONAL AND LEGAL PROCESSES

A. *The Process of Change*

Abel, Albert S.: *Towards a Constitutional Charter for Canada* (University of Toronto Press, Toronto, 1980).

Ackerman, Bruce A. and Robert E. Charney: "Canada at the Constitutional Crossroads," *University of Toronto Law Journal*, vol. 34, no. 2, 1984, pp. 117–135.

Alexander, E. R.: "A Constitutional Strait Jacket for Canada," *Canadian Bar Review*, vol. 43, 1965, pp. 262–313.

Allen, J. G.: "Constitution by Fiat," *Canadian Forum*, vol. 61, no. 710, June 1981, pp. 19, 21.

Angers, F. A.: "Le Problème du repatriement de la Constitution," *L'Action nationale*, vol. 54, novembre 1964, pp. 291–297.

Banting, Keith and Richard Simeon: *And No One Cheered: Federalism, Democracy and the Constitution Act* (Methuen, Toronto, 1983).

—— (eds.): *Redesigning the State: Constitutional Change in Historical Persective* (Macmillan, London, 1984).

Barsh, Russell Laurence and James Youngblood Henderson: "Aboriginal Rights, Treaty Rights, and Human Rights: Indian Tribes and Constitutional Renewal," *Journal of Canadian Studies*, vol. 17, no. 2, 1982, pp. 55–81.

Blache, Pierre: "La Cour suprème et le repatriement de la constitution: l'impact des perceptions différentes de la question," *Les Cahiers de droit*, vol. 22, nos. 3–4, 1981, pp. 649–666.

Boadway, R. W. and K. H. Norrie: "Constitutional Reform Canadian-style: An Economic Perspective," *Canadian Public Policy*, vol. 6, no. 3, 1980, pp. 492–505.

Brady, A.: "Constitutional Amendment and the Federation," *Canadian Journal of Economics and Political Science*, vol. 29, 1963, pp. 486–494.

Cairns, Alan C.: "The Canadian Constitutional Experiment," *Dalhousie Law Journal*, vol. 9, no. 1, 1984, pp. 87–114.

Canada, Prime Minister: *Canada Tomorrow Conference, Nov. 6–9, 1983, Commissioned Papers* (Supply and Services Canada, Ottawa, 1984).

—— *The Constitution and the People of Canada* (Queen's Printer, Ottawa, 1969).

—— : *The Role of the United Kingdom in the Amendment of the Canadian Constitution*, background paper (Publications Canada, Ottawa, 1981).

——, Senate and House of Commons: *Minutes of Procedings and Evidence of the Special Joint Committee on the Constitution of Canada: Report to Parliament*, Feb. 13, 1981 (Supply and Services Canada, Ottawa, 1981).

——, Supreme Court: *The Supreme Court Decisions on the Canadian Constitution* (James Lorimer, Toronto, 1981).

"Canada 1867–1967": *Canadian Bar Review*, vol. 45, no. 3, Sept. 1967 (special issue on the Constitution).

Careless, Anthony G. and Donald W. Stevenson: "Canada: Constitutional Reform as a Policy-making Instrument," *Publius*, vol. 12, no. 3, 1982, pp. 85–98.

Chrétien, J.: *Securing the Canadian Economic Union in the Constitution* (Minister of Supply and Services, Ottawa, 1980).

Clokie, H. M.: "Basic Problems of the Canadian Constitution," *Canadian Journal of Economics and Political Science*, vol. 8, 1942, pp. 1–32.

Close, David: "Federal-Provincal Politics and Constitutional Reform in Canada: A Study in Political Opposition," *Publius*, vol. 15, no. 1, 1985, pp. 161–176.

Cook, Ramsay: *Provincial Autonomy, Minority Rights and the Compact Theory, 1867–1921*, Studies of the Royal Commission on Bilingualism and Biculturalism, no. 4 (Queen's Printer, Ottawa, 1969).

Courchene, T. J.: "The Political Economy of Canadian Constitution Making: The Canadian Economic Union Issue," *Public Choice*, vol. 44, no. 1, 1984, pp. 201–249.

Davenport, Paul and Richard H. Leach: *Reshaping Confederation: The 1982 Reform of the Canadian Constitution* (Duke University Press, Durham, N.C., 1984).

Doerr, Audrey and Micheline Carrier: *Women and the Constitution* (Canadian Advisory Council on the Status of Women, Ottawa, 1981).

Dunn, Sheilagh M.: *The Year in Review, 1981* (Institute of Intergovernmental Relations, Kingston, 1982).

Duplé, Nicole: "La Cour suprême et le repatriement de la constitution: la victoire du compromis sur la rigueur," *Les Cahiers de droit*, vol. 22, nos. 3–4, 1981, pp. 619–648.

Efrat, E. S.: "Federations in Crisis: The Failure of the Old Order," *Western Political Quarterly*, vol. 25, 1972, pp. 589–599.

Favreau, Guy: *The Amendment of the Constitution of Canada* (Department of Justice, Ottawa, 1965).

Forsey, E. A.: "The Constitution Bill," *Queen's Quarterly*, vol. 87, no. 4, Winter 1980, pp. 566–569.

Gaffney, R. E.: *Broken Promises: The Aboriginal Constitutional Conferences* (New Brunswick Association of Métis and Non-status Indians, Fredericton N.B., 1984).

Gérin-Lajoie, P.: *Constitutional Amendment in Canada* (University of Toronto Press, Toronto, 1950).

Government of Alberta: *Constitutional Proposals* (Government of Alberta, Edmonton, 1982).

Grubel, H. G.: "A Canadian Bill of Economic Rights," *Canadian Public Policy*, vol. 8, no. 1, 1982, pp. 57–68.

Hogg, Peter W.: "Constitutional Law — Amendment of the British North America Act — Role of the Provinces: Reference Re Amendment of the Constitution of Canada," *Canadian Bar Review*, vol. 60, no. 2, 1982, pp. 307–334.

—— : "The Theory and Practice of Constitutional Reform," *Alberta Law Review*, vol. 19, no. 3, 1981, pp. 335–351.

Institute of Intergovernmental Relations, Queen's University: *The Response to Quebec: The Other Provinces and the Constitution Debate* (Queen's University, Kingston, 1980).

Jeffrey, Brooke: "The Constitutional Amendment Process: A Case Study of the Policy Process," unpublished Ph.D. thesis (Carleton University, Ottawa, 1983).

Kear, A. R.: "The Unique Character of the Constitution," *Policy Options*, vol. 1, no. 3, Sept./Oct. 1980, pp. 39–41.

Kershaw, Sir Anthony: "The Canadian Constitution and the Foreign Affairs Committee of the U.K. House of Commons, 1980 and 1981," *The Parliamentarian*, vol. 62, no. 3, 1981, pp. 173–182.

Kilgour, D. M. and T. J. Levesque: "The Choice of a Permanent Amending Formula for Canada's Constitution," *Canadian Public Policy*, vol. 10, no. 3, pp. 359–361.

—— : "A Formal Analysis of the Amending Formula of Canada's Constitution Act 1982" (note), *Canadian Journal of Political Science*, vol. 16, 1983, pp. 771–777.

Kome, Penney: *The Taking of Twenty-eight: Women Challenge the Constitution* (Women's Press, Toronto, 1983).

Laselva, Samuel V.: "Federalism and Unanimity: The Supreme Court and Constitutional Amendment," *Canadian Journal of Political Science*, vol. 16, 1983, pp. 757–770.

Laskin, B.: "Amendment of the Constitution: Applying the Fulton-Favreau Formula," *McGill Law Journal*, vol. 11, 1965, pp. 2–18.

Leavy, James: *Mise à jour 1967–1982 de la Cour suprème et la Constitution* (Centre de recherche en droit public, Université de Montréal, 1983).

Lederman, W. R.: "Canada's Current Constitutional Crisis," *The Parliamentarian*, vol. 62, no. 3, 1981, pp. 192–198.

――― : "The Process of Constitutional Amendment for Canada," *McGill Law Journal*, vol. 12, no. 4, 1966.

――― : "The Supreme Court of Canada and Basic Constitutional Change (Comment)," *McGill Law Journal*, vol. 27, no. 3, 1982, pp. 527–540.

Levesque, Terence J. and James W. Moore: "Citizen and Provincial Power under Alternative Amending Formulae: An Extension of Kilgour's Analysis (Comment)," *Canadian Journal of Political Science*, vol. 17, 1984, pp. 157–166.

Livingstone, W. R.: "The Amending Power of the Canadian Parliament," *American Political Science Review*, vol. 34, 1951, pp. 437–439.

Lower, A. R. M.: "Two Ways of Life: The Spirit of Our Institutions," *Canadian Historical Review*, vol. 28, 1947, pp. 383–400.

Lyon, J. N.: "Constitutional Theory and the Martland-Ritchie Dissent," *Queen's Law Journal*, vol. 7, no. 1, 1981, pp. 135–143.

McConnell, W. H.: "Western View of Constitution-building," *Queen's Quarterly*, vol. 87, no. 4, 1980, pp. 570–576.

MacDonald, V. C.: "The Constitution in a Changing World," *Canadian Bar Review*, vol. 26, 1948, pp. 21–45.

McDonald, Virginia: "A Barrel of Fish for a Barrel of Oil," *Canadian Forum*, vol. 61, no. 710, June 1981, pp. 22–23.

Mackay, A. Wayne: "Judicial Process in the Supreme Court of Canada: The Patriation Reference and Its Implications for the Charter of Rights," *Osgoode Hall Law Journal*, vol. 21, no. 1, 1983, pp. 55–81.

MacKinnon, Frank: "Half the Constitutional Story Is Still to Be Told," *Canadian Public Administration*, vol. 26, no. 1, 1983, pp. 113–120.

Marshall, Geoffrey: "The United Kingdom Parliament and the British North America Acts," *Alberta Law Review*, vol. 19, no. 3, 1981, pp. 352–362.

McWhinney, Edward: *Canada and the Constitution 1979–1982* (University of Toronto Press, Toronto, 1982).

――― : *Quebec and the Constitution 1960–1978* (University of Toronto Press, Toronto, 1979).

――― and Gerald-A. Beaudoin: *Mécanismes pour une nouvelle constitution* (Editions de l'Université d'Ottawa, Ottawa, 1981).

Mintz, Eric: "Banzhaf's Power Index and Canada's Constitutional Amending Formula: A Comment on Kilgour's Analysis, *Canadian Journal of Political Science*, vol. 18, 1985, pp. 385–387.

――― : "Changing Canada's Constitutional Amending Formula: A Comment," *Canadian Public Policy*, vol. 11, no. 3, Sept. 1985, pp. 623–624.

Morin, Jacques-Yvan: "Pour une nouvelle constitution du Québec," *McGill Law Journal*, vol. 30, no. 2, 1985, pp. 171–220.

――― : "Le Repatriement de la constitution," *Cité libre*, vol. 26, Dec. 1964, pp. 9–12.

Newfoundland: *Towards the Twenty-first Century Together: The Position of the Government of Newfoundland regarding Constitutional Change* (Queen's Printer, St. John's, 1980).

O'Hearn, Peter J. T.: *Peace, Order and Good Government* (Macmillan, Toronto, 1964).

Olling, R. D. and M. W. Westmacott: *The Confederation Debate: The Constitution in Crisis* (Kendall/Hunt, Dubuque, 1980).

Orban, E. *et al.*: *Mécanismes pour une nouvelle constitution* (Editions de l'Université d'Ottawa, Ottawa, 1981).

Parliament, Senate Standing Committee on Legal and Constitutional Affairs: *Report on Certain Aspects of the Canadian Constitution* (Government Publishing Centre, Ottawa, 1980).

Penner, Norman: "The Left and the Constitution," *Canadian Forum*, vol. 61, no. 710, June 1981, pp. 10–13.

Petter, A.: "Maître chez Who? The Quebec Veto Reference," *Supreme Court Law Review*, vol. 6, 1984, pp. 387–399.

Quebec, Constitutional Committee of the Quebec Liberal Party: *A New Canadian Federation* (The Beige Paper) (Quebec Liberal Party, Montreal, 1980).

Queen's Quarterly: "Canada's Constitutional Turmoil: A Symposium," vol. 87, no. 4, 1980, pp. 560–587.

Romanow, Roy, John Whyte, and Howard Leeson: *Canada . . . Notwithstanding: The Making of the Constitution, 1976–1982* (Methuen, Toronto, 1984).

Rowat, D. C.: "Recent Developments in Canadian Federalism," *Canadian Journal of Economics and Political Science*, vol. 18, 1952, pp. 1–16.

Russell, Peter, Robert Decary, William Lederman, Noel Lyon, and Dan Soberman: *The Court and the Constitution: The Supreme Court Reference on Constitutional Amendment* (Institute of Intergovernmental Relations, Kingston, 1982).

Scott, Stephen Allan: "Law and Convention in the Patriation of the Canadian Constitution," *The Parliamentarian*, vol. 62, no. 3, 1981, pp. 183–191.

—— : "Pussycat, Pussycat; or, Patriation and the New Constitutional Amendment Processes," *University of Western Ontario Law Review*, vol. 247, 1982, pp. 269–275.

Sheppard, Robert and Michael Valpy: *The National Deal: Remaking the Canadian Constitution* (Van Nostrand Reinhold, Toronto, 1982).

Simeon, R.: *A Citizen's Guide to the Constitutional Question* (Business Council on National Issues, Gage Publishing, Toronto, 1980).

—— : "An Overview of the Trudeau Constitutional Proposals," *Alberta Law Review*, vol. 19, no. 3, 1981, pp. 291–400.

Stanley, G. F. G.: "Act or Pact? Another Look at Confederation," in *Canadian Historical Association Annual Report* (Ottawa, 1956).

Stephen, Sir Ninian: *Constitutional Change in Canada: Lessons and Analogies from Across the Pacific* (Australian and New Zealand Association for Canadian Studies, Sydney, 1984).

Stevenson, Garth: "Does the Amending Formula Matter?" *Canadian Forum*, vol. 61, no. 710, June 1980, pp. 20–21.

Tremblay, Guy: "La Cour suprême et l'amendement constitutionnel," *Les Cahiers de droit*, vol. 21, no. 1, 1980, pp. 31–42.

Trudeau, Pierre Elliott: *The Constitution and the People of Canada* (Supply and Services, Ottawa, 1982).

United Kingdom, Parliament, House of Commons, Foreign Affairs Committee: *The British North America Acts: The Role of Parliament* (House of Commons, London, Jan. 30, 1981, April 15, 1981, Jan. 18, 1982).

West, E. G. and S. L. Winer: "The Individual, Political Tension and Canada's Quest for a New Constitution," *Canadian Public Policy*, vol. 6, no. 1, 1980, pp. 3–15.

Woodward, Michael and Bruce George: "The Canadian Indian Lobby of Westminster 1979–1982," *Journal of Canadian Studies*, vol. 18, no. 3, 1983, pp. 119–143.

Zlotkin, Norman K.: *Unfinished Business: Aboriginal Peoples and the 1983 Constitutional Conference* (Institute of Intergovernmental Relations, Queen's University, Kingston, 1983).

Zukowsky, Ronald James: "Struggle over the Constitution from the Quebec Referendum to the Supreme Court: Intergovernmental Relations in Canada," *The Year in Review 1980*, vol. 2 (Institute of Intergovernmental Relations, Queen's University, Kingston, 1981).

B. *The Judicial Process*

Angus, W. H.: "The Individual and the Bureaucracy: Judicial Review — Do We Need It?" *McGill Law Journal*, vol. 20, no. 2, 1974, pp. 177–212.

Arvay, J.: "Newfoundland's Claim to Offshore Mineral Resources: An Overview of the Legal Issues," *Canadian Public Policy*, Winter 1979, pp. 32–44.

Bernier, I. and A. Lajoie (eds.): *The Supreme Court of Canada as an Instrument of Political Change*, study prepared for the Royal Commission on the Economic Union and Development Prospects for Canada, vol. 47 (University of Toronto Press, Toronto, 1986).

Boydell, Craig and Ingrid Arnet Connidis: *The Canadian Criminal Justice System* (Holt Rinehart and Winston, Toronto, 1982).

Brannigan, Augustine: *Crimes, Courts and Corrections: An Introduction to Crime and Social Control in Canada* (Holt Rinehart and Winston, Toronto, 1984).

Bruce, C. J.: "The Calculations of Foregone Lifetime Earnings: Three Decisions of the Supreme Court of Canada," *Canadian Public Policy*, Spring 1979, pp. 155–167.

Bushnell, S. I.: "Leave to Appeal Applications to the Supreme Court of Canada: A Matter of Public Importance," *Supreme Court Law Review*, vol. 3, 1982, pp. 479–558.

Canadian Centre for Justice Statistics: "Legal Aid in Canada: Resource and Caseload Statistics, 1983–84," *Juristat*, vol. 5, 1985, p. 1.

Casswell, Donald: "A Prescriptive Model for Decision-making in the Supreme Court of Canada," *Ottawa Law Review*, vol. 14, 1982, pp. 126–151.

"Chief Justice Bora Laskin: A Tribute," (*University of Toronto Law Journal*) vol. 35, no. 4, 1985 (special issue).

Clark, J. A.: "Appointments to the Bench," *Canadian Bar Review*, vol. 30, 1952, pp. 28–36.

"Comparison of the Role of the Supreme Court in Canada and the United States" (conference proceedings): *Canada-United States Law Journal*, vol. 3, Summer 1980, pp. 1–102 (entire issue).

Cunningham, W. B.: "Labour Relations Boards and the Courts," *Canadian Journal of Political Science*, vol. 30, 1964, pp. 499–511.

Dahl, Robert: "Decision Making in a Democracy: The Supreme Court as a National Policy-maker," *Journal of Public Law*, vol. 6, 1957, pp. 272–295.

——— : "The Too Limited Jurisdiction of the Supreme Court," *Canadian Bar Review*, vol. 25, pp. 573–586.

Dickson, Mr. Justice: "The Judiciary — Law Interpreters or Law Makers?" *Manitoba Law Journal*, vol. 12, no. 1, 1982, pp. 1–8.

Dion, Léon: "Plus de démocratie pour les juges," *La Revue du barreau*, vol. 41, no. 2, 1981, pp. 199–227.

Dussault, René and Micheline Patenaude: "Le Contrôle judiciaire de l'administration: vers une meilleure synthèse des valeurs de liberté individuelle et de justice sociale?" *La Revue du barreau*, vol. 43, no. 2, 1983, pp. 163–276.

Elliot, R.: "Constitutional Law — Judicature: Is Section 96 Binding on Parliament?" *University of British Columbia Law Review*, vol. 16, 1982, p. 314.

Fera, N.: "Review of Administrative Decisions under the Federal Court, October 1970," *Canadian Public Administration*, vol. 14, 1971, pp. 580–594.

Fitzgerald, Patrick and King McShane: *Looking at Law: Canada's Legal System*, 3rd ed. (Bybooks, Ottawa, 1985).

Fouts, D.: "The Supreme Court of Canada, 1950–60," in Glendon A. Schubert and David J. Danelski (eds.), *Comparative Judicial Behaviour* (Oxford University Press, New York, 1969), ch. 10.

Gall, Gerald L.: *The Canadian Legal System*, 2nd ed. (Carswell Legal Publications, Toronto, 1983).

Garant, P. *et al.*: "Le Contrôle politique des organismes autonomes fonctions régulatrices et quasi-judiciaires," *Canadian Public Administration*, vol. 20, 1977, pp. 444–468.

Griffins, C. T., J. F. Klein, and S. N. Verdun-Jones: *Criminal Justice in Canada: An Introductory Text* (Butterworths, Toronto, 1980).

Hogg, Peter: *Constitutional Law of Canada* (Carswell, Toronto, 1978).

——— : "Is the Supreme Court of Canada Biased in Constitutional Cases?" *Canadian Bar Review*, vol. 57, 1979, p. 721.

——— : "Judicial Review: How Much Do We Need?" *McGill Law Journal*, vol. 20, no. 2, 1974, pp. 157–176.

Kinnear, H.: "The County Judge in Ontario," *Canadian Bar Review*, vol. 32, Jan./Feb. 1954.

Knopff, Rainer: "Federalism, the Charter and the Court: Comment on Smith's 'The Origins of Judicial Review in Canada'," *Canadian Journal of Political Science*, vol. 16, 1983, pp. 585–591.

Laskin, Bora: *Canadian Constitutional Law: Cases, Text and Notes on Distribution of Legislative Power*, 4th ed. (Carswell, Toronto, 1973).

——— : *Canadian Constitutional Law*, 4th ed., rev. Albert S. Abel (Toronto, Carswell, 1975).

——— : "Our Civil Liberties: The Role of the Supreme Court," *Queen's Quarterly*, vol. 61, 1954–55, pp. 455–471.

——— : "The Supreme Court of Canada: A Final Court of and for Canadians," *Canadian Bar Review*, vol. 29, 1951, pp. 1038–1079.

Laskin, John B. and Robert J. Sharpe: "Constricting Federal Court Jurisdiction: A Comment on Fuller Construction," *University of Toronto Law Journal*, vol. 30, 1980, pp. 283–306.

Law Reform Commission of Canada: *Judicial Review and the Federal Court* (Supply and Services Canada, Ottawa, 1980).

L'Ecuyer, Gilbert: *La Cour suprême du Canada et le partage des compétences 1949–1978* (Gouvernement du Québec, Ministère des affaires intergouvernementales, Quebec, 1978).

Lederman, William Ralph: *The Courts and the Canadian Constitution* (McClelland and Stewart, Toronto, 1964), pp. 106–175.

——— : "Thoughts on Reform of the Supreme Court of Canada," *Alberta Law Review*, vol. 8, no. 1, 1979, pp. 1–17.

——— : "Thoughts on Reform of the Supreme Court of Canada," in Ontario Advisory Committee on Confederation: *Background Papers and Reports*, vol. 2 (Queen's Printer of Ontario, Toronto, 1970).

Logan, G. R.: "Historical Sketch of the Supreme Court of Canada, *Osgoode Hall Law Journal*, vol. 3, 1964.

Lyon, J. Noel: "A Fresh Approach to Constitutional Law: Use of a Policy-Science Model," *Canadian Bar Review*, vol. 45, 1967, pp. 554–577.

Macdonald, R. A.: "Federal Judicial Review Jurisdiction under the Federal Court Act," *Dalhousie Law Journal*, vol. 6, no. 3, 1981, pp. 449–470.

———— : "Judicial Review and Procedural Fairness in Administrative Law," *McGill Law Journal*, vol. 25, no. 1, 1980, pp. 520–564.

———— : "A Theory of Procedural Fairness," *Windsor Yearbook Access Justice*, vol. 1, 1981, pp. 3–34.

MacDonald, V. C.: "The Privy Council and the Canadian Constitution," *Canadian Bar Review*, Dec. 1951, pp. 1021–1037.

MacKinnon, F.: "The Establishment of the Supreme Court of Canada," *Canadian Historical Review*, vol. 27, pp. 258–274, 1946.

Megarry, Hon. Sir Robert: "The Anatomy of Judicial Appointment: Change but Not Decay," *University of British Columbia Law Review*, vol. 19, no. 1, 1985, pp. 113–132.

Millar, Perry S. and Carl Baar: *Judicial Administration in Canada* (McGill-Queen's University Press, Kingston and Montreal, 1981).

Millward, P. J.: "Judicial Review of Administrative Authorities in Canada," *Canadian Bar Review*, vol. 39, 1961, pp. 351–395.

Morin, Jacques-Yvan: "Le Québec et l'arbitrage constitutionnel: de Charybde en Scylla," *Canadian Bar Review*, vol. 45, 1967, pp. 608–626.

Morley, J. T.: "The Justice Development Commission: Overcoming Bureaucratic Resistance to Innovative Policy-making," *Canadian Public Administration*, vol. 19, 1976, pp. 121–139.

———— : "The Supreme Court of Canada, 1958–1966," *Canadian Bar Review*, vol. 45, 1967, pp. 666–725.

Mullan, D. J.: "The Constitutional Position of Canada's Administrative Appeal Tribunals," *Ottawa Law Review*, vol. 14, 1982, p. 239.

Peck, S. R.: "A Behavioural Approach to the Judicial Process: Scalogram Analysis," *Osgoode Hall Law Journal*, vol. 1, April 1967.

Perry, M. J.: *The Constitution, the Courts, and Human Rights: An Inquiry into the Legitimacy of Policy Making by the Judiciary* (Yale University Press, New Haven, 1982).

Read, H. E.: "The Judicial Process in Common Law Canada," *Canadian Bar Review*, vol. 37, 1959, pp. 265–293.

Reaume, Denise: "The Judicial Philosophy of Bora Laskin," *University of Toronto Law Journal*, vol. 35, no. 4, 1985, pp. 438–468.

Robardet, Patrick: "Le Contrôle judiciare de la procédure administrative: éléments de droit comparé, fédéral, ontarien et québécois," *Les Cahiers de droit*, vol. 23, no. 3, 1982, pp. 651–686.

Russell, Peter H.: *Bilingualism and Biculturalism in the Supreme Court of Canada* (Queen's Printer, Ottawa, 1969).

———— : "Constitutional Reform of the Canadian Judiciary," *Alberta Law Review*, vol. 8, 1970, pp. 1–17.

———— : "Constitutional Reform of the Canadian Judiciary," paper delivered at the A.C.L.T. meetings in Calgary, June 1968.

———— : "Constitutional Reform of the Judicial Branch: Symbolic vs. Operational Considerations," *Canadian Journal of Political Science*, vol. 17, 1984, pp. 227–252.

———— : "The Jurisdiction of the Supreme Court of Canada: Present Policies and a Programme for Reform," *Osgoode Hall Law Journal*, vol. 5, 1968, pp. 1–91.

—— : *Leading Constitutional Decisions: Cases on the British North America Act*, rev. ed. (McClelland and Stewart, Toronto, 1973).

—— : "The Supreme Court and Federal-Provincial Relations: The Political Use of Legal Resources," *Canadian Public Policy*, vol. 11, no. 2, 1985, pp. 161–170.

——, Robert Decary, William Lederman, Noel Lyon, and Dan Soberman: *The Court and the Constitution* (Institute of Intergovernmental Relations, Queen's University, Kingston, 1982).

Scott, Stephen A.: "Canadian Federal Courts and the Constitutional Limits of their Jurisdiction," *McGill Law Journal*, vol. 27, no. 2, 1982, pp. 137–195.

Smith, Jennifer: "The Origins of Judicial Review in Canada," *Canadian Journal of Political Science*, vol. 16, 1983, pp. 115–134.

Snell, James G.: "The West and the Supreme Court of Canada: The Process of Institutional Accommodation of Regional Attitudes and Needs," *Manitoba Law Journal*, vol. 14, no. 3, 1985, pp. 287–304.

—— and Frederick Vaughan: *The Supreme Court of Canada, History of the Institution* (University of Toronto Press for the Osgoode Society, Toronto, 1985).

Solomon, Peter H., Jr.: *Criminal Justice Policy: From Research to Reform* (Butterworths, Toronto, 1983).

Strayer, B. L.: "Comment on 'The Origins of Judicial Review in Canada,' " *Canadian Journal of Political Science*, 16, 1983, pp. 593–596.

—— : *Judicial Review of Legislation in Canada* (University of Toronto Press, Toronto, 1968).

Tarnopolsky, W. S.: *The Canadian Bill of Rights*, 2nd ed. (McClelland and Stewart, Toronto 1975).

Thomas, Paul: "Courts Can't Be Saviours," *Policy Options*, vol. 5, no. 3, May 1984, pp. 24–27.

Weiler, Paul: *In the Last Resort: A Critical Study of the Supreme Court of Canada* (Carswell, Toronto, 1974).

Whyte, J. D. and W. R. Lederman: *Canadian Constitutional Law*, 2nd ed. (Butterworths, Toronto, 1977).

Wilson, Bertha: "Law in Society: The Principle of Sexual Equality," *Manitoba Law Journal*, vol. 13, 1983, pp. 221–233.

FEDERALISM

Aitchison, J. H.: "Interprovincial Cooperation," in James Hermiston Aitchison (ed.), *The Political Process in Canada* (University of Toronto Press, Toronto, 1963), pp. 153–170.

Andrew, C.: "Le Rapport Fullerton: perspective de la science politique," *Canadian Public Policy*, vol. 2, 1975, pp. 162–179.

Angus, H. F.: "Two Restrictions on Provincial Autonomy," *Canadian Journal of Economics and Political Science*, vol. 21, 1955, pp. 445–446.

Armstrong, Christopher: *The Politics of Federalism: Ontario's Relations with the Federal Government 1867–1942* (University of Toronto Press, Toronto, 1981).

Bakvis, Herman: *Federalism and the Organization of Political Life: Canada in Comparative Perspective* (Institute of Intergovernmental Relations, Queen's University, Kingston, 1981).

Baldwin, J. R.: "Transportation Policy and Jurisdictional Issues," *Canadian Public Administration*, vol. 18, no. 4, 1975, pp. 630–641.

Banting, Keith G.: *The Welfare State and Canadian Federalism* (McGill-Queen's University Press, Kingston and Montreal, 1982).

Beaudoin, Gerald A.: *La Partage des pouvoirs*, 3rd ed. (Editions de l'Université d'Ottawa, Ottawa, 1983).

Beck, J. M.: "Canadian Federalism in Ferment," in Richard H. Leach (ed.), *Contemporary Canada* (Duke University Press, Durham, 1968), pp. 148–176.

Beckton, C. F. and A. W. MacKay (eds.): *Recurring Issues in Canadian Federalism*, study prepared for the Royal Commission of the Economic Union and Development Prospects for Canada, vol. 57 (University of Toronto Press, Toronto, 1986).

Bell, D. and L. Tepperman: *The Roots of Disunity: A Look at Canadian Political Culture* (McClelland and Stewart, Toronto, 1979).

Bercuson, David Jay (ed.): *Canada and the Burden of Unity* (Copp Clark Pitman, Toronto, 1985).

—— : *Canada and the Burden of Unity* (Macmillan of Canada, Toronto, 1977).

Bickerton, James and Alain G. Gagnon: "Regional Policy in Historical Perspective: The Federal Role in Regional Economic Development," *American Review of Canadian Studies*, vol. 14, no. 1, 1984, pp. 72–92.

Bissonnette, B.: *Essai sur la Constitution du Canada* (Les Editions du jour, Montreal, 1963).

Black, E. R.: "Federal Strains within a Canadian Party," in H. Thorburn (ed.), *Party Politics in Canada*, 3rd ed. (Prentice-Hall, Toronto, 1972).

—— and Alan C. Cairns: "A Different Perspective on Canadian Federalism," *Canadian Public Administration*, vol. 9, 1966, pp. 27–44.

Brachet, B.: "La Crise du fédéralisme canadien et le problème québécois," *Revue du droit public et de la science politique en France et à l'étranger*, vol. 88, 1972, pp. 303–324.

Brady, Alexander: "Quebec and Canadian Federation," *Canadian Journal of Economics and Political Science*, vol. 25, 1959, pp. 259–270.

Breton, A.: "Federalism versus Centralism in Regional Growth," in D. Biehl *et al.* (eds.), *Public Finance and Economic Growth* (Wayne State University Press, Detroit, 1983).

—— and Anthony Scott: *The Design of Federations* (Institute for Research on Public Policy, Montreal, 1980).

Breton, Raymond, Jeffrey G. Reitz, and Victor Valentine: *Cultural Boundaries and the Cohesion of Canada* (Institute for Research on Public Policy, Montreal, 1980).

Brossard, J.: *L'Immigration: les droits et pouvoirs du Canada et du Québec* (Presses de l'Université de Montreal, Montreal, 1967).

Brown, D. M. and J. Eastman: *The Limits of Consultation: Ottawa, the Provinces and the Private Sector Debate Industrial Policy* (Institute of Intergovernmental Relations, Queen's University, and the Science Council of Canada, Kingston and Ottawa, 1981).

Brown, M. Paul: "Responsiveness versus Accountability in Collaborative Federalism: The Canadian Experience," *Canadian Public Administration*, vol. 26, no. 4, 1983, pp. 628–639.

Browne, G. P.: *The Judicial Committee and the BNA Act* (University of Toronto Press, Toronto, 1967).

Brun, Henri: "Le Labrador à l'heure de la contestation" (bibliogaphical note), *Canadian Journal of Political Science*, vol. 6, 1973, pp. 518–520.

Brunet, J.: "La Croissance de la machine gouvernementale fédérale et le développement de la région de la capitale," *Canadian Public Policy*, vol. 1, 1975, pp. 148–157.

Buck, Arthur Eugene: *Financing Canadian Government* (Public Administration Service, Chicago, 1949), ch. 10, 13, pp. 215–252, 333–348.

Burns, R. M.: *One Country or Two?* (McGill-Queen's University Press, Montreal, 1971).

—— : "The Royal Commission on Dominion-Provincial Relations: The Report in Retrospect," in Robert Mills Clark (ed.), *Canadian Issues* (University of Toronto Press, Toronto, 1961), pp. 143–157.

Bushnell, S. I.: "The Control of Natural Resources through the Trade and Commerce Power and Proprietary Rights," *Canadian Public Policy*, vol. 6, no. 2, 1980, pp. 313–324.

Byers, R. B. and Robert Wm. Reford (eds.): *Canada Challenged: The Viability of Confederation* (Canadian Institute of International Affairs, Toronto, 1979).

Cairns, Alan C.: *From Interstate to Intrastate Federalism in Canada*, discussion paper (Institute of Intergovernmental Relations, Queen's University, Kingston, 1979).

Canada: *Canadian Confederation at the Crossroads: The Search for Federal-Provincial Balance* (The Fraser Institute, Vancouver, 1978).

Canada Committee: *Declaration by English and French-speaking Canadians* (Montreal, 1966).

Canada, Prime Minister: *The Constitution and the People of Canada* (Queen's Printer, Ottawa, 1969).

—— : *Federalism for the Future* (Queen's Printer, Ottawa, 1968).

Canada, Senate: *Report to the Honourable Mr. Speaker relating to the Enactment of the BNA Act, 1867: O'Connor Report* (Queen's Printer, Ottawa, 1939).

Caplan, Neil: "Some Factors affecting the Resolution of a Federal-Provincial Conflict," *Canadian Journal of Economics and Political Science*, vol. 2, 1969, pp. 173–186.

Carson, George Barr, Jr.: "The Spinning Wheel, The Stone Ax, and Sovereignty," *Canadian Journal of Political Science*, vol. 7, 1974, pp. 70–85.

Carter, Voir R.: "Séparation, annexion et fédéralisme," *Actualité économique*, vol. 59, no. 3, 1983, pp. 596–619.

Carty, R. Kenneth and W. Peter Ward (eds.): *National Politics and Community in Canada* (University of British Columbia Press, Vancouver, 1986).

Cheffins, R. I.: *The Constitutional Process in Canada* (McGraw-Hill Ryerson, Toronto, 1976).

Cole, Taylor: *The Canadian Bureaucracy and Federalism, 1947–1965* (University of Denver, Denver, Colorado, 1966).

Cook, R.: *Provincial Autonomy, Minority Rights and the Compact Theory, 1867–1921*, Royal Commission on Bilingualism and Biculturalism Studies, no. 4 (Queen's Printer, Ottawa, 1969).

Corry, J. A.: "Sovereign People or Sovereign Governments," *Policy Options*, vol. 1, no. 1, Mar. 1980, pp. 13–17.

Courchene, T. J.: "Canada's New Equalization Program: Description and Evaluation," *Canadian Public Policy*, vol. 9, no. 4, 1983, pp. 458–475.

—— : *Economic Management and the Division of Powers*, study prepared for the Royal Commission on the Economic Union and Development Prospects for Canada, vol. 67 (University of Toronto Press, Toronto, 1986).

—— : "The Political Economy of Canadian Constitution-making: The Canadian Economic Union Issue," *Public Choice*, vol. 44, 1984, pp. 201–249.

—— , David W. Conklin, and Gail C. A. Cook (eds.): *Ottawa and the Provinces: The Distribution of Money and Power* (Ontario Economic Council, Toronto, 1985).

Creighton, D. G.: *Canada's First Century: 1867–1967* (Macmillan of Canada, Toronto, 1970).

—— : *The Road to Confederation: The Emergence of Canada, 1863–1867* (Macmillan, Toronto, 1964).

Crepeau, Paul André and C. B. Macpherson (eds.): *The Future of Canadian Federalism//l'Avenir du fédéralisme canadien* (University of Toronto Press, Toronto; Les Presses de l'Université de Montréal, Montreal; 1965).

Davenport, Paul and Richard H. Leach (eds.): *Reshaping Confederation: The 1982 Reform of the Canadian Constitution* (Duke University Press, Durham, N. C, 1984).

Dawson, Robert M. (ed.): "Dominion-Provincial Relations" (ch. 9), *Constitutional Issues in Canada, 1900–1931* (Oxford University Press, London, 1933), pp. 431–471.

Desbarats, Peter: *Canada Lost/Canada Found* (McClelland and Stewart, Toronto, 1981).

Doern, G. B.: "Vocational Training and Manpower Policy: A Case Study in Intergovernmental Liaison," *Canadian Public Administration*, vol. 12, 1969, pp. 63–71.

Doerr, Audrey: "Public Administration: Federal and Intergovernmental Relations," *Canadian Public Administration*, vol. 23, no. 4, 1982, pp. 564–579.

Dorval, Brunelle: *L'Etat solide: sociologie du fédéralisme au Canada* (Editions select, Montreal, 1983).

Drache, Daniel and Duncan Cameron: *The Other Macdonald Report* (James Lorimer, Toronto, 1985).

Dubuc, A.: "Une Interprétation économique de la constitution," *Socialisme 66: revue du socialisme internationale et québécoise*, no. 7, janvier 1966, pp. 272–274.

Dufour, André: "Le Statut particulier," *Canadian Bar Review*, vol. 45, 1967, pp. 437–453.

Dunn, Sheilagh M.: "Federalism, Constitutional Reform, and the Economy: The Canadian Experience," *Publius*, vol. 13, no. 2, 1983, pp. 129–142.

Dyck, R.: "The Canada Assistance Plan: The Ultimate in Cooperative Federalism," *Canadian Public Administration*, vol. 19, 1976, pp. 587–602.

Eggleston, Wilfred: "Recent Trends in Federal-Provincial Relations," *The Canadian Banker*, vol. 59, 1952, pp. 66–78.

—— : *The Road to Nationhood: A Chronicle of Dominion-Provincial Relations* (Oxford University Press, Toronto, 1946).

Elazar, Daniel J. (ed.): "Federalism and Consociationalism: A Symposium," *Publius*, vol. 15, no. 2, 1985 (entire issue).

Elton, David, F. C. Engelmann, and Peter McCormick: *Alternatives: Towards the Development of an Effective Federal System for Canada — Amended Report* (Canada West Foundation, Calgary, 1981).

Etudes internationales VII, juin 1977: *Le Canada et le Québec* (Centre des relations internationales, Université Laval).

Fairbault, M. and R. Fowler: *Ten to One: The Confederation Wager* (McClelland and Stewart, Toronto, 1965).

Fearn, Gordon F. N.: "Knowledge, Risk and the Future of the Political Process in Canada," *Canadian Journal of Sociology*, vol. 6, no. 1, 1981, pp. 53–62.

Feldman, Elliot J. and Lily Gardner Feldman: "The Impact of Federalism on the Organization of Canadian Foreign Policy," *Publius*, vol. 14, no. 4, 1984, pp. 33–60.

Forsey, E.: "Canada: Two Nations or One? *Canadian Journal of Economics and Political Science*, vol. 28, 1962, pp. 485–501.

Gagnon, Alain-G.: *Développement régional état et groupes populaires* (Editions Asticou, Montreal, 1986).

Gelinas, A.: "Trois Modes d'approche: la détermination de l'opportunité de la décentralisation de l'organisation politique principalement en système fédéral," *Canadian Public Administration*, vol. 9, 1966, pp. 1–26.

Gettys, Cora Luella: *The Administration of Canadian Conditional Grants: A Study in Dominion-Provincial Relationships* (Public Administration Service, Chicago, 1938).

Gibbins, Roger: *Regionalism: Territorial Politics in Canada and the United States* (Butterworths, Toronto, 1982).

——, Rainer Knopff, and F. L. Morton: "Canadian Federalism, the Charter of Rights, and the 1984 Election," *Publius*, vol. 15, no. 3, 1985, pp. 153–168.

Hall, D. J.: "The Spirit of Confederation: Ralph Heintzman, Professor Creighton, and the Bicultural Compact Theory," *Journal of Canadian Studies*, vol. 9, 1974, pp. 24–42.

Hare, F. K.: "Regionalism and Administration: North American Experiments," *Canadian Journal of Economics and Political Science*, vol. 13, 1947, pp. 563–571.

Hawkins, G. (ed.): *Concepts of Federalism*, proceedings of 34th Couchiching Conference (Canadian Institute on Public Affairs, Toronto, 1965).

—— : *The Idea of Maritime Union*, report of a Conference sponsored by the Canadian Institute on Public Affairs and Mount Allison University (Sackville, N. B., 1965).

House, Peter W. and Wilbur A. Steger: *Modern Federalism* (D. C. Heath, Toronto, 1982).

Hueglin, Thomas O.: *Federalism and Fragmentation: A Comparative View of Political Accommodation in Canada* (Institute of Intergovernmental Relations, Queen's University, Kingston, 1984).

Hutcheson, John: "Harold Innis and the Unity and Diversity of Confederation," *Journal of Canadian Studies*, vol. 17, no. 4, 1982–83, pp. 57–73.

Ismael, Jacqueline S.: *Canadian Social Welfare Policy: Federal and Provincial Dimensions* (McGill-Queen's University Press, Kingston and Montreal, 1985).

Jenkin, Michael: *The Challenge of Diversity: Industrial Policy in the Canadian Federalism* (Science Council of Canada, Ottawa, 1983).

Johnson, A. W.: "The Dynamics of Federalism in Canada," *Canadian Journal of Political Science*, vol. 1, 1968, pp. 18–39.

Kear, A. R.: "Cooperative Federalism: A Study of the Federal-Provincial Continuing Committee on Fiscal and Economic Matters," *Canadian Public Administration*, vol. 6, 1963, pp. 43–56.

King, Preston: *Federalism and Federation* (Johns Hopkins Press, Baltimore, 1982).

Krasnick, M. (ed.): *Case Studies in the Division of Powers*, study prepared for the Royal Commission on the Economic Union and Development Prospects for Canada, vol. 62 (University of Toronto Press, Toronto, 1986).

—— (ed.): *Perspectives on the Canadian Economic Union*, study prepared for the Royal Commission on the Economic Union and Development Prospects for Canada, vol. 60 (University of Toronto Press, Toronto, 1986).

LaForest, G. V.: *Natural Resources and Public Property under the Canadian Constitution* (University of Toronto Press, Toronto, 1969).

Lamontagne, M.: *Le Fédéralisme canadien* (Les Presses universitaires Laval, Quebec, 1954).

Lamy, P.: "Language Planning and Language Use: Canada's National Capital Area," *American Review of Canadian Studies*, vol. 6, no. 1976, pp. 74–87.

La Société Saint-Jean-Baptiste de Montréal: *Le Fédéralisme, l'Acte de l'Amérique du nord britannique et les canadiens français*, memoir au comité parlementaire de la constitution du gouvernement du Québec (Les Editions de l'agence Duvernay, Montreal, 1964).

Laundy, P.: "Report of the Task Force on Canadian Unity," *Parliamentarian*, vol. 60, 1979, pp. 133–140.

Leach, R. H.: "Interprovincial Co-operation: Neglected Aspects of Canadian Federalism," *Canadian Public Administration*, vol. 2, 1969, pp. 83–99.

—— : *Perceptions of Federalism by Canadian and Australian Civil Servants* (Centre for

Research on Federal Financial Relations, Australian National University, Canberra, 1976).

—— (ed.): *Contemporary Canada* (University of Toronto Press, Toronto, 1968).

Lederman, William Ralph: "The Concurrent Operation of Federal and Provincial Laws in Canada," *McGill Law Journal*, vol. 9, no. 1963, pp. 185–199.

—— : "Cooperative Federalism: Constitutional Revision and Parliamentary Government in Canada," *Queen's Quarterly*, vol. 78, 1971, pp. 7–17.

—— : *The Courts and the Canadian Constitution* (McClelland and Stewart, Toronto, 1964).

—— : "Some Forms and Limitations of Cooperative Federalism," *Canadian Bar Review*, vol. 45, 1967, pp. 409–436.

Legaré, Anne: "Towards a Marxian Theory of Canadian Federalism," *Studies in Political Economy*, vol. 8, Summer 1982, pp. 37–58.

Leslie, Peter M.: *Canada: The State of the Federation 1985* (Institute of Intergovernmental Relations, Queen's University, Kingston, 1985).

—— : *Federal State, National Economy* (University of Toronto Press, Toronto, 1986).

Livingston, W. S.: *Federalism and Constitutional Change* (Oxford University Press, Oxford, 1963).

Lortie, Pierre: "The Changing Strains of Federalism," *Policy Options*, vol. 1, no. 3, Sept./Oct. 1980, pp. 25–28.

Lower, A. R. M., F. R. Scott, *et al.*: *Evolving Canadian Federalism* (Duke University Press, Durham, 1958).

McCormick, Peter, Ernest C. Manning, and Gordon Gibson: *Regional Representation: The Canadian Partnership* (Canada West Foundation, Calgary, 1981).

MacEwan, Paul: *Confederation and the Maritimes* (Lancelot Press, Windsor, Nova Scotia, 1976).

Macmahon, A. W.: *Administering Federalism in a Democracy* (Oxford University Press, New York, 1958).

McMillan, M. L. and K. Norrie: "Province-building vs. a Renter Society," *Canadian Public Policy*, vol. 6, 1980, pp. 213–220.

McQueen, Rod: *Leap of Faith: An Abridged Version of the MacDonald Report* (Cowan and Company, Toronto, 1985).

McRae, K. D.: *The Federal Capital: Government Institutions*, Royal Commission on Bilingualism and Biculturalism Studies, no. 1 (Queen's Printer, Ottawa, 1969).

—— : *Switzerland: Example of Cultural Co-existence* (Canadian Institute of International Affairs, Toronto, 1964).

McWhinney, E.: *Comparative Federalism, States' Rights and National Power* (University of Toronto Press, Toronto, 1962).

—— : "The 'Quiet Revolution' in French Canada and Its Constitutional Implications for Canadian Federalism," *Jahrbuch des Öffentlichen Richts der Genewart*, vol. 19, 1970, pp. 331–353.

Mallory, J. R.: The Structure of Canadian Government (Macmillan, Toronto, 1971).

Maxwell, James Ackley: *Federal Subsidies to the Provincial Government in Canada* (Harvard University Press, Cambridge, 1937).

Maxwell, J. and C. Pestieau: *Economic Realities of Contemporary Confederation* (C. D. Howe, Montreal, 1980).

Meekison, J. P. (ed.): *Canadian Federalism: Myth or Reality*, 3rd ed. (Methuen, Toronto, 1977).

Miller, D. R.: "A Shapely Value Analysis of the Proposed Canadian Constitutional Amendment Scheme," *Canadian Journal of Political Science*, vol. 6, 1973, pp. 140–143.

Mintz, Jack and Richard Simeon: *Conflict of Taste and Conflict of Claim in Federal Countries*, Discussion Paper 13, Institute of Intergovernmental Relations (Queen's University, Kingston, 1982).

Monahan, Patrick J.: "At Doctrine's Twilight: The Structure of Canadian Federalism," *University of Toronto Law Journal*, vol. 34, no. 1, Winter 1984, pp. 47–99.

Moore, A. M.: "Fact and Fantasy in the Unity Debate," *Canadian Public Policy*, vol. 5, 1979, pp. 206–222.

—— and J. Harvey Perry: *Financing Canadian Federation: The Federal-Provincial Tax Agreements* (Canadian Tax Foundation, Toronto, 1953).

Morin, Claude: *Le Pouvoir québécois . . . en négociation* (Boréal express, Quebec, 1972).

—— : *Quebec versus Ottawa: The Struggle for Self-government 1960–1972* (University of Toronto Press, Toronto, 1976).

Morisset, Jean: "The Aboriginal Nationhood, The Northern Challenge and the Construction of Canadian Unity," *Queen's Quarterly*, vol. 88, no. 2, Summer 1981, pp. 237–249.

Moull, William D.: "Natural Resources: The Other Crisis in Federalism," *Osgoode Hall Law Journal*, vol. 18, 1980, p. 1.

Murray, Catherine A.: *Managing Diversity* (Queen's University, Kingston, 1984).

Noel, S. J. R.: "Consociational Democracy and Canadian Federalism," *Canadian Journal of Political Science*, vol. 4, 1971, pp. 15–18.

Norrie, K., R. Simeon and M. Krasnick: *Federalism and Economic Union in Canada*, study prepared for the Royal Commission on the Economic Union and Development Prospects for Canada, vol. 59 (University of Toronto Press, Toronto, 1986).

O'Hearn, P.: *Peace and Good Government* (Macmillan, Toronto, 1964).

Oliver, Michael (ed.): *Social Purpose for Canada* (University of Toronto Press, Toronto, 1961).

Olmstead, R. A.: *Decisions relating to the BNA Act, 1867, and the Canadian Constitution, 1867–1954*, 3 vols. (Queen's Printer, Ottawa, 1954).

Options: proceedings of the Conference on the Future of the Canadian Federation (University of Toronto, Toronto 1977).

Pearson, L. B.: *Federalism of the Future* (Queen's Printer, Ottawa, 1968).

Pepin, G.: *Les Tribunaux administratifs et la Constitution: études des articles 96 à 101 de l'A.A.N.B.* (Les Presses de l'Université de Montréal, Montreal, 1969).

Perry, J. H.: "Conditional Grants," in Institute of Public Administration of Canada, *Proceedings of the Annual Conference* (Toronto, 1953), pp. 352–386.

Rémillard, Gil: *Le Fédéralisme canadien* (Québec-Amérique, Montreal, 1980).

Resnick, Philip: "La Gauche et la question nationale (synthèses bibliographiques)," *Canadian Journal of Political Science*, vol. 13, 1980, pp. 377–388.

Riker, W. H.: *Federalism: Origin, Operation, Significance* (Little, Brown, Boston, 1964).

Rioux, Marcel: *Quebec in Question* (James, Lewis & Samuel, Toronto, 1971).

Roberts, S.: "How the West Was Lost," *Policy Options*, vol. 2, no. 2, May/June 1981, pp. 30–31.

Robertson, Gordon: "The Renewal of Federalism," *Policy Options*, vol. 3, no. 6, Nov./Dec. 1982, pp. 27–31.

Robinson, Albert and James Cutt: *Public Finance in Canada: Selected Readings* (Methuen, Toronto, 1968).

Rowat, D. C.: "The Problems of Governing Federal Capitals," *Canadian Journal of Political Science*, vol. 1, 1968, pp. 345–356.

—— : "Recent Developments in Canadian Federalism," *Canadian Journal of Economics and Political Science*, vol. 18, 1952, pp. 1–16.

Royal Commission on the Economic Union and Development Prospects for Canada: *Report, Vols. I–III* (Canadian Government Printing Office, Ottawa, 1985).

Roy, N.: *Mobility of Capital in the Canadian Economic Union*, study prepared for the Royal Commission on the Economic Union and Development Prospects for Canada, vol. 66 (University of Toronto Press, Toronto, 1986).

Russell, P.: *Leading Constitutional Decisions*, rev. ed. (McClelland and Stewart, Toronto, 1973).

—— : *Nationalism in Canada* (McGraw-Hill, Toronto, 1966).

—— : *The Supreme Court of Canada as a Bilingual and Bicultural Institution*, Royal Commission on Bilingualism and Biculturalism Documents, no. 1 (Information Canada, Ottawa, 1970).

Ryerson, S. B.: *Unequal Union: Confederation and the Roots of Conflict in the Canadas 1815–1873*, 2nd ed. (Progress, Toronto, 1973).

—— (ed.): *Philosophers Look at Canadian Confederation* (The Canadian Philosophical Association, Montreal, 1979).

—— et al. (eds.): "The Two Canadas: Towards a New Confederation? A Symposium," *The Marxist Quarterly*, no. 15, Autumn 1965, pp. 56–59.

Sabetti, Filippo and Harold M. Waller (eds.): "Crisis and Continuity in Canadian Federalism," *Publius*, vol. 14, no. 1, 1984.

Saunders, J. Owen (ed.): *Managing Natural Resources in a Federal State* (Carswell, Toronto, 1986).

Savoie, Donald J.: "Co-operative Federalism with Democracy," *Policy Options*, vol. 3, no. 6, Nov./Dec. 1982, pp. 54–58.

—— : *Federal-Provincial Collaboration: The Canada–New Brunswick General Development Agreement* (McGill-Queen's University Press, Kingston and Montreal, 1981).

Scarfe, B. and T. L. Powrie: "The Optimal Savings Question: An Alberta Perspective," *Canadian Public Policy*, vol. 6, Supplement, 1980, pp. 166–179.

Schultz, T.: *Federalism, Bureaucracy and Public Policy: The Politics of Highway Transportation Regulation* (McGill-Queen's University Press, Kingston and Montreal, 1980).

—— and A. Alexandroff: *Economic Regulation and the Federal System*, study prepared for the Royal Commission on the Economic Union and Development Prospects for Canada, vol. 42 (University of Toronto Press, Toronto, 1986).

Scott, Anthony: "The MacDonald Report: Twelve Reviews," *Canadian Public Policy*, vol. 12 (special issue), Supplement, 1986.

Simeon, Richard: "Criteria for Choice in Federal Systems," *Queen's Law Journal*, vol. 18, 1982–83, pp. 131–157.

—— (ed.): *Division of Powers and Public Policy*, study prepared for the Royal Commission on the Economic Union and Development Prospects for Canada, vol. 61 (University of Toronto Press, Toronto, 1986).

—— (ed.): *Must Canada Fail?* (McGill-Queen's University Press, Montreal, 1977).

—— : *Natural Resource Revenues and Canadian Federalism: A Survey of the Issues*, Discussion Paper 9, Institute of Intergovernmental Relations (Queen's University, Kingston, 1980).

—— : *The Political Economy of Canadian Federalism 1940–1984*, study prepared for the Royal Commission on the Economic Union and Development Prospects for Canada, vol. 71 (University of Toronto Press, Toronto, 1986).

Smiley, Donald Victor: *Canada in Question: Federalism in the Seventies*, 3rd ed. (McGraw-Hill Ryerson, Toronto, 1976).

—— : *The Canadian Political Nationality* (Methuen, Toronto, 1967).

——— : "The Challenge of Canadian Ambivalence," *Queen's Quarterly*, vol. 88, no. 1, Spring 1981, pp. 1–12.

——— : *Conditional Grants and Canadian Federalism* (Canadian Tax Foundation, Toronto, 1963).

——— : *Constitutional Adaptation and Canadian Federalism since 1945*, Royal Commission on Bilingualism and Biculturalism Documents, no. 4 (Queen's Printer, Ottawa, 1970).

——— : "Rationalism or Reason: Alternative Approaches to Constitutional Review in Canada," paper delivered at the Progressive Conservative "Priorities for Canada" Conference, Niagara Falls, Ont., Oct. 12, 1969.

——— : *The Rowell-Sirois Report* (Carleton Library, McClelland and Stewart, Toronto, 1963).

——— : "The Structural Problem of Canadian Federalism," *Canadian Public Administration*, vol. 14, 1971, pp. 326–343.

——— : "Territorialism and Canadian Political Institutions," *Canadian Public Policy*, vol. 3, 1977, pp. 449–457.

——— : "The Three Pillars of the Canadian Constitutional Order," *Canadian Public Policy*, vol. 12, Supplement, 1986, pp. 113–121.

——— : "The Two Themes of Canadian Federalism," *Canadian Journal of Economics and Political Science*, vol. 31, 1965, pp. 80–97.

——— and R. L. Watts: *Intrastate Federalism in Canada*, study prepared for the Royal Commission on the Economic Union and Development Prospects for Canada, vol. 39 (University of Toronto Press, Toronto, 1986).

Smith, Denis: *Bleeding Hearts, Bleeding Country* (M. G. Hurtig, Edmonton, 1971).

Smith, Joel and David K. Jackson: *Restructuring the Canadian State: Prospects for Three Political Scenarios*, Duke University Center for International Studies, Occasional Paper Series, no. 11, (Durham, N. C., 1981).

Soucy, E.: "Confédération ou fédéralisme cooperatif?" *L'Action nationale*, vol. 54, octobre 1964, pp. 168–173.

Spector, Norman: "Federal-Provincial Professionalism," *Policy Options*, vol. 5, no. 6, 1984, pp. 44–46.

Stevenson, Garth: "Federalism and Intergovernmental Relations," in Michael S. Whittington and Glen Williams (eds.), *Canadian Politics in the 1980s*, 2nd ed. (Methuen, Toronto, 1984), pp. 371–390.

——— : "Political Constraints and the Province-building Objective," *Canadian Public Policy*, vol. 6, Supplement, 1980, pp. 265–274.

——— : "The Political Economy Tradition and Canadian Federalism," *Studies in Political Economy*, vol. 6, Autumn 1981, pp. 113–133.

——— : *Unfilled Union*, 2nd ed. (Macmillan, Toronto, 1982).

Stewart, W. H.: *Concepts of Federalism* (University Press of America, Lanham, 1984).

Task Force on Canadian Unity: *A Future Together: Observations and Recommendations* (Supply and Services, Ottawa, 1979).

Taylor, M. G.: *Health Insurance and Canadian Public Policy: The Seven Decisions that Created the Canadian Health Insurance System* (McGill-Queen's University Press, Montreal, 1978).

Thorburn, H. G.: *Planning and the Economy: Building Federal-Provincial Consensus* (James Lorimer, Toronto, 1984).

Torrance, Judy: "The Response of Canadian Governments to Violence," *Canadian Journal of Political Science*, vol. 10, 1977, pp. 473–496.

Traves, T. D.: "Some Problems with Peacetime Price Controls: The Case of the Board of

Commerce of Canada, 1919–1920," *Canadian Public Administration*, vol. 17, 1974, pp. 85–95.

Trebilcock, Michael J., J. Robert S. Prichard, Thomas J. Courchene, and John Whalley: *Federalism and the Canadian Economic Union* (University of Toronto Press for the Ontario Economic Council, Toronto, 1983).

Tremblay, A.: *Les Compétences législatives au Canada et les pouvoirs provinciaux en matière de propriété et des droits civils* (Editions de l'Université, Ottawa, 1967).

Trudeau, Pierre Elliott: *The Constitution and the People of Canada* (Queen's Printer, Ottawa, 1969).

────── : *Federalism and the French Canadians* (Macmillan, Toronto, 1968).

────── : *A Time for Action: Towards the Renewal of the Canadian Federation* (Queen's Printer, Ottawa, 1978).

Tupper, Allan: *Bill S-31 and Federalism of State Capitalism* (Institute of Intergovernmental Relations, Queen's University, Kingston, 1983).

Underhill, F. H.: *The Image of Confederation* (CBC, Toronto, 1964).

Usher, D.: "How Should the Redistributive Power of the State Be Divided between Federal and Provincial Governments?" *Canadian Public Policy*, vol. 6, no. 1980, pp. 16–29.

Waines, W. J.: "Dominion-Provincial Financial Arrangements: An Examination of Objectives," *Canadian Journal of Economics and Political Science*, vol. 19, 1953, pp. 304–315.

Waite, P. B.: *The Life and Times of Confederation* (University of Toronto Press, Toronto, 1967).

West, E. D. and S. L. Winer: "The Individual, Political Tension and Canada's Quest for a New Constitution," *Canadian Public Policy*, vol. 6, 1980, pp. 3–15.

Wheare, K. C.: *Federal Government*, 4th ed. (Oxford University Press, London, 1963).

Whitaker, Reginald: *Federalism and Democratic Theory* (Institute of Intergovernmental Relations, Queen's University, Kingston, 1983).

White, W. L., R. H. Wagenberg, R. C. Nelson, and W. C. Soderlund: *Canadian Confederation. A Decision-making Analysis* (Macmillan, Toronto, 1979).

Whyte, John D.: *The Constitution and National Resource Revenues*, Discussion Paper No. 14, Institute of Intergovernmental Relations (Queen's University, Kingston, 1982).

Wiltshire, Kenneth: "Working with Intergovernmental Agreements: The Canadian and Australian Experience," *Canadian Public Administration*, vol. 23, no. 3, 1980, pp. 353–379.

Woodcock, George: *Confederation Betrayed* (Harbour, Madiera Park, B. C., 1981).

Young, R. A., Philippe Faucher, and André Blais: "The Concept of Province Building: A Critique (Field Analysis)," *Canadian Journal of Political Science*, 17, 1984, pp. 783–818.

PARTIES AND ELECTIONS IN CANADA

Note: No attempt has been made to subdivide this part of the bibliography, as most studies of parties bear, at least incidentally, on many themes. For example, it is difficult to discuss minor parties in Canada without also discussing the major ones and vice versa. As well, discussing elections without also discussing parties is virtually impossible.

Abella, Irving M.: *Nationalism, Communism and Canadian Labour: The C.I.O., the Communist Party, and the Canadian Congress of Labour 1935–1956* (University of Toronto Press, Toronto, 1973).

Aitchison, J. H. (ed.): *The Political Process in Canada* (University of Toronto Press, Toronto, 1963).

Albert, Alain: "Conditions économiques et élections: le cas de l'élection provinciale de 1976 au Québec," *Canadian Journal of Political Science*, vol. 13, 1980, pp. 325–345.

―――― : "La Participation politique: les contributions monétaires aux partis politiques québécois" (note), *Canadian Journal of Political Science*, vol. 14, 1981, pp. 397–410.

Alford, Robert R.: *Party and Society: The Anglo-American Democracies* (Rand McNally, Chicago, 1963).

Anderson, Grace M.: "Voting Behaviour and the Ethnic-Religious Variable: A Study of a Federal Election in Hamilton, Ontario," *Canadian Journal of Economics and Political Science*, vol. 32, 1966, pp. 27–37.

Andrews, Ken: "Progressive Counterparts of the CCF: Social Credit and the Conservative Party in Saskatchewan, 1935–1938," *Journal of Canadian Studies*, vol. 17, no. 3, 1982, pp. 58–74.

Archer, Keith: "The Failure of the New Democratic Party: Unions, Unionists and Politics in Canada," *Canadian Journal of Political Science*, vol. 18, no. 2, 1985, pp. 353–366.

―――― and Allan Kornberg: "Issue Perceptions and Electoral Behavior in an Age of Restraint 1974–1980," *American Review of Canadian Studies*, vol. 15, no. 1, 1985, pp. 68–89.

Aube, N. R. Hudson and V. Lemieux: "L'Etude du patronage des partis provinciaux du Québec de 1944 à 1970," *Recherche sociographiques*, vol. 13, 1972, pp. 125–138.

Axworthy, Tom: "After 1984: A Liberal Revival," *Canadian Forum*, vol 64, no. 743, Nov. 1984, pp. 5–7.

Baum, G.: *Catholics and Canadian Socialism: Political Thought in the Thirties and Forties* (James Lorimer, Toronto, 1980).

Beck, J. M.: *Pendulum of Power: Canada's Federal Election* (Prentice-Hall, Toronto, 1968).

―――― : "The Electoral Behaviour of Nova Scotia in 1965," *Dalhousie Review*, vol. 46, 1966, pp. 27–38.

―――― : "Socialist or Democratic Party?" *Dalhousie Review*, vol. 41, 1961, pp. 387–393.

―――― and D. J. Dooley: "Labour Parties New and Old," *Dalhousie Review*, vol. 40, 1960, pp. 323–328.

Beeching, W. C. and M. Lazarus: "Le Socialisme en Saskatchewan: trop ou trop peu," *Socialisme 64: revue du socialisme international et québécois*, no. 2, automne 1964, pp. 16–32.

Bergeron, G.: "Political Parties in Quebec," *University of Toronto Quarterly*, vol. 27, 1958, pp. 352–368.

Blais, André: "Politique agricole et résultats électoraux en milieux agricoles au Québec," *Canadian Journal of Political Sciences*, vol. 11, 1978, pp. 333–381.

―――― : "Third Parties in Canadian Provincial Politics," *Canadian Journal of Political Science*, vol. 6, 1973, pp. 442–438.

―――― , H. Cantin, and J. Crête: "Les Elections comme phénomène de décision collective: les élections fédérales de 1957 à 1965 au Québec, *Canadian Journal of Political Science*, vol. 3, 1970, pp. 522–539.

———, Rachelo Destrosiers, and Francois Renaud: "L'Effet en amont de la carte électorale: le cas de la région du Québec: l'élection fédérale de 1968," *Canadian Journal of Political Science*, vol. 7, 1974, pp. 648–671.

Blake, Donald E.: "The Consistency of Inconsistency: Party Identification in Federal and Provincial Politics," *Canadian Journal of Political Science*, vol. 15, 1982, pp. 691–710.

——— : "Constituency Contexts and Canadian Elections: An Exploratory Study," *Canadian Journal of Political Science*, vol. 11, 1978, pp. 279–305.

——— : "The Measurement of Regionalism in Canadian Voting Patterns," *Canadian Journal of Political Science*, vol. 5, 1972, pp. 55–81.

——— : *Two Political Worlds: Parties and Voting in British Columbia* (University of British Columbia Press, Vancouver, 1985).

———, Richard Johnston, and David J. Elkins: "Sources of Change in the B. C. Party System," *B. C. Studies*, vol. 50, Summer 1981, pp. 3–28.

Blakeney, Allan: "After 1984: The NDP — What Now?" *Canadian Forum*, vol. 64, no. 744, Dec. 1984, pp. 5–7.

Bognador, Vernon and David Butler (eds.): *Democracy and Elections: Electoral Systems and Their Political Consequences* (Cambridge University Press, Cambridge, 1983).

Bordan, H. (ed.): *Robert Laird Borden: His Memoirs* (Macmillan, New York, 1938).

Boudreau, J. A.: "The Medium of the Message of William Aberhart," *American Review of Canadian Studies*, vol. 7, 1978, pp. 18–30.

Boyer, J. Patrick: *Political Rights and the Legal Framework of Elections in Canada* (Butterworths, Toronto, 1982).

Bradley, Michael: *Crisis of Clarity: the New Democratic Party and the Quest for the Holy Grail* (Summerhill Press, Toronto, 1985).

Brady, Alexander: *Democracy in the Dominions*, 3rd ed. (University of Toronto Press, Toronto, 1958).

Brennan, J. William: *Building the Co-operative Commonwealth: Essays on the Democratic Socialist Tradition in Canada* (Canada Plains Research Centre, Regina, 1985).

Brodie, M. Janine and Jane Jenson: *Crisis, Challenge and Change: Party and Class in Canada* (Methuen, Toronto, 1980).

——— : "The Party System," in Michael S. Whittington and Glen Williams (eds.), *Canadian Politics in the 1980s*, 2nd ed. (Methuen, Toronto, 1984), pp. 252–270.

Bullen, John: "The Ontario Waffle and the Struggle for an Independent Socialist Canada: Conflict within the NDP," *Canadian Historical Review*, vol. 64, no. 2, 1983, pp. 188–215.

Butler, David, Howard R. Penniman, and Austin Ranney (eds.): *Democracy at the Polls: A Comparative Study of Competitive National Elections* (American Enterprise Institute, Washington, D. C., 1981).

Cairns, Alan C.: "The Electoral System and the Party System in Canada, 1921–1965," *Canadian Journal of Political Science*, vol. 1, 1968, pp. 55–80.

——— : "The Governments and Societies of Canadian Federalism," *Canadian Journal of Political Science*, vol. 10, 1977, pp. 695–725.

——— : "The NDP and the Waffle," *Canadian Dimension*, vol. 8, no. 8, Special Supplement, April 1971.

Camp, Dalton: *An Eclectic Eel* (Deneau, Ottawa, 1981).
—— : *Points of Departure* (Deneau, Ottawa, 1979).
Canada: *Report of the Committee on Election Expenses* (Queen's Printer, Ottawa, 1966).
Caplan, Gerald L.: *The Dilemma of Canadian Socialism: The CCF in Ontario* (McClelland and Stewart, Toronto, 1973).
Careless, J. M. S.: *Brown of the Globe*: vol. I, *The Voice of Upper Canada 1818–1859* (Macmillan, Toronto, 1959); vol. II, *Statesmen of Confederation 1860–1880* (Macmillan, Toronto, 1963).
Carrigan, O.: *Canadian Party Platforms, 1867–1968* (Copp-Clark, Toronto, 1968).
Carty, R. K.: "The Electoral Boundary Revolution in Canada," *American Review of Canadian Studies*, vol. 15, no. 3, 1985, pp. 273–287.
Casstevens, T. W. and W. A. Denham III: "Turnover and Tenure in the Canadian House of Commons, 1867–1968," *Canadian Journal of Political Science*, vol. 3, 1970, pp. 655–661.
Cherwinksi, W. J. C.: "Bibliographical Note: The Left in Canadian History, 1911–1969," *Journal of Canadian Studies*, vol. 9, Nov. 1969, pp. 51–60.
Christian, William and Colin Campbell: *Political Parties and Ideologies in Canada*, 2nd ed. (McGraw-Hill Ryerson, Toronto, 1983).
Churchill, G.: "Recollections and Comments of Election Strategy," *Queen's Quarterly*, vol. 77, 1970, pp. 499–511.
Clark, S. D.: *Movements of Political Protest in Canada 1640–1840* (University of Toronto Press, Toronto, 1959).
Clarke, Harold D.: "The Parti Québécois and Sources of Partisan Realignment in Contemporary Quebec," *Journal of Politics*, vol. 45, 1983, pp. 64–85.
—— : "Partisanship and the Parti Québécois: The Impact of the Independence Issue," *American Review of Canadian Studies*, vol. 7, 1978, pp. 28–47.
—— , Kai Hildebrandt, Lawrence LeDuc, and Jon Pammett: "Issue Volatility and Partisan Linkages in Canada, Great Britain, the United States and West Germany," *European Journal of Political Research*, vol. 13, no. 3, 1985, pp. 237–264.
—— , Jane Jenson, Lawrence LeDuc, and Jon Pammett: *Absent Mandate: The Politics of Discontent in Canada* (Gage, Toronto, 1984).
—— , Jane Jenson, Lawrence LeDuc, and Jon Pammett: "Voting Behaviour and the Outcome of the 1979 Federal Election: The Impact of Leaders and Issues," *Canadian Journal of Political Science*, vol. 15, 1982, pp. 517–552.
—— , Allan Kornberg, and Marianne C. Stewart: "The Parliament and Political Support in Canada," *American Political Science Review*, vol. 78, no. 2, 1984, pp. 452–469.
—— , Richard Price, and Robert Krause: "Constituency Service Among Canadian Provincial Legislators: Basic Findings and a Test of Three Hypotheses," *Canadian Journal of Political Science*, vol. 8, 1978, pp. 520–542.
Clarkson, Stephen: *City Lib.: Parties and Reform* (A.M. Hakkert, Toronto, 1972).
Comeau, Paul-André: "La Transformation du parti libéral québécois," *Canadian Journal of Economics and Political Science*, vol. 31, 1965, pp. 358–367.
Communist Party of Canada: *Canada's Party of Socialism: History of the Communist Party of Canada 1921–1976* (Progress Books, Toronto, 1982).
Conway, J. F.: "Populism in the United States, Russia and Canada: Explaining the Roots of Canada's Third Parties," *Canadian Journal of Political Science*, vol. 11, 1978, pp. 99–124.
Cook, Ramsay: *The Politics of John W. Dafoe and the Free Press* (University of Toronto Press, Toronto, 1966).

—— (ed.): *Politics of Discontent* (University of Toronto Press, Toronto, 1962).

Copes, P.: "The Fisherman's Vote in Newfoundland," *Canadian Journal of Political Science*, vol. 3, 1970, pp. 577–604.

Cornell, Paul G.: *The Alignment of Political Groups in Canada, 1841–1957* (University of Toronto Press, Toronto, 1962).

Courtney, J. C.: "The Defeat of the Clark Government: The Dissolution of Parliament, Leadership Conventions and the Calling of Elections in Canada," *Journal of Canadian Studies*, vol. 17, no. 2, 1982, pp. 82–90.

—— : "Prime Ministerial Character: An Examination of MacKenzie King's Political Leadership," *Canadian Journal of Political Science*, vol. 9, 1976, pp. 78–100.

—— : "Reflections on Reforming the Canadian Electoral System," *Canadian Public Administration*, vol. 23, no. 3, 1980, pp. 427–457.

—— : *The Selection of National Party Leaders in Canada* (Macmillan, Toronto, 1973).

—— : *Voting in Canada* (Prentice-Hall, Toronto, 1967).

Croisat, M.: "Centralisation et décentralisation au sein des partis politiques canadiens," *Revue française de science politique*, vol. 20, 1970.

Cunningham, Robert: "The Impact of the Local Candidate in Canadian Federal Elections," *Canadian Journal of Political Science*, vol. 4, 1971, pp. 287–290.

Curtis, James E. and Ronald D. Lambert: "Voting, Election Interest, and Age: National Findings for English and French Canadians," *Canadian Journal of Political Science*, vol. 9, 1976, pp. 293–307.

Dalton, Russell J., Scott C. Flanagan, and Paul Allen Beck (eds.); *Electoral Change in Advanced Industrial Democracies: Realignment or Dealignment?* (Princeton University Press, Princeton, 1984).

Davis, Morris: "Ballot Behaviour in Halifax Revisited," *Canadian Journal of Political Science*, vol. 30, 1964, pp. 538–558, 648–671.

Dawson, R. M.: *The Conscription Crisis of 1944* (University of Toronto Press, Toronto, 1970).

—— : *The Government of Canada*, 5th ed. (University of Toronto Press, Toronto, 1970).

Denman, N.: *How to Organize an Election* (Les Editions du jour, Montreal, 1962).

Dion, L.: "A la recherche d'une méthode d'analyse des partis et des groupes d'intérêt," *Canadian Journal of Political Science*, vol. 2, 1969, pp. 45–63.

—— : "The Concept of Political Leadership: An Analysis," *Canadian Journal of Political Science*, vol. 1, 1968, pp. 2–17.

—— : "Politique consultative et système politique," *Canadian Journal of Political Science*, vol. 11, 1978, pp. 419–435.

Dion, l'Abbé G. and l'Abbé L. O'Neill: *Le Chrétien en démocratie* (Les Editions de l'homme, Montreal, 1961).

—— : *Le Chrétien et les élections*, 8th ed. (Les Editions de l'homme, Montreal, 1960).

Dobell, W. M.: "A Limited Corrective to Plurality Voting," *Canadian Public Policy*, vol. 7, no. 1, 1981, pp. 75–81.

Douglas, T. C.: *Tommy Douglas Speaks: Till Power Is Brought to Pooling* (Oolichan Books, Lantzville, B. C. 1979).

Elkins, David J.: "Party Identification: A Conceptual Analysis" (note), *Canadian Journal of Political Science*, vol. 11, 1978, pp. 419–435.

—— : "The Perceived Structure of the Canadian Party Systems," *Canadian Journal of Political Science*, vol. 7, 1974, pp. 502–524.

—— and Donald E. Blake: "Voting Research in Canada: Problems and Prospects," *Canadian Journal of Political Science*, vol. 8, 1975, pp. 313–325.

Elton, David and Roger Gibbins: *Electoral Reform: The Time Is Pressing, the Need Is Now* (Canada West Foundation, Calgary, 1980).

Engelmann, Frederick C.: "Membership Participation in Policy-making in the CCF," *Canadian Journal of Economics and Political Science*, vol. 22, 1956, pp. 161–173.

—— and M. A. Schwartz: *Political Parties and the Canadian Social Structure*, 2nd ed. (Prentice-Hall of Canada, Toronto, 1975).

Epstein, L. D.: "A Comparative Study of Canadian Parties," *American Political Science Review*, vol. 48, 1964, pp. 46–59.

—— : *Political Parties in Western Democracies* (Praeger, New York, 1967).

Ferguson, G. V. and F. H. Underhill: *Press and Party in Canada: Issue of Freedom* (Ryerson, Toronto, 1955).

Filley, Walter O.: "Social Structure and the Canadian Political Parties: The Quebec Case," *Western Political Quarterly*, vol. 9, 1956, pp. 900–914.

Fotheringham, Allan: *Look Ma . . . No Hands: An Affectionate Look at Our Wonderful Tories* (Key Porter Books, Toronto, 1983).

Fox, Paul: "Canada's Most Decisive Federal Election," *Parliamentary Affairs*, vol. 11, 1957–58.

—— : "Early Socialism in Canada," in J. H. Aitchison (ed.), *The Political Process in Canada* (University of Toronto Press, Toronto, 1963).

Fraser, Graham: *PQ, René Lévesque and the Parti Quebecois in Power* (Macmillan, Toronto, 1984).

Frizzell, Alan and Anthony Westell: *The Canadian General Election of 1984* (Carleton University Press, Ottawa, 1985).

Gagne, Wallace and Peter Regenstreif: "Some Aspects of New Democratic Party Urban Support in 1965," *Canadian Journal of Economics and Political Science*, vol. 33, 1967, pp. 529–550.

Gagnon, Alain: "Third Parties: A Theoretical Framework," *American Review of Canadian Studies*, vol. 11, no. 1, 1981, pp. 37–63.

Gerber, Linda M.: "The Federal Election of 1968: Social Class Composition and Party Support in the Electoral Districts of Ontario," *The Canadian Review of Sociology and Anthropology*, vol. 23, no. 1, 1986, pp. 118–135.

Gilsdorf, Robert R.: "Cognitive and Motivational Sources of Voter Susceptibility to Influence" (note), *Canadian Journal of Political Science*, vol. 6, 1973, pp. 624–638.

Graham, Ron: *One-eyed Kings: Promise and Illusion in Canadian Politics* (Collins Publishers, Don Mills, 1986).

Granatstein, J. E.: *The Politics of Survival: The Conservative Party of Canada, 1939–1945* (University of Toronto Press, Toronto, 1967).

Grossman, L. A.: *Les Electeurs québécois* (Groupe de recherches sociales, Montreal, 1960).

—— : " 'Safe' Seats: The Rural Urban Pattern in Ontario," *Canadian Journal of Economics and Political Science* (note), vol. 29, 1963, pp. 367–371.

Guidon, Hubert: "The PQ in the 80s," *Canadian Forum*, vol. 60, no. 707, Mar. 1981, pp. 20–21, 39.

Gwyn, R.: *The Shape of Scandal: A Study of a Government in Crisis* (Clarke Irwin, Toronto, 1965).

Hagy, J. W.: "Le Parti québécois in the 1970 Election," *Queen's Quarterly*, vol. 77, 1970, pp. 266–281.

Hahn, Harlan: "Voting in Canadian Communities: A Taxonomy of Referendum Issues," *Canadian Journal of Political Science*, vol. 1, 1968, pp. 462–469.

Hamelin, Jean Jacques Letarte and Marcel Hamelin: "Les Elections provinciales dans le Québec," *Cahiers de géographie du Québec*, vol. 4, 1958–1960, pp. 5–207.

Hamilton, Richard and Maurice Pinard: "The Basis of Parti Québécois Support in Recent Quebec Elections," *Canadian Journal of Political Science*, vol. 9, 1976, pp. 3–26.

Harbron, J. D.: "The Conservative Party and National Unity," *Queen's Quarterly*, vol. 69, no. 3, 1962–63, pp. 347–360.

Havel, J. E.: *Les Citoyens de Sudbury et la politique* (Laurentian University Press, Sudbury, 1966).

Heasman, D. J.: "The Fragmentation of Canadian Politics," *Parliamentary Affairs*, vols. 16–17, 1963, pp. 419–427.

Higginbotham, C. H.: *Off the Record: The CCF in Saskatchewan* (McClelland and Stewart, Toronto, 1968).

Hoffman, David: "Intra-party Democracy: A Case Study," *Canadian Journal of Economics and Political Science*, vol. 27, 1961, pp. 223–235.

Hogan, G.: *The Conservative in Canada* (McClelland and Stewart, Toronto, 1963).

Hooke, Alf: *Thirty Plus Five: I Know, I Was There* (Institute of Applied Arts, Edmonton, 1971).

Horn, M.: *The League for Social Reconstruction: Intellectual Origins of the Democratic Left in Canada 1930–1942* (University of Toronto Press, Toronto, 1980).

Horowitz, G.: *Canadian Labour in Politics* (University of Toronto Press, Toronto, 1968).

———— : "Conservatism, Liberalism, and Socialism in Canada: An Interpretation," *Canadian Journal of Economics and Political Science*, vol. 32, 1966, pp. 143–171.

———— : "Notes on Conservatism, Liberalism and Socialism in Canada" (note), *Canadian Journal of Political Science*, vol. 11, 1978, pp. 383–399.

———— : "Tories, Socialists and the Demise of Canada," *Canadian Dimension*, vol. 2, no. 4, May/June 1965.

———— : "Toward the Democratic Class Struggle," in Trevor Lloyd and Jack McLeod (eds.), *Agenda 1970* (University of Toronto Press, Toronto, 1968).

Hougham, G. M.: "Canada First: A Minor Party in Microcosm," *Canadian Journal of Economics and Political Science*, vol. 19, 1953, pp. 174–184.

Hunter, W. D. G.: "The New Democratic Party: Antecedents, Policies, Prospects," *Queen's Quarterly*, vol. 69, 1962–63, pp. 361–376.

Irvine, William: *Does Canada Need a New Electoral System?* (Institute of Intergovernmental Relations, Queen's University, Kingston, 1979).

———— : "Does the Candidate Make a Difference? The Macro-politics and Micro-politics of Getting Elected," *Canadian Journal of Political Science*, vol. 15, 1982, pp. 755–782.

———— : "The Puzzle of Liberal Party Success," *Queen's Quarterly*, vol. 89, no. 2, 1982, pp. 340–346.

Irving, J.A.: *The Social Credit Movement in Alberta* (University of Toronto Press, Toronto, 1959).

Isenberg, Seymour: "Can You Spend Your Way into the House of Commons?" *Optimum*, vol. 11, no. 1, 1980, pp. 28–39.

———— : "Spend and Win? Another Look at Federal Election Expenses," *Optimum*, vol. 12, no. 4, 1981, pp. 5–15.

Jacek, H., J. McDonough, R. Shimizu, and P. Smith: "The Congruence of Federal-Provincial Campaign Activity in Party Organizations: The Influence of Recruitment Patterns in Three Hamilton Ridings," *Canadian Journal of Political Science*, vol. 5, 1972, pp. 190–205.

———: "Social Articulation and Aggregation in Political Party Organizations in a Large Canadian City," *Canadian Journal of Political Science*, vol. 8, 1975, pp. 274–298.

Jackman, R. W.: "Political Parties Voting and National Integration," *Comparative Politics*, vol. 4, 1972, pp. 511–536.

Jenson, J.: "Comment: The Filling of Wine Bottles Is Not Easy" (note), *Canadian Journal of Political Science*, vol. 11, 1978, pp. 437–446.

——— and P. Regenstreif: "Some Dimensions of Partisan Choice in Quebec, 1969," *Canadian Journal of Political Science*, vol. 3, 1970, pp. 308–317.

Jewett, Pauline: "Voting in the 1960 Federal By-elections at Peterborough and Niagara Falls: Who Voted New Party and Why?" *Canadian Journal of Economics and Political Science*, vol. 28, 1962, pp. 35–53.

Johnston, Donald: *Up the Hill* (Optimum, Montreal, 1986).

Johnston, Richard and J. Ballantyne: "Geography and the Electoral System" (note), *Canadian Journal of Political Science*, vol. 10, 1977, pp. 857–866.

Joyce, J. G. and H.A. Hosse: *Civic Parties in Canada* (Canadian Federation of Mayors and Municipalities, Toronto, 1970).

Kamin, Leon: "Ethnic and Party Affiliations of Candidates as Determinants of Voting," in S. Sidney Ulmer (ed.), *Introductory Readings in Political Behaviour* (Rand McNally, Chicago, 1961).

Kay, Barry J.: "By-elections as Indicators of Canadian Voting," *Canadian Journal of Political Science*, vol. 14, 1981, pp. 37–52.

——— : "An Examination of Class and Left-Right Party Images in Canadian Voting" (note), *Canadian Journal of Political Science*, vol. 10, 1972, pp. 127–143.

——— : "Voting Patterns in a Non-partisan Legislature: A Study of Toronto City Council," *Canadian Journal of Political Science*, vol. 4, 1971, pp. 224–242.

Keddies, V.: "Class Identification and Party Preference among Manual Workers," *Canadian Review of Sociology and Anthropology*, vol. 17, 1980, pp. 24–36.

Kerr, Donald C.: *Western Canadian Politics: The Radical Tradition* (West Institute for Western Canadian Studies, 1981).

Knopff, Rainer: "Pierre Trudeau and the Problem of Liberal Democratic Statesmanship," *Dalhousie Review*, vol. 10, no. 4, Winter 1980–81, pp. 712–726.

Knowles, S.: *The New Party* (McClelland and Stewart, Toronto, 1961).

Kornberg, A. and W. Mischler: *Influence in Parliament* (Duke University Press, 1976).

——— , J. Smith, and D. Bromley: "Some Differences in the Political Socialization Patterns of Canadian and American Party Officials: A Preliminary Report," *Canadian Journal of Political Science*, vol. 2, 1969, pp. 64–88.

——— , ——— , and H. Clarke: "Attributes of Ascribed Influence in Local Party Organization in Canada and the United States," *Canadian Journal of Political Science*, vol. 5, 1972, pp. 200–233.

——— , ——— , and ——— : *Citizen Politicians—Canada: Party Officials in a Democratic Society* (Carolina Academic Press, Durham, N. C., 1979).

Krashinsky, Michael and William J. Milne: "Additional Evidence on the Effect of Incumbency in Canadian Elections" (note), *Canadian Journal of Political Science*, vol. 18, 1985, pp. 155–165.

——— : "Increasing Incumbency?" *Canadian Public Policy*, vol. 11, no. 1, Mar. 1985, pp. 107–110.

——— : "Some Evidence on the Effect of Incumbency in Ontario Provincial Elections," *Canadian Journal of Political Science*, vol. 16, 1983, pp. 489–500.

LaCalamita, John: "The Equitable Campaign: Party Political Broadcasting Regulation in Canada," *Osgoode Hall Law Journal*, vol. 22, no. 3, Fall 1984, pp. 543–580.

Lambert, R. D. and A. A. Hunter: "Social Stratification, Voting Behaviour, and the Images of Canadian Federal Political Parties," *Canadian Review of Sociology and Anthropology*, vol. 16, no. 3, 1979, pp. 287–304.

Land, Brian: *Eglinton: The Election Study of a Federal Constituency* (Peter Martin Associates, Toronto, 1965).

Landes, Ronald G.: "The Canadian General Election of 1980," *Parliamentary Affairs*, vol. 34, no. 1, 1981, pp. 95–109.

————: "The Canadian General Election of 1984," *Parliamentary Affairs*, vol. 38, no. 1, 1985, pp. 86–96.

Laponce, J. A.: "Canadian Party Labels: An Essay in Semantics and Anthropology," *Canadian Journal of Political Science*, vol. 2, 1969, pp. 141–157.

————: "Non-voting and Non-voters: A Typology," *Canadian Journal of Economics and Political Science*, vol. 33, 1967, pp. 75–87.

————: *People vs. Politics* (University of Toronto Press, Toronto, 1969).

————: "Post-dicting Electoral Cleavages in Canadian Federal Elections, 1949–1968: Material for a Footnote," *Canadian Journal of Political Science*, vol. 5, 1972, pp. 270–286.

Laporte, Pierre: *The True Face of Duplessis* (Harvest House, Montreal, 1960).

Lavau, G.: "Partis et systèmes politiques: interactions et fonctions," *Canadian Journal of Political Science*, vol. 2, 1969, pp. 18–44.

Laxer, J.: "The Socialist Tradition in Canada," *Canadian Dimension*, vol. 6, Dec./Jan. 1960-70, pp. 27–33.

League for Social Reconstruction: *Social Planning for Canada* (Nelson, Toronto, 1935).

Lederle, John W.: "The Liberal Convention of 1893," *Canadian Journal of Political Science*, vol. 16, 1950, pp. 42–52.

————: "The Liberal Convention of 1919 and the Selection of Mackenzie King," *Dalhousie Review*, vol. 27, 1947–1948.

LeDuc, L., Jr.: "Partisan Change and Dealignment in Canada, Great Britain and the United States," *Comparative Politics*, vol. 17, no. 4, 1985, pp. 379–398.

————: "Party Decision-making: Some Empirical Observations on the Leadership Selection Process," *Canadian Journal of Political Science*, vol. 4, 1971, pp. 97–118.

————, Harold Clarke, Jane Jenson, and Jon H. Pammett: "A National Sample Design," *Canadian Journal of Political Science*, vol. 7, 1974, pp. 701–708.

————, ————, ————, and ————: "Partisan Instability in Canada: Evidence from a New Panel Study," *American Political Science Review*, vol. 78, no. 2, 1984, pp. 470–484.

———— and Richard Price: "Great Debates: The Televised Leadership Debates of 1979," *Canadian Journal of Political Science*, vol. 18, 1985, pp. 135–153.

———— and Walter L. White: "The Role of the Opposition in a One-Party Dominant System: The Case of Ontario," *Canadian Journal of Political Science*, vol. 7, 1974, pp. 86–100.

Lemieux, Vincent: "La Composition des préférences partisanes," *Canadian Journal of Political Science*, vol. 2, 1969, pp. 397–418.

————: "Le Patronage politique dans l'Ile d'Orléans," *L'Homme*, vol. 10, no. 2, Apr./June 1970, pp. 22–44.

Leslie, Peter M.: "The Role of Political Parties in Promoting the Interest of Ethnic Minorities," *Canadian Journal of Political Science*, vol. 2, 1969, pp. 419–433.

Levesque, Terence J.: "On the Outcome of the 1983 Conservative Leadership Convention: How They Shot Themselves in the Other Foot" (note), *Canadian Journal of Political Science*, 16, 1983, pp. 779–784.

Levitt, J.: "Henri Bourassa and the Progressive 'Alliance' of 1926," *Journal of Canadian Studies*, vol. 9, 1974, pp. 17–23.

Lightbody, J.: "Electoral Reform in Local Government: The Case of Winnipeg," *Canadian Journal of Political Science*, vol. 11, 1978, pp. 307–332.

—— : "Swords and Ploughshares: The Election Prerogative in Canada," *Canadian Journal of Political Science*, vol. 5, 1972, pp. 287–291.

Lipset, S. M.: *Agrarian Socialism: The Cooperative Commonwealth Federation in Saskatchewan* (Anchor Books, Doubleday, New York, 1968).

—— : *Political Man: The Social Bases of Politics* (Doubleday, New York, 1963).

—— : "Democracy in Alberta," *Canadian Forum*, vol. 34, 1954, pp. 175–177.

Long, J. A.: "Maldistribution in Western Provincial Legislatures: The Case of Alberta," *Canadian Journal of Political Science*, vol. 2, 1969, pp. 345–355.

—— and Brian Slemko: "The Recruitment of Local Decision-makers in Five Canadian Cities: Some Preliminary Findings," *Canadian Journal of Political Science*, vol. 7, 1974, pp. 550–559.

Lorimer, James: *The Real World of City Politics* (James, Lewis and Samuel, Toronto, 1970).

Lovink, J. A. A.: "On Analysing the Impact of the Electoral System on the Party System in Canada," *Canadian Journal of Political Science*, vol. 3, 1970, pp. 497–516.

Lynch, Charles: *Race for the Rose: Election 1984* (Methuen, Toronto, 1984).

Lyon, Vaughan: "The Future of Parties: Inevitable . . . Obsolete?" *Journal of Canadian Studies*, vol. 18, no. 4, 1983–84, pp. 108–131.

Lyons, W. E.: *One Man — One Vote* (McGraw-Hill, Toronto, 1970).

McAllister, James: *The Government of Edward Schreyer: Democratic Socialism in Manitoba* (McGill-Queen's University Press, Kingston, 1984).

McCall-Newman, Christina: *Grits* (Macmillan, Toronto, 1982).

McCormick, Peter: "Is the Liberal Party Declining? Liberals, Conservatives and Provincial Politics 1867–1980," *Journal of Canadian Studies*, vol. 18, no. 4, 1983–84, pp. 88–107.

McDonald, L.: "Social Class and Voting: A Study of the 1968 Canadian Federal Election in Ontario," *British Journal of Sociology*, vol. 22, no. 4, Dec. 1971.

McDonald, Lynn: "A Chance for New Converts: The NDP after 1984," *Canadian Forum*, vol. 64, no. 746, Feb. 1985, pp. 9–11.

McGeer, Pat: *Politics in Paradise* (Peter Martin Associates, Toronto, 1972).

MacGuigan, M. and T. Lloyd: *Liberalism and Socialism* (Exchange for Political Ideas in Canada, Toronto, 1964).

McHenry, D. E.: *The Third Force in Canada: The Cooperative Commonwealth Federation, 1932–1948* (University of California Press, Berkeley, 1950).

McNaught, Kenneth W.: "CCF: Town and Country," *Queen's Quarterly*, vol. 61, 1954–55, pp. 175–177.

—— : *A Prophet in Politics* (University of Toronto Press, Toronto, 1959).

Macpherson, C. B.: *Democracy in Alberta: The Theory and Practice of a Quasi-party System* (University of Toronto Press, Toronto, 1953).

MacQuarrie, Heath N.: *The Conservative Party* (McClelland and Stewart, Toronto, 1965).

—— : "Robert Borden and the Election of 1911," *Canadian Journal of Economics and Political Science*, vol. 25, 1959, pp. 271–286.

Mallory, J. R.: "Style and Fashion: A Note on Alternative Styles in Canadian Political Science," *Canadian Journal of Political Science*, vol. 7, 1974, pp. 129–132.

—— : "The Two Clerks: Parliamentary Discussion of the Role of the Privy Council Office," *Canadian Journal of Political Science*, vol. 10, 1977, pp. 3–19.

Marchak, Patricia: *Ideological Perspectives on Canada* (McGraw-Hill Ryerson, Toronto, 1975).

Marsden, Lorna R.: "After 1984: Controlling the Agenda," *Canadian Forum*, vol. 64, no. 745, Jan. 1985, pp. 6–9.

Martin, Patrick: *Contenders: The Tory Quest for Power* (Prentice-Hall, Scarborough, 1983).

Massam, Bryan H.: "Forms of Local Government in the Montreal Area, 1911–71: A Discriminant Approach," *Canadian Journal of Political Science*, vol. 6, 1973, pp. 243–253.

—— and J. D. Anderson (eds.): *Emerging Party Politics in Urban Canada* (McClelland and Stewart, Toronto, 1972).

Mathews, Robin: "The Terror of Trudeauism," *Canadian Forum*, vol. 61, no. 713, Nov. 1981, pp. 19, 21.

Mayer, L.: "Federalism and Party Behaviour in Australia and Canada," *Western Political Quarterly*, vol. 23, no. 4, Dec. 1970.

Meisel, John: *The Canadian General Election of 1957* (University of Toronto Press, Toronto, 1962).

—— : "Canadian Parties and Politics," in R. H. Leach, *Contemporary Canada* (University of Toronto Press, Toronto, 1968).

—— : "Classic Dilemma," *Canadian Forum*, vol. 59, May 1979, pp. 15–17.

—— : "Cleavages, Parties and Values in Canada," *International Political Science Association*, World Congress, August 1973.

—— : "L'Evolution des partis politiques canadiens," *Cahiers de la société canadienne de science politique*, no. 2, 1966.

—— : "Formulation of Liberal and Conservative Programs in 1957 Canadian General Election," *Canadian Journal of Economics and Political Science*, vol. 26, 1960.

—— : "The June 1962 Election: Break-up of Our Party System," *Queen's Quarterly*, vol. 69, 1962.

—— : "New Challenge to Parliament: Arguing over Wine Lists on the 'Titanic'?" *Journal of Canadian Studies*, vol. 14, 1979, pp. 18–25.

—— : *Papers on the 1962 Election* (University of Toronto Press, Toronto, 1964).

—— (ed.): *Papers on the 1963 Election* (University of Toronto Press, Toronto, 1964).

—— : "Political Culture and the Politics of Culture," *Canadian Journal of Political Science*, vol. 7, 1974, pp. 601–615.

—— : "Religious Affiliation and Electoral Behaviour," *Canadian Journal of Economics and Political Science*, vol. 22, 1956.

—— : "The Stalled Omnibus: Canadian Parties in the 1960s," *Social Research*, vol. 30, no. 3, Sept. 1963.

—— : "Les Transformations des partis politiques canadiens," *Cahiers de la société canadienne de science politique*, no. 2, 1966.

—— : *Working Papers on Canadian Politics*, rev. ed. (McGill-Queen's University Press, Montreal, 1973).

Meynaud, J.: *Agent et politique* (Le Centre de documentation et de recherches politiques, Collège Jean-de-Brébeuf, Montreal, 1966).

Mills, A.: "The Canadian Left and Marxism," *Canadian Journal of Political and Social Theory*, vol. 2, no. 2, 1978, pp. 104–108.

—— : "The Later Thought of J. S. Woodsworth, 1918–1942: An Essay in Revision," *Journal of Canadian Studies*, vol. 17, no. 3, 1982, pp. 75–95.

Morley, J. T.: *Secular Socialists: The CCF/NDP in Ontario — A Biography* (McGill-Queen's University Press, Montreal, 1984).

Morrison, K. L.: "The Businessman Voter in Thunder Bay: The Catalyst to the Federal-Provincial Voting Split?" *Canadian Journal of Political Science*, vol. 6, 1973, pp. 219–229.

Morton, D.: "The Effectiveness of Political Campaigning: The NDP in the 1967 Ontario Election," *Journal of Canadian Studies*, vol. 4, no. 3, Aug. 1969, pp. 21–33.

—— : "Polling the Soldier Vote: The Overseas Campaign in the Canadian General Election of 1917," *Journal of Canadian Studies*, vol. 10, 1975, pp. 39–58.

Morton, W. L.: *The Progressive Party in Canada* (University of Toronto Press, Toronto, 1950).

Muller, Steven: "Federalism and the Party System in Canada," in J. P. Meekison, *Canadian Federalism: Myth or Reality?* (Methuen, Toronto, 1968), pp. 119–132.

—— : "Massive Alternation in Canadian Politics," *Foreign Affairs*, vol. 36, 1958, pp. 633–644.

Mulroney, Brian: *Where I Stand* (McClelland, Toronto, 1983).

Murray, Vera: *Le Parti québécois: de la fondation à la prise du pouvoir* (Hurtubise HMH, Montreal, 1976).

Neill, R. F.: "Social Credit and National Policy in Canada," *Journal of Canadian Studies*, vol. 3, no. 1, Feb. 1968, pp. 3–13.

Newman, P. C.: *The Distemper of Our Times: Canadian Politics in Transition, 1963–1968* (McClelland and Stewart, Toronto, 1968).

—— : *Renegade in Power: The Diefenbaker Years* (McClelland and Stewart, Toronto, 1963).

Nicholson, P.: *Vision and Indecision: Diefenbaker and Pearson* (Longman Canada, Toronto, 1968).

Nixon, Robert (ed.): *The Guelph Papers* (Ontario Liberal Party Conference, Toronto, 1968).

Nurgitz, Nathan: *No Small Measure: The Progressive Conservatives and the Constitution* (Deneau, Ottawa, 1983).

Ogmundson, R.: "Liberal Ideology and the Study of Voting Behaviour," *Canadian Review of Sociology and Anthropology*, vol. 17, 1980, pp. 45–54.

Oliver, M. (ed.): *Social Purpose for Canada* (University of Toronto Press, Toronto, 1961).

Ontario Commission on Election Contributions and Expenses: *Canadian Election Reform: Dialogue on Issues and Effects* (Queen's Printer, Toronto, 1982).

Palda, Kristian S.: "Does Advertising Influence Votes? An Analysis of the 1966 and 1970 Quebec Elections" (note), *Canadian Journal of Political Science*, vol. 6, 1973, pp. 638–655.

—— : "Does Canada's Election Act Impede Voters' Access to Information?" *Canadian Public Policy*, vol. 11, no. 3, Sept. 1985, pp. 533–542.

Paltiel, Khayyam Z.: "Party and Candidate Expenditures in the Canadian General Election of 1972," *Canadian Journal of Political Science*, vol. 7, 1974, pp. 341–352.

—— : *Political Party Financing in Canada* (McGraw-Hill, Toronto, 1970).

Pammett, Jon: "Elections," in Michael S. Whittington and Glen Williams (eds.), *Canadian Politics in the 1980s*, 2nd ed. (Methuen, Toronto, 1984), pp. 271–286.

—— , Lawrence LeDuc, J. Jenson, and Harold D. Clarke: "The Perception and Impact of Issues in the 1974 Federal Election," *Canadian Journal of Political Science*, vol. 10, 1977, pp. 93–126.

Peacock, D.: *Journey to Power: The Story of a Canadian Election* (Ryerson, Toronto, 1968).

Pelletier, Gerard: "The Political Awakening of Pierre Elliott Trudeau," *Saturday Night,* Mar. 1984, pp. 50–56.

Penner, N.: *The Canadian Left* (Prentice-Hall, Toronto, 1977).

—— (ed.): *Winnipeg 1919: The Strikers' Own History of the Winnipeg General Strike* (James, Lewis & Samuel, Toronto, 1973).

Penniman, Howard R. *Canada at the Polls, 1979 and 1980: A Study of the General Elections* (American Enterprise Institute for Public Policy Research, Washington, D. C., 1981).

Perlin, G: "Did the Best Candidate Win? A Comment on Levesque's Analysis" (note), *Canadian Journal of Political Science,* vol. 16, 1983, pp. 791–794.

—— : *The Tory Syndrome* (McGill-Queen's University Press, Montreal, 1980).

—— and Patti Peppin: "Variations in Party Support in Federal and Provincial Elections: Some Hypotheses," *Canadian Journal of Political Science,* vol. 4, 1971, pp. 280–286.

Petryshyn, J.: "R. B. Bennett and the Communists: 1930–1935," *Journal of Canadian Studies,* vol. 9, 1974, pp. 43–54.

Pickersgill, J. W.: *The Liberal Party* (McClelland and Stewart, Toronto, 1962).

Pinard, Maurice: "One Party Dominance and Third Parties," *Canadian Journal of Economics and Political Science,* vol. 33, 1967, pp. 358–373.

—— : *The Rise of the Third Party: A Study in Crisis Politics* (Prentice-Hall, Englewood Cliffs, N. J., 1971).

—— : "Third Parties in Canada Revisited: A Rejoinder and Elaboration of the Theory of One-party Dominance," *Canadian Journal of Political Science,* vol. 6, 1973, pp. 439–460.

—— and Richard Hamilton: "The Independence Issue and the Polarization of the Electorate: The 1973 Quebec Election," *Canadian Journal of Political Science,* vol. 10, 1977, pp. 215–259.

—— and —— : "The Parti Quebecois Comes to Power: An Analysis of the 1976 Quebec Election," *Canadian Journal of Political Science,* vol. 11, 1978, pp. 739–755.

Preece, Rod: "The Anglo-Saxon Conservative Tradition," *Canadian Journal of Political Science,* vol. 13, no. 1, 1980, pp. 3–32.

Punnett, R. M.: "Leadership Selection in Opposition: The Progressive Conservative Party of Canada," *Australian Journal of Politics and History,* vol. 17, 1971, pp. 188–201.

Qualter, T. H.: *The Election Process in Canada* (McGraw-Hill, Toronto, 1970).

—— : "Representation by Population: A Comparative Study," *Canadian Journal of Economics and Political Science,* vol. 33, 1967, pp. 246–268.

—— : "Seats and Votes: An Application of the Cube Law to the Canadian Electoral System," *Canadian Journal of Political Science,* vol. 1, 1968, pp. 336–344.

Quinn, H. F.: "The Role of the Liberal Party in Recent Canadian Politics," *Political Science Quarterly,* vol. 68, 1953, pp. 396–418.

—— : "Third National Convention of the Liberal Party," *Canadian Journal of Economics and Political Science,* vol. 17, 1951, pp. 228–233.

—— : *The Union Nationale: A Study in Quebec Nationalism* (University of Toronto Press, Toronto, 1963).

Raboy, M.: "The Future of Montreal and the MCM," *Our Generation,* vol. 12, no. 4, 1978, pp. 5–18.

Rasmussen, Jorgen: "A Research Note on Canadian Systems," *Canadian Journal of Economics and Political Science*, vol. 33, 1967, pp. 98–106.

Rayside, David M.: "Federalism and the Party System: Provincial and Federal Liberals in the Province of Quebec," *Canadian Journal of Political Science*, vol. 11, 1978, pp. 449–528.

—— : "The Impact of the Linguistic Cleavage on the 'Governing' Parties of Belgium and Canada," *Canadian Journal of Political Science*, vol. 11, no. 1, 1961.

Regenstreif, Peter: "The Canadian General Election of 1958," *Western Political Quarterly*, vol. 13, 1960, pp. 349–373.

—— : *The Diefenbaker Interlude: Parties and Voting in Canada* (Longman Canada, Toronto, 1965).

—— : "Ideology and Leadership in the Canadian Party System," paper preared for delivery to the 1964 Annual Meeting of the American Political Science Association, Chicago, Illinois, Sept. 1964.

—— : "Note on the 'Alternation' of French and English Leaders in the Liberal Party of Canada," *Canadian Journal of Political Science*, vol. 2, 1969, pp. 118–122.

—— : "Some Aspects of National Party Support in Canada," *Canadian Journal of Economics and Political Science*, vol. 29, 1963, pp. 59–74.

Reid, Escott M.: "Canadian Political Parties: A Study of the Economic and Racial Basis of Conservatism and Liberalism in 1930," *Contributions to Canadian Economics*, vol. 6, 1933, pp. 7–39.

Richards, John and Don Kerr (eds.): *Canada: What's Left?* (NuWest Publishers, Edmonton, 1986).

Richardson, B. T.: *Canada and Mr. Diefenbaker* (McClelland and Stewart, Toronto, 1962).

Ricketts, E. F. and H. Waltzer: "Electoral Arrangements and Party System: The Case of Canada," *Western Political Quarterly*, vol. 23, 1970, pp. 695–714.

Roberts, John: *Agenda for Canada: Towards a New Liberalism* (Lester and Orpen Dennys, Toronto, 1985).

Robertson, David and Chuck Rachlis: "The NDP: Replying to Laxer," *Canadian Forum*, vol. 64, no. 740, June/July 1984, pp. 10–14.

Robin, M.: *Canadian Provincial Politics: The Party Systems of the Ten Provinces* (Prentice-Hall, Toronto, 1972).

—— : *Pillars of Profit: The Company Province 1934–1972* (McClelland and Stewart, Toronto, 1973).

—— : *Radical Politics and Canadian Labour, 1880–1930* (Queen's University, Kingston, 1968).

—— : *The Rush for Spoils: The Company Province 1871–1933* (McClelland and Stewart, Toronto, 1972).

—— : "The Social Basis of Party Politics in British Columbia," *Queen's Quarterly*, vol. 72, 1965, pp. 675–690.

Rodney, W.: *Soldiers of the International: A History of the Communist Party of Canada 1919–1929* (University of Toronto Press, Toronto, 1968).

Roussopoulus, D. (ed.): *The New Left in Canada* (Our Generation Press, Montreal, 1970).

Rowat, D. C. (ed.): *Provincial Government and Politics: Comparative Essays*, 2nd ed. (Department of Political Science, Carleton University, Ottawa, 1973).

Sancton, Andrew: "The Application of the 'Senatorial Floor' Rules to the Latest Redistribution of the House of Commons: The Peculiar Case of Nova Scotia," *Canadian Journal of Political Science*, vol. 6, no. 1, Mar. 1973.

Sankoff, David and Koula Mellos: "La Régionalisation électorale et l'amplification des proportions," *Canadian Journal of Political Science*, vol. 6, 1973, pp. 380–398.

Santos, C. R.: "Some Collective Characteristics of the Delegates to the 1968 Liberal Party Leadership Convention," *Canadian Journal of Political Science*, vol. 3, 1970, pp. 299–308.

Scammon, R. M.: "Election of the Canadian House of Commons, May 22, 1979," *World Affairs*, vol. 142, 1979, pp. 135–137.

Scarrow, Howard A.: "By-elections and Public Opinion in Canada," *Public Opinion Quarterly*, vol. 25, 1961, pp. 351–364.

—— : *Canada Votes: A Handbook of Federal and Provincial Election Data* (The Hauser Press, New Orleans, 1962).

—— : "Federal-Provincial Voting Patterns in Canada," *Canadian Journal of Economics and Political Science*, vol. 26, 1960, pp. 289–298.

—— : "Patterns of Voter Turnout in Canada," *Midwest Journal of Political Science*, vol. 5, 1961, pp. 351–364.

—— : "Voting Patterns and the New Party," *Political Science*, vol. 14, 1962, pp. 3–15.

Schindeler, F.: "One Man, One Vote: One Vote, One Value," *Journal of Canadian Studies*, vol. 3, no. 1, Feb. 1968, pp. 13–20.

—— and David Hoffman: "Theological and Political Conservatism: Variations in Attitudes among Clergymen of One Denomination, *Canadian Journal of Political Science*, vol. 2, 1968, pp. 429–441.

Schreiber, E. M.: "Class Awareness and Class Voting in Canada," *Canadian Review of Sociology and Anthropology*, vol. 17, 1980, pp. 37–44.

Schultz, H. J.: "Portrait of a Premier: William Aberhart," *Canadian Historical Review*, vol. 45, 1964, pp. 185–211.

—— : "The Social Credit Back-benchers' Revolt, 1937," *Canadian Historical Review*, vol. 41, 1960, pp. 1–18.

Schwartz, Mildred A.: *Politics and Territory* (McGill-Queen's University Press, Montreal, 1974).

Simmons, James W.: "Voting Behaviour and Socio-economic Characteristics: The Middlesex East Federal Election, 1965," *Canadian Journal of Political Science*, vol. 33, 1967, pp. 389–400.

Simpson, Jeffrey: *Discipline of Power* (Personal Library, Toronto, 1981).

—— : "The Trials of Transition," *Saturday Night*, April 1985, pp. 19–29.

Smiley, Donald V.: "Canada and the Quest for a National Policy," *Canadian Journal of Political Science*, vol. 8, 1975, pp. 40–62.

—— : "Canada's Poujadistes: A New Look at Social Credit," *Canadian Forum*, vol. 42, 1962, pp. 121–123.

—— : "The Two-party System and One-party Dominance in the Liberal Democratic State," *Canadian Journal of Economics and Political Science*, vol. 24, 1958, pp. 312–322.

—— : "The Case against the Canadian Charter of Human Rights," *Canadian Journal of Political Science*, vol. 2, 1969, pp. 277–291.

—— : "Consensus, Conflict and the Canadian Party System," *Canadian Forum*, vol. 40, Jan. 1961, pp. 223–224.

—— : "The National Party Leadership Convention in Canada: A Preliminary Analysis," *Canadian Journal of Political Science*, vol. 1, 1968, pp. 373–397.

—— : "The Left and the New Trudeau," *Canadian Forum*, vol. 61, no. 713, Nov. 1981, pp. 18–20.

Smith, David E.: "A Comparison of Prairie Political Developments in Saskatchewan and Alberta," *Journal of Canadian Studies*, vol. 40, no. 1, Feb. 1969, pp. 17–26.

——— : *Prairie Liberalism: The Liberal Party in Saskatchewan* (University of Toronto Press, Toronto, 1975).

——— : *The Regional Decline of a National Party: Liberals on the Prairies* (University of Toronto Press, Toronto, 1981).

Snider, Norman: *The Changing of the Guard: How the Liberals Fell from Grace and the Tories Rose to Power* (Lester and Orpen Dennys, Toronto, 1985).

Sniderman, Paul M., H. D. Forbes, and Ian Melzer: "Party Loyalty and Electoral Volatility: A Study of the Canadian Party System," *Canadian Journal of Political Science*, vol. 7, 1974, pp. 268–288.

Stark, Frank: "The Prime Minister as Symbol: Unifier and Optimizer" (note), *Canadian Journal of Political Science*, vol. 6, 1973, pp. 514–415.

Stein, Michael B.: "Le Crédit social dans la province du Québec: sommaire et développements," *Canadian Journal of Political Science*, vol. 6, 1973, pp. 563–581.

——— : *The Dynamics of Right-wing Protest: A Political Analysis of the Social Credit in Quebec* (University of Toronto Press, Toronto, 1973).

Stevens, Sinclair: "Inside the 1983 Progressive Conservative Leadership Campaign," *The Parliamentarian*, vol. 65, no. 2, 1984, pp. 117–124.

Stewart, Walter: *Divide and Con: Canadian Politics at Work* (New Press, Toronto, 1973).

——— : *Shrug: Trudeau in Power* (New Press, Toronto, 1971).

Sutherland, S. L. and Eric Tanenbaum: "Rokeach's Value Survey in Use: An Evaluation with Criterion Attitude Scales and Party Identification," *Canadian Review of Sociology and Anthropology*, vol. 12, 1975, pp. 551–564.

Swainson, Donald: "Manitoba's Election: Patterns Confirmed," *Canadian Forum*, vol. 53, Sept. 1973, pp. 4–7.

Taylor, Charles: *The Pattern of Politics* (McClelland and Stewart, Toronto, 1970).

Taylor, K. W. and N. Wiseman: "Class and Ethnic Voting in Winnipeg: The Case of 1941," *Canadian Review of Sociology and Anthropology*, vol. 14, 1977, pp. 174–187.

Teeple, Gary (ed.): *Capitalism and the National Question in Canada* (University of Toronto Press, Toronto, 1972).

Thomas, L. G.: *The Liberal Party in Alberta: A History of Politics in the Province of Alberta, 1905–1921* (University of Toronto Press, Toronto, 1959).

Thorburn, H. G.: *Politics in New Brunswick* (University of Toronto Press, Toronto, 1961).

——— (ed.): *Party Politics in Canada*, 5th ed. (Prentice-Hall, Scarborough, 1985).

Trofimenkoff, Susan Mann: "Thérèse Casgrain and the CCF in Quebec," *Canadian Historical Review*, vol. 66, no. 2, 1985, pp. 125–153.

Troyer, Warner: *200 Days: Joe Clark in Power: The Anatomy of the Rise and Fall of the 21st Government* (Personal Library Publishers, Toronto, 1980).

Tyre, R.: *Douglas in Saskatchewan: The Story of a Socialist Experiment* (Mitchell Press, Vancouver, 1962).

Underhill, F. H.: "Canadian Political Parties," Canadian Historical Association Booklet, no. 8 (Ottawa, 1957).

——— : *In Search of Canadian Liberalism* (Macmillan, Toronto, 1960).

——— : "The Revival of Conservatism in North America," *Transactions of the Royal Society of Canada*, vol. 52, series 3, June 1958, pp. 1–19.

Vallières, P.: "Le Parti socialiste du Québec: l'heure de la révolution tranquille," *Cité libre*, vol. 15, no. 63, janvier 1964, pp. 22–25.

Van Loon, Rick: "Political Participation in Canada: The 1965 Election," *Canadian Journal of Political Science*, vol. 3, 1970, pp. 376–399.

Ward, N.: "A Century of Constituencies," *Canadian Public Administration*, vol. 10, 1967, pp. 105–122.

—— and D. Spafford (eds.): *Politics in Saskatchewan* (Longman Canada, Toronto, 1968).

Wattenberg, Martin P.: "Party Identification and Party Images: A Comparison of Britain, Canada, Australia, and the United States," *Comparative Politics*, vol. 15, no. 1, 1982, pp. 23–40.

Wearing, J.: "A Convention for Professionals: The PCs in Toronto," *Journal of Canadian Studies*, vol. 2, no. 4, Nov. 1967, pp. 3–16.

—— : "How to Predict Canadian Elections," *Canadian Commentator*, vol. 7, no. 2, Feb. 1963, pp. 2–4.

—— : "The Liberal Choice," *Journal of Canadian Studies*, vol. 3, no. 2, May 1968, pp. 3–20.

—— : *The L-shaped Party: The Liberal Party of Canada* (McGraw-Hill Ryerson, Toronto, 1981).

—— : "Party Leadership and the 1966 Conventions," *Journal of Canadian Studies*, vol. 2, no. 1, Feb. 1967, pp. 23–27.

—— : "The Trudeau Phenomenon," *Canadian Journal of Political Science*, vol. 2, 1969, pp. 369–372.

Weisbord, Merrily: *The Strangest Dream: Canadian Communists, the Spy Trials and the Cold War* (Lester and Orpen Dennys, Toronto, 1983).

Westell, Anthony: *Paradox: Trudeau as Prime Minister* (Prentice-Hall, Toronto, 1972).

Whalen, H.: "Social Credit Measures in Alberta," *Canadian Journal of Economics and Political Science*, vol. 18, 1952, pp. 500–517.

Whitaker, R.: *Government Party: Organizing and Financing the Liberal Party of Canada, 1930–1958* (University of Toronto Press, Toronto, 1977).

—— : "The Liberals, Turner and the Trudeau Legacy," *Canadian Forum*, vol. 64, no. 740, June/July 1984, pp. 6–8.

White, Graham: "One Party Dominance and Third Parties: The Pinard Theory Reconsidered," *Canadian Journal of Political Science*, vol. 6, 1973, pp. 399–421.

Williams, J. R.: *The Conservative Party in Canada, 1920–1949* (Duke University Press, Durham, 1956).

Wilson, Barry: *Politics of Defeat: The Decline of the Liberal Party in Saskatchewan* (Western Producer Books, Saskatoon, 1980).

Wilson, Donna (ed.): *Democratic Socialism: The Challenge of the Eighties and Beyond* (New Star Books, Vancouver, 1985).

Wilson, J.: "The Decline of the Liberal Party in Manitoba Politics," *Journal of Canadian Studies*, vol. 10, 1975, pp. 24–41.

—— and D. Hoffman: "The Liberal Party in Contemporary Ontario Politics," *Canadian Journal of Political Science*, vol. 3, 1970, pp. 177–204.

Winham, G. R. and R. B. Cunningham: "Party Leader Images in the 1968 Federal Election," *Canadian Journal of Political Science*, vol. 3, 1970, pp. 37–55.

Winn, Conrad and John McMenemy: "Class and Ethnic Voting in Winnipeg during the Cold War," *Canadian Review of Sociology and Anthropology*, vol. 16, 1979, pp. 60–76.

—— : "Political Alignment in a Polarized City: Electoral Cleavages in Kitchener, Ontario," *Canadian Journal of Political Science*, vol. 6, 1973, pp. 230–242.

Wiseman, Nelson: "An Historical Note on Religion and Parties on the Prairies," *Journal of Canadian Studies*, vol. 16, no. 2, 1981, pp. 109–112.

—— : "The Pattern of Party Voting in Canada," *Public Opinion Quarterly*, vol. 21, 1957, pp. 252–264.

—— : "The Return of the Manitoba NDP," *Canadian Forum*, vol. 61, no. 715, Feb. 1982, pp. 32–33, 42.

—— : *Social Democracy in Manitoba: A History of the CCF/NDP* (University of Manitoba Press, Winnipeg, 1984).

Wrong, Denis H.: "Ontario Provincial Elections 1934–1955: A Preliminary Survey of Voting," *Canadian Journal of Economics and Political Science*, vol. 23, 1957, pp. 395–403.

Young, Walter D.: *The Anatomy of a Party: The National CCF 1932–1961* (University of Toronto Press, Toronto, 1969).

—— : *Democracy and Discontent: Progressivism, Socialism and Social Credit in the Canadian West* (Ryerson, Toronto, 1969).

—— : "The Peterborough By-election: The Success of a Party Image," *Dalhousie Review*, vol. 40, 1960–61, pp. 505–519.

Zakuta, L.: *A Protest Movement Becalmed: A Study of Change in the CCF* (University of Toronto Press, Toronto, 1964).

Zipp, John F.: "Left-Right Dimensions of Canadian Federal Party Identification: A Discriminant Analysis," *Canadian Journal of Political Science*, vol. 11, 1978, pp. 251–277.

POLITICAL BIOGRAPHIES

Note: Political biographies and memoirs are a valuable source of information about political parties and elections. Related references appear in the section on parties and elections.

Archer, J. and J. A. Munro: *One Canada: Memoirs of the Rt. Hon. J. G. Diefenbaker (1895–1979)* (Macmillan, Toronto, 1975).

Barrette, A.: *Mémoires*, vol. 1 (Librairie Beauchemin, Montreal, 1966).

Beal, J. R.: *The Pearson Phenomenon* (Longman, Toronto, 1964).

Beck, J. M.: *Joseph Howe:* vol. I, *Conservative Reformer 1804–1848*; vol. II: *The Briton Becomes Canadian 1848–1873* (McGill-Queen's University Press, Kingston and Montreal, 1982, 1983).

—— : *Joseph Howe, Voice of Nova Scotia* (Carleton Library, McClelland and Stewart, Toronto, 1964).

Benson, N. A.: *None of It Came Easy: The Story of J. G. Gardiner* (Burns and MacEachern, Toronto, 1955).

Bissell, Claude: *The Young Vincent Massey* (University of Toronto Press, Toronto, 1981).

Bordon, H. (ed.): *Robert Laird Borden: His Memoirs*, 2 vols. (Macmillan, Toronto, 1938).

—— (ed.): *Letters to Limbo* (University of Toronto Press, Toronto, 1971).

Bothwell, R. and Wm. Kilburn: *C. S. Howe: A Biography* (McClelland and Stewart, Toronto, 1978).

Bourassa, A., A. Bergevin, and C. Nish (eds.): *Henri Bourassa: Biography, Bibliographical Index and Index of Public Correspondence, 1895–1924* (Les Editions de l'actionale, Montreal, 1966).

Bourassa, R.: *Bourassa/Quebec!* (Les Editions de l'homme, Montreal, 1970).

Brown, R. C.: *Robert Laird Borden: A Biography;* vol. I, *1854–1914*; vol. II, *1914–1937* (Macmillan, Toronto, 1975, 1980).

Brunelle, Dorval: *Les Trois Colombes* (VLB Editeur, Montreal, 1985).

Cahill, Jack: *John Turner: The Long Run* (McClelland and Stewart, Toronto, 1984).

Camp, Dalton: *An Eclectic Eel* (Deneau, Ottawa, 1981).

—— : *Players and Politicians* (McClelland and Stewart, Toronto, 1970).

—— : *Points of Departure* (Deneau and Greenberg, Ottawa, 1979).

Careless, J. M. S.: *Brown of the Globe*: vol. II, *Statesman of Confederation, 1860–1880* (Macmillan, Toronto, 1963).

Casgrain, T.: *Une Femme chez les hommes* (Les Editions du jour, Montreal, 1972).

Chados, R. *et al.*: "David (Lewis): The Centre of His Party," *Last Post*, vol. 1, no. 7, Apr./May 1971.

Chalout, R.: *Mémoires politiques* (McClelland and Stewart, Toronto, 1969).

Colton, Timothy: *Big Daddy: Frederick G. Gardiner and the Building of Metropolitan Toronto* (University of Toronto Press, Toronto, 1980).

Corry, J. A.: *My Life and Work: A Happy Partnership — Memoirs of J. A. Corry* (Queen's University Press, Kingston, 1981).

Creighton, D.: *John A. Macdonald*: vol. 1, *The Young Politician*; vol. 2, *The Old Chieftain* (Macmillan, Toronto, 1955).

Chrétien, Jean: *Straight from the Heart* (Key Porter Books, Toronto, 1985).

Dafoe, J. W.: *Laurier: A Study in Canadian Politics* (Carleton Library, McClelland and Stewart, Toronto, 1963).

Daignault, Richard: *Lesage* (Libre expression, Montreal, 1981).

Dawson, R. M.: *William Lyon Mackenzie King: A Political Biography, 1874–1923*, vol. I (University of Toronto Press, Toronto, 1958).

Dempson, P.: *Assignment Ottawa* (General Publishing, Don Mills, 1968).

Donaldson, G.: *Eighteen Men: The Prime Ministers of Canada* (Doubleday Canada, Toronto, 1985).

—— : *Fifteen Men: Canada's Prime Ministers from Macdonald to Trudeau* (Doubleday, Toronto, 1969).

Drury, E. C.: *Farmer Premier: The Memoirs of the Hon. E. C. Drury* (McClelland and Stewart, Toronto, 1966).

Ferns, H. S.: *Reading from Left to Right: One Man's Political History* (University of Toronto Press, Toronto, 1983).

—— and Ostry, B.: *The Age of Mackenzie King: The Rise of the Leader* (Heinemann, London, 1955).

Fleming, Donald M.: *So Very Near: The Political Memoirs of the Honourable Donald M. Fleming* , 2 vols. (McClelland and Stewart, Toronto, 1985).

Godin, Pierre: *Daniel Johnson: la passion du pouvoir, 1946–1964* (Editions de l'homme, Montreal, 1980).

Gordon, Walter: *A Political Memoir* (McClelland and Stewart, Toronto, 1977).

Graham, R.: *Arthur Meighen*: vol. I, *The Door of Opportunity*; vol. II, *And Fortune Fled*; vol. III, *No Surrender* (Clarke, Irwin, Toronto, 1965).

Granatstein, J. L.: *A Man of Influence: Norman A. Robertson and Canadian Statecraft, 1929–1968* (Deneau Publishers, Ottawa, 1981).

Gruending, Dennis: *Emmett Hall: Establishment Radical* (Macmillan, Toronto, 1985).

Gwyn, R.: *Northern Magus* (McClelland and Stewart, Toronto, 1980).

—— : *Smallwood: The Unlikely Revolutionary*, rev. ed. (McClelland and Stewart, Toronto, 1972).

Gwyn, Sandra: "Sense and Sensibility: Bertha Wilson," *Saturday Night*, June 1985, pp. 13–19.

Haliburton, E. D.: *My Years with Stanfield* (Lancelot, Windsor, N.S., 1972).

Hall, D. J.: *Clifford Sifton*: vol. 1, *The Young Napoleon 1861–1900*; vol. 2, *The Lonely Eminence 1901–1929* (University of British Columbia Press, Vancouver, 1985).

Harrop, Gerry: *Advocate of Compassion: Stanley Knowles in the Political Process* (Lancelott Press, Hantsport, N. S., 1984).

Heaps, L: *The Rebel in the House: The Life and Times of A. A. Heaps, M.P.* (Niccolo, London, England, 1970).
Hoy, Clair: *Bill Davis: The Biography* (Methuen, Toronto, 1985).
Humphries, Charles W.: *Honest Enough to Be Bold: The Life and Times of Sir James Pliny Whitney* (University of Toronto Press for the Ontario Historical Studies Series, Toronto, 1985).
Hutchison, B.: *The Incredible Canadian* (Longman, Green, Toronto, 1952).
—— : *Mr. Prime Minister, 1867–1964* (Longman, Toronto, 1964).
Ignatieff, George: *The Making of a Peacemonger: The Memoirs of George Ignatieff* (University of Toronto Press, Toronto, 1985).
Institut canadien des affaires publiques: *Nos Hommes politiques* (Les Editions du jour, Montreal, 1964).
Johnson, L. P. V. and O. MacNutt: *Aberhart of Alberta* (Institute of Applied Arts, Edmonton, 1970).
Keen, Roger and David Humphreys: *Conversations with W. A. C. Bennett* (Methuen, Toronto, 1980).
Keenleyside, Hugh L.: *Memoirs of Hugh L. Keenleyside* (McClelland and Stewart, Toronto, 1981).
Kendle, John: *John Bracken: A Political Biography* (University of Toronto Press, Toronto, 1980).
King, W. L. M.: *Industry and Humanity* (University of Toronto Press, Toronto, 1973).
LaMarsh, Judy: *Memoirs of a Bird in a Gilded Cage* (McClelland and Stewart, Toronto, 1969).
Lapalme, G. E.: *Mémoires*, vols. 1–3 (Leméac, Montreal, 1969–73).
Laporte, P.: *The True Face of Duplessis* (Harvest House, Montreal, 1960).
LaRogque, H.: *Camilien House: le p'tit gars de Sainte-Marie* (Les Editions de l'homme, Montreal, 1961).
Leclerc, A.: *Claude Ryan: A Biography* (NC Press, Toronto, 1980).
Leger, Jules: *A Selection of His Writings on Canada* (Les Editions La Presse, Montreal, 1982).
Le Sueur, William Dawson (ed.): *William Lyon Mackenzie: A Reinterpretation*, with introduction by A. B. McKillop: (Macmillan, Toronto, 1979).
Lewis, David: *The Good Fight* (Macmillan, Toronto, 1981).
MacDonald, L. Ian: *Mulroney: The Making of the Prime Minister* (McClelland and Stewart, Toronto, 1984).
McDougall, A. K.: *Robarts: His Life and Government* (University of Toronto Press, Toronto, 1986).
McGregor, F. A.: *The Fall and Rise of Mackenzie King: 1911–1919* (Macmillan, Toronto, 1962).
McIlvary, Thad (ed.): *Personal Letters of a Public Man: The Family Letters of John Diefenbaker* (Doubleday, Toronto, 1985).
MacInnis, G.: *J. S. Woodsworth: A Man to Remember* (Macmillan, Toronto, 1953).
McKenna, Brian and Susan Purcell: *Drapeau* (Clarke Irwin and Co., Toronto, 1980).
McKenty, N.: *Mitch Hepburn* (McClelland and Stewart, Toronto, 1967).
McNaught, K.: *A Prophet in Politics: A Biography of J. S. Woodsworth* (University of Toronto Press, Toronto, 1959).
Mardiros, A.: *William Levine: A Life of a Prairie Radical* (Lorimer, Toronto, 1979).
Martin, Paul: *A Very Public Life*, 2 vols. (Deneau, Ottawa, 1985).
Munro, J. A. and A. I. Inglish (eds.): *Mike: The Memoirs of the Right Honourable Lester B. Pearson:* vol. II, *1948–1957* (University of Toronto Press, Toronto, 1973).

Murphy, Rae, Robert Chodos, and Nick Auf der Maur: *Brian Mulroney: The Boy from Baie-Comeau* (James Lorimer, Toronto, 1984).

Nadeau, J.-M.: *Carnets politiques* (Editions Parti pris, Montreal, 1966).

Neatby, H. B.: *Laurier and a Liberal Quebec: A Study in Political Management* (McClelland and Stewart, Toronto, 1973).

——— : *William Lyon Mackenzie King:* vol. 2, *1924–1932: The Lonely Heights* (University of Toronto Press, Toronto, 1963).

——— : *William Lyon Mackenzie King:* vol. 3, *1932–1939: Prism of Unity* (University of Toronto Press, Toronto, 1976).

Newman, P. C.: *Renegade in Power: The Diefenbaker Years* (Carleton Library, McClelland and Stewart, Toronto, 1963).

Oliver, Peter: *G. Howard Ferguson: Ontario Tory* (University of Toronto Press, Toronto, 1977).

——— : *Unlikely Tory: The Life and Politics of Allan Grossman* (Lester and Orpen Dennys, Toronto, 1985).

Ondaatje, Christopher: *The Prime Ministers of Canada: Macdonald to Mulroney 1867–1985* (Pagurian Press, Toronto, 1985).

Pearson, L. B.: *The Memoirs of the Right Honourable Lester B. Pearson:* vol. I, *1897–1948* ; vol. II, *1948–1957*; vol. III, *1957–1968* (University of Toronto Press, Toronto, 1972, 1973, 1975).

Pickersgill, J. W.: *The Mackenzie King Record:* vol. 1, *1939–1944*; vol. 2, with D. Forster, *1944–1945*; vol. 3, *1945–1946*; vol. 4, *1947–1948* (University of Toronto Press, Toronto, 1960, 1968, 1970, 1971).

——— : *My Years with Louis St. Laurent* (University of Toronto Press, Toronto, 1975).

Preece, Rod: "The Political Wisdom of Sir John A. Macdonald," *Canadian Journal of Political Science*, vol. 17, 1984, pp. 459–486.

Provencher, J.: *René Lévesque: portrait d'un québécois* (Les Editions La Presse, Montreal, 1973; English edition: Gage, Toronto, 1975).

Ritchie, Charles: *Diplomatic Passport: More Undiplomatic Diaries 1946–1962* (Macmillan, Toronto, 1981).

Roberts, L.: *C. D.: Life and Time of Clarence Decatur Howe* (Clarke, Irwin, Toronto, 1957).

——— : *The Chief: A Political Biography of Maurice Duplessis* (Clarke, Irwin, Toronto, 1963).

Rolph, W. K.: *Henry Wise Wood of Alberta* (University of Toronto Press, Toronto, 1950).

Ryan, O.: *Tim Buck: A Conscience for Canada* (Progress Books, Toronto, 1975).

Schull, J.: *Edward Blake: Leader and Exile* (Macmillan, Toronto, 1976).

——— : *Edward Blake: The Man of the Other Way* (Macmillan, Toronto, 1975).

——— : *The Great Scot: A Biography of Donald Gordon* (McGill-Queen's University Press, Montreal, 1979).

——— : *Laurier, The First Canadian* (Macmillan, Toronto, 1965).

Schultz, H. J.: "Portrait of a Premier: William Aberhart," *Canadian Historical Review*, vol. 35, no. 3, Sept. 1964.

Sévigny, P.: *This Game of Politics* (McClelland and Stewart, Toronto, 1965).

Shaw, B. (ed.): *The Gospel according to Saint Pierre (Trudeau)* (Richmond Hill Pocket Books, Simon and Schuster, 1969).

Sheppard, C.-A.: *Dossier Wagner* (Les Editions du jour, Montreal, 1972).

Sherman, P.: *Bennett* (McClelland and Stewart, Toronto, 1966). About W. A. C. Bennett.

Shugarman, David: "David Lewis 1909–1981," *Canadian Forum*, vol. 61, no. 712, Sept./Oct. 1981, pp. 4–5.

Smallwood, Hon. J. R.: *I Chose Canada* (Macmillan, Toronto, 1981). Memoirs.
Smith, D.: *Gentle Patriot: A Political Biography of Walter Gordon* (Hurtig, Edmonton, 1973).
Steeves, D. G.: *The Compassionate Rebel: Ernest E. Winch and His Times* (Evergreen Press, Vancouver, 1960).
Stewart, M. and D. Frech: *Ask No Quarter: A Biography of Agnes MacPhail* (Longman, Green, Toronto, 1959).
Stewart, W.: *Shrug: Trudeau in Power* (New Press, Toronto, 1972).
Stinson, L.: *Political Warriors: Recollections of a Social Democrat* (Queenston House, Winnipeg, 1975).
Stursberg, Peter: *Diefenbaker: Leadership Gained, 1956–1962* (University of Toronto Press, Toronto, 1975).
—— : *Diefenbaker: Leadership Lost, 1962–1967* (University of Toronto Press, Toronto, 1976).
—— (ed.): *Lester Pearson and the American Dilemma* (Doubleday, Toronto, 1980).
Thomson, D. C.: *Alexander MacKenzie: Clear Grit* (Macmillan, Toronto, 1960).
—— : *Louis St. Laurent: Canadian* (Macmillan, Toronto, 1967).
Thordarson, B.: *Lester Pearson, Diplomat and Politician* (Oxford University Press, Toronto, 1974).
Trudeau, P. E.: *Conversation with Canadians* (University of Toronto Press, Toronto, 1972).
Van Dusen, T.: *The Chief* (McGraw-Hill, Toronto, 1968). About Diefenbaker.
Vigod, Bernard L.: *Quebec before Duplessis: The Political Career of Louis-Alexandre Taschereau* (McGill-Queen's University Press, Kingston and Montreal, 1986).
Waite, P. B.: *The Man from Halifax: Sir John Thompson, Prime Minister* (University of Toronto Press, Toronto, 1985).
Wallace, W. S.: *The Macmillan Dictionary of Canadian Biography*, 3rd ed. (Macmillan, Toronto, 1963).
Ward, N. (ed.): *A Party Politician: The Memoirs of Chubby Power* (Macmillan, Toronto, 1966).
Watkins, E.: *R. B. Bennett* (Kingswood House, Toronto, 1963).
Westell, A.: *Paradox: Trudeau as Prime Minister* (Prentice-Hall, Toronto, 1972).
Williams, David Ricardo: *Duff: A Life in the Law* (University of British Columbia Press, Vancouver, 1984).
Young, W. D.: "M. J. Coldwell: The Making of a Social Democrat," *Journal of Canadian Studies*, vol. 9, no. 3, Aug. 1974.
Zink, L.: "Trudeaucracy," *Toronto Sun*, 1972.
Zolf, L.: *Dance of the Dialectic* (James, Lewis & Samuel, Toronto, 1973).
—— : *Just Watch Me: Remembering Pierre Trudeau* (James Lorimer, Toronto, 1984).

INTEREST GROUPS

Atkinson, M. and W. Coleman: "Corporatism and Industrial Policy," in A. Cawson (ed.), *Meso-corporatism* (Sage, Beverly Hills, 1985).
Badgley, Robin F. and Samuel Wolfe: *Doctors' Strike* (Macmillan, Toronto, 1967), pp. 133–153.
Beland, F.: "L'Anti-congrès," *Recherches sociographiques*, vol. 13, 1972, pp. 381–397.
Belanger, P. R. and L. Maheu: "Pratique politique étudiante au Québec," *Recherches sociographiques*, vol. 13, 1972, pp. 309–342.

Bentley, A. F.: *The Process of Government*, ed. Peter Odegard (Belknap Press of Harvard University Press, Cambridge, 1967).

Berry, G. R.: "The Oil Lobby and the Energy Crisis," *Canadian Public Administration*, vol. 17, 1974, pp. 600–635.

Boase, Joan: "Regulation and the Paramedical Professions: An Interest Group Study," *Canadian Public Administration*, vol. 25, no. 3, 1982, pp. 332–353.

Bon, Daniel L.: *Lobbying: A Right? A Necessity? A Danger?* (The Conference Board of Canada, Ottawa, 1981).

Cameron *et al.*: "A Crisis in the Organization of Health Care," in Richard Laskin (ed.), *Social Problems: A Canadian Profile* (McGraw-Hill, New York, 1964), pp. 330–360.

Clark, S. D.: *The Canadian Manufacturers' Association* (University of Toronto Press, Toronto, 1939).

—— : "Group Interests in Canadian Politics," in J. H. Aitchison, *The Political Process in Canada* (University of Toronto Press, Toronto, 1963).

Coleman, William D.: "Analysing the Associative Action of Business: Policy Advocacy and Policy Participation," *Canadian Public Administration*, vol. 28, no. 3, 1985, pp. 413–33.

—— and Wyn P. Grant: "Regional Differentiation of Business Interest Associations: A Comparison of Canada and the United Kingdom," *Canadian Journal of Political Science*, vol. 18, 1985, pp. 3–29.

—— and Henry J. Jacek: "The Roles and Activities of Business Interest Associations in Canada," *Canadian Journal of Political Science*, vol. 16, 1983, pp. 257–280.

Dawson, H. J.: "The Canadian Federation of Agriculture," *Canadian Public Administration*, vol. 6, 1963, pp. 92–118.

—— : "The Consumers' Association of Canada," *Canadian Public Administration*, vol. 5, 1963, pp. 92–118.

—— : "Relations between Farm Organizations and Civil Service in Canada and Great Britain," *Canadian Public Administration*, vol. 19, 1967, pp. 470.

Dion, Léon: *Société et politique: la vie des groupes:* vol. 1, *Fondements de la société libérale;* vol. 2, *Dynamique de la société libérale* (Les Presses de l'Université Laval, Quebec, 1971).

Doern, G. B.: *Science and Politics in Canada* (McGill-Queen's Press, Montreal, 1971).

Eckstein, Harry: "Group Theory and Comparative Study of Pressure Groups," in H. Eckstein and D. Apter (eds.), *Comparative Politics* (The Free Press, Glencoe, 1963).

—— : *Pressure Group Politics* (Allen and Unwin, London, 1960).

Forbes, J. D.: *Institutional and Influence Groups in the Canadian Food System Policy Process*, study prepared for the Economic Council of Canada Regulatory Reference (Ottawa, Jan. 1982).

Fulton, M. Jane and W. T. Stanbury: "Comparative Lobbying Strategies in Influencing Health Care Policy," *Canadian Public Adminstration*, vol. 28, no. 2, 1985, pp. 269–300.

Gouldner, Janet W.: "The Doctors' Strike: Change and Resistance to Change in Saskatchewan," in Seymour Martin Lipset (ed.), *Agrarian Socialism* (Anchor Books, Doubleday, Garden City, 1968), pp. 393–404.

Gray, Charlotte: "Friendly Persuasion," *Saturday Night*. vol. 98, Mar. 1983, pp. 11–14.

Heclo, Hugh: "Issue Networks and the Executive Establishment," in Anthony King (ed.), *New American Political System* (American Enterprise Institute Publishers, Washington, D. C., 1978), pp. 87–124.

Horowitz, Gad: *Canadian Labour in Politics* (University of Toronto Press, Toronto, 1968).

Krueger, Cynthia: "Praise Protest: The Medicare Conflict in Saskatchewan," in Seymour Martin Lipset (ed.), *Agrarian Socialism* (Anchor Books, Doubleday, Garden City, 1968), pp. 405–434.

Kwavnick, D.: *Organized Labour and Pressure Politics: The Canadian Labour Congress, 1956–1968* (McGill-Queen's University Press, Montreal and London, 1972).

―――― : "Pressure-group Demands and Organizational Objectives: The CNTU, the Laplame Affair, and National Bargaining Units," *Canadian Journal of Political Science*, vol. 6, 1973, pp. 582–601.

―――― : "Pressure Group Demands and the Struggle for Organizational Status: The Case of Organized Labour in Canada," *Canadian Journal of Political Science*, vol. 3, 1970, pp. 56–72.

Litvak, Isaiah A.: "Lobbying Strategies and Business Interest Groups," *Business Quarterly*, vol. 48, no. 2, 1983, pp. 130–138.

―――― and Christopher J. Maule: "Interest-group Tactics and the Politics of Foreign Investment: The Time–Reader's Digest Case Study," *Canadian Journal of Political Science*, vol. 7, 1974, pp. 616–629.

Lowi, T. M.: *The End of Liberalism* (W. W. Norton, New York, 1969).

McBride, Stephen: "Public Policy as a Determinant of Interest Group Behaviour: The Canadian Labour Congress' Corporatist Initiative, 1976–1978," *Canadian Journal of Political Science*, vol. 16, 1983, pp. 501–517.

MacDonald, David: "Is Lobbying MPs Worth the Effort?" *Parliamentary Government*, vol. 2, no. 1, 1980, pp. 11–12.

Macridis, Roy: "Groups and Group Theory," in R. C. Macridis and B. E. Brown, *Comparative Politics* (Dorsey Press, Homewood, Ill., 1964, pp. 103–117.

Malvern, Paul: *Persuaders: Influence Peddling, Lobbying and Political Corruption in Canada* (Methuen, Toronto, 1985).

Manzer, R.: "Selective Inducements and the Development of Pressure Groups: The Case of the Canadian Teachers' Association," *Canadian Journal of Political Science*, vol. 2, 1969, pp. 103–117.

Park, L. C. and F. W. Park: *Anatomy of Big Business in Canada* (James, Lewis and Samuel, Toronto, 1973).

Pigott, Jean E.: "Lobbyists: Canada's Fifth Estate," *The Canadian Business Review*, Winter 1979–80, pp. 30–32.

Porter, John: *The Vertical Mosaic* (University of Toronto Press, Toronto, 1965), ch. 17, pp. 52–558.

Presthus, Robert: *Elite Accommodation in Canadian Politics* (Macmillan, Toronto, 1973).

―――― : "Interest Groups and the Canadian Parliament: Activities, Interaction, Legitimacy and Influence," *Canadian Journal of Political Science*, vol. 4, 1971, pp. 444–460.

Pross, A. P.: "Canadian Pressure Groups in the 1970s: Their Role and Their Relations with the Public Service," *Canadian Public Administration*, vol. 18, 1975, pp. 121–135.

―――― (ed.): "Governing under Pressure: The Special Interest Groups," *Canadian Public Administration*, vol. 25, no. 2, 1982 (special issue).

―――― : *Group Politics and Public Policy* (Oxford University Press, Toronto, 1986).

―――― : "Pressure Groups: Talking Chameleons," in Michael S. Whittington and Glen Williams (eds.), *Canadian Politics in the 1980s*, 2nd ed. (Methuen, Toronto, 1984), pp. 287–311.

―――― : *Pressure Group Behaviour in Canadian Politics* (McGraw-Hill Ryerson, Toronto, 1975).

Salisbury, R. H.: "Interest Representation: The Dominance of Institutions," *American Political Science Review*, vol. 78, Mar. 1984, pp. 64–76.

Skogstad, Grace: "Interest Groups, Representation and Conflict Management in the Standing Committees of the House of Commons," *Canadian Journal of Political Science*, vol. 18, no. 4, 1985, pp. 739–772.

Stanbury, W. T.: *Business-Government Relations in Canada* (Methuen, Toronto, 1986).

Taylor, Malcolm G.: "The Role of the Medical Profession in the Formulation and Execution of Public Policy," *Canadian Public Administration*, vol. 13, 1970, pp. 233–55.

Thompson, F. and W. T. Stanbury: "Looking Out for No. 1: Incumbency and Interest Group Politics," *Canadian Public Policy*, vol. 2, 1984, pp. 239–144.

———— : *The Political Economy of Interest Groups in the Legislative Process in Canada* (Institute for Research on Public Policy, Montreal, 1979).

Thorburn, H. G.: *Interest Groups in the Canadian Federal System*, study prepared for the Royal Commission on the Economic Union and Development Prospects for Canada (University of Toronto Press, Toronto, 1985).

———— : "Pressure Groups in Canadian Politics," *Canadian Journal of Economics and Political Science*, vol. 30, 1964, pp. 157–174.

Toner, Glen and G. Bruce Doern: "The Two Energy Crises and Canadian Oil and Gas Interest Groups: A Re-examination of Berry's Propositions," *Canadian Journal of Political Science*, vol. 19, no. 2, pp. 467–493.

Truman, David Bicknell: *The Governmental Process* (Knopf, New York, 1951).

Walker, Jack L.: "The Origins and Maintenance of Interest Groups in America," *American Political Science Review*, vol. 77, no. 2, 1983, pp. 390–406.

Zeigler, Harmon: *Interest Groups in American Society* (Prentice-Hall, Englewood Cliffs, 1964).

THE AUTHORITIES AND ELITES OF THE CANADIAN POLITICAL SYSTEM

Note: Many of the political biographies previously listed are relevant here since they present descriptions and background information on many of Canada's more important politicians.

Canada, Prime Minister, Task Force on the Structure of Canadian Industry: *Foreign Ownership and the Structure of Canadian Industry* (The Watkins Report) (Queen's Printer, Ottawa 1968).

Carroll, William: "The Canadian Corporate Elite: Financiers or Finance Capitalists," *Studies in Political Economy*, vol. 8, Summer 1982, pp. 89–114.

Cawson, A.: *Corporatism and Welfare* (Heinemann, London, 1982).

Clement, Wallace: *The Canadian Corporate Elite: An Analysis of Economic Power* (McClelland and Stewart, Toronto, 1975).

———— : "Inequality of Access: Characteristics of the Canadian Corporate Elite," *Canadian Review of Sociology and Anthropology*, vol. 12, 1975, pp. 33–52.

Dion, Léon: "The Concept of Political Leadership: An Analysis," *Canadian Journal of Political Science*, vol. 1, 1968, pp. 2–17.

Fox, Paul: "The Representative Nature of the Canadian Cabinet," in Paul Fox (ed.), *Politics: Canada* (McGraw-Hill, Toronto, 1970), pp. 341–345.

Gibson, F. W. (ed.): *Cabinet Formation and Bicultural Relations*, Royal Commission on Bilingualism and Biculturalism study no. 6 (Queen's Printer, Ottawa, 1970).

Hockin, Thomas A.: *Apex of Power: The Prime Minister and Political Leadership in Canada* (Prentice-Hall, Toronto, 1971).

House, J. D.: "The Social Organization of Multinational Corporations: Canadian Subsidiaries in the Oil Industry," *Canadian Review of Sociology and Anthropology*, vol. 14, 1977, p. 1–14.

Irvine, William P.: *Cultural Conflict in Canada: The Erosion of Consociational Politics* (University Microfilms, Ann Arbor, Mich., 1973).

Kornberg, Alan: *Note:* See also the extensive list of studies by Kornberg and his collaborators in the section "Parliamentary Process," infra.

—— : *Canadian Legislative Behavior: A Study of the 25th Parliament* (Holt Rinehart and Winston, New York, 1967).

—— : "Parliament in Canadian Society," in A. Kornberg, Lloyd A. Musolf *et al.*, *Legislatures in Developmental Perspective* (Duke University Press, Durham, 1970), pp. 55–128.

—— : "The Social Basis of Leadership in a Canadian House of Commons," *Australian Journal of Politics and History*, vol. 11, 1965, pp. 324–334.

—— and Norman C. Thomas: "The Political Socialization of National Legislative Elites in the United States and Canada," *Journal of Politics*, vol. 27, 1965, pp. 761–775.

—— and ——: "Representative Democracy and Political Elites in Canada and the United States," *Parliamentary Affairs*, vol. 19, 1965–66, pp. 91–102.

—— and W. H. Winsbrough: "The Recruitment of Canadian Members of Parliament," *American Political Science Review*, vol. 63, 1968, pp. 1242–1257.

Laponce, J. A.: "The Religious Background of Canadian M.P.'s," *Political Studies*, vol. 1, 1958, pp. 253–258.

Lehmbruch, G. and Philippe C. Schmitter (eds.): *Patterns of Corporatist Policy-making* (Sage, Beverly Hills, 1982).

MacQuarrie, H. N.: "The Formation of Borden's First Cabinet," *Canadian Journal of Economics and Political Science*, vol. 23, 1957, pp. 90–104.

McRae, K. D. (ed.): *Consociational Democracy* (McClelland and Stewart, Toronto, 1974).

Murray, V. V. and C. J. McMillan: "Business-Government Relations in Canada: A Conceptual Map," *Canadian Public Administration*, vol. 26, no. 4, 1983, pp. 591–609.

Newman, P. C.: *The Acquisitors*, 2 vols. (McClelland, Toronto, 1981).

Niosi, Jorge: *Canadian Capitalism* (James Lorimer, Toronto, 1981).

Noel, S. J. R.: "Consociational Democracy and Canadian Federalism," *Canadian Journal of Political Science*, vol. 4, 1971, pp. 15–18.

Olsen, D.: "Power, Elites and Society," *Canadian Review of Sociology and Anthropology*, vol. 18, no. 5, 1981 (special issue in memory of John Porter), pp. 607–614.

—— : *The State Elite* (McClelland and Stewart, Toronto, 1980).

Panitch, Leo: "Corporatism in Canada," *Studies in Political Economy*, vol. 1, Spring 1979, pp. 43–92.

Porter, John: *The Vertical Mosaic* (University of Toronto Press, Toronto, 1965).

Pratt, L. R. and A. Tupper: "The Politics of Accountability: Executive Discretion and Democratic Control," *Canadian Public Policy*, vol. 6, Supplement, 1980, pp. 254–264.

Presthus, Robert: *Elite Accommodation in Canadian Politics* (Macmillan, Toronto, 1974).

Rempel, H. D.: "The Practice and Theory of the Fragile State: Trudeau's Conception of Authority," *Journal of Canadian Studies*, vol. 10, 1975, pp. 24–38.

Rick, H.: "From a Study of Higher Civil Servants in Ontario," *Canadian Public Administration*, vol. 17, 1974, pp. 328–334.

Royal Commission on Bilingualism and Biculturalism, Queen's Printer, Ottawa, 1970: *Note:* Many of the studies and working papers prepared for the Royal Commission bear incidentally on the composition of decision-making élites in Canada. Particularly relevant are (1) Beattie, C. J. Desy and S. Longstaff: *Bureaucratic Careers, Anglophones and Francophones in the Canadian Public Service,* (2) Chartrand, P. J. and K. L. Pond: *A Study of Executive Career Paths in the Public Service of Canada,* and (3) Van Loon, R. J.: *The Structure and Membership of the Canadian Cabinet.* Five copies of all internal studies have been deposited in the National Library, Ottawa and a complete listing is available there. In addition, a nearly complete listing, with a short description of each report, can be found in volume 1 of the report of the Royal Commission. Some studies have been published separately by the Queen's Printer; these are listed under the authors' names in this bibliography.

Santos, C. R.: "A Theory of Bureaucratic Authority," *Canadian Public Administration,* vol. 21, 1978, pp. 243–267.

Schindeler, F.: "The Ontario Cabinet: Definition, Size and Representative Nature," *Canadian Public Administration,* vol. 9, 1966, pp. 334–347.

Smith, David and Lorne Tepperman: "Changes in the Canadian Business and Legal Elites, 1870–1970," *Canadian Review of Sociology and Anthropology,* vol. 11, 1974, pp. 97–109.

Stevenson, Garth: "Foreign Direct Investment and the Provinces: A Study of Elite Attitudes," *Canadian Journal of Political Science,* vol. 7, 1974, pp. 630–647.

Stewart, G. T.: "Political Patronage under Macdonald and Laurier, 1878–1911," *American Review of Canadian Studies,* vol. 19, 1980, pp. 3–26.

Ward, Norman: *The Canadian House of Commons: Representation,* 2nd ed. (University of Toronto Press, Toronto, 1963).

—— and David Hoffman: *Bilingualism and Biculturalism in the Canadian House of Commons,* Royal Commission on Bilingualism and Biculturalism study no. 3 (Queen's Printer, Ottawa, 1970).

CABINET AND POLICY

Abel, Albert S.: "Administrative Secrecy," *Canadian Public Administration,* vol. 11, 1968, pp. 440–448.

Atkinson, M. M. and W. Coleman: "Bureaucrats and Politicians in Canada: An Examination of the Political Administration Model," *Comparative Political Studies,* vol. 18, April 1985, pp. 58–80.

Banks, M. A.: "Privy Council, Cabinet and Ministry in Britain and Canada: A Story of Confusion," *Canadian Journal of Economics and Political Science,* vol. 31, 1965, pp. 193–205. See also "Comments" by Eugene Forsey, in the same volume, p. 575, Trevor Lloyd, in vol. 32, 1966, pp. 88–90, and "Reply" in vol. 32, 1966, pp. 90–93.

Barbe, Raoul P.: "Le Contrôle parlementaire des enterprises publiques au Canada," *Canadian Public Administration,* vol. 12, 1969, pp. 463–480.

Blakeney, Allan: "Goal-setting: Politicians' Expectations of Public Administrators," *Canadian Public Adminstration,* vol. 24, no. 1, 1981, pp. 1–7.

Borins, Sandford F.: "Mandarin Power," *Saturday Night,* Aug. 1982, pp. 7–9.

Campbell, Colin: *Government under Stress: Political Executives and Key Bureaucrats in Washington, London and Ottawa* (University of Toronto Press, Toronto, 1983).

—— and G. Szablowski: *The Super Bureaucrats: Structure and Behaviour in Central Agencies* (Macmillan, Toronto, 1979).

Canada, *Guide to Canadian Ministries since Confederation: July 1, 1867–Feb. 1, 1982* (Supply and Services Canada, Ottawa, 1983).

——, Parliament, House of Commons, Special Commitee on Statutory Instruments: *Third Report* (Queen's Printer, Ottawa, 1969).

——, Royal Commission on Government Organization: *Report:* vol. 1, *Management of the Public Service* (Queen's Printer, Ottawa, 1962–1963).

—— : Treasury Board: *Planning, Programming, Budgeting Guide* (Queen's Printer, Ottawa, 1969).

Chenier, John A.: "Ministers of State to Assist: Weighing the Costs and the Benefits," *Canadian Public Administration*, vol. 28, no. 3, 1985, pp. 397–412.

—— and C. T. Burbridge: "Ministries of State: The Canadian Experience," paper presented to Learned Societies, University of Montreal, 1985.

Clark, Ian D.: "Recent Changes in the Cabinet Decision-making System in Ottawa," *Canadian Public Administration*, vol. 28, no. 2, 1985, pp. 185–201.

Commission of Inquiry concerning Certain Activities of the RCMP: *Ministerial Responsibility for National Security*, Background Study No. 3 (Supply and Services, Ottawa, 1980).

Crowley, Ronald W.: "A New Power Focus in Ottawa: The Ministry of State for Economic and Regional Development," *Optimum*, vol. 13, no. 2, 1982, pp. 5–16.

Doern, G. Bruce: *Political Policy-making: A Commentary on the Economic Council's Eighth Annual Review and the Ritchie Report* (Private Planning Association, Montreal, 1972).

—— : "Recent Changes in the Philosophy of Policy-making in Canada," *Canadian Journal of Political Science*, vol. 4, 1971, pp. 243–264.

—— : "Mr. Trudeau, the Science Council and PPB: Recent Changes in the Philosophy of Policy Making in Canada," paper prepared for the Annual Meeting of the Canadian Political Science Association, June 3, 1970, Winnipeg, Manitoba.

—— and Peter Aucoin: *Public Policy in Canada* (Macmillan, Toronto, 1979).

—— and Richard Phidd: *The Politics and Management of Canadian Economic Policy* (Macmillan, Toronto, 1978).

—— and V. S. Wilson: *Issues in Canadian Public Policy* (Macmillan, Toronto, 1974).

Doerr, Audrey: "The Role of Coloured Papers," *Canadian Public Administration*, vol. 25, no. 3, 1982, pp. 366–379.

Driedger, Elmer A.: *The Composition of Legislation: Legislative Forms and Precedents*, 2nd ed. rev. (Supply and Services, Ottawa, 1976).

Dror, Yehenzkel: "Policy Analyst: A New Professional Role in Government Service," *Public Administration Review*, vol. 27, 1967, pp. 197–203.

—— : *Public Policy Making Re-examined* (Chandler Publishing Co., San Francisco, 1968).

Etzioni, A.: "Mixed Scanning: A 'Third' Approach to Decision-making," *Public Administration Review*, vol. 27, 1967, pp. 385–392.

Forsey, Eugene: "Mr. King and Parliamentary Government," *Canadian Journal of Economics and Political Science*, vol. 17, 1951, pp. 451–467.

French, Richard with Richard van Loon: *How Ottawa Decides: Planning and Industrial Policy Making 1968–84*, rev. ed. (James Lorimer, Toronto, 1984).

Gibson, F. W. (ed.): *Cabinet Formation and Bicultural Relations: Seven Case Studies*, Royal Commission on Bilingualism and Biculturalism study no. 6 (Queen's Printer, Ottawa, 1970).

Gow, Donald John Lutton: *Canadian Federal Administration and Political Institutions: A Role Analysis*, unpublished Ph.D. dissertation (Queen's University, Kingston, 1967).

Granastein, J. L.: "Once but Not Future Kings," *Policy Options*, vol. 3, no. 3, May 1982, pp. 46–51.

——— : *The Ottawa Men: The Civil Service Mandarins 1935–1957* (Oxford University Press, Toronto, 1982).

Hawkins, Freda: *Canada and Immigration: Public Policy and Public Concern* (McGill-Queen's University Press, Montreal, 1972).

Hay, Murray A.: "Understanding the PCO: The Ultimate Facilitator," *Optimum*, vol. 13, no. 1, 1982, pp. 5–21.

Heeney, A. D. P.: "Cabinet Government in Canada and Some Recent Developments in the Machinery of the Central Executive," *Canadian Journal of Economics and Political Science*, vol. 12, 1964, pp. 282–301.

——— : "Mackenzie King and the Cabinet Secretariat," *Canadian Public Administration*, vol. 10, 1967, pp. 366–375.

Hockin, Thomas A. (ed.): *Apex of Power: The Prime Minister and Political Leadership in Canada* (Prentice-Hall, Toronto, 1971).

Hodgetts, J. E.: "The Civil Servant and Policy Formulation," *Canadian Journal of Economics and Political Science*, vol. 23, 1957, pp. 467–479.

——— : "Parliament and the Powers of the Cabinet," *Queen's Quarterly*, vol. 52, 1945, pp. 465–477.

Jackson, Robert J. and Michael M. Atkinson: *The Canadian Legislative System*, 2nd ed. (Macmillan, Toronto, 1980).

Johnson, Andrew F.: "A Minister as an Agent of Policy Change: The Case of Unemployment Insurance in the Seventies," *Canadian Public Administration*, vol. 24, no. 4, 1981, pp. 612–633.

Johnson, A. W.: "The Treasury Board of Canada and the Machinery of Government of the 1970s," *Canadian Journal of Political Science*, vol. 4, 1971, pp. 346–366.

Kersell, John E.: "Parliamentary Debate of Delegated Legislation," *Canadian Public Administration*, vol. 2, 1959, pp. 132–144.

——— : *Parliamentary Supervision of Delegated Legislation: The United Kingdom, Australia, New Zealand and Canada* (Stevens, London, 1960).

Knight, K. W.: "Administrative Secrecy and Ministerial Responsibility," *Canadian Journal of Economics and Political Science*, vol. 32, 1955, pp. 77–83.

Laframboise, H. L.: "Managerial Discretion vs. Central Agency Controls: A Bureaucratic Dilemma," *Optimum*, vol. 11, no. 1, 1980, pp. 67–72.

Lalonde, M.: "The Changing Role of the Prime Minister's Office," *Canadian Public Administration*, vol. 14, 1971, pp. 509–537.

LaMarsh, Judy: *Memoirs of a Bird in a Gilded Cage* (McClelland and Stewart, Toronto, 1969).

Lammers, William W. and Joseph L. Nyomarkay: "The Canadian Cabinet in Comparative Perspective," *Canadian Journal of Political Science*, vol. 15, 1982, pp. 29–46.

Lamontagne, M.: "The Influence of the Politician," *Canadian Public Administration*, vol. 11, 1968, pp. 263–271.

Leger, Paul C.: "The Cabinet Committee System of Policy-making and Resource Allocation in the Government of New Brunswick," *Canadian Public Adminstration*, vol. 26, no. 1, 1983, pp. 16–35.

Lloyd, T.: "The Reform of Parliamentary Proceedings," in Abraham Rotstein, *The Prospect of Change* (McGraw-Hill, Toronto, 1965), pp. 23–39.

McCall-Newman, Christina: "Michael Pitfield and the Politics of Mismanagement," *Saturday Night*, Oct. 1982, pp. 24–44.

MacDonald, Flora: "The Minister and the Mandarins," *Policy Options*, vol. 1, no. 3, Sept./Oct. 1980, pp. 29–31.

McKeough, W. Darcy: "The Relations of Ministers and Civil Servants," *Canadian Public Administration*, vol. 12, no. 1, 1969, pp. 1–8.

MacQuarrie, H. N.: "The Formation of Borden's First Cabinet," *Canadian Journal of Economics and Political Science*, vol. 23, 1957, pp. 263–271.

Mallory, J. R.: "Delegated Legislation in Canada: Recent Changes in Machinery," *Canadian Journal of Economics and Political Science*, vol. 19, 1953, pp. 462–467.

—— : "Mackenzie King and the Origins of the Cabinet Secretariat," *Canadian Public Administration*, vol. 10, 1976, pp. 254–266.

—— : "The Minister's Office Staff: An Unreformed Part of the Public Service," *Canadian Public Administration*, vol. 10, 1967, pp. 25–34.

Morton, W. L.: "The Formation of the First Federal Cabinet," *Canadian Historical Review*, vol. 36, 1955, pp. 113–125.

Newman, Peter C.: *The Distemper of Our Times: Canadian Politics in Transition, 1963–1968* (McClelland and Stewart, Toronto, 1968).

—— : *Renegade in Power: The Diefenbaker Years* (McClelland and Stewart, Toronto, 1963).

"Planning-Programming-Budgeting System: A Symposium," *Public Administration Review*, vol. 26, 1966, pp. 243–310.

Porter, John: *The Vertical Mosaic* (University of Toronto Press, Toronto, 1965), pp. 386–416.

Rabinovitch, Arthur: "The Political Dimension (What Information Should Officials Provide to Assist Ministerial Policy-making?)," *Optimum*, vol. 11, no. 3, 1980, pp. 59–70.

Rankin, Murray: "The Cabinet and the Agencies: Toward Accountability in British Columbia," *University of British Columbia Law Review*, vol. 19, no. 1, 1985, pp. 25–71.

Ritchie, A. Edgar: "Mandarins from Within," *Policy Options*, vol. 3, no. 6, Nov./Dec. 1982, pp. 59–61.

Punnett, R. M.: *The Prime Minister in Canadian Government and Politics* (Macmillan, Toronto, 1977).

Robertson, R. G.: "The Canadian Parliament and Cabinet in the Face of Modern Demands," *Canadian Public Administration*, vol. 11, 1968, pp. 272–279.

—— : "The Changing Role of the Privy Council Office," *Canadian Public Administration*, vol. 14, 1971, pp. 487–508.

Rose, Richard *et al.* (eds.): *Presidents and Prime Ministers* (American Enterprise Institute, Washington, D. C., 1980).

Rowan, M.: "A Conceptual Framework for Government Policy-making," *Canadian Public Administration*, vol. 13, 1970, pp. 277–296.

Rowat, D. C.: "Administrative Secrecy and Ministerial Responsibility: A Reply," *Canadian Journal of Economics and Political Science*, vol. 32, 1966, pp. 84–87.

—— : "How Much Administrative Secrecy?" *Canadian Journal of Economics and Political Science*, vol. 32, 1965, pp. 479–498.

Rutherford, G. S.: "Delegation of Legislative Power to the Lieutenant-Governors in Council," *Canadian Bar Review*, vol. 26, 1948, pp. 533–544.

Savoie, Donald J.: "The Minister's Staff: The Need for Reform," *Canadian Public Administration*, vol. 26, no. 4, 1983, pp. 509–544.

Schindeler, Fred: "The Prime Minister and the Cabinet: History and Development," in T. Hockin (ed.), *Apex of Power* (Prentice-Hall, Toronto, 1971), pp. 22–47.

—— and C. M. Lamphier: "Social Science Research and Participatory Democracy in Canada," *Canadian Public Administration*, vol. 12, 1969, pp. 481–498.

Schultz, Richard, Frank Swedlove, and Katherine Swinton: *The Cabinet as a Regulatory Body: The Case of the Foreign Investment Review Act* (Economic Council of Canada, Ottawa, 1980).

Scott, F. R.: "Administrative Law: 1923–1947," *Canadian Bar Review*, vol. 26, 1948, pp. 268–285.

Sharp, Mitchell: "The Bureaucratic Elite and Policy Formation," in W. D. K. Kernaghan (ed.), *Bureaucracy in Canadian Government* (Methuen, Toronto, 1969), pp. 82–87.

—— : "Neutral Superservants," *Policy Options*, vol. 3, no. 6, Nov./Dec. 1982, pp. 32–34.

—— : "The Role of the Mandarins," *Policy Options*, vol. 2, no. 2, May/June 1981, pp. 43–44.

Simeon, James C.: "Prime Minister Brian Mulroney and Cabinet Decision-making: Political Leadership in Canada in the Post-Trudeau Era," paper presented to the Canadian Political Science Association Meeting, University of Montreal, June 1985.

Smith, David: "The Federal Cabinet in Canadian Politics," in Michael S. Whittington and Glen Williams (eds.), *Canadian Politics in the 1980s*, 2nd ed. (Methuen, Toronto, 1984), pp. 351–370.

Smith, Denis: "President and Parliament: The Transformation of Parliamentary Government in Canada," in O. Kruhlak *et al.* (eds.), *The Canadian Political Process* (Holt Rinehart and Winston, Toronto, 1970), pp. 367–382.

Tennant, P.: "The NDP Government of British Columbia: Unaided Politicians in an Unaided Cabinet," *Canadian Public Policy*, vol. 3, 1977, pp. 367–382.

Ward, Norman: *The Public Purse* (University of Toronto Press, Toronto, 1962).

White, W. L. and J. C. Strick: *Policy, Politics and the Treasury Board in Canadian Government* (Science Research Associates, Don Mills, Ont., 1971).

Wildavsky, Aaron B.: *The Politics of the Budgetary Process* (Little, Brown, Boston, 1964).

Wilson, V. Seymour: "Mandarins and Kibitzers: Men In and Around the Trenches of Political Power in Ottawa," *Canadian Public Administration*, vol. 26, no. 3, 1983, pp. 447–461.

Winn, Conrad: "Cabinet Control of the Public Service," *Canadian Public Policy*, vol. 11, no. 1, Mar. 1985, pp. 126–128.

FEDERALISM AND PUBLIC POLICY

A. *Intergovernmental Institutions*

Atkey, R. G.: "The Role of the Provinces in International Affairs," *International Journal*, vol. 26, 1970–71, pp. 249–273.

Belanger, G.: "Questions de base sur toute réforme du financement municipal," *Canadian Public Administration*, vol. 20, 1977, pp. 370–379.

Black, E. R. and A. C. Cairns: "A Different Perspective on Canadian Federalism," *Canadian Public Administration*, vol. 9, 1966, pp. 27–44.

Brewis, T. N. and Gilles Paquet: "Regional Development and Planning in Canada: An Exploratory Essay," *Canadian Public Administration*, vol. 11, 1968, pp. 123–162.

Cameron, K. (ed.): *Municipal Government in the Intergovernmental Maze* (IPAC, Toronto, 1980).

Canada, Constitutional Conference: *Proceedings*, Ottawa, Feb. 5–7, 1968 (Queen's Printer, Ottawa, 1968).

——, —— : *A Briefing Paper on Discussion within the Continuing Committee of Officials* (Secretariat, Dec. 1968).

——, —— : *Report of the Continuing Committee of Officials to the Constitutional Conference* (Privy Council Office, Dec. 1968).

——, —— : *Proceedings*, Ottawa, Feb. 10–12, 1969 (Queen's Printer, Ottawa, 1969).

——, —— : *Report of the Conclusion of the Meetings*, First Working Session, June 11–12, 1969.

——, Federal-Provincial Relations Division: *Federal-Provincial Grants and the Spending Power of Parliament* (Queen's Printer, Ottawa, June 1969).

——, —— : *Taxing Power and the Constitution of Canada* (Queen's Printer, Ottawa, June 1969).

——, Prime Minister: *Federalism for the Future: A Statement of Policy by the Government of Canada* (Queen's Printer, Ottawa, 1968).

Caplan, Neil: "Some Factors affecting the Resolution of a Federal-Provincial Conflict," *Canadian Journal of Political Science*, vol. 2, 1969, pp. 173–186.

Cody, H: "The Evolution of Federal-Provincial Relations in Canada: Some Reflections," *American Review of Canadian Studies*, vol. 7, 1977, pp. 55–83.

Cole, R. Taylor: "The Universities and Governments under Canadian Federalism," *Journal of Politics*, vol. 34, 1972, pp. 524–553.

Dehem, R.: *Planification économique et fédéralisme* (Laval, Quebec, 1968).

Doern, G. B.: "Canadian Intergovernmental Liaison: Tax Agreements, Fiscal Policy and Conditional Transfers," paper prepared for the Institute of Intergovernmental Relations, Queen's University.

Doerr, Audrey: "Public Administration: Federalism and Intergovernmental Relations," *Canadian Public Administration*, vol. 25, no. 4, 1982, pp. 564–579.

Dupré, J. Stefan, Graeme McKechnie, David M. Cameron, and Theodore B. Rotenberg: *Federalism and Policy Development: The Case of Adult Occupational Training in Ontario* (University of Toronto Press, Toronto, 1973).

Gallant, Edgar: "The Secretariat of the Constitutional Conference," in W. D. K. Kernaghan (ed.), *Bureaucracy in Canadian Government* (Methuen, Toronto, 1969), pp. 47–50.

—— and R. M. Burns: "The Machinery of Federal-Provincial Relations: I and II," *Canadian Public Administration*, vol. 8, 1965, pp. 515–534.

Guindon, H.: "The Social Evolution of Quebec Reconsidered," *Canadian Journal of Economics and Political Science*, vol. 26, 1960, pp. 533–551.

Hodgetts, J. E.: "Regional Interests and Policy in a Federal Structure," *Canadian Journal of Economics and Political Science*, vol. 32, 1966, pp. 3–14.

Johnson, A. W.: "The Dynamics of Federalism in Canada," *Canadian Journal of Political Science*, vol. 1, 1968, pp. 18–39.

Jones, Richard: *Community in Crisis: French-Canadian Nationalism in Perspective* (McClelland and Stewart, Toronto, Montreal, 1967).

Koehler, N. C., Jr.: "The Impact of Canadian Energy Policy on Changing Federal-Provincial Relations: Competition between Alberta and Ottawa," *American Review of Canadian Studies*, vol. 7, 1977, pp. 1–32.

Leach, Richard W.: *Intergovernmental Relations in the 1980s* (Marcel Dekker, New York, 1983).

MacDonald, V. C.: *Legislative Power and the Supreme Court in the Fifties* (Butterworths, Toronto, 1961).

McLarty, R. A.: "Organizing for a Federal-Provincial Fiscal Policy," *Canadian Tax Journal*, vol. 15, 1967, pp. 412–420.

McWhinney, E.: "The New Pluralistic Federalism in Canada," *La Revue juridique Témis*, vol. 2, 1967, pp. 139–149.

Manzer, Ronald A: "The National Organization of Canadian Education," *Canadian Public Administration*, vol. 11, 1968, pp. 492–508.

Neill, R. F.: "National Policy and Regional Development: A Footnote to the Deutsch Report on Maritime Union," *Journal of Canadian Studies*, vol. 9, 1974, pp. 12–19.

Ontario Advisory Committee on Confederation: *Background Papers and Reports*, vols. I and II (title on dust jacket "The Confederation Challenge") (Queen's Printer, Toronto, 1967, 1970).

Ontario Economic Council: *Intergovernmental Relations* (Queen's Printer, Toronto, 1977).

Paltiel, K. Z.: "Federalism and Party Finance: A Preliminary Sounding," in Canada Committee on Election Expenses, *Studies in Canadian Party Finance* (Queen's Printer, Ottawa, 1966), pp. 1–22.

Pollard, Bruce: *The Year in Review 1983: Intergovernmental Relations in Canada* (Institute of Intergovernmental Relations, Queen's University, Kingston, 1984).

Porter, J.: "Post-industrialism, Post-nationalism and Post-secondary Education," *Canadian Public Administration*, vol. 14, 1971, pp. 32–50.

Quebec: *Le Québec dans le Canada de demain*: vol. 1, *Avenir constitutionnel et statut particulier*; vol. 2, *Vers un nouveau partage des pouvoirs*, Publications 62, 63 (Editions du jour, Montreal, 1967).

Reagan, M. D.: *New Federalism* (Oxford University Press, New York, 1972).

—— : *The Report on Maritime Union Commissioned by the Governments of Nova Scotia, New Brunswick and Prince Edward Island* (Queen's Printer, Fredericton, Halifax, Charlottetown, 1970).

Rowat, D. C.: "Relations between Universities and Governments in Canada," *Journal of Constitutional and Parliamentary Studies*, vol. 5, 1971, pp. 8–21.

Russell, Peter H.: *Leading Constitutional Decisions*, 3rd ed. (McClelland and Stewart, Toronto, 1984).

Rutan, G. R.: "Provincial Participation in Canadian Foreign Relations," *Journal of Inter-American Studies and World Affairs*, vol. 13, 1971, pp. 230–245.

Schultz, R.: "Federalism and the Regulatory Process" (mimeo) (Federal-Provincial Relations Office, Ottawa, 1979).

—— : "Intergovernmental Cooperation, Regulatory Agencies and Transportation Regulation in Canada: The Case of Part III of the National Transportation Act," *Canadian Public Administration*, vol. 19, 1978, pp. 183–207.

Sharp, M.: *Federalism and International Conferences on Education* (Queen's Printer, Ottawa, 1968).

Simeon, Richard E. B. (ed.): *Confrontation and Collaboration: Intergovernmental Relations in Canada Today* (Institute of Public Administration of Canada, Toronto, 1979).

—— : *Federal-Provincial Diplomacy: The Making of Public Policy in Canada*, rev. ed. (University of Toronto Press, Toronto, 1982).

—— (ed.): *Intergovernmental Relations*, study prepared for the Royal Commission on the Economic Union and Development Prospects for Canada, vol. 64 (University of Toronto Press, Toronto, 1986).

—— : "Intergovernmental Relations and the Challenges to Canadian Federalism," *Canadian Public Administration*, vol. 23, no. 1, 1980, pp. 14–32.

Smiley, Donald Victor: *Conditional Grants and Canadian Federalism* (Canadian Tax Foundation, Toronto, 1963).

Stein, S. B.: "Environmental Control and Different Levels of Government," *Canadian Public Administration*, vol. 14, 1971, pp. 129–144.

—— : "Symposium on Intergovernmental Relations," *Public Administration Review*, vol. 23, 1968, pp. 3–29.

Torrelli, M.: "Les Relations extérieures du Québec," *Annuaire français de droit interna-tional*, vol. 16, 1970, pp. 275–303.

Veilleux, Gérard: "Intergovernmental Canada: Government by Conference? A Fiscal and Economic Perspective," *Canadian Public Administration*, vol. 23, no. 1, 1980, pp. 33–59.

Weidner, E. W.: "Decision-making in a Federal System," in Aaron B. Wildavsky (ed.), *American Federalism in Perspective* (Little, Brown, Boston, 1967), pp. 229–255.

Wilson, V. Seymour: "Federal-Provincial Relations and Federal Policy Processes," in Bruce Doern and Peter Aucoin, *Public Policy in Canada* (Macmillan, Toronto, 1979), pp. 190–212.

Woolstencroft, Timothy B.: *Organizing Intergovernmental Relations* (Queen's University, Kingston, 1983).

B. *Federal-Provincial Finance*

Ballentine, J. G. and W. R. Thirsky: "The Effects of Revenue Sharing on the Distribu-tion of Disposable Incomes," *Canadian Public Policy*, vol. 6, 1980, pp. 30–40.

Bastien, R.: "La Structure fiscale du fédéralisme cànadien: 1945–73," *Canadian Pub-lic Administration*, vol. 17, 1974, pp. 96–118.

Benson, E. J.: *The Taxing Powers and the Constitution of Canada* (Queen's Printer, Ottawa, 1969).

Birch, A. H.: *Federalism, Finance, and Social Legislation in Canada, Australia and the United States* (Clarendon, Oxford, 1955).

Bird, R. M.: *Financing Canadian Government: A Quantitative Overview* (Canadian Tax Foundation, Toronto, 1979).

—— (ed.): *Fiscal Dimensions of Canadian Federalism* (Canadian Tax Foundation, Toronto, 1980).

—— : "The Incidence of the Property Tax: Old Wine in New Bottles," *Canadian Pub-lic Policy*, vol. 2, 1976, pp. 323–334.

Boadway, R. W.: *Intergovernmental Transfers in Canada* (Canadian Tax Foundation, Toronto, 1980).

—— and Frank Flatters: "Efficiency and Equalization Payments in a Federal System of Government: A Synthesis and Extension of Recent Results," *Canadian Journal of Economics*, vol. 15, 1982, pp. 613–633.

——, —— : *Equalization in a Federal State: An Economic Analysis* (Economic Coun-cil of Canada, Ottawa, 1982).

Boucher, M.: "La Réforme fiscale de l'impôt sur le revenu des particuliers: était-elle nécessaire?" *Canadian Public Policy*, vol. 1, 1975, pp. 527–535.

Break, G. F.: *Financing Government in a Federal System* (Brookings Institute, Washing-ton, D. C., 1980).

—— : *Intergovernmental Fiscal Relations in the U.S.* (Brookings Institute, Washington, 1967).

Breton, A.: "A Theory of Government Grants," *Canadian Journal of Economics and Political Science*, vol. 31, 1965, pp. 175–187. See also J. C. Weldon: "Public Goods (and Federalism)," in vol. 32, 1966, pp. 230–238; reply by Breton: in vol. 32, 1966, pp. 238–242; also Breton: "A Theory of the Demand for Public Goods," in vol. 32, 1966, pp. 455–467; and David M. Winch: "Breton's Theory of Government Grants," in vol. 33, 1967, pp. 115–117.

Brown, Malcolm C.: *Established Program Financing: Evolution or Regression in Cana-dian Fiscal Federalism?* (Australian National University, Canberra, 1984).

Brydon, Marion H.: *Occupancy of Tax Fields in Canada* (Canadian Tax Foundation, Toronto, 1965).

Cameron, N.: "The Taxation of Policyholders' Life Insurance Income," *Canadian Public Policy*, vol. 3, 1977, pp. 129–140.

Canada: *Dominion-Provincial Conference on Reconstruction: Submission and Plenary Conference Discussion* (King's Printer, Ottawa, 1946).

—— : *Fiscal Federalism in Canada* (Minister of Supply and Services, Ottawa, 1981).

—— : *Report of the Royal Commission on Taxation* (Cartier Commission), 6 vols. (Queen's Printer, Ottawa, 1966).

—— : *Report to the Royal Commission on Dominion-Provincial Relations* (Rowell-Sirois Report): Book I, *Canada: 1867–1939*; Book II, *Recommendations*; Book III, *Documentation* (King's Printer, Ottawa, 1940; reprinted in one volume 1954). See also Appendices 1–8.

—— , Minister of Finance: *Report of the Tax Structure Committee to the Federal-Provincial Conference of Prime Ministers and Premiers*, Ottawa, Feb. 16–17, 1970.

Canadian Tax Foundation: *The National Finances 1965–66* (Toronto, 1969–70).

Careless, A. D.: *Initiative and Response: The Adaptation of Canadian Federalism to Regional Development* (McGill-Queen's University Press, Montreal, 1977).

Carter, G. C.: *Canadian Conditional Grants since World War II* (Canadian Tax Foundation, Toronto, 1971).

Christofides, L. N.: "The Federal Government's Budget Constraint 1955–1975," *Canadian Public Policy*, vol. 3, 1977, pp. 291–298.

Clark, D. H.: *Fiscal Need and Revenue Equalization Grants*, Canadian Tax Papers, no. 49 (Canadian Tax Foundation, Toronto, 1969).

Cohen, J. and M. Krashinsky: "Capturing the Rents on Resource Land for the Public Landowner: The Case for a Crown Corporation," *Canadian Public Policy*, vol. 2, 1976, pp. 411–423.

Collings, A. F.: "The A.H.S.T.F.: An Overview of the Issues," *Canadian Public Policy*, vol. 6, 1980, pp. 158–165.

Courchene, Thomas J.: *Equalization Payments: Past, Present and Future* (Ontario Economic Council, Toronto, 1984).

—— and J. R. Velvin: "Energy Revenues: Consequences for the Rest of Canada," *Canadian Public Policy*, vol. 1, 1975, pp. 376–383.

Crowley, R. W.: "Intergovernmental and Fiscal Aspects (Graham Commission)," *Canadian Public Policy*, vol. 1, 1975, pp. 376–383.

Crozier, R. B.: "Deficit Financing and Inflation: A Review of the Evidence," *Canadian Public Policy*, vol. 3, 1977, pp. 270–277.

Dehem, R. and J. N. Wolfe: "The Principles of Federal Finance and the Canadian Case," *Canadian Journal of Economics and Political Science*, vol. 21, 1955, pp. 64–72.

Doern, G. B. (ed.): *Spending Tax Dollars: Federal Expenditures 1980–81* (School of Public Administration, Carleton University, Ottawa, 1980).

Dupre, J. S.: "Contracting Out: A Funny Thing Happened on the Way to the Centennial," *Report of the Proceedings of the Eighteenth Annual Tax Conference* (Canadian Tax Foundation, Toronto, 1965).

—— : "Tax-powers vs. Spending Responsibilities: An Historical Analysis of Federal-Provincial Finance," in A. Rotstein (ed.), *The Prospects of Change* (McGraw-Hill, Toronto, 1965).

Economic Council of Canada: *Financing Confederation* (Minister of Supply and Services, Ottawa, 1982).

Foot, D. K.: "The Demographic Future of Fiscal Federalism in Canada," *Canadian Public Policy*, vol. 10, Dec. 1984, pp. 406–414.

Gainer, W. D. and T. L. Powrie: "Public Revenue from Canadian Crude Petroleum Production," *Canadian Public Policy*, vol. 1, 1975, pp. 1–12.

Gillespie, W. I.: "The June 1975 Budget: Stabilization and Distribution Effects," *Canadian Public Policy*, vol. 1, 1975, pp. 546–556.

Good, D. A.: *The Politics of Anticipation: Making Canadian Federal Tax Policy* (School of Public Administraton, Carleton University, Ottawa, 1980).

Gordon, Roger H.: "An Optimal Taxation Approach to Fiscal Federalism," *Quarterly Journal of Economics*, vol. 98, 1983, pp. 567–586.

Graham, J. F., A. W. Johnson, and J. F. Andrews: *Intergovernmental Fiscal Relationships*, Canadian Tax Papers, no. 40 (Canadian Tax Foundation, Toronto, Dec. 1964).

Grey, R.: "Conditioned Grants in Aid," *Proceedings of the Fifth Annual Conference* (The Institute of Public Administration of Canada, Toronto, 1953).

Grubel, H. G. and S. Sydneysmith: "The Taxation of Windfall Gains on Stocks of Natural Resoures," *Canadian Public Policy*, vol. 1, 1975, pp. 13–29.

Hanson, E. J.: *Fiscal Needs of the Canadian Provinces*, Canadian Tax Papers, no. 23 (Canadian Tax Foundation, Toronto, Feb. 1961).

Hartle, Douglas G.: "The Theory of Rent-seeking: Some Reflections," *Canadian Journal of Economics*, vol. 16, 1983, pp. 539–554.

Institute of Intergovernmental Relations: *Intergovernmental Liaison on Fiscal and Economic Matters* (Queen's Printer, Ottawa, 1968).

Johnson, H. G.: "Inflation, Unemployment and the Floating Rate," *Canadian Public Policy*, vol. 1, 1975, pp. 176–184.

Johnson, J. A.: "Provincial-Municipal Intergovernmental Fiscal Relations," *Canadian Public Administration*, vol. 12, 1968, pp. 166–180.

Kitchin, H. M.: *Local Government Finance in Canada* (Canadian Tax Foundation, Toronto, 1984).

Krasnick, M. (ed.): *Fiscal Federalism*, study prepared for the Royal Commission on the Economic Union and Development Prospects for Canada, vol. 65 (University of Toronto Press, Toronto, 1986).

LaForest, G. V.: *The Allocation of Taxing Powers under the Canadian Constitution* (Canadian Tax Foundation, Toronto, 1967).

———— : *Natural Resources and Public Property under the Canadian Constitution* (University of Toronto Press, Toronto, 1969).

McClure, Charles E., Jr. and Peter Mieszkowski (eds.): *Fiscal Federalism and the Taxation of Natural Resources* (Lexington Books, Lexington, Mass., 1983).

Mackintosh, W. A.: *The Economic Background of Dominion-Provincial Relations* (McClelland and Stewart, Toronto, 1964).

———— : "Federal Finance (Canada)," in G. Sawer (ed.), *Federalism: An Australian Jubilee Study* (F. S. Cheshire, Melbourne, 1952), pp. 80–109.

Maxwell, Judith and Caroline Pestieau: *Réalités économiques de la Confédération* (L'Institut de recherches C. D. Howe, Montreal, 1980).

May, R.: *Federalism and the Fiscal Adjustment* (Queen's Printer, Ottawa, 1968).

Moore, A. M.: "Income Security and Federal Finance," *Canadian Public Policy*, vol. 1, 1975, pp. 473–480.

————, J. H. Perry, and D. I. Beach: *The Financing of Canadian Federation: The First Hundred Years*, Canadian Tax Papers, no. 43 (Canadian Tax Foundation, Toronto, 1966).

Moore, Milton: "Some Proposals for Adapting Federal-Provincial Financial Agreements to Current Conditions," *Canadian Public Administration*, vol. 24, no. 2, 1981, pp. 232–256.

Musgrave, R. A.: *The Theory of Public Policy Finance* (McGraw-Hill, New York, 1959), ch. 8.

Norrie, K. H. and M. B. Percy: *Economic Rents, Province-building and Interregional Adjustment: A Two-region General Equilibrium Analysis* (Economic Council of Canada, Ottawa, 1983).

Nowland, D. M.: "Centrifugally Speaking: Some Economics of Canadian Federalism," in T. Lloyd and J. T. McLeod (eds.), *Agenda 1970* (University of Toronto Press, 1968), pp. 177–196.

Officer, L. H. and L. B. Smith: *Canadian Economic Problems and Policies* (McGraw-Hill, Toronto, 1970).

Ontario: *Report of the Committee on Taxation* (Smith Committee), 3 vols. (Queen's Printer, Toronto, 1967).

—— , Department of Treasury and Economics: *Intergovernmental Policy Coordination and Finance* (Staff Papers, Toronto, 1970).

Pans-Jenssen, A.: "Resource Taxation and the Supreme Court of Canada: The Cigol Case," *Canadian Public Policy*, vol. 5, 1979, pp. 45–58.

Pattison, J. C.: "Government Deficits and Inflation: The Evidence Reconsidered," *Canadian Public Policy*, vol. 3, 1977, pp. 285–290.

Perry, David B.: "The Federal-Provincial Fiscal Arrangements for 1982–87," *Canadian Tax Journal*, vol. 31, 1983, pp. 30–34.

Perry, J. H.: *Taxation in Canada*, 3rd ed. (University of Toronto Press, Toronto, 1961).

—— : *Taxes, Tariffs and Subsidies: A History of Canadian Fiscal Development*, 2 vols. (University of Toronto Press, Toronto, 1955).

—— : "What Price Provincial Autonomy?" *Canadian Journal of Economics and Political Science*, vol. 21, 1955, pp. 432–446.

Plunkett, T. J.: "The Property Tax and the Municipal Case for Fiscal Reform," *Canadian Public Policy*, vol. 2, 1976, pp. 313–322.

Powrie, T. L.: "Natural Resources and Federal Provincial Fiscal Arrangements," *Canadian Tax Journal*, vol. 29, July/Aug. 1981, pp. 449–502.

Quebec: *Report of the Royal Commission on Taxation* (Bélanger Report) (Queen's Printer, Quebec, 1965).

Richardson, R. M.: "Deficit Financing and Inflation: A Reply to the Crozier Report and the Department of Finance," *Canadian Public Policy*, vol. 3, 1977, pp. 278–284.

Robinson, A. J. and J. Cutt (eds.): *Public Finance in Canada: Selected Readings* (Methuen, Toronto, 1968).

Salyzyn, V.: "Federal-Provincial Tax Sharing Schemes," *Canadian Public Administration*, vol. 10, 1967, pp. 161–166.

Saskatchewan: *Report of the Royal Commission on Taxation* (Queen's Printer, Regina, 1965).

Saunders, S. A. and E. Back: *The Rowell-Sirois Commission:* part 1, *A Summary of the Report* (Ryerson, Toronto, 1940).

Scott, Anthony (ed.): "Financing Confederation: Symposia," *Canadian Public Policy*, vol. 8, no. 3, 1982, pp. 283–310.

—— (ed.): *Natural Resource Revenues: A Test for Federalism* (University of British Columbia Press, Vancouver, 1975).

Shearer, Ronald (ed.): *Exploiting Our Economic Potential* (Holt Rinehart and Winston, Toronto, 1968).

Sherbaniuk, D. J.: "Is the Property Tax a Good Tax?" *Canadian Public Policy*, vol. 2, 1976, pp. 310–312.

Simeon, R.: "Fiscal Federalism in Canada: A Review Essay," *Canadian Tax Journal*, vol. 30, Jan./Feb. 1982, pp. 41–51.

——— : "Natural Resource Revenues and Canadian Federalism: A Survey of the Issues," *Canadian Public Policy*, vol. 6, 1980, pp. 182–191.

Smiley, D. V.: "Block Grants to the Provinces: A Realistic Alternative?" *Report of the Proceedings of the Eighteenth Annual Tax Conference* (Canadian Tax Foundation, Toronto, 1965).

——— : *Conditional Grants and Canadian Federalism*, Canadian Tax Papers, no. 32 (Canadian Tax Foundation, Toronto, Feb. 1962).

——— : *Constitutional Adaptation and Canadian Federalism since 1954*, Royal Commission on Bilingualism and Biculturalism Document 4 (Queen's Printer, Ottawa, 1970).

——— : "The Rowell-Sirois Report, Provincial Autonomy, and Post-War Canadian Federalism," *Canadian Journal of Economics and Political Science*, vol. 28, 1962, pp. 54–69.

——— and R. M. Burns: "Canadian Federalism and the Spending Power: Is Constitutional Restriction Necessary?" *Canadian Tax Journal*, vol. 17, 1969, pp. 468–482.

Smith, B.: "Myths and Realities in Mortgage Finance and the Housing Crisis," *Canadian Public Policy*, vol. 2, 1976, pp. 240–248.

Trudeau, P. E.: *Federal-Provincial Grants and the Spending Power of Parliament* (Queen's Printer, Ottawa, 1969).

——— : *Income Security and Social Services* (Queen's Printer, Ottawa, 1969).

Waverman, L.: "The Two-price System in Energy: Subsidies Forgotten," *Canadian Public Policy*, vol. 1, 1975, pp. 76–88.

Woodside, K.: "Tax Incentives vs. Subsidies: Political Considerations in Governmental Choice," *Canadian Public Policy*, vol. 5, 1979, pp. 248–256.

C. The Provinces and Territories

Abele, F. and M. O. Dickerson: "The 1982 Plebiscite on Division of the Northwest Territories: Regional Government and Federal Policy," *Canadian Public Policy*, vol. 11, no. 1, 1985, pp. 1–15.

——— and E. J. Dosman: "Interdepartmental Coordination and Northern Development," *Canadian Public Administration*, vol. 24, no. 3, 1981, pp. 428–451.

Alexander, David G.: *Atlantic Canada and Confederation: Essays in Canadian Political Economy* (University of Toronto Press, Toronto, 1983).

Angers, B.: "Considérations sur le financement des municipalités du Québec," *Canadian Public Policy*, vol. 2, 1976, pp. 599–606.

Antoft, Kell and Jack Novack: *A Guide to Local Government in Nova Scotia*, 2nd ed. (Dalhousie University, Halifax, 1985).

Beaven, Brian P. N.: "Partisanship, Patronage and the Press in Ontario 1880–1914: Myths and Realities," *Canadian Historical Review*, vol. 64, no. 3, 1983, pp. 317–351.

Beck, J. M.: *The Government of Nova Scotia* (University of Toronto Press, Toronto, 1957).

Bellamy, D. *et al.* (eds.): *Provincial Political Systems* (Toronto, Methuen, 1976).

Benajamin, J.: "La Rationalization des choix budgétaires: les cas québécois et canadien," *Revue canadienne de science politique*, vol. 5, 1972, pp. 348–364.

Bishop, O. B. *et al.* (eds.): *Bibliography of Ontario History, 1867–1976: Cultural, Economic, Political, Social*, 2 vols. (University of Toronto Press, Toronto, 1980).

Blais, André and Kenneth McRoberts: "Public Expenditure in Ontario and Quebec 1950–1980: Explaining the Differences," *Journal of Canadian Studies*, vol. 18, no. 1, 1983, pp. 28–53.

Bolduc, Roch: "Incidences du rôle accru de l'état sur la démocratie locale," *Canadian Public Administration*, vol. 23, no. 1, 1980, pp. 60–75.

Bonin, B.: "L'Immigration étrangère du Québec," *Canadian Public Policy*, vol. 1, 1975, pp. 296–301.

Caldarola, Carlo: *Society and Politics in Alberta: Research Papers* (Methuen, Toronto, 1979).

Cameron, David M.: "Provincial Responsibilities for Municipal Government," *Canadian Public Administration*, vol. 23, no. 2, 1980, pp. 222–235.

Canada: *Report of the Advisory Commission on the Development of Government in the Northwest Territories* (Carrothers Report) (Queen's Printer, Ottawa, 1966).

Canadian Arctic Resource Committee: *National and Regional Interest in the North* (Canadian Arctic Resources Committee, Ottawa, 1984).

Canadian Tax Foundation: *Provincial and Municipal Finance* (Canadian Tax Foundation, Toronto, 1983).

Careless, J. M. S. (ed.): *The Pre-Confederation Premiers: Ontario Government Leaders, 1841–1867* (University of Toronto Press, Toronto, 1980).

Chandler, M. A. and W. M. Chandler: *Public Policy and Provincial Politics* (McGraw-Hill Ryerson, Toronto, 1979).

——: "Public Administration in the Provinces," *Canadian Public Administration*, vol. 25, no. 4, 1982, pp. 580–602.

Channing, J. C.: *The Effects of Transition to Confederation on Public Administration in Newfoundland* (University of Toronto Press, Toronto, 1982).

Chorney, Harold and Phillip Hansen: "Neo-conservatism, Social Democracy and 'Province Building': The Manitoba Experience," *Canadian Review of Sociology and Anthropology*, vol. 22, no. 1, 1985, pp. 1–29.

Coates, Kenneth: *Canada's Colonies: A History of the Yukon and Northwest Territories* (James Lorimer, Toronto, 1985).

Conway, John F.: *The West: The History of a Region in Confederation* (James Lorimer, Toronto, 1983).

Dacks, Gurston: *A Choice of Futures: Politics in the Canadian North* (Methuen, Toronto, 1981).

Dobbin, Murray: "Prairies Colonialism: The CCF in Northern Saskatchewan, 1944–1964," *Studies in Political Economy*, vol. 16, Spring 1985, pp. 7–40.

Doern, Russell: *Wednesdays Are Cabinet Days: A Personal Account of the Schreyer Administration* (Queenston House, Winnipeg, 1981).

Donnelly, M. S.: *The Government of Manitoba* (University of Toronto Press, Toronto, 1963).

Dosman, E. J.: *The National Interest: The Politics of Northern Development 1968–1975* (McClelland and Stewart, Toronto, 1975).

Drugge, S. E. and T. S. Veeman: "Industrial Diversification in Alberta: Some Problems and Policies," *Canadian Public Policy*, vol. 6, 1980, pp. 221–235.

Duprat, J.-P.: "Les Institutions québécois," *Revue juridique et économique de Sud-ouest: série juridique*, vol. 22, nos. 1–2, 1971, pp. 3–31; nos. 3–4, pp. 191–223.

Dussault, R. and R. Bernatchez: "La Fonction publique canadienne et québécoise," *Canadian Public Administration*, vol. 15, no. 1, 1972, pp. 74–159.

——: "La Fonction publique candienne et québécoise: suite," *Canadian Public Administration*, vol. 15, no. 2, 1972, pp. 259–374.

Dyck, Rand: *Provincial Politics in Canada* (Prentice-Hall, Scarborough, 1986).

Eager, E.: *Saskatchewan Government: Politics and Pragmatism* (Western Producer Prairie Books, Saskatoon, 1981).

Economic Council of Canada: *Newfoundland: From Dependency to Self-reliance* (Economic Council of Canada, Ottawa, 1980).

—— : *Western Transition* (Supply and Services Canada, Ottawa, 1984).

Elkins, David J. and Richard Simeon: *Small Worlds: Provinces and Parties in Canadian Political Life* (Methuen, Toronto, 1980).

Evans, R. G.: "Health Services in Nova Scotia: A View from the Graham Report," *Canadian Public Policy*, vol. 1, 1975, pp. 355–366.

Feldman, L. D. (ed.): *Politics and Government of Urban Canada: Selected Readings*, 4th ed. (Methuen, Toronto, 1981).

Finbow, Robert: "The State Agenda in Quebec and Ontario, 1960–1980," *Journal of Canadian Studies*, vol. 18, no. 1, 1983, pp. 117–135.

Forman, Debra (ed): *Legislators and Legislatures of Ontario:* vol. I, *1792–1866;* vol. 2, *1867–1929;* vol. III, *1930–1984* (Legislative Library Research and Information Services, Toronto, 1984).

Franks, C. E. S.: "The Public Service in the North," *Canadian Public Administration*, vol. 27, no. 2, 1984, pp. 210–241.

Friesen, Gerald: *The Canadian Prairies: A History* (University of Toronto Press, Toronto, 1984).

Garr, Allen: *Tough Guy Bill Bennett and the Taking of British Columbia* (Key Porter Books, Toronto, 1985).

Gartner, G. J.: "A Review of Cooperation among the Western Provinces," *Canadian Public Administration*, vol. 20, 1977, pp. 174–187.

Gibbins, Roger: *Prairie Politics and Society Regionalism in Decline* (Butterworths, Toronto, 1980).

Gibson, Dale: "The Constitutional Position of Local Government in Canada," *Manitoba Law Journal*, vol. 11, no. 1, 1980, pp. 1–20.

Godrey, Stuart R.: *Human Rights and Social Policy in Newfoundland 1832–1982* (Creative Printers and Publishers, St. John's, 1985).

Goulding, Jay: *The Last Outport: Newfoundland in Crisis* (Sisyphus Press, St. John's, 1982).

Gow, J. I.: "Histoire administrative du Québec et théorie administrative," *Canadian Journal of Political Science*, vol. 4, 1971, pp. 141–145.

—— : "The Modernization of the Quebec Civil Service," *International Review of Administrative Services*, vol. 36, 1970, pp. 234–242.

Graham, J. F.: "An Introduction to the Nova Scotia Royal Commission on Education, Public Services and Provincial-Municipal Relations," *Canadian Public Policy*, vol. 1, 1975, pp. 349–354.

Graham, K. A. *et al.*: *Local and Regional Government in the Northwest Territories* (Institute of Local Government, Queen's University, Kingston, 1980).

Guindon, H.: "Social Unrest, Social Class and Quebec's Bureaucratic Revolution," *Queen's Quarterly*, vol. 17, 1964, pp. 150–162.

Hamelin, Louis-Edmond: "Managing Canada's North: Challenges and Opportunities: Rapporteur's Summary and Comments," *Canadian Public Administration*, vol. 27, no. 2, 1984 (entire issue).

Hourse, J. D.: "The Don Quixote of Canadian Politics? Power In and Power Over Newfoundland Society," *Canadian Journal of Sociology*, vol. 10, no. 2, 1985, pp. 171–188.

Jackson, Robert J.: *Continuity of Discord: Crises and Responses in the Atlantic Community* (Praeger, New York, 1985).

Johannson, P. R.: "Provincial International Activities," *International Journal*, vol. 33, Spring 1984, pp. 357–378.

Johnson, J. A.: "Municipal Tax Reform: Alternatives to the Real Property," *Canadian Public Policy*, vol. 2, 1976, pp. 335–346.

Kavic, Lorne J.: *The 1200 Days: A Shattered Dream — Dave Barrett and the NDP in B. C. 1972–75* (Kaen, Coquitlam, 1979).

Kornberg, Allan, William Mishler, and Harold D. Clarke: *Representative Democracy in the Canadian Provinces* (Prentice-Hall, Scarborough, 1982).

Krueger, R. R.: "The Provincial-Municipal Government Revolution in New Brunswick," *Canadian Public Administration*, vol. 13, 1970, pp. 51–99.

Kwavnick, David (ed.): *The Tremblay Report* (McClelland and Stewart, Toronto, 1973).

Leadbeater, David (ed.): *Essays on the Political Economy of Alberta* (New Hogtown Press, Toronto, 1984).

Leith, J. C.: "What Is Ontario's Mineral Resource Policy?" *Canadian Public Policy*, vol. 4, 1978, pp. 352–363.

Levesque, Terence J. and Kenneth H. Norrie: "Overwhelming Majorities in the Legislature of Alberta," *Canadian Journal of Political Science*, vol. 12, 1979, pp. 451–470.

Lightbody, James: "Dancing with Dinosaurs: Alberta Politics in 1986," *Canadian Forum*, vol. 65, no. 755, Jan. 1986, pp. 6–11.

Lomas, A. A.: "The Council of Maritime Premiers: Report and Evaluation after Five Years," *Canadian Public Administration*, vol. 20, 1977, pp. 188–200.

Lyon, Vaughan: "Minority Government in Ontario 1975–1981: An Assessment," *Canadian Journal of Political Science*, vol. 17, 1984, pp. 685–705.

MacDonald, Donald C.: *Government and Politics of Ontario*, 3rd ed. (Macmillan, Toronto, 1985).

McAllister, James A.: *The Government of Edward Schreyer: Democratic Socialism in Manitoba* (McGill-Queen's University Press, Montreal, 1984).

McCallum, John: *Unequal Beginnings: Agriculture and Economic Development in Quebec and Ontario until 1870* (University of Toronto Press, Toronto, 1980).

MacEwan, Paul: *The Ackerman Years* (Formal, Antigonish, N. S., 1980).

MacKinnon, F.: *The Government of Prince Edward Island* (University of Toronto Press, Toronto, 1951).

MacLean, Deborah: "Bill Bennett's B. C.," *Canadian Forum*, vol. 64, no. 739, May 1984, pp. 6–7.

McMillan, M. L. and K. H. Norrie: "Province-building vs. a Renter Society," *Canadian Public Policy*, Feb. 1980, pp. 213–220.

Macpherson, Ian: *Each for All: A History of the Co-operative Movement in English Canada* (Macmillan, Toronto, 1979).

McWhinney, E. *et al.*: *Municipal Government in a New Canadian Federal System*, report of the Resource Task Force on Constitutional Reform (Federation of Canadian Municipalities, Ottawa, 1980, 1982).

Magnusson, Warren: "The Local State in Canada: Theoretical Perspectives," *Canadian Public Administration*, vol. 28, no. 4, 1985, pp. 575–599.

—— : "Urban Politics and the Local State," *Studies in Political Economy*, vol. 16, Spring 1985, pp. 120–125.

—— and Andrew Sancton (eds.): *City Politics in Canada* (University of Toronto Press, Toronto, 1983).

—— , William K. Carroll, Charles Doyle, Monika Langer, and R. B. J. Walker (eds.): *The New Reality: The Politics of Restraint in British Columbia* (New Star Books, Vancouver, 1984).

Manitoba: *Report of the Royal Commission on Local Government and Finance* (Michener Report) (Winnipeg, 1964).

Mansbridge, S. H.: "Of Social Policy in Alberta: Its Management, Its Modification, Its Evaluation and Its Making," *Canadian Public Administration*, vol. 21, 1978, pp. 311–323.

Mathias, Philip: *Forced Growth* (James, Lewis & Samuel, Toronto, 1971).

Matthews, R.: "Perspectives on Recent Newfoundland Politics," *Journal of Canadian Studies*, vol. 9, 1974, pp. 20–34.

Mayo, H. B.: "Newfoundland's Entry into the Dominion," *Canadian Journal of Economics and Political Science*, vol. 15, 1949, pp. 505–522.

Michelmann, Hans J. and Jeffrey S. Steeves: "The 1982 Transition in Power in Saskatchewan: The Progressive Conservatives and the Public Service," *Canadian Public Administration*, vol. 28, no. 1, 1985, pp. 1–23.

Mitchell, David: *W. A. C. Bennett and the Rise of British Columbia* (Douglas and McIntyre, Vancouver, 1983).

Morley, J. Terence, Norman J. Ruff, Neil A. Swainson, R. Jeremy Wilson, and Walter D. Young: *The Reins of Power: Governing British Columbia* (Douglas and McIntyre, Vancouver, 1983).

Nelles, H. V.: *The Politics of Development: Forests, Mines and Hydro Electric Power in Ontario 1849–1941* (Macmillan, Toronto, 1974).

"Newfoundland: Nation and Province," *Canadian Forum*, Mar. 1974 (special issue).

Noel, S. J. R.: *Politics in Newfoundland* (University of Toronto Press, Toronto, 1971).

Paine, Robert: *Ayatollahs and Turkey Trots: Political Rhetoric in the New Newfoundland — Crosbie, Jamieson and Peckford* (Breakwater Books, St. John's 1981).

Palmer, Howard and Tamara Palmer: "The Alberta Experience," *Journal of Canadian Studies*, vol. 17, no. 3, 1982, pp. 20–34.

——: *People of Alberta Portraits of Cultural Diversity* (Western Producer Prairie Books, Saskatoon, 1986).

Perry, Robert L.: *Galt, U.S.A.* (Maclean-Hunter, Toronto, 1971).

Persky, Stan: *Bennett II: The Decline and Stumbling of Social Credit Government in British Columbia 1979–83* (New Star Books, Vancouver, 1983).

—— : *Son of Socred: Has Bill Bennett's Government Gotten B. C. Moving Again?* (New Star Books, Vancouver, 1979).

Plunkett, T. J. and K. A. Graham: "Whither Municipal Government?" *Canadian Public Administration*, vol. 25, no. 4, 1982, pp. 603–618.

Pratt, Larry and Garth Stevenson (eds.): *Western Separatism: The Myths, Realities and Dangers* (Hurtig Publishers, Edmonton, 1981).

Price, Trevor (ed.): *Regional Government in Ontario* (Science Research Associates, Don Mills, 1971).

Pugh, Robert D. J.: "Are Northern Lands Reserved for the Indians?" *Canadian Bar Review*, vol. 60, no. 1, 1982, pp. 36–80.

Rasporich, A. W. (ed.): *The Making of the Modern West: Western Canada since 1945* (University of Calgary Press, Calgary, 1984).

Rawlyk, George A. (ed.): *The Atlantic Provinces and the Problems of Confederation* (Breakwater Books, St. John's, 1979).

Rea, K. J.: *The Prosperous Years: The Economic History of Ontario 1939–75*, project of the Ontario Historical Studies Series (University of Toronto Press, Toronto, 1985).

Richards, John and Larry Pratt: *Prairie Capitalism: Power and Influence in the New West* (McClelland and Stewart, Toronto, 1979).

Richmond, D. E.: "Some Common Issues in Provincial-Municipal Transfer Systems," *Canadian Public Administration*, vol. 23, Summer 1980, pp. 252–268.

Robertson, Gordon: *Northern Provinces: A Mistaken Goal* (Institute for Research on Public Policy, Montreal, 1985).

Romanow, Roy J., Claude Ryan, and Robert L. Stanfield: *Ottawa and the Provinces: Regional Perspectives* (Ontario Economic Council, Toronto, 1984).

Rowat, D. (ed.): *Provincial Policy-making: Comparative Essays* (Department of Political Science, Carleton University, Ottawa, 1981).

Rowe, Frederick W.: *A History of Newfoundland and Labrador* (McGraw-Hill Ryerson, Toronto, 1980).

———: *The Smallwood Era* (McGraw-Hill Ryerson, Toronto, 1985).

Royal Commission on the Northern Environment (Fahlgren Commission): *Final Report and Recommendations* (Ontario Ministry of Government Services, Toronto, 1985).

Savoie, Donald J.: "The General Development Agreement Approach and the Bureaucratization of Provincial Governments in the Atlantic Provinces," *Canadian Public Administration*, vol. 24, no. 1, 1981, pp. 116–131.

Schindeler, F. F.: *Responsible Government in Ontario* (University of Toronto Press, Toronto, 1969).

Sharman, Campbell: "The Strange Case of a Provincial Constitution: The British Columbia Constitution Act," *Canadian Journal of Political Science*, vol. 17, 1984, pp. 87–108.

Siegel, David: "Provincial-Municipal Relations in Canada: An Overview," *Canadian Public Administration*, vol. 23, no. 2, 1980, pp. 281–317.

Smith, Roger (ed.): "Western Economic Development: Energy Policy and Alternative Strategies," *Canadian Public Policy*, July 1985, supplement.

Smitheram, Verner, David Milne, and Satadal Dasgupta (eds.): *The Garden Transformed: Prince Edward Island 1945–1980* (Ragweed Press, Charlottetown, 1982).

Spafford, D.: "Highway Employment and Provincial Elections," *Canadian Journal of Political Science*, vol. 14, no. 1, 1981, pp. 135–142.

Stevenson, Garth: "Quasi Democracy in Alberta," *Canadian Forum*, vol. 62, no. 725, Feb. 1983, pp. 14–15, 24.

Swainson, Donald (ed.): *Historical Essays on the Prairie Provinces* (McClelland and Stewart, Toronto, 1970).

——— (ed.): *Oliver Mowat's Ontario* (Macmillan, Toronto, 1972).

Thatcher, Colin: *Backrooms: A Story of Politics* (Western Producer Prairie Books, Saskatoon, 1985).

Thompson, M.: "Restraint and Labour Relations: The Case of British Columbia," *Canadian Public Policy*, vol. 11, no. 2, June 1985, pp. 171–179.

Tuohy, C. J.: "Medical Politics after Medicare: The Ontario Case," *Canadian Public Policy*, vol. 2, 1976, pp. 192–210.

Tupper, A.: "Public Enterprise as Social Welfare: The Case of the Cape Breton Development Corporation," *Canadian Public Policy*, vol. 4, 1978, pp. 530–546.

Veeman, Terrence S.: *Water and Economic Growth in Western Canada* (Economic Council of Canada, Ottawa, 1985).

Walsh, Bren: *More than a Poor Majority: The Story of Newfoundland's Confederation with Canada* (Breakwater Books, St. John's, 1985).

White, Randall: *Ontario 1610–1985: A Political Economic History* (Dundurn Press, Toronto, 1985).

Whittington, Michael S. (ed.): *The North*, a study prepared for the Royal Commission on the Economic Union and Development Prospects for Canada, vol. 71 (University of Toronto Press, Toronto, 1986).

———: "Territorial Bureaucracy: Trends in Public Administration in the Northwest Territories," *Canadian Public Administration*, vol. 27, no. 2, 1984, pp. 242–252.

Wilson, R. Jeremy: "Geography, Politics and Culture: Electoral Insularity in British Columbia," *Canadian Journal of Political Science*, vol. 13, 1980, pp. 751–774.

Wiseman, Nelson: "The Pattern of Prairie Politics," *Queen's Quarterly*, vol. 88, no. 2, 1981, pp. 298–315.

Wood, David G.: *The Lougheed Legacy* (Key Porter Books, Toronto, 1985).

Zastow, M.: "Recent Constitutional Developments in Canada's Northern Territories," *Canadian Public Administration*, vol. 10, 1967, pp. 167–180.

CANADIAN BUREAUCRACY

A. *Administrative Process*

Adie, Robert F. and Paul G. Thomas: *Canadian Public Administration: Problematic Perspectives* (Prentice-Hall Canada, Scarborough, 1982).

Arpin, Roland: "L'Evaluation: un moment de vérité dans le développemente de l'enseignement collègial," *Canadian Public Administration*, vol. 28, no. 1, 1985, pp. 120–133.

Arsenault, Frederic J. and Kevin Malone: "L'Innovation dans le secteur public," *Canadian Public Administration*, vol. 28, no. 1, 1985, pp. 143–149.

"Aspects of Municipal Administration: A Symposium," *Canadian Public Administration*, vol. 11, 1968, pp. 18–96.

Atkinson, Michael M. and William D. Coleman: "Bureaucrats and Politicians in Canada: An Examination of the Political Administration Model," *Comparative Political Studies*, vol. 18, no. 1, 1985, pp. 58–80.

—— and K. R. Nossal: "Bureaucratic Politics and the New Fighter Aircraft Decisions," *Canadian Public Administration*, vol. 24, no. 4, 1981, pp. 531–562.

Aucoin, Peter: *The Politics and Management of Restraint in Government* (Institute for Research on Public Policy, Montreal, 1981).

Baar, C.: "Patterns and Strategies of Court Administration in Canada and the United States," *Canadian Public Administration*, vol. 20, 1977, pp. 242–274.

Babe, R. E.: "Public and Private Regulation of Cable Television: A Case Study of Technological Change and Relative Power," *Canadian Public Administration*, vol. 17, 1974, pp. 187–225.

Bailey, A. R. and D. G. Hull: *The Way Out: A More Revenue-dependent Public Sector and How It Might Revitalize the Process of Governing* (Institute for Research on Public Policy, Montreal, 1980).

Baker, Walter A.: "Accountability, Responsiveness and Public Sector Productivity," *Canadian Public Administration*, vol. 23, no. 4, 1980, pp. 542–557.

—— : "Management by Objectives: A Philosophy and Style of Management for the Public Sector," *Canadian Public Administration*, vol. 12, 1969, pp. 427–443.

—— : "The 'Triple E' Movement and Productivity in Canada's Federal Public Service," *Optimum*, vol. 11, no. 3, 1980, pp. 5–20.

Balls, H. R.: "Common Services in Government," *Canadian Public Administration*, vol. 17, 1974, pp. 226–241.

—— : "Decision-making: The Role of the Deputy Minister," *Canadian Public Administration*, vol. 19, 1976, pp. 417–431.

—— : "Improving Performance of Public Enterprise through Financial Management and Control," *Canadian Public Administration*, vol. 13, 1970, pp. 101–123.

Benning, J. A.: "Canadian University Service Overseas and Administrative Decentralization," *Canadian Public Administration*, vol. 12, 1969, pp. 515–550.

Bieler, J. H., R. M. Burns, and A. W. Johnson: "The Role of the Deputy Minister, I, II, and III," *Canadian Public Administration*, vol. 4, 1961, pp. 352–373.

Bolduc, R.: "Le Perfectionnement des cadres," *Canadian Public Administration*, vol. 17, 1974, pp. 482–494.

Bretan, Albert and Ronald Wintrobe: *The Logic of Bureaucratic Conduct* (Cambridge University Press, Cambridge, 1982).

Bridges, The Rt. Hon. Lord: "The Relationship between Ministers and the Permanent Department Head," *Canadian Public Administration*, vol. 7, 1964, pp. 269–281.

Brodtrick, Otto: "Bureaucracy through the Ages," *Optimum*, vol. 12, no. 3, 1981, pp. 5–14.

—— and Richard Patar: "Constraints to Management in the Public Sector," *Optimum*, vol. 15, no. 1, 1984, pp. 7–21.

Brown, Douglas and Julia Eastman: *The Limits of Consultation* (Science Council of Canada, Ottawa, 1981).

Brunet, J. *et al.*: "La Gestion ministérielle et les organismes centraux," *Canadian Public Administration*, vol. 17, 1974, pp. 321–327.

Brunet, M. and A. Vinet: "Le Pouvoir professionnel dans le domaine de la santé et des services sociaux," *Canadian Public Policy*, vol. 5, 1979, pp. 168–180.

Bryden, Kenneth: "Public Input into Policy-making and Administration: The Present Situation and Some Requirements for the Future," *Canadian Public Administration*, vol. 25, no. 1, 1982, pp. 81–107.

Caiden, Gerald E. and Heinrich Siedentopf: *Strategies for Administrative Reform* (D. C. Heath, Toronto, 1982).

Cameron, David: "The Discipline and the Profession of Public Administration: An Academic's Perspective," *Canadian Public Administration*, vol. 25, no. 4, 1982, pp. 496–506.

Cameron, D. M.: "Power and Responsibility in the Public Service: Summary of Discussion," *Canadian Public Administration*, vol. 21, 1978, pp. 358–372.

Canada: *Ethical Conduct in the Public Sector: Report of the Task Force on Conflict of Interest* (Supply and Services, Ottawa, 1984).

Carman, Robert D.: "Accountability of Senior Public Servants to Parliament and Its Committees," *Canadian Public Administration*, vol. 27, no. 4, 1984, pp. 542–555.

Carrothers, A. N. R.: "Quelques Aspects du management du Ministère des affaires extérieures du Canada," *Canadian Public Administration*, vol. 20, 1977, pp. 499–512.

Carter, D. D. and Pradeep Kumar: *Recent Public Sector Restraint Programs: Two Views* (Industrial Relations Centre, Queen's University, Kingston, 1984).

Carter, Richard: "Vers une plus grande décentralisation du financement gouvernemental au Québec," *Canadian Public Administration*, vol. 28, no. 1, 1985, pp. 47–69.

Cassidy, R. Gordon and Edwin H. Neave: "Accountability and Control in the Federal Government," *Queen's Quarterly*, vol. 87, no. 1, 1980, pp. 53–62.

Chartrand, R. and A. Clayton: "Planning a Relocation: The Project Experience," *Optimum*, vol. 8, no. 2, 1977, pp. 19–30.

Commission on Freedom of Information and Individual Privacy: *Access to Information and Policy Making: A Comparative Study* (Commission on Freedom of Information and Individual Privacy, Toronto, 1980).

Cordell, Arthur J.: *The Uneasy Eighties: The Transition to an Information Society and Summary of Background* (Science Council of Canada, Ottawa, 1985).

Coté, N.: "Pour revaloriser la fonction publique," *L'Analyste*, vol. 8, hiver 1984–85, pp. 21–24.

Cutt, James: "Accountability, Efficiency and the 'Bottom Line' in Non-profit Organizations," *Canadian Public Administration*, vol. 25, no. 3, pp. 311–331.

Dahamni, A.: "Quelques Aspects du management du Ministère des affaires extérieures du Canada," *Canadian Public Administration*, vol. 18, 1975, pp. 171–188.

DesRoches, J. M.: "The Evolution of the Organization of Federal Government in Canada," *Canadian Public Administration*, vol. 5, 1962, pp. 408–427.

Dobell, N. M.: "Interdepartmental Management in External Affairs," *Canadian Public Administration*, vol. 21, 1978, pp. 83–102.

Dobell, Rodney and David Zussman: "An Evaluation System for Government: If Politics Is Theatre, Then Evaluation Is (Mostly) Art," *Canadian Public Administration*, vol. 24, no. 3, 1981, pp. 404–427.

Doern, G. Bruce: *The Peripheral Nature of Scientific and Technological Controversy in Federal Policy Formation* (Science Council of Canada, Ottawa, 1981).

—— et al.: "The Structure and Behaviour of Canadian Regulatory Boards and Commissions: Multi-disciplinary Perspectives," *Canadian Public Administration*, vol. 18, 1975, pp. 189–215.

Doerr, Audrey: *The Machinery of Government in Canada* (Methuen, Toronto, 1981).

Dussault, R.: "L'Evolution du professionalisme au Québec," *Canadian Public Administration*, vol. 20, 1977, pp. 275–290.

Dussault, René and Louis Borgeat: "Le Droit administratif: une réalité omniprésente pour l'administrateur public," *Canadian Public Administration*, vol. 25, no. 4, 1982, pp. 653–673.

Dwivedi, O. P. (ed.): *The Administrative State in Canada: Essays in Honour of J. E. Hodgetts* (University of Toronto Press, Toronto, 1982).

—— : "Ethics and Values of Public Responsibility and Accountability," *International Review of Administrative Sciences*, vol. 1, 1985, pp. 61–66.

Dye, Kenneth M.: *Controlling the Public Purse: Is Parliament's Sovereignty Threatened?* (John Porter Memorial Lecture, Carleton University, Ottawa, 1984).

Economic Council of Canada: *The Bottom Line* (Supply and Services Canada, Ottawa, 1983).

Forrest, D. G.: "Performance Appraisal in Government Service," *Canadian Public Administration*, vol. 12, 1969, pp. 444–453.

Fowke, D. V.: Toward a General Theory of Public Administration for Canada," *Canadian Public Administration*, vol. 19, 1976, pp. 34–40.

Fox, D.: *Public Participation in the Administrative Process* (Law Reform Commission, Ottawa, 1980).

Friedmann, Karl A.: "The Public and the Ombudsman: Perceptions and Attitudes in Britain and in Alberta," *Canadian Journal of Political Science*, vol. 10, no. 3, 1977, pp. 497–525.

—— and A. G. Milne: "The Federal Ombudsman Legislation: A Critique of Bill C-43," *Canadian Policy Process*, vol. 6, no. 1, 1980, pp. 63–77.

Gagnon, J.: "Le Cadre général des institutions administratives et la déconcentration territoriale," *Canadian Public Administration*, vol. 18, 1979, pp. 253–268.

—— : "Les Communications administratives," *Canadian Public Administration*, vol. 17, 1974, pp. 495–498.

Gallant, Edgar: "Politicization of the Public Service," *Dialogue*, vol. 7, no. 3, July 1983, pp. 3–4.

Garant, Patrice: *Droit administratif* (Blais, Montreal, 1981).

—— and Huguette Pagé: "L'Ombudsman: première avenue de contrôle de l'administration, ses caractéristiques, son efficacité," *Les Cahiers de droit*, vol. 23, no. 3, 1982, pp. 517–586.

Gélinas, André: "La Commission parlementaire: mécanisme d'imputabilité à l'égard des sous-ministres et des dirigeants d'organismes," *Canadian Public Administration*, vol. 27, no. 3, Fall 1984, pp. 372–398.

———: "Les Parlementaires et l'administration publique au Québec," *Canadian Journal of Political Science*, vol. 1, 1968, pp. 164–179.

Gérin-Lajoie, P.: "CIDA in a Changing Government Organization," *Canadian Public Administration*, vol. 15, 1972, pp. 46–58.

Gibbons, Kenneth and Donald C. Rowat (eds.): *Political Corruption in Canada: Cases, Causes and Cures* (McClelland and Stewart, Toronto, 1976).

Gilbert, M.: "The Glassco Commission Report," *Canadian Public Administration*, vol. 5, 1962, pp. 385–401.

———: "L'Information gouvernementale et les courriéristes parlementaires au Québec," *Canadian Journal of Political Science*, vol. 4, 1971, pp. 26–51.

Gillies, James: *Where Business Fails: Business-Government Relations at the Federal Level in Canada* (Institute for Research on Public Policy, Montreal, 1981).

Goodsell, Charles T.: *The Case for Bureaucracy: A Public Administration Polemic* (Chatham House Publications, Chatham, N. J., 1983).

Gotlieb, C. C. (ed.): *The Information Economy: Its Implications for Canada's Industrial Strategy* (The Royal Society of Canada, Ottawa, 1984).

Hartle, D. G.: "Techniques and Processes of Administration," *Canadian Public Administration*, vol. 19, 1976, pp. 21–33.

Heeney, Arnold D. P.: *Things that Are Caesar's: Memoirs of a Canadian Public Servant* (University of Toronto Press, Toronto, 1972).

Hicks, Michael: "Evaluating Evaluation in Today's Government: Summary of Discussions" (Thirteenth National Seminar), *Canadian Public Administration*, vol. 24, no. 3, Fall 1981, pp. 350–370, 371–427.

Hodgetts, J. E.: "Government Responsiveness to the Public Interest: Has Progress Been Made?" *Canadian Public Administration*, vol. 24, no. 2, 1981, pp. 216–231.

———: "Implicit Values in the Administration of Public Affairs," *Canadian Public Administration*, vol. 25, no. 4, 1982, pp. 471–483.

———: "Managing Money and People in the Public and Private Sectors: Are There More Similarities than Differences?" *Canadian Public Administration*, vol. 26, no. 1, 1983, pp. 80–83.

———: *Parliament and the Bureaucracy: Can We Keep Civil Servants Civil?* Department of Political Science, Occasional Paper No. 1 (University of Guelph, 1980).

Hodgetts, J. F.: *Canadian Public Service: A Physiology of Government 1867–1970* (University of Toronto Press, Toronto, 1973).

———: "The Public Service: Its Past and the Challenges of Its Future," *Canadian Public Administration*, vol. 17, 1974, pp. 17–25.

——— and D. C. Corbett (eds.): *Canadian Public Administration* (Macmillan, Toronto, 1960).

Hodgson, J. S.: "The Impact of Minority Government on the Senior Civil Servant," *Canadian Public Administration*, vol. 19, 1976, pp. 227–237.

Institute of Public Administration of Canada: *Financial Management and Accountability* (Institute of Public Administration of Canada, Toronto, 1980).

Jacques, J. and E. J. Ryan, Jr.: "Does Management by Objectives Stifle Organizational Innovation in the Public Sector?" *Canadian Public Administration*, vol. 21, 1978, pp. 16–25.

Kasurak, P. C.: "American Dollar Diplomats in Canada, 1927–1941: A Study in Bureaucratic Politics," *American Review of Canadian Studies*, vol. 9, 1979, pp. 57–71.

Kemball, P.: "A Scalpel for Government," *Policy Options*, vol. 3, no. 6, Nov. 1984, pp. 15–18.

Kernaghan, Kenneth: *Bureaucracy in Canadian Government*, 2nd ed. (Methuen, Toronto, 1973).

—— : *Canadian Public Administration: Discipline and Profession* (Butterworths, Toronto, 1983).

—— : "Canadian Public Administration: Progress and Prospects," *Canadian Public Administration*, vol. 25, no. 4, Winter 1982, pp. 444–456.

—— : "Changing Concepts of Power and Responsibility in the Canadian Public Service," *Canadian Public Administration*, vol. 21, 1978, pp. 389–406.

—— : "Codes of Ethics and Administrative Responsibility," *Canadian Public Administration*, vol. 17, 1974, pp. 527–541.

—— : "The Conscience of the Bureaucrat: Accomplice or Constraint?" *Canadian Public Administration*, vol. 27, no. 4, 1984, pp. 576–591.

—— : "An Overview of Public Administration in Canada Today," *Canadian Public Administration*, vol. 11, 1968, pp. 291–308.

—— : "Politics, Policy and Public Servants: Political Neutrality Revisited," *Canadian Public Administration*, vol. 19, 1976, pp. 432–456.

—— (ed.): *Public Administration in Canada: Selected Readings*, 5th ed. (Methuen, Toronto, 1985).

—— and O. P. Dwivedi: *Ethics in the Public Service: Comparative Perspectives* (International Institute of Administrative Sciences, Brussels, 1983). See also review by Kenneth W. Gibbons, *Canadian Public Administration*, vol. 28, no. 3, 1985, pp. 499–501.

—— and A. N. Willms (eds.): *Public Administration in Canada: Selected Readings*, 2nd ed. (Methuen, Toronto, 1971).

Kirby, M. J.: *Reflections on the Management of Government in the 1980s* (Alan B. Plaunt Memorial Lecture, Carleton University, Ottawa, 1980).

Kirby, Michael J.: "Shaping the Government of the 80s," *Optimum*, vol. 11, no. 2, 1980, pp. 7–15.

Kirkwood, David: "Accountability and the Deputy Minister," *Optimum*, vol. 13, no. 2, 1982, pp. 17–29.

Kitchen, A.M.: "Some Organizational Implications of Providing an Urban Service: The Case of Water," *Canadian Public Administration*, vol. 14, 1971, pp. 303–325.

Kroeker, H. V. (ed.): *Sovereign People or Sovereign Governments* (Institute for Research on Public Policy, Montreal, 1981).

Laframboise, H. L.: "Administrative Reform in the Federal Public Service: Signs of a Saturation Psychosis," *Canadian Public Administration*, vol. 14, 1971, pp. 303–325.

—— : "Conscience and Conformity: The Uncomfortable Bedfellows of Accountability," *Canadian Public Administration*, vol. 26, no. 3, 1983, pp. 325–343.

—— : "The Future of Public Administration in Canada," *Canadian Public Administration*, vol. 25, no. 4, 1982, pp. 507–519.

—— : "The Responsibilities of a Senior Public Servant: Organization, Profession and Career," *Canadian Public Administration*, vol. 27, no. 4, 1984, pp. 592–600.

Landry, R.: "L'Imputabilité des sociétés d'état," *Journal of Canadian Studies*, vol. 14, 1979, pp. 97–108.

Langford, John W.: "Responsibility in the Senior Public Service: Marching to Several Drummers," *Canadian Public Administration*, vol. 27, no. 4, 1984, pp. 513–521.

Law Reform Commission of Canada: *The Legal Status of the Federal Administration* (Working Paper 40) (Law Reform Commission, Ottawa, 1985).

Legault, A.: "L'Organisation de la défense au Canada," *Etudes internationales*, vol. 3, no. 1972, pp. 198–220.

Lemieux, V.: "L'Information administrative au Québec: faits et interprétations," *Canadian Public Administration*, vol. 18, 1975, pp. 409–427.

—— et al.: "La Régulation des affaires sociales: une analyse politique," *Canadian Public Administration*, vol. 19, 1973, pp. 27–43.

Lemieux, Vincent and Geneviève Ledoux: "Le Contrôle de l'information gouvernementale: le cas du Québec," *Canadian Public Administration*, vol. 26, no. 3, 1983, pp. 402–419.

Lemire, Jean-Marc: "Program Design Guidelines," *Canadian Public Administration*, vol. 20, 1977, pp. 666–678.

Levin, Benjamin: "Squaring a Circle: Strategic Planning in Government," *Canadian Public Administration*, vol. 28, no. 4, 1985, pp. 600–605.

Lindblom, C.: "Still Muddling, Not Yet Through," *Public Administration Review*, vol. 39, 1979, pp. 517–526.

McCamus, John D.: *Freedom of Information: Canadian Perspectives* (Butterworths, Toronto, 1981).

McCallum, Sandra K.: "Personal Liability of Public Servants: An Anachronism," *Canadian Public Administration*, vol. 27, no. 4, 1984, pp. 611–616.

Macdonell, James J.: "Comprehensive Auditing: A New Approach to Public Sector Accounting in Canada," *Optimum*, vol. 12, no. 1, 1981, pp. 35–45.

McKeough, W. Darcy: "The Relations of Ministers and Civil Servants," *Canadian Public Administration*, vol. 12, 1969, pp. 1–8.

McLeod, T. H.: "The Special National Seminar on Financial Management and Accountability: An Appraisal," *Canadian Public Administration*, vol. 23, no. 1, 1980, pp. 105–134.

McQueen, Cameron: "Linking Program Evaluation to Decision Making," *Optimum*, vol. 15, no. 4, 1984, pp. 30–39.

Mallory, J. R.: "The Minister's Office Staff: An Unreformed Part of the Public Service," *Canadian Public Administration*, vol. 10, 1967, pp. 25–34.

Meisel, John: *Bureaucrats and Reformers*, Alan B. Plaunt Memorial Lecture, Carleton University, Ottawa, 1983.

Morgan, Nicole S. with Charles Moubarak: *Nowhere to Go? Possible Consequences of the Demographic Imbalance in Decision-making Groups of the Federal Public Service* (Institute for Research on Public Policy, Montreal, 1981).

Nay, Joe N. and Peg Kay: *Government Oversight and Evaluability Assessment* (D. C. Heath, Toronto, 1982).

Normand, Robert: "Les Relations entre les hauts fonctionnaires et le ministre," *Canadian Public Administration*, vol. 27, no. 4, 1984, pp. 522–541.

Paquet, Gilles: "An Agenda for Change in the Federal Public Service," *Canadian Public Administration*, vol. 28, no. 3, 1985, pp. 455–461.

Pfefter, Jeffrey: *Power in Organizations* (Copp Clark Ltd., Toronto, 1981).

Pitfield, Michael: "The Discipline and the Profession of Public Administration: A Practitioner's Perspective," *Canadian Public Administration*, vol. 25, no. 4, 1982, pp. 484–495.

Pitfield, P. Michael: "The Office of the Auditor General as a Way to Parliamentary Reform," *Optimum*, vol. 15, no. 1, 1984, pp. 22–38.

Plumtre, Timothy: "Perspectives on Accountability in the Public Sector," *Optimum*, vol. 12, no. 1, 1981, pp. 65–72.

Pratt, L. R. and A. Tupper: "The Politics of Accountability: Executive Discretion and Democratic Control," *Canadian Public Administration*, vol. 1, 1980, supplement, pp. 254–264.

Prince, Michael J. and John A. Chenier: "The Rise and Fall of Policy Planning and Research Units: An Organizational Perspective," *Canadian Public Administration*, vol. 23, no. 4, 1980, pp. 519–541.

Privy Council Office: *Ethical Conduct in the Public Sector* (Supply and Services Canada, Ottawa, 1984).

Rankin, T. Murray: "The New Access to Information and Privacy Act: A Critical Annotation," *Ottawa Law Review*, vol. 15, 1983, pp. 1–37.

———— : "Privacy and Technology: A Canadian Perspective," *Alberta Law Review*, vol. 22, no. 3, 1984, pp. 323–347.

Rawson, Bruce: "The Responsibilities of the Public Servant to the Public: Accessibility, Fairness and Efficiency," *Canadian Public Administration*, vol. 27, no. 4, 1984, pp. 601–610.

Rea, K. J. and J. T. McLeod (eds.): *Business and Government in Canada: Selected Readings* (Methuen, Toronto, 1969).

Reuber, Grant: "Better Bureaucracies," *Policy Options*, vol. 3, no. 5, Sept./Oct. 1982, pp. 11–14.

Ridler, N. B.: "PPB: Its Relevance to Financially Constrained Municipalities," *Canadian Public Administration*, vol. 19, 1976, pp. 238–253.

Riley, Tom and Harold C. Relyea (eds.): *Freedom of Information Trends in the Information Age* (Frank Cass and Co., Totawa, N. J., 1983).

Ritchie, Gordon: "Government Aid to Industry: A Public Sector Perspective," *Canadian Public Administration*, vol. 26, no. 1, 1983, pp. 36–46.

Ritchie, R. S., A. D. P. Heeney, M. W. MacKenzie, and M. G. Taylor: "The Glassco Commission Report," *Canadian Public Administration*, vol. 5, 1962, pp. 385–401.

Riverin, Alphonse, André Gagne, Jean Turgeon, and Janon Hamel: *L'Administrateur public: une être "pifométrique"* (Presses de l'Université du Québec, Quebec, 1981).

Robertson, Gordon: "The Deputies' Anonymous Duty," *Policy Options*, July 1983, pp. 11–13.

———— : "The Public Administrator and the Public Interest: A Perspective from Ottawa," *Optimum*, vol. 12, no. 4, 1981, pp. 16–21.

Rogers, Harry G.: "Comptrollership in Departments and Agencies of the Federal Government," *Optimum*, vol. 14, no. 3, 1983, pp. 5–19.

———— : "The Impact of IMPAC," *Optimum*, vol. 11, no. 1, 1980, pp. 40–51.

———— , M. A. Ulrich, and K. L. Traversy: "Evaluation in Practice: The State of the Art in Canadian Governments," *Canadian Public Administration*, vol. 24, no. 3, 1981, pp. 371–386.

Rowat, Donald C.: "Bureaucracy and Policy-making in Developed Democracies: The Decline of Bureaucratic Influence," *International Review of Administrative Sciences*, vol. 51, no. 3, 1985, pp. 189–198.

———— : *Canada's New Access Laws: Public and Personal Access to Government Documents* (Department of Political Science, Carleton University, Ottawa, 1983).

———— (ed.): *Global Comparisons in Public Administration* (Carleton University, Ottawa, 1981).

———— (ed.): *The Making of the Federal Access Act: A Case Study of Policy-making in Canada* (Department of Political Science, Carleton University, Ottawa, 1985).

——— : *The Ombudsman Plan: The Worldwide Spread of an Idea*, 2nd ed. (University Press of America, Lanham, Md., 1985).

——— : "The Right to Government Information in Democracies," *International Review of Administrative Sciences*, vol. 48, no. 1, 1982, pp. 59–69.

Royal Commission on Financial Management and Accountability: *Final Report* (Supply and Services Canada, Ottawa, 1979).

Rudnick, Johan: "Access to Information: Access and the Bureaucratic Milieu," *Optimum*, vol. 13, no. 2, 1982, pp. 49–59.

Sage, G. Arthur: *The Completely Civil Servant: The Bible of Survival and the Key to Prospering in the Civil Service* (Eden Press, Montreal, 1985).

Santos, C. R.: "Public Administration as Politics," *Canadian Public Administration*, vol. 12, 1969, pp. 213–223.

Savoie, Donald J.: "Government Decentralization: A Review of Some Management Considerations," *Canadian Public Administration*, vol. 28, no. 3, 1985, pp. 440–446.

School of Public Administration, Carleton University: *Approaches to the Study of Federal Administrative and Regulatory Agencies, Boards, Commissions and Tribunals* (Carleton University, Ottawa, 1974).

Science Council of Canada: *Planning Now for an Information Society Tomorrow Is Too Late* (Supply and Services Canada, Ottawa, 1982).

Segal, Hugh: "The Accountability of Public Servants," *Policy Options*, Nov./Dec. 1981, pp. 11–12.

Shoyama, T. K.: "Advisory Committees in Administration," *Proceedings of the Ninth Annual Conference* (The Institute of Public Administration of Canada, Toronto, 1957).

Sinclair, Sonja: *Cordial but Not Cosy: A History of the Office of the Auditor General* (McClelland and Stewart, Toronto, 1979).

Smith, L. G.: "Electric Power Planning in Ontario: Public Participation at a Normative Level," *Canadian Public Administration*, vol. 26, no. 3, 1983, pp. 360–377.

——— : "Mechanisms for Public Participation at a Normative Planning Level in Canada," *Canadian Policy Process*, vol. 8, no. 4, 1982, pp. 561–572.

Stead, G. W.: "The Treasury Board of Canada," *Proceedings of the Seventh Annual Conference* (The Institute of Public Administration of Canada, Toronto, 1955).

Steele, G. G. E.: "The Treasury Board as a Control Agency," *Canadian Public Administration*, vol. 4, 1961, pp. 197–205.

Studnicki-Gizbert, K. W.: "The Administration of Transport Policy: The Regulatory Problems," *Canadian Public Administration*, vol. 18, 1975, pp. 642–658.

Sutherland, S. L.: "On the Audit Trail of the Auditor General: Parliament's Servant 1973–1980," *Canadian Public Administration*, vol. 23, no. 4, 1980, pp. 616–645.

——— and G. B. Doern: *Bureaucracy in Canada: Control and Reform*, study prepared for the Royal Commission on the Economic Union and Development Prospects for Canada, vol. 43 (University of Toronto Press, Toronto, 1986).

Szlazak, Anita: "The Public Service in the Eighties," *Optimum*, vol. 12, no. 2, 1981, pp. 41–50.

Taylor, Charles L. (ed.): *Why Governments Grow: Measuring Public Sector Size* (Sage Press, Beverley Hills, 1983). See also review by R. Bird, *Canadian Public Administration*, vol. 28, no. 3, Fall 1985.

Taylor, Claude I.: "Is Comprehensive Auditing Necessary?" *Optimum*, vol. 12, no. 1, 1981, pp. 46–53.

Tellier, P. M.: "Pour une réforme des cabinets de ministres fédéraux," *Canadian Public Administration*, vol. 11, 1968, pp. 414–427.

Théberge, Ghislain: "Relations politico-administratives en période de décroissance," *Canadian Public Administration*, vol. 28, no. 3, 1985, pp. 447–454.

Whitaker, Reg: "Scientific Management Theory as Political Ideology," *Studies in Political Economy*, vol. 2, Autumn 1979, pp. 75–108.

Williams, R. and D. Bates: "Technical Divisions and Public Accountability," *Canadian Public Administration*, vol. 19, 1976, pp. 603–632.

Willis, J., J. E. Eades, H. F. Angus, *et al.*: "The Administrator as Judge," *Proceedings of the Eighth Annual Conference* (The Institute of Public Administration of Canada, Toronto, 1956).

Willms, A. M.: "The Administration of Research on Administration in the Government of Canada," *Canadian Public Administration*, vol. 10, 1967, pp. 405–416.

Wilson, V. Seymour: "The Influence of Organizational Theory in Canadian Public Administration," *Canadian Public Administration*, vol. 25, no. 4, 1982, pp. 545–563.

Winham, G. R.: "Bureaucratic Politics and Canadian Trade Negotiation," *International Journal*, vol. 33, 1978, pp. 64–89.

Wright, Robert D. J.: "The Public Administrator and the Public Interest," *Optimum*, vol. 13, no. 31, 1982, pp. 72–76.

Young, Victor L.: "The Public Administrator and the Public Interest," *Optimum*, vol. 12, no. 4, 1981, pp. 22–28.

Zelman, Maier and Peter Bovie: "The Auditor and Society: Maintaining Public Confidence," *Optimum*, vol. 12, no. 4, 1981, pp. 42–50.

Zussman, David: "The Image of the Public Service in Canada," *Canadian Public Administration*, vol. 25, no. 1, 1982, pp. 63–80.

B. *The Public Service: Personnel Administration*

Anderson, John and Marley Gunderson (eds.): *Union Management Relations in Canada* (Addison-Wesley, Toronto, 1982).

Armstrong, R.: "Some Aspects of Policy Determination in the Development of the Collective Bargaining Legislation in the Public Service of Canada," *Canadian Public Administration*, vol. 11, 1968, pp. 485–493.

Arthurs, H. W., D. D. Carter, and H. J. Glasbeck: *Labour Law and Industrial Relations in Canada* (Butterworths, Toronto, 1982).

Bairstow, F. L.: "Final Position Arbitration," *Canadian Public Administration*, vol. 18, 1, 1975, pp. 55–64.

Bauer, F.: "The Public Service Staff Relations Act and Collective Bargaining 1967–1969," *Civil Service Review*, vol. 43, no. 2, June 1970, pp. 54, 56, 58, 60, 62.

Bernier, I. and A. Lajoie (eds.): *Labour Law and Urban Law in Canada* (University of Toronto Press, Toronto, in cooperation with the Royal Commission on the Economic Union and Development Prospects for Canada, vol. 51, 1986).

Blackburn, G. A.: "A Bilingual and Bicultural Public Service," *Canadian Public Administration*, vol. 12, 1969, pp. 36–44.

Bordeleau, Yvan: "Le Style de gestion du personnel chez les administrateurs publics et privés: une question d'efficacité," *Canadian Public Administration*, vol. 26, no. 4, 1983, pp. 577–590.

Callard, K. B.: *Advanced Training in the Public Service*, Governmental Studies Number 1 (The Institute of Public Administration of Canada, Toronto, 1958).

Canada: *Strikes and Lockouts in Canada, 1983* (Supply and Services Canada, Ottawa, 1984).

————, Civil Service Commission: *Personnel Administration in the Public Service* (Heeney Report) (Queen's Printer, Ottawa, 1959).

————, Preparatory Committee on Collective Bargaining in the Public Service of Canada: *Report* (Queen's Printer, Ottawa, 1965).

————, Task Force on Labour Relations, Canadian Industrial Relations: *Report* (Queen's Printer, Ottawa, 1968).

Carson, J. J.: "The Changing Scope of the Public Servant," *Canadian Public Administration*, vol. 11, 1968, pp. 407–413.

Carson, John J.: "Is There Any Merit in the Merit System Today?" *Optimum*, vol. 12, no. 1, 1981, pp. 73–77.

Christensen, Sandra: *Unions and the Public Interest: Collective Bargaining in the Government Sector* (Fraser Institute, Vancouver, 1980).

Cloutier, S.: "Senior Public Service Officials in a Bicultural Society," *Canadian Public Administration*, vol. 11, 1968, pp. 395–406.

———— : "Le Statut de la fonction publique du Canada: son histoire," *Canadian Public Administration*, vol. 10, 1967, pp. 500–513.

Code, Taylor: *The Canadian Bureaucracy and Federalism, 1947–1965* (University of Denver, Denver, 1966).

———— : *The Canadian Bureaucracy 1939–1947* (Duke University Press, Durham, 1949).

Commission on Equality in Employment: *Equality in Employment* (Supply and Services Canada, Ottawa, 1984).

Coté, E. A.: "The Public Services in a Bicultural Community," *Canadian Public Administration*, vol. 11, 1968, pp. 280–290.

Coulson, Herbert H.: "The Professional Worker and Collective Bargaining," *Civil Service Review*, vol. 41, 1968, pp. 40–42.

Craig, A.: *The System of Industrial Relations in Canada* (Prentice-Hall, Scarborough, 1983).

Craven, P.: *An Impartial Umpire: Industrial Relations and the Canadian State* (University of Toronto Press, Toronto, 1980).

Crispo, John H. B. (ed.): *Collective Bargaining and the Professional Employee* (Centre for Industrial Relations, University of Toronto, Toronto, 1965).

Deslauriers, R. C.: "First Collective Agreements in the Public Service of Canada," *Civil Service Review*, vol. 41, no. 2, June 1968, pp. 24–36.

Deutsch, J. J.: "The Public Service in a Changing Society," *Canadian Public Administration*, vol. 11, 1968, pp. 1–8.

———— : "Some Thoughts on the Public Service," *Canadian Journal of Economics and Political Science*, vol. 23, 1957.

Dowdell, R. H.: "Personnel Administration in the Federal Public Service," in A. M. Willms and W. D. K. Kernaghan (eds.), *Public Administration in Canada: Selected Readings* (Methuen, Toronto, 1968), pp. 360–388.

Edwards, Claude: "Address to the Conference on Collective Bargaining in Public Employment, San Francisco," *Civil Service Review*, vol. 42, no. 1, Mar. 1969, pp. 2, 4, 6, 8, 10, 12, 14, 16.

———— : "Collective Bargaining in Canada between the Federal Government and Its Employees," *Civil Service Review*, vol. 43, no. 2, June 1970, pp. 2, 4, 6, 8, 10, 12.

———— : "Effects of Collective Bargaining on Staff Associations," *Civil Service Review*, vol. 41, Sept. 1968, pp. 24, 26, 28, 30, 32, 34, 36.

Finkelman, Jacob: "Some Aspects of Public Service Bargaining in Canada," *Civil Service Review*, vol. 43, no. 1, Mar. 1970, pp. 18, 20, 22, 24, 26, 28.

———— and Shirley B. Goldenberg: *Collective Bargaining in the Public Service: The Federal Experience in Canada*, 2 vols. (Institute for Research on Public Policy, Montreal, 1983). See also review by A. W. R. Carrothers, *Canadian Public Administration*, vol. 27, no. 4, 1984, pp. 678–690.

Frankel, S. J.: *A Model for Negotiation and Arbitration between the Canadian Government and Its Civil Servants* (McGill University Press, Montreal, 1962).

——— : *Staff Relations in the Civil Service: The Canadian Experience* (McGill University Press, Montreal, 1962).

Gallant, Edgar: "Service above Party," *Policy Options*, vol. 7, no. 2, 1986, pp. 8–9.

Gosselin, E., G. Dozois, R. Boyd, and G. Lalande: "L'Administration publique dans un pays bilingue et bicultural: actualités et propos," *Canadian Public Administration*, vol. 6, 1963, pp. 407–433.

Gow, Donald: "Public Administration Training: For Whom? For What?" *Optimum*, vol. 1, no. 3, Winter 1970, pp. 22–33.

Gunderson, Morley: *Economic Aspects of Interest Arbitration* (Ontario Economic Council, Toronto, 1983).

Heeney, Arnold: "Civil Service Reform 1958," *Canadian Journal of Economics and Political Science*, vol. 25, 1959, pp. 1–10.

——— : *The Things that Are Caesar's: The Memoirs of a Canadian Public Servant* (University of Toronto Press, Toronto, 1972).

Heron, Craig and Robert Storey: *On the Job: Confronting the Labour Process in Canada* (McGill-Queen's University Press, Montreal, 1986).

Hodgetts, J. E.: "Challenge and Response: A Retrospective View of the Public Service of Canada," *Canadian Public Administration*, vol. 7, 1964, pp. 409–421.

——— : *Pioneer Public Service: An Administrative History of the United Canada's, 1841–1867* (University of Toronto Press, Toronto, 1955).

——— and O. P. Dwivedi: "The Growth of Government Employment in Canada," *Canadian Public Administration*, vol. 12, 1969, pp. 224–238.

——— , William McCloskey, Reginald Whitaker, and V. Seymour Wilson: *The Biography of an Institution: The Civil Service Commission of Canada, 1908–1967* (McGill-Queen's University Press, Montreal, 1972).

Kernaghan, Kenneth and P. K. Kuruvilla: "Merit and Motivation: Public Personnel Management in Canada," *Canadian Public Administration*, vol. 25, no. 4, 1982, pp. 696–712.

Kuruvilla, K. P.: "The New Management Category in the Public Service: A Step in the Right Direction," *Optimum*, vol. 12, no. 1, 1981, pp. 77–80.

Kwavnick, D.: "French Canadians and the Civil Service of Canada," *Canadian Public Administration*, vol. 11, 1968, pp. 97–112.

Laberge, E. P.: "Collective Bargaining in the Public Service of Canada," *International Review of Administrative Sciences*, vol. 36, 1970, pp. 234–242.

Laxer, R. M.: *Technological Change and the Workforce* (Ontario Institute for Studies in Education, Toronto, 1978).

——— : *Unions and the Collective Bargaining Process* (Ontario Institute for Studies in Education, Toronto, 1978).

——— : *Union Organization and Strikes* (Ontario Institute for Studies in Education, Toronto, 1978).

Lieberman, Myron: *Public-sector Bargaining* (D. C. Heath, Toronto, 1980).

McQueen, Jennifer: "Integrating Human Resource Planning with Strategic Planning," *Canadian Public Administration*, vol. 27, no. 1, 1984, pp. 1–13.

Maslove, Allan M. and E. Swimmer: *Wage Controls in Canada 1975–78* (Institute for Research on Public Policy, Montreal, 1980).

Menzies, Heather: *Women and the Chip* (Institute for Research on Public Policy, Montreal, 1981).

Morgan, Nicole S.: *Nowhere to Go* (Institute for Research on Public Policy, Montreal, 1981).

Neilson, William A. W.: "Service at the Pleasure of the Crown: The Law of Dismissal of Senior Public Servants," *Canadian Public Administration*, vol. 27, no. 4, 1984, pp. 556–575.

Nethercote, J. R.: "Comments on the 'D'Avignon Report,' " *Optimum*, vol. 11, no. 1, 1980, pp. 5–15.

Panitch, Leo: "Socialist Principles and Collective Bargaining," *Canadian Forum*, vol. 60, no. 700, June/July 1980, pp. 16–17.

Phillips, Gerald E.: *Labour Relations and Collective Bargaining* (Butterworths, Toronto, 1980).

Robinson, K. R.: "Labour Unions in the Armed Forces," *Civil Service Review*, vol. 43, no. 3, Sept. 1970, pp. 2, 4, 6, 8, 10, 12, 14, and 28.

Simmons, C. Gordon and Kenneth P. Swan: *Labour Relations Law in the Public Sector: Cases, Materials and Commentary* (Industrial Relations Centre, Queen's University, Kingston, 1982).

Slivinski, L. W. and B. Desbiens: "Managerial Job Dimensions and Job Profiles in the Canadian Public Service: A Pilot Study," *Studies in Personnel Psychology*, vol. 2, no. 2, October 1970, pp. 36–52.

Special Committee on the Review of Personnel Management and the Merit Principle (D'Avignon Committee): *Report* (Supply and Services Canada, Ottawa, 1979).

Srinivas, Kalburgi M.: *Human Resource Management: Contemporary Perspectives in Canada* (McGraw-Hill Ryerson, Toronto, 1984).

Subramaniam, V.: "Representative Bureaucracy: A Reassessment," *American Political Science Review*, vol. 61, 1967, pp. 1010–1019.

Swan, K. P.: "Public Bargaining in Canada and the U.S.: A Legal View," *Industrial Relations*, vol. 19, no. 3, Fall 1980, pp. 272–291.

Swettenham, John and David Kelly: *Serving the State: A History of the Professional Institute of the Public Service of Canada 1920–1970* (LeDroit, Ottawa, 1970).

Swimmer, G. and M. Thompson (eds.): *Public Sector Industrial Relations in Canada* (Institute for Research on Public Policy, Montreal, 1983).

"Symposium on Collective Negotiations in the Public Service": *Public Administration Review*, vol. 28, 1968, pp. 111–147.

Thompson, Mark and Gene Swimmer (eds.): *Conflict or Compromise: The Future of Public Sector Industrial Relations* (Institute for Research on Public Policy, Montreal, 1984).

Tunnoch, G. V.: "The Bureau of Government Organization: Improvement by Order-in-Council — Committee and Anomaly," *Canadian Public Administration*, vol. 8, 1965, pp. 558–568.

Vaison, R. A.: "Collective Bargaining in the Federal Public Service: The Achievement of a Milestone in Personnel Relations," *Canadian Public Administration*, vol. 12, 1969, pp. 108–122.

Weinfeld, Martin: "The Development of Affirmative Action in Canada," *Canadian Ethnic Studies*, 1981, pp. 23–39.

Werther, William B., Jr., Keith Davis, Hermann F. Schwind, Hari Das, and Frederick C. Miner, Jr.: *Canadian Personnel Management and Human Resources*, 2nd ed. (McGraw-Hill Ryerson, Toronto, 1985).

Wilson, V. Seymour: *Staffing in the Canadian Federal Bureaucracy*, unpublished Ph.D. thesis (Queen's University, Kingston, 1970).

Wood, W. D. and Pradeep Kumar (eds.): *The Current Industrial Relations Scene in Canada* (Industrial Relations Centre, Queen's University, Kingston, 1982).

C. *The Budgetary Process*

Balls, H. R.: "New Techniques in Government Budgeting: Planning, Programming and Budgeting in Canada," *Public Administration*, vol. 48, 1970, pp. 289–305.

Bird, Richard M.: *The Growth of Government Spending in Canada*, Tax Papers, no. 51 (Canadian Tax Foundation, Toronto, July 1970).

Borins, Sanford: *The Theory and Practice of Envelope Budgetting* (York University Press, Toronto, 1980).

Botner, S. B.: "Four Years of PPBS: An Appraisal," *Public Administration Review*, July/Aug. 1970, pp. 423–431.

Brownstone, M.: "The Canadian System of Government in the Face of Modern Demands," *Canadian Public Administration*, vol. 11, 1968, pp. 428–439.

—— : *The Budget Process* (Minister of Finance, Ottawa, April 1982).

Canada: *Estimates: The Blue Book for the Fiscal Year Ending March 31, 1982* (Queen's Printer, Ottawa, 1981 or any other year; they have a certain sameness).

—— : *Guide to the Policy and Expenditure Management System* (Minister of Supply and Services, Ottawa, 1980).

—— , Parliament, House of Commons, Standing Committee on Miscellaneous Estimates: *Minutes of Proceedings and Evidence respecting Bill C–172: An Act to Amend the Financial Administration Act*, nos. 10–12 (Queen's Printer, Ottawa, 1969).

—— , Royal Commission on Government Organization: *Report*, vol. 1 (Queen's Printer, Ottawa, 1962–63).

—— , Task Force on Government Information: *To Know and Be Known* (Queen's Printer, Ottawa, 1969).

—— , Treasury Board, Program Branch: *Program Forecast and Estimates Manual* (Ottawa, 1972, periodically revised).

Canadian Tax Foundation: *The National Finances: An Analysis of the Revenues and Expenditures of the Government of Canada* (Canadian Tax Foundation, Toronto, published annually).

—— : *The National Finances: An Analysis of the Revenues and Expenditures of the Government of Canada, 1982–83* (Canadian Tax Foundation, Toronto, 1983).

—— : *The National Finances: An Analysis of the Revenues and Expenditures of the Government of Canada, 1984–85* (Canadian Tax Foundation, Toronto, 1985).

Carmichael, Edward A.: *Tackling the Federal Deficit* (C. D. Howe Institute, Toronto, 1984).

Clayton, A.: "Brother Could You Spare a Dime?" *Optimum*, vol. 12, no. 1, 1981, pp. 7–19.

Cutt, James: "Efficiency and Effectiveness in Public Sector Spending: The Programme Budgeting Approach," *Canadian Public Administration*, vol. 13, 1970, pp. 396–426.

—— and Richard Ritter: *Public Non-profit Budgeting: The Evolution and Application of Zero-base Budgeting* (Institute of Public Administration of Canada, Toronto, 1984). See also review by David Siegel: *Canadian Public Administration*, vol. 20, no. 3, 1985, pp. 506–507.

Dobell, Rod: "Pressing the Envelope: The Significance of the New, Top-down System of Expenditure Management in Ottawa," *Policy Options*, Nov./Dec. 1981, pp. 13–18.

Doern, G. Bruce: "Mr. Trudeau, The Science Council and PPB: Recent Changes in the Philosophy of Policy Making in Canada," paper presented to 42nd Annual Meeting of the Canadian Political Science Association, June 3, 1970, Winnipeg, Manitoba.

Golembiewski, Robert T. and Jack Rabin: *Public Budgeting and Finance* (Marcel Dekker, New York, 1983).

Harper, E. L. *et al.*: "Implementation and Use of PPB in Sixteen Federal Agencies," *Public Administration Review*, vol. 29, 1969, pp. 623–632.

Hartle, Douglas: *The Expenditure Budget Process in the Government of Canada* (Canadian Tax Foundation, Toronto, 1978).

———: "An Open Letter to R. J. Van Loon," *Canadian Public Administration*, vol. 26, no. 1, pp. 84–94 with replies by Van Loon and French.

———: *The Revenue Budget Process of the Government of Canada* (Canadian Tax Foundation, Toronto, 1982).

Hinrichs, Harley H. and G. M. Taylor (eds.): *Program Budgeting and Cost Benefit Analysis* (Goodyear Publishing Co., Pacific Palisades, 1969).

Hodgetts, J. E.: "The Civil Servant and Policy Formation," *Canadian Journal of Economics and Political Science*, vol. 23, 1957, pp. 467–479.

Johnson, A. W.: "PPB and Decision Making in the Government of Canada," speech to 50th Anniversary Conference of Society of Industrial Accountants, June 18, 1970.

——— : "The Treasury Board of Canada and the Machinery of Government of the 1970's," *Canadian Journal of Political Science*, vol. 4, 1971.

Jones, L. R.: "Phases of Recognition and Management of Financial Crisis in Public Organizations," *Canadian Public Administration*, vol. 27, no. 1, 1984, pp. 48–65.

Kroeker, H. V.: *Accountability and Control: The Government Expenditure Process* (C. D. Howe Research Institute, Montreal, 1978).

Lamontagne, M.: "The Influence of the Politician," *Canadian Public Administration*, vol. 11, 1968, pp. 263–271.

Lévesque, R.: *Program Budgeting in the Canadian Government*, M.A. thesis (Carleton University, 1969).

Lyden, J. F.: *Planning, Programming, Budgeting: A Systems Approach in Management* (Markham, Chicago, 1967).

McCaffery, Jerry: "Canada's Envelope Budgeting System," *American Review of Canadian Studies*, vol. 14, 1, 1984, pp. 45–62.

Malcolmson, Patricia E.: "Zero-base Budgeting: Panacea or Gimmick?" *Optimum*, vol. 14, no. 2, 1983, pp. 34–46.

Maslove, A. M., M. J. Prince, and G. B. Doern: *Federal and Provincial Budgeting*, study prepared for the Royal Commission on the Economic Union and Development Prospects for Canada, vol. 41 (University of Toronto Press, Toronto, 1986).

Normanton, E. L.: *The Accountability and Audit of Governments* (Manchester University Press, Manchester, England; Praeger, New York, 1966).

Novick, David (ed.): *Program Budgeting* (Harvard University Press, Cambridge, 1965).

"Planning-Programming-Budgeting System: A Symposium," *Public Administration Review*, vol. 26, 1966, pp. 243–310.

Robinson, A. J. and James Cutt: *Public Finance in Canada: Selected Readings* (Methuen, Toronto, 1968).

Strick, J. C.: "Recent Developments in Canadian Administration," *Public Administration Review*, vol. 48, 1970, pp. 69–85.

Thomas, Paul G.: "Public Administration and Expenditure Management," *Canadian Public Administration*, vol. 25, no. 4, 1982, pp. 674–695.

Van Loon, Richard: "Ottawa's Expenditure Process: Four Systems in Search of Coordination," in G. B. Doern (ed.), *How Ottawa Spends* (James Lorimer, Toronto, 1983).

———: "The Policy and Expenditure Management System in the Federal Government:

The First Three Years," *Canadian Public Administration*, vol. 26, no. 2, 1983, pp. 255–285.

——: "Stop the Music: The Current Policy and Expenditure Management System in Ottawa," *Canadian Public Administration*, vol. 24, no. 2, 1981, pp. 175–199.

Ward, Norman: *The Public Purse* (University of Toronto Press, Toronto, 1962).

White, W. L. and J. C. Strick: *Policy, Politics and the Treasury Board in Canadian Government* (Science Research Associates, Don Mills, Ontario, 1970).

Wildavsky, Aaron: "From Chaos Comes Opportunity: The Movement toward Spending Limits in American and Canadian Budgeting," *Canadian Public Administration*, vol. 26, no. 2, 1983, pp. 162–181.

——: *The Politics of the Budgetary Process* (Little, Brown, Boston, 1964).

D. Crown Corporations, Regulatory Bodies and Administrative Tribunals

Ashley, C. A.: *The First Twenty-five Years: A Study of Trans-Canada Air Lines* (Macmillan, Toronto, 1965).

—— and R. G. H. Smails: *Canadian Crown Corporations* (Macmillan, Toronto, 1965).

Baldwin, John R.: *The Regulatory Agency and the Public Corporation: The Canadian Air Transport Industry* (Ballinger, Cambridge, Mass., 1975).

Baram, Michael S.: *Alternatives to Regulation* (D. C. Heath, Toronto, 1982).

Barbe, R. P.: "Le Contrôle parlementaire des entreprises au Canada," *Canadian Public Administration*, vol. 12, 1969, pp. 463–480.

Bernier, I. and A. Lajoie (eds.): *Regulations, Crown Corporations and Administrative Tribunals*, study prepared for the Royal Commission on the Economic Union and Development Prospects for Canada, vol. 48 (University of Toronto Press, Toronto, 1986).

Borins, Sandford: "World War Two Crown Corporations: Their Wartime Role and Peacetime Privatization," *Canadian Public Administration*, vol. 5, no. 2, 1982, pp. 380–404.

Brooks, Stephen: "The State as Entrepreneur: From CDC to CDIC," *Canadian Public Administration*, vol. 26, no. 4, Winter 1983, pp. 525–543.

—— and A. Brian Tanguay: "Quebec's Caisse de dépôt et placement: Tool of Nationalism," *Canadian Public Administration*, vol. 28, no. 1, 1983, pp. 99–119.

Brown-John, C. L.: *Canadian Regulatory Agencies* (Butterworths, Toronto, 1981).

——: "Membership in Canadian Regulatory Agencies," *Canadian Public Administration*, vol. 20, no. 3, 1977, pp. 513–533.

Brown-John, Lloyd: "Comprehensive Regulatory Consultation in Canada's Food Processing Industry," *Canadian Public Administration*, vol. 28, no. 1, 1985, pp. 70–98.

Cairns, Robert D.: *Rationale for Regulation*, Regulatory Reference Technical Report No. 2 (Economic Council of Canada, Ottawa, 1980).

Calvert, John: *Government Limited* (Canadian Centre for Policy Alternatives, Ottawa, 1984). See also review by Stephen Brooks, *Canadian Public Administration*, vol. 28, no. 3, Fall 1985.

Campbell, A. E. H.: "Regulations and the Orwellian State," *Canadian Public Administration*, vol. 28, no. 1, 1985, pp. 150–155.

Canada, Committee on Broadcasting: *Report* (Fowler Report) (Queen's Printer, Ottawa, 1965).

Carter, Richard: "Les Entreprises publiques: pourquoi et pour qui?" *Canadian Public Administration*, vol. 26, no. 2, 1983, pp. 239–254.

Cassidy, Michael: "Crown Corporations and the Canadian Legislatures: A Vain Search for Accountability," *The Parliamentarian*, vol. 63, no. 3, 1982, pp. 129–137.

Chandler, Marsha A.: "State Enterprise and Partisanship in Provincial Policies," *Canadian Journal of Political Science*, vol. 15, 1982, pp. 711–740.

Churchill, Gordon: "Toryism and Public Ownership in Canada: A Comment," *Canadian Historical Review*, vol. 64, no. 3, 1983, pp. 404–419.

Corbett, D.: *Politics and the Airlines* (University of Toronto Press, Toronto, 1965).

DeMuth, C. C.: "A Strategy for Regulatory Reform," *Regulation*, Mar./Apr. 1984, pp. 28–29.

Doern, G. B. (ed.): *The Regulatory Process in Canada* (Macmillian, Toronto, 1978).

—— and A. Tupper (eds.): *Public Corporations and Public Policy in Canada* (Institute for Research on Public Policy, Montreal, 1981).

Dussault, René and Louis Borgeat: *Traité de droit administratif*, 2nd ed., vol. 1 (Les Presses de l'Université Laval, Québec, 1984).

Economic Council of Canada: *Reforming Regulation* (Ministry of Supply and Services, Ottawa, 1981).

Forbes, J. D., R. D. Hughes, and T. K. Warley: *Economic Intervention and Regulation in Canadian Agriculture* (Economic Council of Canada and Institute for Research on Public Policy, Ottawa, 1982).

Foster, Peter: "The Power of Petro-Canada," *Saturday Night*, Oct. 1981, pp. 55–56.

Fraser Institute: *Focus on the Insurance Corporation of British Columbia, Public Monopolies and the Public Interest* (Fraser Institute, Vancouver, 1985).

Friedman, W. (ed.): *The Public Corporation: A Comparative Symposium* (Carswell, Toronto, 1954).

Garant, Patrice: "Le Statut légal des tribunaux administratifs et leurs rapports avec le gouvernement," *Canadian Public Administration*, vol. 27, no. 3, 1984, pp. 329–347.

Gordon, Marsha: *Government in Business* (C. D. Howe Research Institute, Montreal, 1981).

Hartle, Douglas G.: *Public Policy Decision Making and Regulation* (Institute for Research on Public Policy, Montreal, 1979).

Hull, W. H. N.: "The Fowler Report Revisited: A Broadcasting Policy for Canada," address to the 38th Annual Meeting of the Canadian Political Science Association, Sherbrooke, Quebec, June 1966.

—— : "The Public Control of Broadcasting: The Canadian and Australian Experiences," *Canadian Journal of Economics and Political Science*, vol. 28, 1962, pp. 114–126.

Janisch, Hudson: "Policy Making in Regulation: Towards a New Definition of the Status of Independent Agencies in Canada," *Osgoode Hall Law Journal*, vol. 17, 1979, pp. 46–106.

Janisch, H. N.: "Administrative Tribunals in the 80s: Rights of Access by Groups and Individuals," *Windsor Yearbook of Access to Justice*, vol. 1, 1981, p. 304.

Janson, H. N.: "The Role of the Independent Regulatory Agency in Canada," *University of New Brunswick Law Journal*, vol. 27, 1978, pp. 83–120.

Kane, T. G.: *Consumers and the Regulators* (Institute for Research on Public Policy, Montreal, 1980).

Kierans, Tom: "Commercial Crowns," *Policy Options*, vol. 5, no. 6, 1984, pp. 23–29.

Kristjanson, K.: "Crown Corporations: Administrative Responsibility and Public Accountability," *Canadian Public Administration*, vol. 11, 1968, pp. 454–459.

Langford, John W.: "The Identification and Classification of Federal Public Corporations: A Preface to Regime Building," *Canadian Public Administration*, vol. 23, no. 1, 1980, pp. 76–104.

—— : "Public Corporations in the 1980s: Moving from Rhetoric to Analysis," *Canadian Public Administration*, vol. 25, no. 4, 1982, pp. 619–637.

—— : "The Question of Quangos: Quasi-public Service Agencies in British Columbia," *Canadian Public Administration*, vol. 26, no. 4, 1983, pp. 563–576.

Laux, Jeanne Kirk: "Public Enterprises and Canadian Foreign Economic Policy," *Publius*, vol. 14, no. 4, 1984, pp. 61–80.

Law Reform Commission of Canada: *Independent Administrative Agencies*, Law Reform Commission Working Paper No. 25 (Ottawa, 1980).

Lesser, B.: "Comments on 'Regulatory Failure and Competition, by G. B. Reschenthaler,' " *Canadian Public Administration*, vol. 20, no. 2, 1977, pp. 389–392.

McGraw, T. (ed.): *Regulation in Perspective: Historical Essays* (Graduate School of Business Administration, Harvard University, Boston, 1981).

MacLean, Gordon: *Public Enterprise in Saskatchewan* (Crown Investments Corporation of Saskatchewan, Regina, 1981).

Mahan, Rianne: "Regulatory Agencies: Captive Agents or Hegemonic Apparatuses," *Studies in Political Economy*, vol. 1, Spring 1979, pp. 162–200.

Ohashi, T. M. *et al.*: *Privatization, Theory and Practice: Distributing Shares in Private and Public Enterprises* (Fraser Institute, Vancouver, 1980).

Osgoode Hall Law Journal: "Regulatory Reform Symposium, Parts I and II," *Osgoode Hall Law Journal*, vol. 20, nos. 3–4, 1982.

Pesando, James E.: *An Economic Analysis of Government Investment Corporations, with Attention to the Caisse de dépôt et placement du Québec and the Alberta Heritage Fund* (Economic Council of Canada, Ottawa, 1985).

Poole, Robert W., Jr. (ed.): *Instead of Regulation: Alternatives to Federal Regulatory Agencies* (Lexington Books/D. C. Heath, Toronto, 1982).

Prichard, J. Robert S.: *Crown Corporations in Canada: The Calculus of Instrument Choice* (Butterworths, Toronto, 1983).

Priest, Margot: *Provision of Information in the Context of Regulation*, Technical Report No. 22 (Economic Council of Canada, Ottawa, 1982).

Prince, Michael J. and G. Bruce Doern: *Federal Policy and the Role of Public Enterprise in the Mining Sector* (Centre for Resource Studies, Queen's University, Kingston, 1985).

—— : *The Origins of Public Enterprise in the Canadian Mineral Sector: Three Provincial Case Studies* (Centre for Resource Studies, Queen's University, Kingston, 1985).

Rea, K. J. and Nelson Wiseman: *Government and Enterprise in Canada* (Methuen, Toronto, 1985).

Reschenthaler, G. B.: "Regulatory Failure and Competition," *Canadian Public Administration*, vol. 19, no. 3, 1976, pp. 466–486.

—— : "Regulatory Failure and Competition: A Reply," *Canadian Public Administration*, vol. 20, no. 2, 1977, pp. 393–394.

Schultz, R. J.: *Federalism and the Regulatory Process* (Institute for Research on Public Policy, Montreal, 1979).

—— : "Regulation and Public Administration," *Canadian Public Administration*, vol. 25, no. 4, 1982, pp. 638–652.

Schultz, Richard (ed.): "Reforming Regulation: Symposium," *Canadian Public Administration*, vol. 25, no. 1982, pp. 24–44.

Science Council of Canada: *Regulating the Regulators: Science, Values and Decisions*, Report No. 35 (Science Council of Canada, Ottawa, Oct. 1982).

Shea, A. A.: *Broadcasting, the Canadian Way* (Harvest House, Montreal, 1963).

Slatter, Frans F.: *Parliament and Administrative Agencies* (Law Reform Commission of Canada, Ottawa, 1982).

Spry, G.: "The Decline and Fall of Canadian Broadcasting," *Queen's Quarterly*, vol. 68, 1961–62, pp. 213–225.

—— (ed.): *Studies on Regulation in Canada* (Institute for Research on Public Policy, Montreal, 1978).

Stanbury, W. T. (ed.): *Government Regulation: Scope, Growth, Process* (Institute for Research on Public Policy, Montreal, 1980).

—— and Thomas E. Kierans: *Papers on Privatization* (Institute for Research on Public Policy, Montreal, 1985).

—— and George Lerner: "Regulation and the Redistribution of Income and Wealth," *Canadian Public Administration*, vol. 26, no. 3, 1983, pp. 378–401.

—— and F. Thompson (eds.): *Managing Public Enterprises* (Praeger Press, New York, 1982).

—— and —— : *Regulatory Reform in Canada* (Institute for Research on Public Policy, Montreal, 1982).

Strong, Maurice: "The Necessary Private-Public Mix," *Policy Options*, vol. 5, no. 6, 1984, pp. 6–12.

Trebilcock, M. J.: "Winners and Losers in the Modern Regulatory System: Must the Consumer Always Lose?" *Osgoode Hall Law Journal*, vol. 13, no. 3, 1975, pp. 619–647.

Tupper, Allan: *Public Money in the Private Sector* (Queen's University, Kingston, 1983).

—— and G. Bruce Doern (eds.): *Public Corporations and Public Policy in Canada* (Institute for Research on Public Policy, Montreal, 1981).

Weir, E. A.: *The Struggle for National Broadcasting in Canada* (McClelland and Stewart, Toronto, 1965).

E. Task Forces, Royal Commissions, and Advisory Councils

Axworthy, L.: "The Housing Task Force: A New Policy Instrument," paper prepared for the 42nd Annual Meeting of the Canadian Political Science Association, Winnipeg, Manitoba, June 4, 1970.

Blair, Cassandra: *Forging Links of Cooperation: The Task Force Approach to Consultation* (Conference Board of Canada, Ottawa, 1984).

Bryden, M. and M. Gurney: "Royal Commission Costs," *Canadian Tax Journal*, vol. 14, 1966, pp. 157–159.

Burns, R. M.: "The Economic Council of Canada: Reflections Prompted by the Fourth Review," *Canadian Tax Journal*, vol. 16, 1968, pp. 600–605.

Canada, Parliament, Senate, Special Committee on Science Policy: *Proceedings*: Phase 1, 27th Parl., 1967–68, or 28th Parl., nos. 1–30, plus subsequent proceedings (Queen's Printer, Ottawa).

Carter, L. A.: "Canadian Science Policy: Doubts Raised about Advisory Apparatus," *Science*, vol. 161, Aug. 2, 1968, pp. 450–451.

Chapman, Ian D. and Farind Chummer: "Accountability and the Social Research Councils," *Journal of Canadian Studies*, vol. 17, no. 4, 1982–83, pp. 3–9.

Cook, Ramsay: "Loyalism, Technology and Canada's Fate," *Journal of Canadian Studies*, vol. 5, no. 3, Aug. 1970, pp. 50–60.

Courtney, J. C.: "In Defense of Royal Commissions," *Canadian Public Administration*, vol. 12, 1969, pp. 198–212.

—— : "Judges as Royal Commissioners," *Canadian Public Administration*, vol. 44, 1964, pp. 413–417.

Cronin, Thomas E. and Sanford D. Greenberg (eds): *The Presidential Advisory System* (Harper and Row, New York, 1969).

Dion, Léon: "Politique consultative et système politique," *Canadian Journal of Political Science*, vol. 2, 1969, pp. 226–244.

Doern, G. Bruce: "The National Research Council: The Causes of Goal Displacement," *Canadian Public Administration*, vol. 13, 1970, pp. 140–184.

—— : "The Political Realities of Science Policy Making in the Federal Government," *Science Forum*, vol. 3, no. 3, June 1970, pp. 21–25.

—— : "Pressure Groups and Canadian Bureaucracy: Scientists and Science Policy Machinery," in W. D. K. Kernaghan (ed.), *Bureaucracy in Canadian Government* (Methuen, Toronto, 1969), pp. 112–119.

—— : "The Role of Royal Commissions in the General Policy Process and in FederalProvincial Relations," *Canadian Public Administration*, vol. 10, 1967, pp. 417–433.

—— : *Science and Politics in Canada* (McGill-Queen's University Press, Montreal, 1972).

—— : "The Senate Report on Science Policy: A Political Assessment," *Journal of Canadian Studies*, vol. 6, no. 2, May 1971, pp. 42–51.

—— : "Scientists and Science Policy Machinery," in W. D. K. Kernaghan (ed.), *Bureaucracy in Canadian Government* (Methuen, Toronto, 1969).

Fowke, V. C.: "Royal Commissions and Canadian Agricultural Policy," *Canadian Journal of Economics and Political Science*, vol. 14, 1948, pp.163–175.

Gillespie, W. I.: "Decision Making by Official Commission," in A. J. Robinson and James Cutt (eds.), *Public Finance in Canada: Selected Readings* (Methuen, Toronto, 1968), pp. 57–60.

Gilpin, Robert and Christopher Wright (eds.): *Scientists and National Policy Making* (Columbia University Press, New York, 1964).

—— : "Technological Strategies and National Purpose," *Science*, vol. 169, July 31, 1970, pp. 441–448.

Glassco Commission: *Scientific Research and Development*, vol. 4, report 23 (Queen's Printer, Ottawa, 1962–63).

Gunning, Harry E.: "Canadian Science Policy and the OECD Report: A Critical Analysis," *Science Forum*, vol. 2, no. 6, Dec. 1969, pp. 3–6.

Hanser, Charles J.: *Guide to Decisions: The Royal Commission* (Bedminster Press, Totawa, N. J., 1965).

Hanson, H. R.: "Inside Royal Commissions," *Canadian Public Administration*, vol. 12, 1969, pp. 356–364.

Heller, Walter W.: "Economic Policy Advisers," in Thomas E. Cronin and S. D. Greenberg (eds.), *The Presidential Advisory System* (Harper and Row, New York, 1969), pp. 29–39.

Henderson, G. F.: *Federal Royal Commissions in Canada 1867–1966: A Checklist* (University of Toronto Press, Toronto, 1967).

Hodgetts, J. E.: "Public Power and Ivory Power," in Trevor Owen Lloyd and Jack McLeod (eds.), *Agenda 1970* (University of Toronto Press, Toronto, 1968), pp. 256–280.

—— : "The Role of Royal Commissions in Canadian Government," *Proceedings of the*

3rd Annual Conference (Institute of Public Administration of Canada, Toronto, 1951).

————— : "Should Canada be De-commissioned? A Commoner's View on Royal Commissions, *Queen's Quarterly*, vol. 70, 1963–64, pp. 475–490.

Jackson, R. W.: "Major Programs in R & D: Where the Means Justify the Ends," *Science Forum*, vol. 2, no. 2, April 1969, pp. 10–14.

Kaliski, S. F. (ed.): *Canadian Economic Policy since the War* (Canadian Trade Committee, Montreal, 1966).

Line, Richard J. and Arthur J. R. Smith: "Economic Planning for Canada," in M. H. Watkins and D. F. Forster (eds.), *Economics Canada* (McGraw-Hill, Toronto, 1963), pp. 35–46. See also pp. 161–167.

Lithwick, N. H.: "Housing in Search of a Crisis," *The Canadian Forum*, Feb. 1969, pp. 250–251.

McLeod, T. H.: "Glassco Commission Report," *Canadian Public Administration*, vol. 6, 1963, pp. 386–406.

New Brunswick: *Participation and Development: The New Brunswick Task Force Report on Social Development and Social Welfare* (Queen's Printer, Fredericton, 1971).

O'Brien, Audrey: "Parliamentary Task Forces in the Canadian House of Commons: A New Approach to Committee Activity," *The Parliamentarian*, vol. 66, no. 1, 1985, pp. 28–32.

Organization for Economic Cooperation and Development (OECD): *Reviews of National Science Policy Canada* (OECD, Paris, 1969).

Paquet, Gilles: "The Economic Council as Phoenix," in Trevor Owen Lloyd and Jack McLeod (eds.), *Agenda 1970* (University of Toronto Press, Toronto, 1968), pp. 135–158.

Phidd, R. W.: "The Economic Council of Canada: Its Establishment, Structure, and Role in the Canadian Policy-making System, 1963–1974," *Canadian Public Administration*, vol. 18, 1975, pp. 428–473.

Salter, Liona and Debra Slaco: *Public Inquiries in Canada* (Science Council of Canada, Ottawa, 1981).

Saywell, John T.: "The Royal Commission on Bilingualism and Biculturalism," *International Journal*, vol. 20, 1964–65, pp. 378–382.

Schindeler, Fred and C. M. Lamphier: "Social Science Research and Participatory Democracy in Canada," *Canadian Public Administration*, vol. 12, no. 4, Winter 1969, pp. 481–498.

Science Council of Canada: *Annual Reports* (Queen's Printer, Ottawa).

————— : *Towards a National Science Policy for Canada*, Report No. 4 (Information Canada, Ottawa, 1968).

————— , Committee on Industrial Policies: *Uncertain Prospects: Canadian Manufacturing Industry, 1971–1977* (Science Council of Canada, Ottawa, 1977).

Silcox, Peter: "To Commission—Or Not To Commission," *Canadian Public Administration*, vol. 5, 1962, pp. 253–304.

————— : "The Proliferation of Boards and Commissions," in Trevor Owen Lloyd and Jack McLeod (eds.), *Agenda 1970* (University of Toronto Press, Toronto, 1968), pp. 115–134.

Thistle, Mel: *The Inner Ring: The Early History of the National Research Council of Canada* (University of Toronto Press, Toronto, 1966).

Trainor, Lynn: "The Americanization of Canadian Science: How We Lose by Default," *Science Forum*, vol. 2, no. 2, April 1970, pp. 3–8.

Tunnoch, G. V.: "The Glassco Commission: Did It Cost More than It Was Worth?" *Canadian Public Administration*, vol. 7, 1964, pp. 389–397.

Verney, D. V.: "The Role of the Private Social Science Research Council of Canada in the Formation of Public Science Policy," *Canadian Public Policy*, vol. 1, 1975, pp. 107–117.

Walls, C. E. S.: "Royal Commissions: Their Influence on Public Policy," *Canadian Public Administration*, vol. 12, 1969, pp. 365–371.

Watkins, M.: "Technology and Nationalism," in Peter Russell (ed.), *Nationalism in Canada* (McGraw-Hill, Toronto, 1966), pp. 284–302.

Willms, A. M.: "The Adminstration of Research on Administration in the Government of Canada," *Canadian Public Administration*, vol. 10, 1967, pp. 405–416.

Wyman, Ken, Robin Mathews, and G. Lermer: "Article Reviewing the Task Force Report on Foreign Ownership," *Canadian Dimension*, vol. 5, no. 4, April/May 1968, pp. 15–20.

PARLIAMENTARY PROCESS

Abel, A. S.: "Administrative Secrecy," *Canadian Public Administration*, vol. 11, 1968, pp. 440–448.

Abrams, Matthew J.: *The Canada-United States Parliamentary Group* (Parliamentary Centre for Foreign Affairs/Canadian Institute for International Affairs, Toronto, 1973).

Aitchison, J. H.: "The Speakership of the Canadian House of Commons," in Robert Mills Clark (ed.), *Canadian Issues* (University of Toronto Press, Toronto, 1961), pp. 23–56.

Albinski, H. S.: "The Canadian Senate: Politics and the Constitution," *American Political Science Review*, vol. 57, pp. 378–391.

Anderson, S. V.: *Canadian Ombudsman Proposals* (University of California Press, Berkeley, 1966).

Atkinson, M.: "Reform and Inertia in the Nova Scotia Assembly," *Journal of Canadian Studies*, vol. 14, 1979, pp. 133–145.

Atkinson, M. M.: "Comparing Legislatures: The Policy Role of Backbenchers in Ontario and Nova Scotia," *Canadian Journal of Political Science*, vol. 13, 1980, pp. 55–74.

—— and Maureen Mancuso: "Do We Need a Code of Conduct for Politicians? The Search for an Elite Political Culture of Corruption in Canada," *Canadian Journal of Political Science*, vol. 18, 1985, pp. 459–480.

—— and Kim Richard Nossal: "Executive Power and Committee Autonomy in the Canadian House of Commons: Leadership Selection, 1968–1979," *Canadian Journal of Political Science*, vol. 13, 1980, pp. 287–308.

Aucoin, P. (ed.): *Institutional Reforms for Representative Government*, study prepared for the Royal Commission on the Economic Union and Development Prospects for Canada, vol. 38 (University of Toronto Press, Toronto, 1986).

—— (ed.): *Party Government and Regional Representation in Canada*, study prepared for the Royal Commission on the Economic Union and Development Prospects for Canada, vol. 36 (University of Toronto Press, Toronto, 1986).

—— (ed.): *Regional Responsiveness and the National Administrative State*, study prepared for the Royal Commission on the Economic Union and Development Prospects for Canada, vol. 37 (University of Toronto Press, Toronto, 1986).

Balinski, M. L. and H. P. Young: "Parliamentary Representation and the Amalgam Method," *Canadian Journal of Political Science*, vol. 14, 1981, pp. 797–812.

Balls, H. R.: "The Watchdog of Parliament: The Centenary of the Legislative Audit," *Canadian Public Administration*, vol. 21, 1978, pp. 584–617.

Bejerm, John: *How Parliament Works* (Borealis Press, Ottawa, 1985).

Brown, Steven D. and John McMenemy: "Generality or Specificity in Political Orientations? A Case Study," *Canadian Journal of Political Science*, vol. 15, 1982, pp. 365–376.

Bryden, K.: "Executive and Legislature in Ontario: A Case Study on Governmental Reform," *Canadian Public Administration*, vol. 18, 1975, pp. 235–252.

Burns, R. M.: "Second Chambers: German Experience and Canadian Needs," *Canadian Public Administration*, vol. 18, 1975, pp. 541–568.

Byers, R. B.: "Perceptions of Parliamentary Surveillance of the Executive: The Case of Canadian Defence Policy," *Canadian Journal of Political Science*, vol. 5, 1972, pp. 234–250.

Byrne, D.: "Some Attendance Patterns Exhibited by Members of Parliament during the 28th Parliament," *Canadian Journal of Political Science*, vol. 5, 1972, pp. 135–141.

Cairns, A. C.: "The Judicial Committee and Its Critics," *Canadian Journal of Political Science*, vol. 4, 1971, pp. 301–345.

Campbell, C.: *The Canadian Senate: Lobby from Within* (Macmillan, Toronto, 1978).

Canada, Minister of Justice: *Reform of the Senate: A Discussion Paper* (Publications Canada, Ottawa, 1983).

Canadian Bar Association: *Report of the Canadian Bar Association Committee on the Reform of Parliament* (Canadian Bar Association, Ottawa, 1982).

Casstevens, Thomas W. and William A. Denham III: "Turnover and Tenure in the Canadian House of Commons, 1867–1969," *Canadian Journal of Political Science*, vol. 3, 1970, pp. 655–661.

Charney, Harold D. and Richard G. Price: "A Note on the Pre-nomination Role: Socialization and Freshmen Members of Parliament," *Canadian Journal of Political Science*, vol. 10, 1977, pp. 391–406.

Cheverett, G.: "The Government Member: His Relationship with Caucus and Cabinet," *Canadian Parliamentary Review*, vol. 4, Spring 1981, pp. 5–8.

Clarke, H. D.: "The Ideological Self-perceptions of Provincial Legislators" (note), *Canadian Journal of Political Science*, vol. 11, 1973, pp. 617–633.

———, Colin Campbell, F. Q. Quo, and Arthur Goddard: *Parliament, Policy and Representation* (Methuen, Toronto, 1980).

——— and R. G. Price: "Freshman M.P.s' Job Images: The Effects of Incumbency, Ambition and Position," *Canadian Journal of Political Science*, vol. 13, 1980, pp. 583–606.

——— and ——— : "Parliamentary Experience and Representational Role Orientations in Canada," *Legislative Studies Quarterly*, vol. 6, no. 3, 1981, pp. 373–390.

Clyne, J. V.: "The Case for a Constitutional Assembly," *Policy Options*, vol. 2, no. 1, Mar./Apr. 1981, pp. 17–21.

Clarkson, S.: "Barriers to Entry of Parties into Toronto's Civic Politics: Towards a Theory of Party Penetration," *Canadian Journal of Political Science*, vol. 4, 1971, pp. 206–223.

Connolly, J. J.: "The Senate of Canada," *The Parliamentarian*, vol. 53, 1972, pp. 95–103.

Courtney, J. C.: "Recognition of Canadian Political Parties in Parliament and in Law," *Canadian Journal of Political Science*, vol. 11, 1978, pp. 33–60.

Courtney, John C. (ed.): *The Canadian House of Commons Essays in Honour of Norman Ward* (University of Calgary Press, Calgary, 1985).

D'Aquino, Thomas *et al.*: *Parliamentary Government in Canada* (Intercounsel, Ottawa, 1979).

———— , G. Bruce Doern, and Cassandra Blair: *Parliamentary Democracy in Canada: Issues for Reform* (Methuen, Toronto, 1983).

Delwarde, Karl: "La Législature québécoise peut-elle implanter un système incomplet d'initiative et de référendum?" *Les Cahiers de droit*, vol. 22, nos. 3–4, 1981, pp. 695–722.

Denham, R. A.: "The Canadian Auditors General: What Is Their Role?" *Canadian Public Administration*, vol. 17, 1974, pp. 259–273.

———— : "New Public-sector Audit Legislation in Canada," *Canadian Public Policy*, vol. 4, 1978, pp. 474–488.

Ducasse, R.: "Les Députés et la fonction parlementaire: éléments d'une enquête à L'Assemblée nationale du Québec," *Journal of Canadian Studies*, vol. 14, 1974, pp. 109–116.

Esberey, J. E.: "Focus on Parliament," *Queen's Quarterly*, vol. 43, 1957, pp. 475–573.

———— : "Personality and Politics: A New Look at the King-Byng Dispute," *Canadian Journal of Political Science*, vol. 6, 1973, pp. 37–55.

Fleming, Robert J. and J. Thomas Mitchinson (eds.): *Canadian Legislatures: The 1982 Comparative Study* (Director of Administration, Queen's Park, Toronto, 1982).

———— (eds.): *Canadian Legislatures: The 1984 Comparative Study* (Legislative Assembly of Ontario, Toronto, 1984).

Forsey, Eugene: "The Extension of the Life of Legislatures," *Canadian Journal of Economics and Political Science*, vol. 29, 1963, pp. 604–616.

———— : "Parliament's Power to Advise," *Canadian Journal of Economics and Political Science*, vol. 29, 1963, pp. 203–210.

———— : "The Problem of 'Minority' Government in Canada," *Canadian Journal of Economics and Political Science*, vol. 30, 1964, pp. 1–11.

———— (Hon.): "The Role and Position of the Monarch in Canada," *The Parliamentarian*, vol. 64, no. 1, 1983, pp. 6–11.

Franks, C. E. S.: "Borrowing from the United States: Is the Canadian Parliamentary System Moving towards the Congressional Model?" *American Review of Canadian Studies*, vol. 13, no. 3, 1983, pp. 201–214.

———— : "The Committee Clerks of the Canadian House of Commons," *The Parliamentarian*, vol. 50, 1969, pp. 159–162.

———— : "Debates and Question Period in the Canadian House of Commons: What Purpose Do They Serve?" *American Review of Canadian Studies*, vol. 15, no. 1, 1985, pp. 1–15.

———— : "The Legislature and Responsible Government," in Norman Ward and Stafford Duff (eds.), *Politics in Saskatchewan* (Longmans Canada, Toronto, 1968), pp. 20–43.

———— : *Parliament and Security Matters*, study prepared for the McDonald Royal Commission on Certain Activities of the RCMP (Supply and Services, Ottawa, 1980).

Fyffe, G.: "The Overhaul that's Overdue," *Policy Options*, vol. 1, no. 4, Dec./Jan. 1980–81, pp. 53–57.

Geller-Schwartz, L.: "Minority Government Reconsidered," *Journal of Canadian Studies*, vol. 14, 1979, pp. 67–79.

Gibbins, Roger: *Senate Reform: Moving towards the Slippery Slope* (Institute of Intergovernmental Affairs, Queen's University, Kingston, 1983).

Gilles, James: "The Parliamentary Imperative," *Saturday Night*, June 1984, pp. 52–56.

———— and Jean Pigott: "Participation in the Legislative Process," *Canadian Public Administration*, vol. 25, no. 2, 1982, pp. 254–264.

Government of Alberta: *A Provincially Appointed Senate: A New Federalism for Canada* (Government Publishing Office, Edmonton, 1982).

Hamel, Jacques and Yvon Thériault: "La Fonction tribunitienne et la députation créditiste à l'Assemblée nationale du Québec: 1970–73," *Canadian Journal of Political Science*, vol. 9, 1975, pp. 3–21.

Hawkins, G. (ed.): *Order and Good Government*, proceedings of the 33rd Couchiching Conference (Canadian Institute on Public Affairs, Toronto, 1965).

Henderson, Maxwell: *Plain Talk: Memoirs of an Auditor General* (McClelland and Stewart, Toronto, 1984).

Hockin, T. A.: "The Advance of Standing Committees in Canada's House of Commons: 1965–1970," *Canadian Public Administration*, vol. 13, 1970, pp. 185–202.

—— : *Apex of Power: The Prime Minister and Political Leadership in Canada* (Prentice-Hall, Toronto, 1971).

—— : "Flexible and Structured Parliamentarianism: From 1848 to Contemporary Party Government," *Journal of Canadian Studies*, vol. 14, 1979, pp. 8–17.

Hoffman, D. and N. Ward: *Bilingualism and Biculturalism in the Canadian House of Commons*, Royal Commission on Bilingualism and Biculturalism, document 3 (Queen's Printer, Ottawa, 1970).

House of Commons, Special Committee on Reform of the House of Commons: *Report* (House of Commons, Ottawa, 1985).

Huntington, Hon. Ron: "Effective Parliamentary Influence and Better Government," *The Parliamentarian*, vol. 65, no. 2, 1984, pp. 99–103.

Irvine, Andrew: "A Potent Senate," *Policy Options*, vol. 5, no. 3, May 1984, pp. 37–40.

Jackson, R. J. and M. M. Atkinson: *The Canadian Legislative System*, 2nd rev. ed. (Macmillan, Toronto, 1980).

Jennings, Sir William Ivor: *Parliament*, 2nd ed. (Cambridge University Press, Cambidge, 1957), ch. 4–6, 10–11.

Jerome, James: *Mr. Speaker* (McClelland and Stewart, Toronto, 1985).

Jewett, P.: "The Reform of Parliament," *Journal of Canadian Studies*, vol. 1, no. 3, Nov. 1966, pp. 11–15.

Johnson, J. K. (ed.): *The Canadian Directory of Parliament, 1867–1967* (Public Archives of Canada, Ottawa, 1968).

Kersell, J. E.: "Statutory and Judicial Control of Administrative Behaviour," *Canadian Public Administration*, vol. 19, 1976, pp. 295–307.

Knowles, Stanley Howard: *The Role of the Opposition in Parliament* (Woodsworth Memorial Foundation, Ontario, 1957).

Konn, Walter S. G.: "Women in the Canadian House of Commons," *American Review of Canadian Studies*, vol. 14, no. 3, 1984, pp. 298–311.

Kornberg, Allan: *Canadian Legislative Behaviour: A Study of the 25th Parliament* (Holt Rinehart and Winston, New York, 1967), ch. 3, pp. 42–62.

—— : "Caucus and Cohesion in Canadian Parliamentary Parties," *American Political Science Review*, vol. 60, Mar. 1966, pp. 83–92.

—— : "Parliament in Canadian Society," in Allan Kornberg and Lloyd D. Musolf (eds.), *Legislatures in Developmental Perspective* (Durham, Duke, 1970), ch. 3, pp. 55–128.

—— : "Representative Democracy and Political Elites in Canada and the United States," *Parliamentary Affairs*, vol. 19, no. 1, Winter 1965–66, pp. 91–102.

—— : "The Rules of the Game in the Canadian House of Commons," *Journal of Politics*, vol. 26, 1964, pp. 358–380.

—— : "The Social Bases of Leadership in a Canadian House of Commons," *Australian Journal of Politics and History*, vol. 11, 1965, pp. 324–334.

—— : *Some Differences in Role Perceptions among Canadian Legislators* (University of Michigan Press, Ann Arbor, 1964).

—— , David Falcone, and William Mischler: "Socio-economic Change, Legislative Composition, and Political System Outputs in Canada, 1867–1968," in *Sage Series in Comparative Legislatures*, no. 1, Nov. 1972.

—— and N. Thomas: "The Purposive Roles of Canadian and American Legislators: Some Comparisons," *Political Science*, vol. 18, no. 2, Sept. 1965, pp. 36–50.

Kunz, E. A.: *The Modern Senate of Canada, 1925–1963: A Re-appraisal* (University of Toronto Press, Toronto, 1965).

Lambert, N.: "Reform of the Senate," pamphlet no. 30 (Winnipeg Free Press, Apr. 1950).

Lamontagne, M.: "The Influence of the Politician," *Canadian Public Administration*, vol. 11, 1968, pp. 263–271.

Laponce, Jean: "The Religious Background of Canadian M.P.s," *Political Science*, vol. 6, no. 1968, pp. 253–258.

Lever, Nora S. *et al.*: "The Parliamentary Task Forces: Committees of the Future," *Canadian Parliamentary Review*, vol. 4, no. 1, 1981, pp. 15–20.

Laundry, Philip: "The Future of the Canadian Speakership," *The Parliamentarian*, vol. 53, 1972, pp. 113–117.

—— : "Procedural Reform in the Canadian House of Commons," *The Parliamentarian*, vol. 50, 1969, pp. 155–157.

—— : *The Table: Being the Journal of the Society of Clerks-at-the-Table in Commonwealth Parliaments*, vol. 34, 1965, pp. 20–30.

Levy, Gary: "Canadian Participation in Parliamentary Associations," *Canadian Journal of Political Science*, vol. 7, 1974, pp. 352–357.

Lloyd, Trevor: "The Reform of Parliamentary Proceedings," in A. Rotstein (ed.), *The Prospect of Change: Proposals for Canada's Future* (McGraw-Hill, Toronto, 1965), pp. 23–39.

Long, John Anthony: "Maldistribution in Western Provincial Legislatures: The Case of Alberta," *Canadian Journal of Political Science*, vol. 2, 1969, pp. 345–355.

Lovink, J. A. A.: "Who Wants Parliamentary Reform?" *Queen's Quarterly*, vol. 79, 1972, pp. 505–513.

Lyon, P. V.: "A New Idea for Senate Reform," *Canadian Commentator*, vol. 6, nos. 7–8, 1962, pp. 24–25.

Macdonald, Donald S.: "Change in the House of Commons: New Rules," *Canadian Public Administration*, vol. 13, 1970, pp. 30–39.

McDonald, D. C.: "The Alberta Ombudsman Act," *University of Toronto Law Journal*, vol. 19, 1969, pp. 257–263.

MacGuigan, Hon. Mark: *Reform of the Senate: A Discussion Paper* (Supply and Services, Ottawa, 1982).

McInnes, S.: "Improving Legislative Surveillance of Provincial Public Expenditures: The Performance of the Public Accounts Committees and Auditors General," *Canadian Pubic Administration*, vol. 20, 1977, pp. 36–86.

MacKay, R. A.: *The Unreformed Senate of Canada*, rev. ed. (McClelland and Stewart, Toronto, 1963).

MacLeod, Alex: "The Reform of the Standing Committees of the Quebec National Assembly: A Preliminary Assessment," *Canadian Journal of Political Science*, vol. 8, 1975, pp. 22–39.

McNaught, Kenneth: "Parliamentary Control of Foreign Policy?" *International Journal*, vol. 11, 1956, pp. 251–260.

Maingot, Joseph P.: *Parliamentary Privilege in Canada* (Butterworths, Toronto, 1982).

Mallory, J. R.: "Delegated Legislation in Canada: Recent Changes in Machinery," *Canadian Journal of Economics and Political Science*, vol. 19, 1953, pp. 462–471.

——— : "Parliamentary Scrutiny of Delegated Legislation in Canada: A Large Step Forward and a Small Step Back," *Public Law*, 1972, pp. 30–42.

——— : "Parliament: Every Reform Creates a New Problem," *Journal of Canadian Studies*, vol. 14, 1979, pp. 26–34.

——— : "The Uses of Legislative Commitees," *Canadian Public Administration*, vol. 6, 1963, pp. 1–14.

——— : "Vacation of Seats in the House of Commons: The Problem of Burnaby-Coquitlam," *Canadian Journal of Economics and Political Science*, vol. 30, 1964, pp. 125–130.

——— and B. A. Smith: "The Legislative Role of Parliamentary Committees in Canada: The Case of the Joint Committee on the Public Service Bills," *Canadian Public Administration*, vol. 15, 1972, pp. 1–23.

Massicotte, Louis: "Le Parlement du Québec en transition," *Canadian Public Administration*, vol. 28, no. 4, 1985, pp. 550–574.

Matheson, W. A.: *Prime Minister and the Cabinet* (Methuen, Toronto, 1976).

Matthews, Donald R.: "Legislative Recruitment and Legislative Careers," *Legislative Studies Quarterly*, vol. 9, no. 4, 1984, pp. 547–585.

Meisel, J.: "New Challenges to Parliament: Arguing over Wine Lists on the Titanic?" *Journal of Canadian Studies*, vol. 14, 1979, pp. 18–25.

Monet, Jacques: *The Canadian Crown* (Clarke, Toronto, 1979).

Morin, J.-Y.: "Un Nouveau Rôle pour un Sénat moribond," *Cité libre*, vol. 15, no. 68, juin/juillet 1964, pp. 3–7.

Neilson, W. A. W. and J. C. MacPherson (eds.): *The Legislative Process in Canada: The Need for Reform* (Institute for Research on Public Policy, Montreal, 1978).

Norton, Philip: "Party Committees in the House of Commons," *Parliamentary Affairs*, vol. 36, no. 1, 1983, pp. 7–27.

Oberle, Frank M. P.: "Caucus Reform in the Canadian Conservative Party," *The Parliamentarian*, vol. 65, no. 1, Jan. 1984, pp. 39–43.

Ogmundson, R.: "A Social Profile of Members of the Manitoba Legislature 1950, 1960, 1970," *Journal of Canadian Studies*, vol. 12, 1977, pp. 79–84.

Organ, E.: *Le Conseil législatif de Québec* (Bellarmin, Montreal, 1967).

Page, D.: "Streamlining the Procedures of the Canadian House of Commons, 1963–66," *Canadian Journal of Economics and Political Science*, vol. 33, 1967, pp. 27–49.

Pasis, Harvey: "Achieving Population Equality among the Constituencies of the Canadian House 1903–1976," *Legislative Studies Quarterley*, vol. 8, no. 1, 1983, pp. 111–115.

——— : "The Inequality of Distribution in the Canadian Provincial Assemblies" (note), *Canadian Journal of Political Science*, 1972, pp. 433–436.

Pelletier, R.: "Le Député: un législateur défaillant?" *Journal of Canadian Studies*, vol. 14, 1979, pp. 48–56.

Poel, Dale H.: "The Diffusion of Legislation among the Canadian Provinces: A Statistical Analysis," *Canadian Journal of Political Science*, vol. 9, 1976, pp. 603–626.

Porter, John: *The Vertical Mosaic: An Analysis of Social Class and Power in Canada* (University of Toronto Press, Toronto, 1965), pp. 386–416.

Pothier, D.: "Parties and Free Votes in the Canadian House of Commons," *Journal of Canadian Studies*, vol. 14, 1979, pp. 80–96 (nine articles on the operation of the legislature). See also K. W. Knight: "Administration Secrecy and Ministerial Responsibility," *ibid.*, vol. 32, 1955, pp. 77–84 and D. C. Rowat: "A Reply," *ibid.*, vol. 32, 1966, pp. 84–87.

Premont, J.: "Publicité de documents officiels," *Canadian Public Administration*, vol. 11, 1968, pp. 449–453.

Pross, A. Paul: "Parliamentary Influence and the Diffusion of Power," *Canadian Journal of Political Science*, vol. 18, no. 2, 1985, pp. 235–266.

Punnett, M.: *Prime Minister in Canadian Politics* (Macmillan, Toronto, 1977).

Randle, Kathryn: "Committees at the Crossroads: Will Innovation Lead to Reform?" *Parliamentary Government*, vol. 2, 1981, p. 3.

Regenstreif, S. P.: "Some Aspects of National Party Support in Canada," *Canadian Journal of Economics and Political Science*, vol. 29, 1963, pp. 59–74.

Reid, Alan D.: "The New Brunswick Ombudsman Act," *University of Toronto Law Journal*, vol. 18, no. 4, 1968, pp. 361–371.

Robertson, Gordon: "New Hope for Federalism," *Policy Options*, vol. 5, no. 2, 1984, pp. 8–11.

Robertson, R. G.: "The Canadian Parliament and Cabinet in the Face of Modern Demands," *Canadian Public Administration*, vol. 11, 1968, pp. 272–279.

Rowat, Donald Cameron: "An Ombudsman Scheme for Canada," *Canadian Journal of Economics and Political Science*, vol. 28, 1962, pp. 543–556.

—— (ed.): *The Ombudsman: Citizen's Defender*, 2nd ed. (University of Toronto Press, Toronto 1968).

—— : "Recent Developments in Ombudsmanship," *Canadian Public Administration*, vol. 10, 1967, pp. 35–46.

Sancton, Andrew: "The Application of the 'Senatorial Floor' Rules to the Latest Redistribution of the House of Commons: The Peculiar Case of Nova Scotia," *Canadian Journal of Political Science*, vol. 6, 1977, pp. 56–64.

Sigelman, Lee and William G. Vanderbok: "Legislators, Bureaucrats and Canadian Democracy: The Long and the Short of It" (note), *Canadian Journal of Political Science*, vol. 10, 1977, pp. 615–623.

Smiley, Donald: *An Elected Senate for Canada? Clues from the Australian Experience* (Intergovernmental Relations, Queen's University, Kingston, 1985).

Smith, D.: *The Speakership of the Canadian House of Commons: Some Proposals*, paper prepared for the House of Commons' Special Committee on Procedure and Organization (Queen's Printer, Ottawa, 1965).

Soldatos, P.: "La Problématique de l'incompatabilité des fonctions ministérielles et du mandat du député en système politique étatique du type parlementaire," *Canadian Journal of Political Science*, vol. 5, no. 1972, pp. 251–269.

Special Committee on Reform of the House of Commons: *Report* (Queen's Printer, Ottawa, 1985).

Special Joint Committee on Senate Reform: *Report* (Canadian Government Publishing Centre, Ottawa, Jan. 1984).

Special Committee on Standing Orders and Procedure: *Report* (House of Commons, Ottawa, Nov. 5, 1982).

Stanfield, Robert: "The Opportunities and Frustrations of Backbenchers," *Canadian Parliamentary Review*, vol. 4, Autumn 1981, pp. 6–9.

Stewart, Ian: "Of Customs and Coalitions: The Formation of Canadian Federal Parliamentary Alliances," *Canadian Journal of Political Science*, vol. 18, 1980, pp. 451–479.

Stewart, John: *The Canadian House of Commons: Procedures and Reform* (McGill-Queen's University Press, Montreal, 1977). The first chapter is a monumental analysis of the parliamentary aspects of the Canadian constitutional system.

—— : "Strengthening the Commons," *Journal of Canadian Studies*, vol 14, 1979, pp. 35–47.

Study Committee on Parliamentary Control of Delegated Legislation: *Parliamentary Control of Delegated Legislation* (The National Assembly of Quebec, Quebec, 1983).

Thomas, P. G.: "The Role of House Leaders in the Canadian House of Commons," *Canadian Journal of Political Science*, vol. 15, 1982, pp. 125–144.

—— : "Theories of Parliament and Parliamentary Reform," *Journal of Canadian Studies*, vol. 14, 1979, pp. 57–66.

Thornburn, H. G.: "Parliament and Policy-making: The Case of the Trans-Canada Gas Pipeline," *Canadian Journal of Economics and Political Science*, vol. 23, 1957, pp. 516–531.

Turner, J. N.: *Politics of Purpose* (McClelland and Stewart, Toronto, 1968), ch. 2.

—— : "The Senate of Canada: Political Conundrum," in R. M. Clark (ed.), *Canadian Issues: Essays in Honour of Henry F. Angus* (University of Toronto Press, Toronto, 1961).

Vaugeois, Denis: "The Parliament of Quebec and Delegated Legislation," *The Parliamentarian*, vol. 66, no. 1, 1985, pp. 14–19.

Walker, H. W.: "Parliamentary Procedure," *Queen's Quarterly*, vol. 58, 1951–52, pp. 228–236.

—— : "Question Time in Parliament," *Queen's Quarterly*, vol. 59, 1952–53, pp. 64–71.

Wallace, D. N.: "Budget Reform in Saskatchewan: A New Approach to Program-based Management," *Canadian Public Administration*, vol. 17, 1974, pp. 586–599.

Ward, John: *The Hansard Chronicles* (Deneau and Greenberg Publishers, Ottawa, 1980).

Ward, N.: "The Committee on Estimates," *Canadian Public Administration*, vol. 6, 1963, pp. 35–42.

—— : "Parliamentary Bilingualism in Canada," *Parliamentary Affairs*, vol. 10, no. 2, Spring 1957, pp. 155–164.

—— : *The Public Purse: A Study in Canadian Democracy*, Canadian Government Series, no. 11 (University of Toronto Press, Toronto, 1962).

—— : "Responsible Government: An Introduction," *Journal of Canadian Studies*, vol. 14, 1979, pp. 3–7.

—— : "The Significance of the Senators (In Representing the West)," *Policy Options*, vol. 2, no. 2, May/June 1981, pp. 32–34.

Ward, Norman: "Called to the Bar of the House of Commons," *Canadian Bar Review*, vol. 35, 1957, pp. 529–546.

—— : *The Canadian House of Commons: Representation* (University of Toronto Press, Toronto, 1950).

Weller, Patrick: *First among Equals: Prime Ministers in Westminster Systems* (George Allen and Unwin, Sydney, Australia, 1985).

White, G.: "Teaching the Mongrel Dog New Tricks: Sources and Directions of Reform in the Ontario Legislature," *Journal of Canadian Studies*, vol. 14, 1979, pp. 117–132.

White, Graham: "Committees in the Ontario Legislature," *The Parliamentarian*, vol. 61, no. 1, 1980, pp. 9–23.

White, Walter L. and Lawrence Leduc: "The Role of Opposition in a One-party Dominant System: The Case of Ontario," *Canadian Journal of Political Science*, vol. 7, 1974, pp. 86–100.

Wilson, R. Jeremy: "Continuity Despite Change: Reform of the British Columbia Legislature," *The Parliamentarian*, vol. 62, 1, 1981, pp. 27–38.

Winn, Conrad and James Twiss: "The Spatial Analysis of Political Cleavages and the Case of the Ontario Legislature," *Canadian Journal of Political Science*, vol. 10, 1977, pp. 287–310.

Woods, Seumas: "Towards a More Federal Parliament," *Saskatchewan Law Review*, vol. 48, no. 1, 1983–84, pp. 91–116.

INDEX